MOSS, FLETCHER AND ISAACS ON THE EU REGULATION ON INSOLVENCY PROCEEDINGS

MOSS, FLETCHER AND ISAACS ON THE EU REGULATION ON INSOLVENCY PROCEEDINGS

THIRD EDITION

Edited by

GABRIEL MOSS QC
IAN F. FLETCHER LLD QC (HON)
STUART ISAACS QC

OXFORD
UNIVERSITY PRESS

OXFORD
UNIVERSITY PRESS

Great Clarendon Street, Oxford, OX2 6DP,
United Kingdom

Oxford University Press is a department of the University of Oxford.
It furthers the University's objective of excellence in research, scholarship,
and education by publishing worldwide. Oxford is a registered trade mark of
Oxford University Press in the UK and in certain other countries

© Gabriel Moss, Ian F. Fletcher, Stuart Isaacs 2016

The moral rights of the authors have been asserted

First Edition published in 2002
Third Edition published in 2016

Impression: 1

Published in the United States of America by Oxford University Press
198 Madison Avenue, New York, NY 10016, United States of America

British Library Cataloguing in Publication Data
Data available

Library of Congress Control Number: 2016930891

ISBN 978–0–19–968780–0

Printed and bound by
CPI Group (UK) Ltd, Croydon, CR0 4YY

FOREWORD

The European Insolvency Regulation is about to enter a new stage. Fifteen years after its existence as a tool for the coordination of cross-border insolvencies the recast Regulation is designed to go beyond that. It represents a great step towards harmonization of the national insolvency laws. Quite a number of norms do change (not always openly) national concepts and so influence the respective systems. It appears even to be justified to assume that this the recast Regulation is only the first step towards even more harmonized legislation—a consequence which can be predicted because of the phrasing of many of the drastically increased number of recitals. As experienced under the 'old' Regulation, the European Court of Justice takes those recitals not only as an expression of a legislative intent; it rather interprets them as a kind of trend setter. Building on this experience, the drafters of the recast Regulation have added ideas and concepts in the recitals which are barely or even not at all reflected in its substantive provisions. It is fair to assume that this was meant to point the Court in certain directions. They have more or less in common a strong tendency towards harmonization.

In these circumstances and in this context, guidance from experts is more necessary than ever, since political wishful thinking must be structured and must be tamed in order to allow the legal population to adapt the new law and to adjust it to the respective systems. As positive as harmonization might be seen, when it comes too fast and too unstructured, the risk of failure is dangerously high and reduces possibly acceptance of the law. Given the European-wide (and even beyond) prominence of this book and its sound reasoning, it appears to be a leading exposition of European insolvency law.

What needs to be kept in mind, though, is the bias necessarily affecting those who are writing and reading this book. Coming from a rescue or insolvency perspective, one's thinking tends to be centered around but also within this universe. Of the many changes that the recast Regulation brings about—suffice it to mention the registration, the attention given to group insolvencies, the undertaking, etc.— the most important one seems to be the enormous extension of the concept of insolvency in Art. 1, which now includes pre-insolvency and insolvency avoidance procedures, with the exception of the English scheme of arrangement. This means that a debt reduction tool is given the status of an insolvency measure. This has a number of advantages but it comes also at a price: debt cancellation is always a violation of the overarching contract rule of *pacta sunt servanda*. By departing from that, the impression of the general public is likely to be that debt accumulation is not that bad since European law provides effective measures for solving the problem. In doing so, however, the Commission might contradict itself. Since as recently as February 2011 it enacted Directive 2011/7/EU on combating late payment in commercial transactions. This means that, on the one hand, payment behaviour is improved whereas, on the other hand, relief from payment is condoned. The least that can be said about these divergent measures is that they do not fit nicely together.

We all may be curious to see in which direction the new Recast Regulation and the present book will push us: more towards compliance with the time-honored principle of *pacta sunt servanda* or more towards a new understanding of kind of floating contract obligations. It is to be assumed that this book will play a rather decisive part in the struggle.

Christoph G. Paulus
Professor of Civil Law, Civil Procedure, Insolvency Law and Roman Law
Humboldt University, Berlin
February 2016

PREFACE TO THE THIRD EDITION

Much has happened in the specialised realm of the EU Regulation on Insolvency Proceedings since the last edition of this work was committed to the press in the early months of 2009. Judicial decisions, both by the Court of Justice of the European Union itself and also by national courts, have been delivered with accelerating frequency, greatly adding to the corpus of jurisprudence relating to the Regulation's meaning and scope. Looming in the background was the prescribed date—1 June 2012—by which the Commission was required to deliver a report on the application of the Regulation, accompanied by any proposals for its reform that were considered to be needed. The prospect that substantial revisions to the original Regulation might be enacted at some point after June 2012 inevitably affected our plans for the timing of this third edition, and also the approach to be adopted. To serve our readers' needs to optimum effect, it was necessary to await the conclusion of the revision process so as to be able to produce a commentary that would provide an up to date account of the original Regulation—to serve during the transitional period during which it would remain applicable—together with a discrete treatment and analysis of the recast Regulation to which users of the work would increasingly need to refer in anticipation of the date when it would replace the text originally adopted in May 2000.

As so often in the history of the EU, target dates and deadlines experienced the phenomenon of elasticity, so that it was not until 20 May 2015 that the agreed, final text of the Recast Regulation, numbered as 2015/848, was formally adopted by the EU Parliament and Council acting in concert under the organisation's current constitutional procedure. In accordance with the 2-year 'grace' period prescribed by Article 92, the Recast Regulation will not commence to apply until 26 June 2017, leaving the original Regulation 1346/2000 to continue to apply to insolvency proceedings opened before that date. Accordingly, we have structured this edition to provide updated commentary on the Regulation as currently in force, complemented by detailed analysis of the provisions of the Recast Regulation indicating the important changes which will enter into effect in a few months' time.

Although the new edition has inevitably expanded by comparison to its predecessor, the overall structure of the book remains essentially unchanged. Chapters 1 to 7 provide the reader with thematic accounts of specific topics bearing upon the Regulation and its impact. The individual authors of these chapters, who are identified in the Contents Summary, remain unchanged with one exception: Professor Matthias Haentjens has assumed responsibility for Chapter 7, which has been completely re-written, and retitled, in the light of major changes to the law governing the insolvency of financial institutions under parallel legislative provisions enacted by the EU. In Chapter 8, which now contains article-by-article commentary to both the original Regulation and to the 2015 Recast, two additional experts—Professors Miguel Virgós and Francisco Garcimartín—have joined the group who provide additional comments to the text written by the two principal authors of the chapter. It is hoped that readers will find these indications of divergent opinions thought-provoking and also illuminating.

We also owe a special debt to several further colleagues at South Square, in addition to named authors of chapters, whose substantial contributions have been essential in enabling us to meet publishing deadlines, namely William Willson, Adam Al-Attar, Robert Amey, Andrew Shaw and Ryan Perkins. Their contributions have been acknowledged at the start of chapters 5 and 8.

For reasons indicated above, this edition has been produced during a period of uncertainty regarding the probable timing of the central event concerning the future shape and content of the EU Regulation. Even as late as May 2015 there was a genuine possibility that many months of inter-institutional negotiation between the EU Commission, Parliament and Council might be frustrated due to a malign combination of internal and external political events. Consequently, considerable demands were placed on all contributors to this book who were unable to finalise their material until the outcome of the revision process was known. We are most grateful to them for their patience and professionalism in completing their contributions in accordance with a timetable that had to be revised several times in response to the unpredictable course of developments within the EU. Our thanks are also due to the editorial and production teams of Oxford University Press, whose own working schedules had to endure the knock-on effects from the shifting fortunes of Euro-politics.

Gabriel Moss QC
Ian Fletcher LLD, QC (Hon.)
Stuart Isaacs QC
1 February 2016

PREFACE TO THE SECOND EDITION

When the first edition of this work appeared in 2002, there was very little case law to cite and the contributors to the book had the difficult task of interpreting the Regulation with the assistance of the Virgos-Schmit Report and the Recitals, together with a limited volume of writings and talks on the subject. Since the first edition, there have been a number of significant cases, not only in the national courts, but also two reported decisions of the European Court of Justice, some further references to the ECJ and, too late to discuss in the text, which refers in detail to the Advocate General's Opinion, the ECJ's decision in the *Frick Teppichboden* case on 12 February 2009. There has also been much further writing and speaking in relation to the Regulation and the case law. The volume of material is now such that it would be impractical to include references to all of it, even if the contributors' linguistic abilities enabled them to do so. The EU has expanded and the Regulation now applies to 26 Member States with 21 language versions.

In order to keep the size of this volume within manageable proportions, and to maintain it as an attempt concisely to state the legal position as we saw it, we have focussed on what we believe to be the main cases and articles available in English or in translation into English, although a number of references to foreign language sources are also included. Not all the case law which touches on the Regulation is of real significance in interpreting it and therefore we have exercised a degree of selection even amongst the material available in English or translation into English. Likewise, in the case of articles and books, we have had to be selective and to focus on what we considered to be the most significant material.

Since the first edition, there have come into force the Directives dealing with credit institutions and insurance undertakings and these have been dealt with in a companion volume published by Oxford University Press in 2006: Moss & Wessels, *EU Banking and Insurance Insolvency*. Unfortunately, no such similar directive has appeared in respect of other types of proceedings excluded by Article 1(2) of the Regulation, namely 'investment undertakings which provide services involving the holding of funds or securities for third parties' and 'collective investment undertakings'. The unfortunate gap left in the case of 'investment undertakings' is illustrated by the recent case of *LBIE*, the principal Lehman Brothers company in the UK, which was an 'investment undertaking' and therefore excluded from the Regulation, but not included in any Directive.

The second edition retains the pattern followed by the first edition of having a series of narrative chapters giving an account of the principal features of the Regulation and a larger chapter providing an article by article commentary on the Regulation as a whole.

Chapter 1 by Professor Fletcher sets out the history of the Regulation and precursors and brings it up-to-date by reference to the Member States, now numbering 26, which are parties to the Regulation.

Chapter 2 by Stuart Isaacs QC and Richard Brent on the mode of interpretation of the Regulation as a community legal instrument is updated.

In Chapter 3, Professor Fletcher sets out the scope and jurisdiction of the Regulation. In Chapter 4 he sets out the choice of law rules. In each case, account is taken of developments in case-law since the first edition.

Chapter 5 by Gabriel Moss QC, Daniel Bayfield and Georgina Peters deals with recognition and enforcement, not only under the Regulation, but under the three other bases available in England for recognizing or assisting foreign proceedings and foreign insolvency practitioners. The changes in statute and case law are taken into account.

In Chapter 6, Stuart Isaacs QC, Felicity Toube, Nick Segal and Jennifer Marshall deal with the effect of the Regulation on cross border security and *quasi* security, updating these subjects in the light of further case-law and analysis.

Chapter 7 by David Marks QC deals with the regulation of financial services and markets in the EU in the light of the implementation of the Directives dealing with the reorganisation and winding up of credit institutions and insurance undertakings. Although the types of proceedings dealt with here are outside the scope of the Regulation, knowledge of these areas is important for understanding the operation of the Regulation and its relationship to credit institution, insurance undertaking and other regulated activity insolvencies.

Chapter 8 by Gabriel Moss QC and Tom Smith, with the assistance of additional commentary by Professor Michael Bogdan, Justice Timo Esko, Professor Ian Fletcher QC, Stuart Isaacs QC, Professor Alberto Piergrossi, Professor Bob Wessels and Alex Wood deals with the Regulation on an article by article basis, adding references to the significant case law developments.

Appendix 1 contains the up-dated text of the Regulation, as amended by reason of the accession of new Member States and changes in the insolvency proceedings in various States. Appendix 2 contains the Virgos-Schmit Report, an essential source of reference in the interpretation of the Regulation. We have been able to include some references to material towards the end of 2008, although in essence the text tries to state the law as at October 2008.

There are two judgments of particular interest which have come too late to be included in the book.

In *Nortel Networks SA* [2009] EWHC 206(Ch) the English High Court, which had opened main proceedings in respect of a number of EU registered companies in the Nortel group, authorised the sending of Letters of Request to local EU courts asking them to ensure that the administrators were given notice of any application to open secondary proceedings. The judgment refers with approval to the view in the *Stojevic* case in Austria to the effect that Article 31(2) implies a duty on courts as well as liquidators to co-operate with each other. The judgment cites the decision of the Versailles Court of Appeal in the *Rover* case to the effect that even where there is jurisdiction to open secondary proceedings, these should not be opened unless they serve a useful purpose. The judgment also refers to the ruling in the Austrian *Collins & Aikman* decision to the effect that a stay under Article 33 is only a stay of the process of liquidation and not the secondary proceeding itself. The three cases cited are dealt with in the book.

The ECJ decision in *Christopher Seagon, in his capacity as liquidator in respect of the assets of Frick Teppichboden Supermärkte GmbH, v Deko Marty Belgium NV*, (Case C-339/07) upheld the Advocate General's Opinion, which is dealt with in the book, in concise terms, holding that the courts of a Member State which opens main proceedings have jurisdiction to try a claim to avoid a transaction brought against a defendant in another Member State.

The first edition enjoyed widespread sales throughout the UK and Europe and has the distinction of being cited by the Advocate General's Opinions in the first two cases on the Regulation in which the ECJ has given judgments, namely *Eurofood* and *Staubitz-Schreiber*. It has also been cited widely in the English case law.

We are very grateful to all our contributors who made the second edition possible. We are also grateful for the continued support and assistance (and patience) of Oxford University Press, including their energetic and able marketing department. We are grateful also to a number of others knowledgeable in this field who have contributed ideas and suggestions, which appear in various places in Chapter 8. We also express our thanks to the organisers of conferences which have facilitated the discussion and debate relating to the Regulation, such as INSOL Europe and the European Academy of Law. We are always happy to receive suggestions relating to the book and any significant case law or articles which any of our readers feel we have overlooked or should take into account in any future edition.

One of the great problems of the subject is that no central registry of cross-frontier EU insolvency proceedings has been set up. This not only leads to situations where purportedly main proceedings can be opened in ignorance of each other in two different Member States, as in the *Stojevic* case, but also makes research and interpretation difficult and uncertain. It is to be hoped that the EU with its vast resources can remedy this situation. Meanwhile, we are happy to both receive and share news of significant case law developments with our readers. The text of this second edition shows the benefits of some of that sharing of information and we hope it will continue into the future.

We should finally mention the unfortunate impression that may have been given at the start of the case law that English courts were unjustifiably ready to find that the 'centre of main interests' of companies registered in other Member States were located in the UK. This misimpression appears to have been rectified by showing that the English courts look at the relevant criteria set out in the Regulation and the case law and make a proper judgment on the evidence available to them without any preference for the English jurisdiction. The fairness of the English procedure has been underlined by cases such as *Stojevic*, in which the opening of bankruptcy proceedings was set aside several years after the opening, on evidence being presented to the English court that there had been no jurisdiction in the UK, and the *Hans Brochier* case where the English court accepted at the prompting of the English administrators themselves that the opening of main administration proceedings in England had been unjustified because COMI had not effectively been moved from Germany.

We would hope that this type of result will reinforce the mutual respect and trust that is necessary for the working of the Regulation.

In practice, mutual trust and cooperation can best be developed by frequent cordial encounters both at conferences and by visits to each other's jurisdictions. Once judges, practitioners and lawyers have met, it is to be hoped that they will be more ready to trust each other and to cooperate in the way envisaged by the Regulation, in the interests of creditors and the public.

Gabriel Moss QC
Ian Fletcher LLD, QC (Hon.)
Stuart Isaacs QC

South Square
Gray's Inn
London
WC1R 5HP
England

17 February 2009

CONTENTS—SUMMARY

CONTENTS

Contents

TABLE OF CASES

TABLE OF EUROPEAN LEGISLATION
AND INTERNATIONAL CONVENTIONS

*Paragraph references in **bold** indicate that the text is reproduced in full*

REGULATIONS

TABLE OF STATUTES

TABLE OF STATUTORY INSTRUMENTS

LIST OF CONTRIBUTORS

Daniel Bayfield QC is a barrister practising from South Square, a business law set with a pre-eminent reputation for insolvency and reorganization work. He specializes in all aspects of corporate insolvency law, including cross-border issues, as well as having a broad chancery commercial practice. Daniel has been involved in a number of high profile insolvencies including *Enron, TXU, Cenargo, Independent Insurance, MG Rover, T&N, PRG Powerhouse, Cheyne Finance, XL, Sigma Finance,* and *MF Global* and is currently advising the administrators of *Lehman Brothers*. He is a contributor to *Lightman & Moss: The Law of Administrators and Receivers of Companies*.

Michael Bogdan is Senior Professor of Comparative and Private International Law at the University of Lund in Sweden. He is the author of nine books and more than 300 articles and reviews on various legal subjects. He was one of the experts invited to address the Legal Affairs Committee of the European Parliament on the draft European Insolvency Convention; the text of the Convention was later enacted as the EC Regulation on Insolvency Proceedings. His e-mail address is Michael. Bogdan@jur.lu.se.

Richard Brent is a barrister practising at 3 Verulam Buildings, one of the leading commercial sets of chambers. He specializes in commercial law (insurance, banking, and financial services as well as general commercial litigation) and has a particular interest in the commercial aspects of European law. Formerly a Fellow of St John's College, Cambridge, and a solicitor in the city, he is the author of *Directives: Rights and Remedies in English and Community Law* (London, 2001) and co-editor (with Mr Justice Blair) and author of *Banks and Financial Crime: The International Law of Tainted Money* (Oxford, 2008).

Mr Timo Esko was appointed member of the Finnish Supreme Court in 2006 and president in 2016. After having defended his thesis on international labour relationships in 1985 he served as Acting Professor in the Law Faculty of Helsinki University and then as director of administration of the University. In 1992 he joined a law office in Helsinki and started his own office with some colleagues in 1996. Insolvency law was one of Mr Esko's main interests as a lawyer. He has been the editor-in-chief of the periodical 'Defensor Legis' published by the Finnish Bar Association and he is also the author of a number of articles in different fields of private international law.

Ian Fletcher LLD QC (Hon) is Emeritus Professor of International Commercial Law and Senior Research Associate at University College London. Previously, he was Professor of Commercial Law at Queen Mary, University of London and

Director of the Centre for Commercial Law Studies from 1994–2000. A graduate of Cambridge University, he undertook postgraduate studies at Tulane University, USA. He was called to the Bar by Lincoln's Inn in 1971, of which he was elected a Bencher in 2003, and is an Academic Member of South Square Chambers, Gray's Inn. He is the author of numerous books and articles including *The Law of Insolvency* (1990; 4th edition 2009); and *Insolvency in Private International Law* (OUP, 1999; 2nd edition 2005; Supplement to Second Edition 2007). He is a member of the American Law Institute, the Insolvency Lawyers' Association, INSOL International, and the International Insolvency Institute, and is an International Fellow of the American College of Bankruptcy. He has been the editor-in-chief of the INSOL *International Insolvency Review* since 1992, and a specialist editor of *Palmer's Company Law* since 1987.

Matthias Haentjens is Professor of Financial Law and director of the Hazelhoff Centre for Financial Law at the University of Leiden. Prior to joining Leiden Law School, he was an attorney with De Brauw Blackstone Westbroek. In this capacity, he was involved in leading banking cases both as a transaction lawyer and as a (supreme court) litigator. He studied Greek and Latin at the University of Amsterdam (BA cum laude), and obtained his Master's degree in 2001. He became a teacher of classics, but subsequently obtained a Master's degree in Law (cum laude) in 2003, also at the University of Amsterdam. He obtained his PhD at the University of Amsterdam in 2007 and was a visiting scholar at Université de Paris II (Panthéon-Assas), Harvard Law School, and New York University School of Law.

Stuart Isaacs QC is a partner in the International Arbitration and Litigation Group of King & Spalding's London office and also has an office in Singapore. He practises from his London Chambers in the fields of commercial law (particularly banking and insurance), international arbitration, and EU law. His practice covers the range of Commercial Court and contentious Chancery work. He has been involved in many reported commercial and EU law cases. Since becoming a Queen's Counsel in 1991, he has been appointed to numerous arbitration tribunals and sits as an accredited mediator. He has a large commercial practice in Asia and visits the region frequently to advise and appear in arbitrations and to act as an arbitrator. He has argued over 20 cases in the European Court of Justice and Court of First Instance in Luxembourg and is the co-author of several works on EU banking and competition law. He was educated at Downing College, Cambridge, and the Université Libre de Bruxelles.

Jennifer Marshall is a partner in the global restructuring group of Allen & Overy LLP. She specializes in a wide range of work in commercial, banking, restructuring, and insolvency law, regularly advising banks and insolvency office-holders in major English and cross-border insolvencies. She has particular expertise in the structuring of transactions to mitigate against the effects of insolvency. She advised over 70 counterparties in relation to the recent Lehmans collapse and has been involved in a number of working groups established by HM Treasury to consider bank and investment firm insolvency and resolution. She is also general editor of the Sweet & Maxwell publication *European Cross Border Insolvency*.

Gabriel Moss QC[1] is a Queen's Counsel pre-eminent in advising and appearing in court in the field of English, EU, and international reorganization and insolvency law. He is also authorized to sit as a deputy High Court judge and decided the case of *Dobb White*. He was one of four experts invited to address the Legal Affairs Committee of the European Parliament on the draft European Insolvency Convention, which led to the introduction of the EC Regulation. He has acted as leading counsel in important cases on the Regulation, including *Enron Directo, Eurofood,* and *Elektrim v Vivendi*. He is the co-editor of *Moss and Wessels: EU Banking and Insurance Insolvency* (OUP, 2006).

Georgina Peters MA (Cantab) History (Christ's College) is a barrister at South Square, Gray's Inn; called to the Bar (Lincoln's Inn) 2005. Georgina specialises in commercial and financial law, with a particular focus on corporate insolvency/restructuring (both domestic and cross-border), banking and finance (including derivatives and securitisations), commercial litigation and company law cases. Before coming to the Bar, Georgina was a référendaire at the European Court of Justice, Luxembourg and worked at a leading French commercial law firm in Paris.

Alberto Piergrossi is an Italian lawyer and Professor. He holds an LLM Degree from Harvard Law School. He is the founder and chairman of the law firm Piergrossi Studio Legale and, formerly, of the Italian firm associated with Eversheds. He is Professor Emeritus of Civil Procedure and of Private and Procedural International Law. He is the author of various publications, mainly on insolvency and arbitration. He specializes in civil and commercial litigation, arbitration, mediation, insolvency and restructuring, commercial, intellectual property, and corporate matters. He has often been appointed as arbitrator and has served as court expert on Italian law. He is a member of the International Insolvency Institute (III) and of many international organizations. He is fluent in Italian, English, and French.

Nick Segal is a partner in the restructuring and insolvency group at Freshfields Bruckhaus Deringer. He also sits as a judge of the Grand Court in the Cayman Islands assigned to the Financial Services Division. Nick was previously a partner at Davis Polk & Wardwell and Allen & Overy. Nick is dual qualified (England and New York) and his practice covers a wide variety of work in commercial and banking law, insolvency and litigation, including bank resolution. Nick was educated at Oxford University where he obtained a first class degree and was awarded the Carl Albert prize. Nick teaches on the BCL course at Oxford and has written and lectured extensively on restructuring, restitution and insolvency law and has contributed to a number of leading textbooks.

---

[1] Further details are available at www.southsquare.com

Tom Smith QC is a barrister practising at South Square. He specializes in all aspects of banking, financial, restructuring, corporate insolvency, and company law. He has been involved in various cross-border restructurings, including schemes of arrangement, and other insolvency proceedings involving cross-border aspects including many involving the application of the EC Regulation. He is also a contributor to Company Directors and The Law of International Finance.

Felicity Toube QC specializes in domestic and cross-border insolvency and restructuring, banking and financial services, commercial litigation, civil fraud, and company law. Felicity appears in the Cayman Islands on a regular basis. She also acts as an expert in international proceedings in English law, as well as the law of other common law jurisdictions. She is asked to speak regularly at conferences, including at INSOL and Offshore Alert. Felicity has acted in relation to most of the recent major corporate restructurings or insolvencies and related litigation including most recently in *Saad, Madoff, Lehman, Stanford, Rastogi, Nortel, SPhinX, Sigma, Landsbanki, MF Global*, and *Rafidain Bank*. Felicity is also an ADR Group Accredited Civil & Commercial Mediator and has been appointed to the INSOL International College of Mediation.

Bob Wessels is a leading insolvency lawyer in the Netherlands. He has his private practice in Dordrecht. He was Professor of International Insolvency Law in Leiden (2007–2014) and of Civil and Commercial Law, Vrije University, Amsterdam (1988–2008). He acted as international consultant to the IMF, the World Bank and is counsel to the European Commission in matters of restructuring and insolvency law. He advises with legal opinions or acted as an expert witness in European or international insolvency related questions in Dutch courts as well as in the courts of New York, London, Warsaw, Alexandria (VA, USA), Vienna, Dublin, Rhodes (Greece), Zürich, Los Angeles, Stockholm and Antwerp. He published hundreds of articles in leading legal journals and (co-)authored some thirty books. Since 1999 he is the single author of: *Wessels Insolventierecht* (Wessels Insolvency Law), a ten Volume series, published by Wolters Kluwer, The Netherlands. In the 4th edition, since 2013 seven volumes have been published, including (in English) *International Insolvency Law Part I. Global Perspectives on Cross-Border Insolvency Law*, 4th edition, 2015. He was a visiting professor at universities in Frankfurt, Pretoria, New York and Riga. He is External Scientific Fellow of the Max Planck Institute Luxembourg for International, European and Regulatory Procedural Law (since 2015), Deputy Justice at the Court of Appeal in The Hague (since 1987); Member of the Joint Board of Appeal of the three European Supervisory Authorities (ESAs; ESMA, EBA and EIOPA respectively) (since 2013); emeritus director of the board of International Insolvency Institute (III), past Chairman of the Netherlands Association for Comparative and International Insolvency Law (NACIIL) and past Chairman of the Academic Forum of INSOL Europe.

Alexander Wood is a partner in the London office of Weil, Gotshal and Manges' business finance and restructuring practice. He has law degrees from both Cambridge and Oxford University. He is experienced in all aspects of business restructuring and insolvency matters. His particular expertise lies in the design and implementation of complex schemes of arrangement, cross-border restructurings, debt restructurings and formal insolvency procedures. Weil is a leading international law firm doing high end work for major international.

LIST OF ABBREVIATIONS

AC	Appeal Cases (law reports of cases in the House of Lords, UK Supreme Court, and UK Privy Council)
AIF	alternative investment fund
BCC	British Company Cases
BCLC	Butterworths Company Law Cases
BPIR	Bankruptcy and Personal Insolvency Reports
BRRD	Bank Recovery and Resolution Directive
CA	Court of Appeal
Ch or Ch. D.	Chancery Division of the High Court of Justice of England and Wales
CJEU	Court of Justice of the European Union
COMI	centre of main interests
Comm	Commercial Court – part of the Queen's Bench Division of the High Court of Justice of England and Wales
CVA	company voluntary arrangement
EBA	European Banking Authority
ECJ	European Court of Justice
EEA	European Economic Area
EWCA	Court of Appeal of England and Wales
EWHC	High Court of England and Wales
ICLQ	International and Comparative Law Quarterly
HL	UK House of Lords (now the UK Supreme Court)
ILPr	International Litigation Procedure
JBL	Journal of Business Law
JOL	joint official liquidator
MiFID	Markets in Financial Instruments Directive
NYULR	New York University Law Review
OR	European Union: Council Regulation (EC) 1346/2000 of 29 May 2000 on Insolvency Proceedings (original Insolvency Regulation)
QBD	Queen's Bench Division of the High Court of Justice of England and Wales
ROT	reservation of title
RR	European Union: Regulation (EU) 2015/848 of the European Parliament and of the Council of 20 May 2015 on Insolvency Proceedings (recast) (recast Insolvency Regulation)
SRM	Single Resolution Mechanism
SRMR	Single Resolution Mechanism Regulation
TFEU	Treaty on the Functioning of the European Union
UCITS	undertakings for collective investment in transferable securities
UKPC	UK Privy Council

UKSC	UK Supreme Court
UNCITRAL	United Nations Commission on International Trade Law
WLR	Weekly Law Reports

1

HISTORICAL OVERVIEW: THE DRAFTING OF THE REGULATION AND ITS PRECURSORS

A. Preliminary

This chapter provides a brief account of the protracted process which resulted in **1.01** the adoption of Council Regulation (EC) 1346/2000.[1] That project had begun as a proposal to conclude a Convention among the Member States of the European Economic Community (EEC), to regulate the conduct of insolvency proceedings as between themselves. The need for such arrangements was foreseen at the time of drafting the Foundation Treaty of the EEC, and was indeed covered by the terms of a specific provision of that Treaty.[2] Successive attempts to implement that provision, pursued first by the Commission and later by the Council, ultimately ended

---

[1] Council Regulation (EC) 1346/2000 of 29 May 2000 on Insolvency Proceedings [2000] OJ L160/1.

[2] Treaty Establishing the European Economic Community, signed in Rome on 25 March 1957, commonly known as the (first) Treaty of Rome. Article 220(4) of that Treaty commits the Member States to negotiating a series of conventions for the benefit of their nationals, including one to secure 'the simplification of formalities governing the reciprocal recognition and enforcement of judgments of courts or tribunals and of arbitral awards'. The logical and legal bases for standardizing the intra-Community treatment of insolvency matters are more fully explored in IF Fletcher, *Conflict of Laws and European Community Law* (1982) chs 1, 2, and 6, esp at 187–90.

in failure although at various times it had seemed possible that agreement could be achieved among the states then participating.

1.02 The last hope of bringing the project to a successful conclusion appeared to have been extinguished when, in May 1996, a finalized Convention that had been signed by 14 of the 15 members of what had by that time become the European Union, failed to come into effect due to the withholding of the signature of the United Kingdom. This had the unfortunate consequence of causing the text, negotiated by and apparently acceptable to all 15 states, to lapse. However, in a final demonstration of collective resolve the Council of Ministers, under the consecutive presidencies of Germany and Finland, revived the project in the form of a Regulation, thereby transforming it into a directly applicable legislative act under Community law. In its final iteration, the text was adopted as a Regulation of the EC Council on 29 May 2000. Having been adopted in that form the Regulation automatically entered into force on the appointed day—31 May 2002—in all the 14 Member States which were then participating in the legislative programme promulgated under the provisions of the EC Treaty (Denmark being for this purpose a non-participating state by virtue of its permanent exemption, under the terms of the Maastricht Treaty, from the effects of legislation adopted under Part IV of the European Community (EC) Treaty in its amended form). Subsequent increases in the membership of the European Union have raised the total number of Member States to 28 at the present time. The augmentations took place, first, in May 2004 (when ten states simultaneously acceded to membership), secondly in January 2007 (when the accessions of Bulgaria and Romania took effect), and most recently in July 2013 (with the accession of Croatia). These developments have brought about the situation where the Regulation on Insolvency Proceedings is currently applicable in 27 states, with the position of Denmark continuing unchanged in this respect.

The principal phases of the evolution of the EC insolvency project are set out below.

B. History of the Convention Project: Evolution of the Text

1.03 Over the period from 1960 to 1996 the Insolvency Convention project featured on the agenda of the institutions of the European Community/European Union, particularly the Commission and the Council. During those years, work advanced in various stages of irregular duration, interspersed by periods of almost total quiescence. As the work progressed, the evolving text bore a succession of different titles, as reflected in the following, abbreviated account. The most intense periods of activity may be broadly divided into two principal phases, of which the first can be subdivided into two parts. The first part of Phase I occurred in the years prior to February 1970, when a group of experts drawn from the original six Member

States,[3] convened by the European Commission, produced a text published as the Preliminary Draft Convention.[4] Following the accession of the first three additional Member States from 1 January 1973,[5] work was resumed on the basis of the 1970 text, with a view to its being adopted by all nine members. During this second part of Phase I, numerous modifications were made to the original text, partly as a reflection of the general thrust of critical comments published after 1970, and partly in response to particular concerns of the new participants in the negotiations. The essential features of the Preliminary Draft were nevertheless largely carried through into the Draft Convention submitted to the Council in April 1980 for further study and potential adoption.[6] However, sustained resistance on the part of several Member States resulted in the discreet abandonment of further attempts to promote the adoption of the 1980 Draft, although no formal announcement was made of this. Several years of inactivity and uncertainty ensued.

The initiative which resulted in a relaunching of the project was taken by the **1.04** Council of Ministers which, in May 1989 with the Community's membership already enlarged to 12 and soon destined to grow to 15,[7] established a new working party on the Bankruptcy Convention under the chairmanship of Dr Manfred Balz. Phase II was pursued with much vigour, and was also characterized by a greater openness in that the emerging versions of the text were given a considerable measure of publicity and exposure to informed comment, in marked contrast

---

[3] The original six members of the European Communities (including the Coal and Steel and Atomic Energy Communities, as well as the Economic Community) were Belgium, France, (West) Germany, Italy, Luxembourg, and the Netherlands.

[4] E Comm Doc 3.327/1/XIV/70–F, dated 16 February 1970. An explanatory report, known as the Noel-Lemontey Report, was published as E Comm Doc 16.775/XIV/70–F. English versions of both texts were later published under the same documentary reference numbers, but substituting the suffix-letter 'E' in place of 'F'. The English version of the text of the Preliminary Draft Convention was published as Appendix 10 to the Report of the Bankruptcy Convention Advisory Committee, in August 1976 (Cmnd 6602). The chairman of the Advisory Committee was Kenneth Cork. He, subsequently, as Sir Kenneth Cork, was chairman of the Insolvency Law Review Committee whose report, generally known as the Cork Report, was published in June 1982 (Cmnd 8558). To avoid confusion, the report of the Advisory Committee is sometimes referred to as the Cork Report No 1.

[5] Denmark, the Republic of Ireland, and the United Kingdom together joined the European Communities as of 1 January 1973. Norway, which had also negotiated terms of accession, resiled from taking up membership following a negative outcome of its national referendum held for that purpose.

[6] E Comm Doc III/D/72/80. The text of the Draft EEC Convention on Bankruptcy, Winding-up, Arrangements, Compositions, and Similar Proceedings was published in EC Bull Supp 2/82, together with a report by J Lemontey. The text was also published by the Department of Trade in April 1980 and is reproduced as Appendix C in Fletcher (n 2 above). See also [1981] OJ L391/23, for the Commission Opinion on its suitability for adoption.

[7] Greece became the tenth member of the EC in January 1981; Spain and Portugal joined in January 1986. A further three accessions took place in January 1993, when Austria, Finland, and Sweden became members of what had, by that time, become known as the European Union, in consequence of the coming into force of the Treaty on European Union (the Maastricht Treaty) of 7 February 1992: [1992] OJ C224/1.

to the prevailing taste for secrecy which had attended most of the developments during Phase I. One source of inspiration for those engaged upon the task of shaping the Phase II text was the recently concluded Istanbul Convention produced under the auspices of the Council of Europe, and opened for signature on 5 June 1990.[8] In addition to adapting some innovations of the Istanbul text, the working party resurrected certain features of the Phase I concept, while expunging or modifying others in the interests of achieving a more workable, and politically acceptable, Convention in terms of the existing realities among a community of 15 states whose domestic laws exhibited, then as now, numerous differences in matters concerning credit, security, and insolvency.

1.05 During the course of the working party's cycle of activity, the European Community officially transformed itself into the European Union (EU) following the ratification of the Treaty of Maastricht, and a further impetus was imparted to such unifying projects as the Convention on Insolvency Proceedings. At a meeting of the EU Council of Ministers on 25 September 1995 the finalized text of the Convention was tabled for approval and, if possible, immediate adoption. The more cautious—and in an EU context somewhat novel—course was taken of an 'initialling' of the text by all 15 Member States, thereby precluding any further negotiation or textual amendment. It was agreed that after a brief interval to allow governments to study this final version the Convention would be opened for signature for a limited period of six months, within which it would have to be signed by all the 15 states, as required by Article 220 of the Treaty of Rome, or otherwise lapse.[9]

1.06 This arrangement was carried into effect at a further meeting in Madrid on 23 November 1995, on which date 12 states signed the Convention.[10] Within the following months, two of the remaining three members—Ireland and the Netherlands—added their signatures. During that period, an approved and revised

---

[8] European Convention on Certain International Aspects of Bankruptcy, ETS No 136. This Convention is discussed in IF Fletcher, *Insolvency in Private International Law* (2nd edn, 2005), ch 6. The text of the Istanbul Convention is reproduced in ibid, app III. Having failed to attract the necessary minimum of three ratifications, the Convention has never entered into force.

[9] Insolvency Convention (1995), Art 49(2), (3) (see also section D below). Community Conventions under Art 220 ECT (as originally numbered; now numbered as Art 293 of the Consolidated EC Treaty) are negotiated by all existing members of the Community (now the EU) as at the time of their adoption, and require the ratification of all members in order to enter into force. Indeed, the Convention of 29 February 1968 on the Mutual Recognition of Companies has never entered into force, for want of the necessary complement of ratifications. Once a Convention is in force, a requirement is imposed upon states which subsequently join the Community/Union to negotiate their accession to it as soon as practicable, as one of the terms of membership. Article 50 of the Insolvency Convention (1995) confirmed this requirement.

[10] The 12 states which signed the EU Convention on the day it was opened for signature (23 November 1995) were: Austria, Belgium, Denmark, Finland, France, Germany, Greece, Italy, Luxembourg, Portugal, Spain, and Sweden. The text of the Convention as opened for signature is reproduced in IF Fletcher, *Insolvency in Private International Law* (1st edn, 1999) app II. See also (1996) 35 International Legal Materials 1223.

version of the Explanatory Report to the Convention was put into circulation, thereby overcoming one of the technical obstacles to acceptance of the text of the Convention that had been raised by some members of the Council at the session in September.[11] The state of uncertainty as to whether the United Kingdom would become a signatory before the expiry of the six-month time limit on 23 May 1996 was maintained by the terms of a Report of the House of Lords Select Committee on the European Communities dated 26 March 1996.[12] The Committee's concluding opinion and recommendation, while acknowledging the generally favourable views of many of those whose evidence it had received, nevertheless advocated a cautious approach, and the need for further study and consideration, before a final decision should be taken by the Government.[13] This proved to be ominous, and when the deadline for completion of signatures passed on 23 May, the signature of the United Kingdom remained outstanding for reasons which only subsequently became fully apparent.[14]

For some time, as already stated, the EU Insolvency Convention languished in an **1.07** uncertain limbo. When, in 1999, the project was revived in the form of a Regulation the substantive provisions of the Convention's text were incorporated with only a handful of alterations, other than essential drafting adjustments. For this reason, the evolution of the provisions during the successive phases of the Convention project—but especially during Phase II—is of more than merely historic interest. Indeed, in the absence of any official guide to the interpretation of the Regulation as finally enacted, the process by which the text of the Convention arrived at its concluded state in the autumn of 1995 merits careful study.

---

[11] The Report on the Convention on Insolvency Proceedings, prepared by Professor M Virgos and Mr E Schmit (hereafter in this book referred to as the 'Virgos-Schmit Report' and reproduced at app 2), was circulated as EU Council Doc 6500/96, DRS 8 (CFC), bearing the date 3 May 1996. It was not officially published, and remains unapproved by the Council, with the consequence that it is technically not of the status of *travaux préparatoires*, either in relation to the Convention itself or to those provisions of Regulation 1346/2000 which are directly derived from the Convention. It is nevertheless a valuable aid to understanding the intended meaning of those provisions. An earlier, English version of the Virgos-Schmit Report, bearing the reference coding 11900/1/95 REV 1, was published as Annexe B to a Consultative Document, *EC Convention on Insolvency Proceedings*, published in February 1996 by the Insolvency Service of the Department of Trade and Industry. The latter version should be regarded as having been superseded by the revised text of 3 May 1996. Many invaluable insights into the Convention's intended effects can be found in M Balz, 'The European Union Convention on Insolvency Proceedings' (1996) 70 American Bankruptcy LJ 485.

[12] *7th Report: Convention on Insolvency Proceedings* (HL Paper (1995–96) 59). The chairman of the Select Committee was Lord Hoffmann.

[13] ibid paras 35–42. The minutes of oral and written evidence supplied to the Select Committee are annexed to the Report, separately paginated (1–52).

[14] Although the pretext for non-signature by the United Kingdom in May 1996 was the disagreement between the United Kingdom and its EC partners over the agricultural crisis caused by the BSE epidemic, it subsequently transpired that the UK Government had concluded that the Convention's failure to make clear and unambiguous provision for its application to the colony of Gibraltar was an insurmountable obstacle to UK acceptance of the text. Regulation 1346/2000, as an Act of the EC Council, applies to Gibraltar under usual principles of Community law.

C. The Phase I Draft Convention (1960–1980): Principal Features

1.08 It might be supposed that, in the light of its subsequent abandonment, the Draft Convention that evolved over the years from 1960 to 1980 is primarily of historic interest. Nevertheless, it is as well that some account of its principal features, and also the reasons for its ultimate failure, should be recorded, partly to provide a better understanding of what was to transpire in Phase II of the project but also in the hope that the same errors will not be repeated in the course of some future project of this kind. A detailed analysis of the text will not be undertaken, however.[15]

1.09 The destiny of this first phase was effectively shaped by the circumstances under which the project began its life, during the early years of existence of the EEC itself. This was a period of rapid advance along the path towards European integration, with a Community of manageable size (consisting of the six founding members) being guided by a Commission whose zeal for the task entrusted to it was, for the first and perhaps only time in its history, matched by a generally favourable political climate across the Community.

---

[15] For detailed discussion of the Preliminary Draft Convention of 1970, see: J Noel and J Lemontey, 'Aperçus sur le projet de convention européenne relative à la faillite, aux concordats et aux procédures analogues' (1968) 4 Revue Trimestrielle de Droit Européen 703; A Hirsch, 'Vers l'universalité de la faillite au sein du marché commun?' (1970) Cahiers de Droit Européen 50; L Ganshof, 'L'élaboration d'un droit européen de la faillite dans le cadre de la CEE' (1971) Cahiers de Droit Européen 146; M Hunter, 'Draft Bankruptcy Convention of the European Economic Community' (1972) 21 ICLQ 682, and 'Draft EEC Bankruptcy Convention—A Further Examination' (1976) 25 ICLQ 310; KH Nadelmann, 'Common Market Bankruptcy Draft Convention—Foreign Assets and Related Problems' in *Conflict of Laws, International and Interstate* (1972) 340, and in (1970) Riv Dir Int Priv e Proc 501; the same author, 'Rehabilitating International Bankruptcy: Lessons Taught by Herstatt and Company' (1977) 52 NYULR 1, 27–32; K Lipstein, *The Law of the European Economic Community* (1974) 284; WC Hillman, 'An American Lawyer Looks at the Common Market Bankruptcy Convention' (1974) 48 American Bankruptcy LJ 369; J Lemontey, 'Perspectives d'unification du droit dans le projet de convention CEE relative à la faillite' (1975) Revue Trimestrielle de Droit Européen 172; J Noel, 'Lignes directrices du projet de convention CEE relative à la faillite' (1975) Revue Trimestrielle de Droit Européen 159; J Farrar, 'EEC Draft Convention on Bankruptcy and Winding Up' [1977] JBL 320; IF Fletcher, 'The Proposed Community Convention on Bankruptcy and Related Matters' in K Lipstein (ed), *Harmonisation of Private International Law by the EEC* (1978) 119 (also published in (1977) 2 EL Rev 15). From the UK perspective, the Report of the Bankruptcy Convention Advisory Committee (n 4 above) is of enduring value: see esp the 'Note of Reservations' by AE Anton at 105–28. For critical assessments of the 1980 version of the Draft Convention, see J Thieme, 'Der Entwurf eines Konkursübereinkommens der EG-Staaten von 1980' (1981) 45 Rabels Z 459; KH Nadelmann, 'A Reflection on Bankruptcy Jurisdiction: News from the European Economic Market, the United States and Canada' (1982) 27 McGill LJ 541; the same author, 'Bankruptcy Jurisdiction: News from the Common Market and a Reflection for Home Consumption' (1982) 56 American Bankruptcy LJ 65; IF Fletcher, *Conflict of Laws and European Community Law* (1982) ch 6 at 187–249; D Lasok and P Stone, *Conflict of Laws in the European Community* (1987) ch 10 at 397–413.

The committee of experts originally formed in July 1960 to undertake the task of   **1.10**
fulfilling the obligations imposed by Article 220 of the Treaty of Rome,[16] took an
early decision to regard insolvency and related matters as a special subject requiring
separate treatment. Thereafter, work continued towards the preparation of what
was to become the Brussels Convention of 27 September 1968 on Jurisdiction
and the Enforcement of Judgments in Civil and Commercial Matters, Article 1(2)
of which expressly declares that the Convention shall not apply to: 'bankruptcy,
proceedings relating to the winding-up of insolvent companies or other legal persons, judicial arrangements, compositions and analogous proceedings'. A parallel
group of experts drawn from the six Member States was therefore convened by the
Commission to develop a Bankruptcy Convention which, it was envisaged, would
complement the Brussels Convention and thereby accomplish the task of 'simplification of formalities governing the reciprocal recognition and enforcement of
judgments' mentioned in the fourth indent of Article 220.

Although it was accepted that the ultimate shape and content of the Bankruptcy   **1.11**
Convention would be determined by the special characteristics of its subject-
matter, the fundamental approach followed by the expert negotiators closely
matched that of the main, and faster-moving, project relating to civil and commercial judgments. In particular, the innovative approach embodied in the Brussels
Convention of superimposing a unitary set of rules of direct jurisdiction in place of
the variety of nationally evolved rules previously applied by the individual Member
States in relation to matters governed by the Convention, was emulated in the
terms of both of the Phase I versions of the Bankruptcy Draft as published in 1970
and in 1980 respectively.[17] Thus, the EEC Convention was conceived as a 'double',
or 'direct' Convention, a radical advance upon anything previously attempted in
the history of multilateral treaties in the field of bankruptcy.

Advocates of the use of a 'direct' type of Convention could legitimately emphasize   **1.12**
its suitability for use within a community of states pursuing an integrationist programme whose aims included the creation of an internal market based upon the
so-called 'four freedoms', namely the free circulation of persons, services, goods,
and capital. To attain this goal, it was necessary to address the problem of distor-
tion caused to the commercial and economic environment of the Community by
differences in the Member States' legislative and administrative provisions. In this
context, both the Brussels Convention and the proposed Bankruptcy Convention
could be viewed as having an important role to play in terms of providing for the
free circulation of judgments in a way that complements the freedoms expressly
established by the Treaty of Rome. By imposing uniform codes of rules for the
exercise of jurisdiction in international cases, the Conventions would enable
the recognition and enforcement of judgments and orders to become virtually

---

[16] See n 2 above.
[17] See 1970 Draft (n 4 above) Title II (Arts 3–17); 1980 Draft (n 6 above) Title II (Arts 3–16).

automatic processes, with minimal scope allowed for parties to challenge or resist at the enforcement stage. The Member States, and the courts and officials operating within them, would be obliged to give 'full faith and credit' to the legal determinations of equivalent institutions belonging to sister states.[18]

1.13 By opting for this more audacious, and dirigiste, model for the Bankruptcy Convention the negotiators simultaneously assumed a more exacting responsibility in the matter of the technical quality of the Convention's design. Under a 'direct' Convention, all interested parties are compelled to rely almost totally on the integrity of the legal process at the point where jurisdiction is first exercised: there is only a limited possibility to rectify any misapplication or misuse of the Convention's provisions, and the expense of doing so can be considerable. Not only must the rules for allocation of jurisdiction be intrinsically sound and sensible, but also they must be well drafted so that their meaning and effects are as clear and unambiguous as possible, in the interests of enabling parties to understand their legal position and arrange their affairs with adequate certainty.

1.14 Unfortunately, the jurisdictional provisions of both of the principal Phase I texts failed to match these exacting, but vital, requirements. What was proposed was a three-tier hierarchy of jurisdictional criteria linking the debtor to the territory of the state in which proceedings could be opened. The first rank was accorded to the contracting state in which the debtor's 'centre of administration' (*centre des affaires*) is situated, the courts of that state being declared to have 'exclusive jurisdiction to declare the debtor bankrupt'.[19] The second rank was intended to apply to situations where the debtor's centre of administration is not located in any of the contracting states. In that event, the courts of any contracting state in which the debtor has an establishment are awarded jurisdiction to declare the debtor bankrupt.[20] Thirdly, where neither the centre of administration nor any establishment is situated in a contracting state, an 'open season' is effectively declared by authorizing the courts of any contracting state whose law so permits to declare the debtor bankrupt. However, whereas the 1970 Draft would have allowed such bankruptcies to enjoy the full advantages of recognition and enforcement throughout the Community, the 1980 text was modified so as to exclude such bankruptcies from falling within the scope of the Convention.[21]

---

[18] The rationale behind the programme of legal harmonization of the EEC/EU, including the 'full faith and credit' concept in relation to civil and commercial judgments, is explored in Fletcher (n 2 above) in chs 1, 2, and 4. The application of these arguments to the area of bankruptcy is addressed in ibid, ch 6 at 187–94.

[19] See Art 3(1) of both the 1970 and 1980 versions of the Draft (the wording is identical).

[20] See Art 4(1) of both the 1970 and 1980 versions (the wording is again identical).

[21] See Art 5 in the respective versions of 1970 and 1980. It may be observed that the earlier text was apparently intended to duplicate the effect of Art 4 of the Brussels Convention of 27 September 1968 (in force from 1 February 1973). The Convention of 1968 was superseded, except as regards Denmark, as from 1 May 2004 by Council Regulation (EC) 44/2001—the Brussels Regulation. That Regulation in turn was superseded and repealed by Regulation (EU) 2015/2012 of 12 December 2012, OJ L351/1, 20 December 2012, which became applicable from 10 January

Even in this modified form, however, the proposed jurisdictional scheme was **1.15**
fraught with perils and uncertainties. Thus, as regards the primary criterion based
upon the location of the debtor's 'centre of administration', there was scope for
divergent approaches to be adopted by the courts of different states when applying
the concept to the facts of actual cases. Although each version of the Draft supplied
a definition of the expression as meaning 'the place where the debtor usually administers his main interests', this merely raises a whole series of further questions.[22]
Similarly, with the secondary tier of jurisdictional competence, based upon the
presence of an establishment, the Draft failed to meet the requirement that it
should embody sensible principles, and above all that it should respect the need for
certainty. The 1970 Draft did not contain any definition of 'establishment', while
the 1980 text merely offered the inadequate pronouncement that 'an establishment
exists in a place where an activity of the debtor comprising a series of transactions
is carried on by him or on his behalf'.[23] Given that this could result in the courts
of several contracting states having concurrent jurisdiction, the sensitive issue of
priority demands a carefully designed rule to promote the fairest and most efficient
solution, rather than one which rewards pre-emptive tactics on a 'winner takes all'
basis. Sadly, the Phase I Drafts promised no such outcome. Instead of a qualitative
test to determine the most appropriate forum, purely mechanical rules were proposed which would have awarded Community-wide supremacy to the proceedings
which were chronologically the first to open.[24] Worse yet—and surely the height
of absurdity as a rule for adoption by a Community of supposedly sophisticated
states—was the 'tie-breaking' provision for cases where proceedings were commenced on the same day in different courts having co-ordinate jurisdiction: it was

---

2015. In both the Brussels Convention and the successive versions of the Brussels Regulation,
Art 4 controversially allows the courts of contracting (or Member) states to deploy their full
repertoire of domestic rules of jurisdiction—including those of an exorbitant nature—against
those defendants in civil or commercial proceedings who happen not to be domiciled in any of
the contracting/Member states. Judgments in such cases are nevertheless accorded the benefit of
full faith and credit throughout the EC/EU territorial area. For trenchant criticism of this aspect
of the original Brussels Convention see eg KH Nadelmann 'Jurisdictionally Improper Fora in
Treaties on Recognition of Judgments: The Common Market Draft' (1967) 67 Columbia L 995;
'The Outer World and the Common Market Experts' Draft of a Convention on Recognition of
Judgments' (1967–68) 5 CML Rev 409; and 'The Common Market Judgments Convention and a
Hague Conference Recommendation: What Steps Next?' (1968) 82 Harvard L Rev 1282; P Hay
'The Common Market Preliminary Draft Convention on the Recognition and Enforcement of
Judgments: Some Considerations of Policy and Interpretation' (1968) 16 AJCL 149, esp at 160–2.

[22] See Art 3(2) of the 1970 Draft; cf Art 3(2) and (3) of the 1980 Draft. Although both versions
embody a rebuttable presumption, in the case of firms, companies, and legal persons, that the registered office is the place where the debtor's main interests are usually administered, the manner
of rebutting this presumption, and the degree of proof needed, are left uncertain. Given the scope
for different views regarding what amount to a debtor's 'main' interests, the potential instability
of this basis of jurisdiction was disturbing. See also the various approaches offered by Arts 6 and 7
of the 1970 and 1980 Drafts respectively for cases where there has been a transfer of the centre of
administration.

[23] See Art 4(2) of the 1980 Draft.

[24] See Arts 15(2) and 52(1) of the 1970 Draft; Arts 13(2) and 58(1) of the 1980 Draft.

solemnly proposed that precedence should be determined by the alphabetical order of the place names of the courts concerned![25]

1.16 The shortcomings of the jurisdictional rules of the Phase I Drafts were compounded by the unsuccessful attempt to simulate the embodiment of the twin principles of unity and universality of bankruptcy, and to misrepresent the degree to which they had genuinely been absorbed into the substance of the provisions to which the contracting states would be committing themselves.[26] If the proclamations within the texts themselves were taken at face value, proceedings opened according to the primary or secondary rules of jurisdiction would constitute the sole proceedings permitted to take place throughout the contracting states, and would have automatic effect in relation to the debtor's property anywhere within those states. By virtue of the choice of law rules within the Draft Convention, whose effect is generally to require the application of the law of the state in which proceedings are opened (the *lex concursus*) for most purposes associated with the proceedings and the administration and distribution of the estate,[27] it ought to follow that the rights of all creditors—secured or unsecured; preferential or non-preferential—would be determined by the provisions of the *lex concursus*. In reality, the negotiators arranged matters somewhat differently, so that the rights of secured and preferential creditors belonging to any of the contracting states could continue to be governed by the law of the *situs* of any secured property, and by the local law of the state under which a creditor's preferential status, and its relative ranking, was generated.[28] The negotiators had discovered at an early stage of their deliberations that the existing domestic laws of the original six Member States of the EEC differed from one another so fundamentally in such matters as their treatment of security, and the rights of preferential creditors, that it was impractical to attempt an alignment and harmonization of substantive laws for the foreseeable future.[29] However, the very same reasons which made it politically unacceptable for the Member States to abandon deeply embedded national traditions towards the treatment of these issues, made it equally unthinkable for any of them to accept the subordination of the rights and expectations of its own, local creditors to the regime of the *lex concursus*, where this happened to be that of some other state.

1.17 The theoretically elegant precepts of the scheme based upon unity and universality therefore yielded to the political imperatives of the shared desire on the part of the

---

[25] See Art 52(2) of the 1970 Draft; Art 58(2) of the 1980 Draft.

[26] See Art 2 (both Drafts), which bears the heading: *Unity of the Bankruptcy*, and Art 33 of the 1970 Draft and Art 34 of the 1980 Draft, both headed *Universality of the Bankruptcy*. For discussion of the two principles of unity and universality, see Fletcher (n 8 above) ch 1 esp at paras 1.11–1.13.

[27] See Arts 17, 18, 19, 20–22, 28, 30, and 32 of the 1970 Draft; Arts 15, 17, 18, 20–22, 29, 31, and 33 of the 1980 Draft.

[28] See Section VI of each of the two Drafts: Arts 40–46 of the 1970 Draft; Arts 43–52 of the 1980 Draft.

[29] See a comparative survey by Professor M Sauveplanne, published in October 1963 as EEC Commission Doc 8838/IV/63–E.

participating states to defend local practices in matters of the preferential treatment of certain types of claim in the process of distribution in an insolvency. This was achieved by means of an inelegant, and cumbersome, arrangement whereby the existence and ranking of preferential rights would be determined by the law of each contracting state under which a creditor was eligible to invoke such personal advantage, but only with respect to such assets as were actually situated in that state on the day when the bankruptcy opened.[30] This would have entailed the creation of a series of sub-estates, for accounting purposes, formed from each pool of assets realized in each of the states concerned. The sheer complexity of the exercise was truly horrifying, and would have resulted in much wasteful expenditure of administrative resources.

Even less palatable, however, was the cynical proposal for the manner of dealing **1.18** with any assets recovered in non-contracting states, and with the claims of creditors from outside the frontiers of the European Community. Here, and here alone, the full rigours of the principles of unity and universality were to be applied, so that assets recovered from third states were to be amalgamated with those located in the *forum concursus* itself, and were likewise to be distributed in accordance with the rules contained in the *lex concursus*. It is surely distasteful, and also embarrassing, to have to acknowledge that such blatantly discriminatory treatment was considered by the authors of the successive versions of the Phase I Draft Convention to be an acceptable approach to the regulation of international insolvency, and was intended to be collectively embraced by an alliance of powerful, but not omnipotent, economically advanced states. Yet such was indeed the case, as the documentary evidence reveals. Fortunately, in the years after 1980, the tide of opposition to this fatally flawed, meretricious, and unworkable Draft gradually grew stronger, and it was consigned to oblivion.

D. Phase II: The Convention on Insolvency Proceedings (1995) and its Relationship to the Original Regulation ('OR') (2000)

As mentioned in section B above, the committee of experts convened by the **1.19** Council in 1989 to relaunch the project for a Bankruptcy Convention[31] adopted an eclectic approach in going about its task. Drawing together the more satisfactory elements from the two models closest to hand—the Phase I Draft EC Convention and the Istanbul Convention which was opened for signature on 5 June 1990—the

---

[30] See Arts 40–46 of the 1970 Draft; Arts 42–52 of the 1980 Draft.
[31] Throughout this section the expression 'the Convention' denotes the European Union Convention on Insolvency Proceedings, opened for signature in Madrid on 23 November 1995 and signed by 14 of the 15 Member States (the exception being the United Kingdom) between that date and 23 May 1996, when the period permitted for signature expired (see paras 1.02 and 1.05–1.06 above).

committee sought to combine these with fresh elements of its own devising. It also appears to have been guided by a strong instinct to provide a workable set of rules that respond to issues actually encountered in practice, rather than to pursue some impossible and almost abstract theory about the way in which to legislate for the problems of international insolvency. The finished text produced by the Balz committee is one which, while by no means devoid of imperfections, has many positive virtues which under normal circumstances would have ensured its implementation by all members of the European Union. Fortunately, despite the unfortunate further setback experienced between 1995 and 1999,[32] the product of the committee's labour was retrieved from limbo and the Convention's substantive provisions were implanted into the text of Regulation 1346/2000. Those provisions will be examined in detail in the subsequent chapters of this work. This account of the history of the project will conclude with a summary of the structure and main features of the Convention as agreed and initialled by all the Member States in November 1995, followed by a brief chronicle of events subsequent to the entry into force of the Regulation itself..

1.20 The finalized text of the Convention consisted of a total of 55 Articles, arranged into six chapters of varying length, together with three Annexes. It was self-evidently the product of an assessment on the part of the committee that there were minimal prospects in the foreseeable future of achieving any fundamental harmonization of the domestic laws of the 15 EU Member States in relation to credit, security, or insolvency matters. That being the case, the most important requirement in the context of the EU internal market was to establish clear rules to determine in which states insolvency proceedings are capable of being commenced, and what choice of law rules are to be applied in those proceedings in relation to the crucial issues typically to be encountered in a cross-border case. In that way, parties can arrange their affairs, and structure their business transactions, on the basis of reasonably dependable predictions concerning the substantive law by which their rights will be governed. The Convention therefore adopted the same strategic approach as the Phase I models, in that it was a 'direct' or 'double' Convention whose effect was to impose a uniform set of jurisdictional rules which must be applied in all the contracting states in cases falling within the ambit of its provisions.[33]

1.21 Having laid the ground rules for jurisdiction and choice of law,[34] the Convention addressed the practical concerns of the office-holder who is responsible for administering the insolvency proceedings (referred to throughout as 'the liquidator'),[35] by provisions for recognition of the proceedings and for enabling the exercise of the

---

[32] See paras 1.02 and 1.04–1.07 above.
[33] See Art 3 of the Convention, further discussed at paras 3.09 et seq below. This contrasts with the Istanbul Convention (n 8 above), which is an 'indirect' Convention containing rules for recognition and enforcement only.
[34] Choice of law rules are contained in Arts 4–15 inclusive, and are discussed in ch 4 below.
[35] Art 2(b) of the Convention.

liquidator's powers in other contracting states.[36] The concerns of creditors involved in a multi-jurisdictional insolvency were also taken into account in various ways, including simplification of the procedure for proving their claims.[37] The special facility under Chapter III to enable secondary proceedings to be opened, with effects restricted to the territory of a single contracting state, offered important advantages for certain types of creditors.[38] Lastly, to ensure that the Convention received a unified interpretation from the outset, provision was made in Chapter V for the European Court of Justice to have jurisdiction to deliver interpretative rulings concerning the Convention and its various Annexes.[39]

From Convention to Regulation

In the transformation from Convention to Regulation, Chapters I to IV inclusive, **1.22** comprising Articles 1 to 42, were directly transposed (with only two specific, albeit significant, exceptions),[40] but with drafting adaptations throughout the text to reflect the altered nature of the legal instrument itself.[41] As an EC legislative act, the Regulation did not need to contain any express provisions relating to its interpretation by the European Court of Justice, and therefore the whole of Chapter V of the Convention was discarded. The concluding chapter of the text, 'Transitional and Final Provisions' (numbered as Chapter VI in the Convention and there comprising Articles 47 to 55) reappears as Chapter V of the Regulation (comprising Articles 43 to 47). Several of the former provisions were only relevant to an instrument in the form of a Convention, and were accordingly omitted from Chapter V of the Regulation. The three Annexes, labelled as A, B, and C, were retained intact in the Regulation as enacted in May 2000, save for the omission of references to Denmark and its legal institutions, and with some rephrasing of the listings of national procedures, reflecting developments during the interval between 1995 and 2000.[42]

---

[36] See Ch II of the Convention (Arts 16–26 inclusive).

[37] Ch IV of the Convention (Arts 39–42 inclusive).

[38] See Arts 27–38 inclusive.

[39] See Arts 43–46 inclusive.

[40] Art 5 was amended by inserting additional wording to indicate that the expression 'rights in rem' includes security effected in relation to 'both specific assets and collections of indefinite assets as a whole which change from time to time'. This amendment, proposed by the United Kingdom, was intended to ensure that the provisions in Art 5 are applicable to floating charges and to such security devices as fixed charges granted over receivables. The wording of Art 42 was amended at the request of Belgium, to accommodate the fact that the state has two official languages. The amendment makes it clear that a creditor is only required to provide a translation of his claim into one of the official languages of such a state.

[41] In addition to the replacement of references to 'this Convention' with 'this Regulation', references to 'the contracting states' (etc) throughout the text are replaced with references to 'the Member States' (etc).

[42] In the case of Austria, in comparison to the Convention, one procedure was eliminated from the entry in Annexe A, relating to insolvency proceedings referred to in Art 2(a) of the Regulation. In the cases of Belgium, the Netherlands, and Sweden, an additional procedure was included in each state's listing in Annexe A of the Regulation. In the case of the United Kingdom, the entry in Annexe A of the Regulation no longer makes express mention of the administration of the

1.23 There is one conspicuous contrast between the Convention and the Regulation which requires special comment. This concerns the elaborate series of numbered 'Recitals' (numbering 33 in all) which are placed at the beginning of the text of the Regulation. By contrast, the substantive Articles of the Convention of 1995 were preceded by a short Preamble, containing four unnumbered and somewhat routine paragraphs declaring the motivation and purposes which were to have supplied the basis for the Convention. The purpose of the extended sequence of Recitals to the Regulation is to furnish assistance in its interpretation by national courts, and by the European Court of Justice. Having apparently determined that it was contrary to settled practice to generate an officially sanctioned 'Explanatory Report' to a Community Act in the form of a Regulation, the EC Council perceived that it was nevertheless desirable to furnish some aids to construction and application of its substantive provisions. This was achieved by extracting a number of propositions from the Virgos-Schmit Report[43] and placing them alongside freshly composed material, so as to provide explanatory statements about certain aspects of the Regulation and its underlying objectives. This has resulted in a somewhat uneven and selective set of guiding statements, which can be employed in the familiar process of 'purposive' interpretation of Community legal instruments.[44] Numerous issues will doubtless arise in practice for which the Recitals offer no clear guidance, thus leaving the Court to formulate its solution in accordance with what it perceives to be the most constructive way of attaining the overall goals mentioned in the Recitals.

E. The Regulation in Force (31 May 2002)

Post-2002 developments

1.24 Since the Regulation entered into force on 31 May 2002 there have been several developments necessitating amendments to the original text. Some of these amendments have been effected on the initiative of one or more of the participating Member States in order to ensure that the provisions of the Regulation are aligned with the current provisions and terminology utilized in the insolvency laws of the states concerned. Internal revisions to domestic insolvency procedures may necessitate amendments to the entries listed in Annexes A, B, or C of the Regulation

---

insolvent estate of a deceased person in England and Wales or in Northern Ireland (or its Scottish equivalent— Administration by a Judicial Factor), but the omission was apparently effected on the basis that such proceedings are included within the references to 'Bankruptcy' (England and Wales, Northern Ireland) and 'Sequestration' (Scotland). On the other hand, the UK entry in Annexe A of the Regulation expressly refers to 'Winding up … subject to the supervision of the court', which is a procedure still available under the law of Gibraltar, although it was abolished within the United Kingdom by the legislative reforms of 1985–86.

[43] See n 11 above.

[44] Issues of interpretation of the Regulation are discussed in ch 2 below.

under the name of that state. Such amendments can be made using the procedure specifically established by Article 45 for amending the Annexes by qualified majority vote of the Council. That procedure was used for the first time on 12 April 2005.[45] Further instances of use of the amending procedure under Article 45 occurred on 27 April 2006,[46] on 13 June 2007,[47] 24 July 2008,[48] 25 February 2010,[49] 9 June 2011,[50] and 5 June 2014.[51] On each occasion since 2006 the convenient practice has been adopted of replacing the entire texts of all three Annexes so as to provide a consolidated version of the text of each one, as in force from the date on which the amending Regulation took effect. As future amendments may be made to the Annexes using the same procedure, care should be taken to consult the most recent version of the text.

Separately from the above amendments made using the in-built procedure of Article 45, the Regulation on Insolvency Proceedings has undergone additional amendments in consequence of the successive enlargements to the membership of the European Union that took effect in 2004, 2007, and 2013 respectively.[52] In each instance, under the terms of the relevant Treaty and Act of Accession the newly joining Member States became fully subject to all existing provisions of Community legislation (the so-called *acquis communautaire*), including Regulation 1346/2000. Accordingly, special provisions were made in or pursuant to the Acts of Accession in each instance to amend the Regulation so that Annexes A, B, and C would include references to the relevant types of insolvency and winding-up proceedings, and also to the relevant types of office-holders under those proceedings, **1.25**

---

[45] Council Regulation (EC) 603/2005 [2005] OJ L100/1 effective from 21 April 2005. Among the amendments made were changes to the entries for the United Kingdom in Annexes A and B (where the words 'including appointments made by filing prescribed documents with the court' were inserted in the references to administration, so as to reflect the amendments to the administration procedure made by the Enterprise Act 2002), and also to Annex C (where the office of provisional liquidator was added to the list of office holders fulfilling the definition of 'liquidator' for the purposes of Art 2(b)). The latter addition appears to have been prompted by the example of the proceedings before the Irish courts, and ultimately the ECJ, during 2004 in *Re Eurofood IFSC Ltd* [2004] BCC 383 (Irish High Court), in which the significance of the inclusion of the office of provisional liquidator in the equivalent entry for Ireland in Annex C became strongly apparent. This point was also a material factor in the subsequent ruling by the ECJ in its judgment dated 2 May 2006 in which the expression 'decision to open insolvency proceedings' for the purposes of Art 16(1) of the Regulation was construed as including a decision involving 'divestment of the debtor and the appointment of a liquidator referred to in Annex C to the Regulation': Case C-341/04 *Re Eurofood IFSC Ltd* [2006] ECR I-3813, at para 54 of the judgment.
[46] Council Regulation (EC) 694/2006 [2006] OJ L121/1 effective from 7 May 2006.
[47] Council Regulation (EC) 681/2007 [2007] OJ L159/1 effective from 21 June 2007.
[48] Council Regulation (EC) 788/2008 [2008] OJ L 213/1 effective from 9 August 2008.
[49] Implementing Regulation of the Council (EU) 210/2010 [2010] OJ L65/1 effective from 2 April 2010.
[50] Council Implementing Regulation (EU) 583/2011 [2011] OJ L160/52 effective from 8 July 2011.
[51] Council Implementing Regulation (EU) 663/2014, [2014] OJ L179/4 effective from 9 July 2014. This text has been incorporated into the text of the Regulation as reproduced in app 1.
[52] See para 1.02 above.

for each new Member State as of the date of entry.[53] The amending provisions also imported additional paragraphs into Article 44(1) of the Regulation to incorporate references to existing conventions to which any of the new Member States was a party, and whose effects were replaced by those of the Regulation in respect of proceedings opened after its entry into force for the state in question.

F. Revision of the Regulation (2012–2015)

1.26 The need for a systematic review and revision of the Regulation was foreseen by its Article 46, which imposes a duty on the Commission to initiate a process whereby reports on the application of the Regulation are to be presented to the European Parliament, Council, and Economic and Social Committee, 'accompanied if need be by a proposal for adaptation of the Regulation'. The first such report was required to be presented 'no later than 1 June 2012, and every five years thereafter'. In preparation for the drawing up of the first report, preliminary consultations and specially commissioned studies were commenced by the Commission in 2011. These were given added impetus by an initiative of the European Parliament resulting in the publication in June 2011 of a Report on insolvency proceedings in the context of EU company law together with recommendations to the Commission.[54] On 12 December 2012 the Commission unveiled its formal response to the duty

---

[53] (a) The following ten states joined the EU with effect from 1 May 2004: Cyprus; Czech Republic; Estonia; Hungary; Latvia; Lithuania; Malta; Poland; Slovakia; and Slovenia. In the Treaty and Act of Accession signed in Athens on 16 April 2003, amendments to Regulation 1346/2000 are made by s 18A of Annex 2 to the Act of Accession, under the heading 'Cooperation in the fields of justice and home affairs': [2003] OJ L236/711–13.

(b) Bulgaria and Romania joined the EU with effect from 1 January 2007. In the Treaty and Act of Accession signed in Luxembourg on 25 April 2005 provision was made in Art 56 of the Act of Accession for the amendment of a large number of elements of EC legislation, including Regulation 1346/2000, by means of further Regulations. This was accomplished through Council Regulation (EC) 1791/2006 [2006] OJ L363/1, Annex 11A ('Judicial Cooperation in Civil and Commercial Matters'). Amendments were made to Art 44(1) of the Regulation on Insolvency Proceedings, and to Annexes A, B, and C thereto, with effect from 1 January 2007 (Art 2).

(c) Croatia joined the EU with effect from 1 July 2013: Treaty and Act of Accession of the Republic of Croatia, Brussels 7 November 2011, Art 3(3). Consequential amendments to Annexes A, B and, C of Regulation 1346/2000 were made by Council Regulation (EU) 517/2013 of 13 May 2013, Art 1(1)(k) together with Section 13.A.1 of the Annex thereto.

[54] European Parliament, Committee on Legal Affairs, Report with Recommendations to the Commission on Insolvency Proceedings in the Context of EU Company Law ('the Lehne Report'), with Motion for a Resolution of the Parliament (6 June 2011, 2011/2006(INI, PE467.008v02-00). In the motion the Parliament confirms 'that the recommendations respect the principle of subsidiarity and the fundamental rights of citizens'. For all related documents, see <http://www.europarl.europa.eu/sides/getDoc.do?type=REPORT&reference=A7-2011-0355&format=XML&language=EN> (accessed 17 December 2015).

See also the Report published by INSOL Europe in May 2012, *Revision of the European Insolvency Regulation, Proposals by INSOL Europe* (Drafting Committee Chairman, Robert van Galen).

imposed under Article 46 by publishing a proposal for a Regulation amending Council Regulation 1346/2000,[55] to which the Parliament responded on 20 December 2013 with a Report containing numerous proposed amendments to the Commission's earlier text.[56] The Parliament voted on 5 February 2014 to adopt its own Legal Affairs Committee's proposed amendments to the Commission's proposals.[57] A process of inter-institutional negotiations then ensued, involving the Parliament, the Council, and the Commission, resulting in a declaration by the Council following its meeting on 5 and 6 June 2014 that agreement had been reached on a 'general approach on the proposal for a regulation amending the existing Council Regulation (1346/2000) on insolvency proceedings'.[58]

An important milestone was attained on Thursday 4 December 2014, when the   **1.27** Council of Justice Ministers adopted a political agreement on the renewed text of the Insolvency Regulation as agreed with the European Parliament.[59] In preparation for the formal adoption of the Regulation a further series of steps took place. First, translations into all the Member States' official languages had to be made, with only technical/linguistic changes to be permitted (ie no changes of substance). The Council then formally adopted this text on 12 March 2015 as its 'first reading position' with a view to its being adopted in turn by the European Parliament (both at committee and plenary level).[60] The process was taken forward at meetings of the Parliament's Legal Affairs Committee, and subsequently at a plenary session of the Parliament itself, on 7 and 20 May 2015 respectively.[61]

---

[55] European Commission, Proposal for a Regulation of the European Parliament and of the Council amending Council Regulation (EC) No 1346/2000 on Insolvency Proceedings, Strasbourg 12 December 2012, COM(2012) 744 final, 2012/0360 (COD).

[56] Report by the European Parliament's Committee of Legal Affairs on the Commission's Proposal for a Regulation amending Council Regulation 1346/2000, reference PE 519.449v02-00; RR\1014200EN.doc, An earlier, Draft Report, was published on 11 September 2013: PE519. 445v01-00.

[57] Legislative resolution adopted by the Parliament as text P7_TA(2014) 0093. See the Europa website at <http://www.europarl.europa.eu/sides/getDoc.do?pubRef=-//EP//TEXT+TA+P7-TA-2014-0093+0+DOC+XML+V0//EN&language=EN> (accessed 17 December 2015).

[58] Press release of the Council of the EU (Provisional Version) 10578/14 (OR.en), PRESSE 328; PRCO 31, on the 3319th Council Meeting—Justice and Home Affairs, Luxembourg, 5 and 6 June 2014, p 3.

[59] The document which formed the basis of the Council's decision at its meeting on 4 December 2014 bears the date Brussels, 20 November 2014, and the reference information Interinstitutional File: 2012/0360/COD; 15414/14, ADD 1; JUSTCIV 285, EJUSTICE 109, CODEC 2225. The document can be viewed at <http://register.consilium.europa.eu/doc/srv?l=EN&f=ST% 2015414%202014%20ADD%201> (accessed 17 December 2015).

[60] The text of the recast Insolvency Regulation as approved by the Council at first reading on 12 March 2015 is published in the EU Official Journal, C series as Position (EU) No 7/2015 of the Council, OJ C 141/1, 28 April 2015.

[61] European Parliament legislative resolution of 20 May 2015 on the Council position at first reading with a view to the adoption of a regulation of the European Parliament and of the Council on insolvency proceedings (recast) (16636/5/2014 – C8-0090/2015 – 2012/0360(COD)) (Ordinary legislative procedure: second reading), viewable on the Europa website at <http://www.europarl. europa.eu/sides/getDoc.do?pubRef=-//EP//TEXT+TA+P8-TA-2015-0203+0+DOC+XML+V0// EN&language=EN> (accessed 17 December 2015).

Both meetings endorsed a proposal that the 'first reading position' of the Council should be adopted, thereby obviating the need for the Council to undertake a second reading and enabling the process of adoption of the revised Regulation to be concluded by the formal act of signing by the respective Presidents of the Parliament and of the Council, which duly took place on the same day, namely 20 May 2015. The recast Regulation was subsequently published in the Official Journal 'L' series on 5 June 2015 as Regulation (EU) 2015/848 and, in accordance with Article 92, entered into force 20 days afterwards on 26 June 2015.[62] However, as further stated in Article 92, the Regulation will only enter into *application* 24 months after its entry into force. Thus the European Insolvency Regulation in its amended form (hereafter referred to as 'RR') will begin to apply to insolvency proceedings opened after 26 June 2017.[63] On that date, the original Regulation 1346/2000 will be repealed in its entirety and will cease to have effect, but in the meanwhile it will continue in force and be applicable to insolvency proceedings which fall within its scope and which have been opened before 26 June 2017.[64]

G. The Recast Insolvency Regulation 2015 ('RR')

1.28 The recast Regulation of 20 May 2015 represents an evolutionary development, based on the foundations of the original Regulation of 29 May 2000 which it will fully replace with effect from 26 June 2017 onwards. While the core principles on which the original Regulation was based have been maintained, the opportunity has been taken to adjust and refine their application, and important additional content has been added. The net effect is to lengthen the text by a considerable amount: the RR comprises 89 initial Recitals (in place of the original 33) and 92 Articles (in place of the original 47). The three Annexes, A, B, and C, which completed the original Regulation have been reduced to two—now lettered as A and B—but this reduction is compensated for by the inclusion of two new Annexes, lettered as C and D, which provide useful information. Annex C lists the official citations of the original Regulation and all successive amendments to it, all of which are repealed as from the effective date of the recast Regulation. Annex D supplies a correlation table to enable comparisons to be made with provisions of the original Regulation, where these are recycled in the RR, as well as indicating those provisions which are completely new. While the provisions of the original Regulation will continue to apply to cases commenced prior to 26 June

---

[62] Regulation (EU) 2015/848 of the European Parliament and of the Council of 20 May 2015 on Insolvency Proceedings (recast), OJ L141/19, 5 June 2015, viewable at: <http://eur-lex.europa.eu/legal-content/EN/TXT/?uri=uriserv:OJ.L_.2015.141.01.0019.01.ENG> (accessed 17 December 2015).

[63] Art 84(1) of the RR.

[64] Arts 84(2) and 91 of the RR.

2015, the provisions of the RR which will become applicable automatically on and after that date must begin to be taken into account in anticipating the potential consequences of an insolvency capable of occurring at a time when the recast Regulation will be applicable. The relevant changes, as they will affect the matters dealt with in the successive chapters of this book, are explained in a concluding section to each chapter.

2

THE INSOLVENCY REGULATION AS AN EU LEGAL INSTRUMENT

A. Introduction

The Insolvency Regulation is a European Union legal instrument. More particularly, it is a form of EU subordinate legislation made under the Treaty on the Functioning of the European Union ('TFEU').[1] As such, its meaning and effects in national law are a matter for EU law. This is because of the doctrine of the supremacy of EU law over national law.[2] In particular, in ascribing meaning, or giving effect, to an EU legal instrument, an English court must do so in accordance with the principles laid down by the European Court of Justice.[3] Accordingly, **2.01**

---

[1] Following the coming into force of the Lisbon Treaty on 1 December 2009, the EC Treaty was amended, re-ordered, re-numbered, and re-named the Treaty on the Functioning of the European Union. The EU also replaced the European Community. There are three principal forms of legislation: Regulations, Directives, and Decisions. See Art 288 TFEU. In addition, the EU's institutions are able to adopt recommendations and opinions.

[2] See, generally, as a matter of EU law, Case 6/64 *Costa v ENEL* [1964] ECR 585; and, as a matter of English law, s 2 of the European Communities Act 1972.

[3] See s 3 of the European Communities Act 1972 and *HP Bulmer v Bollinger* [1974] Ch 401, 425 per Lord Denning MR. Since the coming into force of the Lisbon Treaty and the re-naming of the Court of First Instance as the General Court, the Court of Justice of the European Union is often referred to as 'CJEU', and the acronym 'ECJ' often (but not always) used as a collective term for the CJEU, the General Court, and the Civil Service Tribunal. In this chapter the terms 'CJEU' and 'European Court of Justice' are used interchangeably for the Court of Justice of the European Union.

the purpose of this chapter is to set out the particular legal attributes which the Insolvency Regulation has as an EU measure, and to describe the way in which it is to be understood as a matter of EU law. It also sets out the legal mechanisms established by the EU whereby solutions to questions of validity and interpretation may be obtained.

2.02   The OR itself was adopted under what were then Articles 61(c) and 67(1) of the EC Treaty,[4] on the initiatives of Germany and Finland. Articles 61(c) and 67(1) themselves formed part of Title IV of what was then the EC Treaty.[5] This Title was concerned with the progressive establishment of 'an area of freedom, security and justice'. On 20 May 2015, the European Parliament and Council adopted an amended and recast Insolvency Regulation (RR), this time under Article 81 TFEU (ex Article 65 EC) and in accordance with the ordinary legislative procedure laid down by Article 294 TFEU.[6] The term 'recast' is an EU legislative term of art: it refers to the adoption of a new legal act which incorporates in a single text both the substantive amendments made to an earlier act and the unchanged provisions of that act, which is repealed.[7]

2.03   That the OR was adopted under Articles 61(c) and 67(1), and their subsequent amendment and repeal by the Treaty of Lisbon, is not merely of background interest. It both governs the legal effect and affects the meaning and interpretation of the Regulation. This is also true, *mutatis mutandis*, of the RR and Article 81 TFEU. As the RR, with limited exceptions, does not apply for two years following its coming into force on 26 June 2015,[8] this chapter refers to both the OR and the RR. Where there is no relevant distinction to be made between the two instruments or the relevant Article under consideration, it refers to both as 'the Insolvency Regulation'.

2.04   The TFEU provisions, on the basis of which the Insolvency Regulation was adopted, govern its legal effect in a number of ways. First, they provide the legal basis for the Regulation's adoption by the EU. In the absence of a proper legal basis as provided by the Treaty, the measure would have been invalid. This is because the EU does not have any general competence to legislate, but only particular competences as

---

[4]   See the preamble to the Regulation. However, the Lisbon Treaty substituted a new Art 67 for ex Art 61 EC and repealed ex Art 67 EC, creating a new Title IV with the heading 'Area of Freedom, Security and Justice'. New Title IV includes a new Chapter 3, concerning 'Judicial Cooperation in Civil Matters' and it was under this chapter that the recast Insolvency Regulation was adopted.

[5]   As explained above, old Title IV has now been abolished.

[6]   This was on the initiative of the Commission in the ordinary way.

[7]   This is further set out and explained in an inter-institutional agreement between the European Parliament, the Council, and the Commission dated 28 November 2001 and published in [2002] OJ C77 of 28 March 2002.

[8]   Art 92. The RR was published in the OJ on 5 June 2015, came into force on the twentieth day following publication ie on 26 June and, with limited exceptions, applies from 26 June 2017. See also Art 84(2) which provides that the OR is to continue to apply to insolvency proceedings opened before 26 June 2017.

provided by the governing treaties.[9] Second, by a combination of Article 69 EC[10] and Article 2 of the Protocol on the position of the United Kingdom and Ireland (Protocol 21) annexed to the EC Treaty (and now to the TFEU), measures adopted under Article 61(c) EC (and now Article 81 TFEU) did (and do) not apply to the United Kingdom or Ireland unless these states, in accordance with Articles 3 and 4 of the Protocol, either notify the President of the Council that they wish to participate in its adoption or that they wish to accept the measure. The Insolvency Regulation is binding on the United Kingdom by reason of the fact that the United Kingdom notified its intention to take part in its adoption.[11] Third, neither Article 61(c) nor Article 67(1) EC (nor Article 81 TFEU) prescribed the form that measures adopted pursuant to them had to take. Accordingly, by Article 5 EC (Article 5 TFEU), the Community (and the EU) had to satisfy itself that in adopting the Regulation it was acting both consistently with the principle of subsidiarity and proportionately.[12] If it had not, in theory the Insolvency Regulation was capable of being challenged as being in breach of the EC Treaty (now TFEU) and general principles of Community law.[13] Finally, Article 67(1) EC (Article 81(2) TFEU) prescribed the legislative process that had to be followed for the measure's valid adoption.

The Treaty Articles affect the Insolvency Regulation's meaning and interpretation **2.05** in three principal ways. The first is that they provide the purposive framework within which the Regulation is to be interpreted. This is significant because, as further described below,[14] the Regulation, in accordance with the usual rules of EU law construction, is to be construed purposively. Moreover, this purpose is to be established, in part, by reference to the Community aims as set out in the

---

[9] Title I of Part 1 of the TFEU (Arts 2 to 6) now sets out the categories and areas of competence of the EU. This conferral of powers is generally known as 'the principle of the attribution of powers'.

[10] Now repealed by the Treaty of Lisbon.

[11] Recital (32) OR; see now Recital (87) RR. Ireland gave a similar notification. The Regulation, however, does not apply to Denmark by reason of Arts 1 and 2 of the Protocol on the position of Denmark as annexed to the EC Treaty, now TFEU. See Recital (33) OR (Recital (88) RR). Furthermore, the Insolvency Regulation does not apply to the Channel Islands or the Isle of Man, because those territories are the subject of special arrangements negotiated at the time of UK accession to the European Communities in 1972, whereby only a limited range of EC laws and policies apply to them (Act of Accession, 22 January 1972 (Cmnd 4862-I), Protocol No 3; TFEU, Art 355(5)(c)). Conversely, the Insolvency Regulation does apply to Gibraltar, which is included within the scope of the TFEU by virtue of Art 355(3) as one of the 'European territories for whose external relations a Member State' (in this instance, the UK) 'is responsible'.

[12] See Recital (5) OR as to why it is compatible with the principle of subsidiarity: its objectives 'cannot be achieved to a sufficient degree at national level'; see to similar effect Recital (86) RR; and see Recital (8) of both the OR and the RR as to why a Regulation, as opposed to any other form of Community instrument, is required: 'In order to achieve the aim of improving the efficiency and effectiveness of insolvency proceedings having cross-border effects, it is necessary, and appropriate, that the provisions … should be contained in a [Community/Union] law measure which is binding and directly applicable in Member States.'

[13] The basis on which legislative acts may be challenged in direct actions before the ECJ is set out in Art 263 TFEU.

[14] See section on 'Meaning' at paras 2.19 et seq below.

EC Treaty and now the TFEU and which the Regulation is intended to further. Second, in prescribing the legislative process for the Regulation's adoption, Article 67(1) EC (and Articles 81(2) and 294 TFEU in relation to the RR) not only set out the procedures which had to be observed to ensure the measure's valid adoption by the Community, but they also established the preparatory measures (or *travaux préparatoires*) which preceded it. This is important because, as also further described below, regard may legitimately be had to these measures as aids to its interpretation. Third, in the case of the OR Title IV of the EC Treaty, and in particular Article 68 EC, originally prescribed the role that the European Court of Justice was empowered to play in the interpretation of measures adopted under that Title, which include the Insolvency Regulation. That role, as set out below, has now been expanded following the repeal of Article 68 EC by the Treaty of Lisbon and those restrictions therefore no longer apply either to the OR or to the RR.

B. Legal Attributes

2.06 A Regulation is a creature of the governing treaties of the EU. As such, its attributes are governed by the TFEU, and in particular by Article 288 TFEU. This provides that Regulations shall:

(1) have 'general application';
(2) be 'binding in their entirety'; and
(3) be 'directly applicable in all Member States'.

Other Treaty Articles impose additional requirements. Article 296 TFEU requires Regulations to state the reasons on which they are based[15] and to refer to any proposals, initiatives, recommendations, requests, or opinions which were required to be obtained in accordance with the Treaty.[16] Article 297(1) TFEU provides that Regulations of the Council, such as the Insolvency Regulation, are to be published in the *Official Journal*[17] and, more importantly, shall enter into force on the date specified in them.[18] Each official language

---

[15] These are the reasons set out in the Recitals (or preambles) to the Insolvency Regulation.

[16] Art 67(1) EC provided that the Council was to act, *inter alia*, on the initiative of a Member State, and after consulting the European Parliament. Accordingly, the preamble to the OR refers to the initiative of Germany and Finland (published in [1999] OJ C221/8) and the opinion of the European Parliament. Additionally, the OR refers to the opinion of the Economic and Social Committee which was consulted at the request of the Council. The opinion was adopted on 26 January 2000 and is published in [2000] OJ C75/1. By contrast, the RR refers to the Commission's report on the application of the OR (Recital 1), the Commission's proposal, the transmission of the draft legislation to the national parliaments, the opinion of the Economic and Social Committee (published in [2013] OJ C271/55) and the positions of the European Parliament (of 5 February 2014 and 20 May 2015) and the position of the Council at first reading (of 12 March 2015).

[17] The OR is published in [2000] OJ L160/1 and the RR in [2015] OJ L141/19.

[18] Art 47 OR provides that it was to enter into force on 21 May 2002 and Art 92 RR that it is to enter into force on the twentieth day following its publication. Arts 84 and 92 set out the (later) date for the application of its various Articles and deal with transitional arrangements.

version[19] of a Regulation is equally authentic.[20] Regulations—like all other Community legislative measures—are presumed to be valid unless and until declared invalid by the European Court of Justice.[21]

Having 'general application' means that a Regulation 'applies to objectively deter- **2.07** mined situations and produces its legal effects to categories of persons envisaged in the abstract'.[22] A Regulation will be of general application notwithstanding that it will have different practical effects for the various persons to whom it applies.[23] The importance of this attribute is that it distinguishes a Regulation from other EU measures, and in particular from Decisions, and it does so by the application of a substantive test and not by a test simply of form. The significance of this distinction in turn is that by Article 263 TFEU a 'natural or legal person', as opposed to a Community institution or Member State, may only challenge a Regulation in a direct action by alleging either that it is addressed to that person ie it is a Decision, or that it is of 'direct and individual concern' to that person.[24] In relation to the Insolvency Regulation, there can be no doubt that it is what it purports to be, namely a measure of general application. As a consequence, it is immune to a direct challenge under Article 263 TFEU brought by individuals.[25]

'Binding in their entirety' means no more than that the provisions of a Regulation **2.08** are to apply in identical terms throughout the EU. That is to say, the Insolvency Regulation, like every other Regulation, is meant to be an instrument of uniformity. It is intended to be an instrument of a *single* EU legal order. However, in practice, the extent to which this aim is achieved will vary according to the way in which the interpretation and application of the Insolvency Regulation will vary from Member State to Member State.[26] Nonetheless, the fact that the Insolvency

---

[19] There are 23 official and working languages, but subordinate legislation is translated into only 22 (the exception is Irish). There are 27 Member States.

[20] Case 283/81 *CILFIT Srl v Ministry of Health* [1982] ECR 3415, para 18.

[21] This is subject to the possible exception that a Regulation may be declared 'non-existent', but it remains open to doubt whether legislative (as opposed to administrative) acts of the Community are capable of being declared 'non-existent': see the Opinion of AG Ruiz-Jarabo in Joined Cases C-10 to 22/97 *Ministero delle Finanze v IN.CO.GE.'90 Srl* [1998] ECR I-6307, 6316. AG Sharpston in Case C-345/06 *Heinrich* [2009] ECR I-1659 suggested that a Commission Regulation should be declared non-existent due to its failure to be published in the *Official Journal*, but the ECJ declined to follow this and instead declared that the offending Annex to the Regulation (which had not been published) was of no binding force insofar as it imposed obligations on individuals (judgment of 10 March 2009).

[22] See eg Case C-244/88 *Usines Coopératives de Déshydratation du Vexin v EC Commission* [1989] ECR I-3811 and Case C-299/88 *Cargill v EC Commission* [1990] ECR I-1303.

[23] Case 6/68 *Zuckerfabrik Watenstedt GmbH v Council* [1968] ECR 409; Case 101/76 *Koninklijke Scholten Honig v EC Commission* [1977] ECR 797.

[24] ie distinguishes him or her individually in the same way as an addressee of a Decision: Case C-263/02P *EC Commission v Jégo-Quéré et Cie* [2004] ECR I-3425.

[25] It may nonetheless be the subject of an 'indirect' challenge brought by individuals in national proceedings through the instrumentality of Art 267 TFEU. This is discussed further at paras 2.23–2.39 below.

[26] Attempts have been made to provide a register of national cases on the Insolvency Regulation: see eg <http://www.insolvencycases.eu/>.

Regulation is intended to be an instrument of uniformity, as further discussed below, affects the way in which it should be interpreted in any one Member State.

2.09 'Directly applicable' means that a Regulation takes effect in the domestic legal system of any particular Member State automatically, when it comes into force, without the need for that Member State to transpose it into national legislation.[27] In other words, with effect from 31 May 2002 the OR has formed part of the law of the United Kingdom without further enactment by the UK Parliament. The same will be true from the effective date of the RR, that being for the most part 26 June 2017.[28] From this attribute flow a number of important legal consequences.

'Direct applicability'

2.10 The first is that Member States are under an obligation *not* to introduce national measures intended to give effect to the Regulation,[29] unless implementing measures are required as discussed below. If they did so, they would impose an obstruction between the Regulation and those subject to it. Such national measures would contradict the Regulation's 'direct applicability' and its simultaneous and uniform application in the EU legal order. Thus the Insolvency Regulation has not been transposed into domestic English law, and everyone must look to the same legal instrument, that is the Regulation, in whatever Member State they are domiciled as their source of legal rights.[30]

2.11 Implementing measures may be required in two circumstances. Sometimes a Regulation may expressly require that Member States take steps to implement it. This, however, was not the case with regard to the OR,[31] whereas the RR does expressly contemplate that the conditions for access to information to insolvency registers, which it requires to be established, may vary in the manner contemplated by Article 27. Member States may also adopt detailed rules for the application of a Regulation where this is necessary to give full effect to it in their domestic legal

---

[27] cf the requirement that a Directive be implemented by national measures in the Member States' legal systems.

[28] The exceptions are: Art 86, which applies from 26 June 2016; Art 24(1), which applies from 26 June 2018; and Art 25, which applies from 26 June 2019.

[29] Case 34/73 *Fratelli Variola SpA v Administration des finances italiennes* [1973] ECR 981, esp paras 9–11.

[30] For an example of the direct applicability of the OR, see *Klempka v ISA Daisytek SA* [2003] BCC 984, 990H, where the Court of Appeal of Versailles held that, because Art 17 of the Regulation provides that the judgment opening proceedings produces its effects 'without further formality', the fact that French law requires a judgment opening insolvency proceedings to be published at the relevant Corporate Registry was irrelevant when considering the legal effect of the prior judgment of an English court opening main insolvency proceedings. The Versailles Court of Appeal's judgment was subsequently upheld by the Cour de Cassation: *French Republic v Klempka* [2006] BCC 841.

[31] But note that the Insolvency Regulation does expressly provide that certain matters in connection with its operation are to be reserved to the Member States. See eg Art 4.2 which provides that the conditions for the opening of insolvency proceedings (as defined by Art 2(a) of the Insolvency Regulation) are to be determined by 'the law of the State of the opening of proceedings'.

systems.[32] In the case of the OR, the Insolvency Act 1986 and the Insolvency Rules 1986 were amended[33] so as to give full effect to the rules that the Insolvency Regulation laid down with regard to the allocation of jurisdiction and the enforcement of judgments. In particular, amendments were introduced to modify the definition of 'property' in section 436 of the 1986 Act;[34] to give effect to the extensive role that the Regulation gives to liquidators of other Member States, and in particular their right under Article 37 (now Article 51 RR) to apply to convert (in the context of the United Kingdom) administration and voluntary arrangements into winding-up proceedings;[35] to provide for a procedure (as required by the jurisdictional rules of the Regulation)[36] for liquidators to apply to the court for 'confirmation' of a creditors' voluntary winding-up;[37] and to make clear that administration orders can be made in relation to overseas registered and unregistered companies over which an English court has jurisdiction by virtue of Article 3 of the Regulation.[38]

Amendments to the Insolvency Act 1986 and the Insolvency Rules 1986 must **2.12** themselves comply with the provisions of the Insolvency Regulation[39] as well as complying with general principles of EU law.[40] In particular, they must not alter

---

[32] Case 94/77 *Zerbone v Amministrazione delle Finanze* [1978] ECR 99, para 27.

[33] See, with regard to the 1986 Act, the Insolvency Act 1986 (Amendment) Regulations 2002, SI 2002/1037; the Insolvency Act 1986 (Amendment) (No 2) Regulations 2002, SI 2002/1240; the Insolvency Act 1986 (Amendment) Regulations 2005, SI 2005/879; and, with regard to the 1986 Rules, the Insolvency (Amendment) Rules 2002, SI 2002/1307.

[34] This is because Art 3(2) of the Insolvency Regulation limits the effects of proceedings commenced in a Member State on the basis of an establishment in that state to 'the assets of the debtor situated in the territory of the latter Member State'. Those assets are defined by Art 2(g) (now Art 2(9)). Accordingly, the Insolvency Act 1986 has been amended by the insertion of a new s 436A so that references in that Act to 'property' (as defined in s 436) are deemed to be references to property which, where Art 3 of the Regulation applies, is property that may be dealt with in such proceedings. See reg 18 of the Insolvency Act 1986 (Amendment) (No 2) Regulations 2002, SI 2002/1240.

[35] See eg r 4 of the Insolvency (Amendment) Rules 2002, SI 2002/1307 in relation to company voluntary arrangements, r 5 in relation to administration, and r 7 in relation to individual voluntary arrangements.

[36] Art 2(a) (now Art 2(4)) and Annex A.

[37] Under existing legislation, 'confirmation by the court' was not a step required in relation to a creditors' voluntary winding-up, although it is a requirement for the application of the Insolvency Regulation. Provision for it has now been made by r 9 of the Insolvency (Amendment) Rules 2002, SI 2002/1307.

[38] See *Re BRAC Rent-a-Car International Inc* [2003] BCC 248; *Re The Salvage Association* [2003] BCC 504. See now s 1(4) Insolvency Act 1986 as amended by the Insolvency Act 1986 (Amendment) Regulations 2005 following (and in effect modifying) Blackburne J's judgment in *Re The Salvage Association*.

[39] Case 94/77 *Zerbone v Amministrazione delle Finanze* [1978] ECR 99, para 27. As a matter of English law, these amendments to implement the OR were introduced under powers granted (by way of amendment to the 1986 Act) by the Insolvency Act 1986 (Amendment) Regulations 2002, SI 2002/1037, which instrument was itself adopted under s 2(2), European Communities Act 1972, so as to enable the UK Government to comply with its obligations under the EC Treaty (now the TFEU).

[40] See Case C-327/13 *Burgo Group SpA v Illachroma SA and another* (CJEU, 4 September 2014), [2015] BCC 33, where the CJEU criticized Belgian rules on the opening of secondary proceedings

---

the scope of the Insolvency Regulation[41] or add to its provisions,[42] and they must comply with the aim and objectives of the Regulation.[43] Further, as a matter of EU law, the amendments to domestic legislation adopted to give effect to EU law that is to the 1986 Act and the 1986 Rules are capable of review by the English courts so as to ensure their compatibility with the Insolvency Regulation.[44] To the extent that the amendments do not comply with the Insolvency Regulation, they will also be ultra vires under English law.

2.13 The doctrine of 'direct applicability' also entails a prohibition on Member States introducing new law which has the effect of modifying the legal effects of a Regulation.[45] In addition, in relation to pre-existing national law, it obliges Member States to repeal it. This is so even if it has become obsolete and the Member State in fact acts in a way that is compatible with EU law.[46] This is so as not to infringe the principle of legal certainty, and create what might otherwise be a potentially ambiguous legal situation.

2.14 By way of example, there was a potential conflict between section 117(1) of the Insolvency Act 1986 and the OR. This was because section 117(1) granted the English High Court jurisdiction to wind up *any* company registered in England and Wales. By contrast, by Article 3(1) OR, only the courts of the Member State within whose territory is situated 'the centre of the debtor's main interests' have jurisdiction.[47] Although there is a presumption that the registered office of a company is the centre of a company's main interests, it is capable of being rebutted. Accordingly, although section 117(1) of the Insolvency Act was permissive only, and not mandatory, it was arguable that in the interests of legal certainty it required

---

following the opening of main proceedings insofar as they limited the persons entitled to request such proceedings to creditors resident or with a registered office in Belgium on the basis that such a restriction was inconsistent with the EU general principle of non-discrimination. The CJEU also noted that the exercise of discretion by a national court, when deciding to open secondary proceedings, although governed by the national law of the Member State of the court, must be exercised consistently with the objectives underlying secondary proceedings, the objectives underlying the main proceedings, and consistently with the principle of sincere co-operation as well as with general principles of EU law.

[41] Case 40/69 *Hauptzollamt Hamburg v Bollmann* [1970] ECR 69, para 5.

[42] Case 74/69 *Hauptzollamt Bremen v Kohn* [1970] ECR 451, para 1.

[43] Case 31/78 *Bussone v Italian Ministry for Agriculture* [1978] ECR 2429, para 36. For an example of where implementing measures have not complied with the aims and objectives of the OR, see the CJEU's criticism of Belgian rules regarding the opening of secondary proceedings following the opening of main proceedings in Case C-327/13 *Burgo Group SpA v Illochroma SA and another* (CJEU, 4 September 2014), [2015] BCC 33, referred to at n 40 above.

[44] Case 230/78 *Eridania v Minister of Agriculture and Forestry* [1979] ECR 2749, para 34.

[45] Case 34/73 *Fratelli Variola SpA v Administration des finances italienne* [1973] ECR 981, paras 14–15.

[46] Case C-185/96 *EC Commission v Greece* [1998] ECR I-6601, para 32.

[47] This is subject to the exception that in addition the courts of Member States in which the debtor has an 'establishment' also have jurisdiction to open insolvency proceedings. See Art 3(2). Art 3(1) RR is in similar terms.

amendment to reflect the provisions of the OR. It was therefore amended by the addition of a new subsection (7), which provides that it is subject to Article 3 of the Insolvency Regulation.[48] Other jurisdictional provisions of the Insolvency Act 1986 were similarly amended.[49]

Member States are not only under the negative obligation to ensure that the **2.15** domestic legal order does not contain legislation that contradicts the Insolvency Regulation, they are also, as a matter of EU law, under a positive obligation to ensure that the Regulation will be applied in practice. This obligation now derives from Article 4(3) of the Treaty on European Union which requires Member States to 'take any appropriate measure, general or particular' to ensure the fulfilment of obligations arising both under the treaties and resulting from the acts of the institutions of the Union. The significance of this obligation from the point of view of the Insolvency Regulation is that it falls not simply on national governments, but on all organs of the state. These include the courts[50] as well as administrative and government authorities. That is to say the English courts are bound, as a matter of EU law, to ensure that the Insolvency Regulation is observed and applied. This means that where, for example, the Insolvency Regulation is contradicted by domestic law, or administrative and judicial practices, the English courts are bound as a matter of EU law to disapply those domestic laws or practices, without waiting for them to be set aside by legislative or other means.[51]

Moreover, where a Member State fails to apply the Insolvency Regulation, thereby **2.16** causing loss and damage to an individual, in certain circumstances the individual is entitled, as a matter of EU law, to reparation for the loss and damage under the conditions laid down by the European Court of Justice for Member State liability.[52]

---

[48] Reg 6 of the Insolvency Act 1986 (Amendment) (No 2) Regulations 2002, SI 2002/1240.

[49] See eg regs 7, 9, 10, and 14 of the Insolvency Act 1986 (Amendment) (No 2) Regulations 2002. The Insolvency Rules were amended to ensure that the issue of whether there is jurisdiction under the Regulation is considered at the opening of proceedings. See eg r 4(3) of the Insolvency (Amendment) Rules 2002 in relation to company voluntary arrangements.

[50] The origin of this doctrine is Case 14/83 *Von Colson and Kamann v Land Nordrhein Westfahlen* [1984] ECR 1891, para 26, which concerned the implementation of a Directive. For its application in the context of the OR, see Case C-527/10 *ERSTE Bank Hungary Nyrt v Magyar Allam and others*, judgment of 5 July 2012, para 36, where the CJEU held that from 1 May 2004 (in accordance with the Accession Treaty) Hungarian courts are required in accordance with Art 16(1) to recognize any judgment opening insolvency proceedings handed down by a court of a Member State, without any further formality, including in respect of proceedings opened before 1 May 2004 (in the particular case, in Austria).

[51] Case C-118/00 *Larsy v INASTI* [2001] ECR I-5063, paras 51–53; Case C-173/09 *Elchinov* [2010] ECR I-0000, para 31. But note the limitation on this: it does not require an English court to ignore the orders of a court of another Member State, even where they were improperly adopted (in this case, an order dissolving a company subject to main proceedings in the United Kingdom): see *Re Eurodis Electron Ltd plc and others* [2011] EWHC 1025 (Ch) (Mann J), para 17.

[52] Case C-118/00 *Larsy v INASTI* [2001] ECR I-5063, para 34. Note that the principle of Member State liability in damages was initially established by reference to the failure of Member States to implement Directives (on which there is an extensive case law). However, it is now recognized as a remedy generally for breach of a Member State's obligations under EU law, including those arising under Regulations.

'Direct effect'

2.17 The obligations which the doctrine of 'direct applicability' create, however, have to be distinguished from the doctrine of 'direct effect'. By saying that a particular EU provision has 'direct effect' is meant that it is intended to create rights for individuals which must be protected by the national courts.[53] That is to say individuals may rely on the provision in national courts so as to enforce the right that it is intended to create both as against the state and as against other individuals.[54] Although the European Court of Justice has not expressly ruled on the question whether it is proper to draw a distinction between 'direct applicability' and 'direct effect' in the context of Regulations, and indeed it sometimes uses the words interchangeably, the better view is that such a distinction should be made.[55] Certainly the English courts recognize such a distinction. Thus, Lord Hoffmann has said the fact that a Regulation 'is directly applicable does not necessarily mean that it creates rights and duties enforceable in the courts. It may, like some domestic statutes, create public duties without creating private law rights'.[56]

2.18 Certain provisions of the Insolvency Regulation are clearly not intended to have 'direct effect' in the sense of creating rights for individuals. These include the provisions in the OR empowering the Council to amend the Annexes to the Regulation,[57] and requiring the Commission to report on its application.[58] These are either procedural obligations or powers that are expressly limited to specific persons. But many of the substantive provisions, such as Article 3, which determines which Member States' courts are to have jurisdiction over insolvency proceedings, are likely to have direct effect. This is so notwithstanding that the meaning of certain key concepts, such as the 'centre of main interests' and 'establishment', which determine jurisdiction in accordance with the provisions of that Article, is unclear. There are in fact many expressions in the Regulation of which the meaning is unclear.[59] Such expressions are, however, capable of a single EU meaning which may, in the fullness of time, with the assistance of the jurisprudence of the European Court of Justice, become clear. Similar comments equally apply to other

---

[53] Case 26/62 *Van Gend en Loos v Nederlandse Adminsitratie der Belastingen* [1963] ECR 1.
[54] The provision has both so-called 'horizontal' and 'vertical' direct effect. By contrast, provisions of Directives that have 'direct effect' have only 'vertical direct effect', ie they can only be relied on as against the state, and *not* as against other individuals.
[55] See eg the discussion in S Weatherill and P Beaumont, *EU Law* (3rd edn, 1999) 398–9.
[56] *Consorzio del Prosciutto di Parma v Asda Stores Ltd* [2001] UKHL 7, para 21. But note that he went on to say 'One would normally assume, however, that unless the Regulation contemplated that it would have to be fleshed out by domestic or Community legislation, it was intended to be effective to create rights or duties or both and not be what Lord Simonds once called a "pious aspiration".'
[57] Art 45. In the RR this has been deleted. However, there are similar provisions eg the provision empowering the Commission to adopt implementing acts establishing the interconnection of insolvency registers (Art 87) or to amend standard forms (Art 88).
[58] Art 46 RR; see now Art 90 RR.
[59] The expressions 'right in rem' in Art 5 (OR)/Art 8 (RR); the 'assets' of a debtor, which appears throughout the Regulation; 'act detrimental to all the creditors' and 'any means … in the relevant case' in Art 13 (OR)/Art 16 (RR). There are many other examples.

provisions of the Insolvency Regulation, for example Article 25 OR / Article 32 RR, which governs the recognition and enforceability of judgments, and refers to such potentially unclear concepts as judgments that are 'closely linked' with insolvency proceedings.

C. Meaning

The principles of interpretation that apply as a matter of EU law, when establish- **2.19** ing the meaning of the Insolvency Regulation, reflect its essential characteristics as a piece of EU subordinate legislation. These are that it is a piece of legislation that has to operate within a multilingual community, and that it has to apply uniformly because that community, despite comprising many different Member States, is but a single legal order. Further, as a piece of subordinate legislation, the Insolvency Regulation has to respect and reflect the position that it occupies in the EU's legal hierarchy. These considerations underlie the particular interpretative techniques that have developed in EU law. As further explained below, they differ from the ordinary principles of English statutory interpretation, which themselves traditionally reflect a different legal order. In particular, English principles reflect a legal order which is predominantly monolingual,[60] and where the legislation is the product not of a bargaining process between Member States and the EU's institutions,[61] but the product of a single sovereign legislative assembly.

Interpretation and the European Union legal order

As a piece of subordinate legislation, the Insolvency Regulation must be inter- **2.20** preted consistently with superior EU law rules that govern it. In particular, it must be interpreted consistently with the scheme laid down by the Treaty Articles under which it was adopted[62] and general principles of EU law.[63] 'General principles of EU law' mean those principles of law which have been recognized as such by the

---

[60] But note that this is changing. Subordinate legislation adopted by the Welsh Assembly has to be in both English and Welsh.

[61] The EU does not have a single legislature, but a number of legislative processes that apply in accordance with the provisions of the TFEU.

[62] These were Arts 61(c) and 67(1) EC in the case of the OR and Arts 81 and 294 TFEU in the case of the RR (see para 2.02 above). See eg Case 105/94 *Celestini v Saar-Sektkellerei Faber* [1997] ECR I-2971, para 32 citing in support Joined Cases C-90 and C-91/90 *Neu v Secrétaire d'Etat à l'Agriculture et à la Viticulture* [1991] ECR I-3167, para 12.

[63] See eg Case 105/94 *Celestini v Saar-Sektkellerei Faber* [1997] ECR I-2971, para 32 citing in support Joined Cases C-90 and C-91/90 *Neu v Secrétaire d'Etat à l'Agriculture et à la Viticulture* [1991] ECR I-3167, para 12. For examples of where general principles of EU law were relied upon when construing an Article of the OR, see Case C-341/04 *Eurofoods IFSC Ltd* [2006] ECR I-3813, paras 65–67 (Art 26); Case C-527/10 *ERSTE Bank Hungary Nyrt v Magyar Allam and others*, judgment of 5 July 2012, paras 39–42 (Art 5(1)).

European Court of Justice.[64] These include: the principle of equal treatment or non-discrimination; respect for fundamental rights;[65] the principle of legal certainty; and the principle of proportionality. This means that where a provision of the Regulation is capable of more than one interpretation, in so far as possible an interpretation should be adopted which renders it compatible with these superior sources of EU law.

2.21 By way of example, Article 3 of the Regulation provides that 'The courts of the Member State within the territory of which the centre of a debtor's main interests is situated shall have jurisdiction to open insolvency proceedings.' The term 'Member State' in the Regulation is not defined. In *Re The Arena Corporation Ltd*[66] Arena contended that the centre of its main interests was Denmark, that Denmark was a Member State and therefore prima facie insolvency proceedings should be commenced in Denmark and not in England. Lawrence Collins J rejected the argument that Article 3 was applicable. Having regard to the Treaty Articles under which the Regulation was adopted, the Protocol on the position of Denmark, Denmark's decision not to opt in to the Regulation and Recital (33)[67] of the Regulation, he had no doubt that 'the expression "Member State" in Article 3 is to be interpreted as excluding Denmark'.[68]

2.22 The Insolvency Regulation is also one of a number of measures designed to create 'a European judicial area in civil matters, where citizens have a common sense of justice throughout the Union and where justice is seen as facilitating the day-to-day life of people'.[69] Other existing measures include the recast Council Regulation on jurisdiction and enforcement of judgments in civil and commercial matters ('Brussels I');[70] the Council Regulation on jurisdiction and enforcement of judgments in

---

[64] On general principles of EU law, see in particular T Tridimas, *The General Principles of EC Law* (3rd edn, Nov 2013).

[65] Since the coming into force of the Treaty of Lisbon, the EU has had its own Charter of Fundamental Rights, which has the same status as the EU treaties. However, the United Kingdom (together with Poland) negotiated Protocol 30 to the TFEU, as a result of which the rights set out in the Charter are not justiciable in English courts. (But for a different, and controversial, view see the CJEU's judgment in *Secretary of State for the Home Department v ME and others* (21 December 2011), para 120 and Mostyn J's observations on that judgment in *R (AB) v Secretary of State for the Home Department* [2013] EWHC (Admin), paras 13–14.) The Protocol also provides that the Charter does not extend the ability of the CJEU to find that the United Kingdom's laws, regulations, administrative provisions, or practices are inconsistent with the fundamental rights, freedoms, and principles re-affirmed by the Charter.

[66] [2004] BPIR 377 (Lawrence Collins J).

[67] Now Recital (88) of the RR.

[68] [2004] BPIR 377, 385. The question whether Denmark is to be considered a Member State for the purpose of Art 16 OR (Art 19 RR) was the subject of a reference to the ECJ: Case C-148/08 *Mejnertsen v Barsoe*, but the case was closed and removed from the Register before its determination.

[69] See the Commission's Explanatory Memorandum attached to its Proposal for a Council Regulation establishing a general framework for Community activities to facilitate the implementation of a European judicial area in civil matters (COM/2001/0221 final) [2001] OJ C213/271.

[70] The original Brussels Regulation replaced the 1968 Brussels Convention with effect from 1 March 2002: [2001] OJ L12. It in turn was replaced by Regulation 1215/2012 of 12 December

matrimonial matters (which also covers rights of access to children);[71] and the Taking of Evidence Regulation.[72] The significance of this is that when interpreting the Insolvency Regulation its role as an instrument in a wider EU legal order has to be considered. In other words, it has to be interpreted not only consistently with superior EU law, but also consistently with, and not in isolation from, the EU measures that are intended to complement it.

Of these, the most important is Brussels I.[73] This is because, historically, the **2.23** Brussels Convention that preceded it was originally intended as a Convention concerning civil jurisdiction and judgments in non-insolvency matters that would be adopted in parallel with an insolvency Convention.[74] As a result, the Brussels Convention and Brussels I do not apply to 'bankruptcy, proceedings relating to the winding-up of insolvent companies or other legal persons, judicial arrangements, compositions and analogous proceedings'.[75] The test to be applied for determining whether the action falls within the Insolvency Regulation is whether (i) the right or obligation relied upon 'finds its source in the common rules of civil or commercial law [in which case Brussels I applies] or derogates from them [in which case the

---

2012 [2012] OJ L351 from 10 January 2015 (see Art 81), to which express reference is made in Recital (7) RR.

[71] Council Regulation (EC) 2201/2003 as amended, known as Brussels II.

[72] Council Regulation (EC) 1206/2001.

[73] For an example of where reference to Brussels I and its predecessor, the Brussels Convention, was relied upon to assist in the interpretation of the Regulation, see *Re BRAC Rent-A-Car International Inc* [2003] BCC 248, 253B–D (Lloyd J). Indeed, the ECJ has also held that the Brussels I case law on the public policy exception to the recognition of foreign judgments may be transposed to the public policy exception provided by Art 26 of the Insolvency Regulation: Case C-341/04 *Eurofoods IFSC Ltd* [2006] ECR I-3813, para 64; Case C-444/07 *MG Probud Gdynia* [2010] ECR I-417, para 34. The CA further suggested (but did not decide) that (i) Brussels Convention case law on the meaning of the time when a court is first seised of a matter might be applied where determining 'the time of the opening of [insolvency] proceedings' for the purpose of the Regulation; and (ii) the burden of proof applicable to demonstrating the jurisdiction requirements of the Brussels and Lugano Conventions might also be applicable to the Regulation: see *Shierson v Vlieland-Boddy* [2005] EWCA Civ 974, paras 71–72 (Longmore LJ).

[74] It is because the Brussels Convention was always intended to have its complement in an insolvency regulation that the starting point for any consideration of the scope of the Insolvency Regulation is the ECJ's determination in Case C-133/78 *Gourdain v Nadler* [1979] ECR 733 of the scope of the bankruptcy and winding-up exclusion in the Brussels Convention.

[75] Art 1(2)(b) of Brussels I. For an example of judicial reliance on the complementary purposes of Brussels I and the Insolvency Regulation, see *Re Marann Brooks CSV Ltd* (Ch D, 4 December 2002) (Patten J); *Polymer Vision R&D Ltd v Van Dooren* [2011] EWHC 2951 (Comm) (Beatson J), esp at para 62; and for authoritative judicial discussions of the division of functions between Brussels I and the Insolvency Regulation, and the application of the 'dual criterion' that has to be fulfilled before actions fall within the scope of the Insolvency Regulation (ie they must 'derive directly from insolvency proceedings and are closely connected with them'), see: Case C-339/07 *Seagon* [2009] ECR I-767; Case C-111/08 *SCT Industri v Alpenblume AB* [2009] ECRI-5655; Case C-292/08 *German Graphics Graphische Maschinen GmbH v Alice van der Schee* [2009] ECRI-0842; Case C-213/10 *F-Tex SIA v Lietuvis-Anglijos UAB 'Jadecloud-Vilma'* (CJEU 19 April 2012); Case C-157/13 *Nickel & Goeldner Spedition GmbH v 'Kintra' USAB* (CJEU, 4 September 2014). For an English discussion, see *Byers and others v Yacht Bull Corporation* [2010] EWHC 133 (Ch) (Sir Andrew Morritt C) and more recently *Fondazione Enasarco v Lehman Brothers Finance SA and another* [2014] EWHC 34 (Ch) (David Richards J).

Insolvency Regulation applies]'[76] and (ii) the action is brought 'in the context of' insolvency proceedings.[77] The Insolvency Regulation also makes express reference to other complementary EU regimes by reference to which the scope of its application ought to be determined. In particular, insolvency proceedings relating to financial institutions have their own regimes established by a series of Directives which, unlike the Insolvency Regulation, are not directly applicable, but require to be implemented in the individual legal orders of the Member States. Thus the Insolvency Regulation does not apply[78] to insolvency proceedings concerning insurance undertakings,[79] credit institutions,[80] investment undertakings which provide services involving the holding of funds or securities for third parties, and collective investment undertakings. Further, Article 9 OR, now Article 12 RR, provides that the rights and obligations of parties to a payment or settlement system should be governed solely by the law of the Member State that applies to that system. The purpose of this provision[81] is to preserve the particular insolvency regime that the EU has established by its Directive on settlement finality in payment and securities settlement systems.[82]

Interpretation and the multilingual legal order

2.24   As indicated above,[83] although the Insolvency Regulation by reason of the doctrine of 'direct applicability' is to apply uniformly throughout the Member States, it applies through the medium of texts in 22 of the 23 official languages of the Community,

---

[76] Case C-295/13 *H v HK* (CJEU, 4 December 2014). Note that in this case, in contrast with the earlier judgment in Case C-157/13 *Nickel & Goeldner Spedition GmbH v 'Kintra' USAB* (CJEU, 4 September 2014), the rule of law relied on did not derive directly from insolvency proceedings, with the result that it could be relied on outside the context of insolvency proceedings (ie it was not a rule of law 'specific to insolvency proceedings' (as in the case of *Nickel & Goeldner Spedition GmbH v 'Kintra' USAB*), although the rule of law did require the actual insolvency of the debtor.

[77] Case C-295/13 *H v HK* (CJEU, 4 December 2014). Note that in this case the CJEU considered that, if the same claim had been brought outside the context of insolvency proceedings, it 'may' have fallen within Brussels I.

[78] By Art 1(2).

[79] These are governed by Council Directive (EC) 2001/17 on the reorganisation and winding-up of insurance undertakings [2001] OJ L110/28, implemented by the Insurance (Reorganisation and Winding up) Regulations 2004, SI 2004/353 and for Lloyd's by SI 2005/1998. See *Re AA Mutual Insurance Co Ltd* [2005] 2 BCLC 8 (Lewison J).

[80] These are governed by Council Directive (EC) 2001/24 on the reorganisation and winding-up of credit institutions [2001] OJ L125/15, implemented by the Credit Institutions (Reorganisation and Winding up) Regulations 2004, SI 2004/1045. See *In the matter of Arm Asset Backed Securities S.A.* [2014] EWHC 1097 (Ch), para 12 (Nugee J) for an example of where it was held that the interpretation of Art 10 of the Directive applied equally to Art 4(2) OR (Art 7(2) of the recast Regulation).

[81] See Recital (27) OR and Recital (71) RR.

[82] European Parliament and Council Directive (EC) 98/26 on settlement finality in payment and securities settlement systems [1998] OJ L166/45 implemented in England and Wales by the Financial Markets and Insolvency (Settlement Finality) Regulations 1999. It is suggested, therefore, that terms such as 'payment or settlement systems' that are undefined in Art 9 OR, Art 12 RR should be interpreted consistently with the Directive.

[83] See para 2.09 above.

each of which is authentic.[84] Strictly speaking, therefore, the English language version of the Insolvency Regulation should not be considered in isolation from other language versions. This is in part because of the danger of mistranslation.[85] But more particularly it is to ensure, through comparing language versions, consistency of meaning.[86] In practice, it is neither proportionate nor feasible for national courts to consider all of the different language versions of the Insolvency Regulation.[87] However, it is certainly appropriate, where key concepts are concerned,[88] that they are considered in alternative language versions as well as in the English version.[89] Where the difference between the language versions is crucial to the case, and the point is irresolvable on witness statement evidence, the question should arguably be referred to the European Court of Justice for determination.[90]

However, even where there is consistency across language versions, the meaning of **2.25** any particular provision of the Insolvency Regulation is not necessarily its literal meaning. This is partly because the meaning of the literal term may vary from

---

[84] Case 283/81 *CILFIT Srl v Ministry of Health* [1982] ECR 3415, para 18.

[85] Note in this context the correction to the Finnish version of the OR subsequently published in OJ [2001] L265/42 and the suggestion at para 8.45 of the 2nd edition of this work that the term 'goods' in Art 2(h) of the English language version of the OR is a mistranslation of the French '*biens*' and the German '*Vermögenswerten*', the better translation being 'assets'. The term 'assets' is now used in Art 2(10) of the RR. In *The Trustees of the Olympic Airlines SA Pension and Life Assurance Scheme v Olympic Airlines SA* [2015] UKSC 27, para 3, the Supreme Court stated that it was 'apparent from the equivalent term in the other language versions that ["goods"] means the same as "assets"'. Other possible mistranslations are indicated in the commentary.

[86] eg it was suggested in the 2nd edition of this work that the phrase 'all the creditors' in Art 4(2)(m) OR was better understood to mean 'the creditors as a whole' having regard to the German ('*Gesamtheit*') and French ('*ensemble*') versions. That interpretation has been adopted: see Art 7(2)(m) of the RR, which uses the phrase 'the general body of creditors'. Likewise, the phrase 'having an interest' in Art 34(2) OR, Art 47(2) RR is better understood as meaning 'interested', having regard to the French version ('*les créanciers intéressés*'): see the discussion at para 8.425 below. For an example of the approach of the CJEU (in that case to the interpretation of Art 24(1) (now Art 31(1)) and the meaning of the phrase 'for the benefit of the debtor'), see Case C-251/12 *Christian Van Buggenhout and another v Banque Internationale à Luxembourg SA*, paras 28 and 29, where the Court considered the provision in its Spanish, French, Italian, Dutch, and Portuguese language versions and the relevant preamble in its German, English, and Swedish language versions, on a reference from a Belgian court. Other examples of where, having regard to other language versions, the better view is that the literal meaning of the English version should not be followed are provided in the commentary.

[87] Nor does the ECJ expect them to. See AG Jacobs's Opinion in Case C-338/95 *Wiener SI GmbH v Hauptzollamt Emmerich* [1997] ECR I-6495, para 65.

[88] See, eg in relation to the Insolvency Regulation, the concept of a 'debtor's main interests' in Art 3(1), translated as '*le centre des intérêts principaux*' in the French version, and '*den Mittlepunkt seiner hauptsächlichen Interessen*' in the German version. Note, however, that the RR expands upon the meaning of this term by setting out presumptions in the case of individuals as well as companies and then providing examples in the recitals as to when those presumptions might be rebutted: see Recitals (28)–(31); see also Recitals (27) and (32).

[89] The Court of Appeal has set out how foreign language versions should be put before the court in English proceedings in *R v Customs and Excise Commissioners, ex p Emu Tabac Sarl* [1997] EuLR 153, 160.

[90] ibid. See also *Customs and Excise Commissioners v Samex* [1983] 3 CMLR 194, 210 per Bingham J. On references, see part D below.

Member State to Member State. The consequence of applying a doctrine of 'literalism' in the EU context, unlike the UK statutory context, therefore may well promote divergence rather than uniformity, and so run counter to the legal effects that the measure is intended to produce. But it is also partly because EU law, intended to create a single *EU* legal order, requires an EU interpretation, provided that the provision in question does not make an express reference to the law of the Member States for the purpose of determining its meaning and scope.[91] Thus just as autonomous EU meanings have been given by the European Court of Justice to many of the terms employed by the Brussels Convention on Civil Jurisdiction and Judgments (now Brussels I), so many of the terms employed in the Insolvency Regulation, which is intended to complement this Convention,[92] will require autonomous EU meanings.[93]

2.26 These meanings should be established by adopting a 'purposive'[94] or 'teleological' method of construction.[95] Although this approach differs from ordinary English principles of statutory construction, where the legal meaning of an enactment usually corresponds to its grammatical meaning,[96] it would be wrong to characterize it as simply substituting 'inspiration' for methodology. Even 'a teleological interpretation is an interpretation *intra legem* rather than *extra legem* or *contra legem*'.[97] As a

---

[91] Case C-116/11 *Bank Handlowy w Warszawie SA v Christianpol sp z.o.o.* judgment of CJEU of 22 November 2012, para 49 (a case concerning the interpretation of Art 4(2)(j) OR, Art 7(2)(j) RR). In the context of the Insolvency Regulation, Member State autonomy is expressly preserved in relation to matters such as the law applicable to insolvency proceedings and their effects (save where the Regulation makes express provision): see Art 4(1) OR/Art 7(1) RR. But contrast this with Art 16(1) OR/Art 19(1) RR, where there is no express reference to national law; thus the CJEU held that the Art 16(1)/Art 19(1) concept of a 'judgment opening insolvency proceedings' must be interpreted as encompassing not only decisions that are formally described in national law as opening decisions but also 'a decision handed down following an application, based on the debtor's insolvency, seeking the opening of proceedings … where that decision involves divestment of the debtor and the appointment of the liquidator': Case C-341/04 *Eurofoods IFSC Ltd* [2006] ECR I-3813, para 54.

[92] See Recital (7) of the Insolvency Regulation.

[93] The most obvious example of this is the concept of 'the centre of main interests' which the ECJ has held is to be given an 'autonomous meaning': Case C-341/04 *Eurofoods IFSC Ltd* (ECJ, 2 May 2006), para 31. See also now Case C-396/09 *Interedil Srl v Fallimento Interedil* [2011] ECR I-9915, para 43.

[94] *Re BRAC Rent-A-Car-International Inc* [2003] BCC 248, 254 (Lloyd J). For an example of the ECJ having regard to the 'purpose' of the Insolvency Regulation as set out in its preambles with a view to determining the meaning of a particular provision, see Case C-1/04 *Staubitz-Schreiber* (ECJ, 17 January 2006), esp paras 24–28 and, more recently, Case C-328/12 *Schmid v Hertel* (CJEU, 16 January 2014) (both cases concerning the meaning and scope of Art 3(1)).

[95] See the famous characterization by Lord Diplock in *R v Henn and Darby* [1981] 1 AC 850, 905 and for an example of its express adoption in the context of the Insolvency Regulation, see *Connock and Boyden v Fantozzi* [2011] EWHC 15 (Ch) (Newey J), para 26.

[96] FAR Bennion, *Statutory Interpretation* (5th edn, 2008) section 150, p 441. But note (1) that this is not invariably the case: verbal ambiguity or evidence of a contrary legislative intention may lead to departures from the literal meaning of the words; and (2) the literal or grammatical meaning is accorded precedence on the fiction that it correctly conveys 'the legislative intention', ie the grammatical and legal meanings are the same.

[97] Case C-125/97 *Regeling v Bestuur van de Bedrijfsvereininging voor de Metaalnijverheid* [1998] ECR I-4493 per AG Cosmas at 4504.

result, the interpretation has to be compatible with the wording of the Community law provision. Moreover, establishing the 'teleological' meaning of a Community law provision involves adopting a structured approach. It involves considering the nature of the provision in the Regulation (for example whether it is a derogation or forms part of the general scheme that the Regulation is intended to create).[98] This in turn will require considering the overall scheme and purpose of the Regulation of which it forms part,[99] and understanding it in the context of the system of Treaty provisions and other rules regarding the allocation of jurisdiction and recognition of judgments in civil matters of which it forms part.[100] In particular, in relation to this last matter, it involves having regard to the principle of 'mutual trust which has enabled a compulsory system of jurisdiction to be established'.[101]

---

[98] eg Art 3(4) of the Insolvency Regulation, which permits the opening of territorial insolvency proceedings prior to the opening of main insolvency proceedings in limited cases only, is to be interpreted restrictively, since one of the underlying purposes of the Regulation is the coordination of insolvency proceedings 'to satisfy the need for unity in the European Union' and 'such coordination cannot be ensured if main proceedings have not been opened': Case C-112/10 *Procureur-generaal bij het hof van beroep te Antwerpen v Zaza Retail BV*, judgment of CJEU of 17 November 2011, para 22; Art 26 OR (now Art 33), which provides a 'public policy' exception to the general rule that insolvency proceedings opened in one Member State are to be recognized in another, is to be construed narrowly since it operates by way of an exception to the general scheme of the Regulation, Case C-341/04 *Eurofoods IFSC Ltd* [2006] ECR I-3813, para 64. By contrast the term 'court' eg as in Art 3(1), being the body to which jurisdiction is allocated by the Regulation, will be given a broad meaning (as it is in Recital (10) OR, Recital (20) RR), because it furthers the purpose or scheme of the Regulation, *Re The Salvage Association* [2003] BCC 504, 509 (Blackburne J), where the word 'court' in Art 3(1) of the Regulation was interpreted to encompass any body recognized as competent in a Member State to open insolvency proceedings, with the result that it was held that company voluntary arrangements were capable of falling within Art 3. See also *Re TXU Europe German Finance BV* [2005] BCC 90 (Registrar Baister): a creditors' voluntary winding-up of a foreign company may fall within Art 3(1) of the Regulation.

[99] Case C-116/11 *Bank Handlowy w Warszawie SA v Christianpol sp z.o.o.* judgment of CJEU of 22 November 2012, para 67; as the 'wording' of Art 27(1) OR (Art 34 RR) was 'not entirely clear' (para 66), the CJEU considered it necessary to have regard to the Regulation's 'overall scheme' to determine whether the court of the Member State in which secondary proceedings had been opened was entitled to examine whether the debtor was insolvent, or was bound by the finding of the court of the Member State in which main insolvency proceedings had been opened. The CJEU concluded (para 74) that the examination of the debtor's insolvency by the court having jurisdiction to open main proceedings was binding, given divergent national definitions of insolvency and the absence of a defined concept of insolvency in the Insolvency Regulation. See likewise the Court of Appeal's reliance on 'the rationale of secondary proceedings' as supporting its interpretation of the meaning of 'establishment' as a condition for the opening of secondary proceedings in *Trustees of the Olympic Airlines SA Pension & Life Insurance Scheme v Olympic Airlines SA* [2013] EWCA Civ 643, para 31.

[100] For a 'model' example of such an approach, see the CJEU's consideration of Art 24(1) OR (Art 31(1) RR) in Case C-251/12 *Christian Van Buggenhout and another v Banque Internationale à Luxembourg SA*, where the Court, having set out general EU principles of interpretation (paras 26 and 27), then considered different language versions of the contested provision (paras 28 and 29), the aim of the provision, and finally the 'objectives pursued by the legislation of which it forms part' (paras 33–36).

[101] Case C-341/04 *Eurofoods IFSC Ltd* (ECJ, 2 May 2006), para 40, a principle which the CJEU has emphasized a number of times as a rule to assist interpretation as embodied in Recital (22) OR, Recital (65) RR: Case C-444/07 *MG Probud Gdynia* [2010] ECR-I-417, paras 27 and 28; Case C-527/10 *ERSTE Bank Hungary Nyrt v Magyar Allam and others*, judgment of 5 July 2012, para 34.

2.27 The European Court of Justice has recognized a number of 'aids' to establish the purpose underlying legislative provisions. Of these, the most important is the preamble or statement of reasons which, as indicated above, is a Treaty requirement.[102] For example, Recital (13) OR attempts to explain the meaning of the debtor's 'centre of main interests' in Article 3(1), an important concept that is not defined in that Article.[103] The recitals, however, do not have binding legal force. Where there is a conflict between the preamble and the text of the Regulation itself, the former must give way to the latter.[104]

2.28 In addition, regard may be had to the preparatory measures that preceded the adoption of the Regulation. These measures are not decisive, but only persuasive or confirmatory.[105] Within this category, greater weight is to be given to preparatory measures that are formally required by the legislative process and are referred to in the preamble to the measure. In the case of the OR, as indicated above, these were the initiative of Germany and Finland,[106] the opinion of the European Parliament[107] and the opinion of the Economic and Social Committee.[108] In the case of the RR, these are the proposal from the Commission,[109] the opinion of the European Economic and Social Committee,[110] the positions of the European Parliament and of the Council,[111] and the Commission's report of 12 December 2012 on the application of the OR.[112] Lesser weight (but some weight nonetheless, although this will vary to the extent that the document is publicly available) may

---

[102] Art 296 TFEU (referred to in this chapter as the Recitals). See *Re BRAC Rent-A-Car-International Inc* [2003] BCC 248, 251C (Lloyd J): the recitals 'help to cast light on some of the substantive provisions'. See also the reliance on the recitals by Longmore LJ in *Syska v Vivendi Universal SA* [2009] EWCA Civ 677, para 17 when considering the 'rationale' (para 16) for the Art 15 (Art 18 of the RR) exception to the general rule that the law of the Member State within whose territory proceedings are opened is to determine the effects of opening the proceedings (Art 4/Art 7 of the RR).

[103] See now Recitals (27) to (31) of the RR. Old Recital (13) has now been deleted and superseded by the relevant case law. See likewise Recital (25) OR/Recital (68) RR, which sheds some light on the meaning of 'rights in rem' for the purpose of the Regulation (suggesting that the *lex situs* determines whether a particular right is a right in rem). In the case of the Insolvency Regulation, a number of the recitals have in turn been derived from the Virgos-Schmit Report (on which see below), as a result of which a proper understanding of them requires that they be understood in the context of that report: see the remarks of Registrar Jacques in *Re Stojevic* [2007] BPIR 141, para 33 (in that case concerning Recital (13) OR, which he held had to be understood in the context of para 75 of the report) and *O'Donnell and another v Governor and Company of the Bank of Ireland* [2012] EWHC 3749 (Ch), paras 24–25 (Newey J) (also in relation to former Recital (13)) .

[104] Case C-412/93 *Société d'Importation Edouard Leclerc Siplec v TFI Publicité SA* [1995] ECR I-179, paras 45–47.

[105] See the comments of AG Tesauro in Case C-300/89 *Commission v Council* [1991] ECR I-2867, 2895.

[106] [1999] OJ C221/8.

[107] It was delivered on 2 March 2000.

[108] [2000] OJ C75/1.

[109] COM (2012) 744 final of 12 December 2012.

[110] [2013] OJ C271/55.

[111] The European Parliament positions are dated 5 February 2014 and 20 May 2015 and that of the Council is dated 12 March 2015.

[112] [2000] OJ L160/1.

be given to other preparatory measures. In the case of the Insolvency Regulation, since it is intended to introduce by another means the November 1995 Convention on Insolvency Proceedings, which never came into force, it is legitimate also to have regard to that measure[113] and to the explanatory report that accompanied it,[114] in particular as some of the statements contained in it found their way almost verbatim into the recitals to the Insolvency Regulation.[115] In relation to the RR, some assistance may also be derived from the official documents generated by the Article 294 TFEU procedure for the adoption of legislation, and the exchanges between the European Parliament and the Council.

---

[113] The English version of the Convention is contained in a Consultative Document published in February 1996 by the Insolvency Service of the DTI. English courts also have regard, where the underlying concept is the same, to the UNCITRAL Model Law on Cross-Border Insolvency adopted by the General Assembly of the UN on 15 December 1997 and the case law of other countries which have implemented the UNICTRAL Model Law (eg the US federal bankruptcy code which incorporated the UNCITRAL definition of 'establishment'): *Trustees of the Olympic Airlines SA Pension & Life Insurance Scheme v Olympic Airlines SA* [2013] EWCA Civ 643, paras 17, 23.

[114] This was the basis on which AG Jacobs had regard to the report as 'useful guidance': Case C-341/04 *Eurofoods IFSC Ltd* [2006] ECR I-3813, para 2 (although the ECJ itself did not refer to it in that case). The report is by Professor Virgos and Mr Schmit. A bad translation was attached as Annexe B to the Insolvency Service Consultation Document referred to above. A revised and improved version was produced by the EU Council (Doc 6500/96, DRS 8 (CFC) Brussels 3 May 1996) (see app 2). In the first few years of the Insolvency Regulation there was some, but not universal, judicial scepticism about the use of the report. Thus, although Lloyd J had regard to the report in *Re BRAC Rent-A-Car-International Inc* [2003] BCC 248, 254D–G, he (properly) indicated that he was uncertain as to its status and therefore the weight to be placed on it. Blackburne J in *Re The Salvage Association* [2003] BCC 504, 509 likewise referred to the report as being of 'questionable status', although he was 'encouraged' by the report in adopting in that case a broad approach to questions of interpretation; by contrast Gabriel Moss QC, sitting as a Deputy High Court Judge in *Financial Services Authority v Dobb White & Co & others* [2003] EWHC 3146 (Ch), para 4 referred to it without hesitation. There is now, however, a judicial consensus that the report can be relied on as an aid to interpretation: see most recently *Trustees of the Olympic Airlines SA Pension & Life Insurance Scheme v Olympic Airlines SA* [2013] EWCA Civ 643, para 20 where the Court of Appeal expressly endorsed the view of Sir Andrew Morritt C in *In re Stanford International Bank Ltd* [2010] EWCA Civ 137, para 36 that the report is 'authoritative'. Thus, Lawrence Collins J cited the report without comment in *Re Collins & Aikman Corp Group* [2006] BCC 606, 610D , as did Beatson J *Polymer Vision R&D Ltd v Van Dooren* [2011] EWHC 2951 (Comm), para 49 and Mann J in *Re Office Metro Ltd* [2012] EWHC 1191 (Ch), paras 14–16. See also *Syksa v Vivendi Universal SA* [2009] EWCA Civ 677 where Longmore LJ noted (para 20) that the Virgos-Schmit report had been intended to be the Official Report of the bankruptcy Convention and considered that the fact that the Convention was never agreed and the Regulation was put in its place as not having 'detracted from the authority of that Report'. Likewise, Newey J relied on it in *O'Donnell and another v Governor and Company of the Bank of Ireland* [2012] EWHC 3749 (Ch); Newey J, more questionably, also cited a work co-authored by Professor Virgos on the Insolvency Regulation as did Longmore LJ in *Syksa v Vivendi Universal SA*, paras 22–23. However, the assistance to be derived from the report may vary from case to case and indeed from issue to issue: see the approach of the Court of Appeal in *Shierson v Vlieland-Boddy* [2005] 1 WLR 3966, esp paras 47–50 (where the report was not particularly helpful on the question of the 'immutability' of a debtor's COMI) and 65–68 (where the court had particular regard to the 'guidance' provided by the report on the meaning of 'establishment' within Art 3(2) (Chadwick LJ)).

[115] See further the explanation at fn 23 to AG Jacobs' Opinion in Case C-341/04 *Eurofoods IFSC Ltd* (27 September 2005). As to the consequence of this, see *Re Stojevic* [2007] BPIR 141 as discussed above at n 103 on the need, where relevant, to understand the recitals in the context of the report.

2.29 Finally, although declarations made by the Council cannot be relied on to modify the Regulation any more than any other EU measure,[116] such declarations, since they are now publicly available,[117] may arguably be taken into consideration where interpreting the Regulation. In this respect it is to be noted that when the OR was adopted, the Council minutes record that Portugal made a statement regarding the interpretation of Article 37 (now Article 51 RR, but in a significantly amended form).[118] This has since been published in the *Official Journal*,[119] and was indeed referred to in the footnotes to the published text of the OR.

D. Solving Interpretative Issues and Questions of Validity: The Court of Justice of the European Union

2.30 The European Court of Justice is the supreme court for the purpose of determining questions of the validity of the Insolvency Regulation and of the interpretation of its provisions.[120] Although the decisions of the European Court of Justice do not bind it, its decisions are binding as a matter of EU law on the court which requested its opinion. Further, as a matter of English law, the generally accepted view is that the consequence of section 3(1) of the European Communities Act 1972 is to extend the doctrine of precedent to the decisions of the European Court of Justice. As a result, English courts are bound to give effect when interpreting EU legislation such as the Insolvency Regulation to decisions of the European Court of Justice. In addition, as a matter of EU law, only the European Court of Justice has jurisdiction to declare an EU measure (or particular provisions of such a measure) to be invalid.[121]

2.31 By contrast, the opinions of the Advocates General do not bind national courts. Nonetheless, English courts do regard their Opinions as being persuasive.[122]

---

[116] Case C-306/98 *EC Commission v Greece* [1991] ECR I-5863, para 8.

[117] Art 9 of the Council's Rules of Procedure.

[118] This was that 'Article 37... which mentions the possibility of converting territorial proceedings ... into winding-up proceedings, should be interpreted as meaning that such conversion does not exclude judicial appraisal of the state of the local proceedings (as in the case of Article 36) or of the application of interests of public policy as provided for in Article 26'.

[119] [2000] OJ C183/1.

[120] There have now been a series of references to the CJEU concerning the Insolvency Regulation, the CJEU's first judgment being handed down in January 2006. Although the decisions of the courts of other Member States are not binding on English courts, because the Insolvency Regulation is an EU legal instrument, intended to have the same legal effects in all Member States, it is also appropriate for an English court to have regard to those decisions, in the interests of uniformity, where determining the meaning and effect of the Insolvency Regulation. However, care needs to be taken when citing such cases: see the comments of Mann J in *Re Office Metro Ltd* [2012] EWHC 191 (Ch): '[Counsel] relies on the account of an Estonian case (it cannot be treated as a report) ... appearing in Insolvency Intelligence' (para 23); '[Counsel] also pointed to an English case ... of which no transcript is available' (para 24); 'The authorities [Counsel] relies on are neither clear nor strong' (para 26).

[121] Case 314/85 *Foto-Frost v Hauptzollamt Lübeck Ost* [1987] ECR 4199, paras 15–20.

[122] See the discussion at R Brent, *Directives: Rights and Remedies in English and Community Law* (2001) para 20.05.

The extent to which they are will depend on the relationship between the Opinion and the judgment of the European Court of Justice, that is if the Opinion is referred to in the judgment and the court expressly or impliedly adopts its reasoning,[123] it will be 'persuasive', but if the court rejects it or has not followed it, it will have little or no authority. The Advocate General's Opinion may also be useful where it provides guidance on matters that have not been discussed by the European Court of Justice.[124] Additionally, the opinions of the Advocates General may be helpful sources of academic debate, relevant authorities, and legal argument, thereby indicating the legal framework for the European Court of Justice's judgment, which might not otherwise be apparent, and, by providing its proper legal context, rendering the judgment more intelligible.[125]

Jurisdiction

Historically, the role that the European Court of Justice was entitled to play in interpreting the Regulation or determining the validity of its provisions was somewhat different from the role that it ordinarily plays in relation to other EU secondary legislation. This was because, when the Insolvency Regulation was adopted under Title IV of what was then the EC Treaty, Member State co-operation in the field of 'freedom, security and justice' was not fully developed. In particular, under the reforms introduced by the Treaty of Amsterdam, Member States as well as the Commission were entitled to propose the adoption of legislation; the role of the European Parliament was limited to a right to be consulted and the co-decision

2.32

---

[123] See Case C-116/11 *Bank Handlowy w Warszawie SA v Christianpol sp z.o.o.* judgment of the CJEU of 22 November 2012, paras 48, 66 for express references to the AG's Opinion in the CJEU's judgment.

[124] eg the reliance placed by Lewison J on AG Jacob's Opinion in Case C-341/04 *Eurofood IFSC Ltd* [2006] ECR I-3813 in *Re Lennox Holdings plc* [2009] BCC 155, where the judge relied on the approval by the AG of the 'head office functions test' (sometimes referred to as the 'command and control' test) to displace the presumption that the company's COMI was the state where its registered office was located. He commented 'that the approach of the Advocate-General is a particularly helpful one'. Note, however, that the statement by C Ritter in 'A New Look at the Role and Impact of Advocates-General—Collectively and Individually' (2006) 12 Columbia European Law Review 751–74 that 'In cases where the ECJ did not rule on the substantive issues addressed in the AG's opinion ... [the AG's opinion] constitutes precedent *vis-à-vis* the CFI and *a-fortiori* the Commission' overstates the position. Although the opinion is 'the individual reasoned opinion ... of a Member of the Court of Justice' (Case C-17/98 *Emesa Sugar (Free Zone) NV v Aruba* [2000] ECR I-665, para 14), it forms part of the process of internal deliberation of the Court. Accordingly, it does not have the juridical status of a judgment and should not be relied on as such, even *faut de mieux*.

[125] See further on this C Ritter, 'A New Look at the Role and Impact of Advocates-General—Collectively and Individually' (2006) 12 Columbia European Law Review 751–74, section 3 'The role and influence of Advocates-General'. For an example of an English court's reliance on an Advocate-General's statement of general principle in relation to the Insolvency Regulation, see *Polymer Vision R&D Ltd v Van Dooren* [2011] EWHC 2951 (Comm) (Beatson J), para 62.

procedure did not apply; and Article 68 EC limited the European Court of Justice's jurisdiction to decide questions concerning the interpretation of the Insolvency Regulation to the circumstance where national courts or tribunals 'against whose decisions there is no judicial remedy under national law' considered that a decision was 'necessary' to enable them to give judgment. The European Court of Justice did not have any jurisdiction to accept references from inferior national courts.

2.33 However, the Treaty of Lisbon, which came into force on 1 December 2009, replaced Article 61 EC and repealed Articles 67 and 68 EC (being the Articles under which the OR was adopted). One consequence of this has been that the limitation on the right to refer a question to the Court of Justice disappeared.[126] As a consequence, pursuant to Article 267 TFEU, a court or tribunal against whose decision there is a judicial remedy 'may' refer a question concerning the Insolvency Regulation to the Court of Justice, 'if it considers that a decision on the question is necessary to enable it to give judgment'; whereas a court or tribunal, against whose decision there is no judicial remedy under national law, 'must' make such a reference in these circumstances.

Criteria for references

2.34 There are therefore three considerations for a national court before it requests the European Court of Justice for a ruling on the Insolvency Regulation. They are whether: (i) the court or tribunal is a court or tribunal of last resort; (ii) the ruling is necessary for that body to give judgment; and (iii) if it is necessary, but the court or tribunal is not a court or tribunal of last resort, it should exercise its discretion to refer.[127]

2.35 As a matter of English law, courts of last resort include not only the Supreme Court, but all courts and tribunals from which there is no possibility of appeal. For example, the Court of Appeal will be 'the ultimate court of appeal if leave to appeal to the House of Lords [now the Supreme Court] is not obtainable'.[128] This will be equally true of all courts from which permission to appeal has been refused.

2.36 So far as the condition of 'necessity' is concerned, assuming that the issue is otherwise relevant to the matter to be determined, there are two circumstances in which a court or tribunal is relieved from making the request.[129] They are where the issue

---

[126] Case C-396/09 *Interedil Srl v Fallimento Interedil Srl*, [2011] ECR I-9915, paras 18–19.

[127] There is extensive case law on when a referring body is a 'court or tribunal'. But in the context of references by English bodies applying the Insolvency Regulation this is highly unlikely to be an issue.

[128] *Hagen v Fratelli D&G Moretti* [1980] 3 CMLR 253 per Buckley LJ at 255.

[129] The leading case is still Case 283/81 *Srl CILFIT v Ministry of Health* [1982] ECR 3415. But note that it has been suggested that the guidelines which this case lays down should be reconsidered and relaxed; and that in practice English courts tend to apply them less rigorously than they might so as not to overburden the European Court of Justice with references.

is nonetheless *acte clair*; and where the issue is substantially the same as a question previously raised before the European Court of Justice.

Acte clair means that the correct application of EU law is so obvious as to leave **2.37** no doubt as to the manner in which the question raised is to be resolved.[130] Strictly speaking, before a court can reach such a conclusion, it must be satisfied that the matter is 'equally obvious' to the courts of the other Member States and to the European Court of Justice.[131] This is a high hurdle imposed in the interests of legal uniformity. But it is a hurdle that English courts have approached pragmatically. For example, in considering whether an issue was *acte clair*, the Court of Appeal has taken into account the existence of a body of case law from which it is possible to extrapolate applicable principles of law and the absence of conflicting decisions in other Member States.[132] In relation to the Insolvency Regulation, some concepts (such as 'the centre of main interests' of a debtor) are novel to it and unlikely to be regarded as *acte clair*. But other concepts, which may be novel in the context of insolvency proceedings (such as the term 'establishment' in Article 3(2)) have behind them a body of Community law developed in other contexts.[133]

Strictly speaking, the fact that the same issue has previously been raised before the **2.38** European Court of Justice is not a bar to its being raised again.[134] This follows from the fact that the European Court of Justice is not bound by its own earlier decisions. But the authoritative nature of a previous judgment may be such as to deprive the obligation of the national court to refer of any real purpose. Where the question raised is 'substantially the same as a question which has already been the subject of a preliminary ruling in a similar case'[135] there is thus no necessity to refer. It may,

---

[130] ibid para 16.

[131] ibid paras 16–17.

[132] See *Trinity Mirror plc v Customs and Excise Commissioners* [2001] EWCA Civ 65, paras 53–55.

[133] eg in relation to the meaning of the term 'establishment', in addition to the definition set out at Art 2(h) OR, Art 2(10) RR, see the case law arising out of the right to establishment as provided by Art 49 TFEU, and in particular, in the context of the operation in the single market of EU 'passports', the distinction drawn between operating an 'establishment' in another Member State and the mere provision of cross-border services; and the case law arising out of Art 5(5) of the Brussels Convention, now Brussels I. Case C-396/09 *Interedil Srl v Fallimento Interedil Srl* [2011] ECR I-9915, paras 60–64, however, has now considered the meaning of this term specifically in the context of the Insolvency Regulation; and the Court of Appeal in *Trustees of the Olympic Airlines SA Pension & Life Insurance Scheme v Olympic Airlines SA* [2013] EWCA Civ 646 has considered the meaning of 'establishment' more specifically yet in the context of opening 'secondary proceedings' within the meaning of the Insolvency Regulation. See also now Case C-327/13 *Burgo Group SpA v Illochroma and another* (CJEU, 4 September 2014), [2015] BCC 33.

[134] Case 283/81 *Srl CILFIT v Ministry of Health* [1982] ECR 3415, para 15. However, Art 99 of the CJEU's Rules of Procedure (adopted 25 September 2012) provides that in this circumstance the Court may decide to rule by reasoned order. It may now also do this if the Court considers that the answer can be deduced from existing case law or where the answer to the question admits of no reasonable doubt. This provision was introduced as a means of speeding up the time taken to deal with preliminary references.

[135] Case C-337/95 *Parfums Christian Dior SA v Evora BV* [1997] ECR I-6013, para 29.

however, be a moot point in any given case whether the condition of 'substantial' identity is satisfied.

2.39 So far as concerns the exercise of discretion by an English court (other than a court of last resort), the sort of factors that are relevant are whether the facts are established, such that it would enable a reference to be useful, and the questions to be referred are properly formulated; the time it may take to obtain a judgment; the expense of the reference; the importance of not overwhelming the Court of Justice with references; the need to be able to formulate the question clearly; the difficulty and importance of the point at issue; and the views of the parties.[136]

2.40 The European Court of Justice may itself refuse to entertain a request. This may be for one of five principal reasons.

(a) On the ground that the order for reference is inadequate. The importance of the order for reference is that it is this document, and not the European Court of Justice's file, that is circulated to the Member States and the EU's institutions to give them and the parties the opportunity to submit observations.[137] The criterion that the European Court of Justice will apply to determine this issue is whether it is able to provide a useful answer to the issue referred on the basis of the information supplied.[138]

(b) Although it is up to the national court to determine whether the reference is necessary in order for it to give judgment, the European Court of Justice nonetheless is entitled to refuse to consider it where the reference is 'manifestly irrelevant'. This, however, has happened only in rare cases.[139]

(c) The European Court of Justice will decline jurisdiction where it is asked to give judgment on a hypothetical problem.[140] But again it will refuse a request on these grounds only in rare circumstances.

(d) In isolated cases, where there is evidence that the procedure is being abused (because, for example, the dispute between the parties in the national proceedings has been fabricated), it is entitled to decline jurisdiction.

(e) Where the national procedure has been terminated, or the claims settled, the European Court of Justice must also refuse the request. This is because Article 267 TFEU grants it jurisdiction only in relation to a case that is 'pending' before a national court. However, this is now subject to the important

---

[136] The classic statements remain: *HM Bulmer Ltd v J Bollinger SA* [1974] Ch 401 (Lord Denning MR); *HMRC v APS Samex* [1983] 1 All ER 1042 (Bingham J); *R v Stock Exchange ex p Else Limited* [1993] QB 534 (Sir Thomas Bingham MR).

[137] It should be noted that the reference is from the national court, and not from the parties to proceedings before that court.

[138] Case C-316/93 *Vaneetveld v SA Le Foyer* [1994] ECR I-763, 767 per AG Jacobs.

[139] Case C-319/94 *Jules Dethier Equipement SA v Dassy* [1998] ECR I-1061, para 20.

[140] Case C-83/91 *Meilicke v ADV/ORGA FA Meyer AG* [1992] ECR I-4971. See also Case C-439/08 *VEBIC* [2010] ECR I-12471, para 42.

caveat that, if the withdrawal of the request for the preliminary ruling is made after the CJEU has given notice of the date of delivery of its judgment, the CJEU may nonetheless proceed to give judgment.[141] The purpose behind this reform is to prevent one party from settling the dispute at the last minute because it expects the preliminary ruling to be adverse to its interests, for example after hearing the Advocate General's Opinion.

Procedure

The procedure for making a reference to the European Court of Justice is governed **2.41** by Part 68 of the Civil Procedure Rules 1998 and the Practice Direction to CPR Part 68. An order to refer, however, should not normally be made by a master or district judge (whether of the High Court or the county court).[142] Reference should also be made to the Court of Justice's 'Recommendations to national courts and tribunals in relation to the initiation of preliminary ruling proceedings',[143] as referred to in the Practice Direction.

The European Court of Justice has exclusive jurisdiction to decide requests for **2.42** preliminary rulings.[144] The procedure is essentially non-contentious, reflecting the fact that it is the national court, and not the parties to proceedings, which makes the reference. There are no time limits for making a reference other than the national time limits applicable to the national proceedings. Nor are any specific requirements laid down by the European Court of Justice as to the form of the reference, although (as indicated above) both the case law of that Court and Article 94 of its Rules of Procedure do lay down requirements as to its substantive content and its Recommendations (referred to above) also provide guidance on the form of reference. The Court also publishes 'Notes for the Guidance of Counsel'.[145] The procedures of the European Court of Justice are governed by its own Statute and its Rules of Procedure. In exceptional cases, it is now possible for a national court to request the European Court of Justice to apply an accelerated or expedited procedure.[146] In addition, special provision is made for an 'urgent procedure' in relation to cases falling within Title 5 of Part Three of the TFEU (concerning 'Area of Freedom, Security and Justice'). The Court of Justice has indicated, however,

---

[141] Art 100 of the CJEU's Rules of Procedure, adopted 25 September 2012.

[142] Note that it is a moot point whether this restriction is compatible with EU law; there is no such restriction in Art 267 TFEU.

[143] OJ 2012/ C338/01. They were adopted following the adoption on 25 September 2012 of new Rules of Procedure of the CJEU.

[144] Following the Treaty of Nice, Art 225 EC, now Art 256 TFEU, was amended to permit the General Court (formerly known as the Court of First Instance) to determine requests for preliminary rulings in specific areas to be laid down in the Court's Statute. None has been so far.

[145] Note that there is no automatic oral hearing: it is necessary to submit reasoned requests for an oral hearing and, on a proposal from the Judge-Rapporteur and after hearing the Advocate General, the Court may decide not to hold a hearing: see Art 76 of the Rules of Procedure dated 25 September 2012.

[146] Art 105, Rules of Procedure of the CJEU dated 25 September 2012.

that the expedited and urgent procedures are primarily intended for cases involving people in custody or likely to be deprived of their liberty, or for proceedings concerning parental authority or the custody of children.[147] In 2013 the average length of preliminary reference proceedings before the European Court of Justice was 16.3 months.[148]

---

[147] They are rarely used: in 2013 the expedited procedure was not used at all and the urgent procedure only twice, whereas 699 new cases were brought before the CJEU in that year: Annual Report of the European Court of Justice, pp 9–10 (2013).

[148] Annual Report of the European Court of Justice, Table 12 (2013). This was an improvement on earlier years: eg in 2003 the average length was 25.3 months (the longest annual average in the period 2000–07). To put the CJEU's figures in context, according to the Court of Appeal's Practice Guidance dated 17 June 2015, hear-by dates calculated from the issue of the Appellant's Notice in certain cases (eg where permission to appeal from a final order is granted at an oral hearing) can take up to 19 months.

3

SCOPE AND JURISDICTION

A. The Original Regulation ('OR')

Preliminary

The purpose of section A of this chapter is to explain the scope of operation of **3.01** the EC/EU Regulation on Insolvency Proceedings as currently in force. For this, it is necessary to understand how the provisions in Article 1, which define the Regulation's scope in terms of the types of proceedings to which it does and does not apply, combine with those of Article 3, which prescribe the rules of international jurisdiction for all cases which fall within the Regulation's sphere of application. Section B of this chapter provides a summary of the principal changes which will take effect under the provisions of the recast Regulation adopted on 20 May 2015 when it becomes applicable from 26 June 2017.[1]

Scope of the Regulation

Article 1(1) defines the scope of the Regulation in positive terms, by declaring that **3.02** it 'shall apply to collective insolvency proceedings which entail the partial or total

---

[1] See ch 1 above, section G.

divestment of a debtor and the appointment of a liquidator'. The full effects of Article 1 can only be understood when read in conjunction with Article 2(a)–(c) inclusive, together with Annexes A, B, and C. No formal definition of 'insolvency' is supplied by any of these provisions, however. It is therefore left to each state to administer its own procedures according to the test of insolvency laid down by its national law and practice. On the other hand, the meaning of the expression 'insolvency proceedings' is identified for the purposes of the Regulation. Article 2, which supplies the definitions of a number of the expressions used in the Regulation, states in paragraph (a) that 'insolvency proceedings' means the collective proceedings referred to in Article 1(1) as listed in Annex A. Annex A contains a list of those insolvency proceedings, as contained in the laws of each Member State, which are thereby brought within the ambit of the Regulation. Consequently, the opening of such proceedings in the state in question must take place in conformity with the relevant provisions of the Regulation, and is no longer a matter of unrestricted jurisdictional competence for the courts of that state. Proceedings which, although possibly fulfilling the criteria mentioned in Article 1(1), have not been expressly included in Annex A with respect to the Member State in question, are not affected by the Regulation.[2] Conversely, it appears that proceedings which have succeeded in becoming listed in Annex A after completion of the process specified in Article 45[3] will be accepted as falling within the scope of application of the Regulation even if, strictly speaking, they do not fully meet the criteria mentioned in Article 1(1) together with 2(a).[4]

3.03 In the case of the United Kingdom, the following proceedings are listed in Annex A and thus constitute 'insolvency proceedings' for the purposes of the Regulation:

- winding-up by or subject to the supervision of the court;[5]
- creditors' voluntary winding-up (with confirmation by the court);
- administration, including appointments made by filing prescribed documents with the court;
- voluntary arrangements under insolvency legislation; and
- bankruptcy or sequestration.

3.04 With respect to the above list, it can be noted that none of the types of receivership available under the laws of the various parts of the United Kingdom is

---

[2] C-461/11 *Radziejewsksi v. Kronofogdemyndigheten i Stockholm*, 8 November 2012, CJEU (3rd Chamber) at paras 23 and 24 of the judgment (published in electronic reports of cases at < http://eur-lex.europa.eu/legal-content/EN/TXT/?uri=CELEX:62011CJ0461>) (accessed 19 December 2015).

[3] For commentary on Art 45, see ch 8 below at paras 8.466 et seq.

[4] For example, the French procedure known as *sauvegarde*, which was added to Annex A by amending Regulation 694/2006, is technically a pre-insolvency procedure and, as such, seemingly fails to fulfil the criteria specified in Art 1(1).

[5] The species of proceeding which is technically termed 'winding-up by the court' is also known as 'compulsory winding-up'. The procedure known as 'winding-up under the supervision of the court' was abolished by the legislative reforms of 1985–86 so far as concerns England, Wales, Scotland, and Northern Ireland; it still forms part of the insolvency law in force in Gibraltar.

included.[6] This is to be explained by the fact that such procedures are properly to be considered as remedies invoked by individual creditors and also because, in most instances, the court is not directly involved in the receivership process. It is also the case that schemes of company arrangement concluded under Part 26 of the Companies Act 2006 do not fall within the scope of the Insolvency Regulation, even where a scheme is entered into in relation to an insolvent company, or for the purpose of averting its impending insolvency.[7] The exclusion of administrative receiverships and schemes of arrangement from the ambit of the Regulation are factors to be borne in mind when planning the rescue of a financially ailing business with a cross-border dimension. Although the reforms implemented by the Enterprise Act 2002 have greatly reduced the number of situations in which a holder of floating charge security is entitled to appoint an administrative receiver of a company, the option to do so still survives in respect of specifically excepted cases. Even where such right of appointment survives, however, if there is any likelihood that the office holder may need to take action abroad in any of the EU Member States it may be more effective to resort to administration, to which the Regulation's provisions will be fully applicable, rather than the hitherto more favoured option of administrative receivership.[8] Also noteworthy is the inclusion within the scope of the Regulation of creditors' voluntary liquidations, which are of a collective nature but which do not normally require the active participation of the court. This has been effected subject to the proviso that there must be a judicial confirmation of the voluntary proceedings if they are to enjoy the benefits of extra-territorial recognition and effectiveness by virtue of the Regulation.[9]

---

[6] The exclusion applies to administrative receivership and to other types of receivership under Part III of the Insolvency Act 1986, as well as to receiverships under the Law of Property Act 1925, s 101.

[7] In the event that it is necessary to seek the assistance of other courts of the European Union for purposes related to an approved scheme of arrangement, the provisions of the Brussels Regulation on Jurisdiction and the Recognition and Enforcement of Judgments in Civil and Commercial Matters will be of relevance. That Regulation, formerly in force as Council Regulation (EC) 44/2001, was superseded and repealed by Regulation (EU) 2015/2012 of 12 December 2012, OJ L351/1, 20 December 2012, which became applicable from 10 January 2015. For cases concerned with the impact of the Brussels Regulation on the jurisdiction of English courts to approve schemes of arrangement, see eg *Re Rodenstock GmbH* [2011] EWHC 1851 (Ch), [2011] BCC 459; *Primacom Holding GmbH v A Group of Senior Lenders and Credit Agricole* [2012] EWHC 164 (Ch), [2013] BCC 201; *Re NEF Telecom Co BV* [2012] EWHC 2944 (Ch), [2014] BCC 417; *Re Magyar Telecom BV* [2013] EWHC 3800 (Ch), [2014] BCC 448; *Re Stemcor (Sea) Pte Ltd* [2014] EWHC 1096 (Ch), [2014] 2 BCLC 373.

[8] The radical curtailment of administrative receivership alluded to in the text was effected by s 72A of the Insolvency Act 1986, inserted by s 250 of the Enterprise Act 2002 with effect from 15 September 2003. By ss 72B to 72GA a series of exceptions was created, to which additional exceptions can be added by means of statutory instrument (s 72H). Moreover, rights of appointment conferred on secured lenders under floating charges granted before 15 September 2003, retain their validity for the duration of the lending agreement by virtue of s 72A(3), (4) of the Act as amended, in conjunction with para 14 of Sch B1 thereto.

[9] A new procedure was established in 2002 to enable application to be made to the court for confirmation of a creditors' voluntary winding-up for the purposes of the EC Regulation: Insolvency Rules 1986, rr 7.62, 7.63, inserted by Insolvency (Amendment) Rules 2002, SI 2002/1307, rr 9, 12, and further amended by SI 2003/1730 and by SI 2010/686. The form for making such applications is Form 7.20A.

3.05   As was noted in chapter 1 above, certain species of proceedings under the Insolvency Act 1986, which were listed by name in the original version of Annex A attached to the EC Convention on Insolvency Proceedings 1995, were not expressly included in the modified version of Annex A in the Regulation enacted in May 2000. This was effected as a drafting adjustment, on the understanding that the varieties of special procedures were comprised within the simple references to 'voluntary arrangements under insolvency legislation' and 'bankruptcy or sequestration'. The adjustment was apparently not intended to have the effect of excluding these procedures from the ambit of the Regulation.[10]

3.06   It may be observed that Article 1(1) carefully restricts the application of the Regulation to proceedings which 'entail the partial or total divestment of a debtor and the appointment of a liquidator', thereby excluding any types of insolvency proceeding which, though of a collective nature, leave the debtor in full control of his estate and business under some form of 'debtor in possession' principle. Although partial divestment suffices, there must be some degree of loss of the debtor's powers of administration and control over his affairs, whatever form this may take.[11]

3.07   The term 'liquidator' is defined in Article 2(b) to mean: 'any person or body whose function is to administer or liquidate the assets of which the debtor has been divested or to supervise the administration of his affairs', as listed in Annex C. Annex C (as amended) should therefore be consulted to ascertain, for each Member State respectively, the persons or bodies which qualify to be regarded as 'liquidator' in proceedings commenced under the laws of that state. As is also the case with Annexes A and B, the purpose of this tabloid device is to facilitate the smooth working of the Regulation by eliminating any uncertainty regarding the types of proceedings, and the types of office holders, to which the Regulation applies. The technique of listing all included subject-matter by name has been adapted from the Istanbul Convention.[12] Article 45 of the EC Regulation provides a relatively simple procedure for amendment of the Annexes at any time: the Council, acting by qualified majority on the initiative of one of its members or on a proposal from the Commission, may effect the desired amendment.[13]

Proceedings expressly excluded from the scope of the Regulation

3.08   Article 1(2) sharpens the boundaries of the Regulation's sphere of application, and is expressed in negative terms. It states that the Regulation shall not apply to insolvency proceedings concerning insurance undertakings, credit institutions,

---

[10] See para 1.22 above, n 42 and text thereto.
[11] See Virgos-Schmit Report (app 2 below) para 49(c). See also n 4 above and text thereto.
[12] See para 1.04 above, n 8 and text thereto.
[13] See ch 1 above, paras 1.24–1.25 together with nn 45–52 for information concerning the amendments made to date using Art 45 and also by other means. See also ch 8 below at para 8.466 for commentary on Art 45.

investment undertakings which provide services involving the holding of funds or securities for third parties, or to collective investment undertakings. Entities of the kinds expressly excluded from the ambit of the Regulation are generally subject to special regulatory regimes under national laws, including special procedures in the event of insolvency. It is also the case that specific measures have been developed by the European Union to subject such entities to harmonized standards of regulation by means of Directives. Hence, a separate framework is in place to deal with the insolvencies of these undertakings in the context of the European Union.[14]

International Jurisdiction

Article 3 imposes a uniform set of jurisdictional rules which are applicable to all **3.09** cases which come within the ambit of the Regulation. The direct rules of jurisdiction, which must be respected and applied throughout the Member States as a matter of obligation generated by EU law, are drafted in terms which are somewhat infelicitous as they fail to express the intended effect in clear and positive language. Where the debtor's circumstances place it within the ambit of the Regulation, insolvency proceedings can only be opened in a Member State in accordance with the provisions of Article 3, whose provisions in this respect override any rules of national law whereby such a debtor might otherwise have been amenable to insolvency proceedings in that state. The jurisdictional rules in Article 3 therefore operate in an exclusive manner, and do not merely generate an additional basis of jurisdiction to operate in parallel with national rules. However, the displacement of national rules is limited to those cases where the Regulation properly applies: in other situations, national rules of jurisdiction continue to be applicable. It is therefore of crucial importance to understand the basis on which this distinction depends.

Unfortunately, the substantive text of the Regulation fails to embody the relevant **3.10** information, which may be a source of confusion and misunderstanding. Only in paragraph 14 of the Recitals to the Regulation[15] is there a clear statement that: 'This Regulation applies only to proceedings where the debtor's centre of main interests is located in the Community.' This limitation on the scope of the Regulation is of considerable importance, because it excludes many cross-border insolvencies from the ambit of its provisions even though interested parties and assets may be located within the European Union. The criterion employed for this purpose—the location of the debtor's centre of main interests—is particularly significant because it can produce the effect that insolvency proceedings involving a debtor with quite substantial connections with one or more Member States will nevertheless be

---

[14] See ch 7 below for an account of the regulation of financial services and markets in the EU. See also the commentary to Art 1(2) in ch 8 below, and the Virgos-Schmit Report, paras 54–60 (app 2 below).
[15] See ch 1 above at para 1.23 for the status of the Recitals, and their derivation.

outside the scope of the Regulation, if it so happens that the debtor's centre of main interests is outside the European Union. In such cases, as mentioned above, the pre-existing laws of each Member State apply separately, both in the matter of jurisdiction over the debtor, and in relation to the conduct of the proceedings and their international recognition and enforcement.[16] In consequence, the meaning of the expression 'centre of main interests' (hereinafter referred to as the debtor's COMI) is fundamental to a proper understanding of the Regulation's operation and effects.

Centre of main interests (COMI)

3.11 It is unfortunate, given the vital role played by the concept of the COMI, that the provisions within the main body of the Regulation do not include a definition of the meaning to be ascribed to it. In a belated attempt to atone for this vital omission, a somewhat oblique and abstract indication of the intentions of those who originally drafted the text, as commemorated at somewhat greater length in the pages of the Virgos-Schmit Report, is conveyed by the single sentence of paragraph 13 of the Recitals which states: 'The "centre of main interests" should correspond to the place where the debtor conducts the administration of his interests on a regular basis and is therefore ascertainable by third parties.'[17] While this statement leaves unresolved certain key questions such as the elements which constitute the process of 'administration', and the sense in which the term 'interests' is to be understood, it does indicate that the COMI connecting factor is intended to provide a test in which the attributes of transparency, continuity, and objective ascertainability are dominant factors. This should enable parties who have dealings with a debtor to found their expectations on the reasonable conclusions to be drawn from systematic conduct and arrangements for which the debtor is responsible. In principle therefore it ought not to be possible for a debtor to gain advantages, at creditors' expense, from having resorted to evasive or confusing techniques of organizing his business or personal affairs, in a way calculated to conceal the true location from which interests are systematically administered.

3.12 It therefore seems to be an inherent aspect of the COMI concept that functional realities pertaining to the way in which the debtor's interests are actually administered are capable of displacing the effects of such formal criteria as the place of a company's registration, or its state of incorporation, for the purpose of determining the Regulation's application, and also for the purpose of deciding questions of jurisdiction. This, in effect, amounts to a victory for the civil law-inspired 'real

---

[16] See, eg *Geveran Trading Co Ltd v Kjell Tore Skjevesland* [2003] BCC 209, aff'd [2003] BCC 391; *Re Arena Corporation Ltd* [2004] EWCA Civ 371, [2004] BPIR 415 (CA). The latter case is notable because the COMI of the debtor was in Denmark which, though a Member State of the EU, is not participating in the Regulation—as is stated in Recitals para 33—and is therefore considered as though a non-member for the purposes of applying the jurisdictional regime of its Art 3.
[17] cf Virgos-Schmit Report (app 2 below) para 75.

seat' theory of jurisdictional competence over the 'state of incorporation' theory traditionally espoused by the members of the Anglo-American common law 'family'. However, the spirit expressed in Recital (13) also suggests that this victory of substance over form, in terms of the Regulation's primary rule of jurisdiction, may need to be balanced in some instances by the application of estoppel-like principles to preclude a debtor from pleading that the true location of the COMI is in some different state from that which external parties have been led to suppose. The doctrinal and conceptual issues associated with the notion of COMI, and the case law produced by national courts and by the European Court of Justice (ECJ), are examined in detail in chapter 8 below.[18]

The Regulation is applicable to both natural and legal persons who occupy the role **3.13** of 'debtor'. Although the same connecting factor—the COMI—is utilized in all cases, there is an additional provision within Article 3(1) which should assist in the task of determining the location of the COMI of a company or legal person. That provision states that the place of the registered office shall be presumed to be the centre of its main interests in the absence of proof to the contrary. No further indication is given as to the nature or degree of proof required to overcome this presumption, but it is to be supposed that the burden of proof will rest upon any party wishing to displace the conclusion as to the whereabouts of the COMI of a company or legal person that would otherwise follow from its application. For the future, those who need to calculate commercial or financial risk by reference to the impact of insolvency law upon their rights and interests, cannot simply rely upon an investigation of the law of the state of incorporation of the debtor company. While that is, and will remain, the necessary point of departure, it is essential to conduct diligent inquiry into the current, functional realities of the debtor's corporate administration. If there are indications that the company's interests are administered from the territory of another state on a regular basis, the possibility that the Article 3(1) presumption can be rebutted should be explored, and any necessary precautions taken. This issue has already been considered by the ECJ, first in the case of *Eurofood IFSC Ltd*,[19] in which the location of the COMI of the company in question was central to the question whether jurisdiction to open main insolvency proceedings was vested in the courts of the state of the company's incorporation, or in those of the state in which the COMI of its parent company was located. The ECJ ruled that the 'simple presumption' laid down by Article 3(1) in favour of the registered office of the company as the whereabouts of the COMI 'can be rebutted only if factors which are both objective and ascertainable by third parties enable it to be established that an actual situation exists which is different from that which locating it at that registered office is deemed to reflect'.[20] In its subsequent ruling

---

[18] See ch 8 below, esp commentary to Arts 2(f) and 3.
[19] Case C-341/04, [2006] ECR I-3813, [2006] BCC 397.
[20] ibid para 34 of the ECJ judgment. The *Eurofood* case is examined in detail in ch 8 below, esp in the commentary to Art 3.

in the case of *Interedil Srl* [21] the Court of Justice elaborated upon the nature of the presumption implanted in Article 3(1) and upon the circumstances in which it is capable of being rebutted. The Court first stated that the twin requirements, of objectivity and the possibility of ascertainment by third parties,

> [M]ay be considered to be met where the relevant material factors taken into account for the purpose of establishing the place in which the debtor company conducts the administration of its interests on a regular basis have been made public or, at the very least, made sufficiently accessible to enable third parties, that is to say in particular the company's creditors, to be aware of them. [22]

Secondly, the Court declared that the presumption in Article 3(1) cannot be rebutted '[W]here the bodies responsible for the management and supervision of the company are in the same place as its registered office and the management decisions of the company are taken, *in a manner that is ascertainable by third parties*, in that place'. [23] Conversely, as the Court duly noted, '[T]he presumption … may be rebutted where, from the viewpoint of third parties, the place in which a company's central administration is located is not the same as that of its registered office.' [24]

3.14 The foregoing statements of principle, as contained in leading judgments of the ECJ, are clearly aimed at ensuring legal certainty and foreseeability in relation to the all-important issue of identifying the appropriate forum in which to seek to open insolvency proceedings within the scope of the Regulation. It is therefore apparent that the careful analysis and interpretation of relevant factual information concerning the conduct of corporate activities is a critically important task both for those contemplating the taking of steps to open proceedings and for the court by which any such application is actually considered.

3.15 **The 'mobile COMI' phenomenon.** The very fact that the presumption established by Article 3(1) concerning the location of the COMI of a corporate debtor is expressed to be rebuttable, and the further fact that Article 3(1) is so drafted as to confer jurisdiction on the courts of the country within whose territory the debtor's COMI '*is* situated' (emphasis added) give rise to the logical possibility that the location of the COMI may change from time to time, according to the circumstances actually prevailing at the time when the issue of jurisdictional competence has to be considered. The mobile nature of a debtor's COMI gives rise to important questions of law, as to which the Regulation itself is unfortunately silent, but which carry profound practical implications including the potential wastage of costs through the initiation of proceedings in what may subsequently prove to have been the 'wrong' country. There is the additional possibility that

---

[21] Case C-396/09 *Interedil Srl v Fallimento Interedil Srl* [2011] ECR I-9915, [2012] BCC 851, see esp at paras [41]–[59] of the judgment.
[22] ibid para [49] of the judgment of the Court.
[23] ibid para [50] of the judgment of the Court (emphasis added).
[24] ibid para [51] of the judgment of the Court.

parties may exploit the factor of COMI mobility in order to engage in the practice known as 'forum shopping'.

In the *Staubitz-Schreiber* case,[25] the ECJ delivered a helpful ruling to avert some **3.16** of the negative effects of the mobile COMI phenomenon. The case concerned a debtor who had moved her COMI from Germany to Spain in the interval between the first filing of her application for the German court to open bankruptcy proceedings and the date when a definitive ruling was made at appellate level as to the jurisdictional competence of the German courts. In response to a reference by the German Supreme Court (*Bundesgerichtshof*), the ECJ noted that while Article 3(1) states that the courts of the Member State within whose territory the centre of a debtor's main interests is situated are to have jurisdiction to open insolvency proceedings, it does not specify whether the court originally seised retains jurisdiction if the debtor moves the centre of his or her main interests after submitting the request to open proceedings but before the judgment is delivered.[26] Employing a purposive approach to this question of interpretation, the ECJ referred to Recital (4) to the EC Regulation, which expresses the intention of the Community legislature to avoid incentives for parties to transfer assets or judicial proceedings from one Member State to another, seeking to obtain a more favourable legal position. That objective would not be achieved if the debtor could move his COMI to another Member State between the time when the request to open insolvency proceedings was lodged and the time when the judgment opening the proceedings was delivered, and thereby alter the identity of the court having jurisdiction, and consequently the applicable law. Moreover, such a possibility would result in creditors having to be in continual pursuit of their debtor to the location of the new COMI, and would often mean in practice that the proceedings would be prolonged. Such an outcome would also be contrary to the objectives stated in Recitals (2) and (8) of the Regulation, of achieving efficient and effective cross-border proceedings.[27] Therefore, the ECJ concluded that the cause of greater judicial certainty would be best served by interpreting Article 3(1) to mean that the court of the Member State within whose territory the debtor's COMI is situated at the time when the debtor lodges the request to open insolvency proceedings retains jurisdiction to open those proceedings if the debtor moves the COMI to the territory of another Member State after lodging the request but before the proceedings are opened.[28] It is thought that, by parity of reasoning, the same conclusion should be reached in cases where the request to open proceedings is lodged by one or more creditors, rather than by the debtor herself. It should also be observed that this decision of the

---

[25] Case C-1/04 *Staubitz-Schreiber* [2006] ECR I-701, [2006] BCC 639 ECJ. This was chronologically the first occasion on which the ECJ delivered a ruling on the interpretation of Regulation 1346/2000.

[26] ibid para 23 of the ECJ judgment.

[27] ibid paras 24–26 of the ECJ judgment.

[28] ibid para 29 and also the formal ruling by the Court.

ECJ was concerned with the implications of a removal of COMI *after* the first formal step has been taken to invoke the jurisdiction of the German court: the issues of principle associated with an alleged migration of COMI at some time *before* such first steps are taken still await consideration by the Court of Justice.[29] However, domestic courts have encountered numerous examples of so-called 'bankruptcy tourism' whereby both individual and corporate debtors are found to have resorted to a variety of strategies aimed at relocating their COMI within a relatively short time before seeking to avail themselves of what they consider to be the more favourable, or more commercially suitable, insolvency laws of the target state.[30] With growing awareness of the scale of such exploitative practices, national courts have gradually become more wary of accepting at face value the claims as to the location of their COMI asserted by debtors whose forensic connections with the forum appear to be of very recent origin.[31] Nevertheless, if the advance preparations for a COMI-migration have been executed with scrupulous regard for the requirements of EU law, the treaty-based rights of EU subjects (both individual and corporate) to exercise freedom of movement and establishment ensure that the jurisdictional principles of the Insolvency Regulation will have to be applied by the courts of the state in which the 'new' COMI has been positioned.[32]

---

[29] See however the insightful observations on the subject of 'good' and 'bad' forum-shopping in the opinions of Advocate General Colomer, delivered in the *Staubitz-Schreiber* Case itself (at paras 70–77 of the Advocate General's Opinion), and in Case C-339/07 *Seagon v Deko Marty Belgium NV* [2009] ECR I-767, [2009] 1 WLR 2168 at paras 60–62 of the Advocate General's Opinion. This enlightened approach, involving the distinction between forum-shopping which has the aim of preserving value for the ultimate benefit of creditors (and potentially also for the holders of company shares), and conversely those abusive practices whose purpose is to disadvantage the legitimate interests of creditors, has been endorsed in the expanded interpretative guidance contained in Recitals (29) to (34) of the recast Regulation adopted in May 2015. See para 3.29 below.

[30] Note, however, the problems resulting from one unsuccessful attempt by a debtor to transfer its COMI to a country (the United Kingdom) whose insolvency laws were considered by those in control of the company to be more suited to its immediate requirements. The abortive attempt to relocate the COMI had taken place shortly before the company sought to avail itself of the administration procedure in an attempt to outmanoeuvre creditors who were simultaneously taking steps to open proceedings in the country (Germany) where the COMI had hitherto been located: *Hans Brochier Holdings Ltd v Exner* [2006] EWHC 2594 (Ch), [2007] BCC 127 (Warren J). See the detailed discussion of '*Right to move COMI and forum shopping*' in ch 8 below at paras 8.114 et seq, commentary to Art 3.

[31] For examples of UK cases in which aspects of 'bankruptcy tourism' have been identified or suspected, see *Re Ci4net.com Inc & DBP Holdings Ltd* [2004] EWHC 1941 (Ch), [2005] BCC 277 High Court (Leeds) (HHJ Langan); *Hans Brochier Holdings Ltd v Exner* (n 30 above); *Official Receiver v Eichler* [2007] BPIR 1636 (Registrar Baister); *Re Eichler (No 2)* [2011] BPIR 1293 (Chief Registrar Baister); *Official Receiver v Mitterfellner* [2009] BPIR 1075 (Registrar Baister); *Schrade v Sparkasse Ludenscheid* [2013] BPIR 911 (Chief Registrar Baister); *Irish Bank Resolution Corp Ltd v Quinn* [2012] NI Ch 1 [2012] BCC 608 (Deeny J); *O'Donnell v Bank of Ireland* [2012] EWHC 3749 (Ch), [2013] BPIR 509 (Newey J). cf *O'Mahony v National Irish Bank* [2012] BPIR 1174, where the debtor succeeded in satisfying the court that his COMI was in England. For parallel examples of a successful COMI migration by a company, see cases cited in n 32 below.

[32] See *Re Hellas Telecommunications (Luxembourg) II SCA* [2009] EWHC 3199 (Ch), [2010] BCC 295 (Lewison J) (COMI migration from Luxembourg to London); *Re Kaupthing Capital Partners II Master LP Inc* [2010] EWHC 836 (Ch), [2011] BCC 338 (Proudman J); *Re European Directories (DH6) BV* [2010] EWHC 3472 (Ch), [2012] BCC 46 (HHJ Raynor QC).

The two categories of insolvency proceedings: Main and territorial

The Regulation contemplates only two categories of insolvency proceedings for **3.17** the purposes of its wider scheme of operation, namely main proceedings opened in accordance with Article 3(1) (determined by reference to the location of the centre of the debtor's main interests), and territorial proceedings opened in accordance with Article 3(2) (based upon the presence of an establishment of the debtor within the state in question). Territorial proceedings can occur in two varieties. Under carefully defined circumstances, which are delineated in Article 3(4)(a) and (b), they may be opened in advance of any main proceedings (and it may even happen, in rare cases, that no other insolvency proceedings take place). Where territorial proceedings are opened subsequently to main proceedings, however, then Article 3(2) and (3) together specify that they are to be secondary proceedings and that they must be winding-up proceedings. The latter are specially defined by Article 2(c), which is linked to Annex B where lists are once again provided, state by state, of the proceedings which are classified as 'winding-up proceedings' for this purpose.[33] Proceedings which qualify as main proceedings according to the terms of Article 3(1) are accorded the fullest benefits under the Regulation and enjoy extraterritorial effects throughout all the Member States. The effects of proceedings which qualify as territorial/secondary proceedings under Article 3(2)–(4) are restricted to the assets of the debtor situated in the territory of the state in which they are commenced, but such proceedings are important inasmuch as they amount to a localized derogation from the universal effects otherwise enjoyed by main proceedings involving the same debtor.

If the debtor's circumstances—including the location of the COMI—are such as **3.18** to cause the Regulation to be applicable, the consequence is that no proceedings of the kinds listed in Annex A can be opened in any of the Member States, save in accordance with the rules of international jurisdiction supplied by Article 3. Any court or official which is invited to exercise jurisdiction when this would amount to a contravention of Article 3 should decline to do so—if necessary of its own motion—as this would otherwise constitute a violation of the principle of mutual trust among Member States on which the EU and its legal system is heavily dependent. This is especially important in view of the absence of any procedure or mechanism under the terms of the Regulation itself which could be invoked in cases where there is doubt as to which of two or more states is the proper forum for the opening of main proceedings. Conversely, if the debtor's circumstances give rise to the consequence that the Regulation is not applicable, any proceedings which are opened in any Member State, within the permissible conditions prescribed by its national law, are altogether outside the scope of the Regulation and can derive no benefit from its provisions regarding international effects and

---

[33] For further information about the Annexes to the Regulation, see ch 1 above at paras 1.24, 1.25 and also para 3.02 above.

recognition.[34] Accordingly, they remain subject to national law for purposes of jurisdiction, and are dependent upon the ordinary rules of private international law for such recognition as they may receive from foreign states, including those which are members of the European Union. The precise criteria which are applicable under the Regulation for the opening of main or secondary proceedings therefore require careful consideration.

3.19 **Main proceedings (Article 3(1)).** Article 3(1) enables the courts of the Member State within whose territory the centre of the debtor's main interests is situated to open insolvency proceedings having the character of main proceedings. Such proceedings have universal scope and are intended to encompass the debtor's assets on a worldwide basis and to affect all creditors, wherever located.[35] The principle of unity is also applicable to main proceedings, in that only one set of such proceedings may be opened in the territory covered by the Regulation.

3.20 **Territorial (including secondary) proceedings (Article 3(2)–(4)).** Article 3(2) allows a limited jurisdiction to be exercised by the courts of Member States other than that in which the debtor's centre of main interests is located. Such jurisdiction, while of territorial effect, provides an important exception to the universality of effect accorded to main proceedings opened under Article 3(1). This results from the need to achieve a reconciliation between the aspiration of the authors of the Regulation to subject each given debtor to a unitary insolvency process, and the current reality that, until such time as the material differences between national laws can be eliminated, legitimate expectations of creditors in the various Member States may thereby be unfairly defeated. Such a consequence would undermine the principles of freedom of movement and exchange which are the basis of the internal market of the EU. Consequently, a limited concession to such localized interests was devised.

3.21 Under the terms of Article 3(2), where the centre of the debtor's main interests is situated within the territory of one of the Member States, the courts of another Member State shall have jurisdiction to open insolvency proceedings against that debtor only if he possesses an establishment within the territory of that other Member State. It is expressly stated that the effects of those proceedings shall be restricted to the assets of the debtor situated in the territory of the state in which they are opened. Thus, such proceedings are of purely local effect, and it is appropriate to refer to them as 'territorial'. However where (as will usually be the case) territorial proceedings take place concurrently with main proceedings opened in another Member State, the territorial proceedings are declared to be secondary proceedings.[36] As secondary proceedings, they are subject to the provisions of Chapter III of the Regulation (Articles 27–38 inclusive), which are designed to

---

[34] Virgos-Schmit Report, para 82 (see app 2 below).
[35] ibid para 73.
[36] Art 3(3). See also Recital (17), final sentence.

ensure that secondary proceedings are integrated into the overall process of administering the insolvent debtor's estate for the benefit of creditors generally.[37]

It has already been observed that Article 3(3) declares that secondary proceed-   **3.22** ings must be winding-up proceedings. This has the effect of considerably narrowing the range of options available, in terms of the types of proceedings which can be resorted to, because the definition of 'winding-up proceedings' supplied by Article 2(c) is limited to 'insolvency proceedings (within the meaning of paragraph (a)) involving realizing the assets of the debtor'. The procedures which qualify for this purpose, as listed in Annex B, are considerably fewer than are included in Annex A.[38] The consequence appears to be that in cases where the main proceedings consist of an attempt to bring about the rescue of a business which maintains one or more foreign establishments, the prospects of success could be seriously undermined by any creditors who avail themselves of the opportunity to commence secondary proceedings in the states where the establishments are located. In certain cases such a value-destructive outcome may be averted by the liquidator in the main proceeding having recourse to the device known as a 'synthetic secondary proceeding', whereby parties may be dissuaded from exercising their right to request the opening of secondary proceedings by the liquidator giving an undertaking to ensure that they receive differential treatment under the main proceeding so as to place them in a net position equivalent to that which they would prospectively obtain under the local law governing the secondary proceeding.[39]

In certain situations parties may wish to open territorial insolvency proceedings   **3.23** under Article 3(2) when no main proceedings have been commenced. This may be because, under the law of the state within whose territory the debtor's COMI is situated, the law does not allow such proceedings to be commenced.[40] Alternatively, the opening of main proceedings may be delayed for some technical reason, or simply because those who are eligible to petition for such proceedings delay, or altogether refrain, from doing so. Article 3(4) makes special provision for both these contingencies, by allowing territorial proceedings to be opened prior to any

---

[37] See the commentary to Arts 27–38 in ch 8 below.

[38] In the case of the United Kingdom, the following are listed in Annex B as winding-up proceedings: winding-up by or subject to the supervision of the court; winding-up through administration, including appointments made by filing prescribed documents with the court; creditors' voluntary winding-up (with confirmation by the court); and bankruptcy or sequestration.

[39] For examples of such solutions embodying 'synthetic secondary' proceedings, see *Re Collins & Aikman Europe SA* [2006] BCC 861 (Lindsey J); *Re MG Rover Espana SA* [2006] BCC 599 (Chancery Division, Birmingham DR, HHJ Norris). See also *Re Nortel Networks SA* [2009] BCC 343 (Patten J). See also para 3.33 below.

[40] The laws of a number of Member States follow the tradition whereby insolvency proceedings cannot take place against a debtor who is not classifiable as a trader (*commerçant*). This is the case in Belgium, France, Greece, Italy, Luxembourg, Portugal, and Spain. Indeed, in the case of Italy even small-scale traders (*piccoli imprenditori*) are excluded from the operation of the bankruptcy law by Art 2083 of the Civil Code.

main proceedings being commenced.[41] In the absence of evidence to the effect that main proceedings cannot be opened because of the conditions laid down by the law of the Member State where the debtor's COMI is located, the opening of territorial proceedings can only be requested by a creditor who has his domicile, habitual residence, or registered office within the Member State in whose territory the establishment is situated, or whose claim arises from the operation of that establishment.[42] These restrictions upon the right to request the opening of independent territorial proceedings are clearly aimed at preventing disruptive tactics on the part of creditors who do not have a close personal nexus with the jurisdiction in which the debtor's establishment is located. Accordingly, the ECJ has ruled that the provisions of Article 3(4) must be interpreted strictly so as to limit the cases where the opening of such proceedings can be requested to those where such an exceptional departure is absolutely necessary.[43]

Establishment of the debtor

3.24 The key concept in relation to the opening of secondary (territorial) insolvency proceedings is therefore the existence of an 'establishment' belonging to the debtor. Article 2(h) defines the term as meaning: 'any place of operations where the debtor carries out a non-transitory economic activity with human means and goods'. The significance of the above definition is somewhat clarified by paragraphs 70 and 71 of the Virgos-Schmit Report, which disclose that this provision was the cause of much debate during the negotiations. The exclusion of any possibility for proceedings to be opened on the basis of the mere presence of assets of a debtor without any functional activity to constitute 'an establishment', is the result of a deliberate decision to restrict the number of opportunities for creditors to avail themselves of the personal and tactical advantages to be gained by means of secondary proceedings. A contrast may be drawn between the 'passive' quality of assets (even if of very substantial value), and the 'active' quality of the concept of an establishment. Also to be emphasized are the requirement that the economic activity must be of a 'non-transitory' nature, and be carried out with 'human means *and* goods'.[44] Thus a purely occasional or temporary place of operations could not be classified as an establishment, although there is no indication within the Regulation (nor in the

---

[41] Art 3(4)(a).

[42] Art 3(4)(b).

[43] Case C-112/10 *Procureur-generaal, Antwerpen v Zaza Retail BV* [2011] ECR I-11525, [2012] BPIR 438, judgment of 17 November 2011 (ECJ, First Chamber). Further guidance on the approach to the opening of secondary proceedings was delivered by the Court of Justice in Case C-327/13 *Burgo Group SpA v Illochroma SA*, (CJEU, Judgment 4 September 2014), [2015] BCC 33.

[44] Emphasis added. The test is thus a compound one, requiring both elements to be satisfied. Cf the significant change introduced into the wording of the definition of 'establishment' in Art 2(f) of the UNCITRAL Model Law on Cross-Border Insolvency, where the concluding phrase of the definition (which otherwise follows exactly that in Art 2(h) of the EC Regulation) refers to 'human means and goods *or services*' (emphasis added). The Istanbul Convention of the Council of Europe (not yet in force) would permit the opening of secondary bankruptcy proceedings on the basis of a presence of assets alone: see Art 17. On the Istanbul Convention see ch 1, n 8 and text thereto.

Virgos-Schmit Report) as to the minimum length of time after which an activity ceases to be 'transitory' for this purpose. Similarly, the fact that the debtor happens to have carried out one (or, possibly, several) business transactions within the territory of a Member State would not of itself amount to the maintenance of an establishment there, unless there is further evidence to show that these activities were intended to mark the commencement of a more enduring economic operation in that jurisdiction. It will be a matter of judgment for the court, taken in the light of all relevant circumstances.[45]

Effectively, the court will be seeking to ascertain whether the debtor maintains a **3.25** 'place of business' within its jurisdiction. In their approach, courts should bear in mind that the Regulation's intended purpose is to serve as an integral component in the legal infrastructure sustaining the European Union's internal market. The underlying rationale for allowing insolvency proceedings to be opened on the basis of an establishment is that foreign participants in the economic activities conducted within a given Member State should be subject to equal rules and conditions as compared to national operators with whom they are competing. In this way, potential creditors do not have to concern themselves unduly whether the debtor is ultimately 'foreign' in orientation, provided that the external appearances suggest a locally-established business operation. The external impression is therefore the decisive factor, rather than the subjective intentions of the debtor.[46] This approach was adopted by the ECJ in that part of its ruling in the *Interedil* case which addresses the interpretation of the term 'establishment' within the context of Article 3(2).[47] Noting that the definition of 'establishment' in Article 2(h) links the pursuit of an economic activity to the presence of human resources, the Court declares that 'a minimum level of organisation and a degree of stability are required. ... [C]onversely, the presence of goods alone in isolation or in bank accounts does not, in principle, satisfy the requirements for classification as an "establishment"'.[48] In a further, and most important, statement of principle concerning the test for determining the existence of an establishment, and hence identifying the court or courts with jurisdiction to open secondary or territorial proceedings, the Court ruled: '[I]n order to ensure legal certainty and

---

[45] For a detailed analysis of the term 'establishment', see ch 8 below, commentary to Art 2(h).
[46] Virgos-Schmit Report, para 71 (see app 2 below).
[47] Case C-396/09 *Interedil Srl v Fallimento Interedil Srl* [2011] ECR I-9915, [2012] BCC 851, judgment 20 October 2011 (ECJ, First Chamber), at paras [60]–[64] of the judgment. See also the judgment of the UK Supreme Court in *Trustees of Olympic Airlines SA Pension and Life Assurance Scheme v Olympic Airlines SA* [2015] UKSC 27, [2015] 1 WLR 2399 (SC), in which emphasis was placed on the requirement that the alleged establishment must be operating as such on the date of presentation of a winding-up petition, for which purpose there must be a carrying on of business activity consisting of dealing with third parties. The conduct of acts of a purely internal matter concerning the company's residual administration would not suffice for this purpose.
[48] *Interedil* ibid at para [62] of the judgment. In its concluding formulation at para [64] the Court adopts the somewhat more exacting proposition that an establishment 'must be interpreted as requiring the presence of a structure consisting of a minimum level of organisation and a degree of stability necessary for the purpose of pursuing an economic activity.'

foreseeability … the existence of an establishment must be determined, in the same way as the location of the centre of main interests, on the basis of objective factors which are ascertainable by third parties.'[49]

B. Principal Effects of the Recast Regulation ('RR') When in Force

3.26 The following paragraphs provide a summary of the principal effects relating to matters discussed in the present chapter that will ensue from the entering into effect of the recast Insolvency Regulation (RR) on the appointed date, 26 June 2017.[50] Cross references are made to preceding paragraphs where the affected provisions of the OR are discussed.

Scope

3.27 A major recasting of the scope of the Regulation is proclaimed by the terms of Article 1 RR, which states that

> This Regulation shall apply to public, collective proceedings, including interim proceedings, which are based on laws relating to insolvency and in which, for the purposes of rescue, adjustment of debt, reorganization or liquidation,
> (a) a debtor is totally or partially divested of its assets and an insolvency practitioner is appointed,
> (b) the assets and affairs of a debtor are subject to control or supervision by a court, or
> (c) a temporary stay of individual enforcement proceedings is granted by a court or by operation of law, in order to allow for negotiations between the debtor and its creditors, provided that the proceedings in which the stay is granted provide for suitable measures to protect the general body of creditors, and, where no agreement is reached, are preliminary to one of the proceedings referred to under points (a) or (b).

Thus the recast Regulation will place considerable emphasis on rescue and rehabilitation, and will apply to so-called pre-insolvency procedures as well as to procedures aimed at facilitating business reorganization or debt restructuring. Also notable is the fact that proceedings of the 'debtor in possession' type will be within the scope of the Regulation, provided that the process is subject to control or supervision by a court. To complement the altered focus of this new regime the term 'liquidator' has been omitted in favour of the more open term 'insolvency practitioner', which is defined in Article 2(5) RR and is used throughout the text to denote a person or

---

[49] ibid at para [63] of the judgment. For the complementary elements of the ruling by the ECJ in paras [41]–[59] of the same judgment, dealing with the interpretation of the concept of COMI, see para 3.13 above and also ch 8 below, commentary to Art 3.

[50] See ch 1 above at para 1.27 concerning the provisions governing the entry into *effect* of the recast Regulation.

body whose functions are involved in the conduct of any of the proceedings which fall within the scope of the Regulation. Article 1 of the recast Regulation concludes with a list of proceedings which are excluded from its scope by virtue of the type of corporate entity to which they relate. This list corresponds in substance to that which appears in Article 1(2) OR.

The previous, convoluted provisions delineating the scope of the Regulation **3.28** (see 3.02 above) have been replaced by the singular assertion in Article 1(1) that 'The proceedings referred to in this paragraph *are listed in Annex A*'" (emphasis added). Therefore, if a procedure is listed in Annex A it is definitively included within the scope of the revised Regulation, and conversely if it is not so listed it is excluded. From a United Kingdom perspective, it can be noted that the five entries listed in Annex A of the current Regulation, as set out in paragraph 3.03 above, remain unchanged. Consequently, schemes of arrangement under Part 26 of the Companies Act 2006 do not fall within the scope of the revised Regulation. The newly constituted Annex B to the RR (which replaces the current Annex C listing the office holders who qualify as 'liquidators') lists those who qualify as 'insolvency practitioners' for the purposes of Article 2(5). The list for the United Kingdom replicates that which appears in the current Annex C, with the single addition of the office of 'interim receiver'.[51] It is noteworthy that the provision for periodically revising the Annexes, contained in Article 45 of the current Regulation, has been omitted from the recast Regulation. This will render it more difficult to amend the Annexes in order to keep abreast of new developments in the laws of the Member States. However, there would seem to be no legal impediment to the adoption of an amending regulation of the European Parliament and the Council to bring about such alterations, although this may prove to be difficult in both political and practical terms.[52]

International jurisdiction

Important changes have been made to the key provisions on international jurisdic- **3.29** tion contained in Article 3 RR. These should be carefully compared to the current Article 3 as originally enacted.[53] Although the fundamental principles of jurisdiction, based on main and secondary proceedings, are maintained together with the associated connecting factors of the centre of main interests and establishment of

---

[51] An interim receiver may be appointed by the court pursuant to s 286 of the Insolvency Act 1986 following the presentation of a bankruptcy petition and before the making of a bankruptcy order, for the protection of the debtor's property.

[52] Note the innovative provision in Art 89 RR for the Commission to be assisted by a committee within the meaning of Regulation (EU) 182/2011, of 16 February 2011, OJ L55/13, 28 February 2011. Art 90 RR, bearing the title 'Review clause', does not expressly mention the revision of the Annexes, although the need for any amendments could be included in the periodical reports which the Commission is required to produce on the application of the Regulation according to para 1 of that Article.

[53] See paras 3.09–3.23 above.

the debtor respectively, important amendments are made to the text of Article 3 RR itself, augmented by extensive statements incorporated in Recitals (22) to (38) which are intended to supply guidance on the approach to interpretation of the substantive articles. Notably, as was also the case with the OR, the all-important 'master condition' to the application of the recast Regulation is contained in one of the Recitals, namely number (25), which declares: 'This Regulation applies only to proceedings in respect of a debtor whose centre of main interests is located in the Union'. This is identical in substance to the statement in Recital (14) OR, with the substitution of the term 'the Union' for the previous reference to 'the Community'. The correct ascertainment of the debtor's COMI therefore remains of fundamental importance, first for the purpose of determining whether the recast Regulation will or will not apply, and secondly to determine in which state of the Union main proceedings can be opened. The resolution of the issue of COMI and its location under the recast Regulation will be performed in accordance with the recast provisions of Article 3 taken in conjunction with entirely new provisions enacted as Articles 4 and 5 RR, all of which must be read in the light of the statements contained in Recitals (22) to (38) inclusive. The recast provisions partly reflect the conclusions imparted by the Court of Justice in rulings delivered in relation to the terms of the OR concerning international jurisdiction.[54] Notably, the indicative statement contained in Recital (13) OR has been assimilated into Article 3(1) RR, drafted in more positive terms as follows: 'The centre of main interests shall be the place where the debtor conducts the administration of its interests on a regular basis and which is ascertainable by third parties.' Further indications of the approach to be adopted for this purpose are supplied by Recital (28) RR, which emphasizes: 'special consideration should be given to the creditors and to their perception as to where a debtor conducts the administration of its interests.'

'Mobile COMI'

3.30 The special concerns regarding the potential for abuse of the mobile character of COMI, also known as 'forum shopping' or 'bankruptcy tourism',[55] have been addressed in several ways. Article 4 RR requires a court seised of a request to open insolvency proceedings to examine, of its own motion, whether it has jurisdiction pursuant to Article 3. Moreover any judgment opening insolvency proceedings must specify the grounds on which the jurisdiction is based, and in particular whether it is based on Article 3(1) (main proceedings based on COMI) or 3(2) (territorial proceedings based on the maintenance of an establishment of the debtor). To reinforce the process whereby the court must police the exercise of its own international jurisdiction, Article 5 RR creates a right for the debtor or any creditor to challenge the decision opening main insolvency proceedings by way of judicial

---

[54] Summarized in paras 3.09–3.23 above, and in greater detail in ch 8.
[55] See paras 3.14–3.15 above.

review.[56] Further provisions to combat so-called 'bad forum shopping' have been introduced into unnumbered paragraphs 2, 3, and 4 of Article 3(1) RR. These have the effect of recasting the rebuttable presumption that in the case of a company or legal person the place of the registered office is the location of the COMI, by the addition of a proviso that the presumption shall only apply if the registered office has not been moved to another Member State within three months prior to the request for opening of insolvency proceedings. For the first time, analogous presumptions are included for the benefit of individuals engaged in an independent business or professional activity and for the benefit of individuals who are not so engaged (employed persons or consumers). For the former, there is a rebuttable presumption that the COMI is at the individual's principal place of business, and for the latter the COMI is presumed to be at the individual's habitual residence in the absence of proof to the contrary. In each case, a proviso is appended whereby the presumption shall only apply if the connecting factor on which the COMI presumption is based has not undergone relocation from one Member State to another within close proximity to the request for the opening of insolvency proceedings: the respective periods are three months in the case of those engaged in an independent business or professional activity, and six months in any other case.[57] Recital (30) RR contains further guidance on the factors which should be considered when the court is addressing the question of whether the presumption, where it is initially applicable, should be held to be rebutted.

Territorial (including secondary) proceedings: Establishment of the debtor

The recast Regulation contains some important adjustments to the provisions **3.31** bearing upon international jurisdiction to open territorial, including secondary, proceedings based upon the maintenance of an establishment of the debtor within the Member State concerned.[58] The wording of Article 3(2) RR, which is the root of authority for the opening of territorial proceedings, is identical to that of Article 3(2) OR. However, the definition of 'establishment', now contained in Article 2(10) RR, embodies a crucial amendment as compared to the definition given by Article 2(h) OR.[59] The altered definition reads as follows:

> 'establishment' means any place of operations where a debtor carries out *or has carried out in the three month period prior to the request to open main insolvency proceedings* a non-transitory economic activity with human means and *assets* (the additional or altered wording is italicized).

The significance of the additional words in the first part of the provision is that they remove any doubt about the possibility of opening territorial proceedings provided that the establishment was in active operation in the period immediately preceding

---

[56] See also Recitals (33) and (34) RR.
[57] Art 3(1) RR, paras 3 and 4.
[58] See paras 3.19–3.23 above.
[59] See para 3.23 above.

the request to open main proceedings. Cases have arisen under the original wording of the definition in Article 2(h) where an establishment which was operating at the time of the opening of main proceedings had been shut down, or had ceased to deal with third parties, by the time of the request to open secondary proceedings. National courts have sometimes been influenced by the use of the phrase 'carries out' to assume that jurisdiction under Article 3(2) could only be exercised if the alleged establishment was continuing to operate as a place of business at the time of the request to open territorial proceedings.[60] Some uncertainty remains, however, due to the drafting employed in the recast version of Article 2(10), as it is unclear whether it is necessary that the establishment must have been fully operational *throughout* the three-month period before the request to open main proceedings, or whether it is sufficient to be able to demonstrate that the establishment was in active operation at some time within that period. The second change to the text of Article 2(10) RR when compared to that of the original Article 2(h) consists of the substitution of the final word 'assets' in place of the technical solecism perpetrated by the use of the terms 'goods' in the official English language version. As the commentary to Article 2(h) in chapter 8 below explains, this was an unfortunate mistranslation which has at last been corrected in the recast Regulation.[61]

Secondary proceedings and the rescue culture: Synthetic secondary proceedings

3.32 Two further changes have been accomplished during the course of recasting the provisions on secondary proceedings. The first is the removal of the previous, illogical restriction whereby secondary proceedings were required to be liquidation proceedings, thereby creating a major practical impediment to the conduct of effective corporate rescue under the auspices of the OR.[62] The deletion of the final sentence of Article 3(2) OR, combined with the omission from Article 34 RR of the requirement previously imposed by the terms of Article 27 OR that all secondary proceedings opened under Article 3(2) must be among the proceedings listed in Annex B, has opened the way to a more constructive era in the life of the EU Insolvency Regulation. It has also rendered redundant the original Annex B itself, which is omitted from the recast Regulation with the consequence, as already noted, that the former Annex C becomes Annex B in the RR.

3.33 The second significant change relating to the operation of secondary insolvency proceedings is the inclusion of provisions which incorporate into Union law the practitioner-developed device known as 'synthetic secondary proceedings'.[63] Article 36(1) RR empowers the insolvency practitioner in main insolvency proceedings to

---

[60] This was the basis of the ruling by the UK Supreme Court in *Trustees of Olympic Airlines SA Pension and Life Assurance Scheme v Olympic Airlines SA* [2015] UKSC 27, [2015] 1 WLR 2399 (SC) (see n 47 above).
[61] Ch 8 below at para 8.57.
[62] See paras 3.16 and 3.21 above.
[63] See para 3.21 above, and cases cited at n 39.

avert the opening of secondary proceedings by giving an undertaking in respect
of the assets located in the Member State in which secondary proceedings could
be opened, that when distributing those assets or their realized proceeds he will
comply with the distribution and priority rights under national law that creditors
would have if secondary proceedings were opened in that Member State. Detailed
provisions are made in paragraphs (2) to (11) of Article 36 RR concerning the
operation of this potentially value-saving facility, reinforced by the statements
contained in Recitals (41) to (44) inclusive. It should be noted that by virtue of
its inclusion in the provisions of the recast Regulation the option to engage in a
synthetic secondary proceeding automatically becomes part of the law applicable
in every one of the 27 participating states, and overrides any provision of national
law or policy which might negate such a practice. In particular, this generates an
important exception to the application of the *pari passu* principle of distribution
in cases which are within the scope of the recast Regulation. Moreover this new
procedure is not limited in application to those types of proceedings which are
designed to bring about the rescue or restructuring of the debtor (although that is
likely to be the context in which it will most frequently be employed). It is equally
applicable to liquidation-type proceedings where the possibility of one or more
secondary proceedings could materially affect the ultimate net realization available for distribution among all creditors, having regard to the additional costs
incurred through multiple insolvency proceedings involving the same debtor. One
further, vital practical provision is to be found in the final sentence of Article 36(2)
RR, which states that the relevant point in time for determining the assets referred
to in Article 36(1) shall be the moment at which the undertaking is given by the
insolvency practitioner who is conducting the main proceedings.

*Jurisdiction for actions deriving directly from insolvency proceedings
and closely linked with them*

Article 6 RR, which has no exact counterpart in the OR, creates special rules of **3.34**
international jurisdiction for actions deriving directly from insolvency proceedings and closely linked with them. The courts of the Member State within whose
territory insolvency proceedings have been opened in accordance with Article 3 are
clothed with jurisdiction 'for *any* action which derives *directly* from the insolvency
proceedings *and* is *closely linked* with them, *such as avoidance actions*' (emphasis
added).[64] The terms of this provision are widely drawn ('any action'), but a delimit-
ing feature is injected by the compound condition that for an action to be brought
on the basis of Article 6 RR it must *both* derive directly from the insolvency proceedings *and* be closely linked with them. Significantly, the concluding words of
the provision identify avoidance actions as an example of the kind of proceedings
that can benefit from this extension of the international jurisdiction of a court in
which insolvency proceedings—whether main or secondary—have been opened

---

[64] Art 6(1) RR.

under Article 3. Amplification of the underlying rationale for this provision is to be found in Recital (35) RR, which also mentions avoidance actions as being included within the scope of the extended jurisdiction, together with 'actions concerning obligations that arise in the course of the insolvency proceedings, such as advance payment for costs of the proceedings'. A contrast is drawn between such proceedings and 'actions for the performance of obligations under a contract concluded by the debtor prior to the opening of proceedings'. The latter type of actions 'do not derive directly from the proceedings'. The provisions of Article 6 RR confirm and consolidate the position already established by the case law of the Court of Justice, in the case of *Seagon v Deko Marty Belgium BV*[65] in which the Court, in agreement with the opinion of Advocate General Colomer, adopted a purposive and pragmatic approach to the interpretation of Article 3(1) OR, and to its relationship to the original version of the Brussels Regulation of 22 December 2000.[66]

3.35 Article 6(2) RR further extends the potential scope of the jurisdiction in cases where an action referred to in paragraph 1 is *related to* an action in civil and commercial matters against the same defendant. The insolvency practitioner is allowed to bring *both* actions before the courts of the Member State within whose territory the defendant is domiciled, or where the action is brought against several defendants, before the courts of the Member State within the territory of which any of them is domiciled, provided that those courts have jurisdiction pursuant to the recast Brussels Regulation of 12 December 2012.[67] The proviso to Article 6(2) expressly extends the jurisdiction under paragraph 1 to actions brought by the debtor in possession, provided that national law allows such a party to bring actions on behalf of the insolvency estate. Article 6(3) RR supplies a formula whereby, for the purpose of paragraph 2, 'actions are deemed to be related where they are so closely connected that it is expedient to hear and determine them together to avoid the risk of irreconcilable judgments resulting from separate proceedings'.

3.36 An important adjunct to the extended jurisdiction established by Article 6 RR is the provision in Article 32(1) RR, first proviso (which replicates exactly the terms of the first proviso of Article 25(1) OR), whereby judgments deriving directly from the insolvency proceedings and which are closely linked with them, even if they were handed down by another court, are to be recognized automatically in all other Member States in accordance with Article 19 RR, and are to be enforced in accordance with Articles 39 to 44 and 47 to 57 of the recast Brussels Regulation. One significant consequence of these provisions is that it is made possible for a

---

[65] Case C-339/07 [2009] ECR I-767, discussed in ch 8 below at 8.351.

[66] Council Regulation (EC) 44/2001 of 22 December 2000, on Jurisdiction and the Recognition and Enforcement of Judgments in Civil and Commercial Matters [2001] OJ L12/1, in force from March 2002 until January 2015 (see n 64).

[67] Regulation (EU) 1215/2012 of the European Parliament and of the Council on Jurisdiction and the Recognition and Enforcement of Judgments in Civil and Commercial Matters (recast), OJ L351/1, 20 December 2012, in force from 10 January 2015.

judgment delivered in an action which derives directly from and is closely linked with insolvency proceedings to be eligible for automatic recognition and enforcement throughout the Member States even where the judgment has been given in default of appearance, provided that the defendant was served with the document which instituted proceedings or with an equivalent document in sufficient time and in such a way as to enable him to arrange for his defence.[68] It should be noted that this aspect of the evolutionary development of European Union law constitutes an important exception to the position established by the decision of the UK Supreme Court in *Rubin v Eurofinance SA*[69] whereby it was ruled that English private international law does not permit the enforcement of a foreign judgment delivered in default of appearance in transaction avoidance proceedings brought in the very bankruptcy court whose jurisdictional competence to open the bankruptcy proceedings themselves was fully in accordance with English law rules of recognition. It is submitted that in an analogous case, if insolvency proceedings have been opened in the court of a Member State in accordance with Article 3 OR or RR, a judgment delivered by a court of that same state in an avoidance action, even if given in default of appearance, is enforceable in England in accordance with the recast Brussels Regulation.

---

[68] See recast Brussels Regulation (n 67 above), Arts 45(1)(b), 46 together with Art 41(1), (2).
[69] [2012] UKSC 46, [2013] 1 AC 236 (SC).

4

CHOICE OF LAW RULES

A. The Original Regulation ('OR')

Preliminary

Section A of this chapter provides an overview of the uniform rules of choice of law **4.01** which are applicable to all proceedings governed by the original EC/EU Regulation ('OR'). These rules are contained in Articles 4–15 inclusive. Commentary on the individual Articles is supplied in chapter 8 below. Section B provides a summary of the principal changes which will take effect under the provisions of the RR when it becomes applicable from 26 June 2017 (see chapter 1, section B above at para 1.26).

General principles

Articles 4–15 amount to a miniature code of uniform conflicts rules which are **4.02** integral to the OR's operation. Because the Member States' domestic insolvency

71

laws remain unharmonized at present it is essential that there should be clear, and uniform, rules to determine which state's law is to be applicable to issues which will typically be encountered during the course of insolvency proceedings. This enables affected parties to calculate in advance the legal risks inherent in their relationship with a debtor whose circumstances bring it within the ambit of the OR in the event of insolvency. The uniform rules indicate, as between various Member States and also in relation to third states whose laws may potentially be applicable in a given situation, which state's law shall, in fact, govern. In most cases, the rules contemplate a choice only between the laws of different Member States. In certain situations, however, the drafting of the relevant provision clearly allows for the possibility that the law of some third state may be applicable, if the specified connecting factor leads to that result in the circumstances of a given case. Those instances are noted below in discussing the contents of Articles 5–15.

4.03 Apart from the particular instances just mentioned, however, the OR is so drafted as to confine the scope of the uniform choice of law rules to cases where the relevant contacts give rise to a choice between the laws of different Member States. Consequently, where the facts of a case raise the issue of the potential application of the law of a non-EU state, it is left for each Member State to resolve the conflict according to its own rules of private international law. As is emphasized in paragraph 44 of the Virgos-Schmit Report,[1] in relation to the equivalent provisions embodied in the 1995 version of the Convention, the choice of law provisions are deliberately limited to regulating the 'intra-Community effects' of insolvency proceedings: where non-Member States are concerned it is the responsibility of each Member State to define the appropriate conflict rules. This is, unfortunately, a recipe for instability and uncertainty, particularly where the assets to which the alternating conflicts rules are to apply are mobile, and therefore capable of being subject to different rules according to their whereabouts at the relevant time. Variability of outcome will therefore remain a possibility for cases where the potentially applicable law is that of some third state, as the choice of law rules of different Member States could give rise to the application of different laws in cases with identical material facts. The crucial question will therefore be which Member State's courts have jurisdiction, according to the rules described in chapter 3 above. This is a factor to be borne in mind when calculating the effects of the OR's choice of law rules on such important matters as agreements for the effecting of security, reservation of title agreements, interests in property which is subject to public registration, contracts of employment and contracts relating to immovable property, and on the rights and obligations of parties operating in regulated financial markets.[2]

---

[1] See also para 93 of the Report, and also M Balz, 'The European Union Convention on Insolvency Proceedings' (1996) 70 American Bankruptcy LJ 485, 507. On the Virgos-Schmit Report to the former EC Convention project, and its status as an aid to interpretation of provisions contained in the Regulation on Insolvency Proceedings, see para 1.06 above, n 11 and text thereto.

[2] See section C below.

The rules which are discussed below can also determine whether a creditor will have the benefit of set-off in the event of the insolvency of a counter-party to whom it is simultaneously indebted.[3]

Renvoi

An important general point about the choice of law provisions in the OR is that **4.04** wherever they make reference to 'the law', this denotes the substantive, domestic law of the Member State concerned. The complexities—not to say inconsistencies—of the doctrine of *renvoi* are not intended to form part of the approach to be followed under the OR. In modern treaties which embody uniform conflicts rules it is quite often the case that a specific provision is included to the effect that references to the law of a state or country are not to be interpreted as including a reference to the choice of law rules which are in force there.[4] Indeed, to allow recourse to *renvoi* would defeat the very objective of seeking to harmonize choice of law rules by means of such an international agreement. The OR is intended to follow this approach, although no express provision to that effect was incorporated into the actual text.[5]

B. The Basic Choice of Law Rule (Article 4 OR): *Lex Concursus*

Article 4 expresses the basic principle that the law of the Member State in which **4.05** proceedings are opened according to the OR (referred to as 'the state of opening') is to be applied to those proceedings, and shall determine their effects, except in so far as the OR expressly provides to the contrary. The matters which are to be governed by the law of the state of opening (the *lex concursus*) are mentioned in a non-exhaustive list in Article 4(2), while the particular exceptions to the regime of the *lex concursus* are contained in Articles 5–15. The opening words of Article 4(2) supply a broad proposition stating that the law applicable to insolvency proceedings and their effects shall be that of the Member State within the territory of which such proceedings are opened.[6] Paragraph 2 of the Article further declares that the law of the state of the opening of proceedings shall determine the conditions for

---

[3] See sections B and C below, with reference to Arts 4((2)(d) and 6 respectively, and the further commentary to Art 6 in ch 8 below.

[4] See eg EC Convention on the Law Applicable to Contractual Obligations (the Rome Convention) of 19 June 1980, Art 15 (which has the heading 'Exclusion of *renvoi*'): 'The application of the law of any country specified by this Convention means the application of the rules of law in force in that country *other than its rules of private international law*' (emphasis added). The Rome Convention, which was in force among Member States during the period when the text of the Insolvency Regulation was negotiated and enacted, was replaced in relation to all Member States except Denmark with effect from 17 December 2009 by Regulation (EC) 593/2008 of 17 June 2008 (the Rome I Regulation) [2008] OJ 177/6. Art 20 of that Regulation replicates verbatim the wording of Art 15 of the Rome Convention, save for the addition of the following words at the end of the sentence: '... unless provided otherwise in this Regulation.'

[5] See Virgos-Schmit Report (n 1 above) para 87.

[6] This proposition is qualified by the opening words of Art 4(1): 'Save as otherwise provided by this Regulation ...'. See section C below.

the opening of those proceedings, their conduct, and their closure. Under this formula, many matters of substance are determined by the law of the state of opening, as well as all matters of a procedural nature which, in conformity with accepted principles of conflict of laws, are governed by the *lex fori*.

4.06 Further to this general proposition, 13 particular matters are singled out for special mention in Article 4(2) as being for determination by the *lex concursus*. These are:

(a) against which debtors insolvency proceedings may be brought on account of their capacity;

(b) the assets which form part of the estate and the treatment of assets acquired by or devolving on the debtor after the opening of the insolvency proceedings;

(c) the respective powers of the debtor and the liquidator;

(d) the conditions under which set-offs may be invoked;[7]

(e) the effects of insolvency proceedings on current contracts to which the debtor is party;[8]

(f) the effects of the insolvency proceedings on proceedings brought by individual creditors, with the exception of lawsuits pending;[9]

(g) the claims which are to be lodged against the debtor's estate and the treatment of claims arising after the opening of insolvency proceedings;

(h) the rules governing the lodging, verification, and admission of claims;

(i) the rules governing the distribution of proceeds from the realization of assets, the ranking of claims, and the rights of creditors who have obtained partial satisfaction after the opening of insolvency proceedings by virtue of a right in rem or through a set-off;[10]

(j) the conditions for and the effects of closure of insolvency proceedings, in particular by composition;

(k) creditors' rights after the closure of insolvency proceedings;

(l) who is to bear the costs and expenses incurred in the insolvency proceedings; and

(m) the rules relating to the voidness, voidability, or unenforceability of legal acts detrimental to all the creditors.[11]

4.07 Although many of the matters referred to in paragraphs (a) to (m) above are largely self-explanatory, some comments are appropriate here. Paragraph (a) is particularly significant in view of the wide diversity between the insolvency laws of the 27 participating EU Member States concerning the types of debtors to which the different

---

[7] See however section C below, in relation to the effect of Art 6 (Exception II).

[8] See section C below, in relation to Art 8 (Exception IV).

[9] See section C below, in relation to Art 15 (Exception XI).

[10] See section C below, in relation to Arts 5 and 6 (Exceptions I and II).

[11] The provision in Art 4(2)(m) is given precedence over the special rules in favour of the application of some law other than the *lex concursus*, in Arts 5, 6, and 7: see Arts 5(4), 6(2), and 7(3). However, para (m) is expressly prevented from applying in cases which fall within Art 13 (acts detrimental to all the creditors): see section C below (Exception IX).

kinds of insolvency proceedings are applicable.[12] Variations also occur with regard to the treatment of after-acquired property, the composition of the estate available for distribution among creditors, and the extent to which certain assets are exempt from forming part of it. These are among the issues which paragraph (b) brings under the control of the *lex concursus.* The importance of paragraphs (g), (h), and (i) should also be noted, since they ensure that the law of the state of opening is determinative of each stage of the process of distribution of the estate, including the following matters: what debts are, and are not, provable; the treatment of post-commencement claims against the estate; all aspects bearing upon proof and admission of claims; and the vital question of the ranking of claims for purposes of dividend; and also the treatment of partly-secured creditors who wish to lodge proof for the balance of any claim which has been partly recouped through the enforcement of in rem security or the operation of set-off. By virtue of paragraph (d) the basic approach to be followed in relation to set-off is also that of the state of opening, so that parties' expectations of how the doctrine of set-off will affect their position in the event of their debtor's insolvency are primarily determined by reference to the law of the state where insolvency proceedings can be opened.[13]

Transaction avoidance

The potential for impeachment of an insolvent debtor's pre-bankruptcy transac- **4.08**
tions, and likewise of any acts or dispositions of property carried out after the opening of proceedings, is one of the key aspects of the insolvency process. Moreover, the relevant rules are subject to crucial variations as between different jurisdictions. Hence the importance of Article 4(2)(m), which establishes the basic rule that the *lex concursus* shall be applied to determine the validity or otherwise of the debtor's legal acts detrimental to the general body of creditors. This provision is particularly far-reaching in its effect, because it is intended not merely to determine what procedural steps must be taken to bring about the invalidation or avoidance of such transactions, but also to displace any law which might otherwise have been applicable to govern the transaction, had bankruptcy not supervened.[14] However, Article 13 superimposes a rule whose effect is to disapply Article 4(2)(m) in certain circumstances, with the consequence that the avoidance rule of the *lex concursus* is

---

[12] As stated in para 3.23 above, at n 40 under the laws of Belgium, France, Greece, Italy, Luxembourg, Portugal, and Spain, respectively, insolvency proceedings cannot take place in relation to debtors who are not classified as traders (*commerçants*). In the case of Italy, by Art 1(1) of the Bankruptcy Act (Royal Decree No 267 of 1942) small-scale traders (*piccoli imprenditori*), as defined by Art 2083 of the Civil Code, are excluded from the operation of the bankruptcy law.

[13] See, however, Art 6, discussed in section C below (Exception II).

[14] Virgos-Schmit Report (n 1 above) para 90. See also Balz (n 1 above) 511–12. Note the additional force bestowed on Art 4(2)(m) by the decision of the Court of Justice in Case C-328/12 *Schmid v Hertel* [2014] 1 WLR 633, [2014] BCC 25 (First Chamber, 14 January 2014) affirming that where insolvency proceedings are opened in Germany by virtue of the debtor's German COMI, transaction avoidance proceedings can be brought in that jurisdiction against parties whose place of residence is not within the territory of any Member State.

displaced in favour of the rule of some other state. This important exception to the application of the *lex concursus* is considered in section C below.[15]

4.09 The above account of the dominant role accorded to the *lex concursus* serves to emphasize the substantial benefits which accrue from the opening of proceedings within the scope of application of the OR. The basic choice of law rule established by Article 4 applies both to main proceedings within Article 3(1) and to territorial proceedings (whether secondary or freestanding) within paragraphs 2–4 of that Article.[16] This supplies one of the main reasons why parties may seek to avail themselves of any opportunity to bring about the commencement of secondary insolvency proceedings under the OR, since this will result in the application of the law of that Member State, instead of the law of the state in which the main proceedings have been opened, to the process of administering and distributing the assets located within the state in which the secondary proceedings take place.

C. Exceptions to the Basic Choice of Law Rule (Articles 5–15 OR)

4.10 As noted above, Article 4 opens with the significant words of exception: 'Save as otherwise provided in this Regulation'. The primary rule in favour of the application of the *lex concursus* is therefore subject to displacement under specified circumstances. The provisions which establish the particular cases of exception are contained in Articles 5–15 inclusive. These will be examined in turn.

Exception I: Third parties' rights in rem (Article 5 OR)

4.11 The first major exception to the *lex concursus* rule of Article 4 is provided by Article 5, whose purpose is to confirm the rights of parties to enter into transactions under which proprietary interests are created in favour of a creditor by way of security for the debt or obligation due from the debtor.[17] In practice, the essential purpose of such forms of security is that it enables the secured party to have direct recourse to the collateral in the event that the debtor does not pay or perform—and especially where this occurs by reason of the debtor's insolvency. For this purpose to be achieved, it is vital that the laws of every concerned jurisdiction should fully accept that the right in rem is valid and enforceable even in the event of the debtor's insolvency, provided that it is shown to be valid according to the law of the situs of the collateral.[18] The possibility which has to be confronted in a cross-border case is that the location of the collateral,

---

[15] See section C (Exception IX).

[16] See Recital (23) to the Regulation. On the distinction between main and territorial (secondary) proceedings, and the criteria for opening them, see ch 3, section A above.

[17] For additional commentary on Art 5 and its effects, see ch 8 below. See also M Virgos and F Garcimartin, *The European Insolvency Regulation: Law and Practice* (2004) 91–108; B Wessels, *International Insolvency Law* (3rd edn, 2012) paras 10639–60.

[18] See the propositions embodied in Recital (25) to the Regulation.

either at the time of opening of proceedings or at some other material time, may be in a different state from that in which insolvency proceedings are opened. In that event, given the variations between national laws concerning real security and the impact of insolvency upon such arrangements, there is a very real prospect that different conclusions as to the secured creditor's rights may be reached under the *lex concursus* and the *lex situs*. Such uncertainty is a commercial anathema, and has serious repercussions for the stability and cost of transactions concluded in a transnational context. Also of concern to a secured creditor is the extent to which, even if the right in rem is recognized, its enforcement or realization may be inhibited in some way which may erode its economic value, for example through the application of a comprehensive stay and moratorium during the course of a reorganization procedure.

Article 5 supplies a rule which significantly reinforces the position of the secured credi-   **4.12**
tor whose collateral is situated, at the time of opening of proceedings, in a different Member State from that in which insolvency proceedings take place. To the extent that the *lex situs* upholds the rights of the secured creditor, and allows him to enforce those rights over the collateral, for example through sale or foreclosure, in spite of the debtor's insolvency, such rights are to be respected even if this is contrary to the effects that would be produced according to the *lex concursus*.[19] Article 5(1) states:

> The opening of insolvency proceedings shall not affect the rights in rem of creditors or third parties in respect of tangible or intangible, moveable or immoveable assets (both specific assets and collections of indefinite assets as a whole which change from time to time) belonging to the debtor which are situated within the territory of another Member State at the time of the opening of proceedings.

It should be noted how widely the terms of this provision are drawn in relation to the   **4.13**
types of assets to which it can have application. All types of property are capable of being affected, including such commercially important items as book debts and other receivables, and assets that are of a future character at the time the security interest is created but which have come into existence by the time insolvency proceedings are opened. However, an asset is only within the ambit of this Article if it is located within the territory of one of the Member States at the time of opening: where the *situs* of the asset at the relevant time is in some third state,[20] Article 5 is not applicable and it is left to the *lex concursus* alone to determine to what extent, if at all, rights which are dependent on the law of the *situs* can be respected or in some way taken into account.[21]

---

[19] See Recital (25) to the Regulation.
[20] In this context, the expression 'third state' must be taken to include Denmark: see ch 3 above at para 3.10, n 16.
[21] Note the possibility that Art 5 may operate with retrospective effect in the case of insolvency proceedings commenced before the accession of a newly-joining Member State, provided that the assets in question to which a right in rem is asserted were situated in that state at the time of its accession to the EU: Case C-527/10 *ERSTE Bank Hungary Nyrt v Republic of Hungary* [2012] ILPr 38 (First Chamber, 21 December 2012 (not yet reported in ECR)). The text of the judgment can be accessed online at <http://eur-lex.europa.eu/legal-content/EN/TXT/PDF/?uri=CELEX:62010CJ0527> (accessed 22 April 2015).

4.14 **The *situs* of property.** There is an obvious need for certainty with regard to the method of identifying the location of an asset for the purposes of applying the rule in Article 5. Some assistance is provided by Article 2(g), which defines the expression, 'the Member State in which assets are situated' in the case of three particular kinds of property, namely tangible property, registrable property, and 'claims'. In the case of tangible property, the physical location of the property is, somewhat prosaically, identified as the *situs*. In the case of property and rights to which there attaches a requirement of public registration, the *situs* is in the Member State under whose authority the register is kept. In the case of 'claims' (in the sense of liabilities that are enforceable by the insolvent debtor against some other party), these are declared to be situated in the Member State in which the obligated party has his centre of main interests, to be determined according to the test employed under Article 3(1).[22] Consequently, the place at which a debt is expressed to be payable, or at which the debtor expressly agreed to be sued in the event of non-payment, does not constitute the *situs* of the debt for the purposes of Article 5.

4.15 **The time factor.** The relevant time at which the situation of an asset is to be determined, according to the terms of Article 5(1), is the opening of insolvency proceedings. This could give rise to difficulties if the asset is of a movable nature and its location has changed between the time at which the right in rem was created and the time when proceedings are opened. The rule could work to the disadvantage of the supposedly secured party if the asset happens to be located at the relevant time in a jurisdiction whose law does not afford protection to the security interest in question. Conversely, it would be a cause for concern as far as the interests of unsecured parties are concerned if it should transpire that the consequence of such a relocation is that the asset in question has been removed from the territory over which the *lex concursus* is applicable, with the possibility that the rights of the secured creditor are less susceptible to impeachment than they would otherwise have been. This contingency is countered by the provision in Article 5(4), which preserves the applicability of the actions for avoidance of antecedent transactions that form part of the *lex concursus*, as laid down in Article 4(2)(m).[23] Conversely, a creditor who takes security over movable property on the basis that the law of its current *situs* confers satisfactory protection in the event of the debtor's insolvency, must consider the possibility that the asset may be moved to another Member State, or to some third state, and thereby

---

[22] On the centre of main interests, see ch 3, section A above.
[23] See the decision of the CJEU in Case C-557/13 *Lutz v Bäuerle*, 16 April 2015 [2015] BCC 413 (not yet reported but viewable at <http://curia.europa.eu/juris/celex.jsf?celex=62013CJ0557&langl=en&type=TXT&ancre=>) in which the Court, while confirming that Art 5 enables the creditor to assert, even after the opening of insolvency proceedings, a right in rem established before the opening of those proceedings, noted that Art 5(4) preserves the possibility of avoidance proceedings being brought under the *lex concursus*, in which event the defence provided under Art 13 may become applicable (see para 4.38 below).

become subject to a different legal regime at the relevant time. If possible, the terms of the transaction should be so designed as to minimize the consequent risks of such relocation.

It should also be noted that the rule in Article 5(1) is so drafted as to confine its **4.16** effects to cases where the subject-matter of the security is situated within the territory of another Member State at the time of opening of proceedings: where assets are situated in a third state, the effect of the opening of insolvency proceedings upon the rights of the secured party is not determined by Article 5. In such cases, the law of the state of opening of proceedings, including its rules of private international law, will primarily determine the rights of any parties which are amenable to the jurisdiction of the *lex concursus*. However, according to standard conflict of laws principles, the *lex situs* (at the material time) may be referred to for the purpose of determining the validity of the security interest as at the time of its creation, and also for assessing the effect of insolvency proceedings on the rights of the secured party. Conversely, the rights of any parties which are not so subject to the authority of the law of the state of opening will in practice be determined by the extent to which the *lex situs* is prepared to recognize and give effect to the foreign insolvency proceedings. If the rights of the secured creditor are held to prevail over the claims of the liquidator appointed in the foreign proceedings, the secured creditor may be able to retain the fruits of exercising the rights previously bargained for, unless it proves necessary to participate in the insolvency process in respect of any unsecured balance of claim. In such circumstances, the duty to account for the fruits of the enforcement of security will arise, in accordance with the principle of hotchpot.[24]

Meaning of 'rights in rem'. The OR does not supply an exhaustive definition **4.17** of the expression 'rights in rem'. However, Article 5(2) and (3) furnish some indication of the meaning to be attributed to the expression, while supplementary guidance, albeit of a persuasive character only, can be found in the Virgos-Schmit Report.[25] Article 5(2) is essentially concerned to describe the nature and content of rights which qualify as rights in rem within Article 5(1). It states that they shall, in particular, mean:

(a) the right to dispose of assets or have them disposed of and to obtain satisfaction from the proceeds of or income from those assets, in particular by virtue of a lien or a mortgage;

---

[24] See Art 20 of the Regulation, on which there is commentary in ch 8 below.
[25] See n 1 above, at paras 94–106 inclusive. For critical discussion of the treatment of secured creditors under the substantially identical provisions of the proposed EC Convention of 1995, see J Garrido, 'Some Reflections on the EU Bankruptcy Convention and its Implications for Secured Creditors' (1998) 7 International Insolvency Review 79. For a comprehensive study of security interests in the context of the Regulation, see M Veder, *Cross-Border Insolvency Proceedings and Security Rights* (2004) esp ch 4. See further in ch 6 below.

(b) the exclusive right to have a claim met, in particular a right guaranteed by a lien in respect of the claim or by assignment of the claim by way of a guarantee;

(c) the right to demand the assets from, and/or to require restitution by, anyone having possession or use of them contrary to the wishes of the party so entitled; and

(d) a right in rem to the beneficial use of assets.

The above list of attributes that are associated with various kinds of rights in rem is intended as a guide to the task of characterization, which, however, remains a matter for the state where the assets are located. The OR, following the policy adopted by the draftsmen of the former Convention text of 1995, has deliberately refrained from imposing its own definition of a right in rem which could result in assets having to be classified in a way which is in conflict with the approach followed by the law of the *situs*.[26] Nevertheless, a more *dirigiste* approach is taken by Article 5(3) in respect of rights which are recorded in a public register and enforceable against third parties, whereby a right in rem may be obtained. Such a right is to be considered a right in rem throughout all Member States, irrespective of any contrary conclusions to be derived from the provisions of national law.[27] The Virgos-Schmit Report to the Convention emphasized that the provisions of Article 5 only protect pre-existing rights which were created before the insolvency proceedings were opened.[28] Therefore, creditors who have not succeeded in perfecting their right to be treated as secured under the law of the *lex situs* before the time of opening of insolvency proceedings in another Member State, are subject to the effects of the *lex concursus*, in accordance with the basic principle of Article 4. This would be the case, for example, with creditors who have commenced such processes as distress or execution which are incomplete at the time of opening of insolvency.[29]

4.18 **Floating charge security, etc.** In the absence of an exhaustive definition of 'rights in rem', either for the specific purposes of Article 5 or more generally, it is necessary to establish whether certain types of security, such as the floating charge, fall within the ambit of this important exception to the regime of the *lex concursus*. Since this form of security is recognized under the laws of only a minority of the Member States—notably the United Kingdom and Ireland—the possibility of conflicting classifications by courts in states belonging to the civil and common law traditions respectively is an issue of no little practical importance. Similar conflicts of characterization may occur in relation to other kinds of security devices developed in recent times, such as the practice of creating a fixed charge over future book debts, which can be analysed as purporting to create a

---

[26] Virgos-Schmit Report (n 1 above) para 100.
[27] ibid para 101.
[28] ibid paras 96, 103.
[29] See eg Insolvency Act 1986, ss 130(2), 183, 184, 346, and 347.

present right in rem without either surrender of possession or even an existing subject-matter to which the right can attach.

Paragraph 104 of the Virgos-Schmit Report[30] (written with reference to the pro- **4.19** posed Convention of 1995) attempted to clarify the position as follows:

> A right in rem may not only be established with regard to specific assets but also with regard to assets as a whole. Security rights such as the 'floating charge' recognized in United Kingdom and Irish law can, therefore, be characterized as a right in rem for the purposes of the Convention. Likewise, rights characterized under national law as rights in rem over intangible assets or over rights are also included.

The above passage supplied the inspiration for the insertion of an additional phrase **4.20** into Article 5(1) during the process of converting the Convention text of 1995 into that of the Regulation adopted on 29 May 2000 by the EC Council. Although very few substantive changes were made to the text as settled in 1995, the following words were inserted into Article 5(1): 'both specific assets and collections of indefinite assets as a whole which change from time to time'. The extra words are primarily intended to remove any uncertainty as to whether Article 5 applies to floating charge security. It is submitted that they can also apply, and were intended to apply, to those cases where, under the approach followed in the common law systems of the United Kingdom and Ireland, a fixed charge is created in relation to receivables, present and/or future, whose precise contents will also change from time to time.

One final observation may be made with respect to Article 5 and its effects. **4.21** Although it can provide protection for the secured creditor against the direct disturbance of expectations founded upon the provisions of the *lex situs*, it does not immunize the creditor against the invocation of processes which may be available under the law of the *situs* itself in the event of the debtor's insolvency. In order to bring such remedies into operation, however, it would be necessary for the liquidator in the main proceedings, or some other qualified party, to procure the opening of secondary bankruptcy proceedings under the *lex situs*, and in this way provoke such consequences for the holder of the right in rem as may be available under the insolvency law of that state. Naturally, such secondary proceedings can only be commenced if the debtor has an establishment in that Member State.[31]

Exception II: Set-off (Article 6 OR)

The laws of the Member States diverge sharply over the operation of set-off in the **4.22** event of a debtor's insolvency. In the United Kingdom, set-off is treated as a mandatory process which must be applied, as a matter of public policy, in both individual and corporate insolvencies in which the necessary requirement of mutuality

---

[30] See n 1 above.
[31] Virgos-Schmit Report (n 1 above) para 98. On the meaning of 'establishment', see ch 3, section C above.

is present.[32] In most civil law systems, on the other hand, the prevailing view is that insolvency set-off constitutes a violation of the principle of *pari passu* distribution, and that as a matter of public policy it must be confined to the most carefully limited circumstances, as where the cross-liabilities arise out of one and the same contract or obligation. Therefore, in a cross-border insolvency, the outcome for any creditor who is also a debtor to the estate can be drastically affected by the way in which the issue of applicable law is resolved, if the competing laws happen to represent the different schools of opinion with regard to set-off.[33] Particularly in major commercial operations where large sums of money are involved, the ability to predict the applicable law and to take its provisions on set-off fully into account is vitally important in the assessment of risk. Clear, and uniformly applicable, choice of law rules are therefore essential.

4.23 We have seen above that Article 4(2)(d) establishes a basic rule to the effect that it is for the *lex concursus* to determine the conditions under which set-offs may be invoked. Accordingly, any party to an international transaction who wishes to calculate the consequences of the other party's insolvency in the event that there are subsisting debts or liabilities in both directions must first determine which Member State is destined to become the forum for main bankruptcy proceedings, or for any secondary proceedings, involving the other party as the insolvent debtor. It is of course perfectly possible that the mutual dealings between the parties may have as their respective governing laws either the same country's law, or the laws of different countries, and that these may or may not happen to be Member States of the European Union. The possible variations are therefore very numerous. Under the primary rule of Article 4(2)(d), however, it is entirely a matter for the *lex concursus* to determine whether, in the course of applying its doctrine of set-off, any account will be taken of the fact (if such is the case) that either of the cross-obligations is governed by a foreign law under which a different approach is followed. Clearly, there are latent perils for the unwary, whose assumptions may be founded upon familiar rules of the law of the state in which their own business has been conducted, and of the law or laws by which their contractual relationships are designed to be governed.

4.24 Although the fate of any creditor who is simultaneously a debtor to the insolvent estate is primarily controlled by the set-off rule of the *lex concursus*, Article 6 establishes one, carefully limited, exception to this. If the result produced by application of the *lex concursus* is that set-off is not applicable to the cross-claims in question, the creditor may have recourse in the alternative to the exception supplied by Article 6(1),

---

[32] See *Stein v Blake* [1996] AC 243, HL; *Secretary of State for Trade and Industry v Frid* [2004] 2 AC 506, HL. For authoritative accounts of the subject of set-off, see PR Wood, *English and International Set-Off* (1989); R Derham, *Set-Off* (4th edn, 2010).

[33] For a vivid illustration of this problem, see *Re Bank of Credit and Commerce International SA (No 10)* [1997] Ch 213. For comment on that case, see IF Fletcher [1997] Journal of Business Law 471–6; S Shandro (1998) 7 International Insolvency Review 63.

which provides that the creditor shall not be deprived of the right to demand the set-off of his claims against the claims of the debtor, 'where such a set-off is permitted by the law applicable to the insolvent debtor's claim'. This somewhat ponderous phrase is intended to denote 'the law applicable to the claim where the insolvent debtor is the creditor in relation to the other party'.[34] To establish the law by which the relevant claim is governed (assuming it to be contractual), a common set of choice of law rules is supplied by the Rome I Regulation on the Law Applicable to Contractual Obligations, which is applicable in all Member States of the European Union, with the exception of Denmark.[35]. The Rome I Regulation, as a legislative act of the EU, is confined in its application to those states which are members of the European Union and which participated in its adoption.[36] Like its predecessor the Rome Convention, the Rome I Regulation is based upon the principle that the governing law of any contract to which its provisions apply may be that of some third state, rather than being limited to the laws of the Member States themselves.[37] The Regulation applies to contracts concluded after 17 December 2009.[38]

Significantly, Article 6 of the Regulation on Insolvency Proceedings omits any reference to 'the Member States', or their respective laws, in creating the exception in favour of the rule of set-off that is operated by 'the law applicable to the insolvent debtor's claim'. It therefore follows that in this instance the law of some third state could furnish the basis for allowing the creditor to have the benefit of set-off which would otherwise be excluded under the regime of the *lex concursus*.[39] **4.25**

---

[34] Virgos-Schmit Report (n 1 above) para 108. The rationale expressed in that paragraph is epitomized in Recital (26) to the Regulation. Some writers employ the expression 'the passive claim' to denote the insolvent debtor's claim against the proving creditor (ie the claim where the insolvent debtor is the creditor in relation to the other party), to be contrasted with the 'active' claim owed to that creditor by the estate (ie the claim in respect of which proof will be lodged in the insolvency).

[35] Regulation (EC) 593/2008 of the European Parliament and Council of 17 June 2008 on the law applicable to contractual obligations [2008] OJ L177/6 (see n 4 above). By Recital (46) to the Regulation it is declared that by virtue of its opt-out granted under the Maastricht Treaty on European Union, Denmark does not participate in the adoption of the Regulation and is not bound by it or subject to its application. By virtue of Art 24, the Rome Convention continues to apply to Denmark.

[36] Although at the time of adoption of the Rome I Regulation the United Kingdom exercised its own opt-out facility (as recorded in Recital (45)) a subsequent change of position by the United Kingdom came about following further negotiations. In July 2008 the Government formally notified the EU Commission that it would opt in to the Regulation and by Decision 2009/26/EC [2009] OJ L10/22 the Commission decided that the Rome I Regulation would apply to the United Kingdom. Ireland separately chose to take part in the adoption and application of the Regulation: Recital (44).

[37] Art 2 of the Rome I Regulation states: 'Any law specified by this Regulation shall be applied whether or not it is the law of a Member State'. Art 2 of the Rome Convention is identical in substance, save that the expressions 'Convention' and 'Contracting State' are used instead of 'Regulation' and 'Member State'.

[38] ibid, Art 28.

[39] This conclusion, based on the unrestricted terms in which Art 6 is drafted, is not universally accepted. Some commentators have sought to claim that an implied restriction must be read into the text to limit its scope of application to cases where the claim in question is governed by the law of an EU Member State. See eg Virgos-Schmit Report, para 93; M Virgos and F Garcimartin, *The European Insolvency Regulation: Law and Practice* (2004) 91 (§137) and 117 (§189); cf B Wessels,

With this possibility in mind therefore, where parties are in a position to choose the law by which their transactions are governed they may well deem it expedient to ensure that a clear, express choice is made in favour of the law of a country whose rule concerning set-off is most suited to their requirements. Article 3 of the Rome I Regulation gives effect to such an act of choice, which can be made with respect to the whole or to a particular part of the contract.[40]

4.26 One notable feature of Article 6 OR is that it can only operate, if at all, in such a way as to allow a set-off to be invoked in circumstances where otherwise it would be excluded: it does not allow a creditor to be denied the benefit of a set-off which is already available under the *lex concursus* in accordance with the rule in Article 4(2)(d). Once again, it is to be observed that Article 6(2) preserves the application of Article 4(2)(m) in relation to cases benefiting from the exception created under Article 6(1). Consequently, the avoidance rules of the *lex concursus* continue to be applicable to any challenge to the validity or enforceability of any claim to which the doctrine of set-off may otherwise be applicable by virtue of Article 6(1).

Exception III: Reservation of title (Article 7 OR)

4.27 The practice of including a reservation of title clause within a contract of sale, as a means of affording protection to an unpaid seller in the event of the buyer's insolvency, is treated in different ways under the laws of the Member States of the European Union.[41] To minimize the uncertainty associated with cross-border cases, special rules are needed. Article 7 provides two such rules, which introduce exceptions to the application of the *lex concursus* in relation to contracts to which the insolvent debtor is a party. The rules deal, respectively, with the insolvency of the buyer or of the seller, and in each instance the relevant factor is the *situs* of the subject-matter of the contract of sale at the time of opening of insolvency proceedings. Where this is in a Member State other than the state of opening, the provisions of the *lex concursus* are displaced by the rules respectively contained in Article 7(1) or (2), as the case may be.

International Insolvency Law (2012) para 10665, where the various writers' views are surveyed, with the author affirming a personal position aligned with that stated in the present text. In view of the diversity of opinion, currently unresolved by definitive judicial decision, the most prudent course, wherever practicable, is to ensure that the governing law of a claim which may in due course occupy the role of 'insolvent debtor's claim' is that of a Member State which supports the operation of set-off, as is the case within the United Kingdom or Ireland.

[40] Rome I Regulation, Art 3(1). Note also that Art 3(2) allows the parties to agree at any time to subject their contract to a law other than that which previously governed it, whether as a result of earlier choice or by reason of absence of choice as to governing law. There is a proviso to Art 3(2) whose effect is to prevent such subsequent changes of governing law from adversely affecting third parties (such as creditors generally), and it is also the case that any change of this nature would have to be effected prior to the opening of insolvency proceedings.

[41] On the inability of the EU Member States to agree on terms of harmonization of their treatment of reservation of title, see G McCormack, *Reservation of Title* (1990) 210–20.

Article 7(1) applies in a case where insolvency proceedings are opened against the **4.28** purchaser of an asset for which the price has not been paid in full. It provides that the seller's rights based on a reservation of title ('ROT') clause shall not be affected by the opening of proceedings where the asset in question is at that time situated within the territory of a Member State other than the state of opening.[42] Therefore, any provisions within the *lex concursus* whereby the ROT clause is rendered ineffective as against the claims of the liquidator—for example due to lack of formal registration, or on other grounds—would not affect the seller's right to retake the asset provided that such a right is conferred by the *lex situs* under the circumstances existing at the relevant time. The terms of Article 7(1) are such as to make it irrelevant, apparently, whether the asset in question is moved to the territory of some other Member State subsequent to the opening of proceedings.[43] However, the exact way in which this provision will operate in practice is far from clear. It is to be noted that there is no positive provision to the effect that the *lex situs* is to apply: all that is stated is that the opening of proceedings, 'shall not affect the seller's rights based on a reservation of title'. This phrase implies that the determinative factors are the provisions of the contract itself and—of necessity—the law by which it is governed. It seems to be envisaged that these factors will be assimilated into the process of determination under the law of the Member State in which the asset happens to be situated, although the details are not explained.

Article 7(2) is concerned with the position where it is the seller of an asset who, **4.29** following its delivery, is the subject of insolvency proceedings. Where, due to the effects of a ROT clause, the seller retains ownership of the asset even after delivery, the consequence might be that the asset is regarded as part of the insolvent estate and thus liable to repossession by the liquidator, leaving the buyer to lodge proof for any damages occasioned through the loss of bargain.[44] The provision in Article 7(2) alleviates the buyer's predicament by declaring that the opening of insolvency proceedings shall not constitute grounds for rescinding or terminating the sale, and shall not prevent the buyer from acquiring title, where at the time of opening the asset sold is situated within the territory of a Member State other than the *forum concursus*. This provision is not a choice of law rule, but is a uniform rule of substantive law whose application is confined to specially defined circumstances.

Finally, Article 7(3) preserves the application of the avoidance rules of the *lex* **4.30** *concursus* in cases falling within the ambit of either Article 7(1) or (2). The fact that in each of those paragraphs reference is made to the *situs* of the asset as being within

---

[42] Cf the ruling of the CJEU in Case C-292/08 *German Graphics GmbH v van der Schee* [2009] ECR I-8421, where the asset covered by the ROT clause was situated, at the relevant time, in the Member State of the opening of insolvency proceedings concerning the purchaser of the asset. Consequently, Art 7(1) provided no protection to the unpaid seller.
[43] This is the view expressed in the Virgos-Schmit Report (n 1 above) para 113.
[44] Such a claim would of course be subject to deduction of the price due from the buyer.

the territory of a Member State necessarily means that Article 7 has no application to cases where the asset is situated in some third state at the relevant time.

Exception IV: Contracts relating to immovable property (Article 8 OR)

4.31 It is usually the case that a liquidator is empowered to elect whether to confirm or to terminate any executory contract to which the debtor is a party at the time of commencement of insolvency proceedings.[45] Article 4(2)(e) asserts the basic principle that the *lex concursus* determines the effects of insolvency upon current contracts to which the debtor is a party. However, Article 8 creates an exception to this rule for cases of contracts conferring the right to acquire or make use of immovable property which is situated within the territory of a Member State other than the state of opening. The Article provides that the effect of insolvency upon such contracts will be governed solely by the *lex situs*. The Virgos-Schmit Report explains at paragraph 118 that the reference to the exclusive application of the law of the *situs* includes the insolvency law of that state, so that parties to an international contract for the sale of land or the leasing of immovable property need to inform themselves about the relevant provisions of the insolvency law of the Member State in which the property is situated, in order to discover the consequences of the insolvency of the other party. This provision is not applicable to cases where the property is situated in some third state, and it is therefore left to the *lex concursus*, including the conflicts rules of that system, to resolve the issue. However, according to standard principles of conflict of laws it is generally the case that questions concerning rights over, and succession to, immovable property are referred to the *lex situs*.

Exception V: Payment systems and financial markets (Article 9 OR)

4.32 An especially sensitive area, in view of its commercial importance, is the effect of insolvency upon executory contracts between parties operating within an organized payment or settlement system, or a particular financial market. In the interest of sustaining confidence in the integrity of the arrangements to which the participants have originally assented upon joining the system or market in question, Article 9(1) imposes a special choice of law rule whereby the effects of insolvency proceedings on the rights and obligations of parties to a payment or settlement system or to a financial market will be governed solely by the law of the Member State applicable to that system or market.[46] This rule in favour of the

---

[45] For analysis of the problems of executory contracts (a neglected topic in the literature of insolvency under UK law), see the writings of authors commenting from the standpoint of American law: JL Westbrook, 'A Functional Analysis of Executory Contracts' (1989) 74 Minnesota L Rev 227; V Countryman, 'Executory Contracts in Bankruptcy' (Parts 1 and 2) (1973) 57 Minnesota L Rev 439, and (1974) 58 Minnesota L Rev 479.

[46] See Recital (27) to the Regulation. Examples of such special markets, whose rules contain provisions for closing out contracts and netting in the event of insolvency of a member, are the London International Financial Futures and Options Exchange (LIFFE); the International Stock Exchange of the United Kingdom and Republic of Ireland; the London Metal Exchange, and the London Commodity Exchange. See ch 7 below. See Companies Act 1989, Part VII (*Financial Markets and*

exclusive application of the systemic law is reinforced by the provision in Article 9(2) whereby any action for voidness, voidability or unenforceability of payments or transactions carried out under the system or market in question, and which may be detrimental to creditors generally, is nevertheless declared to be subject to the law applicable to the relevant payment system or financial market. The practice followed in Articles 5, 6, and 7 OR, of reserving the application of the avoidance rule of the *lex concursus* as referred to in Article 4(2)(m), is here relinquished in favour of the total prevalence of the law which is applicable to the payment system or market, thereby enabling parties to base their expectations purely upon a single set of rules without having to take into account the various national laws to which counter-parties may be personally subject, and by which the insolvency of any of them may happen to be governed. It must be emphasized, however, that the rules of Article 9 are only applicable in a situation where the system or market is operating under the law of one of the Member States. Moreover, there is a special proviso in Article 9(1) to the effect that it is without prejudice to the effect of Article 5, which subjects the protection of rights in rem over assets belonging to the debtor to the law of the *situs*.[47]

Exception VI: Contracts of employment (Article 10 OR)

A further category of executory contracts for which special considerations arise **4.33** is the employment relationship. Indeed, special rules are already operative under the Brussels Regulation[48] and the Rome I Regulation[49] to regulate jurisdictional and choice of law aspects of contracts of employment. To protect the interests of employees, Article 10 OR stipulates that the effects of such proceedings on employment contracts and relationships shall be governed solely by the law of the Member State applicable to the contract of employment.[50] To ascertain the applicable law, the courts of all Member States will apply the provisions of the Rome I Regulation, notably Articles 3, 8, and 9 thereof. If this produces the conclusion that the contract is governed by the law of one of the Member States, the rule of Article 10 OR will apply. If the law of some third state is indicated, however, the

---

Insolvency), as amended by and under the Financial Services and Markets Act 2000, together with the Financial Markets and Insolvency Regulations 1991, SI 1991/880, as amended, and Council Directive (EC) 98/26 (the Settlement Finality Directive [1998] OJ L166/45) as transposed for UK purposes by SI 1999/2979 (the Financial Markets and Insolvency (Settlement Finality) Regulations 1999).

[47] See Exception 1 at paras 4.11–4.21 above.

[48] Regulation (EU) 2015/2012 of 12 December 2012, on Jurisdiction and the Recognition and Enforcement of Judgments in Civil and Commercial Matters (recast) OJ L351/1, 20 December 2012, which became applicable from 10 January 2015, Arts 20–23. The Regulation of 2012 replaced Council Regulation (EC) 44/2001, of 22 December 2000, [2001] OJ L12/1. The latter Regulation replaced, with effect from 1 March 2002, the Brussels Convention (originally concluded on 27 September 1968 and several times subsequently amended and expanded) with respect to 27 of the 28 EU Member States (the exception being Denmark).

[49] Regulation (EC) 593/2008 of the European Parliament and Council of 17 June 2008 on the law applicable to contractual obligations [2008] OJ L177/6, nn 4 and 35 above, Art 8.

[50] See Recital (28) to the Regulation on Insolvency Proceedings.

effects of insolvency will be determined by the *lex concursus*, with reference as appropriate to any provisions of the private international law of that system.

4.34 It should also be emphasized that Article 10 is confined to the question of the effect of insolvency upon the contract of employment as such, including the issue as to whether the contract is automatically terminated by the insolvency of either party to it, or whether the liquidator has the option to affirm or rescind the contract, subject to specified terms. Article 10 does not purport to regulate other issues such as the ranking of employees' claims for unpaid wages or salaries, and the mode of treatment to be accorded to these claims. Such questions remain subject to the *lex concursus*, in accordance with Article 4(2)(h).[51] It is also the case that in many states nowadays there is a statutory scheme under which, in the event of their employer's insolvency, employees are guaranteed a measure of payment out of a national fund, with the state then becoming subrogated to the employee in respect of that portion of the latter's claim against the employer. Paragraph 128 of the Virgos-Schmit Report asserts that such guaranteed payments, since they are maintained under provisions of the national law of the Member State concerned, are subject to the law of that state.

Exception VII: Rights subject to registration (Article 11 OR)

4.35 National laws usually operate a system of public registration for many kinds of right or interest over immovable property. Such registration forms an essential aspect of the safeguards for other parties who may have or acquire interests in the same property. Certain kinds of movable property, including ships and aircraft, are likewise subject to public registration in the state in which they are principally kept, or from which they are operated. Such registers play important roles in the protection of trade and the maintenance of certainty, and in ensuring compliance with health and safety regulations affecting the assets in question. The casual location of such assets, which may be of very large value, should not be the decisive criterion by which to determine the effects of insolvency proceedings upon the rights of the debtor in relation to them. Both with immovable property and with movables of this kind, there is the possibility of a conflict between the provisions of the law of the state under whose authority the register is maintained and the provisions of the *lex concursus*.

4.36 Article 11 provides that, where the register is kept under the authority of a Member State, it is the law of that state, and not the *lex concursus*, which shall determine the effects of insolvency proceedings on the rights of the debtor in immovable property, a ship, or an aircraft subject to public registration. However, it should be noted that this choice of law provision does not include the word 'solely', and that this omission is intended to enable the *lex concursus* to continue to play a part in the process of determining the net effect of insolvency upon the rights which

---

[51] Virgos-Schmit Report (n 1 above) para 128.

are the subject of registration. In the words of paragraph 130 of the Virgos-Schmit Report, 'a sort of cumulative application of both laws is necessary'. What appears to be envisaged is that there should be an interaction between the liquidator and the official by whom the relevant register is maintained, to arrange for appropriate entries to be made in the register that will reflect the fact that insolvency proceedings are taking place in a different Member State. It will remain a matter for the law of the state of registration to determine what effects this process shall have upon the rights of the debtor in the property concerned.

Exception VIII: Community patents and trade marks (Article 12 OR)

In view of the fact that arrangements are already in force within the European **4.37** Union to regulate patents, trade marks, and the rights of plant breeders throughout the whole territory of the Union,[52] it is appropriate that the OR should endeavour to complement the provisions already operating with regard to the treatment of such forms of intellectual property in cases of insolvency of those who own or have interests in the rights concerned. Each of the existing arrangements concluded under EC law contains a rule to the effect that a Community right arising thereunder may be included only in the first proceedings that are opened in a contracting state.[53] Under the provisions of the OR, however, it can sometimes happen that the first proceedings to be opened are not main proceedings under Article 3(1), but are territorial proceedings within the meaning of Article 3(2) and (4).[54] This has necessitated a special rule, contained in Article 12, whereby a Community patent, a Community trademark or any similar right established by Community law may be included only in main insolvency proceedings which are opened under Article 3(1). This provision is operative only when the debtor has his centre of main interests in a Member State, for this is an essential condition to the opening of proceedings under Article 3(1). Where the debtor's centre of main interests is located outside the Union, the rules of the individual enactments relating to intellectual property are applicable without modification, with the consequence that the right in question is included in the insolvent estate of the first proceedings to be opened in a Member State.[55]

Exception IX: Detrimental acts protected from avoidance (Article 13 OR)

According to Article 4(2)(m) the law of the state of the opening of proceedings **4.38** shall determine the rules relating to voidness, voidability, or unenforceability of

---

[52] Community Patent Convention [1975] OJ L17/1, as modified by the Luxembourg Agreement of 30 December 1989 [1989] OJ L401/10; Council Directive (EEC) 89/104 [1989] OJ L207/44, and Council Regulation (EC) 40/94 on the Community Trademark [1994] OJ L11/1; Council Regulation (EC) 2100/94 on Community Plant Variety Rights [1994] OJ L227/1.

[53] Luxembourg Agreement, Art 41; Trademark Regulation, Art 21; Regulation on Plant Variety Rights, Art 25 (all previous footnote).

[54] See ch 3, section A above.

[55] See Virgos-Schmit Report (n 1 above) paras 133, 134.

legal acts detrimental to all the creditors. However, Article 13 supplies a rule which operates by way of exception to this general proposition, to the effect that Article 4(2)(m) shall not apply where the person who benefited from a legal act detrimental to all the creditors provides proof that:

(i)   the act in question is subject to the law of a Member State other than that of the state of opening of proceedings; and

(ii) that law does not allow any means of challenging that act in the relevant case.

Protection is thereby given to parties who have reasonably relied upon the validity of a transaction whose governing law happens to be that of a Member State, and which is unimpeachable under the concrete circumstances of the case according to both the insolvency law and the general law of that state.[56] It should be observed that if the governing law of the transaction is that of a non-EU Member State the exception under Article 13 does not apply, and that the avoidance rule of the *lex concursus* can then be applied irrespective of whether the transaction would be unimpeachable under the general and insolvency laws of the other state. The supporting rationale of this Article is the protection of a party's legitimate expectations formed with reference to the circumstances prevailing at the time of entering into a transaction which is subsequently impeached under the legal provisions of the state in which the counterparty is later the subject of insolvency proceedings. The Court of Justice has affirmed that the special protection afforded by Article 13 is not available in the case where the acts which are impeached took place after the opening of insolvency proceedings. Such extended application would go beyond what is necessary to protect legitimate expectations and the certainty of transactions in Member States other than that in which proceedings are opened. This is because, in the Court's reasoning, as from the opening of insolvency proceedings the creditors of the debtor concerned are able to predict the effects of the application of the *lex fori concursus* on the legal relations which they maintain with that debtor. However, in a case concerning the exercise of a right in rem to which the protective provision of Article 5(1) was applicable, the Court ruled that in order that the main purpose of Article 5 may be attained it is necessary for the creditor to be able to exercise rights validly established prior to the opening of insolvency proceedings even after the date of opening. Accordingly it must be possible for the creditor to rely on the protective defence offered by Article 13 in a situation in which a payment, challenged by an insolvency administrator, of a sum of money attached before the opening of the insolvency proceedings was made only after the opening of those proceedings.[57]

---

[56] ibid paras 135–39.

[57] Case C-557/13 *Lutz v Bäuerle*, 16 April 2015 [2015] BCC 413 (not yet reported but viewable at <http://curia.europa.eu/juris/celex.jsf?celex=62013CJ0557&lang1=en&type=TXT&ancre=>). See the judgment of the CJEU at paras 32–43.

A further notable effect of Article 4(2)(m) is that it has been designed to surmount **4.39** one of the controversial aspects of the application of transaction avoidance rules in cases of conflict of laws, namely the possibility of cumulative application of the rules of more than one system in order to decide whether the transaction is valid. The rule supplied by paragraph (m) ensures that under most circumstances only a single avoidance rule—that of the *lex concursus*—is applicable. This greatly simplifies the task of the liquidator in seeking to bring about the avoidance of such transactions. However, in the special situation covered by Article 13 the other party to the transaction with the debtor is effectively allowed to interpose, by way of defence to any attack based upon the avoidance rule of the *lex concursus*, the fact that it is valid and unimpeachable according to the law by which it is properly governed, always provided that the law in question is that of another Member State which is participating in the OR. In this respect it should be remembered that Denmark, although a member of the EU, does not count as a 'Member State' for the purposes of the OR due to its having secured a permanent opt-out from this sector of EU legislation, as stated in Recital (33).[58] Therefore the benefit of Article 13 cannot be claimed in a case where the transaction in question is governed by Danish law.

Exception X: Protection of third-party purchasers (Article 14 OR)

It is usually the case that under the provisions of national law the opening **4.40** of insolvency proceedings causes the debtor to be deprived of the capacity to deal with or dispose of property to the detriment of the general body of creditors. According to the circumstances of the disposition, such transactions may be declared to be void under all circumstances, or in other instances may be subject to validation by the court at its discretion, or subject to defined conditions.[59]

However, where the property which is improperly disposed of by the debtor is **4.41** subject to some form of public registration, a policy dilemma is caused by the possibility that the transaction with the third party may take place before the fact of the insolvency is placed upon the record. Such parties, consulting the record in its unamended state, may be prejudiced by their reliance upon the information thereby obtained. Consequently, in the interest of maintaining confidence in the integrity of the public register, the national law of the state in which the register is maintained may embody a rule to protect a party who has dealt in good faith and for valuable consideration, and in reliance upon the information carried on the face of the register at the time in question. In cases of international insolvency, where the state of opening of proceedings and the state where the register is maintained are separate from each other, the interval before the register can be amended may

---

[58] See para 1.02 above.
[59] Insolvency Act 1986, s 127.

be even longer, thus allowing more time in which such transactions may take place. If the protection to be accorded to the third party is made to depend upon the *lex concursus*, that party may suffer injustice due to reliance that was originally and reasonably placed upon the rule contained in the *lex situs* (in the case of immovable property), or in the law of the state in which the register is maintained (in the case of ships or aircraft, or of securities whose existence is dependent upon registration). Article 14 OR accordingly creates a rule to protect third-party purchasers to whom the debtor, other than gratuitously, has disposed of any of these kinds of assets by an act concluded after the opening of insolvency proceedings. The validity of the act of disposal is governed by the *lex situs* in the case of an immovable asset, and in the case of registrable assets by the law of the state under whose authority the register is kept.

4.42 The drafting of Article 14 omits any reference to 'Member State' in its provision regarding the law to govern the validity of the acts to which it is applicable, and it would therefore appear that the provision can be applied to cases where the *situs* of the immovable property, or the place where the register is maintained, is located in some third state. However, the Virgos-Schmit Report, written with reference to the provisions of the corresponding Article of the 1995 version of the proposed Convention, appears to contradict the indications conveyed by the terms of the Article itself, by consistently referring to 'contracting state' in relation to the scope of its application.[60] Conversely, the scope of Article 14 is widened in another respect by a further statement in the Report that: 'An act of disposal must be understood to include not only transfers of ownership but also the constitution of a right in rem relating to such property.'[61]

Exception XI: Effects on pending lawsuits (Article 15 OR)

4.43 The laws of the Member States of the European Union differ from one another with regard to the effect of insolvency proceedings on a pending lawsuit to which the debtor is a party. These differences concern not only the forcible interruption of proceedings by virtue of an automatic stay, but also the possible removal of litigation from the civil or commercial court which would normally have jurisdiction, into the exclusive control of the bankruptcy court, under the principle known as *vis attractiva concursus*. This principle is by no means universally, or even uniformly, applied, and there are likewise variations of approach to such matters as the possible lifting of the stay upon proceedings at the discretion of the bankruptcy court. Potentially, much confusion and uncertainty could result in a given case due to the presence of conflicting rules contained respectively in the *lex concursus* and in the law of the state in which the litigation is pending.

---

[60] Virgos-Schmit Report (n 1 above) paras 140, 141.
[61] ibid para 141.

Article 15 imposes a uniform choice of law rule in favour of the sole application **4.44** of the law of the forum in which the lawsuit is pending. The scope of this rule is likely to be of considerable practical importance, and hence the terms of the Article should be noted with some care. First, a distinction is to be made between the effects of insolvency on individual enforcement actions (such as distress, execution, attachment, and sequestration), as opposed to pending lawsuits. The former are governed by the law of the state of opening, as provided by Article 4(2)(f), whereas only the latter are affected by Article 15. The Article refers expressly to 'a lawsuit pending concerning an asset or a right of which the debtor has been divested'. Accordingly, if the asset happens to be excluded from the effects of insolvency according to the *lex concursus*, it would be unaffected by Article 15.[62] It is also essential to the application of Article 15 that the lawsuit in question should be pending in another Member State: litigation in third states is not within the ambit of this provision. Where the rule applies, it is for the law of the state where litigation is pending (including the procedural law of that state) to determine whether or not the proceedings are to be suspended or whether they may continue subject to terms or conditions, including any procedural modifications which may be necessary in view of the fact that the debtor has been deprived of the powers of administration and disposal of his property, with the liquidator having been substituted in his place.[63]

As currently drafted, Article 15 gives rise to a degree of uncertainty as to its true scope of application. The expression 'a lawsuit pending' (which is employed twice in the body of the Article itself as well as forming part of the title heading) is undoubtedly applicable to a broad spectrum of matters and proceedings which may be conducted before a duly constituted court or tribunal. What is not made clear is whether the expression 'lawsuit pending' is also intended to apply to arbitration proceedings. Although the point awaits a definitive ruling by the European Court of Justice, the English Court of Appeal has delivered a carefully reasoned judgment in which it concluded that 'lawsuit pending' in the context of Article 15 must be taken to include pending references to arbitration.[64]

---

[62] For an account of the position under English law concerning property in the ownership of a bankrupt individual which does not vest in the trustee in bankruptcy, see IF Fletcher, *The Law of Insolvency* (4th edn, 2009, with Second Cumulative Supplement 2014) paras 8-055–8-085.

[63] See further the commentary to Art 15 in ch 8 below.

[64] *Syska v Vivendi Universal SA* [2009] EWCA Civ 677, [2010] BCC 348. See comments on the proceedings by Fletcher in (2009) 22 Insolvency Intelligence 60–62; 155–57. For an extensive review of the literature and national case law relating to Art 15 see B Wessels, *International Insolvency Law* (3rd edn, 2012) paras 10710–13. The Virgos-Schmit Report, which refers briefly to Art 15 at para 142, unfortunately omits to deal with this point explicitly, although the reference therein to 'legal proceedings concerning the assets or rights of the estate' may be thought to carry connotations of court-based procedures. In the recast version of the Insolvency Regulation, adopted in May 2015 and destined to enter into effect in June 2017, the revised version of Art 15 (now numbered as Art 18) is drafted so as to make it expressly applicable to both pending lawsuits and pending arbitral proceedings. See para 4.50 below.

D. Principal Effects of the Recast Regulation ('RR') when in Force

The Basic Choice of Law Rule (Article 7 RR): *Lex Concursus*

4.45 The basic choice of law rule, titled 'Applicable law', is contained in Article 7 RR. In substance it remains identical to Article 4 OR (discussed above at paras 4.05–4.10), subject to a small number of drafting adjustments such as that in Article 7(2)(c) where the term 'insolvency practitioner' is substituted for 'liquidator'. A welcome correction has been made to the wording of the former Article 4(2)(m)—now numbered as Article 7(2)(m)—where the illogical reference to 'acts detrimental to all the creditors' has been replaced with the more appropriate phrase 'acts detrimental to the general body of creditors'.

Exceptions to the Basic Choice of Law Rule (Articles 8–18 RR)

4.46 No changes of substance are made to the provisions now enacted as Article 8 RR (Third parties' rights in rem);[65] Article 9 RR (Set-off);[66] or Article 10 RR (Reservation of title).[67] Note should be taken however of the amended definition in Article 2(9) RR of the expression 'the Member State in which assets are situated', as this has relevance to the operation of those Articles in which the phrase appears, including Articles 8 and 10 RR, and also Article 11 RR (Contracts relating to immoveable property).[68] The text of Article 11(1) is identical to that of Article 8 OR, but an additional provision has been inserted as Article 11(2) to enable the court which opened main proceedings to exercise jurisdiction to approve the termination or modification of such contracts subject to certain conditions.

4.47 No changes of substance are made in Article 12 RR (Payment systems and financial markets),[69] and Article 13(1) (Contracts of employment) maintains the same wording as that employed in Article 10 OR.[70] However, an entirely new paragraph is added as Article 13(2) to enable the courts of the Member State in which secondary proceedings could be opened to retain jurisdiction to approve the termination or modification of those contracts of employment which are governed by the law of that state even if no insolvency proceedings have been opened in that Member State. This provides a safeguard for the interests of employees, for example in the event of recourse to a synthetic secondary proceeding as described in chapter 3.[71]

---

[65] Discussed at paras 4.11–4.21 above.
[66] See paras 4.22–4.26 above.
[67] See paras 4.27–4.30 above.
[68] See para 4.31 above.
[69] See para 4.32 above.
[70] See paras 4.33–4.34 above.
[71] See paras 3.21 and 3.32 above.

Article 14 RR (Effects on rights subject to registration) is unchanged from the **4.48** provision of Article 11 OR.[72] The drafting of Article 15 RR has merely been amended so that the references are made to 'a European Patent with unitary effect, a Community trade mark or any other similar right established by Union law'. The new wording reflects the changes in terminology brought about by the evolution of the European Union since Article 12 OR was drawn up in the year 2000.[73]

Both Article 16 RR (Detrimental acts) and Article 17 RR (Protection of third- **4.49** party purchasers) are unchanged in substance by comparison with their counter-parts in Articles 13 and 14 respectively of the OR.[74]

A welcome amendment has been made in the enactment of Article 18 RR (Effects **4.50** of insolvency proceedings on pending lawsuits or arbitral proceedings). As the title sufficiently indicates, the uncertainty regarding the application of the equivalent provision in Article 15 OR to arbitral proceedings as well as to pending lawsuits has been resolved by the inclusion of explicit reference to both forms of dispute resolu-tion.[75] This outcome is in line with the conclusion formed by the English Court of Appeal, applying a purposive approach to the interpretation of Article 15 OR.[76]

---

[72] See paras 4.35–4.36 above.
[73] See para 4.37 above.
[74] See paras 4.38–4.39, and 4.40–4.42 above respectively.
[75] See paras 4.43–4.44 above.
[76] *Syska v Vivendi Universal SA* [2009] EWCA Civ 677, [2010] BCC 348 (CA), para 4.44 above.

5

RECOGNITION AND ENFORCEMENT

---

[1] Contributed by Daniel Bayfield QC and Georgina Peters, barristers at South Square, Gray's Inn, London, with the assistance of Andrew Shaw, barrister at South Square, Gray's Inn, London.

[2] Contributed by William Willson and Ryan Perkins, barristers at South Square, Gray's Inn, London.

[3] Contributed by Daniel Bayfield QC and Georgina Peters, barristers at South Square, Gray's Inn, London, with the assistance of Andrew Shaw, barrister at South Square, Gray's Inn, London.

[4] Contributed by Robert Amey, barrister at South Square, Gray's Inn, London.

[5] Contributed by Daniel Bayfield QC and Georgina Peters, barristers at South Square, Gray's Inn, London, with the assistance of Andrew Shaw, barrister at South Square, Gray's Inn, London.

A. Introduction

5.01 This chapter considers the recognition of insolvency proceedings and the enforcement of the rights and powers of liquidators under the Regulation.[6]

5.02 The Regulation has been repealed by a recast version of the Regulation, being Regulation (EU) 2015/848 of the European Parliament and of the Council of 20 May 2015 on Insolvency Proceedings (recast) (the 'RR')[7]. The RR applies with effect from 26 June 2017.[8] It applies only to insolvency proceedings opened on or after 26 June 2017.[9] The original Regulation ('OR') will continue to apply to insolvency proceedings which fall within its scope, having been opened prior to 26 June 2017.[10]

5.03 This chapter therefore also considers the recognition of insolvency proceedings and the enforcement of the rights and powers of insolvency practitioners under the RR.[11] The rights and powers of insolvency practitioners have been substantially amplified by the RR, in two major respects. First, more detailed provision has been made in relation to the duty of co-operation and co-ordination in cases where both

---

[6] In particular, as dealt with under the Regulation, Arts 16–22, Arts 31–38.

[7] OJ L141/19, 5 June 2015.

[8] Art 92 RR. That is subject to three exceptions, specified in Art 92 RR, of which two exceptions are directly relevant to this chapter. They concern the establishment and interconnection of insolvency registers (Arts 24(1) and 25 RR, which apply with effect, respectively, from 26 June 2018 and 26 June 2019: see further paras 5.129 to 5.134 below). The remaining exception concerns the obligations to which Member States are now subject to provide and regularly update a short description of their national legislation and procedures relating to insolvency (Art 86 RR), which applies with effect from 26 June 2016.

[9] Art 84(1) RR; see commentary on that Article in ch 8 below.

[10] Art 84(2) RR.

[11] In particular, as dealt with under Arts 19–29, Arts 41–52, Arts 56–77 RR.

main and secondary proceedings have been opened in different Member States. Second, a new set of rules has been implemented relating to co-operation and communication in proceedings concerning groups of companies.

B. Recognition and Enforcement Outside the Regulation

Where the OR and RR do not apply,[12] the law of recognition and judicial assistance **5.04** derives from three main sources: the common law, section 426 of the Insolvency Act 1986 (the '1986 Act'), and the Cross-Border Insolvency Regulations 2006, SI 2006/1030 (the 'Cross-Border Regulations').[13] This chapter examines each source in turn. The common law is supplemented (rather than superseded) by the Cross-Border Regulations and section 426, and all three sources of law are concurrently applicable.[14] However, for reasons explained below, the practical importance of the common law in England has been significantly reduced in recent years.

The common law

Following the publication of the previous edition of this book, two major judg- **5.05** ments have been delivered by the Supreme Court and the Privy Council (respectively), which have reshaped the common law of recognition and judicial assistance: *Rubin v Eurofinance SA*[15] and *Singularis Holdings Ltd v PwC*.[16] Between *Rubin* and *Singularis*, almost everything that Lord Hoffmann said in the Privy Council case of *Cambridge Gas Transport Corp v Official Committee of Unsecured Creditors of Navigator Holdings plc*,[17] which was previously the leading authority in this area, has now been overruled.

It is sometimes said that the common law of recognition and judicial assistance **5.06** is underwritten by the concept of universalism, which was explained by Lord Hoffmann in *Cambridge Gas* as follows:[18]

> The English common law has traditionally taken the view that fairness between creditors requires that, ideally, bankruptcy proceedings should have universal application. There should be a single bankruptcy in which all creditors are entitled and required to prove. No one should have an advantage because he happens to live in a jurisdiction where more of the assets or fewer of the creditors are situated.

---

[12] For example, because the debtor's centre of main interests is situated outside of the EU, or because the debtor is one of the exempt entities specified in Art 1 OR or RR, or because the proceedings against the debtor are not listed in Annex A OR or RR.

[13] If the debtor is a credit institution or an insurer, specialist EU Directives will apply: see ch 7 below and G Moss and B Wessels, *EU Banking and Insurance Insolvency* (1st edn, 2006).

[14] See Art 7 of Sch 1 to the Cross-Border Regulations.

[15] [2013] 1 AC 236.

[16] [2015] 2 WLR 971.

[17] [2007] 1 AC 508.

[18] At [16].

5.07 However, the principle of universalism is heavily qualified on pragmatic grounds. English law makes no real attempt to ensure that there is only one insolvency proceeding per debtor, and it is relatively straightforward to commence insolvency proceedings in England even if insolvency proceedings in the debtor's domicile are already underway abroad (see below).

5.08 The terminology of recognition and judicial assistance can be confusing, and is not used in a consistent manner throughout the cases (or the legislation). For present purposes, it is important to distinguish between (i) the recognition of a foreign office-holder's authority to act on behalf of the debtor, and (ii) the recognition of an order made by a foreign court against third parties in the course of insolvency proceedings. The preconditions for (and consequences of) the first form of recognition are very different from the preconditions for (and consequences of) the second form of recognition. In turn, both forms of recognition must be distinguished from judicial assistance, which involves the grant of additional relief beyond mere recognition in support of foreign insolvency proceedings. Each concept is considered below.

Recognizing the authority of a foreign office-holder

5.09 If an office-holder ('O') is appointed in foreign insolvency proceedings, the law of the relevant foreign state ('S') will ordinarily grant O extensive authority to act on behalf of the debtor ('D'). For example, O will often have authority under the law of S to deal with and dispose of D's worldwide assets, and authority to cause D to bring legal proceedings against third parties in D's own name. The English court will recognize O's authority to act on D's behalf (in accordance with the law of S), provided that D was domiciled in S at the time when insolvency proceedings commenced in S.[19] There are a number of standard bars to recognition at common law, such as fraud, public policy, and prejudice to local creditors.[20]

5.10 Traditionally, a corporation is deemed to be domiciled in the place of its incorporation. This test is ill-suited to the modern world, where corporations are frequently registered in low-tax jurisdictions with which they have no real connection. In *Cambridge Gas*, Lord Hoffmann proposed a development of the common law, whereby a corporation would be deemed to be domiciled in its centre of main interests (which may diverge from its place of incorporation). This sensible suggestion would have brought the common law into harmony with the Regulation, the RR, and the Model Law. However, the Supreme Court in *Rubin* rejected Lord Hoffmann's suggestion in *Cambridge Gas*.[21] It therefore appears that the place of incorporation retains its traditional connection with the concept of domicile, and that this role can only be modified by legislative intervention. (The domicile of

---

[19] See *Rubin* (n 17 above) at [13] and *Dicey, Morris & Collins on The Conflict of Laws* (15th edn, 2015) at 30R-100.

[20] See *Re a Debtor, ex p Viscount of the Royal Court of Jersey* [1981] Ch 384 at 402 (Goulding J) and R Sheldon, *Cross-Border Insolvency* (4th edn, 2015) at ch 11.

[21] See *Rubin* (n 17 above) at [121]–[129].

an individual is determined by a more fact-sensitive test: readers should refer to specialist commentaries.[22])

Where an individual is subject to insolvency proceedings, many jurisdictions **5.11** provide for his property (wherever situated) to vest in a specified office-holder, such as a trustee in bankruptcy. In these circumstances, the English court will recognize that the debtor's movable property situated in England has vested in the office-holder, provided that the latter was appointed in the place of the debtor's domicile.[23] This doctrine does not apply to immovable property.[24]

If the English court recognizes the authority of a foreign office-holder, he will be **5.12** permitted to sue in his own name before the English court.[25]

If the English court declines to recognize an office-holder's authority to act on the **5.13** debtor's behalf, a number of consequences may follow. Where the debtor owns land or goods situated in England, the office-holder may be liable for trespass or conversion. The office-holder may be liable for procuring breaches of contract to which the debtor is a party. There may also be scope for criminal liability, depending on the facts.

Even if the English court recognizes the authority of a foreign office-holder to **5.14** act on the debtor's behalf, the office-holder faces two potential problems. First, under section 389 of the 1986 Act, it is a criminal offence to act as 'an insolvency practitioner'[26] without proper authorization, if acting outside the OR.[27] Few foreign insolvency practitioners will have such authorization. The criminal offence applies to acting not only in respect of English incorporated companies, but also in respect of foreign companies which the English court has jurisdiction to wind up.[28] It is thought that the authorities in England do not regard a liquidator or other insolvency administrator appointed by a foreign court as coming within the criminal offence. However, such a person can never be completely certain that if he acts in England he is not committing a criminal offence (even if his authority has been recognized by the English court), unless he has or obtains authorization under the English provisions.

---

[22] See R Sheldon, *Cross-Border Insolvency* (4th edn, 2015) at paras 8.13 *ff.*

[23] See *Singularis* (n 18 above) at [12], and the authorities cited therein.

[24] ibid.

[25] See *Alivon v Furnival* [1902] 2 KB 312; *Macaulay v Guaranty Trust Co of New York* (1927) 44 TLR 99; *Re Borovsky* [1902] 2 KB 312.

[26] Acting as an insolvency practitioner covers acting as liquidator, trustee in bankruptcy, administrator, administrative receiver, and supervisor. It does not cover acting as a court-appointed receiver appointed by the English court without any insolvency proceedings in England, even where the company or individual is insolvent.

[27] The 1986 Act, s 388(6) read with the s 436 definition of 'the EC Regulation'. There will undoubtedly be an amendment to extend this immunity to the RR.

[28] See s 388(4) of the 1986 Act. Where the Regulation applies, there is an exception contained in s 388(6) of the 1986 Act. Where the Cross-Border Regulations apply, there is a similar exception provided by Art 8 thereof.

5.15 The court can provide a degree of protection to a foreign office-holder by appointing him as a receiver of the debtor's property. Such an appointment is not an insolvency proceeding in England, and derives from a special statutory power conferred on the court in civil litigation.[29] A court-appointed receiver does not need to acquire special authorization as an insolvency practitioner under English domestic law.[30] A receiver is an officer of the English court, and interference with him is a contempt of court.[31] The receiver must act according to the directions of the English court, and must accept its jurisdiction.

5.16 Second, section 234 of the 1986 Act provides administrators, administrative receivers, liquidators, and provisional liquidators with special statutory protection in the event that such a person seizes or disposes of property which does not belong to the insolvent company. There is a similar immunity for trustees in bankruptcy, pursuant to section 304(3) of the 1986 Act. The statutory protection does not extend to a seizure or disposal which results from the insolvency practitioner's own negligence. The persons included in the statutory protection are all authorized insolvency practitioners. The protections do not apply to a foreign office-holder. It is possible, however, that they could be applied pursuant to the Cross-Border Regulations, which is discussed below.

5.17 Even if the English court has appointed the foreign office-holder as a receiver, sections 234 and 304 of the 1986 Act do not apply. However, the court has the power, upon the release or discharge of a receiver, to protect him from liability for acts done in the course of his duties (after investigating any known claims).[32]

Recognizing foreign orders against third parties

5.18 It is common for judgments to be entered against third parties in the course of insolvency proceedings. In all developed jurisdictions, transactions effected by the debtor prior to the onset of insolvency are liable to be avoided in certain circumstances, and transferees may be ordered to restore money or other assets to the estate. Therefore, it is necessary to identify the circumstances in which foreign judgments against third parties in the course of insolvency proceedings can be recognized in England. (Where the English court has recognized the authority of an office-holder appointed by a foreign court, it does not automatically follow that judgments entered by the foreign court against third parties will also be recognized in England.)

5.19 Outside the context of insolvency, the recognition of foreign judgments is a substantial topic within private international law. Traditionally, English law distinguishes between two categories of judgments: judgments in rem and judgments

---

[29] Senior Courts Act 1981, s 37(1).
[30] Because he is not within the 1986 Act, s 388.
[31] See G Lightman and G Moss, *The Law of Administrators and Receivers of Companies* (5th edn, 2014) ch 29.
[32] ibid para 29-015.

in personam. A judgment in personam binds only the parties to the proceedings in which the judgment was made, whereas a judgment in rem is binding on all persons, whether parties or not.[33] In general, judgments in rem relate to the ownership of property (or the status of a person), whereas judgments in personam require specified persons to pay a sum of money or to perform an action.

Rule 43 of *Dicey, Morris & Collins on the Conflict of Laws* (15th edition) ('*Dicey*') **5.20** describes the circumstances in which a judgment in personam will be recognized at common law:

> A court of a foreign country outside the United Kingdom has jurisdiction to give a judgment *in personam* capable of enforcement or recognition as against the person against whom it was given in the following cases:
>
> First Case—If the person against whom the judgment was given was, at the time the proceedings were instituted, present in the foreign country.
>
> Second Case—If the person against whom the judgment was given was claimant, or counterclaimed, in the proceedings in the foreign court.
>
> Third Case—If the person against whom the judgment was given submitted to the jurisdiction of that court by voluntarily appearing in the proceedings.
>
> Fourth Case—If the person against whom the judgment was given had before the commencement of the proceedings agreed, in respect of the subject matter of the proceedings, to submit to the jurisdiction of that court or of the courts of that country.

By contrast, a judgment in rem will only be recognized at common law if the rel- **5.21** evant property was situated in the jurisdiction where the judgment was made at the time thereof: see Rule 40 of *Dicey*.

In *Cambridge Gas*, Lord Hoffmann suggested that judgments delivered in the **5.22** course of insolvency proceedings fall into a *sui generis* third category, being neither judgments in personam nor judgments in rem. Applying this analysis, Lord Hoffmann held that an order of the US Bankruptcy Court for the confiscation of shares belonging to a third party could be recognized in the Isle of Man, notwithstanding that the third party was not present in the US and had not submitted to the jurisdiction of the US Bankruptcy Court, and notwithstanding that the shares were situated outside of the US. In short, the normal grounds for the recognition of a judgment in personam or in rem did not exist.

However, Lord Hoffmann's analysis was rejected by the Supreme Court in *Rubin*. **5.23** Lord Collins, who gave the leading speech, held that judgments in insolvency proceedings must be either judgments in rem or judgments in personam, and that the ordinary principles of recognition under English private international law (embodied in Rules 40 and 43 of *Dicey*) apply equally within the context of insolvency. There is no 'third category' of judgments, with special rules of recognition.

---

[33] See *Pattni v Ali* [2007] 2 AC 85 and *Dicey, Morris & Collins on the Conflict of Laws* (15th edn, 2015) ch 14.

5.24 The facts of *Rubin* illustrate the impact of this analysis. An insolvent trust ('TCT') had entered into insolvency proceedings under Chapter 11 of the US Bankruptcy Code. A claw-back action was brought against the officers and promoters of TCT before the US Bankruptcy Court. The defendants were not present in the United States at any material time, did not submit to the jurisdiction of the US Bankruptcy Court and did not defend the proceedings. The US Bankruptcy Court entered judgment against the defendants. Lord Collins held that this constituted a judgment in personam. Applying Rule 43 of *Dicey*, recognition was impossible.

5.25 In the Supreme Court, the *Rubin* case was joined to the case of *New Cap Reinsurance Corp Ltd v AE Grant*, which raised similar issues. The company had entered into liquidation in Australia. A claw-back action was brought against a Lloyd's syndicate before the Supreme Court of New South Wales. The latter court entered judgment against the syndicate. The syndicate was not present in Australia at any material time, and did not defend the proceedings. However, the syndicate had previously participated in the liquidation by filing proofs of debt and participating in creditors' meetings. This proved to be crucial. Lord Collins held that such conduct constituted a submission to the jurisdiction of the Australian court, with the consequence that the judgment against the syndicate fell to be recognized in England. Thus, a defendant (or potential defendant) in a foreign claw-back action should think very carefully before submitting a proof of debt in the foreign insolvency proceedings: this may render his English assets liable to attachment and seizure.

5.26 Technically, the judgment of the Australian court was required to be registered under the Foreign Judgments (Reciprocal Enforcement) Act 1933, rather than being recognized or enforced at common law. The 1933 Act applies to judgments given by the courts of various Commonwealth nations, including judgments in 'civil and commercial matters' given by the courts of Australia.[34] The grounds for registration under the 1933 Act are substantially the same as the grounds for recognition at common law.[35] Lord Collins held that judgments in claw-back proceedings constitute 'civil and commercial matters'.[36]

Judicial assistance: General principles

5.27 Judicial assistance involves the grant of relief (beyond mere recognition) in support of foreign insolvency proceedings. Judicial assistance is only available at common law for insolvency proceedings in the place of the debtor's domicile, as explained above.[37] Judicial assistance is sometimes sought by way of a formal letter of request from the foreign court conducting the insolvency proceedings.

---

[34] See the Reciprocal Enforcement of Judgments (Australia) Order 1994, SI 1994/1901.
[35] See Rule 54 of *Dicey*.
[36] See *Rubin* (n 17 above) at [175].
[37] See *Rubin* (n 17 above) at [31].

Under section 25 of the Civil Jurisdiction and Judgments Act 1982, the court has **5.28** the power to assist foreign proceedings by granting interim relief (such as a freezing injunction). However, section 25 only applies to proceedings within the Brussels Regulation (Recast).[38] Insolvency proceedings, including avoidance actions based on insolvency law, fall outside the Brussels Regulation (Recast).[39] But an ordinary civil action to recover a debt or damages falls within the Brussels Regulation (Recast), even if the action is brought by an insolvency office-holder.[40] In such cases, the court has the power to grant assistance under section 25. (Readers should refer to specialist works for commentary.[41])

At common law, the standard forms of judicial assistance in the context of insol- **5.29** vency include (i) an order for the stay of proceedings against the debtor, (ii) an order requiring a third party to provide relevant information (in oral or documentary form) to the foreign office-holder, and (iii) an order for the remission of assets situated in England to the foreign office-holder, for distribution in the foreign insolvency proceedings. All three forms of judicial assistance are discussed below. However, the categories of judicial assistance are not closed, and the common law may develop new forms of judicial assistance to meet new challenges.[42] Indeed, 'the courts have repeatedly recognised not just a right but a duty to assist in whatever way they properly can'.[43] This has been described as the principle of 'modified universalism',[44] which 'has not been discredited'.[45]

In *Cambridge Gas*, Lord Hoffmann sought to identify the permissible scope of **5.30** judicial assistance. He said:[46]

> What are the limits of the assistance which the court can give? In cases in which there is statutory authority for providing assistance, the statute specifies what the court may do ... At common law, their Lordships think it is doubtful whether assistance could take the form of applying provisions of the foreign insolvency law which form no part of the domestic system. But the domestic court must at least be able to provide assistance by doing whatever it could have done in the case of a domestic insolvency. The purpose of recognition is to enable the foreign office holder or the creditors to avoid having to start parallel insolvency proceedings and to give them the remedies to which they

---

[38] Regulation (EU) 1215/2012 on jurisdiction and the recognition and enforcement of judgments in civil and commercial matters.

[39] See Art 1(2)(b) of the Brussels Regulation (Recast) and Case C-339/07 *Seagon v Deko Marty Belgium NV* [2009] 1 WLR 2168. See also Art 6 RR, which provides for 'any action which derives directly from ... insolvency proceedings and is closely linked with them, such as avoidance actions' to fall within the RR (and, therefore, to fall outside the scope of the Brussels Regulation (Recast)).

[40] Case C-157/13 *Nickel & Goeldner Spedition GmbH v Kintra UAB* [2015] QB 96.

[41] See *Dicey, Morris & Collins on the Conflict of Laws* (15th edn, 2015) ch 8.

[42] See *Singularis* (n 18 above) at [19].

[43] ibid at [23].

[44] ibid at [15] ('the principle of modified universalism, namely that the court has a common law power to assist foreign winding up proceedings so far as it properly can').

[45] See *Singularis* (n 18 above) at [19].

[46] See *Cambridge Gas* (n 19 above) at [22].

would have been entitled if the equivalent proceedings had taken place in the domestic forum.

5.31 This has been described as the 'as if' basis for judicial assistance, whereby domestic insolvency law is applied 'by analogy'. In *Singularis*, the Privy Council unanimously rejected Lord Hoffmann's analysis. Lord Collins, with whom the entire court agreed, said that Lord Hoffmann had engaged in a 'plain usurpation of the legislative function'.[47] To that extent, *Singularis* represents the overruling of *Cambridge Gas*, as well as the overruling or disapproval of several subsequent decisions applying the reasoning therein—including *Re Phoenix Kapitaldienst GmbH*[48] and the judgment at first instance in the Cayman case of *Picard v Primeo Fund*.[49]

5.32 When the court grants judicial assistance in support of foreign insolvency proceedings, it is not, according to the Privy Council, applying domestic legislation 'by analogy'.[50] Rather, the court is simply exercising its common law powers. As Lord Sumption said in *Singularis*:[51]

> First, there is a principle of the common law that the court has the power to recognise and grant assistance to foreign insolvency proceedings. Second, that power is primarily exercised through the existing powers of the court. Third, those powers can be extended or developed from existing powers through the traditional judicial law-making techniques of the common law. Fourth, the very limited application of legislation by analogy does not allow the judiciary to extend the scope of insolvency legislation to cases where it does not apply. Fifth, in consequence, those powers do not extend to the application, by analogy 'as if' the foreign insolvency were a domestic insolvency, of statutory powers which do not actually apply in the instant case.[52]

5.33 Lord Sumption declined to provide a general account of the circumstances in which the common law should be extended to facilitate judicial assistance: this issue 'does not admit of a single, universal answer'.[53] Lord Sumption did, however, identify five basic constraints on the availability of judicial assistance. First, the court is not entitled to provide assistance in support of a voluntary liquidation, or any other proceedings which are not conducted by an officer of the court.[54] Second, judicial assistance cannot be used to enable a foreign office-holder to do something that he cannot do under the law by which he was appointed. (This constraint is discussed

---

[47] See *Singularis* (n 18 above) at [64].
[48] [2013] Ch 61.
[49] [2013] (1) CILR 16.
[50] Although the practical result looks very similar to the local statutory provisions applying in domestic cases.
[51] See *Singularis* (n 18 above) at [38].
[52] The reasoning in this paragraph is open to criticism: see G Moss and I Fletcher, 'A Saad Affair' (2015) 28(4) Insolv Int 49–55.
[53] See *Singularis* (n 18 above) at [19].
[54] There is no obvious basis for this proposition. Lord Sumption said that a voluntary liquidation is 'essentially a private arrangement' [25], but this is incorrect: in all known jurisdictions, a voluntary liquidation brings into effect a statutory scheme which radically affects the rights of third parties (especially creditors), involving a high level of actual or potential judicial scrutiny and oversight.

in greater detail below.) Third, judicial assistance is only available when it is necessary for the performance of the office-holder's functions. Fourth, the exercise of judicial assistance must be consistent with the substantive law and public policy of the assisting court. Finally, where the office-holder seeks an order which requires actions to be taken by a third party, he must be prepared to pay the third party's reasonable costs of compliance.

Judicial assistance: Stay of proceedings and related relief

Historically, one of the most common forms of judicial assistance involved impos- **5.34**
ing a stay of proceedings brought against the debtor in England (or related relief, such as discharging or refusing to grant an injunction affecting the debtor or his property). The importance of such relief has been greatly reduced by the provisions of the implementation of the UNCITRAL Model Law in Great Britain by means of the Cross-Border Regulations 2006, which enable foreign office-holders to obtain a stay of English proceedings by making a straightforward application to the court (see below). However, this aspect of common law judicial assistance remains significant in several offshore jurisdictions (such as Bermuda) which have not enacted any version of the Model Law and in all other cases where the Cross-Border Regulations, section 426, and the OR/RR (or Directives) do not apply.[55]

Thus, in *Firswood Ltd v Petra Bank*,[56] a Jordanian bank had entered into liquida- **5.35**
tion. One of the bank's creditors assigned its claim to a party who had knowledge of the liquidation. The assignee attempted to sue the bank in England. The Court of Appeal refused to allow the action to proceed, thereby (in effect) giving judicial assistance to the liquidation in Jordan.

Likewise, in *Banque Indosuez v Ferromet*,[57] Hoffmann J held that he should do **5.36**
his utmost to cooperate with the US Bankruptcy Court and prevent any action which might disturb the orderly administration of the company in US Chapter 11 proceedings. An action had been brought in England for an injunction against property belonging to the company, over which a bank asserted rights of security. Such claims would have been impossible in the US, pursuant to the statutory stay created by the Chapter 11 proceedings. Hoffmann J thought it right to co-operate with the US Bankruptcy Court by refusing to grant an injunction which would undermine the stay of creditors' remedies.

In *Felixstowe Dock v US Lines*,[58] a creditor in England had obtained an interim **5.37**
freezing order against the assets of a US corporation. The corporation went into Chapter 11 bankruptcy, and applied for the injunction to be discharged (so that

---

[55] For example, where the debtor falls within one of the carve-outs in Art 1(2) of Sch 1 to the Cross-Border Regulations.
[56] [1996] CLC 608.
[57] [1993] BCLC 112.
[58] [1989] QB 360.

the assets could be repatriated to the United States and used in the restructuring). Hirst J dismissed the application. This case can be explained on the basis that Hirst J regarded the restructuring as being biased in favour of US creditors and as being discriminatory against European creditors.[59]

Judicial assistance: Obtaining information

5.38 A foreign office-holder can seek judicial assistance to obtain information (whether oral or documentary) from a third party. *Singularis* is the leading case on this form of judicial assistance.

5.39 *Singularis* was an appeal brought by the Joint Official Liquidators ('JOLs') of the company. A winding-up order had been made against the company in the Cayman Islands, its place of incorporation. The JOLs believed that PwC, the company's former auditors, had information which would assist in tracing its assets. To that end, the JOLs sought to obtain (*inter alia*) PwC's working papers. Under section 103 of the Cayman Islands Companies Law, the Grand Court of the Cayman Islands was empowered to compel the production of 'documents belonging to the company'. However, the latter provision did not assist the JOLs, who accepted that PwC's working papers did not belong to the company. In an attempt to circumvent this difficulty, the JOLs sought judicial assistance in Bermuda, where the relevant PwC entity was registered. If the company had been wound up in Bermuda, PwC could have been compelled to produce its working papers pursuant to section 195 of Bermuda's Companies Act 1981, which is drafted in much broader terms than section 103 of the Cayman Islands Companies Law. However, no attempt was made in relation to this company to obtain a winding-up order in Bermuda, and the Privy Council held in a related appeal that the Supreme Court of Bermuda had no jurisdiction to make such an order.[60] As a result, the JOLs did not directly rely on section 195. Instead, the JOLs argued that the Supreme Court of Bermuda had a common law power to order the production of the relevant information.

5.40 By a bare majority,[61] the Privy Council held that there is 'a power at common law to assist a foreign court of insolvency jurisdiction by ordering the production of information in oral or documentary form which is necessary for the administration of a foreign winding up'.[62] As Lord Sumption observed, 'the recognition by a domestic court of the status of a foreign liquidator would mean very little if it entitled him to take possession of the company's assets but left him with no effective means of

---

[59] Lord Hoffmann, 'Cross-Border Insolvency', the 1996 Denning Lecture. See also G Moss, 'Comparative Bankruptcy Cultures: Rescue or Liquidation? Comparison of Trends in National Law—England' (1997) 115 Brooklyn Journal of International Law 135–36.
[60] *PricewaterhouseCoopers v Saad Investments Company Limited* [2014] UKPC 35.
[61] Lords Sumption, Collins, and Clarke comprised the majority. Lords Mance and Neuberger dissented on this point, the former in fairly strong terms (see [130]–[148]). Unusually, all five members of the Privy Council delivered an opinion.
[62] Per Lord Sumption at [25]. See also Lord Collins at [33] and Lord Clarke at [112].

identifying or locating them'.[63] Lord Sumption emphasized that the Privy Council 'would not wish to encourage the promiscuous creation of other common law powers to compel the production of information',[64] and emphasizsed the limitations and constraints on judicial assistance (discussed above).

For present purposes, the basic problem identified by Lord Sumption was that **5.41** judicial assistance cannot enable a foreign office-holder to do something which he cannot do under the law by which he was appointed. Since the Grand Court of the Cayman Islands had no power to require third parties to provide documents to the JOLs which did not belong to the company itself, it would be improper to grant the assistance sought.[65] The JOLs were engaged in 'forum-shopping',[66] which Lord Sumption sought to discourage.

Lord Sumption's reasoning is open to criticism.[67] The insolvency laws of different **5.42** jurisdictions (even within the common law world) are very far from homogeneous. In order to determine whether a foreign office-holder seeks to do something which he cannot do under the law by which he was appointed, extensive (and expensive) expert evidence may be required. Applying Lord Sumption's reasoning, small differences between the insolvency laws of two jurisdictions (such as the length of a claw-back period or the permissible scope of a private examination) may result in the denial of judicial assistance. This can hardly be said to promote the universalist vision. However, there is little prospect that *Singularis* will be overruled at the present time.

Judicial assistance: Claw-back claims

For a number of reasons, a foreign office-holder may wish to bring claw-back pro- **5.43** ceedings before the English court (rather than the court which appointed him). The proposed defendant may be present in England, and unwilling to submit to the jurisdiction of foreign courts; or the proposed defendant may have assets situated in England available for execution; or the office-holder may consider the claw-back provisions in his home jurisdiction to be inadequate; or the office-holder may wish to avail himself of England's relatively quick and efficient civil procedure.

It is submitted that the English court can provide judicial assistance at common **5.44** law to a foreign office-holder by permitting him to bring claw-back proceedings in England. However, this gives rise to a difficult question: what substantive law should the English court apply? There are several possibilities: (i) the English claw-back provisions in the 1986 Act (such as sections 238, 239, and 423), (ii) the claw-back provisions under the foreign law by which the office-holder was appointed,

---

[63] See *Singularis* (n 18 above) at [23].
[64] ibid at [25].
[65] ibid at [29].
[66] ibid.
[67] See G Moss and I Fletcher, 'A Saad Affair' (2015) 28(4) Insolv Int 49–55.

and (iii) English common law avoidance provisions. Both of the first two options face difficulties. As to the first option, the claw-back provisions of the 1986 Act only apply expressly if an English liquidation or administration has actually commenced. *Singularis* has held that the statutory provisions cannot be applied on an 'as if' basis or by analogy (see above). As to the second option, even Lord Hoffmann in *Cambridge Gas* had rejected the idea of being able to apply foreign law. As Lord Loreburn said in *Galbraith v Galbraith* [1910] AC 508 at 510, '[a] foreign [insolvency] law ... has no operation in England, while the English law ... applies only to cases of English bankruptcy, and therefore the [foreign] trustee may find himself (as in this case) falling between two stools'.

5.45   As explained below, both the Cross-Border Regulations and section 426 of the 1986 Act provide simple solutions to this problem. However, where the Cross-Border Regulations and section 426 are inapplicable, the difficulty remains.

5.46   Prior to *Singularis*, the English court was prepared to apply the claw-back provisions in the 1986 Act by analogy, 'as if' English insolvency proceedings had commenced at the time of the foreign insolvency proceedings.[68] This approach was based on Lord Hoffmann's speech in *Cambridge Gas*, discussed above. Following *Singularis*, any such approach is no longer tenable. The English court can only provide judicial assistance by exercising its existing powers at common law.

5.47   Fortunately, it appears that the English court has a longstanding common law power to avoid preferences and transactions defrauding creditors. As Bowen LJ said in *Ex p Wilcoxon* (1883) 23 Ch D 69 at 74:

> Everybody knows that originally there was no express statutory enactment in regard to fraudulent preference. But from the time of Lord Mansfield down to 1869 the courts considered that certain transfers of property were frauds upon the bankruptcy law, though there was no statutory enactment upon the subject.[69]

5.48   In a purely domestic context, the court's inherent power to avoid preferences and transactions defrauding creditors is no longer relevant, and has been superseded by the relevant provisions of the 1986 Act. But in the context of common law judicial assistance (where the 1986 Act does not apply), there is no reason to believe that the 1986 Act extinguished the court's inherent claw-back powers.[70] If this analysis is correct, then the English court can provide judicial assistance to a foreign

---

[68]   See *Re Pheonix Kapitaldienst GmbH* [2013] Ch 61. See also the Cayman case of *Picard v Primeo Fund* [2013] (1) CILR 16. Both authorities were disapproved in *Singularis*.

[69]   See also *Lewis v Hyde* [1997] BCC 976 at 980; *Worsley v De Mattos* (1758) 1 Bun 467; *Alderson v Temple* (1768) 4 Burr 2235. The latter authorities relate to preferential transactions. As to transactions defrauding creditors, see *Ryall v Rolle* (1749) 1 Atkyns 165; *Hamilton v Russell* (1803) 1 Cranch 309; *Meeker v Wilson* (1813) 1 Gall 419.

[70]   As Lord Wilberforce said in *Shiloh Spinners Ltd v Harding* [1973] AC 691 at 723, 'where the courts have established a general principle of law or equity, and the legislature steps in with particular legislation in a particular area, it must, unless showing a contrary intention, be taken to have left cases outside that area where they were under the influence of the general law'.

office-holder by avoiding preferences and transactions defrauding creditors at common law. Such assistance would appear to be entirely consistent with *Singularis*, because the relevant avoidance powers have an independent existence under the common law: domestic legislation need not be applied 'by analogy'. However, the foreign office-holder will not be granted relief which he would not be able to obtain under the law by which he was appointed.[71]

Likewise, it appears that the English court can give judicial assistance to a foreign   **5.49**
office-holder by avoiding contracts that contravene the anti-deprivation rule, even if insolvency proceedings have not commenced in England.[72]

Ancillary insolvency proceedings

It may be desirable to commence English insolvency proceedings against a debtor,   **5.50**
even though insolvency proceedings have already commenced in his place of domicile. In such cases, the English proceedings are said to be 'ancillary' to the 'principal' proceedings abroad. One advantage of ancillary proceedings is that the foreign office-holder reduces his risk of personal liability (as described above).

In order for insolvency proceedings to be commenced in England against a debtor   **5.51**
domiciled elsewhere, certain criteria must be satisfied at common law. Most importantly, there will, save in exceptional cases, have to be shown a sufficient connection between the foreign company and the English jurisdiction. This must be proved by the presence of assets or a business or at least sufficient points of contact with England.[73] In *Stocznia Gdanska v Latreefers* the underlying dispute was between a Polish shipyard and the Latvian state shipping company. The Latvian shipping company had used an 'off-the-shelf' Liberian company to enter into certain ship-building contracts and the Liberian company subsequently defaulted. On the facts before the Court of Appeal there were sufficient points of contact with the English jurisdiction to make it right for the English court to assume jurisdiction to wind up the company. The default arose under contracts governed by English law and the Liberian company had been controlled through agents in London. The judgment debt upon which the insolvency proceedings were based had been created by a judgment of the English court.

Where the English court declares English insolvency proceedings shall be 'ancil-   **5.52**
lary' to principal proceedings abroad, no fixed or rigid course of conduct is thereby

---

[71] See *Singularis* (n 18 above) at [25].

[72] See *Money Markets International Stockbrokers Ltd v London Stock Exchange Ltd* [2002] 1 WLR 1150 at [40]–[41] and *Perpetual Trustee Co Ltd v BNY Corporate Trustee Services Ltd* [2009] EWHC 1912 (Ch) at [27]–[28] and [47]–[48].

[73] *Stocznia Gdanska v Latreefers* [2001] BCC 174 (CA). Where the OR or RR applies, the English courts will have to apply the jurisdictional rules of the Regulation: see ch 3 above. See also: *Re Drax Holdings Ltd, Re Inpower Ltd* [2003] EWHC 2743 (Ch) at [26] in which Lawrence Collins J held that the criteria went to the discretion of the court, rather than to its jurisdiction; *Re Sovereign Marine and General Insurance Co Ltd* [2007] 1 BCLC 228; *Re OJSC Ank Yugraneft* [2010] BCC 475.

set in motion.[74] However, in a classic ancillary winding-up, the essential function of the English liquidator is to collect assets belonging to the debtor which are situated in England (but not the assets situated abroad), and to remit those assets to the principal proceedings for *pari passu* distribution among the debtor's world-wide creditors.[75] The ancillary liquidator also collects claims against the debtor in England and remits those to the main proceedings. Subject to those exceptions, the full scope of domestic English insolvency law applies to the principal liquidation. Although in the express terms of the Insolvency Act 1986 an English liquidator has a duty to get in assets belonging to the company 'wherever situated',[76] the concept of this being in effect modified by the directions of the English court to the liquidator is well-established.[77] The *situs* of the debtor's assets will be determined in accordance with the general rules of private international law.[78]

5.53 However, an English ancillary liquidator may not remit assets to the principal proceedings where such remission would be contrary to 'justice' or 'public policy'. The scope of this exception is somewhat unclear, and is illustrated by two important cases: *Re BCCI (No 10)*[79] and *Re HIH Casualty and General Insurance Ltd*.[80]

5.54 In *Re BCCI (No 10)*, the insolvent bank entered into liquidation in Luxembourg (where it was incorporated) and in England, among other places. There were significant differences between the law of set-off in England and in Luxembourg, which Sir Richard Scott VC explained at 252:

> A creditor has a deposit of £1,000 and an outstanding loan of £200. He is a net creditor for £800 and, in England, would receive £320 if a 40% dividend were declared. In Luxembourg, the creditor would be entitled to a dividend of £400 but the £400 would be applied in discharging the £200 loan. So the creditor would receive only £200.

5.55 The English liquidators applied for directions as to whether the English assets should be remitted to Luxembourg for distribution in the principal liquidation. Sir Richard Scott VC directed the English liquidators to remit the English assets to the Luxembourg liquidators, but to retain sufficient funds to compensate creditors who would otherwise be disadvantaged by the Luxembourg set-off rules. In

---

[74] See R Sheldon, *Cross-Border Insolvency* (4th edn, 2015) at para 7.16.

[75] *Re Commercial Bank of South Australia* (1886) 33 Ch D 174; *Re Queensland Mercantile Agency Co Ltd* (1888) 58 LT 878; *North Australian Territory Co Ltd v Goldsborough, Mort & Co Ltd* (1889) 61 LT 716; *Re Federal Bank of Australia Ltd* (1893) 62 LJ Ch 561; *Re English, Scottish and Australian Chartered Bank* [1893] 3 Ch 385; *Re Alfred Shaw & Co Ltd* (1897) 8 QLJ 93; *Sedgwick Collins & Co v Rossia Insurance Co of Petrograd (Employers' Liability Assurance Corp garnishees)* [1926] 1 KB 1; *Re Vocalion (Foreign) Ltd* [1932] 2 Ch 196; *Re Hibernian Merchants Ltd* [1958] Ch 76; *Re Suidair International Airways Ltd* [1951] Ch 165.

[76] See ss 143(1) and 436(1) of the 1986 Act.

[77] See *Re HIH Casualty and General Insurance Ltd* [2008] 1 WLR 852 and *Re BCCI (No 10)* [1997] Ch 213.

[78] See ch 22 of *Dicey* (n 21 above) for a summary of the relevant rules.

[79] [1997] Ch 213.

[80] [2008] 1 WLR 852.

effect, the retained funds were designed to ensure that creditors who proved in the English liquidation received the same amount as they would have received if the English assets had not been remitted to Luxembourg.

This result was justified on the basis that the ancillary nature of an English winding- **5.56**
up did not relieve the English court of its obligation to apply mandatory rules of English insolvency law (and, in particular, rule 4.90 of the Insolvency Rules 1986 containing the rules on set-off in an English liquidation). Remitting the English assets without retaining the sums described above would amount to a *de facto* dis-application of rule 4.90. The essential principles to be derived from *BCCI (No 10)* were summarized by Sir Richard Scott VC at 246:

> (1) Where a foreign company is in liquidation in its country of incorporation, a winding up order made in England will normally be regarded as giving rise to a winding up ancillary to that being conducted in the country of incorporation. (2) The winding up in England will be ancillary in the sense that it will not be within the power of the English liquidators to get in and realise all the assets of the company worldwide. They will necessarily have to concentrate on getting in and realising the English assets. (3) Since in order to achieve a *pari passu* distribution between all the company's creditors it will be necessary for there to be a pooling of the company's assets worldwide and for a dividend to be declared out of the assets comprised in that pool, the winding up in England will be ancillary in the sense, also, that it will be the liquidators in the principal liquidation who will be best placed to declare the dividend and to distribute the assets in the pool accordingly. (4) None the less, the ancillary character of an English winding up does not relieve an English court of the obligation to apply English law, including English insolvency law, to the resolution of any issue arising in the winding up which is brought before the court. It may be, of course, that English conflicts of law rules will lead to the application of some foreign law principle in order to resolve a particular issue.

In *Re HIH*, the House of Lords revisited the issue of remission. The issue con- **5.57**
sidered by the House of Lords was whether English ancillary liquidators should be directed to remit the English assets of an insolvent insurance company to the Australian principal liquidators, to be distributed in accordance with priorities applicable under Australian domestic law. The Australian priorities were radically different from the priorities which prevailed under English law at the time the English proceedings were opened: among other things, the proceeds of reinsur-ance policies held by the company would be applied in discharge of the underlying liabilities of the company which had been reinsured, rather than being distributed *pari passu* among the company's general creditors.

There were two possible grounds for remission. First, an Australian court had **5.58**
written a letter of request to the English court asking for the English assets to be remitted under section 426 of the 1986 Act. Second, the Australian liquidators argued that remission could be ordered by way of common law judicial assistance. (Following the enactment of the Cross-Border Regulations, remission might also have been sought thereunder: see below.) The House of Lords unanimously agreed that the English assets should be remitted to Australia, but differed as to

the theoretical basis for such remission. By a majority, the House of Lords held that all of the English assets should be remitted to Australia pursuant to section 426 of the 1986 Act, notwithstanding the substantial differences between the English priorities and the Australian priorities.[81] This aspect of *HIH* is considered below. However, the House of Lords was divided on the question of whether the English assets could also be remitted to the Australian liquidation by way of common law judicial assistance. Lords Hoffmann and Walker held that the remission could and should be directed at common law; Lords Scott and Neuberger rejected this proposition; and Lord Phillips declined to express a view. In short, there was a '2.5 to 2.5' split.[82]

5.59 Lord Scott's reasoning in *HIH* on the issue of common law judicial assistance is similar to his reasoning in *BCCI (No 10)*. The radical differences between English and Australian law meant that remission would, in substance, involve the disapplication of the English statutory scheme. As a matter of basic constitutional theory, the English court has no power to override an Act of Parliament: therefore, remission could not be ordered at common law.[83] (The same problem did not arise in relation to section 426, which is why Lord Scott was content to order remission on that basis.) Lord Neuberger adopted a similar analysis.[84]

5.60 By contrast, Lord Hoffmann held that:[85]

> The whole doctrine of ancillary winding up is based upon the premise that in such cases the English court may 'disapply' parts of the statutory scheme by authorising the English liquidator to allow actions which he is obliged by statute to perform according to English law to be performed instead by the foreign liquidator according to the foreign law (including its rules of the conflict of laws). These may or may not be the same as English law.

5.61 On this footing, Lord Hoffmann held that the English court has a common law discretion (quite apart from its powers under section 426) to remit English assets in an ancillary liquidation to the principal liquidation, to be distributed within a different system of priorities (which may be substantially different from the English insolvency waterfall). Indeed, the principle of universalism:[86]

> ... requires that English courts should, so far as is consistent with justice and UK public policy, co-operate with the courts in the country of the principal liquidation

---

[81] Excluding Lord Hoffmann (who considered that s 426 was irrelevant to the issue of remission) and Lord Walker (who agreed with Lord Hoffmann).

[82] This phrase is derived from Lord Neuberger's speech to the Insolvency Lawyers Association on 16 November 2008, entitled 'Insolvency, Internationalism and Supreme Court Judgments'. For a fuller consideration of the judgment, see G Moss, '"Modified Universalism" And The Quest For The Golden Thread' (2008) 21 Insolv Int 145, and the conclusions reached at 146 and 151.

[83] See *HIH* (n 82 above) at [59]–[61].

[84] ibid at [75].

[85] ibid at [19].

[86] ibid at [30].

to ensure that all the company's assets are distributed to its creditors under a single system of distribution.

Lord Hoffmann explained the result in *BCCI (No 10)* on the basis that it had **5.62** not been just for the Luxembourg rules of set-off to apply to claims which were governed by English law.[87] He did not consider that Australian exceptions to the *pari passu* principle suffered from any such defect. Lord Hoffmann was influenced by recent amendments to the English statutory scheme for insolvent insurance companies,[88] which also create dramatic exceptions to the *pari passu* principle (although those exceptions are rather different from the exceptions established by the Australian legislation).[89]

In light of *Singularis* and *Rubin*, it is questionable whether Lord Hoffmann's **5.63** analysis based on the common law will be followed, despite its obvious merits. The Supreme Court has recently held (in a different context) that it would be 'extraordinary' and 'highly problematic' for an English court to modify the statutory order of priorities in insolvency.[90]

It appears, therefore, that *BCCI (No 10)* may still be a guide to the circumstances **5.64** in which the court will remit assets in an ancillary liquidation by way of common law judicial assistance (as opposed to the use of statutory powers). It has been confirmed that there is nothing in *HIH* which calls into question the long-established principle that the court has the power to order the remittal of assets to a foreign liquidation where the local law provides for a *pari passu* distribution.[91] The mere fact that foreign priorities are not completely identical to English priorities should not be treated as an automatic bar to remission, provided that the *pari passu* principle is respected.

Section 426, Insolvency Act 1986

Section 426 obliges the English courts to assist insolvency proceedings from **5.65** countries specified by delegated legislation where a request has been made for assistance by the relevant foreign court. The English Court of Appeal has held that the giving of assistance under section 426 is not mandatory, although the

---

[87] See *HIH* (n 82 above) at [17].
[88] ibid at [32].
[89] See the Insurers (Reorganisation and Winding Up) Regulations 2004, SI 2004/353, implementing Directive (EC) 2001/17 on the reorganisation and winding up of insurance undertakings. The latter Regulations were not yet in force at the time the *HIH* proceedings commenced. In brief, the Regulations ensure that retail policyholders in a direct insurance business have priority over all other ordinary unsecured creditors. For further details, see G Moss and B Wessels, *EU Banking and Insurance Insolvency* (1st edn, 2006).
[90] *Re Nortel GmbH* [2014] AC 209 at [116] *ff* (the Nortel/Lehman pensions case).
[91] *Re SwissAir Schweizerische Luftverkehr-Aktiengesellschaft* [2010] BCC 667 at [10].

court should assist if it is properly able to do so.[92] The designated countries are, except for the Republic of Ireland and (since the handover to China) Hong Kong, all members of the Commonwealth.[93]

5.66 Section 426(4) of the 1986 Act provides that: 'The courts having jurisdiction in relation to insolvency law in any part of the United Kingdom shall assist the courts having the corresponding jurisdiction in … any relevant country'. Under subsection 11 the Channel Islands and the Isle of Man are automatically within section 426. The Secretary of State has in addition power under section 426(11) to designate further countries as 'relevant' and has so designated a number of present and former colonies and Commonwealth countries. It might have been expected that designation would be based on the availability of reciprocal judicial assistance, but no such check appears to have been carried out prior to designation.

5.67 Section 426(5) describes the assistance which a UK court may give. A request from the court of a relevant country is 'authority for the court to which the request is made to apply, in relation to any matters specified in the request, the insolvency law which is applicable by either court in relation to comparable matters falling within its jurisdiction. In exercising its discretion under this subsection, a court shall have regard in particular to the rules of private international law'.

5.68 This permits the English court to apply English law or foreign law, as it deems it appropriate, albeit that in determining which law to apply, the court is required to have regard to the rules of private international law.[94]

5.69 The English court has jurisdiction to grant relief under section 426(4) even if no insolvency proceedings have commenced in the requesting country.[95] Section 426(4) is to be given a broad interpretation: provided that the request relates to insolvency in some way, the section 426(4) jurisdiction is engaged. It follows that the English court had jurisdiction to accede to a letter of request from the Royal

---

[92] *Hughes v Hannover Ruckversicherungs AG* [1996] 1 BCLC 497. See also *Re Southern Equities Corp; England v Smith* [2000] 2 BCLC 21, CA, the reasoning of which is not easy to reconcile with *Hughes*, although it affirms the non-mandatory nature of s 426.

[93] The Co-operation of Insolvency Courts (Designation of Relevant Countries and Territories) Order 1986, SI 1986/2123 designated (1) the Republic of Ireland, (2) the ten UK Overseas Territories (Anguilla, Bermuda, Cayman Islands, Falkland Islands, Gibraltar, Hong Kong, Montserrat, St Helena, Turks and Caicos Islands, and the Virgin Islands), and (3) six independent members of the Commonwealth (Australia, the Bahamas, Botswana, Canada, New Zealand, and Tuvalu). The Co-operation of Insolvency Courts (Designation of Relevant Countries) Order 1996, SI 1996/253 designated South Africa and Malaysia and the Co-operation of Insolvency Courts (Designation of Relevant Countries) Order 1998, SI 1998/2766 designated Brunei Darussalam, all three countries being independent members of the Commonwealth. However, when Hong Kong rejoined the People's Republic of China as a Special Administrative Region, it ceased to be part of the Commonwealth.

[94] A cross-reference which has been criticized as unclear both by Lawrence Collins J in *Re Television Trade Rentals Ltd* [2002] BCC 807 and by the Chancellor (Sir Andrew Morritt) in the Court of Appeal in *McGrath v Riddell (sub nom Re HIH Casualty and General Insurance Ltd)* [2007] 1 All ER 177.

[95] *Re Tambrook Jersey Ltd* [2014] Ch 252 (CA).

Court of Jersey to appoint administrators over a company incorporated in Jersey (where no analogous procedure was available) under Schedule B1 to the Insolvency Act 1986.[96]

Although section 426(4) must be construed in a broad manner, a foreign judgment **5.70** cannot be recognized or enforced thereunder. Section 426(4) is not concerned with recognition or enforcement, but with judicial assistance (which is a different concept).[97] In this respect, section 426(4) of the 1986 Act contrasts with section 426(1) and (2), which deals with the enforcement of orders from one part of the United Kingdom in another part of the same.

Since its enactment, a considerable body of authority has developed on the mean- **5.71** ing and workings of section 426. As discussed above, one of the leading cases on section 426 is the decision of the House of Lords in *Re HIH Casualty and General Insurance Ltd*.[98] The House of Lords unanimously agreed that the English assets should be remitted to Australia, but differed as to the theoretical basis for such remission. By a majority,[99] the House of Lords held that all of the English assets should be remitted to Australia pursuant to section 426 of the 1986 Act, not-withstanding the substantial differences between the English priorities and the Australian priorities (and regardless of whether remission was possible by way of common law judicial assistance).

More generally, it is suggested that *HIH* is authority for the proposition that in a case **5.72** to which section 426 applies and the foreign court makes a request for assistance, remission can and probably will be ordered of assets (net of costs and preferential claims) from an English ancillary liquidation to the principal liquidation unless such remission is negatived by considerations of justice or public policy. The precise con-tent of 'justice' in this context is not clear, but a different system of priorities in the case of insurance liquidation does not of itself make remission 'unjust' or contrary to English public policy. By contrast, a material difference in the rules of set-off in rela-tion to creditors whose debts are governed by English law may make such remission unjust, as in *BCCI (No 10)*.[100] Unfair discrimination, for example on the grounds of nationality or residence, may violate English public policy and prevent remission.

It is suggested that in the light of the law as it stood at the beginning of the *HIH* **5.73** liquidation proceedings, a remission into the Australian system of priorities, to the extent that it prejudiced creditors in the English proceedings, was very arguably 'unjust', but that, if the matter were judged in the light of insurance liquidation priorities after the coming into effect of the UK implementation of the European

---

[96] ibid.
[97] See *Rubin* (n 17 above) at [152].
[98] [2008] BCC 349.
[99] Excluding Lord Hoffmann (who considered that s 426 was irrelevant to the issue of remis-sion) and Lord Walker (who agreed with Lord Hoffmann).
[100] [1997] Ch 213.

Directive relating to reorganization and winding-up of insurance companies,[101] no such 'injustice' can be perceived, given that the interference with pari passu distribution is probably greater under English law than under Australian law. English law's conception of what is 'just' has changed in this context.

5.74 Article 44(3)(b) OR/Article 85 RR provides that the Regulation does not apply 'to the extent that is irreconcilable with the obligations arising in relation to bankruptcy and the winding-up of insolvent companies from any arrangements with the Commonwealth existing at the time this Regulation enters into force'. This appears to be a rather oblique reference to section 426 of the 1986 Act. The effect of Article 44(3)(b) therefore appears to be that section 426 will take precedence over the provisions of the Regulation in relation to requests for assistance from the courts of Commonwealth countries or territories designated under section 426 at the time the Regulation came into force. In relation to the Republic of Ireland and Hong Kong, not being members of the Commonwealth at the time the Regulation came into force, it appears that the provisions of the Regulation will prevail, in the event of any conflict, over any request for assistance made in accordance with section 426 so that any assistance may only be granted to the extent consistent with the provisions of the Regulation.

UNCITRAL Model Law[102]

5.75 In May 1997 the United Nations Commission on International Trade Law, UNCITRAL, adopted a Model Law on Cross-Border Insolvency.[103] Provision was included in the Insolvency Act 2000 for the Model Law to be given effect in the United Kingdom by regulations made by statutory instrument.[104] The enabling provision allowed for implementation with or without modification and it further allowed for amendment of any provision of section 426 of the Insolvency Act 1986.

5.76 The Model Law was enacted in Great Britain,[105] on 4 April 2006, by the Cross-Border Insolvency Regulations 2006 ('the Cross-Border Regulations')[106] and in

---

[101] See above.

[102] For a detailed consideration of the Model Law see G Lightman and G Moss, *The Law of Administrators and Receivers of Companies* (5th edn, 2014) ch 34.

[103] UNCITRAL 30th Session, 12–30 May 1997: Official Records of the General Assembly of the United Nations, 52nd Session, Supplement No 17 (A152/17), Part II, paras 12–225. The text of the Model Law as adopted is included in that document as Annex I (68–78).

[104] Insolvency Act 2000, s 14.

[105] In this context, this means the jurisdictions of (i) England and Wales and (ii) Scotland.

[106] SI 2006/1030. There have been dozens of applications under the Cross-Border Insolvency Regulations in recent years. In addition to the cases cited below, see (among many others) *Re Sanko Steamship Co Ltd* [2015] EWHC 1031 (Ch); *Re Kombinat Aluminjuma Podgorica AD* [2015] EWHC 750 (Ch); *American Energy Group Ltd v Hycarbex Asia Pte Ltd* [2014] EWHC 1091 (Ch); *Fondazione Enasarco v Lehman Brothers Finance SA* [2014] 2 BCLC 662; *United Drug (UK) Holdings Ltd v Bilcare Singapore Ltd* [2013] EWHC 4335 (Ch); *Kemsley v Barclays Bank plc* [2013] EWHC 1274 (Ch); *Re Pan Oceanic Maritime Inc* [2010] EWHC 1734 (Comm); *Samsun Logic Corp v DEF* [2009] BPIR 1502; *Warner v Verfides* [2008] EWHC 2609 (Ch).

Northern Ireland, on 12 April 2007, by the Cross-Border Insolvency Regulations (Northern Ireland) 2007.[107] The Cross-Border Regulations are composed of six parts: (1) the enacting provisions themselves (Regulations 1–8); and (2) five Schedules. The text of the Model Law in the modified form in which it applies in Great Britain is contained in Schedule 1. Various procedural matters are dealt with in the remaining Schedules.

The policy was to adopt the Model Law in a form which tracked the UNCITRAL **5.77** version as closely as possible but there have been important changes, especially those relating to the position of secured creditors (see below).

The Model Law enables a 'foreign representative'[108] of a debtor to apply for recog- **5.78** nition in the courts of an enacting state. While its scope is more modest than the Regulation, being limited to questions of 'recognition' of foreign proceedings[109] (in fact, mainly judicial assistance to them) and of the rights of the 'foreign representative' to obtain access to, and assistance from, the courts of enacting states, the impact of the Model Law is unrestricted in geographical terms. For example, it applies in Great Britain and in Northern Ireland in respect of all foreign countries without any requirement of reciprocity. The philosophy here is that the United Kingdom should set an example for other countries.

Unlike the Regulation, the Model Law and the Cross-Border Regulations do not **5.79** embody any rules of jurisdiction or choice of law. On the other hand, 'recognition' of foreign proceedings under the Model Law and the Cross-Border Regulations is based on the criteria employed in the Regulation to differentiate between main proceedings and secondary, or territorial, proceedings. The Cross-Border Regulations utilize similar criteria to designate foreign insolvency proceedings as either 'foreign main' or 'foreign non-main' proceedings for the purposes of recognition and assistance (Article 17(2)).[110] Very importantly, however, the COMI and 'establishment' criteria are intended in the Cross-Border Regulations to be *additional* bases for giving

---

[107] Statutory Rules of Northern Ireland 2007/115.

[108] 'Foreign representative' is defined under Art 2(j) of the Cross-Border Regulations and Art 2(d) of the Model Law as 'a person or body, including one appointed on an interim basis, authorised in a foreign proceeding to administer the reorganisation or the liquidation of the debtor's assets or affairs or to act as a representative of the foreign proceeding'.

[109] 'Foreign proceeding' is defined under Art 2(i) of the Cross-Border Regulations and Art 2(a) of the Model Law as 'a collective judicial or administrative proceeding in a foreign State, including an interim proceeding, pursuant to a law relating to insolvency in which proceeding the assets and affairs of the debtor are subject to control or supervision by a foreign court, for the purpose of reorganisation or liquidation'. It seems therefore that cases of provisional liquidations will fall within the ambit of the Model Law, by reason of the reference to 'interim proceeding'. The latter proposition was confirmed by in *Re Stanford International Bank Ltd* [2011] Ch 33 (CA) at [28]. In that case, the Court of Appeal also held that the appointment of a receiver by the Securities and Exchange Commission in the United States did not constitute a 'foreign proceeding', because (i) the essential function of the receivership was to protect a particular class of creditors (*viz.* investors) rather than creditors generally, and (ii) the receivership was not designed to effect a reorganization or a liquidation of the company, and did not provide for the possibility of a *pari passu* distribution to creditors.

[110] Which is in terms identical to those of Art 17(2) of the Model Law.

judicial assistance beyond pre-existing bases for 'recognition'.[111] Unfortunately, in the United States enactment of the Model Law in Chapter 15 of the US Bankruptcy Code the COMI and establishment criteria have been so far treated as exclusive bases for 'recognition'[112] and have restricted rather than enlarged the ability of the US courts to assist foreign insolvency and rescue proceedings.

5.80 The concept of COMI under the Model Law should be construed in substantially the same way as the concept of COMI under the Regulation.[113] Of course, this does not mean that all of the provisions in the Regulation regarding COMI can be 'read into' the Model Law. Although the new provisions regarding COMI in the RR have no equivalent in the Model Law, they are intended to codify the CJEU case law under the OR, and should therefore be followed by UK courts.

5.81 A foreign main proceeding is a 'foreign proceeding taking place in the State where the debtor has the centre of its main interests' (Article 2(g) of the Cross-Border Regulations).[114] A foreign non-main proceeding is a 'foreign proceeding, other than a foreign main proceeding, taking place in a State where the debtor has an establishment' (Article 2(h) of the Cross-Border Regulations).[115] Whilst there is once again no definition of the centre of main interests in the Cross-Border Regulations, 'establishment' is defined as 'any place of operations where the debtor carries out a non-transitory economic activity with human means and assets or services' (Article 2(e) of the Cross-Border Regulations).[116] This excludes the possibility that the mere presence of assets belonging to the debtor can be regarded as founding the exercise of insolvency jurisdiction capable of international recognition. Nor will a purely temporary or occasional place of operations provide a basis for the exercise of jurisdiction. Furthermore, Article 16(3) of the Cross-Border Regulations[117] lays down a rebuttable presumption that the debtor's registered office, or habitual residence in the case of an individual, is presumed to be the COMI.

5.82 Following *Stanford*, it is likely that the court will construe the term 'establishment' in substantially the same manner under the Regulation and the Model Law.[118] Of course, this does not mean that all of the provisions in the Regulation regarding establishments can be 'read into' the Model Law. Furthermore, there are crucial differences between the new definition of 'establishment' in the RR

---

[111] And are treated in the same way under the Model Law. See Art 7 of the Cross-Border Regulations and of the Model Law and para 90 of the Guide to Enactment.

[112] Moss, 'Bitter Pill Delivered by Judge Sweet' (2008) 21 Insolvency Intelligence 118.

[113] *Re Stanford International Bank Ltd* [2011] Ch 33 (CA) at [54].

[114] Which is in terms identical to those of Art 2(b) of the Model Law.

[115] Which is in terms identical to those of Art 2(c) of the Model Law.

[116] Although in largely similar terms to those of Art 2(f) of the Model Law, Art 2(e) of the Cross-Border Regulations replaces the term 'goods' with 'assets' to correct the faulty English version of the definition in the Regulation: see commentary on Art 2(h) of the Regulation in ch 8 below. The definition thus clearly embraces both tangible and intangible assets.

[117] Which is in terms identical to those of Art 16(3) of the Model Law.

[118] As to the concept of an establishment, see the leading Supreme Court case of *Trustees of the Olympic Airlines SA Pension & Life Assurance Scheme v Olympic Airlines SA* [2015] 1 WLR 2399.

and the definition of the same term in the Model Law: the definition in the RR includes a 'look back' period of three months, which has no equivalent under the Model Law.

By Article 15(1) of the Cross-Border Regulations,[119] a foreign representative may **5.83** apply to the court of an enacting state for recognition of the foreign proceeding in which he has been appointed.[120] Recognition will be accorded where the grounds set out in Article 17(1) of the Cross-Border Regulations[121] can be shown to exist. In like vein to the Regulation, Article 6 of the Cross-Border Regulations[122] allows recognition or assistance to be refused where it would be 'manifestly contrary' to the public policy of Great Britain or any part of it.[123] Further, by Article 17(4) of the Cross-Border Regulations[124] recognition which has already been granted by the court of an enacting state may be modified or terminated by that court, in the event of changed circumstances or further information coming to the notice of the court which reveals that the grounds for granting recognition were in fact fully or partially lacking.

The more direct and automatic effects (including an automatic stay) are accorded **5.84** in the case of foreign main proceedings, whereas relief and assistance is placed upon a discretionary basis in the case of foreign non-main proceedings. Article 20(1) of the Cross-Border Regulations[125] lists the effects of recognition of a foreign main proceeding which are automatic and do not depend on the exercise of judicial discretion. Specifically:

(a) a stay on the commencement or continuation of individual actions or proceedings concerning the debtor's assets, rights, obligations, or liabilities;
(b) a stay on execution against the debtor's assets; and
(c) a suspension of the debtor's right to transfer, encumber, or otherwise dispose of any assets.

---

[119] Which is in terms identical to those of Art 15(1) of the Model Law.
[120] See Art 15(2)–(4) for the documentation to be provided in support of the application and Art 16 which sets out certain presumptions in this respect.
[121] Although the grounds are for the most part the same as those specified by Art 17(1) of the Model Law, Art 17(1)(c) of the Cross-Border Regulations imposes the additional requirement for recognition that Art 15(3) of the same is satisfied. That provision differs from its counterpart in the Model Law, in its requirement that the application be accompanied by a statement identifying not simply all foreign proceedings in respect of the debtor that are known to the foreign representative, but also all proceedings under British insolvency law and s 426 requests known to the foreign representative.
[122] Art 6 of the Model Law institutes the same public policy exception.
[123] That notwithstanding, Art 8 promotes international uniformity of application and the observance of good faith. As in the case of the Regulation, the underlying intention is to ensure that comity is achieved in the context of cross-border insolvency proceedings.
[124] Art 17(4) of the Model Law accords the courts the same power. However, Art 17(4) of the Cross-Border Regulations extends yet further in also providing that in such a case, the court may, on the application of the foreign representative or a person affected by recognition or of its own motion, modify or terminate recognition either altogether or for a limited time, on such terms and conditions as the court thinks fit.
[125] Which is the same as Art 20(1) of the Model Law.

Article 20(2) of the Cross-Border Regulations[126] delineates the extent of the automatic stay and suspension, which are to be the same in scope and effect as if the debtor had been subject to analogous proceedings under the Insolvency Act 1986 and are to be subject to the same powers of the court and the same prohibitions, limitations, exceptions, and conditions as would apply under the law of Great Britain in such a case.[127] Article 20(5) provides that the stay does not affect the right to request or otherwise initiate the commencement of a proceeding under British insolvency law, or the right to file claims in such a proceeding.[128]

5.85 Of much significance are the additional provisions instituted by the Cross-Border Regulations, in particular those contained in Article 20(3), which provides that the automatic stay and suspension does not affect a number of specified rights. That includes the right to take any steps to enforce security over the debtor's property, or to take any steps to repossess goods in the debtor's possession under a hire purchase agreement,[129] or the right of a creditor to set off its claim against a claim of the debtor, if such rights would have been exercisable in the event of the debtor's bankruptcy, sequestration, or winding-up (as the case may be). It is also provided that the stay will not affect any right exercisable under a financial market contract in connection with the provisions of UK legislation which are excluded from the scope of the Model Law by Article 1(4). In addition, Article 20(6) allows an application to be made to the court by the foreign representative or a person affected by the automatic stay and suspension for an order that the stay or suspension be modified or terminated, in whole or in part. The court may grant the same relief of its own motion.

5.86 Article 21 of the Cross-Border Regulations[130] sets out the forms of relief which may be granted upon recognition of a foreign proceeding, whether main or non-main. It confers a general discretionary power upon the court of the enacting state to grant 'any appropriate relief', including the forms of relief instanced at Article 21(1)(a)–(g). The effects set out in Article 20(1) are repeated. The relief specified at Article 21(1) (d)–(g) will thus be discretionary even in the case of a foreign main proceeding. Article 21(1)(d) enables the court on the application of the foreign representative to provide for the examination of witnesses, the taking of evidence, and the delivery of information concerning the debtor's assets. So, for example, in *Re Bernard L Madoff Investment Securities LLC*,[131] the court concluded that the provision had both a jurisdictional and a discretionary component: the court had to be satisfied that the

---

[126] By Art 20(2) of the Model Law the enacting state may impose any exceptions to the automatic stay and suspension which are found elsewhere in its domestic insolvency law.

[127] The legal principles governing the exercise of discretion in relation to applications for lifting the stay were considered by Briggs J in *Cosco Bulk Carrier Co Ltd v Armada Shipping SA* [2011] EWHC 216 (Ch).

[128] See the equivalent provisions at Art 20(3) and (4) of the Model Law.

[129] Defined under Art 2(k).

[130] Which provides for the same relief as Art 21 of the Model Law.

[131] [2010] BCC 328. For a case in relation to Art 21(1)(g), which enables the office-holder to obtain orders for an examination, see *Re Chesterfield United Inc* [2012] BCC 786.

information sought concerned the debtor's assets, affairs, rights, and obligations, and that, having regard to all the circumstances of the case, the interests of the persons against whom the order was sought were sufficiently protected.

Of much significance is Article 21(2). That provision allows the foreign representa- **5.87**
tive to apply to the court of the enacting state for an order entrusting the distribution of assets located in that state to him or to another person designated by the court. Article 21(2) provides another mechanism for the court to remit assets to a foreign office-holder, in addition to its powers at common law and under section 426 of the 1986 Act. The court has ordered remittal under Article 21(2) on at least one occasion since the previous edition of this book.[132] It remains unclear whether the English court would (or could) use Article 21(2) to order the remission of assets to a jurisdiction with substantially different priorities than the priorities which prevail in England. However, the mere fact that foreign priorities are not identical to English priorities is not a bar to remittal, provided that the *pari passu* principle is respected.

The scope of Article 21(1)(g), which empowers the court to grant 'any appropri- **5.88**
ate relief' upon the recognition of a foreign proceeding, has been the subject of recent consideration in two important cases: *Re Atlas Bulk Shipping A/S*[133] and *Pan Ocean Ltd v Fibria Celulose S/A*.[134] In *Atlas Bulk*, the Danish liquidators commenced proceedings against a third party (Navios) for the recovery of sums due under forward freight agreements (FFAs) governed by English law and subject to exclusive English jurisdiction. In its defence, Navios relied on a number of purported set-offs. The set-offs were founded on cross-claims which were either (i) non-mutual or (ii) acquired by assignment after the Danish insolvency proceedings had already commenced. Such set-offs are forbidden under Danish insolvency law. Furthermore, such set-offs would also be prohibited in an English liquidation: see rule 4.90 of the Insolvency Rules 1986. Norris J granted relief to the Danish liquidators under Article 21(1)(g) by declaring that Navios was not entitled to rely on the set-offs pleaded in its defence. The judge said:[135]

> Navios contracted with a Danish entity. The Danish bankruptcy law recognises the principle of equal distribution and strikes a balance between the interests of the person having a claim capable of amounting to a set-off and the interests of the general body of creditors. Those who contract with a Danish entity might expect that balance to govern their relationships inter se when insolvency supervenes. The only reason it does not do so automatically in the present case is the fortuitous circumstance that the FFAs happen to be governed by English law and justiciable in England. But English law in fact strikes the same balance. The public policy of Denmark and England both say that non-mutual set-offs and post-insolvency assignment set-offs do not hold good against the general body of creditors, and the

---

132 *Re SwissAir Schweizerische Luftverkehr-Aktiengesellschaft* [2010] BCC 667.
133 [2012] Bus LR 1124.
134 [2014] Bus LR 1041.
135 See *Atlas Bulk* (n 194 above) at [26].

assets of the debtor and the interests of the general body of unsecured creditors are to be protected accordingly. There is no reason why the recognising court in England should not regard as 'necessary' the protection which both Danish and English law afford to the general body of creditors.

5.89 However, in *Pan Ocean*, Morgan J refused to grant relief under Article 21(1)(g) in an application brought by Korean administrators. Pan Ocean had entered into a charterparty with a third party (Fibria), expressly governed by English law. The appointment of the administrators constituted an event of default, which entitled Fibria to terminate the charterparty by written notice under clause 28 thereof. The judge proceeded on the basis that Korean insolvency law prohibited the termination of a contract on such grounds, but that English law contained no such prohibition. The administrators made an application under Article 21(1)(g) for an injunction restraining Fibria from serving a termination notice. In short, the object of the injunction was to give effect to Korean law in an English court. In a lengthy judgment (citing numerous authorities from the United States and elsewhere), Morgan J rejected the application. The judge held that Article 21(1)(g), despite its apparent breadth, does not authorize the court to grant relief which would not be available in a domestic English insolvency. The approach to interpretation favoured by the US Bankruptcy Court in *Re Condor Insurance Ltd*,[136] based on a very different legislative history, was not followed.

5.90 Provision is also made for temporary relief. Article 19 of the Cross-Border Regulations[137] provides for discretionary relief under the law of the enacting state from the time of the filing of the application for recognition, until its determination. A non-exhaustive list of examples of such relief is provided under Article 19(a)–(c). By Article 22(2) of the Cross-Border Regulations,[138] the court may also attach conditions to any relief granted under Article 19 or 21.

5.91 Article 11 of the Cross-Border Regulations[139] confers on the foreign representative the right to apply to commence a proceeding under the Insolvency Act 1986 as if he were an office-holder appointed under the Act, whether or not recognition has been granted.[140] For those purposes, the foreign representative may have been appointed in a foreign main proceeding or a foreign non-main proceeding (but must have been appointed in one or the other).[141] Under Article 23 of the Cross-Border Regulations,[142] a foreign

---

[136] 601 F.3d 319.

[137] Which is identical to Art 19 of the Model Law.

[138] The same provision is contained in Art 22(2) of the Model Law, save that Art 22(2) of the Cross-Border Regulations extends further in providing that such conditions may include provision by the foreign representative of security or caution for the proper performance of his functions.

[139] As permitted by Art 11 of the Model Law.

[140] The right of direct access to the court is accorded by Art 9 of both the Cross-Border Regulations and the Model Law and is of much significance in promoting the timely and effective operation of cross-border insolvency proceedings.

[141] Art 11 of the Model Law refers simply to a foreign representative without requiring his appointment in foreign main or non-main proceedings.

[142] As permitted by Art 23 of the Model Law.

representative has standing to apply to obtain an order under the avoidance provisions contained in the Insolvency Act 1986. This right exists regardless of whether or not there are concurrent proceedings in this jurisdiction. Where there are, the foreign representative will first require the court's permission.[143] Under Article 24 of the Cross-Border Regulations,[144] upon recognition of a foreign proceeding the foreign representative acquires standing to intervene in any proceedings in which the debtor is a party. In this connection, Article 12 of the Cross-Border Regulations[145] allows the foreign representative to participate in a proceeding regarding the debtor under the local insolvency laws. The Cross-Border Regulations also cater for co-operation between courts and office-holders. By virtue of Articles 25–27,[146] the courts of Great Britain may rely on provisions entitling them to co-operate with foreign courts and foreign representatives. A list of the forms of co-operation is set out under Article 27 and expressed in general terms. Articles 28–32 of the Cross-Border Regulations[147] operate to co-ordinate concurrent proceedings, by directing the types of procedures to be followed in such cases. The principle of hotchpot (explained below) is applicable by reason of Article 32.

The Model Law modified what is described as British insolvency law[148] and, in the case of any conflict, the provisions of the Cross-Border Regulations are to prevail.[149] However, as against the Model Law, the EC Regulation on Insolvency Proceedings prevails: Article 3 of the Model Law as enacted by Schedule 1 to the Cross-Border Regulations[150] provides that: 'To the extent that this Law conflicts with an obligation of the United Kingdom under the EC Insolvency Regulation, the requirements of the EC Insolvency Regulation prevail.' That notwithstanding, the objectives of the respective Regulations are for the most part complementary and mutually reinforcing, aided by the use of similar criteria and terminology for the purposes of securing recognition and judicial assistance. That, combined with the wide geographical scope for the putative representative, provides a wide-ranging terrain for recognition and judicial assistance.

5.92

---

[143] See further Art 23(6) and also Art 23(2)–(4) and (7)–(9) of the Cross-Border Regulations, which contain provisions additional to those contained in Art 23 of the Model Law. Both the Cross-Border Regulations (para 5) and the Model Law (para 2) provide that when the foreign proceeding is a foreign non-main proceeding, the court must be satisfied that the Art 23 application relates to assets that, under the law of Great Britain, should be administered in the foreign non-main proceeding.

[144] Standing to intervene is also given by Art 24 of the Model Law.

[145] Entitlement to participate is provided for under Art 12 of the Model Law.

[146] Also Arts 25–27 of the Model Law in almost identical terms: Art 26(1) of the Cross-Border Regulations ensures that a British insolvency office-holder will co-operate with foreign courts or foreign representatives only to the extent consistent with his other duties under the law of Great Britain.

[147] Arts 28–32 of the Model Law are broadly the same. The Cross-Border Regulations have inserted an additional provision at Art 29(b)(iii), which states that when a concurrent proceeding under British insolvency law commences after the filing of the application for recognition of the foreign proceeding, any proceedings brought by the foreign representative by virtue of Art 23(1) before the proceeding in Great Britain commenced shall be reviewed by the court, which may give such directions as it thinks fit as to the continuance of those proceedings.

[148] Defined in Art 2(a) of the Cross-Border Regulations.

[149] Reg 3(2) of the Cross-Border Regulations.

[150] As provided by Art 3 of the Model Law.

C. Recognition under the Original Regulation ('OR')/Recast Regulation ('RR') (Articles 16 and 17 OR/Articles 19 and 20 RR)

Use of terms

5.93   In the discussion of the OR in this chapter:[151]

- 'liquidator' refers to the relevant insolvency administrator in proceedings covered by the Regulation: Article 2(b) OR;
- 'judgment' in relation to the opening of insolvency proceedings or the appointment of a liquidator includes the decision of any court empowered to open insolvency proceedings or to appoint a liquidator covered by the Regulation: Article 2(e) OR;
- 'court' means not only a judicial body but also any other competent body empowered by national law to open insolvency proceedings: Article 2(d) OR and Recital (10) OR;
- references to 'Member States', the 'European Union', or 'EU' refer to all Member States except Denmark;[152]
- references to the 'Virgos-Schmit Report' are to the report on the failed Convention on Insolvency Proceedings by Professor Miguel Virgos[153] and Etienne Schmit;[154] [155]
- the *opening* of insolvency proceedings, in an English context, where there is a filing of an application followed by a court order, means the making of an order of the court pursuant to which the debtor enters into the insolvency proceeding, for example, the making of a winding-up order, and not the filing of the application or petition pursuant to which the order is made. The application or petition in such a case is referred to as the *request* for the opening of proceedings. In the case of a Creditors' Voluntary Liquidation ('CVL'), *opening* probably refers to the court order confirming the CVL, since it is only with such confirmation that a CVL falls within the Regulation;[156]

---

[151] See also insolvency rule r 13.13, as modified by the Insolvency (Amendment) Rules 2002, SI 2002/1307 and the Insolvency (Amendment) Rules 2010, SI 2010/686, which provides definitions of terms used in the amended Insolvency Rules 1986, SI 1986/1925.

[152] See Recital (33)OR.

[153] Of the Universidad Autonoma of Madrid.

[154] Magistrate, Deputy Public Prosecutor, Luxembourg.

[155] The full text of the Report is set out in app 2 below.

[156] For a contrary view, see the commentary to Art 16 at paras 8.288–8.298 below. The Insolvency (Amendment) Rules 2002 add a new r 7.62 into the Insolvency Rules 1986 providing that a liquidator may apply to the court for an order confirming the CVL. The application must be made in writing and verified by written evidence by the liquidator. The court may confirm the CVL without a hearing. See also Form 7.20A in the 2010 Rules.

- references to the 'UK' include Gibraltar but exclude the Channel Islands and the Isle of Man;
- references to 'territorial' proceedings, unless the context otherwise requires, are to proceedings opened pursuant to Article 3(2) and (4) OR *prior* to the opening of main proceedings; this usage is also adopted in the amended Insolvency Rules: see rule 13.13(14) of the Insolvency Rules 1986. Paragraph 25 of the Virgos-Schmit Report uses the term 'independent territorial proceedings', as does the Commentary in chapter 8 below;
- references to 'secondary' proceedings, unless the context otherwise requires, are to Article 3(2) proceedings opened *after* the opening of main proceedings; this accords with the definition adopted in the amended insolvency rules: see Insolvency Rule 13.13(12) of the Insolvency Rules 1986.

In the discussion of the RR in this chapter: **5.94**

- 'insolvency practitioner' has replaced the term liquidator and is now given a more detailed definition in Article 2(5) RR;
- 'debtor in possession' is defined for the first time to mean a debtor in respect of which insolvency proceedings have been opened which do not necessarily involve the appointment of an insolvency practitioner or the complete transfer of the rights and duties to administer the debtor's assets to an insolvency practitioner and where, therefore, the debtor remains totally or at least partially in control of its assets and affairs: Article 2(3) RR;
- 'judgment opening insolvency proceedings' is now specifically defined to include: (i) the decision of any court to open insolvency proceedings or to confirm the opening of such proceedings; and (ii) the decision of a court to appoint an insolvency practitioner: Article 2(7) RR;
- 'court' has a substantially similar definition to that provided by the Regulation: Article 2(6) RR;
- references to 'territorial' proceedings, unless the context otherwise requires, continue to refer to proceedings opened pursuant to, Article 3(2) and (4) RR prior to the opening of main proceedings;
- references to 'secondary' proceedings, unless the context otherwise requires, continue to refer to Article 3(2) RR proceedings opened after the opening of main proceedings.

The following new definitions are included in the RR, necessitated by its more   **5.95**
detailed provisions for co-operation between main and secondary proceedings and its provisions for co-operation and communication concerning members of a group of companies:

- 'local creditor' means a creditor whose claims arose from or in connection with the operation of an establishment situated in a Member State other than that in which the debtor's centre of main interests is located: Article 2(10) RR;

127

- 'foreign creditor' means a creditor which has its habitual residence, domicile, or registered office in a Member State other than the Member State in which the proceedings were opened: Article 2(12) RR;
- 'group of companies' means a parent undertaking and all its subsidiary undertakings: Article 2(13) RR;
- 'parent undertaking' means an undertaking which controls, directly or indirectly, one or more subsidiary undertakings:, Article 2(14) RR. Article 2(14) refers expressly to an undertaking which prepares consolidated financial statements in accordance with Directive 2013/34/EU,[157] which is deemed to be a parent undertaking by and within the meaning of the RR.

General approach to recognition

5.96 Recital (22) of the OR[158] sets the scene as follows:

> This Regulation should provide for immediate recognition of judgments concerning the opening, conduct and closure of insolvency proceedings which come within its scope and of judgments handed down in direct connection with such insolvency proceedings. Automatic recognition should therefore mean that the effects attributed to the proceedings by the law of the State in which the proceedings were opened extend to all other Member States. Recognition of judgments delivered by the courts of the Member States should be based on the principle of mutual trust. To that end, grounds for non-recognition should be reduced to the minimum necessary. This is also the basis on which any dispute should be resolved where the courts of two Member States both claim competence to open the main insolvency proceedings. The decision of the first court to open proceedings should be recognised in the other Member States without those Member States having the power to scrutinise the court's decision.

5.97 Article 16(1) OR/Article 19 RR establishes the principle of immediate and universal (throughout the EU) recognition of insolvency proceedings opened in accordance with the jurisdictional scheme of Article 3 OR/RR.[159] Article 16(1) OR/Article 19(1) RR provides that: 'Any judgment opening insolvency proceedings handed down by a court of a Member State *shall be recognised in all other Member States from the time that it becomes effective in the state of the opening of proceedings*' (emphasis added).

5.98 Article 16(2) OR/Article 19(2) RR provides that recognition of the main proceedings opened pursuant to Article 3(1) OR/RR shall not preclude the opening of secondary proceedings by the courts of another Member State pursuant to Article 3(2) OR.

---

[157] Directive 2013/34/EU of the European Parliament and of the Council of 26 June 2013 on the annual financial statements, consolidated financial statements and related reports of certain types of undertaking (OJ L182, 29 June 2013, p 19).

[158] For the RR, see Recital (65).

[159] The question of jurisdiction is dealt with in ch 3 above.

The OR/RR afford immediate recognition of judgments concerning the opening, **5.99** course, and closure of insolvency proceedings which fall within its remit. The general principle of recognition is valid for all proceedings covered by the Regulation which are opened in a Member State.[160]

Article 16 OR has been replicated by Article 19 RR in identical terms. **5.100**

The effects of recognition of main, territorial, and secondary proceedings

Whereas Article 16 OR/Article 19 RR establishes the general principle of the rec- **5.101** ognition of a judgment opening insolvency proceedings, Article 17 OR/Article 20 RR under the heading of 'effects of recognition' distinguishes between the effects of recognition of main, territorial, and secondary proceedings.

Article 16 OR/Article 19 RR provides the basic principle of recognition for judg- **5.102** ments opening insolvency proceedings. Recognition takes place from the time that the 'judgment' becomes effective in the state of the opening of proceedings. In *Re Eurofood IFSC Ltd*,[161] the ECJ held that on the proper interpretation of the first sentence of Article 16(1) OR, the main insolvency proceedings opened by a court of a Member State had to be recognized by the courts of the other Member States without those courts being able to review the jurisdiction of the court of the opening state.

Article 17(1) OR/Article 20(1) RR provides that the judgment opening the main **5.103** proceedings under Article 3(1) OR shall, 'with no further formalities', produce the same effects in any other Member State as under the law of the state of the opening of proceedings, except where the Regulation provides otherwise and as long as no secondary proceedings are opened in the other Member State under Article 3(2) OR/RR.

Recognition has its effects under Article 17 OR/Article 20 RR 'with no further **5.104** formalities'. This means without any need to issue local proceedings to create such effects. The 'effects' are not spelt out and depend on the law of the proceedings, the *lex concursus*.[162] In English law terms, such 'effects' include the vesting of property

---

[160] In this connection, the ECJ has yet to determine whether Denmark constitutes a Member State within the meaning of the Regulation, Art 16. It seems clear that Denmark is not a 'Member State' for the purposes of Art 16: see the English and German decisions referred to in the commentary to Art 16 OR at paras 8.288–8.298 below. However, on 9 April 2008, the Juzgado de lo Mercantil No 1 referred this question to the ECJ in the case of Case C-148/08 *Finn Mejnertsen v Betina Mandal Barsoe*. It asked whether Denmark is a Member State within the meaning of Art 16 and, in particular, whether other Member States are obliged, unless they have made derogations, to apply the Regulation when a judicial declaration of insolvency is handed down in Denmark and presented for recognition and enforcement in those other Member States (see [2008] OJ C142/19–20). The reference was not ultimately determined by the ECJ.
[161] Case C-341/04 *Re Eurofood IFSC Ltd* [2006] BCC 397, ECJ (Grand Chamber).
[162] See Recital (23).

in a trustee in bankruptcy, the replacement of the agency of directors of a company in liquidation with that of the liquidator, the statutory stay on creditors' remedies in administration, etc. As the Virgos-Schmit Report explains in paragraph 154 (see Appendix 2):

> From the time fixed by the law of the State of the opening, the judgment opening proceedings produces its effects with equal force in all [Member States]. The divestment of the debtor, the appointment of the liquidator, the prohibition on individual executions, the inclusion of the debtor's assets in the estate regardless of the State in which they are situated, the obligation to return what has been obtained by individual creditors after opening, etc, are all effects laid down by the law of the State of the opening which are simultaneously applicable in all [Member States].

5.105 For example, if main proceedings are opened in England by means of an administration order,[163] the mandatory statutory stay on execution by judgment creditors would extend throughout the European Union, subject to the exceptions set out in the Regulation.[164]

5.106 The analogous regime for recognition under the Credit Institutions Directive was considered by the Supreme Court in *Heritable Bank plc v Landsbanki Islands hf*.[165] The decision arose in the context of similar provisions contained in Directive 2001/24/EC of 4 April 2001 on the reorganisation and winding-up of credit institutions,[166] which derive in significant part from the Regulation. The issue, broadly speaking, was the recognition and effect in the administration of Heritable of any extinction of Heritable's claims as a matter of the insolvency law of Iceland in Landsbanki's winding-up. The continued existence of those claims was critical to Heritable being able to rely on them as being available for set-off against Landsbanki's claims in its administration. Thus, the issue depended on the proper construction of the regime for recognition contained in Directive 2001/24/EC (and UK Regulations implementing the Directive).[167] Landsbanki, in effect, sought recognition in Heritable's Scottish law-governed administration of the discharge of Heritable's claims which had, as a matter of Icelandic law, occurred in Landsbanki's winding-up.

---

[163] See further the commentary to Art 16 at paras 8.288 et seq below.

[164] The qualification 'unless this Regulation provides otherwise' must include a reference to Art 15 OR, which provides that the effects of insolvency proceedings on a pending lawsuit concerning an asset or right of which the debtor has been divested shall be governed solely by the law of the Member State in which that lawsuit is pending: see further paras 8.270–8.287 below.

[165] [2013] 1 WLR 725, paras 44 et seq.

[166] OJ 2001 L125, p 15. It has been explained above that the scope of application of the OR (and RR) expressly excludes, *inter alia,* credit institutions (Art 1(2) OR, Art 1(2)(b) RR) which are dealt with separately under Directive 2001/24/EC. Directive 2001/24/EC differs from the Regulation in that it has effect throughout the European Economic Area, which includes Iceland. Also, it does not allow secondary proceedings.

[167] Directive 2001/24/EC has been transposed into English law by the Credit Institutions (Reorganisation and Winding up) Regulations 2004, SI 2004/1045.

The Supreme Court rejected Landsbanki's contention that the Directive required **5.107** the effects of Icelandic insolvency law on Heritable's claims lodged in (but subsequently withdrawn from) its winding-up to extend to Heritable's administration and held that the claims subsisted for set-off purposes in Heritable's administration.

The decision was based on the Court's interpretation of the provisions and scheme **5.108** of the Directive, as implemented, which permitted not only Landsbanki's winding-up board to adjudicate on claims and apply set-off, but also permitted Heritable's office-holders, being a company subject to insolvency proceedings itself, to apply set-off in its adjudication of claims. The fact that Heritable was also subject to insolvency proceedings governed by the Directive was not, it is considered, critical to the conclusion that the discharge of a debt under the insolvency law of a Member State is effective only for the purpose of the creditor's right to a dividend in those proceedings and does not have the effect of discharging it for all purposes.[168] In this respect, Lord Hope stated at paragraph 60:

> As the Lord President observed in para 32, the logic of Landsbanki's argument is that Heritable's claims against Landsbanki would have been extinguished even if Heritable had been a wholly solvent company. It might have decided that there was no point in pursuing a claim in Landsbanki's winding up because the prospects of a dividend were remote and the costs of doing that outweighed any possible advantage. However sound that assessment might have been, its effect would have been that Heritable would have been unable to set off its claim by way of a defence to a claim pursued against it in Scotland by Landsbanki. The only way for a creditor to avoid that result would be to lodge and maintain its claim in the insolvency proceedings in the other member state, even if the prospects of recovering anything were nil. This would also be, as the Lord President said in para 40, to give universal priority to the process in which a decision happened to be made first. That would encourage forum shopping, especially where there was a prospect of inconsistent findings as to the validity of a claim in different member states. It is hard to believe that this was intended by the framers of the Directive.

The recognition of main proceedings under Article 3(1) OR or RR will be limited **5.109** by the opening of secondary proceedings in accordance with Article 3(2) OR or RR. The main proceedings cannot produce its effects in respect of the assets and legal situations which come within the jurisdiction of the secondary proceedings. The secondary proceedings, *inter alia,* protect local interests[169] and for this purpose

---

[168] Separately, there is a general principle of English law that a discharge from any debt or liability under the bankruptcy law of a foreign country is effective in England if, and only if, it is a discharge under the law applicable to the contract: *Gibbs v Société Industrielle des Métaux* (1890) 25 QBD 399, approved by the House of Lords in *National Bank of Greece and Athens SA v Metliss* [1985] AC 509, 523. This rule accords with the position that existed prior to the commencement of a foreign bankruptcy (*cf Wight v Eckhardt Marine GmbH* [2004] 1 AC 509, 523).

[169] Recital (19) OR, which points out that secondary proceedings can also assist in the administration of an 'estate' where it is too complex to administer as one unit.

the national law applies.[170] However, the main proceedings may influence the conduct of the secondary proceedings as a result of the co-ordination and subordination rules set out in the OR or RR. Secondary proceedings and, to a lesser extent, territorial proceedings opened prior to the main proceedings, are subject to these rules (as to which see below).[171]

5.110 Territorial and secondary proceedings affect only the assets situated in the state opening those proceedings. Recognition of territorial and secondary proceedings pursuant to Article 16(1) OR or Article 19(1) RR does not imply the extension of the effects of the secondary proceedings to property situated in other Member States. Their effects cannot be challenged in other Member States but any restrictions on creditors' rights can only affect assets in another Member State if the creditors consent: Article 17(2) OR. Article 17 has been replicated by the RR, Article 20 in identical terms.

Potential conflict with English law

5.111 The restriction on what assets are covered by territorial and secondary proceedings (ie assets situated in the territory of the Member State in which those territorial or secondary proceedings have been opened)[172] would have conflicted with the pre-31 May 2002 wording of section 436 of the Insolvency Act 1986 which, although it does not define 'property', provides that 'property' includes 'property wherever situated'. Article 3(2) OR/Article 3(2) RR does not seek to redefine property, but does limit the effects of territorial and secondary proceedings to territorial assets. Consequently, a new section 436A has been added[173] to modify the definition of property in the application of the 1986 Act to proceedings by virtue of Article 3 of the Regulation, to refer to property as property which may be dealt with in the proceedings.

5.112 In relation to personal insolvency, section 283 of the 1986 Act provides that a bankrupt's estate comprises 'all property belonging to or vested in the bankrupt'. By section 306 of the 1986 Act the bankrupt's estate automatically vests in his trustee in bankruptcy immediately on that trustee's appointment. The operation of section 306 as a matter of English domestic insolvency law is to vest all of the bankrupt's assets, wherever situated, in his trustee who may be the 'liquidator' in terms of the OR/'insolvency practitioner' in terms of the RR in territorial or secondary proceedings. This would have to be read subject to Article 3(2) OR/RR and given only territorial effect in the case of territorial or secondary proceedings.

---

[170] Art 4 OR.
[171] The need for co-operation is emphasized in Recital (20) OR.
[172] Art 3(2) OR.
[173] By the Insolvency Act 1986 (Amendment) (No 2) Regulations 2002, SI 2002/1240, reg 18.

Public policy exception to recognition

The OR and RR are based on a presumption that a judgment opening insolvency **5.113** proceedings is valid. The only ground for opposing recognition is that the foreign judgment is contrary to the public policy of the requested state. The public policy exception will only operate in exceptional cases,[174] Article 26 OR/Article 33 RR (in identical terms) setting a high threshold by providing that a state may refuse to recognize insolvency proceedings where 'the effects of such recognition or enforcement would be *manifestly contrary to that State's public policy*, in particular its fundamental principles or the constitutional rights and liberties of the individual' (emphasis added). The Virgos-Schmit Report states in paragraph 206 (see Appendix 2):

> Public policy operates as a general clause as regards recognition and enforcement, covering fundamental principles of both substance and procedure.
>
> Public policy may thus protect participants or persons concerned by the proceedings against failures to observe due process. Public policy does not involve a general control of the correctness of the procedure followed in another [Member] State, but rather of essential procedural guarantees such as the adequate opportunity to be heard and the rights of participation in the proceedings ...

Public policy derives from national law and, therefore, the concept does not neces- **5.114** sarily have a uniform content throughout the European Union. In the past, a refusal of recognition and enforcement of foreign tax laws was part of English law public policy. Since Article 39 OR expressly permits tax and social security authorities in one Member State to claim in an insolvency in another Member State, it may well now be that for the purposes of the OR the tax and social security claims of one EU state cannot be regarded as being within an Article 26 OR public policy exception in the courts of another. In the RR, the equivalent article, Article 53 RR, does not expressly refer to tax and social security claims, but presumably those are intended to remain claimable in proceedings under the RR opened in other Member States. This seems to be confirmed by Recital (63) RR, which expressly refers to the right of 'tax authorities and social insurance institutions' to lodge claims.

The question of the public policy exception was dealt with in some detail by the **5.115** ECJ in *Re Eurofood IFSC Ltd*:[175]

> 62. In the context of the Brussels Convention, the Court of Justice has held that, since it constitutes an obstacle to the achievement of one of the fundamental aims of that Convention, namely to facilitate the free movement of judgments, recourse to the public policy clause contained in Art. 27(1) of the Convention is reserved for exceptional cases (*Bamberski v Krombach* (Case C-7/98) [2000] E.C.R. I-1935; [2001] Q.B. 709, paras 19 and 21).

---

[174] The limited scope of the public policy exception was considered for the first time by the ECJ in C-341/04 *Re Eurofood IFSC Ltd* [2006] BCC 397. See further the commentary to Art 26 OR / Art 33 RR at paras 8.362 et seq and 8.649 below.

[175] C-341/04 *Re Eurofood IFSC Ltd* [2006] BCC 397.

63. Considering itself competent to review the limits within which the courts of a Contracting State may have recourse to that concept for the purpose of refusing recognition to a judgment emanating from a court in another Contracting State, the Court of Justice had held, in the context of the Brussels Convention, that recourse to that clause can be envisaged only where recognition or enforcement of the judgment delivered in another Contracting State would be at variance to an unacceptable degree with the legal order of the State in which enforcement is sought inasmuch as it infringes a fundamental principle. The infringement would have to constitute a manifest breach of a rule of law regarded as essential in the legal order of the State in which enforcement is sought or of a right recognised as being fundamental within that legal order (*Bamberski v Krombach* (above), paras 23 and 37).

64. That case-law is transposable to the interpretation of Art. 26 of the regulation.

65. In the procedural area, the CJEU has expressly recognised the general principle of Community law that everyone is entitled to a fair legal process (*Baustahlgewebe GmbH v Commission of the European Communities* (Case C-185/95 P) [1998] E.C.R. I-8417, paras 20 and 21; *Netherlands and Van der Wal v Commission of the European Communities* (Joined Cases C-174/98 P and C-189/98 P) [2000] E.C.R. I-1; [2002] 1 C.M.L.R. 16, para.17; and *Bamberski v Krombach*, para.26). That principle is inspired by the fundamental rights which form an integral part of the general principles of Community law which the Court of Justice enforces, drawing inspiration from the constitutional traditions common to the Member States and from the guidelines supplied, in particular, by the European Convention for the Protection of Human Rights and Fundamental Freedoms, signed in Rome on November 4, 1950.

66. Concerning more particularly the right to be notified of procedural documents and, more generally, the right to be heard, referred to in the referring court's fifth question, these rights occupy an eminent position in the organisation and conduct of a fair legal process. In the context of insolvency proceedings, the right of creditors or their representatives to participate in accordance with the equality of arms principle is of particular importance. Though the specific detailed rules concerning the right to be heard may vary according to the urgency for a ruling to be given, any restriction on the exercise of that right must be duly justified and surrounded by procedural guarantees ensuring that persons concerned by such proceedings actually have the opportunity to challenge the measures adopted in urgency.

67. In the light of those considerations, the answer to the fifth question must be that, on a proper interpretation of Art.26 of the Regulation, a Member State may refuse to recognise insolvency proceedings opened in another Member State where the decision to open the proceedings was taken in flagrant breach of the fundamental right to be heard, which a person concerned by such proceedings enjoys.

68. Should occasion arise, it will be for the referring court to establish whether, in the main proceedings, that has been the case with the conduct of the proceedings before the Tribunale civile e penale di Parma. In that respect, it should be observed that the latter court cannot confine itself to transposing its own conception of the requirement for an oral hearing and of how fundamental that requirement is in its legal order, but must assess, having regard to the whole of the circumstances, whether or not the provisional liquidator appointed by the High Court was given sufficient opportunity to be heard.

The EU Charter of Fundamental Rights, which became binding on the EU with **5.116** the entry into force of the Treaty of Lisbon in December 2009, is a modern codification consistent with the European Convention.[176]

Proof of the liquidator's appointment (Article 19 OR/Article 22 RR)

In order to remove any formal obstacles to the recognition of a foreign 'liquidator' **5.117** (as defined by Article 2(b) OR)/'insolvency practitioner' (as defined by Article 2(5) RR) under local law, thus enabling the liquidator to take timely and effective action, Article 19 OR/Article 22 RR overrides local formal requirements. It establishes a simple means of providing proof of appointment, by means of a certified copy of the original decision appointing the liquidator, or by any other certificate issued by the court which has jurisdiction. The local jurisdiction can, however, require a translation of the relevant document into one or more of the local official languages.[177]

The Article derives from Article 2 of the 1990 Istanbul Convention. It was not **5.118** thought necessary to establish a uniform model for the certificate attesting the appointment of the liquidator. For example, if main proceedings are commenced in England by means of an administration order, a certified copy of the order will provide evidence of appointment throughout the European Union.

Article 19 OR/Article 22 RR is of practical importance as it limits the costs that **5.119** the liquidator will have to incur before acting outside the territory of the court in which he has been appointed and it enables the liquidator to take action quickly and effectively in relation to assets situated in another Member State.

Article 19 OR has been replicated by Article 22 RR in identical terms, save that ref- **5.120** erences to the 'insolvency practitioner' have replaced references to the 'liquidator'.

Publication and registration (Articles 21 and 22 OR)

Under the OR, the ability of a 'liquidator' to rely on the effects of the insolvency **5.121** proceedings in other Member States may to an extent depend on the existence of actual or constructive notice in that state of the proceedings or of his appointment. For example, in English law the authority of agents to deal with third parties ceases from the date of the winding-up order but it has been held in case law that this only affects a third party abroad when he gets notice of the court order.[178]

The liquidator therefore may wish to publish an official notice of the proceedings **5.122** or his appointment in an official journal or newspaper or may wish to register the proceedings or his appointment at a land or other registry. At the same time, the

---

[176] See http://ec.europa.eu/justice/fundamental-rights/charter/index_en.htm
[177] Art 19, second paragraph.
[178] *Re Oriental Bank Corp, ex p Guillemain* (1885) 28 Ch D 634.

local jurisdiction may be concerned that local persons dealing with the debtor should have the benefit of official notification or registration. However, in relation to proceedings covered by the RR, more prescriptive protections have now been implemented (see paragraphs 5.129 et seq below).

5.123 Article 21(1) OR enables a liquidator in main, territorial, or secondary proceedings to request that notice of the 'judgment'[179] opening the insolvency proceedings and, where appropriate, the decision appointing him, be published in other Member States. The publication will be effected in accordance with the publication procedure provided for in the Member State in which publication is requested. Article 21(1) OR specifically provides that the publication shall specify the liquidator appointed and whether the jurisdiction rule applied was that of Article 3(1) or (2) OR, that is whether or not the proceedings are main proceedings.[180]

5.124 Article 21(2) OR adds that any Member State in which the debtor has an establishment may require mandatory publication. In that case, there is an obligation on the liquidator, or any authority empowered to that effect in the Member State where the main proceedings are opened, to take all necessary measures to ensure such publication.

5.125 Article 22(1) OR provides that a liquidator may request that the judgment opening the main proceedings under Article 3(1) OR be registered in the land register, the trade register, and any other public register kept in the other Member States.

5.126 Again, any Member State may require mandatory registration (Article 22(2) OR) and where mandatory registration is required, the liquidator or any authority empowered to that effect in the Member State where the main proceedings are opened is obliged to take all necessary measures to ensure such registration.

5.127 Neither publication nor registration is laid down as a condition precedent to recognition in the Regulation and it is considered that neither should be regarded as such even when compulsory under the local law.[181]

5.128 The OR also requires immediate individual notice to be given by a 'court' or 'liquidator' to creditors who have their habitual residences, domiciles, or registered offices in other Member States: Article 40(1) OR.[182] Again, compliance with this obligation is not laid down as a condition precedent to recognition under the Regulation.

---

[179] In the OR, this expression includes the decision of any court empowered to open insolvency proceedings covered by the OR: Art 2(e) OR. 'Court' here means not only a judicial body but also any other competent body empowered by national law to open insolvency proceedings: Art 2(d) OR and Recital (10) OR.
[180] The Insolvency (Amendment) Rules 2002 introduced many amended forms. Petitions and orders are now required to state whether proceedings are main, secondary, or territorial.
[181] Insol Europe has produced a practical guide for publishing and registering the opening of insolvency proceedings in particular EU Member States at: *www.insol-europe.org*.
[182] The particular matters which have to be dealt with are listed in Art 40(2) OR/Art 54 RR.

Articles 24–29 RR

Articles 24–27 RR contain new provisions for the establishment, interconnection, **5.129** and accessing of insolvency registers. Article 24(1) RR imposes a mandatory obligation on Member States to establish and maintain in their territory one or several registers in which information concerning insolvency proceedings is published ('insolvency registers'). That information is required to be published as soon as possible after the opening of insolvency proceedings.

Article 24(1) RR requires such information to be made publically available, sub- **5.130** ject to the conditions laid down in Article 27 RR. It identifies a list of 'mandatory information' which is required to be included in the insolvency register, although Member States are expressly permitted to include other documents or additional information in their national insolvency registers, such as directors' disqualifications related to insolvency (Article 24(3) RR).

There is, however, an exception prescribed by Article 24(4) RR, paragraph 1, in the **5.131** case of individuals not exercising an independent business or professional activity, provided that known foreign creditors are informed, pursuant to Article 54 RR, of the court before which and, where applicable, the time limit within which a challenge of the decision opening insolvency proceedings is to be lodged in accordance with Article 5 RR. If a Member State makes use of that exception, the insolvency proceedings cannot affect the claims of foreign creditors who have not received such information (Article 24(4) RR, paragraph 2).

There is a limitation imposed on the legal effects which information that is pub- **5.132** lished in the insolvency registers may have, being confined to those set out by the national law and by Article 55(6) RR (time limit for lodging claims by foreign creditors).

Articles 25–27 RR make detailed provision for the establishment and intercon- **5.133** nection of insolvency registers by the Commission, and enabling access to the insolvency registers by Member States.

Article 28 RR substantially reprises Article 21OR, subject to three key changes: **5.134** (i) it is not only the 'insolvency practitioner', but also the 'debtor in possession' that is subject to such publication provisions; (ii) the power to request that notice of the judgment opening insolvency proceedings[183] in any other Member State is expressly stated to apply where the insolvency practitioner deems it necessary in accordance with the publication procedures provided for in that Member State;

---

[183] In the RR, 'judgment opening insolvency proceedings' is defined to include a decision by a court to open or confirm proceedings or to appoint an insolvency practitioner: Art 2(7) RR. 'Court' is defined very broadly for this purpose and includes either a judicial body or any other competent body of a Member State empowered to open or confirm an opening or to take decisions in the course of proceedings: Art 2(6)(ii) RR. Note that for some other purposes 'court' is restricted in the RR to a judicial body: Art 2(6)(i) RR.

and (iii) in the case of any other Member State where an establishment of the debtor is located, the insolvency practitioner is now subject to a mandatory obligation to request such publication. Similarly, Article 29 RR differs from Article 22 OR, in that, in summary, a mandatory obligation has been imposed on the insolvency practitioner or debtor in possession to take all necessary measures to ensure registration in a land register, company register, or any other public register, in the case of another Member State where an establishment of the debtor is located.

D. Recognition of Judgments under the Original Regulation ('OR')/Recast Regulation ('RR') (Article 25 OR/Article 32 RR)

Recognition and enforceability of other judgments (Article 25 OR and Article 32 RR)

5.135 Following on from Articles 16–24 OR (Articles 19–31 RR), which deal with recognition of the opening of insolvency proceedings and its effects, Article 25 OR (Article 32 RR) deals with the recognition of judgments relating to the conduct and closure of insolvency proceedings and of judgments made in the framework of those proceedings.

Impact of the RR

5.136 Authorities concerning Article 25 OR will continue to be relevant to the interpretation of Article 32 RR, since the provisions are identical except for three changes, two of which are purely administrative. First, the reference to Article 16 OR is now a reference to Article 19 RR. Secondly, references to the Brussels Convention on Jurisdiction and the Enforcement of Judgments in Civil and Commercial Matters have been replaced with references to the equivalent provisions of Regulation (EU) 1215/2012. Thirdly, the saving at Article 25(3) for judgments which 'might result in a limitation of personal freedom or postal secrecy' no longer appears in Article 32 RR.[184] This provision was arguably redundant anyway, since Article 33 RR provides (as did Article 26 OR) that:

> Any Member State may refuse to recognise insolvency proceedings opened in another Member State or to enforce a judgment handed down in the context of such proceedings where the effects of such recognition or enforcement would be manifestly contrary to that State's public policy, in particular its fundamental principles or the constitutional rights and liberties of the individual.[185]

---

[184] Nor has this saving been moved to the preamble, as has been done in other instances where text in the main body of the OR has been removed from the main body of the RR.

[185] The Virgós-Schmit Report para 193 described the right of postal secrecy as 'an area which relates directly to fundamental rights', and stated at para 208 that there would be no need to rely on (what later became) Article 26 OR in such circumstances, because (what became) Article 25(3) OR contained an express provision on the point. Although there is an argument that the removal

Recognition

Where a court has jurisdiction under Article 3 OR (Article 3 RR) to open insol-   **5.137**
vency proceedings, Article 25(1) OR (Article 32(1) RR) provides for automatic
recognition, without any further formalities, of judgments given by that court
concerning the course and closure of insolvency proceedings, and compositions[186]
approved by that court. The same applies to judgments deriving directly from the
insolvency proceedings and which are closely linked with them,[187] even if they
were handed down by another court,[188] and also to judgments relating to preservation measures[189] taken after the request for the opening of insolvency proceedings
or in connection with it. The judgment relating to preservation measures is effective from the moment a request for the opening of insolvency proceedings is made,
even if proceedings have not yet been opened.[190] Recognition is, of course, subject
to a public policy exception under Article 26 OR (re-enacted in identical terms in
Article 33 RR).[191] It follows from the fact of automatic recognition that if the same
issue is pending before courts in two different Member States, both of which would
otherwise have jurisdiction, the first judgment in time will prevail, since the other
court will be bound to recognize it.[192]

It follows, from the limited grounds on which recognition can be refused, that a   **5.138**
judgment falling within Article 25(1) OR (Article 32(1) RR) cannot be reviewed as
to its substance in a court of the Member State in which recognition or enforcement
is sought. Matters of substance must be taken before the courts of the Member

---

of Art 25(3) OR from the RR was a deliberate attempt to remove the postal secrecy exception, since
the right of postal secrecy is enshrined as a fundamental right in the constitutions of many Member
States, the better view is that circumstances which would have justified refusal of recognition under
Art 25(3) will similarly justify refusal of recognition under Art 33 RR.

[186] Such as, for example, a scheme of arrangement under Part 26 of the Companies Act 2006
proposed by an administrator under Insolvency Act 1986, Sch B1, para 49(3), although the same
scheme of arrangement sanctioned outside of formal insolvency proceedings would not fall within
the scope of the Insolvency Regulation: *Re Rodenstock GmbH* [2011] Bus LR 1245.

[187] A formulation which closely follows the language in C-133/78 *Gourdain v Nadler* [1979] ER
733, which decided that proceedings commenced in a court not specializing in bankruptcy can still
be bankruptcy proceedings if they 'derive directly from the bankruptcy' and are 'closely connected'
with the bankruptcy.

[188] It has been said that such a court can be in the same or even a different Member State as the
court seised of the insolvency proceedings: C-339/07 *Seagon v Deko Marty Belgium NV* [2009] 1
WLR 2168, 2186 per Advocate General Ruiz-Jarabo Colomer at [67].

[189] Such measures take their character from the nature of the right they serve to protect (see
C-143/78 *De Cavel v De Cavel* [1979] ECR 1055 for a case concerning the matrimonial property
exclusion to the Brussels Convention) and therefore fall outside the scope of the Brussels Regime
(see Virgós-Schmit Report para 199).

[190] Virgós-Schmit Report para 198.

[191] See paras 8.362 et seq below.

[192] C-649/13 *Comité d'entreprise de Nortel Networks SA and others* v *Rogeau*. Where there is a
conflict of jurisdictions under the Insolvency Regulation, the general rule is that it is the first judgment in time which prevails, see for example *Re X* [2014] ILPr 35 in the context of the opening of
main proceedings. This may be contrasted with the position under the Brussels Regime, where it is
generally the court first seised which has jurisdiction.

State in which proceedings are opened.[193] Moreover, the court of the Member State in which recognition or enforcement is sought may not impugn the jurisdiction of the court of the Member State in which proceedings are opened. [194] That challenge too must be taken in the Member State in which proceedings are opened.[195]

Enforcement

5.139 Although recognition is automatic, subsequent enforcement is to be effected in accordance with the Brussels Regime for enforcement of civil judgments. Accordingly, Article 25(1) OR provides that enforcement shall be in accordance with Articles 31–51 (except Article 34(2))[196] of the Brussels Convention on Jurisdiction and the Enforcement of Judgments in Civil and Commercial Matters (the 'Brussels Convention'). It was suggested that, following the replacement of the Brussels Convention with Regulation (EC) 44/2001, references to the Brussels Convention should be instead be understood as references to Articles 38–58 (except Article 45(2)) of Regulation (EC) 44/2001.[197] By the same reasoning, it would appear that, following the enactment of Regulation (EU) 1215/2012, references to the Brussels Convention should (where the relevant judgment was given on or after 10 January 2015)[198] now be understood as references to Articles 39–44 and 47–57 of Regulation (EU) 1215/2012. As one would expect, Article 32(1) RR already refers to Regulation (EU) 1215/2012.

Interaction with the Brussels Regime for the enforcement of civil judgments

5.140 The Insolvency Regulation and the Judgments Regulation are intended to be mutually exclusive, but also to 'dovetail almost completely with each other … [t]o avoid, as far as possible, leaving lacunae between the scope of the two [regulations]'.[199] Accordingly, Article 32(2) RR (replacing Article 25(2) OR, which was in materially the same terms) provides that the recognition and enforcement of judgments that do not fall within paragraph 1 shall be governed by Regulation (EU) 1215/2012. Article 25(2) OR contains a corresponding reference to the Brussels Convention, which, as above, should now be read as a reference either to Regulation (EC) 44/2001 or, if the relevant judgment was entered on or after 10 January 2015, Regulation (EU) 1215/2012.

---

[193] Virgós-Schmit Report para 202(1).

[194] ibid para 202(2).

[195] C-341/04 *Re Eurofood IFSC Ltd* [2005] BCC 1021; *French Republic v Klempka* [2006] BCC 841.

[196] The relevance of the exclusion is that the numerous grounds for refusing recognition which are available under the Brussels Regime will not be available in the context of the Insolvency Regulation. The only ground for refusing recognition is that in Art 26 OR (Article 33 RR): public policy.

[197] B Wessels, 'Article 23 of the Insolvency Regulation' (2008) 21 Insolvency Intelligence 135. See also Art 68(2) of Regulation (EC) 44/2001, which provides that 'In so far as this Regulation replaces the provisions of the 1968 Brussels Convention between the Member States, any reference to that Convention shall be understood as a reference to this Regulation'. Art 68(2) of Regulation (EU) 1215/2012 is in identical terms.

[198] See Art 66 of Regulation (EU) 1215/2012

[199] Schlosser Report on the Brussels Convention [1979] OJ C59/91, [53]. See also *In re Rodenstock GmbH* [2011] Bus LR 1245 [47].

The distinction between proceedings falling within Article 25(1) OR, and ordi- **5.141**
nary commercial proceedings which happen to arise in the context of insolvency, is
not always an easy one to draw. In C-295/13 *H (Liquidator of GT GmbH) v HK*,[200]
the ECJ held that a claim by a liquidator against the former director of the debtor
company concerning payments made by the company after the onset of insolvency
did fall within the scope of the Insolvency Regulation, even though the relevant
cause of action was capable of being asserted without formal insolvency proceedings being commenced. Other illustrative cases in which the court found the necessary connection to the conduct of insolvency proceedings include C-111/08 *SCT
Industri v Alpenblume*,[201] *Polymer Vision R&D Ltd v Van Dooren*[202] and *Fondazione
Enasarco v Lehman Brothers Finance SA*.[203]

It appears, however, that if the office-holder assigns such a cause of action to a third **5.142**
party, who then commences proceedings, those proceedings will not fall under the
Insolvency Regulation.[204] There are also numerous instances of actions brought by
office-holders which, although plainly arising in the context of an insolvency process, did not fall within the Insolvency Regulation. In C-292/08 *German Graphics
Graphische Maschinen GmbH v Schee*,[205] an action concerning a reservation of title
clause was held to be an independent claim, as it was not based on insolvency law
and could be brought without the involvement of an office-holder or the opening of insolvency proceedings. Similarly, in C-157/13 *Nickel & Goeldner Spedition
GmbH v 'Kintra' UAB*,[206] the ECJ held that an action for payment of a debt based
on the provision of carriage services which happened to have been brought by an
insolvency office-holder did not fall within the Insolvency Regulation. Finally, in
Byers v Yacht Bull Corp,[207] a claim for a declaration as to the beneficial ownership
of a yacht brought by an officeholder arose under general law and, if good, accrued
to the company before the opening of insolvency proceedings. Consequently, the
Insolvency Regulation did not apply.

As for actions brought by an English office-holder, proceedings for fraudulent or **5.143**
wrongful trading or for preference would fall within the scope of the Insolvency
Regulation.[208] It has also been held by the Supreme Court of the Netherlands that
an order under section 366 of the 1986 Act falls under the Insolvency Regulation.[209]

---

[200] [2015] OJ C 46/9.
[201] [2010] Bus LR 559.
[202] [2012] ILPr 14.
[203] [2014] EWHC 34 (Ch).
[204] C-213/10 *F-Tex SIA v Lietuvos-Anglijos UAB 'Jadecloud-Vilma'* [2013] Bus LR 232.
[205] [2009] ECR I-8421.
[206] [2015] QB 96.
[207] [2010] 2 BCLC 169.
[208] *Byers v Yacht Bull Corp* [2010] 2 BCLC 169, although note the result of that case, which was
that the Insolvency Act claims were dependent or alternative to the principal cause of action, which
was independent of the insolvency. The Insolvency Act claims were therefore stayed until after the
foreign court had determined the principal cause of action.
[209] *Handelsveem BV v Hill* [2011] BPIR 1024.

Confusingly, it has been suggested that claw-back actions under section 423 of the 1986 Act (which may be commenced regardless of whether insolvency proceedings are afoot), even where brought by a liquidator, do not fall within the definition of 'insolvency proceedings': see *Re Baillies Ltd*.[210] However, the judge's reasoning in that case was based upon *Jyske Bank (Gibraltar) Ltd v Spjeldnaes (No 2)*[211] and *TSB Bank plc v Katz*,[212] both cases where the transferor was not in an insolvency process. It appears that following the ECJ's judgment in *H v HK*, a section 423 action brought by an office-holder will fall within the Insolvency Regulation and not the Judgments Regulation. This analysis is also supported by the opinion of Advocate General Ruiz-Jarabo Colomer in *Seagon v Deko Marty Belgium NV*.[213]

5.144 In *Re Hayward*[214] an office-holder sought an order that he was entitled to the bankrupt's interest in real property in Spain, which the bankrupt's wife had purported to transfer to a third party. The court concluded that such an action could be pursued quite outside the bankruptcy jurisdiction, and the fact that the office-holder could have sought the same relief under the 1986 Act made no difference. Accordingly, the Insolvency Regulation did not apply. The result was approved by the Court of Appeal in *Ashurst v Pollard*,[215] which considered the correct test to be whether the bankruptcy was the principal subject-matter of the proceedings, and went on to follow the result of *Hayward* in the context of an application by an office-holder for an order for sale of a villa in Portugal registered in the names of the bankrupt and his wife.

5.145 A members' voluntary solvent winding-up has been held in England not to fall within the Insolvency Regulation.[216] Nor will a solvent scheme of arrangement under the Companies Act.[217]

E. Enforcement of the Rights and Powers of Liquidators within the EU and their Duties and Obligations

The powers of the 'liquidator' (Article 18 OR/Article 21 RR)

Article 18 OR

5.146 Article 18(1) OR provides, subject to very important exceptions, that the 'liquidator' appointed by the opening of the main proceedings may exercise 'all the powers

---

[210] [2012] BPIR 665 [13].
[211] [1999] 2 BCLC 101.
[212] [1997] BPIR 147.
[213] [2009] 1 WLR 2168.
[214] [1997] Ch 45.
[215] [2001] Ch 595.
[216] *Re Cover Europe Ltd* [2002] 2 BCLC 61 [11]. Following Art 22 of Regulation (EC) 44/2001, re-enacted as Art 24 of Regulation (EU) 1215/2012, the courts of the jurisdiction where the company has its seat have exclusive jurisdiction.
[217] *Re Rodenstock* [2012] BCC 459 [38].

conferred on him by the law of the State of opening of proceedings in another Member State'. The liquidator's powers will be determined by the law of the state of the proceedings in respect of which he has been appointed. Likewise, his obligations are determined by the law of the same state.

Thus, in the case of main proceedings opened in England, unless and to the extent **5.147** one of the exceptions applies, the powers of the 'liquidator' will automatically be exercisable in all other Member States.

Article 18(1) OR specifically mentions the power of the liquidator in the main **5.148** proceedings to remove the debtor's assets from the territory of the Member State in which they are situated, subject to Article 5 OR (third parties' rights in rem) and Article 7 OR (reservation of title) (as to which, see below). For example, an English administrator will be able to collect assets in other EU states, such as a Rolls Royce owned by the debtor company and kept by the managing director outside his apartment in Paris, subject to any security rights that are held by third parties in respect of that asset.

The main exceptions built into Article 18(1) OR are the existence of local pro- **5.149** ceedings or of any preservation measure further to a request for the opening of insolvency proceedings which negates the exercise of the powers of the liquidator appointed in the main proceedings. The limitation based on the existence of local proceedings mirrors the restriction on the effects of recognition of the main proceedings in Article 17(1) OR.

In addition to the general exceptions to situations where the powers can be exer- **5.150** cised, there are also important restrictions in those situations where the powers can be exercised:

(a) Article 18(3) OR provides that the liquidator must comply with the law of the Member State within whose territory he acts, in particular with regard to procedures for the realization of assets and that his powers exercisable there do not include 'coercive powers' or the right to rule on legal proceedings or disputes;[218]
(b) the removal of property in another Member State is subject to Articles 5 and 7 OR.

The restriction on the use of coercive powers pursuant to the law of the main proceedings means that the 'liquidator' may himself wish to request the opening of secondary proceedings in order to make use of coercive powers under local law. He has the right to do that under Article 29(a) OR.

Any party who, under the local law, has power to request the opening of insolvency **5.151** proceedings can try to stop property being removed by the liquidator in the main

---

[218] See the commentary on Art 18(3) OR in ch 8 below.

proceedings by requesting the opening of secondary proceedings in the state in which the property is located: Article 29 OR.

5.152 Article 5 OR preserves the position of rights in rem, that is proprietary rights.[219] It provides that the opening of insolvency proceedings shall not affect the rights in rem of creditors or third parties in relation to assets of the debtor situated in another Member State. It is an important feature of English law that a floating charge 'security interest' is regarded in English law as a proprietary right. The foreign liquidator's ability to remove assets may, therefore, be severely limited if such a charge is in place over all the assets of the debtor. Article 5(2) OR sets out particular examples of rights in rem which include, amongst others, liens and mortgages. The absence of a definition appears to be deliberate and designed to leave the question of what constitutes a right in rem to the law of the Member State where the assets in question are located.

5.153 It is clear that the floating charge satisfies the requirements of a right in rem within the meaning of the Regulation. The inclusion in Article 5 OR of the words 'both specific assets and collections of indefinite assets as a whole which change from time to time' ensures that the floating charge is adequately covered.

5.154 It should also be noted that rights in rem are not entirely immune from the effect of proceedings to which the Regulation relates. If, for example, the law of the Member State where the assets are located imposes a stay on the enforcement of security following the commencement of a local insolvency proceeding, the liquidator in the main proceedings or any other person empowered to do so might request secondary insolvency proceedings to be opened in that Member State if the debtor has an establishment there. The secondary proceedings would be conducted according to local law and affect the rights of secured creditors with assets in that jurisdiction in the same way as in purely domestic proceedings.

5.155 Article 7 OR refers to reservation of title. Article 7(1) OR provides that the opening of insolvency proceedings against the purchaser of an asset shall not affect the seller's rights to that asset founded on a reservation of title clause where, at the time of the opening of the insolvency proceedings, the asset is situated in a Member State which is not the Member State in which those proceedings were opened. Accordingly, an effective reservation of title is also a limitation on the ability of the foreign liquidator to remove assets.

5.156 The OR does not provide any immunity from suit for the wrongful removal of or wrongful interference with property or contracts. Thus if a foreign liquidator

---

[219] The importance of protecting creditors who have rights in rem in relation to the debtor's assets is expressly recognized in Recital (25) of the OR. It is recognized that such protection is crucial to banks and other lenders in the granting of credit.

appointed in main proceedings removes assets from England which, unknown to him, are subject to third-party rights or reservation of title, he may still be personally liable and his liability will not be limited by reference to English statutory immunities referred to above. This is a significant risk because retention of title rights against corporate debtors to tangible movables do not have to be registered in any public registry in England, nor do certain other types of rights in rem. Accordingly, even with the Regulation in force, a foreign insolvency practitioner will still be running the risk of personal liability, since liability in tort (delict) for the removal of or interference with someone else's movables is, in English law, strict and not dependent on any proof of knowledge or negligence.

Thus a foreign liquidator may, as long as there is an establishment here, find it necessary or useful to bring or procure secondary insolvency proceedings in England. As explained above, under Article 29 OR he himself will have express authority to request the opening of secondary proceedings. **5.157**

There is an interesting question whether the non-extension, of statutory immunities enjoyed by English 'liquidators', to their counterparts in other EU states when they are acting in England and subject to English law (Article 18(3)) as liquidators under a main proceedings exercising powers in England pursuant to the OR or RR, is not a form of discrimination outlawed by EU law. **5.158**

Article 7(2) OR provides that the opening of insolvency proceedings against the seller of an asset, *after* its delivery, shall not constitute grounds for rescinding or terminating the sale and shall not prevent the purchaser from acquiring title where, at the time of the opening of insolvency proceedings, the asset sold is situated in a Member State which is not the Member State in which those proceedings were opened. The buyer will not, therefore, be prevented from acquiring title where, at the time of the opening of the proceedings, the purchased asset is located within the territory of a Member State other than the state of the opening of proceedings. **5.159**

Article 21 RR

Article 18 has been replicated by Article 21 RR in substantially similar terms. The provisions addressing third parties' rights in rem (Article 5 OR) and reservation of title (Article 7 OR) are now contained in Articles 8 and 10 RR. **5.160**

Equal treatment of creditors—'hotchpot' (Article 20 OR/Article 23 RR)

Article 20 OR

One purpose of the Regulation is that main proceedings should produce similar effects within the whole of the territory of the Member States. Article 20 of the Regulation seeks to guarantee the equal treatment of all of the creditors of a single debtor. **5.161**

5.162   Article 20(1) OR provides that where a creditor, after the opening of the main insolvency proceedings under Article 3(1) OR, by any means (including enforcement) obtains total or partial satisfaction of his claim out of assets of the debtor situated in another Member State, he shall return what he has obtained to the liquidator, subject to Articles 5 and 7 OR.[220] This rule of 'return'[221] has as its clear aim the furtherance of the pari passu principle: a creditor who, after the opening of proceedings, obtains total or partial satisfaction of his claim individually breaches the principle of collective satisfaction on which the insolvency proceedings are based. The liquidator may demand either the return of the assets or the equivalent in money.

5.163   The rule of 'return' operates subject to Articles 5 and 7 OR. Where those Articles apply, a creditor who obtains satisfaction of claims secured by rights in rem created before the opening of insolvency proceedings is realizing his own proprietary interest and does not enrich himself to the detriment of the estate. He therefore cannot be said to be acting in breach of the principle of collective satisfaction. However, in *Lutz v Bäuerle, acting as liquidator of ECZ Autohandel GmbH* (Case -557/13)[222] the CJEU held that Article 5 OR combined with Article 13 OR could protect a right in rem acquired after the opening of main insolvency proceedings if the time for challenging the creation of the right in rem under the law governing its creation had passed.

5.164   Article 20(2) OR further (and expressly) reinforces that principle by providing that:

> In order to ensure equal treatment of creditors a creditor who has, in the course of insolvency proceedings, obtained a dividend on his claim shall share in distributions made in other proceedings only where creditors of the same ranking or category have, in those other proceedings, obtained an equivalent dividend.

5.165   The Virgos-Schmit Report in paragraph 175 (see Appendix 2) isolates four rules which apply to distribution:

(a) no creditor may obtain more than 100 per cent of his claim;

(b) the total original amount of the claim (100 per cent of its initial value) is to be taken into account where a dividend has already been paid and not the remaining amount;

(c) a claim is not taken into account in the distribution until such time as the creditors with the same ranking have obtained an equal percentage of satisfaction in these proceedings as that obtained by its holder in the first proceedings;

---

[220] Arts 5 and 7 are discussed above.
[221] Art 20 is entitled 'return and imputation'. The similar rule of 'return' in English domestic law is known as 'hotchpot'.
[222] [2015] BCC 413.

(d) the ranking or category of each claim is determined for each of the proceedings by the law of the state of the opening, hence the ranking of the same claim lodged in two different proceedings may not be the same in both. The only ranking or category which is taken into account in order to apply Article 20(2) is that given to the claim by the law governing proceedings in which distribution is to be effected.

Article 23 RR

Article 20 has been replicated by Article 23 RR in substantially similar terms.   **5.166**

Duty of co-operation (Article 31 OR/Article 41 RR)

Article 31 OR

Where there are at the same time main and either territorial or secondary proceedings, co-operation and information between liquidators is vital to ensure efficient insolvency administration across the Member States and to avoid conflict or wasteful duplication.   **5.167**

Article 31 imposes upon liquidators a duty to cooperate with one another. The duty is made subject to the rules restricting the communication of information which are assumed to exist in each jurisdiction.[223] Article 31(1) states that liquidators 'shall be duty bound to communicate information to each other. They shall immediately communicate any information which may be relevant to the other proceedings, in particular the progress made in lodging and verifying claims and all measures aimed at terminating the proceedings'. The rationale behind this Article is clear and is explained in Recital (20). The purpose behind having main and secondary proceedings is the effective realization of the total assets of the debtor within the European Union. That can only happen if the liquidators cooperate with each other and share information.   **5.168**

Article 31(2) imposes upon the liquidator in the main proceedings and the liquidators in secondary proceedings a duty to cooperate with each other. The Insolvency Rules 1986 have been amended to ensure that the duty of co-operation is expressly provided for.[224] Where the Rules have been amended, it is expressly stated that the new obligations specified by the Rules are without prejudice to the generality of the obligations imposed by Article 31.[225]   **5.169**

---

[223] Art 31(1).
[224] By the Insolvency (Amendment) Rules 2002.
[225] An example of the duty of co-operation being catered for in the amended Rules is the new r 1.34, which provides that where a supervisor of a company voluntary arrangement is obliged to give notice, or provide a copy of a document, to the court, the registrar of companies, or the official receiver, the supervisor shall give notice or provide copies (as the case may be) to the Member State liquidator. Materially identical new rules apply to administrators (r 2.133(5)), liquidators (r 4.231(5)), supervisors of individual voluntary arrangements (r 5.65(2)), and trustees (r 6.238(5)).

5.170   Article 31(3) provides that the liquidator in secondary proceedings is obliged to give the liquidator in the main proceedings an early opportunity to submit proposals on the realization or use of assets in the secondary proceedings.[226] Article 31(3) demonstrates that the main proceedings are of primary importance. It may enable the liquidator in the main proceedings to prevent the liquidator in secondary proceedings from doing something which would be detrimental to that which the main liquidator is attempting to achieve. In appropriate circumstances he may seek a stay of the secondary proceedings pursuant to Article 33 (as to which see below) to assist him in securing his aims.

5.171   Article 31 does not expressly place a duty of co-operation on the courts of Member States, but such an obligation is to be implied.[227] This case law has been codified by the RR in Article 42 (see below).

Article 41 RR

5.172   Article 31 OR has been replaced by Article 41 RR, which makes provision for co-operation and communication between insolvency practitioners in modified terms. Article 41 RR departs from its predecessor in the following, key respects: (i) the requirement to co-operate is still expressed in mandatory terms, although the words 'duty bound' are no longer employed (Articles 41(1) and (2) RR); (ii) it is expressly stated that such co-operation may take any form, including the conclusion of agreements or protocols (Article 41(1) RR); and (iii) the duty of co-operation is extended to main, secondary, or territorial proceedings in which the debtor remains in possession of its assets (Article 41(3) RR).

5.173   Further, Article 41(2) RR expressly identifies three categories of co-operation which insolvency practitioners are required, where relevant, to pursue, namely to;

(a)   as soon as possible communicate to each other any information which may be relevant to the other proceedings, in particular any progress made in lodging

---

[226] The extent to which the liquidator in main proceedings may influence the conduct of secondary proceedings was considered in *Re Alitalia Linee Aeree Italiane SpA; Connock & another v Fantozzi* [2011] 1 BCLC 606. In that case, the opening of extraordinary administration proceedings in Italy (the main proceedings) were followed by the opening of winding-up proceedings (the secondary proceedings) in England. The issue in dispute concerned the manner in which monies held in a bank account in England were to be applied. The Italian administrator contended that the duty of cooperation prescribed by Art 31 required the English liquidators to pay those monies to employees in order to carry into effect a sale arranged by the Italian administrator in the main proceedings. The court rejected that contention, holding that the claims of former employees were unsecured and ranked *pari passu* with other debts of the company for the purpose of the English proceedings. The court considered that the duty of co-operation imposed by Art 31 OR did not extend to requiring the English liquidators to apply assets otherwise than in accordance with English law, as the law applicable to the secondary proceedings.
[227] *Re Nortel Networks SA* [2009] BCC 343, *Re Stojevic* (Higher Regional Court, Vienna, 9 November 2004) 28 R 225/04 w. See also the discussion of this question in Vallender, 'Judicial Co-operation within the EC Insolvency Regulation' Eurofenix, Issue 30, Winter 2007–2008, 8 et seq.

and verifying claims and all measures aimed at rescuing or restructuring the debtor, or at terminating the proceedings, provided appropriate arrangements are made to protect confidential information;

(b) explore the possibility of restructuring the debtor and, where such a possibility exists, co-ordinate the elaboration and implementation of a restructuring plan;

(c) co-ordinate the administration of the realization or use of the debtor's assets and affairs; the insolvency practitioner in the secondary insolvency proceedings shall give the insolvency practitioner in the main insolvency proceedings an early opportunity to submit proposals on the realization or use of the assets in the secondary insolvency proceedings.

Article 42 RR is a new provision which for the first time expressly imposes a duty **5.174** of co-operation and communication between courts before which a request to open insolvency proceedings is pending, or which have opened such proceedings. The duty exists to the extent that such co-operation is not incompatible with the rules applicable to each of the proceedings (Article 42(1) RR). For that purpose, the courts are expressly empowered, where appropriate, to appoint an independent person or body acting on its instructions, provided that it is not incompatible with the rules applicable in the relevant jurisdictions (Article 42(1) RR).

It is made clear by Article 42(2) RR that in complying with this duty of co- **5.175** operation, the courts, or any appointed person or body acting on their behalf, may communicate directly with, or request information or assistance directly from, each other provided that such communication respects the procedural rights of the parties to the proceedings and the confidentiality of information. Further, the courts may comply with this duty of co-operation 'by any means that the court considers appropriate'. Article 42(3) RR identifies the following categories of co-operation:

(a) co-ordination in the appointment of the insolvency practitioners;

(b) communication of information by any means considered appropriate by the court;

(c) co-ordination of the administration and supervision of the debtor's assets and affairs;

(d) co-ordination of the conduct of hearings;

(e) co-ordination in the approval of protocols, where necessary.

Article 43 RR is a further, new provision which extends the duty of co-operation **5.176** and communication to the relationship between insolvency practitioners and courts.

Chapter V, Articles 56–77 RR, contain new provisions dealing expressly with **5.177** insolvency proceedings of members of a group of companies. Detailed provision is made for the duty of co-operation, communication, and co-ordination between insolvency practitioners and courts in proceedings concerning members of a group of companies.[228] Those provisions are set out and commented on in chapter 8 below.

Exercise of creditors' rights (Article 32 OR/Article 45 RR)

Article 32 OR

5.178 Article 32(1) OR provides that any creditor may lodge his claim in the main proceedings and in any secondary proceedings. Article 32(2) OR provides that:

> The liquidators in the main and any secondary proceedings shall lodge in other proceedings claims which have already been lodged in the proceedings for which they were appointed, provided that the interests of creditors in the latter proceedings are served thereby, subject to the right of creditors to oppose that or to withdraw the lodgement of the claims where the law applicable so provides.

Finally, Article 32(3) OR provides that the liquidator in the main or secondary proceedings shall be empowered to participate in other proceedings on the same basis as a creditor,[229] in particular by attending creditors' meetings.[230]

---

[228] Such provision is particularly pertinent in light of the decision in *Re Nortel Networks SA* [2009] BCC 343. In that case, administration orders had been made in relation to 19 companies forming the Europe, Middle East, and Africa ('EMEA') arm of the global Nortel Networks group. The main reason for seeking administration orders in respect of each of the Nortel EMEA companies was to facilitate the implementation of a co-ordinated programme with the Canadian and US companies for restructuring or disposing of all or some of Nortel's global operations, with a view to maximizing the returns to creditors generally. Although each of the Nortel EMEA companies had its COMI in England, many of the companies were incorporated or had establishments in Member States other than the United Kingdom. It was thus recognized that local creditors might commence secondary proceedings under the Regulation if they considered that they might be more favourably treated under applicable local law.

In order to pre-empt this possibility, the court made orders which expressly acknowledged the ability of the proposed administrators to make payments, first, to employees and preferential creditors of the relevant Nortel EMEA company, such that they would receive the same amount as if secondary proceedings were commenced under Art 27 OR, and secondly, in respect of pre-administration liabilities, provided in each case that they considered such payments were likely to achieve the purpose of the administration of the relevant company.

Subsequently, further steps were taken with a view to preventing the opening of secondary proceedings. The court authorized the sending of letters of request to the courts of a number of Member States, asking those courts to put in place arrangements under which the English administrators would be given notice of any request or application for the opening of secondary insolvency proceedings in respect of any of the companies in administration. The intended purpose was to ensure that the English administrator would be entitled to be heard on any such application. In ordering such letters of request to be sent, the court was influenced in its view that Art 31(2) OR extended the duty of co-operation between liquidators to the courts exercising control over insolvency proceedings in their respective jurisdictions. The express provisions for such individual debtor and group co-ordination in the RR, Chapter V, including a duty of co-operation between courts in Art 57 RR, could now be directly tailored to co-ordinating the insolvency proceedings of a group or sub-group such as the European Nortel companies.

[229] In England, participation 'on the same basis as a creditor' will include a right to inspect the court file, an excellent source of information about the proceedings: r 7.64, introduced by the Insolvency (Amendment) Rules 2002.

[230] See in relation to England the Insolvency Rules 1986 (as amended by the Insolvency (Amendment) Rules 2002) rr 2.38 and 2.133 (in relation to administration), 4.67 and 4.231 (in

The aim of Article 32 OR is: **5.179**

(a) to facilitate the exercise of the rights of those creditors who lodge claims in particular proceedings;
(b) to facilitate that their claims are also lodged by the liquidator in other proceedings; and
(c) to permit the liquidators to reinforce their influence in other proceedings. The rights of the creditors are preserved in so far as they may oppose the lodging of their claims in other proceedings by the liquidator or withdraw any previous lodgement in other proceedings.[231]

The Insolvency Rules 1986 were extensively amended to reflect Article 32.[232]   **5.180**
A Member State liquidator is deemed to be a creditor for many purposes.[233]
The amended Rules are expressly without prejudice to the generality of the right to participate referred to in Article 32.

Article 45 RR

Article 32 has been replicated by Article 45 RR in identical terms.   **5.181**

Staying the secondary proceedings (Article 33 OR/Article 46 RR)

Article 33 OR

Article 33 OR, which further demonstrates the primacy of the main proceedings,   **5.182**
provides that the liquidator of the main proceedings may apply to the court of the Member State where secondary proceedings have been opened to stay the liquidation proceedings in whole or in part. The court shall stay the process of liquidation on receipt of the liquidator's request but may require him to take suitable measures to guarantee the interests of the creditors in the secondary proceedings and any class of them. The court is entitled to refuse the liquidator's request only if it is manifestly of no interest to the creditors in the main proceedings. The stay may only be made for a period of up to three months but is renewable thereafter for further three-month periods.

---

relation to liquidation), and 6.93, 6.238, and 6.239 (in relation to bankruptcy). See also rr 7.64, 8.8, and 11.1.

[231] The Virgos-Schmit Report deals with creditors' rights under Art 32 of the Convention (which was the forerunner of the Regulation) in some detail at paras 235–240 of the Report (see app 2 below).

[232] By the Insolvency (Amendment) Rules 2002 and, subsequently, further amendments were made by the Insolvency (Amendment) Rules 2010.

[233] See new rr 2.38 (entitlement to vote) and 2.133 (generally) in relation to administration; rr 4.67 (entitlement to vote) and 4.231 (generally) in relation to winding-up; and rr 6.93 (entitlement to vote), 6.238, and 6.239 (generally) in relation to bankruptcy. See also new rr 7.64 (right to inspect court file and right of attendance); 8.8 (right of inspection of proxies); 11.2(1) (notice of intended dividend); 11.3(4) (final admission or rejection of proofs); 11.6(1) (declaration of dividends); and 12A.54(2) (list of creditors).

5.183 The liquidator in the main proceedings is similarly entitled to request that the stay be terminated, as may a creditor and the liquidator of the secondary proceedings.[234] The touchstone of whether the court will make such an order is whether it is justified, in particular, by the interests of the creditors in the main proceedings, giving the court an apparent discretion on such an application.

5.184 Although the powers of the local court in considering a request for a stay are limited, the court does have the power, as the price of the stay, to require the liquidator in the main proceedings to ensure that the interests of the creditors in the secondary proceedings (and individual classes of them) are protected. This may involve setting up a mechanism to ensure that the local creditors as a whole and each class of local creditors are better off than they would have been in a liquidation.[235]

5.185 In the context of the cases involving the Collins & Aikman group of companies, the Austrian Higher Regional Court (Court of Appeal) in Graz[236] has held that Article 33 only stays the process of liquidating assets and not the secondary proceedings as a whole.

Article 46 RR

5.186 Article 33 OR has been replicated by Article 46 RR in identical terms, save that the fact that secondary proceedings may now comprise any of the (permitted) forms of insolvency proceeding is reflected in the replacement of the term 'liquidation' by the words 'realization of assets'.

Closure of the secondary proceedings other than by liquidation (Article 34 OR/Article 47 RR)

Article 34 OR

5.187 The liquidator has power by virtue of Article 34(1) OR to propose a rescue composition such as a voluntary arrangement or scheme of arrangement, or other comparable measure (avoiding liquidation) where the law of the Member State in which secondary proceedings have been opened allows for such closure of the proceedings.

5.188 Further, the consent of the liquidator in the main proceedings is necessary before the closure of secondary proceedings through such a route can become final,

---

[234] Art 33(2).

[235] The measures could be analogous to those used in *Re Collins & Aikman Europe SA* [2006] BCC 861, HCJ; *Re MG Rover España SA* [2006] BCC 599, High Court, Birmingham, and *Re MG Rover Belux SA/NV* [2007] BCC 446, High Court, Birmingham.

[236] (Oberlandesgericht, 20 October 2005), 3 R 149/05, NZI (Neue Zeitschrift fur Insolvenz und Sanierung) 2006, vol 11, 660 on appeal from the Landesgericht Leoben, 31 August 2005, 17 p 56/05, NZI 2005, vol 11, 646. We are grateful to Christian Köhler-Ma of Leonhardt Westhelle & Partner Rechtsanwälte—Insolvency administrators—Notaries Kurfürstendamm 212 10719 Berlin for supplying an English translation of this judgment, the judgment at first instance, and the subsequent judgment lifting the stay (mentioned below).

unless the financial interests of the creditors in the main proceedings are not affected by the proposed measure. In making his decision, the liquidator may take into consideration all the interests of the creditors in the main proceedings, including (in appropriate cases) the interests in reorganizing and continuing the main business.

The Virgos-Schmit Report comments in paragraph 249 that: 'The financial inter-   **5.189**
ests are estimated by evaluating the effects which the rescue plan or the composition has on the dividend to be paid to the creditors in the main proceedings.' The effects of such a measure on a creditor's rights (for example by way of a stay or discharge) will not extend beyond the assets in the secondary proceedings unless all the creditors with an interest consent.

Where the process of liquidation in the secondary proceedings has been stayed   **5.190**
under Article 33 OR, only the liquidator in the main proceedings (and the debtor with the liquidator's consent) may propose the closure of the secondary proceedings without liquidation. The stay would have been ordered at the request of the liquidator in the main proceedings on the account of the interests of the creditors in the main proceedings; during the period of the stay, the main proceedings should not be disrupted except at the instigation of, or with the agreement of, the liquidator in the main proceedings.

Article 47 RR

Article 34 OR has been has been substantially modified by Article 47 RR. One   **5.191**
minor difference is that a rescue plan is now referred to as a restructuring plan. The major differences are that: (i) the ability of the insolvency practitioner in main proceedings to veto the restructuring plan proposed in respect of secondary proceedings, subject to the question whether creditors' financial interests in the main proceedings are affected, has not been reprised by Article 47 RR; and (ii) the insolvency practitioner's power to propose a restructuring plan in respect of secondary proceedings during a stay of such proceedings, has also not been reprised by Article 47 RR.

Further, Article 48 RR is a new provision addressing the impact of the closure of   **5.192**
insolvency proceedings. Article 48(1) RR provides that the closure of insolvency proceedings shall not prevent the continuation of other insolvency proceedings concerning the same debtor which are still open at that point in time. That is stated to be without prejudice to Article 49 RR (Assets remaining in the secondary insolvency proceedings), which is dealt with below. Article 48(2) RR also makes clear that the dissolution of a legal person or company by reason of insolvency proceedings in the Member State of that person's or company's registered office, will not take effect until any other insolvency proceedings concerning the same debtor have been closed, or the insolvency practitioner(s) in such proceedings have given consent to the dissolution.

Surplus assets in the secondary proceedings (Article 35 OR/Article 49 RR)

5.193 Where the liquidator in the secondary proceedings succeeds in meeting all of the creditors' claims in those proceedings and holds surplus monies or other assets, he is under a duty to transfer that surplus to the liquidator in the main proceedings. In practice, no doubt, the limited pool of assets comprising the available estate in the secondary proceedings will in most cases be exhausted. Article 35 has been replicated by Article 49 RR in identical terms.

Conversion of earlier proceedings (Article 37 OR/Article 51 RR)

Article 37 OR

5.194 The liquidator in the main proceedings may request that proceedings listed in Annex A to the Regulation previously opened in another Member State be converted into winding-up proceedings listed in Annexe B OR if this proves to be in the interests of the creditors in the main proceedings.

5.195 New Rules 1.31–1.33 were added to the Insolvency Rules 1986 which set out what a Member State liquidator is required to do to seek conversion of a voluntary arrangement into a winding-up.[237] The application shall be by originating application, supported by written evidence served on the debtor company and its supervisor containing the matters listed in Rule 1.32(1). The Member State liquidator must, amongst other things, state his belief that the conversion would prove to be in the interests of the creditors in the main proceedings. Similar insertions were made into the 1986 Rules in relation to converting individual voluntary arrangements into bankruptcies by virtue of new Rules 5.62–5.64.

5.196 New rules were also inserted to set out the requirements which a Member State liquidator must meet to convert an administration into a winding-up.[238] Again, the application must be made by originating application, supported by written evidence. The Member State liquidator's evidence must contain those matters listed in new Rule 2.131 including his opinion that the conversion would prove to be in the interests of the creditors in the main proceedings.

Article 51 RR

5.197 Under the RR, the list of winding-up proceedings in Annex B OR has been removed, as it is no longer a requirement that secondary proceedings be

[237] New r 1.33(3) states that an order converting a voluntary arrangement into a winding-up may provide that the company be wound up as if a resolution for voluntary winding-up under the Insolvency Act 1986, s 84 were passed on the day on which the order is made. Where an order converting a voluntary arrangement into a winding-up is made, new r 1.33(4) provides that any expenses properly incurred as expenses of the administration of the voluntary arrangement shall be a first charge on the company's assets.

[238] New r 2.132(3) states that an order converting an administration into a winding-up may provide that the company be wound up as if a resolution for voluntary winding-up under the Insolvency Act 1986, s 84 were passed on the day on which the order is made.

winding-up proceedings. Otherwise, Article 37 OR has been replicated by Article 51 RR in substantially similar terms, save that the following, more detailed conditions are stipulated for the conversion of secondary proceedings into another type of insolvency proceeding listed in Annex A: (i) that the conditions for opening that type of proceeding under national law are fulfilled; and (ii) that the proposed type of proceeding is the most appropriate as regards the interests of the local creditors and coherence between the main and secondary insolvency proceedings.

Preservation measures (Article 38 OR/Article 52 RR)

Article 38 OR

In order to preserve the debtor's assets during the period between the request for the opening of a proceeding and the decision on that application, the Regulation envisages the appointment of a temporary administrator. **5.198**

Article 38 OR provides that where the court of a Member State which has the jurisdiction to open the main proceedings pursuant to Article 3(1) appoints a temporary administrator in order to ensure the preservation of the debtor's assets, that temporary administrator may request any measures to secure and preserve any of the debtor's assets situated in another Member State provided for under the law of that state. That order operates between the date of the application requesting the opening of insolvency proceedings and the judgment opening them. **5.199**

To understand what Article 38 OR intended, it is helpful to read it together with Recital (16) of the OR. This explains that preservation measures are important, both prior to and after the commencement of insolvency proceedings, 'to guarantee the effectiveness of the insolvency proceedings'. It also stresses the importance of the availability of such measures both to the liquidator once proceedings have been opened and also to a temporary administrator appointed *before the judgment opening the proceedings*. The 'temporary administrator' in Article 38 OR seems to be the same person as the 'liquidator appointed temporarily prior to the opening' in Recital (16). However, the CJEU has rejected this interpretation. **5.200**

In *Re Eurofood IFSC Ltd*,[239] the ECJ stated: **5.201**

> 57. In that respect, it should be noted that Art.38 of the Regulation must be read in combination with Art.29, according to which the liquidator in the main proceedings is entitled to request the opening of secondary proceedings in another Member State. That Art.38 thus concerns the situation in which the competent court of a Member State has had main insolvency proceedings brought before it and has appointed a person or body to watch over the debtor's assets on a provisional basis, but has not yet ordered that that debtor be divested or appointed a liquidator referred to in Annex C to the Regulation. In that case, the person or body in question, though not empowered to initiate secondary insolvency proceedings in

---

[239] Case C-341/04 *Re Eurofood IFSC Ltd* [2006] BCC 397, ECJ (Grand Chamber).

another Member State, may request that preservation measures be taken over the assets of the debtor situated in that Member State.

5.202 The Grand Chamber went on to hold that Article 38 OR did not apply to a situation where the court had appointed a provisional liquidator listed in Annex C and had divested the debtor of control of his business, since that opened the proceeding and gave rise to the application of Article 29 OR, which would enable the provisional liquidator to apply for the opening of proceedings in the other Member State. This unfortunately ignores the fact that by the express terms of Recital (16) OR the concept of 'temporary administrator' in Article 38 OR is meant to be understood as 'a *liquidator* temporarily appointed *prior to the opening* of the main insolvency proceedings' (emphasis added).[240]

Article 52 RR

5.203 Article 38 OR has been replicated by Article 52 RR in identical terms.

5.204 Further commentary on this Article and the other Articles considered above is contained in chapter 8 below.

---

[240] See also the commentary under Art 3 OR at paras 8.60 et seq below, esp at paras 8.80 et seq.

6

THE EFFECT OF THE REGULATION ON CROSS-BORDER SECURITY AND QUASI-SECURITY

A. Introduction

This chapter deals with the impact of insolvency proceedings recognized by **6.01** the Regulation on the rights of secured creditors, particularly the rights of such creditors to enforce their security and participate in the relevant insolvency proceedings. Although this chapter refers to the Regulation as currently in force, in certain places, the authors refer to the changes that will be made by Regulation (EU) 2015/848 of the European Parliament and of the Council on insolvency proceedings (RR). It is anticipated that the RR will come into force in 2017.

6.02 Throughout this chapter, there are references to the rights and position of banks as secured creditors. The Regulation does not address the position of banks as a separate class of creditor, but does impact on the rights of secured creditors as a whole. However, as the holders of security will often include banks in the context of commercial lending arrangements, this chapter refers to, and considers the impact of the Regulation on, banks which hold security or quasi-security.

6.03 As the Regulation does not apply to the insolvency procedures which can be commenced in respect of banks and other credit institutions (Article 1), this chapter does not address the regime which applies to bank insolvencies under EC law. This regime is addressed in chapter 7 below.

6.04 Instead, the chapter addresses, in particular:

(a) the cross-frontier security rights of banks which hold security over the assets of companies or persons who enter into insolvency proceedings regulated by the Regulation; and

(b) the effect of those insolvency proceedings on the banks' security interests.

6.05 This chapter identifies those Articles of the Regulation which are particularly relevant to the position of a bank as a secured creditor, addresses the interpretation of those provisions (including the identification of difficult points of construction), and considers the practical aspects and the issues which are likely to face banks seeking to enforce security following the Regulation coming into force.

6.06 As set out below, the basic principle, as Article 4(1) makes clear, is that the law of the place where insolvency proceedings are opened (the inelegantly termed 'state of the opening of proceedings') governs each of the sub-paragraphs which are set out in Article 4(1). Although choice of law questions are generally dealt with in chapter 4 above, this chapter looks at Article 4(1) in the context of security and quasi-security. As the judgment opening main proceedings is to produce the same effects in any other Member State as under the state of the opening of proceedings unless the Regulation provides otherwise (Article 17), main proceedings opened in one Member State could potentially affect the bank's rights to enforce its security in another Member State subject to the exceptions discussed below.

6.07 At the end of this chapter, 11 hypothetical factual examples are set out. Together, these examples explore, from a practical perspective, some of the ways in which the Regulation may impact on the rights of secured creditors (or creditors with quasi-security). In each case, there is a brief description of the facts, a summary (by way of a number of brief statements) of the key issues raised, and a commentary on those issues.

So far as the authors are aware, there are only a few cases which touch upon the **6.08** impact of the Regulation on the rights of secured creditors (each of which is discussed below), including one decision of the Court of Justice of the European Union (CJEU). In the light of the limited case law available on this issue, the analysis in this chapter merely reflects the authors' views. In many cases, the lack of clarity as to the meaning of relevant provisions of the Regulation means that further questions of interpretation are likely to be referred by national courts to the CJEU for a preliminary ruling.

The focus of the practical examples tends to be primarily, although not solely, on **6.09** English law[1] insolvency or enforcement procedures and on rights in rem which would be recognized as a matter of English law.

In general, a bank will be concerned with whether it can enforce its security **6.10** in a particular jurisdiction and about the effect which the opening of insolvency proceedings in respect of the borrower will have on the bank's rights as secured lender. These overriding concerns can be broken down into a number of key questions which are explored through the practical examples in the final section of this chapter. In particular, a bank may have the following questions:

(a) Will a receiver appointed in England under a security agreement governed by English law and which purports to cover assets in another Member State be recognized in that other Member State? (See Examples 1 and 2.)
(b) Will a security agreement governed by English law be recognized as creating a valid right in rem in another Member State for the purposes of Article 5? (See Example 2.)
(c) What impact will the opening of main proceedings have on the enforcement of security over assets located: (i) in the jurisdiction where those proceedings are opened; and (ii) in other Member States and, in particular, what will be the effect of the statutory moratorium on the enforcement of security which arises in the main proceedings of many Member States (including, for example, an English administration)? (See Examples 1 and 3.)
(d) Where is a secured asset located for the purposes of the Regulation and which court will determine this issue? (See Example 2.)

---

[1] In this context, references to English law should be construed as to the law of England and Wales as England and Wales comprise a single legal jurisdiction. References to England should also be construed as to England and Wales.

(e) What impact will the opening of secondary proceedings have on the enforcement of security over assets located: (i) in the jurisdiction where those proceedings are opened; and (ii) in other Member States? (See Example 1.)

(f) In the case of either main or secondary proceedings, what will the effect be if different rules apply regarding the priority of secured and unsecured claims under: (i) the insolvency law of the jurisdiction where the insolvency proceedings are opened; and (ii) the law applicable to the relevant right in rem? (See Examples 1 and 3.)

(g) What impact will the opening of main or secondary proceedings have on the enforcement of security over assets in a jurisdiction outside the European Union and what impact will insolvency proceedings commenced in a jurisdiction outside the European Union have on the enforcement of security in a Member State? (See Example 4.)

(h) What types of rights in rem are covered by Article 5 and what law will determine whether a right in rem exists for the purposes of Article 5? (See Example 5.)

(i) Could either main or secondary proceedings have the effect of discharging secured liabilities and, if so, what effect will this have on the enforcement of security over assets located: (i) in the jurisdiction where those proceedings have commenced; and (ii) in other Member States? (See Examples 6, 7, and 8.)

(j) What impact will main or secondary proceedings have on an intercreditor agreement between the secured creditors, particularly where that agreement is governed by a different law from that of the Member State in which the insolvency proceedings are commenced? (See Example 8.)

(k) What is the impact of the provisions in the Regulation regarding its applicability in time and, in particular, will the Regulation have the same impact on security created prior to 31 May 2002? (See Example 9.)

(l) What is the effect on security or quasi-security of a challenge made under the rules relating to the voidness, voidability, and unenforceability of legal acts detrimental to all the creditors[2] and what is the impact of Article 13 in this regard? (See Example 10.)

(m) How will the opening of main or secondary proceedings affect rights of set-off and which law will determine whether such a right exists? (See Example 11.)

B. The Purposes of the Regulation

6.11 As the recitals to the Regulation demonstrate, the Regulation attempts to strike a balance between giving extra-territorial effect to the main proceedings and the

---

[2] This wording is from Art 4(2)(m).

need to preserve the predictability of secured transactions entered into in accordance with the laws of a particular Member State.[3]

In particular the recitals reveal that the purposes of the Regulation are: **6.12**

(a) to enable cross-border insolvency proceedings to operate efficiently and effectively;
(b) to provide for co-ordination of the measures to be taken regarding an insolvent debtor's assets;
(c) to avoid forum shopping.[4]

In addition, insolvency proceedings relating to the winding-up of insolvent com- **6.13** panies or other legal persons, judicial arrangements, compositions, and analogous proceedings are excluded from the Brussels Convention. The Regulation therefore provides an additional element of predictability and certainty as to matters of jurisdiction and governing law concerning insolvency proceedings.

Against this background, however, the 'interest of each State in protecting its market's **6.14** trade, in the form of respect of rights in rem acquired over assets of the debtor located in that country under the law that is applicable before the opening of the insolvency proceedings' is acknowledged (paragraph 100 of the Virgos-Schmit Report).[5] The challenge for those drafting the Regulation was the divergence of views regarding the impact of insolvency proceedings on security, with some Member States (such as the United Kingdom) being traditionally more pro-secured creditor than others. The compromise adopted in the Regulation is that, whereas under Article 4 the law of the state of opening generally applies to issues arising in the insolvency proceedings, by virtue of Article 5, that law shall not affect creditors' rights in rem in relation to assets located in a different Member State (discussed below).

C. The Effect of the Regulation on the Rights of Banks

Insolvency proceedings to which the Regulation applies

As stated elsewhere in this book, Annex A of the Regulation sets out those main **6.15** proceedings to which the Regulation applies:

(a) If the debtor's centre of main interests is in England, a compulsory liquidation, creditors' voluntary liquidation, administration (including out-of-court

---

[3] See Recitals (11), (24), and (25).
[4] Recitals (29) and (31) of the RR will clarify that it is only the avoidance of fraudulent or abusive forum shopping (where the purpose is to obtain a more favourable legal position to the detriment of the general body of creditors) which is against the purpose of the Regulation.
[5] See app 2 below. See para 2.28 above and n 96 thereto regarding whether it is legitimate to have regard to the Report as an aid to interpretation of the Regulation and the problems with the translation of the Report.

administration), voluntary arrangement, or bankruptcy of the debtor in England will constitute main proceedings for the purposes of the Regulation; main proceedings can have an impact on security granted by the relevant debtor as discussed below. The Regulation will govern the effects of any main proceedings opened in England on the realization of secured assets located in England and in another Member State.

(b) However, importantly for banks seeking to enforce their rights under English law governed security agreements, a receivership (including both administrative receivership and Law of Property Act receivership) is not recognized as main proceedings under the Regulation and therefore receivership will not be subject to, or have the benefit of, the recognition provisions of the Regulation. This is crucial as receivership has traditionally been the most common method of security enforcement for banks (although the reforms introduced by the Enterprise Act 2002 have significantly reduced the availability of administrative receivership as a mechanism for security enforcement).

6.16 In addition, under Article 27, secondary proceedings are limited to those procedures listed in Annex B of the Regulation:[6]

(a) In England, Annex B is confined to compulsory liquidation, creditors' voluntary liquidation, and bankruptcy.

(b) The combined effect of Article 3(1) and Article 27 is therefore that a receivership will not be recognized as main or secondary proceedings under the Regulation.

Articles which are of particular relevance to a bank

Article 4 (choice of law)

6.17 The text of Article 4[7] is as follows (emphasis added):

1. **Save as otherwise provided in this Regulation, the law applicable to insolvency proceedings and their effects shall be that of the Member State within the territory of which such proceedings are opened**, hereafter referred to as the 'State of the opening of proceedings'.

2. The law of the State of the opening of proceedings shall determine the conditions for the opening of those proceedings, their conduct and their closure. It shall determine in particular:

    (a) against which debtors insolvency proceedings may be brought on account of their capacity;

    (b) **the assets which form part of the estate** and the treatment of assets acquired by or devolving on the debtor after the opening of the insolvency proceedings;

---

[6] This will cease to be the case when the RR comes into force and Annex B will become redundant.
[7] This will become Art 7 in the RR but otherwise there are no substantive amendments.

(c) the respective powers of the debtor and the liquidator;

(d) **the conditions under which set-offs may be invoked;**

(e) the effects of insolvency proceedings on current contracts to which the debtor is party;

(f) **the effects of the insolvency proceedings on proceedings brought by individual creditors,** with the exception of lawsuits pending;

(g) **the claims which are to be lodged against the debtor's estate and the treatment of claims arising after the opening of insolvency proceedings;**

(h) **the rules governing the lodging, verification and admission of claims;**

(i) **the rules governing the distribution of proceeds from the realisation of assets, the ranking of claims and the rights of creditors who have obtained partial satisfaction after the opening of insolvency proceedings by virtue of a right in rem or through a set-off;**

(j) the conditions for **and the effects of closure of insolvency proceedings,** in particular by composition;

(k) **creditors' rights after the closure of insolvency proceedings;**

(l) **who is to bear the costs and expenses incurred in the insolvency proceedings;**

(m) **the rules relating to the voidness, voidability or unenforceability of legal acts detrimental to all the creditors.**

A bank will be interested, in particular, in those Articles which are emphasized in bold type in paragraph 6.17 above. Each of these Articles is discussed in further detail below. **6.18**

Article 4(2)(b): The assets which form part of the estate.   It is essential for a bank which is a secured creditor to be able to maintain its security rights in an insolvency procedure which is governed by the Regulation. Subject to the discussion of Article 5 below, it seems likely that, under Article 4, it will be the law of the country in which insolvency proceedings have been opened which will determine whether the secured assets: **6.19**

(a) are excluded from the estate as a result of the bank's security right (such as, in England, assets which are subject to a fixed charge); or

(b) form part of the estate which will be divided pari passu between all creditors (in England, assets which are subject to no security right); or

(c) form part of the estate, but nevertheless remain subject to the security right (such as, in England, a floating charge).[8]

---

[8] However, this issue is made more difficult by the fact that laws other than the insolvency laws of a particular jurisdiction may have an effect on, or determine, whether secured assets form part of the insolvent estate. For example, in England, the rights of a secured creditor to enforce its security following the commencement of insolvency proceedings are determined by both the insolvency code and the law relating to security interests.

6.20 **Article 4(2)(d): The conditions under which set-offs may be invoked.**   A right to set-off may well be relevant, for example, if a bank wishes to net or combine accounts. Again, the validity of rights of set-off, or the extent to which set-offs are permitted, will be determined in the first instance by the law of the state of the opening of proceedings (subject to Article 6 discussed below). Whether such a set-off is permitted will depend upon the answers to two separate questions:

(a) is there a right of set-off under the applicable law; and
(b) is such a right of set-off valid after the commencement of insolvency proceedings?

6.21 However, by virtue of Article 6,[9] the opening of insolvency proceedings will not affect the right to set-off, where set-off is permitted by the law applicable to the insolvent debtor's claim. This goes to the first of the two questions referred to above. Article 6 is likely to have little effect where winding-up proceedings are opened in England, because of the mandatory operation of wide insolvency set-off rules in an English liquidation. However, Article 6 will be of great value to a bank against whom the insolvent debtor has a cross-claim governed by English law if that bank is a creditor in a foreign insolvency proceeding that has been opened in a Member State whose laws do not allow set-off and where no insolvency proceedings are commenced in England.

6.22 Article 6 raises some difficult questions of interpretation, some of which are considered in chapter 8 below. In particular, Article 6 raises the question of what law will be applicable to the insolvent debtor's claim and this is explored further in Example 11 below. For example, it may be that set-off would be permitted in insolvency proceedings in relation to the debtor in the Member State whose law is applicable to the insolvent debtor's claim but a right of set-off is not available outside such insolvency proceedings. Article 6 does not make any reference to the fact that different set-off rules may apply before and after an insolvency of the debtor in a particular Member State and this issue is also explored further in Example 11. Unfortunately, none of these issues is addressed by the RR.

6.23 **Article 4(2)(f): The effects of the insolvency proceedings on proceedings brought by individual creditors, with the exception of lawsuits pending.**   This Article addresses the question of the stay of proceedings which arises under (for example) an English administration. Under the law of the state of the opening of proceedings, there may well be a stay on certain methods of enforcement such as peaceable re-entry, distress, or the commencement or continuation of legal proceedings. The question arises as to whether such a stay could affect the ability of the bank to enforce its security, or to commence litigation, in a Member State

---

[9] This will become Art 9 in the RR but there are no substantive amendments.

where main or secondary proceedings have been opened. The issue can be broken down into two separate but related questions:

(a) Does the action which is proposed by the bank as secured creditor fall within the meaning of the expression 'proceedings' for the purposes of Article 4(2)(f)? This will be a question of characterization. It is unclear from the Regulation whether the word 'proceedings' in Article 4(2)(f) is limited to judicial or quasi-judicial proceedings. In England, a bank may appoint a receiver to enforce its security without the assistance of the court and it is not clear whether this type of action would constitute 'proceedings' for the purposes of Article 4(2)(f).[10] This is considered further in Example 1.

(b) If there is a moratorium on the particular enforcement action, in what circumstances would the court be prepared to lift such a stay? This is a matter at the discretion of the court of the Member State where proceedings are opened.

The effect of insolvency proceedings on pending lawsuits concerning the divest-   **6.24** ment of an asset or right is governed by Article 15 and not by Article 4(2)(f). The effect of insolvency proceedings on pending lawsuits which concern an asset or a right of which the debtor has been divested will be governed by the law of the Member State where the lawsuit is pending. In other words, the law of the forum where such lawsuit is pending will determine the effect on the proceedings before it of any main and secondary insolvency proceedings, applying its own conflict of law rules.[11] This will not prevent an insolvency office-holder from seeking a stay of the proceedings in the relevant Member State but the question of whether such stay will be granted will be a matter for the discretion of the Member State where the proceedings have been commenced. Under English insolvency law, an office-holder may make a request for a stay under section 426 of the Insolvency Act 1986

---

[10] In an English administration (but not a liquidation), there is a statutory moratorium on the appointment of an administrative receiver or the taking of other steps to enforce security as well as the commencement or continuation of proceedings: paras 41(1) and 43(2) of Sch B1 to the Insolvency Act 1986. Hence the moratorium may be much wider than the expression 'proceedings' used in Art 4(2)(f). In England, the meaning of the expression 'proceedings' in the context of the administration moratorium was considered in *Re Olympia & York Canary Wharf Ltd* [1993] BCC 154 although this decision did not concern the expression used in Art 4(2)(f) of the Regulation and so will be of limited use in interpreting this expression. The Irish High Court has considered Art 4(2)(f) of the Regulation, and its interrelation with Art 15, in *Re Flightlease (Ireland) Ltd* [2005] IEHC 275. The Irish Court considered that the effects of insolvency proceedings on individual enforcement actions are governed by the law of the state of opening under Art 4(2)(f) (thus giving this expression a wider meaning than legal proceedings). However, this matter will ultimately be determined by decisions of the CJEU rather than decisions under the laws of Member States.

[11] See *Mazur Media Ltd v Mazur Media GmbH* [2005] 1 BCLC 305 and *Re Flightlease (Ireland) Ltd* [2005] IEHC 275. In addition to decisions from a number of other Member States' courts, the Austrian Supreme Court has handed down a number of decisions on Art 15. Divergences exist in the case law on a number of interpretation issues which arise in relation to Art 15; such issues are beyond the scope of this chapter.

if he is appointed under the law of a 'relevant country or territory' as that expression is defined in section 426.

6.25 **Articles 4(2)(g) and (h): Proof of debt.**   Under this Article, the law of the state of the opening of proceedings will govern the manner in which the proof of debt procedure is operated. The proof of debt procedure is, of course, relevant to the question of when a debt is admissible to proof, the manner in which it should be dealt with, the ability of a creditor to appeal such proof, and the ability of a creditor to make an application which attacks the proof of another. Of particular relevance to a bank's security rights will be the question of the manner in which the bank will be able to value the security and prove for the unsecured portion of the debt. In addition, the law of the state of the opening of proceedings will govern the issue of whether such security can be revalued at any time.

6.26 Chapter IV of the Regulation (Articles 39–42) sets out a number of uniform rules which relate to the provision of information for creditors and lodgement of their claims:

(a) Article 39 provides that any creditor who has his habitual residence, domicile, or registered office in a Member State other than the state of the opening of proceedings, including the tax and social security authorities, has the right to lodge claims in the insolvency proceedings in writing.

(b) Article 40 provides for the duty of the liquidator to inform known creditors in other states of various matters, including time limits for lodging of claims. This information is (by virtue of Article 42(1)) to be provided in the official language or one of the official languages of the state of the opening of proceedings.

(c) Article 41 provides that the creditor shall send copies of supporting documents, if any, and shall indicate the nature of the claim, the date on which it arose, and its amount, as well as whether the creditor alleges preference, security in rem, or a reservation of title in respect of the claim, and what assets are covered by the guarantee which the creditor invokes. This information is (by virtue of Article 42(2)) to be provided in the official language or one of the official languages of the state where the creditor has his habitual residence, domicile, or registered office, but the heading 'Lodgement of claim' must be in the official language or one of the official languages of the state of the opening of proceedings. (A creditor may also be required to provide a translation of his proof.)

6.27 **Articles 4(2)(i) and (l): Distribution of proceeds (questions of priority).**   The law of the state of the opening of proceedings will govern the question of when and how distributions of proceeds will take place. It will also govern the question of whether distributions can be made at all in certain insolvency proceedings.[12]

---

[12] Under English law, for example, an administrator needs the leave of the court to make distributions to unsecured creditors under para 65(3) of Sch B1 to the Insolvency Act 1986.

The governing law will also determine the ranking and treatment of claims in the insolvency proceedings (including, for example, whether any claims are to be given preferential status in the insolvency proceedings).[13] Article 4(2)(i) also determines whether a secured creditor that has obtained partial satisfaction of its claim, either through the exercise of a right in rem or by way of set-off, may make a claim in the insolvency proceedings for the balance of its claim.

Questions regarding the ranking and treatment of claims can be very significant **6.28** where there are insufficient monies to pay the creditors in full. Where a person or a company is insolvent, there will not be enough money to pay all of its liabilities, whether incurred pre- or post-insolvency procedure. Under English law, the insolvency practitioner is only entitled to pay monies out of the estate which fall within certain prescribed categories: such as expenses of the administration; dividends to creditors in respect of provable debts; or return of any surplus to the shareholders of the company. All of these questions will be governed by the law of the state of the opening of proceedings.[14]

Under English law, certain categories of preferential claims have priority to the **6.29** claims of a floating charge-holder but not to the claims of a fixed charge-holder.[15] It is not clear whether these rules of priority fall within Article 4(2)(i). Although the priority given to preferential debts arises, generally, pursuant to the insolvency legislation, it is at least arguable that these rules relate to the priority of security (since they regulate the relationship between secured creditors and preferential creditors) and are not therefore an effect of the insolvency procedure. This is considered further in the context of Example 1 (in paragraph 6.93 below). Furthermore, difficult questions arise regarding the effect on Article 4(2)(i) of Article 5 (discussed below) if there are different rules regarding the ranking of secured claims under

---

[13] The priority of secured claims *inter se* will be determined by other matters such as the date of registration of the security or any deed of priorities.

[14] In *Re MG Rover Belux SA* [2006] EWHC 1296 (Ch) and *Re Collins & Aikman Europe SA* [2006] EWHC 1343 (Ch), the English High Court made orders, within the context of English administrations, allowing the English administrators to make distributions to creditors in other Member States in accordance with the local priority rules (rather than in accordance with the order of priority that applies in an English administration). In each case, the administrators were seeking to avoid the costs of secondary proceedings in the relevant jurisdictions. The two judges relied on different grounds for making the orders but those of the court in the *Collins & Aikman* case are to be preferred (ie an English administrator has the power, under para 66 of Sch B1 to the Insolvency Act 1986, to make a payment otherwise than in accordance with the usual order of priority if he or she considers that such payment is likely to assist the purpose of the administration).

[15] See Companies Act 2006, s 754 which applies outside a winding-up and provides that, if possession is taken, by or on behalf of a debenture-holder, of any property subject to a floating charge, the company's preferential debts are to be paid out of the assets coming into the hands of the person taking possession in priority to the claims for principal and interest in respect of the debenture. Section 175 of the Insolvency Act 1986 applies in a winding-up and provides that preferential debts have priority over the claims of floating charge-holders. In both cases, a floating charge is defined as a charge which, as created, is a floating charge and the preferential debts are set out in Sch 6 to the Insolvency Act 1986 (generally speaking, certain claims of employees within a relevant period).

the law of the state of the opening of proceedings and the law of the Member State where the secured assets are located. This issue is explored further in Example 1.

6.30 **Article 4(2)(j): The effects of closure of insolvency proceedings, in particular by composition.** Main proceedings may have the effect of varying or discharging creditor claims even in circumstances where a particular creditor has not consented to that variation or discharge. For example, an English voluntary arrangement under the insolvency legislation is available under the Regulation as main proceedings. If approved by the requisite majority of members and creditors, a voluntary arrangement will bind all unsecured creditors whether or not they had notice of the creditors' meeting called to consider the proposals for the voluntary arrangement.[16] Such a voluntary arrangement cannot affect the right of a secured creditor to enforce its security except with the concurrence of the creditor concerned.[17] The compromise proceedings that are available as main proceedings in other Member States, however, may (as a matter of the law of the state of opening) purport to bind secured creditors, even if such creditors do not vote in favour of the compromise proceedings (an example is the compromise plan in French safeguard proceedings which will be approved if the requisite majorities of creditors approve the plan). The question of whether a discharge or variation of the bank's secured debt through such a compromise would affect its rights in rem for the purposes of Article 5 is considered further below and is explored in Examples 6, 7, and 8.

6.31 **Article 4(2)(m): Rules relating to the voidness, voidability, or unenforceability of legal acts detrimental to all the creditors.** The law of the state of the opening of proceedings governs questions of void, voidable, or unenforceable legal acts detrimental to all the creditors such as, under English law, transactions at undervalue, preferences, and void floating charges. This may, of course, affect a bank where, for example, a charge is to be granted at a date which is proximate to insolvency proceedings particularly where no new monies are advanced by the bank at the time the charge is granted.

6.32 By virtue of Article 13,[18] Article 4(2)(m) does not apply where the person who benefited from an act detrimental to all the creditors provides proof that:

(a) the act in question is subject to the law of a Member State other than that of the state of the opening of proceedings; and

(b) that law does not allow any means of challenging that act in the relevant case.

6.33 Article 13 raises a number of questions. For example, what law will be the applicable law of the act in question? In other words, what is the meaning of the expression 'subject to' in Article 13? How does the expression 'any means' relate to the

---

[16] Insolvency Act 1986, s 5(2).
[17] ibid, s 4(3).
[18] This has become Art 16 in the RR but no substantive amendments have been made.

expression 'in the relevant case'? The Article appears to mean that the court may only have regard to the facts as at the time of the opening of proceedings. Does this mean that the English court would have to ignore the English insolvency rules if there were no main or secondary proceedings in England? Consider, for example, a payment made pursuant to a contract governed by English law by a company which subsequently becomes subject to insolvency proceedings in France. There may be no means of challenging the payment under English law outside the insolvency legislation but the payment may constitute a preference if the company were to go into liquidation or administration in England. When determining whether Article 13 applies, would the English preference provisions be irrelevant on the basis that there were no insolvency proceedings in England and so there was no means of challenging the payment in the relevant case? Unfortunately none of these issues are addressed by the RR. These questions are explored further in Example 10.

Other matters not expressly covered by Article 4(2).   The list in Article 4(2) **6.34** is not exhaustive and there may be other procedural and substantive effects of the main proceedings which are to be determined by the law of the state of the opening of proceedings. For example, that law may determine what voting rights and other opportunities to participate in the proceedings are given to creditors. In an English liquidation or administration, a bank can only vote in respect of the unsecured portion of its debt (unless it wishes to surrender its security and prove as an unsecured creditor) and a bank will wish to know what rights it has to participate in main proceedings opened in other Member States.

Article 5

The text of Article 5 is as follows: **6.35**

1. The opening of insolvency proceedings shall not affect the rights in rem of creditors or third parties in respect of tangible or intangible, moveable or immoveable assets—both specific assets and collections of indefinite assets as a whole which change from time to time—belonging to the debtor which are situated within the territory of another Member State at the time of the opening of proceedings.
2. The rights referred to in paragraph 1 shall in particular mean:
    (a) the right to dispose of assets or have them disposed of and to obtain satisfaction from the proceeds of income from those assets, in particular by virtue of a lien or a mortgage;
    (b) the exclusive right to have a claim met, in particular a right guaranteed by a lien in respect of the claim or by assignment of the claim by way of a guarantee;
    (c) the right to demand the assets from, and/or to require restitution by anyone having possession or use of them contrary to the wishes of the party so entitled;
    (d) a right in rem to the beneficial use of assets.

3. The right, recorded in a public register and enforceable against third parties, under which a right in rem within the meaning of paragraph 1 may be obtained, shall be considered a right in rem.

4. Paragraph 1 shall not preclude actions for voidness, voidability or unenforceability as referred to in Article 4(2)(m).[19]

6.36 Article 5 is clearly relevant to banks. Rights in rem, including those security rights which will often be held by a bank, are not affected by the opening of insolvency proceedings provided that the rights in rem relate to assets situated outside the Member State in which proceedings are opened. As the CJEU put it in *Lutz v Bäuerle*[20] Article 5 seeks 'to enable the creditor to assert effectively, and even after the opening of insolvency proceedings, a right in rem established before the opening of those proceedings'. These rights in rem include floating charges, a matter which is of some importance to an English bank. As paragraph 94 of the Virgos-Schmit Report notes,[21] in order to understand the functioning of Article 5 account should be taken of the fact that main insolvency proceedings based on Article 3(1) have a universal scope and, under Article 17, the judgment opening the proceedings is to have the same effect throughout the whole European Union. All the assets of a debtor are subject to the main proceedings, irrespective of the state where they are situated, unless secondary proceedings are opened. Therefore some protection is required in relation to certain transactions completed in other Member States.

6.37 Article 5 does not determine whether assets which are subject to rights in rem are to be excluded from or included in the insolvent estate in the main proceedings, but rather the Regulation allows a bank to enforce those rights in rem over assets which are located in a Member State other than the Member State where the main proceedings have been opened. Therefore, although the law of the main proceedings stipulates that all assets are part of the estate, in fact the holder of the right in rem retains certain rights with respect to the assets over which the holder's debt is secured (subject to the matters discussed below).

6.38 As the Virgos-Schmit Report suggests,[22] at paragraph 97, the fundamental policy behind Article 5 is to protect the trade in the Member State where the assets are situated, and legal certainty in relation to the rights over those assets. Rights in rem have a very important function with respect to credit and the mobilization of wealth. They insulate their holders against the risk of insolvency of the debtor and the interference of third parties. They allow credit to be obtained under conditions which would not be possible without provisions which protect the

---

[19] This text has become Art 8 in the RR but there are no substantive amendments.
[20] CJEU, 16 April 2015.
[21] See app 2 below.
[22] See app 2 below.

provision of this credit by way of security. Rights in rem can only properly fulfil their function if they are not adversely affected by the opening of main proceedings in other Member States.

Article 5 only applies to the rights in rem which are created before the opening **6.39** of proceedings. If they are created after the opening of proceedings, Article 4 applies. However, the CJEU has held that there is no such limitation on the reference in Article 5(4) to actions for voidness, voidability, or unenforceability—see paragraph 6.69 below.

Article 5 is unclear. It gives rise to difficulties of interpretation in a number of **6.40** important respects including:

(a) What is a right in rem and what law determines this?
(b) Where is a secured asset located and what law determines this?
(c) What does it mean to say that the insolvency proceedings shall not 'affect' the right in rem? In particular:
   (i) Is a liquidator entitled to discharge the security by paying the secured creditor a sum equal to the value of the secured asset?
   (ii) Does the protection given by Article 5 extend to the secured debt or merely the security interest over the relevant assets?
   (iii) What impact does Article 5 have on an intercreditor agreement between the secured creditors?
(d) As Article 5 requires the secured asset to be located in another Member State at the time of opening of the relevant insolvency proceedings, how is this expression to be interpreted?
(e) Article 5 does not protect a right in rem from any claw-back challenge under the law of the relevant insolvency proceedings but how does Article 5 relate to Article 13 in this regard?
(f) How do the provisions in Article 43 regarding the Regulation's applicability in time relate to Article 5?

Each of these questions is explored through the 11 factual examples in this chapter **6.41** but is summarized briefly below.

What is a right in rem?

Article 5 raises the question of what 'rights in rem' are the subject of the protection **6.42** given by Article 5 and what law is to determine whether a right is to be regarded as a right in rem for the purposes of Article 5. Does this expression include all types of security and quasi-security interest (such as retention of title clauses, flawed asset arrangements, finance leases, and sale and repurchase agreements)? What about powers of attorney which may be given to support or protect the security interest— do these form part of the right in rem? And what about rights in rem which may be recognized by one Member State but not others (such as the beneficial interest under a trust)?

6.43 The Regulation provides no definition of a right in rem, except that Article 5(3) states that a right which is entered in a public register and is enforceable against third parties shall be considered to be a right in rem. The Virgos-Schmit Report states that the failure to provide a definition (at least in respect of the November 1995 Convention on Insolvency Proceedings) was deliberate, allowing the law of the state where the assets are located to determine the question of whether a right is a right in rem.[23]

6.44 Paragraphs 102–104 of the Virgos-Schmit Report may provide some guidance in relation to what will constitute a right in rem. Those paragraphs are more explicit in their indication of the intended scope of the Article (at least in the form which that Article took when the Regulation was to be issued as a Convention). It appears that:

(a) a right in rem is not to be given an unreasonably wide interpretation. It should not include, for instance, rights simply reinforced by a right to claim preferential payment;

(b) in particular, a right in rem may not only be established with respect to floating charge assets but also rights which are characterized under national law as rights in rem over intangible assets or over other rights.

6.45 Of course, whether the court will construe the scope of an Article in the Regulation by reference to the Virgos-Schmit Report on the November 1995 Convention on Insolvency Proceedings is by no means clear.[24]

6.46 The following provisions of Article 5 will also be helpful in determining whether particular rights in rem fall within Article 5:

Article 5(a) Both specific assets and collections of indefinite assets

6.47 For a UK bank, Article 5 clearly applies to both fixed charge assets ('specific assets') and floating charge assets ('collections of indefinite assets'). This means that a bank with a floating charge which may not be recognized in the Member State where insolvency proceedings are opened will still be able to enforce that floating charge in another Member State where the floating charge is recognized, provided that the security is properly created and perfected according to the law of the *situs* of the secured assets in question. This is of particular importance as a floating charge is not a security interest familiar to other European jurisdictions. It is not clear, however, whether the same analysis would apply in relation to, for example, the beneficial interests created by a constructive or remedial trust where such a trust is not recognized in the Member State where insolvency proceedings are opened. This is considered further in Example 5.

---

[23] See Virgos-Schmit Report, para 100.
[24] See para 2.27 above and n 87 thereto regarding problems with the translation of the Report.

Article 5(b) The right to dispose of assets and to obtain satisfaction from the proceeds

It is unclear whether it is intended that this right, under Article 5(2)(a), includes the **6.48** right to appoint a receiver to dispose of the assets, although this may be included in the right to have assets disposed of. There does not seem to be any reason why this right should not be included. The Virgos-Schmit Report suggests that, for example, the owner of the right in rem may exercise the right to separate the security from the estate and, where necessary, to realize the asset individually to satisfy the claim. In addition, the office-holder, even if he is in possession of the asset, cannot take any decision in relation to that asset which might affect the right in rem created over it, without the consent of its holder.[25]

Article 5(c) Other rights expressly set out in Article 5

Article 5(2) provides a list of the types of rights which are normally considered **6.49** by national laws to be rights in rem. According to the Virgos-Schmit Report, the comparable list in the November 1995 Convention on Insolvency Proceedings was influenced by two main considerations:

(i) a right in rem which comes into existence only after insolvency proceedings have been opened (ie that did not exist prior to that time) is not covered by Article 5;

(ii) in determining whether a right is a right in rem for the purposes of Article 5, a right in rem has two essential characteristics:
   • its direct and immediate relationship with the asset to which it relates, which remains linked until the debt has been satisfied (without depending upon the asset belonging to a person's estate, or on the relationship between the holder of the right in rem and another person);
   • the absolute nature of the allocation of the right to the holder. In other words, the person who holds a right in rem can enforce it against anyone who interferes with his right without his consent. Such rights are typically protected by actions to recover the property which is subject to the right in rem. The right in rem survives a transfer of the asset to a third party (in other words, it can be claimed against a purchaser, unless that purchaser is acting bona fide).[26]

Although Article 5(2) sets out those rights to which Article 5 refers in particular, **6.50** the Article does not regulate all matters which may be of interest to secured creditors, for example priorities as between banks and as between floating charges and preferential creditors. As referred to above, some priority issues (in particular, the ranking of claims of preferential creditors and floating charge-holders) may be within the scope of Article 4(2) but this is not clear.

---

[25] Virgos-Schmit Report, para 95.
[26] ibid para 103.

6.51   Examples 2 and 5 explore some of the issues surrounding what rights are to be construed as rights in rem for the purposes of Article 5.

Where is a secured asset located?

6.52   The protection given by Article 5 only applies where the secured asset is situated within the territory of a Member State other than the one in which the insolvency proceedings are commenced. Hence the location of a secured asset is crucial. Article 5, however, leaves open the question of when assets are situated within the territory of another Member State. In the context of certain assets (such as real property) it may be easy to determine their location but where are debts and other intangibles situated for this purpose? The conflicts rules of the forum where this issue is litigated could be relevant in determining this issue.

6.53   The Virgos-Schmit Report states that the applicable rules governing the creation, validity, and scope of these rights in rem are those of their own applicable law (in general the *lex rei sitae* at the relevant time) and are not affected by the opening of insolvency proceedings.[27] However, there is no assistance as to which law should determine the *lex rei sitae*, and therefore the applicable law, and it is possible that conflicts may arise. Some of these issues are considered in Example 2 below.

6.54   Article 2(g) of the Regulation gives some guidance as to where certain types of assets are located for the purposes of the Regulation:

   (a) in the case of tangible property, the assets will be located in the Member State within which the property is situated;
   (b) in the case of property and rights where ownership or entitlement must be entered in a public register, those assets will be situated in the Member State under whose authority the register is kept; and
   (c) in the case of claims, the claim will be situated in the Member State where the third party required to meet the claim has its centre of main interests.

6.55   It is not clear whether all assets are intended to fall under one of the three categories listed in Article 2(g) or whether the conflicts rules outside the Regulation are intended to determine the situs of assets which do not readily fall within the categories listed in Article 2(g). For example, are private company shares to be treated as a bundle of claims falling within the third category or do shares fall outside the scope of Article 2(g)? Another question is what happens if an asset falls within more than one category? A ship, for example, is tangible property falling within the first limb of Article 2(g), but ownership of that ship could also be recorded in a public register as per the second limb of Article 2(g). In such a case, it is not clear whether the three limbs of Article 2(g) create an order of priority so that the 'tangible property' limb trumps the 'public register' limb.

---

[27] ibid para 95.

These definitions could lead to surprising results in respect of certain intangi- **6.56** ble assets. For example, if the insolvent debtor has a bank account in England with the English branch of an overseas bank, Article 2(g) would seem to suggest that the bank account will not be situated in England but instead will be situated in the Member State in which the bank has its centre of main interests. This does not appear to be the view of Professor Virgos who has stated that:

> In the case of *current accounts* and *deposits* in banking institutions, for these pur- poses each branch must be considered as an *autonomous entity* (i.e. as if it were a distinct debtor) in accordance with the special structure of these institutions; con- sequently the claim will be considered situated in the State where the office serving the customer account is located.[28]

Unfortunately, the Virgos-Schmit Report does not contain such an assertion. The location of assets is considered further in the context of Example 2.

It should be noted that Article 5 does not appear to apply where the assets are situ- **6.57** ated in a non-Member State (even though the private international laws of that non-Member State may have a similar effect).

Article 5 does apply where: (a) insolvency proceedings have been opened in an exist- **6.58** ing Member State prior to the accession of a new Member State to the European Union; and (b) the assets which are subject to the right in rem are situated in the new Member State on the date it accedes to the European Union.[29]

Some but not all of the issues highlighted above concerning the location of assets **6.59** have been addressed by the RR. Article 2(9) RR will provide a number of addi- tional definitions of where assets are located for the purpose of the RR. These, include, among others:

(i) registered shares in companies (other than those which are financial instru- ments) which will be located in the Member State within the territory of which the company having issued the shares has its registered office;[30]

(ii) financial instruments (where title is evidenced by entries in a register or account maintained by or on behalf of an intermediary, that is book entry securities) which will be situated in the Member State in which the register or account in which the entries are made is maintained; and

(iii) cash held in accounts with a credit institution which will be located in the Member State indicated in the account's IBAN (or for cash held in accounts

---

[28] M Virgos and F Garcimartin, *The European Insolvency Regulation: Law and Practice* (2004) 168 (original emphasis).

[29] C-527/10 *ERSTE Bank Hungary Nyrt v Magyar Allam, BCL Trading GmbH, ERSTE Befektetesi Zrt,*.

[30] The new definition of registered shares in companies may create its own interpretation issues. For example, does the rule for 'registered shares' apply: (i) even if the registered shares are held through a chain of intermediaries; and (ii) to registered preference shares as well as registered ordi- nary shares?

with a credit institution which does not have an IBAN, the Member State in which the credit institution holding the account has its central administration or where the account is held with a branch, agency, or other establishment, the Member State in which the branch, agency, or other establishment is located).

The inclusion of a definition of cash held in accounts with a credit institution will mean that it will no longer be necessary to look to the centre of main interests of the credit institution in which the deposit has been made to establish where that cash is situated for the purpose of the RR when this comes into force. However, other than to make clear that cash held in accounts with a credit institution are not claims, no changes have been made in relation to the location of 'claims'. While the amendments in the RR do not set out whether the new list provided for in Article 2(9) RR is intended to be exhaustive, the amendments should clarify that, where an asset falls within more than one category, there will be no overlap between the various limbs of the definition (to use the earlier example of a ship whose ownership was recorded in a public register, the RR makes it clear that the ship will be located in the Member State under whose authority the register is kept).

What does 'shall not affect' mean?

6.60 Article 5 states that the opening of insolvency proceedings shall not affect the rights in rem of creditors or third parties. The Article therefore raises the question of the meaning of the word 'affect'. No definition is provided by the Regulation, but it is to be expected that the word will be construed in order to give effect to the purpose of the Article, namely to protect third-party rights in rem. Some indication of the intention of the Regulation in this regard is given by Recital (25). This states that the basis, validity, and extent of a right in rem should normally be determined according to the *lex rei sitae* and should not be affected by the opening of insolvency proceedings. The Recital states that the proprietor of the right in rem should be able to continue to assert his right to segregation or separate settlement of the collateral security. The Recital also indicates that the liquidator in the main proceedings should be able to open secondary proceedings in the jurisdiction where the rights in rem arise if the debtor has an establishment there—such secondary proceedings may have an impact on the enforcement of security and this is discussed further in Example 1.

6.61 The mere vesting of title to the asset over which security exists in the insolvency officeholder in the main proceedings does not, at least according to the German Supreme Court,[31] affect the rights in rem of creditors. This seems likely to be followed in other Member States because the rights in rem are not affected; there has merely been a change in the person against whom they can be enforced.

---

[31] V ZB 54/10, German Federal Court of Justice (BGH), 3 February 2011.

One important question is unanswered by the Regulation and is not addressed in **6.62** the Virgos-Schmit Report.[32] Does the Article merely protect the right in rem in the strict sense (ie the security interest over the relevant assets) or does it also protect the underlying secured debt? In other words, does Article 5 prevent a composition plan or proceeding which would be effective under the state of the opening of proceedings from amending or discharging the debtor's secured indebtedness and therefore protect the bank's rights to enforce its security in respect of that indebtedness over assets located in another Member State? Although an English voluntary arrangement (which is available as a main proceeding in the United Kingdom) cannot, by virtue of section 4(3) of the Insolvency Act 1986, affect the right of a secured creditor to enforce its security without its concurrence, it may well be that main proceedings opened in another Member State could provide for the variation or discharge of a secured debt governed by English law[33] without the express consent of the secured creditor and this could have an effect on the enforcement of security in England. Although such a result would seem to be far from the intentions of the draftsman, it cannot be excluded.[34] This issue is explored further in Examples 6, 7, and 8.

A second question which arises from the use of the words 'shall not affect the rights **6.63** in rem of creditors' is what effect (if any) Article 5 would have on the turnover trust provisions in an intercreditor agreement between the secured creditors *inter se*. This is also explored through Example 8. This is likely to depend on whether (but for Article 5) the insolvency proceedings in question purport to affect the rights of the secured creditors as between themselves (rather than merely affecting the position as between the insolvent debtor and its creditors). Following the decision in *Prudential Assurance Company Ltd v PRG Powerhouse*,[35] it is clear that an English company voluntary arrangement (if properly drafted) could affect the position between a creditor and a third party (such as another creditor) and it is theoretically possible that main proceedings commenced in other Member States could purport to have the same effect.

Finally in this context, the question arises as to whether Article 5 would prevent **6.64** a liquidator in the main proceedings from 'paying off' the bank, thereby gaining control of the secured asset. The Virgos-Schmit Report makes it clear that, if the value of the security is greater than the value of the secured claim, the creditor will be obliged to surrender to the insolvent estate any surplus proceeds of sale [36] and

---

[32] See app 2 below.

[33] By way of analogy, an English voluntary arrangement provides for the variation or discharge of all (unsecured) debt, whatever the governing law.

[34] While the authors of this chapter are not aware of any case law on this point, it is helpful that one of the authors of the European Convention on Insolvency Proceedings, Professor Balz, considers that secured creditors may not be impaired by a plan: see M Balz, 'The European Convention on Insolvency Proceedings' (1996) 70 ABLJ 485, 509.

[35] [2007] EWHC 1002 (Ch).

[36] Para 99 (see app 2).

this is unobjectionable. The Report also states that the liquidator has the power to decide on the immediate payment of the secured claim and thus to avoid any loss in value that certain assets could suffer if they were to be realized separately.[37] This is more problematic as it could be argued that such a right on the part of the liquidator affects the right in rem of the secured creditor, particularly in circumstances where the security is underwater. For example, if the secured debt is 100 but the secured asset (at the current time) is only worth 80, the secured creditor would be deprived of its chance to wait and see if the value of the secured asset might increase in the future if the liquidator in the main proceedings were able to discharge the security by paying the secured creditor 80.

What does the time of opening of proceedings mean?

6.65 This expression is relevant in two contexts. First it appears that only rights in rem that are in existence at the time of the opening of the relevant insolvency proceedings are protected by Article 5.[38] Secondly, Article 5 only applies in relation to assets which are located in another Member State at the time of opening of proceedings.

6.66 The time of the opening of proceedings is defined by Article 2 as 'the time at which the judgment opening proceedings becomes effective, whether it is a final judgment or not'. At present, there is no such 'judgment' opening proceedings for many English insolvency procedures such as the company voluntary arrangement and creditors' voluntary liquidation. These are extra-judicial procedures. By the Insolvency (Amendment) Rules 2002, rule 7.62, rules have been introduced in the United Kingdom to ensure that there is confirmation of these procedures, so that there can be a 'judgment' which becomes 'effective'. A list of these rules can be found in Appendix 3 to this book.

6.67 It is unclear, however, what the position should be if (as a matter of the insolvency law of the Member State in which insolvency proceedings are commenced) there is a concept of 'relation-back' so that the relevant insolvency proceedings are deemed to commence on the date the petition or application is filed (rather than the date on which the order is made). In this regard, reference is made to chapter 8 below.

6.68 The Article does not address the question as to what happens if assets are moved from one state to another after proceedings have started. It appears from the wording of Article 5 that it is sufficient for the assets to be located in another Member State at the time of the opening of proceedings, even if the assets are subsequently moved out of the European Union or to the Member State where proceedings have been opened.

---

[37] ibid.
[38] ibid para 96.

Relationship between Article 5 and Article 13

Article 5(4) states that Article 5(1) shall not preclude actions for voidness, void- **6.69**
ability, or unenforceability as referred to in Article 4(2)(m). The general rule is
that such matters are determined by the law of the Member State in which the
insolvency proceedings are commenced. However, this is subject to the defence
in Article 13 where the act in question is subject to the law of another Member
State and that law does not allow any means of challenging that act in the relevant
case. The relationship between Articles 5 and 13 is considered in Example 10. It
was also considered by the CJEU in *Lutz v Bäuerle*.[39] The CJEU held that while
Article 13 is not, in principle, applicable to acts which take place after the opening of the insolvency proceedings, in certain circumstances, Article 13 would be
applicable if an act takes place after the opening of insolvency proceedings on the
basis of rights established before the opening of the insolvency proceedings. The
CJEU's decision related to a payment made post-insolvency in respect of a right
in rem created pre-insolvency and was reached on the basis of the wording of
Article 5 of the Regulation. While Article 5 provides protection for rights in rem
of creditors or third parties in respect of property situated within the territory of
another Member State at the time of the opening of the insolvency proceedings,
Article 5(4) specifically provides that it shall not preclude actions for voidness,
voidability, or unenforceability as referred to in Article 4(2)(m) of the Regulation.
Therefore, even where a payment is made after the commencement of the insolvency proceedings, if the payment is made pursuant to a right in rem granted prior
to the insolvency proceedings being commenced, Article 13 may still provide a
defence to a challenge of the underlying agreement under which the payment has
been made and therefore ultimately the post-insolvency payment.

Relationship between Article 5 and Article 43

Article 43 of the Regulation states that the provisions of the Regulation shall apply **6.70**
only to insolvency proceedings opened after its entry into force and 'Acts done by a
debtor before the entry into force of this Regulation shall continue to be governed
by the law which was applicable to them at the time they were done'.[40] The question therefore arises as to whether Article 5 will protect security created pursuant
to agreements entered into prior to 31 May 2002, using a broad interpretation of
the words 'acts done' to encompass the entry into of the security. This is considered
further in Example 9. Although there is no case law yet on this issue, the authors
do not consider that Article 5 should be disapplied in the context of security created prior to 31 May 2002 (although the contrary view is possible). In our view, the

---

[39] CJEU, 16 April 2015.
[40] A similar transitional issue arises in respect of the RR. Art 84 RR provides that acts committed
by the debtor before the coming into force of the RR shall continue to be governed by the law which
was applicable to them at the time they were committed.

relevant 'acts done' refer to actions undertaken to place a debtor into insolvency proceedings and not other 'acts' more generally. If a wider interpretation was to be applied, this would (for example) prevent voidable transactions from being treated under the choice of law rules set out in the Regulation (if those transactions were entered into prior to 31 May 2002) and the authors do not consider that this could be correct. If (contrary to the views of the authors) the expression 'acts done' were to encompass the entry into of the security, a possible interpretation of Article 43 is that the creation, validity, and scope of any right in rem created by a security agreement or act pre-dating 31 May 2002 should be determined by the applicable law applying conflicts rules outside the Regulation. So, for example, if the security was created prior to 31 May 2002 and the English court were to determine the *lex rei sitae* of a secured asset that comprised a debt, it may well apply the general rule under English common law that a debt is situate where it is expressly or impliedly payable (rather than applying the *lex rei sitae* rules in Article 2(g) of the Regulation).

Other case law concerning Article 5

6.71 In addition to the *ERSTE* and German Federal Court cases referred to in paragraphs 6.58 and 6.61 above and the *Lutz v Bäuerle* CJEU decision referred to in paragraph 6.69 above, the authors are only aware of two other decisions.

The first is the decision of the Antwerp Court of Appeal in *Stella Europe SA v Apex International NV*.[41] Unfortunately that decision does not answer any of the issues of interpretation set out above and, indeed, Article 5 was not referred to in the judgment, even though it would have provided an obvious answer (and the same result) in the *Stella* case. The case concerned main insolvency proceedings (*redressement judiciare* proceedings) which were opened in France in respect of Stella Europe SA, a French registered company. Following the commencement of such proceedings, the Commercial Court of Antwerp allowed Apex International NV, a Belgian creditor of Stella Europe SA, to enforce a '*gage commercial*' under Belgian law [42] over goods belonging to the French registered company. The goods were in transit within the Belgian jurisdiction.

6.72 The French registered company appealed and the Belgian Court of Appeal in principle suspended the enforcement procedure but held that the creditor could pursue the enforcement of the '*gage commercial*' in Belgium. The Court of Appeal's reasoning was as follows:

(a) the effect of the Regulation was that the French insolvency proceedings must be recognized in Belgium;

---

[41] 2004/RK/274, RGDC/TBBR 2006, 558 (Antwerp Court of Appeal, 23 August 2004).
[42] This gives a creditor the right to get paid in priority from the proceeds of the sale of goods when the goods have remained in the creditor's possession. The creditor is deemed to be in possession when the goods have not reached the debtor and the creditor holds the bills of lading over the goods.

(b) however, the effects of the French insolvency procedure on the enforcement of the *'gage commercial'* in Belgium must be determined according to what the position would have been in Belgium had judicial composition proceedings been opened in Belgium. This conclusion was reached on the basis that judicial composition proceedings were the closest Belgian equivalent to a French *redressement judiciare* proceeding; and

(c) as the creditor could have enforced the *'gage commercial'* in a Belgian judicial composition proceeding, the creditor therefore had a right to pursue enforcement over the goods.

The Belgian court did not, however, refer to Article 5 and it is not clear why the **6.73** Belgian court considered the position under the equivalent Belgian insolvency proceeding to the main proceedings opened in France.

The second case is that of *Avukat Louis Pullicion as mandatory and in the name of* **6.74** *The Foreign Economic & Technical Co-Operation Company of China, Changjiang National Shipping Group u Qingshan Shipyard of China Changjiang National Shipping Group v Il-Bastiment M.V. Beluga Sydney*,[43] a decision at first instance in the Court of Malta. The facts and decision of that case were as follows:

(a) On 14 June 2011, the Maltese court issued a warrant for the arrest of a sea vessel. The warrant was issued as security for the in personam and in rem claims of the claimant ('L') against a German registered company ('D'). The claims were for the balance of the price incurred for the construction of the vessel. The vessel was registered in Germany. On the dates both when the warrant was issued and later when the vessel was arrested, the vessel was located in Maltese waters, and was flying a Liberian flag.

(b) The vessel was built in L's shipyards in 2006. Ownership had been transferred to D on 26 April 2010. An agreement was later reached between D and L in relation to payment for the vessel. The full amount was never paid. On 12 July 2011, D was placed into insolvency proceedings in Germany.

(c) D applied to the Maltese court to revoke the arrest warrant. One of the grounds on which D relied was that the commencement of the German insolvency proceedings in respect to D was a sufficient ground in and of itself for the Maltese court to revoke the warrant. It was contended by D that once the German insolvency proceedings were commenced, then there was a moratorium on creditor action, and that (pursuant to the Regulation) the moratorium had to be recognized in all Member States.

(d) The Maltese court held that Article 5, interpreted in accordance with Recital (25) of the Regulation, meant that the opening of the German insolvency proceedings could not affect L's rights to request the warrant

---

[43] In the acts of warrant of arrest of sea vessels exceeding ten metres, No 803/11, Application Number 1136/2011; First Hall, Civil Court, 30 December 2011.

of arrest against the vessel in Malta as a safeguard for its rights in rem in respect of the vessel.

(e) The Maltese court did not consider the question of whether the vessel was (for the purposes of the Regulation) located in Germany because that was its place of registration at the time of the opening of proceedings. Under Article 2(g), assets may be situated either in 'the Member State within which the property is situated' (Malta) or in the Member State where there is a public register where 'property and rights of ownership of or entitlement to which must be entered in a public register' (Germany). The Maltese court did not answer the question of whether the 'tangible property' limb of Article 2(g) has priority over the 'public register' limb but this seems to be the assumption on which its decision is based. Notably, once the RR comes into force, the question of whether the 'tangible property' limb will trump the 'public register' limb will be answered. The RR will make it clear that it is the 'public register' limb which takes priority. See paragraph 6.59 above for further information on this issue.

D. Practical Examples

Example 1

6.75 Borrower A has its centre of main interests in England and a branch office in Ireland. It has assets in both of these jurisdictions and also in Germany although it has no branch office there. The bank takes full fixed and floating security over all the assets in England, Ireland, and Germany pursuant to an English law governed debenture and also takes local security in Germany and Ireland under the laws of these jurisdictions. The bank complies with all perfection requirements in all relevant jurisdictions. There are no grounds for challenging the security under English, Irish, or German law. Borrower A becomes insolvent and the security becomes enforceable. What are the options for the bank in respect of the security over the assets in each jurisdiction and how would these options be affected if insolvency proceedings were opened in respect of A in a particular jurisdiction?

Issues arising: Summary

6.76 **Assets in England**
- Main proceedings would need to be opened in England as the centre of main interests is there.
- If no main proceedings have been commenced in England, the bank may be able to appoint a receiver or administrative receiver as a matter of English law, depending on when the security was created or whether an exception to the general prohibition on appointing an administrative receiver applies.

The receivership would not be recognized as insolvency proceedings for the purposes of the Regulation.

- If an administrative receiver is appointed, this will affect the types of insolvency proceedings that can subsequently be opened as main proceedings in England. This is not an aspect of the Regulation but a consequence of the provisions of the Insolvency Act 1986.

- If an administrator is appointed at main proceedings in England, this will affect the bank's ability to enforce its security over assets in England and Article 5 will not be relevant in this context as the assets are located in the same Member State as the state where proceedings are opened.

Assets in Ireland   6.77

- If the branch in Ireland is sufficient for there to be an establishment there, territorial or secondary insolvency proceedings could be opened in Ireland.

- The opening of territorial or secondary proceedings could in theory have an impact on the enforcement of security in that jurisdiction but the types of proceedings that could be opened in Ireland as secondary proceedings will not have such an impact. Accordingly, even if secondary proceedings are opened in Ireland, the bank will be able to enforce its security over assets in Ireland. This is very different from the position under the old law where an examinership could have been commenced which would have had an impact on the enforcement of security in Ireland.

- If no territorial or secondary proceedings have been commenced in Ireland, but an administrator had been appointed in England, Article 5 should allow the bank to enforce its security over assets in Ireland notwithstanding the moratorium on security enforcement which arises in an English administration.

- Any surplus monies following the enforcement of the security in Ireland should be handed to the office-holder in the main proceedings.

Assets in Germany   6.78

- As there is no establishment in Germany, there can be no secondary proceedings there.

- Article 5 should allow the bank to enforce its security over assets in Germany in accordance with German law and procedure notwithstanding any moratorium which may arise in either the main or the secondary proceedings.

Issues arising: Commentary

Assets in England.   As A's centre of main interests is in England, any main   6.79
insolvency proceedings which are opened would need to be opened in England.
The types of proceedings which could be opened as main proceedings in England
are liquidation (either compulsory or voluntary with confirmation of the court),
administration, or a voluntary arrangement.

6.80 **No main proceedings opened in England.** If no such proceedings have been opened at the time the security becomes enforceable and, in particular, if no administrator has been appointed in England in respect of A, the bank will be able to take steps to enforce the security in accordance with English substantive and procedural law. This could include appointing a receiver under the Law of Property Act 1925 or possibly an administrative receiver under the Insolvency Act 1986 but only if the security agreement was entered into prior to 15 September 2003 or one of the exceptions to the general prohibition on appointing an administrative receiver were to apply.[44]

6.81 As receivership and administrative receivership are not 'insolvency proceedings' for the purposes of the Regulation, the appointment of the receiver or administrative receiver over the assets in England would be outside the scope of the Regulation and would not automatically be recognized in other Member States pursuant to Article 17 of the Regulation. Therefore the questions of whether the receiver or administrative receiver would be recognized in Germany and Ireland, and whether the receiver would be able to take possession of assets located in those jurisdictions pursuant to the security agreement governed by English law, will be a matter of German or Irish private international law (as the case may be) and will not be governed by the Regulation. This is considered further in the context of Example 2. This illustrates that there may be an advantage to the secured creditor in consenting to the making of an administration order or the appointment of an administrator, as administration is an 'insolvency proceeding' for the purposes of the Regulation, rather than appointing an administrative receiver; in this way, the secured creditor could take advantage of the recognition provisions in the Regulation in respect of the administration.

6.82 Administration is one of the insolvency proceedings set out in Annex A of the Regulation and the centre of main interests is in England and so there would be jurisdiction under the Regulation to appoint an administrator. However, under English insolvency law, if an administrative receiver is appointed in England over the assets of A, it will not subsequently be possible for the English court to make an administration order in respect of A[45] or for the directors to appoint an administrator by filing documents with the court.[46] On the face of it, there might be said to be a conflict between domestic law and the Regulation. This is not, in fact, the case. The Regulation is merely enabling. It allows insolvency proceedings to be opened in a particular jurisdiction if the domestic criteria are met. Here, there would be no jurisdiction under the Insolvency Act 1986

---

[44] See Insolvency Act 1986, s 72A.
[45] Sch B1, para 39 to the Insolvency Act 1986. There would be an exception if the security could be avoided under certain provisions of the Insolvency Act 1986 relating to transactions at an undervalue, preferences, and avoidance of floating charges.
[46] Sch B1, para 25(c) to the Insolvency Act 1986.

to appoint an administrator because of the appointment of the administrative receiver.

Liquidation as main proceedings. It would still be possible to open the other types of insolvency proceedings listed in Annex A to the Regulation in England (for example a compulsory liquidation or a creditors' voluntary liquidation with confirmation from the court). These proceedings do not affect the enforcement of security in England as, generally speaking, a liquidator has no right to deal with the secured assets in England and there is no moratorium on the appointment of a receiver, or the taking of other steps to enforce security, following the commencement of an English winding-up. **6.83**

However, the commencement of a liquidation would affect the priority of the claims of the floating charge-holder (as certain categories of preferential debt and the expenses of the liquidation will rank ahead of the claims of the floating charge-holder).[47] In this example, as English law governs both the security agreement and the ranking of claims in the liquidation, there will not be any conflict. This issue is considered further in paragraph 6.93 below in the context of the security agreement governed by Irish law where different rules may apply under Irish law (as the law governing the security agreement) and English insolvency law (as the law of the main proceedings). **6.84**

Administration as main proceedings. If the bank is not able to or does not appoint an administrative receiver on receiving notice of an administration application (or a notice of intention to appoint an administrator by the company or its directors), and an administration order is subsequently made (or an administrator appointed), a statutory moratorium arises which will prevent the bank from appointing a receiver or administrative receiver or taking any other steps to enforce its security over A's property.[48] **6.85**

Article 5 of the Regulation is not relevant in relation to the security over the assets in England because those assets are not situated within the territory of another Member State at the time of the opening of the main proceedings in England. **6.86**

Assets in Ireland No territorial or secondary proceedings in Ireland—administration in England. If the moratorium which arises in the main proceedings does not prevent the enforcement of security in another Member State (a matter which is considered below), it will be necessary to open secondary proceedings in the Member State where the secured assets are located in order to take advantage of any stay which may arise in those secondary proceedings. In some circumstances (as in this example), it may not be possible under the Regulation to open **6.87**

---

[47] Insolvency Act 1986, ss 175 and 175ZA. See also the House of Lords decision in *Kahn v IRC* [2002] UKHL 6 where corporation tax on notional interest income which was not actually received by the company was treated as an expense of the liquidation.

[48] Sch B1, para 43(2) to the Insolvency Act 1986.

as secondary proceedings the types of insolvency proceedings which would give rise to a stay, and this is discussed further below.

6.88 If an administrator is appointed in respect of A in England pursuant to main proceedings, and no secondary proceedings have been opened in Ireland, the question arises whether the moratorium on the enforcement of security which arises in the English administration should be recognized across the European Union and so affect the enforcement of security in Ireland. This depends in part on the construction of paragraph 43 of Schedule B1 to the Insolvency Act 1986 and in part on the effect of the Regulation:

(a) It has been suggested by the Court of Appeal that, as a matter of domestic insolvency law, the administration moratorium has no extra-territorial effect and so does not prevent the attachment of assets overseas, although the Court of Appeal did not give a definitive ruling on this point.[49] The separate question of the English court's equitable or in personam jurisdiction is considered below.

(b) Even if paragraph 43 of Schedule B1 to the Insolvency Act 1986 has extra-territorial effect (which seems unlikely), that extra-territorial effect will be subject to Article 5 (discussed below). In the absence of Article 5, Article 17(1) provides that the judgment opening the main proceedings is to produce the same effects in any other Member State as under the law of the state of opening (unless the Regulation states otherwise). Therefore, in relation to matters governed by the Regulation, the better question is not whether the administration moratorium has extra-territorial effect, but whether the Regulation has the effect of exporting the moratorium which applies in England to other Member States. It is not clear whether a moratorium on the enforcement of security (such as the stay which arises on the making of an administration order or the appointment of an administrator) falls expressly within Article 4(2), although this list is not exclusive.[50] However, even if the moratorium on security enforcement is not a matter which is expressly listed in Article 4(2) as a matter which is to be determined by the law of the state of the opening of proceedings, it should still have extra-territorial effect by virtue of Article 17(1). As the matter is not entirely clear, this is a question which, therefore, it might be desirable to refer to the CJEU.

(c) However, Article 5 protects extra-territorial rights in rem and so should allow a secured creditor to enforce its security over assets located in another Member State notwithstanding any moratorium on security enforcement

---

[49] *Harms Offshore AHT Taurus GmbH & Co KG v Bloom* [2009] EWCA Civ 632.

[50] A secured creditor can appoint a receiver under English law pursuant to a security agreement without an application to court and so such an appointment is likely to fall outside the definition of 'proceedings' in Art 4(2)(f). It is possible that the moratorium on security enforcement could fall within Art 4(2)(e)—the effect of insolvency proceedings on current contracts—on the basis that the security agreement is a contractual arrangement but this is not entirely clear.

which arises in the state where proceedings are opened, even if that moratorium purports to have extra-territorial effect. Article 5 provides that the opening of insolvency proceedings will not affect the rights in rem of creditors—although the moratorium which arises in an English administration does not destroy rights in rem, it does prevent a secured creditor from enforcing its security and in this sense could be seen as 'affecting' the rights in rem. Hence it is to be expected that Article 5 would be construed as allowing a secured creditor to enforce its security in another Member State, notwithstanding any moratorium which arises as a consequence of the main proceedings.[51]

6.89 Applying this analysis to the facts of Example 1, as the assets in Ireland are situated within the territory of another Member State at the time of the opening of proceedings in England, and assuming the bank has effective security over those assets as a matter of Irish law, Article 5 should allow the bank to enforce its security in Ireland.

6.90 Article 5 refers to rights in rem in respect of specific assets or collections of indefinite assets as a whole which change from time to time, and so the rights in rem covered by Article 5 would include the bank's floating security over the assets in Ireland.

6.91 As mentioned above, there is also a question as to whether the English court may, acting in personam, restrain an English creditor (or a foreign creditor who is subject to the jurisdiction of the English court) from taking action to enforce security abroad. In the context of a creditor who wishes to commence or continue proceedings abroad, it has been suggested that there is no scope for the English court to exercise any equitable jurisdiction to restrain such proceedings since the administration order or appointment of an administrator does not result in any vested right on the part of the unsecured creditors.[52] However, this has been doubted by another leading commentator.[53] If the English court does have such an equitable jurisdiction to grant an 'anti-suit' injunction in respect of foreign proceedings, if it were not for Article 5, the principles generally established in relation to antisuit injunctions would apply. Although antisuit injunctions are not referred to specifically in Article 5, the ability to grant such an injunction would seem to be inconsistent with Article 5. Discussion of antisuit injunctions generally falls outside the scope of this work.

---

[51] This is certainly the view taken by Balz (n 24 above) 509: 'These [ie secured] creditors are not affected by a stay issued in connection with foreign insolvency proceedings and they may not be impaired by a plan.'

[52] See G Lightman and G Moss, *The Law of Receivers and Administrators of Companies* (4th edn, 2007) para 32-011.

[53] See PS Smart, *Cross-Border Insolvency* (2nd edn, 1998) 296–8 where it is suggested that such an equitable jurisdiction *could* be invoked in the case of an administration.

6.92   In conclusion, for the reasons given above, it seems unlikely that the moratorium which arises in an English administration would prevent the bank from enforcing its security over the assets in Ireland and, if A wished to prevent the enforcement of security over its assets in Ireland, it would be necessary for it to commence secondary proceedings in Ireland in order to take advantage of any stay which may arise as a matter of Irish law. This is considered further in paragraphs 6.95–6.97 below.

6.93   **No territorial or secondary proceedings in Ireland—English liquidation.** If there were a liquidation of A as main proceedings, the question arises as to which rules regarding the priority of claims should apply. Article 4(2)(i) states that the law of the state where proceedings are opened will determine the rules governing the distribution of proceeds from the realization of assets and the ranking of claims. Under English law, certain categories of preferential debt and the expenses of the liquidation rank ahead of the claims of the floating charge-holder[54] (although, as stated in paragraph 6.29 above, it is not clear whether this is an aspect of English insolvency law or security law and therefore it is not clear whether Article 4(2)(i) applies).

6.94   However, Article 5 states that the opening of insolvency proceedings is not to affect the rights in rem of creditors in respect of assets situated in another Member State and a right to have a claim met out of secured assets in priority to other unsecured creditors may be an incident of the right in rem. Therefore, although the Regulation is not clear, it seems likely that Irish law, as the applicable law of the security, would determine the priority of payments as between the bank and any preferential creditors. This is a matter which it might be appropriate to refer to the CJEU.

6.95   **Territorial or secondary proceedings in Ireland.** As A has an establishment in Ireland, territorial or secondary proceedings may be opened in Ireland. These proceedings would be conducted according to Irish law and will affect rights in rem in Ireland in exactly the same way as those proceedings would have affected rights in rem in Ireland if the proceedings had been purely domestic proceedings.

6.96   Under Irish law, a company examinership would give rise to a moratorium on the enforcement of security in a similar manner to an English administration. However, company examinership is not available as secondary proceedings under the Regulation. It does not appear that the types of insolvency proceedings which could be opened in Ireland as secondary proceedings (i.e. compulsory winding-up and creditors' voluntary winding-up with confirmation of the court) would affect the enforcement of security although, as with the English assets, they may impact on the priority of payments pursuant to that security. Hence, on the facts of this example, the Regulation would prevent A from opening any proceedings in Ireland as secondary proceedings which would prevent the bank from enforcing its security over the assets in Ireland.

---

[54]   Insolvency Act 1986, ss 175 and 175ZA.

If the value of the secured assets in Ireland is greater than the value of the bank's **6.97** secured liability, and the bank takes steps to enforce its security over the Irish assets, the bank will be obliged to surrender to the office-holder of the secondary proceedings in Ireland any surplus proceeds of sale. This is because Article 5 states that the proceedings shall not affect rights in rem in respect of assets located in another Member State and does not state that the proceedings shall not affect *assets* located in another state.[55] This also means that the office-holder in either the main proceedings or the secondary proceedings could choose to pay the secured claim and thus avoid any loss in value that the secured assets might suffer if they were to be realized separately.

Assets in Germany The main difference here is that, as there is no establish- **6.98** ment in Germany, it will not be possible to open territorial or secondary proceedings in Germany to impact on the enforcement of security in that Member State.

Article 5 should enable the bank to enforce its security notwithstanding any mora- **6.99** torium on enforcement which might arise as a consequence of an English administration. For the reasons given above, it seems that the types of proceedings that could be opened as secondary proceedings in Ireland would not give rise to a stay on the enforcement of security but, were those secondary proceedings to have this effect, Article 5 would enable the bank to enforce its security in Germany notwithstanding such a moratorium. However, the bank must enforce its security in accordance with German law and procedure. So, for example, under German law, where the security is over land, the security must be enforced by means of public auction or court administration.

If the secured assets in Germany are worth more than the secured liability, any **6.100** surplus proceeds of sale would need to be handed over to the office-holder in the main proceedings in England.

Example 2

Borrower B has its centre of main interests in England and a branch office in **6.101** Ireland. It has granted security over its assets in England, Ireland, and Germany under an English law governed debenture but the bank has not taken local security under agreements governed by Irish or German law. B becomes insolvent. Would the bank be able to enforce its security over the assets in all three jurisdictions and what would be the impact of the opening of main or secondary proceedings?

Issues arising: summary

- As with Example 1, main proceedings can be commenced in England and **6.102** secondary proceedings can be commenced in Ireland (if the Irish branch office gives rise to an establishment) but not in Germany.

---

[55] See the Virgos-Schmit Report, para 99 (app 2 below).

- The issue here is whether the English law governed debenture would be recognized as giving rise to a valid security interest over the assets in Ireland and Germany for the purposes of Article 5. It appears that issues relating to the creation, validity, and scope of the security as a right in rem will be determined by the applicable law under the usual conflict of laws rules regarding security interests.
- Some of these issues regarding the characterization of a right in rem are explored in more detail in Example 5.

Issues arising: commentary

6.103   **Assets in England**   The analysis will be as set out in paragraphs 6.76–6.86 above.

6.104   **Assets in Ireland   No secondary or territorial proceedings in Ireland**. As mentioned above, receivership and administrative receivership are not insolvency proceedings for the purposes of the Regulation and so any receiver or administrative receiver appointed in England pursuant to the security agreement governed by English law will not automatically be recognized in other Member States pursuant to the Regulation. Irish private international rules will determine whether the receiver or administrative receiver is recognized in Ireland, and whether the receiver is able to take possession of assets located there pursuant to the security agreement governed by English law.

6.105   It is a separate question whether the security agreement governed by English law would give rise to a right in rem over the assets in Ireland to which Article 5 would apply. Article 5 does not define what is a right in rem for the purposes of the Regulation and does not state the law of which jurisdiction is to determine the matter. This might be a matter which is suitable for reference to the CJEU. The Virgos-Schmit Report suggests that the characterization of a right as a right in rem must be sought in the national law which, according to normal pre-insolvency conflict of laws rules, governs the security interest. In general, this will be the *lex rei sitae* at the relevant time.[56] However, neither the Regulation nor the Virgos-Schmit Report gives any guidance as to which court is to apply its normal pre-insolvency conflict of laws rules. It is possible (though perhaps unlikely) that the English court (as the court of the Member State where the main proceedings are opened or whose law is expressed to govern the security agreement) and the Irish court (as the court of the Member State where the assets appear to be located or where secondary proceedings could be commenced) could come to different conclusions regarding the applicable law governing the security interest.

6.106   Furthermore, a number of different laws could be relevant to the question of whether there is a valid right in rem. For example, as both parties are based in Member States, the contractual aspects of the security (including such matters as whether an agreement exists at all, the formalities of the agreement, and its

---

[56] ibid para 100.

interpretation) will be governed by the Convention on the Law Applicable to Contractual Obligations 1980 (the 'Rome Convention'). However, the validity of the security will also depend on whether it has been properly registered in the relevant jurisdiction, whether any perfection requirements (such as notifying a debtor of an assignment of receivables) have been complied with and whether title can pass by mere agreement or whether there needs to be physical delivery: these issues will generally (though not always) be determined by the *lex rei sitae* of the relevant asset[57] and this will depend in turn on the nature of the asset in question.

In respect of tangible property where rights of ownership do not have to be regis-   **6.107** tered in a public register, the Regulation provides that the property will be treated as being located in the Member State where it is located.[58] Therefore, in the case of real or immovable property located in Ireland, Irish law (as the *lex rei sitae*) will determine the proprietary effects of the security (including such factors as the registration and perfection requirements).[59] However, jurisdictions differ greatly in their approach to determining the *lex rei sitae* of movable goods. Under English conflict of laws rules, the validity of a transfer of a tangible movable asset, and its effect on the proprietary rights of the parties to the transfer, are governed by the law of the country where the movable asset is at the time of the transfer.[60] However, it is first necessary to determine whether the asset is properly characterized as a movable or an immovable asset and different courts may reach different views on this preliminary issue.[61] In the case of property and rights which are registered in a public register located in Ireland, Article 2(g) states that these assets will be located in Ireland as the Member State under the authority of which the register is kept. However, in the case of security taken over intangible rights (such as choses in action or bank accounts), the position may be more complex. The Regulation states that, for the purposes of the Regulation, a 'claim' is located in the Member State where the third party required to meet the claim has its centre of main interests.[62] Therefore, in the case of a contractual right, the home jurisdiction of the third-party debtor is likely to be relevant rather than the governing law of the contract. In the case of a bank account held with an Irish branch of an overseas bank, the bank account may not be located in Ireland for the purposes of the Regulation but may be located in the home jurisdiction of the overseas bank (although see paragraphs 6.56 and 6.59 above in this regard).

There may also be an issue regarding whether the type of security interest cre-   **6.108** ated by the English law security document is recognized by the foreign court.

---

[57] An exception, for example, would be security over a contractual debt: under Art 12 of the Rome Convention, the proper law of the assigned debt, and not the *lex rei sitae*, will determine the validity of the assignment and the form of notice to be given to the debtor.

[58] Art 2(g).

[59] See Dicey and Morris, *Conflict of Laws* (13th edn, 1999) rr 113 and 114.

[60] ibid r 116.

[61] ibid r 111(1).

[62] Art 2(g).

For example, an English floating charge may not be recognized in all Member States (although, for the purposes of Example 2, a floating charge is recognized in Ireland). Article 5 refers specifically to 'collections of indefinite assets as a whole which change from time to time' and so a floating charge is capable of falling within Article 5. However, this does not necessarily mean that a secured lender would be able to rely on Article 5 in order to enforce a floating charge which was recognized in the jurisdiction of the governing law of the security agreement but which was not recognized in the *lex rei sitae* of the secured assets, particularly if the relevant registration and perfection requirements in the *lex rei sitae* are not complied with or it is not possible to take security over future property in that jurisdiction.

6.109   **Territorial or secondary proceedings in Ireland**. As with Example 1, if territorial or secondary insolvency proceedings are commenced in Ireland and these proceedings (as a matter of Irish law) impose a stay on the enforcement of security, the enforcement of the security over the Irish assets will be affected by such a stay notwithstanding the fact that the security is expressed to be governed by English law. However, as stated above, it does not appear that the types of proceedings which can be opened in Ireland as secondary proceedings would have this effect (although they could impact on the priority of payments to the bank).

6.110   **Assets in Germany**   The analysis will be as above in relation to the assets in Ireland—assuming that German law is the applicable law according to the normal pre-insolvency conflict of law rules, German law will determine whether the security which is expressed to be governed by English law is effective to create a security interest over the assets located in Germany. The key difference (as with Example 1) is that it will not be possible to have secondary proceedings in Germany which could have any effect on the enforcement of the security.

Example 3

6.111   Borrower C has its centre of main interests in France and has assets located in France and in England. There is no branch in England and the assets located there are not sufficient for C to have an establishment in England. The bank has taken full fixed and floating security over the assets in England and France pursuant to a security agreement governed by English law and this security has been perfected in England. The bank has lent on the basis of the assets in England and is not concerned about enforcing its security over the assets in France. Can the bank appoint a receiver in England and how would the commencement of main proceedings in France affect the enforcement of security in England?

Issues arising: summary

6.112   • As the centre of main interests is in France, main proceedings would need to be opened there and no secondary proceedings could be opened in England as there is no establishment there.

- By virtue of Article 5, the opening of main proceedings in France should have no impact on the enforcement of security over the assets in England.
- Following amendments to the definition of company for the purpose of the Insolvency Act 1986[63] it is now the case that an administrative receiver cannot be appointed in respect of a foreign registered company, although it is unclear whether an administrative receiver can be appointed in respect of an overseas company which has registered particulars under Part 34 of the Companies Act 2006.

Issues arising: commentary

As the centre of main interests is in France, main insolvency proceedings will **6.113** be in that jurisdiction. These can either be rehabilitation proceedings ('*redresse-ment judicaire*'), safeguard ('*sauvegarde*'), or judicial liquidation proceedings ('*liquidation judicaire*'). All three proceedings give rise to a stay on enforcement of security for a certain period and so will affect the enforcement of the security over the assets in France. However, the bank should be able to enforce its secu-rity in England pursuant to Article 5 notwithstanding the stay on enforcement in France. The bank will need to enforce its security over the assets in England in accordance with English law and procedure.

As the bank has taken security (including floating charge security) over all or sub- **6.114** stantially all of the assets of C, the issue arises as to whether a receiver appointed by the bank in England would be deemed to be an administrative receiver under the Insolvency Act 1986. Prior to the changes to the Insolvency Act 1986 that were made by the Enterprise Act 2002, this question was likely to have been of academic interest only. From a practical perspective, the only advantage of the receiver being an administrative receiver is that he or she would have additional rights and powers under the English insolvency legislation but any well-drafted security agreement is likely to give the receiver wide powers (including the power to manage the business) in any event. In a domestic situation, the main advan-tage to a lender of being able to appoint an administrative receiver was (and still is, where an exception to the general prohibition on appointing an administra-tive receiver applies) that such a lender can prevent the appointment of an admin-istrator as an administrator cannot be appointed if an administrative receiver is in office.[64] However, as the centre of main interests of C is not in England in the current example, it would not be possible to appoint an administrator in respect of C in any event and so this advantage of the receiver being an administrative receiver will be irrelevant.

---

[63] The Companies Act 2006 (Consequential Amendments, Transitional Provisions, Savings) Order 2009, SI 2009/1941.

[64] Insolvency Act 1986, Sch B1, paras 25(c) and 39.

6.115 Following the changes to the Insolvency Act 1986 that were made by the Enterprise Act 2002, there is now a general prohibition on appointing an administrative receiver unless the floating charge was created prior to the date on which the relevant provisions of the Enterprise Act 2002 came into force (i.e. 15 September 2003) or one of a limited number of exceptions to the general prohibition applies.[65] The question as to whether any receiver appointed over all or substantially all of the assets of the company would be deemed to be an administrative receiver is therefore now highly relevant. If such a receiver were to be deemed to be an administrative receiver, the appointment may be contrary to the prohibition in section 72A. The Insolvency Act 1986 does not deal with the consequences of an appointment being in breach of section 72A but there is a risk that such an appointment would be invalid, in which case the receiver may be a trespasser.

6.116 However, it is no longer possible to appoint an administrative receiver in respect of a foreign registered company.[66] Despite this, in this example, although C has its centre of main interests in France, it may still be incorporated in England (although the presumption under the Regulation is that the centre of main interests is the place of incorporation). If C is incorporated in England, any receiver appointed by the bank over all the assets would clearly be an administrative receiver and so the security agreement would need to have been created prior to 15 September 2003, or one of the exceptions to the general prohibition on appointing an administrative receiver would need to apply, before the bank could appoint such an receiver. If C is incorporated in France, as stated above it would not be possible to appoint an administrative receiver in respect of C (and this is probably also the case if C has registered particulars in England and Wales under Part 34 of the Companies Act 2006). No doubt a bank would wish to appoint a receiver over all the assets but to maintain that such an appointment did not amount to the appointment of an administrative receiver. Given the uncertainties the bank may wish to seek the direction of the court to clarify the position. Alternatively the bank could seek to rely on the fixed charge security and simply appoint a fixed charge receiver. Much will depend on whether the assets subject to the fixed charge are sufficient to pay the amount owing to the bank..

6.117 In a French *redressement*, preferential creditors (including post-order expenses and contracts) rank ahead of all security interests, including the claims of fixed

---

[65] Insolvency Act 1986, s 72A.

[66] This is the effect of the Companies Act 2006 (Consequential Amendments, Transitional Provisions and Savings) Order SI 2009/1941 which amended the definition of company for the purpose of the Insolvency Act 1986 to an 'entity registered under the Companies Act 2006 in England and Wales or Scotland'. There is some doubt as to whether an administrative receiver could be appointed in respect of a foreign registered company which has registered particulars under Part 34 of the Companies Act 2006. However, the better view is that such a foreign registered company would not fall within the new definition of company (as registering particulars is not the same as being an entity registered under the Companies Act 2006).

charge-holders. It could be argued that Article 4(2)(i) should have the effect of giving recognition to these priority rules across the European Union. However, for the reasons given above in paragraph 6.29 and paragraphs 6.93–6.94, English priority rules would apply in relation to the enforcement of the English law governed security rather than the priority rules in the main proceedings.

Example 4

Borrower D has its centre of main interests in France and assets located in France **6.118** and England. It also has a branch and assets in New York and the bank has taken security over the New York assets in a security agreement governed by, and perfected in accordance with, New York law. Would any insolvency proceedings commenced in France affect the bank's ability to enforce its security in New York? Could any bankruptcy proceedings commenced in New York have an effect on the enforcement of security in England?

Issues arising: summary

- The Regulation is only binding on Member States and so it would be a matter **6.119** of New York law (or US bankruptcy law) as to what effect the French insolvency proceedings had on the enforcement of security in New York.
- It may be possible to file for relief under chapter 7 or 11 of the US Bankruptcy Code on the basis of the branch in New York. As a matter of US law, the moratorium on creditor action as a consequence of the filing of a petition under the Bankruptcy Code would have a worldwide effect but it will be a matter for the English court to determine what effect the US bankruptcy proceedings have on the enforcement of security in England.
- Alternatively, the liquidator in the French insolvency proceedings may apply for recognition of those proceedings in the United States under chapter 15 of the US Bankruptcy Code. If such recognition is granted, there would be an automatic stay on the enforcement of the security over the assets in New York unless the US bankruptcy court ordered otherwise.

Issues arising: commentary

Article 5 will not apply in relation to the security granted over assets in New York. **6.120** As the Regulation is only binding on Member States of which the United States is, of course, not one, the New York court would not be required by the Regulation to recognize the insolvency proceedings opened in France. However, it may be possible for D to file a bankruptcy petition in New York or for the French liquidator to apply for recognition of the French insolvency proceedings under chapter 15 of the US Bankruptcy Code (which implemented in the United States the UNCITRAL Model Law on insolvency proceedings). It will then be a matter of US bankruptcy law as to what effect a full bankruptcy proceeding or an order recognizing the French proceedings under chapter 15 would have on the enforcement of the security over the assets located in New York.

6.121   Once main insolvency proceedings under the Regulation have been commenced in France, one option would be for the French liquidator to apply for recognition of the French insolvency proceedings as 'foreign main proceedings' under chapter 15 of the US Bankruptcy Code on the basis that D has its centre of main interests in France. Provided that the New York bankruptcy court is satisfied that D does indeed have its centre of main interests in France, the court would be obliged to recognize the proceedings as foreign main proceedings with the consequence that there would be an automatic stay on the enforcement of security over the assets in New York unless the court ordered otherwise. Unlike the former provisions of section 304 of the Bankruptcy Code, the US bankruptcy court would not need to be satisfied that, as a matter of French insolvency law, the stay on enforcement of security would extend to the assets in New York as chapter 15 expressly provides for a stay equivalent to that which would arise if bankruptcy proceedings were commenced under chapters 7 and 11 of the US Bankruptcy Code (see below) upon recognition of foreign main proceedings under chapter 15 of the US bankruptcy code.

6.122   Alternatively, D, or a creditor of D, may file a petition for bankruptcy proceedings under chapter 7 or 11 of the US Bankruptcy Code. The filing of a petition under chapter 7 or 11 of the US Bankruptcy Code creates and operates as an immediate continuing injunction against virtually all creditor actions against the debtor and so would prevent the enforcement of security in the United States (unless the secured creditor were to seek and obtain relief from the automatic stay).

6.123   In respect of the assets in England, if full bankruptcy proceedings were commenced in the United States, as a matter of US law, the stay would have extra-territorial effect but it would be a matter for the English court to determine whether it recognized the extra-territorial effect of the stay. If the bank had a presence in the United States, the bank would be subject to the in personam jurisdiction of the US bankruptcy court although the bank may be able to get relief from the stay.

Example 5

6.124   Company E has its centre of main interests in France and assets in both France and England. There is no establishment in England. The bank has lent monies to E to be applied for a particular purpose and that purpose has failed. As a matter of English law, a 'Quistclose trust'[67] has arisen in favour of the bank over monies in a bank account held through the English branch of a French bank. Can the

---

[67] Named after the decision in *Quistclose Investments Ltd v Rolls Razor Ltd* [1970] AC 567, considered by Lord Millett in the decision in *Twinsectra Ltd v Yardley* [2002] UKHL 12 and recently by the Court of Appeal in *Gabriel v Little* [2013] EWCA Civ 1513.

bank enforce its beneficial interest under the Quistclose trust notwithstanding any insolvency proceedings which may be opened in France?

Issues arising: summary

- The main proceedings would be in France and it would not be possible to open insolvency proceedings in England.   **6.125**
- The question here is whether Article 5 is intended to cover more than the rights which are traditionally considered to be security rights (such as the pledge, mortgage, charge, or lien). There is nothing in Article 5 which suggests that the meaning of a right in rem should be restricted in this way.
- The issue also arises as to which law should determine whether a right in rem arises. According to the Virgos-Schmit Report, this matter should be determined by the *lex rei sitae* of the bank account as the Regulation does not define what is meant by a right in rem. It is consistent with the general principle of the Regulation that proprietary rights which are recognized by the *lex rei sitae* of the assets should not be disturbed by the Regulation. However, in certain cases, different Member States may reach different views as to where the *lex rei sitae* is to be found, particularly in the case of intangible assets. In this particular example, it is not clear whether the bank account should be deemed to be located in England (as the place of the branch holding the account) or France (as the place where the bank is likely to have its centre of main interests).

Issues arising: commentary

The question arises in this case whether Article 5 would allow the bank to rely on and enforce rights in rem which may be recognized as a matter of English law but which may not be recognized under French law as the law governing the effects of the main proceedings pursuant to Article 4. In the example given, it is not clear whether rights under a Quistclose trust would be recognized in French insolvency proceedings but it is assumed for the purposes of this example that they would not be.[68]   **6.126**

The Regulation does not define 'rights in rem' (as this may run the risk of describing as a right in rem something which would not be so regarded by the Member State where the assets are located).[69] The Virgos-Schmit Report suggests that the characterization of a right as a right in rem must be sought in the national law which, according to normal pre-insolvency conflict of laws rules, governs rights   **6.127**

---

[68] It is generally accepted that a trust of any kind cannot arise under French law although the French court has been prepared to recognize the effects of a trust between the trustee and beneficiary and, to a certain extent, has been prepared to accept the enforceability of the trust as against third parties, where that trust arises as a matter of the law of another jurisdiction. It is less clear whether such a trust would be recognized in French insolvency proceedings, particularly if, as a matter of the law of the jurisdiction where the trust arose, the trust purported to extend to assets in France.

[69] Virgos-Schmit Report, para 100 (app 2 below).

in rem (in general, the *lex rei sitae* at the relevant time).[70] However, neither the Regulation nor the Virgos-Schmit Report gives any guidance as to which court is to apply its normal pre-insolvency conflict of laws rules in determining this issue. In the current example, it is unclear whether a declaration should be sought from the English court (if that is where the constructive trust arises) or from the French court (as the jurisdiction of the main proceedings). In the case of a right in respect of a movable or intangible asset, it is possible that different courts could reach different decisions regarding the location of the *lex rei sitae* and the Regulation does not give any guidance as to where the parties should go for such a declaration. This may be a matter which is suitable for a reference to the CJEU.

6.128 In the current case, applying the general rule under English common law, the asset in question (ie the chose in action created by the bank account in which the relevant monies are held) would be deemed to be situate in England as the place where that chose in action is payable. However, if the bank account constitutes a 'claim' for the purposes of Article 2(g) of the Regulation, the application of that Article would appear to result in the asset being deemed to be situate in France (as the place where the bank through which the account is held has its centre of main interests). However, see paragraph 6.56 above for a contrary view and paragraph 6.59 above for how the RR will affect this issue). Hence in this example, the *lex rei sitae* of the asset, and therefore the law that is to determine whether there is a valid right in rem in respect of that asset, is unclear.

6.129 As a procedural matter, the bank should seek a declaration from the English court as to (i) the location of the asset; and (ii) the validity of the rights in rem under the Quistclose trust as a matter of English law. The bank may be able to rely on this declaration for the purposes of Article 5 in the absence of any challenge of the jurisdiction of the English court to decide this matter.

Example 6

6.130 Borrower F has its centre of main interests in England and assets in England and the Netherlands. There is no establishment in the Netherlands. The bank has entered into a Dutch law governed loan agreement and has taken security over the assets in the Netherlands pursuant to Dutch law. A company voluntary arrangement ('CVA') is proposed in respect of F in England which would have the effect of discharging F's debts. What effect would the CVA have on the bank's ability to enforce its security in the Netherlands?

Issues arising: summary

6.131 • As the centre of main interests is in England, a CVA can be implemented as main proceedings and the effects of the CVA would be recognized by all Member States.

---

[70] ibid.

- Under English insolvency law, a CVA can only affect the rights of a secured creditor to enforce its security if the secured creditor consents to the proposals. Hence the bank is unlikely to consent to the CVA unless it considers that its position is protected in both England and the Netherlands. There is an academic question, however, as to whether Article 5 would still enable the bank to enforce its security in the Netherlands if the bank did consent to the CVA in England and the CVA has the effect of discharging F's debt to the bank. The Regulation is not clear in this regard.

Issues arising: commentary

Prior to the Regulation coming into force, as a matter of English insolvency law, the discharge or variation of contractual rights which arose pursuant to a CVA or scheme of arrangement was effective in relation to all the obligations of the debtor, no matter what the governing law of the debt in question was and regardless of the domicile of the creditor concerned. Hence, an English CVA (as a matter of English law) would be effective to discharge or vary any liabilities owed by F to the bank under the Dutch law governed loan agreement. **6.132**

This will still be the case now that the Regulation has come into force. Where the main insolvency proceeding in question is a CVA under English law and the arrangement has the effect of varying or discharging the obligations of F, then English law (as the law of the Member State where the main proceedings are opened) will determine the conditions for and the effects of closure of the insolvency proceedings, in particular by composition, and creditors' rights after the closure of insolvency proceedings.[71] Furthermore, the CVA will have the same effect in any other Member State as it does under English law.[72] Hence English law will determine the effectiveness of the discharge or variation of the bank's contractual rights and not Dutch law as the proper law of the loan agreement. **6.133**

However, as the bank is a secured creditor, under English insolvency law, the CVA can only affect the rights of the bank to enforce its security if it consents to the proposals.[73] It is unlikely that the bank would be advised to do so unless the terms of the CVA provided that the bank was to be paid in priority to unsecured creditors in accordance with its security rights. **6.134**

However, main proceedings commenced in a Member State other than the United Kingdom could make provision for the variation or discharge of the obligations of the debtor and could potentially, as a matter of the insolvency law of the relevant Member State, affect the rights of secured creditors to enforce their security (even if they did not consent to the proceedings) (see Example 8 below). It appears that, but **6.135**

---

[71] Arts 4(2)(j) and (k).
[72] Art 17(1) applies to judgments opening proceedings. Where a CVA is approved within an administration, there will be a court judgment but otherwise the 'judgment opening the CVA' for the purposes of Art 17(1) will have to be the decision of the meeting of creditors.
[73] Insolvency Act 1986, s 4(3).

for Article 5, the effect of the Regulation would be that the English courts would have to recognize and give effect to the discharge even in cases where the underlying obligation is governed by English law.[74] As far as the authors are aware this issue is yet to be tested before the courts.

6.136 If, as a matter of the insolvency law of the relevant Member State referred to above, the main proceeding has the effect of discharging the obligations of the debtor in all jurisdictions, the question arises whether Article 5 would allow a secured creditor to enforce its security in another Member State notwithstanding the discharge of the secured liability pursuant to the main proceedings. The Regulation is not clear in this regard. Whilst Article 5 states that the opening of proceedings shall not 'affect' the rights in rem of creditors in respect of assets in another Member State, it could be argued that this does not prevent the discharge of the secured liability. However, without any underlying secured liability for the security to secure, the rights in rem would be worthless. This is a matter which it might be appropriate to refer to the CJEU. See also paragraph 6.62 above.

6.137 The practical advice to the bank in this example must be to take great care before consenting to a CVA which could have the effect of discharging secured liabilities, even if the bank is relying on its rights to enforce its security over assets outside the United Kingdom.

Example 7

6.138 Borrower G has its centre of main interests in Spain and an establishment in England. The bank has security over assets in Italy (where there is no establishment) under a security document governed by Italian law. Is it possible to have a CVA in England and, if so, what effect will this have on the bank's ability to enforce its security in Italy?

Issues arising: summary

6.139 • Main proceedings will need to be commenced in Spain but secondary proceedings can be commenced in England. If G is a company, these proceedings would have to be voluntary or compulsory liquidation proceedings.
   • Whilst it is not possible to have a CVA as secondary proceedings, Article 34 allows secondary proceedings to be closed by way of composition proceedings. It is unclear whether this permits an exit to be made by way of an English CVA (which might be said to be contrary to the decision not to list a CVA in Annex B

---

[74] In the context of the discharge or compromise of an unsecured claim where the protection given by Art 5 is not available, this would seem to overturn the basic English rule currently applied by the English courts that only a variation or discharge under English law is effective to discharge obligations governed by English law. See Dicey and Morris (n 59 above) r 170, *Gibbs & Sons v Societe Industrielle et Commerciale de Metaux* [1886–90] All ER Rep 804 and *National Bank of Greece v Metliss* [1958] AC 509.

of the Regulation as a secondary proceeding in the United Kingdom) or whether the only potential exit route is by way of a scheme. For the purposes of this example, it is assumed that it is possible to have an English CVA under Article 34 if a liquidation is commenced in England.

• It is unclear what effect such a CVA would have on assets located outside England. This will be a matter of construction of both the Insolvency Act 1986 and the Regulation.

Issues arising: commentary

As there is an establishment in England, it will be possible to open territorial or secondary proceedings in that jurisdiction. It is not possible to carry out a CVA by way of secondary proceedings and these proceedings are limited to liquidation proceedings. **6.140**

However, Article 34 allows secondary proceedings to be closed by means of a res- **6.141** cue plan, composition, or comparable measure to the extent that such a measure is available in the local jurisdiction. The office-holder in the main proceedings in Spain must consent to the rescue plan, composition, or comparable measure unless the financial interests of the creditors in the main proceedings are not affected by the measure proposed. It is, however, unclear whether such a 'rescue plan, composition, or comparable measure' includes the proposal of an English CVA by the Spanish liquidator (or at least his consent to it), or whether it is limited to a scheme of arrangement (which is a composition which is not included as main proceedings for the United Kingdom and therefore, unlike a CVA, appears not to be considered to be an 'insolvency proceeding' for the purposes of the Regulation at all). If it were possible to open liquidation proceedings as secondary proceedings, and then exit from them via a CVA, it might be said to be contrary to the decision of the European Council not to list the English CVA as secondary proceedings in Annex B of the Regulation. This is a matter which may be suitable for a reference to the CJEU. However, for present purposes, it is considered to be at least a possible exit route. The other, perhaps more straightforward, composition which could be used to close the liquidation, would be a scheme of arrangement. Both are therefore suggested in this example as possible alternatives to close the liquidation.

Article 34(2) states that any restriction of creditors' rights arising from a com- **6.142** position or rescue will only apply to assets covered by the secondary proceedings and not to the debtor's other assets situated outside that Member State (unless creditors having an interest agree to the restriction of rights over assets in other Member States). Again, similar issues arise to those discussed in the context of Example 6. If the effect of the CVA or scheme of arrangement (as a matter of English insolvency law) is to release all claims (including those governed by laws other than English law and, in particular, the secured liabilities under the Italian security agreement), does this mean that a bank with a loan agreement governed

201

by Italian law would be prevented from pursuing assets outside England notwithstanding the provisions of Article 34(2) because the secured debt had been discharged? This does not appear to be the intention but the Regulation is not clear in this regard. Again, this issue is unlikely to arise in practice because the English CVA can only affect the rights of a secured creditor to enforce its security if it consents to the CVA. Whether a scheme can affect such rights will depend upon the wording of the scheme. In any event, this inability of a composition to affect security rights may not be the case in respect of other compromise proceedings in other Member States.

Example 8

6.143 Company H has its centre of main interests in France and assets (but not an establishment) in England. H has granted security over its assets to both senior and junior lenders. The financing agreements are governed by English law and include an intercreditor agreement which provides that, if the junior lenders recover any monies at a time when amounts are still due to the senior lenders, the junior lenders will hold those recoveries on trust for the senior lenders (ie standard turnover trust wording). The facility agreements require the unanimous consent of the lenders to any reduction in the amount of the secured indebtedness. H is placed into safeguard proceedings in France and the requisite majorities of creditors approve a plan whereby H's indebtedness under the facility agreements is reduced. Under the plan, it is proposed that the senior lenders will only receive 45 per cent of their indebtedness and the junior creditors will receive five per cent of their indebtedness. Notwithstanding the plan, can the senior lenders enforce their security over the assets in England and would the junior lenders be required to turn over to the senior lenders any amounts they receive pursuant to the terms of the intercreditor agreement?

Issues arising: summary

6.144 • Under Article 25 of the Regulation, a composition approved by the French court (as the court that commenced main insolvency proceedings in relation to H) must be recognized in all Member States. As with all main proceedings, the effect of the safeguard procedure is subject to Article 5. The question therefore arises as to whether Article 5 would enable the senior creditors: (i) to enforce their security over the assets in England notwithstanding the French composition; and (ii) to enforce their rights pursuant to the intercreditor agreement.

• For the reasons given in paragraph 6.62 above, it is not clear whether Article 5 merely protects the right in rem in the strict sense (ie the security interest over the relevant assets) or whether it also protects the underlying secured debt. Article 5 may be thought to enable a secured creditor to enforce its security over assets in another Member State notwithstanding a compromise of the secured indebtedness pursuant to the main proceedings, subject to the question of whether the rights in rem have in fact been compromised by the safeguard procedure.

- The impact of the composition on any intercreditor arrangements between the junior and senior lenders will depend upon French insolvency law (and whether such a composition purports to affect the rights of creditors *inter se* as a matter of French insolvency law). If the turnover trust provisions do not create rights in rem in favour of the senior lenders over H's assets, it is hard to see how the senior lenders could rely on Article 5 in order to enforce their rights pursuant to the intercreditor agreement.

Issues arising: commentary

The issues arising in relation to a compromise as part of main insolvency proceed- **6.145** ings, and its impact on rights in rem over assets in another Member State, are discussed in paragraphs 6.62 and 6.136 above. Although such a compromise must be recognized in all Member States pursuant to Article 25 of the Regulation, the authors consider that such recognition must be subject to Article 5.[75] Although there is a question as to whether a distinction can be drawn between the right in rem itself and the underlying secured debt (and there is a further factual and legal question as to whether this right itself has been compromised), assuming that there has been no compromise of the right in rem, it would seem to rob Article 5 of any purpose if the secured debt could be compromised to 45 per cent (or even 99.9 per cent) of its face value though a compromise in the main proceedings and the secured creditor could only enforce its security over assets in another Member State to the extent of the compromised debt.[76] Making these assumptions, the authors consider that Article 5 would enable the senior lenders to enforce their security over the assets in England notwithstanding the compromise as part of the French safeguard proceedings. This is subject, of course, to any 'no action' clauses in the security or other finance documents which may prevent the lenders taking any enforcement action otherwise than through the security trustee.

If, contrary to the view expressed above, Article 5 does not enable the senior lend- **6.146** ers to enforce their security over the assets in England (or if the senior lenders choose not to do so or are prevented from doing so by any 'no action' clauses), the question arises as to whether, pursuant to the intercreditor agreement, the senior lenders could require the junior lenders to turn over to them any recoveries which the junior lenders may make pursuant to the French main proceedings or whether the French main proceedings could affect the terms of the intercreditor agreement in this regard. The first question which arises is whether, as a matter of

---

[75] The contrary view has been taken by Professor Wessels in his article 'The Secured Creditor in Cross Border Finance Transactions under the EU Insolvency Regulation' (2003) 18 JIBL & Reg 135, 140.

[76] This is certainly the view of Philip Smart in 'Rights in Rem, Article 5 and the EC Insolvency Regulation: An English Perspective' (2006) 15 International Insolvency Review 17, 33.

French law, the safeguard proceedings are capable of affecting the rights of credi-tors *inter se* or whether such proceedings can only affect the position as between H and its creditors. If the French proceedings could have an impact on the position between creditors, the second question to ask is whether the senior lenders could rely on Regulation (including Article 5) to protect their rights under the intercredi-tor agreement.

6.147 It is understood that, as a matter of French law, a French compromise plan may seek to take effect so as to override the rights and priorities contained within an inter-creditor agreement. This is consistent with the position under English law where, if properly drafted, an English CVA may purport to release the claims of creditors against third parties (such as guarantors).[77] It will be a matter of French law as to whether such a release has extra-territorial effect and can affect rights and priori-ties under an English law governed agreement. If it does, it is arguable that, under Article 25, such effect would need to be recognized in England. It is difficult to see how Article 5 could protect the rights of the senior lenders under the intercreditor agreement. Article 5 refers to rights in rem over assets of the insolvent debtor; as a matter of English law, the turnover trust created by the inter-creditor agreement would create a right in rem over assets of the junior lenders (ie any recoveries made by them pursuant to the French compromise plan) but would not create rights in rem over assets of H.

Example 9

6.148 Company I has its centre of main interests in Germany and no establishments in any other Member State. In April 2002, it granted security to bank J over a bank account held through the English branch of Deutsche Bank AG pursuant to an English law security agreement. In 2008, I becomes insolvent and is placed into self-management proceedings in Germany. Such proceedings give rise to a stay on the enforcement of security. Can J enforce its security over the bank account not-withstanding the German stay?

Issues arising: summary

6.149 • The security agreement in this example was created before 31 May 2002 (ie the date on which the Regulation came into force). The issue arises as to what effect the second sentence of Article 43 of the Regulation will have in this regard. This is unclear.
   • In addition to issues and protections arising under the Regulation, J may also be able to rely on the Financial Collateral Directive (and the English and/or German law implementing such directive) in order to enforce its security not-withstanding the German moratorium.

---

[77] *Prudential Assurance Co Ltd v PRG Powerhouse Ltd* [2007] EWCH 1002.

Issues arising: commentary

The German insolvency proceedings in this example are opened after the coming **6.150** into force of the Regulation and therefore, pursuant to the first sentence of Article 43, the Regulation will apply in relation to those insolvency proceedings. Hence, pursuant to Articles 17 and 25, the effects of the German proceedings (including most probably the stay on security enforcement) are to be recognized in all other Member States.

However, the question arises as to whether the entry into of the security agreement **6.151** is an 'act done by the debtor before the entry into force of [the] Regulation'. For the reasons given in paragraph 6.70 above, we consider that the expression 'acts done' should be construed as actions undertaken to place a debtor into insolvency proceedings and not other 'acts' more generally. However, if this is not correct, and 'acts done' could extend to the entering into of a security agreement, by virtue of the second sentence of Article 43, the entry into of the security shall continue to be governed by the law which was applicable to it at the time it was done.

The interpretation of Article 43 in this regard is unclear and this is a matter which **6.152** may ultimately need to be referred to the CJEU. Using a broad interpretation of the expression 'acts done', Article 43 may have the effect that Article 5 does not apply in relation to the right in rem created by the English law security agreement and, instead, the extra-territorial effect of the German stay is to be determined by the law which was applicable to the security at the time it was created (which may be either English law as the governing law of the security agreement or the *lex rei sitae* of the secured asset). However, this interpretation could lead to arbitrary results with the German liquidator having to apply different choice of law rules regarding the impact of the German insolvency proceedings on rights in rem in other Member States depending on when those rights were created.

Alternatively, still using the broad interpretation, Article 43 may have the effect **6.153** that the creation, validity, and scope of the right in rem created pursuant to the security agreement are to be determined by the law that would have been applicable to determining such matters (ie generally the *lex rei sitae*) prior to the entry into force of the Regulation. The problems of interpretation regarding the *lex rei sitae* of bank accounts pursuant to the Regulation are discussed in paragraph 6.56 above. In the current example, the application of Article 2(g) of the Regulation could lead to the conclusion that the bank account is located in Germany (as the place of Deutsche Bank AG's centre of main interests) rather than England (as the place of the branch holding the account). On this analysis, the secured asset would not be located in a Member State other than the one in which the main insolvency proceedings are commenced. However, if (in any enforcement proceedings brought in England) English conflict laws outside the Regulation were to be applied on the basis of Article 43, this may lead to the conclusion that the secured asset was located in England.

6.154   Leaving aside the issues that arise under the Regulation, J may also be able to rely on Council Directive (EC) 2002/47 of 6 June 2002 on financial collateral arrangements (the 'Financial Collateral Directive') in order to enforce its security over the bank account (which would constitute 'financial collateral' for these purposes) notwithstanding the German moratorium. The application of the Financial Collateral Directive is beyond the scope of this book but, in brief, J's ability to rely on such legislation will depend upon how it has been implemented in Germany (and possibly England if the secured asset is deemed to be located there) and whether J has possession or control of the bank account.

Example 10

6.155   Company K has its centre of main interests in France and a number of bank accounts in England with English banks, including a deposit account which has been drafted as a 'flawed asset' (ie there is a contractual limitation on K's right to withdraw the deposit, eg if K becomes insolvent, thus qualifying the bank's repayment obligation). Will the contractual limitation on K's right to withdraw the deposit be recognized and upheld in the French insolvency proceedings?

Issues arising: summary

6.156   • The contractual limitation on the right to withdraw the deposit is not a right in rem (although it has the effect of security) and so would not fall within Article 5.

  • Although it is not entirely clear, a contractual limitation of this nature may be invalid as a matter of French insolvency law if it were deemed to be a termination of an outstanding contract by virtue of insolvency.

  • However, Article 13 may possibly give the bank a defence in any action brought by the French office-holder to recover the amount of the deposit. Whilst this Article may appear to be aimed primarily at fraudulent preferences, transactions at an undervalue, and other grounds for challenging antecedent transactions, it could have wider scope.

  • The question arises whether the bank would be able to rely on Article 13 in circumstances where there could be grounds on which a similar arrangement could be challenged as a matter of English insolvency law in circumstances where K is not in liquidation in England. The bank may be able to seek a declaration in England regarding the validity of the flawed deposit arrangement; Article 13 suggests that such a declaration would be upheld in France.

Issues arising: commentary

6.157   **Flawed deposits under English law** The flawed deposit arrangement described above is commonly used by banks in England as a form of quasi-security although the arrangement would usually restrict K's right to withdraw the amount of the deposit whilst any amounts remained outstanding from K rather than restricting these rights specifically on an insolvency of K. Under the usual arrangements, the bank is protected in the depositor's insolvency because, to the extent that there are any amounts outstanding from the depositor to the bank under other agreements, the depositor is not entitled to have the amount of the deposit returned to it. However, the flaw operates by way of a contractual limitation on, or qualification of, the depositor's rights in respect of the deposit and the arrangement does not create any right in rem in favour of the bank. Hence, although much would depend on the drafting, the arrangement would be unlikely to fall within Article 5.

As a matter of English law, it is possible that the contractual limitation would be **6.158** upheld on the insolvency of the depositor. The main concern would be that the contractual restriction on K's right to withdraw the deposit might be in breach of the anti-deprivation principle[78] if it was triggered by a liquidation of K and was seen as having the effect of removing from K's insolvent estate an asset (ie the deposit) which would otherwise have been available for the general body of creditors.[79] The fact that the asset was 'flawed' from the outset will not mean that the limitation will be automatically upheld by the English court. In particular, if the flawed asset is drafted so that it determines or changes on the insolvency of K, the English court has confirmed that the anti-deprivation principle is capable of applying. In such circumstances very broadly, the provision will only be effective if it can be shown that: (i) the transaction was commercially sensible and entered into good faith; and (ii) that the predominant purpose (or one of the main purposes) of the transaction was not to evade English insolvency law. As such questions go to matters of intention they may be challenging to determine in practice.

Main proceedings in France   As the centre of main interests is in France, main **6.159** proceedings would need to be opened in that jurisdiction. In those proceedings, French law will determine whether the deposit is an asset which forms part of K's estate (Article 4(2)(b)). French law will also govern the rules relating to the voidness, voidability, or unenforceability of the 'flaw' or contractual limitation on K's right to withdraw the deposit which may be detrimental to all the creditors (Article 4(2)(m)). However, English law, as the applicable law of the contract, will

---

[78] As set out by the Supreme Court in *Belmont Park Investments PTY Limited v BNY Corporate Trustee Services Limited and Lehman Brothers Special Financing Inc* [2011] UKSC 38. The broad effect of the anti-deprivation principle is that an agreement that provides that assets are to belong to a company until its insolvency, but are then to be taken away from the insolvent estate, is invalid as a matter of public policy. This is distinct from the *pari passu* principle considered in *British Eagle* [1975] 1 WLR 758 which reflects the principle that statutory provisions for pro rata distribution may not be excluded by a contract which gives one creditor more than its proper share.

[79] There is a similar concern that there may be an invalid disposition of H's assets for the purposes of the Insolvency Act 1986, s 127.

apply to the construction of the terms of the bank mandate which will determine the circumstances in which K is entitled to withdraw the deposit.

6.160 For the purposes of this example, we have assumed that French law would prevent the bank from relying on the termination provisions in the mandate, although this would depend on the specific drafting of the deposit arrangement.[80]

6.161 **Article 13** The question arises whether Article 13 can be used as a defence by the bank in any action bought by the French office-holder to recover the amount of the deposit. The Virgos-Schmit Report states that 'Article 13 acts as a veto against the invalidity of the act decreed by the law of the State of the opening' (ie in this case French law) and that the aim of the Article is to uphold the legitimate expectations of creditors or third parties regarding the validity of the act under the normally applicable national law and to prevent interference from a different '*lex concursus*'.[81]

6.162 In order for the defence to be available, it would be necessary for the bank to establish:

(a) that the contractual limitation on K's right to withdraw the deposit was 'subject to' English law and not French law (ie the law of a Member State other than the state of the opening of the proceedings). It is likely that reference would be made to English law as the governing law of the contract concerning the deposit;

(b) that English law does not allow a challenge first by 'any means' and secondly 'in the relevant case'. It is not clear how the expression 'any means' in Article 13 relates to the expression 'in the relevant case'. For example, where the transaction is governed by English law, and, as may be the case in this example, may be challengeable by a liquidator or administrator of the debtor in England (but is not challengeable outside of such insolvency proceedings), is there a 'means' of challenging the transaction 'in the relevant case' where, in the relevant case, it might not be possible to commence English insolvency proceedings (as would be the case here as K does not have an establishment in England—the mere presence of assets does not amount to an

---

[80] Under French law, the contractual limitation on K's right to withdraw the deposit may not be upheld by the French court if it is triggered by K's insolvency and is deemed to be a termination of an existing contract (*contrats en cours*). A termination clause pursuant to which a contract is automatically terminated in the case of the opening of formal insolvency proceedings is null and void under French insolvency law and, notwithstanding any contractual provision to the contrary, the insolvency office-holder may elect either to continue or to terminate the existing contract. As a matter of French law, the French office-holder may be entitled to require performance of such contracts even if the contracts are governed by foreign law (Art L.621-28 of the Commercial Code). There are a number of exceptions (eg in relation to close-out netting in an insolvency situation) but these are unlikely to apply.

[81] Virgos-Schmit Report, paras 135–139 (app 2 below).

establishment)?[82] Furthermore, if the challenge in France is being made on the basis of, for example, French transaction at an undervalue provisions, is it only necessary to consider the equivalent English transaction at an undervalue provisions (on the basis that this is the means of challenge in the relevant case) or can other English provisions be taken into account (both other insolvency provisions and non-insolvency specific provisions)?[83] Given the above, the application of Article 13 in practice is currently far from clear and, despite the decision of the EFTA court referred to in footnote 83, the issues would benefit from a referral to the CJEU.

What is not clear is whether the bank would be able to rely on Article 13 in order **6.163** to establish that there was not a disposal of an asset pursuant to English law as the law governing K's entitlement to the return of the deposit. This is a question which might be appropriate for reference to the CJEU.

Example 11

The centre of main interests of borrower L is in Luxembourg and it has an estab- **6.164** lishment in England. The bank has a claim against L under an English law governed unsecured loan agreement but also has an obligation to L in respect of a deposit account located in England and governed by English law terms and conditions. L becomes insolvent and the bank wants to be able to set-off against

---

[82] Para 137 of the Virgos-Schmit Report suggests that regard must be had to the insolvency and general rules of the applicable law but this may require some juggling to decide when the 'deemed' English proceedings would have been commenced in order to determine whether the transaction is within the relevant claw-back period.

[83] Para 137 of the Virgos-Schmit Report indicates that such a restriction should not be read into Art 13 and that 'any means' should be interpreted to mean that the act or transaction in question cannot be challenged by using either rules applicable on an insolvency or other general rules of English law. This view is supported by a decision of the EFTA court in Case E-28/13 *In the matter of LBI hf v Merrill Lynch International Ltd* which concerned Art 30 of Directive 2001/24/EC on the reorganisation and winding up of credit institutions (CIWUD). Art 30 is the equivalent provision in CIWUD to Art 13 of the Regulation and is in substantially the same form as Art 13. Accordingly, decisions on Art 30 of CIWUD will be persuasive when a court is considering Art 13 of the Regulation. The EFTA court confirmed that, as long as the act is regarded as detrimental to the entire mass of creditors, it does not matter whether the possibility of challenge is classified as part of the insolvency law. This indicates that, when considering the words 'any means of challenge', all grounds of challenge should be considered, both insolvency and contractual (and potentially wider). The EFTA court also confirmed that where the act detrimental to all the creditors is capable of challenge in principle only under the law of the state governing the act (eg where for example in theory the act could be challenged as a transaction at an undervalue but for the expiry of the relevant hardening period) then this alone will not cause a defence under Art 30 to fail. It is necessary to consider the precise facts of the case in question, including any procedural laws which mean that the claim would, for example, be time barred. Therefore, even where the act may be challenged in principle under the law of the state governing it, it will be sufficient for the defendant to prove that the requirements for such a challenge are not fulfilled in the specific case in hand in order to be able to rely on the defence. While a decision of the EFTA court is not binding in EU Member States, such decisions are seen as highly persuasive and it is expected that the European Court of Justice and EU Member States' courts will have regard to the EFTA court's decision when considering Art 13 of the Regulation.

its obligation in respect of the deposit account the amounts owed to it by L under the loan agreement.[84]

Issues arising: summary

6.165
- Main proceedings in respect of L must be commenced in Luxembourg but secondary proceedings can be commenced in England.
- The conditions in which rights of set-off may be invoked in the main proceedings will be a matter of Luxembourg insolvency law.
- However, Article 6 provides additional protection for certain rights of set-off which are not available in the main proceedings. Rights of set-off which are permitted by and arise in accordance with the law applicable to L's claim cannot be affected by the opening of insolvency proceedings. This leads to questions regarding the law applicable to L's claim.
- If the set-off rights which are relied upon under Article 6 are only available in a liquidation of L in England, it may be necessary to commence liquidation proceedings as secondary proceedings under the Regulation in order to make use of those set-off rights, although this is not clear.

Issues arising: commentary

6.166 As the centre of main interests is in Luxembourg, main insolvency proceedings would be opened in this jurisdiction and Luxembourg law would determine the conditions under which rights of set-off could be invoked in the main proceedings.[85] However, this will not be attractive to the bank because rights of set-off are very limited under Luxembourg law. The bank will not wish to pay over to L the amount of the deposit and then claim for the full amount owing by L pursuant to the loan agreement.

6.167 Article 6 may provide an answer for the bank. This Article states that the opening of insolvency proceedings shall not affect the right of creditors to demand the set-off of their claims against the claims of the debtor where such a set-off is permitted by the law applicable to the insolvent debtor's claim. In the case of L's claim in respect of the deposit, it is likely that the applicable law will be English law as the governing law of the deposit agreement.[86] The position may be less clear in relation to a cross-claim which arises as a matter of tort; there may be an issue regarding which choice of law rules should decide the applicable law in a case involving a foreign element.

---

[84] These facts are based on the decision in *Re Bank of Credit and Commerce International SA (No 10)* [1997] Ch 213, although that case involved the insolvency of a credit institution which would not be subject to the Regulation.

[85] Art 4(2)(d).

[86] The nature and type of set-off seem to be irrelevant for the purposes of Art 6 which simply focuses on the cross-claim which forms the basis of the creditor's set-off and the law relating to it.

Depending on the terms of the deposit agreement, it may be that, as a matter of **6.168** English law, the bank does not have a right of pre-insolvency set-off (for example because the bank has agreed to repay the amount of the deposit without set-off or counterclaim). However, on an English liquidation, the bank may well have a right of set-off under Rule 4.90 of the Insolvency Rules 1986 (which is mandatory and overrides any contractual exclusions of set-off if the requisite conditions for set-off under Rule 4.90 are met). This raises the question whether the bank will need to open secondary insolvency proceedings (ie liquidation proceedings) in respect of L in England in order to benefit from the safe-harbour provisions in Article 6. Although Article 6 is silent in this regard, it is possible that the bank could not rely on a right of insolvency set-off unless L were in liquidation in England (although this is not clear).

Where there is an establishment in England (as is the case in this example), the **6.169** bank will be able to open secondary, liquidation proceedings in England. Hence, the Regulation will not change the position which arose in *Re Bank of Credit and Commerce International SA (No 10)*[87] in which the court held that, even though winding-up proceedings in England were ancillary to the Luxembourg proceedings (because BCCI was incorporated there), certain mandatory English rules applied including the application of the set-off provisions under rule 4.90 of the Insolvency Rules 1986.

However, if I does not have an establishment in England, so that secondary pro- **6.170** ceedings cannot be opened there, it is possible that Article 6 would entitle the bank to rely on the provisions of rule 4.90 (although this is not clear and as such is a matter that would benefit from a referral to the CJEU).

---

[87] [1997] Ch 213.

7

FINANCIAL INSTITUTIONS

A. General and Background

General

Article 1(2) of Regulation (EU) 2015/848 of the European Parliament and of the Council of 20 May 2015 on insolvency proceedings (recast) (the Recast Regulation, 'RR'[1]) provides that: **7.01**

---

[1] The RR is a recast of Council Regulation (EC) 1346/2000 of 29 May 2000 on insolvency proceedings, [2000] OJ L160 (Original Regulation, OR). The RR will apply to insolvency proceedings (as defined in the RR) opened after 26 June 2017 (see Article 84(1) RR). Prior to that date, the OR will continue to apply. In the following paragraphs, reference is therefore made to both the OR and RR.

This Regulation shall not apply to proceedings referred to in paragraph 1 that concern:
(a) insurance undertakings;
(b) credit institutions;
(c) investment firms and other firms, institutions and undertakings to the extent that they are covered by Directive 2001/24/EC; or
(d) collective investment undertakings.

Before turning to a consideration of the regime or regimes which might be said to apply to each of the entities set out in this Article 1(2) taking into account the effect of Articles 9(1) and 12(1) RR (equivalent to Articles 6 and 9 OR, respectively),[2] it is proposed to review the major legal and policy elements behind the need to segregate these aspects of the financial services markets designated by these Articles from the general ambit of the Insolvency Regulation.[3]

Basic EU framework for financial institution insolvencies

7.02 For all of the categories of financial institutions listed above, European regulation has been adopted so that they can and must make use of a single authorization granted by the home Member State's supervisory authority. This form of authorization has often been referred to as the European passport. In practical terms it means that the financial institution is allowed to operate branches in other Member States without further authorization from the relevant host state or states.

7.03 The original regulation introducing the European passport for insurance undertakings and credit institutions, however, did not contain coordination rules in the event of the insurance undertaking's or credit institution's reorganization or winding-up. To fill this gap, the European legislature introduced in 2001 both the Council Directive (EC) 2001/17 (Insurance Directive)[4] and the Council Directive (EC) 2001/24 on the reorganisation and winding up of credit institutions (the Credit Institutions Directive or Winding-up Directive).[5]

7.04 Recitals (1) and (2) of the Credit Institutions Directive expressly state that it is in the interests of the proper functioning of the internal market first that coordination rules be established at Community level in order to regulate reorganization measures or winding-up proceedings with regard to credit institutions and secondly, that any obstacles otherwise set up in the face of the freedom of establishment and of the provision of services within the Community be alleviated or

---

[2] For a fuller review of these provisions, see ch 8 below.
[3] [2015] OJ L 141. The subject matter of this chapter is covered extensively in a related publication, G Moss and B Wessels (ed), *EU Banking and Insurance Insolvency* (2006). A completely revised new edition of this book will be published by OUP in the course of 2016/2017.
[4] [2001] OJ L110.
[5] [2001] OJ L125.

removed, especially in the case of institutions holding or operating branches in other Member States.

There is a difference of approach with regard to the Insurance Directive. In par- **7.05** ticular, Recital (3), while promoting the benefits of the establishment of coordination rules, if anything militates against the need to engage in a 'winding-up situation'.[6]

As a consequence of the financial crisis, a so-called Banking Union has been **7.06** established, which consists of three legs. First, a Single Supervisory Mechanism has been put in place, under which the European Central Bank acts as the single prudential supervisor responsible (directly or indirectly) for all credit institutions in the Eurozone and states that wish to accede.[7] This should contribute to the prevention of bank insolvencies and will be discussed more extensively below. A harmonized bank insolvency regime for the EU forms the Banking Union's second leg. Initially, the Commission proposed to create a common European deposit guarantee scheme as the third leg of the Banking Union, but this has proven too ambitious politically. A recast of the deposit guarantee scheme Directive, however, has been adopted on 16 April 2014.[8]

The EU harmonized bank insolvency regime, or Banking Union's second leg **7.07** represents a major overhaul of the rules governing credit institutions and investment firms that experience financial difficulties. It provides for a comprehensive framework with an aim to 'provide authorities with a credible set of tools to intervene sufficiently early and quickly in an unsound or failing institution so as to ensure the continuity of the institution's critical financial and economic functions, while minimising the impact of an institution's failure on the economy and financial system'.[9] It consists both of a Bank Recovery and Resolution Directive (BRRD)[10] and a Single Resolution Mechanism (SRM). While the BRRD applies to all EU Member States, its application in the Eurozone has been unified by means of the SRM. Under this mechanism, established by a Single Resolution

---

[6] Cf Recital (6) in the Credit Institutions Directive which expressly states that it is 'necessary to establish mutual recognition by the Member States of the measures taken by each of them to restore to viability the credit institutions which it has authorised'.

[7] Council Regulation (EU) 1024/2013 of 15 October 2013 conferring specific tasks on the European Central Bank concerning policies relating to the prudential supervision of credit institutions, OJ L287/63.

[8] Directive 2014/49/EU of the European Parliament and of the Council of 16 April 2014 on deposit guarantee schemes, OJ L173.

[9] Recital (5) Bank Recovery and Resolution Directive.

[10] Directive 2014/59/EU of the European Parliament and of the Council of 15 May 2014 establishing a framework for the recovery and resolution of credit institutions and investment firms and amending Council Directive 82/891/EEC, and Directives 2001/24/EC, 2002/47/EC, 2004/25/EC, 2005/56/EC, 2007/36/EC, 2011/35/EU, 2012/30/EU and 2013/36/EU, and Regulations (EU) No 1093/2010 and (EU) No 648/2012, of the European Parliament and of the Council, OJ L173.

Mechanism Regulation (SRMR),[11] 'a centralised power of resolution is established and entrusted to the Single Resolution Board [...] and to the national resolution authorities.'[12]

Overview

7.08 At the moment of writing, the reorganization and winding-up of insurance undertakings still is the subject of the Insurance Directive. As of 1 January 2016, this Directive will have been repealed by Directive 2009/138/EC of the European Parliament and of the Council of 25 November 2009 on the taking-up and pursuit of the business of Insurance and Reinsurance (Solvency II).[13] In essence, the Insurance Directive has been transposed to Title IV (Articles 267–296) of Solvency II. For the purposes of this chapter, both the Insurance Directive and Solvency II will be referred to. In particular the second Recital of the Insurance Directive stated that insurance Directives providing for a single authorization system within a 'Community scope' for insurance undertakings do not contain coordination rules in the event of there being winding-up proceedings. It added that the internal market and the protection of creditors were best served by a separate regime in respect of insurance undertakings.

7.09 The same principle underlies the relevant Directive regarding credit institutions. This Directive being Council Directive (EC) 2001/24 on the reorganisation and winding up of credit institutions (the Credit Institutions Directive or Winding-up Directive)[14] had to be implemented by Member States by 5 May 2004 and has, most recently, been amended by the BRRD. The Credit Institutions Directive in effect grew out of the 2000 Banking Directive.[15]

7.10 As stated above, the BRRD and SRM have been adopted as a consequence of the financial crisis and represent a comprehensive framework of rules governing credit institutions and investment firms that experience financial difficulties.

7.11 However, the European legislature still has not addressed financial institution insolvencies in a comprehensive manner but rather tailors instruments to

---

[11] Regulation (EU) 806/2014 of the European Parliament and of the Council of 15 July 2014 establishing uniform rules and a uniform procedure for the resolution of credit institutions and certain investment firms in the framework of a Single Resolution Mechanism and a Single Resolution Fund and amending Regulation (EU) No 1093/2010, OJ L225.

[12] Recital (11) SRMR.

[13] [2009] OJ L335, as amended by Directive 2013/58/EU of the European Parliament and of the Council of 11 December 2013 amending Directive 2009/138/EC (Solvency II) as regards the date for its transposition and the date of its application, and the date of repeal of certain Directives (Solvency I), OJ L341.

[14] [2001] OJ L125.

[15] [2000] OJ L12. In turn amended by Directive (EC) 2000/28 [2000] OJ L275. The Banking Directive has been recast in European Parliament and Council Directive (EC) 2006/48. However, for the purposes of this chapter reference will continue to be made to the 2000 Directive and its terms.

specific institutions or to specific functions these institutions perform. More specifically, it has regulated financial institutions where they act as participants in market infrastructures and as counterparties in certain financial collateral transactions. It concerns Directive 98/26/EC of the European Parliament and of the Council of 19 May 1998 on settlement finality in payment and securities settlement systems[16] and Directive 2002/47/EC of the European Parliament and of the Council of 6 June 2002 on financial collateral arrangements,[17] respectively.

Earlier background

For a brief survey of the evolution of the earlier Directives in particular Council **7.12** Directive (EC) 88/361,[18] see the corresponding chapter in the first edition of this work.[19]

B. Financial Institutions excluded from the Insolvency Regulation

Recital (9) RR requires that the Regulation should apply to insolvency proceedings **7.13** concerning national and legal persons,[20] whereas Recital (19) specifically excludes four categories of financial institutions and related entities, namely:

(i)   insurance undertakings;
(ii) credit institutions;
(iii) investment firms and other firms, institutions and undertakings to the extent that they are covered by Directive 2001/24/EC of the European Parliament and of the Council; and
(iv) collective investment undertakings.[21]

The same Recital (19) stresses that these four categories are subject to special arrangements and notes that 'the national supervisory authorities have wide-ranging powers of intervention'. The four categories in question, however, are not further considered, let alone defined by the RR. One has to turn to other instruments of Community law for that purpose.[22]

---

[16] [1998] OJ L 166.
[17] [2002] OJ L 168.
[18] [1988] OJ L178/5.
[19] See pp 132–33 entitled 'Background: the treaty framework'.
[20] The insolvency proceedings to which the Insolvency Regulation applies are set out in Annex A.
[21] The same provision can be found in Art 1(2) RR. Cf. Art 1(2) OR.
[22] Note, however, *FSA v Dobb White & Co* [2004] BPIR 479 which stresses that insofar as an entity otherwise caught by the four categories but not otherwise subject to a discrete Community regime is concerned, the Insolvency Regulation will apply.

Insurance undertakings

7.14   Insurance undertakings are the subject of the Insurance Directive and Solvency II. Most of the matters provided for by those Directives are reflected in the Credit Institutions Directive and vice versa.

7.15   Unfortunately, the Insurance Directive did not contain a definition of an 'insurance undertaking'. An 'insurance undertaking' is any entity covered by the First Council Directive (EEC) 73/239, which dealt with direct insurance other than life insurance as well as by Council Directive (EEC) 79/267 (Direct Life Insurance Directive), which dealt with direct life assurance. Both of these Directives were supplemented by Council Directive (EEC) 92/96 as further supplemented (the so-called Third Life Assurance Directive), which was, in its turn, repealed and replaced by Directive 2002/83/EC of the European Parliament and of the Council of 5 November 2002 concerning life assurance.[23]

7.16   Solvency II covers direct life and non-life insurance undertakings as well as reinsurance undertakings. It also contains a definition of 'insurance undertaking' in Article 13(1), which directs the reader via Article 14 to Article 2(2) for non-life insurance (which directs, in part, to activities of the classes set out in Part A of Annex I), and to Article 2(3) for life insurance (which provision also contains a list of activities).

Credit institutions

7.17   Under Article 4(1)(1) of Regulation (EU) 575/2013 of the European Parliament and of the Council of 26 June 2013 on prudential requirements for credit institutions and investment firms and amending Regulation (EU) 648/2012 (CRR),[24] a 'credit institution' is 'an undertaking the business of which is to take deposits or other repayable funds from the public and to grant credits for its own account'. Article 2(5) of Directive 2013/36/EU of the European Parliament and of the Council of 26 June 2013 on access to the activity of credit institutions and the prudential supervision of credit institutions and investment firms, amending Directive 2002/87/EC and repealing Directives 2006/48/EC and 2006/49/EC (CRD IV)[25] excludes certain institutions, principally central banks of the Member States and other financial institutions such as friendly societies and post office giro institutions from this definition. Article 4(1)(17) CRR defines a 'branch' as meaning 'a place of business which forms a legally dependent part of an institution and which carries out directly all or some of the transactions inherent in the business of institutions'.

7.18   Article 1 Credit Institutions Directive refers to a precursor of CRD IV for the definition of 'credit institution' (which was, in pertinent part, identical to the

---

[23] [2002] OJ L 345.
[24] [2014] OJ L 176.
[25] [2014] OJ L 176.

definition quoted above), whilst Article 2 Credit Institutions Directive points to
CRR for the definition of 'branch' (Article 2).

Investment firms

Article 1(2)(c) RR (equivalent to Recital (9) OR) excludes from its scope 'invest-   **7.19**
ment firms and other firms, institutions and undertakings to the extent that they
are covered by Directive 2001/24/EC of the European Parliament and of the
Council'. Directive 2001/24/EC (the Credit Institutions Directive), however, does
not define, nor (directly) concern investment firms. It concerns credit institutions,
which nonetheless may also function as investment firms or other categories of
financial institutions. For the definition of 'investment firm', reference must be
had to Article 4(1)(1) of Directive 2014/65/EU of the European Parliament and of
the Council of 15 May 2014 on markets in financial instruments and amending
Directive 2002/92/EC and Directive 2011/61/EU (MiFID II),[26] which says that
an 'investment firm' 'means any legal person whose regular occupation or business
is the provision of one or more investment services to third parties and/or the performance of one or more investment activities on a professional basis'. 'Investment
services and activities' are then defined as 'any of the services and activities listed
in Section A of Annex I [of MiFID II] relating to any of the instruments listed in
Section C of Annex I [of MiFID II]'. In general terms, this will cover any enterprise
which regularly carries out a professional activity consisting of supplying third
parties with an investment service concerning securities as well as instruments
used in the money markets. This would include receiving or dealing with securities
either on the undertaking's own behalf or on behalf of third parties, and managing
investment portfolios on the same bases.

Collective investment undertakings

A 'collective investment undertaking' as such is not defined in EU legislation.   **7.20**
Yet the EU legislator has adopted two instruments that cover the most important (sub)categories of collective investment undertakings, viz. undertakings for
collective investment in transferable securities (UCITS) and alternative investment funds (AIFs). UCITS are regulated by means of Directive 2009/65/EC
of the European Parliament and of the Council of 13 July 2009 on the coordination of laws, regulations and administrative provisions relating to undertakings for collective investment in transferable securities (UCITS) (UCITS IV),[27]
and AIFs by means of Directive 2011/61/EU of the European Parliament and
of the Council of 8 June 2011 on Alternative Investment Fund Managers and

---

[26] [2014] OJ L 173. Confusingly, Art 1(3) Credit Institutions Directive, as added by Art 117
BRRD refers to investment firms as defined in CRR, which redirected to Directive 2004/39/EC,
the precursor of MiFID II.
[27] [2009] OJ L 302.

amending Directives 2003/41/EC and 2009/65/EC and Regulations (EC) 1060/2009 and (EU) 1095/2010 (AIFMD).[28]

7.21 Article 1(2) UCITS IV defines a UCITS as

> an undertaking: (a) with the sole object of collective investment in transferable securities or in other liquid financial assets referred to in Article 50(1) of capital raised from the public and which operate on the principle of risk-spreading; and (b) with units which are, at the request of holders, repurchased or redeemed, directly or indirectly, out of those undertakings' assets. Action taken by a UCITS to ensure that the stock exchange value of its units does not significantly vary from their net asset value shall be regarded as equivalent to such repurchase or redemption.

In short: open-ended collective investment funds, or any body whose sole aim is to deal with the collective investments of so called 'transferable securities' from capital raised from the public and whose operations are subject to the principles of risk spreading and risk sharing and the shares or units of which are, on the bearer's request, bought or paid back directly or indirectly from the assets of those bodies.[29]

7.22 Pursuant to Article 4(1)(a) AIFMD, alternative investment funds are 'collective investment undertakings, including investment compartments thereof which raise capital from a number of investors, with a view to investing it in accordance with a defined investment policy for the benefit of those investors and do not require authorisation pursuant to [UCITS IV].'

7.23 For purposes of the Insolvency Regulation, both in its original and recast versions, most probably both UCITS and AIFs as just defined are excluded from its scope, but maybe also other collective investment undertakings not so defined.

C. Settlement Finality and Collateral Directive

Settlement Finality Directive

7.24 In this context settlement in effect represents the satisfaction or payment of a monetary obligation owed or owing by a counterparty to a financial institution.

7.25 The Council Directive (EC) 98/26 on settlement finality in payment and securities settlement systems (Settlement Finality Directive)[30] had as its objective the reduction of settlement risk by providing principally for the finality of settlement of the transfers of funds and securities through payment and securities settlement systems, including cases where the insolvency of one party arises.

---

[28] [2011] OJ L 174.
[29] See the Virgos-Schmit Report 1996, para 60.
[30] [1998] OJ L166.

The netting or setting-off of claims will be enforceable after the opening of insol-   **7.26**
vency proceedings when there has been a prior 'transfer order'.[31] Also and importantly, insolvency proceedings shall not have retroactive effects on the rights and
obligations of a participant arising from, or in connection with, its participation
in a system before the moment of opening of such proceedings.[32] In words, the so-
called 00-hours rule is disapplied for this specific instance.

The RR expressly recognizes[33] that the specific provisions of the Settlement Finality   **7.27**
Directive in general take precedence over the general rules in the RR. As a major
derogation, the rights and obligations arising from, or in connection with, the participation of a participant in a settlement system is determined by the law governing
that system, should insolvency proceedings be opened against that participant.[34]
In addition, the rights of a system operator or of a participant to collateral security
provided to them in connection with a system, and the rights of central banks of
the Member States or the European Central Bank to collateral security provided
to them, are not to be affected by insolvency proceedings against the participant,
the system operator, a counterparty to central banks of the Member States or the
European Central Bank, or any third party which provided the collateral security,
whilst such collateral security may be realized for the satisfaction of those rights.[35]

Collateral Directive

The Collateral Directive addresses the complexities that can arise whenever repur-   **7.28**
chase agreements and similar transfers of title instruments are entered into. If the
creditor is exposed to a fall in the value of his or its collateral, provision is generally
made for the provision of top-up or substitute collateral. Also, a creditor may commonly terminate the contract and net all outstanding obligations upon the commencement of his counterparty's insolvency.

In June 2002, the European Parliament and Council Directive on financial col-   **7.29**
lateral arrangements (EC) 2002/47[36] (the Collateral Directive) was issued. It seeks
to address the form of potential imbalance described in the preceding paragraph
in relation to transactions which occur across or between EU Member States. For
instance, it aims to ensure that the operation of close-out netting provisions is
not hindered by, in short, insolvency law prescriptions.[37] Also, insolvency provisions are disapplied which declare invalid or void or reverse financial collateral
arrangements, as well as the provision of financial collateral on the sole basis
that the financial collateral arrangement has come into existence, or the financial

---

[31] Art 3(1) Settlement Finality Directive.
[32] Art 7 Settlement Finality Directive.
[33] Recital (27) and Art 9 RR (equivalent to Art 6 OR).
[34] Art 8 Settlement Finality Directive.
[35] Art 9(1) Settlement Finality Directive.
[36] [2002] OJ L168/43.
[37] Art 7 Collateral Directive.

collateral has been provided on the day of the commencement of winding-up proceedings or reorganization measures, or in a prescribed period prior to, and defined by reference to, the commencement of such proceedings or measures. Similarly, the provision of top-up or substitute collateral is thus safeguarded from insolvency provisions.[38]

D. Credit Institutions Directive

Common principles for bank and insurance company insolvencies

7.30 Although this is not the place to discuss the finer aspects of these principles, regard should be had to a number of important governing principles, which, to a greater or lesser extent, may affect an insolvency which spans more than one jurisdiction.

7.31 First, the concept inherent in the so-called principle of unity means that only one state, namely that state in which the registered seat, head office, or centre of main interests is located, should determine the course of the insolvency. In consequence, an overseas branch of a foreign company would be subject to the latter's laws and regulations. The governing law is referred to as the *lex concursus*.

7.32 Second, regard may be had to the principle of universality. Here the *lex concursus* will govern all the terms and effects of the insolvency and will do so beyond the territorial frontiers of the state where the insolvency proceedings have been opened. This is to be compared with the principle of territoriality which is self-explanatory. There may, however, be variations of one or both approaches in any given case. In general terms the Insurance Directive/Solvency II Title IV and the Credit Institutions Directive adopt the universalist approach.

7.33 Third, note should be taken of the principle of single entity. In practical terms, the insolvent entity will be wound up as a single legal entity by its home state. The assets of a branch will fall to be administered by the insolvency procedures instigated by that state's jurisdiction.[39]

7.34 If not capable of being elevated to the rank of relatively well recognized principles such as the ones discussed above, there are at least three other concepts which need to be borne in mind whenever insolvency-related issues arise with regard to financial institutions.

---

[38] Art 8 Collateral Directive.
[39] For the more nuanced BRRD approach, see below, para 7.57. Art 4(1)(43) CRR (defined below) provides that the home state means 'the Member State in which an institution has been granted authorization', while Art 4(1)(44) of the same CRR provides that the host state is 'the Member State in which an institution has a branch or in which it provides services'. Art 4(1)(17) CRR defines a branch as 'a place of business which forms a legally dependent part of an institution and which carries out directly all or some of the transactions inherent in the business of institutions'.

The first concept reflects a feature of some types of Community legislation which **7.35** seeks to ensure that a special group of persons or interests are protected in the event of financial difficulties in turn affecting the entity which deals with such persons: see, for example, Directive 2014/49/EU of the European Parliament and of the Council of 16 April 2014 on deposit guarantee schemes,[40] aimed to ensure that all branches of the same financial institutions are covered by means of a single guarantee scheme.

Analogous to the above concept is the type of measure whereby specific types **7.36** of financial or contractual positions are rendered exempt from the rules in certain Directives, for example the rules in the Settlement Finality and Collateral Directive discussed above.[41]

Finally, note should be taken of what is generally called the hotchpot rule. Basically, **7.37** this rule prevents a creditor from 'shopping around' for the best return whenever connected or parallel proceedings are opened or are in play. If such a creditor obtains more as a result of participation in one set of foreign proceedings than he would have got in the local or main jurisdiction, he should give credit or equalize matters in the former proceedings in respect of what he may have obtained in the latter proceedings.

Credit Institutions Directive: Scope and definitions

Pursuant to Article 1 Credit Institutions Directive, this Directive applies to credit **7.38** institutions, and, since BRRD, also to investment firms.

As indicated above,[42] the definition of 'credit institution' has to be gleaned from **7.39** Article 4(1)(1) CRR, namely 'an undertaking the business of which is to take deposits or other repayable funds from the public and to grant credits for its own account'.

For the definition of 'investment firm', reference must be had, as stated above, to **7.40** Article 4(1)(1) MiFID II, which says that an 'investment firm' 'means any legal person whose regular occupation or business is the provision of one or more investment services to third parties and/or the performance of one or more investment activities on a professional basis'. 'Investment services and activities' are then defined as 'any of the services and activities listed in Section A of Annex I [of MiFID II] relating to any of the instruments listed in Section C of Annex I [of MiFID II]'. Article 1(4) Credit Institutions Directive now states that in as far as resolution tools are applied and resolution powers are exercised to 'financial institutions, firms and parent undertakings' as covered by BRRD, the Credit Institutions Directive also applies to the same. These institutions are further defined (via Article 2 BRRD)

---

[40] [2014] OJ L 173.
[41] See above at paras 7.24 et seq.
[42] See above at para 7.17.

in Article 4 CRR. More notable for these purposes, financial institutions may be subsidiaries of, in short, a credit institution or investment firm, a (parent) financial holding company, or (parent) mixed holding company (Article 1(1)(b) BRRD).

7.41   A 'branch' is defined in Article 4(1)(17) CRR as meaning:

> a place of business which forms a legally dependent part of an institution and which carries out directly all or some of the transactions inherent in the business of institutions.[43]

7.42   Recital (3) makes it clear that the Credit Institutions Directive takes a single entity approach but only as between a credit institution and its branches. As a matter of principle, no such approach is taken as between the institution and its subsidiaries. The latter are treated as legally self-standing entities and thus subject to the laws of the Member States in which they are incorporated or by which they are regulated. In general terms, European law does not treat groups of companies as a single entity either for the purposes of general corporate law or with regard to insolvency law. Under the BRRD however, relevant authorities will have to co-operate.[44]

7.43   In the case of non-EU banks, it is only where such institutions have branches 'in at least some Member States of the Community' that the Directive will apply.[45]

7.44   Of equal, if not greater, importance are some of the major definitions in the Credit Institutions Directive. Two of the critical concepts in the Directive are 'reorganisation measures' and 'winding-up proceedings'.

7.45   The Directive defines 'reorganisation measures' in much the same terms as the Insurance Directive/Solvency II,[46] but it also employs the term 'administrator' to describe any person or body appointed by the administrative or judicial authorities whose task it is to administer such measures.[47] A 'liquidator' shall mean any person or body appointed by the administrative or judicial authorities 'whose task it is to administer winding-up proceedings'.[48]

7.46   Such 'winding-up proceedings' are defined as meaning 'collective proceedings opened and monitored by the administrative or judicial authorities of a Member State with the aim of realising assets under the supervision of those authorities,

---

[43] This is on the basis that the reference to 'headquarters' can be taken to mean 'head office'; reference should again be made to Art 6(2) of the 2000 Banking Directive which stipulates that each Member State shall require that 'any credit institution which is a legal person and which, under its national law, has a registered office shall have its head office in the same Member State as its registered office': now see Art 4 of Directive (EC) 2006/48.

[44] See below at paras 7.239–7.241.

[45] See Art 1(2) and Recital (22). Recital (22) appears to make it clear that the liquidations or administrations of both branches should in the event of concurrent insolvencies endeavour to coordinate their activities. Such language does not without more infer any element of binding obligation to cooperate.

[46] See below at para. 7.114.

[47] Art 2, fifth definition.

[48] Art 2, eighth dash.

including where the proceedings are terminated by a composition or other similar measure'.

The Credit Institutions Directive, unlike the Insurance Directive/Solvency II, **7.47** lists only two elements which constitute 'reorganisation measures' namely, first the aim of the measures must be to preserve or restore the financial situation of a credit institution and secondly, the effect of the measures is such that it must have a potential for affecting third parties' pre-existing rights, including measures involving the possibility of a suspension of payments, suspension of enforcement measures, or the reduction of claims.

Prior to the BRRD, the above definitions seemed to exclude formal regulatory inter- **7.48** vention designed to stem or stop a bank's increasingly worsening financial position: if nothing else such a step would not directly entail any direct effect upon the pre-existing rights of third parties.[49] Since BRRD, 'reorganisation measures' also include 'the application of the resolution tools and the exercise of resolution powers' provided for in the BRRD, to be discussed below.[50] As a consequence of those tools and powers, third parties' pre-existing rights are not necessarily affected.[51]

In relation to the definition of 'winding-up proceedings', the requisite elements **7.49** appear to be three-fold. First there must be a collective proceeding; secondly, such a proceeding must be opened and monitored by the administrative or judicial authorities of a Member State; and thirdly, they should be opened with the aim of realizing assets under the supervision of those authorities including where the proceedings are terminated by a composition or other similar means.

It can be seen that there are material differences between the above definitions and **7.50** those afforded to the same expressions in the Insurance Directive/Solvency II Title IV, the principal difference being that the present definition refers specifically to the winding-up process 'by a composition or other similar measure' without any specific reference to the absence or otherwise of a demonstrable insolvency (as is the case in the Insurance Directive/Solvency II Title IV).

Recital (5) of the Insurance Directive confirms that the approach in that Directive **7.51** to the concept of a winding-up is extremely open-ended and to that extent perhaps not entirely clear.[52] Indeed, it is not immediately apparent when a reorganization measure might be said to end and a winding-up proceeding begin. A line of demarcation might emerge on account of the fact that the latter type of proceeding must, in the case of a credit institution, be opened and monitored by a Member State's administrative or judicial authority.

---

[49] This view seems reinforced by Recitals (8)–(10).
[50] At paras 7.182 et seq.
[51] Cf the 'resolution objectives' set out in Art 31(2) BRRD.
[52] It is not, for example, clear whether a partial voluntary liquidation would be covered, that is one involving some form of limitation upon the liquidation as a whole.

7.52 What is clear, however, is the unqualified effect of Article 3 of the Credit Institutions Directive which provides that the 'administrative or judicial authorities of the home Member State must have sole power to decide upon and to implement the reorganisation measures' provided for in the law and practices in force in that Member State.[53]

7.53 Reverting to the various general principles set out above,[54] Article 3 affirms not only the principle of unity but also the principles of universality and single entity with regard to the effect of reorganization measures applicable to credit institutions.[55] Moreover, the same Article clothes the home Member State with exclusive jurisdiction exercised via its administrative or judicial authority to decide upon the implementation of one or more reorganization measures.[56]

7.54 Moreover, the Credit Institutions Directive ensures equality of treatment as between creditors. It does so by providing for one collective proceeding and it requires the authorities of the home Member State to adopt measures it considers necessary for creditors or other Member States to exercise such rights and to take such steps as the lodging of claims: see Article 16. Article 18 of the same Directive imposes an obligation on the liquidator to keep the creditors regularly informed.

Credit Institutions Directive: Selective commentary

7.55 Articles 1 and 2 of the Credit Institutions Directive determine the scope of the Directive. See on its scope the immediate preceding paragraphs.

7.56 Overall the Directive applies to the financial position of an EU bank with at least one branch within a Member State other than the state in which it has its head office. If, however, what purports to be a bank within a given national system does not satisfy the definition of a credit institution set out above, the Directive will not apply. Should that entity be subject to a form of collective proceeding, the Insolvency Regulation will generally apply.

7.57 It has already been pointed out[57] that the Credit Institutions Directive embraces the so-called single entity principle. This means that a credit institution and its branches will constitute a single entity. However, foreign subsidiaries of a credit institution are excluded: they will be subject to the law of the Member State in which they are authorized. As stated above, subsidiaries are included

---

[53] See Recital (6), first sentence, Credit Institutions Directive. See, for example EU Court of Justice judgement in Case C-85/12 *re LBI hf vs Kepler Capital Markets SA and Frédéric Giraux*, 24 October 2013, ECLI:EU:C:2013:697 for an extensive interpretation of Arts 3 and 9.

[54] At paras 7.30–7.37.

[55] See also Recital (16).

[56] This exclusiveness is nuanced by the introduction of resolution colleges under the BRRD. See below at para 7.164.

[57] See above at para 7.33.

in as far as resolution tools are applied or resolution powers are exercised under the BRRD and SRMR.

Other than under the BRRD and SRMR, as for groups of companies, there were **7.58** no principles of EU corporate and insolvency law which addressed themselves to entities larger than single corporate vehicles. On the other hand, principles of supervision within the EU banking sector may well address group economic interests. Also, the RR now contains provisions that resemble the rules of the BRRD and cater for the cooperation and communication where there are insolvency proceedings which relate to two or more members of a group of companies, as well as for 'group co-coordination proceedings'.[58] This is not to say that the courts across Member States may not still agree or arrange to entrust a reorganization measure to the same person or group of persons in respect of a group of interrelated entities operating within a particular Member State.

The aim reflected in this latter respect is explained in Recital (22), second sentence, **7.59** which addresses the operation of more than one branch within the European Union.[59] In such a case it is provided that 'the administrative or judicial authorities and the competent authorities as well as the administrators and liquidators should endeavour to co-ordinate their activities'.

Article 2 deals with some important definitions. The most important are 'home **7.60** Member State' and 'host Member State'. Both terms find their meanings in the CRR. A 'home Member State' means the Member State of origin, that is the state which grants authorization to the credit institution.[60] That is the state in which a reorganization measure or winding-up proceeding in respect of a credit institution must be opened. A 'host Member State' is a Member State in which a credit institution has a branch or in which it provides services.[61] A 'branch' according to the CRR is a 'place of business which forms a legally dependent part of an institution and which carries out directly all or some of the transactions inherent in the business of institutions'.

A number of other terms are defined in the Directive itself. For example, an 'admin- **7.61** istrator' is a person or body appointed by the administrative or judicial authorities whose task it is to administer reorganization measures. The latter are measures 'which are intended to preserve or restore the financial situation of a credit institution which could affect third parties' pre-existing rights, including measures involving the possibility of a suspension of payments, suspension of enforcement measures or reduction of claims'.

---

[58] See generally below at paras 8.746–8.806.
[59] As noted above at para 7.43, the Directive applies to the branches of a non-EU bank where such bank 'has branches in at least two Member States of the Community' Art 1(2): this is the so-called de minimis rule.
[60] Art 4(1)(43) CRR.
[61] Art 4(1)(44) CRR.

7.62 A 'liquidator' means any person or body appointed by the administrative or judicial authorities whose task it is to administer winding-up proceedings. This last expression means 'collective proceedings opened and monitored by the administrative or judicial authorities of a Member State with the aim of realizing assets under the supervision of those authorities including where the proceedings are terminated by a composition or other similar means'.

7.63 'Administrative or judicial authorities' are such administrative or judicial authorities of a Member State 'as are competent for the purposes of reorganisation measures or winding-up proceedings'. This will clearly cover a single centralized body in which all of these functions are vested, as well as a single body dealing with various aspects of the competencies under consideration. The way in which the competencies are divided up in a given case will depend on the particular Member State involved.

7.64 Article 3 emphasizes that the administrative or judicial authorities of the home Member State alone shall be empowered to decide on the implementation of one or more reorganization measures affecting credit institutions. The same Article makes it clear that once implemented such measures are to be fully effective throughout the Community without further formality.

7.65 Article 4 confirms that the administrative or judicial authorities of the home Member State shall, without delay, inform the competent authorities of the host Member State or States of their decision to adopt any reorganization measures 'including the practical effects which such measures may have, if possible before it is adopted or otherwise immediately thereafter'. There seems to be no restriction on the methods by which the information can be given.

7.66 Article 6 imposes on the administrative or judicial authorities in a home Member State an obligation to publish notice of the implementation of any reorganization measures which have been implemented where they are 'likely to affect the rights of third parties in a host Member State'. An extract of the relevant decision must be published in the Official Journal of the EC and in two newspapers in each host Member State. The other precondition to the obligation to publish is that an appeal 'may be brought' in the home Member State against the decision ordering the measures.

7.67 In addition to the overall requirement that due publication be made in accordance with Article 6, Article 7 imposes the additional obligation on the administrative or judicial authorities to inform 'known creditors' who have their domiciles, normal places of residence, or head offices in other Member States. This information is to be given in accordance with the procedures laid down in Articles 14 and 17(1).[62]

---

[62] Which address the provision of information to known creditors as issues of the relevant languages respectively.

The duty to inform specific creditors does not, however, exist in the situation **7.68** described in Article 7(2), that is where the home Member State's laws or rules provide for the creditors domiciled or resident in that state to lodge claims: in such a case non-home Member State creditors shall enjoy the same rights.

Much the same rules and principles as are found in Articles 3–8 inclusive with **7.69** regard to reorganization measures apply equally to the opening of and publication relating to winding-up proceedings in Articles 9 and 13 respectively.

However Article 10 contains a critical provision regarding the applicable law to **7.70** the winding-up proceedings. A credit institution is to be wound up 'in accordance with the laws, regulations and procedures applicable to its home Member State insofar as this Directive does not provide otherwise'. This is almost an identical provision to that set out in Article 7 of the Insolvency Regulation save that in Article 10(1) reference is made to the 'laws', etc of the home Member State (*lex domus*), whilst in the context of the Insolvency Regulation, the applicable law is that of the law of the state of the opening of proceedings (*lex concursus*). Under both regimes, the *lex domus* and *lex concursus* respectively have universal application within the European Union (subject to the specified exceptions).

Pursuant to Article 14(1), when winding-up proceedings are opened, the adminis- **7.71** trative or judicial authority of the home Member State or the liquidator shall without delay individually inform known creditors who have their domiciles, normal places of residence or head offices in other Member States, except in cases where the legislation of the home state does not require lodgement of the claim with a view to its recognition. This provision of information is critical for the possibility to lodge claims under Article 16, to be discussed below. In that context, the EFTA Court has defined 'known creditor' as meaning:

> those who are already known by the credit institution to be creditors, those creditors who may be discovered by a reasonably diligent responsible winding up authority, such as by requesting information on the identity of creditors from a securities holding service, and those creditors who bring themselves to the attention of the credit institution at any stage prior to the final date imposed by national law for submission of claims to the responsible winding-up authority.[63]

Perhaps even more importantly, it held that:

> [a]rticle 14 [...] precludes a rule of national law which, following the publication of an invitation to lodge claims directed towards known creditors who have their domicile, permanent residence or head offices in other EEA States, allows for the cancellation of claims that have not been lodged even if these creditors have not been individually notified and the national legislation requires the lodgement of the claim with a view to its recognition.[64]

---

[63] EFTA Court, Case E-18/11 *Irish Bank Resolution Corporation Ltd and Kaupthing Bank hf,* 28 September 2012, at [98].
[64] ibid at [99].

7.72   Article 10(2) then provides that the lex domus is to determine 'in particular' a non-exhaustive list of specific matters and questions such as the powers of the credit institution and of the liquidator, the claims and treatment of such claims, the rules governing distributions, and the question and incidence of costs and expenses. The list is similar to the list found in Article 7(2) RR (equivalent to Article 4 OR).[65]

7.73   However, there is no equivalent in this Directive to the provisions of Articles 8–18 RR (equivalent to Articles 5–15 OR) which list those subjects excluded from the *lex concursus*. In such exceptional cases both in the case of credit institutions as well as in the case of insurance undertakings, there are specific Articles which address the question of the applicable law.

7.74   A word should be said at this point regarding Article 15. It is conceivable that some persons may be unaware of the opening of proceedings affecting a credit institution. In such circumstances they might act in good faith but they do so in the face of otherwise valid winding-up proceedings. Article 15 provides that where an obligation has been honoured in a Member State for the benefit of a credit institution, not being a legal person,[66] which is subject to winding-up proceedings opened in a home Member State, when it should have been honoured for the benefit of the liquidator in those proceedings, the person honouring the obligation will be deemed to have discharged it if he was unaware of the opening of proceedings.[67] Article 15 contains two rebuttable presumptions. If such an obligation is honoured before the publication provided for in Article 13 has been effected, the person honouring the obligation shall be presumed in the absence of proof to the contrary, to have been unaware of the opening of insolvency proceedings: where the obligation is honoured after such publication has been effected, the person honouring the obligation is presumed, again in the absence of proof to the contrary, to have been unaware of the opening of proceedings.

7.75   Article 16 deals with the right to lodge claims. This Article reflects Articles 53 and 55 of the RR (equivalent to Articles 39 and 41 OR respectively).[68] Article 10(2)(g) provides that the law of the home Member State shall determine the rules governing the lodging, etc of claims. Article 16(1) and (2) address the cases of claims by creditors whose domiciles, places of residence, etc are in Member States other than the home Member State. Admittedly it is provided that such creditors are to be treated in the same way and are to be accorded the same ranking as claims of an equivalent nature lodged by home Member State-based creditors, but Article

---

[65] See generally below at paras 8.590–8.592 (RR) and 8.196–8.212 (OR).

[66] This appears to refer to a debtor honouring his obligation towards an individual banker but it may equally refer to a branch.

[67] This reflects the terms of Art 31 RR (equivalent to Art 24(1) OR): see generally below at paras 8.643 (RR) and 8.347–8.350 (OR).

[68] See generally below at 8.726–8.728 and 8.736–8.745 (RR), and 8.442–8.446 and 8.450–8.454 (OR), respectively.

16 represents a clear derogation from the terms and effect of Article 10(2)(g). The notion of equal treatment in Article 16(2) has no corresponding provision in the Insolvency Regulation (either in the OR or the RR).

Title IV

This heading relates to Title IV and is accompanied by the sub-heading 'Provisions   **7.76**
Common to Reorganisation Measures and Winding-up Proceedings'. The entirety
of this Title is, in effect, a derogation from the application of the law of the home
Member State (*lex domus*), similar to the exceptions to the application of the *lex
concursus* contained in the Insolvency Regulation.

Title IV comprises Articles 20–33 inclusive. There are, however, two types of   **7.77**
exceptions built into that Title. The first consists of situations in which the *lex
domus* is not to affect certain rights: the second represents cases where a choice of
law other than the *lex domus* is stipulated. The former group comprises Articles 21,
22, and 23: the latter, Articles 20, 24, 25, 26, and 27.

Article 21 states that the adoption of reorganization measures or the opening of   **7.78**
winding-up proceedings 'shall not affect the rights in re of creditors or third parties in respect of tangible or intangible, moveable or immoveable assets' which
belong to the credit institutions which are situated within the territory of another
Member State at the time of the adoption of the measures or the opening of the
proceedings. Reference to 'rights in re' is no doubt the same as one made to 'rights
in rem' and it can therefore be assumed that the legal position of third parties in
this respect is in effect the same as that provided for by Article 8 RR (equivalent
to Article 5 OR).

Article 21 excludes from the effects of the adoption of any measures or the open-   **7.79**
ing of winding-up proceedings rights in rem of creditors or third parties regarding
assets belonging to credit institutions which at those times are situated within the
territory of another Member State. It is, however, important to note that the Article
does not say that the measures or proceedings shall never affect assets located in
another state. Much, if not all, depends on the law of the state where the assets are
located. Moreover, in addition, Article 21 does not impose its own definition of a
right in rem: in fact, it provides a list of types of rights which most national laws
would generally properly regard as rights in rem.

Article 22 deals with reservation of title. It therefore covers the same content as   **7.80**
Article 10 of the RR (equivalent to Article 7 OR).[69] Article 21(1) addresses the case
where a credit institution, which is otherwise subject to reorganization measures
or the opening of winding-up proceedings, and as a purchaser, is obliged to allow
a seller to preserve his rights based on the reservation of title. In such a case and for

---

[69] See generally below at paras 8.595 (RR) and 8.236 (OR).

the provision to apply, the asset must be located at the relevant time (ie when the measures are adopted or the proceedings opened) in a Member State other than the state in which the measures or proceedings take place.[70]

7.81 Article 22(2) deals with the analogous case where the credit institution acts as the seller after delivery of the asset. In such a case, the provision effectively allows the sale to remain valid. If the purchaser continues to make payment, he will be allowed to acquire title at the end of the period prescribed by the contract. As in the case of Article 22(1) the asset must be located in a Member State other than the state of opening, at the time the measures are adopted or the proceedings opened.

7.82 Actions for voidness, voidability, or unenforceability can nevertheless be brought in respect of the legal acts which involve reservation of title.[71]

7.83 Finally, with regard to the first group of excepted cases, Article 23 deals with set-off. It provides in Article 23(1) that the adoption of reorganization measures or the opening of winding-up proceedings shall not affect the right of a creditor to demand a set-off where set-off is permitted. This reflects the rule in Article 9 RR, corresponding to Article 6 OR.[72] Article 10(2)(c) of the Directive determines whether the laws, regulations, and procedures of the home Member State, that is the *lex domus*, allow the set-off. Article 23 deals with the effect of the adoption of a reorganization measure or the opening of winding-up proceedings. It in effect allows for the operation of the set-off to the extent 'permitted' by the law applicable to the credit institution's claim.[73]

7.84 The second group of Articles in Title IV referred to above consists of Articles 20, and 24–27 inclusive. Article 20(c) deals with employment contracts and reflects a similar exemption put forward in Article 13(1) RR (corresponding to Article 10 OR).[74] Recitals (23) and (24) of the Directive recognize that contracts of employment with credit institutions need to be protected. Article 20(c) therefore provides that 'employment contracts and relationships' shall be governed solely by the law of the Member State applicable to the contract and relationship. To that extent there is a derogation to the general applicability of the *lex domus*.

7.85 Article 20(b) applies an analogous rule with regard to contracts which confer 'the right to make use of or acquire' immovable property, that is the applicable law is the law of the Member State within the territory in which the immovable property is situated.

---

[70] It seems difficult to imagine many cases in practice in which a bank would act as a buyer subject to a payment instalment plan or similar arrangement.
[71] See Art 22(3).
[72] See generally below at paras 8.594 (RR) and 8.227–8.235 (OR).
[73] On set-off rights under the BRRD, see below at paras 7.215–7.216.
[74] See generally below at paras 8.600–8.601 (RR) and 8.245–8.247 (OR).

Article 20(c) provides that rights subject to registration in respect of immovable **7.86** property, ships, or aircraft are to be governed, as in the case of Article 20(b), 'solely' by the law of the Member State under the authority of which the register is kept.

This is a convenient point at which to observe that even as regards the subject- **7.87** matter of Article 20, there may well be a considerable degree of overlap between the rule set out in Article 20 on the one hand and on the other certain other Articles either within the same group of Articles or drawn from the earlier group of Articles already considered. So, for example, a right in rem may well have to be considered within the ambits of both Article 20(c) and Article 21.

Articles 24–27 inclusive deal with the *lex rei sitae*, netting agreements, repurchase **7.88** agreements, and regulated markets respectively. Article 24 deals in effect with financial rights and more particularly 'the enforcement of proprietary rights in instruments or other rights in such instruments the existence or transfer of which presupposes their recording in a register'. In such cases the law of the Member State where that register is held or located will apply. The applicable law could therefore quite easily be the law of a Member State other than the home Member State or even that of a host Member State. This provision mimics Article 9(2) Settlement Finality Directive.[75]

Article 25, which deals with netting agreements, provides that such agreements **7.89** 'shall be given solely by the law of the contract which governs such agreements'. Although the term 'netting' is not defined, Recital (25) appears to indicate that the netting agreements alluded to by Article 25 are restricted to transactions carried out within the framework of a payment and settlement system covered by the Settlement Finality Directive.[76] In addition Recital (26) states that the adoption of the Credit Institutions Directive does not call into question the provisions of the Settlement Finality Directive which in effect remain immune from the effect of any insolvency proceedings upon the enforceability of orders. Since the enactment of the BRRD, Article 25 of the Credit Institutions Directive is without prejudice to Articles 68 and 71 BRRD, which in essence say that the mere taking of a 'crisis prevention measure or a crisis management measure' (as defined under the BRRD) may not, in itself, lead to termination (Article 68) and that resolution authorities have the power to temporarily suspend termination rights (Article 71). BRRD thus disapplies certain contractual termination grounds that might otherwise have remained immune as they were to be governed solely by the law of the contract which governs such agreements.

---

[75] But compare Art 9(1) Collateral Directive, which is similar, but not identical. For a more detailed account, see M Haentjens, *The Law Applicable to Indirectly Held Securities: The Plumbing of International Securities Transactions* (2006) pp 30–38.

[76] See above at para 7.24.

7.90 Article 26 provides that without prejudice to Article 24, repurchase agreements 'shall be governed solely by the law of the contract which governs such agreements'. Where Article 26 concerns contractual rights following from repos, Article 24 concerns the proprietary rights or rights in rem in securities. However, proprietary rights regarding securities in repos have their own, specialist conflicts of law rule, viz. Article 9(2) Collateral Directive. Also as regards repos, Articles 68 and 71 BRRD disapply certain contractual termination grounds that might otherwise have remained immune as they were to be governed solely by the law of the contract which governs such agreements.

7.91 Finally with regard to this second group of Articles, Article 27 provides that 'transactions carried out in the context of a regulated market shall be governed solely by the law of the contract which governs such transactions'.

Credit Institutions Directive: Final provisions

7.92 Article 28 deals with proof of a liquidator's appointment. This generally takes the form of a certified copy of the original appointment decision issued by the administrative or judicial authorities of the home Member State. This is in keeping with the general principle that the nature and scope of the administrator's or liquidator's powers will be governed by the *lex domus*.

7.93 Article 29 allows for the possibility that the reorganization measure or decision to open winding-up proceedings can be registered in non-home Member State registers such as land and trade registers.

7.94 Article 30 provides an exception to the primacy of the *lex domus* when it comes to considering so-called detrimental acts. Under this provision, the *lex domus* does not apply to the rules relating to the voidness, voidability, or unenforceability of legal acts detrimental to the creditors as a whole, where the beneficiary of these acts provides proof that the act detrimental to the creditors as a whole is subject to the law of a Member State other than the home Member State, and that law does not allow any means of challenging that act in the case in point.[77] Article 31 protects third parties dealing with a credit institution after the adoption of measures or of winding-up proceedings in respect of assets such as ships, immovable assets, and other assets which are normally the subject of public registration.

7.95 Article 32 provides that the effects of measures or winding-up proceedings in pending lawsuits are to be governed by the *lex domus*.

---

[77] See for example EFTA Court Case E-28/13 *re. LBI hf. vs Merrill Lynch International Ltd (Landsbanki insolvency)*, 17 October 2014 holding that 'The expression "voidness, voidability or unenforceability of legal acts" in Article 30(1) of [the Credit Institutions Directive] also refers to rescission in bankruptcy law on the basis of avoidance rules' [46] and that 'It must be assessed according to the rules of the home EEA State whether or not the beneficiary has proved that the law applicable to the act does not allow any means of challenge' [81].

Finally Article 34 confirms that Member States were to bring the Directive into force by the appropriate laws, regulations, and administrative procedures by or on 5 May 2004. **7.96**

E. Insurance Directive/Solvency II

Insurance Directive/Solvency II: scope

Article 1(1) Insurance Directive and Article 267 caput and under (a) Solvency II have [effect so that] the insolvency regime of, respectively, the Insurance Directive and Solvency II Title IV apply to 'insurance undertakings'. Such an undertaking is in turn defined as one 'which has received official authorisation'.[78] The upshot of this is that an 'insurance undertaking' is one which is authorized to write direct insurance, both life as well as non-life insurance, as distinct from reinsurance business. Reinsurance companies are not authorized to write direct insurance as a normal rule.[79] On this basis such companies would therefore be governed by the Insolvency Regulation.[80] **7.97**

Article 1(2) Insurance Directive and Article 267 caput and under (b) Solvency II have [effect so that] the insolvency regime of, respectively, the Insurance Directive and Solvency II Title IV also apply to 'branches' albeit within the Community but whose head offices are situated outside the Community. Article 2(b) Insurance Directive defines a branch as 'any permanent presence of an insurance undertaking in the territory of a Member State which carries out insurance business'.[81] Article 268(b) Solvency II is materially the same. **7.98**

As in the Credit Institutions Directive, the Insurance Directive/Solvency II Title IV applies to 'reorganisation measures' and 'winding-up proceedings'. The first of these two expressions in turn embodies four elements, namely: **7.99**

(a) intervention,
(b) by an administrative body or judicial authority,
(c) which is intended to preserve or restore the financial situation, and
(d) which has an effect upon the pre-existing rights of parties other than the insurance undertaking itself, such as the suspension of payments, the suspension of enforcement measures or the reduction of claims.

---

[78] Art 4 of Directive 2002/83/EC/Article 14 Solvency II.
[79] Whilst this is true on the continent, the UK practice is different, where insurance regulation covers both direct insurance and reinsurance and the same companies/Lloyds syndicates do both.
[80] It is submitted that this is possible by way of an approach: the term 'insurance undertaking' is not defined by the Insolvency Regulation (neither in OR nor RR).
[81] It appears likely but not certain that if all branches are within the same Member State, each branch must be treated separately: see Recital (29), Art 30(1) and (2) Insurance Directive.

From the point of view of English law, the applicability of the first of these elements is not without difficulty. On the one hand statutory compositions for insolvency insurers have been viewed as outside the scope of such 'measures', even though a court order is required for sanction; on the other hand, it is not clear why an English company voluntary arrangement should also be excluded since it remains at all material times subject to potential judicial oversight.

7.100 It is perhaps easier to see why a solvent scheme under UK law should be excluded; here there could be said to be no 'intervention' but also that there would be an absence of any intention to preserve or restore financial stability. However, some solvent schemes do seek to preserve or restore financial stability.[82]

7.101 With regard to the term 'winding-up proceedings', the same appears to be a notion which involves six components. First, they must constitute collective proceedings; secondly, such proceedings should involve the realization and distribution of assets and their proceeds; thirdly, there must be 'intervention' by the appropriate administrative or judicial authority; fourthly, such intervention can involve termination by means of composition or by some other analogous measure; fifthly, such intervention and termination need not be founded on insolvency; and sixthly and finally, such intervention and/or termination can be voluntary.

Insurance Directive/Solvency II: Selective commentary

7.102 Article 1 Insurance Directive/Articles 1, 2(2), 2(3), and 267 Solvency II set out their scope. Apart from undertakings which operate solely within the Community, Article 1(2) Insurance Directive/Article 267 caput and under (b) Solvency II makes it plain that their regime also applies to branches of undertakings which have their head office outside the Community.

7.103 The overall aim of the Insurance Directive and Solvency II Title IV is perhaps best encapsulated in Recital (117) Solvency II which states:

> Since national legislation concerning reorganisation measures and winding-up proceedings is not harmonised, it is appropriate, in the framework of the internal market, to ensure the mutual recognition of reorganisation measures and winding-up legislation of the Member States concerning insurance undertakings, as well as the necessary cooperation, taking into account the need for unity, universality, coordination and publicity for such measures and the equivalent treatment and protection of insurance creditors.

It might perhaps be conceded that to some extent the Insurance Directive/Solvency II does succeed in altering substantive national law in relation to the last item referred to in the quoted passage, namely the protection of insurance creditors.

---

[82] For example, the Equitable Life scheme sought to stabilize the direct insurer. See also the Insurers (Reorganisation and Winding Up) Regulations 2004, specifically Art 5(5).

On the definition of 'insurance undertakings', see above, paragraph 7.97.[83] **7.104**

In the United Kingdom, the term 'insurance' usually connotes and includes 'rein- **7.105**
surance'. Much the same approach is taken by a number of EU Member States,
for example Finland, Denmark, and Luxembourg. However, the Directive on
Reinsurance[84] (now: Solvency II) had as its stated aim the creation of an EU-wide
market based on the regime introduced by earlier Insurance Directives. Under
Solvency II reinsurance across the Union is subject to a common system of authorization, prudential regulation, and solvency and, like direct insurers, reinsurers
have a single home state authorization valid for the whole of the EU.

Whether a particular reinsurance company is within the scope of the Insurance **7.106**
Directive/Solvency II Title IV will depend on whether it is in receipt of authorization to write direct business. If it in fact does write such business, there is no reason
in principle why the Insurance Directive/Solvency II Title IV should not apply
to it. If despite the fact of authorization, in fact no direct business is conducted,
the position is not clear. The practical solution is for such a company, when facing
insolvency, to delimit its own powers so as to exclude the writing of direct business, if it wishes to place itself within the ambit and applicability of the Insolvency
Regulation. Pending the institution of a full-blown regime with regard to insolvent
reinsurers, such may be the best solution currently available.

As in the case of credit institutions, the Insurance Directive/Solvency II Title IV **7.107**
covers EU undertakings authorized in a Member State as well as branches of a
non-EU undertaking set up in one or more Member States. In the case of the latter
type of undertaking, the home Member State is a state in which the branch has
been granted authorization: if there are two or more branches, each branch will be
treated separately.

As in the case of the Credit Institutions Directive, the Insurance Directive/Solvency **7.108**
II Title IV applies to 'reorganisation measures' as well as 'winding-up proceedings'.
The fourfold aspects of the former measures have already been considered above.[85]
From what has already been said, identification of the element of 'intervention' by
an administrative body or judicial authority is a key component in the equation.
Hence in terms of English law at least, it is arguable that a company voluntary
arrangement attracts a suitable degree of court scrutiny whilst a formal scheme
of arrangement, albeit containing as it does formal court approval, nonetheless
remains essentially a concordat between the company and its creditors and therefore outside the scope of the Insurance Directive.

---

[83] See Art 6 of Directive (EC) 73/239 and Directive (EC) 79/267 respectively. The Insurance
Directive was adopted by the European Council on 19 March 2001. It came into force on 20 April
2001. EU Member States had to comply with it by bringing in appropriate laws and regulations on
or before 20 April 2003.

[84] Directive (EC) 2005/68 [2005] OJ L327/1, amended by Directive (EC) 2007/44.

[85] See above at para 7.99.

7.109 With regard to winding-up proceedings, it is worth revisiting the observations made above that the Insurance Directive/Solvency II Title IV applies to all winding-up proceedings whether or not they are founded on insolvency[86] and indeed whether they are voluntary or compulsory. It is equally important to note that the Insurance Directive/Solvency II Title IV also provides that the adoption of reorganization measures in relation to an undertaking will not preclude the opening of winding-up proceedings.

7.110 Article 2 Insurance Directive/Article 268 Solvency II sets out various important definitions. The word 'branch' is defined in Article 268 Solvency II as 'any permanent presence of an insurance undertaking in the territory of a Member State other than the home Member State which pursues insurance business'. There is an echo in that definition of the definition accorded to the term 'establishment' for the purposes of the OR and RR.[87] Other terms are more self-explanatory. The definition of 'Home Member State' is now to be found in Article 13(8) Solvency II and says, in pertinent part, that it means any of: (a) for non-life insurance, the Member State in which the head office of the insurance undertaking covering the risk is situated; and (b) for life insurance, the Member State in which the head office of the insurance undertaking covering the commitment is situated.

7.111 The position with regard to an undertaking with its head office outside the European Union but with branches in more than one Member State is similar to that in the case of credit institutions.[88]

7.112 In such a case Article 3 Insurance Directive/296(1) Solvency II indicates that each such branch must be treated independently.

7.113 Other main terms employed, namely 'host Member State' (to be found in Article 13(9) Solvency II), 'competent authorities', 'administrator', and 'liquidator' (all to be found in Article 268(1) Solvency II) are again largely self-explanatory.

7.114 The term 'reorganisation measures' is not only defined as a separate term in Article 2 Insurance Directive/Article 268(1)(c) Solvency II but is the subject of Title II Insurance Directive which covers Articles 3–7 inclusive/Chapter II which covers Articles 269–272 inclusive Solvency II. The definition is the same as that afforded to the same term in the Credit Institutions Directive.[89] Article 4 Insurance Directive/Article 269 Solvency II confirms that only the 'competent authorities' of the home Member State are entitled to decide on such measures with regard to an insurance undertaking and that such measures 'shall not preclude the opening of winding-up proceedings' by the same home Member State; Article 4(3) Insurance Directive/Article 269(4) Solvency II further confirms that

---

[86] See Art 2(d) Insurance Directive/Art 268(d) Solvency II.
[87] See generally below at 8.546–8.554 (RR) and 8.37–8.42 (OR).
[88] See above at para 7.43.
[89] See above at paras 7.45–7.48.

the reorganization measures 'shall be fully effective' throughout the Community 'without any further formalities' including as against third parties in other Member States, even if the legislation of those other Member States does not provide for such measures or alternatively makes the implementation subject to conditions which are not fulfilled. Article 4(4) Insurance Directive/Article 269(5) Solvency II reinforces this provision by establishing that the Community-wide effect of the reorganization measures will arise at the same time as they take effect under the relevant national law, that is the law of the home Member State.

Article 5 Insurance Directive/Article 270 Solvency II confirms that the compe- **7.115** tent authorities in the home Member State must inform the same state's supervisory authorities regarding the former's decision. The latter authorities must then inform the supervisory authorities of all other Member States and not simply such of those states as reflect the particular commercial relationships of the undertaking in question.

Article 5 Insurance Directive/Article 270 Solvency II talks of informing other **7.116** states of a decision on a reorganization measure taking place 'where possible before the adoption of such a measure and failing that immediately thereafter'. This suggests that it is necessary for only the notice of the measure to be communicated.

Article 6 Insurance Directive/Article 271 Solvency II provides for the publication **7.117** of the measures but only where an appeal is 'possible' in the home Member State, which refers to an appeal by parties other than the insurance undertaking itself.[90] Furthermore such publication should be made only if the relevant national law requires it. Reference to an appeal seems wide enough to encompass an appeal to an administrative as well as to a judicial body. Article 6 Insurance Directive/Article 271 Solvency II also contains a requirement to publish an extract from the document establishing the measures in the *Official Journal* of the Community. As far as Member States other than the home Member State are concerned, there exists a discretion to publish the decision.

Article 7 Insurance Directive/Article 272 Solvency II reflects the terms of Article 7 **7.118** of the Credit Institutions Directive.[91]

Title III of the Insurance Directive/Chapter III Solvency II deals with winding-up **7.119** proceedings and covers Articles 8–18/273–284. As already pointed out,[92] such proceedings need not be founded on insolvency and can be voluntary or compulsory in nature. Article 8(1) Insurance Directive/Article 273(1) Solvency II confirms that the entitlement to decide to open winding-up proceedings rests solely with the competent authorities within the home Member State. It also stresses that

---

[90] See Recital (22) of the Insurance Directive.
[91] See above at paras 7.67 and 7.68.
[92] See above at paras 7.101 and 7.109.

winding-up proceedings can take place whether or not prior reorganization meas-ures have been adopted.

7.120 Article 8(2) Insurance Directive/Article 273(2) Solvency II echoes Article 4 Insurance Directive/Article 269 Solvency II and confirms that decisions to open winding-up proceedings are to be recognized without further formality in other Member States and are to be effective in such other states the moment they are effective in the home Member State.

7.121 Article 8(3) Insurance Directive/Article 273 Solvency II deals with the provision of information regarding the relevant decision and mirrors Article 5 Insurance Directive/Article 270 Solvency II.[93] First, the competent authorities of the home Member State must inform the supervisory authorities of the home Member State and then must inform the equivalent authorities in other Member States.

7.122 Article 9 Insurance Directive/Article 274 Solvency II deals with the *lex domus* in terms which are similar to those contained in Article 10 of the Credit Institutions Directive. It therefore deals not only with the question of jurisdiction but also with those conflict of law rules which replace the various national rules of private international law in so far as the latter apply to the winding-up of insurance under-takings. Recital (23) of the Insurance Directive, however, makes it clear that the Directive does not seek to govern the applicable rules regarding the existence of a contract, the rights and obligations of parties, and the evaluation of debts. This Recital has not returned in Solvency II, for this Directive does contain substantive rules on the rights and obligations of insurance undertakings.

7.123 The principal requirement in Article 9(1) Insurance Directive/Article 274(1) Solvency II is that the law applicable is that of the home Member State or *lex domus*. That law is to apply to the decision which opens the proceedings, the proceedings themselves, and their effects. Again, as in the case of the Credit Institutions Directive, this overriding rule is subject to a number of exceptions as set out in Articles 19–26 inclusive Insurance Directive/Article 285–292 inclusive Solvency II which deal with such matters as third parties' rights in rem, reserva-tion of title, and set-off.[94]

7.124 The list of matters to which the *lex domus* applies contained in Article 9(2) Insurance Directive/Article 274(2) Solvency II is, as in the case of Article 10 of the Credit Institutions Directive, non-exhaustive.

7.125 Article 10 Insurance Directive/Article 275 Solvency II is a key provision in the Directive. It provides by Article 10(1) Insurance Directive/Article 275(1) Solvency II that Member States shall ensure that insurance claims take precedence over

---

[93] See above at para 7.115.
[94] Recital (24) of the Insurance Directive justifies these exceptions as being ones which 'protect the legitimate expectations and the certainty of transactions in [non-home] Member States'.

other claims on the insurance undertaking by reference to one of two distinct approaches. First, the Member State can provide for insurance claims to be given absolute preference over all other claims with regard to assets which represent the technical provisions of the relevant undertaking (Article 10(1)(a) Insurance Directive/Article 275(1)(a) Solvency II). Alternatively the Member State can accord insurance claims priority over all other claims with respect to all of their assets except for claims by employees, public bodies in relation to taxes, claims by social security systems, and claims on assets subject to rights in rem (Article 10(1)(b) Insurance Directive/Article 275(1)(b) Solvency II).

Furthermore, Member States can provide that the whole or part of the expenses **7.126** of a winding-up proceeding can take priority over insurance claims (Article 10(2) Insurance Directive/Article 275(2) Solvency II).

The term 'insurance claim' is defined in Article 2 Insurance Directive/Article 268(1)(g) **7.127** Solvency II as meaning any amount which is owed by an insurance undertaking to insured persons, policy-holders, beneficiaries, or to any injured party having a direct right of action against the insurance undertaking and which arises out of an insurance contract in relation to direct insurance business, including amounts set aside for such persons when some elements of the debt are not yet known. The definition also includes premium refunds due from an insurer.

It appears to follow from Article 10 Insurance Directive/Article 275 Solvency II **7.128** that reinsurance creditors would fall to be dealt with after insurance claims, that is they would be treated as general creditors.

Article 10(3) Insurance Directive/Article 275(3) Solvency II requires Member **7.129** States who adopt the first of these two approaches in Article 10 to maintain a special register of the assets used to cover technical provisions.[95]

Article 11 Insurance Directive/Article 277 Solvency II states that the home **7.130** Member State may provide that where the rights of insurance creditors have been subrogated to a guarantee scheme established in that Member State, claims by the scheme shall not benefit from the provisions of Article 10(1) Insurance Directive/Article 275(1) Solvency II. Although Article 11 clearly clothes the Member State with a discretion, it in effect reinforces the protection afforded to insurance creditors by Article 10 Insurance Directive/Article 275 Solvency II.

Article 12 revisits Article 10(1)(b) Insurance Directive/Article 275(1)(b) Solvency **7.131** II by providing that insurance undertakings must indicate in their accounts at all times those claims recorded in the accounts which might take precedence over insurance claims.

---

[95] Details of the contents of such a register and details of the manner in which it should be held are set out in the Annex to the Directive.

7.132   Article 13 Insurance Directive/Article 279 Solvency II deals with withdrawal of authorization in the event of the opening of winding-up proceedings. However, it allows a liquidator or other appointee of the competent authorities to pursue the business of the insurance undertaking if required for the purposes of the winding-up.

7.133   Article 14 Insurance Directive/Article 280 Solvency II gives effect to the principle of publicity in similar terms to that which applies to reorganization measures in Article 6 Insurance Directive/Article 271 Solvency II.[96] Here, however, publication would be required whether or not an appeal is possible. However, Article 14 Insurance Directive/Article 280 Solvency II does not in terms provide that the winding-up proceedings will have effect regardless of whether the requirements for publicity set out in Article 14(1) and (2) Insurance Directive/Article 280(1) and (2) Solvency II are satisfied. This is not to say that publicity is a precondition to the effectiveness of reorganization or winding-up provisions across the Community.[97]

7.134   Article 15 Insurance Directive/Article 281 Solvency II reflects one of the prime motives of the Directive, namely that as much information as possible be given to creditors in relation to the opening of the reorganization measures or winding-up proceedings as well as with regard to the manner in which they unfold. The Article specifically requires the creditors of the particular undertaking in other Member States to be individually informed of the opening of the winding-up proceedings without delay. Article 15(2) Insurance Directive/Article 271(2) Solvency II prescribes that the details which form the notification should include such matters as time limits, etc. However, it also provides that in the case of insurance claims as defined in Article 2(k) Insurance Directive/Article 268(1)(g) Solvency II,[98] the notice must indicate the general effect of the winding-up proceedings on the insurance contracts, including the date on which the insurance contracts, etc will cease 'to produce effects'.

7.135   Article 16 Insurance Directive/Article 282 Solvency II deals with the right to lodge claims. The basic aim is to ensure equality of treatment between creditors as between those in the home Member State and those in non-home Member States.[99] Although the entitlement under the Insurance Directive/Solvency II Title IV to lodge claims extends only to creditors with a habitual residence, domicile, or head office within a Member State, the law governing the proceedings may well allow creditors from other states to lodge claims. Article 16(1) Insurance Directive/Article 282(1) Solvency II specifically extends the right to lodge claims to public

---

[96] See above at para 7.117.
[97] This is on account of Art 8(2) Insurance Directive/Art 273(2) Solvency II: see above at para 7.120.
[98] As to Art 2 Insurance Directive/Art 268 Solvency II, see above at para 7.110.
[99] See Recital (21) of the Insurance Directive.

authorities which operate within a Member State. This last entitlement represents an exception to the general rule that foreign tax laws will not be enforced.

As in the case of the Credit Institutions Directive,[100] although Article 16 Insurance Directive/Article 282 Solvency II provides for a general right for Community-wide creditors to be able to lodge claims and proceedings regarding an insurance undertaking, it would certainly be the law applicable to the proceedings, that is the *lex domus*, which in accordance with Article 9(2)(g) Insurance Directive/Article 274(2)(g) Solvency II will determine the rules governing the lodging, verification, and admission of claims. **7.136**

Article 17 Insurance Directive/Article 283 Solvency II deals with the question of which language is to be used in relation to the manner in which notification must be made to creditors and the manner in which claims are lodged.[101] The information in the notice to creditors need be only in the official language of the home Member State although the heading of the form which is used must be in all the official languages of the Union. However, in the case of insurance creditors, the notice must be provided in the official language of the Member State where the insurer has its habitual residence, domicile, or head office. **7.137**

As far as creditors are concerned, a creditor from a Member State other than the home Member State can lodge his claim in the official language of his own Member State. Again, however, the form used in order to lodge the claim must be headed in the official language of the home Member State. **7.138**

Article 18 Insurance Directive/Article 283 Solvency II ends Title III/Chapter III by imposing a requirement that liquidators must keep all creditors in all other Member States informed as to the progress of the winding-up proceedings. **7.139**

Title IV Insurance Directive/Chapter IV of Title IV Solvency II sets out various provisions which are common to both reorganization measures and winding-up proceedings. Whilst Articles 4 and 9 Insurance Directive/Article 269 and 274 Solvency II provide for the general principle that the applicable law to reorganization measures and winding-up proceedings is the *lex domus*, there are, as in the case of the Credit Institutions Directive, some important exceptions. **7.140**

The first principal exception is provided by Article 19 Insurance Directive/Article 285 Solvency II. Employment contracts are governed (in Solvency II: exclusively) by the law of the Member State 'applicable' to such contracts. This law will generally be determined by reference to Article 8 Rome I Regulation.[102] It is important to note that the exception contained in Article 19(a) Insurance **7.141**

---

[100] See above at para 7.75.

[101] There is a strong resemblance to Art 54 RR (equivalent to Arts 40 and 42(1) OR): see generally below at paras 8.729–8.735 (RR), and 8.447–8.449 and 8.455–8.459 (OR), respectively.

[102] Regulation (EC) No 593/2008 of the European Parliament and of the Council of 17 June 2008 on the law applicable to contractual obligations (Rome I), OJ L177.

Directive/Article 285(a) Solvency II means that the relevant national law will apply only to determine the effect of the opening of the reorganization measures or winding-up proceedings on the employment contract and any employment relationship. All other matters regarding the employment contract, etc will remain governed by the law of the home Member State, for example the lodging, verification, and admission of claims, etc.

7.142 Article 19(b) Insurance Directive/Article 285(b) Solvency II addresses contracts conferring the right to use or acquire immovable property. Such contracts are to be governed solely by the law of the Member State in whose territory the immovable property is situated. The width of Article 19(b) Insurance Directive/Article 285(b) Solvency II suggests that all forms of immovable-related contracts are included, for example leases and agreements for sale.

7.143 Article 19(c) Insurance Directive/Article 285(c) Solvency II deals with the publicly registered rights of an insurance undertaking in relation not only to immovable property but also to property, ships, and aircraft. The latter types of assets must be 'subject' to registration. If they are, the law of the home Member State should be incapable of affecting the systems for registration which exist or are in force in other Member States.

7.144 Article 20 Insurance Directive/Article 286 Solvency II deals with third parties' rights in rem. Such rights insofar as they exist in respect of an insurance undertaking's assets situated within the territory of another Member State at the time of the opening of the relevant measures or proceedings, are not to be affected by such opening. In other words, secured creditors can exercise their security rights over an insurance undertaking's local assets in accordance with the local law irrespective of the effect of the *lex domus*.

7.145 No definition of a 'right in rem' appears anywhere in the Insurance Directive/Solvency II Title IV.[103] Article 20(1) Insurance Directive/Article 286(1) Solvency II refers to 'specific assets' as well as to 'collections of indefinite assets as a whole which change from time to time'. The latter phrase appears to cover the case of a floating charge under English law.

7.146 Article 21 Insurance Directive/Article 287 Solvency II deals with reservation of title. Its terms reflect the contents of Article 22 of the Credit Institutions Directive.[104] This exception applies whenever a seller has rights based on a reservation of title claim regarding an asset which at the time of the opening of the reorganization measures or winding-up proceeding is located in the Member State other than the home Member State. In such a case the seller's rights are governed by the relevant national law. However, as with third parties' rights in rem, such reservation of title

---

[103] The same omission occurs in the case of both the OR and RR.
[104] See above at paras 7.80–7.82.

rights may still remain impeachable under the law of the home Member State as being void, voidable, or unenforceable. This will still leave a seller with the right to raise a defence to claims brought under the law of the home Member State if Article 24 Insurance Directive/Article 290 Solvency II (dealing with detrimental acts) is relied upon.[105] That Article provides a defence to such a claim which would be brought under the law of the home Member State, by allowing the defendant to rely on the law of a Member State other than that of the home Member State if the latter governed the act in question. As will be pointed out in relation to Article 24 Insurance Directive/Article 290 Solvency II such a defence in effect protects the legitimate expectations of creditors and third parties who acted in accordance with the law which governed that act and who therefore would not have expected that the law of the home Member State might invalidate or otherwise impeach that act.

Article 21(2) Insurance Directive/Article 287(2) Solvency II resembles Article **7.147** 10(2) RR (which is equivalent to Article 7(2) OR).[106] It prevents an office-holder appointed in connection with the reorganization measure or winding-up proceeding from using the commencement of the measure or proceeding as a ground for rescinding a sale or transaction in a case where the relevant asset is at the time of the opening of the measure or proceeding situated in a Member State other than the home Member State. That clearly represents a substantive rule of law which would override not only any contractual provision to the contrary but also any national law which was also to such contrary effect.

Article 22 Insurance Directive/Article 288 Solvency II deals with set-off. If set-off **7.148** of a creditor's claim and an insurance undertaking's claim is allowed according to the law which governs the latter's claim, Article 22 Insurance Directive/Article 288 Solvency II confirms that the opening of the measure or the proceedings is not to affect such right. For this purpose the law applicable to the creditor's claim is not relevant. Although Article 22 Insurance Directive/Article 288 Solvency II provides that the conditions under which the set-off may be invoked remains a matter for the law of the home Member State, the latter law will apply to determine the availability of set-off regarding claims incurred following upon the opening of the relevant measure or the proceeding and also, more importantly, where set-off is disallowed under the law applicable to the claim of the insurance undertaking.

Article 23 Insurance Directive/Article 289 Solvency II deals with regulated mar- **7.149** kets. It provides that the law of the home Member State will not apply in respect of the rights and obligations of parties to a regulated market. The term 'regulated market' is defined (not in the Insurance Directive, but) in Article 13(22) Solvency II. In general terms, a 'regulated market' is defined as either (in the case of a market situated in a Member State), a multilateral system operated and/or managed by a

---

[105] See below at para 7.152.
[106] See generally below at paras 8.595 (RR) and 8.238–8.239 (OR).

market operator, which brings together or facilitates the bringing together of multiple third-party buying and selling interests in financial instruments (as defined under Article 4(1)(21) MiFID II), or (in the case of a market situated in a third country) a financial market which is regarded by an undertaking's home Member State as a regulated market and the fact that the financial instruments dealt in on that market are of a quality comparable to that of the instruments dealt in on the regulated market or markets of the Home Member State.[107]

7.150 Unlike the Insurance Directive/Solvency II Title IV, the Credit Institutions Directive deals with an equivalent exception for netting agreements and repurchase agreements, whilst it also provides a conflict of laws rule for rights recorded in a 'register, account or centralised deposit system' (Articles 24, 25, and 26 of that Directive).[108] This no doubt reflects the reality that insurance undertakings are less likely than banks to be involved in the various forms of payments or settlement systems referred to.

7.151 The exceptions set out in Article 23 Insurance Directive/Article 289 Solvency II apply to the rights and obligations of parties in relation to a market. This is unlike the scope of the equivalent Article, namely Article 27, in the Credit Institutions Directive[109] which applies only to contractual transactions carried out in the context of a regulated market. In consequence, Article 23 Insurance Directive/Article 289 Solvency II appears to be broader and to cover all aspects relating to the relationship of an insurance undertaking to a market.

7.152 Article 24 Insurance Directive/Article 290 Solvency II deals with detrimental acts. The general rule is that the law of the home Member State governs the rules relating to the nullity, voidability, and unenforceability of legal acts detrimental to all creditors of an insurance undertaking.[110] There may be a challenge in the home Member State, for example to the creation of a security interest over assets in a non-home Member State. Article 24 Insurance Directive/Article 290 Solvency II would provide a defence if the act in question was subject to non-home Member State law when that law did not permit such a challenge.

7.153 Moreover such a defence must be raised by the parties seeking to rely on it. The defence only applies in relation to acts carried out prior to the opening of the relevant measures or proceedings. If the act in question is carried out after that time, the law of the home Member State will apply.[111]

---

[107] [2009] OJ L335, as amended by Directive 2013/58/EU of the European Parliament and of the Council of 11 December 2013 amending Directive 2009/138/EC (Solvency II) as regards the date for its transposition and the date of its application, and the date of repeal of certain Directives (Solvency I), OJ L341.
[108] See above at paras 7.88–7.90.
[109] See above at para 7.91.
[110] See Art 9(2)(l) Insurance Directive/Art 274(2)(1) Solvency II.
[111] On account of Art 13 Insurance Directive/Article 279 Solvency II.

Article 25 Insurance Directive/Article 291 Solvency II revisits the protection **7.154** afforded to immovable assets and publicly registered assets such as ships and aircraft, insofar as third party purchasers are concerned. It provides that if by an act concluded after adoption of the reorganization measures or the winding-up proceedings an insurance undertaking disposes of such an asset 'for a consideration', 'the validity of that act shall be governed by the law of the Member State within whose territory the immoveable asset is situated or under whose authority the register account or system is kept'.

It should be noted that Article 25 Insurance Directive/Article 291 Solvency II does **7.155** not state that the relevant national law is to apply 'solely'. In other words both the law of the home Member State and the national law will apply.

The final exception to the applicability of the law of the home Member State is **7.156** in Article 26 Insurance Directive/Article 292 Solvency II. This provides that the effect of reorganization measures or winding-up proceedings or a pending lawsuit concerning an asset or right of which the insurance undertaking has been divested shall be governed solely by the law of the Member State in which the lawsuit is pending.[112] Article 26 Insurance Directive/Article 292 Solvency II does not extend to any enforcement proceeding arising out of a pending lawsuit. That is a matter for the home Member State.[113]

Articles 27–29 Insurance Directive/Article 293–295 Solvency II deal with pre- **7.157** dominantly formal matters. The first of these Articles states that an administrator's or liquidator's appointment shall be evidenced by a certified copy of the original decision of appointment or by any other certificate issued by the competent authorities of the home Member State. Article 27(2) and (3) Insurance Directive/ Article 293(2) and (3) Solvency II confirm that administrators and liquidators can exercise in all Member States all the powers that they can exercise in the home Member State but that with regard to acting in a non-home Member State, they shall comply with that law 'in particular with regard to procedures for the realisation of assets and the informing of employees'.

Article 28 Insurance Directive/Article 294 Solvency II entitles an administrator, **7.158** liquidator, or duly authorized person in the home Member State to require that the reorganization measure or decision to open winding-up proceedings be registered in a suitable public register such as a land or trade register, in the absence of a binding obligation to effect such a registration.

Article 29 Insurance Directive/Article 295 Solvency II preserves professional **7.159** secrecy otherwise applicable to those persons or parties who have worked or otherwise been formally associated with insurance undertakings but note should

---

[112] See the commentary on Art 18 RR (equivalent to Art 15 OR) at 8.609–8.615 (RR) and 8.270–8.287 (OR) below as well as *Mazur Media Ltd v Mazur Media GmbH* [2004] 1 WLR 2966.
[113] See Recital (26) of the Insurance Directive.

be taken of the obligations of professional secrecy in Articles 64–69 Solvency II. The said Articles do allow the disclosure of information which does not concern third parties involved in attempts to rescue an undertaking where the undertaking is declared bankrupt or is otherwise the subject of a compulsory winding-up.

7.160   Article 30 Insurance Directive/Article 296 Solvency II deals with the position of an insurance undertaking in a non-Member State, ie where the head office is situated outside the Community, but which has branches in one or more Member States. In such a case the Member State or States in which the branch or branches of the undertaking is or are situated will be treated as the respective home Member State and the authorities of that state are to be treated as the competent authorities in relation to that undertaking.

7.161   If there are branches in more than one Member State, then each such branch will be treated separately. Article 30(2) Insurance Directive/Article 296 second and third sentences Solvency II provides that in such circumstances the competent authorities and the supervisory authorities in the home Member State should endeavour to coordinate their actions: equally any duly appointed administrators and liquidators should coordinate their actions accordingly.

F. Bank Recovery and Resolution Directive

Title I: Scope and definitions

7.162   As stated above[114] the EU harmonized bank insolvency regime recently adopted represents a major overhaul of the rules governing credit institutions and investment firms that experience financial difficulties.[115] It consists both of a Bank Recovery and Resolution Directive (BRRD) and a Single Resolution Mechanism (SRM). While BRRD applies to all EU Member States and has to be implemented into national laws, SRM has been adopted by means of the Single Resolution Mechanism Regulation (SRMR), which may not be implemented but works directly. It applies only to the countries that use the euro as a currency or wish to accede to SRM. Moreover, where BRRD provides for the harmonization of substantive rules of bank insolvency law in the broadest sense, SRMR specifically concerns the application of a unified resolution regime by the Single Resolution Board.[116]

---

[114] At para 7.07.

[115] This paragraph and the following ones have been based, in part, on M Haentjens et al., *New Bank Insolvency Law for China and Europe, Inventory Report I (Europe)*—a project funded by the Royal Netherlands Academy of Arts and Sciences and the China Ministry for Education (on file with the author, to be published 2016). See also generally M Haentjens and B Wessels (ed), *Crisis Management in the Banking Sector* (2015).

[116] The SRMR mainly contains materially the same provisions as the BRRD. For that reason, and also because of SRMR's more limited remit, the following paragraphs will follow the BRRD's

It can be assumed that in practice, BRRD and SRMR are or will become the **7.163** predominant instruments for credit institutions and investment firms in financial distress. Not only do BRRD and SRMR harmonize and unify substantive rules of European bank insolvency law, but the BRRD also prescribes rules that apply in going concern and in the earliest stages of financial difficulties, as it involves three pillars: preparatory and preventive measures, early intervention measures, and resolution tools and powers. In contrast, SRMR concerns only resolution. Resolution here is understood as a process of orderly restructuring and if necessary the winding down of it as a whole or a part of it.

As a matter of principle, the BRRD and SRMR harmonize and unify substantive **7.164** law whilst the Credit Institutions Directive focuses on coordination and conflict of law rules. The BRRD and SRMR will therefore leave the principles set out above[117] intact. Yet for purposes of the Credit Institutions Directive, 'reorganisation measures' now also include 'the application of the resolution tools and the exercise of resolution powers' provided for in the BRRD, while the Credit Institutions Directive's definition of 'winding-up proceedings' echoes what BRRD calls 'normal insolvency proceedings', viz. 'collective insolvency proceedings which entail the partial or total divestment of a debtor and the appointment of a liquidator or an administrator normally applicable to institutions under national law and either specific to those institutions or generally applicable to any natural or legal person' (Article 2(1)(47) BRRD). In the regime accomplished by BRRD (and SRMR) these latter 'normal insolvency proceedings' will play only a secondary, if not marginal role as predominance is given to administrative intervention in the earliest stages and collective proceedings are avoided. As one of the consequences thereof, for instance, the BRRD nuances the principle of unity discussed above,[118] through the introduction of 'resolution colleges', of which not only the home state group-level resolution authority is a member, but also, *inter alia*, the resolution authorities of member states in which significant branches are located (Article 88(2)(d) BRRD). This college may eg have to reach an agreement on a resolution scheme for the entire group (Article 88(1)(f) BRRD).

Pursuant to Article 1(1)(a) and Article 2(1)(23) BRRD/Article 2 SRMR, this **7.165** Directive and Regulation apply to credit institutions and investment firms. As indicated above,[119] the definition of 'credit institution' has to be gleaned from Article 4(1)(1) CRR, namely 'an undertaking the business of which is to take deposits or other repayable funds from the public and to grant credits for its own account'.

---

set-up and principally discuss the BRRD's provisions. Nonetheless, references to SRMR will be made where appropriate.

[117] At paras 7.30–7.37.
[118] At para 7.31.
[119] See above at para 7.17.

7.166 For the definition of 'investment firm', reference must be had, as stated above, to Article 4(1)(1) MiFID II, which says that an 'investment firm' 'means any legal person whose regular occupation or business is the provision of one or more investment services to third parties and/or the performance of one or more investment activities on a professional basis'. 'Investment services and activities' are then defined as 'any of the services and activities listed in Section A of Annex I [of MiFID II] relating to any of the instruments listed in Section C of Annex I [of MiFID II]'.

7.167 Whilst European law generally does not treat groups of companies as a single entity either for the purposes of general corporate law or with regard to insolvency law, SRMR radically derogates from that approach as under this Regulation, the Single Resolution Board is empowered to take decisions in relation to certain categories of groups as a whole, as the Board shall be responsible for adopting all decisions relating to resolution for those groups pursuant to Article 7(2) SRMR. Under Article 1(1) BRRD, also 'financial institutions' that are a subsidiary of a credit institution, investment firm, or of, in short, a holding company of a financial group are covered. A financial institution is further defined (via Article 2(1)(4) BRRD/Article 3(1)(15) SRMR) in Article 4(1)(26) CRR, which says that a 'financial institution' means:

> an undertaking other than an institution [ie a credit institution or investment firm, MH], the principal activity of which is to acquire holdings or to pursue one or more of the activities listed in points 2 to 12 and point 15 of Annex I to Directive 2013/36/EU, including a financial holding company, a mixed financial holding company, a payment institution within the meaning of Directive 2007/64/EC of the European Parliament and of the Council of 13 November 2007 on payment services in the internal market, and an asset management company, but excluding insurance holding companies and mixed-activity insurance holding companies as defined in point (g) of Article 212(1) of Directive 2009/138/E.

7.168 A 'subsidiary' is defined (via Article 2(1)(5) BRRD/Article 3(1)(21) SRMR) as meaning:

> (a) a subsidiary undertaking within the meaning of Articles 1 and 2 of Directive 83/349/EEC; (b) a subsidiary undertaking within the meaning of Article 1(1) of Directive 83/349/EEC and any undertaking over which a parent undertaking effectively exercises a dominant influence. Subsidiaries of subsidiaries shall also be considered to be subsidiaries of the undertaking that is their original parent undertaking.[120]

7.169 BRRD and SRMR also apply to, in short, a holding company of a financial group (Article 1(1)(c) and (d) BRRD/Article 2(b) SRMR).

7.170 Finally, Article 1(1)(e) BRRD has the BRRD also apply, under certain circumstances, to 'branches' outside of the Union. A 'branch' is defined (via Article 2 BRRD) as meaning 'a place of business which forms a legally dependent part of an

---

[120] Directive 83/349/EEC is the Seventh Council Directive of 13 June 1983 based on Article 54(3)(g) of the Treaty on consolidated accounts, OJ L193. On the definitions of branches see also above, at paras 7.41 and 7.110.

institution and which carries out directly all or some of the transactions inherent in the business of institutions' (Article 4(1)(17) CRR).

Article 2 BRRD and Article 3 SRMR contain too many definitions to be discussed   **7.171**
here. Noteworthy is the definition of 'resolution' of Article 2(1)(1) BRRD, which
reads: 'the application of a resolution tool or a tool referred to in Article 37(9) in
order to achieve one or more of the resolution objectives referred to in Article
31(2)'. The resolution tools listed in Article 37(3) BRRD[121]/Article 22(2) SRMR
form some of the central elements of the BRRD and SRMR and the regime these
instruments create. Pursuant to Article 37(3) BRRD/Article 22(2) SRMR, the
resolution tools are: the sale of business tool, the bridge institution tool, the asset
separation tool, and the bail-in tool. 'Special management' as defined in Article 35
BRRD may be considered to represent an additional resolution tool. These 'resolution tools' will be discussed below.[122]

To apply the resolution tools just listed, resolution authorities need to be con-   **7.172**
ferred 'resolution powers' which are listed in Articles 63–72 inclusive BRRD
(Article 2(1)(20) BRRD).

Title II: Preparation

Article 3 provides that, in short, Member States must designate 'resolution authori-   **7.173**
ties' to apply the resolution tools and exercise the resolution powers.

Under Title II (Preparation) of the BRRD, institutions must draw up 'recovery   **7.174**
plans' whilst resolution authorities must have 'resolution plans' in place. Recovery
plans must provide 'for measures to be taken by the institution to restore its financial position following a significant deterioration of its financial situation' (Article
5(1) BRRD). Resolution plans must provide 'for the resolution actions which the
resolution authority may take where the institution meets the conditions for resolution' (Article 10(1) BRRD). Recovery plans must be drawn up for groups by
the 'Union parent undertaking' (Article 7(1) BRRD), that is a parent institution
in a Member State which is not a subsidiary of another institution authorized in
any Member State, or of a financial holding company or mixed financial holding
company set up in any Member State (Article 4(1)(29) CRR via Article 2(1)(50)
BRRD). Group resolution plans must be drafted by the 'group-level resolution
authority' (Article 12(1) BRRD), that is the resolution authority in the Member
State in which the consolidating supervisor is situated (Article 2(1)(44) BRRD).
The 'consolidating supervisor' is defined as meaning a competent authority responsible for the exercise of supervision on a consolidated basis of EU parent institutions and of institutions controlled by EU parent financial holding companies or

---

[121] The reference to Art 37(9) in the BRRD definition is probably erroneous, also considering the definition of 'resolution tool' in Art 2(1)(19) BRRD which redirects to Art 37(3) BRRD.
[122] At paras 7.191–7.208.

EU parent mixed financial holding companies (Article 4(1)(41) CRR via Article 2(1)(37) BRRD). With regard to cross-border groups and significant entities and groups in the Member States participating in the SRM, the Single Resolution Board draws up the resolution plans just discussed (Article 7(2) SRMR).

7.175 The Single Resolution Board and the (national) resolution authorities are required to assess constantly the extent to which a credit institution or a group of credit institutions is 'resolvable' by either liquidating it under normal insolvency proceedings or resolving it by applying the different resolution tools and powers, while avoiding significant adverse consequences for the financial systems and ensuring the continuity of the critical functions of the credit institution or the group entities (Article 15(1) and 16(1) BRRD/Article 10(1) SRMR).[123] The national resolution authorities are empowered to demand measures necessary to reduce or remove impediments to the resolvability of the group or entity, such as the requirement to divest specific assets, to limit or cease specific activities, or to change legal or operational structures (Article 17(4) and (5) BRRD/Article 10(10)-(11) SRMR).[124]

7.176 Title II also contains a Chapter III under which, in short, parent institutions may enter into an agreement to provide financial support to group companies in financial difficulties.

Title III: Early intervention

7.177 In Title III of the BRRD (Early Intervention) supervisory authorities (rather than resolution authorities) are granted early intervention powers in order to intervene before the deterioration of the institution's financial and economic situation reaches a point at which authorities have no other alternative than resolution (Recital (40) BRRD).[125] The early intervention measures may be taken where the institution is in breach of, or is likely in the near future to be in breach of, certain prudential requirements (Article 27(1) BRRD).[126] The ECB and the national supervisory authorities have to inform the Single Resolution Board and the national resolution authorities about the early intervention in order for them to update the resolution plan and to prepare for a possible resolution (Article 27(2) BRRD/Article 13 SRMR).

7.178 The early intervention measures that may be taken by the supervisory authorities are (not exhaustively) (Article 27(1) BRRD): (a) require the management body

---

[123] Annex Section C BRRD sets out the matters that the resolution authority must examine when assessing the resolvability of an institution or a group.

[124] With regard to a group outside the scope of the SRM, the group-level resolution authority together with the resolution authority of the subsidiaries shall take reasonable steps to reach a joint decision on the application of measures to address or remove impediment to resolvability; Art 18 BRRD.

[125] The early intervention powers supplement the measures already provided for in Section IV CRD IV.

[126] These are the prudential requirements of CRR and CRD IV. The European Banking Authority shall develop guidelines, adopted by the European Commission, to promote consistent application of the trigger for use of the early intervention measures (Art 27(4) BRRD).

of the institution to implement one or more of the arrangements or measures set out in the recovery plan or to update such a recovery plan and implement one or more of the arrangements or measures set out in the updated plan; (b) require the management body of the institution to examine the situation, identify measures to overcome any problems identified and draw up an action programme to overcome those problems and a timetable for its implementation; (c) require the management body of the institution to convene, or if the management body fails to comply with that requirement convene directly, a meeting of shareholders of the institution, and in both cases set the agenda and require certain decisions to be considered for adoption by the shareholders; (d) require one or more members of the management body or senior management to be removed or replaced if those persons are found unfit to perform their duties; (e) require the management body of the institution to draw up a plan for negotiation on restructuring of debt with some or all of its creditors according to the recovery plan, where applicable; (f) require changes to the institution's business strategy; (g) require changes to the legal or operational structures of the institution; and (h) acquire, including through on-site inspections and provide to the resolution authority, all the information necessary in order to update the resolution plan and prepare for the possible resolution of the institution and for valuation of the assets and liabilities of the institution (Article 27(1) BRRD).

If these arrangements and measures do not provide for a sufficient solution, the relevant supervisory authority may also remove and replace the management body or senior management (Article 28 BRRD). **7.179**

Moreover, where the replacement of the management body or the senior management is deemed to be insufficient, the supervisory authorities may appoint a temporary administrator to replace the management of the institution or to work with this management (Article 29 BRRD). **7.180**

If, as regards groups, early intervention measures can be taken in relation to the Union parent undertaking, the consolidating supervisor must notify the European Banking Authority (EBA) and consult the other competent authorities within the 'supervisory college', ie the college in which the competent authorities of the home and host Member States co-operate[127] (Article 30(1) BRRD). The same applies for any subsidiary (Article 30(3) BRRD). **7.181**

Title IV: Resolution

Title IV of the BRRD concerns resolution. If 'conditions for resolution' are met, resolution authorities may place any entity covered by BRRD under resolution, apply the resolution tools and exercise the resolution powers as listed above.[128] **7.182**

---

[127] Art 2(1)(52) BRRD and Art 116 CRD IV.
[128] At paras 7.171–7.172.

7.183   The application of resolution tools and the exercise of resolution powers must have regard to the five following 'resolution objectives' listed in Article 31(2) BRRD/Article 14(2) SRMR: to ensure the continuity of critical functions; to avoid a significant adverse effect on the financial system, in particular by preventing contagion, including to market infrastructures, and by maintaining market discipline; to protect public funds by minimizing reliance on extraordinary public financial support; to protect depositors covered by Directive 2014/49/EU and investors covered by Directive 97/9/EC; and to protect client funds and client assets. These resolution objectives are of equal significance and must be balanced by the resolution authorities in each case (Article 31(3) BRRD/Article 14(3) SRMR).

7.184   Pursuant to Article 32(1) BRRD/Article 18(1) SRMR the conditions for resolution are that the institution is failing or likely to fail, that there is no reasonable prospect that any alternative private sector measures or supervisory action would prevent the failure of the institution within a reasonable timeframe, and that the resolution action is necessary in the public interest. In case of the resolution of a group, these conditions must be met, in principle, with regard to both the failing subsidiary and its parent company. Nonetheless, resolution action may also be taken with regard to a parent company that does not meet the resolution conditions, but one or more subsidiaries do, if the assets and liabilities of the relevant subsidiary are such that its failure threatens the institution or group as a whole or if the insolvency law of the Member State requires that the group be treated as a whole, and such resolution action is necessary (Article 33(4) BRRD).

7.185   An institution is deemed to be failing or likely to fail if the institution infringes, or it will infringe in the near future, the requirements for continuing authorization in a way that would justify the withdrawal of the authorization by the ECB or national supervisory authority. Authorization can be withdrawn, for instance, if the institution has incurred or is likely to incur losses that will deplete all or a significant amount of its own funds.[129] An institution is also deemed failing or likely to fail if its assets are, or will be in the near future, less than its liabilities; if the institution is, or it will be in the near future, unable to pay its debts or other liabilities as they fall due; or if it requires extraordinary public financial support (Article 32(4) BRRD/Article 18(4) SRMR).

7.186   A resolution action will be in the public interest if it achieves and is proportionate to one or more of the resolution objectives and winding-up of the institution under normal insolvency proceedings would not meet those resolution objectives to the same extent (Article 32(5) BRRD/Article 18(5) SRMR). As a consequence,

---

[129] 'Own funds' means 'the sum of Tier 1 capital and Tier 2 capital' (Art 2(1)(38) BRRD and Art 4(1)(118) CRR).

prior to the application of the resolution tools, the winding-up of the failing institution through normal insolvency proceedings has to be considered by the authorities. It could be hypothesized that in view of these resolution objectives,[130] such insolvency proceedings may prove to remain only suitable for the smaller credit institutions and investment firms.[131]

Under Article 34(1) BRRD/Article 15(1) SRMR, the resolution authorities must take appropriate measures to ensure that resolution actions are taken in accordance with the following general principles: **7.187**

(a) the shareholders of the institution under resolution bear the first losses;
(b) the creditors bear the losses after the shareholders, in accordance with the order of priority provided in national insolvency law (as partly harmonized by the BRRD);[132]
(c) where appropriate, senior management of the institution under resolution is replaced;
(d) the management body and senior management provides all necessary assistance for the achievement of the resolution objectives;
(e) natural or legal persons are made liable under civil law or criminal law in the Member States for their responsibility for the failure of the institution;
(f) creditors of the same class are treated equitably;
(g) no creditor incurs greater losses than would have been incurred if the institution or entity would have been wound up under normal insolvency proceedings. The shareholders and creditors who received less are compensated by the Single Resolution Fund in case the SRM applies or by the national financing arrangements;[133]
(h) deposits covered by the national deposit guarantee schemes[134] are fully protected; and
(i) the resolution action is taken in accordance with the safeguards of the SRMR and the BRRD. For example, in case of only a partial transfer of the assets, rights, or liabilities of the institution under resolution to another entity, the transactions under the same netting arrangements are protected against a separation.[135]

---

[130] See para 7.183 above.

[131] Cf Recital (45) of the BRRD which says that '[a] failing institution should in principle be liquidated under normal insolvency proceedings. However, liquidation under normal insolvency proceedings might jeopardise financial stability, interrupt the provision of critical functions, and affect the protection of depositors. In such a case it is highly likely that there would be a public interest in placing the institution under resolution and applying resolution tools rather than resorting to normal insolvency proceedings.'

[132] Especially Art 108 BRRD.

[133] Art 73 BRRD.

[134] See Directive 2014/49/EU of the European Parliament and of the Council of 16 April 2014 on deposit guarantee schemes, OJ L173.

[135] See paras 7.227 and 7.228 below.

7.188   Chapter II of Title IV BRRD consists of a single provision (Article 35 BRRD/
Article 23 SRMR) which concerns what may be considered an additional resolution tool: special management. The resolution authorities can appoint a 'special
manager' for a maximum period of one year to replace the management body of
the institution under resolution, which appointment has to be made public. In case
of an insolvency of the institution and the relevant national insolvency law provides for a so-called 'insolvency management', this management may constitute
the special management as established by the BRRD.[136] The BRRD specifies that
the special manager is required to have the qualifications, ability, and knowledge
to carry out his functions. He shall have the powers of the institution's shareholders and the management body, although the exercise of these powers is subject
to the control of the resolution authority. The special manager has the duty to
take the necessary measures to promote the BRRD's resolution objectives and to
implement the resolution actions in accordance with the decisions of the resolution
authority. In line with the provisions on the temporary administrator in the stage
of early intervention (see above, para 7.180),[137] the special manager can be removed
by the resolution authority at any time and its actions can be made subject to the
prior approval of or be limited by the resolution authority. Yet in contrast to the
tasks and powers of the temporary administrator, the duty of the special manager
in resolution may override any other duty of the management under the statute of
the institution or under national law, in case they are not consistent. Possible measures include an increase of capital, reorganization of the ownership structure of the
institution or takeovers by institutions that are financially and organizationally
sound, in accordance with the resolution tools provided for in the BRRD (Article
35(3) BRRD). With regard to entities operating in a group, the competent resolution authorities have to consider together whether it is appropriate to appoint the
same special manager for all entities concerned (Article 35(7) BRRD/Article 23
SRMR).[138]

7.189   The application of resolution tools and the exercise of resolution powers requires
an *ex-ante* valuation of the assets and liabilities of the failing institution. This valuation should provide a factual basis for several determinations with regard to the
resolution process, such as whether the conditions for resolution are met, which
resolution action is to be taken, and, in case of the application of the bail-in tool
(to be discussed more extensively below), to what extent liabilities must be written
down or converted. Another purpose of the valuation is to ensure that any losses on
the assets of the institution are fully recognized at the moment the resolution tools

---

[136] Art 35(8) BRRD. Under Dutch law, for instance, this would be a 'curator', and under French
law 'un administrateur en charge de la gestion de l'insolvabilité'.
[137] See para 7.180 above.
[138] Under the SRM, the Single Resolution Board can appoint the same special manager for all
entities in a group in case that is necessary to facilitate solution to redress the financial situation of
those entities.

are applied (Article 36(4) BRRD/Article 20(5)(g) SRMR). Article 36(1) BRRD/ Article 20(1) SRMR prescribes that such valuation is to be carried out by an independent third party.

Moreover, before any other resolution action is taken, capital instruments issued by **7.190** the institution must fully absorb the losses of the institution by writing them down or converting them into equity, in accordance with the priority of claims under normal insolvency proceedings (Recital (81) and Articles 59 and 60 BRRD/Article 20 SRMR). This write-down or conversion of capital instruments, however, is not only required prior to the application of any resolution tools and the exercise of resolution powers, but also at the point the relevant authority decides that the institution in question ceases to be viable without the exercise of this power, regardless of the application of any subsequent resolution action (Article 37(2) and 59(1) BRRD/Article 20(1) SRMR).

Chapter IV of Title IV BRRD contains a substantiation of the resolution tools, **7.191** viz the sale of business tool, the bridge institution tool, the asset separation tool, and the bail-in tool (as listed in Article 37(3) BRRD/Article 22(2) SRMR, see also above, para 7.171),[139] which will be commented on subsequently. Notably, resolution authorities may apply the asset separation tool only together with another resolution tool (Article 37(5) BRRD/Article 22(4) SRMR).

In order to maintain critical functions or viable parts of the institution in resolu- **7.192** tion, the resolution authorities are empowered by 'the sale of the business tool' to effect a sale of the institution or a part thereof to one or more private sector purchasers, by transferring shares or other instruments of ownership[140] issued by the institution under resolution or all or any of its assets, rights, or liabilities (Article 38(1) BRRD/Article 24 SRMR). Obtaining the consent of the shareholders or any third party other than the purchaser is not required for the transfer and any company or securities law procedural requirements may be suspended (Article 38(1) BRRD).[141]

Unless this would undermine the resolution objectives, the resolution authority **7.193** is required to market the assets, rights, liabilities, and shares of the institution in a way that is transparent, is free from any conflict of interest, aims at maximizing the sale prices, and shall take into account the need for a fast resolution action (Article 39 BRRD).

For the transfer commercial terms are to be obtained, with any consideration going **7.194** to the shareholders who have been deprived of their shares, or to the institution

---

[139] See also para 7.171 above.

[140] Art 2(1)(61) BRRD defines 'instruments of ownership' as '[…] shares, other instruments that confer ownership, instruments that are convertible into or give the right to acquire shares or other instruments of ownership, and instruments representing interests in shares or other instruments of ownership.'

[141] Art 38(8) and (9) BRRD detail how some securities law requirements may be suspended.

under resolution, in case of only a partial transfer of the business to the purchaser (Article 38(3)–(4) BRRD). In case of only a partial sale of the business of the institution, the residual institution from which the assets, rights, or liabilities have been transferred, shall be wound down under normal insolvency proceedings (Article 37(6) and Recital (50) BRRD/Article 22(5) SRMR).

7.195 In case no private buyer is quickly available or the failing institution is too big to merge with another institution, 'the bridge institution tool' enables the resolution authorities to transfer all or a part of the business of the institution under resolution to a temporary bridge institution, without consent of the shareholders or any third party other than the bridge institution itself (Article 40(1) and (2) BRRD/Article 25 SRMR).[142] This bridge institution is a legal entity wholly or partially owned by one or more public authorities, which may include the resolution authority, and is controlled by the resolution authority (Article 40(2) BRRD). It is created and must be operated with a view to maintaining access to critical functions and selling the business to a private sector purchaser when conditions are appropriate (Articles 40(2)(b) and 41(2) BRRD). The bridge institution may be considered as a continuation of the rights, functions, services, and activities of the institution under resolution, including the right to operate in another Member State. It must have the necessary authorization to carry on these activities and services and must comply with prudential requirements (Articles 40(9), (10), and 41(1) BRRD).

7.196 The resolution authorities have the power to force a transfer of shares, rights, assets, or liabilities from the distressed institution to the bridge institution, but may in certain circumstances also transfer these shares, rights, assets, or liabilities back to the institution under resolution (Article 40(1) and (7) BRRD—as in the case of the sale of business tool: Article 38(6) BRRD). As with the sale of business tool, in case of only a partial transfer of the business of the institution to the bridge institution, the residual institution from which the assets, rights, or liabilities have been transferred, shall be wound down under normal insolvency proceedings (Article 37(6) and Recital (50) BRRD/Article 22(5) SRMR).

7.197 The operations of the bridge institution are to be terminated when the bridge institution merges with another entity, it ceases to meet specific requirements, when all or substantially all its assets, rights, or liabilities are sold to a third party, or when the assets of the bridge institution are wound down and its liabilities are all discharged (Article 41(3) BRRD). If none of these outcomes occur within a reasonable period of time, ie in any event within two years, which may be extended with one or more additional one-year periods, the operations of the bridge institution shall be terminated as soon as possible and the business shall be wound down. Any

---

[142] S Madaus, 'Bank Failure and pre-emptive Planning' in M Haentjens and B Wessels (eds), *Bank Recovery and Resolution: A Conference Book* (2014) 61–62.

proceeds as a result of the termination shall benefit the shareholders of the bridge institution (Article 41(3)(d) and 41(5)–(8) BRRD).

The asset separation tool is a resolution tool that authorizes the resolution authori- **7.198**
ties to transfer, without consent of the shareholders or any third party, certain assets, rights, and liabilities of the institution under resolution or a bridge institution to an asset management vehicle, a so-called 'bad bank' (Article 42(1) BRRD/Article 26 SRMR). As with the bridge institution tool, this is a legal entity wholly or partially owned by one or more public authorities, which may include the resolution authority, and is controlled by the resolution authority (Article 42(2)(a) BRRD). The tool may only be used if the liquidation of the transferred assets under normal insolvency proceedings would have an adverse effect on the financial markets, the transfer of the assets, rights, or liabilities to the vehicle is necessary to ensure the proper functioning of the credit institutions under resolution or the bridge institution, or the transfer is necessary to maximize liquidation proceeds (Article 42(5) BRRD). Thus, an asset separation tool can serve to separate underperforming or toxic assets from the failing institution in order to cleanse that institution's balance sheet.[143] The asset management vehicle shall manage the assets transferred to the vehicle with the objective of maximizing their value through eventual sale or orderly wind-down (Article 42(3) BRRD). To prevent moral hazard (the institution has been offloaded of its riskiest assets), the asset separation tool may only be applied together with another resolution tool (Article 37(5) BRRD).

Recital (67) BRRD states: **7.199**

> An effective resolution regime should minimise the costs of the resolution of a failing institution borne by the taxpayers. It should also ensure that systemic institutions can be resolved without jeopardising financial stability. The bail-in tool achieves that objective by ensuring that shareholders and creditors of the failing institution suffer appropriate losses and bear an appropriate part of those costs arising from the failure of the institution. The bail-in tool will therefore give shareholders and creditors of institutions a stronger incentive to monitor the health of an institution during normal circumstances [...]

Article 2(1)(57) BRRD/Article 3(1)(33) SRMR defines the 'bail-in tool' as '[...] **7.200**
the mechanism for effecting by a resolution authority of the write-down and conversion powers in relation to liabilities of an institution under resolution [...]' However, it only applies to the liabilities of an institution that are not so excluded in Articles 44(2) and (3) and 2(1)(71) BRRD, and therefore classify as 'eligible liabilities' (Article 27(3) SRMR). Article 45 BRRD defines the amount of 'own funds' and eligible liabilities (also known as 'MREL' or minimum requirement of eligible liabilities) institutions must meet. The resolution authorities may use the tool only for two purposes: (i) to recapitalize an

---

[143] M Schillig, 'Bank Resolution Regimes in Europe II–Resolution Tools and Powers' (2012) (available at: <http://papers.ssrn.com/sol3/papers.cfm?abstract_id=2136084>) 28.

institution as a whole in order to restore its ability to comply with the conditions for authorization and to carry on its activities, and to sustain sufficient market confidence in the institution; or (ii) to guarantee financing a bridge institution, a sale of a business or an asset separation tool by converting to equity or reducing the principal amount of claims or debt instruments that are transferred (Article 43(2) BRRD/Article 27(1) SRMR).[144] In the first scenario the bail-in tool may only be applied if there is a reasonable prospect that the application of the tool, together with other relevant measures and in addition to achieving the relevant resolution objectives, will restore the institution to financial soundness and long-term viability (Article 43(3) BRRD/Article 27(2) SRMR).

7.201 Article 44(2) BRRD/Article 27(3) SRMR excludes the following liabilities:

(i) deposits covered by the national deposit guarantee schemes up to the coverage level;[145]

(ii) liabilities which are secured by a charge, pledge, lien, or title transfer collateral, including covered bonds, up to the amount of the value of the collateral;[146]

(iii) liabilities arising from the holding of client assets or client money or from the institution acting as a fiduciary in a fiduciary relationship, provided that the client or beneficiary is protected under applicable insolvency law or civil law;[147]

(iv) liabilities to institutions (except entities in the same group) with an original maturity of less than seven days;

(v) liabilities with a remaining maturity of less than seven days, owed to (operators of) systems designated according to the Settlement Finality Directive 1998 or to participants and arising from the participation in such a system;[148]

(vi) certain liabilities owed to an employee (for instance in relation to accrued salary), to a commercial or trade creditor (only if they arise from the provisions of goods and services that are critical to the daily functioning of the institution under resolution), to tax and social security authorities (if those liabilities are preferred under the applicable law) and to deposit guarantee schemes.

7.202 The above list however is subject to some flexibility, since the resolution authority in exceptional circumstances and under specific conditions may also exclude or partially exclude certain other liabilities from bail-in. The list of exclusions may for example be extended if it is not possible to bail in that liability within a reasonable time or if the exclusion is strictly necessary and is proportionate to achieve

---

[144] FJ Garcimartín, 'Resolution tools and derivatives' in M Haentjens and B Wessels (eds), *Bank Recovery and Resolution: A Conference Book* (2014) 182–83.

[145] Art 2(1)(94) BRRD. The current uniform coverage level is EUR 100,000.

[146] Art 2(1)(96) BRRD and Art 52(4) Directive 2009/65/EC.

[147] See Art 1(2) Directive 2009/65/EC ('UCITS IV') and Art 4(1) Directive 2011/61/EU ('AIFMD') for such protection.

[148] For a discussion of the Settlement Finality Directive see above, paras 7.24–7.27.

the continuity of critical functions and core business lines (Article 44(3) BRRD/ Article 27(5) SRMR). Thus, the flexibility is provided to ensure the effective rescue and continuance of key functions of the institution under resolution and to avoid disturbances to financial markets.

As a matter of principle, derivatives are included within the eligible obligations. **7.203** Yet the write-down and conversion powers with regard to liabilities that arise from derivatives are only to be exercised after a closing out of the derivatives. For that purpose, the resolution authorities are empowered to terminate and close out any derivative contract. With regard to derivatives transactions that are subject to the same master agreement, the value shall be calculated on a net basis (Article 49 BRRD).

The national resolution authorities determine on an individual basis the required **7.204** minimum funds and eligible liabilities, expressed as a percentage of the total liabilities and own funds of the institution (Article 45 BRRD).

Articles 48 and 60 BRRD determine the following sequence for exercising the **7.205** write-down of and conversion powers with regard to the eligible liabilities, either in resolution (the bail-in tool) or at the point of non-viability (the write-down and conversion powers which can also be applied independently,[149] see below, para 7.211), respectively:

(1) Common Equity Tier 1 (eg the share capital) must be reduced first;
(2) then Additional Tier 1 instruments;
(3) then Tier 2 instruments (eg subordinated medium term bonds);
(4) then other subordinated debt, consistent with the normal insolvency sequence; and
(5) finally other eligible liabilities, consistent with the normal insolvency sequence (as harmonized by Article 108 BRRD).

When applying the write-down or conversion powers, the resolution authorities **7.206** have to allocate the losses equally between the shares or other instruments of ownership and eligible liabilities of the same rank. Thus, provided that they have not been put on the list of exclusions, the principal amount of or outstanding amount payable in respect of those instruments or liabilities is reduced to the same extent pro rata to their value (Article 48(2) BRRD).

Article 47 BRRD requires specific actions in respect of the institution's sharehold- **7.207** ers and holders of other instruments of ownership when the bail-in tool is applied. The resolution authorities are required to either cancel the existing shares or other instruments of ownership or transfer them to the bailed-in creditors, or dilute those instruments of ownership as a result of the conversion of the capital instruments or eligible liabilities into instruments of ownership.

---

[149] See para 7.211 below.

7.208 When the bail-in tool is applied, the management body or an administrator must draw up a business reorganization plan that sets out measures aimed at restoring the long-term viability of the institution or parts of its business within a reasonable timescale, such as the withdrawal from loss-making activities, changes to the operational systems and infrastructure within the institution or the sale of assets or business lines (Article 52 BRRD/Article 27(16) SRMR).

7.209 To enhance the effectiveness of the bail-in powers and to facilitate cross-border recognition, Article 55 BRRD requires a contractual recognition of bail-in. Institutions are required to include a contractual provision as regards eligible liabilities governed by the law of a third country, by which the creditors recognize that liability may be subject to the write-down and conversion powers, and agree to be bound by any reduction of the principal or outstanding amount due, any conversion or any cancellation as a consequence of the exercise of the powers.

7.210 Articles 56–58 BRRD preserve government 'financial stabilisation tools' by means of extraordinary public financial support through either public equity support or temporary public ownership. The government financial stabilization tools may only be used as a last resort (Article 56(3) BRRD). Public equity support means the provision of capital by the government to a failing institution in exchange for defined capital instruments (Article 57 BRRD). Temporary public ownership means, in short, nationalization (Article 58 BRRD).

7.211 Chapter V of Title IV BRRD confers to resolution authorities the power to write down or convert (into Common Equity Tier 1 instruments) 'relevant capital instruments', that is Additional Tier 1 instruments and Tier 2 instruments. This power has to be exercised, *inter alia*, at the point the conditions for resolution are met but before any resolution action is taken, if the institution ceases to be viable (as defined in Article 59(4) BRRD) unless the power would be exercised, or in case extraordinary public support would be required by the institution (Article 59(a), (b) and (e) BRRD, respectively/Article 21(1) SRMR). As a result, the relevant capital instruments fully absorb the losses of the issuing institution prior to or without subsequent application of any resolution tools and exercise of resolution powers (Recital (81) BRRD).

7.212 In Chapter V of Title IV BRRD, resolution authorities are conferred the powers needed to apply the resolution tools discussed above. Article 63(1) lists the resolution powers, while Article 64(1) enumerates the so-called 'ancillary powers' which are granted to resolution authorities to exercise the resolution powers.

7.213 Article 66–67 BRRD requires Member States to ensure that the exercise of the transfer powers or write-down or conversion powers of the resolution authorities of another Member State has effect under their own laws, and that in case resolution actions are taken with regard to assets, shares, rights, and liabilities under the law of a third country, necessary steps are taken that the actions become effective under the law of that third country.

The European legislator has deemed the interests of market stability and effective **7.214** resolution of a failing institution to be of greater value than the interests of counterparties to limit their risk by having their contracts (automatically) terminated. Hence, early termination rights can be subject either to (permanent) disapplication under Article 68 BRRD, or to a temporary stay under Article 71 BRRD (the latter to be ordered by the resolution authorities). Resolution authorities would be authorized to invoke a temporary stay on termination rights under Article 71, if, Article 68 notwithstanding, counterparties would continue to remain entitled to employ early termination rights, for instance because these termination rights are not triggered by resolution measures per se.

More specifically, Article 68(3) BRRD provides, most notably, that contractual **7.215** terms that allow for the termination, suspension, modification, netting, or set-off rights upon the occurrence of a 'crisis prevention measure',[150] 'crisis management measure',[151] or 'any event directly linked to the application of such a measure' (together: 'BRRD measures') cannot be exercised. Hence, this provision intends to permanently prevent that the very measures directed at a recovery or orderly resolution of a failing institution result in the collective termination of its contractual relationships, which obviously would have the opposite result. However, should the failing institution cease to perform its substantive contractual obligations, all rights of termination, set-off etc remain applicable as usual (Article 68(3)(caput) and (4) BRRD).

In addition, Article 68(1) precludes that a crisis prevention measure, crisis manage- **7.216** ment measure, or any event directly linked to the application of such a measure, qualifies as an 'enforcement event' or as 'insolvency proceedings' in the context of the Financial Collateral Directive and the Settlement Finality Directive, respectively. Pursuant to the Collateral Directive, an 'enforcement event' means an event of default as agreed between parties. One of the consequences of the occurrence of such an event of default, is that close-out netting provisions become operable. In short, the occurrence of an enforcement event will prompt the operation of netting or set-off proceedings.[152] Consequently, the preclusion of a qualification of

---

[150] Pursuant to Art 1(1)(101) BRRD, '"crisis prevention measure" means the exercise of powers to direct removal of deficiencies or impediments to recoverability under Article 6(6), the exercise of powers to address or remove impediments to resolvability under Article 17 or 18, the application of an early intervention measure under Article 27, the appointment of a temporary administrator under Article 29 or the exercise of the write down or conversion powers under Article 59.'

[151] Pursuant to Art 1(1)(102), '"crisis management measure" means a resolution action or the appointment of a special manager under Article 35 or a person under Article 51(2) or under Article 72(1).'

[152] Arts 2(l) and 2(n), and 4(1) Collateral Directive.

BRRD measures as an enforcement event under the Financial Collateral Directive prevents that termination rights are triggered.

7.217 Under the Settlement Finality Directive, 'insolvency proceedings' are defined as any legal collective measure intended to wind up or reorganize the institution.[153] By disapplying all provisions of the Settlement Finality Directive relating to insolvency proceedings as defined in that Directive, the BRRD indicates that, in short, contractual relationships with clearing and settlement systems may continue to function as usual, while stressing that BRRD measures are not to be regarded as proceedings involving 'the suspending of, or imposing limitations on, transfers or payments'.[154]

7.218 For the same reasons that early termination rights can be (permanently) disapplied, viz market stability and the orderly and effective resolution of a failing institution, the European legislator has empowered resolution authorities to impose a temporary stay on certain contractual certain rights and obligations. The temporary stay powers consist of three separate but related powers, each representing a power that the resolution authorities may employ at their discretion. First, Article 69 BRRD stipulates that authorities have the power to suspend certain obligations. Second, Article 70 BRRD defines the power to restrict the enforcement of security interests. Third, Article 71 BRRD codifies the power to temporarily suspend termination rights.

7.219 All three powers have been restricted in several ways. First, they all are limited in temporal scope. The temporary stay starts as soon as the resolution authority has published a notice of the specific power employed.[155] The temporary stay lasts until midnight of the next business day. Midnight here, more specifically, means the midnight in the Member State of the resolution authority of the institution under resolution. A second means by which the resolution authorities' discretion to use the temporary stay powers is reined in (albeit not very strictly), is through the requirement of proportionality. For that reason, resolution authorities must have regard to the impact the exercise of this power has on 'the orderly functioning of financial markets'.[156] Third, to the exercise of all temporary stay powers, exceptions are made for important categories of contracts. In general, exceptions are always made for rights and obligations arising in the context of, in short, the failing institution's participation in market infrastructure systems. More specifically, market infrastructure systems are, in this context: systems of trading, clearing and settlement systems, central counterparties, and central banks. Consequently, where the Settlement Finality Directive derogates from normal insolvency laws with an

---

[153] Art 2(j) Settlement Finality Directive.
[154] ibid.
[155] Arts 69(1), 71(1), and 70(1) BRRD for the power to suspend certain obligations, termination rights, and enforcement of security interests, respectively.
[156] ibid Arts 69(5), 71(6) and 70(4) BRRD.

aim to reduce the risk related to participating in payment and securities settlement systems,[157] these derogations are respected by the BRRD.[158]

In contrast to the continuation of market infrastructures' exceptional position, the **7.220** derogations for collateralized finance transactions such as repurchase agreements and securities lending agreements, and derivatives have not been maintained. Thus, the temporary stay powers do not grant special status to these types of transactions, whilst the Collateral Directive had created specific rules for this category of transactions that oftentimes derogated from the normal insolvency laws in Member States.[159] The BRRD therefore rescinds these derogatory provisions insofar as they concern, in short, resolution measures (Article 118 BRRD).

Pursuant to Article 69(1) BRRD, authorities must have the power to suspend 'any **7.221** payment or delivery obligations pursuant to any contract to which an institution under resolution is a party'. Article 69(2) BRRD explains that this means that if during the suspension period any of the failing institution's contractual payment or delivery obligations elapse, these payments or deliveries shall not be due until immediately upon expiry of the suspension period. Under Article 69(3) BRRD, the suspension power not only alters commitments on the part of the financial institution in resolution, but also works reciprocally. Counterparties that have payment or delivery obligations towards the institution will see their obligations suspended for the same period of time.

A second power conferred upon the authorities charged with the orderly resolu- **7.222** tion of a failing institution is laid down in Article 70 BRRD, and this provision involves the power to temporarily restrict the enforcement of security interests. The authorities may invoke this power to prevent secured creditors of the institution under resolution from enforcing security interests in relation to any assets of that institution (Article 70(1) BRRD).

Under the BRRD, resolution authorities have been conferred the powers to trans- **7.223** fer assets and liabilities of a failing institution to a private purchaser or to a bridge institution. When that happens, the authorities need to be able to assess which contracts need to be transferred and determine the true value of the institution's assets and values.[160] Whilst Article 68 generally excludes (automatic) early termination rights in so far as they are triggered by resolution measures, early termination rights could also be triggered by other causes. In those situations, the value and scope of the balance sheet of the institution could change significantly and thus form an obstacle to the authorities' resolution strategy.[161] Consequently, Article 71 BRRD

---

[157] Recital (2) Settlement Finality Directive.
[158] See above at paras 7.26 and 7.27.
[159] See above at para 7.29.
[160] Recital (94) BRRD.
[161] See also FSB, Key Attributes 2014, I-Annex 5, para 1.1. and SN Grünewald, *Resolution Cross-Border Banking Crisis in the European Union* (2014) 96.

introduced the power of the resolution authorities to temporarily suspend a coun-terparty's right to terminate his contract(s) with an institution under resolution.

7.224 When applying the resolution tools and exercising the resolution powers, the reso-lution authorities are not subject to requirements to notify any person or to obtain approval or consent of any person, including the shareholders and the creditors of the institution (Article 63(2) BRRD). However, the BRRD provides several safeguards to protect the interests of the persons affected, such as shareholders, creditors, and counterparties (Article 63(4) BRRD).

7.225 If resolution tools are applied, shareholders and creditors are protected by the 'no creditor worse off'-principle (cf Article 34(1)(g) BBRD/Article 15(1)(g) SRMR), which means that where resolution authorities transfer only parts of the rights, assets, and liabilities of the institution under resolution, the shareholders and those creditors whose claims have not been transferred, receive in satisfaction of their claims at least as much as what they would have received if the institution under resolution had been wound up under normal insolvency proceedings. Also, where resolution authorities apply the bail-in tool, the shareholders and creditors whose claims have been written down or converted to equity may not incur greater losses than they would have incurred if the institution under resolution had been wound up under normal insolvency proceedings (Article 73 BRRD).

7.226 To assess whether shareholders and creditors would have received better treatment if the institution under resolution had entered into normal insolvency proceedings, a valuation must be carried out by an independent person (Article 74(1) BRRD). Should the valuation find that shareholders and creditors would have received bet-ter treatment if the institution under resolution had entered into normal insolvency proceedings, they are entitled to the payment of the difference from the resolution financing arrangements (Article 75 BRRD).

7.227 Furthermore, in case of a partial transfer of assets, rights, and liabilities from the institution under resolution, the bridge institution or the asset management vehicle to another entity, Articles 76–80 BRRD seek to prevent the separation of transactions that are economically and functionally linked. These transactions include security arrangements, title transfer financial collateral arrangements, set-off and netting arrangements, covered bonds and structured finance arrangements (including securitizations) (Article 76(1) BRRD).

7.228 Article 76 BRRD states as a general rule that the secured transactions discussed above should be awarded 'appropriate protection'. What such protection means is further clarified in the following Articles 77–80 BRRD, but these provisions all have in common that they prohibit partial transfers or the exercise of the contract modification power (see above, para 7.227).[162] Partial transfers may occur if the

---

[162] See para 7.227 above.

relevant resolution authorities would choose to transfer only some of the assets, rights, or liabilities of the institution they are resolving to another entity ('cherry-picking'). Also, they could choose to transfer just part of the assets, rights, or liabilities from a bridge institution or asset management vehicle to another person. Protection is also awarded against the exercise of the contract modification power, that is the power to 'cancel or modify the terms of a contract to which the institution under resolution is a party or substitute recipient as a party' (Articles 76(1)(a), (b) and 64(1)(f) BRRD). The safeguards of Articles 76–80 apply irrespective of the number of parties involved, how the secured transactions are created, and by which laws these transactions are governed (Article 76(3) BRRD).

Articles 77, 78, and 79 of the Directive provide specific rules for each of the three cat- **7.229** egories of secured transactions discussed above, viz title transfer financial collateral arrangements, set-off arrangements, and netting arrangements (Article 77), security arrangements (Article 78), and covered bonds and structured finance arrangements (Article 79). As stated above, all three provisions prohibit partial transfers or the exercise of the contract modification power, but all three contain an exception for covered deposits, ie for deposits guaranteed under a Deposit Guarantee Scheme. Thus, should an integral transfer of the secured transaction concerned result in there not being sufficient covered deposits left available, either with the transferor/bank under resolution or with the transferee, the resolution authorities are allowed to effectuate a partial transfer. As a result, the authorities may either transfer covered deposits without transferring 'other assets, rights or liabilities that are part of the same arrangement' or transfer 'those assets, rights or liabilities without transferring the covered deposits' (Articles 77(2), 78(2), and 79(2) BRRD). Also, under all three provisions, Member States are to ensure 'appropriate protection' whilst the Directive does not specify what this requirement exactly entails. In the absence of a specific description, an amount of flexibility is given to the Member States in order to properly adapt protective measures to the existing national regulation and legislation.[163]

Finally, trading, clearing, and settlement systems are also protected from par- **7.230** tial transfers. More specifically, when applying a resolution tool the use of which requires a partial transfer, Member States are required to ensure that these market infrastructure systems can continue to operate unaffected as provided for in the Settlement Finality Directive (Article 80(2) BRRD).

Chapter VIII of Title IV BRRD prescribes several procedural obligations for **7.231** both (the management body of) failing institutions, supervisory authorities, and

---

[163] ISDA, Possible EU Framework for Bank Recovery and Resolution, Comment Letter to EC Directorate-General Internal Market and Services, 3 March 2011, 14. Under Dutch and English law, partial transfers are not void by law. Under the same jurisdictions, a partial transfer that has been effectuated contrary to the prohibition just discussed, would not result in setting aside any netting rights.

resolution authorities. More specifically, it contains notification requirements (Articles 81 and 83 BRRD), requirements regarding the decision of the resolution authority whether the conditions for resolution have been met (Article 82 BRRD), and confidentiality requirements (Article 84 BRRD).

7.232 Title IV Chapter IX BRRD contains only two but important provisions. Article 85(1) BBRD recognizes the right for *ex-ante* judicial review at the national level and states that Member States may require that a decision to take a crisis prevention measure or a crisis management measure is subject to (*ex-ante*) judicial approval, provided that in respect of a decision to take a crisis management measure, according to national law, the procedure relating to the application for approval and the court's consideration are expeditious. BBRD Recital (92) substantiates that the court should give its decision within 24 hours and the relevant authority should take its decision immediately after the court has given its approval, without prejudice to the rights that interested parties might have in requesting the court to set aside the decision for a limited period after the resolution authority has taken the crisis management measure.

7.233 Under Article 85(2) and (3) BRRD, Member States' national law shall provide for a right of (*ex-post*) appeal against a decision to take a crisis prevention or a crisis management measure, respectively. The review shall be expeditious and national courts shall use, as a basis for their own assessment, the complex economic assessments of the facts undertaken by the resolution authority.

7.234 However, Article 85(4) BRRD provides that this right of appeal shall be subject to two limitations, given that it intends to address situations of extreme urgency, and the suspension of any decision of the resolution authorities might impede the continuity of critical functions.[164] First, the lodging of an appeal shall not automatically suspend the effects of the challenged decision (Article 85(4)(a) BRRD). Second, the resolution authority's decision shall become immediately enforceable with a rebuttable presumption that a suspension of its enforcement would be against the public interest (Article 85(4)(b) BRRD).

7.235 In order to protect the interests of third parties acting in good faith who have acquired shares, other instruments of ownership, assets, rights, or liabilities of an institution under resolution, the annulment of a resolution authority's decision shall not affect any subsequent administrative acts or transactions concluded by that resolution authority on the basis of the annulled decision. Compensation for the loss suffered by the applicant caused by the decision or act is the only type of remedy available for a wrongful decision or action by the resolution authorities (Article 85(4) BRRD).

---

[164] Recital (90) BRRD.

Article 86 BRRD prescribes that, in short, normal insolvency proceedings may not **7.236**
be commenced except at the initiative of the resolution authority and that a decision placing an institution into normal insolvency proceedings shall be taken only
with the consent of the resolution authority.

Article 85 SRMR provides for the establishment of an Appeal Panel with which **7.237**
any natural or legal person, including resolution authorities, may appeal the
decisions of the Single Resolution Board as listed in Article 85(3) SRMR. Also
these appeals have no suspensive effect (Article 85(6) SRMR). Against the decisions taken by the Appeal Panel or, where there is no right of appeal to the Appeal
Panel, by the Board, proceedings may be brought before the Court of Justice
(Article 86 SRMR).

Title V: Cross-border group resolution

Title V BRRD concerns cross-border group resolution. For purposes of this Title V, **7.238**
a 'group' means a parent undertaking and its subsidiaries (Article 2(26) BRRD).
A parent undertaking is further defined as a 'Union parent undertaking' meaning
a Union parent institution, a Union parent financial holding company, or a Union
parent mixed financial holding company, and a 'third-country parent undertaking' meaning a parent undertaking, a parent financial holding company, or a parent mixed financial holding company, established in a third country (ie outside
the EU) (Articles 2(85) and 2(87) BRRD respectively). A 'subsidiary' is defined as
'Union subsidiary', which means an institution which is established in a Member
State and which is a subsidiary of a third-country institution or a third-country
parent undertaking (Article 2(84) BRRD). Similarly, a 'branch' means a 'Union
branch', being a branch located in a Member State of a third-country institution
(Article 2(89) BRRD). In addition, the BRRD uses the term 'group entity' meaning a legal person that is part of a group (Article 2(31) BRRD), while a 'group' is
further specified a 'cross-border group'. This means a group 'having group entities
established in more than one Member State' (Article 2(27) BRRD). 'Group resolution' means either of the following: (a) the taking of resolution action at the level of
a parent undertaking or of an institution subject to consolidated supervision, or (b)
the coordination of the application of resolution tools and the exercise of resolution
powers by resolution authorities in relation to group entities that meet the conditions for resolution.[165]

The central provision of Title V BRRD seems to be Article 88 BRRD, which **7.239**
provides that group-level resolution authorities shall establish resolution colleges
to carry out, in short, BRRD tasks and, where appropriate, to ensure cooperation
and coordination with third-country resolution authorities. Resolution colleges
shall in particular provide a framework for the group-level resolution authority,

---

[165] See Art 2(42) BRRD.

the other resolution authorities and, where appropriate, competent authorities and consolidating supervisors concerned.

7.240 Article 88(2) BRRD prescribes that resolution colleges should be populated by: the group-level resolution authority; the resolution authorities of each Member State in which a subsidiary covered by consolidated supervision is established; the resolution authorities of Member States where a parent undertaking of one or more institutions of the group is established; the resolution authorities of Member States in which significant branches are located; the consolidating supervisor and the competent authorities of the Member States where the resolution authority is a member of the resolution college; the competent ministries, where the resolution authorities which are members of the resolution college are not the competent ministries; the authority that is responsible for the deposit guarantee scheme of a Member State, where the resolution authority of that Member State is a member of a resolution college; and EBA (but which has no voting rights; Article 88(4) BRRD).

7.241 Under Article 88(3) BRRD, resolution authorities of third countries where a parent undertaking or an institution established in the Union has a subsidiary institution or a branch that would be considered to be significant were it located in the Union may, at their request, be invited to participate in the resolution college as observers. The group-level resolution authority shall be the chair of the resolution college (Article 88(5) BRRD).

7.242 Article 89(1) BRRD provides that where a third country institution or third country parent undertaking has Union subsidiaries established in two or more Member States, or two or more Union branches that are regarded as significant by two or more Member States, the resolution authorities of Member States where those Union subsidiaries are established or where those significant branches are located shall establish a 'European resolution college'. In such a case the European resolution college shall perform the functions and carry out the tasks specified in Article 88 with respect to the subsidiary institutions and, in so far as those tasks are relevant, to branches (Article 89(2) BRRD). However, the requirement to establish a European resolution college may be waived (Article 89(4) BRRD).

7.243 Article 90(1) BRRD provides that subject to Article 84 ('Confidentiality') BRRD resolution authorities and competent authorities shall provide one another on request with all the information relevant for the exercise of the other authorities' tasks under the BRRD. It is for the group-level resolution authority to coordinate the flow of all relevant information between resolution authorities (Article 90(2) BRRD).

7.244 When the group-level resolution authority receives a notification that an institution or any entity that is a subsidiary in a group, meets the conditions referred to in Article 32 ('Conditions for resolution') or Article 33 ('Conditions for resolution with regard to financial institutions and holding companies') (see above, at paras 7.184-7.186),[166] it will consult the other members of the relevant resolution college and shall determine whether the resolution actions or other measures notified would make it likely that the conditions laid down in Article 32 or 33 BRRD would be satisfied in relation to a group entity in another Member State. If not, the resolution authority responsible for that institution or that entity may take the resolution actions or other measures notified. If so, the group-level resolution authority shall, no later than 24 hours after receiving the notification propose a group resolution scheme and submit it to the resolution college (Article 91(2)–(5) BRRD).

Article 92 BRRD concerns group resolution and generally follows the structure **7.245** Article 91 BRRD provides in relation to a subsidiary in a group. Where a group-level resolution authority decides that a Union parent undertaking for which it is responsible meets the conditions referred to in Article 32 or 33 BRRD it shall notify the consolidating supervisor, if different, and to the other members of the resolution college of the group in question. The group-level resolution authority may then decide to propose a group resolution scheme, on which a joint decision must be agreed between the group-level resolution authority and resolution authorities of responsible for the relevant subsidiaries (Article 92(3) BRRD)—who may disagree, depart from the scheme, or take independent resolution actions or measures (Article 92(4) BRRD). Where the actions proposed by the group-level resolution authority under Article 92(1) BRRD do not include a group resolution scheme, the group-level resolution authority shall take its decision after consulting the members of the resolution college (Article 92(2) BRRD).

As stated above,[167] SRMR radically deviates from the above approach which **7.246** reflects the traditional European view that generally does not treat groups of companies as a single entity, for under this Regulation, the Single Resolution Board is empowered to take decisions in relation to the groups covered by the Regulation as a whole. More specifically, and as a derogation of Title V of BRRD, Article 7(2) SRMR requires that the Single Resolution Board be responsible for adopting all decisions relating to the resolution for those groups.

Title VI: Relations with third countries

Title VI of BRRD ('Relations with third countries') contains six provisions. Article **7.247** 93(1) BRRD introduces the possibility of international agreements on cooperation between the resolution authorities and the relevant third country authorities. In the absence of such agreements Member States may enter into bilateral agreements with a third country until the entry into force of an agreement as just referred to (Article 93(4) BRRD).

---

[166] See paras 7.184–7.186 above.
[167] At para 7.167.

7.248　Article 94 BRRD/Article 33 SRMR sets out rules for recognition and enforcement of third-country resolution proceedings in respect of third-country resolution proceedings unless and until an international agreement with the relevant third country enters into force, or following the entry into force of such an international agreement to the extent that recognition and enforcement of third-country resolution proceedings is not governed by that agreement. In essence, when there is a European resolution college, it must take a joint decision to recognize third-country resolution proceedings (Article 94(2) BRRD). If no joint decision has been reached or in the absence of a European resolution college each resolution college concerned makes its own decision on whether to recognize and enforce such proceedings (Article 94(3) BRRD).

7.249　On the grounds listed in Article 95 BRRD/Article 33(3) SRMR, a recognition or enforcement of third-country resolution proceedings may be refused.

7.250　Article 96 BRRD provides that (EU) resolution authorities may exercise resolution powers in relation to a Union branch that is not subject to any third-country resolution proceedings or against whom recognition is refused.

7.251　Article 97 BRRD introduces 'non-binding framework cooperation agreements', to be concluded by EBA with relevant third country authorities unless and until an international agreement with the relevant third country enters into force, or following the entry into force of such an international agreement to the extent that, in short, the framework cooperation agreement is not governed by that international agreement. The non-binding framework co-operation agreements are not to make provisions in relation to specific institutions and nor impose legal obligations upon Member States (Article 97(2) BRRD). Instead, they are intended to establish processes and arrangements between the participating authorities for sharing information and co-operation (Article 97(3) BRRD). It is foreseen that competent authorities or resolution authorities (including the Single Resolution Board, see Article 32(4) SRMR), where appropriate, shall conclude non-binding co-operation arrangements in line with the EBA framework arrangement with the relevant third-country authorities (Article 97(4) BRRD).

7.252　Finally, Article 98 BRRD sets rules for exchanging information with relevant third-country authorities. As a matter of principle, the provision prescribes that (EU) resolution authorities, competent authorities, and competent ministries may not exchange confidential information with third country authorities, unless certain listed conditions are met.

Title VII: Financing arrangements

7.253　Title VII of BRRD ('Financing Arrangements') concerns the financing of resolutions, for there are circumstances when the effectiveness of the resolution tools applied may depend on the availability of short-term funding for an institution or a bridge institution, the provision of guarantees to potential purchasers, or the provision of capital to the bridge institution (Recital (103) BRRD). Also, government financial stabilization tools, such as temporary public ownership may require short-term funding (Recital (8) BRRD). Title VII sets up a system for: (a) national financing arrangements; (b) the borrowing between national financing arrangements; and (c) the mutualization of national financing arrangements in the case of a group resolution (Article 99 BRRD).

Under Article 100 BRRD, all Member States must establish at least one financing **7.254** arrangement for the purpose of ensuring the effective application by the resolution authority of the resolution tools and powers. Such an arrangement will be funded through: (a) *ex-ante* contributions with a view to reaching a target level of at least 1 per cent of the amount of covered deposits of all the institutions authorized in a certain territory; (b) *ex-post* extraordinary contributions as where the contributions specified in point (a) are insufficient; and (c) contract borrowings (Article 100(4) BRRD).

Article 101(1) BRRD lists exhaustively the purposes for which the financing **7.255** arrangements may be used. Article 103 BRRD prescribes that Member States must raise contributions to the financing arrangement at least annually from the institutions authorized in their territory, and how those contributions should be calculated. Under Article 104 BRRD, extraordinary *ex-post* contributions may be raised from the institutions authorized in a certain territory, where the available financial means are not sufficient to cover the losses, costs, or other expenses incurred by the use of the financing arrangements.

Articles 105–107 BRRD elaborate on the borrowing between national financing **7.256** arrangements (Article 106 BRRD) and the mutualization of national financing arrangements in the case of a group resolution (Article 107 BRRD). For purposes of such mutualization, the national financing arrangement of each institution that is part of a group contributes to the financing of the group resolution (Article 107(1) BRRD), and the group-level resolution authority, after consulting the resolution authorities of the institutions that are part of the group, shall propose a financing plan as part of the group resolution scheme provided for in Articles 91 and 92 (see above, paras 7.244-7.245).[168] Under Article 109 BRRD, also the deposit guarantee scheme to which an institution is affiliated may be used for its resolution under certain circumstances.

As regards the SRM, the 'national financing arrangements' discussed above merge **7.257** into a Single Resolution Fund, owned and managed by the Single Resolution Board (Articles 67–79 SRMR).

---

[168] See paras 7.244–7.245 above.

7.258 Somewhat hidden but most importantly, Article 108 BRRD requires that Member States amend (if necessary) their national law governing normal insolvency proceedings so that: (i) that part of eligible deposits from natural persons and micro, small, and medium-sized enterprises which exceeds the coverage level provided for in Article 6 of Directive 2014/49/EU (now: EUR 100,000); and (ii) deposits that would be eligible deposits from natural persons, micro, small, and medium-sized enterprises were they not made through branches located outside the Union of institutions established within the Union, rank higher than the ranking provided for the claims of ordinary unsecured, non-preferred creditors. Moreover, covered deposits and deposit guarantee schemes subrogating to the rights and obligations of covered depositors in insolvency rank higher than the claims just referred to. Thus, this provision represents the EU harmonization of substantive national insolvency law, which is otherwise virtually absent in European law.

Title VIII: Penalties

7.259 Articles 110–114 BRRD require that, in short, administrative penalties and other administrative measures be applied by resolution authorities or (where different) supervisory authorities where the national provisions transposing BRRD have not been complied with (Article 110(1) and (3) BRRD). Such administrative penalties must be published (Article 112 BRRD).

7.260 Articles 38–41 SRMR contain substantive rules on the penalties the Single Resolution Board may impose, including their amounts, the aggravating or mitigating factors the Board must take into account, procedural safeguards, and disclosure and enforcement regulations.

8

COMMENTARY ON REGULATION
1346/2000 AND RECAST REGULATION
2015/848 ON INSOLVENCY PROCEEDINGS

Commentary by Gabriel Moss QC[1] and Tom Smith QC.[2]

Additional commentary by: Professor Michael Bogdan (**MB**); Justice Timo Esko (**TE**); Professor Ian Fletcher LLD QC (Hon) (**IF**); Professor Francisco Garcimartin (**FG**); Stuart Isaacs QC (**SI**); Professor Alberto Piergrossi (**AP**); Professor Miguel Virgos (**MV**); Professor Bob Wessels (**Wess**); and Alex Wood (**AW**).

Details of the authors of the commentary and additional commentary are to be found in the List of Contributors at the start of this book.

This chapter first provides a commentary on the original Regulation ('OR')[3] on insolvency proceedings (1346/2000), which applies to proceedings opened before 26 June 2017, and then a commentary on the Recast Regulation ('RR'),[4] which applies to proceedings opened on or after 26 June 2017.[5] Despite the repeal of the OR, proceedings opened prior to 26 June 2017 will continue to be governed by the Original Regulation.[6]

The Recitals[7] to the OR and the RR are not reproduced here and can be found at Appendix 1 (OR) and Appendix 3 (RR).

---

[1] Gabriel Moss QC was a member of a panel of experts which advised the European Commission on the proposed changes.

[2] Assisted by Adam Al-Attar, Robert Amey, Andrew Shaw, Ryan Perkins, barristers, of 3–4 South Square, Gray's Inn, London.

[3] Council Regulation 1346/2000 of 29 May 2000, OJ L160 (30 June 200) p 1.

[4] Regulation (EU) 2015/848 of the European Parliament and of the Council of 20 May 2015 on insolvency proceedings, OJ L141, (5 June 2015) p 19.

[5] Article 84 RR.

[6] Article 84(2) RR. On a literal reading of Article 84 RR, there is a lacuna affecting insolvency proceedings opened on 26 June 2017 itself. To make sense of the provisions, Article 84(1) RR needs to be interpreted so as to make the RR applicable to proceedings opened *on or after* 26 June 2017: see the commentary on Article 84 RR below.

[7] 'Recitals' is the English legal expression for the numbered paragraphs which are preceded by 'Whereas'. The section with the Recitals can also be called the 'Preamble', *Josef Syska acting as the Administrator of Elektrim SA (In bankruptcy) v Vivendi Universal SA* (hereinafter referred to as *Elektrim v Vivendi*) [2008] EWHC 2155 (Comm), [2009] 1 All ER (Comm) 244.

The applicable principles of interpretation are dealt with in chapter 2 above. The principal tools of interpretation used here are the Recitals to the OR and RR, printed respectively in Appendices 1 and 3, and the Virgos-Schmit Report ('VS'), referred to below and printed in Appendix 2. With regard to using the Recitals to OR, care must be taken, since they are often copied or adapted from VS[8] and in such a case need to be considered in the context from which they are taken.[9]

VS was elaborated in relation to the OR in Virgos and Garcimartin, *The European Insolvency Regulation: Law and Practice* (Kluwer, 2004) ('VG').

The Court of Justice of the European Union is variously referred to as 'CJEU' or 'ECJ'.

The concept 'centre of main interests' is sometimes abbreviated as 'COMI'.

---

[8] Set out in app 2 below; see also n 15 below.
[9] See eg in relation to Recital (13), which is taken from para 75 of the Virgos-Schmit Report, *Re Stojevic* [2007] BPIR 141, HCJ.

Council Regulation 1346/2000
on Insolvency Proceedings ('OR')

A. Chapter I: General Provisions

(OR) Article 1—Scope

1. This Regulation shall apply to collective insolvency proceedings which entail the partial or total divestment of a debtor and the appointment of a liquidator.
2. This Regulation shall not apply to insolvency proceedings concerning insurance undertakings, credit institutions, investment undertakings which provide services involving the holding of funds or securities for third parties, or to collective investment undertakings.

General principles

8.01 Article 1 sets out the scope and subject-matter of the OR. This should be read in the light of the 'Recitals' to the OR which set out in some detail the rationale behind the OR. In particular, it is apparent that the OR is not only intended to deal with the fact that insolvencies increasingly have cross-border aspects but is also intended to be one element in the progress towards a complete and free internal market between all the Member States. This purpose should always be borne in mind given that national courts, taking their cue from the approach to legislation of the CJEU, are bound to adopt a purposive approach to the construction of the OR.[10]

---

[10] On the interpretation of the OR generally, see ch 2 above. In *Trustees of the Olympic Airlines SA Pension & Life Assurance Scheme v Olympic Airlines SA* [2015] 1 WLR 2399, counsel for the respondent submitted that the RR could be used as an aid to the interpretation of the OR. The Supreme Court did not address this submission in its judgment. It is considered that the RR should not be

The Recitals note that insolvencies and cross-border insolvency proceedings are **8.02** factors which can affect the proper functioning of the European internal market. Accordingly, it is desirable that cross-border insolvency proceedings should operate efficiently and effectively.[11] In order to achieve this there is a need for the co-ordination of the various measures which may be taken in relation to an insolvent debtor's assets across the European Union.[12] In addition it is said to be necessary for the proper functioning of the internal market that any incentives for parties to transfer assets or proceedings from one Member State to another (forum shopping) are avoided.[13] Furthermore, bankruptcy, proceedings relating to the winding-up of insolvent companies or other legal persons, judicial arrangements, compositions, and analogous proceedings[14] are excluded from the scope of the Convention on Jurisdiction and the Enforcement of Judgments in Civil and Commercial Matters signed in Brussels on 27 September 1968 (the Brussels Convention).[15]

It is therefore stated that the purpose of the OR is to be a Community law meas- **8.03** ure, binding[16] and directly applicable in Member States, containing provisions relating to jurisdiction, recognition, and applicable law in respect of insolvency proceedings.[17] It is important to bear these statements of general principle in

---

used as an aid to the interpretation of the OR, although the OR can plainly be used as an aid to the interpretation of the RR. Accordingly, there is minimal discussion of the RR in the commentary on the OR.

[11] Recitals (2), (3).

[12] Recital (3).

[13] Recital (4). Unfortunately, the Recital does not distinguish between 'good' forum shopping, ie seeking a forum which is likely to give the best outcome for creditors, from 'bad' forum shopping, where the debtor seeks to do the best for himself at the expense of his creditors. This is discussed further under *Right to move COMI and 'forum shopping'* at paras 8.114 et seq below. [Emphasis was placed on the objective expressed in Recital (4) by the ECJ in its judgment in Case C1/04 *Staubitz-Schreiber* [2006] ECR I-701, para 25, to support the court's purposive approach to its ruling on the capability of a debtor to move its COMI between the date when a request to open insolvency proceedings is lodged and the date when the court is able to deliver its judgment opening the proceedings. The thesis that it is the objective of the OR to counter 'opportunistic' and 'fraudulent' forum shopping, while accepting that it is appropriate 'on occasions' to encourage practices which have a beneficent purpose, was concisely stated by AG Colomer in his submissions to the ECJ in Case C-339/07 *Seagon v Deko Marty Belgium NV* [2009] ECR I-767 at para 60. (IF)]

[14] The expression 'judicial arrangements, compositions and analogous proceedings' may be restricted to situations of actual or threatened insolvency: see the Jenard Report [1979] OJ C59/1 and the Schlosser Report [1979] OJ C59/71. The point was left open in *Re Sovereign Marine & General Insurance Co Ltd* [2006] BCC 774, HCJ, para 62.

[15] Recital (7). See Art 1(2) of the Brussels Convention implemented into English law by the Civil Jurisdiction and Judgments Act 1982, s 2(1), Sch 1. The Brussels Convention was replaced within the EU (except Denmark) by Regulation 44/01 and then by Regulation 1215/2012 on jurisdiction and the recognition and enforcement of judgments in civil and commercial matters (referred to hereinafter as the Recast Regulation on Civil Jurisdiction and Judgments). Art 1(2)(b) of Regulation 1215/2012 states that this Regulation does not apply to 'bankruptcy, proceedings relating to the winding-up of insolvent companies or other legal persons, judicial arrangements, compositions and analogous proceedings'.

[16] [Being a Regulation, it has general application and is binding and directly applicable: Art 249 EC. (**SI**)] See also ch 2 above and app 4 below in connection with Art 249 EC.

[17] Recital (8).

mind when considering the effect of the individual Articles. In general terms, the correct interpretation will be the one which promotes the general purpose of the OR.

8.04 Turning to the text of Article 1 itself, Article 1(1) states that the OR applies to collective insolvency proceedings which entail the partial or total divestment of a debtor and the appointment of a liquidator. Article 1(1) thus encompasses four elements:

- Proceedings must be *collective*. The OR therefore does not apply to those proceedings which are commenced by one creditor only for his sole benefit. It follows that the OR does not apply to English administrative receiverships or to foreign equivalents.[18] Equally it does not include execution or debt collection proceedings commenced against a debtor by an individual creditor. On the other hand, winding-up petitions and administration applications by creditors, which may be driven by a subjective motivation of recovering a debt, are nevertheless regarded by English law as requests for administration or winding-up orders as class remedies.[19]

- The proceedings must be *insolvency* proceedings. It is said that this means that the proceedings must be based on the debtor's insolvency (as determined by national law) and not on any other grounds.[20] However, the question of whether or not a debtor is insolvent is a matter to be determined by national law; the OR is not aiming to create uniform legislation in this regard.[21] It follows that as a matter of English law the OR would not apply, for example, where a winding-up order is made on the grounds of public interest or on other 'non-insolvency' grounds.[22] However, a regulator's petition which is

---

[18] [And a fortiori, Law of Property Act receiverships are excluded from the scope of the OR. (**IF**)]

[19] *Re Leigh Estates (UK) Ltd* [1994] BCC 292.

[20] The Report on the Convention of Insolvency Proceedings by Miguel Virgos and Etienne Schmit (the 'Virgos-Schmit Report') para 49(b). The Report deals with the OR when it was in the form of a proposed Convention. As described above, it did not prove possible to bring the Convention into force. However, the OR is modelled almost entirely on the terms of the Convention signed in November 1995 by 14 of the 15 states of the EU. A copy of the Virgos-Schmit Report is at app 2 below. It has been cited in a number of national decisions, and also by AG Jacobs in his opinion in Case C-341/04 *Re Eurofood IFSC Ltd* [2006] ECR I-3813, and by AG Colomer in his Opinion in Case C-1/04 *Re Staubitz-Schreiber* [2006] ECR I-701. In *Trustees of the Olympic Airlines SA Pension & Life Assurance Scheme v Olympic Airlines SA* [2015] 1 WLR 2399, Lord Sumption described the Virgos-Schmit Report as an 'authoritative commentary' on the Convention (see [9] of the judgment), and held that it provided 'much the most useful source of guidance' on the interpretation of Article 2(h) (see [10] of the judgment).

[21] J-L Vallens, 'Procédures d'insolvabilité: présentation du règlement sur les procédures d'insolvabilité' Lamy Droit Commercial, No 125, August–September, 2. The laws of some Member States in this regard focus more on the strict accountancy test of whether assets exceed liabilities while others place greater emphasis on the failure to pay debts over a period of time.

[22] See *Re Marann Brooks CSV Ltd* [2003] BPIR 1159 where the court held that winding-up petitions presented on public interest grounds are not within the scope of the OR. The OR also does not apply to a resolution opening a members' voluntary winding-up proceeding ('MVL'), since an MVL

necessarily based on an allegation of insolvency will be covered.[23] Member States (such as the United Kingdom) which have proceedings which can be utilized either as insolvency proceedings or on grounds other than insolvency must ensure that their courts are aware of the requirement to make clear the grounds on which each of those proceedings has been commenced (ie based on insolvency or not) so that it can be easily determined whether or not the OR applies in each case. However, since the OR applies to rescue and reconstruction proceedings as well as traditional insolvency proceedings, even a threat or danger of insolvency will be sufficient to bring a proceeding within the OR. Thus, in *Bank Handlowy*,[24] the ECJ treated a French rescue procedure known as *sauveguarde* as an insolvency proceeding—even though *sauveguarde* is designed to prevent insolvency, and cannot be opened if the debtor has already become insolvent under French law. *Sauvegarde* is listed as an insolvency proceeding in Annex A of the OR, and the parties did not challenge its inclusion on the list.[25]

[In this respect the United Kingdom has led the way in taking the necessary steps to ensure that the authorized forms of judicial orders to be made when opening insolvency proceedings are so designed as to make it a requirement that the court expressly declares whether the OR will apply to the proceedings and whether, if so, the proceedings will be main, secondary, or territorial proceedings as defined in Article 3. (**IF**)]

• The proceedings must entail the *total or partial divestment of the debtor*. 'Divestment' means the transfer to the liquidator of the power of administration and disposal over all or part of the debtor's assets or the limitation of those powers through the intervention and control of the debtor's actions.[26] It follows that it is sufficient that an insolvency proceeding involves a partial divestment of the debtor's assets for the OR to apply.[27]

---

is required to commence on the footing that the company is or will be solvent: Insolvency Act 1986, ss 89, 90. However, if insolvency ensues and the MVL is converted under s 96 to a creditors' voluntary liquidation ('CVL'), upon confirmation by the court the OR will apply.

[23] *FSA v Dobb White* [2004] BPIR 479 (regulator's petition for winding-up grounded on an allegation of insolvency required by the relevant statute).

[24] Case C-116/11 *Bank Handlowy w Warszawie SA v Christianapol sp. z o.o.* [2013] Bus LR 956, ECLI: EU:C 2012:739.

[25] ibid at [31]–[35].

[26] Virgos-Schmit Report para 49(c).

[27] Accordingly the OR applies to cover voluntary arrangements since these typically involve divesting a debtor of at least some of his assets: see Annex A. But would the position be different in the case of an individual voluntary arrangement where all the contributions were provided by a third party? This may be a case where the fact that the proceeding is listed in Annex A takes precedence over strict compliance with the principles set out in Art 1(1): see also the discussion at para 8.07 below. The mechanism of *surrendement* in French law whereby a private individual may reach a settlement with his creditors is not included because of the absence of divestiture and also because of the amicable and contractual nature of the mechanism: see Vallens (n 21 above).

[The divestment may be partial with regard to the assets or with regard to the debtor's powers (he may, for example, retain certain authority to dispose of his assets subject to the supervision and approval by the liquidator). (**MB**)]

• The proceedings must entail the *appointment of a liquidator*. For the purposes of the OR, a 'liquidator' is a broad concept and certainly goes much beyond the idea of a liquidator as understood in English insolvency law. Indeed, Article 2(b) of the OR states that a 'liquidator' is any person or body whose function is to administer or liquidate assets of which the debtor has been divested or to supervise the administration of his affairs. Those persons and bodies considered to be 'liquidators' for the purposes of the OR are set out in Annex C.[28] In relation to England and Wales ('England'): these are a liquidator, a supervisor of a voluntary arrangement, an administrator (including—as a result of a change to Annex C—administrators appointed out of court), the official receiver (acting as liquidator or trustee in bankruptcy), a trustee (in bankruptcy), and (as a result of a change to Annex C) a provisional liquidator.

Debtor

8.05 In addition to the four requirements above it is axiomatic that in all insolvency proceedings there must be a debtor. The reference to a 'debtor' in Article 1(1) is to any natural or legal person of that status and accordingly the OR applies to the insolvencies of individuals and companies and other legal entities.[29] Moreover, there is no distinction between the capacities in which individuals may have incurred liabilities.[30] However, the general rules defining jurisdiction only apply in respect of a debtor who has his 'centre of main interests' in one of the Member States.[31] Thus the OR does not apply at all where a debtor's centre of main interests is located outside the European Union or in Denmark.[32] For example, a company registered in England whose centre of main interests was in New York would be outside the OR.

---

[28] See app 1 below.

[29] See Recital (9).

[30] Some Member States only apply insolvency proceedings to individuals when they are acting in the capacity of a trader. Under the OR each Member State in which proceedings are sought to be opened in respect of a debtor remains free to apply its own rules of national law to determine whether the proceedings should be opened.

[31] Art 3(1); Recital (14).

[32] See Recital (14). In *Re Arena Corp Ltd* [2004] BPIR 375, [2003] EWHC 3032 (Ch) the English court made a winding-up order in relation to a company which had its COMI in Denmark since Denmark had not opted into the OR (see Recital (33)) and therefore the OR did not apply so as to preclude the English court from making a winding-up order in respect of the company. [Note: see the questions referred to the CJEU in Case C-148/08 *Finn Mejnertsen v Betina Mandal Barsoe*, reference by the Spanish Commercial Court concerning the position of Denmark. (The case was subsequently removed from the register: [2009] OJ C 69/32) (**IF**)]

It should be noted that there is no requirement that the insolvency proceedings **8.06** result in the realization of the debtor's assets for the benefit of creditors. Thus the OR extends in principle to all forms of insolvency proceeding including both those which result in the winding-up of the debtor and those which result in the reorganization or restructuring of the debtor's affairs.

Defined insolvency proceedings

However, although these statements of general principle are important in under- **8.07** standing the OR, it will not generally be necessary for the courts to apply these principles and determine whether particular proceedings fall within the scope of the OR. The particular insolvency proceedings to which the OR applies are detailed in Annex A to the OR. In *Bank Handlowy*,[33] the CJEU considered the relationship between Annex A and Article 1(1), and established an important principle:

> [33] … Once proceedings are listed in Annex A to the Regulation, they must be regarded as coming within the scope of the Regulation. Inclusion in the list has the direct, binding effect attaching to the provisions of a Regulation.

The relevant proceedings in Annex A to the OR are set out in list form in order to provide for greater certainty in the application of the OR.[34] As such the principal practical importance of Article 1(1) is in determining whether such new insolvency proceedings as may be developed in the future should also be brought within in the scope of the OR.[35]

English insolvency proceedings

As regards the jurisdiction of England, the OR applies to the following insolvency **8.08** proceedings as listed in Annex A:

- Winding-up by the court.
- Creditors' voluntary winding-up (with confirmation by the court).[36]

---

[33] Case C-116/11 *Bank Handlowy w Warszawie SA v Christianapol sp. z o.o.* [2013] Bus LR 956, ECLI: EU:C 2012:739, at [31]–[35].

[34] J-L Vallens notes that whilst the draftsmen opted for this approach in the interests of certainty, it does heighten the risk that there may be certain proceedings which both fall outside the scope of the OR and are also excluded from the scope of the Regulation on Civil Jurisdiction and Judgments by Art 1(2)(b) of that Regulation: 'Le droit européen de la faillite: la Convention relative aux procédures d'insolvabilité' (1995) Actualité Legislative Dalloz 239.

[35] See Art 45 which sets out the procedure for the amendment of the annexes. Amendments were made to the annexes in 2004 upon the accession of the ten new Member States to the EU and further amendments were made between 2005 and 2014 pursuant to the procedure in Art 45: see Council Implementing Regulation (EU) 663/2014 of 5 June 2014. (Full references for all the amendments to the OR and to the three Annexes so far made under the Art 45 procedure are set out in ch 1 above at para 1.24: see at nn 45–51 and text thereto. See also ibid at nn 52–53, concerning additional amendments made on the occasions of enlargement of the membership of the EU.)

[36] The restriction of the application of the OR to only those creditors' voluntary liquidations which have been confirmed by the court reflects the fact that insolvency administrators in Europe are

- Administration, including appointments made by filing prescribed documents with the court.
- Voluntary arrangements under insolvency legislation.
- Bankruptcy.

Excluded undertakings

8.09 Particular categories of undertaking have deliberately been left outside the scope of the OR. Article 1(2) states that the OR does not apply to insolvency proceedings in relation to insurance undertakings,[37] credit institutions (ie banks and similar entities),[38] investment undertakings which provide services involving the holding of funds or securities for third parties,[39] or to collective investment undertakings.[40] These entities were excluded from the scope of the OR because they are already subject to specific EU regulation and because it was envisaged that insolvencies of these undertakings which have cross-border elements will be co-ordinated by means of separate Directives.

Insurance undertakings

8.10 Council Directive (EC) 2001/17 on the reorganization and winding-up of insurance undertakings dealt with insolvency proceedings for insurers. This Directive was implemented into English law principally by the Insurers (Reorganisation and Winding up) Regulations 2004.[41] The provisions of the Directive have been subsumed into Directive 2009/138/EC ('Solvency II') under Title IV.

8.11 Although by its terms the OR does not apply to insolvency proceedings concerning insurance undertakings, there is no definition of 'insurance undertaking' in the OR. The scope of the exclusion has therefore to be worked out from the

---

normally appointed by a court or other official body. For the confirmation of creditors' voluntary liquidation by the court see r 7.62 of the Insolvency Rules 1986 added by the Insolvency (Amendment) Rules 2002.

[37] See paras 8.10–8.13 below and see ch 7 above.

[38] A 'credit institution' is any entity covered by the definition in Council Directive (EEC) 77/780 [1977] OJ L 322/30 (as amended by Council Directive (EC) 95/26): 'any undertaking whose activity is to receive deposits or other refundable funds and to grant loans for its own account'. See ch 7 above and M Dassesse, S Isaacs, and G Penn, *EC Banking Law* (2nd edn, 1999).

[39] An 'investment undertaking' is any entity covered by the definition in Council Directive (EC) 93/22 [1993] OJ L141/27 (as amended by Council Directive (EC) 95/26). See ch 7 above. In *Byers v Yacht Bull Corp* [2010] BCC 368, Sir Andrew Morritt C emphasized that an investment undertaking must provide services involving the 'holding of funds or securities for third parties' in order to fall within the Article 1(2) exception: other types of investment undertakings do not qualify (see [37] of the judgment).

[40] A 'collective investment undertaking' is any undertaking covered by the definition in Council Directive (EEC) 85/611[1985] OJ L375/3 (as amended by Council Directive (EC) 95/26). See also ch 7 above. The exclusion refers to bodies which are authorized to carry on that type of business pursuant to the relevant directives and not to unauthorized collective investment undertakings: *FSA v Dobb White* [2004] BPIR 479.

[41] SI 2004/353. The other implementing legislation is referred to in Moss and Smith (see n 42 below).

terms of the Directives.[42] Recital (2) to Directive 2001/17 points out that insurance undertakings are expressly excluded from the scope of the Regulation on insolvency proceedings. It seems, therefore, that what is excluded from the OR can be taken to be that which is *included* in the Directives. It is generally understood that the Directives are meant to plug a gap left by the OR. For the purposes of Solvency II, 'insurance undertaking' means a direct life or non-life insurance undertaking which has received official authorization under Article 14 of Solvency II: see Article 13(1). The reorganization and winding up provisions of the Directives thus do not apply to reinsurers as such.

The result in relation to reinsurance is not very clear. It may well be that those **8.12** reinsurers who have been authorized to conduct direct insurance will be included in the insolvency aspects of the Directives and excluded from the OR but that any reinsurer who is *not* authorized to conduct direct insurance business is not included in the insolvency aspects of the Directives and therefore should be taken to be included in the OR. A further possibility is that a reinsurer who is authorized to write direct insurance is subject to the OR in respect of its reinsurance business and subject to the Directive in respect of its direct insurance business.

[An argument against the latter possibility is the fact that it would be difficult to imagine insolvency proceedings regarding only some of the debtor's activities. (**MB**)]

Credit institutions

Council Directive (EC) 2001/24 on the reorganisation and winding up of credit **8.13** institutions as amended deals with insolvency proceedings for banks and investment firms and with bank resolution proceedings.[43] This Directive has been implemented into English law by the Credit Institutions (Reorganisation and Winding Up) Regulations 2004.[44]

Intra-Union effects

It should be noted that the OR applies generally only to the intra-European Union **8.14** *effects* of insolvency proceedings. It generally only creates effects as between Member States and not between Member States and non-Member States in relation to insolvency proceedings.[45]

---

[42] Directive 2001/17 is set out and discussed in detail by G Moss and T Smith in G Moss and B Wessels, *EU Banking and Insurance Insolvency* (2006). See also G Moss *et al, Cross Frontier Insolvency of Insurance Companies* (2001).
[43] See ch 7 above at 7.38–7.48.
[44] SI 2004/1045.
[45] Member States for the purposes of the OR do not include Denmark, which is not bound by the OR: see Recital (33).

8.15 It was also originally thought generally that the OR applied only to international jurisdiction and so did not regulate the domestic law position within a Member State.[46] However, the CJEU in *Schmid (as liquidator of the assets of Zimmermann) v Hertel* (Case C-328/12)[47] held that the German courts had jurisdiction under Article 3 to hear an avoidance action against a Swiss resident, even though there was no jurisdiction to do so under German domestic law.[48] It now seems to be the case that where a court has international jurisdiction to open insolvency proceedings within the OR and hear a case against a party outside the EU as part of such proceedings, it cannot refuse jurisdiction on the grounds of any limitation in domestic jurisdiction based on the residence of the defendant.

(OR) Article 2—Definitions

For the purposes of this Regulation:

(a) 'insolvency proceedings' shall mean the collective proceedings referred to in Article 1(1). These proceedings are listed in Annex A;

(b) 'liquidator' shall mean any person or body whose function is to administer or liquidate assets of which the debtor has been divested or to supervise the administration of his affairs. Those persons and bodies are listed in Annex C;

(c) 'winding-up proceedings' shall mean insolvency proceedings within the meaning of point (a) involving realising the assets of the debtor, including where the proceedings have been closed by a composition or other measure terminating the insolvency, or closed by reason of the insufficiency of the assets. Those proceedings are listed in Annex B;

(d) 'court' shall mean the judicial body or any other competent body of a Member State empowered to open insolvency proceedings or to take decisions in the course of such proceedings;

(e) 'judgment' in relation to the opening of insolvency proceedings or the appointment of a liquidator shall include the decision of any court empowered to open such proceedings or to appoint a liquidator;

(f) 'the time of the opening of proceedings' shall mean the time at which the judgment opening proceedings becomes effective, whether it is a final judgment or not;

(g) 'the Member State in which assets are situated' shall mean, in the case of:
- tangible property, the Member State within the territory of which the property is situated,

---

[46] Recital (15).

[47] [2014] 1 WLR 633, [2014] ILPr 11, [2014] BPIR 504.

[48] See the debate about the merits of this decision in C Paulus, 'The ECJ's Understanding of the Universality Principle' (2014) 27(5) Insolvency Intelligence 70 and G Moss, 'ECJ Takes Worldwide Jurisdiction' (2015) 28(1) Insolvency Intelligence 6. The CJEU justified its interpretation by reference to the principles of universalism, effectiveness, foreseeability, and legal certainty, as to which, see G Moss, 'Principles of EU Insolvency Law' (2015) 28(3) Insolvency Intelligence 40. See also Case C-295/13 *H v HK* (CJEU, Sixth Chamber) 4 December 2014, ECLI:EU:C:2014:2410.

- property and rights ownership of or entitlement to which must be entered in a public register, the Member State under the authority of which the register is kept,
- claims, the Member State within the territory of which the third party required to meet them has the centre of his main interests, as determined in Article 3(1);

(h) 'establishment' shall mean any place of operations where the debtor carries out a non-transitory economic activity with human means and goods.

Article 2 OR sets out the definitions which apply in interpreting and applying the **8.16** OR. Articles 2(a), 2(b), and 2(c) OR defining the meanings of 'insolvency proceedings', 'liquidator',[49] and 'winding-up proceedings' respectively have already been discussed in relation to Article 1.

'Court'

Article 2(d) OR sets out the definition of 'court' as the judicial body or any other **8.17** competent body of a Member State empowered to open insolvency proceedings or to take decisions in the course of such proceedings. Since in certain Member States bodies other than the courts may commence insolvency proceedings and make decisions in the course of such proceedings, these bodies may, for these purposes, constitute courts.[50]

In the case of a voluntary arrangement under the Insolvency Act 1986 in England, **8.18** which is listed in Annex A to the OR, the question arises whether the meetings of members and creditors which are empowered to make the decision to place the company into a voluntary arrangement are to be regarded as a 'court' for the purposes of the OR. At first sight this seems unlikely, since a meeting of creditors is not in any ordinary sense a competent body *of a Member State*. One would expect this phrase to refer to tribunals or other entities which are constituted and regulated by law or by the state.

However, a broader interpretation has been adopted with regard to the mean- **8.19** ing of 'court' in Article 3(1) in order to make sense of the OR. In particular, since supervisors of voluntary arrangements come within the extended meaning of 'liquidator', if the voluntary arrangement is a main proceeding, in order to have his powers extend to other Member States as envisaged by Article 18, the supervisor will, under the terms of that Article, have to have been appointed by a 'court' having Article 3(1) jurisdiction. This can only refer to the meeting of creditors.

---

[49] R 13.13(11) of the English Insolvency Rules 1986 (added by the Insolvency (Amendment) Rules 2002) provides that for the purposes of the Rules a person who falls within the definition of 'liquidator' as set out in Art 2(b) of the OR can be referred to as a 'member state liquidator'.

[50] See Virgos-Schmit Report para 66, which also cross-refers to para 52 of that Report.

8.20   As was pointed out by Blackburne J in the *Salvage Association* case:[51]

> 21. The answer lies, in my view, in avoiding a too-literal approach to the application of the definition of 'court' in the Regulation and in understanding the reference in that definition to 'other competent body of a Member State' as applying not merely to some organ of the state but, more widely, to any body recognised as competent in that Member State to resolve upon (i.e. 'open') the insolvency proceedings in question. In this connection it is not without interest that para.66 of a Report by Miguel Virgos and Etienne Schmit published in July 1996 on the Convention on Insolvency Proceedings referred, in a commentary on the definition article of the Convention, in particular the Convention's definition of the expression 'court' (which, I understand, is word for word the same as in the Regulation), to the expression having 'a very broad sense' and as covering 'not only the judiciary or an authority which plays a similar role to that of a court or public authority ... but also a person or body empowered by national law to open proceedings or make decisions in the course of those proceedings ...

8.21   [According to the Italian Council of State—the most prominent national jurisdictional authority for review of public agencies' acts—the Italian competent ministry or governmental department, in declaring the insolvency of a foreign company, must be considered as a *'court'* within the meaning of Article 2(d): see Council of State [Cons Stato], 6th Session, 25 January 2007, 267/2006, para 4.3 (published only in Italian in 21 *Diritto del commercio internazionale* 513 (2007). (**AP**)]

8.22   A more difficult question arises in relation to appointments of administrators in England by directors or secured creditors under paragraphs 14 and 22 of Schedule B1 to the Insolvency Act 1986 which are now listed in Annex A. A person who makes such an appointment is obliged by paragraph 29 to file a notice of appointment with the court together with any other documents that may be required by the rules applying to such proceedings. However, as in the case of voluntary arrangements, the role of the court is only potential and is not necessary for the opening of the proceeding. In any case which may involve a non-UK element, it is best to avoid any out of court appointment of an administrator.[52]

8.23   [If, after an initial appointment of an administrator has taken place out of court, a need arises to take action abroad in an EU Member State, a possible means of confirming or reinforcing the authority of the administrator in the eyes of courts or officials in other states unaccustomed to out of court procedures for opening insolvency may be by using paragraph 63 of Schedule B1 to the Insolvency Act 1986. The court's order giving directions to the effect that

---

[51] *Re The Salvage Association* [2003] BCC 504. [The meeting of creditors will not, however, be a 'court' for the purposes of Art 234 EC (jurisdiction to seek preliminary rulings). (**SI**)] See also Virgos-Schmit Report para 52 (decisions by non-court entities not to be treated as court rulings).

[52] G Moss, 'On the Edge of Non-Recognition? Appointments of Administrators Under the Enterprise Act and the EC Regulation' (2004) 17 Insolvency Intelligence 13.

certain actions should be carried out abroad would simultaneously serve as proof of the administrator's status as an officer of the English court. It should also be noted that the wording of the UK entries in Annexes A and B were specially amended in 2005 to indicate that an administration is both an 'insolvency proceeding' and a 'winding-up proceeding' for the purposes of the OR, even where the initial appointment was made out of court. Although the efficacy of such an approach, using the 'directions application' facility in Schedule B1, may need to be tested before the courts in the first instance, it is submitted that it has the attraction of avoiding the initial expense involved in applying for an administration order in those cases where an out of court appointment is otherwise more convenient. (**IF**)]

[In relation to English out of court administration appointments (by both the **8.24** debtor or the holder of a qualifying floating charge), the appointor is simply required to identify if the OR applies and, if so, whether the proceeding is main or territorial[53] when completing the appointment documents to be filed with the court (following which, the appointment becomes effective). Under the out of court route, the English court does not make any determination concerning the location of the debtor's COMI or establishment, as the case may be. It is submitted that, irrespective of the existence of this self-certifying process or the absence of a formal 'judgment' from the court, the filing of the requisite documentation with the court constitutes a 'judgment opening insolvency proceedings' which requires recognition under Article 16. If a party wishes to dispute the jurisdictional basis on which the out of court appointment has been made, it must do so by recourse to the English court. Nevertheless, any risk of non-recognition of the appointment by another Member State or of an application to set aside or vary the appointment before the English court can be reduced by seeking the appointment of an administrator in court and ensuring that matters relating to jurisdiction are fully ventilated before the court. (**AW**)]

'Judgment'

Article 2(e) defines 'judgment' to *include* the decision of any court empowered to **8.25** open insolvency proceedings or to appoint a 'liquidator'. This suggests that persons or bodies other than courts, even on the wide definition of this term, may open insolvency proceedings or appoint liquidators within the OR.

The purpose of referring to decisions of courts in this context appears to be to men- **8.26** tion the typical case, but also to make it clear that the reference is not exclusive. It

---

[53] [It will be recalled that territorial proceedings include secondary proceedings, the latter being territorial proceedings opened under Art 3(2) subsequent to the opening of main proceedings and which, under Art 3(3), must be winding-up proceedings. An out of court administration appointment is now possible as a secondary proceeding as a result of the changes to Annex B. (**AW**)]

is suggested that there is no scope here for the application by English courts of the '*expressio unius*' approach to statutory interpretation.

8.27 If a proceeding within the OR is opened by a person or body other than a 'court', the recognition provisions in Articles 16–18 OR do not, at least on their literal terms, apply. 'Court' itself, however, has a very wide meaning; see paras 8.17–8.24 above.

Time of the opening of proceedings

8.28 Article 2(f) OR deals with the important question of the time at which insolvency proceedings are held to have been opened. This question is important because, as will be seen, many other aspects of the OR turn on the question of whether or not insolvency proceedings have been opened. Article 2(f) OR says that the time of opening of proceedings is the time at which the judgment opening the proceedings becomes effective, whether it is a final judgment or not.[54]

8.29 In *Shierson v Vlieland-Boddy*[55] the English Court of Appeal applied Article 2(f) and held that as a result the time at which the location of the COMI was to be determined for the purposes of Article 3 was the time at which at the judgment opening the proceedings would become effective. Thus before a court of a Member State can assume jurisdiction to open main insolvency proceedings, it must be satisfied that, at the time that it does so, the debtor's COMI is situated within the territory of that state.

8.30 However, that decision must now be read subject to the CJEU's subsequent decisions in *Staubitz Schreiber*[56] and *Interedil*.[57] In the former case, the debtor had moved her COMI, which was in Germany at the time of her request to open proceedings, to Spain, after the request but prior to any opening. The CJEU held that this did not deprive the German courts of jurisdiction. It would have been contrary to the objectives of the OR to allow a debtor to move the COMI to another Member State, and thereby deprive the original court of its jurisdiction, after a request to open insolvency proceedings had been issued but prior to the determination of that request by the court. It would have encouraged debtors to move to more favourable jurisdictions and would have involved creditors in the time and expense of having to chase after debtors. *Staubitz Schreiber* was cited by the CJEU in *Interedil* for the

---

[54] In relation to a CVL, a question arises as to whether the proceedings are opened when the meeting of members passes a resolution for the company to be wound up (at which point the company goes into liquidation under English law: s 247(2), Insolvency Act 1986) or when there is subsequent court confirmation of the liquidation (as required by Annex A of the OR). Since without court confirmation the CVL would not be a proceeding within the OR at all, the better view seems to be that for the purposes of the OR the proceedings will not be regarded as opened until there has been court confirmation of the CVL. Note, however, the contrary view set out by Professor Ian Fletcher at para 8.294 below.
[55] [2006] 2 BCLC 9.
[56] Case C-1/04 [2006] ECR I-701, [2006] BCC 639.
[57] Case C-396/09 *Interedil Srl, in liquidation v Fallimento Interedil Srl and Intesa Gestione Crediti SpA* [2011] ECR I-9915, [2012] BCC 851.

proposition that the correct time for judging the location of COMI was 'at the time when the request was lodged' to open insolvency proceedings (at para 55). In that case the debtor had been removed from the company register, but it was held that COMI should be judged as at the time the debtor was removed from the register (at para 58).

In some Member States, the 'effects' of opening under domestic law are retrospec-   **8.31** tive, but this does not mean that the 'time of opening' under the OR should be regarded as having taken place earlier. The Irish courts at first instance[58] and the Advocate General in *Eurofood*[59] appear to have regarded the time of opening as having taken place retrospectively in such a case but the point was left open by the ECJ[60] and it is suggested that a domestic law relation back of 'effects' cannot retrospectively alter the 'time of opening' under the OR for the purposes of the international allocation of jurisdiction between Member States.[61]

In the *BenQ* case[62] there were two successive Dutch proceedings, both within   **8.32** the OR, where the 'effects' of the second related under Dutch law back to the start of the first. The Dutch court held that the opening of the second proceeding was to be regarded as having taken place when the first was opened, and thus ahead of a German opening which was regarded by the Dutch court as having taken place in between. In such a case it is a practical and sensible interpretation of the OR to treat the time of opening of the second proceeding as the time of opening of the first, even for the purposes of the allocation of international jurisdiction, since the transition from one proceeding to the other can be seen as a mere technicality and in substance there has only been one proceeding for the purposes of the OR.

Member State in which assets are situated

Article 2(g) deals with the problem of identifying the Member State in which a   **8.33** debtor's assets are situated as follows:

- In the case of tangible property, it is the Member State within the territory of which the property is situated.
- In the case of property and rights, ownership of or entitlement to which must be entered in a public register, it is the Member State under the authority of

---

[58] *Re Eurofood IFSC Ltd* [2004] BCC 383, Irish High Court, Kelly J (left open and referred to the ECJ by the Irish Supreme Court at [2005] BCC 999.
[59] Case C-341/04 *Re Eurofood IFSC Ltd* [2006] ECR I-3813, [2005] BCC 1021.
[60] Case C-341/04 *Re Eurofood IFSC Ltd* [2006] BCC 397, [2006] ECR I-3813, ECJ (Grand Chamber).
[61] G Moss, 'When is a Proceeding Opened?' (2008) 21 Insolvency Intelligence 33, 37–9.
[62] *BenQ Mobile Holding BV* [2008] BCC 489, District Court of Amsterdam; G Moss, 'When is a Proceeding Opened?' (2008) 21 Insolvency Intelligence 33, 38–9; C Paulus, 'The Aftermath of Eurofood—BenQ Holding BV and the Deficiencies of the ECJ Decision' (2007) 20 Insolvency Intelligence 85; B Wessels, 'BenQ Mobile Holding BV Battlefield Leaves Important Questions Unresolved' (2007) 20 Insolvency Intelligence 103.

which the register is kept. This provision deals with the position of tangible property which is registered, such as aircraft and ships, and also of registered intangible property, such as patents and securities.[63]

- In the case of claims, it is the Member State within the territory of which the third party required to meet the claim has his centre of main interests (as determined under Article 3(1)). For example, in the *Stojevic* litigation in Austria, the debtor's claim against a Czech bank was held to be located in the Czech Republic and therefore fell within the main bankruptcy proceedings in the United Kingdom, which the Austrian courts held they were obliged to recognize, and not in the subsequently opened Austrian bankruptcy, and therefore could not be assigned by the Austrian trustee back to the debtor.[64]

8.34 These criteria leave some areas of doubt, which are resolved by the RR: (i) are registered shares, which are registered in a private and not public register, to be treated as 'claims' for this purpose? (ii) Are bank accounts treated as 'claims' and those deemed located at the COMI of the bank, which may be in another Member State or outside the EU?

8.35 In the case of registered shares, VG at paragraph 313 suggests that they should be located where the company has its COMI and bearer shares should be treated like negotiable instruments. Where shares are held in the indirect holding system, they should be deemed located at the place where the account containing the shares is kept.

8.36 VG suggests at paragraph 312 that for the purposes of current and deposit bank accounts, each branch should be treated as if it were a separate entity and the claim should be deemed located at the branch serving the customer.

Where there is a dispute as to whether assets are located in the main or the secondary proceedings, both the court of the main proceeding and that of the secondary proceeding have jurisdiction to decide the issue and where one court makes a decision, that must be respected by the other court.[65] In deciding the dispute, the criteria in Article 2(g) OR must be used and not the national law criteria of the court hearing the case,[66] even if the asset is said to be outside the EU.[67] This decision fails to give precedence to the main proceeding and potentially encourages a rush to court to obtain the first decision.

---

[63] A company will sometimes keep a subsidiary share register in a state other than the place of its own registration. In such a situation the relevant Member State may be the one under whose authority the main register is kept.

[64] (Austrian Supreme Court, 17 March 2005), 8 Ob 135/04t.

[65] Case 649/13 *Comité d'entreprise de Nortel Networks and Others* ECLI:EU:C:2015:384 (Judgment) and ECLI:EU:C:2015:44 (Opinion).

[66] ibid.

[67] ibid.

'Establishment'

Article 2(h) OR defines an 'establishment' as any place of operations where the **8.37**
debtor carries out a non-transitory economic activity with human means and
goods. This definition is important because of the distinction in the OR between
main and Article 3(2) insolvency proceedings: Article 3(2) proceedings[68] can only
be commenced against a debtor if he has an establishment in the Member State
concerned (see Article 3(2)).[69]

Apparently, several states had wished to be able to commence territorial proceed- **8.38**
ings not only on the basis of the debtor having an establishment in the Member
State but also if the debtor had assets in the Member State. In the negotiations
surrounding the agreement of the OR, this ground for territorial proceedings was
dropped and the mere presence of a debtor's assets within a Member State does not
enable territorial proceedings to be commenced in that Member State where the
OR applies. However, the concerns of those Member States who desired there to be
such a jurisdiction are meant to be reflected in the particularly broad definition of
'establishment' adopted.[70]

The approach taken by the UK Supreme Court is that the definition of 'establish- **8.39**
ment' must be read as a whole, because each element of the definition colours the
other elements.[71] The debtor's activities must be 'economic', 'non-transitory', and
carried on from a 'place of operations' using the debtor's assets and human agents.

In *Interedil*,[72] the ECJ explained the concept of an establishment in the follow- **8.40**
ing terms:

> 62. The fact that [the definition of 'establishment'] links the pursuit of an economic
> activity to the presence of human resources shows that a minimum level of organi-
> sation and a degree of stability are required. It follows that, conversely, the pres-
> ence alone of goods in isolation or bank accounts does not, in principle, satisfy the
> requirements for classification as an 'establishment'.

---

[68] The English statutory instruments define 'territorial proceedings' as Art 3(2) proceedings
opened *prior* to the opening of main proceedings, by contrast to 'secondary' proceedings opened
after the opening of main proceedings Insolvency Rules 1986, r 13.13(14) added by the Insolvency
(Amendment) Rules 2002, SI 2002/1307. To avoid the confusion that could arise from the possible
ambiguity over the meaning of 'territorial proceedings', a term not defined in the OR itself, we have
avoided the expression and used the term 'independent territorial proceedings' when referring to
non-main proceedings opened before the opening of main proceedings and 'secondary proceedings'
when referring to those opened after the opening of main proceedings. We use 'Article 3(2) proceedings' to cover both.

[69] ['Territorial insolvency proceeding' is the general concept for two categories of proceedings
the OR distinguishes: secondary proceedings (Art 3(3), Art 27(f)) and (without a specific wording
in the OR) 'independent' territorial insolvency proceedings as meant in Art 3(4). (Wess)]

[70] See the Virgos-Schmit Report para 70.

[71] See *Trustees of the Olympic Airlines SA Pension & Life Assurance Scheme v Olympic Airlines SA*
[2015] 1 WLR 2399 at [13].

[72] Case C-396/09 *Interedil Srl v Fallimento Interedil Srl and Intesa Gestione Crediti SpA* [2011]
ECR I-9915, [2012] BCC 851.

63. Since, in accordance with Article 3(2) of the Regulation, the presence of an establishment in the territory of a Member State confers jurisdiction on the courts of that State to open secondary insolvency proceedings against the debtor, it must be concluded that, in order to ensure legal certainty and foreseeability concerning the determination of the courts with jurisdiction, the existence of an establishment must be determined, in the same way as the location of the centre of main interests, on the basis of objective factors which are ascertainable by third parties.

8.41 This approach was followed by the CJEU in the *Burgo* case.[73] The CJEU also held in that case that there is nothing in the OR to rule out the possibility that an 'establishment' can also be at the place of the registered office or in the same member State.[74]

8.42 The objective nature of the test for the presence of an 'establishment' is also emphasized in paragraph 71 of the Virgos-Schmit report, which states that a 'purely occasional place of operations cannot be classified as an "establishment" … The decisive factor is how the activity appears externally, and not the intention of the debtor'. The foregoing passages from *Interedil* and the Virgos-Schmit Report were cited and applied by the UK Supreme Court in *Olympic Airlines*,[75] which is discussed below.

Place of operations

8.43 In order for a debtor to have an 'establishment' in a Member State there must be a place of operations from which the debtor carries on economic activities. It follows that an office[76] or a shop from which the debtor carries on operations will be an establishment but the fact that a debtor has assets in a Member State will not of itself be sufficient.[77] Accordingly, if a debtor has goods held in a warehouse operated by a third party this will not be an establishment and equally a holiday home operated by an individual debtor should not generally be considered an establishment since this is not usually a place where economic activity is carried on, at least not on a stable footing. [A question might arise requiring judicial determination if the owner of a holiday home, in addition to maintaining it for personal and/or family use, adopts a practice of renting it out at other times to third parties on a commercial basis. **(IF)**]

---

[73] Case 327/13 *Burgo Group SpA v Illochrama SA (in liquidaton)* at [31], citing Case C-396/09 *Interedil* EU:C:2011:671 at [62].

[74] Case 327/13 *Burgo Group SpA v Illochrama SA (in liquidaton)*, ruling 1.

[75] *Trustees of the Olympic Airlines SA Pension & Life Assurance Scheme v Olympic Airlines SA* [2015] 1 WLR 2399.

[76] Even an office with a secretary (one-man office) would do: *Re Stojevic* (Higher Regional Court (Court of Appeal) of Vienna, 9 November 2004), 28 R 225/04w (not reversed on this point by the Supreme Court).

[77] See Case C-396/09 *Interedil Srl v Fallimento Interedil Srl and Intesa Gestione Crediti SpA* [2012] BCC 851 at [62] and *Re Stojevic* (Higher Regional Court (Court of Appeal) of Vienna, 9 November 2004), 28 R 225/04w (not reversed on this point by the Supreme Court).

It is arguable that it would be different if the individual also had a non-temporary **8.44** interest-earning bank account in the state in which he also had a holiday home since this might be argued to be an economic activity. However, the reference to economic activity being carried on with 'human means' is probably intended to distinguish between the situation where a debtor has a passive investment in a state from the situation where the debtor or a person or persons on his behalf are actively engaged in generating economic returns.

In addition, in order to qualify as an establishment a debtor's place of operations **8.45** must have a certain level of organization and stability.[78] Accordingly, a purely occasional place of operations will not constitute an 'establishment'.

In England, the decision of the UK Supreme Court in *Olympic Airlines*[79] is the most **8.46** recent case on the concept of an 'establishment'. A main liquidation proceeding had been opened in Greece (the centre of main interests) in October 2009. Prior to October 2009, the company carried on business from a number of offices in the UK with the assistance of several dozen members of staff. However, after the winding-up of the company in Greece, the company's presence in the UK began to decline. In July 2010, the trustees of the company's pension scheme presented a petition against the company in England, with the intention of opening secondary proceedings. By that time, the company occupied only one office in the UK, where three members of staff on *ad hoc* contracts assisted the Greek liquidators to wind up the company's affairs.

Lord Sumption, who gave the only judgment in the UK Supreme Court, held that **8.47** the presence of an establishment must be determined as at the date of the petition (being July 2010).[80] He stated that Article 2(h) does not simply require the debtor to be locatable or identifiable by a brass plate on a door. Rather, the debtor must carry on activities which, by their nature, involve business dealings with third parties.[81] Some activities which a company in liquidation might carry on may satisfy this requirement—for example, where a liquidator carries on business with a view to its disposal, or disposes of stock in trade on the market. However, where a company has no subsisting business, it is clearly not the case that the mere internal administration of its winding-up will qualify.[82] On this basis, Lord Sumption held that the company did not have an establishment in the UK.

This conclusion is consistent with *Office Metro*,[83] which Lord Sumption cited **8.48** with apparent approval. In that case, the company's centre of main interests was in Luxembourg, where it had been placed into liquidation. The company had an

[78] ibid.
[79] *Trustees of the Olympic Airlines SA Pension & Life Assurance Scheme v Olympic Airlines SA* [2015] 1 WLR 2399 (SC).
[80] ibid at [5].
[81] ibid at [13].
[82] ibid at [14].
[83] *Re Office Metro Ltd* [2012] BCC 829.

English office, which the Luxembourg liquidators used to arrange the settlement of liabilities to associated companies, the forwarding of post and the taking of legal and accountancy advice. Mann J held that these facts were insufficient to constitute an establishment.

8.49 [In general an 'establishment' requires any 'place' of 'operations' where the 'debtor' carries out 'a non-transitory economic activity with human means and goods'. Possession of a bank account does not constitute having a 'place', or 'operations'.[84] A lorry or truck, operated by a Belgian company and on its way through France to Belgium does not constitute a 'place'; a mobile caravan belonging to the same company, which is placed for two months in Toulon to support merger negotiations with the management of a Spanish company would be considered a 'place', but probably not qualify as a place of 'operations'. Also raw material from the Belgian company, located/stored near Lyon for making end products by a French company, will not qualify as a 'place'. (**Wess**)]

8.50 It has been said that the concept of 'establishment' adopted in the OR is intended to be less restrictive than that which has been adopted by the ECJ in its interpretation of the expression 'branch, agency or any other establishment' in Article 5(5) of the Brussels Convention.[85] In this context the ECJ has held that the concept of an establishment implies a place of business which has the appearance of permanency so that third parties do not have to deal directly with the parent body.[86] However, one consequence of this definition has been that subsidiaries of a parent company could be considered to be establishments of the parent.[87] In this way the Article 5(5) definition is in fact too wide for the purposes of the OR since such a definition of establishment would interfere with the general jurisdictional rules which treat all companies as separate entities.[88] It is submitted that the definition of 'establishment' for the purposes of the OR will be similar to that developed for Article 5(5) save that separate subsidiary companies will not be considered to be establishments of the parent.[89]

---

[84] See Case C-396/09 *Interedil Srl v Fallimento Interedil Srl and Intesa Gestione Crediti SpA* [2012] BCC 851 at [62].

[85] ibid. Art 5(5) provided that the courts of a contracting state have jurisdiction to determine disputes arising out of the operations of a branch, agency, or other establishment situated within that state. A similar provision is contained in the Regulation on Jurisdiction and the Recognition and Enforcement of Judgments in Civil and Commercial Matters, Council Regulation (EC) 44/2001 [2001] OJ L12/1, which superseded the Brussels Convention of 1968 for all Member States except Denmark. The relevant provision of Regulation 44/2001 is also numbered as Art 5(5). The equivalent provision in the Recast Regulation on Jurisdiction and Judgments (Regulation (EU) 1215/2012 is Article 7(5).

[86] Case 33/78 *Somafer SA v Saar-Ferngas AG* [1978] ECR 2183. In this regard entities such as exclusive distributorships have been held not be establishments for the purposes of Art 5(5): Case 14/76 *De Bloos SPRL v Bouyer SA* [1976] ECR 1497.

[87] See Case 218/86 *Schotte v Parfums Rothschild* [1987] ECR 4905. [In this case it was, in fact, the parent company that was held to be an establishment of its own subsidiary. (**MB**)]

[88] See Vallens (n 21 above).

[89] Vallens (n 21 above) supports the view that the notion of establishment in the OR is intended to be close to that in Art 5(5). See also *Telia AB v Hillcourt (Docklands) Ltd* [2002] EWHC 2377 (Ch), [2003] BCC 856 (Park J) (see below).

In *Shierson v Vlieland-Boddy*[90] the English Court of Appeal held that the fact **8.51** that a debtor owned and controlled a property in England in the name of a letterbox BVI company nominee, which he let out to other parties, amounted to having an 'establishment' in England within the meaning of the OR. This conclusion is not easy to support.[91] As noted above, an 'establishment' is a place of operations with a degree of organization and stability from where the debtor carries on economic activities with human means and goods. The mere letting of a property does not constitute an 'establishment' in a case where the debtor does not have a 'place of operations' at the property which he lets out. It would be different if there were, for example, a block of flats or a complex of retail outlets and a letting office at the site. It is also not clear what the 'human means' were, unless that is a reference to letting agents used to rent the property. Even then, there is no suggestion that the agents had an office at the property. As far as the requirement of 'goods' is concerned, it is explained below that this should be read as a reference to 'assets', and ownership of or an interest in land should be sufficient.

In the case of groups of companies, an establishment of a subsidiary company **8.52** will not automatically also constitute an establishment of the parent company. In *Telia AB v Hilcourt (Docklands) Ltd* [92] the English High Court correctly held that the business premises in England of a Swedish debtor company's UK premises did not constitute an 'establishment' of the debtor.

In *Burgo Group*,[93] the CJEU held that the definition of 'establishment' in **8.53** Article 2(h) does not rule out the possibility that an establishment could possess legal personality, or that an establishment could be situated in the Member State where the company has its registered office, provided it meets the criteria in Article 2(h).[94]

Human means

[The 'human' means referred to in Article 2(h) must, it is submitted, be under- **8.54** stood as referring to activities conducted by persons for whom the debtor is legally responsible, either as employer or as principal. (IF)][95]

In *Re Stojevic* (Higher Regional Court of Vienna, 9 November 2004), 28 R 225/ **8.55** 04w the Austrian court rejected the idea that if a main proceeding had been opened previously in another Member State but the Austrian court thought that COMI was really in Austria, this would be sufficient, even in the absence of employees, to

---

90 [2006] 2 BCLC 9.
91 See G Moss, 'A Very Peculiar Establishment' (2006) 19 Insolvency Intelligence 20.
92 [2003] BCC 856.
93 Case 327/13 *Burgo Group SpA v Illochroma SA* [2015] 1 WLR 1046.
94 ibid at [32].
95 Cited with approval in *Re Stojevic* (Higher Regional Court of Vienna, 9 November 2004) 28 R 225/04w.

297

open a secondary proceeding in Austria as a 'countermeasure'. It further held that the activity of a human debtor himself was not enough to constitute 'human means' in this context, although an office with a secretary would suffice. Work done by an individual debtor for an Austrian corporation would also not suffice to constitute an establishment in Austria.

8.56 In the *BenQ* case in Germany,[96] where secondary proceedings were opened, it was held sufficient for the 'human means' requirement that work was done for the debtor by employees of another group company, i.e. it was not necessary for the 'human means' to be employees of the debtor itself.[97] In the *Office Metro* case,[98] it was held that the employees for this purpose could be employees of the debtor company, employees of a group company, or even independent contractors.

Goods

8.57 The use of the word 'goods' in Article 2(h) appears to be a mistranslation of *'biens'* in the French or *'Vermogenswerten'* in the German.[99] Those expressions would have been better rendered as 'assets',[100] since 'goods' are strictly speaking restricted to tangible movables. In another EU legislative context, *'biens'* has been held to refer to movable and immovable property.[101] Since each language version of the OR is equally authoritative, UK courts should read the definition as referring to 'assets' and not 'goods'. The correctness of this analysis was confirmed in *Olympic Airlines*,[102] where Lord Sumption said that the word 'goods' is 'hardly a satisfactory English word to use in this context. It is apparent from the equivalent term in the other language versions that it means the same as "assets"'.[103]

8.58 The mistranslation has been carried through to the English language version of the UNCITRAL Model Law, although there the words 'and services' have been added to broaden the concept of 'establishment'. However, in the enactment of

---

96 ZIP 10/2007 p 495 (District Court of Munich, 5 February 2007).

97 See also Professor Paulus 'The Aftermath of "Eurofood"—BenQ Holdings BV and the Deficiencies of the ECJ Decision' (2007) 20 Insolvency Intelligence 85, 85–86; Professor Wessels 'BenQ Mobile Holding BV Battlefield leaves important questions unresolved' (2007) 20 Insolvency Intelligence 103, 105.

98 *Re Office Metro Ltd, Trillium Nelson Properties Ltd v |Office Metro Ltd* [2011] EWHC 1191, [2012] BCC 829.

99 See *Re Stojevic* (Higher Regional Court of Vienna, 9 November 2004) 28 R 225/04w.

100 See the linguistic discussion in the English Court of Appeal case of *Newham v Khatun* [2005] 1 QB 37, paras 68–70, 78.

101 See *Newham v Khatum* above and Case 283/81 *CILFIT v Ministry of Health* [1982] ECR 3415.

102 *Trustees of the Olympic Airlines SA Pension & Life Assurance Scheme v Olympic Airlines SA* [2015] 1 WLR 2399.

103 ibid at [3]. See also *Re Office Metro Ltd, Trillium Nelson Properties Ltd v |Office Metro Ltd* [2011] EWHC 1191, [2012] BCC 829. The mistake is to be corrected in the RR.

the Model Law in Britain (England and Scotland) by the Cross-Border Insolvency Regulations 2006, the mistranslation has finally been corrected, on the recommendation of a Review Panel set up by the Insolvency Lawyers' Association,[104] in Article 2(e) of Schedule 1, where 'establishment' is defined as 'any place of operations where the debtor carries out a non-transitory economic activity with human means and assets or services'.

In the case of *R AB*,[105] the Tallinn Court of Appeal in Estonia opened secondary **8.59** proceedings in a case where the facts did not appear to disclose any 'goods' in the narrow sense of personal movables but there was land belonging to the debtor company which was contracted to be developed into a hunting lodge for tourists. The Tallinn Court of Appeal referred to a requirement to have 'assets' as part of the definition of 'establishment' (ie, rather than 'goods').

(OR) Article 3—International jurisdiction

1. The courts of the Member State within the territory of which the centre of a debtor's main interests is situated shall have jurisdiction to open insolvency proceedings. In the case of a company or legal person, the place of the registered office shall be presumed to be the centre of its main interests in the absence of proof to the contrary.
2. Where the centre of a debtor's main interests is situated within the territory of a Member State, the courts of another Member State shall have jurisdiction to open insolvency proceedings against that debtor only if he possesses an establishment within the territory of that other Member State. The effects of those proceedings shall be restricted to the assets of the debtor situated in the territory of the latter Member State.
3. Where insolvency proceedings have been opened under paragraph 1, any proceedings opened subsequently under paragraph 2 shall be secondary proceedings. These latter proceedings must be winding-up proceedings.
4. Territorial insolvency proceedings referred to in paragraph 2 may be opened prior to the opening of main insolvency proceedings in accordance with paragraph 1 only:
   (a) where insolvency proceedings under paragraph 1 cannot be opened because of the conditions laid down by the law of the Member State within the territory of which the centre of the debtor's main interests is situated; or
   (b) where the opening of territorial insolvency proceedings is requested by a creditor who has his domicile, habitual residence or registered office in the Member State within the territory of which the establishment is situated, or whose claim arises from the operation of that establishment.

Article 3 OR sets out the fundamental principles in relation to the allocation of **8.60** international jurisdiction in respect of insolvency proceedings. It does not deal

---

[104] Professor Ian Fletcher and Gabriel Moss QC were two of the members of this panel.
[105] 14 June 2006.

with the allocation of jurisdiction within a Member State.[106] It does not set out the criteria for exercising jurisdiction under domestic law:[107] see Article 4(2) OR. It does however override domestic law limitations on taking jurisdiction in cases affecting a non-Member State.[108]

8.61 Some Member States, such as the United Kingdom, are multi-jurisdictional states containing different law countries. In the United Kingdom, for the purposes of the OR, these are England (including Wales), Scotland, Northern Ireland, and Gibraltar. The allocation of jurisdiction to open proceedings as between those jurisdictions is a matter for the laws of the United Kingdom. The criteria for opening insolvency proceedings are governed by the domestic law of each law-country.

8.62 Article 3 OR also illustrates the tension which is at the heart of the OR: the reconciliation of the desire that in relation to each debtor there should just be a single set of insolvency proceedings which has universal effect with the pragmatic requirement to give effect to the demands of individual Member States to retain some control of proceedings commenced in respect of debtors who have interests within their jurisdiction.

The ideal: Single proceedings with a universal effect

8.63 The main principle underlying the OR is that of the 'universality' of insolvency proceedings. This principle requires that when insolvency proceedings are commenced in relation to a debtor then those proceedings should comprise all of that debtor's assets [wherever they might be located in the Member States **(Wess)**] and that furthermore no further separate insolvency proceedings should be permitted to be commenced.

The reality: Separate proceedings are permitted

8.64 However, the general principle of universality has been compromised in the OR and is limited by the possibility of the opening of one or more sets of insolvency proceedings, having territorial effect, in other Member States where the debtor has an 'establishment'[as defined in Article 2(h), as interpreted by the CJEU in *Interedil*. **(Wess)**]. These Article 3(2) proceedings are limited in effect to the

---

[106] G Moss, 'Group Insolvency—Choice of Forum and Law: the European Experience under the Influence of English Pragmatism' (2007) 32 Brooklyn Journal of International Law 1005, 1007; G Moss, 'Group Insolvency—Forum —EC Regulation and Model Law Under The Influence of English Pragmatism Revisited' (2014) 9(1) Brooklyn Journal of Corporate, Financial & Commercial Law 250.

[107] *Re The Salvage Association* [2003] BCC 504, [2004] 1 WLR 174, para 13, Blackburne J. See also Case 327/13 *Burgo Group SpA v Illochroma SA* [2015] 1 WLR 1046 at [63].

[108] Case C-328/12 *Schmid v Hertel*[2014] 1 WLR 633, [2014] ILPr 11, [2014] BPIR 504. For contrasting commentaries on this case by C Paulus, 'The ECJ's Understanding of the Universality Principle' (2014) 27(5) Insolvency Intelligence 70; G Moss, 'ECJ Takes Worldwide Jurisdiction' (2015) 28(1) Insolvency Intelligence 1.

particular Member State in which they are commenced[109] and are subject to rules of co-ordination with the main proceedings.[110] Nevertheless they represent a major incursion on the principle of universality.[111]

The concept of 'opening'[112]

Although the concept of 'opening' is central to Article 3, the word is not defined in the OR. Yet it is crucial for many purposes to know when an 'opening' has taken place. As noted above under Article 2(f) OR, the definition of 'the time of the opening of proceedings' only helps in a very limited way. **8.65**

An 'opening' will often follow a 'request' for an opening. The concept of 'request' is used in various places in the OR, such as Articles 3(4)(b), 25(1), and 38, and Recital (16) OR. It is, however, not defined. **8.66**

The main importance of being able to judge when there has been an 'opening' in the autonomous sense used in the OR is where a court in one Member State is asked to recognize the opening of a proceeding in another Member State. Although the use of 'open' in relation to insolvency proceedings may be familiar in Continental jurisdictions, it was unknown in the United Kingdom and Ireland prior to the OR and had no definite meaning. **8.67**

The automatic recognition provisions of Article 16 OR and following means that it is important to identify when proceedings are 'opened' for the purposes of the OR by the courts of a Member State. In the *Eurofood* case (*Re Eurofood IFSC Ltd*, Case C-341/04) the CJEU confirmed that the filing of a petition (request) seeking a winding-up order in Ireland on the grounds of insolvency, together with the appointment of a provisional liquidator (who displaced the directors) on an *ex parte* (without notice) application, without notice even to the company or its directors, represented the 'opening' of proceedings. In the *BenQ Mobile Holding BV* case[113] the opening of a *surséance van betaling* (temporary respite) proceeding in the Netherlands on an *ex parte* basis was held to be an opening for the purposes of the OR. In that case, BenQ Mobile Holding BV filed a request seeking *surséance van betaling* in Amsterdam on 27 December 2006 which the same day granted a temporary moratorium on payments. This was followed by a separate application made on 29 December to a Munich court **8.68**

---

[109] Art 3(2).

[110] See eg Arts 31, 33, and 37.

[111] In contrast, in relation to insolvent insurers and banks, the regimes under the relevant Directives make no provision for secondary proceedings but instead provide for true universality pursuant to which insolvency proceedings can be opened in, and only in, the home Member State of the insurer or bank: see ch 7 above and G Moss and B Wessels, *EU Banking and Insurance Insolvency* (2006).

[112] See generally G Moss, 'When is a Proceeding Opened?' (2008) 21 Insolvency Intelligence 33; Backner, 'The Battle over Jurisdiction in European Insolvency Law' (2006) 3 European Company & Financial Law Review 310. In relation to opening and the meaning of 'court', see under Art 2 OR above.

[113] *BenQ Mobile Holding BV* [2008] BCC 489, District Court of Amsterdam.

for the opening of proceedings in Germany which ordered the opening of proceedings (*vorläufiges Insolvenzverfahren*) in Germany, which can be translated as 'preliminary', 'provisional', or 'temporary'. On 31 January 2007 the Amsterdam court opened final proceedings as main proceedings in the Netherlands. On 5 February 2007 the German court opened secondary proceedings in Germany recognizing that main proceedings had been opened in the Netherlands on 27 December 2006.

8.69 It is suggested that the rational interpretation of 'opening' would have accorded with its principal function of extending the 'effects' of the proceedings to other Member States pursuant to Article 16 OR and following, subject to the exceptions set out in the OR. On this basis, an 'opening' would take place, in accordance with the autonomous meaning used in the OR, when the general 'effects' of the proceeding applied, as opposed to partial or limited 'effects' which in some systems of law apply, usually as a safeguard for creditors, from either the date of the 'request' or from the date of the appointment of a provisional liquidator or temporary administrator etc. The stage at which the general effects apply is usually very easy to ascertain.

8.70 However, the ECJ in the *Eurofood* case[114] took a completely different view and held that the autonomous meaning of 'opening' in the OR meant either:

(a) 'a decision which is formally described as an opening decision by the legislation of the Member State of the court that handed it down' or

(b) a decision handed down following an application, based on the debtor's insolvency, seeking the opening of proceedings referred to in Annex A to the OR, where that decision involves divestment of the debtor and the appointment of a liquidator referred to in Annex C to the OR. Such divestment involves the debtor losing the powers of management which he has over his assets.'[115]

8.71 This approach brings considerable problems and uncertainties. With regard to 'opening' type (a) the domestic legislation of a state may not use the term 'opening'. For example, prior to the OR, neither the United Kingdom nor Ireland used the concept. The United Kingdom has legislated the use of the expression to harmonize with the OR, but Ireland has not. In principle, no part of the autonomous concept of 'opening' should depend on any description supplied by domestic law.

8.72 With regard to opening type (b), the 'extended' meaning of the concept, this requires the coincidence of a number of factors:

(i) a decision;

(ii) following an application;

---

[114] Case C-341/04 *Re Eurofood IFSC Ltd* [2006] ECR I-3813, [2006] BCC 397, ECJ (Grand Chamber). Gabriel Moss QC acted as leading counsel for the Italian special administrator, Dott. Bondi, at the ECJ oral hearing and in the submission of written observations prior to the hearing.
[115] Case C-341/04 *Re Eurofood IFSC Ltd* [2006] ECR I-3813, [2006] BCC 397, para 54.

(iii) based on the debtor's insolvency;

(iv) seeking the opening of proceedings listed in Annex A;

(v) where that decision involves the divestment of the debtor in the sense of losing the powers of management which he has over his assets; and

(vi) the appointment of a liquidator listed in Annex C.

The main problems and anomalies connected this approach stem from the uncer- **8.73**
tainties arising from requirements (v) and (vi), the lack of any requirement of finding that the debtor is insolvent (or likely to become insolvent without a rescue or
reorganization), and the lack of any requirement of a proper *inter partes* hearing in
which those affected (and in particular the debtor in a hostile or 'involuntary' case)
can be heard by the court.

With regard to 'divestment', the appointment of a provisional liquidator in some **8.74**
Member States usually, but not necessarily, amounts to complete divestment (as in
the United Kingdom and Ireland) but in others usually, but not always, amounts
to only partial divestment and complete divestment only occurs on 'opening' in the
(a) sense (as in Germany). A court in another Member State would have to obtain
a copy of the decision and have it translated, sometimes together with the relevant
statute and/or case law to see what the effect is. Even then it is not clear whether
total or partial divestment is required or something in between. Since this is an
extended type of opening created by the ECJ, this question is not solved simply by
referring to the fact that a proceeding within the OR may involve total or partial
divestment under Article 1(1). The *BenQ* case[116] appears to suggest that partial
divestment will suffice.

With regard to the requirement that the provisional liquidator be included **8.75**
in Annex C, at the time of the *Eurofood* decision there was no uniformity
of practice: for example Ireland included him in Annex C but the United
Kingdom did not.[117] Since the start of the *Eurofood* case there has been some
catching up to ensure that advantage was taken of the *Eurofood* decision, for
example by the United Kingdom,[118] and the amended Annex C at Appendix

---

[116] *BenQ Mobile Holding BV* [2008] BCC 489, District Court of Amsterdam; See C Paulus, 'The Aftermath of Eurofood—BenQ Holding BV and the Deficiencies of the ECJ Decision' (2007) 20 Insolvency Intelligence 85; B Wessels, 'BenQ Mobile Holding BV Battlefield Leaves Important Questions Unresolved' (2007) 20 Insolvency Intelligence 103.

[117] [Although, paradoxically, the positions of the UK and Ireland were exactly reversed in their respective lists included in Annex B to the Council of Europe Convention on Certain International Aspects of Bankruptcy (the Istanbul Convention 5 June 1990, *not yet in force*). The entry for the UK, listing the titles of those who are 'liquidators' for the purposes of Art 1(3) of that Convention, includes 'provisional liquidator'; the list for Ireland makes no mention of that office-holder. The reason for the omission of provisional liquidator from the UK list in the original Annex A to the EC Convention, and subsequently to Regulation 1346/2000 as first adopted, has never been officially disclosed. Cyprus included the office of provisional liquidator in its entry in Annex C from the time of joining the EU on 1 May 2004. (IF)]

[118] [The UK entry in Annex C was amended so as to include provisional liquidators by Council Regulation (EC) 694/2006 [2006] OJ L121/1 with effect from 7 May 2006. (IF)]

1 of this work should be consulted and then checked against the European Union's website.[119]

8.76 In the case of Germany, Annex C OR lists a provisional liquidator.[120] These can be 'weak' or 'strong' depending on the degree of control given over the debtor's assets. However, even the appointment of a 'weak' provisional liquidator has been held to be an opening of an insolvency proceeding.[121]

8.77 With regard to the lack of any need for a finding of insolvency or threatened insolvency, such a requirement is, as we have seen above in relation to Article 1, absolutely fundamental to the whole concept of insolvency proceedings. To allow 'insolvency' proceedings to be held to be opened within the meaning of the OR merely on the basis of an *allegation* of insolvency (as in the *Eurofood* case) is wrong in principle. For example, if a creditor requests the opening of a liquidation proceeding against a debtor company, alleging insolvency, and has a provisional liquidator appointed, this is counted by the ECJ as an opening (in the extended (b) sense) of an insolvency proceeding within the OR. However, if it later turns out that the debtor is and has throughout been solvent, the proceeding should never have been within the OR because it has never in reality been an insolvency proceeding. On the other hand, if the request was based on solvency and made as shareholder, and a provisional liquidator is appointed the extended meaning of opening invented by the ECJ does not apply, even if the debtor company turns out later to be and to have been at all times insolvent.

8.78 With regard to the lack of any need for a proper *inter partes* hearing, this will give rise to potential problems which are dealt with under Article 26 OR below.

8.79 **The principle of effectiveness.**[122] The ECJ's concern in setting out their 'extended' type of 'opening' was to promote the 'effectiveness' of the proceedings.[123] It is impossible to see, however, why the principle of effectiveness should lead to this 'extended' form of opening. After the request for the opening of proceedings, any 'judgment'[124] by way of a preservation measure (ie pending the opening) given by a 'court' whose judgment has to be recognized in accordance with Article 16 (ie a judgment opening main proceedings) must automatically be recognized in other Member States pursuant to Article 25. This includes the appointment of a provisional liquidator, so it is completely unnecessary to

---

[119] [Amendments to the OR, and especially to the Annexes, down to the date of this book going to press are cited in ch 1 above at paras 1.24, 1.25: see nn 42, 45–53. (IF)]

[120] 'Vorläufiger Insolvenzverwalter'.

[121] *LG Patra*, Beschl.v.2.5.2007-316/06, ZIP 2007, 1875 (LS); *Westwood Shipping Lines Inc v Universal* [2012] EWHC 1394 (Comm).

[122] See also G Moss, 'Principles of EU Insolvency Law' (2015) 28(3) Insolvency Intelligence 40,

[123] Case C-341/04 *Eurofood IFSC Ltd* [2006] ECJ I-3813, [2006] BCC 397, ECJ (Grand Chamber), paras 52–54.

[124] See the wide interpretation given to this expression under Art 2(e) above.

hold that such an appointment constitutes an opening in order to make the OR effective.

Argument based on Article 38 OR. The ECJ considered the argument against **8.80** its extended interpretation of opening based on Article 38 OR:

> 56. Both Mr Bondi and the Italian Government acknowledge that, in the main proceedings, the 'provisional liquidator' appointed by the High Court, by decision of January 27, 2004, appears amongst the liquidators mentioned in Annex C to the Regulation in relation to Ireland. They argue, however, that this is a case of a provisional liquidator, in respect of whom the Regulation contains a specific provision. They note that Art.38 of the Regulation [OR] empowers the provisional liquidator, defined in the 16th recital as the liquidator 'appointed prior to the opening of the main insolvency proceedings', to apply for preservation measures on the assets of the debtor situated in another Member State for the period between the request for the opening of insolvency proceedings and the judgment opening the proceedings. Mr Bondi and the Italian Government infer from that that the appointment of a provisional liquidator cannot open the main insolvency proceedings.
>
> 57. In that respect, it should be noted that Art.38 of the Regulation must be read in combination with Art.29, according to which the liquidator in the main proceedings is entitled to request the opening of secondary proceedings in another Member State. That Art.38 thus concerns the situation in which the competent court of a Member State has had main insolvency proceedings brought before it and has appointed a person or body to watch over the debtor's assets on a provisional basis, but has not yet ordered that that debtor be divested or appointed a liquidator referred to in Annex C to the Regulation. In that case, the person or body in question, though not empowered to initiate secondary insolvency proceedings in another Member State, may request that preservation measures be taken over the assets of the debtor situated in that Member State. That is, however, not the case in the main proceedings here, where the High Court has appointed a provisional liquidator referred to in Annex C to the Regulation and ordered that the debtor be divested.

With respect to the CJEU, its argument is mistaken. Article 29 refers to 'the liq- **8.81** uidator in the main proceedings', in other words where a main proceeding has been opened. Article 38, as the CJEU says, deals with the earlier situation after the request but before the opening. However, it is clear that 'temporary administrator' in Article 38 OR has the same meaning as 'liquidator temporarily appointed *prior to the opening*' [emphasis added] in Recital (16),[125] which deals with the same subject matter. The appointment of such a liquidator *may or may not* divest the debtor— therefore 'divestment' cannot be the critical trigger for 'opening'. Also, such a liquidator may or may not be listed in Annex C OR,[126] so that cannot be the critical trigger either.

---

[125] Note that Recital (16) does not use the 'temporary administrator' wording used by Art 38 and paras 262, 263 of the Virgos-Schmit Report, so the deliberate use of 'liquidator temporarily appointed prior to the opening' as the equivalent concept is a very forceful and clear statement by the community legislator that that is what is meant by 'temporary administrator' in Art 38.

[126] Virgos-Schmit Report para 263.

8.82 The simpler and more satisfactory answer is that the autonomous meaning of 'opening' in the OR is the point at which the proceeding listed in Annex A has its general 'effects' which require to be recognized in other Member States under Article 16. However, unless and until the CJEU revises its view, we must struggle to apply the CJEU's normal and extended concepts of opening, with the resulting confusion and uncertainty.

8.83 [Note, however, that a perverse incentive could be created if the appointment of a provisional liquidator by a court were held not to mark the point in time from which the jurisdiction of that court is to be measured in any circumstances in which it becomes necessary to assess the competing claims of the courts of two Member States to be recognized as the 'first to open proceedings'. If a party who wishes to cause proceedings to be based in a different Member State, so as to be governed by its insolvency law, succeeds in persuading a court of that state that the debtor's COMI is located there, and that it should open insolvency proceedings with immediate effect, this could subvert the more orderly approach being undertaken in the court which has taken the initial step of appointing a provisional liquidator for purposes which may include the carrying out of an investigation into the full circumstances of the case before a decision is taken whether a winding-up order is appropriate. If it were to become legally possible for pre-emptive tactics undertaken in other Member States to circumvent the process in the state first engaged, those making the initial application might deem it more expedient to seek a winding-up order immediately, rather than to proceed via provisional liquidation in the first instance. This could give rise to less than satisfactory results in some circumstances, with potential wastage of costs. (**IF**)]

8.84 **The 'relation back' theory.**   Although the ECJ itself did not deal with this, the Advocate General also expressed the view that because of the relation back of the winding-up order under Irish law to the filing of the petition, the date of filing was the date of 'opening' for the purposes of the OR.[127] With respect this is wrong for a number of reasons. Firstly, the Irish law relation back only provides that the proceedings are 'treated' (deemed) as if they began at the petition filing date, not that they actually did so, and the doctrine only exists for limited purposes such as the avoidance of dispositions by the debtor company between the filing and the opening. Secondly, the Advocate General has, in the *Eurofood* case itself, overlooked the effect under the OR of the intervening Italian opening of main proceedings. Ignoring the appointment of the provisional liquidator, the order of events was: (i) Irish petition filed, (ii) Italian opening, (iii) Irish winding-up order. Ignoring also the public policy argument for this purpose, the Advocate General has forgotten that when the matter returned to Ireland the Irish court was, under Article 16, bound to recognize the Italian opening and could not itself open a

---

[127] [2005] BCC 1021, paras 89–95.

main proceeding. Any 'relation back' could only create the opening of a territorial proceeding. Thirdly and most fundamentally, it is a completely unacceptable notion that a domestic law relation back should be able to dictate the answer to a question of international jurisdiction.

Main insolvency proceedings

Centre of main interests.[128]   Article 3(1) provides that the courts of the Member **8.85** State within the territory of which 'the centre of a debtor's main interests' (COMI) is situated have jurisdiction to open insolvency proceedings. These are the *main proceedings* which in principle have universal scope and encompass all of the debtor's assets wherever located within the European Union (with the exception of Denmark).

[The OR neither requires nor forbids the extension of the scope of Article 3(1) **8.86** proceedings to assets located beyond the European Union, but such universalist ambition will usually be present pursuant to the national law of the Member State of the opening of the proceedings. (**MB**)]

The concept of COMI is therefore an important one since it lies at the heart of the **8.87** OR's principal jurisdictional rule. The concept is not, however, defined in the OR.

The role of Recital (13).   Recital (13) suggests COMI is the place where the **8.88** debtor conducts the administration of his interests on a regular basis and is therefore ascertainable by third parties.

The wording of Recital (13) is taken from the first sub-paragraph of paragraph 75 **8.89** of the Virgos-Schmit Report. That is a general statement about COMI (and not a definition), before the Report goes on to discuss the COMI of different types of debtors.

The ECJ in *Re Eurofood IFSC Ltd*[129] used the word 'definition' in relation to Recital **8.90** (13) (paragraph 33), but in the context this is the equivalent of the phrase '[t]he scope of the concept is highlighted' in paragraph 32. In other words, Recital (13) provides clarification and not definition in any strict sense.

In *Re Stojevic*[130] the English court rejected an argument that Recital (13) was a **8.91** definition of COMI:

> [31] In my judgment Recital (13) does not define the expression 'centre of main interests' and I do not understand the European Court of Justice to have said otherwise. The Regulation contains definitions of various expressions used in the

---

[128] English Insolvency Rules 1986, r 13.13(8) (added by the Insolvency (Amendment) Rules 2002) provides that for the purposes of the Rules 'centre of main interests' has the same meaning as in the OR.
[129] [2006] ECR I-3813, [2006] Ch 508.
[130] [2007] BPIR 141, HCJ.

Regulation, such as 'establishment', in Art 2, which is headed 'Definitions'. It is significant that the expression 'centre of main interests' does not appear amongst the expressions collected in that Article.

[32] I agree with Mr Moss and Mr Fuller, when they submitted that, in the context of the *Eurofood* case, the word 'definition' is used, in para [33] of the judgment, as the equivalent of the phrase '[t]he scope of that concept is highlighted', which is the language adopted in para [32] of the judgment, ie more in the nature of what we would call 'a description'. I reject Mr Robins' submission that Recital (13) contains a definition of the expression 'centre of main interests'.

[33] I also agree with Mr Moss and Mr Fuller, when they submitted that Recital (13) can only be properly understood by putting it back in its original context, namely para 75 of the Virgos-Schmit Report.

8.92 **Legal persons.** In the case of a company or 'legal person' the place of the registered office is presumed to be the COMI in the absence of proof to the contrary.[131] The circumstances in which the presumption will be rebutted were considered by the ECJ in *Re Eurofood IFSC Ltd*.[132] That case concerned Eurofood, an Irish incorporated subsidiary of Parmalat SpA which was itself incorporated in Italy. In this context, the CJEU considered the test for identifying the COMI of a subsidiary company where it and its parent have their registered offices in two different Member States. The CJEU referred to Recital (13) of the OR and stated that the Recital showed that the COMI had to be identified by reference to criteria that are both objective and ascertainable by third parties in order to ensure legal certainty and foreseeability concerning the determination of the court with jurisdiction to open main insolvency proceedings. The CJEU held that it followed that, in determining the COMI of a debtor company, the presumption in favour of the registered office of that company could be rebutted only if factors which are both objective and ascertainable by third parties enable it to be established that an actual situation existed which was different from that which locating it at that registered office was deemed to reflect.[133] Importantly, the CJEU then went on specifically to comment that one of the situations where the presumption could be rebutted is in the case of (in the court's words) a *'letterbox'* company.

8.93 The rationale for the presumption in the case of a legal person that a debtor's COMI will be found in the place of its registered office is that the registered office 'normally corresponds to the debtor's head office'.[134] It follows that any inquiry as to whether the COMI is in fact located in a Member State other than that in which the registered office is located, must centre on whether or not the head office functions of the debtor are carried out in that other state. The inquiry is more correctly focused

---

[131] Art 3(1). See also B Wessels, 'The place of the registered office of a company: a cornerstone in the application of the EC Insolvency Regulation' (2006) 3 European Company Law, August 183–90.
[132] [2006] ECR I-3813, [2006] Ch 508.
[133] The ECJ approved and expanded upon this analysis in Case C-396/09 *Interedil Srl v Fallimento Interedil Srl and Intesa Gestione Crediti SpA* [2011] ECR I-9915, [2012] BCC 851 at [51]. *Interedil* is discussed in greater detail below.
[134] Virgos-Schmit Report para 75, last sub-paragraph.

on the question of the location of the place where head office functions are carried out than on the location of the head office since, in modern business conditions, the two are not necessarily in the same place. Furthermore, a company in a group of companies may not have its own head office, but its head office functions may be carried on at the group headquarters. It is where the head office functions are carried out that the company conducts the administration of its interests on a regular basis within the approach of Recital (13).

Head office functions test.[135]   In practice, therefore, in the case of legal persons, **8.94** the place where a debtor administers his interests on a regular basis (and which is therefore ascertainable by third parties) has been equated with the place where the '*head office functions*' of the debtor are carried out. The head office functions test has been adopted and followed in the case law. In particular, the head office functions test was adopted (at least implicitly) by the ECJ in *Interedil*:[136]

> 50. ... where the bodies responsible for the management and supervision of a company are located in the same place as its registered office and the management decisions that the company are taken, in a manner that is ascertainable by third parties, in that place, the presumption ... that the centre of the company's main interests is located in that place is wholly applicable.

This 'presumption' may be rebutted if 'from the viewpoint of third parties, the place in which a company's central administration is located is not the same as that of its registered office'.[137] The factors to be taken into account include the places where the debtor pursues economic activities and the places where the debtor's assets are situated, insofar as those places are ascertainable by third parties (although the matter must be determined in light of the individual circumstances of each case). Ultimately, however, it is the 'company's actual centre of management and supervision' which is the crucial criterion.[138] It is suggested that this is simply a statement of the head office functions test.

The head office functions test was implicitly accepted by the English High **8.95** Court in *Re Enron Directo SA*[139] in the case of a Spanish incorporated Enron company trading in Spain but whose headquarters functions were carried out in London.

---

[135] Professor Wessels has criticized the head office functions approach and, instead, has advocated a 'contact with creditors' approach, as better reflecting the description of COMI given in Recital (13): see B Wessels, *International Insolvency Law* (2006) para 10597, and B Wessels, 'The place of the registered office of a company: a cornerstone in the application of the EC Insolvency Regulation' (2006) 3 European Company Law, August, 183–90.

[136] Case C-396/09 *Interedil Srl v Fallimento Interedil Srl and Intesa Gestione Crediti SpA* [2011] ECR I-9915, [2012] BCC 851.

[137] ibid at [51].

[138] ibid at [53].

[139] Lightman J, 4 July 2002, no judgment given. A summary of the decision is available on the website of the International Insolvency Institute at <http://www.iiiglobal.org/> under 'European Union—Articles'.

8.96 In *Re BRAC Rent-A-Car International Inc*[140] the English High Court held that it had jurisdiction to make an administration order in respect of a company incorporated in the United States on the grounds that its COMI was in England and Wales. In particular, the court found on the evidence that the COMI of the company was in England since, although its registered office was in the United States, it had never traded there and its operations were concluded almost entirely in the United Kingdom. The company traded from an address in England and had for a long time been registered under the Companies Acts as an oversea company. It had no employees in the United States, with virtually all its employees working in England, under contracts of employment governed by English law.[141]

8.97 *Re Daisytek-ISA Ltd* [142] concerned an English incorporated company which was a subsidiary of a United States company which had gone into Chapter 11 proceedings. The English company itself had subsidiaries incorporated in Germany and France. The English High Court made administration orders in respect of the European subsidiaries on the basis that their COMIs were in England, principally on the basis that their activities were co-ordinated from the head office in Bradford. The court also placed reliance on the fact that it appeared that a large majority of creditors knew (by virtue of the fact that the funding was supplied by the factoring agreement with the subsidiary of a United Kingdom bank and the fact that 70 per cent of purchase contracts were dealt with from Bradford) that Bradford was where many important functions of the German companies were carried out. Similar reasoning was applied in relation to the French company.

8.98 The head office functions test has been followed in various other cases both in England[143] and in other EU states including France[144], Germany,[145] and

---

[140] [2003] 2 All ER 201, [2003] 1 WLR 1421.

[141] It should be noted that in one respect the reasoning in the *BRAC* decision was erroneous. The judge held that the OR itself had brought about an extension of the jurisdiction of the English court to make an administration order to any company whose COMI was in the UK. In fact, under the OR, the conditions for the opening of proceedings are left to the law of the relevant Member State (Art 4(2)(f) OR) and, accordingly, the provisions of the Insolvency Act 1986 had been amended to empower the English court to make an administration order over a company whose COMI is within the UK (see now Insolvency Act 1986, SchB1, para 111(1A)). This analysis was adopted in *Re The Salvage Association* [2003] BCC 504.

[142] [2004] BPIR 30.

[143] *Re Energy Group Overseas BV and Energy Group Holdings BV* (20 November 2003), no judgment given; *Re Aim Underwriting Agencies (Ireland) Ltd* [2004] EWHC 2114 (Ch); *Re Ci4net.com Inc* [2005] BCC 277; *Re TXU German Finance BV* [2005] BPIR 209; *Re Collins & Aikman* [2006] BCC 606; *Re Damovo Group SA* (25 April 2007), no written judgment given but noted in *European Cross-Border Insolvency* at 4.46; *Re Lennox Holdings Plc* (HCJ, 20 June 2008).

[144] *Re MPOTEC GmbH* [2006] BCC 681, Tribunal de Commerce de Nanterre; *Re Energotech Sarl*, Tribunal de Grande Instance de Lure, 29 March 2006; *Re ISA Daisytek SAS* [2006] BCC 841, Cour de Cassation; *Re Eurotunnel Finance Ltd* (Paris Commercial Court, 2 August 2006) application to set aside dismissed on 15 January 2007 and appeal from refusal to set aside dismissed 29 November 2007.

[145] *Re Hettlage-Austria* (Amtsgericht, Munich, 4 May 2004). See <http://www.eir-database.com>

Hungary[146], and was also endorsed by the Advocate General in *Eurofood* [147] in referring to the arguments put forward on behalf the Italian administrator and the Italian Government:

> 111. Those two parties rely principally on the Virgós-Schmit Report, para.75, which states:
>
> 'Where companies and legal persons are concerned, the Convention presumes, unless proved to the contrary, that the debtor's centre of main interests is the place of his registered office. This place normally corresponds to the debtor's head office.' (Balz puts it in somewhat different terms: 'In the case of a mere mailbox registration, the headquarters will be treated as the centre of main interests' (p 504).)
>
> Dr Bondi and the Italian Government submit that if it is to be demonstrated that the centre of main interests is somewhere other than the State where a company's registered office is located, it consequently needs to be shown that the 'head office' type of functions are performed elsewhere. The focus must be on the head office functions rather than simply on the location of the head office because a 'head office' can be just as nominal as a registered office if head office functions are not carried out there. In transnational business the registered office is often chosen for tax or regulatory reasons and has no real connection with the place where head office functions are actually carried out. That is particularly so in the case of groups of companies, where the head office functions for the subsidiary are often carried out at the place where the head office functions of the parent of the group are carried out.
>
> 112. I find those submissions sensible and convincing ...

8.99 In *Re MPOTEC GmbH*[148] the Tribunal de Commerce of Nanterre noted that the courts of Member States had applied the concept of 'headquarters functions' in determining COMI and considered that, in the context of a group of companies, the concept of 'head-office functions' should be used to determine the location of the company's COMI.

8.100 In *Eurotunnel*[149] the Paris Tribunal de Commerce adopted a similar approach which focused on the fact that the strategic and operational management of the companies was run by a single committee based in Paris and that the financial management was also carried out there.

8.101 The CJEU has held that the mere fact that two companies use intermingled bank accounts (or transfer assets between each other without consideration) does not entail that the companies have the same COMI. Such facts may be difficult to ascertain by third parties, and have no direct relevance to the determination of COMI.[150]

---

[146] *Re Parmalat Slovakia* (Municipal Court of Fejer/Székesfehérvár, 14 June 2004).

[147] Case C-341/04 *Eurofood IFSC Ltd* [2005] BCC 1021, paras 111–112. This passage was cited and applied in *Re Lennox Holdings Plc* (HCJ, 20 June 2008). See also Paulus, 'A Vision of the European Insolvency Law' (2008) 17 Norton Journal of Bankruptcy Law and Practice 607, 610.

[148] *Re MPOTEC GmbH* [2006] BCC 681, Tribunal de Commerce de Nanterre.

[149] 2 August 2006.

[150] See Case C-191/10 *Rastelli Davide e C. Snc v Hidoux* [2011] ECR I-13209, [2013] 1 BCLC 329 at [38]–[39]. Under French law such confusion of assets can give the French court, which is

8.102 **Groups of companies.** One of the notable aspects of the OR is that it does not deal with the position of groups consisting of a number of related companies.[151] Under the OR it would be possible to open main insolvency proceedings in relation to each individual company and there are no provisions in the OR which provide for any degree of co-operation between the different proceedings.[152] Nor is there any express provision similar to the US concept of 'substantive consolidation', which sometimes enables separate corporate entities to be treated as one. Thus, in *Rastelli Davide*,[153] the ECJ considered a rule of French insolvency law, which enables two or more companies to be joined to a single insolvency proceeding where their assets have become 'intermixed'. The ECJ held that the COMI of each legal entity must be determined on an individual basis, notwithstanding any rule of domestic law which provides for consolidation in the event of insolvency.[154]

8.103 The ECJ in *Eurofood* emphasized that in the case of groups of companies it is necessary to examine the location of each company's COMI individually and that there can be no automatic assumption that the location of a subsidiary's COMI will be the same as that of its parent. Nevertheless, it may well be the case that this inquiry leads to the conclusion that the location of each company's COMI is in fact in the same place, by virtue of the head office functions test in *Interedil*.[155] In many corporate structures, the head office functions for the entire group, consisting of the parent company and its subsidiaries, may be carried out from a single group head office. Applying *Interedil*, the COMI of each of the group companies may well be located at that head office. This was the conclusion reached by the English court in *Re Daisytek-ISA Ltd* (see above at para 8.97), *Re Crisscross Telecommunications Group*,[156] *Re Collins & Aikman*,[157] *Re MG Rover*,[158] and by the French courts in *Re MPOTEC GmbH, Re Energotech,* and *Eurotunnel* (the citations for each of which appear in note 144 above).

---

conducting one set of insolvency proceedings over one debtor, jurisdiction to open insolvency proceedings in respect of another debtor. However, as this case decides, this domestic law French doctrine does not give the French court international jurisdiction within the OR to open the second proceedings if the COMI or an establishment is not located in France.

[151] See Virgos-Schmit Report para 76. See generally G Moss, 'Group Insolvency—Choice of Forum and Law: the European Experience under the Influence of English Pragmatism' (2007) 32 Brooklyn Journal of International Law 1005; G Moss, 'Group Insolvency—Forum—EC Regulation and Model Law Under The Influence of English Pragmatism Revisited' (2014) 9(1) Brooklyn Journal of Corporate, Financial & Commercial Law 250.

[152] In English law based jurisdictions co-operation is often ensured by having the same insolvency practitioners, or insolvency practitioners from the same major firm of accountants, appointed as liquidators in the separate insolvency proceedings for different companies in the same group.

[153] Case C-191/10 *Rastelli Davide e C. Snc v Hidoux* [2011] ECR I-13209, [2013] 1 BCLC 329.

[154] ibid at [29].

[155] Case C-396/09 *Interedil Srl v Fallimento Interedil Srl and Intesa Gestione Crediti SpA* [2011] ECR I-9915, [2012] BCC 851.

[156] (20 May 2003), Rimer J.

[157] [2006] BCC 606.

[158] [2005] EWHC 874, Ch.

The practical advantage of such a conclusion is that, subject to the possibility **8.104** of secondary proceedings, the insolvent group of companies may be subject to a de facto single set of insolvency proceedings with common office-holders in place. The benefits of this in terms of the efficient running of the proceedings and maximizing returns for creditors are obvious. Strictly, such considerations are not themselves factors relevant to the determination by the court of the location of the companies' COMIs, though there is suggestion in the French cases in particular that they have influenced the approach adopted.[159] In any event, it is suggested that the ECJ's implicit approval of the head office functions test in *Interedil* should be welcomed, and is likely to lead to sensible results for groups of companies.

[It should, however, be noted that in a case 'where the estate of the debtor is **8.105** too complex to administer as a unit or where differences in the legal systems concerned are so great that difficulties may arise from the extension of effects deriving from the law of the state of the opening to the other states where the assets are located', the liquidator in the main proceedings may request the opening of secondary proceedings 'when the efficient administration of the estate so requires' (Recital (19)). This Recital may provide grounds to request the opening of secondary proceedings for, for example, a wholly owned subsidiary in another state, when the financial and commercial administration, the IT-platform, etc are shared with the debtor. (**Wess**)]

[It is noteworthy that domestic courts often attempt to administer multinational **8.106** enterprise failures by including in the same insolvency proceedings both the parent and the subsidiaries. Besides the above-mentioned *ISA-Daisytek* case, there are several other cases involving multinational enterprise failures, in which the insolvency process significantly involved the whole enterprise, regardless of the circumstance that the different subsidiaries' COMIs were located in different countries.[160] The presumption established by Article 3(2) was not plainly and regularly respected by domestic courts before the ECJ rendered the *Eurofood* decision. From this standpoint, as one scholar has recently argued 'the adjudication of transnational bankruptcy proceedings increasingly resembles a race against time in which creditors and debtors rush to choose the most favourable forum and courts compete to adjudicate the case'.[161] In fact, 'with billions of dollars at stake for bankruptcy

---

[159] See in particular the *MPOTEC* and *Eurotunnel* decisions cited above, and subsequently, *Sobieski Sp. Zo O* (a Polish registered company which is part of the French Belvedere SA group) (Tribunal de Commerce of Beaune, 16 July 2008).

[160] See in particular Tribunal of Rome, 26 November 2004, *Cirio Finance Luxembourg SA*, 2004 Foro it. 1567 (in Italian); Tribunal of Parma, 20 February 2004, *Eurofood IFSC Ltd*, ibid.

[161] M M Winkler, 'From Whipped Cream to Multibillion Euro Financial Collapse: The European Regulation on Translation Insolvency in Action' (2008) 26 Berkeley Journal of International Law 352, 369.

professionals competing courts cannot be counted on to determine fairly and in good faith whether they are the home court of multinationals'.[162] This problem affects also the European context. In fact, '*Eurofood* indicated the actual status of the EC Regulation: that the lacunae of its regulatory framework run so deep that future insolvency proceedings in Europe would scarcely be efficient'.[163] (**AP**)]

8.107 **The presumption under the UNCITRAL Model Law.** The presumption that COMI is located in the place of the registered office has also been adopted by the UNCITRAL Model Law on Cross-Border Insolvency, which has been enacted with different modifications in several countries. The presumption has been discussed in several decided cases in the United States, where the Model Law was enacted, with significant variations, as Chapter 15 of the US Bankruptcy Code. The US courts have given the presumption little weight and if there is *any* evidence before the court that the COMI may be elsewhere they will require proof that COMI is in the place of the registered office, even in an unopposed case.[164]

8.108 **Natural persons.** The use of the term 'interests' is intended to encompass a wide spread of activities extending beyond commercial, industrial, and professional activities to the general economic activities of private individuals.[165] The concept of a debtor's COMI therefore applies equally to private individuals who do not carry on business as it does to corporate entities engaged in trade.

8.109 The COMI for natural persons will generally be their place of habitual residence.[166] In the case of 'professionals', however, it will be the place of their professional domicile.[167] This suggests that the centre of main interests is linked to the type of activity from which the insolvency or need for rescue/reconstruction arises. Thus, where an individual is carrying on business activities and it is the business that is at the root of the insolvency or need for rescue/restructuring, the centre of main interests may well be in the place of business rather than the place of habitual residence (if different).[168]

---

[162] L LoPucki, *Courting Failure: How Competition for Big Cases is Corrupting the Bankruptcy Courts* (2005) 209.

[163] Winkler (n 161 above) 369.

[164] *In Re Bear Stearns High-Grade Structured Credit Strategies Master Fund* 389 BR 325 (SDNY 2008) (US District Court of New York, 22 May 2008) (Chapter 15 case No 07-12383, Sweet DJ).

[165] Virgos-Schmit Report para 75.

[166] ibid para 75 fourth sub-paragraph; *Re Stojevic* [2007] BPIR 141, HCJ.

[167] Virgos-Schmit Report para 75.

[168] Cited with approval in *Re Stojevic* [2007] BPIR 141, HCJ. This point is also the correct explanation of the decision of *Vennink v Fortis Bank* (Dutch Supreme Court, 9 January 2004): Vennink's centre of main interests was held to be located where he was carrying on business, which was the Netherlands, and not where he habitually resided, which was in Belgium. The English courts have also adopted the same, pragmatic analysis when deciding whether a debtor's COMI should be determined by reference to his personal domestic arrangements (principally linked to Spain) or his professional orientation as a self-proclaimed 'Swiss banker': *Skjevesland v Geveran Trading Co Ltd* [2003] BCC 391 (Jaques R), aff'd [2003] BCC 391 (Ch D, Judge Howarth) (holding that the debtor's COMI was in Switzerland).

In England, one court has drawn a doubtful distinction between cases where an **8.110** individual administers his affairs *in* a particular Member State, and cases where an individual administers his affairs *from* a particular Member State. Thus, in *Re Eichler (No 2)*,[169] Chief Registrar Baister said:

> 149. Generally, it seems to me, [the debtor] sought to arrange his affairs so as to spend as little money as possible in England and remit as much as possible to Germany, which must mean that the latter was the place where he continued to undertake the bulk of his personal and economic activity in euros rather than pounds. It is no answer to say that he was able to administer them from a laptop computer. The fact that he may have been using a laptop in England for some or even the majority of those transactions did not constitute administering them *in* England as opposed to administering them *from* England. The majority of transactions plainly took place in Germany and in local rather than British currency.

Work done by a natural person on behalf of a legal person constitutes the carry- **8.111** ing on of the business of the legal person and does not go towards establishing the place of COMI of the natural person.[170] Nor are the 'interests' of the legal person to be confused with the interests of the natural person, even if the natural person is a director or controller of the legal person.[171] 'Habitual residence' in this context must be distinguished from 'ordinary residence', as explained in *Re Stojevic*:[172]

> 59. The two concepts, habitual residence and ordinary residence, are very different and must not be confused. The difference is easier to ascertain, than it is to explain. Essentially, however, a man's habitual residence is his settled, permanent home, the place where he lives with his wife and family, until, in the case of the younger members of the family, they grow up and leave home, the place to which he returns from business trips elsewhere or abroad. A man's ordinary residence is a place where he lives, which is not his settled, permanent home, the place where he lives, when away from home on business or on holiday with his wife and family. Depending on the nature of his work, a man may well live away from his settled, permanent home for a greater number of days in any given year than he spends there with his wife and family.

Where a debtor resides in one Member State but is imprisoned in another, his **8.112** COMI does not simply by reason of such imprisonment move to the second

---

[169] [2011] BPIR 1293.

[170] *Re Stojevic* [2007] BPIR 141, HCJ. The point seems to have been overlooked in *Official Receiver v Eichler* [2007] BPIR 1636, HCJ (German doctor working for company in England. See however the subsequent re-hearing of this case, *Re Eichler (No 2)*, considered immediately above and also below at 8.116. See also *Re Stojevic* (Higher Regional Court, Vienna (Court of Appeal, 9 November 2004) 28 R 225/04w. A dictum to the contrary by Lewison J in *Cross Construction Sussex Ltd v Tseliki* [2006] BPIR 888, appears to have been given without the learned judge's attention being drawn to the Virgos-Schmit Report, in particular para 75. See also *Re Stojevic* (Higher Regional Court (Court of Appeal) of Vienna, 9 November 2004) 28 R 225/04w, making the same point in relation to 'establishment'.

[171] *Re Stojevic* [2007] BPIR 141, HCJ paras 56–57 (Croatian debtor with habitual residence in Austria controlled companies in the UK).

[172] [2007] BPIR 141, HCJ.

Member State.[173] [In this case, the debtor had kept this residence in Luxembourg during the time he was kept in custody in Germany. Hence, there was not even a shadow of a doubt that the COMI of this individual was in Luxembourg and not in Germany. Consequently, this decision clarifies that the residence is a very strong criterion to define the COMI of an individual; that this criterion is very hard to overrule and, in particular, that it is not sufficient to be in custody to effectively establish a new residence and therefore, a new COMI. (**Wess**)]

8.113 The fact that the debtors' activities are illegal does not appear to affect the COMI.[174]

8.114 **Right to move COMI and 'forum shopping'.** It has been held by the Court of Appeal in England that a debtor has a right to move his COMI, even in a case where he is trying to remove himself from the Member State where he has incurred the debt and where his creditors are located.[175]

8.115 The courts in England have not, thus far, drawn a clear distinction between 'good' forum shopping (usually by a legal person) which occurs where a debtor moves COMI to benefit creditors and 'bad' forum shopping (usually by a natural person) where the debtor moves COMI to escape creditors. Advocate General Colomer has pointed out in his Opinions in *Staubitz-Schreiber*[176] and *Seagon v Deko Marty Belgium* (also known as *Frick Teppichboden*)[177] that Community law combats opportunistic and fraudulent choices of jurisdiction and not 'forum shopping' per se.

8.116 However, the English courts have begun in recent years to scrutinize bankruptcy (individual insolvency) petitions involving apparent COMI shopping with greater care. In *Re Eichler (No 2)*,[178] Chief Registrar Baister said:

> 190. This is one of a number of cases in which the courts have annulled bankruptcy orders made on petitions presented by German debtors where it has been established that the court had no jurisdiction to open the proceedings. The scope of the inquiries the court can make when faced with a debtor's bankruptcy petition and doubts about the truth of what a debtor says about where his centre of main interests is situated is limited, not least of all because there is an understandable reluctance to depart from the long established principle that evidence given on oath (or nowadays in a witness statement verified by a statement of truth) should not be disbelieved unless it is properly challenged or is inherently incredible.

---

[173] German Federal Court of Justice (Bundesgerichtshof), 8 November 2007, NZI 2008, 121.

[174] See *Re Tricontinental Exchange Ltd* 2006 WL 2671336, 349 BR 627 (Bankr E.D. Cal. 2006) where the debtor was recognized under Chapter 15 of the US Bankruptcy Code (the US Enactment of the UNCITRAL Model Law) as having its COMI in St Vincent and the Grenadines, even though the insurance business run from there was unauthorized and illegal.

[175] *Shierson v Vlieland-Boddy* [2006] 2 BCLC 9, CA (UK debtor moved to Spain). See also *Official Receiver v Eichler* [2007] BPIR 1636, HCJ (German doctor with creditors in Germany moved to UK).

[176] C-1/04 [2006] ECR I-701, paras 7–77.

[177] C-339/07 [2009] ECR I-767, at para 49.

[178] [2011] BPIR 1293.

191. In the light of persistent abuse of its jurisdiction, however, this court has now developed two practices when dealing with petitions where it has doubts about its jurisdiction. Before a bankruptcy order is made, a debtor may be required to file more detailed evidence than is required by rr 6.38 and 6.41 of the Insolvency Rules in order to establish that his centre of main interests really is in this country, exhibiting documentary evidence in support of his claim that it is situated here; and/or the court may adjourn the petition and require that notice of the hearing be given to the debtor's creditors so that they can appear and make representations at that stage in opposition to the making of the order instead of having to apply after the order has been made. It is hoped that in future those steps (and perhaps others which may develop in the future) will ensure that bankruptcy orders founded on sham claims as to jurisdiction or supported by a false statement of affairs are not made in the future.

A debtor may choose to move COMI in order to take advantage of more favour- **8.117** able restructuring laws which exist in a particular Member State.[179] Despite Recital (4) OR, which mentions the policy against 'forum shopping', there is nothing objectionable in principle with this if it is done with a view to benefiting creditors and not to prejudice them.[180] The ability to move COMI is also consistent with the principle of freedom of establishment within the EU.

To be successful, any movement of COMI must have sufficient substance to be **8.118** credible and must also satisfy the requirements of Recital (13) that the COMI be the place where the debtor conducts the administration of his interests on a 'regular basis' and is therefore ascertainable by third parties. In *Official Receiver v Eichler,*[181] where a German doctor with German creditors had moved to the United Kingdom, it was said that while there was no minimum period of presence laid down in order to establish a move of COMI to another Member State, 'Common sense would seem to indicate that a few days (or even a few weeks) would be unlikely to suffice because that would be at odds with conducting the administration of one's interests in a place "on a regular basis ...".'

[Accordingly, the cases appear to emphasize that while COMI may be transferred, it **8.119** nonetheless requires an 'element of permanence', as stated in *Re Ci4net.com Inc.*[182] In that case, the fact that the director of a company moved around frequently was not capable of moving the company's COMI. The court in *Shierson v Vlieland-Boddy,*[183] while recognizing the right of debtors to move their interests around the EU, applied the 'element of permanence' test to determine COMI and added that the court had a duty to scrutinize carefully situations where it appeared the move had been made with impending insolvency in mind. (**AW**)]

---

[179] See A Marshall and C Pardiwala, 'Changing COMI Prior to Insolvency is Fair Game!' (2007) 4 International Corporate Rescue 318. This appears to have occurred in *PIN Group SA* (Amtsgericht Köln, 19 February) (73 IE 1-08), where there was a move of COMI to Germany from Luxembourg.
[180] This approach is accepted in the RR.
[181] [2007] BPIR 1636, HCJ.
[182] [2004] EWHC 1941, [2005] BCC 277.
[183] [2006] 2 BCLC 9, CA.

8.120 Where a debtor moves COMI, prior to any request for an opening in the original place of COMI, to another Member State, in order to avoid the original jurisdiction, the courts in England so far have failed to regard COMI as continuing in the original Member State and have accepted the move: *Shierson v Vlieland-Boddy*.[184] In the first edition of this work at paragraph 8.44 it was suggested that the OR could be interpreted in such a way as to treat a debtor who leaves his COMI to avoid his creditors as retaining the COMI, by analogy to the English law principle that a debtor who carries on business in England is treated as continuing that business until he has made arrangements to pay his debts.[185] In the case of a move of COMI within the EU, as in the *Shierson* case, this suggestion is complicated by the principle of freedom of establishment within the EU.

8.121 A similar issue arises where a debtor seeks to move its COMI outside the EU in order to avoid the commencement of insolvency proceedings in any Member State and to prejudice creditors in the EU. However, in such a case, there is no question of freedom of establishment within the EU and a more acute tension arises between the principle that COMI falls to be assessed as at the date of the opening of the proceedings with the need to prevent abuse of the OR by debtors. Where it can be shown that the steps to move COMI outside the EU are plainly abusive and for the purpose of avoiding insolvency proceedings under the OR, such steps should arguably be ignored.[186]

8.122 **Terminated activities.** What is the correct approach where the debtor has not moved COMI but has simply terminated its activities? Here again, it would seem to make sense to regard those activities as continuing for the purpose of assessing COMI.[187] This conclusion is consistent with the ECJ's analysis in *Interedil*,[188] in which the debtor company had ceased all economic activity (and, indeed, had been formally dissolved). The ECJ held that it was 'logical' to focus on the last COMI which the debtor had before being dissolved.[189]

8.123 **Risk of conflicting decisions.** Basing the jurisdiction to commence main proceedings on the concept of COMI is said to be beneficial to creditors since it is

---

[184] ibid.

[185] *Re A Debtor (No 784 of 1991)* [1992] Ch 554; *Re Theophile* [1950] AC 186, HL.

[186] cf *Hans Brochier Holdings Ltd v Exner* [2006] EWHC 2594 (Ch), [2007] BCC 127, at para 8.372 below, and in ch 3 above at n 30. See also the discussion below under the heading 'Statutory Changes in England'.

[187] See Dr Andrea Csöke, *A Határon Átnyúló Fizetésképtelenségi Eljárások (Cross-Frontier Insolvency Proceedings)* (HVG-Orac, Budapest, 2008) 75.

[188] Case C-396/09 *Interedil Srl v Fallimento Interedil Srl and Intesa Gestione Crediti* SpA [2011] ECR I-9915, [2012] BCC 851.

[189] ibid at [58]. Every debtor has to have a COMI for the OR (or the RR) to be able to work and therefore a practical solution had to be found for cases of terminated activities or even terminated existence. Note however that this approach has not been applied to the concept of 'establishment' (see the commentary above to Article 2(h) OR, presumably because it is not *necessary* for any debtor to have an 'establishment' as defined by the OR: the OR (and RR) can work on the basis of there only being a main proceeding.

said to be easily ascertainable by them and therefore enables creditors to identify easily the Member State in which main proceedings would be commenced against a debtor.[190] It is possible that the courts of the various individual Member States might take different views on the application of the concept to the facts of a particular case. However, conflicting decisions in the same case should not occur because any finding by the court which deals with the matter first should be respected by any subsequent court.[191] As the ECJ said in *Burgo Group*:[192]

> 28. ... the decision taken by the court of a Member State to open main proceedings in respect of a debtor company, and the finding, at least by implication, that the centre of the debtor company's main interests is situated in that Member State, cannot, in principle, be called into question by the courts of the other Member States.

In particular, under Article 16 of the OR the judgment of the court opening pro-   **8.124**
ceedings is to be recognized and enforced in other Member States without further formality. This means that it is not possible for this decision to be reviewed in the courts of another Member State except in exceptional circumstances on grounds of public policy. This principle has been respected by the courts of the Member States, an approach which has been fundamental to the proper functioning of the OR. In *MG Probud*, the ECJ emphasized the importance of this principle, which is founded on the concept of mutual trust.[193]

In *Re ISA-Daisytek SAS*[194] the French appellate courts held that they were not enti-   **8.125**
tled to review the decision of the English court opening main insolvency proceedings in relation to a French company which the English court had found had its COMI in England. In *Daisytek* the German courts came to the same result.[195] The same conclusion was also reached by the French courts in *Re Rover France SAS*,[196] again concerning a French company which had been placed into administration in England. The French court held that it was obliged to recognize the decision of the English court opening proceedings and, in particular, that it was not open to the French court to refuse recognition on grounds of public policy under Article 26 of the OR. The Versailles Court of Appeal did point out that the judge in England had examined its jurisdiction by applying the relevant criterion, and stated that the English court had thus fulfilled the condition necessary for recognition. There may be a hint in the judgment that if the English court had not examined its

---

[190] Virgos-Schmit Report para 75.
[191] Recital (22).
[192] Case 327/13 *Burgo Group SpA v Illochroma SA* [2015] 1 WLR 1046.
[193] Case C-444/07 *MG Probud Gdynia sp. z o.o* [2010] ECR I-417, [2010] BCC 453 at [27]–[29]. See also *Re Eurodis Electron plc* [2012] BCC 57 at [17] and Case 327/13 *Burgo Group SpA v Illochroma SA* [2015] 1 WLR 1046.
[194] [2003] BCC 984 (Court of Appeal of Versailles, 4 September 2003) and [2006] BCC 841 (Cour de Cassation, 27 June 2006).
[195] *Re ISA-Daisytek Deutschland GmbH* (Higher Regional Court of Dusseldorf, 9 July 2004).
[196] Commercial Court of Nanterre, 19 May 2005; Court of Appeal of Versailles, 15 December 2005.

jurisdiction or if it had not applied the relevant criterion, recognition may not have been forthcoming.

8.126 In *Eurofood* the ECJ held that on the proper interpretation of the first sentence of Article 16(1) OR, the main insolvency proceedings opened by a court of a Member State had to be recognized by the courts of the other Member States without those courts being able to review the jurisdiction of the court of the opening state. Both the Advocate General and the ECJ also referred to the narrow scope of the public policy exception in Article 26 OR. The ECJ held that, on the proper interpretation of Article 26, a Member State could refuse to recognize insolvency proceedings opened in another Member State where the decision to open the proceedings had been taken in flagrant breach of the fundamental right to be heard which a person concerned by such proceedings enjoyed. However, short of such a manifest breach of the principles of natural justice, Article 26 will not be applicable and the decision of the court opening the proceedings will fall to be recognized.

8.127 Accordingly, the remedy for any person who is concerned that a court of a Member State may have mistakenly opened insolvency proceedings is to pursue the matter in accordance with the procedure for appeal and review under the law of that Member State with the ultimate possibility of a reference to the ECJ. Absent some serious irregularity which falls within the narrow scope of Article 26, the courts of other Member States will be bound to recognize the decision without review.

8.128 [It is unfortunate that the OR makes no provision to enable conflicts between courts in different Member States regarding questions of jurisdictional competence to be resolved in an orderly and cost-efficient manner while proceedings are still at a relatively early stage. This is in marked contrast to the approach of the Brussels Convention (now Recast Regulation 1215/2012) on jurisdiction and recognition of judgments,[197] where Articles 29–32 lay down a set of rules, some mandatory and others discretionary, which apply when proceedings involving the same cause of action, or related actions, are brought in the courts of different Member States. It is submitted that there is a strong case for amendment of the OR to be made, designed by analogy with Article 29 of Regulation 1215/2012, whereby a doctrine of *lis pendens* could be imposed to prevent any court other than 'the court first seised' from exercising jurisdiction to open insolvency proceedings until such time as the jurisdiction of the court first seised of an application for the opening of insolvency proceedings is established. For this purpose, the presentation of a petition for a winding-up by the court, combined with an application for the appointment of a provisional liquidator, could be regarded as a step whereby the court in question

---

[197] See also B Wessels 'Mutual, Comity and Respect among States in International Insolvency Matters' in *Norton Annual Survey of Bankruptcy Law* (2005) 569–86.

becomes 'seised' of the matter. It would be essential to include a provision requiring the court first seised to make the determination as to its own jurisdictional competence at the earliest possible time, and in fidelity to the principle of mutual trust mentioned in Recital (22), given the special factors of urgency that are attendant upon cases of insolvency. There is a powerful need for national courts to be scrupulous and conscientious in approaching their exercise of jurisdiction, mindful of the impact of their decisions in an EU-wide dimension. The principle of 'mutual trust', alluded to in Recital (22), is fundamental to ensuring that the OR operates in a way which is fair, and lacking in oppressive side-effects. The provision in Article 57 RR for cooperation between courts could furnish a platform for the resolution of conflicts of jurisdiction, provided that timely initiatives are taken by those concerned. (**IF**)]

[Paragraph 79 of the Virgos-Schmit Report discusses the problem where two **8.129** Member States claim concurrent jurisdiction. Of interest, it is suggested that the courts will be able to take account of, among others, the general principles of procedural law which are valid in all Member States, including those derived from other Community Conventions, including the Brussels Convention (now Brussels Regulation). The ECJ in *Re Eurofood IFSC Ltd* [198] referred to *Erich Gasser v Misat Srl* [199] but did not take the opportunity to import the 'court first seised' doctrine. (**AW**)]

The intention of the OR was that the 'first court seised' doctrine should be imported **8.130** into the OR,[200] as part of '…the general principles of procedural law which are valid in all…'[201] Member States but the implications of para 79(3) of the V-S Report were overlooked by the ECJ in *Eurofood*. If the foreign debtor was included in the insolvency proceedings already opened abroad, the domestic administrative authority has no power to retain jurisdiction—unless the *ordre public* (public policy) exception to recognition operates—and must therefore decline its jurisdiction in favour of the foreign judge, even if the latter was wrong in assessing the debtor's COMI.[202] This in turn involves the already mentioned problem of courts competing to deal with large insolvency cases. (**AP**)]

[If the 'judgment opening proceedings' does not make clear that it constitutes **8.131** main proceedings and does not deal with the basis on which the court has determined it has jurisdiction to open main proceedings (for example there is no judicial determination concerning the location of the debtor's COMI), then query

---

[198] [2006] Ch 508.
[199] Case C-116/02 [2005] QB 1, [2003] ECR I-14693.
[200] See V-S Report at para 79(3) and VG at para 70 on p 52, where the point is explained in detail.
[201] V-S Report at para 79(3).
[202] [Council of State (Cons. Stato), 6th Session, 25 January 2007, No 267/2006, para 4.3 (published only in Italian in 21 Diritto del Commercio Internazionale 513 (2007) para 18, 18b. (**AP**)]

whether the court of another Member State would be free to determine that the debtor's COMI is in its own jurisdiction and that it is therefore free to open main proceedings (this might be possible if the first judgment could be said to constitute the opening of territorial proceedings, such that opening of the subsequent proceedings as main proceedings does not infringe the obligation to recognize the judgment of the first court under Article 16). Similarly, if the determination of the court's jurisdiction has been made without a proper *inter partes* hearing (the location of the debtor's COMI might be controversial), then query whether this would allow a court in another Member State to rely on Article 26 OR to refuse to give recognition to that judgment and to allow it to open its own main proceedings. This could be an issue in relation to English out of court applications, although the ability to apply to set aside the appointment before the English court is likely to be a relevant factor against the availability of Article 26 OR in such circumstances. (AW)]

8.132 **The time at which COMI is assessed** The terms of the OR contrast the 'opening' of insolvency proceedings with a 'request' for the opening of insolvency proceedings. Under Article 3(1), jurisdiction to open main proceedings is conferred on the courts of the Member State where the debtor's COMI is situated. The location of COMI is however to be assessed as at the time of the request for the opening of the proceedings.[203]

8.133 In *Staubitz-Schreiber*,[204] the debtor had moved her COMI, which was in Germany at the time of her request to open proceedings, to Spain, prior to any opening. The ECJ held that this did not deprive the German courts of jurisdiction.[205] It would have been contrary to the objectives of the OR to allow a debtor to move jurisdiction after a request to open insolvency proceedings had been issued but prior to the determination of that request by the court. It would have encouraged debtors to move to more favourable jurisdictions and would have involved creditors in the time and expense of having to chase after debtors.

8.134 In principle, this means that it is open to a debtor to move its COMI and alter the place where there is jurisdiction to open main proceedings prior to the filing of the request for the opening of proceedings: see paragraphs 8.114 et seq above.

---

[203] Case C-396/09 *Interedil Srl v Fallimento Interedil Srl and Intesa Gestione Crediti* SpA [2011] ECR-I 9915, [2012] BCC 851 at [55]. (Case C-396/09) [2012] BCC 851, following Case C-1/04 *Staubitz-Schreiber* [2006] ECR I-701, [2006] BCC 639 at [29]. In *Shierson v Vlieland-Boddy* the English Court of Appeal had held that the time at which the location of the COMI was to be determined was the time at which at the judgment opening the proceedings would become effective (see Article 2(f) OR). This case can no longer be relied on in respect of the relevant time for judging COMI.

[204] Case C-1/04 [2006] ECR I-701, [2006] BCC 639.

[205] This may be referred to as the principle of *perpetuatio fori*: see VG at para 68, p 50 and G Moss, 'Principles of EU Insolvency Law' (2015) 28(3) Insolvency Intelligence 40.

The ruling in *Staubitz-Schreiber* was applied by the Court of Appeal in Paris in **8.135** *Tendance Edition Ltd v L'URSSAF de Paris.*[206] In that case the English registered company had its 'seat' in Paris and was enrolled in the commercial register in Paris at the time of the request to open proceedings made by the creditor. Prior to the opening, the debtor company moved its seat to England. It was held that the French courts retained jurisdiction.

In *Interedil,*[207] the CJEU confirmed the reasoning in *Staubitz-Schreiber*: **8.136**

> 55. … The court has held that, where the centre of a debtor's main interests is trans-
> ferred after the lodging of a request to open insolvency proceedings, but before the
> proceedings are opened, the courts of the member state within the territory of which
> the centre of main interests was situated at the time when the request was lodged
> retain jurisdiction to rule on those proceedings: In re Staubitz-Schreiber (Case C-1/
> 04) [2006] ECR I-701, para 29. It must be inferred from this that, in principle, it is
> the location of the debtor's main centre of interests at the date on which the request
> to open insolvency proceedings was lodged that is relevant for the purpose of deter-
> mining the court having jurisdiction.

Specifying type of proceeding requested. In England the request for opening **8.137** and the judgment opening proceedings are required to specify whether main or territorial proceedings are sought to be opened but that is not the case at least in some other Member States. Where the judgment opening does not specify the type of proceeding being opened, it may be open to the courts of other Member States to recognize the proceedings as either main or territorial, depending on the evidence as to the place of COMI.

[It seems that the OR leaves it to the law of the Member State of the forum to **8.138** decide whether the applicant must specify whether he is applying for main proceed-ings pursuant to Article 3(1) or territorial proceedings pursuant to Article 3(2). A Swedish appellate court (RH[208] 2006:25) has held that a request for territorial proceedings, in a case where the COMI was in Sweden, had to be rejected. It could not result in the opening of main proceedings, as the court was not allowed to go beyond the applicant's request. (**MB**)]

Although the OR does not expressly require a court opening insolvency proceed- **8.139** ings under the OR to specify whether or not it is opening main or territorial pro-ceedings, it must logically have been the intention of the OR that this should be specified, otherwise creditors and courts in other Member States will have no cer-tainty as to the nature of the proceedings opened. VG is adamant that '…the court must *expressly record* whether it bases its jurisdiction on Articles 3.1 or 3.2….i.e. it

---

[206] 20 May 2008.
[207] Case C-396/09 *Interedil Srl v Fallimento Interedil Srl and Intesa Gestione Crediti* SpA [2011] ECR-I 9915, [2012] BCC 851 at [55].
[208] ['RH' is an abbreviation of 'Rättsfall från hovrätterna', meaning reports of decisions of Swedish courts of appeal (there are several appellate courts). (**MB**)]

must disclose whether the proceedings in question are main proceedings or territorial proceedings (see Article 21.1) [footnote omitted].' Article 21.1 OR requires the liquidator, when he requests notice of the opening to be published in another Member State, to specify whether his proceedings are main or territorial.

8.140 **Potential conflict with non-EU jurisdictions.** In most non-EU jurisdictions, 'main' or potentially universal proceedings can be opened on the basis of the existence of a registered office, assets or business or, in the United States, even the placing of a relatively small sum in a special account for this purpose. In a case where COMI is held by an EU court to be in the European Union, the OR requires recognition of this proceeding and its liquidator on a mandatory basis. Accordingly, unless one of the exceptions in the OR applies, courts in other Member States must recognize the EU proceeding in preference to any non-EU proceeding.

8.141 **Evidence required by an English court.** One issue which arises concerns the nature and extent of the evidence which will be required by an English court when opening insolvency proceedings in respect of a debtor in order to be satisfied that the debtor's centre of main interests is located in England and not in another Member State. Although not set out as an express requirement in the OR, the English court, like any other Member State court, must of its own motion (*ex officio*) examine the question of its own jurisdiction.[209]

8.142 In the case of companies, given the presumption contained in Article 3(1), it should be sufficient in the first instance to prove that the registered office of the company is in England and to confirm that there are no facts which would tend to rebut the presumption that the COMI is at the same place.[210] In the case of bankruptcy, the onus of proving the location of the debtor's centre of main interests or establishment (as the case may be) will be on the petitioning creditor.[211] However, in cases of suspicious forum shopping designed to disadvantage creditors, the English courts should require the debtor to present more detailed evidence than that which would ordinarily be required, and should, if appropriate, adjourn the petition to ensure that all interested creditors can make representations before the court.[212]

8.143 However, where a creditor is attempting to persuade an English court to open proceedings in respect of a company whose registered office is located outside England on the basis that the company's COMI is in England, it will obviously be

---

[209] VG para 65.

[210] See Practice Note, Insolvency Proceedings, 1/2002, 10 May 2002, [2002] BCC 572.

[211] cf the old law relating to proof of a debtor's domicile: the onus of proving the debtor's domicile is on the petitioning creditor but prima facie evidence can be adduced so as to throw the burden on the debtor: *Re Mitchell, ex p Cunningham* (1884) 13 QBD 418.

[212] *Re Eichler (No 2)* [2011] BPIR 1293 at [190]–[191]. This procedure was applied in *O'Donnell v Bank of Ireland* [2012] EWHC 3749 (Ch), a case of Irish bankruptcy tourism in England by Irish property developers, where the allegation of a successful COMI shift from Ireland to the UK was suspicious and was eventually rejected after notification to the principal creditors and a trial with cross-examination of the petitioners.

necessary to adduce evidence to rebut the presumption arising from the place of its registered office.

In principle, it is possible to use the out of court procedure to place a company **8.144** into administration in England, even where the company is incorporated outside England, on grounds that the company's COMI is located in England. However, taking this route presents several risks.[213] In particular, since there will have been no judicial determination of the company's COMI, there is a risk that aggrieved creditors might seek to set aside the appointment. This obviously raises issues for the office-holder who cannot be sure that his appointment will be effective. It is suggested that where there is any doubt about the location of a company's COMI the better approach will nearly always be to make an application to the court making full disclosure of all the relevant facts.

Statutory changes in England   The concept of COMI potentially conflicted **8.145** with the jurisdictional rules in the Insolvency Act 1986 and, in particular, in relation to individual debtors, with section 265 of the Act. For example, there may well be cases where a debtor is domiciled in England in the English law sense, but he has no 'establishment' in England and his centre of main interests is located in another Member State. Nevertheless, a literal application of section 265 would allow the English court to make a bankruptcy order against the debtor.[214] As a result, section 265 was amended to avoid any such conflict.[215]

There is no similar amendment in the case of corporate insolvency. In the case of **8.146** winding-up by the court, section 221 of the Insolvency Act 1986 creates a general jurisdiction over foreign registered companies. The restrictions on jurisdiction are judge-made and the case law will now have to apply the OR. With regard to

---

[213] cf the problems which arose in *Re Hans Brochier Holdings Ltd* [2006] EWHC 2594 (Ch) [2007] BCC 127. Although the company was incorporated in England, its operations were located in Germany and an attempt to place the company into administration in England by the out of court route was held to be invalid because its COMI was in Germany. In a further decision, the High Court held that the company did not even have an establishment in England. [Those seeking to make an out of court administration appointment should consider carefully whether the company's COMI or establishment is in the UK. If it is not, any appointment will be invalid and the purported appointor may be liable to the administrator under the court's discretion to impose a statutory indemnity for the invalid appointment. Note, also, that if the appointor is the debtor, the ability to commence administration as territorial proceedings prior to the opening of main proceedings elsewhere will be limited under Art 3(4). Therefore, seeking to rely on the existence of an establishment in the UK to justify the appointment at least in the UK may be of no use. It would, however, be possible for the debtor to open administration as *subsequent* territorial proceedings (such proceedings would then have to be secondary proceedings and be limited to winding-up proceedings), provided there was an establishment in the UK. (AW)]

[214] See *Henwood v Barlow Clowes International Ltd* [2008] EWCA Civ 577, [2008] All ER (D) 330. Note (by F Toube) in (2008) 21 Insolvency Intelligence 121.

[215] S 265(3) was added by reg 14 of the Insolvency Act 1986 (Amendment) (No 2) Regulations 2002, SI 2002/1240: 'This section is subject to Article 3 of the EC Regulation. See also r 6.7(1)(f) of the Insolvency Rules 1986 (added by the Insolvency (Amendment) Rules 2002), which requires a bankruptcy petition to state whether the debtor has his centre of main interests or an establishment in another Member State, and see the new form bankruptcy petitions (forms 6.7, 6.8, 6.9, and 6.27).

voluntary winding-up, section 221(4) contains a general bar on voluntary wind-ing-up for foreign registered companies, but was amended to introduce an excep-tion for cases covered by the OR.[216] In the case of corporate voluntary arrangements and administration, the former ambiguity as to whether these proceedings were available to foreign registered companies has been removed in relation to proceed-ings covered by the OR.[217]

8.147 There is a further complication in English law to the effect that a person who has carried on business in England is treated as continuing the business for the purposes of bankruptcy jurisdiction until he has made arrangements to settle his business debts.[218] The question of how far such an approach is possible under the OR is discussed above at paragraphs 8.120 and 8.121.

8.148 [In this instance, it may be necessary to await the pronouncement of the European Court of Justice on the precise meaning to be ascribed to 'centre of main interests' in the context of the OR. It is unquestionably an 'autonomous' term within the sense employed by European Union law, whose meaning cannot be taken from the legal vocabulary of any single, national system alone. On the other hand, a 'purposive' approach to interpretation of the term within the OR's sphere of application would suggest that a rule analogous to that deployed in the *Theophile* case (see paragraph 8.120 above) might prove adaptable to an EC-wide instrument under which the fiscal authorities of all the Member States are now eligible to participate. As noted at paragraph 8.122, the decision of the CJEU in the *Interedil* case provides some support for the argument that where a debtor attempts to change COMI under circumstances where creditors' interests are likely to be prejudiced by its subse-quently undergoing a legal procedure pursuant to the law of the state into which the COMI has allegedly migrated, such evasive tactics may be defeated through the attaching of greater importance to the location of the last centre of main inter-ests, thereby enabling the courts of the erstwhile COMI to retain jurisdictional competence.[219] (**IF**)]

8.149 **Scope of insolvency proceedings** Although Article 3(1) provides a rule to deter-mine which Member State is to have jurisdiction to open insolvency proceedings in relation to a debtor, it does not determine the *extent* of that jurisdiction. In particular, there is a question about the scope of insolvency proceedings: does the concept of insolvency proceedings extend to all ancillary actions commenced within the context of an insolvency or is it confined to the core proceeding itself? This question is important because it determines which regime is to provide the

---

[216] Insolvency Act 1986 (Amendment) (No 2) Regulations 2002, reg 9. See *Re TXU German Finance BV* [2005] BPIR 209.
[217] Insolvency Act 1986, s 1(4); Insolvency Act 1986, Sch B1, para 111(1A).
[218] *Re a Debtor (No 784 of 1991)* [1992] Ch 554; *Theophile v Solicitor-General* [1950] AC 186, HL.
[219] See Case C-396/09 *Interedil Srl v Fallimento Interedil Srl and Intesa Gestione Crediti* SpA [2011] ECR-I 9915, [2012] BCC 85, at [54]–[59], esp. at [58].

jurisdictional rules governing the action: the OR or the Recast Regulation on Civil Jurisdiction and Judgments 1215/2012.

This issue is dealt with by applying the principle that the OR and the Recast **8.150** Regulation on Civil Jurisdiction and Judgments are complementary so that they do not overlap or leave gaps in their application. The ECJ has endorsed this principle in several recent cases, including *Nickel & Goeldner*[220] and *F-Tex*.[221] Thus, the scope of the OR can be identified by reference to the exceptions to the application of the Regulation on Civil Jurisdiction and Judgments. In this regard, Article 1(2)(b) of the Recast Regulation on Civil Jurisdiction and Judgments provides that the Regulation does not apply to: 'bankruptcy, proceedings relating to the winding up of insolvent companies or other legal persons, judicial arrangements, compositions and analogous proceedings'.

The ECJ has held that proceedings relating to bankruptcy and winding-up will fall **8.151** within the scope of this exception if they derive directly from the bankruptcy or winding-up and are closely connected with the insolvency proceedings.[222]

In the English case law it has been held that claims by a liquidator to recover pre- **8.152** liquidation debts are not sufficiently closely connected.[223] By contrast, proceedings to set aside a vulnerable transaction or in respect of wrongful or fraudulent trading would be sufficiently connected.[224]

In recent years, the ECJ has heard numerous cases concerning the scope of what is **8.153** now Article 1(2)(b) of the Recast Regulation on Civil Jurisdiction and Judgments (and, by implication, the scope of Article 3(1) of the OR). This appears to be a fertile ground for satellite litigation. In *Seagon*,[225] the ECJ held that a German law avoidance action fell within the OR, and that the German court had jurisdiction over the Belgian corporate defendant against which the avoidance action had been brought. The key factors were (i) that the action was founded on German insolvency law, and (ii) that the German liquidator brought the action in the interests of the general body of creditors of the estate.[226]

In *SCT Industri*,[227] the ECJ held that an action before an Austrian court did not fall within **8.154** the scope of what is now the Recast Regulation on Civil Jurisdiction and Judgments, because it had a 'particularly close' link to Swedish insolvency proceedings.[228]

---

[220] Case C-157/13 *Nickel & Goeldner Spedition GmbH v 'Kintra' UAB* [2015] QB 96 at [21].
[221] Case C-213/10 *F-Tex SIA v Lietuvos-Anglijos UAB* [2013] Bus LR 232 at [21], [29], and [48].
[222] Case 133/78 *Gourdain v Nadler* [1979] ECR 733. The ECJ has applied the same principle in a number of subsequent cases (cited below).
[223] *Re Hayward (Deceased)* [1997] Ch 45; *UBS AG v OminiHolding AG* [2001] 1 WLR 916, [2000] BCC 593; *Re Ultra Motorhomes International Ltd* [2006] BCC 57, 42–43.
[224] *Re Ultra Motorhomes International Ltd* [2006] BCC 57, 42.
[225] Case C-339/07 *Seagon v Deko Marty Belgium NV* [2009] ECR I-767, [2009] 1 WLR 2168.
[226] ibid at [16].
[227] Case C-111/08 *SCT Industri AB v Alpenblume AB* [2009] ECR I-5655, [2010] Bus LR 559.
[228] ibid at [26].

The crucial factor was that the Austrian action related to the powers of a Swedish liquidator to dispose of certain assets belonging to the debtor, pursuant to provisions of Swedish insolvency law which derogated from the general rules of Swedish private law.[229] Accordingly, the exception in Article 1(2)(b) applied–notwithstanding that the Swedish insolvency proceedings had closed prior to the commencement of the Austrian action, and notwithstanding that the OR was not in force when the Swedish insolvency proceedings opened in 1993.[230]

8.155 In *German Graphics*,[231] the debtor company contracted to sell certain machines to a Dutch company. The contract contained a reservation of title clause. After the contract was made (but before the purchase price had been paid), a Dutch court placed the purchaser into compulsory liquidation. The vendor brought an action in Germany to recover the machines. The Dutch liquidator contended that the German action fell outside what is now the Recast Regulation on Civil Jurisdiction and Judgments. However, the ECJ held that the exception in Article 1(2)(b) did not apply, because there was an insufficiently close link between the German action and the Dutch insolvency proceedings. The only issue before the German court related to the ownership of the machines. This issue of ownership can arise outside the context of insolvency, and does not depend on insolvency law (properly so-called).[232] The mere fact that the Dutch liquidator was a party to the proceedings was insufficient.[233] The ECJ held that the scope of the OR should be construed narrowly, whereas the scope of what is now the Recast Regulation on Civil Jurisdiction and Judgments (and, in particular, the term 'civil and commercial matters') should be construed in a broad manner.[234] The reasoning in *German Graphics* was applied by the English High Court in *Byers v Yacht Bull*.[235]

8.156 In *F-Tex*,[236] the German liquidator asserted rights of action against a payee of the debtor's money, pursuant to claw-back provisions of the German insolvency code. Under German law, only the liquidator is entitled to bring such an action, unless the liquidator assigns his rights of action to a third party for the benefit of the general body of creditors. In this case, the liquidator assigned his rights of action to F-Tex (the sole creditor) in return for a share of the proceeds. F-Tex commenced proceedings in Lithuania, being the place of the payee's registered office. If the liquidator had brought the action himself, it would clearly have fallen within the Article 1(2)(b) exception. However, the ECJ held that the assignment to F-Tex severed the

[229] ibid at [27]–[30].
[230] ibid at [18] and [30].
[231] Case C-292/08 *German Graphics Graphische Maschinen GmbH v Alice van der Schee* [2009] ECR I-8421, [2010] ILPr 1.
[232] ibid at [32].
[233] ibid at [33].
[234] ibid at [23]–[25].
[235] *Byers v Yacht Bull* [2010] BCC 368 at [22] *ff.* See also *Polymer Vision R&D Ltd v Van Dooren* [2012] ILPr 14 at [46] *ff.*
[236] Case C-213/10 *F-Tex SIA v Lietuvos-Anglijos UAB* [2013] Bus LR 232.

link between the claw-back action and the German insolvency proceedings, so that what is now the Recast Regulation on Civil Jurisdiction and Judgments applied instead of the OR. The following factors were particularly significant: (i) unlike the liquidator, F-Tex was not required to act in the creditors' interests;[237] (ii) F-Tex could freely decide whether to bring the action;[238] and (iii) the closure of the insolvency proceedings would have no effect on F-Tex's ability to bring the action.[239]

In *Nickel & Goeldner*,[240] the ECJ reiterated that, if an action is based on principles **8.157** of insolvency law which derogate from the normal principles of private law, it falls within the Article 1(2)(b) exception.[241] The decisive criterion is not the procedural context of the action, but rather its legal basis.[242] Therefore, an action for the recovery of an ordinary debt brought by the liquidator of an company did not fall within the Article 1(2)(b) exception: the debt arose under a contract of carriage, and the action could have been brought by the company itself prior to the opening of insolvency proceedings.

In *H v HK*,[243] the German liquidator of a company brought an action in Germany **8.158** against its managing director under paragraph 64 of the Law on Limited Liability Companies, which provides as follows: 'the managing directors of a company are obliged to reimburse to the company payments made after the company is declared insolvent or after it has been established that its liabilities exceed its assets. That does not apply to payments, even those made after those events, that are compatible with the care to be expected of a prudent businessman'. The managing director was domiciled in Switzerland, and argued the action fell within what is now the Recast Regulation on Civil Jurisdiction and Judgments. The liquidator contended that the action fell within the exception in Article 1(2)(b) (and, therefore, within Article 3(1) of the OR). The ECJ accepted the liquidator's argument, holding that it would be artificial to distinguish between claw-back actions (as in *Seagon* and *F-Tex*) and the action in the present case.[244] Paragraph 64 of the Law on Limited Liability Companies derogated from the ordinary rules of civil and commercial law, specifically because of the insolvency of the debtor company,[245] and therefore satisfied the test in *Nickel & Goeldner*.

In summary, when insolvency proceedings are commenced in a Member State, **8.159** the jurisdiction of that state to open those proceedings is governed by the OR. However, other proceedings arising within the insolvency proceedings will only

---

[237] ibid at [44].
[238] ibid at [43].
[239] ibid at [46]. This may arguably be inconsistent with the ECJ's reasoning in Case C-111/08 *SCT Industri AB v Alpenblume AB* at [30].
[240] Case C-157/13 *Nickel & Goeldner Spedition GmbH v 'Kintra' UAB* [2015] QB 96.
[241] ibid at [24].
[242] ibid at [27].
[243] Case C-295/13 *H v HK*.
[244] ibid at [24].
[245] ibid at [23].

be within the OR and outside the scope of what is now the Recast Regulation on Civil Jurisdiction and Judgments by Article 1(2)(b) if they derive directly from the bankruptcy or winding-up and are closely connected with the insolvency proceedings. Thus actions by a liquidator to recover debts due to an insolvent company would not be excluded[246] and neither would claims against directors for breach of duty.[247] However, claims by a liquidator in respect of wrongful trading, preferences, or transactions at an undervalue will fall outside the scope of what is now the recast Regulation on Civil Jurisdiction and Judgments and therefore fall within the scope of insolvency proceedings governed by the OR.[248] Likewise, an application for information and documents under section 236 of the Insolvency Act 1986 has been held to be outside the Brussels 1 Regulation and would have been within the OR had the debtor's administration proceeding been subject to it.[249]

8.160 The identification of the basis of jurisdiction for legal proceedings relating to an insolvency may be important since it will determine whether or not the rules and jurisprudence of the Recast Regulation on Civil Jurisdiction and Judgments applies to those proceedings. For example, where, on analysis, proceedings before an English court fall within the insolvency exception, then the English court would be free to apply its discretionary powers to stay such proceedings, whereas the exercise of such powers is circumscribed where jurisdiction arises under the Recast Regulation on Civil Jurisdiction and Judgments.[250]

8.161 It should be noted that the possession of Article 3(1) jurisdiction enables the court having such jurisdiction to order protective measures from the time of the request to open proceedings.[251] In England, this would include the granting of injunctive relief such as a freezing order. In addition, under the English procedure, the court may appoint a provisional liquidator. In the light of the decision in *Eurofood* a decision to appoint a provisional liquidator will itself be a decision

---

[246] *Re Hayward (Deceased)* [1997] Ch 45. See also Case C-157/13 *Nickel & Goeldner Spedition GmbH v 'Kintra' UAB* [2015] QB 96.

[247] *Grupo Torras SA v Sheikh Fahad Mohammad Al-Sabah* [1995] 1 Lloyd's Rep 374, Case C-295/13 *H v HK*. Note also the judgment of the ECJ in Case C-267/97 *Coursier v Fortis Bank SA* [1999] ECR I-2543 that the question of the enforceability of a judgment obtained in foreign insolvency proceedings which was sought to be enforced pursuant to Art 36 of the Brussels Convention was to be determined by reference to the rules of private international law of the Member State in which enforcement was sought and not necessarily by the law governing the insolvency proceedings.

[248] Case 133/78 *Gourdain v Nadler* [1979] 1 ECR 733 (considered in *Re Hayward (Deceased)* [1997] Ch 45) and Case C-339/07 *Seagon v Deko Marty Belgium NV* [2009] ECR I-767, [2009] 1 WLR 2168.

[249] *Re MFGlobal UK Ltd In Special Administration)* [2015] EWHC 2319, a special administration proceeding relating to an investment undertaking which was not a credit institution. An insolvency proceeding of this type will fall under the RR: see Article 1 RR below.

[250] cf *Owusu v Jackson* [2005] QB 801.

[251] Virgos-Schmit Report para 78. See also Art 38 of the OR.

opening proceedings for the purposes of Article 3 if a provisional liquidator is a 'liquidator' for the purposes of the OR. Annex C to the OR has been amended to include a provisional liquidator as a 'liquidator' in the case of the UK.

Finally, it is important to bear in mind that Article 3(1) jurisdiction can be asserted **8.162** against defendants residing outside of the EU. In *Schmid v Hertel*,[252] main proceedings had commenced in Germany. The liquidator brought a claw-back action in a German court against a defendant residing in Switzerland. The ECJ held that the German court had jurisdiction to hear and determine the action. Article 3(1) jurisdiction extends to all defendants, residing anywhere in the world. It is irrelevant whether the defendant resides in a Lugano State.[253]

Insolvency proceedings limited to the territory of a Member State

In addition to the main insolvency proceedings, Article 3(2) gives the courts of a **8.163** Member State in which the debtor does not have his centre of main interests but has an 'establishment', jurisdiction to open insolvency proceedings in relation to that debtor. The critical point to note is that, in contrast to the main insolvency proceedings which have a universal effect, the effect of Article 3(2) insolvency proceedings is restricted to the assets of the debtor situated in the territory of the particular Member State.[254] Despite this, Article 3(2) proceedings represent an important exception to the general principle that the main insolvency proceedings are to have effect over all of the debtor's assets wherever situated (universal effect).[255]

[Where both main and secondary proceedings are opened, the OR leaves unclear **8.164** the consequences on the benefit of a current contract which is due to be performed in the Member State where secondary proceedings are opened. Article 4(2)(e) provides for the applicability of the *lex concursus* in such a case (save for the exceptions in Articles 5–15). However, under Article 3(2) the effects of the secondary proceedings are restricted to assets situated in that Member State. Article 2(g) provides that a claim is situated in the Member State where the third party required to meet the claim has his centre of main interests, and this could be the Member State in which main proceedings are opened. (**Wess**)]

'**Establishment**'.[256]   The definition of 'establishment' is set out in Article 2(h) **8.165** (see paragraphs 8.37–8.59 above) which defines an 'establishment' as any place of

---

[252] Case C-328/12 *Schmid v Hertel* [2014] 1 WLR 633. See also the commentary under Article 1 OR.

[253] Case C-295/13 *H v HK* at [32].

[254] [It should be noted that the effects of the secondary proceedings, based on that Member State's *lex fori* must be recognized in the other Member States. (**Wess**)]

[255] There are other specific exceptions to the principle of universal effect created by Arts 5, 6, and 7.

[256] English Insolvency Rules 1986, r 13.13(9) (added by the Insolvency (Amendment) Rules 2002) provides that for the purposes of the Rules 'establishment' has the meaning given to it by Art 2(h) of the OR.

operations where the debtor carries out a non-transitory economic activity with human means and goods. The effect of this is that it is insufficient for a debtor to have assets within a Member State; there must be a *place of operations* within the state in order for the courts of that state to have jurisdiction to open territorial proceedings.

8.166 **Terminated activities.** The question arises as to whether jurisdiction is retained to open secondary proceedings in a Member State where there has been an 'establishment' as defined by Article 2(h) but activities at the place of operations have ceased at the time of the request to open proceedings.[257] The answer to this question appears to be negative. In the UK Supreme Court case of *Olympic Airlines*,[258] the debtor had an establishment in England at the time when main proceedings opened in Greece. Over nine months later, the appellants presented a winding-up petition against the debtor in England. The UK Supreme Court held that the debtor had ceased to carry on any significant economic activities in England at the date of the petition. Accordingly, the debtor did not have an establishment in England at that date, and the English courts lacked jurisdiction to open secondary proceedings. It follows from *Olympic Airlines* that, if economic activities at the debtor's place of operations in a given Member State have ceased at the time of the request to open proceedings, the relevant Member State does not retain jurisdiction to open secondary proceedings against the debtor. (However, it is important to note that the new definition of 'establishment' in Article 2(10) RR has the effect of reversing the decision in *Olympic Airlines* in relation to similar facts. Under Article 2(10) RR, 'establishment' is defined as 'any place of operations where a debtor carries out or has carried out in the 3-month period prior to the request to open main insolvency proceedings a non-transitory economic activity with human means and assets'.)

8.167 There is in principle no limit on the number of Article 3(2) proceedings which may be commenced; if a debtor has a number of establishments in different Member States then a corresponding number of territorial insolvency proceedings can be commenced in each of those states.

8.168 There is a question here whether Article 3(2) jurisdiction can be taken even if the 'establishment' has been moved or disbanded in order to avoid jurisdiction. Similar points are considered in the commentary relating to main proceedings at paragraphs 8.114–8.121 above. The decision of the ECJ in *Staubitz-Schreiber*[259] in relation to COMI and the policy of the OR against forum shopping, indicates that a debtor will not be able to disband an establishment after a request to open

---

[257] See Dr Andrea Csöke, *A Határon Átnyúló Fizetésképtelenségi Eljárások (Cross-Frontier Insolvency Proceedings)* (HVG-Orac, Budapest, 2008) 75.

[258] *Trustees of the Olympic Airlines SA Pension and Life Assurance Scheme v Olympic Airlines SA* [2015] 1 WLR 2399. See also n 189 above.

[259] Case C-1/04, *Staubitz-Schreiber* [2006] ECR I-701, [2006] BCC 639, ECJ.

insolvency proceedings has been made in order to avoid jurisdiction. However, prior to the making of a request to open proceedings, a debtor should be free to move or disband an establishment.[260] This is consistent with the principle of freedom of establishment and it will remain open to creditors to open main proceedings in the Member State where the debtor has its COMI.

Secondary Article 3(2) proceedings.   Article 3(2) insolvency proceedings can   **8.169** be commenced even if main insolvency proceedings have previously been commenced in relation to the debtor. However, if main insolvency proceedings have already commenced, then Article 3(3) provides that the local insolvency proceedings can only be winding-up proceedings[261] (as opposed to reorganization proceedings) and are also in that case to be termed 'secondary proceedings'.

In England, winding-up proceedings for this purpose are compulsory winding-up,   **8.170** CVL, bankruptcy, and (as a result of an amendment to Annex B) administration.[262]

The restriction of secondary proceedings to winding-up proceedings can have   **8.171** unpleasant consequences. The example given prior to the amendment of Annex B was as follows. Suppose a corporate debtor's centre of main interests is in France, where the company's business is not viable, but there is an establishment and a separate, profitable business in England. It might well be desirable to place the company into administration in England. Prior to the amendment, unless the English jurisdiction opened proceedings first under Article 3(2), it was not possible to have administration proceedings in England. In the case of the United Kingdom, this has fortunately changed by the addition of administration to Annex B on the grounds that since the changes to domestic law under the Enterprise Act 2002 it is possible for administration to function as a liquidation proceeding. However, it may still be a problem in some of the other Member States.

[Secondary proceedings under the OR must be 'winding-up proceedings', this is   **8.172** defined as proceedings which involve the realizing of the assets of the debtor, being those proceedings listed in Annex B OR. In the case of an English administration, the amended Annex B OR refers to 'winding up through administration, including appointments made by filing prescribed documents with the court'. It is not clear if it would be possible to use an administration as a secondary proceeding to rescue the company as a going concern (being the first objective of an English

---

[260] This is consistent with the approach of the UK Supreme Court in *Olympic Airlines SA Pensions & Life Assurance Scheme v Olympic Airlines SA* [2015] 1 WLR 2399 (SC).

[261] For those insolvency proceedings which are 'winding-up proceedings' for the purposes of the OR see Annex B of the OR. See app 1 below.

[262] ibid Annex B, which refers to 'winding-up through administration, including appointments made by filing prescribed documents with the court'. Since it is impossible to tell at the start of an administration whether it will include 'winding-up', and since every administration is potentially a winding-up, it is thought that every administration will now qualify.

administration) if that does not involve some realization of the assets of the debtor. Further, it will not be possible to state at the outset whether such an administration will involve a realization of assets or not. (AW)]

8.173 The ability to open secondary proceedings in Member States where a debtor has an establishment, notwithstanding that main proceedings have already been opened in the Member State where the debtor has its COMI, may be problematic in practice. The initiation of secondary proceedings introduces multiple insolvency proceedings in relation to the debtor which will inevitably lead to increased costs and may also prejudice the successful achievement of the purposes of the main insolvency proceedings. Further, under the OR, a creditor does not need to satisfy any requirements in order to be able open secondary proceedings;[263] the issue as to whether the requirements for the opening of secondary proceedings are satisfied is one for the relevant local law.

8.174 However, under English law, the question whether to open insolvency proceedings is ultimately one for the discretion of the court. It can be expected that the English court would decline to exercise its discretion to open proceedings, notwithstanding that the formal requirements for the opening of proceedings were satisfied, if it could be shown that the opening of proceedings would prejudice the main proceedings and that the applicant creditor had no proper interest in the opening of secondary proceedings sufficient to override this consideration. A similar approach has been taken France: see paragraph 8.179 below.

8.175 In *Burgo Group*,[264] the ECJ confirmed the propriety of this approach. The ECJ held that the OR does not create a 'right' to open secondary proceedings in any Member State where the debtor has an establishment. Rather, the courts of each Member State where the debtor has an establishment can exercise a discretion to refuse the opening of secondary proceedings, provided that the exercise of such a discretion is permitted by the domestic law of the relevant Member State.[265] Clearly, the risk of undermining main proceedings in another Member State is a factor which can be taken into account. However, Member States must not establish conditions for the opening of secondary proceedings which discriminate between creditors from different Member States, and national courts must take into account the purpose of secondary proceedings as described in the OR.[266]

---

[263] See the Virgos-Schmit Report para 227 which notes that the right of creditors to commence secondary proceedings is not limited by the requirement of a specific interest and that the draft provision which envisaged that a creditor would only be able to open secondary proceedings if he could show that he would benefit from a more favourable legal status in those proceedings was deleted from the final text. See also Tschauner and Desch, 'Secondary Insolvency Proceedings in Germany over the Estate of a Dutch BV' (2007) 4 International Corporate Rescue 232.

[264] Case 327/13 *Burgo Group SpA v Illochroma SA* [2015] 1 WLR 1046.

[265] ibid at [63].

[266] ibid at [64]–[65] and [34].

In *Bank Handlowy*,[267] the ECJ commented on the possibility of opening second-   **8.176**
ary proceedings where a detailed plan of reorganization was already being implemented under main proceedings in a different Member State. The ECJ observed
that the opening of secondary proceedings in such a situation 'risks running counter to the purpose served by main proceedings, which are of a protective nature'.[268]
The ECJ referred to the principle of sincere co-operation, which requires a court
with jurisdiction to open secondary proceedings to have regard to the objectives of
the main proceedings and to take account of the scheme of the OR, which has the
aim of ensuring efficient and effective cross-border insolvency proceedings through
mandatory co-ordination of the main and secondary proceedings, guaranteeing the
priority of the main proceedings.[269]

Avoiding secondary proceedings.[270]   Secondary proceedings can disrupt the   **8.177**
beneficial rescue or realization of a business. Particularly in the case of a group
which had traded prior to insolvency as one organization, it makes practical sense
for the rescue, reconstruction, or insolvency proceedings to be run as a unity. In
some situations, local creditors can be persuaded to abstain from starting secondary proceedings in the interests of a better realization by promising to respect local
law priorities in the eventual distribution.

In *Collins & Aikman*[271] the administrators appointed by the English courts in   **8.178**
main proceedings promised creditors in other Member States that if they did not
cause secondary proceedings to be opened in their own states the administrators
would respect local law priorities in making distributions. In most Member States
the local creditors did not cause secondary proceedings to be opened and the
English court agreed with the administrators that English domestic law allowed
distributions to respect local law priorities in those cases. This resulted in a more
beneficial realization of the businesses of the Collins & Aikman companies incorporated outside the United Kingdom and is a useful model in situations where
the domestic law of a main proceeding is sufficiently flexible to follow the *Collins
& Aikman* model.[272] The *Collins & Aikman* model is now enshrined in Article 36
of the RR.

---

[267] Case C-116/11 *Bank Handlowy w Warszawie SA v Christianapol sp. z o.o.* [2013] Bus LR 956.
[268] ibid at [59].
[269] ibid at [62].
[270] See also G Moss, 'Group Insolvency—Choice of Forum and Law: the European Experience
under the Influence of English Pragmatism' (2007) 32 Brooklyn Journal of International Law
1005, 1017–18; G Moss, 'Group Insolvency—Forum—EC Regulation and Model Law Under the
Influence of English Pragmatism Revisited' (2014) 9(1) Brooklyn Journal of Corporate, Financial &
Commercial Law 250.
[271] [2007] 1 BCLC 182, [2006] BCC 861, HCJ. See also *Re Nortel Networks SA* [2009] EWHC
206 (Ch), [2009] BCC 343.
[272] A Schroeder, 'Secondary Insolvency Proceedings' in Schultze and Braun, *Insolvency and
Restructuring in Germany* (2008) 35, 37–38.

8.179   In *Public Prosecutor v Segard (as Administrator for Rover SAS)* the Versailles Court of Appeal[273] stated that in order to have secondary proceedings opened the applicant must show a valid purpose for such opening, such as improving the protection of local interests or the realization of assets.[274] In that case the court refused to open secondary proceedings because the existence of single proceedings was beneficial to the sale of assets and co-ordination of proceedings throughout Europe and the opening of secondary proceedings would multiply costs and formalities for no good purpose.[275]

8.180   **Pre-main Article 3(2) proceedings.**   If main insolvency proceedings have not yet been commenced in relation to the debtor, then Article 3(4) provides that Article 3(2) proceedings (in this commentary referred to as 'independent territorial proceedings') may only be commenced upon one of two conditions being satisfied.[276] Condition (a) of Article 3(4) provides for the situation where main insolvency proceedings cannot be commenced against a debtor.[277] In such circumstances there is no reason why there should be a restraint on the opening of territorial proceedings in other Member States.

8.181   Condition (b) is likely to be used more widely in practice. This condition permits a creditor who is domiciled or who has his habitual residence or registered office (as the case may be) in the Member State where an establishment of the debtor is situated to commence independent territorial insolvency proceedings against that debtor prior to main insolvency proceedings being commenced. In addition, a creditor whose claim arises from the operation of the establishment has a similar power to commence independent territorial proceedings.

8.182   [It must be stressed that condition (b) merely restricts the right to *commence* independent territorial insolvency proceedings. After such proceedings have been opened, even other creditors are in principle permitted to participate by filing their claims etc. (**MB**)]

8.183   It follows that where a debtor has its centre of main interests in another Member State, and no proceedings have been opened there, creditors will be restricted, even where under the ordinary national law the creditor would be able to open insolvency proceedings in relation to the debtor, by the need to fulfil one or other of the conditions.

---

[273] 15 December 2005.

[274] At paras 44–47.

[275] ibid.

[276] However, in contrast to territorial proceedings commenced after the main proceedings, territorial proceedings commenced before main proceedings have been commenced can be either winding-up or reorganization proceedings.

[277] This might be the case where, eg, the law of the Member State in which the centre of the debtor's main interests is located requires a debtor to be a trader in order to be subject to insolvency proceedings and the debtor is not a trader.

The aim of this rule is to give effect to the fundamental principle of the OR that the **8.184** main insolvency proceedings in relation to a debtor should be in the state where his 'centre of main interests' is situated whilst recognizing that local creditors may have a legitimate interest in pursuing insolvency proceedings against a debtor in their own Member State.[278] The conditions set by Article 3(4) are intended to achieve this aim.

One important advantage, already mentioned, of opening independent territo- **8.185** rial proceedings before the opening of any main proceedings is the ability to have non-winding-up proceedings.[279] Another important consequence is that a series of provisions in Articles 31–35 which regulate the relationship of main and secondary proceedings and ensure the primacy of the main proceedings, only apply to independent territorial proceedings in so far as the progress of the main and independent territorial proceedings permit: Article 36.

[Article 37 provides for the possibility that the liquidator in the main proceed- **8.186** ings may make a request to convert the independent territorial proceeding into winding-up proceedings. (**Wess**)]

The ruling of the ECJ in *Zaza Retail*[280] is the leading case on independent territorial **8.187** proceedings. In that case, the debtor had an establishment in Belgium, but had its COMI in the Netherlands. On the application of the Belgian prosecution service (which was acting in the public interest, and was not a creditor in the conventional sense), a Belgian court opened independent territorial proceedings against the debtor. On a preliminary reference to the ECJ, the Belgian prosecution service argued that Article 3(4)(a) conferred jurisdiction on the Belgian court to open independent territorial proceedings, because the Belgian prosecution service lacked *locus standi* to apply for the opening of insolvency proceedings in the Netherlands. The ECJ rejected this argument. From the mere fact that a specific person (in this case, the Belgian prosecution service) has no standing to apply for the opening of main insolvency proceedings, it does not follow that such proceedings 'cannot be opened'.[281] The impossibility of opening main proceedings must be determined objectively, and does not depend on the identity of the applicant.[282] Since other persons (such as ordinary creditors) had standing to apply for the opening of main proceedings in the Netherlands at all material times, Article 3(4)(a) had no

---

[278] See Virgos-Schmit Report para 84.

[279] In England the insolvency forms require the petitioner to state whether he is seeking to open main, secondary, or territorial proceedings and the court order opening the proceedings will also state whether the proceedings opened are main, secondary, or territorial. See the Insolvency Rules 1986, r 13.13(10), (12), and (14) (added by the Insolvency (Amendment) Rules 2002) for the formal definitions of main, secondary, and territorial proceedings for the purposes of the Rules.

[280] Case C-112/10 *Procureur-generaal bij het hof van beroep te Antwerpen v Zaza Retail BV* [2011] ECR I-11525.

[281] ibid at [24].

[282] ibid at [21].

application. The ECJ emphasized the importance of Recital (17), which states that independent territorial proceedings should be limited to what is 'absolutely necessary'.[283] Further, the ECJ held that the Belgian prosecution service could not be treated as a 'creditor' within Article 3(4)(b), because it had no right to lodge a claim against the debtor's estate,[284] and did not act as a representative of the creditors.[285] The concept of a 'creditor' should be construed strictly,[286] and does not include public authorities which act in the public interest rather than as creditors (or in the name or on behalf of creditors).[287]

(OR) Article 4—Law applicable

1. Save as otherwise provided in this Regulation, the law applicable to insolvency proceedings and their effects shall be that of the Member State within the territory of which such proceedings are opened, hereafter referred to as the 'State of the opening of proceedings'.
2. The law of the State of the opening of proceedings shall determine the conditions for the opening of those proceedings, their conduct and their closure. It shall determine in particular:
   (a) against which debtors insolvency proceedings may be brought on account of their capacity;
   (b) the assets which form part of the estate and the treatment of assets acquired by or devolving on the debtor after the opening of the insolvency proceedings;
   (c) the respective powers of the debtor and the liquidator;
   (d) the conditions under which set-offs may be invoked;
   (e) the effects of insolvency proceedings on current contracts to which the debtor is party;
   (f) the effects of the insolvency proceedings on proceedings brought by individual creditors, with the exception of lawsuits pending;
   (g) the claims which are to be lodged against the debtor's estate and the treatment of claims arising after the opening of insolvency proceedings;
   (h) the rules governing the lodging, verification and admission of claims;
   (i) the rules governing the distribution of proceeds from the realisation of assets, the ranking of claims and the rights of creditors who have obtained partial satisfaction after the opening of insolvency proceedings by virtue of a right in rem or through a set-off;
   (j) the conditions for and the effects of closure of insolvency proceedings, in particular by composition;
   (k) creditors' rights after the closure of insolvency proceedings;
   (l) who is to bear the costs and expenses incurred in the insolvency proceedings;
   (m) the rules relating to the voidness, voidability or unenforceability of legal acts detrimental to all the creditors.

---

[283] ibid at [22].
[284] ibid at [31].
[285] ibid at [32].
[286] ibid at [29].
[287] ibid at [34].

In contrast to the Brussels Regulation on Civil Jurisdiction and Judgments 44/ **8.188**
2001 (and the Recast Brussels Regulation (EU) 1215/2012[288]) which deals with
the questions of jurisdiction, recognition, and enforcement, the OR also contains
conflict of laws rules which replace the various national rules of private international law in relation to insolvency proceedings. The reasons for this are set out
in the Virgos-Schmit Report. In particular, it is said that insolvency proceedings
are collective proceedings and in order for collective proceedings to function
effectively it is necessary for there to be clear legal positions. It follows that international insolvency proceedings can only be effectively conducted if the relevant
states recognize not only the jurisdiction of the state in which the main proceedings were commenced but also the powers of the liquidators in those proceedings
and the effect of any judgments given by the courts in those proceedings. This
can only happen if there are harmonized rules on conflict of laws which provide
a degree of certainty that, in the event of insolvency, rights created or granted
in insolvency proceedings will be recognized throughout the Member States. In
German Graphics,[289] the ECJ emphasized that the choice of law rules in Article 4
OR are conceptually independent from the jurisdiction rules in the Regulation on
Civil Jurisdiction and Judgments, such that the former rules have 'no effect'[290] on
the latter rules.

The general rule given effect to by Article 4(1) OR is that the law applicable to **8.189**
insolvency proceedings is that of the state where the proceedings are commenced
('the state of the opening of proceedings') (*lex concursus*). This general rule applies
to both main insolvency proceedings and Article 3(2) OR insolvency proceedings
(whether secondary proceedings or independent territorial proceedings).[291]

In relation to the general rule, it appears that the law of the state of the opening of **8.190**
proceedings applies to both matters of substantive law and matters of procedure
which arise in the context of the insolvency proceedings.[292]

Since Article 4 is a conflict of laws provision,[293] it is probably meant to be a reference **8.191**
only to domestic insolvency law, excluding rules of private international law.[294]

---

[288] Regulation (EU) 1215/2012 of the European Parliament and of the Council of 12 December
2012 on jurisdiction and the recognition and enforcement of judgments in civil and commercial
matters.
[289] Case C-292/08 *German Graphics Graphische Maschinen GmbH v Alice van der Schee* [2010]
ILPr 1.
[290] ibid at [37].
[291] Art 28 OR specifically deals with the position in relation to secondary proceedings. However,
since Art 4(1) OR is stated as a general rule it must be taken as applying to independent territorial
proceedings. See also the Virgos-Schmit Report para 89.
[292] Virgos-Schmit Report para 90. However, if a particular matter arises in the context of insolvency proceedings which falls outside the scope of the OR, then the Recast Brussels Regulation
(EU) 1215/2012 will apply and accordingly the ordinary rules of private international law will be
applicable.
[293] Virgos-Schmit Report para 88.
[294] ibid para 87.

8.192 The application of such domestic insolvency law under Article 4 OR can, however, in special cases, indirectly lead to the application of the law of another Member State. In *Collins & Aikman Europe SA*[295] the English court held that where the English court had opened main proceedings in respect of a number of companies incorporated in other Member States, the promises made by the administrators to local creditors to the effect that local law priorities would be respected if they did not cause secondary proceedings to be opened, led the English court to direct, as a matter of English law principles of justice, to apply, in the main proceedings, local law priorities to the claims of the creditors of each company.[296] This holds out the possibility of having a single main proceeding in relation to a debtor, without the need for secondary proceedings, whilst at the same time respecting the substantive rights which local creditors would have in secondary proceedings under the relevant local law.[297]

8.193 As noted above, under the jurisdictional rules contained in Article 3 of the OR, the court of a Member State may be empowered to make an order commencing insolvency proceedings in relation to a company incorporated in a different Member State but whose COMI is in the first state. Under Article 4, the law of the state where the proceedings are commenced will apply to the insolvency. However, because national insolvency law may be designed to apply to a company which is incorporated in that state or which has it operations there, this may give rise to difficulties when it is sought to apply this law to a company which is incorporated or has its operations elsewhere. Since in such a case, the application of the national law stems from Article 4, the national law ought to be interpreted purposively and in such a way as to give effect to the purpose of the OR.[298]

8.194 [Directors of a company incorporated under the law of one jurisdiction might find that they are exposed to the insolvency laws of other jurisdictions (ie the law(s) of the Member State(s) where the proceedings are opened). This important point will be relevant when advising directors of their duties in the twilight of insolvency. Further, such liability is not subject to the potential protection afforded by Article 13 OR (unless the source of the directors' liability relates to a matter falling within Article 4(2)(m)) OR. (**AW**)]

---

[295] [2007] 1 BCLC 182.
[296] The decision reflects the fact that the English Insolvency Act is not a mandatory code which requires the application of English substantive law in all circumstances.
[297] Amrei Schroeder, Secondary Insolvency Proceedings, in Schultze & Braun's *Insolvency and Restructuring Yearbook* (2008) 35, 37–8.
[298] eg s 233 of the English Insolvency Act 1986 deals with the disconnection of utility services to an insolvent company by UK utilities. On its face, this would not apply in relation to a foreign company which had its head office and COMI in England but its trading operations in a different Member State. In *Appell v Essent Netwerk BV* (District Court of Hertogenbosch, 31 October 2005), the Dutch Court held that s 233 would apply in relation to a Dutch company in administration in England so as to prohibit a Dutch utility from terminating supply.

The view has been expressed that the question of whether or not a director should **8.195** be disqualified from acting as a director is outside the scope of Article 4 OR.[299]

Article 4(2) OR

Article 4(2) OR provides for a (non-exhaustive) list of specific matters in relation to **8.196** the opening of proceedings, their conduct, and their closure to which the law of the state of the opening of proceedings applies. This list effectively represents examples of the application of the general rule in Article 4(1) OR and should not be taken as limiting the application of that rule in any way.

Article 4(2)(e) OR

Article 4(2)(e) provides that the law of the state of the opening of the proceedings **8.197** determines the effect of the insolvency proceedings on current contracts to which the debtor is a party. This covers matters such as the termination of such contracts as a result of the opening of the proceedings and for these purposes the law which would otherwise be applicable to the contract may be displaced.[300] There are exceptions for contracts relating to immovable property and employment contracts (Articles 8 and 10).

[The law of the state of the opening of the proceedings governs the effects on current **8.198** contracts irrespective of whether such effects are invoked by the administrator (for example in order to escape some of the debtor's contractual obligations) or by the other party to the contract (for example a seller refusing to deliver goods because of anticipated non-payment). The latter effect would be more appropriately governed by the law applicable to the contract in question, but that seems to be incompatible with the wording of Article 4(2)(e). (**MB**)]

The term '*current contracts*' has been held by the English Commercial Court to **8.199** include arbitration clauses.[301] It was also held that a pending arbitration claim falls within the exception to Article 4(2)(f) OR and into Article 15 OR (ie 'lawsuits pending') and that aspect was also confirmed by the Court of Appeal. The combined effect of the provisions is discussed further under Article 15 OR.

Article 4(2)(f) OR

Article 4(2)(f) provides that the law of the state of the opening will determine the **8.200** effects of the proceedings on 'proceedings brought by individual creditors'. All of

---

[299] Professor Michael Bogdan at the European Academy of Law (ERA) in Trier on 18 September 2006.

[300] Virgos-Schmit Report para 91(e).

[301] *Elektrim v Vivendi* [2008] EWHC 2155 (Comm), aff'd (CA) sub nom *Syska v Vivendi Universal SA* [2009] EWCA Civ 677, [2010] BCC 348. [See I Fletcher, 'Effect on Arbitration of the EU Regulation' (2009) 22 Insolvency Intelligence 60–62, and I Fletcher, 'The EU Insolvency Regulation and Pending Arbitration Proceedings: The Court of Appeal Ruling on Article 15' (2009) 22 Insolvency Intelligence 155–7. Notably, this sensible approach by the English courts to the interpretation of Article 15 OR has been explicitly endorsed by the amended wording of Article 18 RR. (**IF**)]

the national laws of the Member States are believed to provide for an interruption or suspension of proceedings or at least executions or seizures of property by means of a stay of steps by individual creditors against the debtor or his assets upon insolvency (as opposed to reorganization) proceedings being opened in relation to that debtor and some also provide greater or lesser stays for reorganization proceedings. Where such a stay on actions against the debtor arises under the law of the state where main proceedings were opened, then such stay will have automatic effect across all Member States pursuant to Article 17 of the OR so as to preclude actions against the debtor otherwise than in accordance with the terms of that stay. [See, for example, *Merrill Lynch International Bank Ltd v Winterthur Swiss Insurance Co: Re Eurotunnel Finance Ltd* (HCJ, 30 November 2006) concerning the application of the stay under a French insolvency procedure in the United Kingdom. (**AW**)]

8.201   Although put in very general terms, 'proceedings brought by individual creditors' in Article 4(2)(f) OR may be limited to 'individual enforcement actions',[302] that is against assets in the estate.[303] It must be remembered, however, that Article 4(2)(f) is simply part of a list of examples of the general rule in Article 4(2) that in accordance with Articles 4(1) and 4(2) the *lex concursus* governs the effects and conduct of the insolvency proceeedings, including any stay of non-enforcement proceedings, subject to the exceptions such as Article 15 set out in the OR.

8.202   The exception in Article 4(2)(f) for 'lawsuits pending' appears to contain an implied cross-reference to Article 15 and presumably covers the same ground as Article 15, in respect of which see the commentary under Article 15 below. As mentioned above under Article 4(2)(e) arbitration proceedings have been held to be covered by the expression 'lawsuits pending'.

8.203   The application of Article 4(2)(f) OR is illustrated by the ruling of the ECJ in *MG Probud*.[304] In that case, a Polish court opened main proceedings against the eponymous debtor. Under Polish law, post-insolvency attachments are prohibited. Two days after the opening of main proceedings in Poland, administrative authorities in Germany made an attachment order against assets belonging to the debtor situated

---

[302] Virgos-Schmit Report para 142; Fletcher at para 4.42 of the first edition of this work; Virgos and Garcimartin, *The European Insolvency Regulation: Law and Practice* (2004) paras 253–255. Note that para 91(f) of the Report refers to 'executions brought by individual creditors', which appears to be based on the use of '*ejecuciones*' (executions) in the Spanish version. In English terminology, 'execution' refers only to a process *after* judgment (see *Re Overseas Aviation Engineering Ltd* [1963] 1 Ch 24, 39 (per Lord Denning MR)) whereas here processes before and after judgment are intended. In some Continental jurisdictions it is possible to obtain a seizure of a debtor's property before or without judgment: see for example the attachment in France in Case C-85/12 *LBI hf v Kepler Capital Markets SA*.

[303] In the light of the words 'concerning an asset or right of which the debtor has been divested' in Art 15. See also commentary under Art 15 below.

[304] Case C-444/07 *MG Probud Gydnia sp. z o.o* [2010] ECR I-417, [2010] BCC 453.

in Germany. The ECJ emphasized that the Polish main proceedings enjoyed universal effect, which could only be curtailed by the opening of secondary insolvency proceedings in Germany. No such secondary proceedings had been opened. Therefore, by virtue of Article 4(2)(f) (and also Article 4(2)(b)), the attachment order had been wrongly made.

Article 4(2)(h) OR

The rules relating to the lodging, verification, and admission of claims are governed **8.204** by the law of the state of the opening of the proceedings. This covers matters such as the formal requirements for submitting a claim in the insolvency, the time limits for so doing and the burden of proof. This is so even where the substantive law applicable to such claims is a different law.[305] However, the applicability of the law of the state of the opening of the proceedings subject to the rules relating to the lodgement of claims contained in the OR itself (see Articles 32 and 39–42 OR) will override national law to the contrary.

The Court of Appeal of Aix-en-Provence held in *Dawson International Trading Ltd* **8.205** *v SARL Regimentals*[306] that whilst lodging, verification, and admission of claims are governed by the law of the proceeding (in this case, French law), the question of who is the proper authorized representative of a corporate creditor for the purposes of lodging a claim is determined by the national law of the company (in this case, Scots law).

Article 4(2)(i) OR

The law of the state of opening sets out 'the rules governing the distribution of **8.206** proceeds from the realization of assets, the ranking of claims'. In special situations, however, the domestic law of the state of opening main proceedings may allow for distributions to respect local law priorities in another Member State. In *Collins & Aikman*[307] the administrators appointed by the English courts in main proceedings promised creditors in other Member States that if they did not cause secondary proceedings to be opened in their own states the administrators would respect local law priorities in making distributions. In most Member States the local creditors did not cause secondary proceedings to be opened and the English court agreed with the administrators that English domestic law allowed distributions to respect local law priorities in those cases. This resulted in a more beneficial realization of the businesses of the Collins & Aikman companies incorporated outside the United Kingdom and is a useful model in situations where the domestic law of a main proceeding is sufficiently flexible to follow the *Collins & Aikman* model.

---

[305] So, the admissibility of a claim arising under a French law contract in an English administration is governed by English law not French law.
[306] 13 September 2007.
[307] [2006] BCC 861, HCJ.

Article 4(2)(j) OR

8.207 The rules relating to the conditions for and the effects of closure of insolvency proceedings are governed by the *lex concursus*. In *Bank Handlowy*,[308] the ECJ ruled that (by virtue of Article 4(2)(j)) the concept of closure cannot be given an autonomous interpretation under EU law. Rather, the concept of closure must be interpreted in accordance with the *lex concursus*. In this respect, the concept of closure differs from the concept of opening, which (by virtue of Article 16(1)) must be given an autonomous interpretation under EU law.[309]

Article 4(2)(m) OR

8.208 With regard to Article 4(2)(m) OR, a literal reading of the phrase 'all the creditors' in the English version would lead to an absurd result. It is suggested that in the context it means 'creditors as a whole' or 'general body of creditors'. This approach may be supported by the French and German versions which use the terms '*ensemble*' and '*Gesamtheit*' respectively.

8.209 A literal reading would be unworkable for a number of reasons. It would require proof that the act in question was detrimental to every single creditor. First, the act will almost certainly not be detrimental to the creditor who gets the relevant benefit. Even excluding that creditor by necessary implication, there are a number of situations plainly intended to be covered which do not involve every creditor other than the benefited creditor receiving a detriment.

8.210 For example, if the debtor gives a creditor security in the nature of a right in rem which ranks in priority behind another secured creditor, this may well not be detrimental to the prior security holder, but it is detrimental to creditors generally. Likewise, if there are sufficient assets to pay preferential creditors in full, a voidable payment or security given to one creditor may not have a detrimental effect on preferential creditors but will again be detrimental to the general body of creditors.

Exceptions to the general rule

8.211 However, the general rule stated in Article 4(1) is subject to a considerable number of exceptions set out in Articles 5–15 of the OR:

(a) In certain cases the OR excludes some rights over assets located in another Member State, or the right of creditors to demand set-off accorded to them under the law of another state, from the effects of the main insolvency proceedings.[310] These rights are governed by the relevant national law and

---

[308] Case C-116/11 *Bank Handlowy w Warszawie SA and another v Christianapol sp. z o.o* [2013] Bus LR 956.
[309] ibid at [50]–[51].
[310] Virgos-Schmit Report para 92(1).

not by the law of the state of the opening of proceedings. See in this regard Article 5 (Third parties' rights in rem), Article 6 (Set-off) and Article 7 (Reservation of title).

(b) In other cases the OR specifically provides for the effects of insolvency proceedings to be governed not by the law of the state of the opening of proceedings but by the law of the particular state indicated by means of a specific connecting factor (which may or may not coincide with the state of the opening of proceedings).[311] See in this regard Article 8 OR (Contracts relating to immoveable property), Article 9 OR (Payment systems and financial markets), Article 10 OR (Contracts of employment), Article 11 OR (Effects on rights subject to registration), Article 14 OR (Protection of third-party purchasers) and Article 15 OR (Effects of insolvency proceedings in lawsuits pending). In this context, the law of the particular state concerned refers not to the general law but to the legal effects of the nearest equivalent insolvency procedure in that Member State.[312]

(c) [In one case a specific asset may only be included in the main proceedings, see the EC intellectual property rights as mentioned in Article 12. (**Wess**)]

In this way the law of the insolvency proceedings will be combined with different national laws which are applicable to particular matters which arise in the insolvency. Consequently the OR will require a degree of co-ordination and co-operation between foreign courts.

Where one of the exceptions to Article 4 OR applies, presumably this covers proceedings required to enforce rights which fall under such exception.[313] For example, if a secured creditor has rights in rem excluded from Article 4 OR by Article 5 OR, the secured creditor must be able to take proceedings to enforce his rights. Moreover, such a right to take proceedings to enforce excluded rights must apply notwithstanding any stay of proceedings or *vis attractiva concursus* which might otherwise apply under the *lex concursus* by the application of Article 4(2)(f).[314] **8.212**

(OR) Article 5—Third parties' rights in rem

1. **The opening of insolvency proceedings shall not affect the rights in rem of creditors or third parties in respect of tangible or intangible, moveable or immoveable assets—both specific assets and collections of indefinite assets**

---

[311] ibid para 92(2).

[312] See ibid para 92(2) and the Austrian Supreme Court cases cited under Art 15 below. In England, in the case of *Mazur Media Ltd v Mazur Media GmbH* [2004] 1 WLR 2966 no reference was made to the Virgos-Schmit Report and the judgment mistakenly proceeds on the basis that the English court can only apply its general discretion: see further the commentary to Art 15 below.

[313] We are obliged to Stephen Robins, barrister of 3–4 South Square, Gray's Inn, London for drawing our attention to this issue.

[314] See now Case C-327/13 *Burgo group SpA v Illochrama SA* [2015] 1 WLR 1046.

as a whole which change from time to time—belonging to the debtor which are situated within the territory of another Member State at the time of the opening of proceedings.

2. The rights referred to in paragraph 1 shall in particular mean:
   (a) the right to dispose of assets or have them disposed of and to obtain satisfaction from the proceeds of or income from those assets, in particular by virtue of a lien or a mortgage;
   (b) the exclusive right to have a claim met, in particular a right guaranteed by a lien in respect of the claim or by assignment of the claim by way of a guarantee;
   (c) the right to demand the assets from, and/or to require restitution by, anyone having possession or use of them contrary to the wishes of the party so entitled;
   (d) a right in rem to the beneficial use of assets.

3. The right, recorded in a public register and enforceable against third parties, under which a right in rem within the meaning of paragraph 1 may be obtained, shall be considered a right in rem.

4. Paragraph 1 shall not preclude actions for voidness, voidability or unenforceability as referred to in Article 4(2)(m).

8.213 As noted above, Article 5 OR creates an exception to the general rule stated in Article 4(1) OR that the law applicable to insolvency proceedings is that of the law of the state of the opening of proceedings. It also creates an exception to the general principle that the main insolvency proceedings are to have a universal scope (ie to have effect over all of the debtor's assets wherever situated). (The other exception to this principle is of course the fact that local assets may be subject to separate Article 3(2) OR proceedings.) This exception is part of a series of exceptions protecting legitimate expectations and certainty in relation to transactions in Member States other than the one in which proceedings are opened.[315]

8.214 There was felt to be a particular need for an exception in relation to rights in rem, since such rights 'are of considerable importance for the granting of credit'[316] and because the laws on security interests, and in particular on the creation, validity, and scope of security interests, differ widely across Member States.[317] Article 5 OR therefore provides, as an exception to the general rule under the Regulation that insolvency proceedings and their effects are governed by the law of the Member State in which they were opened,[318] that rights in rem shall not be affected by the effects of the insolvency proceedings under this law. Article 5 OR can be understood as a *'negative conflict'* rule[319] in that it provides that rights in rem shall not be

---

[315] Recital (24).
[316] Recital (25).
[317] Recital (11).
[318] Art 4(1).
[319] Per Virgos and Garcimartin (n 302 above) 163.

subject to the effects of the main proceedings arising under the law governing those proceedings.

The effect of Article 5(1) OR is to exclude third parties' rights in rem over local **8.215** assets (ie situated in a state other than the state of the opening of proceedings) from the universal scope of the main insolvency proceedings. Equally, the general rule as to applicable law set out by Article 4(1) OR does not apply and matters relating to rights in rem are governed by their own applicable law.

The practical effect of Article 5(1) OR is that although the law of the state of the **8.216** opening of main proceedings may claim local assets as part of the debtor's estate in those proceedings, the rights in rem of any third parties in relation to those assets are preserved in accordance with local law. This means, for example, that the holder of a security right can exercise that security over the debtor's local assets (in accordance with local law) regardless of whether or not the law governing the main insolvency proceedings permits this. However, because the local assets themselves (as opposed to the rights in rem over them) remain subject to the universal scope of the main proceedings, then any surplus remaining after the exercise of rights in rem will be subject to the law and scope of the main proceedings.

It should also be noted that Article 5(1) OR does not prevent secondary proceed- **8.217** ings being commenced in respect of local assets which may prevent the enforcement of rights in rem over local assets (according to the local law applicable to the secondary proceedings). In addition Article 5(1) OR applies only to rights in rem created before the commencement of the main proceedings; any such rights created afterwards are subject to law and the scope of the main insolvency proceedings.[320] The requirement in Article 5(1) OR that the assets be 'situated within the territory of another Member State at the time of the opening of proceedings' must be read in the light of the principle of effectiveness. In the *ERSTE Bank* case,[321] the security interest was over shares situated in Hungary, which was not a Member State at the time of the opening of the relevant main insolvency proceedings in Austria, but which was a Member State by the time declaratory relief was sought in Hungary. The CJEU held that the OR could only be made effective if the security over assets in Hungary qualified for protection under Article 5, even though Hungary was not a Member State when the main insolvency proceedings were opened and therefore the assets did not in a literal sense fall within Article 5 OR.

There is no general definition of a 'right in rem' in the Regulation and it appears **8.218** that this is a matter to be determined by national law.[322] However, it must follow

---

[320] V-S Report para 96.
[321] Case C-527/10 *ERSTE Bank Hungary v Hungarian State* [2012] ILPr 38. See also G Moss, 'Principles of EU Insolvency Law' (2015) 28(3) Insolvency Intelligence 40.
[322] V-S Report para 100. [The national law in question is the law determined by the normal conflict of law rules of the forum, generally pointing to the *lex rei sitae* at the relevant time. (**MB**)]

from the general scheme of the Regulation that an unreasonably wide definition of rights in rem should not be adopted since the effect of this would be to abrogate the fundamental principle behind the Regulation (that the main insolvency proceedings have universal scope) to an unacceptable extent. In these circumstances, it is probable that 'rights in rem' are to be construed narrowly as an exception to the general rule.

8.219 Furthermore, Article 5(2) OR does provide a list of rights which are to be regarded as being rights in rem within the meaning of Article 5(1). This list reflects the narrow definition which should be given to rights in rem. In particular, it is said that the list is based on the concept that a right in rem has two fundamental characteristics:[323]

(a) a direct and immediate relationship between the right and the asset or assets it covers with the asset or assets being attached to the satisfaction of the right; and

(b) the absolute right of the holder of the right in rem to have the asset allocated to satisfaction of the right. This encompasses a requirement that the right be enforceable against third parties.

8.220 It seems appropriate that when considering whether a right constitutes a 'right in rem' within the meaning of Article 5(1) OR, a court should consider whether the right has these two characteristics. It has been held by the CJEU that the right of a judgment creditor arising from attachment of a bank account by way of enforcement of a judgment will amount to a right in rem provided that under the national law concerned (usually the *lex situs* pursuant to Recital (25)), that right is exclusive in relation to the other creditors of the debtor company.[324] In relation to the position in England (and also, in this context, Scotland, Northern Ireland, Gibraltar, and Ireland), it is noteworthy that the Virgos-Schmit Report at paragraph 104 expressly indicates that a floating charge is to be considered as a right in rem. This conclusion would in any event appear to follow from the fact that a floating charge satisfies the two fundamental characteristics of a right in rem set out above.

8.221 The exception in favour of rights in rem should only apply as far as necessary to protect the holder of the rights in rem. If he has been satisfied in full from the asset or its proceeds, the balance should be available, in the absence of local Article OR 3(2) proceedings, to the 'liquidator' in main proceedings.[325] [This seems logical, where it should be noted that Article 5 itself does not interfere with the ownership of the goods, subject to the right in rem itself. (**Wess**)]

8.222 [In certain jurisdictions the domestic insolvency legislation may provide the liquidator with the power to pay an equivalent amount representing the fair

---

[323] ibid para 103.
[324] Case C-557/13 *Lutz v Bäuerle* [2015] ILPr 21.
[325] Recital (25).

market value of the asset that is subject to the right in rem (for example in the Netherlands the liquidator has a *lossingsrecht*, a power to release). A literal reading of Article 5 OR allows the creditor to maximize his rights, but one could argue that the equivalent payment provision does not materially 'affect' the rights in rem of the holder. (**Wess**)]

The combined effect of Article 5(4) OR and Article 4(2)(m) OR should be noted. **8.223**
Article 4(2)(m) OR elaborates on the general rule in Article 4(1) and specifically provides that rules relating to the voidness, voidability, or unenforceability of legal acts detrimental to all creditors are to be governed by the law of the state of the opening of proceedings. Article 5(4) OR makes it clear that the specific exception to the general rule in Article 4(1) OR created by Article 5(1) OR does not operate so as to preclude any of the actions envisaged by Article 4(2)(m) (ie in relation to the voidness, voidability, or unenforceability of legal acts).

The Virgos-Schmit Report suggests that this means that the act by which a right **8.224**
in rem is created might be subject to challenge by an action which would be governed by the law of the state of the opening of the main proceedings (on the basis that the creation of a right in rem is detrimental to the unsecured creditors of a debtor).

These provisions must be considered with Article 13 OR (see below), which **8.225**
creates a kind of 'double actionability' test.

The combined effect of Articles 4(2)(m), 5, and 13 OR is illustrated by the *Lutz* **8.226**
case in the CJEU described in the commentary under Article 13 OR below.

(OR) Article 6—Set-off

1. The opening of insolvency proceedings shall not affect the right of creditors to demand the set-off of their claims against the claims of the debtor, where such a set-off is permitted by the law applicable to the insolvent debtor's claim.
2. Paragraph 1 shall not preclude actions for voidness, voidability or unenforceability as referred to in Article 4(2)(m).

Article 6 OR provides that the opening of insolvency proceedings does not affect a **8.227**
creditor's rights of set-off where they are permitted under the law applicable to the debtor's claim. Therefore such rights remain effective regardless of whether or not the law of the insolvency proceedings permits set-off in those proceedings. This is a very significant exception to the general rule set out in Article 4(2)(d) OR that the law governing the proceedings determines the conditions under which set-off may be invoked.

The combined effect of Article 4(2)(d) OR and Article 6 OR is that a creditor may **8.228**
be able to take advantage of rights of set-off either where this is permitted under the law of the *lex concursus* (pursuant to Article 4(2)(d)) OR or where this is permitted under the law applicable to the debtor's claim (pursuant to Article 6 OR).

8.229 It is important to note that the law which has to permit rights of set-off is the law applicable to the *debtor's* claim (and not to the creditor's claim).[326] [The wording of OR Article 6 does not require that the law in question be the law of a Member State, but it seems that such requirement is implied: see the Virgos-Schmit Report at paragraph 93. (**MB**)][327]

8.230 It would appear that in determining the national law applicable to the debtor's claim the normal rules of private international law are to apply including, in particular, the 1980 Rome Convention on the Law Applicable to Contractual Obligations ('the Rome Convention'), which was superseded from 17 December 2009 by Regulation 593/2008 ('Rome I') within the European Union.[328] A question may arise as to the courts in which the law applicable to a debtor's claim falls to be determined. On the face of it, the jurisdiction to adjudicate on a debtor's claim, including the determination of the law applicable to the claim, will fall to be decided in accordance with the Recast Brussels Regulation (EU) 1215/2012[329] (replacing the Regulation on Civil Jurisdiction and Judgments (44/2001)), since the debtor's claim is itself unlikely to be a matter relating to bankruptcy or the winding-up of companies or to fall within one of the other exceptions to the application of that Regulation. However, where the sole question to be determined by the court in relation to the debtor's claim is the applicable law for the purposes of Article 6 OR of the Insolvency Regulation then it seems likely that this will be considered as a matter relating to the insolvency proceedings so that the courts of the state of the opening of the proceedings will have jurisdiction to determine the issue.

8.231 [Although the text of Article 6 OR is not clear, it seems most likely that the provision implies that 'law applicable' is the applicable law of a Member State. Is 'law' the general (civil or common) law of one Member State or does 'law' also encompass that Member State's insolvency law? For example, under Dutch 'general civil law' a creditor is, according to the Civil Code of the Netherlands (Article 6:127), not able to set off a claim which has not yet matured, since maturity (payability) of the claim is a prerequisite. In Dutch insolvency law (Article 53, Bankruptcy Act), however, maturity is not a precondition. Authors

---

[326] cf Art 10 of the Rome Convention.

[327] [See however ch 4 above at paras 4.24–4.25 where it is argued that the omission of any limiting words from the drafting of Art 6 OR as finally enacted should be construed as an indication that this provision is intended to allow a wider spectrum of laws to be applicable, including those of third states, in order to respect parties' legitimate expectations as to the availability of set-off arising under their previously concluded, contractual agreements. (**IF**)]

[328] Regulation (EC) 593/2008 of the European Parliament and of the Council of 17 June 2008 on the law applicable to contractual obligations (Rome I), OJ L177/6, 4 July 2008.

[329] Regulation (EU) 1215/2012 of the European Parliament and of the Council of 12 December 2012 on jurisdiction and the recognition and enforcement of judgments in civil and commercial matters OJ L351/1, 20 December 2012.

defending the latter view hold the opinion that the creditor indeed can set-off. In other circumstances the former view would give the creditor a right to set-off, for example in general French law, that provides for relatively wide criteria to set-off. In the latter view—applying the 'double standard' of both civil law and insolvency law of France—the creditor can not set off his claim, as French insolvency law applies quite narrow conditions. The example shows that with engineering of financial transactions, 'forum shopping' could raise the possibilities for set-off, although this seems to go against the rationale of the Regulation (see Recital (4)) indicating that for the proper functioning of the internal market it is necessary to avoid 'incentives for the parties to transfer assets or judicial proceedings from one member state to another, seeking to obtain a more favourable legal position (forum-shopping)'. (**Wess**)]

['Law applicable' does include the Member State's insolvency law. When the **8.232** Regulation refers to the 'law' of a Member State, is it not natural that 'law' includes all the rules applicable in an insolvency situation? (**TE**)]

Article 6 OR makes it both possible and important for creditors who are likely to **8.233** benefit from set-offs to try to ensure that the debtor's claim against them is governed by a law which permits the widest possible rights of set-off. For example, if an English lender lends money to a borrower who has his centre of main interests in France, in a French main insolvency proceeding there would be significantly narrower rights of set-off than in English law. The English lender can therefore try to insist that any dealing which may give rise to a claim against him by the debtor be governed by English law. If it is, the creditor can by reason of Article 6 OR rely on the wider rights of set-off permitted by English law.

It is considered that Article 6 OR covers only rights to set-off arising in respect of **8.234** mutual claims incurred prior to the opening of the main insolvency proceedings. In respect of claims incurred after the opening of proceedings, the right to set-off should be determined in accordance with the law of the relevant insolvency proceedings pursuant to Article 4(2)(d) OR.

Article 9 OR provides for a specific case of set-off, between the parties to a payment **8.235** or settlement system or to a financial market, to be governed solely by the law of the Member State applicable to the system or market concerned.

(OR) Article 7—Reservation of title

1. The opening of insolvency proceedings against the purchaser of an asset shall not affect the seller's rights based on a reservation of title where at the time of the opening of proceedings the asset is situated within the territory of a Member State other than the State of opening of proceedings.
2. The opening of insolvency proceedings against the seller of an asset, after delivery of the asset, shall not constitute grounds for rescinding or terminating the sale and shall not prevent the purchaser from acquiring title where at the time

of the opening of proceedings the asset sold is situated within the territory of a Member State other than the State of the opening of proceedings.
3. Paragraphs 1 and 2 shall not preclude actions for voidness, voidability or unenforceability as referred to in Article 4(2)(m).

8.236 Article 7(1) OR excludes from the scope of the main insolvency proceedings a seller's rights based on a reservation of title where the asset is situated in a Member State other than the state of opening of the proceedings.[330] Although the seller's right will be rights in rem and therefore already covered by Article 5 OR, the separate mention in Article 7 OR settles any doubt which may arise in any Member State's law.[331]

8.237 Thus if there are main winding-up proceedings in England and the company had, prior to the winding-up order, bought some goods from a supplier in France, and the goods are still in France, the French seller can enforce his reservation of title in respect of the goods, whether or not that reservation of title would be valid in England under English law.

8.238 Article 7(2) OR appears to be designed to prevent the 'liquidator' of a seller using the commencement of insolvency proceedings as grounds for keeping or getting title back to goods which have been delivered to another Member State. It provides for a substantive rule of law to be applied in the Member States. It provides that after delivery of assets being sold, the commencement of insolvency proceedings against the seller are not to constitute grounds for rescission or termination of the sale and do not prevent the purchaser acquiring title, as long as the assets are, at the time of opening of the proceedings, in the territory of a member state other than the state of the opening of proceedings. This rule takes precedence over any contrary rules of national law. Presumably it overrides any contractual provision to the contrary.

8.239 As with Articles 5 and 6 OR, Article 4(2)(m) OR applies in relation to actions for voidness, voidability, or unenforceability. Thus in the example given above, if the agreement to create reservation of title were voidable under English law as a result of the making of the winding-up order, the seller could not successfully rely on the reservation of title.

(OR) Article 8—Contracts relating to immoveable property

The effects of insolvency proceedings on a contract conferring the right to acquire or make use of immoveable property shall be governed solely by the law of the Member State within the territory of which the immoveable property is situated.

---

[330] It will not apply where the asset is situated in the state of opening of the proceedings: Case C-292/08 *German Graphics Graphische Maschinen GmbH* v *van der Schee* [2009] ECR I-8421, [2010] ILPr 1.

[331] Dr Oliver Liersch, head of the Hannover Branch of Schultze & Braun mentioned this point at the European Academy of Law (ERA) on 18 September 2006.

The general principle of the Regulation is that the law of the Member State of the   **8.240**
opening of proceedings applies to govern those proceedings including determining
the effects of the proceedings on any contracts to which the debtor is a party (see in
particular Article 4(2)(e) OR). However, it was recognized that there is an equally
important interest in permitting the relevant national law to apply to contracts
concerning immovable property.[332] In particular, contracts relating to immovable
property encompass a number of special factors, including of course the fact that
the property is permanently located within a particular state, and the fact that
contracts relating to immovable property are subject to special rules in many states,
which make the application of relevant national law desirable.[333] Article 8 OR
therefore gives effect to this by providing that effects of insolvency proceedings on
a contract conferring the right to acquire or make use of immoveable property shall
be governed solely by the law of the Member State within the territory of which
the immoveable property is situated. The reference to the law of that Member State
includes a reference to its insolvency law.[334]

Article 8 OR applies to contracts to 'acquire' or 'make use' of immovable property   **8.241**
and it therefore applies to both contracts for the use of immovable property (such
as leases) and contracts covering the sale and transfer of immovable property.[335]

In English law, an unconditional contract for the purchase of land gives the pur-   **8.242**
chaser a right in rem in the land and therefore the exception in Article 5 OR may
also on occasions apply in addition to Article 8 OR.

(OR) Article 9—Payment systems and financial markets

1. **Without prejudice to Article 5, the effects of insolvency proceedings on the
   rights and obligations of the parties to a payment or settlement system or to a
   financial market shall be governed solely by the law of the Member State applicable to that system or market.**
2. **Paragraph 1 shall not preclude any action for voidness, voidability or unenforceability which may be taken to set aside payments or transactions under the
   law applicable to the relevant payment system or financial market.**

Article 9 OR provides for a further exception to the general conflict of laws rule   **8.243**
stated in Article 4 OR. This time the law of the relevant Member State is to apply
to govern the effects of insolvency proceedings on the rights and obligations of the
parties to a payment or settlement system or to a financial market. Essentially the
idea here is to prevent any confusion or lack of certainty which might result if
the law of the state of the opening of proceedings was applied to financial market

---

[332] Virgos-Schmit Report para 118.
[333] The mode of applying national law is described in the Virgos-Schmit Report at para 92(2).
See also on this point the commentary under Art 15 below.
[334] V-S Report para 118, third sub-paragraph.
[335] See also ibid para 119.

mechanisms such as the closing out of contracts, netting, and the realization of securities.[336] On the mode of applying national law, see paragraph 8.211 above.

8.244 The key terms 'payment or settlement system' and 'financial market' are not defined in the Regulation. The reference to payment and settlement systems is amplified in Recital (27) by a reference to Council Directive (EC) 98/26 on settlement finality in payment and securities systems. However, the term 'financial market' itself is potentially more ambiguous. In this regard, the Virgos-Schmit Report comments that a 'financial market' is understood to be a market where financial instruments, other financial assets or commodity futures and options are traded. Such a market is said to be characterized by regular trading and conditions of operation and access.[337]

(OR) Article 10—Contracts of employment

The effects of insolvency proceedings on employment contracts and relationships shall be governed solely by the law of the Member State applicable to the contract of employment.

8.245 Article 10 OR provides that the effects of insolvency proceedings on contracts of employment are to be governed solely by the national law applicable to the contract of employment. Again this provision recognizes that there is a legitimate interest in contracts of employment and labour relations being governed only by the relevant national law. The mode of applying national law is described in paragraph 92(2) of the Virgos-Schmit Report. See also on this point the commentary under Article 15 OR below.

8.246 However, it is important to note the limits of this exception to the general rule. It applies only to the effects of the insolvency proceedings on contracts of employment. Thus other matters which may arise out of contracts of employment in the context of insolvency proceedings (such as the admission of claims and, importantly, the priority of any claims)[338] will be governed by the law of the state of the opening of proceedings.

8.247 The question of which national law is applicable to a contract of employment will fall to be determined by the Rome I Regulation (formerly the Rome Convention):[339] see in particular Articles 8 and 9 of the Rome I Regulation (replacing Articles 6 and 7 of the Rome Convention). [It is possible that under certain circumstances employees working in one Member State and employed by a debtor who went insolvent in another Member State, will have less protection than the employees

---

[336] See ibid para 120 and Recital (27) OR. See also ch 7 above.

[337] See the Virgos-Schmit Report para 120.

[338] See also Art 4(2)(h).

[339] See comments to Art 6 above, at 8.230, regarding the replacement of the Rome Convention by the Rome I Regulation.

who are located in that other Member State, in which the *lex concursus* applies to the termination of employment contracts. If, for example, a German liquidator in main proceedings terminates the contracts of employees who fulfil their labour in the Netherlands, the German court must apply Dutch insolvency law (specific termination provisions in Article 40, Dutch Bankruptcy Act), given that Dutch law applies in these contracts. Article 68 of the Dutch Bankruptcy Act provides that a liquidator needs permission from the supervisory judge ('*rechter-commissaris*') to terminate contracts of employment. According to German law, no specific permission is required. As the nature of the act of the German liquidator is of German origin, the Dutch supervisory judge will probably refuse to take jurisdiction. This would result in a termination of employment contracts in the Netherlands without a previous, independent check. In practice this problem will in most cases be solved, as the Dutch employees will work in an 'establishment', and they for the protection of their rights may request a secondary proceeding, in which Dutch law will apply. (**Wess**)]

(OR) Article 11—Effects on rights subject to registration

The effects of insolvency proceedings on the rights of the debtor in immoveable property, a ship or an aircraft subject to registration in a public register shall be determined by the law of the Member State under the authority of which the register is kept.

Article 11 OR recognizes an important legal and commercial reality: the fact that in many Member States rights in immovable property, ships, and aircraft are subject to schemes of registration. [Such schemes of registration are themselves often the result of international arrangements. (**SI**)] **8.248**

Article 11 OR therefore provides that such rights are to be subject to the law of the state under whose authority the register is kept so as to uphold the integrity and effectiveness of such schemes of registration. There is clearly a justifiable interest in this since, as the Virgos-Schmit Report acknowledges, '[t]he systems for the registration of property play a significant role in protecting trade and legal certainty'.[340] **8.249**

But there is a material difference between Article 11 OR and Articles 8, 9, and 10 OR. Those Articles state that the relevant matters are to be governed 'solely' by the law of the relevant Member State. Article 11 OR does not contain this word but instead states that the rights are to be determined by the law of relevant state (see also paragraph 8.23 and n 43 thereto above). **8.250**

The effect of this deliberate change is explained in the Virgos-Schmit Report as being that the general applicability of the law of the state of the opening of **8.251**

---

[340] Virgos-Schmit Report para 130.

proceedings is not displaced and that both this law and that of the relevant Member State apply cumulatively. In particular, it is said that the law of the state of registration will determine which, if any, aspects of the law of the state of the opening of proceedings are to apply.[341]

8.252 It has been suggested that Article 11 OR is designed to prevent rights which may be alien to the national registration system having to be registered.

8.253 It is important to note the limits of the Article 11 OR exception. For example, it does not extend to those rights over the assets of companies which are in England generally required to be registered at Companies House.[342] However, to the extent that such rights constitute rights in rem then they may fall under the Article 5 OR exception.

(OR) Article 12—Community patents and trade marks

> For the purposes of this Regulation, a Community patent, a Community trade mark or any other similar right established by Community law may be included only in the proceedings referred to in Article 3(1).

8.254 This Article is designed to replace certain rules contained in the Community Patent Convention[343] and the Council Regulation on Trademarks[344] relating to the insolvency proceedings in which Community-wide patent and trade mark rights could be included.[345] It was apparent that the inclusion of these Community-wide rights in different national insolvency proceedings in relation to the same debtor could give rise to difficulties. The rules in the Convention and the Regulation therefore provided that until such times as common rules for Member States in relation to insolvency proceedings were in force, the only Member State in which a Community patent or trade mark could be involved in insolvency proceedings was the state in which such proceedings were first brought.[346] These rules clearly lapsed upon the Insolvency Regulation coming into force and, accordingly, Article 12 OR introduces a new rule that Community intellectual property rights may only be included in the main insolvency proceedings commenced in relation to the debtor.[347]

---

[341] ibid para 130. On the mode of applying national law, see 8.211 above.

[342] See the Companies Act 2006 (Amendment of Part 25) Regulations 2013.

[343] The European Patent Convention 1973, which was implemented into English law by the Patents Act 1977, did not create a Community-wide patent but rather enabled various national rights to be granted at the same time. Subsequent developments are dealt with under Article 15 RR below.

[344] Council Regulation (EC) 94/40 [1994] OJ L11/1.

[345] There is a further updating in Article 15 RR: see that provision and the commentary on it below.

[346] Art 41 of the Community Patent Convention; Art 21 of the Trade Marks Regulation.

[347] The new rule extends beyond patents and trade marks to other intellectual property rights established by Community law such as plant variety rights: Council Regulation (EC) 94/2100 [1994] OJ L227/1.

(OR) Article 13—Detrimental acts

Article 4(2)(m) shall not apply where the person who benefited from an act detrimental to all the creditors provides proof that:
- the said act is subject to the law of a Member State other than that of the State of the opening of proceedings; and
- that law does not allow any means of challenging that act in the relevant case.

Article 13 OR relates back to Article 4(2)(m). As noted above, Article 4(2)(m) **8.255** OR elaborates on the general rule in Article 4(1) OR that insolvency proceedings are to be governed by the law of the Member State of the opening of the proceedings. In this regard Article 4(2)(m) OR specifically provides that the law of the state of the opening of proceedings is to apply in determining the rules relating to the voidness, voidability, or unenforceability of legal acts detrimental to all creditors. Furthermore, Articles 5, 6, 7, and 9 OR which provide for specific exceptions to the general rule in Article 4(1) OR expressly provide that the effect of the exceptions is not to preclude any of the actions envisaged by Article 4(2)(m) OR. The probable effect of these provisions is explained above in relation to Article 5(4) OR.[348]

Article 13 OR provides that Article 4(2)(m) OR shall not in any event apply where **8.256** the creditor satisfies the two conditions stated in Article 13. As to these conditions, the reference to 'any means' in the second condition is said to indicate that the act must not be capable of being challenged either under rules relating to insolvency or under the general law of the relevant Member State.[349] Furthermore, the act must actually be capable of being challenged in fact in the particular case and not just as a matter of principle; this is indicated by the reference in Article 13 to 'in the relevant case'.[350]

The CJEU has held in the *Lutz* case[351] that, in a German bankruptcy, where a det- **8.257** rimental act was governed by Austrian law, Article 13 applied to give the Austrian defendant a defence, because claw-back proceedings were brought outside the one-year limitation period mandated by Austrian law.[352] It did not matter that the bar was procedural.[353] and that Austrian law did otherwise provide for claw-back proceedings in similar cases. The Regulation does not distinguish between substantive

---

[348] See paras 8.223–8.226 above. The meaning of 'all the creditors' is discussed at paras 8.208–8.209 above.

[349] Virgos-Schmit Report para 137; Lombardi Molinari, 'Avoidance of Transactions Under the E.U. Insolvency Regulation' (2008) Top Legal International I at V. See now *Nike v Sportland Oy* (Case C-310/14).

[350] ibid. See also *LBI hf v Merrill Lynch International*, EFTA Court, Case E 28/13 on Art 30 of Directive 2001/24 (the equivalent of Article 13 OR) at para 75. The onus of proof in relying on Article 13 is on the defendant: *Nike* (supra).

[351] Case C-557/12 *Lutz v Bäuerle* [2015] ILPr 21.

[352] See also *LBI hf v Merrill Lynch International*, EFTA Court, Case E 28/13 on Art 30 of Directive 2001/24/EC, which is in similar terms to Art 13 OR, at para 77.

[353] ibid at para 74.

and procedural defences. Consequently, it is necessary not only that the *lex fori concursus* and the *lex causae* both have a means of challenging the relevant transaction, but that the relevant transaction could in fact be attacked under both systems of law, including compliance with any limitation periods.

8.258 The CJEU in the same case considered that the Article 13 OR defence did not in principle apply to acts which take place after the opening of insolvency proceedings. However, the CJEU considered that a right in rem was a special case, referring to Recital (25) OR, 'since these rights are of considerable importance for the granting of credit'. Article 5 OR enables a creditor to assert rights in rem *which had been acquired before the opening of insolvency proceedings*, even after the opening of insolvency proceedings. This was the only way to assert his right in rem effectively. Article 5 OR was thus a special case because it sought to protect acts taking place after the opening of insolvency proceedings. In order to ensure the effectiveness of Article 5(1) OR, the creditor is entitled to rely on Article 13 OR to protect the payment over of monies pursuant to the creation of a right in rem before such opening.

8.259 In the *Lutz* case, the creditor had attached monies of the debtor prior to the opening of insolvency proceedings and the monies were paid over to the creditor after the opening. That payment could not be recovered under German law because Article 13 OR gave the creditor a defence under Austrian law, which governed the creation of the security in Austria and the payment made under it.

8.260 The potential challenge under the *lex causae* need not be under insolvency law:[354] Article 13 OR creates no such restriction.

8.261 The standard of proof required and the question of whether the *lex causae* is treated as a matter of law or fact would seem to be a matter for the law of the Member State which has opened the main proceedings and whose court is hearing an application to avoid a transaction.[355]

8.262 [Difficult situations may occur. For example under Finnish law the *actio Pauliana*[356] can be instituted within six months from a certain date. It is possible to have a three-month extension of the time from the date the liquidator has become or should have become aware of the relevant facts. Thus the question of whether an act is capable of being challenged 'in the relevant case' under Finnish law may depend on a judge's assessment of the situation. (TE)]

---

[354] *LBI hf v Merrill Lynch International*, EFTA Court, Case E 28/13 on Art 30 of Directive, at para 74; see now *Nike v Sportland Oy* (Case C-310/14).
[355] ibid at para 78; see now *Nike v Sportland Oy* (Case C-310/14).
[356] A common fraudulent transfer provision in Roman law based systems, analogous to Insolvency Act 1986, s 423 in England.

In considering the question of challengeability under insolvency law, it will be nec- **8.263** essary to assume for the purposes of the domestic law, on the basis of the opening of the otherwise applicable insolvency proceeding, some basic aspects of the criteria for challenging the act in question, such as a finding of insolvency.[357]

Article 13 OR thus operates as an exception to the general applicability of the **8.264** *lex fori concursus* and the onus is on the defendant to produce evidence which makes out the exception.[358] This will involve not only proving the relevant foreign law but also the relevant facts.[359] This may be quite difficult, since it may involve attempting to prove a negative, such as lack of knowledge of wrongdoing by the debtor.[360]

The aim of the exception is to uphold the legitimate expectations of creditors or **8.265** third parties with regard to the validity of the act in accordance with the normally applicable law.[361]

Article 13 OR applies only to acts carried out prior to the commencement of insol- **8.266** vency proceedings. Once insolvency proceedings are commenced the law of the state of those proceedings will apply and the assets of the debtor (wherever situated) will fall to be treated in accordance with that law. A creditor will not be able to rely on Article 13 to defeat this consequence.

[Article 13 OR leads to the undesirable result that the parties to a contract detri- **8.267** mental to the general body of creditors may succeed in protecting it from being challenged by introducing into it a choice-of-law clause in favour of a legal system not permitting the challenge. The law thus chosen must be the law of a Member State but need not have any natural connection with the contract in question: no such connection is required by the 1980 Rome Convention on the Law Applicable to Contractual Obligations, nor by its successor, the Rome I Regulation. (**MB**)]

(OR) Article 14—Protection of third-party purchasers

> Where, by an act concluded after the opening of insolvency proceedings, the debtor disposes, for consideration, of:
> - an immoveable asset, or
> - a ship or an aircraft subject to registration in a public register, or
> - securities whose existence presupposes registration in a register laid down by law,

---

[357] Lombardi Molinari (n 349 above) VI.
[358] Virgos-Schmit Report para 136; Lombardi Molinari (n 349 above) V.
[359] ibid V.
[360] ibid VII.
[361] Recital (24); Virgos-Schmit Report para 138; Lombardi Molinari (n 349 above) V.

the validity of that act shall be governed by the law of the State within the territory of which the immoveable asset is situated or under the authority of which the register is kept.

8.268 Article 14 OR represents another exception to the general rule in Article 4(1) OR by providing that the law of the national state applies in relation to dispositions of certain property by a debtor to a third party after insolvency proceedings have been commenced. However, as is apparent from the terms of the Article, it applies only to dispositions of immovable assets, ships, or aircraft which are registered and securities 'whose existence presupposes registration in a register laid down by law'. The mode of applying national law is described in paragraph 92(2) of the Virgos-Schmit Report. See also on this point the commentary under Article 15 OR below.

8.269 [It appears that even the registration of immovable assets and securities must be in a register that is public (see Article 2(g) OR). Similarly to Article 6 OR, Article 14 OR does not explicitly require that the applicable law be that of a Member State but such requirement seems to be implied (Virgos-Schmit Report paragraph 93).[362] Together with Article 11 OR, Article 14 OR deviates from most of the Regulation's conflict rules by omitting the word 'solely'. (**MB**)]

(OR) Article 15—Effects of insolvency proceedings on lawsuits pending

The effects of insolvency proceedings on a lawsuit pending concerning an asset or a right of which the debtor has been divested shall be governed solely by the law of the Member State in which that lawsuit is pending.

8.270 Article 15 OR establishes the final exception to the general rule that insolvency proceedings are governed by the law of the state of the opening of the insolvency proceedings (*lex fori concursus*). This is that the relevant domestic law of the forum (*lex fori processus*) applies to determine the effect of insolvency proceedings on pending 'lawsuits' 'concerning an asset or a right of which the debtor has been divested'.

8.271 As noted above, all of the national laws of the Member States are believed to provide for an interruption or suspension of proceedings or enforcement by means of a stay of steps by individual creditors against the debtor or his assets upon insolvency (as opposed to reorganization) proceedings being opened in relation to that debtor and some also provide stays for reorganization proceedings. Upon the opening of proceedings such a stay will operate automatically across the European Union by virtue of Articles 4(1), 4(2), and 17 OR.

---

[362] [The English, French, and German versions of the text refer to 'state' (*l'état, Staates*), whilst the Dutch text reads '*lidstaat*' (Member State). The scheme of the Regulation implies that Art 14 is limited to the law of the respective Member State. (**Wess**)] This may well be the correct approach in the context, although the Spanish and Portuguese ('*estado*') and Italian ('*stato*') versions also fail to specify 'Member' State.

However, as noted under Article 4(2)(f) OR, Article 15 OR provides an excep- **8.272**
tion to this[363] in the case of lawsuits which are already pending when the insolvency proceedings are opened which concern an asset or a right of which the
debtor has been divested. Such pending lawsuits are to be dealt with solely
under the law of the Member State in which the lawsuit is pending. One possible effect of this provision is to avoid the application of the rule of *vis attractiva
concursus* which sometimes applies under the law of Member States pursuant to
which pending proceedings may be removed from the civil or commercial court
in which they are pursued into the exclusive control of the relevant bankruptcy
court.[364]

It is important to note that Article 15 OR applies only to 'lawsuits pending' **8.273**
at the time the insolvency proceedings are opened. Accordingly, it does not
apply to lawsuits commenced after the opening of the insolvency proceedings (which will, therefore, be subject to any stay or *vis attractiva concursus*
(see above) imposed under the law of the state of the opening of the proceedings). However, the text refers to 'lawsuits pending' not 'causes of action pending'. It follows that where a lawsuit is pending in England in relation to a
Luxembourg company which subsequently enters a bankruptcy process, the
question whether the existing particulars of claim can be amended to allege a
fresh cause of action is governed by English law as the law of the place where
the lawsuit is pending.[365]

In the earlier context of Article 4(2)(f) OR, the grammatical construction reads as if **8.274**
'lawsuits pending' are intended to be a subset of 'proceedings brought by individual
creditors'. This has not however been accepted as a correct interpretation of Article
15 OR by the CJEU.

The alternative approach is to contrast individual enforcement actions (such as **8.275**
distress, execution, attachment, or sequestration) with 'lawsuits pending', the latter
being directed at obtaining a decision on the merits rather than enforcing against
the debtor's assets.[366] Individual enforcement actions do not fall within Article 15
irrespective of whether or not they were pending at the time the insolvency proceedings were opened and are therefore governed by the *lex concursus*. On this
approach, any pending actions can continue to judgment, for example to be used to

---

[363] In principle, the exception in Art 15 is meant to be 'interpreted strictly': Case C-85/12 *LBI hf v
Kepler Capital Markets SA* ECLI:EU:C:2013:697, a case on Art 32 of Directive 2001/24, which is in
similar terms to Article 15 OR, at para 52.

[364] See para 4.43 above.

[365] *Fortress Value Recovery Fund I LLC v Blue Skye Special Opportunities Fund LP* [2013] 2 BCLC
351. See also *Isis Investments Ltd v Oscatello Investments Ltd* [2014] Bus LR 341 (CA), which reached
the same result under the similarly worded Directive 2001/24/EC on the reorganisation and winding
up of credit institutions Art 32.

[366] Virgos-Schmit Report para 142; Virgos & Garcimartin, paras 252–55; *Syska v Vivendi* [2010]
1 BCLC 467 (CA) at [16].

make a claim to a distribution in the insolvency proceedings, but may not be used to seize or enforce judgment on any assets of the debtor if such recourse is barred by the *lex concursus*.[367]

8.276 This approach was adopted by the CJEU in *Kepler*,[368] where the CJEU made a distinction between 'lawsuits pending', which were held to cover 'only proceedings on the substance' (paragraph 54) and 'individual enforcement actions'[369] such as the pre-judgment attachments in that case. In *Kepler*, the creditor on 10 November 2008 obtained French law attachments in France against monies of the debtor, Landsbanki hf, (later LBI hf), held by a third party. On 5 December 2008, the Icelandic court granted Landsbanki a moratorium. On 22 November 2010 a winding-up order was made. Icelandic law retrospectively invalidated the attachments and effect had to be given to this invalidation in France. It is suggested that the same would have applied if the insolvency proceeding had been a main proceeding in one EU Member State (except Denmark) and the attachments had been made in another Member State, pursuant to Articles 4(2) (f) and 15 OR.

8.277 In *SAS Frontrange Solutions France v Van der Schee as liquidator of WOCL BV* the Court of Appeal in Paris[370] appears to have held that a French summary and provisional disclosure procedure designed to quantify a claim against the debtor was not within 'lawsuit pending' in Article 15 and the proceeding was dismissed on the basis that the claim should be lodged in the supervening Dutch liquidation.

The effect of applying Article 15 OR

8.278 Under Article 15 OR, the effect of a foreign insolvency on the proceedings concerning an asset or a right of which the debtor has been divested pending in a Member State is '*governed solely*' by the law of the Member State. As to this, the Virgos - Schmit Report states in a passage dealing generally with the exceptions contained in Articles 8–15:[371]

> ... the effects to be given to the proceedings opened in other [Member States] are the same effects attributed to a domestic proceedings of equivalent nature (liquidation, composition or reorganisation proceedings) by the law of the State concerned ...

---

[367] See Case C-85/12 *LBI hf v Kepler Capital Markets SA* ECLI:EU:C:2013:697, discussed below. That was a case on Art 32 of Directive 2001/24, which is in similar terms to Art 15 OR.

[368] ibid.

[369] See also *Elektrim v Vivendi* [2008] EWHC 2155 (Comm), [2008] Lloyd's Rep 636, aff'd (CA) sub nom *Syska v Vivendi Universal SA* [2009] EWCA Civ 677, [2010] BCC 348. See notes by I Fletcher in (2009) 22 Insolvency Intelligence 60–62, and 155–57.

[370] 15 June 2007.

[371] Virgos-Schmit Report para 92(2).

This approach has been followed in three Austrian Supreme Court cases.[372] If **8.279** that approach is correct, then in a case in which Article 15 OR applies, the court before which a 'lawsuit' is proceeding needs to consider what would be the equivalent *type* of proceeding (ie not necessarily an exactly equivalent proceeding) and to apply the effects of such proceeding under local law. To take a simple example, if during a 'lawsuit' proceeding in England covered by Article 15 OR the defendant has liquidation proceedings opened in respect of it in the Member State where its COMI is located, the English mandatory and automatic liquidation stay of proceedings (section 130(2) of the Insolvency Act 1986) will apply, subject to the discretion given by that English statutory provision to the English court to allow proceedings to continue in special cases, subject to any conditions the court might impose.

Unfortunately, however, the explanation in the Virgos-Schmit Report was over- **8.280** looked in the English case of *Mazur Media Ltd v Mazur Media GmbH*,[373] which predated the Austrian Supreme Court decisions. In *Mazur Media* the defendant went into liquidation as a main proceeding in Germany but the general English law discretionary stay jurisdiction was held to apply instead of the statutory automatic stay which applies in English liquidation.

It is suggested that given the lack of any consideration of the Virgos-Schmit Report, **8.281** that case cannot be taken to establish any real precedent. Moreover, the end result in that case may well have been the same in any event, even if the correct approach had been applied. It seems from the judgment that the judge would in the circumstances probably have given special permission, as he is entitled to do under the English statute, for the English action to proceed, despite the general automatic stay under English law.

In *Mazur Media* the relevant question was whether an action proceeding in **8.282** England was automatically interrupted by the opening of liquidation proceedings against the defendant, a German company, in Germany. The judge held that the English liquidation law automatic stay did not apply. He held that he had, however, a general discretion to stay but should not use the discretion where the effect would have been to get round the normal rule of allocation of jurisdiction under the Judgments Regulation (44/2001). Had he been referred to paragraph 92(2) of the Virgos-Schmit Report he would, it is suggested, have held that the English law liquidation automatic stay did apply, but, since that stay is subject to a discretion vested in the court to allow the action to continue, on the special facts of that case he

---

[372] 24 January 2006, 10 Ob 80/05w; 23 February 2006 9 Ob 135/04z; 17 March 2005, 8 Ob 131/04d. In the second of these cases, which cites an article which in turn cites the Virgos-Schmit Report, the Austrian Supreme Court states that 'the Austrian court must operate the rules of the Austrian insolvency proceedings which are closest to the nature of the insolvency proceedings in the opening State and must suspend them or not on that basis'.

[373] [2004] 1 WLR 2966.

might have exercised his discretion to allow the proceedings to continue in England in any event.

8.283 Where the *lex concursus* imposes a stay but the *lex fori processus* does not, then where Article 15 applies, there is no stay. On the other hand if the *lex concursus* does not impose a stay but the *lex fori* does, a stay is imposed.[374]

Article 15 OR is not limited to proprietary claims

8.284 It is not clear from the literal wording in English whether the phrase 'concerning an asset or a right of which the debtor has been divested' means that the lawsuit, in order to fall within the Article 15 OR exception, has to concern some claim of proprietary right in or over an asset of the estate in order to be within Article 15 OR[375] or whether the claim can simply be one to a share in the estate. The English and some other language versions can be read as suggesting that Article 15 OR applies only to recovery of assets[376] whereas other language versions clearly refer to assets which are part of the debtor's 'estate'.[377] The English Commercial Court in the case of *Elektrim v Vivendi* [378] has ruled in favour of the wider interpretation refusing to limit Article 15 to proprietary claims.

8.285 It is, however, clear that lawsuits concerning assets which are not part of the estate are not covered by Article 15 OR because they do not concern an asset of the estate.[379] Furthermore, the reference to an asset or right of which the debtor 'has been divested' refers to divestment by reason of the insolvency proceedings.[380]

Article 15 OR and arbitrations

8.286 It is not clear from a literal reading of Article 15 OR whether 'lawsuits' covers arbitration proceedings: in English and some other languages the expression suggests

---

[374] Austrian Supreme Court, 23 February 2006, 9 Ob 135/04z.

[375] As held by Murphy J in the Irish High Court on 27 July 2005 in *Flightlease Ireland Ltd* [2005] IEHC 274, in relation to a proceeding in France which was merely a money claim. *Mazur Media Ltd v Mazur Media GmbH* [2004] 1 WLR 2966 was distinguished by Murphy J as a case where there was a proprietary claim. Note that the point does not appear to have been argued in the Austrian Supreme Court cases mentioned here under Art 15 OR, perhaps because the German version refers to '*Masse*' or 'estate' and not to divestment: see below.

[376] eg the French '*concernant un bien ou un droit dont le debiteur est dessaisie*', or Italian '*relativo a un bene o a un diritto del quale il debitore e spossessato*'.

[377] eg the versions which refer to the Continental concept of 'mass', ie 'estate', such as Spanish ('*masa*'), or German '*Masse*'. In the light of the Spanish version, the Virgos-Schmit Report unsurprisingly refers to 'estate' at para 142 (third sub-para). Note also the concept of 'divestment' in Art 1(1).

[378] [2008] EWHC 2155 (Comm) [2008] Lloyd's Rep 636, aff'd (CA) sub nom *Syska v Vivendi Universal SA* [2009] EWCA Civ 677, [2010] BCC 348, refusing to follow the Irish case of *Flightlease Ireland Ltd* [2005] IEHC 274.

[379] Austrian Supreme Court, 17 March 2005, 8 Ob 131/04d.

[380] *Syska v Vivendi* [2009] BPIR 163 [38] per Christopher Clarke J, *Rawlinson & Hunter Trustees SA v Kaupthing Bank* HF [2012] BCC 441 [33] per Burton J.

proceedings in court[381] but other language versions may be thought to be ambiguous on this point.[382] A policy distinction could be drawn between protecting court proceedings, which closely involve national sovereignty, and not protecting arbitration proceedings, which do not. On the other hand, it could be argued that extending the protection of Article 15 OR to arbitration would further the policy of protecting legitimate expectations, a policy goal set out in Recital (24) OR. This English Commercial Court in *Elektrim v Vivendi*[383] refused to draw a distinction between court and arbitral proceedings in this context and rejected this policy argument in favour of excluding arbitration from 'lawsuits pending'. Although there was no appeal against this finding, the Court of Appeal accepted the correctness of the proposition that an existing arbitration is a pending lawsuit within the meaning of Articles 15 and 4(2)(f) OR.[384]

It was also held at first instance in *Elektrim v Vivendi* that there was a con- **8.287**
flict in that case between the effect of Article 4(2)(e) OR on the one hand and Article 4(2)(f) OR (exception) and Article 15 OR on the other. This was because the effect of applying Polish law as the *lex concursus* under Article 4(2)(e) OR was to nullify the arbitration agreement as a 'current contract' and terminate the ongoing arbitration reference, whereas the effect of applying English law as the *lex fori processus* of the arbitration was to allow it to continue. On appeal, the Court of Appeal reached the same result as the Commercial Court, but rejected the notion that there was a conflict between Articles 4 and 15 OR, saying that each Article had its own sphere of operation.[385]

B. Chapter II: Recognition of Insolvency Proceedings

(OR) Article 16—Principle

1. **Any judgment opening insolvency proceedings handed down by a court of a Member State which has jurisdiction pursuant to Article 3 shall be recognised in all the other Member States from the time that it becomes effective in the State of the opening of proceedings.**
   This rule shall also apply where, on account of his capacity, insolvency proceedings cannot be brought against the debtor in other Member States.

---

[381] eg the German '*Rechtsstreit*' means 'lawsuit'.

[382] eg the French '*instance*' can if suitably qualified refer to arbitral proceedings as in '*instance arbitral*'. On the other hand, in English one can refer to 'court of arbitration' but still be aware that a court is very different from an arbitral tribunal.

[383] [2008] EWHC 2155 (Comm), [2008] Lloyd's Rep 636, aff'd (CA) sub nom *Syska v Vivendi Universal SA* [2009] EWCA Civ 677, [2010] BCC 348, [2010] 1 BCLC 467. See notes by I Fletcher in (2009) 22 Insolvency Intelligence 60–62, and 155–57.

[384] Note that this rational conclusion has been adopted in the wording of the equivalent provision to Art 15 OR in the Recast Regulation. Art 18 RR bears the heading: 'Effects of insolvency proceedings on pending lawsuits or arbitral proceedings'.

[385] *Syska v Vivendi Universal SA* [2009] EWCA Civ 677, [2010] BCC 348, [2010] 1 BCLC 467.

> 2. **Recognition of the proceedings referred to in Article 3(1) shall not preclude the opening of the proceedings referred to in Article 3(2) by a court in another Member State. The latter proceedings shall be secondary insolvency proceedings within the meaning of Chapter III.**

8.288 Article 16 OR provides the basic principle of recognition for judgments[386] opening insolvency proceedings.[387] Recognition takes place from the time that the 'judgment' (as defined) becomes effective in the state of the opening of proceedings.

8.289 Recognition must be provided without preconditions under local law.[388] The Regulation therefore operates a system of automatic recognition: once insolvency proceedings have been commenced in one Member State then [the opening of the insolvency proceedings and their effects (**Wess**)] are immediately recognized in all other Member States without any further steps having to be taken.

8.290 Moreover, it is important to note that the OR imposes an obligation on a Member State to recognize proceedings opened in another Member State even when those proceedings could not have been commenced in the recognizing Member State.[389] For example, the laws of some states do not provide for insolvency proceedings to be brought against an individual who is not a trader; however, if such proceedings are opened in another Member State then those proceedings must be recognized regardless of the fact that it would not have been possible to have commenced those proceedings under domestic law. The recognizing state can, however, in certain limited circumstances invoke grounds of public policy to refuse recognition (see Article 26 OR).

8.291 The recognition of insolvency proceedings probably extends not only to judgments of 'courts' in the usual sense opening insolvency proceedings but also to the decisions of other bodies where the law of the state of the opening of proceedings empowers those bodies to commence insolvency proceedings.[390] A 'court' is defined in Article 2(d) OR as meaning 'the judicial body or any other competent body of a member state empowered to open insolvency proceedings or to take decisions in the course of such proceedings'.[391]

---

[386] See commentary under Art 2 OR at paras 8.25–8.27 above.

[387] I Fletcher, *The Law of Insolvency* (4th edn, 2009, with 2nd Supplement, 2014) para 31-049.

[388] Eg there is no requirement that the decision to open the insolvency proceedings be published locally before the proceedings will be recognized; although publication can be required by any Member State where a debtor has an establishment (Art 21(2) OR), this is not a precondition of the proceedings being recognized. However, the liquidator appointed in the proceedings is required to procure a certificate evidencing his appointment so that he is then in a position to prove his position as liquidator: see Art 19 OR below.

[389] Virgos-Schmit Report para 148.

[390] ibid. See also Vallens, *European Insolvency Law: the Convention Relating to Insolvency Proceedings* (Actualité Legislative Dalloz, 1995).

[391] See Virgos-Schmit Report para 52. See also the discussion of this question at paras 8.17–8.24 above.

England

In the case of English law, a decision by meetings of a company's members and credi-   **8.292**
tors to place the company into a company voluntary arrangement ('CVA')[392] would
on this basis attract automatic recognition under the Regulation. A CVA comes
within the phrase 'Voluntary arrangements under insolvency legislation' in Annex
A and there is no court judgment (in an English law sense) opening the proceedings.[393]

In the case of creditors' voluntary liquidation ('CVL') the position is complicated   **8.293**
by the fact that Annex A to the Regulation expressly states that the insolvency
proceeding is 'creditors' voluntary winding-up (*with confirmation by the court*)'
(emphasis added).[394] This suggests that although the meeting of the company's
members might otherwise be a competent body to open the proceedings, court
confirmation is a necessary element of the proceeding governed by the Regulation
and therefore it is the court confirmation that opens the proceedings.

[*Sed quaere*. The Virgos-Schmit Report, paragraph 68, explains the position intended   **8.294**
by the authors of Article 2(f) OR, which defines 'the time of the opening of proceedings' as 'the time when the decision begins to be effective under the law of the state
of the opening of the proceedings'. Paragraph 68 explains that 'in the case of non-
judicial proceedings of the "company voluntary winding-up" type, the Working Party
discussed whether, in order to fix the time of opening, the same rule should be used or
whether the date of confirmation by the court of the nature of the proceedings and the
appointment of the liquidator should be taken as the reference point. Only in order
to allow the liquidator to exercise his powers on the territory of another contracting
state would it be necessary to take the date of confirmation by the court as the reference (see paragraph 52). *For all other matters, the general rule given in this paragraph
stands*' (emphasis added). (**IF**)] A better analysis may therefore be that the opening
takes place at the time of the Resolution to wind up but that it has no effect outside
the UK under the OR until court confirmation.

Extent of recognition

The principle of automatic recognition extends to both main and Article 3(2)   **8.295**
OR insolvency proceedings which fall within the scope of the Regulation.
Its principal effect is in relation to main proceedings, since Article 3(2) OR

---

[392] Under Insolvency Act 1986, Part I.

[393] See discussion at paras 8.18–8.20 above. Note also that there is some court aspect in
every case, since recourse is available for any interested party to challenge the propriety of CVA
proceedings, whether at their inception or during their subsequent course of implementation,
by application to the court under Insolvency Act 1986, s 6. Also, there is some court involvement in CVAs in every case in the sense that the chairman of the meetings of the company's
members and creditors is obliged to report the results of the meetings to the court: Insolvency
Act 1986, s 4(6).

[394] See Insolvency Rules 1986, r 7.62 (inserted by the Insolvency (Amendment) Rules 2002),
which sets out the procedure in England for an application for confirmation. See also para 8.23 n 36
above.

proceedings are in any event limited in effect to the territory of the Member State in which they are commenced, [but note Article 18(2) OR authorizes the liquidator in Article 3(2) proceedings to act in other Member States in some situations. (**MB**)]

8.296 The principle that main insolvency proceedings, once commenced, should be automatically recognized reflects the principle that these proceedings are to have universal effect over all of a debtor's assets wherever situated within the European Union (except Denmark).[395] The general principle is subject to important qualifications set out in the Regulation.[396]

8.297 Article 16(2) OR provides that the recognition by a Member State of main insolvency proceedings commenced in another Member State shall not preclude the opening of subsequent Article 3(2) OR proceedings (which would be 'secondary' proceedings[397]) in that Member State.[398] In all cases the question of whether or not secondary proceedings can be commenced after main proceedings have been commenced elsewhere falls to be determined by local law.[399]

8.298 [There is no time limit for the opening of secondary proceedings. This is unfortunate, since the liquidator in the main proceedings runs the risk at all times that important assets may be taken over by secondary proceedings. In order to avoid this, the liquidator in the main proceedings may have to move, as soon as possible, all assets to his own country. Regardless of his choice of action, he will find it difficult to negotiate the sale of a whole enterprise, with establishments and assets in several Member States, as a going concern. (**MB**)]

(OR) Article 17—Effects of recognition

1. The judgment opening the proceedings referred to in Article 3(1) shall, with no further formalities, produce the same effects in any other Member State

---

[395] Although it seems clear that Denmark is not a 'Member State' for the purposes of Art 16, as the English courts have already held in relation to Art 3 (*Re Arena Corp. Ltd* [2004] BCC 375) and the German courts in relation to Art 25 ((District Court of Frankfurt, 24 January 2005), ZinsO (2005) 715), the Spanish Supreme Court referred this question to the ECJ in relation to Art 16 in Case C-148/08*Finn Mejnersten v Betina Mandal Barsoe*. This reference was subsequently withdrawn.

[396] It has also been held in England that the principle of automatic recognition prevents a court of one Member State from treating an order of a court in another Member State as a nullity even if it appears to have been made without jurisdiction. In *Re Eurodis Electron Plc* [2012] BCC 57, *main proceedings* had been opened in England but a Belgian court erroneously wound up and then dissolved the company. The time limit for setting aside the dissolution in Belgium having expired, the English administrators argued *inter alia* that the effect of Art 3, 16, and 17 OR was that the orders of the Belgian court winding up and dissolving the company should be ignored. Mann J rejected this argument.

[397] Art 3(3) OR.

[398] See also the commentary to Art 3 OR above.

[399] Art 4(2) OR, and see also Art 28 OR.

as under this[400] law of the State of the opening of proceedings, unless this Regulation provides otherwise and as long as no proceedings referred to in Article 3(2) are opened in that other Member State.

2. The effects of the proceedings referred to in Article 3(2) may not be challenged in other Member States. Any restriction of the creditors' rights, in particular a stay or discharge, shall produce effects vis-à-vis assets situated within the territory of another Member State only in the case of those creditors who have given their consent.

Article 17 OR spells out the effects of automatic recognition set out in Article 16 in **8.299** relation to main insolvency proceedings and Article 3(2) OR proceedings. Under Article 17(1) OR the 'judgment'[401] opening the Article 3(1) OR proceedings is to have the same effects in all Member States as under the law of the state of the opening of proceedings.[402] [This means, in fact, that the judgment may have more far-reaching effects in other Member States than their own proceedings would have had. (**MB**)]

The 'effects' of a judgment opening proceedings would appear to include the **8.300** divestment of the debtor, the appointment of a liquidator, the prohibition of individual executions, the inclusion of the debtor's assets in the estate, and the obligation on individual creditors to return what they have received after proceedings have been commenced.[403] [The effects may be both procedural and substantive in nature. (**Wess**)]

However, in this regard, it should be noted that the applicability of the law of **8.301** the state of the opening of proceedings is subject to the various exceptions stated in Articles 5–15 OR. Furthermore, the automatic recognition of the effects of a judgment commencing *main proceedings* is subject to two specific types of exceptions:

- where the Regulation provides otherwise (for example the exceptions relating to the rights in rem of third parties (Article 5 OR), the set-off of mutual debts (Article 6 OR), and to retention of title (Article 7 OR));[404]
- where Article 3(2) OR proceedings have been commenced in a Member State.

---

[400] [The original Art 17.1 of the Convention had 'the' instead of 'this': 'the' is clearly correct. The error has been corrected in Art 20(1) RR, which reinstates the word 'the'. (**IF**)] The French and German versions use the equivalents of 'the'.

[401] The extended meaning of this term is dealt with in the commentary to Art 2(e) see paras 8.25 and 8.27 above.

[402] The CJEU has decided that where a Member State has joined the EU after a judgment opening proceedings has been made in another Member State, that judgment produces effects in the new Member State, pursuant to Art 17(1) OR, from the date of its accession (Case C-527/10 *ERSTE Bank Hungary NYRT v Hungary* [2012] ILPr 38 at [36]). The decision was based on the principle of effectiveness: see also G Moss, 'Principles of EU Insolvency Law' (2015) 28(3) Insolvency Intelligence 40.

[403] Virgos-Schmit Report para 154.

[404] In addition, Art 26 OR might give rise to an exception where recognition of the insolvency proceeding is opposed by a Member State on the grounds of public policy.

8.302 [One weakness of the OR is that it does not oblige the court opening the proceedings to specify in its decision whether the proceedings are based on Article 3(1) or 3(2) OR, or are not covered by the Regulation at all (for example if the centre of the debtor's main interests is not situated within the European Union). This may cause confusion, in particular in other Member States. The Member States may, however, make such specifications obligatory by their national law.[405] (**MB**)]

8.303 In relation to Article 3(2) OR proceedings, it follows from the fact that these proceedings are intended to protect local interests, that the effects of main insolvency proceedings will not be recognized in relation to local assets. Once Article 3(2) OR proceedings are commenced, the local assets form part of those proceedings and are governed by local law. This enables local expectations with regard to such matters as local law priorities in respect of dividends and the validity of locally perfected security to be met.[406] However, the primary position of main insolvency proceedings is reflected in the rules relating to co-ordination between main and Article 3(2) OR proceedings: see Articles 29–38 OR.

8.304 Article 17(2) OR provides for the recognition of Article 3(2) OR proceedings. Since these proceedings are limited in their effects to local assets, there is no need for their effects to be recognized over assets located in other Member States.[407] However, it is necessary for the effect of the territorial proceedings over the local assets to be recognized in other Member States; thus Article 17(2) OR provides that these effects cannot be challenged in other Member States.

8.305 The second sentence of Article 17(2) OR deals primarily with two types of situations. The first is where the Article 3(2) OR proceedings have produced a stay of creditors' remedies. That stay cannot extend beyond the Member State where those proceedings have been opened save in respect of creditors outside who have consented.

8.306 The second specified situation is where Article 3(2) OR proceedings are concluded by creditors agreeing to discharge the debtor, for example by a compromise of their claims against the debtor.[408] Article 17(2) OR provides that, in the absence

---

[405] As has been done in the new English forms of order.
[406] Fletcher (n 387 above) para 31-054.
[407] [One might argue that recognition of an Art 3(2) OR proceeding need not be provided for in positive wording in Art 17(1) OR. However, a secondary proceeding may affect another proceeding, eg in a case where an asset, belonging to the debtor, has been transferred to the other proceeding, and there is an application of the equal treatment principle in Art 20 OR re sharing and returning certain dividends. (**Wess**)]
[408] See also Art 34(4) OR.

of specific consent from the creditor, the effect of any such discharge is limited to the debtor's assets situated in the Member State in which the territorial proceedings were commenced, leaving the creditor free to pursue the balance of his claim against the debtor's assets in other Member States.

It is not clear whether 'consent' in this context is restricted to individual con-   **8.307** sents or whether it would include legal mechanisms whereby a consent binding a minority can be given through a sufficient majority vote with the approval of a court.[409] It is suggested that there would have been little practical point in adding the consent exception unless a locally acceptable means of majority voting so as to bind a minority could supply the necessary consent. There is an analogous question arising from Article 34(2) OR which refers to a stay or discharge arising from a measure closing a secondary proceeding. The measure is not to have effect in respect of the debtor's assets not covered by the secondary proceedings without the consent of 'all'[410] the creditors having an interest. It may be intended that the consent of 'all' can, if need be, be acquired by the use of an appropriate legal mechanism, or the use of the word may suggest that such a process is ruled out.[411]

(OR) Article 18—Powers of the liquidator

1. The liquidator appointed by a court which has jurisdiction pursuant to Article 3(1) may exercise all the powers conferred on him by the law of the State of the opening of proceedings in another Member State, as long as no other insolvency proceedings have been opened there nor any preservation measure to the contrary has been taken there further to a request for the opening of insolvency proceedings in that State. He may in particular remove the debtor's assets from the territory of the Member State in which they are situated, subject to Articles 5 and 7.
2. The liquidator appointed by a court which has jurisdiction pursuant to Article 3(2) may in any other Member State claim through the courts or out of court that moveable property was removed from the territory of the State of the opening of proceedings to the territory of that other Member State after the opening of the insolvency proceedings. He may also bring any action to set aside which is in the interests of the creditors.
3. In exercising his powers, the liquidator shall comply with the law of the Member State within the territory of which he intends to take action, in particular with regard to procedures for the realisation of assets. Those powers may not include coercive measures or the right to rule on legal proceedings or disputes.

---

[409] As in the case of an English law 'scheme' (statutory compromise) under Part 26 of the Companies Act 2006 (formerly Companies Act 1985, s 425).

[410] In the French version 'tous' and in the German version 'alle'.

[411] See also the commentary under that provision at para 8.425 below.

Main proceedings

8.308   A key and very sensitive effect of recognition of the effects of main proceedings lies in the exercise of a liquidator's powers in other Member States.[412] This important area is set out expressly in Article 18 OR. For the meaning of 'court', see the commentary under Article 2 OR at paragraphs 8.17–8.24 above.

8.309   A 'liquidator' in a main proceeding cannot be required to obtain an *exequatur* before seeking to exercise his powers in the various Member States.[413] Some civil law countries in the European Union would, apart from the Regulation, require such an *exequatur*, a formal judgment of the local court authorizing the execution of a foreign judgment after an exhaustive legal process amounting to a retrial.[414]

8.310   The power of the liquidator that is specifically mentioned is the power to remove the debtor's assets from the territory of the Member State in which they are situated. This is perhaps the most common reason for attempting to exercise powers abroad and perhaps the most sensitive in terms of local interests.

8.311   The power is specifically made subject to the effects of Article 5 OR (Third parties' rights in rem) and Article 7 OR (Reservation of title). Parties with such rights rely on their title and to that extent stand outside the main insolvency proceedings. In addition to this, the powers of a liquidator may not be exercisable in another Member State in one of two sets of circumstances:

- when there are Article 3(2) OR proceedings in that Member State in relation to the debtor;
- when a preservation measure 'to the contrary' has been taken in relation to the assets of the debtor pursuant to a request to open Article 3(2) OR proceedings.

8.312   The first exception follows from the nature of Article 3(2) OR proceedings, which must be recognized as having effect in the relevant territory.[415] Once commenced, they take effect in relation to the local assets of the debtor and it follows that the powers of the liquidator in the main proceedings will not be effective as against those assets.[416]

8.313   The second exception is effectively an extension of the first and deals with the situation where a provisional protective measure has been taken pursuant to a request to open Article 3(2) OR proceedings (for example a request under

---

[412]   In all cases those powers must be exercised in accordance with the law of the Member State in which they are sought to be exercised: Art 18(3) OR (see paras 8.315 et seq below).
[413]   Fletcher (n 387 above) para 31-050.
[414]   ibid.
[415]   Art 17(2).
[416]   Though the co-ordination measures contained in the Regulation may apply (see Arts 31–37 OR).

Article 29 OR)[417] and such measure is inconsistent with the recognition of the powers of the liquidator in the main proceedings.

Two further important restrictions on the exercise by a liquidator in main **8.314** proceedings of his powers in the other Member States are contained in Article 18(3) OR.

The first is that in all cases a liquidator must exercise his powers in compliance with **8315** the law of the Member State within whose territory he seeks to take action. There are two different interpretations of this requirement.

One analysis suggests that the restriction simply provides that the manner in which **8.316** a liquidator is to exercise his powers is to be determined by local law but that the nature and extent of those powers will be determined by the law of the opening of proceedings (subject to the express prohibition on coercive measures and the power to rule on legal proceedings and disputes). The alternative view is that local law effectively determines the powers which a liquidator can exercise on the basis that if the exercise of a particular power is barred by local law then the liquidator will not be able to exercise that power in that state.

The better view is that under Article 18(3) OR the nature, content, and extent of **8.317** a liquidator's powers will be determined by reference to the law of the state of the opening of the proceedings but that the manner in which those powers are to be exercised must be in accordance with the relevant local law. In particular, this is consistent with the policy of the Regulation which provides that subject to specific exceptions, the law applicable to insolvency proceedings is that of the state of the opening of the proceedings. It probably also follows from the language of Article 18(3) OR which appears to draw a distinction between procedures (governed by local law) and substantive powers (governed by the law of the opening state subject to express bars on coercive measures and rights to rule on legal proceedings and disputes).[418]

The exercise by a liquidator of his powers under the law of the opening state is **8.318** not specifically referred to in the public policy exception in Article 26 OR. That Article seems to be referring to insolvency proceedings as a whole, but probably should be read as referring also to individual acts. Article 18 OR does not restrict the way in which a liquidator appointed in proceedings commenced in one state can exercise powers in another state by reference to any restriction on such powers had the liquidator been appointed pursuant to proceedings commenced in the latter state.

---

[417] The liquidator in main proceedings can himself request the opening of territorial proceedings in a Member State where the debtor has an 'establishment': Art 29(a) OR.

[418] Leggatt J took an approach consistent with this view in *Aria Inc v Credit Agricole Corporate and Investment Bank* [2014] EWHC 872 (Comm) at [60] in relation to Greek insolvency proceedings, where he interpreted Art 18(3) as meaning that English law applied to procedural matters.

8.319 As noted above, Article 18(3) OR contains complete bars on liquidators exercising certain powers at all in foreign Member States:

- A liquidator is not able to take coercive 'measures' in another Member State. While it is not clear whether this restriction applies only to self-help measures or extends also to requests to a court to apply coercive measures, there appears to be no reason in principle why a liquidator should not be able to apply to a local court for such assistance if available under local law. Also, as a matter of principle, local law and courts should as far as possible make available to liquidators in main proceedings all the remedies available to local liquidators, so as to avoid discrimination against an EU citizen. This may sometimes necessitate the opening of secondary proceedings.
- Alternatively, it seems that a liquidator in a main proceeding can apply to his own court for an order applying coercive measures and then seek to have that order enforced in another Member State via Article 25 OR.[419]
- A liquidator is not able to rule on legal proceedings or disputes in a foreign Member State. Under the pre-Regulation law of some Member States, such as France, the same person can act both as insolvency administrator and as 'judge', ruling on disputes, subject to a right of appeal to a court. This is inimical to the legal policy of other Member States, including Germany, Ireland, and the United Kingdom, which take a strict attitude to any person being a judge in his own case.[420]

8.320 [It seems that complaints alleging that a foreign liquidator has violated local rules (and thereby Article 18(3) OR) should be addressed to the supervising authorities in the Member State opening the proceedings rather than to the authorities in the Member State the rules of which have been violated. (**MB**)]

Article 3(2) OR proceedings

8.321 Article 18(2) OR deals with the powers of 'liquidators'[421] in Article 3(2) OR proceedings. Clearly such liquidators have powers, as determined by the relevant national law, in relation to the local assets of the debtor. Generally speaking, such powers are limited to the Member State in which Article 3(2) OR proceedings are

---

[419] In *Handelsveem BV v Hill* [2011] BPIR 1024, the Dutch Supreme Court held that an order by the English court, which had opened main proceedings, for the compulsory provision of information under s 366 of the Insolvency Act 1986 derived directly from insolvency proceedings for the purposes of Art 25(1) OR and was to be recognized. Consequently, the restriction on the use of coercive measures by a trustee in bankruptcy in Art 18(3) OR did not prohibit the English trustee in bankruptcy from seeking recognition and enforcement of the order of the English court in the Netherlands, if necessary with the application of coercive measures available under Dutch law.

[420] In English law this would be a breach of the principle of natural justice, '*nemo judex in sua causa*': see *Ex p Pinochet* [2000] AC 119 (HL).

[421] As defined in the Regulation: see the commentary to Art 1 OR at para 8.04 above.

opened.[422] However, there are two areas where the powers of such a liquidator are extended to other Member States.

First, Article 18(2) OR provides that a liquidator appointed in Article 3(2) OR **8.322** proceedings has the power to claim in any other Member State that movable property belonging to the debtor was removed from the state where the territorial proceedings were commenced after those proceedings had been commenced. This protects the integrity of the Article 3(2) OR proceedings. It also conforms to the policy against fraudulent or abusive forum shopping[423] which is embodied in the Regulation. Recital (4) OR states:

> It is necessary for the proper functioning of the internal market to avoid incentives for the parties to transfer assets or judicial proceedings from one Member State to another, seeking to obtain a more favourable legal position (forum shopping).

Secondly, the liquidator in Article 3(2) OR proceedings may bring, in any **8.323** Member State, any action to set aside which is in the interests of the creditors.[424] The expression 'action to set aside' is said to encompass all actions for a declaration that an act or contract, entered into prior to the commencement of insolvency proceedings, is void or enforceable on the ground that the act or contract was for the benefit of one creditor and prejudiced the collective interests of the other creditors as a whole.[425]

(OR) Article 19—Proof of the liquidator's appointment

> The liquidator's appointment shall be evidenced by a certified copy of the original decision appointing him or by any other certificate issued by the court which has jurisdiction.
>
> A translation into the official language or one of the official languages of the Member State within the territory of which he intends to act may be required. No legalisation or other similar formality shall be required.

This Article provides for a simple, quick, and inexpensive mode of proof of appoint- **8.324** ment. However, it should be noted that there is no corresponding rule relating to proof of the extent of powers of a liquidator. The Virgos-Schmit Report suggests that the scope of a liquidator's powers might be proved by way of a certificate issued by the court appointing him.[426] Such certificates may be a useful mode of providing at least prima facie evidence.

---

[422] For a discussion of the point of time at which proceedings are 'opened' in the context of the Regulation, see the commentary to Art 2 OR at para 8.28–32 above.

[423] See commentary in respect of Art 3 OR above.

[424] The specific inclusion of this power in Art 18(2) does not mean that actions to set aside are otherwise excluded from the scope of Art 3(1), which does not expressly mention such actions (Case 339/07 *Seagon v Deko Marty Belgium NV* [2009] ECR I-767, [2009] 1 WLR 2168 at [45] to [47]).

[425] See Vallens (n 21 above) at n 144.

[426] Virgos-Schmit Report para 170.

(OR) Article 20—Return and imputation

> 1. A creditor who, after the opening of the proceedings referred to in Article 3(1) obtains by any means, in particular through enforcement, total or partial satisfaction of his claim on the assets belonging to the debtor situated within the territory of another Member State, shall return what he has obtained to the liquidator, subject to Articles 5 and 7.
> 2. In order to ensure equal treatment of creditors a creditor who has, in the course of insolvency proceedings, obtained a dividend on his claim shall share in distributions made in other proceedings only where creditors of the same ranking or category have, in those other proceedings, obtained an equivalent dividend.

8.325 The aim of Article 20 OR is to ensure the equal treatment of non-preferential, unsecured creditors throughout all states to which the Regulation applies. The policy of *pari passu* distribution for all creditors with the same ranking throughout the European Union (except Denmark) is one of the fundamental policies of the Regulation.

8.326 Article 20(1) OR establishes the opening of main proceedings as a base line after which an unsecured creditor cannot improve his position by going against the debtor's assets in another Member State. If he obtains satisfaction, he has to return what he has obtained to the liquidator in the main proceedings. The assumption appears to be that no such improvement is available under the law governing the main proceedings.

8.327 The obligation to return is subject to the proprietary rights safeguarded by Articles 5 and 7 OR.

8.328 [In spite of the formulation 'by any means', Article 20(1) OR does not apply to dividends obtained in parallel insolvency proceedings. Such dividends are dealt with in Article 20(2). (**MB**)]

8.329 Article 20(2) OR directly addresses the fact that separate sets of insolvency proceedings in respect of the same debtor are permitted under the Regulation and may lead to disparities between the returns to creditors. Article 20(2) OR does attempt to minimize the potential unfairness to creditors by restricting those creditors who receive a dividend in one set of proceedings from obtaining dividends in other proceedings until the creditors with the same ranking or in the same category in those other proceedings have received an equivalent dividend. In applying Article 20(2) OR, the Virgos-Schmit Report indicates that four rules are relevant:[427]

- No creditor may obtain more than 100 per cent of his claim.
- When a creditor is admitted for proof, the total amount of his claim is to be admitted (and not the amount as reduced by any dividend in other proceedings).

---

[427] Virgos-Schmit Report para 175.

- A claim is not to be admitted for a distribution until such time as the creditors with the same ranking have obtained an equal percentage of satisfaction as that obtained by the creditor in the first set of proceedings. [Whether the ranking is the same depends on the law governing the second set of proceedings, ie the proceedings in which Article 20(2) OR is applied. (**MB**)]
- The ranking of each claim is determined for each of the proceedings by the law of the state of the opening of proceedings.[428]

The principle underlying Article 20(2) OR will be familiar to lawyers in **8.330** England as the 'hotchpot' principle, set out in detail in *Cleaver v Delta American Reinsurance*.[429]

(OR) Article 21—Publication

1. The liquidator may request that notice of the judgment opening insolvency proceedings and, where appropriate, the decision appointing him, be published in any other Member State in accordance with the publication procedures provided for in that State. Such publication shall also specify the liquidator appointed and whether the jurisdiction rule applied is that pursuant to Article 3(1) or Article 3(2).
2. However, any Member State within the territory of which the debtor has an establishment may require mandatory publication. In such cases, the liquidator or any authority empowered to that effect in the Member State where the proceedings referred to in Article 3(1) are opened shall take all necessary measures to ensure such publication.

Publication is not necessary for recognition of insolvency proceedings, of their **8.331** effects, or of the appointment of a liquidator in other Member States. However, in the interests of openness and certainty, it was considered that provision should be made for publication of the commencement of insolvency proceedings.[430]

Though it is very unfortunate that no central register of insolvency proceedings **8.332** has been set up in the European Union, this omission has been addressed in the RR, which mandates the establishment of insolvency registers in Member States and provides for the implementation of a system to connect these registers.[431]

[Article 21 OR may give rise to more detailed domestic legislation in Member **8.333** States for the possibility of publication (by whom, what, what languages, right to oppose by certain interested parties etc). (**Wess**)]

Under Article 21(1) OR, it is up to the liquidator to decide whether or not **8.334** to request that notice of the judgment commencing the insolvency proceedings

---

[428] Art 4(2)(i) OR.
[429] [2001] 2 AC 328, PC.
[430] See Virgos-Schmit Report para 177.
[431] See the commentary to Art 24–27 RR in paras 8.625–8.636 below.

and the decision appointing him be published in another Member State. However, Article 21(2) OR provides that any Member State in which the debtor has an establishment (a term defined in Article 2(h) OR) may itself require publication.

8.335 In either case, Article 21 OR sets out the basic information which the publication must contain:

- the identity of the liquidator appointed;
- whether the proceedings are Article 3(1) OR (main) proceedings or Article 3(2) OR proceedings.

8.336 There may be an important advantage in terms of Article 24(2) OR for the liquidator to publish the judgment opening proceedings in other Member States. After publication, a person honouring an obligation for the benefit of the debtor which should have been honoured for the benefit of the liquidator will be presumed, in the absence of proof to the contrary, to have been aware of the opening of proceedings and will therefore not have the protection of the deemed discharge of the obligation under Article 24(1) OR.[432]

8.337 It may be desirable for Member States to require local publication so as to protect local creditors from having to return benefits under Article 20(1) OR that might be acquired in ignorance of the opening of main proceedings in another Member State.

8.338 [The absence of publication will in some Member States have as a consequence that a third party will be protected against a claim re ownership of property the third party has acquired. (**Wess**)]

8.339 Insol Europe has a practical guide for publishing and registering the opening of insolvency proceedings in particular EU Member States at: <http://www.insol-europe.org/technical-content/european-insolvency-regulation-articles-21-22>

(OR) Article 22—Registration in a public register

1. The liquidator may request that the judgment opening the proceedings referred to in Article 3(1) be registered in the land register, the trade register and any other public register kept in the other Member States.
2. However, any Member State may require mandatory registration. In such cases, the liquidator or any authority empowered to that effect in the Member State where the proceedings referred to in Article 3(1) have been opened shall take all necessary measures to ensure such registration.

8.340 Article 22 OR is the corresponding provision to Article 21 OR, this time dealing with the registration of insolvency proceedings in a public register, but it deals only

---

[432] See also the commentary under Art 24 OR in paras 8.347 and 8.348 below.

with the registration of *main* proceedings (not Article 3(2) OR proceedings) and only with the *judgment* opening main proceedings, not the appointment of the liquidator.

As with Article 21 OR, the Regulation provides that a liquidator may request reg- **8.341** istration of the judgment opening the proceedings, this time in the land register, trade register, and any other public register kept in Member States. The idea here is that registration of insolvency proceedings may protect the interests of third parties and help give full effect to insolvency proceedings.[433]

In addition, Article 22(2) OR provides that any Member State may require registra- **8.342** tion to take place.

[Article 22 OR may give rise to more detailed domestic legislation in Member **8.343** States for the possibility of registration (by whom, what, what languages, right to oppose by certain interested parties etc. (**Wess**)]

The reason that Article 22 OR applies only to main insolvency proceedings (ie **8.344** those commenced under Article 3(1) OR) and not to Article 3(2) OR proceedings seems to be that Article 3(2) OR proceedings do not affect assets located outside the relevant Member States.

[It should be noted that in some Member States for a specific type of registration **8.345** several actual registers, in different locations, may be held. The Regulation does not provide a clear rule regarding in which register in a specific Member State the opening judgment may be registered. Domestic law should provide specific rules or need amending for that purpose. (**Wess**)]

(OR) Article 23—Costs

> The costs of the publication and registration provided for in Articles 21 and 22 shall be regarded as costs and expenses incurred in the proceedings.

It can be inferred from this that the liquidator has to pay the cost of any publica- **8.346** tion and any applicable fee for any registration, whether voluntary or mandatory. He will normally have an indemnity from the estate and be able to recover such expenditure from the assets of the estate.

(OR) Article 24—Honouring of an obligation to a debtor

> 1. Where an obligation has been honoured in a Member State for the bene-fit of a debtor who is subject to insolvency proceedings opened in another Member State, when it should have been honoured for the benefit of the liquidator in those proceedings, the person honouring the obligation shall be deemed to have discharged it if he was unaware of the opening of proceedings.

---

[433] Virgos-Schmit Report para 182.

2. Where such an obligation is honoured before the publication provided for in Article 21 has been effected, the person honouring the obligation shall be presumed, in the absence of proof to the contrary, to have been unaware of the opening of insolvency proceedings; where the obligation is honoured after such publication has been effected, the person honouring the obligation shall be presumed, in the absence of proof to the contrary, to have been aware of the opening of proceedings.

8.347 Article 24 OR assumes that, under the insolvency law of the relevant proceedings, the honouring for the benefit of the debtor of an obligation which should have been honoured for the benefit of the liquidator will not normally discharge that obligation. The honouring would normally consist of the payment of a debt. Injustice could result where an obligation is honoured for the benefit of the debtor in another Member State in ignorance of the opening of insolvency proceedings. Accordingly, Article 24 OR provides that the person honouring the obligation in another Member State shall be deemed to have discharged it if he was unaware of the opening of proceedings.

8.348 In relation to awareness of proceedings, Article 24 OR sets up two presumptions based on the provisions as to publication set out in Article 21 OR. Article 24(2) OR states that if the obligation was honoured before the insolvency proceedings were published then there is a presumption that the person honouring the obligation was not aware of the insolvency proceedings. Conversely, if the obligation was honoured after the commencement of the insolvency proceedings had been published then it is presumed that the person was aware of those proceedings. In both cases the presumptions are rebuttable by producing proof to the contrary. [The publication can reasonably have the above-mentioned effects only in relation to payments made in, or by persons residing in, the country where the publication took place. (**MB**)]

8.349 The CJEU has held that Article 24 OR is not a conflict of laws rule, but a provision of substantive law that applies in each Member State independently of the law of the Member State in which insolvency proceedings were opened.[434] Interpreted in the light of Recital (30) OR, its purpose is to protect debtors of the insolvent debtor who have indirectly or directly honoured an obligation to the insolvent debtor in good faith.[435]

8.350 Where, however, an insolvent entity has requested that one of its debtors pay one of its creditors, such a payment is outside the scope of the protection provided by Article 24(1) OR; this is the case even where the paying debtor is a bank.[436] Were it otherwise, the assets of the insolvent entity could be transferred

---

[434] Case 251/12 *Van Buggenhout v Banque Internationale à Luxembourg SA* [2014] ILPr 28 at [23].
[435] Ibid at [26]–[31].
[436] Ibid at [32]–[38]. Although in this case the payment by the bank to a creditor of the insolvent entity at the latter's instigation fell outside the scope of Art 24, it did not necessarily follow that the

to specific creditors via unaware third parties and thus denude the assets available to the general body of creditors. This would be contrary to one of the principal objectives of the OR, as set out in Recital (4) OR, which is to prevent forum shopping.

(OR) Article 25—Recognition and enforceability of other judgments[437]

1. Judgments handed down by a court whose judgment concerning the opening of proceedings is recognised in accordance with Article 16 and which concern the course and closure of insolvency proceedings, and compositions approved by that court shall also be recognised with no further formalities. Such judgments shall be enforced in accordance with Articles 31 to 51, with the exception of Article 34(2), of the Brussels Convention on Jurisdiction and the Enforcement of Judgments in Civil and Commercial Matters, as amended by the Conventions of Accession to this Convention.
   The first subparagraph shall also apply to judgments deriving directly from the insolvency proceedings and which are closely linked with them, even if they were handed down by another court. The first subparagraph shall also apply to judgments relating to preservation measures taken after the request for the opening of insolvency proceedings.
2. The recognition and enforcement of judgments other than those referred to in paragraph 1 shall be governed by the Convention referred to in paragraph 1, provided that that Convention is applicable.
3. The Member States shall not be obliged to recognise or enforce a judgment referred to in paragraph 1 which might result in a limitation of personal freedom or postal secrecy.

Recognition of insolvency judgments

The OR in earlier Articles provides for the automatic recognition of judgments **8.351** opening insolvency proceedings (Article 16 OR), of the effects of insolvency proceedings (Article 17 OR), and of the powers of a liquidator (Article 18 OR). Article 25 OR completes the picture by providing for the general recognition and enforcement of judgments relating to the conduct and closure of insolvency proceedings, where the judgment opening those proceedings has to be recognized under Article 16 OR. Two specific cases are mentioned, presumably for the avoidance of doubt:

(1) Judgments deriving directly from the insolvency proceedings and which are closely linked with them,[438] even if they were handed down by another

---

bank had to reimburse the monies paid to the general body of creditors; the liability of the bank in this regard would be governed by the applicable national law.

[437] See generally B Wessels, 'Article 25 of the Insolvency Regulation; a hornet's nest' (2008) 21 Insolvency Intelligence 135.

[438] This reflects the decision of the CJEU in Case 133/78 *Gourdain v Nadler* [1979] ECR 733 (decided in relation to Art 1(2) of the Brussels Convention of 1968) that proceedings can be bankruptcy proceedings, if their nature properly indicates them to be such, even if not commenced in a bankruptcy court. The character of the judicial body which determines the action is not

court.[439] These are said to include actions to set aside voidable transactions, actions seeking the personal liability of directors under insolvency law, disputes about the admission or ranking of claims, and disputes as to whether property is part of the debtor's estate.[440]

(2) Judgments relating to preservation measures taken after a request for the opening of insolvency proceedings.[441]

8.352 Article 25(1) OR also specifically provides for the recognition of compositions approved by the court whose judgment opened the insolvency proceedings. Accordingly, pursuant to Article 25, a composition between the company and its creditors approved by the court in the main proceedings can, without further formality, have binding effect between the company and the creditors in all other Member States. A composition for these purposes may, for example, include a scheme of arrangement pursuant to Part 26 of the Companies Act 2006 (formerly section 425 of the Companies Act 1985).

8.353 There is a question as to whether these effects are subject to the provisions contained in Chapter I of the OR and, in particular, Articles 5–15 OR which modify the general principle in Article 17 OR that the judgment opening proceedings shall produce the same effects in all Member States as it does in the Member State where the proceedings were opened.

---

determinative of the nature of the action itself. See Virgos-Schmit Report para 195. A similar conclusion was reached in relation to the OR in Case 339/07 *Seagon v Deko Marty Belgium NV* [2009] ECR I-767, [2009] 1 WLR 2168, in which the CJEU held that the courts of a Member State where insolvency proceedings have been opened have jurisdiction to decide an avoidance action against an entity whose registered office is in another Member State. Such actions fell within the scope of Art 3(1) of the Regulation.

[439] Wessels (n 437 above) 139 points out that the Dutch version uses words which mean 'other judge'. However, the French version has '*une autre juridiction*' and the German '*einem anderen Gericht*', which make it clear that a court is being referred to, in the sense that the judgment may be that of a court other than the court which opened the insolvency proceedings. In Case C-339/07 *Seagon v Deko Marty Belgium NV* [2009] ECR I-767 at [27] the CJEU confirmed that these words mean that it is for the Member State to determine the court with territorial and substantive jurisdiction and that this need not be the court which opened the insolvency proceedings.

[440] Virgos-Schmit Report para 196. See also Case 157/13 *Nickel & Goeldner Spedition GmbH v 'Kintra' UAB* [2015] QB 96, in which the CJEU held that only actions which derive directly from and are closely connected to insolvency proceedings fall within the scope of the Regulation. They stated that the 'decisive criterion' was '…not the procedural context of which that action is part, but the legal basis thereof…it must be determined whether the right or the obligation which respects the basis of the action finds its source in the common rules of civil and commercial law or in the derogating rules specific to insolvency proceedings.' (at para 27). In Case C-295/13 *H v HK* the CJEU held that an action brought by a liquidator under German law requiring directors to reimburse to the company payments made after the company was declared insolvent fell within the OR and outside Brussels 1, even though such an action can be brought even in the absence of insolvency proceedings. The fact that the action was being brought in the context of insolvency proceedings was regarded as critical.

[441] Such measures do not fall within the scope of the Brussels Convention/Brussels 1 Regulation/Brussels 1 recast Regulation: Case 143/78 *De Cavel v De Cavel* [1979] ECR 1055.

Of particular relevance in this context is Article 5 OR which provides that the **8.354** opening of insolvency proceedings shall not affect the rights in rem of creditors or third parties. On its face, Article 5 OR applies only to the effects of the opening of insolvency proceedings and therefore, on a literal reading, would not apply to the effects of the recognition of a composition under Article 25 OR. However, it has been argued that Article 5 should be seen as protecting the rights of secured creditors generally[442] and, in the context of the recognition of compositions under Article 25, it has been suggested that the effects of such compositions will be subject to Article 5.[443] Balz has commented that secured creditors may not be impaired by a plan issued in connection with foreign insolvency proceedings.[444]

Recognition of non-insolvency judgments

Article 25(2) OR of the Insolvency Regulation expressly provides for the **8.355** Brussels Convention to apply to the recognition and enforcement of these judgments which do not fall under Article 25(1). The purpose of this provision is to avoid any gaps between the Insolvency Regulation and the Convention in this regard.[445] The reference to the Brussels Convention should now be read as a reference to the equivalent provisions of the recast Brussels 1 Regulation, Regulation (EU) 1215/2012 of the European Parliament and the Council on jurisdiction and the recognition and enforcement of judgments in civil and commercial matters (recast).[446]

Mode of enforcement of insolvency judgments

Article 25(1) OR also provides that any judgments recognized pursuant to that **8.356** provision are to be enforceable in accordance with Articles 31–51 of the Brussels Convention (except Article 34(2)). This should have been read after 1 March 2002 as referring to Articles 38–58 except for Article 45(2) of the Regulation on Civil Jurisdiction and Judgments (44/2001)[447] which came into effect on 1 March 2002 and which replaced the Brussels Convention for all cases except those involving relations between Denmark and the other EU Member States: see Article 68(2) of

---

[442] See Smart, 'Rights In Rem, Article 5 and the EC Insolvency Regulation: An English Perspective' (2006) International Insolvency Review 17, 23–4 and 33–4 and see the Virgos-Schmit Report para 95.

[443] See Virgos and Garcimartin 384. But cf B Wessels, 'The Secured Creditor in Cross Border Finance Transactions Under the EU Insolvency Regulation' (2003) 18 JIBL & Reg 135, 140 who takes a different view arguing that the court in the main proceedings could hand down a judgment imposing a stay on the enforcement of rights in rem over assets in other Member States which could then be recognized and enforced under Art 25.

[444] M Balz, 'The European Convention on Insolvency Proceedings' (1996) 70 ABLJ 485, 509.

[445] Virgos-Schmit Report para 197.

[446] OJ L351/1, 20 December 2012. The Recast Brussels Regulation was adopted on 12 December 2012 and commenced to apply from 10 January 2015.

[447] See to same effect Wessels, 'Article 25 of the Insolvency Regulation' (2008) 21 Insolvency Intelligence 135.

that Regulation It should now be read as referring to the equivalent articles in the Brussels 1 recast Regulation (see above). This approach has the advantage of using the system of enforcement contained in the Brussels 1 Regulation recast, derived from the system which was in place under the Brussels Convention, which has already been in practice for more than 45 years and will be familiar to practitioners and to the courts.

Categorization of judgments

8.357 Before considering whether a judgment must be recognized and enforced under the OR via the recast Brussels 1 Regulation, or under the recast Brussels 1 Regulation alone, it is first necessary to determine whether the judgment falls outside the scope of the recast Regulation on Jurisdiction and Judgments. This is indicated *inter alia* by the use of the words 'provided that that Convention is applicable' in Article 25(2) OR.[448]

8.358 The simple fact that a liquidator is party to proceedings is not enough to bring a judgment in those proceedings outside the scope of the Recast Regulation on Civil Jurisdiction and Judgments, and thus allow its recognition and enforcement under Article 25 OR.[449] Conversely, where a liquidator exercises his powers in insolvency proceedings for the benefit of the creditors as a whole, such proceedings would fall outside the scope of the Recast Regulation on Civil Jurisdiction and Judgments and, *prima facie*, Article 25 would apply.[450]

Further points

8.359 Article 25(1) OR expressly requires recognition without further formalities of judgments relating to preservation measures. This would seem to cover, for example, the appointment of an interim manager (in administration order proceedings) by the court.

8.360 Article 25(1) OR also expressly requires the recognition without further formalities of a composition approved by the court. It seems therefore, that if, for example in England, an administration order results in a scheme sanctioned by the court which amounts to a 'composition' under Part 26 of the Companies Act 2006 (formerly section 425 of the Companies Act 1985), that scheme will be entitled to automatic recognition.

8.361 Courts often have power to make a confiscation order against a person who has been convicted of a criminal offence when it can be shown that his/her assets include the

---

[448] Case 292/08 *Graphische Maschinen GmbH v Van der Schee* [2009] ECR I-8421, [2010] ILPr 1 at [20].

[449] Ibid at [33].

[450] Case 111/08 *SCT Industri AB v Alpenblume AB* [2009] ECR I-5655, [2010] Bus LR 559. In this case, the Regulation did not in fact apply because insolvency proceedings had been opened before its entry into force. See also the decision of the CJEU in Case C-444/07 *MG Probud Gdynia sp z.o.o.* [2010] ECR I-417, [2010] BCC 453.

proceeds of crime. If that person also has ordinary unsecured debts when a problem arises as to whether the state—the beneficiary of the confiscation order—should have priority over the ordinary creditors. If the convicted person (or company) is already in some form of insolvency process, the state would seem not to have any priority at all and indeed it would not seem possible for a confiscation order to be made because the assets of the convicted person/company no longer belong beneficially to that person/company but are held for the creditors acting through the insolvency practitioner. This has subsequently been confirmed by the CJEU in Case 444/07 *MG Probud Gdynia Sp Zoo v Hauptzollamt Saarbrucken*,[451] a case in which concerned the lawfulness of an attachment of an entity's assets in Germany pursuant to an enforcement order after insolvency proceedings had been opened in Poland. The CJEU held that since main proceedings had been opened in Poland, Polish law was applicable to those proceedings and their effects. Polish law did not permit enforcement proceedings to be brought against a debtor's assets after the opening of insolvency proceedings and so such enforcement proceedings could not take place under the law of another Member State.

(OR) Article 26—Public policy

Any Member State may refuse to recognise insolvency proceedings opened in another Member State or to enforce a judgment handed down in the context of such proceedings where the effects of such recognition or enforcement would be manifestly contrary to that State's public policy, in particular its fundamental principles or the constitutional rights and liberties of the individual.

Article 26 of the OR echoes what is now Article 45 of the Recast Brussels Regulation **8.362** 1215/2012[452] (which has replaced Article 34(1) of the Civil Jurisdiction Regulation 44/2001, which in turn replaced Article 27 of the Brussels Convention of 1968) which permits a state to refuse to recognize a judgment given in another Member State where to do so would be manifestly contrary to the public policy of the recognizing state.

[However, it should be noted that there are significant differences between the pro- **8.363** visions of the Recast Civil Jurisdiction Regulation and the Insolvency Regulation which affect the scope and effect of the 'public policy' exception to recognition. Thus, whereas Article 45(1)(a) of the former declares that a judgment *shall* not be recognized if to do so would be manifestly contrary to public policy (emphasis added), the drafting of Article 26 of the OR employs the word 'may', thus making it a matter of discretion whether to refuse recognition or enforcement on the public policy ground.[453] Moreover, the concluding words of Article 26

---

[451] [2010] ECR I-417, [2010] BCC 453.

[452] Regulation (EU) 1215/2012 of the European Parliament and of the Council, of 12 December 2012, on jurisdiction and the recognition and enforcement of judgments in civil and commercial matters (recast), OJ L351/1, 20. December 2012, replaced the former version of the Brussels Regulation 44/2001 with effect from 10 January 2015.

[453] Cited with approval in *Re Stojevic* (Vienna Higher Regional Court, 9 November 2004), 28 R 225/04w.

OR of the Insolvency Regulation, not replicated anywhere in either iteration of the Civil Jurisdiction Regulation, focus upon two specific aspects of the public policy of the recognizing state, namely its fundamental principles or the constitutional rights and liberties of the individual. This additional language in the Insolvency Regulation reinforces the conclusion that the public policy exception embodied in Article 26 OR is intended to be of restricted application, and should only be invoked in cases where there are grave implications for the maintenance of basic rights and freedoms within the recognizing state. It may be further observed that the public policy exception, where invocable, need not result in the total rejection of the judgment emanating from the other Member State: it may be possible to refuse recognition or enforcement of the invidious portions of the judgment, while allowing other parts to enjoy effect.[454] The extent to which this may be possible will depend on the exact circumstances of the individual case. (**IF**)].

8.364 In relation to the enforcement of judgments, many of the same principles which underpinned the Brussels Convention should apply. Thus:

- A recognizing state cannot review the merits of a judgment.[455]
- A recognizing state cannot review the jurisdiction of the court which gave judgment.[456] In this regard, it is for the judicial authorities of the state in which judgment was given to verify the jurisdiction of the courts which gave judgment.[457]

8.365 Furthermore, the 'public policy' exception is a narrow one and should be used in only exceptional circumstances. This is emphasized by the use of the word 'manifestly'.[458]

8.366 In relation to 'public policy' itself, this is a national law concept and, accordingly, its meaning may vary from state to state. However, given the need to uphold the

---

[454] See Virgos-Schmit Report para 209.

[455] cf Art 52 of the Recast Civil Jurisdiction Regulation 1215/2012 (which corresponds to Art 36 of the former version of the Regulation, 44/2001): 'Under no circumstances may a foreign judgment be reviewed as to its substance in the Member State addressed.' (So also Art 29 of the Brussels Convention of 1968). The same approach has been taken by the ECJ in relation to the Regulation: Case C-341/04 *Re Eurofood IFSC Ltd* [2006] ECR I-3813, [2006] Ch 508. See also *Public Prosecutor v Segard (as Administrator for Rover France SAS)* (Versailles Court of Appeal, 15 December 2005) para 37.

[456] Case C-341/04 *Re Eurofood IFSC Ltd* [2006] ECR I-3813, [2006] Ch 508; cf Art 45(3) of the Recast Civil Jurisdiction Regulation.

[457] See Virgos-Schmit Report para 202(2).

[458] In matters re what is now the Recast Civil Jurisdiction Regulation the ECJ is of the opinion that the public policy exception should be interpreted strictly and can only apply in exceptional cases: see Case C-7/98 *Krombach v Bamberski* [2000] ECR I-1935, and Case C-38/98 *Renault SA v Maxicar SpA* [2000] ECR I-2973. In *Krombach* the ECJ stated that there needed to be 'a manifest breach of a rule of law regarded as essential in the legal order of the state in which enforcement is sought, or of a right recognized as being fundamental within that legal order' for the exception to apply (para 37 of the judgment). In *Re Eurofood IFSC Ltd* the ECJ held that this case law applied to the interpretation of Art 26 OR: para 64 of the judgment.

purpose of the Regulation, 'public policy' should be interpreted strictly[459] and lim-ited to those particularly important and fundamental principles of national law.[460] In this vein, the Virgos-Schmit Report refers to 'constitutionally protected rights and freedoms and fundamental policies of the requested state, including those of the Community'.[461]

[In addition one can think of refusing recognition based on the fact that the rec-   **8.367** ognition or enforcement is manifestly contrary to a Member State's legitimate public interest, like the availability of a minimum quantity of energy (oil and gas). (**Wess**)]

In *Re Stojevic*,[462] the Austrian Supreme Court, upholding the Higher Regional of   **8.368** Vienna (Court of Appeal), held that recognition could not be refused under Article 26 merely on the grounds that it was thought that the court opening prior main proceedings had taken jurisdiction without any proper basis. The point was suf-ficiently clear not to be referred to the ECJ for a preliminary ruling.

In *Re Eurofood IFSC Ltd*,[463] both the Advocate General and the ECJ itself referred   **8.369** to the narrow scope of Article 26. The Advocate General stated:[464]

> In my view it is clear, first, and as Dr Bondi and the Italian Government stress, that the public policy exemption in Art 26 is intended to be of limited scope. That is borne out by the inclusion in that provision of the requirement that the effects of recognition should be 'manifestly' contrary to public policy, by the statement in recital 22 in the preamble to the Regulation that 'grounds for non-recognition should be reduced to the minimum necessary', and by the Virgos-Schmit Report, which states: 'The public policy exception ought to operate only in exceptional cases'. 33 (Point 204.)

The Court of Justice itself in the *Eurofood* case held that the Article 26 OR exception would apply where insolvency proceedings were opened in another Member State where the decision to open the proceedings '*was taken in flagrant breach of the fundamental right to be heard*'.[465] Importantly, however, the ECJ pointed out that the Irish court in that case could not hold that there was a breach of this fundamental right simply because there was no fair *oral* hearing, even though that might be fundamental to Irish notions of a fair hearing, if in all the circumstances (ie the ability to file written submissions) there was a fair hearing.[466]

---

[459] *Public Prosecutor v Segard (as Administrator for Rover France SAS)* (Versailles Court of Appeal, 15 December 2005) para 41, citing Recital (22) 'grounds for non-recognition should be reduced to the minimum necessary'.
[460] Case C-341/04 *Re Eurofood IFSC Ltd* [2006] ECR I-3813, [2006] Ch 508.
[461] Virgos-Schmit Report para 205.
[462] (Austrian Supreme Court, 17 March 2005), 8 Ob 135/04t.
[463] C-341/04 [2006] ECR I-3813, [2006] Ch 508.
[464] Para 131.
[465] Para 67 of the judgment.
[466] Case C-341/04 *Re Eurofood IFSC Ltd* [2006] ECR I-3813, [2006] Ch 508, para 68.

8.370 Likewise, the special importance attached to employee protection by French insolvency law does not afford the French courts a ground for non-recognition on the basis of public policy where English main proceedings offer much less protection.[467]

8.371 It has been suggested by Dr Gerald Mäsch,[468] that if jurisdiction to open main proceedings has been taken on the basis of a move of COMI designed to avoid creditors then this may not be recognized in other Member States on the basis of Article 26.

8.372 In the *Hans Brochier* case, administrators were appointed out of court in England in respect of a German company on the basis of an assertion by the directors that COMI was in the United Kingdom. The German court[469] refused to recognize the opening in the United Kingdom on the grounds that COMI was in Germany, the UK opening was fraudulent and that Article 26 OR applied. Subsequently, the UK administrators obtained a declaration from the English court that, in the light of further information from Germany, COMI was in Germany.[470] It followed that the opening of main proceedings had been invalid.

C. Chapter III: Secondary Insolvency Proceedings[471]

8.373 Chapter III of the Regulation deals with 'secondary' insolvency proceedings. Secondary proceedings are Article 3(2) OR proceedings which are opened in a Member State after main insolvency proceedings have already been commenced in another Member State (see Article 3(3) OR). These proceedings must be winding-up proceedings as listed in Annex B of the Regulation. In the case of England, these proceedings are winding-up by the court, winding-up through administration (including out of court appointments), creditors' voluntary winding-up (with confirmation by the court), and bankruptcy.[472]

8.374 Although some of the provisions in Chapter III of the Regulation relate only to secondary proceedings, Articles 31–35 OR are also applied by Article 36 OR to independent territorial proceedings,[473] ie those opened prior to the opening of main proceedings, 'in so far as the progress of those proceedings so permits'.

---

[467] *Public Prosecutor v Segard (as Administrator for Rover France SAS)* Versailles Court of Appeal, 15 December 2005) paras 39–43.

[468] At the European Academy of Law (ERA) on 19 September 2006.

[469] Amtsgericht Nürnberg, ZIP 2/2007 81.

[470] *Hans Brochier Holdings Ltd v Exner* [2007] BCC 127.

[471] See also the commentary to Art 3 OR at paras 8.59 et seq above.

[472] Two further types of Annex B proceedings are listed for the 'UK': sequestration for Scotland and voluntary winding-up subject to the supervision of the court for Gibraltar. See app 1 below.

[473] Referred to in English statutory instruments simply as 'territorial proceedings'.

(OR) Article 27—Opening of proceedings

The opening of the proceedings referred to in Article 3(1) by a court of a Member State and which is recognised in another Member State (main proceedings) shall permit the opening in that other Member State, a court of which has jurisdiction pursuant to Article 3(2), of secondary insolvency proceedings without the debtor's insolvency being examined in that other State. These latter proceedings must be among the proceedings listed in Annex B. Their effects shall be restricted to the assets of the debtor situated within the territory of that other Member State.

As a general principle, secondary proceedings once commenced are governed by the relevant national law (Article 4 OR). However, Article OR 27 modifies this principle to an extent by providing that where main proceedings have been commenced in relation to a debtor which is recognized in another Member State, then secondary proceedings can be commenced without the insolvency of the debtor having to be established. This exception to the application of national law obviously represents a significant change from the standard practice adopted by English law in relation to the winding-up of companies and the bankruptcy of debtors. It also reflects the fact that local secondary proceedings are to be regarded as being very much ancillary and subordinate to the main proceedings. **8.375**

In such circumstances the principal role of the local court requested to open secondary proceedings is to examine whether main proceedings have been commenced in another Member State in relation to the relevant debtor, and whether those proceedings are insolvency proceedings within the meaning of Article 3(1) OR so that the Regulation applies. In this regard it is probably also open to the local court to examine whether or not the court opening the main proceedings based its judgment on a finding that the centre of the debtor's main interests was in that state. The local court will also have concurrent jurisdiction with the court of the main proceedings to determine what assets fall within the scope of any secondary proceedings that should be opened.[474] However, it should not be open to the local court to investigate whether or not a finding as to the centre of the debtor's main interests was correct; this is a matter which must be dealt with by the judicial authorities of the state concerned.[475] Recital (22) OR suggests that the decision of the first court which holds that it is opening main proceedings should be recognized in other Member States [on the basis of 'the principle of mutual trust' between courts in different Member States. (**Wess**)] **8.376**

[Most importantly, the public policy exception under Article 26 OR should not be invoked as a ground for refusing to recognize or enforce a judgment that has **8.377**

---

[474] Case C-649/13 *Comité d'entreprise de Nortel networks SA and others v Rogeau* (2015) () ECLI:EU:C:2015:384

[475] Virgos-Schmit Report para 215 refers to 'the trust placed in judgments given by Community courts'.

been based on a finding that the centre of main interests is in the Member State from which the judgment emanates.[476] Any party wishing to challenge the finding of the court of origin should utilize the available channels of appeal within the legal system of that state. (IF)]

8.378 If, however, the first 'court' as defined in the Regulation,[477] which may not be a court in any usual sense, does not make a finding that the debtor's centre of main interests was located in that state or that the proceedings are main proceedings (which would imply that the centre of main interests was in that state), it would seem to be open to courts in other Member States to make their own findings on the question until one 'court' makes such a finding in relation to its own proceeding. It is clearly desirable that 'courts' should always specify the type of proceeding they are opening.

8.379 In England, forms of order were introduced to make it clear whether the court considers the proceedings to be main, secondary, or 'territorial' (defined to mean territorial proceedings opened prior to the opening of main proceedings).[478]

8.380 The ability to open secondary proceedings without proof of insolvency once main proceedings have been opened and are to be recognized, appears to assume that insolvency will have been established in the main proceedings. However, three of the potential main proceedings in England, administration orders and individual and corporate voluntary arrangements, do not require proof of insolvency. In practice, voluntary arrangements always involve insolvent debtors, either in the sense that assets are less than liabilities or in the sense that debts cannot be paid in full as they fall due, otherwise there would be no incentive for creditors to agree to a composition. On the other hand, administration orders can expressly be made and sometimes are made on the basis that the debtor company is 'likely to become' insolvent. The direction in Article 27(1) OR that the opening of main insolvency proceedings in a Member State 'shall permit the opening' of secondary proceedings in another Member State within the territory of which the debtor has an establishment 'without the debtor's insolvency being examined in that other State' has however been interpreted by the CJEU to mean that the local court cannot examine the insolvency of a debtor, even where the main proceedings do not require proof of insolvency under local law and have a protective purpose.[479]

---

[476] ibid para 202, where emphasis is placed upon the 'principle of Community trust and on the general legal presumption that the judgment handed down in another [member] state is valid'.

[477] See Art 2(d) OR and the commentary to Art 2 at OR paras 8.17–8.24 above.

[478] Referred to in this commentary as 'independent territorial proceedings'. For the forms, see the Insolvency (Amendment) Rules 2002, SI 2002/1307.

[479] Case C-116/11 *Bank Handlowy w Warszawie SA v Christanapol sp. zoo* ECLI:EU:C:2012:739, [2013] BPIR 174, at [64]–[74]. In this case the *procédure de sauvegarde* under French law required only that the debtor 'demonstrate the existence of difficulties, which he is not able to overcome, such as to lead to the cessation of payments': see Arts L.620-2 of the French Commercial Code.

The reference in Article 27 OR to recognition appears to import the notion that if **8.381** recognition is not afforded to the Article 3(1) OR proceeding because it would be manifestly contrary to the other Member State's public policy pursuant to Article 26 OR, Article 27 OR will not apply. The local court must also be satisfied that it itself has jurisdiction to open Article 3(2) OR proceedings in relation to the debtor by reason of the debtor having an 'establishment' as defined in Article 2(h) OR in the Member State (see Article 3(2) OR).[480] The question of whether a debtor has an establishment in the local state is a question of fact to be determined by the local court.

The conditions for opening Article 3(2) OR proceedings in respect of a debtor are **8.382** to be determined by the local court applying its national law, in accordance with Article 4(2) OR. Thus it is possible that in certain states it may not be possible to commence secondary proceedings against a debtor even though main proceedings have been commenced in another state, have to be recognized, and the debtor has an establishment in the state concerned. This may occur, for example, because the national law of that state prohibits insolvency proceedings being commenced against that debtor. For example, in certain states it is not possible to commence insolvency proceedings against public undertakings or against debtors who are not traders.[481]

The application of national law to govern the opening of secondary proceedings **8.383** entails that the local court may exercise its discretion as to whether or not to open such proceedings, including consideration of whether it is appropriate to do so.[482] The framework of EU law however places constraints upon the exercise of any such discretion. For example, the principle of non-discrimination[483] precludes conditions for the opening of secondary proceedings which draw a distinction between creditors seeking the opening of such proceedings on the basis of their place of residence or registered office.[484] Correspondingly the local court must exercise its discretion with regard to the purpose of secondary proceedings,[485] as explained above, and also the objective of the main proceedings and the principle of sincere co-operation.[486] In principle then the local court may open secondary proceedings even if all the assets of the debtor are within that Member State and the purpose of the main proceedings is protective. In such a case the local court must however consider the purpose of the main proceedings

---

[480] See the commentary under those OR Articles at paras 8.37–8.59 and 8.163–8.176 above.
[481] See commentary to Art 1 OR ('General Principles') at para 8.05 above.
[482] Case C-327/13 *Burgo Group SpA v Illochroma SA* (in liquidation) (2014) ECLI:EU: 2158 at [59]–[63] and [67]
[483] See Case C-109/09 *Deutsche Lufthansa* (2011) EU:C:2011:129 at [37] and the case law cited.
[484] *Burgo group* at n 482 above at [64].
[485] Ibid at [65].
[486] Ibid at [66].

and the effect of the opening of secondary proceedings on the achievement of that purpose.[487]

8.384 Article 27 OR also repeats the principle set out in Article 3(2) OR that the effects of secondary proceedings are limited to the assets of the debtor located in the Member State in which the secondary proceedings are commenced. However, Article 18(2) OR does provide that a liquidator in Article 3(2) proceedings has the power to act in any other Member State in order to recover any assets of the debtor which were moved out of the territory after the commencement of the Article 3(2) OR proceedings and, in addition, can bring any action to set aside a transaction which is in the interests of the creditors.

8.385 The jurisdiction to determine the Member State in which assets are situated, in accordance with Article 2(g) OR, is concurrent as between the court of the main proceedings and that of the secondary proceedings. This follows from the construction of Articles 3(2) and 25(1) OR, as interpreted by the CJEU in the *Nortel* case.[488] A consequence of a concurrent jurisdiction is that, inevitably, there will be a racetojudgment as between liquidators in certain instances. The principal justification for the construction in favour of a concurrent jurisdiction is that, on the one hand, the protection of local interests (which is the object of a secondary proceeding) would not be realized if, for example, a related action or other action integral to the secondary proceeding could not be adjudicated on by the local court;[489] and, on the other hand, that the utility of a main proceeding with capacity to decide all issues would be diminished, contrary to Article 3(1) OR and Article 4 OR, if that jurisdiction were exclusive and the court with control of the main proceedings did not also have jurisdiction.[490] This approach however fails to give effect to the superiority of the main proceedings.

8.386 In the *Nortel* case the Court of Justice explained that the situation of an asset within a given Member State was a question not to be determined applying the law application under national choice of law rules. Article 2(g) OR provided an autonomous set of rules for the determination of an asset's *situs*, which rules displaced any which would otherwise be applicable under national rules of private international law.[491]

---

[487] Case C-116/11 *Bank Handlowy w Warszawie SA v Christianapol sp. z o.o.* [2013] Bus LR 956, ECLI: EU:C 2012:739at [53]–[63].
[488] C-649/13 *Comité d'entreprise de Nortel networks SA and others v Rogeau* (2015) ECLI:EU: C:2015:384.
[489] Ibid at [34]–[38].
[490] Ibid at [40]–[42].
[491] Ibid at [49]–[55].

(OR) Article 28—Applicable law

> Save as otherwise provided in this Regulation, the law applicable to secondary proceedings shall be that of the Member State within the territory of which the secondary proceedings are opened.

Article 28 OR is a specific instance of the general rule in Article 4 that the law **8.387** applicable to insolvency proceedings is the law of the state of the opening of the proceedings.

(OR) Article 29—Right to request the opening of proceedings

The opening of secondary proceedings may be requested by:

(a) the liquidator in the main proceedings;
(b) any other person or authority empowered to request the opening of insolvency proceedings under the law of the Member State within the territory of which the opening of secondary proceedings is requested.

Article 29(a) OR establishes a right of the 'liquidator', as defined by Article 2(b) **8.388** OR, in the main proceedings to request the opening of secondary proceedings whether or not the local law gives him that right. This may be a useful power for example where the liquidator needs to exercise powers, which cannot be exercised simply by reason of his appointment in the main proceedings, such as 'coercive measures'.[492]

A liquidator in main proceedings will be able to request the opening of second- **8.389** ary proceedings in other Member States simply by producing a certified copy of the original decision appointing him (see Article 19 OR), probably together with a translation into one of the official languages of the Member State in which he wishes to make the application.

The courts in the relevant Member State will not be able to dismiss the application **8.390** on the grounds that the debtor is solvent, since it is expressly provided that there should be no examination of the debtor's solvency on a request to open secondary proceedings (Article 27 OR).

Article 29(b) OR provides a specific instance of the general rule in Article 4(2) **8.391** that the conditions for opening proceedings are governed by the law of the state of the opening of the proceedings. In other words, the question as to which person or authority is empowered to seek the opening of secondary proceedings must be determined on the basis of the national law of the Member State within the territory of which the opening of such proceedings is sought.[493] In practice, this rule gives local creditors the ability to request the opening of local

---

[492] Art 18(3).
[493] Case C-327/13 *Burgo Group SpA v Illochroma SA (in liquidation)* (2014) ECLI:EU: 2158 at [51].

proceedings in order to protect local interests and prevent the removal of assets by the liquidator in the main proceedings. The right to seek the opening of secondary proceedings cannot, however, be restricted to creditors who have their domicile or registered office within the Member State in whose territory the relevant establishment is situated, or to creditors whose claims arise from the operation of that establishment.[494]

8.392 The Polish Supreme Court has held, on the basis of the Polish, German, and Lithuanian language versions of Article 29(b) OR that only persons who can request the opening of *secondary* proceedings under the relevant Member State law will fall within Article 29(b) OR.[495]

(OR) Article 30—Advance payment of costs and expenses

> Where the law of the Member State in which the opening of secondary proceedings is requested requires that the debtor's assets be sufficient to cover in whole or in part the costs and expenses of the proceedings, the court may, when it receives such a request, require the applicant to make an advance payment of costs or to provide appropriate security.

8.393 This provision provides for the fact that in certain jurisdictions insolvency proceedings cannot be commenced in relation to a debtor unless the debtor has sufficient assets to cover the costs and expenses of the proceedings. It is important to note that any such requirement must be part of the general law of the Member State concerned and cannot be introduced specifically for secondary proceedings commenced pursuant to the Regulation.[496]

(OR) Article 31—Duty to co-operate and communicate information

> 1. Subject to the rules restricting the communication of information, the liquidator in the main proceedings and the liquidators in the secondary proceedings shall be duty bound to communicate information to each other. They shall immediately communicate any information which may be relevant to the other proceedings, in particular the progress made in lodging and verifying claims and all measures aimed at terminating the proceedings.
> 2. Subject to the rules applicable to each of the proceedings, the liquidator in the main proceedings and the liquidators in the secondary proceedings shall be duty bound to cooperate with each other.
> 3. The liquidator in the secondary proceedings shall give the liquidator in the main proceedings an early opportunity of submitting proposals on the liquidation or use of the assets in the secondary proceedings.

8.394 Article 31 OR deals with a recurring problem in cross-frontier insolvencies relating to the same debtor, namely how to co-ordinate different proceedings in different

---

[494] Ibid.

[495] *Polmos Lancut SA* C III CZP 115/09, 20 Jan 2010; see Barlowski, 'Practical Problems in Applying Regulation 1346/2000' (2011) 8 Corporate Rescue 172.

[496] See the Virgos-Schmit Report para 228.

jurisdictions. Prior to and outside the Regulation, solutions have to be developed between different insolvency administrators and their national courts.[497] Where the OR applies, there are mandatory provisions.

As the Virgos-Schmit Report states, co-operation between the various liquida- **8.395** tors is necessary to ensure the smooth course of operations in the proceedings.[498] Article 31(1) OR therefore provides that as a general principle the liquidator in the main proceedings and the liquidators in any secondary proceedings should communicate information to each other (subject to any rules of national law restricting such communication) and in particular should immediately communicate any information which might be relevant to the other proceedings. The provision goes on to state that such information to be communicated includes information relating to the lodging and verification of claims and relating to the termination of the proceedings.[499] The duty to co-operate is however expressed as being '[s]ubject to the rules applicable to each of the proceedings'. Accordingly, the duty has not been construed as a freestanding obligation capable of overriding other mandatory features of the Regulation or the applicable law under the Regulation, for example the rules applicable to the distribution of assets.[500]

The Virgos-Schmit Report itself gives more detail about the type of information **8.396** which it is envisaged is to be provided and exchanged.[501] This includes information relating to:

• the assets of the debtor;
• any actions planned or under way to recover assets or to obtain payment or to set aside transactions;
• the liquidation of assets;
• the lodging of claims;
• the verification of claims and any disputes arising;
• the ranking of creditors;
• planned reorganization measures;
• proposed compositions;
• allocation and payment of dividends;
• the progress of the proceedings.

---

[497] See ch 5 above.

[498] Virgos-Schmit Report para 229.

[499] See also Insolvency Rules 1986, rr 1.34, 2.62(5), 4.231(5), 5.34, and 6.238(5) (inserted by the Insolvency (Amendment) Rules 2002), which impose specific duties on the supervisors of CVAs and IVAs, administrators, liquidators, and trustees in bankruptcy to send certain types of information to 'Member State liquidators', a term defined in the 1986 Rules, r 13.13(11) (inserted by the Insolvency (Amendment) Rules 2002) as being a 'liquidator' within Art 2(b) of the Regulation appointed in another Member State.

[500] *Re Alitalia Linee Aeree Italiane SpA* [2011] 1 BCLC 606 at [42]–[43].

[501] Virgo-Schmit Report para 230.

[The wording at the beginning of Article 31(1) 'Subject to the rules restricting the communication of information' refers to domestic rules with regard to the registration of privacy-sensitive data. (**Wess**)]

8.397 Article 31(2) OR adds to the duty to communicate information by introducing a general duty on liquidators in proceedings relating to the same debtor to co-operate with each other. It clearly makes sense that where 'liquidators'[502] are seeking to achieve a common goal (to maximize the return to the creditors of the debtor) then they should co-operate to try to achieve this aim. A use of Article 31(2) OR developed by the English court is to issue a letter of request to the courts of other Member States following the opening of main proceedings in order to secure a means by which the Member State liquidator is to be notified of any application to open secondary insolvency proceedings.[503] However, there will undoubtedly be circumstances where there is a tension between the aims of a liquidator in secondary proceedings and the aims of a liquidator in the main proceedings. For example, there may be a dispute as to whether or not a particular asset is a local asset (so falling under the secondary proceedings) or an asset in relation to which the main proceedings take effect.

8.398 Article 31(3) OR develops one particular aspect of the duty to co-operate by imposing a duty on the liquidator in secondary proceedings to permit the liquidator in the main proceedings an early opportunity to submit proposals on the secondary liquidation and the use of the debtor's assets in those proceedings. The Virgos-Schmit Report states that this mechanism might enable the liquidator in the main proceedings to prevent, for example, the sale of assets in the secondary proceedings. However, there is no indication in Article 31(3) OR that the liquidator in the secondary proceedings is bound to comply with any proposals submitted to him by the main liquidator. Presumably the liquidator in the main proceedings could challenge any decision made by the liquidator in the secondary proceedings upon submitted proposals under the relevant national law.

8.399 In the case of England, a liquidator in main proceedings commenced in another Member State would appear to have locus under the Insolvency Act 1986 to challenge a decision of a liquidator in English secondary proceedings in the Companies Court. In particular, section 168(5) of the Insolvency Act 1986 allows any person aggrieved by an act or decision of a liquidator to apply to the court for relief.

8.400 The liquidator in the main proceedings may be able to lodge the claims of all those creditors who have lodged claims in the main proceedings in any secondary proceedings (see Article 32(2) OR) and will in any event be able to participate in the secondary proceedings 'on the same basis as a creditor' (Article 32(3) OR). This

---

502 As defined in Art 2(b).
503 *Re Nortel Networks SA* [2009] EWHC 206 (Ch), [2009] BCC 343, at [10]. This is on the basis that courts as well as liquidators have a duty to co-operate: see 8.402 below.

might itself give the liquidator in the main proceedings an influential role in the secondary proceedings.

[Where a liquidator fails to comply with the duty to co-operate or to communi- **8.401** cate information, the *lex concursus* of the Member State in which proceedings are opened and in which he is appointed, governs the question of his liability. (**Wess**)]

Article 31 OR does not expressly place a duty of co-operation on the courts of **8.402** Member States, but such an obligation is to be implied.[504] The obligation on courts to co-operate is expressly spelt out in the UNCITRAL Model Law.[505] Professors Wessels and Virgos have drafted Guidelines to be used in EU Communication and Co-operation.[506] Guidelines for Court-to-Court Communications in International Insolvency Cases, drafted by Professors Wessels and Fletcher, were included in a Report devoted to Transnational Insolvency produced for the American Law Institute and the International Insolvency Institute in 2012.[507] The foregoing texts were further developed between 2013 and 2014 in a project, chaired by Professor Wessels, specifically designed to develop EU Cross-Border Insolvency Cooperation Principles for use by all courts operating under the aegis of the EU Insolvency Regulation (both the OR and the RR). The resulting Report was published in 2015.[508]

(OR) Article 32—Exercise of creditors' rights

1. Any creditor may lodge his claim in the main proceedings and in any secondary proceedings.
2. The liquidators in the main and any secondary proceedings shall lodge in other proceedings claims which have already been lodged in the proceedings for which they were appointed, provided that the interests of creditors in the latter proceedings are served thereby, subject to the right of creditors to oppose that or to withdraw the lodgement of their claims where the law applicable so provides.
3. The liquidator in the main or secondary proceedings shall be empowered to participate in other proceedings on the same basis as a creditor, in particular by attending creditors' meetings.

---

[504] *Re Nortel Networks SA* [2009] BCC 343; *Re Collins & Aikman* (Higher Regional Court of Graz, 20 October 2005) 3 R 149/05 reported at NZI 2006 vol 11, p 660, Re *Stojevic* (Higher Regional Court, Vienna, 9 November 2004), 28 R 225/04w. See also the discussion of this question in Vallender, 'Judicial Co-operation within the EC Insolvency Regulation' (Winter 2007) 30 Eurofenix Insol Europe 8 et seq.

[505] UNCITRAL Model Law on Cross-Border Insolvency (May 1997), Art 25.

[506] 'European Communication & Cooperation Guidelines for Cross-Border Insolvency' (July 2007, INSOL Europe publications), See Van Nielen, 'The CoCo Guidelines versus Real-World Experience' (Winter 2007) Eurofenix Insol Europe 12.

[507] The American Law Institute and the International Insolvency Institute, 'Transnational Insolvency: Global Principles for Cooperation in International Insolvency Cases', Reporters Ian F Fletcher and Bob Wessels, dated March 2012. The Report can be accessed on the website of the III at <http://iiiglobal.org/component/jdownloads/viewdownload/36/5897.html>.

[508] B Wessels (ed), *EU Cross-Border Insolvency Court-to-Court Cooperation Principles* (2015).

8.403 Since Article 4(2)(h) OR provides that the law of the state of the opening of the proceedings governs the lodging of claims, Article 32(1) OR only applies to claims which are admissible under the law governing the proceedings in question (*lex concursus*).

8.404 It is necessary to allow creditors to claim in both main and secondary proceedings because the assets will be different and the priorities are likely to be different. These differences cannot completely be compensated for by the 'imputation' (hotchpot) provision in Article 20(2) OR.

8.405 It has been suggested that the ability to claim in both proceedings 'may engender considerable administrative complexity in cross-accounting and record keeping'.[509] If that proves to be the case in relation to a debtor, consideration should be given to simplifying the claims and distribution procedure by means of parallel compositions in the main and secondary proceedings.[510]

8.406 The creditors entitled to lodge claims in both proceedings pursuant to the Regulation are those creditors who have their habitual residence, domicile, or registered office in a Member State (Article 39 OR): of course the law governing the main or secondary proceedings may well allow creditors from other states to lodge claims. Creditors who are entitled to lodge claims include the tax and social security authorities of other Member States (Article 39 OR).

8.407 Article 32(2) OR avoids the need for individual creditors in main or secondary proceedings to come to grips with the linguistic and legal difficulties that may be found in trying to claim in the other type of proceeding.

8.408 Article 32(3) OR provides that a liquidator in each type of proceeding is entitled to participate[511] in the other type of proceeding on the same basis as a creditor, including participation by attending creditors' meetings.[512] It might be thought from the wording of Article 32(3) OR that this would include a liquidator being

---

[509] Fletcher (n 387 above) para 31-056.

[510] See also Art 34 OR. A technique used in one case was for the English court in charge of the main proceedings to authorize the liquidator to delegate to the foreign trustee in charge of the secondary insolvency proceedings in another Member State the distribution under the main proceeding, so that he could conduct a *de facto* joint distribution in both estates. This was possible because English law allows liquidators etc to delegate the performance of duties to an agent and because the creditor priorities in the two proceedings were the same. It was convenient because most creditors were in the secondary jurisdiction and claimed under the law of that jurisdiction.

[511] [The English, French and Dutch texts refer to 'participate'. The German text, however, has '*mitzuwirken*' (to co-operate). The latter wording suggests that the power vested in the liquidator by Art 32(3) OR only exists when he has lodged the creditor's claims pursuant to Art 32(2). This limitation does not make sense given the central principle of co-operation and communication. (**Wess**)]

[512] See in relation to England the Insolvency Rules 1986 (as amended by the Insolvency (Amendment) Rules 2002) rr 2.22 and 2.62 (in relation to administration), rr 4.67 and 4.231 (in relation to liquidation), and rr 6.93, 6.238, and 6.239 (in relation to bankruptcy). See also rr 7.64, 8.8, and 11.1.

entitled to exercise the voting rights attaching to the claims which he lodges in proceedings on behalf of creditors who have lodged claims in his proceedings.[513] However, the Virgos-Schmit Report indicates that such a proposal was specifically rejected during the negotiations leading up to the agreement of the Regulation.[514]

The Regulation does not prevent the creditors in each of main and secondary **8.409** proceedings themselves lodging claims in each proceeding. It is not clear in terms of the Regulation what is to happen if both the liquidator and one or more creditors in one proceeding lodge identical or overlapping claims in the other. Since pari passu treatment for creditors of equal standing is a fundamental principle of the Regulation, the claim (and each part of the claim) can only be counted once.[515] The apparent ability for the same claim to be lodged by both creditors and liquidator suggests that if that happens the claims remain the creditors' claims and only the creditors can vote on them and receive dividends in respect of them.[516]

In England, participation 'on the same basis as a creditor' will include a right to **8.410** inspect the court file, an excellent source of information about the proceedings: Insolvency Rule 7.64, introduced by the Insolvency (Amendment) Rules 2002.

It is not clear in what circumstances creditors would want to exercise their **8.411** rights under Article 32(2) OR to oppose their claims being lodged in other proceedings by the liquidator or to exercise any right given by the applicable law to withdraw a claim previously lodged in proceedings. One possible situation might be where a claim has been made by a creditor with a right in rem which the creditor has inadvertently omitted to disclose, and the omission might under the applicable law have the effect of waiving the right in rem.[517] [The lodging of a claim may also result in the creditor incurring certain costs. (**MB**)]

(OR) Article 33—Stay of liquidation

1. **The court, which opened the secondary proceedings, shall stay the process of liquidation in whole or in part on receipt of a request from the liquidator in the**

---

[513] This assumption appears to have been made in the amendments to the Insolvency Rules in England: see rr 2.62 (administration orders), 4.231 (liquidation), and 6.238 (bankruptcy); but where the same claim has also been put in by a liquidator and a creditor, there can only be one vote and usually it will be the creditor who can vote: rr 2.22, 4.67, and 6.93 of the Insolvency Rules 1986 (as amended by the Insolvency (Amendment) Rules 2002).

[514] Virgos-Schmit Report para 240.

[515] This is the subject of specific provision in England: Insolvency Rules 1986, rr 2.22(6), 4.67(6), and 6.93 (6) (added by the Insolvency (Amendment) Rules 2002).

[516] This is also the actual result achieved by the English amended rules: see the Insolvency Rules 1986, rr 2.22, 4.67, and 6.93 (as amended by the Insolvency (Amendment) Rules 2002).

[517] In England, see the Insolvency Rules 1986, r 4.96(3) (added by the Insolvency (Amendment) Rules 2002).

main proceedings, provided that in that event it may require the liquidator in the main proceedings to take any suitable measure to guarantee the interests of the creditors in the secondary proceedings and of individual classes of creditors. Such a request from the liquidator may be rejected only if it is manifestly of no interest to the creditors in the main proceedings. Such a stay of the process of liquidation may be ordered for up to three months. It may be continued or renewed for similar periods.

2. The court referred to in paragraph 1 shall terminate the stay of the process of liquidation:
   - at the request of the liquidator in the main proceedings,
   - of its own motion, at the request of a creditor or at the request of the liquidator in the secondary proceedings if that measure no longer appears justified, in particular, by the interests of creditors in the main proceedings or in the secondary proceedings.

8.412 There is an initial question as to whether Article 33 OR, in referring to the 'process of liquidation', is referring to the secondary proceedings or merely to the process of liquidation of assets within the secondary proceeding. In the series of cases involving the Collins & Aikman group of companies, the Austrian Higher Regional Court (Court of Appeal) in Graz[518] held that Article 33 only stays the process of liquidating assets and not the secondary proceedings as a whole. This result is consistent with the comment of MB in the first edition of this work set out at paragraph 8.418 below.

8.413 It is likely that the most common situation where a stay is requested is where the 'liquidator' in the main proceedings is seeking to rescue, reorganize, or sell the business or assets of the debtor as a whole (as in the *Collins & Aikman* case mentioned above) and therefore needs to avoid a liquidation of assets in the secondary proceedings.

8.414 Although the powers of the local court in considering a request for a stay are limited, the court does have the power, as the price of the stay, to require the liquidator in the main proceedings to ensure that the interests of the creditors in the secondary proceedings (and individual classes of them) are properly looked after.[519] This may involve setting up a mechanism to ensure that the local creditors as a whole and each class of local creditors are better off than they would have been in a liquidation.[520]

---

[518] (Oberlandesgericht, 20 October 2005), 3 R 149/05, NZI (Neue Zeitschrift für Insolvenz und Sanierung) 2006, vol 11, 660 on appeal from the Landesgericht Leoben, 31 August 2005, 17 p 56/05, NZI 2005, vol 11, 646. We are grateful to Christian Köhler-Ma of Leonhardt Westhelle & Partner Rechtsanwälte—Insolvency administrators—Notaries Kurfürstendamm 212 10719 Berlin for supplying an English translation of this judgment, the judgment at first instance, and the subsequent judgment lifting the stay (mentioned below).

[519] The limitations on the court's obligation to grant a stay have been described as 'unclear': Fletcher (n 387 above) para 31-053.

[520] The measures could be analogous to those used in *Re Collins & Aikman Europe SA* [2007] 1 BCLC 182, [2006] BCC 861; *Re MG Rover España SA* [2006] BCC 599, and *Re MG Rover Belux SA/NV* [2007] BCC 446.

The local court can only reject the request 'if it is manifestly of no interest to the **8.415** creditors in the main proceedings'. The use of the word 'manifestly', as in the public policy exception in Article 26 OR, suggests that if a request is made it should only be rejected in a wholly exceptional case. The liquidator in the main proceedings should be allowed a margin of appreciation on his application as to whether a stay of the secondary proceedings is of any interest to the creditors in the main proceedings.

A stay may only be granted initially for a period of time up to three months, a **8.416** period normally too short in practice for a rescue, reorganization, or sale as a going concern. However, there is no limit to the number of extensions of the stay for up to three months at a time. The effect of this seems to be to enable the local court to require reporting back to it by the liquidator in the main proceedings, through the mechanism of the extension applications, at intervals of no greater than three months at a time.

[The Regulation is silent with regard to requests for reconsideration or an appeal **8.417** against the (affirmative or negative) decision on a stay. Domestic law should fill in this gap. (**Wess**)]

[The granting of a stay stops the liquidation of assets in the secondary proceedings, **8.418** but it does not entitle the liquidator in the main proceedings to dispose of the same assets. (**MB**)]

The local court is bound to terminate the stay on the application of the liquidator **8.419** in the main proceedings: Article 33(2) OR. This refers to the stay granted under Article 33(1) OR; no doubt a different stay could then be granted under the local law governing the local proceedings if justified under it, for example if it were in the interests of local creditors: Article 4(2) OR.

The test under Article 33(2) OR on an application by a creditor or by the liquidator **8.420** in the secondary proceedings for the termination of the stay is different from the approach to granting the stay. The stay has to be terminated if it is no longer justified in accordance with the interests of the creditors in the main proceedings and the interests of the creditors in the secondary proceedings. This test was held to be satisfied in the case of the Austrian proceedings relating to Collins & Aikman on the grounds that:

(i) the creditors in the main and secondary proceedings were the same;
(ii) the creditors would be paid in full by the proposed sale in the secondary proceeding; and
(iii) the purchaser had good economic reasons for saying it could not keep its offer open until a later date and therefore any delay would threaten the ability to pay creditors of this company in full.[521]

---

[521] (Leoben Landesgericht, 1 December 2005) 17 p 56/05 m, NZI 2006, vol 11, 663.

(OR) Article 34—Measures ending secondary insolvency proceedings

1. Where the law applicable to secondary proceedings allows for such proceedings to be closed without liquidation by a rescue plan, a composition or a comparable measure, the liquidator in the main proceedings shall be empowered to propose such a measure himself. Closure of the secondary proceedings by a measure referred to in the first subparagraph shall not become final without the consent of the liquidator in the main proceedings; failing his agreement, however, it may become final if the financial interests of the creditors in the main proceedings are not affected by the measure proposed.

2. Any restriction of creditors' rights arising from a measure referred to in paragraph 1 which is proposed in secondary proceedings, such as a stay of payment or discharge of debt, may not have effect in respect of the debtor's assets not covered by those proceedings without the consent of all the creditors having an interest.

3. During a stay of the process of liquidation ordered pursuant to Article 33, only the liquidator in the main proceedings or the debtor, with the former's consent, may propose measures laid down in paragraph 1 of this Article in the secondary proceedings; no other proposal for such a measure shall be put to the vote or approved.

8.421 A rescue plan or composition closing secondary proceedings is clearly a measure which may affect the main proceedings themselves. Article 34(1) OR recognizes the primacy of the main proceedings by giving special powers to the liquidator in the main proceedings in relation to the closure of secondary proceedings.

8.422 The liquidator in the main proceedings is himself empowered to propose a rescue plan, composition, or comparable measure available under the relevant national law to close secondary proceedings. This ensures that he has standing (*locus standi*) to make such an application, which he might otherwise not have under law governing the secondary proceedings.

8.423 Where any such measure is proposed by another person, then the liquidator in the main proceedings has a right of veto on the measure becoming final unless the financial interests of the creditors in the main proceedings are not affected by the proposed measure (Article 34(1) OR). This right of veto enables the liquidator in the main proceedings to assert the primacy of those proceedings. In relation to the question of whether or not the 'financial interests' of the creditors in the main proceedings are affected by the proposed composition, it appears that the reference to 'financial interests' means specifically whether or not the proposed measure will affect the dividend which the creditors in the main proceedings are likely to receive.[522]

---

[522] Virgos-Schmit Report para 249.

Where the liquidator in the main proceedings has obtained a stay of the secondary **8.424** proceedings in place pursuant to Article 33 OR, then Article 34(3) OR provides that only the liquidator in the main proceedings or the debtor with the liquidator's consent, may propose such a measure. This exclusivity provision gives the liquidator in the main proceedings an important degree of control over the secondary proceedings.

Just as all Article 3(2) OR proceedings cannot restrict creditors' rights in rela- **8.425** tion to assets in other Member States save in respect of 'those creditors who have given their consent' (Article 17(2) OR),[523] rescue/composition/comparable measures relating to a secondary proceeding cannot restrict creditors' rights in respect of assets not covered by the secondary proceedings without 'the consent of all the creditors having an interest' (Article 34(2) OR). It is not entirely clear why different language is used. It may be that in the case of Article 17(2) OR it is envisaged that there may be a mechanism for a majority to bind a minority so that all creditors or a class or group of creditors in one or more other Member States can become bound by the restriction, whereas the use of the word 'all' in Article 34(2) OR requires unanimity amongst creditors 'having an interest' in the foreign assets. It is not clear, however, that the use of the word 'all' is intended to have this effect. The phrase 'having an interest' is also different and presumably extends not only to interests in rem and rights to retention of title but also interests in a prospective dividend as an unsecured creditor. One suspects the translator did not appreciate that 'having an interest' in English law often refers to a proprietary interest and the phrase 'having an interest' should probably have read 'interested': compare the French version: '*les créanciers intéressés*'.[524]

In the case of English law, it is possible to 'close' secondary proceedings commenced **8.426** in England (ie winding-up by the court, creditors' voluntary liquidation with confirmation by the court, and bankruptcy) by various means without liquidation. The phrase 'a rescue plan, a composition or a comparable measure' seems to fit a compromise or reorganization by means of a 'scheme' (plan) under Part 26 of the Companies Act 2006. Such an exit would be recognized under Article 25 OR in other Member States as a composition approved by the court which opened the secondary proceedings.

Company voluntary arrangements ('CVAs') and individual voluntary arrange- **8.427** ments ('IVAs') will also fit the phrase if their terms amount to a rescue or composition, which they normally would. However, these are proceedings covered by the Regulation as 'voluntary arrangements under insolvency legislation' in Annex A, and since they are not 'winding-up' proceedings listed in Annex B,

---

[523] See the commentary on this provision in paras 8.304–8.307 above.
[524] Note however that the text of Art 47(2) RR (the counterpart of Art 34(2) OR), employs the same form of words: '... without the consent of all the creditors having an interest.'

they cannot be opened as secondary proceedings (ie Article 3(2) OR proceedings opened after the opening of main proceedings): Article 3(3) OR. If that were to stop CVAs and IVAs being used pursuant to Article 34 OR to end secondary proceedings it would be very unfortunate and contrary to the interests of creditors. The point of limiting secondary proceedings to winding-up proceedings is to maintain the primacy of the main proceedings; once the secondary proceedings start as winding-up proceedings, that primacy is maintained, in relation to rescues and compromises etc, by Article 34 OR. Therefore there is no reason to exclude CVAs and IVAs from the exit routes available, even if the result may look odd, in that it could lead to an exit via a procedure which could not be opened as a secondary proceeding in its own right and which would have to be recognized under Article 25 OR as a judgment concerning the 'closure' of the secondary proceeding. Pursuant to OR Article 36, Article 34 OR will also apply to Article 3(2) OR proceedings where main proceedings are opened subsequently. In such cases, schemes could undoubtedly be used to 'close' administration order proceedings. It is submitted that CVAs can also be so used, for the reasons suggested above.

(OR) Article 35—Assets remaining in the secondary proceedings

> If by the liquidation of assets in the secondary proceedings it is possible to meet all claims allowed under those proceedings, the liquidator appointed in those proceedings shall immediately transfer any assets remaining to the liquidator in the main proceedings.

8.428 Since the liquidator in the main proceedings will have had to lodge in the secondary proceedings the claims of creditors in the main proceedings, there may not often be a surplus in the secondary proceedings to be passed over to the main proceedings. However, the law governing the secondary proceedings may be more restrictive as to the types and amounts of claims admissible in those proceedings and that may lead to a surplus.

8.429 It is consistent with the primacy of the main proceedings that the surplus in the secondary proceedings should go to pay claims admissible in the main proceedings rather than go to the debtor. By contrast, there is no provision for any surplus in the main proceedings to go to creditors in any secondary proceedings, reflecting the supremacy of the main proceedings. In certain cases this may cause injustice: for example, if the main proceedings exclude the claims of certain creditors or part of the quantum of such claims, and they can only claim in the secondary proceedings, the surplus in the main proceedings will go to the debtor and not to the creditors in the secondary proceedings.

(OR) Article 36—Subsequent opening of the main proceedings

> When the proceedings referred to in Article 3(1) are opened following the opening of the proceedings referred to in Article 3(2) in another Member State, Articles 31

to 35 shall apply to those opened first, in so far as the progress of those proceedings so permits.

Where Article 3(2) OR proceedings are commenced prior to the commencement **8.430** of main proceedings (in accordance with Article 3(4) OR), they are not 'secondary' proceedings and may be referred to as 'independent territorial proceedings' or simply 'territorial' proceedings.[525]

[Recital (17)OR states, however, that if main proceedings are opened 'the ter- **8.431** ritorial proceedings become secondary'. The Virgos-Schmit Report similarly indicates that in such circumstances 'the proceedings opened at the place of the centre of main interests will be the main proceedings, while the proceedings previously opened at the place of the establishment *will have to be necessarily regarded as secondary proceedings*'[526] (emphasis added). This is a logical and realistic approach to the state of affairs resulting from the chronological sequence of opening of the relevant proceedings, but it can be observed that there is no formal provision within the body of the Regulation to the effect that the subsequent opening of main proceedings causes the previously-opened, Article 3(2) OR proceedings to be transformed into '*secondary proceedings*' as such. Article 36 thus provides a pragmatic solution to the problem of co-ordination between the two proceedings, while Article 37 OR enables the liquidator in the main proceedings to procure the conversion of territorial proceedings which do not qualify as 'winding-up' proceedings into one of the more limited range of proceedings listed in Annex B. In principle, however, rescue proceedings which have been commenced in the state where the debtor has an establishment, and which have been opened first in time, could continue on that basis in conjunction with rescue proceedings later opened at the debtor's centre of main interests, provided that the officeholder in the main proceedings does not choose to invoke the power available under Article 37 OR. A 'cross-border' rescue process could therefore be inaugurated, without the problems potentially engendered by the Regulation's somewhat inflexible rule that 'secondary proceedings must be winding-up proceedings'.[527] If time and circumstances so permit, it may be worthwhile in appropriate cases to arrange for the opening of concurrent, rescue-type proceedings to be co-ordinated in such a way that proceedings are first opened in those locations where the debtor has establishments, thereby enabling the 'lead' office-holder in the main proceedings to have the maximum flexibility in terms of the future conduct of the rescue process. (**IF**)]

Independent territorial proceedings cannot simply be subject to Articles 31–35 **8.432** OR in the same way as secondary proceedings, since their application may not

---

[525] As in the English statutory instruments and forms: see r 10(7) of the Insolvency (Amendment) Rules 2002, adding r 13.13(14) to the Insolvency Rules 1986.
[526] Virgos-Schmit Report para 254.
[527] Art 3(3) OR and see also Art 27 OR.

be practical in the light of how far the independent territorial proceedings have progressed. Hence, Article 36 OR provides that Articles 31–35 OR are to apply to the territorial proceedings 'in so far as the progress of those proceedings so permits'.

8.433 The more limited application of Articles 31–35 OR in such cases illustrates another tactical advantage for local creditors in requesting, where there is an establishment in the Member State, the opening of Article 3(2) OR proceedings before main proceedings are opened.

(OR) Article 37—Conversion of earlier proceedings

The liquidator in the main proceedings may request that proceedings listed in Annex A previously opened in another Member State be converted into winding-up proceedings if this proves to be in the interests of the creditors in the main proceedings.

The court with jurisdiction under Article 3(2) shall order conversion into one of the proceedings listed in Annex B.

8.434 This Article, like Article 36 OR, applies to independent territorial proceedings, which can be reorganization proceedings, whereas 'secondary' proceedings can only be winding-up proceedings listed in Annex B of the Regulation.

8.435 As part of the primary role of main proceedings, Article 37 OR provides that the liquidator in the main proceedings can request the court with jurisdiction over the independent territorial proceedings to convert them into winding-up proceedings if that proves to be in the interests of the creditors in the main proceedings. This undoubtedly gives the liquidator standing to make such an application, even where he might not have had any under the local law.[528]

8.436 Article 37 OR, in the English version, states in mandatory terms that the local court 'shall' order the conversion. This is a mistranslation, since the Virgos-Schmit Report at paragraph 258 makes it clear that conversion is not mandatory and, for example, neither the French nor German versions have the equivalent of 'shall'.[529] The amendments to the English Insolvency Rules have not treated conversion as being mandatory and in fact have given the court an express discretion as to whether to order conversion or not.[530] If conversion is ordered, it is mandatory that the proceedings be converted into a winding-up

---

[528] In England, the Insolvency Rules 1986 were amended by the Insolvency (Amendment) Rules 2002 to deal with such applications: see rr 1.31–1.33 (CVA to winding-up), 2.59–2.61 (administration order to winding-up), and 5.31–5.33 (IVA to bankruptcy).

[529] The French has *'ordonne'* (orders) and the German *'ordnet'* (orders). Notably, the English version of the equivalent provision of RR (Art 51(1)) states that '... the court ... *may* order the conversion of the secondary proceedings into another type of insolvency proceedings ...' (emphasis added).

[530] rr 1.33, 2.61, and 5.33.

proceeding and perhaps the word 'shall' in the English version can be understood in that sense.

There was plainly concern about this provision, because Portugal made a special **8.437** declaration about Article 37 OR as follows:

> Article 37 of Council Regulation (EC) No 1346/2000 of 29 May 2000 on insolvency proceedings, which mentions the possibility of converting territorial proceedings opened prior to the main proceedings into winding up proceedings, should be interpreted as meaning that such conversion does not exclude judicial appreciation of the state of the local proceedings (as is the case in Article 36) or of the application of the interests of public policy as provided for in Article 26.[531]

Thus it seems that Portugal considers that the local court can take into account the state of progress of the local proceedings in considering whether to convert them.

(OR) Article 38—Preservation measures[532]

> **Where the court of a Member State which has jurisdiction pursuant to Article 3(1) appoints a temporary administrator in order to ensure the preservation of the debtor's assets, that temporary administrator shall be empowered to request any measures to secure and preserve any of the debtor's assets situated in another Member State, provided for under the law of that State, for the period between the request for the opening of insolvency proceedings and the judgment opening the proceedings.**

There is often a gap between the 'request' (application) to open insolvency proceed- **8.438** ings and the actual 'opening'. In the meanwhile, it may well be necessary to take urgent steps both in the state of proposed opening and elsewhere. A 'temporary administrator' may well be appointed in such a situation and empowered by the appointing court to take urgent steps to safeguard assets. In the *Eurofood* case,[533] the ECJ stated:

> 57. In that respect, it should be noted that Art.38 of the Regulation must be read in combination with Art.29, according to which the liquidator in the main proceedings is entitled to request the opening of secondary proceedings in another Member State. That Art.38 thus concerns the situation in which the competent court of a Member State has had main insolvency proceedings brought before it and has appointed a person or body to watch over the debtor's assets on a provisional basis, but has not yet ordered that that debtor be divested or appointed a liquidator referred to in Annex C to the Regulation. In that case, the person or body in question, though not empowered to initiate secondary insolvency proceedings in

---

[531] The Portuguese Declaration is published at [2000] OJ C183/1.
[532] See also the discussion at paras 8.65 et seq above.
[533] Case C-341/04 *Re Eurofood IFSC Ltd* [2006] ECR I-3813, [2006] Ch 508, ECJ (Grand Chamber).

another Member State, may request that preservation measures be taken over the assets of the debtor situated in that Member State.

8.439 They went on to hold that Article 38 OR did not apply to a situation where the court had appointed a provisional liquidator listed in Annex C OR and had divested the debtor of control of his business, since that opened the proceeding and gave rise to the application of Article 29 OR, which would enable the provisional liquidator to apply for the opening of proceedings in the other Member State. This ignores the fact that by the express terms of Recital (16) OR the concept of 'temporary administrator' in Article 38 OR is meant to be understood as 'a *liquidator* temporarily appointed *prior to the opening* of the main insolvency proceedings' (emphasis added).[534] A 'temporary administrator' within Article 38 OR need not in any event be within the definition of 'liquidator' in Article 2(b) OR or be listed in Annex C.[535]

8.440 Article 38 OR specifically gives a temporary administrator in main proceedings the power to apply in another Member State for measures to secure and preserve the debtor's assets in that state available under the local law until the opening of the main proceedings. This is an important step forward in that the temporary administrator now has standing (*locus standi*) to apply in the local court, regardless of whether he had it under the local law, and he is not hindered by the fact that his appointment is only interim.

8.441 The approach of the ECJ quoted above appears to confirm the view of the Virgos-Schmit Report that this power vested in a temporary administrator can only be exercised in relation to Member States where the debtor has an 'establishment', thereby corresponding with the jurisdictional requirement for the commencement of secondary proceedings.[536] There is no such limitation expressed in the language and it may be arguable that no such limitation should be implied. It would seem to be more practical for the powers of the temporary administrator to request preservation measures to be exercisable in all Member States where the debtor has assets. Assets of the debtor in Member States where there is no establishment are just as much or more in need of being secured and preserved than those in Member States where there is an establishment. It would make more practical sense if, contrary to the apparent view of the ECJ, Articles 38 and 29 OR were regarded as having independent operation, with Article 29 applying (as a result of its express reference to opening 'secondary proceedings') only to cases where there is an 'establishment' in the other Member State and Article 38 applying more generally.

---

[534] See also the commentary under Art 3, sub-heading 'The concept of Opening' at paras 8.80 et seq above.
[535] Virgos-Schmit Report para 263.
[536] ibid para 262.

D. Chapter IV: Provision of Information for Creditors and Lodgement of their Claims

(OR) Article 39—Right to lodge claims

> Any creditor who has his habitual residence, domicile or registered office in a Member State other than the State of the opening of proceedings, including the tax authorities and social security authorities of Member States, shall have the right to lodge claims in the insolvency proceedings in writing.

Article 32(1) OR read with Article 36 OR has already provided for the right **8.442** of creditors to lodge claims in both the main and Article 3(2) OR proceedings. Article 39 OR identifies the type of non-domestic creditor who is entitled to lodge claims in the proceedings in question. The right to lodge claims is linked, not to nationality, but to residence and domicile. It prevents discrimination against creditors resident or domiciled or incorporated in other Member States.

There is a considerable advance in Article 39 OR in that the tax and social **8.443** security authorities of other Member States are expressly entitled to lodge claims; therefore the principle, which can be found in the law of most states, that foreign tax laws will not be enforced does not apply to the lodging of claims by creditors in proceedings to which the Regulation applies.[537] The Regulation in this regard stands in contrast to the successive iterations of the Regulation on Civil Jurisdiction and Judgments which expressly exclude revenue and customs matters from its scope.[538] It is considered that as a result of the specific inclusion of tax and social security authorities of other Member States the Article 26 OR public policy exception cannot be used to block such claims.

[On the other hand, Article 39 OR does not grant foreign tax claims the prior- **8.444** ity they may enjoy in their countries of origin (priority for domestic tax claims exists in, for example, Swedish law). This means that the tax authorities of such countries will probably request, whenever possible, the opening of secondary proceedings in order to preserve their priority rights at least in relation to the local assets. (**MB**)]

Although the right to lodge claims is a substantive right under the Regulation, all **8.445** procedural matters governing the process of lodging are governed by the relevant

---

[537] As to the rule against the enforcement of foreign revenue laws see Dicey, Morris, and Collins, *The Conflict of Laws* (14th edn, 2006) paras 5-020 et seq.

[538] Art 1(1) of the EU Regulation on Civil Jurisdiction and Judgments (recast) (1215/2012), which has applied since 10 January 2015, and which is identically worded to Art 1(1) of the original version of the Civil Jurisdiction and Judgments Regulation (44/2001).

national law which applies to the proceedings in question (Article 4(2)(h) OR). Thus matters such as time limits for lodging claims and the conditions for admissibility of claims are to be dealt with under the law governing the proceedings (*lex concursus*).

[The same applies to the form of lodging of claims: Article 39 OR speaks of lodging 'in writing', but this means merely that the written submission of a claim must be accepted as if done in proper form. The law governing the proceedings may accept a submission in another form. (**MB**)]

8.446 It is important to note that Article 39 OR is concerned only with the rights of those creditors who have a habitual residence, domicile, or registered office in a Member State.[539] The rights of creditors situated outside the European Union and in Denmark are governed, like the rights of domestic creditors, solely by the law governing the proceedings.

(OR) Article 40—Duty to inform creditors

> 1. As soon as insolvency proceedings are opened in a Member State, the court of that State having jurisdiction or the liquidator appointed by it shall immediately inform known creditors who have their habitual residences, domiciles or registered offices in the other Member States.
> 2. That information, provided by an individual notice, shall in particular include time limits, the penalties laid down in regard to those time limits, the body or authority empowered to accept the lodgement of claims and the other measures laid down. Such notice shall also indicate whether creditors whose claims are preferential or secured in rem need lodge their claims.

8.447 Since there is as yet no EU register of insolvency proceedings,[540] it is particularly important that either the court opening the proceedings or the liquidator[541] appointed should be obliged to inform all known creditors situated in other Member States.

8.448 [The law governing the proceedings may prescribe that creditors shall be given additional information, not listed in Article 40(2) OR, but it cannot dispense with any of the requirements listed there. (**MB**)]

---

[539] In considering the domicile of companies and other legal persons it will probably be helpful to have regard to Art 63 of the recast Jurisdiction and Judgments Regulation 1215/2012 (Art 60 of the Regulation on Civil Jurisdiction and Judgments 44/2001). This provides that any such entity will be domiciled at the place where it has its (a) statutory seat or (b) central administration, or (c) principal place of business. Art 63(2) of Regulation 1215/2012 provides that in the case of Ireland, Cyprus, and the UK 'statutory seat' means the registered office (or if none, the place of incorporation). The expression 'registered office' used in Art 40 OR is probably equivalent to the expression 'statutory seat' used in Regulations 1215/2012 and 44/2001.

[540] Provisions are made for registers in the RR – see below.

[541] [Without aligning domestic legislation it will be unclear whether the obligation to inform rests on the court or on the liquidator. (**Wess**)]

The sensitive question of the language of notification is dealt with in **8.449**
Article 42(1) OR.

(OR) Article 41—Content of the lodgement of a claim

A creditor shall send copies of supporting documents, if any, and shall indicate the
nature of the claim, the date on which it arose and its amount, as well as whether
he alleges preference, security in rem or a reservation of title in respect of the claim
and what assets are covered by the guarantee he is invoking.

Article 41 OR constitutes an exception to the rule stated in Article 4(2)(h) OR that **8.450**
the lodging of claims is a matter governed by the national law applying to the proceedings in question (see also Article 39 OR and Article 42(2) OR). This provision
is intended to facilitate the exercise by creditors in Member States other than the
state where the proceedings were commenced to exercise their right under Article
39 OR to lodge a claim in those proceedings.[542] Accordingly, Article 41 OR prevents the relevant national law from imposing restrictions, other than those stated
in Article 41 OR itself, on the lodging of claims. However, Article 41 does require
a creditor to submit all that information which is necessary for the liquidator to
identify and deal with his claim.

The English text once again has linguistic problems and should not be read **8.451**
literally.

'Alleges preference'

'Preference' in this context cannot have the usual English insolvency law meaning **8.452**
of better treatment of one out of a class of creditors having the *same* ranking. In this
context the phrase here must mean 'claim preferential ranking'.

'Security in rem'

Taken literally, this would be a tautology in English insolvency law terms, since a **8.453**
'security' within section 248(b)(i) of the Insolvency Act 1986 would be a right *in
rem*, ie a proprietary right. In this context, 'security' must include non-proprietary
rights, so that the entire phrase means 'security' in the English insolvency law sense.

'Guarantee'

In English law, this would normally refer to a contract of suretyship creating a **8.454**
secondary personal liability.[543] In the present context it refers to the means of
ensuring payment, whether by means of preferential ranking, proprietary security,
or retention of title.[544]

---

[542] Virgos-Schmit Report para 273.
[543] See Rowlatt, *Principal and Surety* (6th edn, 2011) ch 1.
[544] In the German version *'sicherheit'* ('security' in a wide sense) is used both for 'security' in the
phrase corresponding to 'security in rem' and for 'guarantee'.

(OR) Article 42—Languages

1. The information provided for in Article 40 shall be provided in the official language or one of the official languages of the State of the opening of proceedings. For that purpose a form shall be used bearing the heading 'Invitation to lodge a claim. Time limits to be observed' in all the official languages of the institutions of the European Union.
2. Any creditor who has his habitual residence, domicile or registered office in a Member State other than the State of the opening of proceedings may lodge his claim in the official language or one of the official languages of that other State. In that event, however, the lodgement of his claim shall bear the heading 'Lodgement of claim' in the official language or one of the official languages of the State of the opening of proceedings. In addition, he may be required to provide a translation into the official language or one of the official languages of the State of the opening of proceedings.

8.455 Article 42 provides for rules governing the language in which creditors are to be notified of proceedings and in which they can lodge their claims. Again the aim of this provision is to facilitate the exercise by creditors in all Member States of their rights in relation to all proceedings wherever commenced. The provision tries to balance the difficulties for the 'liquidator' on the one hand in dealing with foreign language documents against the difficulties faced by a creditor in trying to claim in foreign language proceedings.

8.456 Article 42(1) OR deals with the notices to be sent to creditors informing them of proceedings pursuant to Article 40 OR. Such notices are to be provided in the official language (or one of the official languages) of the state of the opening of proceedings. The liquidator cannot tell whether any particular creditor will be able to understand this language and the onus is on creditors to obtain translations where necessary. [The creditor will, in any case, become aware of the nature of the notification, as it must be made on a form bearing the heading 'Invitation to lodge a claim. Time limits to be observed' in all the official languages of the European Union. The form will be produced by the Secretariat of the Council. (**MB**)]

8.457 Article 42(2) OR deals with the lodging of claims by creditors. In relation to this, it is open to a creditor who is situated in a state other than the state of the relevant proceedings to submit his claim in an official language of the state in which he is situated. In this way the Regulation makes it easier for creditors in other Member States to exercise their rights in insolvency proceedings.

8.458 However, Article 42(2) OR also provides that any claim must be headed 'Lodgement of claim' in the official language of the state of the opening of proceedings. This means that even if the liquidator does not understand the language in which the claim is lodged he knows that the document is the lodging of a claim. He can then, under Article 42(2) OR, require a translation into an official language of the state of the opening of proceedings.

In *R Jung GmbH v SIFA SA*,[545] SIFA was in French administration proceedings **8.459** and under French law claims had to be lodged by creditors within four months of the official date for the onset of insolvency, 5 December 2003. The German creditor Jung had lodged a claim document on 10 November 2003. The time for lodging the claim expired on 5 April 2004. On 12 May 2004 the creditors' representative informed Jung that he would be recommending rejection of the claim as not being valid under French law because of a failure to prove the authority of the person lodging the claim. On 24 May 2004 Jung's claim was lodged again signed by an officer of Jung and in a subsequent letter it was explained that this officer was the managing director (*Geschäftsführer*) of Jung. Although Jung's claim was not contested on its merits, the Tribunal de Commerce[546] of Orleans rejected the claim. The Court of Appeal in Orleans reversed this decision and allowed the claim on the basis that there had been a failure to comply with Article 42: the invitation to make claims had only been in French and the heading 'Invitation to lodge a claim. Time limits to be observed' required by Article 42 had not been supplied in the official languages of the European Union and in particular had not been supplied in the language of the creditor, German. The Court of Appeal held that in these circumstances the only remedy which would give effect to Articles 40(1) and 42 OR was to extend the time allowed by French law for the lodging of the German creditor's claim. Jung's claim was thus accepted as being valid.

E. Chapter V: Transitional and Final Provisions

(OR) Article 43—Applicability in time

> The provisions of this Regulation shall apply only to insolvency proceedings opened after its entry into force. Acts done by a debtor before the entry into force of this Regulation shall continue to be governed by the law which was applicable to them at the time they were done.

The OR applies only to insolvency proceedings commenced after 31 May 2002 **8.460** (for the commencement date see Article 47 OR). It has no retrospective application. Although repealed by the RR, the OR will continue to govern insolvency proceedings within the scope of the OR opened before 26 June 2017: Article 84(2) RR.

[As the Regulation is based on a sophisticated interplay between main and sec- **8.461** ondary proceedings, it must be assumed that it applies only if both proceedings

---

[545] [2006] BCC 678.
[546] This type of court is not a 'commercial' court in the English sense, as the judges are part-time and not legally qualified.

were commenced after the Regulation's entry into force. Even after the entry into force it is, therefore, impossible to open secondary proceedings governed by the Regulation, if there are no main proceedings opened after 31 May 2002. (**MB**)]

8.462 [Some uncertainty may arise for acts of the debtor (or his representatives and employees) done before 31 May 2002, but done conditionally, coming in fact into effect after 31 May 2002. (**Wess**)]

8.463 In *Re Ultra Motorhomes International Ltd* [547] a CVA proceeding listed in Annex A was opened prior to the coming into force of the Regulation and a liquidation proceeding was opened in respect of the same debtor after the Regulation came into force. Under English law the two proceedings can in principle both continue, no automatic relation back to the start of the CVA takes place, and the Supervisor of the CVA (listed as a 'liquidator' in Annex C OR) can operate independently of the liquidation. It was held that proceedings by the Supervisor could not fall within the Regulation, even if they took place during the liquidation, which was a main proceeding under the Regulation.

(OR) Article 44—Relationship to Conventions

1. After its entry into force, this Regulation replaces, in respect of the matters referred to therein, in the relations between Member States, the Conventions concluded between two or more Member States, in particular:
   (a) the Convention between Belgium and France on Jurisdiction and the Validity and Enforcement of Judgments, Arbitration Awards and Authentic Instruments, signed at Paris on 8 July 1899;
   (b) the Convention between Belgium and Austria on Bankruptcy, Winding-up, Arrangements, Compositions and Suspension of Payments (with Additional Protocol of 13 June 1973), signed at Brussels on 16 July 1969;
   (c) the Convention between Belgium and the Netherlands on Territorial Jurisdiction, Bankruptcy and the Validity and Enforcement of Judgments, Arbitration Awards and Authentic Instruments, signed at Brussels on 28 March 1925;
   (d) the Treaty between Germany and Austriaon Bankruptcy, Winding-up, Arrangements and Compositions, signed at Vienna on 25 May 1979;
   (e) the Convention between France and Austria on Jurisdiction, Recognition and Enforcement of Judgments on Bankruptcy, signed at Vienna on 27 February 1979;
   (f) the Convention between France and Italy on the Enforcement of Judgments in Civil and Commercial Matters, signed at Rome on 3 June 1930;
   (g) the Convention between Italy and Austriaon Bankruptcy, Winding-up, Arrangements and Compositions, signed at Rome on 12 July 1977;
   (h) the Convention between the Kingdom of the Netherlands and the Federal Republic of Germany on the Mutual Recognition and Enforcement of

---

[547] [2006] BCC 57.

Judgments and other Enforceable Instruments in Civil and Commercial Matters, signed at The Hague on 30 August 1962;

(i) the Convention between the United Kingdom and the Kingdom of Belgium providing for the Reciprocal Enforcement of Judgments in Civil and Commercial Matters, with Protocol, signed at Brussels on 2 May 1934;

(j) the Convention between Denmark, Finland, Norway, Sweden and Iceland on Bankruptcy, signed at Copenhagen on 7 November 1933;

(k) the European Convention on Certain International Aspects of Bankruptcy, signed at Istanbul on 5 June 1990.

(l) the Convention between the Federative People's Republic of Yugoslavia and the Kingdom of Greece on the Mutual Recognition and Enforcement of Judgments, signed at Athens on 18 June1959;[548]

(m) the Agreement between the Federative People's Republic of Yugoslavia and the Republic of Austria on the Mutual Recognition and Enforcement of Arbitral Awards and Arbitral Settlements in Commercial Matters, signed at Belgrade on 18 March 1960;

(n) the Convention between the Federative People's Republic of Yugoslavia and the Republic of Italy on Mutual Judicial Cooperation in Civil and Administrative Matters, signed at Rome on 3 December1960;

(o) the Agreement between the Socialist Federative Republic of Yugoslavia and the Kingdom of Belgium on Judicial Cooperation in Civil and Commercial Matters, signed at Belgrade on 24 September1971;

(p) the Convention between the Governments of Yugoslavia and France on the Recognition and Enforcement of Judgments in Civil and Commercial Matters, signed at Paris on 18 May1971;

(q) the Agreement between the Czechoslovak Socialist Republic and the Hellenic Republic on Legal Aid in Civil and Criminal Matters, signed at Athens on 22 October1980, still in force between the Czech Republic and Greece;

(r) the Agreement between the Czechoslovak Socialist Republic and the Republic of Cypruson Legal Aid in Civil and Criminal Matters, signed at Nicosiaon 23 April 1982, still in force between the Czech Republic and Cyprus;

(s) the Treaty between the Government of the Czechoslovak Socialist Republic and the Government of the Republic of France on Legal Aid and the Recognition and Enforcement of Judgments in Civil, Family and Commercial Matters, signed at Paris on 10 May1984, still in force between the Czech Republic and France;

(t) the Treaty between the Czechoslovak Socialist Republic and the Italian Republic on Legal Aid in Civil and Criminal Matters, signed at Prague on 6 December 1985, still in force between the Czech Republic and Italy;

(u) the Agreement between the Republic of Latvia, the Republic of Estonia and the Republic of Lithuania on Legal Assistance and Legal Relationships, signed at Tallinn on 11 November 1992;

---

[548] S 18A of Annex 2 to the Act of Accession relating to the accession of Cyprus, the Czech Republic, Estonia, Hungary, Latvia, Lithuania, Malta, Poland, Slovakia, and Slovenia, under the heading 'Cooperation in the fields of justice and home affairs': [2003] OJ L236/711–13 added sub-paras (l)–(w) to Art 44(1).

(v)   the Agreement between Estonia and Poland on Granting Legal Aid and Legal Relations on Civil, Labour and Criminal Matters, signed at Tallinn on 27 November 1998;

(w) the Agreement between the Republic of Lithuania and the Republic of Poland on Legal Assistance and Legal Relations in Civil, Family, Labour and Criminal Matters, signed in Warsaw on 26 January 1993;

(x)   the Convention between Socialist Republic of Romania and the Hellenic Republic on legal assistance in civil and criminal matters and its Protocol, signed at Bucharest on 19 October 1972;

(y)   the Convention between Socialist Republic of Romania and the French Republic on legal assistance in civil and commercial matters, signed at Paris on 5 November 1974;

(z)   the Agreement between the People's Republic of Bulgaria and the Hellenic Republic on Legal Assistance in Civil and Criminal Matters, signed at Athens on 10 April 1976;

(aa) the Agreement between the People's Republic of Bulgaria and the Republic of Cyprus on Legal Assistance in Civil and Criminal Matters, signed at Nicosia on 29 April 1983;

(ab) the Agreement between the Government of the People's Republic of Bulgaria and the Government of the French Republicon Mutual Legal Assistance in Civil Matters, signed at Sofia on 18 January 1989;

(ac) the Treaty between Romania and the Czech Republic on judicial assistance in civil matters, signed at Bucharest on 11 July 1994;

(ad) the Treaty between Romania and Poland on legal assistance and legal relations in civil cases, signed at Bucharest on 15 May 1999.

2. The Conventions referred to in paragraph 1 shall continue to have effect with regard to proceedings opened before the entry into force of this Regulation.

3. This Regulation shall not apply:

(a)   in any Member State, to the extent that it is irreconcilable with the obligations arising in relation to bankruptcy from a convention concluded by that State with one or more third countries before the entry into force of this Regulation;

(b)   in the United Kingdom of Great Britain and Northern Ireland, to the extent that is irreconcilable with the obligations arising in relation to bankruptcy and the winding-up of insolvent companies from any arrangements with the Commonwealth existing at the time this Regulation enters into force.

8.464   Article 43(3)(b) OR, as far as England is concerned, appears to be a rather oblique reference to section 426 of the Insolvency Act 1986. Section 426 obliges the English courts to assist insolvency proceedings from countries specified by delegated legislation where a request has been made for assistance by the relevant foreign court. The English Court of Appeal has held that the giving of assistance under section 426 is not mandatory although the court should assist if it is properly able to do so.[549]

---

[549]   *Hughes v Hannover Ruckversicherungs AG* [1996] 1 BCLC 497. See also *Re Southern Equities Corp; England v Smith* [2000] 2 BCLC 21, CA, the reasoning of which is not easy to reconcile with *Hughes*. See also the discussion of s 426 in ch 5 above.

The designated countries are, except for the Republic of Ireland and (since the hand- **8.465** over to China) Hong Kong, all members of the Commonwealth.[550] The effect of Article 43(3)(b) therefore appears to be that section 426 will take precedence over the provisions of the Regulation in relation to requests for assistance from the courts of Commonwealth countries or territories which were designated under section 426 on 31 May 2002. In relation to the Republic of Ireland and Hong Kong, it appears that the provisions of the Regulation will prevail, in the event of any conflict, over any request for assistance made in accordance with section 426 so that any assistance may only be granted to the extent consistent with the provisions of the Regulation.

(OR) Article 45—Amendment of the Annexes

> The Council, acting by qualified majority on the initiative of one of its members or on a proposal from the Commission, may amend the Annexes.

The Annexes, which detail the various insolvency proceedings governed by the **8.466** Regulation, can be amended from time to time. This covers the possibility that new insolvency procedures may be introduced in Member States which will then need to be regulated by the Regulation.

The Annexes have in fact been amended by means of amending or implementing **8.467** Regulations[551] several times and a consolidated version appears in Appendix 1. Additional changes have resulted from the accession of new Member States and changes to insolvency proceedings in Member States.

[It must be stressed that the Member State concerned does not have the right **8.468** to amend the Annexes by itself, but must ask the Council to do so. In fact, the Annexes can be amended even against the will of the Member State in question. (**MB**)]

(OR) Article 46—Reports

> No later than 1 June 2012, and every five years thereafter, the Commission shall present to the European Parliament, the Council and the Economic and Social

---

[550] The Co-operation of Insolvency Courts (Designation of Relevant Countries and Territories) Order 1986, SI 1986/2123 designated (1) the Republic of Ireland, (2) the 10 UK Overseas Territories (Anguilla, Bermuda, Cayman Islands, Falkland Islands, Gibraltar, Hong Kong, Montserrat, St Helena, Turks and Caicos Islands, and the Virgin Islands), and (3) 6 independent members of the Commonwealth (Australia, the Bahamas, Botswana, Canada, New Zealand, and Tuvalu). The Co-operation of Insolvency Courts (Designation of Relevant Countries) Order 1996, SI 1996/253 designated South Africa and Malaysia, and the Co-operation of Insolvency Courts (Designation of Relevant Countries) Order 1998, SI 1998/2766 designated Brunei Darussalam, all three countries being independent members of the Commonwealth. However, when Hong Kong rejoined the People's Republic of China as a Special Administrative Region, it ceased to be part of the Commonwealth.

[551] Council Regulations (EC) 603/2005, 694/2006, 1791/2006, 681/2007, 788/2008, 210/2010, and 663/2014. Full references to these amending Regulations are supplied in ch 1, Section E, above, in nn 45–51. See also n 53.

Committee a report on the application of this Regulation. The report shall be accompanied if need be by a proposal for adaptation of this Regulation.

8.469   This automatic review provision compares favourably to legislation in England, where such a provision is not usually found. The report was in fact submitted on 12 December 2012 (12/12/12). This sytem of review is being displaced by the new system in the RR—see below.

(OR) Article 47—Entry into force

This Regulation shall enter into force on 31 May 2002.

8.470   [See also Article 43 OR, which provides that the Regulation has no retrospective effect. **(IF)**]

8.471   The concluding sentence of the Regulation declares that it is binding in its entirety and directly applicable in the Member States in accordance with the Treaty establishing the European Community.[552]

---

[552] See Art 249 EC reproduced at app 4 below.

Recast Regulation 2015/848 on Insolvency Proceedings ('RR')

A. Chapter I: General Provisions

(RR) Article 1—Scope

1. This Regulation shall apply to public collective proceedings, including interim proceedings, which are based on laws relating to insolvency and in which, for the purpose of rescue, adjustment of debt, reorganisation or liquidation:

(a) a debtor is totally or partially divested of its assets and an insolvency practitioner is appointed;

(b) the assets and affairs of a debtor are subject to control or supervision by a court; or

(c) a temporary stay of individual enforcement proceedings is granted by a court or by operation of law, in order to allow for negotiations between the debtor and its creditors, provided that the proceedings in which the stay is granted provide for suitable measures to protect the general body of creditors, and, where no agreement is reached, are preliminary to one of the proceedings referred to in point (a) or (b).

Where the proceedings referred to in this paragraph may be commenced in situations where there is only a likelihood of insolvency, their purpose shall be to avoid the debtor's insolvency or the cessation of the debtor's business activities.

The proceedings referred to in this paragraph are listed in Annex A.

2. This Regulation shall not apply to proceedings referred to in paragraph 1 that concern:

    (a) insurance undertakings;

    (b) credit institutions

    (c) investment firms and other firms, institutions and undertakings to the extent that they are covered by Directive 2001/24/EC; or

    (d) collective investment undertakings.

8.472 Despite the original Article 1 confining the scope of the OR to 'insolvency proceedings', the list of such proceedings in Annex A OR was not, even at the start, limited to insolvency proceedings in any strict sense. For example, Annex A OR included UK administration proceedings, which do not require proof of actual insolvency but only that the corporate debtor was likely to become insolvent.

8.473 Despite the original definition in the original Article 1, even more clearly pre-insolvency proceedings such as the French *sauvegarde* proceeding were added by amendment to Annex A OR. *Sauvegarde* is in fact a proceeding which the debtor must not be insolvent in the French law sense when the proceeding is opened.

8.474 The newly worded Article 1 brings the position up to date and covers both insolvency and pre-insolvency proceedings. It also clearly brings within the scope of the Recast Regulation (RR) proceedings which involve a debtor in possession.

8.475 Very importantly, the RR has kept the principle established by the *Bank Handlowy* case (C-116/11) of the CJEU to the effect that, in the case of a conflict between the definition in Article 1 and Annex A, Annex A will prevail: see the definition of 'insolvency proceedings' in Article 2(4) RR and Recital (9) RR which provides, in so far as material:

> Those insolvency proceedings are listed exhaustively in Annex A. In respect of the national procedures contained in Annex A, this Regulation should apply without any further examination by the courts of another Member State as to whether the conditions set out in this Regulation are met. National insolvency procedures not listed in Annex A should not be covered by this Regulation.

The conditions set out in the new Article 1 will however still be significant when questions arise as to whether any further national insolvency or pre-insolvency proceeding should be added to RR Annex A.[1]

Proceedings must be public

8.476 The first condition that must be fulfilled by proceedings to fall within the Regulation is that they must be public. The intention of the Council in proposing this was that proceedings within the scope of the Regulation should be subject to publicity in

---

[1] A Commission proposal to act as gatekeeper in relation to the addition of proceedings to Annex A was not accepted and additions will have to be made by Amending Regulation(s). The original Regulation Art 45 procedure for amending annexes by qualified majority has not been retained by the RR.

order to identify the claims and creditors and, by that means ensure the collective nature of the proceedings and give creditors a possibility to challenge the jurisdiction of the court. This point is now made by Recital (12) RR.

This requirement causes no particular problems in England, where the public is **8.477** already admitted into all insolvency proceedings hearings, unless there is some special reason to do with commercial confidentiality for excluding the public from all or part of the hearing. The actual opening of an insolvency proceeding will always be a public matter.

One aspect of the requirement that the proceedings should be public is the Council's **8.478** wish to exclude insolvency proceedings which are confidential. Some proceedings under the laws of some Member States, such as France, take the form of negotiations between the debtor and certain creditors with a view to reaching an agreement on the debtor's refinancing or reorganization. Such proceedings are notified to the court but are not made public. The Council considered that the confidential nature of such proceedings made it impossible for a creditor or a court in another Member State to know that such proceedings were pending. In the light of this, it would be difficult to provide for the recognition of their effects throughout the EU. This point is made in Recital (13) RR.

Proceedings must be collective

This was an express requirement of the original text[2] and is therefore not a change. **8.479** Proceedings such as receivership, when it takes the form of a secured creditor's remedy, in England or Ireland, remain outside the scope of the Recast Regulation.

The term 'collective' was not defined in the OR but is now defined in Article 2(1) **8.480** RR. As well as the obvious case of proceedings including all of the debtor's creditors, the definition covers proceedings which include 'a significant part' of a debtor's creditors, with the proviso that the proceedings do not affect the claims of creditors which are not involved in them. The wider definition is particularly significant for pre-insolvency restructuring proceedings, which may for example only affect financial creditors, but not trade creditors. That potential situation is expressly referred to in Recital (14) RR.

The term 'a significant part' is rather vague, but Recital (14) RR suggests that it **8.481** refers to creditors to whom the debtor 'owes … a substantial proportion of the debtor's outstanding debts …'. Presumably, 'outstanding' does not imply that the debts have to be immediately due and payable, otherwise that would seriously restrict the ability of pre-insolvency proceedings to fall within the RR.

Recital (14) RR also suggests that proceedings which do not include all the credi- **8.482** tors '… should be proceedings aimed at rescuing the debtor'. That is contrasted

---

[2] See the commentary above on the original text of the Regulation.

with proceedings which lead to the 'definitive' cessation of business or liquidation of assets, which ought to include all creditors.

8.483 Recital (14) RR further suggests that in the case of natural persons the proceedings will be regarded as collective even if certain types of claims, such as maintenance claims, are not discharged. In English law as in the systems of other Member States there are exceptions to the general discharge of debts in individual insolvency and Recital (14) RR ensures that these will still be regarded as collective proceedings.

Proceedings can be 'interim proceedings'

8.484 The Council proposed the express inclusion of 'interim proceedings', so as expressly to cover proceedings which, under the law of some Member States, could be opened and conducted for a certain period of time on an interim or provisional basis, before the court issues an order confirming the continuation of the proceedings on a non-interim basis. The Council however wished it to be clear that such interim proceedings need to comply with all the criteria set out in Article 1 RR, and that the only difference was that the proceedings would be conducted for a period of time on an interim or provisional basis. This point is now made in Recital (15) RR.

8.485 Presumably the concept of interim proceedings is meant to cover such things as the appointment of a provisional liquidator under English, Irish, or German law. The appointment of a provisional liquidator under Irish law was held in the circumstances of the *Eurofood* case (C-341/04) to constitute the opening of a proceeding within the OR.[3]

Proceedings must be 'based on laws relating to insolvency'

8.486 The Recast Regulation requires proceedings covered by the RR to be 'based on laws relating to insolvency', but this does not prevent pre-insolvency proceedings being included, as long as they are provided by laws relating to insolvency. The Council's proposal here was to clarify the fact that proceedings not based on a law relating to insolvency but which are based on general company law not designed exclusively for insolvency situations should not be included in the Regulation. This point is now made in Recital (16) RR. Recital (16) RR also suggests the exclusion of specific types of proceedings in which the debts of an individual of very low income and low asset value are written off, as long as there is no provision for payment to creditors.

8.487 The requirement that proceedings be based on laws relating to insolvency and the express exclusion in Recital (16) RR of proceedings based on general company law not designed exclusively for insolvency situations is very significant for England. That is because the proceeding known in England as a Scheme of Arrangement,

---

[3] See the commentary to Art 3 of the original Regulation.

currently under Part 26 of the Companies Act 2006, often operates *de facto* as a pre-insolvency proceeding for companies. However, the proceedings are provided by general company law and not by any insolvency law and Schemes of Arrangement are also available in situations of complete and undoubted insolvency, including situations where only the shareholders and not the creditors are involved. Schemes of Arrangement will therefore not fall under the Regulation.

The purpose of proceedings must be rescue, adjustment of debt, reorganization, or liquidation

The Council wished to have a Recital clarifying that the term 'adjustment of debt' should cover *inter alia* a reduction in the amount to be paid by the debtor or an extension of the payment period granted to the debtor. In the text of the OR, an adjustment of debt or composition was mentioned only as a mode of closing an insolvency proceeding: see the old Article 25(1). However in England, as a result of voluntary arrangements being added to Annex A OR, proceedings for adjustment of debt were already included in the Regulation. **8.488**

Recital (10) RR clarifies that the scope of the RR extends to rescue and restructuring proceedings, including those where the debtor remains in possession. The Recital also makes it clear that such proceedings include those for a debt discharge or a debt adjustment in relation to consumers and self-employed persons. **8.489**

Proceedings must be one of three types

As well as the requirement that the purpose of proceedings within the RR must be for 'rescue, adjustment of debt, reorganisation or liquidation', proceedings, to be within the RR, must be one of three kinds. **8.490**

Proceeding type (a) is one in which the debtor is totally or partially divested of its assets and an insolvency practitioner is appointed. The divesting requirement was present in the original Article 1(1). The reference in the old provision to a 'liquidator' being appointed has been replaced by the broader and more inclusive 'insolvency practitioner', which is already used in the UK to cover the different types of insolvency administrator who can come within the Regulation.[4] The definitive list of such persons was contained in the original Annex C and is now contained in Annex B RR. The term 'insolvency practitioner' is defined in Article 2(5) RR. When considering whether or not an 'insolvency practitioner' has been appointed in a particular proceeding in an EU Member State, a court in another Member State should only have to consult the new Annex B and should not be obliged to consider whether an 'insolvency practitioner' in fact has any of the functions set out **8.491**

---

[4] See Annex C of the original Regulation and RR Annex B. See also Insolvency Act 1986, Part XIII (ss 388–398) which bears the heading: 'Insolvency Practitioners and their Qualification'. Although the expression 'insolvency practitioner' is thus familiar to those with knowledge of UK insolvency law, it must be remembered that for the purposes of the RR its meaning is controlled by Art 2(5) RR together with Annex B RR, as explained below.

in Article 2(5)(i)–(v) RR. That is because the definition itself cross-refers to Annex B. A similar cross-reference in the OR led to the list in Annex A OR being regarded as conclusive by the CJEU: *Bank Handlowy* (C-116/11).

8.492 A type (b) proceeding is one in which the assets and affairs of the debtor are subject to 'control or supervision by a court'. Some proceedings already listed in Annex A do not necessarily involve 'control or supervision' by a court, for example voluntary liquidation in the UK and voluntary arrangements in the UK. Recital (10) RR explains that proceedings can be within the RR on the basis that in this context 'control' includes situations where the court only intervenes on an 'appeal' by a creditor or other interested party. Here, the word 'appeal' must be a reference to an application. In some countries, such as France, the equivalent word to 'appeal' refers to or includes an application by a third party such as a creditor or other interested party. For the UK and Ireland, the expression is unfortunate, because 'appeal' is only used to refer to applications to a higher court and not to the same court or a court of co-ordinate jurisdiction.

8.493 Nevertheless, Recital (10) RR makes it clear that proceedings such as voluntary liquidation and voluntary arrangements are correctly included in the RR, assuming other criteria are met.

8.494 The word 'court' is defined in Article 2(6) below RR.[5] Importantly, it includes both judicial and other competent bodies of a Member State empowered to either open proceedings, to confirm such an opening, or to take decisions in the course of such proceedings. So for example in the case of a voluntary liquidation confirmed by the court, the role of the judicial body in England is to confirm the opening, if it is to fall within the Regulation. In the case of corporate voluntary arrangements, the court's role is to take decisions in the course of the proceedings if an application is made to it by a party with standing to do so.

8.495 A type (c) proceeding involves a temporary stay of individual enforcement proceedings granted by a court or by operation of law, in order to allow for negotiations between the debtor and its creditors. There is a proviso that the proceedings in which the stay is granted must provide for suitable measures to protect the general body of creditors and, where no agreement is reached, the proceedings must be preliminary to a type (a) or (b) proceeding.

8.496 The Council proposal suggested that a Recital should clarify that the scope of the RR should extend to procedures where the court orders a temporary moratorium on enforcement actions brought by individual creditors where such actions may adversely affect negotiations and hamper the prospects of a restructuring of the debtor's business. This is now Recital (11) RR. That Recital also states that such procedures should not be detrimental to the general body of creditors and that, if

---

[5] See also Recital (20) RR.

no agreement on the restructuring plan can be reached, should be preliminary to other procedures covered by the RR.

Type (c) proceedings may often occur where there is no present insolvency in the **8.497** sense of the law of the relevant Member State and only a 'likelihood of insolvency'. In such cases, the coda to Article 1(1) RR specifies that the purpose of the proceedings 'shall be to avoid the debtor's insolvency or the cessation of the debtor's business activities'. This should not be a difficult criterion to meet in most cases of this kind.

Recital (10) RR specifically refers to cases within the RR where there is only a 'likeli- **8.498** hood of insolvency' and links it to cases where there may be a debtor in possession.

[Article 1(1)(c) RR refers to pre-insolvency proceedings where the debtor remains **8.499** in full control of his assets and affairs, ie without any court supervision, but restricts the creditors' individual rights with a temporary moratorium on enforcement actions to allow for negotiations between the debtor and his creditors to reach a refinancing or restructuring agreement. In this case, however, the RR lays down additional safeguards: (i) the proceedings must provide for suitable measures to protect the general body of creditors and (ii) they must be preliminary to one of the other two types of proceedings if no agreement is reached. Spanish pre-insolvency proceedings are a typical example of the proceedings envisaged by Article 1(1)(c). According to Article 5bis (1) and (4) of the Spanish Insolvency Act,

> (T)he debtor may notify the Court which is competent to open insolvency proceedings that it has started negotiations with a view to reach a refinancing agreement [...]. From the submission of the notification, no judicial or extrajudicial enforcement proceedings may be initiated on assets or rights that are necessary for the continuation of the debtor's professional or corporate activity until [...] the formalization of the refinancing agreement.

If no agreement is reached within three months from such notification, the debtor must file for insolvency (Article 5bis(5) of the Spanish Insolvency Act).

The jurisdiction to open these types of pre-insolvency proceedings is now governed **8.500** by Article 3 RR and their cross-border effects by Articles 19 and 32 RR. Thus, for example, if a Spanish company has entered into negotiations with its creditors to restructure its liabilities in accordance with Article 5bis of the Spanish Insolvency Act (and included in Annex A), the affected creditors will be prevented from initiating individual enforcement proceedings not only in Spain but also in other Member States, and no main insolvency proceedings may be opened in other Member States. A judgment confirming a restructuring plan or a debt discharge will also be recognized and produce effects in the rest of the Member States under those provisions. However, a temporary moratorium: (i) may not affect the rights in rem of creditors or third parties over assets located in other Member States (see Article 8 RR); and (ii) it may only temporarily stay the opening of secondary proceedings in accordance with Article 38(3) RR for a maximum period of three months and provided that suitable measures to protect the interests of the local creditors are in place. (**MV/FG**)]

'Non-financial' difficulties

8.501 The Council proposal suggested that a Recital be added clarifying that the scope of the RR may extend to cover proceedings which are triggered by situations in which the debtor faces what are referred to as 'non-financial' difficulties, provided that such difficulties give rise to a real and serious threat to the debtor's actual or future ability to pay his debts as they fall due. The time horizon for the determination of such a threat may extend to a period of several months or even longer. The example that is given is where the debtor has lost a contract which is of key importance to him. These points are now set out in Recital (17) RR.

The oddity from the point of view of English law is that what are described as non-financial difficulties, such as losing a key contract, would in England be categorized as falling within financial difficulties. The word 'financial' in this context appears in fact to refer to 'financing' difficulties, ie situations where it is the borrowing of money or taking on of credit that causes difficulties. By contrast, 'non-financial' appears to refer to difficulties which do not arise from the borrowing of money or the obtaining of credit.

English administration proceedings

8.502 The opening of English administration proceedings only require there to be a likelihood of insolvency.[6] To be within the RR, the Article 1(1) RR coda requires the purpose to be the avoidance of insolvency or the cessation of the debtor's business activities. There is a potential mismatch of purposes here, since the purposes of an administration are (a) rescuing the company as a going concern, or (b) achieving a better result for creditors as a whole than would be likely in a liquidation, or (c) realizing property in order to make a distribution to one or more secured or preferential creditors, although the administrator can only pursue (b) if (a) is not possible and so on. There is clearly a lot of overlap between the purposes required by Article 1(1) RR and those required by English law and in all cases the administrator's primary goal is (a), which is wholly compatible with RR. Where, however, the eventual purpose of the administration does not match the required purpose in Article 1(1) RR, the administration proceeding will nevertheless be within the RR. Not only is the initial and primary purpose of administration within the RR, but the listing of administration in Annex A RR is conclusive in the light of the terms of Article 1(1) RR and Recital (9) RR which in effect tells courts of other Member States simply to look at Annex A and not to attempt to test the proceeding they are looking at against the criteria in Article 1(1).

The Article 1(2) exclusions

8.503 The exclusions remain generally similar to those set out in the OR and reference should be made to the commentary under the original Article 1(2). There is,

---

[6] Para 11(a) of Sch B1 to the UK Insolvency Act 1986.

however, one important and radical change in that the Article 1(2) OR exclusion of 'investment undertakings which provide services involving the holding of funds or securities for third parties' is replaced by the exclusion in Article 1(2)(c) RR of 'investment firms and other firms, institutions and undertakings to the extent that they are covered by Directive 2001/24/EC…'. In other words, by limiting the exclusion to investment and other firms to those covered by the credit institutions reorganisation and winding-up Directive, the RR is *including* previously excluded investment undertakings which are not covered by the Directive. For example, during the recent major financial crisis it was found that certain major debtors which were thought to be 'banks' were not in fact credit institutions but investment firms, lacking any applicable Directive. However, it should be noted that the Directive itself has been amended by Directive 2014/59/EU of the Parliament and the Council of 15 May 2015[7] (known as the 'BRRD', see chapter 7) so as to apply to 'investment firms as defined in point (2) of Article 4(1) of Regulation (EU) No 575/2013 of the European Parliament and of the Council [footnote omitted] and their branches located in Member States other than those in which they have their head offices.' In addition, there is an amendment which applies the Directive in 'the event of application of the resolution tools and exercise of the resolution powers provided for in Directive 2014/59/EU of the European Parliament and of the Council… to the financial institutions, firms and parent undertakings falling within the scope of Directive 2014/59/EU.' Thus the number of investment firms to which the Directive applies (and therefore the OR/RR does not), has been increased.[8]

The rationale for the remaining exclusions in Recital (19) RR, which refers to 'special arrangements' and wide-ranging powers of intervention by national supervisory authorities does not provide a satisfactory reason for the exclusion of, and the failure to provide a Directive for, collective investment undertakings. **8.504**

(RR) Article 2—Definitions

For the purposes of this Regulation:
1. 'collective proceedings' means proceedings which include all or a significant part of a debtor's creditors, provided that, in the latter case, the proceedings do not affect the claims of creditors which are not involved in them;
2. 'collective investment undertakings' means undertakings for collective investment in transferable securities (UCITS) as defined in Directive 2009/65/EC of the European Parliament and of the Council and alternative investment funds (AIFs) as defined in Directive 2011/61/EU of the European Parliament and of the Council;
3. 'debtor in possession' means a debtor in respect of which insolvency proceedings have been opened which do not necessarily involve the appointment of an insolvency practitioner or the complete transfer of the rights and duties to administer

---

[7] OJ L 173/190.
[8] See paras 7.38–7.41 and 7.48 above.

the debtor's assets to an insolvency practitioner and where, therefore, the debtor remains totally or at least partially in control of its assets and affairs;

4. 'insolvency proceedings' means the proceedings listed in Annex A;

5. 'insolvency practitioner' means any person or body whose function, including on an interim basis, is to:
   (i) verify and admit claims submitted in insolvency proceedings;
   (ii) represent the collective interest of the creditors;
   (iii) administer, either in full or in part, assets of which the debtor has been divested;
   (iv) liquidate the assets referred to in point (iii); or
   (v) supervise the administration of the debtor's affairs.

The persons and bodies referred to in the first subparagraph are listed in Annex B;

6. 'court' means:
   (i) in points (b) and (c) of Article 1(1), Article 4(2), Articles 5 and 6, Article 21(3), point (j) of Article 24(2), Articles 36 and 39, and Articles 61 to 77, the judicial body of a Member State;
   (ii) in all other articles, the judicial body or any other competent body of a Member State empowered to open insolvency proceedings, to confirm such opening or to take decisions in the course of such proceedings;

7. 'judgment opening insolvency proceedings' includes:
   (i) the decision of any court to open insolvency proceedings or to confirm the opening of such proceedings; and
   (ii) the decision of a court to appoint an insolvency practitioner;

8. 'the time of the opening of proceedings' means the time at which the judgment opening insolvency proceedings becomes effective, regardless of whether the judgment is final or not;

9. 'the Member State in which assets are situated' means, in the case of:
   (i) registered shares in companies other than those referred to in point (ii), the Member State within the territory of which the company having issued the shares has its registered office;
   (ii) financial instruments, the title to which is evidenced by entries in a register or account maintained by or on behalf of an intermediary ('book entry securities'), the Member State in which the register or account in which the entries are made is maintained;
   (iii) cash held in accounts with a credit institution, the Member State indicated in the account's IBAN, or, for cash held in accounts with a credit institution which does not have an IBAN, the Member State in which the credit institution holding the account has its central administration or, where the account is held with a branch, agency or other establishment, the Member State in which the branch, agency or other establishment is located;
   (iv) property and rights, ownership of or entitlement to which is entered in a public register other than those referred to in point (i), the Member State under the authority of which the register is kept;
   (v) European patents, the Member State for which the European patent is granted;
   (vi) copyright and related rights, the Member State within the territory of which the owner of such rights has its habitual residence or registered office;
   (vii) tangible property, other than that referred to in points (i) to (iv), the Member State within the territory of which the property is situated;

(viii) claims against third parties, other than those relating to assets referred to in point (iii), the Member State within the territory of which the third party required to meet the claims has the centre of its main interests, as determined in accordance with Article 3(1);

10. 'establishment' means any place of operations where a debtor carries out or has carried out in the 3-month period prior to the request to open main insolvency proceedings a non-transitory economic activity with human means and assets;

11. 'local creditor' means a creditor whose claims against a debtor arose from or in connection with the operation of an establishment situated in a Member State other than the Member State in which the centre of the debtor's main interests is located;

12. 'foreign creditor' means a creditor which has its habitual residence, domicile or registered office in a Member State other than the State of the opening of proceedings, including the tax authorities and social security authorities of Member States;

13. 'group of companies' means a parent undertaking and all its subsidiary undertakings;

14. 'parent undertaking' means an undertaking which controls, either directly or indirectly, one or more subsidiary undertakings. An undertaking which prepares consolidated financial statements in accordance with Directive 2013/34/EU of the European Parliament and of the Council shall be deemed to be a parent undertaking.

Introduction

Many of the definitions in Article 2 RR are new. Among other changes, there are **8.505** new definitions of 'collective proceedings', 'collective investment undertakings', 'debtor in possession', 'insolvency practitioner', 'court', 'the Member State in which assets are situated', 'establishment', and several other terms.

'Collective proceedings'

Article 1 OR stated that the OR applied to 'collective insolvency proceedings' **8.506** without defining the term. Reference should be made to the commentary under Article 1 OR above.

The definition in Article 2 RR is in effect elaborated in Recital (14) RR. It makes the **8.507** point that proceedings which involve only financial creditors should also be covered. This is an important practical point, since a number of viable, basically profitable companies can suffer from being overloaded with financial debt (eg resulting from a leveraged buy-out) and need to have the financial debt reorganized, without affecting the payment of trade creditors.

The elaboration in Recital (14) RR also makes the point that proceedings which do **8.508** not include all the creditors should be aimed at rescuing the debtor. Presumably, 'rescue' in this context includes similar concepts such as 'reorganization' and 'restructuring'. This is consistent with the further point made in Recital (14) RR that proceedings which lead to the 'definitive cessation of the debtor's activities or the liquidation of the debtor's assets should include all the debtor's creditors.' That appears to be the case contrasted with 'rescue' cases.

8.509 What if it is the *business* of the debtor that is rescued and not the debtor itself? On a literal reading of Recital (14) RR, such proceedings should include all the debtor's creditors. In practice, this should not cause problems as the proceedings, in so far as they affect the debtor, will normally include all the creditors from a legal point of view, even if unsecured or junior creditors do not get a distribution.

'Collective investment undertakings'

8.510 The RR does not apply to collective investment undertakings: see Article 1(2)(d) RR. Collective investment undertakings were also excluded from the scope of the OR: see Article 1(2) OR. The OR did not include a definition of 'collective investment undertakings'. This omission has been remedied under the RR.

8.511 Article 2(2) RR provides that two types of entity qualify as collective investment undertakings: undertakings for collective investment in transferable securities (known as 'UCITS') and alternative investment funds (known as 'AIFs'). The RR adopts the definition of UCITS in the UCITS IV Directive,[9] and adopts the definition of AIF in the AFIM Directive.[10]

8.512 In brief (and with a degree of over-simplification), UCITS are retail mutual funds. More precisely, Article 1(2) of the UCITS IV Directive states that:

> ... UCITS means an undertaking:
> (a) with the sole object of collective investment in transferable securities or in other liquid financial assets referred to in Article 50(1) of capital raised from the public and which operate on the principle of risk-spreading; and
> (b) with units which are, at the request of holders, repurchased or redeemed, directly or indirectly, out of those undertakings' assets. Action taken by a UCITS to ensure that the stock exchange value of its units does not significantly vary from their net asset value shall be regarded as equivalent to such repurchase or redemption.

All UCITS must be authorized in accordance with the UCITS IV Directive: see Article 5(1) thereof.

8.513 In brief (and with a degree of over-simplification), AIFs comprise all collective investment undertakings which are not UCITS. More precisely, Article 4(1)(a) of the AIFM Directive defines AIFs as:

> ... collective investment undertakings, including investment compartments thereof, which:
> (i) raise capital from a number of investors, with a view to investing it in accordance with a defined investment policy for the benefit of those investors; and
> (ii) do not require authorisation pursuant to Article 5 of [the UCITS Directive].

---

[9] Directive 2009/65/EC of the European Parliament and of the Council.
[10] Directive 2011/61/EU of the European Parliament and of the Council.

Ultimately, the definition of 'collective investment undertakings' in Article 2(2) RR can fairly be said to involve an element of circularity, since the very same term is used (but not defined) in the provisions of the UCITS IV Directive and the AFIM Directive to which the RR cross-refers. For further commentary on the definitions of UCITS and AIFs in the respective Directives, readers should refer to specialist commentaries.[11]

'Debtor in possession'

RR Article 2(3) introduces the concept of a debtor in possession, which means: **8.514**

> ... a debtor in respect of which insolvency proceedings have been opened which do not necessarily involve the appointment of an insolvency practitioner or the complete transfer of the rights and duties to administer the debtor's assets to an insolvency practitioner and where, therefore, the debtor remains totally or at least partially in control of its assets and affairs.

The concept of a debtor in possession does not feature expressly in the OR. This is because in express terms the OR does not apply to insolvency proceedings unless such proceedings 'entail ... the appointment of a liquidator': see Article 1(1) OR. Thus, insolvency proceedings involving a debtor in possession will generally fall outside the scope of the OR.[12] By contrast, debtor in possession proceedings are expressly included within the scope of the RR. As Recital (10) RR explains:

> The scope of this Regulation should extend to proceedings which promote the rescue of economically viable but distressed businesses and which give a second chance to entrepreneurs. It should, in particular, extend to proceedings which provide for restructuring of a debtor at a stage where there is only a likelihood of insolvency, and to proceedings which leave the debtor fully or partially in control of its assets and affairs. It should also extend to proceedings providing for a debt discharge or a debt adjustment in relation to consumers and self-employed persons, for example by reducing the amount to be paid by the debtor or by extending the payment period granted to the debtor. Since such proceedings do not necessarily entail the appointment of an insolvency practitioner, they should be covered by this Regulation if they take place under the control or supervision of a court. In this context, the term 'control' should include situations where the court only intervenes on appeal by a creditor or other interested parties.

Accordingly, Article 1(1) RR identifies three types of insolvency proceedings which fall within the scope of the RR: (a) proceedings in which a debtor is totally or partially divested of its assets; (b) proceedings in which the assets and affairs of a debtor are subject to control or supervision by a court; and (c) proceedings in which a temporary stay of individual enforcement proceedings is granted by a court or by

---

[11] See eg G Walker and R Purves, *Financial Services Law* (3rd edn, 2014) at ch 18.
[12] But note the inclusion of a CVA in Annex A OR.

operation of law, in order to allow for negotiations between the debtor and its creditors. Evidently, proceedings falling within categories (b) or (c) need not involve the appointment of an insolvency practitioner, and proceedings falling within category (a) can involve a debtor in 'partial' possession. This is an important change from the position which formerly prevailed under the OR.

8.515 There are a number of other new provisions in the RR dealing with the rights of debtors in possession. It would be wrong to suggest that the RR confers the same powers on debtors in possession and insolvency practitioners: this is not so.[13] However, debtors in possession and insolvency practitioners share some of the same powers. For example, where a debtor in possession can bring avoidance proceedings under national law, Article 6(2) RR ensures that the jurisdictional scheme for such actions applies equally to insolvency practitioners and debtors in possession. By Articles 28 and 29 RR, a debtor in possession has the same rights and duties as an insolvency practitioner vis-à-vis publication and registration. Likewise, almost all of the provisions relating to prospective secondary proceedings in Article 38 RR apply to insolvency practitioners and debtors in possession alike.[14] In the same vein, Article 76 RR ensures that all the provisions of Chapter V apply both to insolvency practitioners and debtors in possession.

'Insolvency proceedings'

8.516 Article 2(4) RR defines insolvency proceedings as 'the proceedings listed in Annex A'. If a proceeding is included in Annex A RR, then it is within the scope of the RR even if it does not in fact meet the criteria laid down by the RR: Recital (9) RR. If it is not in RR Annex A, then it is not within the scope of the RR, even if it does meet those criteria: Recital (9) RR.

8.517 The forms of UK insolvency proceedings listed in Annex A are winding-up by or subject to the supervision of the court, creditors' voluntary winding-up (but only with confirmation by the court under rule 7.62 of the Insolvency Rules 1986), administration (including appointments made by filing documents at court), company voluntary arrangements, individual voluntary arrangements, bankruptcy, and sequestration.

8.518 The court has the power to appoint an administrator under paragraph 11 of Schedule B1 to the Insolvency Act 1986. However, an administrator can also be appointed by the holder of a qualified floating charge (paragraph 14 of Schedule B1), the insolvent company itself (paragraph 22(1) of Schedule B1) or its directors (paragraph 22(2) of Schedule B1). The procedure for such appointments involves the filing of prescribed documents at court.[15] Under the OR, it was arguably unclear whether

---

[13] See, among many other provisions, Art 21 RR (dealing with the powers of an insolvency practitioner), which does not apply to debtors in possession).

[14] Though see Art 38(4) RR, which only applies to insolvency practitioners.

[15] See paras 14–29 of Sch B1 to the Insolvency Act 1986.

the appointment of an administrator by a floating chargee, the company, or its directors was going to be recognized in other Member States, as a result of their unfamiliarity with appointments out of court.[16] This difficulty has been remedied by the RR. Where an administrator is appointed by a floating chargee, the company or its directors, the relevant appointer is deemed to be a 'court' for certain purposes under the RR.

The most notable absence from Annex A is the scheme of arrangement under Part 26 of the Companies Act 2006 when used as a tool for pre-insolvency proceedings (in a way analogous to a reorganization under Chapter 11 of the US Bankruptcy Code), to which the RR does not apply. The English court has asserted an increasingly long-arm jurisdiction to sanction schemes of arrangement in respect of foreign companies,[17] which would have been radically curtailed if schemes had been included in Annex A.   **8.519**

The RR also does not apply to members' voluntary winding-up, since that is not listed in Annex A.   **8.520**

If there is a conflict between the definition in Article 1 RR and Annex A, Annex A prevails: the very fact that a proceeding appears in Annex A conclusively establishes that it constitutes an 'insolvency proceeding' to which the RR applies. The CJEU so held in the *Bank Handlowy* case[18] (decided under the OR), which remains good law under the RR. As Recital (9) explains: **8.521**

> This Regulation should apply to insolvency proceedings which meet the conditions set out in it, irrespective of whether the debtor is a natural person or a legal person, a trader or an individual. Those insolvency proceedings are listed exhaustively in Annex A. In respect of the national procedures contained in Annex A, this Regulation should apply without any further examination by the courts of another Member State as to whether the conditions set out in this Regulation are met. National insolvency procedures not listed in Annex A should not be covered by this Regulation.

However, the conditions set out in Article 1 RR will be significant when questions arise as to whether an insolvency proceeding should be added to Annex A in the future.[19]

'Insolvency practitioner'

The concept of a 'liquidator', which performed an essential function under the OR, has been replaced with the new concept of an 'insolvency practitioner' under the RR. Article 2(5) RR defines an insolvency practitioner as a person or body whose function (whether on a permanent or interim basis) is to (i) verify and admit claims submitted   **8.522**

---

[16] See G Moss, 'On the Edge of Non-Recognition? Appointments of Administrators Under the Enterprise Act and the EC Regulation' [2004] 17 Insolv Int 13.

[17] See *Re Apcoa Parking Holdings GmbH* [2015] Bus LR 374.

[18] Case C-116/11 *Bank Handlowy w Warszawie SA v Christianapol sp. z o.o.* [2013] Bus LR 956.

[19] A Commission proposal to act as 'gatekeeper' in relation to the addition of proceedings to Annex A was rejected, and additions will have to be made by amending the RR. The Art 45 OR procedure for amending annexes by qualified majority has not been retained by the RR.

in insolvency proceedings; (ii) represent the collective interest of the creditors; (iii) administer, either in full or in part, assets of which the debtor has been divested; (iv) liquidate the assets referred to in point (iii); or (v) supervise the administration of the debtor's affairs. The language of Article 2(5) RR clearly indicates that it is sufficient if the relevant person performs one of the five identified functions.

8.523 Article 2(5) RR expressly provides for the possibility that an insolvency practitioner will perform his functions on an 'interim' basis only. This removes any doubt as to whether the RR applies to provisional liquidators (or other office-holders who act on an interim basis). As Recital (15) explains:

> This Regulation should also apply to proceedings that, under the law of some Member States, are opened and conducted for a certain period of time on an interim or provisional basis before a court issues an order confirming the continuation of the proceedings on a non-interim basis. Although labelled as 'interim', such proceedings should meet all other requirements of this Regulation.

Article 2(5) RR states that the categories of insolvency practitioners are 'listed in Annex B'. The UK insolvency practitioners identified in Annex B are liquidators, supervisors of voluntary arrangements, administrators, the Official Receiver, trustees in bankruptcy, provisional liquidators, interim receivers, and judicial factors.

8.524 Article 2(5) is supplemented by Recital (21), which states that:

> Insolvency practitioners are defined in this Regulation and listed in Annex B. Insolvency practitioners who are appointed without the involvement of a judicial body should, under national law, be appropriately regulated and authorised to act in insolvency proceedings. The national regulatory framework should provide for proper arrangements to deal with potential conflicts of interest.

By analogy to the approach to 'insolvency proceedings' in *Bank Handlowy,*[20] it seems that inclusion in Annex B RR is conclusive in favour of being within the definition and not being included in Annex B RR is conclusive as to exclusion from the concept. Complications have arisen under the OR and can continue to arise under the RR if for example an 'administrator' is listed in Annex A (as in the case of the UK) and a 'special administrator' is appointed in a specialist proceeding. If the relevant Member State court treats such a 'special administrator' as being within the concept of 'administrator', it would seem that that will also have to be accepted in the courts of other Member States, on the basis of mutual trust.

'Court'

8.525 There is a new definition of 'court' in Article 2(6) RR. The background to the new definition is explained in Recital (20):

> Insolvency proceedings do not necessarily involve the intervention of a judicial authority. Therefore, the term 'court' in this Regulation should, in certain provisions,

---

[20] Case C-116/11 *Bank Handlowy w Warszawie SA v Christianapol sp. z o.o.* [2013] Bus LR 956.

be given a broad meaning and include a person or body empowered by national law to open insolvency proceedings. In order for this Regulation to apply, proceedings (comprising acts and formalities set down in law) should not only have to comply with the provisions of this Regulation, but they should also be officially recognised and legally effective in the Member State in which the insolvency proceedings are opened.

Article 2(6) RR distinguishes between two possible meanings of the term 'court'. The first meaning is 'the judicial body of a Member State': see Article 2(6)(i) RR. The second meaning is 'the judicial body or any other competent body of a Member State empowered to open insolvency proceedings, to confirm such opening or to take decisions in the course of such proceedings': see Article 2(6)(ii) RR.

In order to reduce potential ambiguity, Article 2(6)(i) RR lists the provisions of **8.526** the RR in which 'court' should be construed in accordance with the first meaning. Those provisions are Articles 1(1)(b) and 1(1)(c) (dealing with the scope of the RR), Article 4(2) (dealing with determinations of jurisdiction by insolvency practitioners), Articles 5 and 6 (dealing with other jurisdictional matters), Article 21(3) (dealing with the powers of an insolvency practitioner), Article 24(2)(j) (dealing with the establishment of insolvency registers), Articles 36 and 39 (dealing with secondary proceedings), and Articles 61 to 77 (dealing with matters of co-ordination). In all other Articles of the RR, 'court' should be construed in accordance with the second meaning set out above: see Article 2(6)(ii) RR.

A creditors' meeting which approves a CVA has been held to be a 'court or other **8.527** competent body' within Article 2(d) OR and should therefore be recognized as a 'competent body of a Member State empowered to open insolvency proceedings' within Article 2(6) RR.[21] By parity of reasoning, the same must apply to a shareholders' meeting which places a company into creditors' voluntary winding-up. Likewise, where an administrator is appointed by a floating chargee (or by the company or its directors), it is submitted that the relevant appointer must be treated as a 'competent body of a Member State empowered to open insolvency proceedings'. After all, Annex A RR ensures that appointments made in these ways constitute insolvency proceedings: so the appointer must logically be regarded as a 'court' within the RR.

'Judgment opening insolvency proceedings'
The definition of 'judgment opening insolvency proceedings' is very similar to the **8.528** definition of 'judgment' in the OR. Article 2(7) RR states that a 'judgment opening insolvency proceedings includes: (i) the decision of any court to open insolvency proceedings or to confirm the opening of such proceedings; and (ii) the decision of a court to appoint an insolvency practitioner'.

---

[21] See *Re Salvage Association* [2003] EWHC 1028 (Ch), and see commentary under Art 2(d) OR above.

8.529 In Article 2(7) RR, 'court' means 'the judicial body or any other competent body of a Member State empowered to open insolvency proceedings, to confirm such opening or to take decisions in the course of such proceedings': see Article 2(6). As observed above, where an administrator is appointed by a floating chargee (or by the company or its directors), the relevant appointer must be treated as a 'competent body of a Member State empowered to open insolvency proceedings'. Therefore, the filing of a notice of appointment under paragraph 18 or 29 of Schedule B1 to the Insolvency Act 1986 must logically be regarded as a 'decision of a court to appoint an insolvency practitioner' within Article 2(7) RR.

8.530 Article 19 RR provides that 'any judgment opening insolvency proceedings handed down by a court of a Member State which has jurisdiction pursuant to Article 3 shall be recognised in all other Member States from the moment that it becomes effective in the State of the opening of proceedings.'

8.531 The 'time of the opening of proceedings' is defined in Article 2(8) RR. The definition is much the same as to the definition of the same term in Article 2(f) OR and reference should be made to the commentary on Article 2(f) OR above.

'The time of the opening of proceedings'

8.532 This is in the same terms as the definition of the same words in Article 2(f) OR. Reference should be made to the commentary on Article 2(f) OR above.

'The Member State in which assets are situated'

8.533 Territorial proceedings only affect assets of the debtor which are situated in the Member State where the territorial proceedings were opened: see Article 3(2) RR. Article 2(9) RR contains a series of rules for determining the Member State in which the debtor's assets are located or treated as being located.[22] This will determine whether particular assets are within the main or territorial/secondary proceedings.

8.534 Article 2(g) OR is the predecessor of Article 2(9) RR. However, the latter provision is more complex than the former provision. Under the OR, definition of 'the Member State where assets are situated' had only three limbs; under the RR, it has seven. Limbs (i), (ii), and (iii) of the OR definition are equivalent to limbs (vii), (iv) and (viii) of the RR definition (respectively). Limbs (i), (ii), (iii), (v) and (vi) of the RR definition are new.

8.535 The Article 2(g) OR trichotomy of (i) tangible property, (ii) rights which were required to be entered on a public register under the authority of a Member State, and (iii) 'claims' gave rise to uncertainty. Were the three categories intended to be exclusive, so that every asset had to be fitted into one of them? What was the

---

[22] Strictly speaking, an intangible cannot have a location, but intangibles are treated as a matter of law as having a location determined by legal rules, a 'deemed' location.

position of registered shares? Did bank accounts fall under 'claims'? Where were intermediated securities located?

The RR does not clear up the question as to whether the definitions are exclusive in **8.536** the sense of every asset having to be fitted into one category or another. However, new definitions deal with cases of uncertainty previously identified and therefore the risk of there being an asset not clearly included in one definition or another may be small.

[In both Article 2(g) OR and the Article 2(9) RR the fact that the lists are preceded **8.537** by the words 'in the case of:' suggests that the lists themselves are not intended to be exclusive in the sense that all types of asset must somehow be fitted into one or other of the cases listed, but rather that the lists simply provide rules to resolve questions of *situs* in respect of those classes of asset which are included in the lists. IF]

Under the RR, the basic rules of the OR remain the same: tangible property is **8.538** deemed to be situated in the Member State where the property is physically located; property rights which must be entered in a public register are deemed to be situated in the Member State which has 'authority' over the register; and claims against third parties (*choses in action*) other than money in bank accounts are deemed to be situated in the Member State where the obligor's centre of main interests is located.

However, these general principles are subject to a number of more specific rules, **8.539** which seek to deal with the uncertainties created by the OR rules.

Registered shares

Article 2(9)(i) RR deems registered shares in a company to be situated in the place **8.540** of the company's registered office. In practice, this rule is similar to the traditional rule under English law that registered shares are situated in the place where the share register is kept: see *Macmillan Inc v Bishopsgate Investment Trust plc (No 3)*,[23] since that will normally be at the registered office.

The question arises whether a debtor who holds shares in an account with an equities **8.541** broker owns 'registered shares' governed by Article 2(9)(i) RR or 'book entry securities' governed by Article 2(9)(ii) RR. Since (i) applies expressly to 'registered shares in companies other than those referred to in point (ii)', the implication is that registered shares can be 'book entry securities' within (ii) and that therefore an asset in the form of a right against an intermediary to shares held in an account will fall under (ii).[24]

---

[23] [1996] 1 WLR 387 at 411.
[24] In the UK and Ireland, the situation may be further complicated if the shares in the account are held by the intermediary (or its nominee) on trust for the debtor. Under company law the company would only recognize the registered holder as legal owner of the shares and the debtor would not have an asset as against the company unless and until it became the registered owner. The asset of the debtor pending any such registration would be its right against the intermediary as trustee and against any third party who acquired the shares with notice of the trust. See *Re LBIE* [2010] EWHC 2914 (Ch) at [226] and Moss, 'Intermediated Securities: Issues Arising From Insolvency', Ch 3 of *Intermediated Securities: Legal Problems and Practical Issues* ed. Gullifer and Payne (Hart Publishing, 2010).

Book entry securities

8.542   Article 2(9)(ii) RR deems 'book entry securities' to be situated in the place where the register or account in which the entries are made is maintained. Book entry securities are 'financial instruments, the title to which is evidenced by entries in a register or account maintained by or on behalf of an intermediary'. In practice, most securities traded on the international capital markets are book entry securities. For example, where the debtor holds bonds through a clearing house (such as Euroclear or Clearstream), the debtor's interest in the bonds will constitute 'book entry securities' within the RR.

8.543   This brings the RR into line with other EU financial services legislation. For example, Article 9 of the Financial Collateral Arrangements Directive[25] provides for proprietary issues relating to 'book entry securities collateral' to be governed by the 'law of the country in which the relevant account is maintained'. Article 9(2) of the Settlement Finality Directive[26] contains a similar provision. It is suggested that the *situs* of book entry securities should be determined in the same way under the RR, the Financial Collateral Arrangements Directive, and the Settlement Finality Directive.

Bank accounts

8.544   Article 2(9)(iii) RR deems cash held in a bank account to be situated in the Member State indicated on the account's IBAN (international bank account number). The vast majority of bank accounts have an IBAN. Where an IBAN does not exist, Article 2(9)(iii) RR contains various fall-back rules.

8.545   Finally, Article 2(9)(v) and 2(9)(vi) RR contain special provisions for determining the *situs* of intellectual property, including European patents and copyright.

'Establishment'

8.546   Article 2(10) RR contains a revised definition of the term 'establishment', which builds on the OR definition in Article 2(h) OR.

8.547   As explained in the commentary on Article 3 RR (below), the concept of an establishment is essential to the allocation of territorial jurisdiction under the RR. If a debtor's centre of main interests is situated in one Member State, but the debtor has an establishment in another Member State, then the courts of the latter Member State have jurisdiction to open territorial proceedings against the debtor. Where territorial proceedings are opened after main proceedings have already opened in the debtor's centre of main interests, they are known as 'secondary insolvency proceedings'. Where territorial proceedings are opened before main proceedings have

---

[25]   Directive 2002/47/EC of the European Parliament and of the Council of 6 June 2002 on financial collateral arrangements.

[26]   Directive 98/26/EC of the European Parliament and of the Council of 19 May 1998 on settlement finality in payment and securities settlement systems.

opened in the debtor's centre of main interests, they are known as 'independent territorial proceedings'.

The RR defines an establishment as a place of operations where either:　　　　**8.548**

(1) the debtor currently carries out a non-transitory economic activity with human means and assets (the 'first limb'); or
(2) the debtor carried out a non-transitory economic activity with human means and assets within the three-month period prior to the request to open main proceedings (the 'second limb').

The first limb is derived from the definition of 'establishment' in Article 2(h) OR, and reference should be made to the commentary on Article 2(h) OR above. It does however confirm English case law to the effect that 'goods' in the OR version should be read as 'assets'.[27]

However, the second limb is new. The second limb was inserted at the request of　**8.549** the European Parliament, in a report prepared by Mr Klaus-Heiner Lehne (acting as rapporteur of the Committee on Legal Affairs) dated 20 December 2013. Most of the amendments proposed in the Lehne report are supported by a list of reasons. Unfortunately (and inexplicably), the Lehne report does not explain the reasons for inserting the second limb into the definition of 'establishment'. The likelihood is that the change is driven by a suspicion that the insolvency practitioner or debtor in possession in the main proceedings, or management prior to the opening of main proceedings, may close down the operations in the secondary jurisdiction in order to prevent the opening of a secondary proceeding and thus thwart the interests of local creditors.[28]

The second limb does not apply unless a request has been made to open main　**8.550** proceedings in the debtor's centre of main interests. Thus, under the second limb, the existence of an establishment is dependent on (and relative to) the time of a particular request to open main proceedings. Where a request has not been made to open main proceedings against the debtor, the second limb of the definition does not apply. (This situation may arise where a creditor makes a request to open independent territorial proceedings.) Further, it is suggested that the second limb does not apply unless main proceedings have actually been opened against the

---

[27] The English case law, in particular *Re Olympic Airlines SA* [2015] 1 BCLC 589 (SC) at [3], is referred to in the commentary on Art 2(h) OR above.

[28] In *Re Olympic Airlines SA* [2015] 1 BCLC 589 (SC), the UK Supreme Court refused to open a secondary UK proceeding in the case of the Greek airline in main liquidation proceedings in Greece on the basis that the London branch was no longer carrying on any business activity at the London office at the time of the request to open secondary proceedings in England. While it was not suggested that in that case the operations were closed in order to thwart the opening, that was the effect. As explained below, if the same facts were to be repeated in a case arising under the RR, the winding down of operations at the company's English establishment following the opening of main proceedings in Greece would not preclude the opening of secondary proceedings in England based on the former existence of an active establishment there.

debtor. If a request to open main proceedings is dismissed, the second limb cannot apply: it would be absurd for the existence of an establishment to be determined by reference to the time of a failed request to open main proceedings. By parity of reasoning, if a request to open main proceedings is pending (but has not been granted), it should not be possible to prove that an establishment exists by relying on the second limb of the definition: after all, the request to open main proceedings might be dismissed in due course. More generally, it is suggested that 'the request to open main proceedings' in Article 2(10) RR means 'the successful request to open main proceedings'. That would also accord with the rationale suggested for the new timing provision: if no main proceeding is actually opened, it is unlikely that an establishment would be closed in order to prevent the opening of territorial proceedings.

8.551 The second limb is one of several 'look-back periods' introduced by the RR. For example, Article 3(1) RR provides that if a debtor moves its registered office within three months of a request to open insolvency proceedings, the presumption that the debtor's centre of main interests is situated in the place of its registered office does not apply for the purposes of that request. (See the commentary below.) The essential function of the 'look-back periods' in the RR is to prevent fraudulent or abusive forum shopping: see Recital (29) RR. It is suggested that the second limb of the definition of 'establishment' also attempts to combat fraudulent or abusive forum shopping. For example, if a professional person plans or expects to become bankrupt in England, the second limb ensures that he cannot prevent his creditors from opening territorial proceedings merely by closing his establishments in other Member States shortly before the presentation of a petition in England. In short, the second limb aims to prevent a debtor from impeding territorial proceedings by closing his establishments within the three-month 'look-back period'.

8.552 The importance of the second limb can be illustrated by reference to the judgment of the UK Supreme Court in the *Olympic Airlines* case,[29] which was decided under the OR. Olympic Airlines had been put into liquidation in Greece (being its centre of main interests) in October 2009. Prior to October 2009, the company carried on business from a number of offices in the UK with the assistance of several dozen members of staff. However, after the winding-up of the company in Greece, the company's presence in the UK began to decline. In July 2010, the trustees of the company's pension scheme presented a petition against the company in England, with the intention of opening secondary proceedings. By that time, the company occupied only one office in the UK, where three members of staff on ad hoc contracts assisted the Greek liquidators to wind up the company's affairs. Lord Sumption, who gave the only judgment in the Supreme Court, held that the presence of an establishment must be determined at the date of the English petition

---

[29] *Trustees of the Olympic Airlines SA Pension and Life Assurance Scheme v Olympic Airlines SA* [2015] 1 WLR 2399.

(being July 2010). He held that the debtor had ceased to carry on any significant economic activities in England at that date. Accordingly, the debtor did not have an establishment in the England within Article 2(h) OR.

The new second limb of the definition of 'establishment' in the RR has the effect **8.553** of reversing the decision in *Olympic Airlines* for cases under the RR. The company clearly had an establishment in the UK within three months prior to the date when the request was made to open main proceedings in Greece. That is sufficient for the purposes of Article 2(10) RR. The principle stated by Lord Sumption, *viz.* that the presence of an establishment must be determined at the date of the request for opening territorial proceedings, is no longer good law under the RR.

[The date for assessing whether an establishment exists in any given Member State **8.554** has now changed from the original date of the opening of the secondary proceedings to two dates, namely the date on which the main insolvency proceedings were opened and three months before that date. This now makes it clear, therefore, that it will not be possible to 'change' a debtor's establishment after the opening of main proceedings. While this may prevent 'bad' forum shopping, it may also prevent 'good' forum shopping, eg by the debtor (likely to be acting through the office holder of the main insolvency proceedings) who might wish to move the establishment in order to allow a 'controlled' secondary proceeding for the benefit of the estate as a whole. Given that creditors remain free to seek to open a secondary proceeding at any time, the restriction on the prior ability to move the debtor's establishment in this way is questionable (**AW**)].

(RR) Article 3—International jurisdiction

1. The courts of the Member State within the territory of which the centre of the debtor's main interests is situated shall have jurisdiction to open insolvency proceedings ('main insolvency proceedings'). The centre of main interests shall be the place where the debtor conducts the administration of its interests on a regular basis and which is ascertainable by third parties.
   In the case of a company or legal person, the place of the registered office shall be presumed to be the centre of its main interests in the absence of proof to the contrary. That presumption shall only apply if the registered office has not been moved to another Member State within the 3-month period prior to the request for the opening of insolvency proceedings.
   In the case of an individual exercising an independent business or professional activity, the centre of main interests shall be presumed to be that individual's principal place of business in the absence of proof to the contrary. That presumption shall only apply if the individual's principal place of business has not been moved to another Member State within the 3-month period prior to the request for the opening of insolvency proceedings.
   In the case of any other individual, the centre of main interests shall be presumed to be the place of the individual's habitual residence in the absence of proof to the contrary. This presumption shall only apply if the habitual residence has not been moved to another Member State within the 6-month period prior to the request for the opening of insolvency proceedings.

2. Where the centre of the debtor's main interests is situated within the territory of a Member State, the courts of another Member State shall have jurisdiction to open insolvency proceedings against that debtor only if it possesses an establishment within the territory of that other Member State. The effects of those proceedings shall be restricted to the assets of the debtor situated in the territory of the latter Member State.

3. Where insolvency proceedings have been opened in accordance with paragraph 1, any proceedings opened subsequently in accordance with paragraph 2 shall be secondary insolvency proceedings.

4. The territorial insolvency proceedings referred to in paragraph 2 may only be opened prior to the opening of main insolvency proceedings in accordance with paragraph 1 where

(a) insolvency proceedings under paragraph 1 cannot be opened because of the conditions laid down by the law of the Member State within the territory of which the centre of the debtor's main interests is situated; or

(b) the opening of territorial insolvency proceedings is requested by:

(i) a creditor whose claim arises from or is in connection with the operation of an establishment situated within the territory of the Member State where the opening of territorial proceedings is requested; or

(ii) a public authority which, under the law of the Member State within the territory of which the establishment is situated, has the right to request the opening of insolvency proceedings.

When main insolvency proceedings are opened, the territorial insolvency proceedings shall become secondary insolvency proceedings.

Introduction

8.555 Article 3 RR contains the fundamental rules on the allocation of international jurisdiction for insolvency proceedings. Article 3 RR is based on Article 3 OR, and the basic scheme remains much the same as before. However, there are several significant differences between Article 3 RR and Article 3 OR, which are discussed in detail below.

8.556 Article 3(1) introduces the concept of a debtor's centre of main interests ('COMI'), which is defined as 'the place where the debtor conducts the administration of its interests on a regular basis and which is ascertainable by third parties'. The latter phrase is derived from Recital (13) OR. It is doubtful that the draftsman's decision to transfer the phrase from the Recitals into the main body of Article 3(1) has any real significance. Indeed, subject to the specific modifications identified below, it is suggested that the concept of COMI should be construed in substantially the same manner under the RR and the OR. The commentary on Article 3 OR above deals with pre-RR jurisprudence.

8.557 The basic scheme of Article 3 is relatively straightforward. In summary:

(1) If a debtor has its COMI within the EU (with the exception of Denmark), then the courts of the Member State where the debtor's COMI is situated have exclusive jurisdiction to open 'main insolvency proceedings': see

Article 3(1) RR. Main proceedings enjoy universal effect across the EU: see Articles 19 and 20 RR.

(2) Where the debtor's COMI is situated in a Member State (MS1), but the debtor has an establishment in another Member State (MS2), the courts of MS2 have jurisdiction to open 'territorial insolvency proceedings': see Article 3(2) RR. Territorial proceedings are restricted to assets of the debtor which are situated in MS2.

(3) If the debtor does not have its COMI within the EU, or if the COMI is in Denmark, then the RR has no application, and the domestic rules of jurisdiction prevail.

Under the OR, it was possible (and wholly legitimate) for a debtor to shift its COMI **8.558** in order to utilize the insolvency proceedings available in a different Member State, if the purpose was to benefit his creditors.[30] This remains the position under the RR. However, the debtor's COMI should always be readily identifiable by its creditors, especially where the debtor purports to move its COMI. This is reinforced by Recital (28), which is new:

When determining whether the centre of the debtor's main interests is ascertainable by third parties, special consideration should be given to the creditors and to their perception as to where a debtor conducts the administration of its interests. This may require, in the event of a shift of centre of main interests, informing creditors of the new location from which the debtor is carrying out its activities in due course, for example by drawing attention to the change of address in commercial correspondence, or by making the new location public through other appropriate means.'[31]

The RR contains several new provisions which are designed to make fraudulent or abusive COMI-shifting more difficult. These provisions are considered below.

Three presumptions

The second paragraph of Article 3(1) provides that, in the absence of proof to the **8.559** contrary, the COMI of a company (or other legal person) is presumed to be the place of its registered office (the 'registered office presumption'). This is the same as the presumption under Article 3(1) OR. Recital (30) identifies the circumstances in which the registered office presumption can be rebutted:

In the case of a company, it should be possible to rebut this presumption where the company's central administration is located in a Member State other than that of its registered office, and where a comprehensive assessment of all the relevant factors establishes, in a manner that is ascertainable by third parties, that the company's

---

[30] See the commentary under Art 3 OR.
[31] The approach here follows case-law under the OR—see for example Case C-396/09 *Interedil Srl v Fallimento Interedil Srl* [2011] ECR I-9915, [2012] BCC 851 and *Irish Bank Resolution Corp Ltd v Quinn* [2012] BCC 608.

actual centre of management and supervision and of the management of its interests is located in that other Member State.

This passage was included in the RR at the request of the European Commission,[32] and was designed as a restatement of the CJEU's reasoning in *Interedil*.[33]

8.560   The registered office presumption is expressly disapplied (by the second sentence of the second paragraph of Article 3(1)) if the company moved its registered office to another Member State within three months of the 'request for the opening of insolvency proceedings'. This is a novel addition to Article 3(1) RR, which is designed to prevent fraudulent or abusive forum shopping: see Recital (31) RR. Fraudulent and abusive forum shopping was a particular concern of the European Parliament, which had wanted an arbitrary time-limit restraint on moves of COMI. The disapplication of the presumption represents a compromise reached between the Parliament and the Council.

8.561   Thus, the registered office presumption is now dependent on (and relative to) the time of a particular request to open insolvency proceedings. If two requests are made at slightly different times to open insolvency proceedings against the same company, the registered office presumption may only apply in relation to one such request.

8.562   Importantly, the RR does not make it impossible for a company to move its COMI in less than three months. This was possible under the OR, and remains possible under the RR. Furthermore, the RR does not prevent a company from relying on a relocation of its registered office as evidence that its COMI has moved, even if the relocation occurred less than three months prior to the request to open insolvency proceedings. The RR merely prevents reliance on the registered office *presumption* if the company moved its registered office within three months of the request.

8.563   The OR did not contain any express presumptions concerning the COMI of a natural person, although approaches were suggested by way of interpretation by V-S and VG (see p 276 *ante* for the full names of these sources) and by way of legislation in the UNCITRAL Model Law.

8.564   This gap has been filled in by the RR. The second paragraph of Article 3(1) RR provides that, in the absence of proof to the contrary, the COMI of an individual exercising an independent business or professional activity is presumed to be his principal place of business. The professional activity presumption comes originally from paragraph 75 of the Virgos-Schmit Report, which states that 'in principle, the centre of main interests will in the case of professionals be the place of their

---

[32]   See the Proposal of the European Commission dated 12 December 2012 (2012/0360 (COD)), at 3.1.2 of the Explanatory Memorandum.

[33]   Case C-396/09 *Interedil Srl v Fallimento Interedil Srl and Intesa Gestione Crediti SpA* [2011] ECR I-9915, [2012] BCC 851. In some countries bankruptcy judges may not keep up to date with insolvency law decisions of the CJEU and it was thought preferable to put some basic points decided by case law in the text of the RR or in the Recitals to the RR.

professional domicile'. The expression 'independent business or professional activity' comes from VG at para 56(c).

The concept of an 'independent business or professional activity' is not completely **8.565** clear. It seems to cover business or professional activities other than as an employee of an enterprise. VG at para 56(c) contrasts it with '*dependent* work'. It also excludes activities which are merely facets of the debtor's personal life (such as managing his own financial affairs). As in the case of companies and legal persons, the foregoing presumption is expressly disapplied if the relevant individual moved his principal place of business to a new Member State within three months of the request to open insolvency proceedings.

If an individual does not exercise an independent business or professional activity, **8.566** his COMI is presumed (in the absence of proof to the contrary) to be the place of his habitual residence: see the third paragraph of Article 3(1) RR. This presumption also comes originally from paragraph 75 of the Virgos-Schmit Report, which states that 'for natural persons in general, the place of their habitual residence' should be treated as their COMI. VG refers to it at para 56(c).

The foregoing presumption is expressly disapplied if the individual moved his **8.567** habitual residence to a new Member State within six months of the request for the opening of insolvency proceedings. The restriction on the normal presumption is once again the product of a compromise between the European Parliament (which wanted an arbitrary time limit) and the Council. The longer restriction on the presumption (being six months rather than three months) perhaps reflects the fact that a habitual residence is easier to move than a registered office or a principal place of business.

The editors of *Dicey, Morris & Collins on the Conflict of Laws* (15th edition) observe **8.568** that 'habitual residence plays a key role in European private international law'.[34] The concept of habitual residence features in numerous EU instruments, including (among others) the OR, the Brussels Regulation (Recast),[35] and legislation dealing with family law. Habitual residence must be given an autonomous interpretation under EU law,[36] which need not coincide with the traditional English concept of habitual residence. Reference may be made to Rule 18 of *Dicey, Morris & Collins* for a comprehensive discussion of this topic.

Territorial insolvency proceedings

As noted above, where the debtor's COMI is situated in a Member State (MS1), but **8.569** the debtor also has an establishment in another Member State (MS2), the courts of

---

[34] *Dicey, Morris & Collins on the Conflict of Laws* (15th edn, 2015) at para 6–146.
[35] Regulation (EU) No 1215/2012 of the European Parliament and of the Council of 12 December 2012 on jurisdiction and the recognition and enforcement of judgments in civil and commercial matters (recast), OJ L 351/1, 20 December 2012.
[36] Case C-523/07 *Proceedings brought by A* [2009] ECR I-2805.

MS2 have jurisdiction to open territorial proceedings. Where territorial proceedings are opened after main proceedings have already opened, they are known as 'secondary insolvency proceedings': see Article 3(3) RR. All territorial proceedings must be secondary proceedings, unless the exceptions in Article 3(4) RR apply. There is no material change in this respect from the OR.

8.570 An 'establishment' is defined as 'any place of operations where a debtor carries out or has carried out in the 3-month period prior to the request to open main insolvency proceedings a non-transitory economic activity with human means and assets': see RR Article 2(10) RR. This is a new and important definition, the effect of which is discussed in the commentary on Article 2 above RR.

8.571 Under the OR, secondary proceedings were required to be winding-up proceedings (as defined in Annex B OR, which excluded many restructuring, rescue or pre-insolvency proceedings). The idea was to reinforce the supremacy of the main proceeding.

However, this was an unfortunate and unpopular requirement, with potentially damaging consequences referred to in the commentary in respect of OR (above).

8.572 In a welcome development, the RR abolishes the requirement for secondary proceedings to be winding-up proceedings. Annex B OR, which contains a list of winding-up proceedings in each Member State, has been excised in its entirety from the RR.[37] It follows that the full array of insolvency proceedings listed in Annex A RR can (in principle) be used as secondary proceedings, provided that the necessary conditions under domestic law are satisfied. This ensures that 'the opening of secondary proceedings does not automatically thwart the rescue or restructuring of a debtor as a whole'.[38]

8.573 Where territorial proceedings are opened prior to the opening of main proceedings, they are known as 'independent territorial proceedings'. Such proceedings 'are intended to be limited to what is absolutely necessary' (Recital (37) RR), and may be opened in three circumstances.

8.574 First, Article 3(4)(a) RR permits independent territorial proceedings to be opened if it is impossible to open main proceedings because of the conditions laid down by the law of the Member State where the debtor's COMI is situated. For example, if the law of the COMI prevents non-traders from entering into insolvency proceedings, and the debtor is not a trader, then independent territorial proceedings can (at least in principle) be opened in any Member State where the debtor has an establishment. Article 3(4)(a) RR is identical to Article 3(4)(a) OR, and should be

---

[37] Annex B RR now contains a list of insolvency practitioners, formerly listed in Annex C OR: see Art 2(5) RR.
[38] See the Proposal of the European Commission dated 12 December 2012 (2012/0360 (COD)), at 3.1.2 of the Explanatory Memorandum.

interpreted in the same manner. Reference should be made to the commentary on Article 3(4)(a) OR above.

Second, Article 3(4)(b)(i) RR permits independent territorial proceedings to be **8.575** opened in a particular Member State upon the request of a creditor whose claim arises from (or is in connection with) the operation of an establishment in that Member State. Under the equivalent provision of the OR, it was sufficient if the requesting creditor had his domicile, habitual residence, or registered office in the relevant Member State. This is no longer sufficient under the RR: it is necessary for the creditor's claim to arise from the operation of the relevant establishment, regardless of the creditor's domicile.

Third, Article 3(4)(b)(ii) RR permits independent territorial proceedings to be **8.576** opened in a particular Member State upon the request of a public authority which, under the law of that Member State, has the right to request the opening of insolvency proceedings. This is a novel provision, which appears to be designed as a response to the decision of the CJEU in *Zaza Retail*.[39] In that case, the debtor had its COMI in the Netherlands and an establishment in Belgium. Upon the application of the Belgian prosecution service (which was acting in the public interest, and was not a creditor in the conventional sense), a Belgian court opened independent territorial proceedings against the debtor. The CJEU ruled that the Belgian court had no jurisdiction to open such proceedings. In particular:

(1) The Belgian prosecution service argued that Article 3(4)(a) OR conferred jurisdiction on the Belgian court to open independent territorial proceedings, because the Belgian prosecution service lacked *locus standi* to apply for the opening of insolvency proceedings in the Netherlands. The CJEU rejected this argument. From the mere fact that a specific person (in this case, the Belgian prosecution service) has no standing to apply for the opening of main insolvency proceedings, it does not follow that such proceedings 'cannot be opened'. Other persons (namely, ordinary creditors) had standing to apply for the opening of main proceedings in the Netherlands at all material times, so Article 3(4)(a) OR had no application.
(2) Further, the CJEU held that the Belgian prosecution service could not be treated as a 'creditor' within Article 3(4)(b) OR, because it had no right to lodge a claim against the debtor's estate, and did not act as a representative of the creditors. The concept of a 'creditor' must be construed strictly, and does not include public authorities which act in the public interest rather than as creditors (or in the name or on behalf of creditors).

The foregoing principles remain good law. However, *Zaza Retail* would be decided differently under the RR. The Belgian prosecution service, being a public authority, would be entitled to rely on Article 3(4)(b)(ii) RR of the RR before the Belgian

---

[39] Case C-112/10 *Procureur-generaal bij het hof van beroep te Antwerpen v Zaza Retail BV* [2011] ECR I-11525.

court. Although the Belgian prosecution is not a 'creditor' within Article 3(4)(b)(i) RR, this is irrelevant for the purposes of Article 3(4)(b)(ii) RR.

(RR) Article 4—Examination as to jurisdiction

1. A court seised of a request to open insolvency proceedings shall of its own motion examine whether it has jurisdiction pursuant to Article 3. The judgment opening insolvency proceedings shall specify the grounds on which the jurisdiction of the court is based, and, in particular, whether jurisdiction is based on Article 3(1) or (2).

2. Notwithstanding paragraph 1, where insolvency proceedings are opened in accordance with national law without a decision by a court, Member States may entrust the insolvency practitioner appointed in such proceedings to examine whether the Member State in which a request for the opening of proceedings is pending has jurisdiction pursuant to Article 3. Where this is the case, the insolvency practitioner shall specify in the decision opening the proceedings the grounds on which jurisdiction is based and, in particular, whether jurisdiction is based on Article 3(1) or (2).

8.577 Article 4 RR is a new provision. It is derived from the European Commission's original legislative proposal,[40] which includes the following explanatory statement:[41]

> The proposal also improves the procedural framework for determining jurisdiction for the opening of proceedings. The proposal requires the court to examine its jurisdiction ex officio prior to opening insolvency proceedings and to specify in its decision on which grounds it based its jurisdiction … These changes aim at ensuring that proceedings are only opened if the Member State concerned actually has jurisdiction. It should therefore reduce the cases of forum shopping through abusive and non-genuine relocation of the COMI.

The proposal reflects the suspicion in relation to cases under the OR that the courts of some Member States were not considering the question of international jurisdiction under the OR with sufficient care, thereby facilitating abusive or fraudulent forum shopping.

8.578 Article 4(1) RR reflects good practice under the OR. In England, the court has always sought to determine (of its own volition) whether it has jurisdiction to determine any matter of which it is seised. Furthermore, all advocates in *ex parte* proceedings have a duty to draw to the court's attention any factor which suggests that the court may lack jurisdiction.

8.579 A question may however arise as to the degree of examination required. In a busy court list where the evidence suggests a purely national case, the examination may not have to be very detailed. In any case where there is a foreign element and

---

[40] See the Proposal of the European Commission dated 12 December 2012 (2012/0360 (COD)).
[41] Ibid at 3.1.2 of the Explanatory Memorandum.

suspicious circumstances suggesting eg 'bankruptcy tourism', the question of jurisdiction will need to be looked at much more carefully.

Article 4(2) RR enables Member States to empower insolvency practitioners (who **8.580**
have been appointed out of court) to determine whether the relevant Member State
has jurisdiction pursuant to Article 3 RR. It is doubtful that this provision will
have any impact in England. Under English law, administrators and liquidators
(whether appointed out of court or otherwise) have no power to make a binding
determination as to the debtor's centre of main interests, the existence of an establishment, or any other jurisdictional issue. Where a problem of jurisdiction arises,
the office-holder's only option is to apply to the court for directions.[42] There is no
indication that English law is likely to change in this respect.

[Self-certified procedures (eg an out of court administration appointment) are still **8.581**
possible. The Member State may entrust the office-holder to determine whether the
Member State has jurisdiction following his purported appointment. It is assumed
that the consequences of an invalid appointment will be sufficiently serious to
encourage an office-holder to do this promptly after appointment where there is any
uncertainty, but that may not be guaranteed in all jurisdictions. Of course, any creditor in any Member State (or even the debtor) now has the ability to challenge the
opening of main proceedings on jurisdictional grounds and there is no time limit on
a creditor being able to do so (a three-month time limit had been proposed but was
not adopted). The absence of a time limit may of course leave the proceedings vulnerable to attack much later on although if there is doubt, the office-holder should
make his determination (and seek court directions as necessary) promptly. (**AW**)]

(RR) Article 5—Judicial review of the decision to open main insolvency proceedings

1. **The debtor or any creditor may challenge before a court the decision opening main insolvency proceedings on grounds of international jurisdiction.**
2. **The decision opening main insolvency proceedings may be challenged by par-ties other than those referred to in paragraph 1 or on grounds other than a lack of international jurisdiction where national law so provides.**

Article 5 RR is a new provision. It is derived from the European Commission's **8.582**
original legislative proposal,[43] and is designed to ensure that all creditors (including foreign creditors) have *locus standi* to challenge a decision opening insolvency
proceedings. Article 5 RR reflects the existing practice in England.

---

[42] The liquidator of a company in creditors' voluntary liquidation can make an application under
r 7.62 of the Insolvency Rules 1986 for 'an order confirming the creditors' voluntary winding up for
the purposes of the EC Regulation'.
[43] See the Proposal of the European Commission dated 12 December 2012 (2012/0360 (COD))
at 3.1.2 of the Explanatory Memorandum.

8.583 Under the OR there was a concern that in some Member States an insolvency proceeding could be opened without notice to the debtor or without notice to creditors and there may not be recourse. Article 5 RR provides that regardless of national law rules, such recourse will be available.

8.584 Article 5(2) RR ensures that this right of challenge created by the RR is not interpreted as excluding a challenge under national law by a party or on a basis not provided for by the RR.

8.585 The use in the heading of 'judicial review' is unfortunate, as in English legal practice that refers to proceedings challenging administrative actions and subordinate legislation and not applications to court generally or in insolvency cases. However, the meaning of Article 5 RR is clear from the text.

(RR) Article 6—Jurisdiction for actions deriving directly from insolvency proceedings and closely linked with them

1. The courts of the Member State within the territory of which insolvency proceedings have been opened in accordance with Article 3 shall have jurisdiction for any action which derives directly from the insolvency proceedings and is closely linked with them, such as avoidance actions.
2. Where an action referred to in paragraph 1 is related to an action in civil and commercial matters against the same defendant, the insolvency practitioner may bring both actions before the courts of the Member State within the territory of which the defendant is domiciled, or, where the action is brought against several defendants, before the courts of the Member State within the territory of which any of them is domiciled, provided that those courts have jurisdiction pursuant to Regulation (EU) No 1215/2012.
   The first subparagraph shall apply to the debtor in possession, provided that national law allows the debtor in possession to bring actions on behalf of the insolvency estate.
3. For the purpose of paragraph 2, actions are deemed to be related where they are so closely connected that it is expedient to hear and determine them together to avoid the risk of irreconcilable judgments resulting from separate proceedings.

8.586 Article 6 RR is a new provision, which clarifies the relationship between the RR and the Brussels Regulation (Recast).[44] It is derived from the European Commission's original legislative proposal,[45] which includes the following explanatory statement:[46]

> … the proposal clarifies that the courts opening insolvency proceedings also have jurisdiction for actions which derive directly from insolvency proceedings or are

---

[44] That is, Regulation (EU) 1215/2012 of the European Parliament and of the Council of 12 December 2012 on jurisdiction and the recognition of judgments in civil and commercial matters (recast).

[45] See the Proposal of the European Commission dated 12 December 2012 (2012/0360 (COD)).

[46] Ibid at 3.1.2 of the Explanatory Memorandum.

closely linked with them such as avoidance actions. This amendment codifies the case-law of the CJEU in the 'DekoMarty' decision.[47] Where such an action is related to another action against the same defendant which is based on general civil and commercial law, the proposal gives the liquidator the possibility to bring both actions in the courts of the defendant's domicile if these courts are competent pursuant to [the Judgments Regulation]. This rule would allow a liquidator to bring, for example, an action for directors' liability based on insolvency law together with an action against that director based on tort law or company law in the same court.

Thus, Article 6(1) RR is not designed to modify the law, but to codify the existing principles governing the relationship between the Brussels Regulation (Recast) and the OR, as set out in the case law under the OR.

Recital (35) RR also explains the purpose of Article 6 RR: **8.587**

> The courts of the Member State within the territory of which insolvency proceedings have been opened should also have jurisdiction for actions which derive directly from the insolvency proceedings and are closely linked with them. Such actions should include avoidance actions against defendants in other Member States and actions concerning obligations that arise in the course of the insolvency proceedings, such as advance payment for costs of the proceedings. In contrast, actions for the performance of the obligations under a contract concluded by the debtor prior to the opening of proceedings do not derive directly from the proceedings. Where such an action is related to another action based on general civil and commercial law, the insolvency practitioner should be able to bring both actions in the courts of the defendant's domicile if he considers it more efficient to bring the action in that forum. This could, for example, be the case where the insolvency practitioner wishes to combine an action for director's liability on the basis of insolvency law with an action based on company law or general tort law.

Recital (7) RR states that: **8.588**

> Bankruptcy, proceedings relating to the winding-up of insolvent companies or other legal persons, judicial arrangements, compositions and analogous proceedings and actions related to such proceedings are excluded from the scope of [the Brussels Regulation (Recast)]. Those proceedings should be covered by this Regulation. The interpretation of this Regulation should as much as possible avoid regulatory loopholes between the two instruments. However, the mere fact that a national procedure is not listed in Annex A to this Regulation should not imply that it is covered by [the Brussels Regulation (Recast)].

This confirms the well-established principle that the RR and the Brussels Regulation (Recast) are intended to be complementary, so that they do not (at least in principle[48])

---

[47] That is, Case C-339/07 *Seagon v Deko Marty Belgium NV* [2009] ECR I-767, [2009] 1 WLR 2168.

[48] There are in fact some obvious gaps, even after allowing for the effect of Directive 2001/24/EC on the reorganisation and winding up of credit institutions as amended and Solvency II: see 8.10–8.13 above. The gaps include insolvency proceedings for investment undertakings in the case

overlap or leave gaps in their application. The ECJ has endorsed this principle in several recent cases, including *Nickel & Goeldner*[49] and *F-Tex*.[50]

8.589 However, this principle must be construed subject to Article 6(2) RR, which is not a mere codification of the existing law. In summary: where an 'insolvency action' (A1) is related to a 'civil or commercial action' (A2) against the same defendant(s), the insolvency practitioner may bring both actions together in the Member State(s) where any of the defendants are domiciled, provided that such Member State(s) have jurisdiction in respect of A2 under the Brussels Regulation (Recast). The same rule applies to debtors in possession, provided that national law allows the debtor in possession to bring actions on behalf of the estate. The definition of 'related actions' in Article 6(3) RR is identical to the definition of the same term in Article 30(3) of the Brussels Regulation (Recast), and should be construed in the same manner.

(RR) Article 7—Applicable law

1. Save as otherwise provided in this Regulation, the law applicable to insolvency proceedings and their effects shall be that of the Member State within the territory of which such proceedings are opened (the 'State of the opening of proceedings').
2. The law of the State of the opening of proceedings shall determine the conditions for the opening of those proceedings, their conduct and their closure. In particular, it shall determine the following:
   (a) the debtors against which insolvency proceedings may be brought on account of their capacity;
   (b) the assets which form part of the insolvency estate and the treatment of assets acquired by or devolving on the debtor after the opening of the insolvency proceedings;
   (c) the respective powers of the debtor and the insolvency practitioner;
   (d) the conditions under which set-offs may be invoked;
   (e) the effects of insolvency proceedings on current contracts to which the debtor is party;
   (f) the effects of the insolvency proceedings on proceedings brought by individual creditors, with the exception of pending lawsuits;
   (g) the claims which are to be lodged against the debtor's insolvency estate and the treatment of claims arising after the opening of insolvency proceedings;
   (h) the rules governing the lodging, verification and admission of claims;
   (i) the rules governing the distribution of proceeds from the realisation of assets, the ranking of claims and the rights of creditors who have obtained

---

of the OR, and collective investment undertakings in the case of both the OR and RR, all of which are excluded from both Brussels Regulation (Recast) and the OR/RR as the case may be.

[49] Case C-157/13 *Nickel & Goeldner Spendition GmbH v 'Kintra' UAB* [2015] QB 96 at [21].
[50] Case C-213/10 *F-Tex SIA v Lietuvos-Anglijos UAB* [2013] Bus LR 232 at [21], [29], and [48].

partial satisfaction after the opening of insolvency proceedings by virtue of a right in rem or through a set-off;

(j)   the conditions for, and the effects of closure of, insolvency proceedings, in particular by composition;

(k) creditors' rights after the closure of insolvency proceedings;

(l)   who is to bear the costs and expenses incurred in the insolvency proceedings;

(m) the rules relating to the voidness, voidability or unenforceability of legal acts detrimental to the general body of creditors.

Article 7 RR is copied from Article 4 OR, and reference should be made to the com- **8.590** mentary under Article 4 OR above.

However, it should be noted that 'lawsuits pending' in Article 7(2)(f) RR in effect **8.591** cross-refers to Article 18 RR, just as Article 4(2)(f) OR in effect cross-referred to Article 15 OR. The changes to Article 15 OR contained in Article 18 RR are commented on below under Article 18 RR.

It should also be noted that just as Article 4(2)(m) OR was qualified by the 'double **8.592** actionability' defence in Article 13 OR, Article 7(2)(m) RR is similarly qualified by Article 16 RR.

(RR) Article 8—Third parties' rights in rem

1. The opening of insolvency proceedings shall not affect the rights in rem of creditors or third parties in respect of tangible or intangible, moveable or immoveable assets, both specific assets and collections of indefinite assets as a whole which change from time to time, belonging to the debtor which are situated within the territory of another Member State at the time of the opening of proceedings.

2. The rights referred to in paragraph 1 shall, in particular, mean:

(a) the right to dispose of assets or have them disposed of and to obtain satisfaction from the proceeds of or income from those assets, in particular by virtue of a lien or a mortgage;

(b) the exclusive right to have a claim met, in particular a right guaranteed by a lien in respect of the claim or by assignment of the claim by way of a guarantee;

(c) the right to demand assets from, and/or to require restitution by, anyone having possession or use of them contrary to the wishes of the party so entitled;

(d) a right in rem to the beneficial use of assets.

3. The right, recorded in a public register and enforceable against third parties, based on which a right in rem within the meaning of paragraph 1 may be obtained shall be considered to be a right in rem.

4. Paragraph 1 shall not preclude actions for voidness, voidability or unenforceability as referred to in point (m) of Article 7(2).

This Article simply copies Article 5 OR without any material changes. There is **8.593** a change to the cross-reference in Article 8(4) RR from a cross-reference to Article 4(2)(m) OR to a cross-reference to Article 7(2)(m) RR. Reference should be made to the commentary on Article 5 OR above.

(RR) Article 9—Set-off

1. The opening of insolvency proceedings shall not affect the right of creditors to demand the set-off of their claims against the claims of a debtor, where such a set-off is permitted by the law applicable to the insolvent debtor's claim.
2. Paragraph 1 shall not preclude actions for voidness, voidability or unenforceability as referred to in point (m) of Article 7(2).

8.594 Article 9 RR is copied from Article 6 OR without any material change. There is simply a change in Article 9(2) RR in changing the cross-reference from Article 4(2)(m) OR to Article 7(2)(m) RR. Reference should be made to the commentary on Article 6 OR above.

(RR) Article 10—Reservation of title

1. The opening of insolvency proceedings against the purchaser of an asset shall not affect sellers' rights that are based on a reservation of title where at the time of the opening of proceedings the asset is situated within the territory of a Member State other than the State of the opening of proceedings.
2. The opening of insolvency proceedings against the seller of an asset, after delivery of the asset, shall not constitute grounds for rescinding or terminating the sale and shall not prevent the purchaser from acquiring title where at the time of the opening of proceedings the asset sold is situated within the territory of a Member State other than the State of the opening of proceedings.
3. Paragraphs 1 and 2 shall not preclude actions for voidness, voidability or unenforceability as referred to in point (m) of Article 7(2).

8.595 Article 10 RR is copied from Article 7 OR without any material change. The only alteration is in the cross-reference in Article 10(3) RR from a cross-reference to Article 4(2)(m) OR to a cross-reference to Article 7(2)(m) RR. Reference should be made to the commentary on Article 7 OR above.

(RR) Article 11—Contracts relating to immoveable property

1. The effects of insolvency proceedings on a contract conferring the right to acquire or make use of immoveable property shall be governed solely by the law of the Member State within the territory of which the immoveable property is situated.
2. The court which opened main insolvency proceedings shall have jurisdiction to approve the termination or modification of the contracts referred to in this Article where:
   (a) the law of the Member State applicable to those contracts requires that such a contract may only be terminated or modified with the approval of the court opening insolvency proceedings; and
   (b) no insolvency proceedings have been opened in that Member State.

8.596 Article 11(1) RR is copied from Article 8 OR without any material change. Reference should be made to the commentary on Article 8 OR above.

The change is contained in the additional paragraph Article 11(2) RR. Whereas **8.597** Article 11(1) is a general exclusion from the effects of insolvency proceedings on a contract relating to immoveable property, causing the contract to be governed solely by the law of the Member State within the territory of which the immoveable property is situated, Article 11(2) RR creates an exception to that exception. It confers jurisdiction on the court which has opened main insolvency proceedings to approve the termination or modification of contracts relating to immoveable property in certain circumstances. The relevant circumstances are where the law of the Member State applicable to the contract requires that the contract may only be terminated or modified with the approval of the court opening insolvency proceedings and where no insolvency proceedings have been opened in that Member State. Without this conferral of jurisdiction, a serious problem may have arisen in such a case, if, for example, it were not possible to open secondary proceedings in the Member State within the territory of which the moveable property was situated. In any event, even where the opening of local territorial proceedings is possible in such a case, it would be an unnecessary expense and complication, which is avoided by this additional provision.

(RR) Article 12—Payment systems and financial markets

1. Without prejudice to Article 8, the effects of insolvency proceedings on the rights and obligations of the parties to a payment or settlement system or to a financial market shall be governed solely by the law of the Member State applicable to that system or market.
2. Paragraph 1 shall not preclude any action for voidness, voidability or unenforceability which may be taken to set aside payments or transactions under the law applicable to the relevant payment system or financial market.

Article 12 RR is copied from Article 9 OR and contains no material change. The **8.598** only change is the change in the cross-reference in Article 12(1) RR from a cross-reference to Article 5 OR to a cross-reference to Article 8 RR. Reference should be made to the commentary on Article 9 OR above.

[The concept of payment or settlement systems in Article 12 is closely linked to **8.599** the Directive 98/26/EC on settlement finality in payment and securities settlement systems ('Finality Directive'). However, a relatively widespread view is that the scope of Article 12 is broader than that of the Directive and also covers formal netting arrangements between three or more participants such as inter-company netting arrangements. The absence in the Recast Regulation of an express rule on netting may help to explain this broad understanding of Article 12. Giving the economic importance of netting, the question of whether and to what extent netting arrangements are governed by Article 9 (set-off) and/or Article 12 (payment and settlement systems) could end up before the ECJ for clarification. (**MV/FG**)]

(RR) Article 13—Contracts of employment

1. The effects of insolvency proceedings on employment contracts and relationships shall be governed solely by the law of the Member State applicable to the contract of employment.
2. The courts of the Member State in which secondary insolvency proceedings may be opened shall retain jurisdiction to approve the termination or modification of the contracts referred to in this Article even if no insolvency proceedings have been opened in that Member State.
   The first subparagraph shall also apply to an authority competent under national law to approve the termination or modification of the contracts referred to in this Article.

8.600 Article 13(1) RR is copied from Article 10 OR and reference should be made to the commentary on Article 10 OR above.

8.601 The changes are contained in the new Article 13(2) RR. Under the OR, it was occasionally found necessary to apply for the opening of secondary proceedings simply in order to assist with the termination or modification of employment contracts.[51] The opening of secondary proceedings, which might be disruptive to the main proceedings and in any event would involve additional expense and potential delay, can now be avoided by the conferment of this power. The word 'retain' in this context should be read as 'have', since this type of jurisdiction usually arises in connection with local insolvency proceedings. The coda to Article 13(2) RR, which extends the same power to an authority competent under national law to approve the termination or modification of employment contracts in the case of insolvency proceedings, deals with the situation where the approval of the termination or modification during local insolvency proceedings lies with an authority other than the court in charge of the insolvency proceedings.

(RR) Article 14—Effects on rights subject to registration

The effects of insolvency proceedings on the rights of a debtor in immoveable property, a ship or an aircraft subject to registration in a public register shall be determined by the law of the Member State under the authority of which the register is kept.

8.602 Article 14 RR is copied from Article 11 OR and the commentary on Article 11 OR above should be referred to.

---

[51] For example, in *Re Nortel Networks SA* [2009] EWHC 1482 (Ch), [2010] BCC 21, where the English High Court gave the English administrators of the French registered debtor company permission to apply to the Versailles *tribunal de commerce* to open secondary proceedings to assist with redundancy of employees in France.

**(RR) Article 15—European patents with unitary effect
and Community trade marks**

> For the purposes of this Regulation, a European patent with unitary effect, a
> Community trade mark or any other similar right established by Union law may
> be included only in the proceedings referred to in Article 3(1).

Article 15 RR is based on the text of Article 11 OR, but the reference to 'a   **8.603**
Community patent' has been replaced by 'a European patent with unitary effect'
and the reference to 'Community Law' has been replaced by 'Union Law'.[52]

The changes are in effect an updating to take account of developments in   **8.604**
European patent law. For several decades the Member States of the European
Union have been negotiating the creation of a European patent with uni-
tary effect and a unified European patent court. In 2012, representatives of
the EU Member States achieved a breakthrough agreement. The 'European
Patent with Unitary Effect' is a European patent, granted by the European
Patent Office (EPO) under the rules and procedures of the European Patent
Convention, to which, upon request of the patent proprietor, unitary effect
is given for the territory of the 25 Member States participating in the unitary patent scheme. The unitary patent will co-exist with national patents
and with classical European patents. Patent proprietors will in future be able
to choose between various combinations of classical European patents and
unitary patents. The new patent regime is set out in Regulations 1257/2012
and 1260/2012.

[Some Member States (eg Spain and Italy) do not participate in Regulation   **8.605**
1257/2012 implementing enhanced co-operation in the area of the creation
of unitary patent protection. However Article 15 is also applicable in these
Member States in order to determine which assets belong to the estate of the
main proceedings and which belong to the estate of the territorial proceedings
(MV/FG)].

(RR) Article 16—Detrimental acts

> Point (m) of Article 7(2) shall not apply where the person who benefited from
> an act detrimental to all the creditors provides proof that:
> (a) the act is subject to the law of a Member State other than that of the State
>   of the opening of proceedings; and
> (b) the law of that Member State does not allow any means of challenging that
>   act in the relevant case.

Article 16 RR is copied from Article 13 OR with no material change. The only   **8.606**
change is a change in the cross-reference from a cross-reference to Article 4(2)(m)

---

[52] See the Treaty on European Law (TEU) and the Treaty of the Functioning of the European
Union (TFEU).

OR to Article 7(2)(m) RR. Reference should be made to the commentary on Article 13 OR above.

8.607 [Article 16 can be invoked against the provisions of insolvency law on fraudulent or undervalued transfers. It is worth noting that Article 16 RR may also be applicable to rules of the *lex fori concursus* that fulfil an equivalent function to avoidance actions, but do not require the setting-aside of the challenged act. That is the case, for instance of rules that leave the transaction valid but give the insolvency practitioner the right to apply for a court order reversing its effects, or impose the subordination of the rights arisen out of the challenged act (eg the insolvency subordination of loans given by shareholders or insiders under some national laws) (**MV/FG**)].

(RR) Article 17—Protection of third-party purchasers

Where, by an act concluded after the opening of insolvency proceedings, a debtor disposes, for consideration, of:
(a) an immoveable asset;
(b) a ship or an aircraft subject to registration in a public register; or
(c) securities the existence of which requires registration in a register laid down by law;
the validity of that act shall be governed by the law of the State within the territory of which the immoveable asset is situated or under the authority of which the register is kept.

8.608 Article 17 RR is copied from Article 14 OR and reference should be made to the commentary on Article 14 OR above.

(RR) Article 18—Effects of insolvency proceedings on pending lawsuits or arbitral proceedings

The effects of insolvency proceedings on a pending lawsuit or pending arbitral proceedings concerning an asset or a right which forms part of a debtor's insolvency estate shall be governed solely by the law of the Member State in which that lawsuit is pending or in which the arbitral tribunal has its seat.

8.609 Article 18 RR is based on Article 15 OR but contains clarifications of its meaning and effect. The commenatry on Article 15 OR above should be consulted for the background.

8.610 In Article 15 OR, the question arose whether 'lawsuit pending' included arbitration proceedings. Different language versions suggested different answers but the English Commercial Court in *Elektrim v Vivendi*[53] held that

---

[53] [2008] EWHC 2155 (Comm), [2008] 2 Lloyd's Rep 636, aff'd (CA) [2009] EWCA Civ 677, [2010] BCC 348.

Article 15 OR included arbitration proceedings. This result is confirmed in the text of Article 18 RR.

The wording of Article 15 OR also gave rise to a question of whether Article 15 **8.611** OR was (i) limited to proprietary claims and/or (ii) limited to claims that property belonged to the debtor: see the commentary relating to Article 15 OR above.

The English commercial court in the case of *Elektrim v Vivendi* (cited above) ruled **8.612** that Article 15 OR was not limited to proprietary claims. The view was taken that Article 15 OR applied to any claim to a share in the estate.

The suggestion that Article 15 OR applied only to proprietary claims originated **8.613** from the expression 'concerning an asset or a right of which the debtor has been divested'. This was actually a reference back to the formation of an estate by means of the 'divestment' of a debtor mentioned in Article 1(1) OR. Although the English text might have suggested, if read literally, that Article 15 OR only applied to the recovery of assets belonging, or formerly belonging, to the debtor, other language versions referred to assets which were part of the estate: see the commentary on Article 15 OR above.

By removing the reference to divesting, and making an express reference to the **8.614** insolvency estate, Article 18 RR clarifies the fact that, as had been held in the English commercial court case of *Elektrim v Vivendi*, the provision is not restricted to proprietary claims. That, at least, appears to be the intention of the change in wording, although the reference is still to 'concerning an asset or a right which forms part of the debtor's insolvency estate',[54] which could be read as making a claim to ownership of some asset within the debtor's estate. It is suggested that the broader interpretation in *Elektrim v Vivendi*, namely that any claim which affects the insolvency estate by seeking a share of it, is the correct interpretation of the provision.

[The reference in Article 18 to the law of the Member State where the dispute **8.615** is pending does not extend to questions of international jurisdiction, which are subject to a uniform regime under the Recast Regulation. The jurisdiction of the insolvency courts *only* extends to actions which are based on insolvency rules and are directly linked to the insolvency proceedings (see Article 6 RR). Conversely, actions based on general civil and commercial law (eg contract law) are subject to the Brussels I Regulation (see Recital 35 RR). This may have an indirect effect upon the validity and efficacy of arbitration agreements. Some national laws do not recognise the validity or efficacy of arbitration clauses in the case of insolvency in order to allow for the centralization

---

[54] See also the same wording in Recital (73) RR.

of all disputes affecting the estate in the insolvency courts. However, this justification does not hold in the EU context, as with regard to actions based on general civil and commercial law such centralization is not possible: if the validity of the arbitration agreement is nullified or its efficacy suspended by the insolvency proceedings, it would not mean that the dispute could be joined to the insolvency proceedings, but merely that the general rules on jurisdiction apply, in particular the Brussels I Regulation. Therefore, if the main justification of the national rule invalidating or rendering inoperative the arbitration agreement is the concentration of disputes before the insolvency court, that justification does not hold when the RR governs the insolvency proceedings. (**MV/FG**)].

B. Chapter II: Recognition of Insolvency Proceedings

(RR) Article 19—Principle

1. Any judgment opening insolvency proceedings handed down by a court of a Member State which has jurisdiction pursuant to Article 3 shall be recognised in all other Member States from the moment that it becomes effective in the State of the opening of proceedings.
   The rule laid down in the first subparagraph shall also apply where, on account of a debtor's capacity, insolvency proceedings cannot be brought against that debtor in other Member States.
2. Recognition of the proceedings referred to in Article 3(1) shall not preclude the opening of the proceedings referred to in Article 3(2) by a court in another Member State. The latter proceedings shall be secondary insolvency proceedings within the meaning of Chapter III.

8.616 Article 19 RR is copied from Article 16 OR and reference should be made to the commentary on Article 16 OR above. Note however the RR provisions relating to the meaning of 'court' in Article 2(6) RR above.

(RR) Article 20—Effects of recognition

1. The judgment opening insolvency proceedings as referred to in Article 3(1) shall, with no further formalities, produce the same effects in any other Member State as under the law of the State of the opening of proceedings, unless this Regulation provides otherwise and as long as no proceedings referred to in Article 3(2) are opened in that other Member State.
2. The effects of the proceedings referred to in Article 3(2) may not be challenged in other Member States. Any restriction of creditors' rights, in particular a stay or discharge, shall produce effects vis-à-vis assets situated within the territory of another Member State only in the case of those creditors who have given their consent.

Article 20 RR is copied from Article 17 OR and reference should be made to the **8.617** commentary under Article 17 OR above.

(RR) Article 21—Powers of the insolvency practitioner

1. The insolvency practitioner appointed by a court which has jurisdiction pursuant to Article 3(1) may exercise all the powers conferred on it, by the law of the State of the opening of proceedings, in another Member State, as long as no other insolvency proceedings have been opened there and no preservation measure to the contrary has been taken there further to a request for the opening of insolvency proceedings in that State. Subject to Articles 8 and 10, the insolvency practitioner may, in particular, remove the debtor's assets from the territory of the Member State in which they are situated.
2. The insolvency practitioner appointed by a court which has jurisdiction pursuant to Article 3(2) may in any other Member State claim through the courts or out of court that moveable property was removed from the territory of the State of the opening of proceedings to the territory of that other Member State after the opening of the insolvency proceedings. The insolvency practitioner may also bring any action to set aside which is in the interests of the creditors.
3. In exercising its powers, the insolvency practitioner shall comply with the law of the Member State within the territory of which it intends to take action, in particular with regard to procedures for the realization of assets. Those powers may not include coercive measures, unless ordered by a court of that Member State, or the right to rule on legal proceedings or disputes.

There is a change of terminology here, as there is throughout the RR, in that the **8.618** expression 'liquidator' as defined in the OR has been replaced by 'insolvency practitioner' as defined in Article 2(5) RR and listed in Annex B.

Otherwise Article 21(1) RR is copied in all material respects from Article 18(1) **8.619** OR and the commentary to that Article should be referred to above. The cross-references in Article 18(1) OR to Articles 5 and 7 OR have been replaced by cross-references to Articles 8 and 10 RR.

Article 21(2) RR, apart from exchanging 'liquidator' for 'insolvency practi- **8.620** tioner' is identical to Article 18(2) OR and reference should be made to the commentary on Article 18 OR above.

Article 21(3) RR is similar to Article 18(3) OR, but there is a significant change **8.621** in the last sentence. The last sentence of both Article 18 OR and Article 21 RR state that the powers exercised by the insolvency administrator 'may not include coercive measures' or the right to rule on legal proceedings or disputes. With regard to the text of the OR, there is a question as to whether the prohibition on coercive measures applied to situations where (i) such measures were ordered by the court conducting the main insolvency proceedings and therefore in principle enforceable via Article 25 OR (see now Article

32 RR)[55] and/or (ii) the measures were ordered by a local court in another Member State.

8.622   Article 21(3) RR makes it clear that the liquidator in the main proceeding may exercise coercive measures in another Member State if they are ordered by a court of that Member State.[56] The change in the text has not however resolved whether the bar on coercive measures extends to orders of the court conducting the main insolvency proceedings which are required to be recognized under the RR equivalent of Article 25 OR, namely Article 32 RR. That issue remains to be decided by the CJEU.

(RR) Article 22—Proof of the insolvency practitioner's appointment

The insolvency practitioner's appointment shall be evidenced by a certified copy of the original decision appointing it or by any other certificate issued by the court which has jurisdiction.

A translation into the official language or one of the official languages of the Member State within the territory of which it intends to act may be required. No legalisation or other similar formality shall be required.

8.623   Article 22 RR is copied from Article 19 OR, save for the substitution of 'insolvency practitioner' for 'liquidator'. Reference should therefore be made to the commentary to Article 19 OR above.

(RR) Article 23—Return and imputation

1. A creditor which, after the opening of the proceedings referred to in Article 3(1), obtains by any means, in particular through enforcement, total or partial satisfaction of its claim on the assets belonging to a debtor situated within the territory of another Member State, shall return what it has obtained to the insolvency practitioner, subject to Articles 8 and 10.
2. In order to ensure the equal treatment of creditors, a creditor which has, in the course of insolvency proceedings, obtained a dividend on its claim shall share in distributions made in other proceedings only where creditors of the same ranking or category have, in those other proceedings, obtained an equivalent dividend.

8.624   Article 23 RR is copied from Article 20 OR and is identical to it, save for the substitution of 'insolvency practitioner' for 'liquidator' and for the alteration of the cross-references from Articles 5 and 7 OR to Articles 8 and 10 RR. Reference should be made to the commentary under Article 20 OR.

(RR) Article 24—Establishment of insolvency registers

1. Member States shall establish and maintain in their territory one or several registers in which information concerning insolvency proceedings is published

---

[55] In *Handelsveem BV v Hill* [2011] BPIR 1024 the Netherlands Supreme Court held that Art 18(3) OR did not apply to prevent a coercive measure ordered by the English court being recognized and enforced by the Netherlands courts via Art 25 OR.

[56] Note that 'court' for this purpose is restricted to a 'judicial body': Art 2(6)(i) RR.

('insolvency registers'). That information shall be published as soon as possible after the opening of such proceedings.

2. The information referred to in paragraph 1 shall be made publicly available, subject to the conditions laid down in Article 27, and shall include the following ('mandatory information'):

(a) the date of the opening of insolvency proceedings;

(b) the court opening insolvency proceedings and the case reference number, if any;

(c) the type of insolvency proceedings referred to in Annex A that were opened and, where applicable, any relevant subtype of such proceedings opened in accordance with national law;

(d) whether jurisdiction for opening proceedings is based on Article 3(1), 3(2) or 3(4);

(e) if the debtor is a company or a legal person, the debtor's name, registration number, registered office or, if different, postal address;

(f) if the debtor is an individual whether or not exercising an independent business or professional activity, the debtor's name, registration number, if any, and postal address or, where the address is protected, the debtor's place and date of birth;

(g) the name, postal address or e-mail address of the insolvency practitioner, if any, appointed in the proceedings;

(h) the time limit for lodging claims, if any, or a reference to the criteria for calculating that time limit;

(i) the date of closing main insolvency proceedings, if any;

(j) the court before which and, where applicable, the time limit within which a challenge of the decision opening insolvency proceedings is to be lodged in accordance with Article 5, or a reference to the criteria for calculating that time limit.

3. Paragraph 2 shall not preclude Member States from including documents or additional information in their national insolvency registers, such as directors' disqualifications related to insolvency.

4. Member States shall not be obliged to include in the insolvency registers the information referred to in paragraph 1 of this Article in relation to individuals not exercising an independent business or professional activity, or to make such information publicly available through the system of interconnection of those registers, provided that known foreign creditors are informed, pursuant to Article 54, of the elements referred to under point (j) of paragraph 2 of this Article.

Where a Member State makes use of the possibility referred to in the first subparagraph, the insolvency proceedings shall not affect the claims of foreign creditors who have not received the information referred to in the first subparagraph.

5. The publication of information in the registers under this Regulation shall not have any legal effects other than those set out in national law and in Article 55(6).

Article 24 RR is entirely new and stems from the proposal of the European **8.625** Commission to establish national insolvency registers which will in time be interconnected.

8.626 Commentators have for a long period pointed out the difficulties that are caused by the lack of insolvency registers which can be searched electronically from other Member States and which preferably should be interconnected across the European Union.

8.627 One example of the difficulties created by the lack of searchable electronic registers is illustrated by the *Stojevic* case,[57] where shortly after the opening of main insolvency proceedings in the UK, a further, purportedly main, proceeding was opened in respect of the same debtor by the Austrian courts.

8.628 Article 24(1) RR lays down the obligation on Member States to establish and maintain one or more registers about insolvency proceedings. Although this is not spelt out, the implication from the following Articles is that the registers must be electronic and available on the internet.

8.629 Article 24(2) RR sets out in detail the information that should be contained in the register, although Member States are not precluded from including documents or additional information: Article 24(3) RR.

8.630 There is an exception to the detailed information required to be placed on the register in relation to what could be described as 'non-traders', ie 'individuals not exercising an independent business or professional activity'. In such a case, the bare bones information set out in Article 24(2)(j) RR is sufficient.

8.631 The date of publication in the register may have a significance under national law. As far as EU law is concerned, in accordance with Article 24(5) RR the time limit for lodging claims under Article 55(6) RR is required to be not less than 30 days following the publication of the opening of the insolvency proceedings in the register of the Member State of opening. There is an exception for cases within Article 24(4) RR, which allows for the publication of minimal information in relation to non-traders: the period for lodging claims is required to be not less than 30 days following the notice required to be given under Article 54 RR requiring the lodging of claims.

(RR) Article 25—Interconnection of insolvency registers

1. The Commission shall establish a decentralised system for the interconnection of insolvency registers by means of implementing acts. That system shall be composed of the insolvency registers and the European e-Justice Portal, which shall serve as a central public electronic access point to information in the system. The system shall provide a search service in all the official languages of the institutions of the Union in order to make available the mandatory information and any other documents or information included in the insolvency registers

---

[57] Referred to at various points in the commentary on the OR—see the index of cases at the front of this work.

which the Member States choose to make available through the European
e-Justice Portal.

2. By means of implementing acts in accordance with the procedure referred
   to in Article 87, the Commission shall adopt the following by 26 June
   2019:
   (a) the technical specification defining the methods of communication and
       information exchange by electronic means on the basis of the established
       interface specification for the system of interconnection of insolvency
       registers;
   (b) the technical measures ensuring the minimum information technology
       security standards for communication and distribution of information
       within the system of interconnection of insolvency registers;
   (c) minimum criteria for the search service provided by the European e-Justice
       Portal based on the information set out in Article 24;
   (d) minimum criteria for the presentation of the results of such searches based
       on the information set out in Article 24;
   (e) the means and the technical conditions of availability of services provided
       by the system of interconnection; and
   (f) a glossary containing a basic explanation of the national insolvency pro-
       ceedings listed in Annex A.

Article 25 RR requires the European Commission to establish a decentralized **8.632**
system for the interconnection of insolvency registers. The system will have to
provide a search service in all the official languages of the institutions of the
European Union in relation to the mandated information and any other documents for information included in the insolvency registers which the Member
States choose to make available through the European e-Justice Portal.

Article 25(2) RR requires the European Commission to adopt a number of steps **8.633**
by 26 June 2019. The interconnectivity of national registers is thus still a long way
away at the time of writing.

(RR) Article 26—Costs of establishing and interconnecting
insolvency registers

1. The establishment, maintenance and future development of the system of interconnection of insolvency registers shall be financed from the general budget of
   the Union.
2. Each Member State shall bear the costs of establishing and adjusting its
   national insolvency registers to make them interoperable with the European
   e-Justice Portal, as well as the costs of administering, operating and maintaining those registers. This shall be without prejudice to the possibility
   to apply for grants to support such activities under the Union's financial
   programmes.

One of the questions raised when interconnecting insolvency registers were sug- **8.634**
gested, was the source of finance. Article 26(1) RR provides that the establishment, maintenance, and future development of the system of interconnection of

insolvency registers is to be financed from the general budget of the European Union. By contrast, Article 27(2) RR provides that each Member State shall bear the costs of establishing and adjusting its national insolvency registers to make them interoperable with the European e-Justice Portal and are to bear their own costs of administering, operating, and maintaining the national registers. That responsibility is 'without prejudice' to the possibility of applying for grants to support such activities under the EU's financial programmes.

(RR) Article 27—Conditions of access to information via the system of interconnection

1. Member States shall ensure that the mandatory information referred to in points (a) to (j) of Article 24(2) is available free of charge via the system of interconnection of insolvency registers.
2. This Regulation shall not preclude Member States from charging a reasonable fee for access to the documents or additional information referred to in Article 24(3) via the system of interconnection of insolvency registers.
3. Member States may make access to mandatory information concerning individuals who are not exercising an independent business or professional activity, and concerning individuals exercising an independent business or professional activity when the insolvency proceedings are not related to that activity, subject to supplementary search criteria relating to the debtor in addition to the minimum criteria referred to in point (c) of Article 25(2).
4. Member States may require that access to the information referred to in paragraph 3 be made conditional upon a request to the competent authority. Member States may make access conditional upon the verification of the existence of a legitimate interest for accessing such information. The requesting person shall be able to submit the request for information electronically by means of a standard form via the European e-Justice Portal. Where a legitimate interest is required, it shall be permissible for the requesting person to justify his request by electronic copies of relevant documents. The requesting person shall be provided with an answer by the competent authority within 3 working days.
   The requesting person shall not be obliged to provide translations of the documents justifying his request, or to bear any costs of translation which the competent authority may incur.

8.635 Article 27(1) RR requires the information required to be registered by the RR to be available free of charge via the system of interconnected insolvency registers. By contrast, Member States which register non-mandatory documents or information may charge a 'reasonable fee' for access to those.

8.636 Article 27(3) and (4) RR make special provision where the individual debtors 'who are not exercising an independent business or professional activity' and where the insolvency proceedings are not related to an independent business or professional activity. In such cases searches can be restricted or access made conditional upon a request to the competent authority. Member States may make access conditional upon the verification of the existence of legitimate interests for accessing such information.

(RR) Article 28—Publication in another Member State

1. The insolvency practitioner or the debtor in possession shall request that notice of the judgment opening insolvency proceedings and, where appropriate, the decision appointing the insolvency practitioner be published in any other Member State where an establishment of the debtor is located in accordance with the publication procedures provided for in that Member State. Such publication shall specify, where appropriate, the insolvency practitioner appointed and whether the jurisdiction rule applied is that pursuant to Article 3(1) or (2).
2. The insolvency practitioner or the debtor in possession may request that the information referred to in paragraph 1 be published in any other Member State where the insolvency practitioner or the debtor in possession deems it necessary in accordance with the publication procedures provided for in that Member State.

Pending the establishment of interconnected EU-wide searchable registers in the future, the question of publication in other Member States of the opening of insolvency proceedings remains significant. **8.637**

Article 28 RR is in some ways modelled on Article 21 OR, but there are significant changes. **8.638**

Article 21 OR provided that the insolvency administrator 'may' request notice of the judgment of opening of proceedings and, where appropriate, the decision appointing him, be published in any other Member State, and allowed Member States in which the debtor had an establishment to require publication; Article 28(1) RR requires the insolvency practitioner or the debtor in possession to request publication in any other Member State where the debtor has an establishment. In addition, Article 28(2) RR allows the insolvency practitioner or the debtor in possession to request publication in any other Member State where they think it necessary. **8.639**

Article 28(1) RR, second sentence, requires what is now the mandatory publication in any other Member State where the debtor has an establishment to specify, where appropriate, the insolvency practitioner appointed and whether the opening is a main proceeding under Article 3(1) RR or a territorial proceeding under Article 3(2) RR. **8.640**

(RR) Article 29—Registration in public registers of another Member State

1. Where the law of a Member State in which an establishment of the debtor is located and this establishment has been entered into a public register of that Member State, or the law of a Member State in which immovable property belonging to the debtor is located, requires information on the opening of

insolvency proceedings referred to in Article 28 to be published in the land register, company register or any other public register, the insolvency practitioner or the debtor in possession shall take all the necessary measures to ensure such a registration.

2. The insolvency practitioner or the debtor in possession may request such registration in any other Member State, provided that the law of the Member State where the register is kept allows such registration.

8.641 Article 29 RR is new. It requires registration of information in Article 28 RR regarding insolvency proceedings to be effected by the insolvency practitioner or debtor in possession where local law requires such registration in a public register. This may relate to a public register of establishments, immoveable property, company register, or any other public register.

(RR) Article 30—Costs

The costs of the publication and registration provided for in Articles 28 and 29 shall be regarded as costs and expenses incurred in the proceedings.

8.642 Article 30 RR is copied from Article 23 OR, but the cross-references to Articles 21 and 22 OR have been updated to cross-references to Articles 28 and 29 RR. Reference should be made to the commentary on Article 23 OR above.

(RR) Article 31—Honouring of an obligation to a debtor

1. Where an obligation has been honoured in a Member State for the benefit of a debtor who is subject to insolvency proceedings opened in another Member State, when it should have been honoured for the benefit of the insolvency practitioner in those proceedings, the person honouring the obligation shall be deemed to have discharged it if he was unaware of the opening of the proceedings.

2. Where such an obligation is honoured before the publication provided for in Article 28 has been effected, the person honouring the obligation shall be presumed, in the absence of proof to the contrary, to have been unaware of the opening of insolvency proceedings. Where the obligation is honoured after such publication has been effected, the person honouring the obligation shall be presumed, in the absence of proof to the contrary, to have been aware of the opening of proceedings.

8.643 Article 31 RR is copied from Article 24 OR, save for the substitution of 'insolvency practitioner' for 'liquidator' in Article 31(1) RR and the cross-reference in Article 24(2) OR to Article 21 OR being changed to Article 28 RR in Article 31(2) RR. Reference should be made to the commentary on Article 24 OR above.

(RR) Article 32—Recognition and enforceability of other judgments

1. Judgments handed down by a court whose judgment concerning the opening of proceedings is recognised in accordance with Article 19 and which concern the course and closure of insolvency proceedings, and compositions approved by that court, shall also be recognised with no further formalities.

Such judgments shall be enforced in accordance with Articles 39 to 44 and 47 to 57 of Regulation (EU) No 1215/2012.

The first subparagraph shall also apply to judgments deriving directly from the insolvency proceedings and which are closely linked with them, even if they were handed down by another court.

The first subparagraph shall also apply to judgments relating to preservation measures taken after the request for the opening of insolvency proceedings or in connection with it.

2. The recognition and enforcement of judgments other than those referred to in paragraph 1 of this Article shall be governed by Regulation (EU) No 1215/2012 provided that that Regulation is applicable.

Article 32 RR essentially copies Article 25 OR, but updates it, apart from the changes mentioned below. **8.644**

Article 32(1) RR is in essence a copy of Article 25(1) OR, save as follows. In Article 32(1) RR the cross-reference to Article 16 OR is replaced by cross-reference to Article 19 RR and the reference to the Brussels Convention on Jurisdiction and the Enforcement of Judgments in Civil and Commercial Matters as amended is replaced by a reference to the relevant Articles of the Recast Brussels Regulation (EU) 1215/2012. **8.645**

Likewise in Article 32(2) RR the cross-reference to the Convention is replaced by cross-reference to the Regulation referred to in Article 32(1) RR. **8.646**

Note that for the purpose of this provision the 'court' need not be a judicial body: Article 2(6) RR. **8.647**

[It should not be forgotten that English schemes of arrangement promulgated as part of a compromise through a main proceeding will be entitled to recognition under Article 32. (AW)] **8.648**

(RR) Article 33—Public policy

Any Member State may refuse to recognise insolvency proceedings opened in another Member State or to enforce a judgment handed down in the context of such proceedings where the effects of such recognition or enforcement would be manifestly contrary to that State's public policy, in particular its fundamental principles or the constitutional rights and liberties of the individual.

Article 33 RR is copied from Article 26 OR and the commentary on Article 26 OR should be referred to above. **8.649**

C. Chapter III: Secondary Insolvency Proceedings

(RR) Article 34—Opening of proceedings

Where main insolvency proceedings have been opened by a court of a Member State and recognised in another Member State, a court of that other Member

State which has jurisdiction pursuant to Article 3(2) may open secondary insolvency proceedings in accordance with the provisions set out in this Chapter. Where the main insolvency proceedings required that the debtor be insolvent, the debtor's insolvency shall not be re-examined in the Member State in which secondary insolvency proceedings may be opened. The effects of secondary insolvency proceedings shall be restricted to the assets of the debtor situated within the territory of the Member State in which those proceedings have been opened.

8.650 Article 34 RR is essentially similar in effect to Article 27 OR. It allows for the opening of secondary proceedings after main proceedings have been opened in another Member State.

8.651 In the *Bank Handlowy* case (C-116/11), the rather absurd conclusion had to be reached, as a matter of practicality, that even if the main proceedings were pre-insolvency proceedings, which could not take place if the debtor were insolvent, nevertheless Article 27 OR required courts in other Member States where there was an establishment to treat the debtor as insolvent for the purposes of opening secondary insolvency proceedings. This type of absurdity is now avoided, since the bar on re-examining the debtor's insolvency is now restricted to cases where the main proceedings require the debtor to be insolvent.

8.652 Article 27 OR had required any secondary proceeding to be a winding-up proceeding listed in Annex B OR. This requirement was widely criticized and appeared to be impractical. It was designed to emphasize the pre-eminence of the main proceedings, but opened up the danger of anomaly and injustice in cases where for example a rescue proceeding was needed in the secondary Member State. Article 34 RR does away with this restriction on the types of possible secondary proceedings. The list of winding-up proceedings in Annex B OR has disappeared and the list of insolvency practitioners formerly set out in Annex C OR has been moved to Annex B RR.

(RR) Article 35—Applicable law

Save as otherwise provided for in this Regulation, the law applicable to secondary insolvency proceedings shall be that of the Member State within the territory of which the secondary insolvency proceedings are opened.

8.653 Article 35 RR is copied from Article 28 OR and reference should be had to the commentary relating to Article 28 OR above.

(RR) Article 36—Right to give an undertaking in order to avoid secondary insolvency proceedings

1. In order to avoid the opening of secondary insolvency proceedings, the insolvency practitioner in the main insolvency proceedings may give a unilateral undertaking (the 'undertaking') in respect of the assets located in the

Member State in which secondary insolvency proceedings could be opened, that when distributing those assets or the proceeds received as a result of their realisation, it will comply with the distribution and priority rights under national law that creditors would have if secondary insolvency proceedings were opened in that Member State. The undertaking shall specify the factual assumptions on which it is based, in particular in respect of the value of the assets located in the Member State concerned and the options available to realise such assets.

2. Where an undertaking has been given in accordance with this Article, the law applicable to the distribution of proceeds from the realisation of assets referred to in paragraph 1, to the ranking of creditors' claims, and to the rights of creditors in relation to the assets referred to in paragraph 1 shall be the law of the Member State in which secondary insolvency proceedings could have been opened. The relevant point in time for determining the assets referred to in paragraph 1 shall be the moment at which the undertaking is given.

3. The undertaking shall be made in the official language or one of the official languages of the Member State where secondary insolvency proceedings could have been opened, or, where there are several official languages in that Member State, the official language or one of the official languages of the place in which secondary insolvency proceedings could have been opened.

4. The undertaking shall be made in writing. It shall be subject to any other requirements relating to form and approval requirements as to distributions, if any, of the State of the opening of the main insolvency proceedings.

5. The undertaking shall be approved by the known local creditors. The rules on qualified majority and voting that apply to the adoption of restructuring plans under the law of the Member State where secondary insolvency proceedings could have been opened shall also apply to the approval of the undertaking. Creditors shall be able to participate in the vote by distance means of communication, where national law so permits. The insolvency practitioner shall inform the known local creditors of the undertaking, of the rules and procedures for its approval, and of the approval or rejection of the undertaking.

6. An undertaking given and approved in accordance with this Article shall be binding on the estate. If secondary insolvency proceedings are opened in accordance with Articles 37 and 38, the insolvency practitioner in the main insolvency proceedings shall transfer any assets which it removed from the territory of that Member State after the undertaking was given or, where those assets have already been realised, their proceeds, to the insolvency practitioner in the secondary insolvency proceedings.

7. Where the insolvency practitioner has given an undertaking, it shall inform local creditors about the intended distributions prior to distributing the assets and proceeds referred to in paragraph 1. If that information does not comply with the terms of the undertaking or the applicable law, any local creditor may challenge such distribution before the courts of the Member State in which main insolvency proceedings have been opened in order to obtain a distribution in accordance with the terms of the undertaking and the applicable law. In such cases, no distribution shall take place until the court has taken a decision on the challenge.

8. Local creditors may apply to the courts of the Member State in which main insolvency proceedings have been opened, in order to require the insolvency practitioner in the main insolvency proceedings to take any suitable measures necessary to ensure compliance with the terms of the undertaking available under the law of the State of the opening of main insolvency proceedings.

9. Local creditors may also apply to the courts of the Member State in which secondary insolvency proceedings could have been opened in order to require the court to take provisional or protective measures to ensure compliance by the insolvency practitioner with the terms of the undertaking.

10. The insolvency practitioner shall be liable for any damage caused to local creditors as a result of its non-compliance with the obligations and requirements set out in this Article.

11. For the purpose of this Article, an authority which is established in the Member State where secondary insolvency proceedings could have been opened and which is obliged under Directive 2008/94/EC of the European Parliament and of the Council to guarantee the payment of employees' outstanding claims resulting from contracts of employment or employment relationships shall be considered to be a local creditor, where the national law so provides.

8.654 Article 36 RR is an entirely new provision and provides for what have been referred to as 'virtual secondaries'.

8.655 Where the main proceedings are pre-insolvency rescue restructuring or reorganization proceedings, with or without a composition, they can be badly disrupted by the opening of secondary proceedings in another Member State.

8.656 As a practical matter, it is often best to avoid secondary proceedings being opened. As we point out in Moss, Fletcher & Isaacs: *The EC Regulation on Insolvency Proceedings* (2nd edn, 2009) at paragraph 8.151:

> Secondary proceedings can disrupt the beneficial rescue or realisation of the business. Particularly in the case of a group which had traded prior to insolvency as one organisation, it makes practical sense for the rescue, reconstruction or insolvency proceedings to be run as a unity. In some situations, local creditors can be persuaded to abstain from starting secondary proceedings in the interests of a better realisation by promising to respect local law priorities in the eventual distribution.

There is then a citation of the *Collins & Aikman* Case,[58] which was subsequently followed by the *Nortel* Case.[59] In both those cases, a promise was made by the UK main administrator to respect local priorities in respect of distributions from assets which would have fallen into a secondary proceeding, *if* no request was made by local creditors to open a secondary proceeding. In *Collins & Aikman* the undertaking was given first and the court approved of this technique subsequently and held

---

[58] [2007] 1 BCLC 182.
[59] [2009] BCC 343.

it to be legally effective. In *Nortel* the judge gave advanced permission and equally regarded the process as effective.

Subsequently in *Nortel* the judge agreed to reinforce the position by sending **8.657** out letters of request to potential secondary jurisdictions to ask them to ensure that the main administrators were given notice of any request to open a secondary. An express provision requiring such notice to be given is now provided as Article 38(1) RR.

There was however a concern that the insolvency laws of some Member States **8.658** were not flexible enough to overcome the apparent obstacle of the mandatory choice of law rules in Article 4 OR (see now Article 7 RR), which require distributions in the main proceeding to be carried out under the law of the main proceeding. English insolvency law is flexible enough to provide that in some cases, even applying English law pursuant to Article 4 OR (see now Article 7 RR), the normal priorities can be departed from, including situations where an undertaking had been given to local creditors to respect their local priorities, in the interests of better realizations for creditors generally, provided that local creditors did not request the opening of local insolvency proceedings.

The European Council proposal, based on the original Commission proposal, **8.659** included a new provision for the creation of such 'virtual secondaries', which is now contained in Article 36 RR. This creates a right on the part of the insolvency practitioner in the main proceeding to give an undertaking in order to avoid secondary proceedings. There are a series of detailed rules laid down and of course the provision has self-executing, mandatory effect throughout the EU (except Denmark). It thus overrides any provision of national law or practice whereby it is forbidden to depart from the national statutory scheme of distribution in any species of insolvency proceeding conducted under the laws of a given EU Member State.

Article 36 RR empowers an insolvency practitioner to give a written 'unilateral' **8.660** undertaking to comply with local law priorities that would apply in a secondary in relation to assets which are located in the local jurisdiction. The relevant time for looking at the assets is at the time the undertaking is given. Presumably, the word 'unilateral' is used to emphasize that the undertaking is not a matter of contract.

Article 36(2) RR then makes the local law applicable to the distribution of local **8.661** assets, thereby avoiding any problem with what is now Article 7 RR.

Article 36(5) RR states that the undertaking 'shall be approved by the known local **8.662** creditors.' This reads rather oddly in English, as if the known local creditors were being ordered to approve the undertaking. However, there is then a statement about the voting rules that are to be applied, namely those applicable for the adoption of restructuring plans in the local jurisdiction. This seems to imply that the proposal is making the undertaking *subject* to approval by 'the known local creditors'. This accords with the text of Article 36(6) RR, which states that an undertaking given *and approved* under Article 36 'shall be binding on the estate.'

8.663 Enforcement of the undertaking is to take place, under the proposal, in the main proceedings (Article 36(8) RR), but provisional or protective measures can also be sought in the secondary jurisdiction (Article 36(9) RR). Rather worryingly for the insolvency practitioner in the main proceeding, he is to be made personally liable for not complying with the requirements of Article 36 (Article 36(10) RR).

8.664 There does not seem to be any scope for the insolvency practitioner to make his undertaking conditional upon the local creditors not requesting the opening of local proceedings. However, Article 38(2) RR requires a court facing such a request to turn it down if an undertaking 'in accordance with Article 36' has been given '…if it is satisfied that the undertaking adequately protects the general interests of local creditors.' Presumably the words 'in accordance with Article 36' import the need for local creditor approval under Article 36(5) RR, so that it is only undertakings given *and approved by local creditors* and therefore binding on the estate under RR Article 36(6) that can block the opening of a secondary proceeding.

8.665 Even if secondary proceedings are in fact opened, if an undertaking has been given and approved, it remains binding on the estate and the insolvency practitioner in the main proceeding is required to return to the secondary proceeding any assets (or their proceeds) which he has removed since the undertaking was given (Article 36(6) RR).

8.666 The requirement of approval by local creditors (Article 36(5) RR), may give rise to some paradoxical results. In some countries it may well be against the interests of the majority of local creditors for local priorities to apply, because of the priority awarded to governmental preferential creditors.[60] In such cases it would make sense for the local creditors to vote down the approval of the undertaking and rely on the priorities in the main proceeding, if that is likely to give them a better result.

8.667 The proposal expressly gives the insolvency practitioner in the main proceeding standing to apply to challenge a decision opening a secondary proceeding (Article 39 RR) on the grounds that the court did not comply with the conditions and requirements of Article 38 RR. This seems to cover for example a case where the local court opens a secondary despite the giving and acceptance by local creditors of an Article 36 RR undertaking which adequately protects the general interests

---

[60] This may for example occur in relation to Italy.

of local creditors. Since Article 38(1) RR requires notice to be given of a request to open a secondary, the insolvency practitioner in the main proceeding should be able simply to oppose the opening rather than have to challenge it subsequently. However, if no notice has been given, that would seem to be an obvious case for a subsequent challenge.

The heading of Article 39 RR, giving standing as mentioned, reads rather oddly **8.668** in English because it refers to 'judicial review' of the decision to open secondary proceedings. As a matter of legal English, 'judicial review' is only used for court challenges against administrative (or delegated legislative) decisions or regulations and not court decisions. Legal English would refer to an application to 'set aside' the opening, but the true meaning of 'judicial review' here appears to be clear from the context and the actual text of Article 39 RR, which refers to challenging the decision opening the proceedings before the courts of the Member State in which secondary proceedings have been opened.

[Under Article 33 OR, the office-holder of the main proceedings was able to **8.669** seek a stay of any secondary proceedings (in the court in which the secondary proceedings were opened). Such a stay was within the discretion of the court, the court having the power to require the office holder of the main proceeding to guarantee the interests of the local creditors. Now, the office-holder of the main proceedings has the 'right' to provide an undertaking and to put that to the local creditors in that secondary jurisdiction for approval. There are a number of issues with this change. First, this enfranchises local creditors and allows them to refuse the undertaking and to therefore strengthen their ability to seek secondary proceedings (including in circumstances where a local court might have exercised its discretion to stay under the previous Regulations). The undertaking has to be approved by reference to 'the rules on qualified majority and voting that apply for the adoption of restructuring plans under the law of the Member State where secondary proceedings could have been opened' (Article 36(5) RR). It is not clear what those rules might be given that in certain jurisdictions, different voting regimes might apply. Also, given that the undertaking and 'local protection' might only need to cover a limited category of creditors (for example, those that have preferential status under that local law), it is not clear if this means that all creditors in that jurisdiction would have to vote on the undertaking, including those not affected by it or the opening of secondary proceedings. Third, the court seised of the request to open the secondary proceedings still retains the discretion to do so, although the court should take into account the fact that an undertaking has been approved. Article 33 OR remains (in a new Article 46 RR) albeit the stay is limited to staying 'the process of realisation of assets in whole or in part' as opposed to 'the process of liquidation in whole or in part' under old Article 33. It will be interesting to see whether new Article 36 is used in preference to the amended provisions of old Article 33. (AW)]

(RR) Article 37—Right to request the opening of secondary insolvency proceedings

1. The opening of secondary insolvency proceedings may be requested by:
   (a) the insolvency practitioner in the main insolvency proceedings;
   (b) any other person or authority empowered to request the opening of insolvency proceedings under the law of the Member State within the territory of which the opening of secondary insolvency proceedings is requested.
2. Where an undertaking has become binding in accordance with Article 36, the request for opening secondary insolvency proceedings shall be lodged within 30 days of having received notice of the approval of the undertaking.

8.670 Article 37(1) RR is based on Article 29 OR.

8.671 The reference in Article 29(a) OR to 'liquidator' has been replaced in Article 37(1)(a) RR by 'insolvency practitioner'.

8.672 The text of Article 37(1)(b) RR is copied from the text of Article 29(b) OR. In relation to this wording, a question arose as to whether the person who can request the opening of secondary proceedings under what is now Article 37(1)(b) RR has to be a person or authority who can request the opening of *secondary* proceedings under the relevant law of the Member State in question.[61] This question has not been resolved by the RR.

8.673 Article 37(2) RR is a new provision which ties in with the subject of 'virtual secondaries' discussed under Article 36 RR. Article 37(2) RR provides that where an undertaking has become binding in accordance with Article 36, a request to open secondary proceedings must be lodged within 30 days of having received notice of the approval of the undertaking. This ability in effect to challenge the undertaking must be read subject to Article 38 RR below.

(RR) Article 38—Decision to open secondary insolvency proceedings

1. A court seised of a request to open secondary insolvency proceedings shall immediately give notice to the insolvency practitioner or the debtor in possession in the main insolvency proceedings and give it an opportunity to be heard on the request.
2. Where the insolvency practitioner in the main insolvency proceedings has given an undertaking in accordance with Article 36, the court referred to in paragraph 1 of this Article shall, at the request of the insolvency practitioner, not open secondary insolvency proceedings if it is satisfied that the undertaking adequately protects the general interests of local creditors.

---

[61] In *Polmos Lancut SA*, the Polish Supreme Court on 20 January 2010 held on the basis of the Polish German and Lithuanian versions of Art 29(b) OR that only persons who can request the opening of *secondary* proceedings under the relevant Member State law fall within Art 29(b) OR. See 8.392 above.

3. Where a temporary stay of individual enforcement proceedings has been granted in order to allow for negotiations between the debtor and its creditors, the court, at the request of the insolvency practitioner or the debtor in possession, may stay the opening of secondary insolvency proceedings for a period not exceeding 3 months, provided that suitable measures are in place to protect the interests of local creditors.

   The court referred to in paragraph 1 may order protective measures to protect the interests of local creditors by requiring the insolvency practitioner or the debtor in possession not to remove or dispose of any assets which are located in the Member State where its establishment is located unless this is done in the ordinary course of business. The court may also order other measures to protect the interest of local creditors during a stay, unless this is incompatible with the national rules on civil procedure.

   The stay of the opening of secondary insolvency proceedings shall be lifted by the court of its own motion or at the request of any creditor if, during the stay, an agreement in the negotiations referred to in the first subparagraph has been concluded.

   The stay may be lifted by the court of its own motion or at the request of any creditor if the continuation of the stay is detrimental to the creditor's rights, in particular if the negotiations have been disrupted or it has become evident that they are unlikely to be concluded, or if the insolvency practitioner or the debtor in possession has infringed the prohibition on disposal of its assets or on removal of them from the territory of the Member State where the establishment is located.

4. At the request of the insolvency practitioner in the main insolvency proceedings, the court referred to in paragraph 1 may open a type of insolvency proceedings as listed in Annex A other than the type initially requested, provided that the conditions for opening that type of proceedings under national law are fulfilled and that that type of proceedings is the most appropriate as regards the interests of the local creditors and coherence between the main and secondary insolvency proceedings. The second sentence of Article 34 shall apply.

Article 38 RR is an entirely new provision. Under the OR, there is a potential difficulty in avoiding the unnecessary opening of secondary proceedings in that, in some Member States, there was no requirement for notice to be given to a main liquidator of a request to open a secondary proceedings in that Member State. A partial remedy was used in England, in the case of *Re Nortel Networks SA*.[62] In this case, at the request of the administrators to the main proceedings in England, the English High Court Judge sent letters of request to foreign courts where there might have been a request to open secondary proceedings asking them to ensure that notice was given to the main proceeding administrator before any secondary proceeding was opened. **8.674**

Article 38(1) RR now requires the court, seised of a request to open a secondary proceeding, immediately to give notice to the insolvency practitioner or the debtor **8.675**

---

[62] [2009] BCC 343.

in possession in the main proceedings and give him an opportunity to be heard on the request.

8.676 Article 38(2) RR is linked to the topic of 'virtual secondaries' in Article 36 RR. Where the relevant undertaking in accordance with Article 36 RR has been given, the court seised of a request to open secondary proceedings shall, at the request of the insolvency practitioner, not open secondary proceedings if it is satisfied that the undertaking adequately protects the general interests of local creditors. Note that the same protection is not given to a main proceeding where there is a debtor in possession and no insolvency practitioner.

8.677 The introduction of an 'adequate protection' standard in Article 38 RR may give rise to some uncertainty. It is difficult to think what further may be needed, for there to be adequate protection of local creditors, than an undertaking to comply with local distribution and priority rights under the national law that the creditors would have if secondary proceedings were opened.

8.678 Article 38(3) RR is also a new provision. The first sub-paragraph deals with the type of pre-insolvency proceeding where there is a temporary stay of individual enforcement proceedings to allow for negotiations between the debtor and his creditors, being the type (c) proceedings referred to in Article 1 RR. In the case of such a type (c) proceeding, the court, at the request of the insolvency practitioner or the debtor in possession, has a discretion to stay the opening of secondary proceedings for not longer than three months, providing that suitable measures are in place to protect the interests of local creditors. In this case, the reference to the interests of local creditors presumably means the safeguarding of their potential rights in respect of the business and assets of the debtor.

8.679 Specifically, the second sub-paragraph provides for a discretion to order protective measures to protect the interests of local creditors by requiring the insolvency practitioner or the debtor in possession not to remove or dispose of any assets located in the Member State where his establishment is located, unless this is done in the ordinary course of business. This is intended to deal with the risk that the insolvency practitioner or debtor in possession running the main proceeding may, during the temporary stay of the opening of secondary proceedings, remove assets which would fall into such secondary proceedings.

8.680 The second sub-paragraph also gives the local court a discretion to order other measures to protect the interests of local creditors during a stay of the opening of secondary proceedings, unless this is incompatible with the national rules on civil procedure.

8.681 The third sub-paragraph provides a supplementary provision to the effect that the stay of the opening of secondary proceedings must be revoked by the court of its own motion or at the request of any creditor if, during the stay, an agreement in the negotiations has been concluded. Additionally, under the fourth sub-paragraph, the stay of the opening of secondary proceedings may be revoked in the court's discretion of its own motion or at the request of any creditor if the continuation of the stay is detrimental to the creditors' rights. Particular examples given are when negotiations have been disrupted or it has become evident that they are unlikely to be concluded or if the insolvency practitioner or debtor in possession has infringed the prohibition on disposal of assets or on removing them from the territory of the Member State where the establishment is located.

Article 38(4) RR is a new provision enabling the local court, at the request of **8.682** the insolvency practitioner in the main proceedings to open a secondary proceeding of a different type from that initially requested as long as it is within the list of proceedings in Annex A. This can also only be done if the conditions for opening the other type of procedure under national law are fulfilled. Such a step should only be taken if the alternative procedure is the most appropriate taking account of the interests of the local creditors and/or of 'coherence' between the main and secondary proceedings. In such a case there is a cross-reference to Article 34 RR, second sentence, so that the debtor's insolvency is not to be re-examined, as long as the main proceedings require that the debtor be insolvent.

(RR) Article 39—Judicial review of the decision to open secondary insolvency proceedings

> The insolvency practitioner in the main insolvency proceedings may challenge the decision to open secondary insolvency proceedings before the courts of the Member State in which secondary insolvency proceedings have been opened on the ground that the court did not comply with the conditions and requirements of Article 38.

This is a new provision, in respect of which see the commentary under Article 36 **8.683** RR above.

'Judicial review' in the heading is once again a misnomer, since in English legal **8.684** usage it refers to challenges to administrative action or delegated legislation, but the meaning is clear from the text.

(RR) Article 40—Advance payment of costs and expenses

> Where the law of the Member State in which the opening of secondary insolvency proceedings is requested requires that the debtor's assets be sufficient to cover in whole or in part the costs and expenses of the proceedings, the court may, when it receives such a request, require the applicant to make an advance payment of costs or to provide appropriate security.

8.685   Article 40 RR is copied from Article 30 OR. Reference should be made to the commentary under Article 30 OR above.

(RR) Article 41—Co-operation and communication between insolvency practitioners

1. The insolvency practitioner in the main insolvency proceedings and the insolvency practitioner or practitioners in secondary insolvency proceedings concerning the same debtor shall cooperate with each other to the extent such cooperation is not incompatible with the rules applicable to the respective proceedings. Such cooperation may take any form, including the conclusion of agreements or protocols.
2. In implementing the cooperation set out in paragraph 1, the insolvency practitioners shall:
    (a) as soon as possible communicate to each other any information which may be relevant to the other proceedings, in particular any progress made in lodging and verifying claims and all measures aimed at rescuing or restructuring the debtor, or at terminating the proceedings, provided appropriate arrangements are made to protect confidential information;
    (b) explore the possibility of restructuring the debtor and, where such a possibility exists, coordinate the elaboration and implementation of a restructuring plan;
    (c) coordinate the administration of the realisation or use of the debtor's assets and affairs; the insolvency practitioner in the secondary insolvency proceedings shall give the insolvency practitioner in the main insolvency proceedings an early opportunity to submit proposals on the realisation or use of the assets in the secondary insolvency proceedings.
3. Paragraphs 1 and 2 shall apply mutatis mutandis to situations where, in the main or in the secondary insolvency proceedings or in any territorial insolvency proceedings concerning the same debtor and open at the same time, the debtor remains in possession of its assets.

8.686   Article 41 RR builds on and has essentially the same theme as Article 31 OR, with the differences explained below.

8.687   First of all, the general change from 'liquidator' to 'insolvency practitioner' is made. Secondly, whereas Article 31 OR began with the duty to communicate information between insolvency administrators, and then set out a duty to co-operate, Article 41 RR begins with a general duty to co-operate and then goes on to mention communication as one branch of co-operation. The general duty of co-operation in Article 41 RR is only to the extent that such co-operation 'is not incompatible with the rules applicable to the respective proceedings'.

8.688   Article 41(1) RR makes specific mention of protocols, which have been used as a tool of co-operation in a number of international groups, often between the UK and the United States and/or Canada. Specific mention is made of protocols in Article 41(1) RR, probably because Continental judges may be reluctant to approve protocols unless there is express mention of them under the heading of the duty to co-operate.

Article 41(2) RR sets out three specific types of co-operation. Type (a) is the communication 'as soon as possible' of information relevant to the other proceedings. Type (b) requires the exploration of the possibility of restructuring the debtor and, where such restructuring is possible, the co-ordination of 'the elaboration and implementation of a restructuring plan'. Type (c) requires the co-ordination of the administration of the realization or use of the debtor's assets and affairs. The insolvency practitioner in the secondary insolvency proceedings is required to give the insolvency practitioner in the main insolvency proceedings an early opportunity to submit proposals on the realization or use of the assets in the secondary insolvency proceedings. **8.689**

Article 41(3) RR is an entirely new provision, designed to take account of the fact that under the RR there may not be an insolvency practitioner, but rather a debtor in possession. Article 41(3) RR provides that Article 41(1) and (2) are to apply *mutatis mutandis*. **8.690**

(RR) Article 42—Co-operation and communication between courts

1. In order to facilitate the coordination of main, territorial and secondary insolvency proceedings concerning the same debtor, a court before which a request to open insolvency proceedings is pending, or which has opened such proceedings, shall cooperate with any other court before which a request to open insolvency proceedings is pending, or which has opened such proceedings, to the extent that such cooperation is not incompatible with the rules applicable to each of the proceedings. For that purpose, the courts may, where appropriate, appoint an independent person or body acting on its instructions, provided that it is not incompatible with the rules applicable to them.
2. In implementing the cooperation set out in paragraph 1, the courts, or any appointed person or body acting on their behalf, as referred to in paragraph 1, may communicate directly with, or request information or assistance directly from, each other provided that such communication respects the procedural rights of the parties to the proceedings and the confidentiality of information.
3. The cooperation referred to in paragraph 1 may be implemented by any means that the court considers appropriate. It may, in particular, concern:
   (a) coordination in the appointment of the insolvency practitioners;
   (b) communication of information by any means considered appropriate by the court;
   (c) coordination of the administration and supervision of the debtor's assets and affairs;
   (d) coordination of the conduct of hearings;
   (e) coordination in the approval of protocols, where necessary.

The OR text in Article 31 OR did not expressly require courts, as opposed to insolvency administrators, to co-operate in relation to main and secondary proceedings **8.691** in respect of the same debtor. However, judicial interpretation in national courts[63] interpreted Article 31 OR as implying a duty of co-operation between courts. Absent any express duty in the text of OR, however, there was a doubt as to whether all national courts would adopt the same interpretation. Accordingly, Article 42 RR contains a new text expressly requiring co-operation and communication between courts.

8.692 Article 42(1) RR pushes the time at which co-operation is required back to the time that a court has before it to request to open insolvency proceedings. Once again the duty to co-operate is subject to the limitation that it must not be 'incompatible with the rules applicable to each of the proceedings'.

8.693 In considering the question of co-operation and communication between national courts, various issues have been raised, including the question of whether the courts will have a common language. If the judges themselves do not have a common language, Article 42 RR provides a solution in that it gives an express power to 'appoint an independent person or body' acting on the instructions of the court, providing that that is not incompatible with the rules applicable to that court. The court can thus appoint a person or body which has a common language with either the judge or independent person appointed by the court in the other proceeding.

8.694 Although there is a duty on the two or more courts to co-operate, there is no duty, but only a discretion to communicate directly with, or request information or assistance from, the other court. This discretion applies to any person or body appointed to act on behalf of either court. The communication, if any, is required to respect the procedural rights of the parties and the confidentiality of information.

8.695 It is suggested that such procedural rights should be safeguarded by allowing the parties and their legal advisers to be present, either in person or by telephone or by video link in any communication between the two courts. Whereas as between the United States and Canada there have been communications between judges in the absence of parties, this would not seem to accord with European procedural rights and principles.

6.696 Article 42(3) RR sets out five particular means of implementing the duty to co-operate, giving the courts a discretion as to which they use.

8.697 Type (a) involves co-ordination in the appointment of insolvency practitioners. Where there is no problem of conflict, or any conflict issue can be resolved in some satisfactory way, it may often be cheaper and simpler to appoint partners of the same accountancy firm as insolvency practitioners in each proceeding. This is a

---

[63] *Re Nortel Networks SA* [2009] BCC 343; *Re Stojevic* 28 R 225/04w (Vienna Higher Regional Court, 9 November 2004).

common practice in the UK for insolvency practitioners in the case of different group companies.

Type (b) is the communication of information 'by any means considered appropri- **8.698**
ate by the court'. In the limited number of communications that have so far taken place in relation to Europe, communication has been by telephone. However, with the advance of technology, courts should no doubt consider whether a video link could usefully be employed.

Type (c) involves the co-ordination of the administration and supervision of the **8.699**
debtor's assets and affairs. In many cases, such administration will be simpler and cheaper if the assets which fall within both the main and the secondary proceedings can be treated *de facto* as a unity.

Type (d) refers to the co-ordination of the conduct of hearings. It is important to **8.700**
note here that this is not a power to conduct joint hearings, which have sometimes taken place between US and Canadian judges.[64] Co-ordination would cover such matters as (i) the avoidance or clearing up of misunderstandings about procedure in each court, (ii) the co-ordination of proceedings so as to prevent one from under-mining or pre-empting the other, (iii) agreement on which issues are suitable to be heard in each court, so as to avoid as far as possible any conflict in the decisions of each court.

Type (e) involves co-ordination in the approval of protocols, 'where necessary'. **8.701**
Such protocols will often be conditional on the approval of each court and it may be useful to co-ordinate approval so that it happens either simultaneously or very close together in time. Protocols have in the past been common between the courts of common law countries such as England, US, Canada, Bermuda, and Cayman. They have for example dealt with the division and co-ordination of the work of rescue or reconstruction or with the question of the payment of fees for insolvency practitioners.

(RR) Article 43—Co-operation and communication between insolvency practitioners and courts

1. In order to facilitate the co-ordination of main, territorial and secondary insol-vency proceedings opened in respect of the same debtor:
   (a) an insolvency practitioner in main insolvency proceedings shall coop-erate and communicate with any court before which a request to open secondary insolvency proceedings is pending or which has opened such proceedings;
   (b) an insolvency practitioner in territorial or secondary insolvency pro-ceedings shall cooperate and communicate with the court before which a request to open main insolvency proceedings is pending or which has opened such proceedings; and

---

[64] Recently in the US and Canadian proceedings concerning the Nortel group.

> (c) an insolvency practitioner in territorial or secondary insolvency proceedings shall cooperate and communicate with the court before which a request to open other territorial or secondary insolvency proceedings is pending or which has opened such proceedings;
> to the extent that such cooperation and communication are not incompatible with the rules applicable to each of the proceedings and do not entail any conflict of interest.
> 2. The cooperation referred to in paragraph 1 may be implemented by any appropriate means, such as those set out in Article 42(3).

8.702 Having laid down duties of co-operation (i) between insolvency practitioners and (ii) between courts, Article 43 RR sets out a duty of co-operation and communication between insolvency practitioners on the one hand and courts on the other. This again is completely new text.

8.703 The duty of co-operation is created expressly in order to facilitate the co-ordination of main, independent territorial and secondary insolvency proceedings opened in respect of the same debtor. Three specific types of duty are set out.

8.704 Type (a) requires an insolvency practitioner in the main proceedings to co-operate and communicate with any court before which a request to open secondary proceedings is pending or which has opened such proceedings. Once again, the point at which the duty arises has been pushed back to the time when a request to open secondary proceedings has been made. A court presented with a request to open secondary proceedings may well have to consider whether such an opening is necessary or even beneficial in the interests of the general body of creditors. The court may well need information from the insolvency practitioner in the main proceedings in relation to this issue.

8.705 Type (b) is a requirement on an insolvency practitioner in territorial or secondary proceedings to co-operate and communicate with a court before which a request to open main proceedings is pending or which has opened such proceedings. Again the relevant point in time has been pushed back to the time a court is hearing a request to open main proceedings. In such a situation, there is likely to be less of a question whether main proceedings are necessary or useful, but it is conceivable that such situations will arise. If so, information from the insolvency practitioner in the territorial proceedings may be essential or at least useful. Once main proceedings have actually been opened, it may also be very important to receive information from the insolvency practitioner in any secondary insolvency proceedings in relation to business and assets in the territory of the secondary proceedings.

8.706 Type (c) is a duty on the insolvency practitioner in territorial or secondary insolvency proceedings to co-operate and communicate with a court before which there is a request to open yet another territorial or secondary proceeding or which has opened such a proceeding. The potential point of co-operation is again pushed back to the date of the request to open such other territorial or secondary proceedings. Once again it may be that the opening of the further territorial or secondary proceeding could damage the interests of creditors and once again the further court considering such a request may need or at least find useful information from the insolvency practitioner in other territorial or secondary proceedings.

Types (a)–(c) are each duties expressly subject to the relevant co-operation or **8.707** communication not being incompatible with the rules applicable to each of the proceedings. They are also expressly subject to the question of any conflict of interest.

Article 43(2) RR makes applicable to the duty to co-operate in Article 43(1) RR the **8.708** general ability to implement co-operation 'by any means that the court considers appropriate' provided in Article 42(3)RR, including the five particular means of co-operation set out in Article 42(3) RR.

(RR) Article 44—Costs of co-operation and communication

> The requirements laid down in Articles 42 and 43 shall not result in courts charg-ing costs to each other for cooperation and communication.

The new provisions in Articles 42 and 43 RR spelling out the express duty of **8.709** co-operation between courts and between insolvency practitioners and courts also gives rise to a new question as to whether courts can charge costs to each other for co-operation and communication. Article 44 RR specifically states that they may not.

(RR) Article 45—Exercise of creditors' rights

1. Any creditor may lodge its claim in the main insolvency proceedings and in any secondary insolvency proceedings.
2. The insolvency practitioners in the main and any secondary insolvency proceedings shall lodge in other proceedings claims which have already been lodged in the proceedings for which they were appointed, provided that the interests of creditors in the latter proceedings are served by doing so, subject to the right of creditors to oppose such lodgement or to withdraw the lodgement of their claims where the law applicable so provides.
3. The insolvency practitioner in the main or secondary insolvency proceedings shall be entitled to participate in other proceedings on the same basis as a creditor, in particular by attending creditors' meetings.

Article 45 RR is copied from Article 32 OR, with the substitution of the new term **8.710** 'insolvency practitioners' instead of 'liquidators'. Reference should be made to the commentary on Article 32 OR above.

(RR) Article 46—Stay of the process of realisation of assets

1. The court which opened the secondary insolvency proceedings shall stay the process of realisation of assets in whole or in part on receipt of a request from the insolvency practitioner in the main insolvency proceedings. In such a case, it may require the insolvency practitioner in the main insolvency proceedings to take any suitable measure to guarantee the interests of the creditors in the secondary insolvency proceedings and of individual classes of creditors. Such a request from the insolvency practitioner may be rejected only if it is manifestly of no interest to the creditors in the main insolvency proceedings. Such a stay of the process of realisation of assets may be ordered for up to 3 months. It may be continued or renewed for similar periods.

2. The court referred to in paragraph 1 shall terminate the stay of the process of realisation of assets:

   (a) at the request of the insolvency practitioner in the main insolvency proceedings;

   (b) of its own motion, at the request of a creditor or at the request of the insolvency practitioner in the secondary insolvency proceedings if that measure no longer appears justified, in particular, by the interests of creditors in the main insolvency proceedings or in the secondary insolvency proceedings.

8.711 The text of Article 46 RR is largely taken from the text of Article 33 OR and reference should be made to the commentary on Article 33 OR above. There is however one clarification. The OR text referred to staying 'the process of liquidation'. This was held by a national court to refer only to a stay of the process of liquidation *of assets* and not the secondary proceedings as a whole.[65] This interpretation has now been adopted in the text of Article 46 RR, which now refers, not to a stay on the process of 'liquidation' but to a stay of the process of 'realization of assets'. Article 33 OR was headed 'Stay of Liquidation', reflecting the fact that the OR only permitted liquidation proceedings as secondary proceedings. Under RR, secondary proceedings need not be liquidation proceedings. It would therefore no longer be appropriate to refer to a stay of liquidation in any event. Otherwise the only change is the usual switch from 'liquidator' to 'insolvency practitioner'.

(RR) Article 47—Power of the insolvency practitioner to propose restructuring plans

1. Where the law of the Member State where secondary insolvency proceedings have been opened allows for such proceedings to be closed without liquidation by a restructuring plan, a composition or a comparable measure, the insolvency practitioner in the main insolvency proceedings shall be empowered to propose such a measure in accordance with the procedure of that Member State.

---

[65] See the *Collins & Aikman* case referred to in the commentary to Art 33 OR.

2. Any restriction of creditors' rights arising from a measure referred to in paragraph 1 which is proposed in secondary insolvency proceedings, such as a stay of payment or discharge of debt, shall have no effect in respect of assets of a debtor that are not covered by those proceedings, without the consent of all the creditors having an interest.

Article 47(1) and (2) RR are to a large extent taken from Article 34(1) and (2) OR, subject to the following changes.   **8.712**

The first sentence of Article 47(1) RR is much the same as the first sentence of Article 34(1) OR, with the substitution of 'insolvency practitioner' for 'liquidator' and the qualification, added in Article 47 RR that the power of the main proceeding insolvency practitioner to propose a rescue plan, composition etc. must be 'in accordance with the procedure of that Member State'. However, Article 47(1) RR omits the second sentence of Article 34(1) OR. The former restriction on the closure of the secondary proceeding by a rescue plan composition or a comparable measure becoming final without the consent of the insolvency administrator in the main proceeding, subject to a further caveat, has been abolished. This change does represent a change in the balance of powers between the insolvency practitioners running the main and secondary proceedings respectively. The former restriction was part of a system which in several provisions placed emphasis on the supremacy of the main proceedings.   **8.713**

Article 47(2) RR is copied from Article 34(2) OR. It is simply a corollary from the fact that the secondary proceedings are territorial and therefore have no effect on assets of a debtor not covered by the secondary proceedings.   **8.714**

[Article 47 RR now requires the office-holder of the main proceedings to comply with the procedure of the law of the Member State in which secondary proceedings have been opened in relation to any restructuring plan, composition, or comparable measure. This is a missed opportunity—allowing the office-holder to use a restructuring plan in accordance with the law of the Member State in which the main proceedings have been opened would have provided for significant cost and time savings. (**AW**)]   **8.715**

(RR) Article 48—Impact of closure of insolvency proceedings

1. Without prejudice to Article 49, the closure of insolvency proceedings shall not prevent the continuation of other insolvency proceedings concerning the same debtor which are still open at that point in time.
2. Where insolvency proceedings concerning a legal person or a company in the Member State of that person's or company's registered office would entail the dissolution of the legal person or of the company, that legal person or company shall not cease to exist until any other insolvency proceedings concerning the same debtor have been closed, or the insolvency practitioner or practitioners in such proceedings have given consent to the dissolution.

8.716 This is a new provision. Article 48(1) RR states the obvious that the closure of insolvency proceedings does not prevent the continuation of other insolvency proceedings concerning the same debtor which is still open.

8.717 The real point comes in Article 48(2) RR, which makes provision for a problem which arose under the OR. Where a company registered in one Member State had its centre of main interests ('COMI') in another Member State and main proceedings were opened in the place of COMI, these could be undermined by the dissolution of the company, eg after the closure of a secondary proceeding, in the Member State of registration.[66] To avoid this kind of problem, Article 48(2) RR expressly provides that in such a case the relevant legal person or company 'shall not cease to exist' until any other insolvency proceeding concerning the same debtor has been closed or the insolvency practitioner or practitioners in such proceedings have given their consent to the dissolution. Such consent might be forthcoming if for example, as in England, where a company is in liquidation, that liquidation is deemed to continue even if the company is dissolved and ceases to exist.

(RR) Article 49—Assets remaining in the secondary insolvency proceedings

If, by the liquidation of assets in the secondary insolvency proceedings, it is possible to meet all claims allowed under those proceedings, the insolvency practitioner appointed in those proceedings shall immediately transfer any assets remaining to the insolvency practitioner in the main insolvency proceedings.

8.718 Article 49 RR is in effect a copy of Article 35 OR, apart from the usual change from 'liquidator' to 'insolvency practitioner'. In view of the fact that secondary proceedings no longer have to be liquidation proceedings, it might have been more appropriate to change 'liquidation' to realization, and that had been done in a previous draft, but 'liquidation' has reappeared for a reason we are not aware of. In other respects, reference may be made to the commentary to Article 35 OR above.

(RR) Article 50—Subsequent opening of the main insolvency proceedings

Where the proceedings referred to in Article 3(1) are opened following the opening of the proceedings referred to in Article 3(2) in another Member State, Articles 41, 45, 46, 47 and 49 shall apply to those opened first, in so far as the progress of those proceedings so permits.

8.719 Article 50 RR is copied from Article 36 OR, except that the previous cross-references to Articles 31 to 35 OR are replaced by cross-references to Articles 41, 45 to 47, and 49 RR.

---

[66] *Re Eurodis Electron Plc* [2012] BCC 57.

(RR) Article 51—Conversion of secondary insolvency proceedings

1. At the request of the insolvency practitioner in the main insolvency proceedings, the court of the Member State in which secondary insolvency proceedings have been opened may order the conversion of the secondary insolvency proceedings into another type of insolvency proceedings listed in Annex A, provided that the conditions for opening that type of proceedings under national law are fulfilled and that that type of proceedings is the most appropriate as regards the interests of the local creditors and coherence between the main and secondary insolvency proceedings.
2. When considering the request referred to in paragraph 1, the court may seek information from the insolvency practitioners involved in both proceedings.

This is a new conversion provision, replacing the old one in Article 37 OR. **8.720**

Whereas Article 37 OR was concerned with the conversion of territorial pro- **8.721** ceedings into winding-up proceedings, since secondary proceedings are no longer required to be winding-up proceedings, this form of conversion has become redundant.

The new provision is a general power to convert secondary proceedings into another **8.722** type of insolvency proceeding listed in Annex A and therefore within the scope of the RR. The proviso is the obvious one that the conditions for opening the new type of procedure under national law are fulfilled and that the other type of procedure is the 'most appropriate for taking account of the interests of the local creditors and of coherence between the main and secondary insolvency proceeding'.

This is a useful power. For example where rescue type proceedings have been **8.723** opened in the main jurisdiction and liquidation proceedings in the secondary jurisdiction, it may be convenient for there to be parallel rescue proceedings in both Member States.

Article 51(2) RR contains a new discretion to seek information from the insolvency **8.724** practitioners in both proceedings. This again is very useful, in order to make sure that the court considering the request from the insolvency practitioner in the main proceedings for conversion is fully informed.

(RR) Article 52—Preservation measures

Where the court of a Member State which has jurisdiction pursuant to Article 3(1) appoints a temporary administrator in order to ensure the preservation of a debtor's assets, that temporary administrator shall be empowered to request any measures to secure and preserve any of the debtor's assets situated in another Member State, provided for under the law of that Member State, for the period between the request for the opening of insolvency proceedings and the judgment opening the proceedings.

Article 52 RR is identical to Article 38 OR and reference should be made to the **8.725** commentary under Article 38 OR.

D. Chapter IV: Provision of Information for Creditors and Lodgement of their Claims

(RR) Article 53—Right to lodge claims

> Any foreign creditor may lodge claims in insolvency proceedings by any means of communication, which are accepted by the law of the State of the opening of proceedings. Representation by a lawyer or another legal professional shall not be mandatory for the sole purpose of lodging of claims.

8.726 Article 53 RR is an updated version of Article 39 OR and reference should be made to the commentary on Article 39 OR above.

8.727 The updating concerns the method of lodging claims. In the last edition of this work at paragraph 8.405 Professor Michael Bogdan suggested that, despite the reference to claims being lodged 'in writing' the law governing the proceedings might accept a submission in another form. This is now put into an express statutory form in Article 53 RR. The text now states that the creditors within Article 53 RR may lodge claims 'by any means of communication, which are accepted by the law of the State of opening'.

8.728 In addition, there is a new and useful express provision which makes it clear that representation by a lawyer or other legal professional is not to be required for the purpose of lodging claims. That avoids the further expense and complication of hiring a legal professional where that is otherwise required by local law.

(RR) Article 54—Duty to inform creditors

> 1. As soon as insolvency proceedings are opened in a Member State, the court of that State having jurisdiction or the insolvency practitioner appointed by that court shall immediately inform the known foreign creditors.
> 2. The information referred to in paragraph 1, provided by an individual notice, shall in particular include time limits, the penalties laid down with regard to those time limits, the body or authority empowered to accept the lodgement of claims and any other measures laid down. Such notice shall also indicate whether creditors whose claims are preferential or secured in rem need to lodge their claims. The notice shall also include a copy of the standard form for lodging of claims referred to in Article 55 or information on where that form is available.
> 3. The information referred to in paragraphs 1 and 2 of this Article shall be provided using the standard notice form to be established in accordance with Article 88. The form shall be published in the European e-Justice Portal and shall bear the heading 'Notice of insolvency proceedings' in all the official languages of the institutions of the Union. It shall be transmitted in the official language of the State of the opening of proceedings or, if there are several official languages in that Member State, in the official language or one of the official languages of the place where insolvency proceedings have been opened, or

in another language which that State has indicated it can accept, in accordance with Article 55(5), if it can be assumed that that language is easier to understand for the foreign creditors.

4. In insolvency proceedings relating to an individual not exercising a business or professional activity, the use of the standard form referred to in this Article shall not be obligatory if creditors are not required to lodge their claims in order to have their claims taken into account in the proceedings.

Article 54 RR begins by essentially copying Article 40(1) and (2) OR into Article 54(1) and (2) RR, with usual substitution of 'insolvency practitioner' for 'liquidator'. There are however certain additions.   **8.729**

Firstly, the notice required to be sent to creditors in other Member States is required to include a copy of the new standard form for lodging of claims referred to in Article 55 RR, or information on where that form is available.   **8.730**

Furthermore, Article 54(3) RR requires the information required to be given under Article 54 to be provided using the standard notice form to be established in accordance with Article 88 RR. This form is to be published in the European e-Justice Portal and is to bear the heading 'Notice of Insolvency Proceedings' in all the official languages of the institutions of the Union.   **8.731**

Article 54(3) RR also provides that the notice must be transmitted in the official language of the State of the opening or, if there are several official languages in the official language or one of the official languages of the place where insolvency proceedings are being opened, or in another language which that State has indicated it can accept in accordance with Article 55(5) RR if it can be assumed that that language is easier to understand for the foreign creditors.   **8.732**

So for example if insolvency proceedings are opened in Wales, one of the official languages is Welsh. That language is not widely understood, even in the UK outside Wales. The notice can be given in English, which is another official language in Wales. In cases where the relevant official language is little understood outside the Member State, the Member State can under Article 55(5) RR indicate that it accepts any official language of the institutions of the Union other than its own. Thus for example a notice by a Dutch, Finnish, Latvian, Estonian, or Hungarian insolvency practitioner might be able to use English if that has been accepted by their relevant Member State under Article 55(5) RR. It could certainly be assumed that English would be easier to understand for the foreign creditors.   **8.733**

There is a special exception in Article 54(4) RR with regard to insolvency proceedings relating to an individual not exercising a business or professional activity. In such a case the use of the standard form is not obligatory, provided that creditors are not required to lodge their claims in order to have their debts taken into account in the proceedings.   **8.734**

8.735 Thus for example in England, where there is no difference in procedure depending on whether an individual is exercising a business or professional activity, and all creditors are required to lodge claims in order to have their debts taken into account, the exception will not apply.

(RR) Article 55—Procedure for lodging claims

1. Any foreign creditor may lodge its claim using the standard claims form to be established in accordance with Article 88. The form shall bear the heading 'Lodgement of claims' in all the official languages of the institutions of the Union.
2. The standard claims form referred to in paragraph 1 shall include the following information:
    (a) the name, postal address, e-mail address, if any, personal identification number, if any, and bank details of the foreign creditor referred to in paragraph 1;
    (b) the amount of the claim, specifying the principal and, where applicable, interest and the date on which it arose and the date on which it became due, if different;
    (c) if interest is claimed, the interest rate, whether the interest is of a legal or contractual nature, the period of time for which the interest is claimed and the capitalised amount of interest;
    (d) if costs incurred in asserting the claim prior to the opening of proceedings are claimed, the amount and the details of those costs;
    (e) the nature of the claim;
    (f) whether any preferential creditor status is claimed and the basis of such a claim;
    (g) whether security in rem or a reservation of title is alleged in respect of the claim and if so, what assets are covered by the security interest being invoked, the date on which the security was granted and, where the security has been registered, the registration number; and
    (h) whether any set-off is claimed and, if so, the amounts of the mutual claims existing on the date when insolvency proceedings were opened, the date on which they arose and the amount net of set-off claimed.
    The standard claims form shall be accompanied by copies of any supporting documents.
3. The standard claims form shall indicate that the provision of information concerning the bank details and the personal identification number of the creditor referred to in point (a) of paragraph 2 is not compulsory.
4. When a creditor lodges its claim by means other than the standard form referred to in paragraph 1, the claim shall contain the information referred to in paragraph 2.
5. Claims may be lodged in any official language of the institutions of the Union. The court, the insolvency practitioner or the debtor in possession may require the creditor to provide a translation in the official language of the State of the opening of proceedings or, if there are several official languages in that Member State, in the official language or one of the official languages of the place where insolvency proceedings have been opened, or in another language which that Member State has indicated it can accept. Each Member State shall indicate whether it accepts any official language of the institutions of the Union other than its own for the purpose of the lodging of claims.

6. Claims shall be lodged within the period stipulated by the law of the State of the opening of proceedings. In the case of a foreign creditor, that period shall not be less than 30 days following the publication of the opening of insolvency proceedings in the insolvency register of the State of the opening of proceedings. Where a Member State relies on Article 24(4), that period shall not be less than 30 days following a creditor having been informed pursuant to Article 54.

7. Where the court, the insolvency practitioner or the debtor in possession has doubts in relation to a claim lodged in accordance with this Article, it shall give the creditor the opportunity to provide additional evidence on the existence and the amount of the claim.

This is a new provision replacing the much simpler and shorter provision con- **8.736** tained in Article 41 OR.

There was a concern under the OR that foreign creditors might be put to con- **8.737** siderable expense and trouble in lodging claims. Article 55(1) RR provides that any foreign creditor may lodge his claim using the standard claims form to be established in accordance with Article 88.

Two points are then taken over from OR Article 42(2) RR. First of all, Article **8.738** 55(5) RR provides, as did Article 42(2) OR, that claims may be lodged in any official language of the Union. As before, the insolvency practitioner, and now also, the debtor in possession, may however require the creditor to provide a translation into the official language of the Member State of the opening of proceedings or, if there are several official languages in that Member State, the official language or one of the official languages of the place where insolvency proceedings have been opened or any other language which the Member State has indicated it can accept.

Going back to the example of a proceeding opened in Wales, the translation **8.739** could in theory be into Welsh or English as being official languages of the place of opening, although in practice one would expect the translation to be into English.

Under Article 42(2) OR it was only where a creditor lodged a claim in his own **8.740** Member State language that the claim had to bear the heading 'Lodgement of Claim' in the official language or one of the official languages of the State of the opening of proceedings. Under Article 55(1) RR the new standard form is to have the heading 'Lodgement of Claims' in all the official languages of the institutions of the Union.

Article 55(2) RR provides for eight headings of information to be provided in the **8.741** standard claim form, being much more extensive than the basic points formerly required under Article 41 OR.

Article 55 RR requires claims forms to be accompanied by copies of supporting **8.742** documents, if any, as did Article 41 OR. Article 55(1) RR uses the word 'may' in respect of a foreign creditor lodging his claim using the standard claim form. This, together with Article 55(4) RR, which expressly refers to a creditor lodging his claim by 'other means than the standard form' show that the use of the standard form is optional and not mandatory.

8.743 There was a concern under the OR that time limits in some member States were very short and also inflexible. Article 55 RR has an entirely new provision setting down a minimum period of 30 days during which a foreign creditor can lodge a claim after the publication of the opening of insolvency proceedings in the insolvency register of the Member State of opening.

8.744 In cases where a Member State is making use of the exception in Article 24(4) RR which permits a Member State to avoid making certain information publicly available through a system of interconnection of insolvency registers, in the case of individuals not exercising an independent business or professional activity, Article 55(6) RR requires a minimum period of 30 days from the foreign creditor being informed pursuant to the insolvency practitioner's duty to inform known creditors with habitual residences, domiciles or registered offices in other Member States pursuant to Article 54 RR.

8.745 Article 55(7) RR lays down a minimum standard of conduct for an insolvency practitioner in relation to claims. Where he has 'doubts' in relation to a claim lodged pursuant to Article 55 RR, then the insolvency practitioner is obliged to give the creditor an opportunity to provide additional evidence of the existence and the amount of the claim.

E. Chapter V: Groups of Companies

Introduction

8.746 One of the key changes made in the RR has been to introduce a new Chapter V dealing specifically with insolvency proceedings involving a group of companies. In practice, many corporate insolvencies will involve a group of companies often located across different jurisdictions, rather than a single corporate entity, and one of the perceived deficiencies of the OR as originally enacted was a lack of any provision to deal specifically with the insolvency of a group of companies. In the case of a group insolvency, it is likely to be inefficient and destructive of value for there to be separate unco-ordinated insolvency proceedings in respect of each of the individual corporate entities which comprise the group, as opposed to a single group-wide process.

8.747 In practice, in a number of cases such as *Collins & Aikman* and *Nortel*,[67] the issue has been dealt with by the Court concluding that the COMI of each of the

---

[67] *Collins & Aikman* [2007] 1 BCLC 182; *Re Nortel Networks SA* [2009] BCC 343.

companies within the group was located in a single jurisdiction. The effect of this conclusion was that co-ordinated insolvency processes in a single jurisdiction and involving the same insolvency office-holders could then be put in place. In both *Collins & Aikman* and *Nortel*, the English Court found that the COMIs of each of the companies within the European groups was located in England so that English administration proceedings were opened in relation to each of the European companies as main proceedings with the same insolvency office-holders appointed. This meant that the insolvency proceedings in respect of the group could be closely co-ordinated and managed. In both cases, this approach worked successfully.

However, this approach is obviously dependent on the COMI of each of the companies within the group being in a single jurisdiction. Depending on the corporate organization of the group of companies in question, this may or may not be the case. Moreover, the approach adopted in *Collins & Aikman* and *Nortel* does not preclude the possibility of secondary proceedings being opened in other jurisdictions. **8.748**

One of the possible techniques in dealing with the insolvencies of groups of companies is to substantively consolidate the insolvency proceedings in respect of the individual corporate entities into a single insolvency proceeding. This is a technique which may be adopted in Chapter 11 bankruptcy cases in the United States. The revisions to the RR dealing with groups do not, however, go as far as allowing for substantive consolidation of the insolvencies of individual corporate entities. Rather two approaches have been adopted: **8.749**

1. a general requirement for co-operation and communication where there are insolvency proceedings which relate to two or more members of a group of companies; and
2. a new concept of 'group co-ordination proceedings' which is intended to provide for the co-ordination of insolvency proceedings in respect of members of a group of companies.

It is important to note, however, that the new provisions do not preclude the possibility previously adopted in cases like *Collins & Aikman* and *Nortel* of finding that the COMIs of all of the group companies are in the same Member State and appointing the same insolvency office-holder in the proceedings relating to each company. Recital (50) to the RR makes clear that this possibility remains open, and it may still be the most effective approach in many cases provided that it is justified on the facts.

[Any office-holder appointed over any entity in a group insolvency will be able to request group co-ordination proceedings. The Regulations adopt a principle of 'court first seised' in relation to an application to open such proceedings. The Regulations eschew a principle which might otherwise require the jurisdiction of the 'most important' insolvency proceeding in the group to be identified (eg based on where a group's most crucial functions are performed). While this militates in favour of simplicity, it may result in more minor office-holders rushing to their **8.750** courts to seek to open group co-ordination proceedings. This risk is mitigated by the ability of at least two-thirds of the insolvency office-holders appointed over the group companies to pre-agree that one particular jurisdiction is the most appropriate, in which case that jurisdiction will have exclusive jurisdiction. Furthermore, the court first seised must notify other office-holders (who are to be affected by the group plan) and be satisfied that (i) it is appropriate to open group co-ordination proceedings and (ii) that no creditor of any group member anticipated to participate in the proceeding is likely to be financially disadvantaged by the inclusion of such member in the proceedings. How one will be able to demonstrate that (ii) has or has not been satisfied (depending on whether one is seeking or opposing the application) is far from clear in evidentiary terms. Ultimately, participation in the group proceeding is voluntary (and non-participation means that that group member will not have to bear any costs), see Article 65 RR. This may significantly undermine the utility of the procedure and even allow an element of bargaining by office-holders for their preferred jurisdiction on account of a threat not to participate. Further, even if a local proceeding is included in the group proceedings, the local office-holder of such proceeding is not obliged to follow in whole or in part the co-ordinator's recommendation or the group co-ordination plan (although it must then give reasons to the persons it is required to report to under local law and the co-ordinator), see Article 70 RR. Again, this may significantly undermine the utility of the group procedure. (**AW**)]

Groups of companies

8.751 Chapter V applies to groups of companies, and it is therefore important to understand the meaning and scope of this. This term is defined in Article 2(11) RR as meaning 'a parent undertaking and its subsidiary undertakings'. In turn:

- 'Parent undertaking' is defined as meaning 'an undertaking which controls, either directly or indirectly, one or more subsidiary undertakings'.
- An undertaking which prepares consolidated financial statements pursuant to Directive 2013/34/EU of 26 June 2013 is deemed to be a parent undertaking.
- The term 'subsidiary undertaking' is not defined in the Regulation. However, it appears to follow from the definition of 'parent undertaking' that an entity which is controlled (directly or indirectly) by a second entity will be a subsidiary undertaking vis-à-vis that second entity (and that the second entity will be a parent undertaking).

It follows from these definitions that the concept of a 'group of companies' is based on the concept of control (direct and indirect). Accordingly, where one company controls (directly or indirectly) another company there will be a 'group of companies' for the purposes of Chapter V of the RR. Further guidance as to the meaning of 'control' in this context can also be derived from Directive 2013/34/EU on annual financial statements (which, as noted above, is referenced in the definition of 'parent undertaking'). Recital (31) of that Directive provides that:

> Consolidated financial statements should present the activities of a parent undertaking and its subsidiaries as a single economic entity (a group). Undertakings controlled by the parent undertaking should be considered as subsidiary undertakings. Control should be based on holding a majority of voting rights, but control may also exist where there are agreements with fellow shareholders or members. In certain circumstances control may be effectively exercised where the parent holds a minority or none of the shares in the subsidiary.

In other words, 'control' is likely to exist where one company controls a majority of voting rights in another company. However, 'control' may also arise in other circumstances where the relevant company does not hold a majority of the shares but there are other agreements in place conferring control. In practice, this means that the question of whether there is a 'group of companies' is likely to be fact-sensitive and will depend on evidence of the existence of control between the relevant entities.

Finally, the rules in Chapter V relating to groups of companies only apply to the **8.752** extent that proceedings relating to different members of the same group of companies have been opened in more than one Member State (Recital (58) RR). In other words, they have no application to insolvency proceedings taking place in respect of members of the same group of companies within the same Member State.

Co-operation and communication

Section 1 of Chapter V (Articles 56 to 60 RR) deals with co-operation and commu- **8.753** nication where there are insolvencies of the members of a group of companies. The basic structure of the legislation is to impose duties to co-operate and communicate: (1) duties on insolvency office-holders appointed in respect of group companies to co-operate and communicate with each other (Article 56 RR), (2) duties on courts seised of insolvency proceedings in respect of group companies to co-operate and communicate with each other (Article 57 RR), and (3) duties on insolvency office-holders appointed in respect of group companies to co-operate and communicate with courts seised of insolvency proceedings in respect of other group members (Article 58 RR). In addition, insolvency office-holders are given rights and powers in relation to the insolvency proceedings of other group companies (Article 60 RR).

(RR) Article 56—Co-operation and communication between insolvency practitioners

1. Where insolvency proceedings relate to two or more members of a group of companies, an insolvency practitioner appointed in proceedings concerning a member of the group shall cooperate with any insolvency practitioner appointed in proceedings concerning another member of the same group

to the extent that such cooperation is appropriate to facilitate the effective administration of those proceedings, is not incompatible with the rules applicable to such proceedings and does not entail any conflict of interest. That cooperation may take any form, including the conclusion of agreements or protocols.

2. In implementing the cooperation set out in paragraph 1, insolvency practitioners shall:

   (a) as soon as possible communicate to each other any information which may be relevant to the other proceedings, provided appropriate arrangements are made to protect confidential information;

   (b) consider whether possibilities exist for coordinating the administration and supervision of the affairs of the group members which are subject to insolvency proceedings, and if so, coordinate such administration and supervision;

   (c) consider whether possibilities exist for restructuring group members which are subject to insolvency proceedings and, if so, coordinate with regard to the proposal and negotiation of a coordinated restructuring plan.

   For the purposes of points (b) and (c), all or some of the insolvency practitioners referred to in paragraph 1 may agree to grant additional powers to an insolvency practitioner appointed in one of the proceedings where such an agreement is permitted by the rules applicable to each of the proceedings. They may also agree on the allocation of certain tasks amongst them, where such allocation of tasks is permitted by the rules applicable to each of the proceedings.

8.754 Article 56 RR contains the core obligation for insolvency officeholders to co-operate where there are insolvency proceedings in relation to members of the same group of companies. It is important to note that the obligation to co-operate is mandatory ('shall'). However, the obligation is qualified in three important respects:

1. the obligation to co-operate is limited to the extent appropriate 'to facilitate the effective administration of the proceedings'—in other words, on its face, the focus is on the efficient administration of the insolvency proceedings, rather than on a broader obligation to co-operate to (for example) enhance returns to creditors;

2. the obligation to co-operate is subject to the rules applicable to the relevant insolvency proceeding;

3. the obligation to cooperate is also subject to the principle that it should not entail any conflict of interest—this presumably reflects the point that where (for example) there is a disputed claim between the two estates then the obligation of the insolvency officeholders to co-operate will need to be circumscribed accordingly.

In relation to the content of the obligation to co-operate, as noted above, it is on its face primarily focussed on furthering the effective administration of the insolvencies. This would no doubt encompass matters such as the sharing of information and co-operation in relation to claims made by the estates and incoming claims into the estates.

This is consistent with Article 56(2)(a) RR which imposes a mandatory obligation **8.755** on insolvency office-holders to communicate to each other, as soon as possible, any information which may be relevant to the other proceedings (provided appropriate arrangements are made to protect confidential information). It is to be noted that this obligation is again mandatory ('shall') and cast in very broad terms ('any' information which 'may' be relevant to the other proceedings). The intention appears to be that, in practice, there should be a free flow of information between the different insolvency proceedings.[68] A key issue for office-holders appointed in relation to companies within a group of companies would be to consider how best to facilitate this exchange of information.

The first of the other aspects of co-operation which are specifically mentioned in **8.756** Article 56(2) RR is to consider whether it is possible to co-ordinate the administration and supervision of the affairs of group companies which are subject to insolvency proceedings. This is consistent with the obligation in Article 56(1) RR to facilitate the 'effective administration' of the proceedings. The question is the scope of the concepts of 'administration' and 'supervision' for these purposes. They would appear to encompass the management of the business of the group where it is continuing to trade, but they may arguably also extend to encompass the realization of assets where a group is being wound down. In practice, a co-ordinated approach to the realization of assets may be the area where co-operation between the different insolvency office-holders of group companies is most required, given that many groups are organized on the basis of business lines or divisions rather than on the basis of legal entities. In order to obtain full value of the sale of assets which span different legal entities, a co-operative approach is likely to be essential. The recitals to the RR note the importance of a co-ordinated approach to asset realization where there are main and secondary proceedings in relation to a single debtor (see Recital (45) RR); the same considerations will often apply in relation to groups of companies.

The final specific area of co-operation set out in Article 56(2) RR is an obliga- **8.757** tion on office-holders to consider whether possibilities exist for restructuring group members and, if so, to co-ordinate with respect to the proposal and negotiation of a co-ordinated restructuring plan. This obligation is complemented by Article 60(1)(b) RR which allows an office-holder to apply for a stay of the realization of assets in a foreign proceeding in order to allow a restructuring plan to be implemented.

Article 56 RR suggests that the cooperation may take the form of agreements or **8.758** protocols. Recital (46) RR provides further guidance as to the type of agreements and protocols envisaged ranging from simple generic agreements to more detailed

---

[68] Art 56(2) RR does not say anything about the language in which information is to be provided or how the costs of translations are to be borne.

and specific agreements which establish a framework of principles to govern multiple insolvency proceedings.

(RR) Article 57—Co-operation and communication between courts

1. Where insolvency proceedings relate to two or more members of a group of companies, a court which has opened such proceedings shall cooperate with any other court before which a request to open proceedings concerning another member of the same group is pending or which has opened such proceedings to the extent that such cooperation is appropriate to facilitate the effective administration of the proceedings, is not incompatible with the rules applicable to them and does not entail any conflict of interest. For that purpose, the courts may, where appropriate, appoint an independent person or body to act on its instructions, provided that this is not incompatible with the rules applicable to them.
2. In implementing the cooperation set out in paragraph 1, courts, or any appointed person or body acting on their behalf, as referred to in paragraph 1, may communicate directly with each other, or request information or assistance directly from each other, provided that such communication respects the procedural rights of the parties to the proceedings and the confidentiality of information.
3. The cooperation referred to in paragraph 1 may be implemented by any means that the court considers appropriate. It may, in particular, concern:
   (a) coordination in the appointment of insolvency practitioners;
   (b) communication of information by any means considered appropriate by the court;
   (c) coordination of the administration and supervision of the assets and affairs of the members of the group;
   (d) coordination of the conduct of hearings;
   (e) coordination in the approval of protocols where necessary.

8.759 Whereas Article 56 RR provides for co-operation between insolvency office-holders, RR Article 57 provides for co-operation between courts. As with Article 56 RR, the mandatory obligation imposed by Article 57(1) RR to co-operate is cast in broad and general terms, although subject to the same qualifications as those contained in Article 56(1) RR which qualify the obligations on insolvency office-holders to co-operate with each other. Although Article 57(1) RR imposes a general duty on courts to co-operate, in practice the duty is only likely to be invoked when an application is made by a party (for example, an office-holder in insolvency proceedings relating to another group company) for relief.

8.760 The scope of the obligation to cooperate is likely to depend on what is understood by facilitating 'the effective administration of the proceedings' and the qualification relieving the Court from the obligation to co-operate where this is 'incompatible with the rules applicable' to the insolvency proceeding. These provisions both suggest that co-operation cannot affect the substantive rights of creditors in the relevant insolvency proceeding; as noted in relation to Article 56 RR, the concept of co-operation appears to be primarily focussed on matters such as information sharing, rather than on matters which go to substantive rights.

As to the methods of implementing co-operation, Article 57(2) RR empowers **8.761** the court to communicate directly with the other court or to request information or assistance directly, subject to the procedural rights of the parties and the confidentiality of information. In practice, this appears to be similar to the 'letter of request' procedure, which is a feature of cross-border insolvency in common law jurisdictions, under which the courts of one country where an insolvency is taking place may request assistance from the courts of another state.

In addition, Article 57(3) RR identifies a number of specific methods through **8.762** which co-operation can be achieved. Notably, this includes co-ordination in the appointment of insolvency practitioners. The recitals to the RR envisage the possibility that the courts in different Member States may co-operate by appointing the same office-holders in insolvency proceedings in respect of different companies in the same group (Recital (47)), although this is expressly subject to local rules concerning the qualification and licensing of insolvency practitioners.

(RR) Article 58—Co-operation and communication between insolvency practitioners and courts

An insolvency practitioner appointed in insolvency proceedings concerning a member of a group of companies:
(a) shall cooperate and communicate with any court before which a request for the opening of proceedings in respect of another member of the same group of companies is pending or which has opened such proceedings; and
(b) may request information from that court concerning the proceedings regarding the other member of the group or request assistance concerning the proceedings in which he has been appointed;
to the extent that such cooperation and communication are appropriate to facilitate the effective administration of the proceedings, do not entail any conflict of interest and are not incompatible with the rules applicable to them.

RR Article 58 is the final of the three provisions in Chapter V requiring co- **8.763** operation and communication; it requires co-operation and communication between an insolvency office-holder appointed in an insolvency proceeding in respect of a group member and the courts in other states where insolvency proceedings in respect of other group members are taking place. The obligation to co-operate is again mandatory but subject to the same qualifications as contained in Articles 56 and 57 RR.

Article 58(b) RR additionally enables the office-holder appointed in the insol- **8.764** vency proceeding of one group company to apply directly to a foreign court seised of the insolvency proceeding in respect of another group company without having first to apply to the court for a letter of request addressed to the foreign court. The office-holder may request either information or assistance. This may mean that, in practice, the more efficient route for an insolvency office-holder seeking assistance from a foreign court seised of an insolvency proceeding in respect of another group company is to approach that court directly, rather than applying to his own court for a request to made to the foreign court for assistance pursuant to Article 57 RR.

(RR) Article 59—Costs of co-operation and communication in proceedings concerning members of a group of companies

> The costs of the cooperation and communication provided for in Articles 56 to 60 incurred by an insolvency practitioner or a court shall be regarded as costs and expenses incurred in the respective proceedings.

8.765 Article 59 RR provides that the costs of co-operation and communication which are incurred are to be a cost and expense of the relevant insolvency proceeding. To this extent, Article 59 RR may have the effect of enlarging the categories of expense allowed for under the relevant domestic legislation.

(RR) Article 60—Powers of the insolvency practitioner in proceedings concerning members of a group of companies

1. An insolvency practitioner appointed in insolvency proceedings opened in respect of a member of a group of companies may, to the extent appropriate to facilitate the effective administration of the proceedings:
    (a) be heard in any of the proceedings opened in respect of any other member of the same group;
    (b) request a stay of any measure related to the realisation of the assets in the proceedings opened with respect to any other member of the same group, provided that:
        (i)   a restructuring plan for all or some members of the group for which insolvency proceedings have been opened has been proposed under point (c) of Article 56(2) and presents a reasonable chance of success;
        (ii) such a stay is necessary in order to ensure the proper implementation of the restructuring plan;
        (iii) the restructuring plan would be to the benefit of the creditors in the proceedings for which the stay is requested; and
        (iv) neither the insolvency proceedings in which the insolvency practitioner referred to in paragraph 1 of this Article has been appointed nor the proceedings in respect of which the stay is requested are subject to coordination under Section 2 of this Chapter;
    (c) apply for the opening of group coordination proceedings in accordance with Article 61.
2. The court having opened proceedings referred to in point (b) of paragraph 1 shall stay any measure related to the realisation of the assets in the proceedings in whole or in part if it is satisfied that the conditions referred to in point (b) of paragraph 1 are fulfilled.

Before ordering the stay, the court shall hear the insolvency practitioner appointed in the proceedings for which the stay is requested. Such a stay may be ordered for any period, not exceeding 3 months, which the court considers appropriate and which is compatible with the rules applicable to the proceedings.

The court ordering the stay may require the insolvency practitioner referred to in paragraph 1 to take any suitable measure available under national law to guarantee the interests of the creditors in the proceedings.

The court may extend the duration of the stay by such further period or periods as it considers appropriate and which are compatible with the rules applicable to the proceedings, provided that the conditions referred to in points (b)(ii) to (iv) of paragraph 1 continue to be fulfilled and that the total duration of the stay (the initial period together with any such extensions) does not exceed 6 months.

8.766 To complete the provisions dealing with co-operation and communication in relation to insolvency proceedings in respect of group companies, Article 60 RR confers powers and rights on an office-holder appointed in an insolvency of a group company. These rights comprise:

- A right to be heard in insolvency proceedings relating to other members of the same group of companies
- A right to request a stay of the realization of assets in insolvency proceedings relating to any other member of the same group of companies.
- A right to apply for the opening of group co-ordinating proceedings.

8.767 The right to request a stay of realization of assets ties in with the concept of a co-ordinated restructuring plan provided for by Article 56(2)(c) RR. Pursuant to that Article, insolvency office-holders in insolvency proceedings relating to group companies are obliged to consider whether group companies can be restructured through a co-ordinated restructuring plan. Article 60(1)(b) RR then provides that, where such a plan has been proposed and stands a reasonable prospect of success, a stay of the realization of assets may be imposed in order to allow the proper implementation of the plan.

8.768 The imposition of such a stay is subject to the four conditions mentioned in Article 60(1)(b)(i)–(iv) RR. However, where these conditions are satisfied, then the court is obliged to grant the stay that is it is not discretionary. The stay is to be for any period, not exceeding three months, which the court considers to be appropriate. The stay may then be extended provided that the total duration of the stay does not exceed six months.

8.769 [An office-holder appointed over any group member may be heard in any proceeding concerning another member within the same group. Crucially, such office-holder can also request a stay, up to a maximum of six months, of any measure taken by another office-holder to realize assets in the proceedings of another group company, subject to certain conditions. Again, this may represent an incursion on one office-holder's powers to administer the estate in favour of allowing another office-holder to seek a stay in order to impose a degree of co-ordination. Again, it is clear that one can foresee differences of opinion between office-holders as to the most appropriate strategy with further recourse to the courts to resolve such matters. (AW)]

Co-ordination

8.770 The second technique adopted in the RR for dealing with groups of companies is the new concept of 'group coordination proceedings' which is intended to provide for the co-ordination of insolvency proceedings in respect of members of a group of companies. In essence, these proceedings involve the appointment of a 'group coordinator' to oversee the insolvency proceedings or restructuring of a group of companies and to facilitate a 'group coordination plan'. However, there are a number of detailed procedural rules which govern participation in group co-ordination proceedings.

(RR) Article 61—Request to open group co-ordination proceedings

1. Group coordination proceedings may be requested before any court having jurisdiction over the insolvency proceedings of a member of the group, by an insolvency practitioner appointed in insolvency proceedings opened in relation to a member of the group.
2. The request referred to in paragraph 1 shall be made in accordance with the conditions provided for by the law applicable to the proceedings in which the insolvency practitioner has been appointed.
3. The request referred to in paragraph 1 shall be accompanied by:
   (a) a proposal as to the person to be nominated as the group coordinator ('the coordinator'), details of his or her eligibility pursuant to Article 71, details of his or her qualifications and his or her written agreement to act as coordinator;
   (b) an outline of the proposed group coordination, and in particular the reasons why the conditions set out in Article 63(1) are fulfilled;
   (c) a list of the insolvency practitioners appointed in relation to the members of the group and, where relevant, the courts and competent authorities involved in the insolvency proceedings of the members of the group;
   (d) an outline of the estimated costs of the proposed group coordination and the estimation of the share of those costs to be paid by each member of the group.

8.771 Article 61 RR confers jurisdiction on the courts of Member States to consider requests for the opening of group co-ordination proceedings. Any court having jurisdiction over the insolvency proceeding in respect of a member of the relevant group of companies may consider such a request. The request may be made by an office-holder appointed in any insolvency proceeding in respect of a member of the group. However, a creditor does not itself have standing to make a request for the opening of group co-ordination proceedings. Article 61(2) RR also envisages that the law under which an insolvency office-holder has been appointed may impose conditions regulating the ability of that office-holder to apply to open group co-ordination proceedings.[69]

Article 61(3) RR sets out the material which is required to accompany such an application. As envisaged by Article 61(2) RR, it is likely that requests for the opening of group co-ordination proceedings will also be subject to procedural rules laid down under the relevant national laws. **8.772**

(RR) Article 62—Priority rule

> **Without prejudice to Article 66, where the opening of group coordination proceedings is requested before courts of different Member States, any court other than the court first seised shall decline jurisdiction in favour of that court.**

Article 62 RR introduces the 'first seised' rule, a central part of the Judgments Regulation dealing with jurisdiction in civil proceedings, into the RR. It provides that where the opening of group co-ordination proceedings is requested in the courts of different Member States, then only the court first seised will have jurisdiction in relation to that request. Although this rule has the benefit of simplicity and clarity, it does mean that in practice there may well be a rush to file requests for group co-ordination proceedings in order to render a particular court first seised. The question of when the court is 'seised' for these purposes is likely to determined in the same way as under the Judgments Regulation that is when the application is issued rather than served. **8.773**

Article 62 RR is subject to the effect of Article 66 RR which, as noted below, allows the requisite majority of insolvency office-holders appointed in insolvencies of members of a group of companies to agree that the courts of a single Member State should have exclusive jurisdiction to deal with group co-ordination proceedings. **8.774**

[The potential hazards resulting from the inclusion into the RR of the 'court first seised' principle which has long been a feature of the EU Judgments Regulation (and its predecessor, the Brussels Convention) should not be underestimated. It is likely that, when matters of interpretation of this expression in the context of the RR come to be considered by the CJEU, it will replicate the commercially obtuse interpretation developed in that Court's own previous case decisions interpreting the Brussels Convention of 1968 and the more recent Brussels Regulation 44/2001 and the Recast Regulation 1215/2012. In the most notorious of these decisions, the *Erich Gasser* case, the CJEU adamantly refused to accept the long-established proposition that a valid agreement on jurisdiction should prevail over a party's recourse to tactics designed to defeat or delay the proper course of justice by launching illegitimate proceedings in the courts of some other country whose judicial processes could be expected to occupy a great deal of time before reaching **8.775**

---

[69] See also Recital (52) RR: 'where the law applicable to the insolvency so requires, this insolvency practitioner should obtain the necessary authorisation before making such a request.'

the conclusion that the terms of the jurisdiction clause must be respected.[70] While it is of course the case that Article 62 is expressed to operate 'subject to Article 66' (which is dealt with below), there may a period of delay due to the practical difficulty in co-ordinating the views of the various insolvency practitioners appointed in the respective insolvency proceedings of the members of the group so as to arrive at an agreement whereby at least two-thirds of them concur in the designation of the most appropriate court for the opening of group co-ordination proceedings. This could result in value-destructive uncertainty while the 'court first seised' awaits the outcome of efforts aimed at over-reaching the priority rule of Article 62 RR via the exception created by Article 66 RR. **(IF)**]

(RR) Article 63—Notice by the court seised

1. The court seised of a request to open group coordination proceedings shall give notice as soon as possible of the request for the opening of group coordination proceedings and of the proposed coordinator to the insolvency practitioners appointed in relation to the members of the group as indicated in the request referred to in point (c) of Article 61(3), if it is satisfied that:
   (a) the opening of such proceedings is appropriate to facilitate the effective administration of the insolvency proceedings relating to the different group members;
   (b) no creditor of any group member expected to participate in the proceedings is likely to be financially disadvantaged by the inclusion of that member in such proceedings; and
   (c) the proposed coordinator fulfils the requirements laid down in Article 71.
2. The notice referred to in paragraph 1 of this Article shall list the elements referred to in points (a) to (d) of Article 61(3).
3. The notice referred to in paragraph 1 shall be sent by registered letter, attested by an acknowledgment of receipt.
4. The court seised shall give the insolvency practitioners involved the opportunity to be heard.

8.776 Article 63 RR deals with the procedure for the opening of group co-ordination proceedings. This provides for a two-stage process. The first stage is an initial consideration of the request made by the relevant insolvency office-holder for the opening of group co-ordination proceedings. At this stage, the court to whom the request has been addressed must consider whether the request satisfies requirements (a) to (c) in Article 63(1) RR.

8.777 The requirements in (a) to (c) of Article 63(1) RR focus on the central questions of (1) whether group co-ordination proceedings will assist with the effective administration of the different insolvency proceedings, (2) whether any creditor will be financially disadvantaged by group co-ordination proceedings and (3) whether the proposed coordinator satisfies the relevant requirements. The second requirement, in particular, appears to be focussed on the question of whether group co-ordination

---

[70] Case C-116/02 *Erich Gasser GmbH v MISAT srl* [2003] ECR I-14693, [2005] QB 1.

proceedings will be likely to have a net positive benefit for creditors after allowing for the costs of those proceedings. As stated in Recital (54) RR, group coordination proceedings should 'have a generally positive impact on the creditors'. Recital (55) RR also makes clear that 'the advantages of group coordination proceedings should never be outweighed by the costs of these proceedings'.

If the court is satisfied that these requirements are met, then the request will move to **8.778** the second stage of the process. For these purposes, the court will require notice to be given of the request to all the insolvency practitioners appointed in insolvency proceedings of members of the group of companies. The notice must contain the information prescribed in Article 61(3)(a)–(d) RR and must be sent by registered letter. Following the giving of such notice, a further hearing will take place, at which the various insolvency office-holders will have opportunity to the heard, and at which the court will decide whether or not to open group co-ordination proceedings.

(RR) Article 64—Objections by insolvency practitioners

1. **An insolvency practitioner appointed in respect of any group member may object to:**
   (a) **the inclusion within group coordination proceedings of the insolvency proceedings in respect of which it has been appointed; or**
   (b) **the person proposed as a coordinator.**
2. **Objections pursuant to paragraph 1 of this Article shall be lodged with the court referred to in Article 63 within 30 days of receipt of notice of the request for the opening of group coordination proceedings by the insolvency practitioner referred to in paragraph 1 of this Article.**
   The objection may be made by means of the standard form established in accordance with Article 88.
3. **Prior to taking the decision to participate or not to participate in the coordination in accordance with point (a) of paragraph 1, an insolvency practitioner shall obtain any approval which may be required under the law of the State of the opening of proceedings for which it has been appointed.**

Following receipt of a notice sent following the first stage of the process established **8.779** under Article 63 RR, any insolvency office-holder appointed in the insolvency of a group member may lodge an objection to (a) the inclusion of that group member in the group co-ordination proceedings and/or (b) to the choice of the co-ordinator. The objection must be sent within 30 days of receipt of the notice and may be made on the standard form established by the Commission pursuant to Article 88 RR.

As explained by Article 65 RR, the consequences of an objection to the inclusion of **8.780** the insolvency group member in coordination proceedings is that the co-ordination proceedings will necessarily not apply to that group member. Accordingly, before lodging any such objection, the relevant insolvency office-holder must first obtain any authorization which is required under the law applicable to that insolvency. On the other hand, an objection to the choice of co-ordinator does not have any automatic effect; rather, it is for the court to whom the request to open co-ordination proceedings has been addressed to decide on the appointment of the co-ordinator in light of any such objections (see further Article 67 RR below).

(RR) Article 65—Consequences of objection to the inclusion in group co-ordination

1. Where an insolvency practitioner has objected to the inclusion of the proceedings in respect of which it has been appointed in group coordination proceedings, those proceedings shall not be included in the group coordination proceedings.
2. The powers of the court referred to in Article 68 or of the coordinator arising from those proceedings shall have no effect as regards that member, and shall entail no costs for that member.

8.781 Article 65 RR provides that where the relevant insolvency office-holder has objected to the inclusion of the insolvency proceedings of group member in respect of which he has been appointed in co-ordination proceedings, then the co-ordination proceedings shall not apply to such insolvency proceedings. This is an automatic rule, and does not involve any element of discretion or judgment by the court to whom the request for the opening of co-ordination proceedings has been made. According to Recital (53) RR, the right to object reflects the essentially 'voluntary nature' of group co-ordination proceedings.

8.782 As noted below, Article 69 RR provides for a subsequent right to request 'opt in' where an insolvency office-holder has originally objected to inclusion of insolvency proceedings within co-ordination proceedings.

(RR) Article 66—Choice of court for group co-ordination proceedings

1. Where at least two-thirds of all insolvency practitioners appointed in insolvency proceedings of the members of the group have agreed that a court of another Member State having jurisdiction is the most appropriate court for the opening of group coordination proceedings, that court shall have exclusive jurisdiction.
2. The choice of court shall be made by joint agreement in writing or evidenced in writing. It may be made until such time as group coordination proceedings have been opened in accordance with Article 68.
3. Any court other than the court seised under paragraph 1 shall decline jurisdiction in favour of that court.
4. The request for the opening of group coordination proceedings shall be submitted to the court agreed in accordance with Article 61.

8.783 Article 66 RR qualifies the 'first seised' rule provided for in Article 62 RR. It allows the requisite majority of office-holders appointed in insolvencies of members of a group of companies to agree that the courts of a single Member State should have exclusive jurisdiction to deal with group co-ordination proceedings. For these purposes, the requisite majority is two-thirds of the relevant insolvency office-holders. It is to be noted that the relevant majority is based on a simple poll of the relevant insolvency office-holders and is not, for example, weighted to take account of the different value of claims or assets in the different insolvency proceedings of group members.

Pursuant to Article 66(2) RR, such an agreement may be made at any time until **8.784** group co-ordination proceedings have actually been opened. In other words, the agreement may be made after a request for the opening of group co-ordination proceedings has been lodged until such time as the court actually adjudicates in favour of the request.

(RR) Article 67—Consequences of objections to the proposed co-ordinator

Where objections to the person proposed as coordinator have been received from an insolvency practitioner which does not also object to the inclusion in the group coordination proceedings of the member in respect of which it has been appointed, the court may refrain from appointing that person and invite the objecting insolvency practitioner to submit a new request in accordance with Article 61(3).

Article 67 RR deals with the situation where an insolvency office-holder has not **8.785** objected to the inclusion of the insolvency of the group member in respect of which he has been appointed in the co-ordination proceedings, but has objected to the proposed co-ordinator. As noted above, such an objection does not have the automatic effect of disqualifying the proposed co-ordinator from appointment; rather it is for the Court to whom the request for co-ordination proceedings has been addressed to consider whether the person has been appointed. No doubt, the court would consider the grounds for the objection, as well as assessing whether the proposed co-ordinator satisfies the requirements of Article 71 RR. Given the voluntary nature of co-ordination proceedings and the purpose of co-ordination proceedings as facilitating the more efficient administration of the insolvencies of the group members, it is obviously important that a co-ordinator commands the confidence of the insolvency office-holders appointed in the insolvencies of the group members.

(RR) Article 68—Decision to open group co-ordination proceedings

1. After the period referred to in Article 64(2) has elapsed, the court may open group coordination proceedings where it is satisfied that the conditions of Article 63(1) are met. In such a case, the court shall:
   (a) appoint a coordinator;
   (b) decide on the outline of the coordination; and
   (c) decide on the estimation of costs and the share to be paid by the group members.
2. The decision opening group coordination proceedings shall be brought to the notice of the participating insolvency practitioners and of the coordinator.

Article 68 RR deals with the second stage of the process for the commencement **8.786** of co-ordination proceedings. As noted above, pursuant to Article 63 RR, if the court is satisfied that the requirements in Article 63(1)(a)–(c) RR are satisfied, then a notice is to be sent to all of the relevant insolvency office-holders. Following the expiration of 30 days following the receipt of such notices by the insolvency office-holders, the court will then hold a further hearing to decide whether to open co-ordination proceedings. At this hearing, the insolvency office-holders will have a right to be represented and heard.

8.787 The court will no doubt consider whether its initial views as to the satisfaction of the requirements in Article 63(1)(a)–(c) RR remain justified in light of any representations made by the insolvency office-holders and in light of any further information. A relevant factor may well be the extent to which objections have been lodged pursuant to Article 64(1)(a) RR with the effect that insolvency proceedings in respect of individual group members will not be included within any co-ordination proceedings.

8.788 If the court decides to open co-ordination proceedings then, pursuant to Article 68(1)(a)–(c) RR, it must appoint a co-ordinator, decide on the outline of the co-ordination and decide on the estimated costs and the share to be paid by the various group members. These requirements reflect the matters required to be contained in the application for the commencement of co-ordination proceedings pursuant to Article 61(3) RR.

8.789 The language in Article 68(1)(c) RR which requires the court to 'decide on the estimation of costs' is somewhat vague but appears to encompass the idea that the court should, when opening the co-ordination proceedings, approve an estimate of the costs of those proceedings. The Recitals to the RR and the provisions of the RR envisage that if it becomes apparent subsequently that the estimated costs will be exceeded by more than 10 per cent the co-ordinator should inform the insolvency office-holders of the participating group companies and should return to the court for prior approval of the additional costs to be incurred above the original estimate (Recital (55) RR and Article 72(6) RR).

8.790 The RR does not provide any guidance as to the manner in which costs should be shared as between the estates of the group members participating in the co-ordination proceedings. An obvious yardstick would be by reference to the relative gross assets in the relevant estates. Such an approach would appear to be fairer to the relevant creditors than simply splitting the costs between the relevant insolvency estates pro rata.

(RR) Article 69—Subsequent opt-in by insolvency practitioners

1. In accordance with its national law, any insolvency practitioner may request, after the court decision referred to in Article 68, the inclusion of the proceedings in respect of which it has been appointed, where:
   (a) there has been an objection to the inclusion of the insolvency proceedings within the group coordination proceedings; or
   (b) insolvency proceedings with respect to a member of the group have been opened after the court has opened group coordination proceedings.

2. Without prejudice to paragraph 4, the coordinator may accede to such a request, after consulting the insolvency practitioners involved, where
   (a) he or she is satisfied that, taking into account the stage that the group coordination proceedings has reached at the time of the request, the criteria set out in points (a) and (b) of Article 63(1) are met; or
   (b) all insolvency practitioners involved agree, subject to the conditions in their national law.
3. The coordinator shall inform the court and the participating insolvency practitioners of his or her decision pursuant to paragraph 2 and of the reasons on which it is based.
4. Any participating insolvency practitioner or any insolvency practitioner whose request for inclusion in the group coordination proceedings has been rejected may challenge the decision referred to in paragraph 2 in accordance with the procedure set out under the law of the Member State in which the group coordination proceedings have been opened.

Article 69 RR provides for a right to request 'opt in' to co-ordination proceedings **8.791** in two circumstances. The first is whether there was originally an objection to inclusion of a particular insolvency proceeding within the co-ordination proceeding. As noted above, the automatic effect of such an objection pursuant to Article 65 RR is that the relevant insolvency proceeding will not be included in the group co-ordination proceedings. The second circumstance is whether insolvency proceedings in respect of a group member were opened after the commencement of co-ordination proceedings.

In either of these circumstances, the relevant insolvency office-holder may request **8.792** the inclusion of the relevant insolvency proceedings in the co-ordination proceedings. The co-ordinator must consult with all the insolvency office-holders in the insolvency proceedings currently comprised in the co-ordination proceedings. The co-ordinator may then accede to such a request provided either that:

- the criteria in Article 63(1)(a) and (b) RR are satisfied (ie whether group co-ordination proceedings will assist with the effective administration of the different insolvency proceedings and whether any creditor will be financially disadvantaged by group co-ordination proceedings) bearing in mind the stage of the co-ordination proceedings; or
- all the insolvency office-holders in the insolvency proceedings currently comprised in the co-ordination proceedings agree.

Any request for inclusion in co-ordination proceedings which is refused may be subject to challenge in accordance with the law of the Member State where the group co-ordination proceedings were opened.

(RR) Article 70—Recommendations and group co-ordination plan

1. When conducting their insolvency proceedings, insolvency practitioners shall consider the recommendations of the coordinator and the content of the group coordination plan referred to in Article 72(1).

2. An insolvency practitioner shall not be obliged to follow in whole or in part the coordinator's recommendations or the group coordination plan.
If it does not follow the coordinator's recommendations or the group coordination plan, it shall give reasons for not doing so to the persons or bodies that it is to report to under its national law, and to the coordinator.

8.793 Article 70 RR deals with the impact of co-ordination proceedings on the insolvency proceedings in respect of the participating group members. Pursuant to Article 70(1) RR, the relevant insolvency office-holders are required to 'consider' the recommendations made by the co-ordinator and the group co-ordination plan. There is, however, no obligation to abide by and follow such recommendations and plan. Indeed, Article 70(2) RR makes expressly clear that there is no such obligation.

8.794 That said, in circumstances where the insolvency proceedings of a group member are subject to co-ordination proceedings (because there has been no objection made pursuant to Article 65 RR), then the expectation would be that in the ordinary course the insolvency office-holder would follow the recommendations of the co-ordinator and the contents of the co-ordination plan. Article 70(2) RR recognizes this since it provides that, if an insolvency office-holder does not follow the recommendations or the plan, then he must give his reasons for not doing so. These are to be provided to the relevant bodies specified in national law and to the co-ordinator himself.

(RR) Article 71—The co-ordinator

1. The coordinator shall be a person eligible under the law of a Member State to act as an insolvency practitioner.
2. The coordinator shall not be one of the insolvency practitioners appointed to act in respect of any of the group members, and shall have no conflict of interest in respect of the group members, their creditors and the insolvency practitioners appointed in respect of any of the group members.

8.795 Article 71 RR sets out the requirements which need to be satisfied for a person to be appointed as co-ordinator. First of all, the relevant person must be authorized under the law of a Member State to act as an insolvency practitioner. Secondly, no person who is already an insolvency office-holder in respect of any group member can be appointed as co-ordinator. Thirdly, the person must not have any conflict of interest in respect of any of (a) any group members, (b) any creditors of group members, or (c) the insolvency office-holders appointed in respect of any group members.

(RR) Article 72—Tasks and rights of the co-ordinator

1. The coordinator shall:
   (a) identify and outline recommendations for the coordinated conduct of the insolvency proceedings;

    (b) propose a group coordination plan that identifies, describes and recommends a comprehensive set of measures appropriate to an integrated approach to the resolution of the group members' insolvencies. In particular, the plan may contain proposals for:

2. The coordinator may also:

    (a) be heard and participate, in particular by attending creditors' meetings, in any of the proceedings opened in respect of any member of the group;

    (b) mediate any dispute arising between two or more insolvency practitioners of group members;

    (c) present and explain his or her group coordination plan to the persons or bodies that he or she is to report to under his or her national law;

    (d) request information from any insolvency practitioner in respect of any member of the group where that information is or might be of use when identifying and outlining strategies and measures in order to coordinate the proceedings; and

    (e) request a stay for a period of up to 6 months of the proceedings opened in respect of any member of the group, provided that such a stay is necessary in order to ensure the proper implementation of the plan and would be to the benefit of the creditors in the proceedings for which the stay is requested; or request the lifting of any existing stay. Such a request shall be made to the court that opened the proceedings for which a stay is requested.

3. The plan referred to in point (b) of paragraph 1 shall not include recommendations as to any consolidation of proceedings or insolvency estates.

4. The coordinator's tasks and rights as defined under this Article shall not extend to any member of the group not participating in group coordination proceedings.

5. The coordinator shall perform his or her duties impartially and with due care.

6. Where the coordinator considers that the fulfilment of his or her tasks requires a significant increase in the costs compared to the cost estimate referred to in point (d) of Article 61(3), and in any case, where the costs exceed 10 % of the estimated costs, the coordinator shall:

    (a) inform without delay the participating insolvency practitioners; and

    (b) seek the prior approval of the court opening group coordination proceedings.

Article 72 RR is an important provision which sets out the tasks which the co-ordinator is required to undertake and the rights conferred on him to enable him to perform those tasks. The co-ordinator's tasks form into two broad categories: **8.796**

- first, to produce recommendations for the co-ordinated conduct of the various insolvency proceedings;
- secondly to produce a group co-ordination plan.

The group co-ordination plan is likely to be the centrepiece of any co-ordination proceedings. In the case of insolvency proceedings which are directed at rehabilitating and restructuring the relevant group companies and/or their businesses, the plan may include measures applicable across the relevant companies for restructuring liabilities and operations. In the case of insolvency proceedings which are directed at realizing assets for distribution to creditors, the plan may include co-ordinated measures for realizing assets and dealing with inter-group liabilities and claims.

8.797 However, it is important to note that the RR makes expressly clear that a plan may not involve the consolidation of proceedings or estates (Article 72(3) RR). This reflects the general approach of the RR in rejecting substantive consolidation as an approach for dealing with the insolvencies of groups of companies.

8.798 As a counterpoint to Article 72(1) RR, Article 72(2) RR confers various rights and powers on the co-ordinator. These include:

1. A right to participate at both hearings and creditors' meetings in the insolvency proceedings of any group member, providing such group member is participating in the co-ordination proceedings: Article 72(4) RR.

2. A power to mediate any dispute between the insolvency office-holders of group members, providing such group members are participating in the co-ordination proceedings: Article 72(4) RR. This raises the question of whether, where there is a dispute between two such insolvency office-holders, it is a prerequisite to seek to mediate the dispute through the co-ordinator (where one has been appointed) before commencing court proceedings. The better view is probably that it is not, on the footing that Article 72(2)(b) RR confers a power on the co-ordinator to mediate disputes rather than making such mediation compulsory.

3. A power to present the co-ordination plan to relevant persons as required under the national law applicable to the co-ordinator.

4. A right to request information from any insolvency office-holder in respect of any group members participating in group co-ordination proceedings: Article 72(4) RR. The condition is that the relevant information is or might be of use when identifying and outlining strategies and measures in order to co-ordinate the proceedings. Given the terms of Article 72(2)(d) RR (it is sufficient that the information 'might' be of use), this represents a broad information gathering power.

5. A right to request a stay (for up to six months) of any insolvency proceeding of a group member participating in group co-ordination proceedings: Article 72(4) RR. This is the counterpart of the power conferred on individual office-holders under Article 60(1) RR to request a stay in order to implement a restructuring plan, although, unlike the power under Article 60(1) RR, the power conferred by Article 72(2)(e) RR is not limited to a stay of the realization of assets but extends to a stay of the relevant insolvency proceedings generally.

Article 72(5) RR expresses the general duty imposed on co-ordinators to perform his or her duties impartially and with due care. The Article does not identify whether the duty is owed to the company or to the creditors (or both), or whether it could be subject to an action brought by one or more creditors.

[The group co-ordinator's substantial powers (including the power to stay pro-   **8.799**
ceedings in respect of any group member, albeit subject to conditions) could interfere with the other office-holders' ability to administer their respective proceedings. Disputes on this will invariably increase costs to the estate. This aspect of the co-ordinator's power and its potential impact on creditors will need to be monitored. It is clear that one can foresee differences in opinion between local office-holders and a co-ordinator as to what may be in the best interests of the local office-holders' creditors and what may be in the best interests of the group as a whole. This may also increase the risk that office-holders will opt out of such proceedings until the plan is clear and acceptable to them and opt in under Article 69 at a later stage. See also Article 72(4) RR which makes it clear that the co-ordinator's tasks and rights do not extend to any member of the group not participating in group co-ordination proceedings. In terms of role, the co-ordinator must be a person who could act as an insolvency practitioner under the laws of any Member State (the regulation of such persons may vary widely from state to state). The co-ordinator's tasks and rights are set out in Article 72 RR and the grounds for the revocation of his appointment in Article 75 RR. However, it is clear that the co-ordinator is a pure creature of the Regulation—while the co-ordinator is required to perform his duties impartially and with due care, it is not clear to whom his duties are owed (the office-holders, the debtor, the creditors?) and what the avenues of recourse against him or her might be. (AW)

(RR) Article 73—Languages

1. The coordinator shall communicate with the insolvency practitioner of a participating group member in the language agreed with the insolvency practitioner or, in the absence of an agreement, in the official language or one of the official languages of the institutions of the Union, and of the court which opened the proceedings in respect of that group member.
2. The coordinator shall communicate with a court in the official language applicable to that court.

Article 73 RR deals with the issue of the language of communications in co-   **8.800**
ordination proceedings. It provides for two options. Either communications take place in the language agreed between the co-ordinator and the relevant insolvency office-holder. Alternatively, absent agreement, communications are to be in the language which is one of the official languages of the Union and of the court which opened the relevant insolvency proceedings in which

the insolvency office-holder is appointed. In practice, it would no doubt be most efficient for the co-ordinator and all of the relevant insolvency office-holders to agree that all communications should take place in a single language. Absent agreement, Article 73 RR imposes a potentially expensive burden on co-ordinators to translate all communications into the home languages of each of the relevant insolvency office-holders.

(RR) Article 74—Co-operation between insolvency practitioners and the co-ordinator

1. Insolvency practitioners appointed in relation to members of a group and the coordinator shall cooperate with each other to the extent that such cooperation is not incompatible with the rules applicable to the respective proceedings.
2. In particular, insolvency practitioners shall communicate any information that is relevant for the coordinator to perform his or her tasks.

8.801 Article 74 RR imposes an obligation on the relevant insolvency office-holders and the co-ordinator himself to co-operate with each other. The notion of co-operation is inherent in co-ordination proceedings, and it is therefore unsurprising to find such an obligation imposed. Article 74(2) RR amplifies the co-operation obligation as extending to a requirement to communicate 'any' information that is relevant to the performance by the co-ordinator of his tasks.

(RR) Article 75—Revocation of the appointment of the co-ordinator

The court shall revoke the appointment of the coordinator of its own motion or at the request of the insolvency practitioner of a participating group member where:
(a) the coordinator acts to the detriment of the creditors of a participating group member; or
(b) the coordinator fails to comply with his or her obligations under this Chapter.

8.802 Article 75 RR imposes on the Court which opened the co-ordination proceedings an obligation to revoke the appointment of a co-ordinator either of its own motion or on the request of an insolvency office-holder of a group participating in the proceeding. The conditions for such a removal are either that the co-ordinator has acted to the detriment of the creditors of a participating group member or has failed to comply with his obligations under Chapter V of the RR.

8.803 There is, however, no ability for a creditor of a participating group company to request the removal of a co-ordinator.

(RR) Article 76—Debtor in possession

The provisions applicable, under this Chapter, to the insolvency practitioner shall also apply, where appropriate, to the debtor in possession.

Article 76 makes clear that the provisions in relation to co-ordination proceedings **8.804** also apply to a group member which is the subject of debtor in possession proceeding within the scope of the RR.

(RR) Article 77—Costs and distribution

1. The remuneration for the coordinator shall be adequate, proportionate to the tasks fulfilled and reflect reasonable expenses.
2. On having completed his or her tasks, the coordinator shall establish the final statement of costs and the share to be paid by each member, and submit this statement to each participating insolvency practitioner and to the court opening coordination proceedings.
3. In the absence of objections by the insolvency practitioners within 30 days of receipt of the statement referred to in paragraph 2, the costs and the share to be paid by each member shall be deemed to be agreed. The statement shall be submitted to the court opening coordination proceedings for confirmation.
4. In the event of an objection, the court that opened the group coordination proceedings shall, upon the application of the coordinator or any participating insolvency practitioner, decide on the costs and the share to be paid by each member in accordance with the criteria set out in paragraph 1 of this Article, and taking into account the estimation of costs referred to in Article 68(1) and, where applicable, Article 72(6).
5. Any participating insolvency practitioner may challenge the decision referred to in paragraph 4 in accordance with the procedure set out under the law of the Member State where group coordination proceedings have been opened.

Article 77 RR deals with the costs of co-ordination proceedings. As noted above, **8.805** one of the key criteria for determining whether co-ordination proceedings are appropriate is whether the benefits of the co-ordination proceedings outweigh the costs. Where the court opens co-ordination proceedings, it must approve an estimate of costs for those proceedings and determine the shares to be paid by the relevant group companies participating in the co-ordination proceedings.

Article 77(1) RR establishes the general principle that the co-ordinator should **8.806** receive adequate and proportionate remuneration for his work and be entitled to recover reasonable expenses. In terms of procedure, following the completion of the co-ordination work, the co-ordinator is to produce a final statement of costs detailing the share to be paid by each participating group member. The statement is deemed to be agreed absent an objection being received from the relevant insolvency office-holder within 30 days of its receipt. In the event of any objection, the court which opened the co-ordination proceedings will determine the matter pursuant to Article 77(4) RR.

F. Chapter VI: Data Protection

(RR) Article 78—Data protection

1. National rules implementing Directive 95/46/EC shall apply to the processing of personal data carried out in the Member States pursuant to this Regulation, provided that processing operations referred to in Article 3(2) of Directive 95/46/EC are not concerned.
2. Regulation (EC) No 45/2001 shall apply to the processing of personal data carried out by the Commission pursuant to this Regulation.

(RR) Article 79—Responsibilities of Member States regarding the processing of personal data in national insolvency registers

1. Each Member State shall communicate to the Commission the name of the natural or legal person, public authority, agency or any other body designated by national law to exercise the functions of controller in accordance with point (d) of Article 2 of Directive 95/46/EC, with a view to its publication on the European e-Justice Portal.
2. Member States shall ensure that the technical measures for ensuring the security of personal data processed in their national insolvency registers referred to in Article 24 are implemented.
3. Member States shall be responsible for verifying that the controller, designated by national law in accordance with point (d) of Article 2 of Directive 95/46/EC, ensures compliance with the principles of data quality, in particular the accuracy and the updating of data stored in national insolvency registers.
4. Member States shall be responsible, in accordance with Directive 95/46/EC, for the collection and storage of data in national databases and for decisions taken to make such data available in the interconnected register that can be consulted via the European e-Justice Portal.
5. As part of the information that should be provided to data subjects to enable them to exercise their rights, and in particular the right to the erasure of data, Member States shall inform data subjects of the accessibility period set for personal data stored in insolvency registers.

(RR) Article 80—Responsibilities of the Commission in connection with the processing of personal data

1. The Commission shall exercise the responsibilities of controller pursuant to Article 2(d) of Regulation (EC) No 45/2001 in accordance with its respective responsibilities defined in this Article.
2. The Commission shall define the necessary policies and apply the necessary technical solutions to fulfil its responsibilities within the scope of the function of controller.
3. The Commission shall implement the technical measures required to ensure the security of personal data while in transit, in particular the confidentiality and integrity of any transmission to and from the European e-Justice Portal.

4. The obligations of the Commission shall not affect the responsibilities of the Member States and other bodies for the content and operation of the interconnected national databases run by them.

(RR) Article 81—Information obligations

Without prejudice to the information to be given to data subjects in accordance with Articles 11 and 12 of Regulation (EC) No 45/2001, the Commission shall inform data subjects, by means of publication through the European e-Justice Portal, about its role in the processing of data and the purposes for which those data will be processed.

(RR) Article 82—Storage of personal data

As regards information from interconnected national databases, no personal data relating to data subjects shall be stored in the European e-Justice Portal. All such data shall be stored in the national databases operated by the Member States or other bodies.

(RR) Article 83—Access to personal data via the European e-Justice Portal

Personal data stored in the national insolvency registers referred to in Article 24 shall be accessible via the European e-Justice Portal for as long as they remain accessible under national law.

These provisions are entirely new and deal with data protection. This is a subject **8.807** beyond the scope of this work and a specialist source on data protection should be consulted.

G. Chapter VII: Transitional and Final Provisions

(RR) Article 84—Applicability in time

1. The provisions of this Regulation shall apply only to insolvency proceedings opened after 26 June 2017. Acts committed by a debtor before that date shall continue to be governed by the law which was applicable to them at the time they were committed.
2. Notwithstanding Article 91 of this Regulation, Regulation (EC) No 1346/2000 shall continue to apply to insolvency proceedings which fall within the scope of that Regulation and which have been opened before 26 June 2017.

Article 84(1) RR provides that the RR will only apply to insolvency proceedings **8.808** opened 'after' 26 June 2017. Article 84(2) RR provides that OR will continue to apply to insolvency proceedings within the scope of the OR and which were opened before 26 June 2017. This leaves the rather odd position that nothing on the face of this Article seems to be provided for any insolvency proceeding opened on 26 June 2017. However, it seems clear from Article 92 (which is dealt with below) that 'after' needs to be read as 'on or after', so that a proceeding opened on 26 June 2017 will be governed by the RR.

8.809   Article 84 RR provides that acts 'committed' by a debtor before 26 June 2017 will continue to be governed by the law which was applicable to them at the time they were committed. This appears to be in accord with the general principle of non-retroactivity. Again, the wording is odd, because it is not clear what law would apply to an act done by a debtor on 26 June 2017. However, the words 'after 26 June 2017' should in the light of Article 92 (which is dealt with below) be interpreted as 'on or after 26 June 2017'.

(RR) Article 85—Relationship to Conventions

1. This Regulation replaces, in respect of the matters referred to therein, and as regards relations between Member States, the Conventions concluded between two or more Member States, in particular:
   (a) the Convention between Belgium and France on Jurisdiction and the Validity and Enforcement of Judgments, Arbitration Awards and Authentic Instruments, signed at Paris on 8 July 1899;
   (b) the Convention between Belgium and Austria on Bankruptcy, Winding-up, Arrangements, Compositions and Suspension of Payments (with Additional Protocol of 13 June 1973), signed at Brussels on 16 July 1969;
   (c) the Convention between Belgium and the Netherlands on Territorial Jurisdiction, Bankruptcy and the Validity and Enforcement of Judgments, Arbitration Awards and Authentic Instruments, signed at Brussels on 28 March 1925;
   (d) the Treaty between Germany and Austria on Bankruptcy, Winding-up, Arrangements and Compositions, signed at Vienna on 25 May 1979;
   (e) the Convention between France and Austria on Jurisdiction, Recognition and Enforcement of Judgments on Bankruptcy, signed at Vienna on 27 February 1979;
   (f) the Convention between France and Italy on the Enforcement of Judgments in Civil and Commercial Matters, signed at Rome on 3 June 1930;
   (g) the Convention between Italy and Austria on Bankruptcy, Winding-up, Arrangements and Compositions, signed at Rome on 12 July 1977;
   (h) the Convention between the Kingdom of the Netherlands and the Federal Republic of Germany on the Mutual Recognition and Enforcement of Judgments and other Enforceable Instruments in Civil and Commercial Matters, signed at The Hague on 30 August 1962;
   (i) the Convention between the United Kingdom and the Kingdom of Belgium providing for the Reciprocal Enforcement of Judgments in Civil and Commercial Matters, with Protocol, signed at Brussels on 2 May 1934;
   (j) the Convention between Denmark, Finland, Norway, Sweden and Iceland on Bankruptcy, signed at Copenhagen on 7 November 1933;
   (k) the European Convention on Certain International Aspects of Bankruptcy, signed at Istanbul on 5 June 1990;
   (l) the Convention between the Federative People's Republic of Yugoslavia and the Kingdom of Greece on the Mutual Recognition and Enforcement of Judgments, signed at Athens on 18 June 1959;

(m) the Agreement between the Federative People's Republic of Yugoslavia and the Republic of Austria on the Mutual Recognition and Enforcement of Arbitral Awards and Arbitral Settlements in Commercial Matters, signed at Belgrade on 18 March 1960;

(n) the Convention between the Federative People's Republic of Yugoslavia and the Italian Republic on Mutual Judicial Cooperation in Civil and Administrative Matters, signed at Rome on 3 December 1960;

(o) the Agreement between the Socialist Federative Republic of Yugoslavia and the Kingdom of Belgium on Judicial Cooperation in Civil and Commercial Matters, signed at Belgrade on 24 September 1971;

(p) the Convention between the Governments of Yugoslavia and France on the Recognition and Enforcement of Judgments in Civil and Commercial Matters, signed at Paris on 18 May 1971;

(q) the Agreement between the Czechoslovak Socialist Republic and the Hellenic Republic on Legal Aid in Civil and Criminal Matters, signed at Athens on 22 October 1980, still in force between the Czech Republic and Greece;

(r) the Agreement between the Czechoslovak Socialist Republic and the Republic of Cyprus on Legal Aid in Civil and Criminal Matters, signed at Nicosia on 23 April 1982, still in force between the Czech Republic and Cyprus;

(s) the Treaty between the Government of the Czechoslovak Socialist Republic and the Government of the Republic of France on Legal Aid and the Recognition and Enforcement of Judgments in Civil, Family and Commercial Matters, signed at Paris on 10 May 1984, still in force between the Czech Republic and France;

(t) the Treaty between the Czechoslovak Socialist Republic and the Italian Republic on Legal Aid in Civil and Criminal Matters, signed at Prague on 6 December 1985, still in force between the Czech Republic and Italy;

(u) the Agreement between the Republic of Latvia, the Republic of Estonia and the Republic of Lithuania on Legal Assistance and Legal Relationships, signed at Tallinn on 11 November 1992;

(v) the Agreement between Estonia and Poland on Granting Legal Aid and Legal Relations on Civil, Labour and Criminal Matters, signed at Tallinn on 27 November 1998;

(w) the Agreement between the Republic of Lithuania and the Republic of Poland on Legal Assistance and Legal Relations in Civil, Family, Labour and Criminal Matters, signed at Warsaw on 26 January 1993;

(x) the Convention between the Socialist Republic of Romania and the Hellenic Republic on legal assistance in civil and criminal matters and its Protocol, signed at Bucharest on 19 October 1972;

(y) the Convention between the Socialist Republic of Romania and the French Republic on legal assistance in civil and commercial matters, signed at Paris on 5 November 1974;

(z) the Agreement between the People's Republic of Bulgaria and the Hellenic Republic on Legal Assistance in Civil and Criminal Matters, signed at Athens on 10 April 1976;

(aa) the Agreement between the People's Republic of Bulgaria and the Republic of Cyprus on Legal Assistance in Civil and Criminal Matters, signed at Nicosia on 29 April 1983;

    (ab) the Agreement between the Government of the People's Republic of Bulgaria and the Government of the French Republic on Mutual Legal Assistance in Civil Matters, signed at Sofia on 18 January 1989;

    (ac) the Treaty between Romania and the Czech Republic on judicial assistance in civil matters, signed at Bucharest on 11 July 1994;

    (ad) the Treaty between Romania and the Republic of Poland on legal assistance and legal relations in civil cases, signed at Bucharest on 15 May 1999

2. The Conventions referred to in paragraph 1 shall continue to have effect with regard to proceedings opened before the entry into force of Regulation (EC) No 1346/2000.

3. This Regulation shall not apply:

    (a) in any Member State, to the extent that it is irreconcilable with the obligations arising in relation to bankruptcy from a convention concluded by that Member State with one or more third countries before the entry into force of Regulation (EC) No 1346/2000;

    (b) in the United Kingdom of Great Britain and Northern Ireland, to the extent that is irreconcilable with the obligations arising in relation to bankruptcy and the winding-up of insolvent companies from any arrangements with the Commonwealth existing at the time Regulation (EC) No 1346/2000 entered into force.

8.810 The text of Article 85 is, apart from small adjustments referred to below, copied from Article 44 OR (as amended from time to time when new countries acceded) and reference should be generally be made to the commentary on Article 44 OR above.

8.811 There are slight adjustments in Article 85(2) and (3) RR as a result of the transition from the OR to the RR, but they do not alter the original effect of the OR. Thus, for example, in the case of the UK the exception which appears to refer to Section 426 of the UK Insolvency Act 1986 (Article 85(3)(b) RR) has simply been adjusted to ensure that the reference is to the time of the entry into force of the OR and not the RR.

(RR) Article 86—Information on national and Union insolvency law

1. The Member States shall provide, within the framework of the European Judicial Network in civil and commercial matters established by Council Decision 2001/470/EC [footnote omitted]), and with a view to making the information available to the public, a short description of their national legislation and procedures relating to insolvency, in particular relating to the matters listed in Article 7(2).

2. The Member States shall update the information referred to in paragraph 1 regularly.

3. The Commission shall make information concerning this Regulation available to the public.

8.812 This is an entirely new provision requiring Member States to provide a short description of their national legislation and procedures relating to insolvency and in particular relating to the matters listed in Article 7(2) RR, which refers in detail to the conditions for opening and closing insolvency proceedings and their conduct. Member States are required to update the information regularly. The provision of such information is with a view to making the information available to the public. Article 86(3) RR places the duty on the European Commission to make information concerning RR itself available to the public.

(RR) Article 87—Establishment of the interconnection of registers

> The Commission shall adopt implementing acts establishing the interconnection of insolvency registers as referred to in Article 25. Those implementing acts shall be adopted in accordance with the examination procedure referred to in Article 89(3).

This is a new provision requiring the European Commission to adopt implement- **8.813** ing Acts establishing the interconnection of the national insolvency registers. Those implementing Acts are to be adopted in accordance with the 'examination' procedure referred to in Article 89(3) RR, which is dealt with below.

(RR) Article 88—Establishment and subsequent amendment of standard forms

> The Commission shall adopt implementing acts establishing and, where necessary, amending the forms referred to in Article 27(4), Articles 54 and 55 and Article 64(2). Those implementing acts shall be adopted in accordance with the advisory procedure referred to in Article 89(2).

This is a new provision requiring the European Commission to adopt implement- **8.814** ing Acts establishing and, where necessary, amending the standard forms referred to in Articles 27(4), 54, 55, and 64(2) RR. These implementing Acts are to be adopted in accordance with the advisory procedure referred to in Article 89(2) RR, which is dealt with below.

(RR) Article 89—Committee procedure

1. The Commission shall be assisted by a committee. That committee shall be a committee within the meaning of Regulation (EU) No 182/2011.
2. Where reference is made to this paragraph, Article 4 of Regulation (EU) No 182/2011 shall apply.
3. Where reference is made to this paragraph, Article 5 of Regulation (EU) No 182/2011 shall apply.

Article 89 RR provides that the European Commission is to be assisted by a com- **8.815** mittee within the meaning of Regulation (EU) Number 182/2011 laying down rules and general principles concerning mechanisms for control by Member States of the Commission's exercise of implementing powers.

(RR) Article 90—Review clause

1. No later than 27 June 2027, and every 5 years thereafter, the Commission shall present to the European Parliament, the Council and the European Economic

and Social Committee a report on the application of this Regulation. The report shall be accompanied where necessary by a proposal for adaptation of this Regulation.

2. No later than 27 June 2022, the Commission shall present to the European Parliament, the Council and the European Economic and Social Committee a report on the application of the group coordination proceedings. The report shall be accompanied where necessary by a proposal for adaptation of this Regulation.

3. No later than 1 January 2016, the Commission shall submit to the European Parliament, the Council and the European Economic and Social Committee a study on the cross-border issues in the area of directors' liability and disqualifications.

4. No later than 27 June 2020, the Commission shall submit to the European Parliament, the Council and the European Economic and Social Committee a study on the issue of abusive forum shopping.

8.816 Article 46 OR provided for reports to be prepared by the Commission on the application of the OR with any proposals for 'adaptation' of the OR. In the case of Article 90 RR, Article 90(1) RR provides that no later than 27 June 2027 and every five years thereafter the European Commission is to present a report on the application of the RR. It is to be accompanied where necessary by a proposal for 'adaptation' of the RR.

8.817 In the case of group co-ordination proceedings in particular, a new type of procedure brought in by the RR, the European Commission is required to present a report no later than 27 June 2022.

8.818 Article 90(3) RR requires that as soon as 1 January 2016 the European Commission is to submit a study on the cross-border issues in the area of directors' liability and disqualifications.

8.819 Article 90(4) RR deals with a particular concern of the European Parliament, namely abusive forum shopping. A study on this subject is required to be presented by the European Commission no later than 27 June 2020.

8.820 All the reports referred to are required to be presented to the European Parliament, the Council, and the European Economic and Social Committee.

(RR) Article 91—Repeal

Regulation (EC) No 1346/2000 is repealed.

References to the repealed Regulation shall be construed as references to this Regulation and shall be read in accordance with the correlation table set out in Annex D to this Regulation.

8.821 This is necessarily a new provision, since it provides for the repeal of the OR. It has to be borne in mind however that pursuant to Article 84(2) RR the repealed OR is to continue to apply to insolvency proceedings within the scope of the OR which had been opened before 26 June 2017.

There is a further helpful interpretational provision to the effect that references to **8.822**
the OR are to be construed as references to the RR and are to be read in accordance
with the correlation table set out in Annex D to the RR. This is significant because it
means that references in other legislation or in contracts are to be read as references
to the equivalent provisions in the RR. Although this is not clearly spelt out, presumably this interpretational provision will not take effect until the RR itself takes
effect, ie on 26 June 2017: see the commentary to Article 84 RR above.

(RR) Article 92—Entry into force

This Regulation shall enter into force on the twentieth day following that of its
publication in the Official Journal of the European Union.

It shall apply from 26 June 2017, with the exception of:
(a) Article 86, which shall apply from 26 June 2016;
(b) Article 24(1), which shall apply from 26 June 2018; and
(c) Article 25, which shall apply from 26 June 2019.

Article 92 RR provides that the RR is to enter into force on the 20th day following **8.823**
that of its publication in the Official Journal of the European Union. That publication took place on 5 June 2015.

Article 92 RR further provides that generally RR provisions will apply 'from 26 June **8.824**
2017' with certain exceptions. The provision that it will apply 'from' 26 June 2017
suggests that the reading of Article 84(1) as if it read 'on or after 26 June 2017' is
correct.

There are three exceptions to the application of the RR from 26 June 2017. Exception **8.825**
(a) is that Article 86 RR, which requires Member States to provide information by
way of a short description of their national legislation and procedures relating to
insolvency takes effect 'from 26 June 2016'. Exception (b) relates to Article 24(1)
RR, which relates to the establishment of national insolvency registers by Member
States and that provision is to apply 'from 26 June 2018'. Exception (c) relates to
Article 25 RR, which relates to the Commission's obligation to establish a system
for the interconnection of national insolvency registers and that provision is to
apply 'from 26 June 2019'.

Appendices

APPENDIX 1

European Union: Council Regulation (EC) No. 1346/2000 of 29 May 2000 on Insolvency Proceedings

The Council of the European Union,

Having regard to the Treaty establishing the European Community, and in particular Article 61(c) and 67(1) thereof,

Having regard to the initiative of the Federal Republic of Germany and the Republic of Finland,

Having regard to the opinion of the European Parliament,[1]

Having regard to the opinion of the Economic and Social Committee,[2]

Whereas:

(1) The European Union has set out the aim of establishing an area of freedom, security and justice.

(2) The proper functioning of the internal market requires that cross-border insolvency proceedings should operate efficiently and effectively and this Regulation needs to be adopted in order to achieve this objective which comes within the scope of judicial cooperation in civil matters within the meaning of Article 65 of the Treaty.

(3) The activities of undertakings have more and more cross-border effects and are therefore increasingly being regulated by Community law. While the insolvency of such undertakings also affects the proper functioning of the internal market, there is a need for a Community act requiring coordination of the measures to be taken regarding an insolvent debtor's assets.

(4) It is necessary for the proper functioning of the internal market to avoid incentives for the parties to transfer assets or judicial proceedings from one Member State to another, seeking to obtain a more favourable legal position (forum shopping).

(5) These objectives cannot be achieved to a sufficient degree at national level and action at Community level is therefore justified.

(6) In accordance with the principle of proportionality this Regulation should be confined to provisions governing jurisdiction for opening insolvency proceedings and judgments which are delivered directly on the basis of the insolvency proceedings and are closely connected with such proceedings. In addition, this Regulation should contain provisions regarding the recognition of those judgments and the applicable law which also satisfy that principle.

(7) Insolvency proceedings relating to the winding-up of insolvent companies or other legal persons, judicial arrangements, compositions and analogous proceedings are excluded from the scope of the 1968 Brussels Convention on Jurisdiction and the Enforcement of Judgments in Civil and Commercial Matters,[3] as amended by the Conventions on Accession to this Convention.[4]

(8) In order to achieve the aim of improving the efficiency and effectiveness of insolvency proceedings having cross-border effects, it is necessary, and appropriate, that the provisions on jurisdiction, recognition and applicable law in this area should be contained in a Community law measure which is binding and directly applicable in Member States.

---

[1] Opinion delivered on 2 March 2000 (not yet published in the Official Journal).
[2] Opinion delivered on 26 January 2000 (not yet published in the Official Journal).
[3] [1972] OJ L299, p 32.
[4] [1975] OJ L204, p 28; [1978] OJ L304, p 1; [1982] OJ L388, p 1; [1989] OJ L285, p 1; [1997] OJ C15, p 1.

(9) This Regulation should apply to insolvency proceedings, whether the debtor is a natural person or a legal person, a trader or an individual. The insolvency proceedings to which this Regulation applies are listed in the Annexes. Insolvency proceedings concerning insurance undertakings, credit institutions, investment undertakings holding funds or securities for third parties and collective investment undertakings should be excluded from the scope of this Regulation. Such undertakings should not be covered by this Regulation since they are subject to special arrangements and, to some extent, the national supervisory authorities have extremely wide-ranging powers of intervention.

(10) Insolvency proceedings do not necessarily involve the intervention of a judicial authority; the expression 'court' in this Regulation should be given a broad meaning and include a person or body empowered by national law to open insolvency proceedings. In order for this Regulation to apply, proceedings (comprising acts and formalities set down in law) should not only have to comply with the provisions of this Regulation, but they should also be officially recognized and legally effective in the Member State in which the insolvency proceedings are opened and should be collective insolvency proceedings which entail the partial or total divestment of the debtor and the appointment of a liquidator.

(11) This Regulation acknowledges the fact that as a result of widely differing substantive laws it is not practical to introduce insolvency proceedings with universal scope in the entire Community. The application without exception of the law of the State of opening of proceedings would, against this background, frequently lead to difficulties. This applies, for example, to the widely differing laws on security interests to be found in the Community. Furthermore, the preferential rights enjoyed by some creditors in the insolvency proceedings are, in some cases, completely different. This Regulation should take account of this in two different ways. On the one hand, provision should be made for special rules on applicable law in the case of particularly significant rights and legal relationships (e.g. rights in rem and contracts of employment). On the other hand, national proceedings covering only assets situated in the State of opening should also be allowed alongside main insolvency proceedings with universal scope.

(12) This Regulation enables the main insolvency proceedings to be opened in the Member State where the debtor has the centre of his main interests. These proceedings have universal scope and aim at encompassing all the debtor's assets. To protect the diversity of interests, this Regulation permits secondary proceedings to be opened to run in parallel with the main proceedings. Secondary proceedings may be opened in the Member State where the debtor has an establishment. The effects of secondary proceedings are limited to the assets located in that State. Mandatory rules of coordination with the main proceedings satisfy the need for unity in the Community.

(13) The 'centre of main interests' should correspond to the place where the debtor conducts the administration of his interests on a regular basis and is therefore ascertainable by third parties.

(14) This Regulation applies only to proceedings where the centre of the debtor's main interests is located in the Community.

(15) The rules of jurisdiction set out in this Regulation establish only international jurisdiction, that is to say, they designate the Member State the courts of which may open insolvency proceedings. Territorial jurisdiction within that Member State must be established by the national law of the Member State concerned.

(16) The court having jurisdiction to open the main insolvency proceedings should be enabled to order provisional and protective measures from the time of the request to open proceedings. Preservation measures both prior to and after the commencement of the insolvency proceedings are very important to guarantee the effectiveness of the insolvency proceedings. In that connection this Regulation should afford different possibilities. On the one hand, the court competent for the main insolvency proceedings should be able also to order provisional protective measures covering assets situated in the territory of other Member States. On the other hand, a liquidator temporarily appointed prior to the opening of the main insolvency proceedings should be able, in the Member States in which an establishment belonging to the debtor is to be found, to apply for the preservation measures which are possible under the law of those States.

(17) Prior to the opening of the main insolvency proceedings, the right to request the opening of insolvency proceedings in the Member State where the debtor has an establishment should be limited

to local creditors and creditors of the local establishment or to cases where main proceedings cannot be opened under the law of the Member State where the debtor has the centre of his main interest. The reason for this restriction is that cases where territorial insolvency proceedings are requested before the main insolvency proceedings are intended to be limited to what is absolutely necessary. If the main insolvency proceedings are opened, the territorial proceedings become secondary.

(18) Following the opening of the main insolvency proceedings, the right to request the opening of insolvency proceedings in a Member State where the debtor has an establishment is not restricted by this Regulation. The liquidator in the main proceedings or any other person empowered under the national law of that Member State may request the opening of secondary insolvency proceedings.

(19) Secondary insolvency proceedings may serve different purposes, besides the protection of local interests. Cases may arise where the estate of the debtor is too complex to administer as a unit or where differences in the legal systems concerned are so great that difficulties may arise from the extension of effects deriving from the law of the State of the opening to the other States where the assets are located. For this reason the liquidator in the main proceedings may request the opening of secondary proceedings when the efficient administration of the estate so requires.

(20) Main insolvency proceedings and secondary proceedings can, however, contribute to the effective realisation of the total assets only if all the concurrent proceedings pending are coordinated. The main condition here is that the various liquidators must cooperate closely, in particular by exchanging a sufficient amount of information. In order to ensure the dominant role of the main insolvency proceedings, the liquidator in such proceedings should be given several possibilities for intervening in secondary insolvency proceedings which are pending at the same time. For example, he should be able to propose a restructuring plan or composition or apply for realisation of the assets in the secondary insolvency proceedings to be suspended.

(21) Every creditor, who has his habitual residence, domicile or registered office in the Community, should have the right to lodge his claims in each of the insolvency proceedings pending in the Community relating to the debtor's assets. This should also apply to tax authorities and social insurance institutions. However, in order to ensure equal treatment of creditors, the distribution of proceeds must be coordinated. Every creditor should be able to keep what he has received in the course of insolvency proceedings but should be entitled only to participate in the distribution of total assets in other proceedings if creditors with the same standing have obtained the same proportion of their claims.

(22) This Regulation should provide for immediate recognition of judgments concerning the opening, conduct and closure of insolvency proceedings which come within its scope and of judgments handed down in direct connection with such insolvency proceedings. Automatic recognition should therefore mean that the effects attributed to the proceedings by the law of the State in which the proceedings were opened extend to all other Member States. Recognition of judgments delivered by the courts of the Member States should be based on the principle of mutual trust. To that end, grounds for non-recognition should be reduced to the minimum necessary. This is also the basis on which any dispute should be resolved where the courts of two Member States both claim competence to open the main insolvency proceedings. The decision of the first court to open proceedings should be recognized in the other Member States without those Member States having the power to scrutinize the court's decision.

(23) This Regulation should set out, for the matters covered by it, uniform rules on conflict of laws which replace, within their scope of application, national rules of private international law. Unless otherwise stated, the law of the Member State of the opening of the proceedings should be applicable (lex concursus). This rule on conflict of laws should be valid both for the main proceedings and for local proceedings; the lex concursus determines all the effects of the insolvency proceedings, both procedural and substantive, on the persons and legal relations concerned. It governs all the conditions for the opening, conduct and closure of the insolvency proceedings.

(24) Automatic recognition of insolvency proceedings to which the law of the opening State normally applies may interfere with the rules under which transactions are carried out in other Member States. To protect legitimate expectations and the certainty of transactions in Member States other

than that in which proceedings are opened, provisions should be made for a number of exceptions to the general rule.

(25) There is a particular need for a special reference diverging from the law of the opening State in the case of rights in rem, since these are of considerable importance for the granting of credit. The basis, validity and extent of such a right in rem should therefore normally be determined according to the lex situs and not be affected by the opening of insolvency proceedings. The proprietor of the right in rem should therefore be able to continue to assert his right to segregation or separate settlement of the collateral security. Where assets are subject to rights in rem under the lex situs in one Member State but the main proceedings are being carried out in another Member State, the liquidator in the main proceedings should be able to request the opening of secondary proceedings in the jurisdiction where the rights in rem arise if the debtor has an establishment there. If a secondary proceeding is not opened, the surplus on sale of the asset covered by rights in rem must be paid to the liquidator in the main proceedings.

(26) If a set-off is not permitted under the law of the opening State, a creditor should nevertheless be entitled to the set-off if it is possible under the law applicable to the claim of the insolvent debtor. In this way, set-off will acquire a kind of guarantee function based on legal provisions on which the creditor concerned can rely at the time when the claim arises.

(27) There is also a need for special protection in the case of payment systems and financial markets. This applies for example to the position-closing agreements and netting agreements to be found in such systems as well as to the sale of securities and to the guarantees provided for such transactions as governed in particular by Directive 98/26/EC of the European Parliament and of the Council of 19 May 1998 on settlement finality in payment and securities settlement systems.[5] For such transactions, the only law which is material should thus be that applicable to the system or market concerned. This provision is intended to prevent the possibility of mechanisms for the payment and settlement of transactions provided for in the payment and set-off systems or on the regulated financial markets of the Member States being altered in the case of insolvency of a business partner. Directive 98/26/EC contains special provisions which should take precedence over the general rules in this Regulation.

(28) In order to protect employees and jobs, the effects of insolvency proceedings on the continuation or termination of employment and on the rights and obligations of all parties to such employment must be determined by the law applicable to the agreement in accordance with the general rules on conflict of law. Any other insolvency-law questions, such as whether the employees' claims are protected by preferential rights and what status such preferential rights may have, should be determined by the law of the opening State.

(29) For business considerations, the main content of the decision opening the proceedings should be published in the other Member States at the request of the liquidator. If there is an establishment in the Member State concerned, there may be a requirement that publication is compulsory. In neither case, however, should publication be a prior condition for recognition of the foreign proceedings.

(30) It may be the case that some of the persons concerned are not in fact aware that proceedings have been opened and act in good faith in a way that conflicts with the new situation. In order to protect such persons who make a payment to the debtor because they are unaware that foreign proceedings have been opened when they should in fact have made the payment to the foreign liquidator, it should be provided that such a payment is to have a debt-discharging effect.

(31) This Regulation should include Annexes relating to the organisation of insolvency proceedings. As these Annexes relate exclusively to the legislation of Member States, there are specific and substantiated reasons for the Council to reserve the right to amend these Annexes in order to take account of any amendments to the domestic law of the Member States.

(32) The United Kingdom and Ireland, in accordance with Article 3 of the Protocol on the position of the United Kingdom and Ireland annexed to the Treaty on European Union and the Treaty establishing the European Community, have given notice of their wish to take part in the adoption and application of this Regulation.

---

[5] [1988] OJ L166, p 45.

(33) Denmark, in accordance with Articles 1 and 2 of the Protocol on the position of Denmark annexed to the Treaty on European Union and the Treaty establishing the European Community, is not participating in the adoption of this Regulation, and is therefore not bound by it nor subject to its application.

HAS ADOPTED THIS REGULATION:

CHAPTER I: GENERAL PROVISIONS

Article 1
Scope

1. This Regulation shall apply to collective insolvency proceedings which entail the partial or total divestment of a debtor and the appointment of a liquidator.

2. This Regulation shall not apply to insolvency proceedings concerning insurance undertakings, credit institutions, investment undertakings which provide services involving the holding of funds or securities for third parties, or to collective investment undertakings.

Article 2
Definitions

For the purposes of this Regulation:

(a) 'insolvency proceedings' shall mean the collective proceedings referred to in Article 1(1). These proceedings are listed in Annex A;

(b) 'liquidator' shall mean any person or body whose function is to administer or liquidate assets of which the debtor has been divested or to supervise the administration of his affairs. Those persons and bodies are listed in Annex C;

(c) 'winding-up proceedings' shall mean insolvency proceedings within the meaning of point (a) involving realising the assets of the debtor, including where the proceedings have been closed by a composition or other measure terminating the insolvency, or closed by reason of the insufficiency of the assets. Those proceedings are listed in Annex B;

(d) 'court' shall mean the judicial body or any other competent body of a Member State empowered to open insolvency proceedings or to take decisions in the course of such proceedings;

(e) 'judgment' in relation to the opening of insolvency proceedings or the appointment of a liquidator shall include the decision of any court empowered to open such proceedings or to appoint a liquidator;

(f) 'the time of the opening of proceedings' shall mean the time at which the judgment opening proceedings becomes effective, whether it is a final judgment or not;

(g) 'the Member State in which assets are situated' shall mean, in the case of:

— tangible property, the Member State within the territory of which the property is situated,

— property and rights ownership of or entitlement to which must be entered in a public register, the Member State under the authority of which the register is kept,

— claims, the Member State within the territory of which the third party required to meet them has the centre of his main interests, as determined in Article 3(1);

(h) 'establishment' shall mean any place of operations where the debtor carries out a non-transitory economic activity with human means and goods.

Article 3
International jurisdiction

1. The courts of the Member State within the territory of which the centre of a debtor's main interests is situated shall have jurisdiction to open insolvency proceedings. In the case of a company or legal person, the place of the registered office shall be presumed to be the centre of its main interests in the absence of proof to the contrary.

2. Where the centre of a debtor's main interests is situated within the territory of a Member State, the courts of another Member State shall have jurisdiction to open insolvency proceedings against that debtor only if he possesses an establishment within the territory of that other Member State. The

effects of those proceedings shall be restricted to the assets of the debtor situated in the territory of the latter Member State.

3. Where insolvency proceedings have been opened under paragraph 1, any proceedings opened subsequently under paragraph 2 shall be secondary proceedings. These latter proceedings must be winding-up proceedings.

4. Territorial insolvency proceedings referred to in paragraph 2 may be opened prior to the opening of main insolvency proceedings in accordance with paragraph 1 only:

  (a) where insolvency proceedings under paragraph 1 cannot be opened because of the conditions laid down by the law of the Member State within the territory of which the centre of the debtor's main interests is situated; or
  (b) where the opening of territorial insolvency proceedings is requested by a creditor who has his domicile, habitual residence or registered office in the Member State within the territory of which the establishment is situated, or whose claim arises from the operation of that establishment.

Article 4
Law applicable

1. Save as otherwise provided in this Regulation, the law applicable to insolvency proceedings and their effects shall be that of the Member State within the territory of which such proceedings are opened, hereafter referred to as the 'State of the opening of proceedings'.

2. The law of the State of the opening of proceedings shall determine the conditions for the opening of those proceedings, their conduct and their closure. It shall determine in particular:

  (a) against which debtors insolvency proceedings may be brought on account of their capacity;
  (b) the assets which form part of the estate and the treatment of assets acquired by or devolving on the debtor after the opening of the insolvency proceedings;
  (c) the respective powers of the debtor and the liquidator;
  (d) the conditions under which set-offs may be invoked;
  (e) the effects of insolvency proceedings on current contracts to which the debtor is party;
  (f) the effects of the insolvency proceedings on proceedings brought by individual creditors, with the exception of lawsuits pending;
  (g) the claims which are to be lodged against the debtor's estate and the treatment of claims arising after the opening of insolvency proceedings;
  (h) the rules governing the lodging, verification and admission of claims;
  (i) the rules governing the distribution of proceeds from the realisation of assets, the ranking of claims and the rights of creditors who have obtained partial satisfaction after the opening of insolvency proceedings by virtue of a right in rem or through a set-off;
  (j) the conditions for and the effects of closure of insolvency proceedings, in particular by composition;
  (k) creditors' rights after the closure of insolvency proceedings;
  (l) who is to bear the costs and expenses incurred in the insolvency proceedings;
  (m) the rules relating to the voidness, voidability or unenforceability of legal acts detrimental to all the creditors.

Article 5
Third parties' rights in rem

1. The opening of insolvency proceedings shall not affect the rights in rem of creditors or third parties in respect of tangible or intangible, moveable or immoveable assets—both specific assets and collections of indefinite assets as a whole which change from time to time—belonging to the debtor which are situated within the territory of another Member State at the time of the opening of proceedings.

2. The rights referred to in paragraph 1 shall in particular mean:

  (a) the right to dispose of assets or have them disposed of and to obtain satisfaction from the proceeds of or income from those assets, in particular by virtue of a lien or a mortgage;
  (b) the exclusive right to have a claim met, in particular a right guaranteed by a lien in respect of the claim or by assignment of the claim by way of a guarantee;

(c) the right to demand the assets from, and/or to require restitution by, anyone having possession or use of them contrary to the wishes of the party so entitled;

(d) a right in rem to the beneficial use of assets.

3. The right, recorded in a public register and enforceable against third parties, under which a right in rem within the meaning of paragraph 1 may be obtained, shall be considered a right in rem.

4. Paragraph 1 shall not preclude actions for voidness, voidability or unenforceability as referred to in Article 4(2)(m).

Article 6
Set-off

1. The opening of insolvency proceedings shall not affect the right of creditors to demand the setoff of their claims against the claims of the debtor, where such a set-off is permitted by the law applicable to the insolvent debtor's claim.

2. Paragraph 1 shall not preclude actions for voidness, voidability or unenforceability as referred to in Article 4(2)(m).

Article 7
Reservation of title

1. The opening of insolvency proceedings against the purchaser of an asset shall not affect the seller's rights based on a reservation of title where at the time of the opening of proceedings the asset is situated within the territory of a Member State other than the State of opening of proceedings.

2. The opening of insolvency proceedings against the seller of an asset, after delivery of the asset, shall not constitute grounds for rescinding or terminating the sale and shall not prevent the purchaser from acquiring title where at the time of the opening of proceedings the asset sold is situated within the territory of a Member State other than the State of the opening of proceedings.

3. Paragraphs 1 and 2 shall not preclude actions for voidness, voidability or unenforceability as referred to in Article 4(2)(m).

Article 8
Contracts relating to immoveable property

The effects of insolvency proceedings on a contract conferring the right to acquire or make use of immoveable property shall be governed solely by the law of the Member State within the territory of which the immoveable property is situated.

Article 9
Payment systems and financial markets

1. Without prejudice to Article 5, the effects of insolvency proceedings on the rights and obligations of the parties to a payment or settlement system or to a financial market shall be governed solely by the law of the Member State applicable to that system or market.

2. Paragraph 1 shall not preclude any action for voidness, voidability or unenforceability which may be taken to set aside payments or transactions under the law applicable to the relevant payment system or financial market.

Article 10
Contracts of employment

The effects of insolvency proceedings on employment contracts and relationships shall be governed solely by the law of the Member State applicable to the contract of employment.

Article 11
Effects on rights subject to registration

The effects of insolvency proceedings on the rights of the debtor in immoveable property, a ship or an aircraft subject to registration in a public register shall be determined by the law of the Member State under the authority of which the register is kept.

Article 12
Community patents and trade marks

For the purposes of this Regulation, a Community patent, a Community trade mark or any other similar right established by Community law may be included only in the proceedings referred to in Article 3(1).

Article 13
Detrimental acts

Article 4(2)(m) shall not apply where the person who benefited from an act detrimental to all the creditors provides proof that:

— he said act is subject to the law of a Member State other than that of the State of the opening of proceedings, and
— that law does not allow any means of challenging that act in the relevant case.

Article 14
Protection of third-party purchasers

Where, by an act concluded after the opening of insolvency proceedings, the debtor disposes, for consideration, of:

— an immoveable asset, or
— a ship or an aircraft subject to registration in a public register, or
— securities whose existence presupposes registration in a register laid down by law, the validity of that act shall be governed by the law of the State within the territory of which the immoveable asset is situated or under the authority of which the register is kept.

Article 15
Effects of insolvency proceedings on lawsuits pending

The effects of insolvency proceedings on a lawsuit pending concerning an asset or a right of which the debtor has been divested shall be governed solely by the law of the Member State in which that lawsuit is pending.

CHAPTER II: RECOGNITION OF INSOLVENCY PROCEEDINGS

Article 16
Principle

1. Any judgment opening insolvency proceedings handed down by a court of a Member State which has jurisdiction pursuant to Article 3 shall be recognized in all the other Member States from the time that it becomes effective in the State of the opening of proceedings.

This rule shall also apply where, on account of his capacity, insolvency proceedings cannot be brought against the debtor in other Member States.

2. Recognition of the proceedings referred to in Article 3(1) shall not preclude the opening of the proceedings referred to in Article 3(2) by a court in another Member State. The latter proceedings shall be secondary insolvency proceedings within the meaning of Chapter III.

Article 17
Effects of recognition

1. The judgment opening the proceedings referred to in Article 3(1) shall, with no further formalities, produce the same effects in any other Member State as under this law of the State of the opening of proceedings, unless this Regulation provides otherwise and as long as no proceedings referred to in Article 3(2) are opened in that other Member State.

2. The effects of the proceedings referred to in Article 3(2) may not be challenged in other Member States. Any restriction of the creditors' rights, in particular a stay or discharge, shall produce effects vis-à-vis assets situated within the territory of another Member State only in the case of those creditors who have given their consent.

Article 18
Powers of the liquidator

1. The liquidator appointed by a court which has jurisdiction pursuant to Article 3(1) may exercise all the powers conferred on him by the law of the State of the opening of proceedings in another Member State, as long as no other insolvency proceedings have been opened there nor any preservation measure to the contrary has been taken there further to a request for the opening of insolvency proceedings in that State. He may in particular remove the debtor's assets from the territory of the Member State in which they are situated, subject to Articles 5 and 7.

2. The liquidator appointed by a court which has jurisdiction pursuant to Article 3(2) may in any other Member State claim through the courts or out of court that moveable property was removed from the territory of the State of the opening of proceedings to the territory of that other Member State after the opening of the insolvency proceedings. He may also bring any action to set aside which is in the interests of the creditors.

3. In exercising his powers, the liquidator shall comply with the law of the Member State within the territory of which he intends to take action, in particular with regard to procedures for the realisation of assets. Those powers may not include coercive measures or the right to rule on legal proceedings or disputes.

Article 19
Proof of the liquidator's appointment

The liquidator's appointment shall be evidenced by a certified copy of the original decision appointing him or by any other certificate issued by the court which has jurisdiction.

A translation into the official language or one of the official languages of the Member State within the territory of which he intends to act may be required. No legalisation or other similar formality shall be required.

Article 20
Return and imputation

1. A creditor who, after the opening of the proceedings referred to in Article 3(1) obtains by any means, in particular through enforcement, total or partial satisfaction of his claim on the assets belonging to the debtor situated within the territory of another Member State, shall return what he has obtained to the liquidator, subject to Articles 5 and 7.

2. In order to ensure equal treatment of creditors a creditor who has, in the course of insolvency proceedings, obtained a dividend on his claim shall share in distributions made in other proceedings only where creditors of the same ranking or category have, in those other proceedings, obtained an equivalent dividend.

Article 21
Publication

1. The liquidator may request that notice of the judgment opening insolvency proceedings and, where appropriate, the decision appointing him, be published in any other Member State in accordance with the publication procedures provided for in that State. Such publication shall also specify the liquidator appointed and whether the jurisdiction rule applied is that pursuant to Article 3(1) or Article 3(2).

2. However, any Member State within the territory of which the debtor has an establishment may require mandatory publication. In such cases, the liquidator or any authority empowered to that effect in the Member State where the proceedings referred to in Article 3(1) are opened shall take all necessary measures to ensure such publication.

Article 22
Registration in a public register

1. The liquidator may request that the judgment opening the proceedings referred to in Article 3(1) be registered in the land register, the trade register and any other public register kept in the other Member States.

2. However, any Member State may require mandatory registration. In such cases, the liquidator or any authority empowered to that effect in the Member State where the proceedings referred to in Article 3(1) have been opened shall take all necessary measures to ensure such registration.

Article 23
Costs

The costs of the publication and registration provided for in Articles 21 and 22 shall be regarded as costs and expenses incurred in the proceedings.

Article 24
Honouring of an obligation to a debtor

1. Where an obligation has been honoured in a Member State for the benefit of a debtor who is subject to insolvency proceedings opened in another Member State, when it should have been honoured for the benefit of the liquidator in those proceedings, the person honouring the obligation shall be deemed to have discharged it if he was unaware of the opening of proceedings.

2. Where such an obligation is honoured before the publication provided for in Article 21 has been effected, the person honouring the obligation shall be presumed, in the absence of proof to the contrary, to have been unaware of the opening of insolvency proceedings; where the obligation is honoured after such publication has been effected, the person honouring the obligation shall be presumed, in the absence of proof to the contrary, to have been aware of the opening of proceedings.

Article 25
Recognition and enforceability of other judgments

1. Judgments handed down by a court whose judgment concerning the opening of proceedings is recognized in accordance with Article 16 and which concern the course and closure of insolvency proceedings, and compositions approved by that court shall also be recognized with no further formalities. Such judgments shall be enforced in accordance with Articles 31 to 51, with the exception of Article 34(2), of the Brussels Convention on Jurisdiction and the Enforcement of Judgments in Civil and Commercial Matters, as amended by the Conventions of Accession to this Convention.

The first subparagraph shall also apply to judgments deriving directly from the insolvency proceedings and which are closely linked with them, even if they were handed down by another court.

The first subparagraph shall also apply to judgments relating to preservation measures taken after the request for the opening of insolvency proceedings.

2. The recognition and enforcement of judgments other than those referred to in paragraph 1 shall be governed by the Convention referred to in paragraph 1, provided that that Convention is applicable.

3. The Member States shall not be obliged to recognize or enforce a judgment referred to in paragraph 1 which might result in a limitation of personal freedom or postal secrecy.

Article 26 [6]
Public policy

Any Member State may refuse to recognize insolvency proceedings opened in another Member State or to enforce a judgment handed down in the context of such proceedings where the effects of such recognition or enforcement would be manifestly contrary to that State's public policy, in particular its fundamental principles or the constitutional rights and liberties of the individual.

---

[6] Note the Declaration by Portugal concerning the application of Arts 26 and 37 [2000] OJ C183, p 1. [2007] OJ C183, p1.

Article 27

Opening of proceedings

The opening of the proceedings referred to in Article 3(1) by a court of a Member State and which is recognized in another Member State (main proceedings) shall permit the opening in that other Member State, a court of which has jurisdiction pursuant to Article 3(2), of secondary insolvency proceedings without the debtor's insolvency being examined in that other State. These latter proceedings must be among the proceedings listed in Annex B. Their effects shall be restricted to the assets of the debtor situated within the territory of that other Member State.

Article 28

Applicable law

Save as otherwise provided in this Regulation, the law applicable to secondary proceedings shall be that of the Member State within the territory of which the secondary proceedings are opened.

Article 29

Right to request the opening of proceedings

The opening of secondary proceedings may be requested by:
- (a) the liquidator in the main proceedings;
- (b) any other person or authority empowered to request the opening of insolvency proceedings under the law of the Member State within the territory of which the opening of secondary proceedings is requested.

Article 30

Advance payment of costs and expenses

Where the law of the Member State in which the opening of secondary proceedings is requested requires that the debtor's assets be sufficient to cover in whole or in part the costs and expenses of the proceedings, the court may, when it receives such a request, require the applicant to make an advance payment of costs or to provide appropriate security.

Article 31

Duty to cooperate and communicate information

1. Subject to the rules restricting the communication of information, the liquidator in the main proceedings and the liquidators in the secondary proceedings shall be duty bound to communicate information to each other. They shall immediately communicate any information which may be relevant to the other proceedings, in particular the progress made in lodging and verifying claims and all measures aimed at terminating the proceedings.

2. Subject to the rules applicable to each of the proceedings, the liquidator in the main proceedings and the liquidators in the secondary proceedings shall be duty bound to cooperate with each other.

3. The liquidator in the secondary proceedings shall give the liquidator in the main proceedings an early opportunity of submitting proposals on the liquidation or use of the assets in the secondary proceedings.

Article 32

Exercise of creditors' rights

1. Any creditor may lodge his claim in the main proceedings and in any secondary proceedings.

2. The liquidators in the main and any secondary proceedings shall lodge in other proceedings claims which have already been lodged in the proceedings for which they were appointed, provided that the interests of creditors in the latter proceedings are served thereby, subject to the right of creditors to oppose that or to withdraw the lodgement of their claims where the law applicable so provides.

3. The liquidator in the main or secondary proceedings shall be empowered to participate in other proceedings on the same basis as a creditor, in particular by attending creditors' meetings.

Article 33

Stay of liquidation

1. The court, which opened the secondary proceedings, shall stay the process of liquidation in whole or in part on receipt of a request from the liquidator in the main proceedings, provided that in that event it may require the liquidator in the main proceedings to take any suitable measure to guarantee the interests of the creditors in the secondary proceedings and of individual classes of creditors. Such a request from the liquidator may be rejected only if it is manifestly of no interest to the creditors in the main proceedings. Such a stay of the process of liquidation may be ordered for up to three months. It may be continued or renewed for similar periods.

2. The court referred to in paragraph 1 shall terminate the stay of the process of liquidation:
    — at the request of the liquidator in the main proceedings,
    — of its own motion, at the request of a creditor or at the request of the liquidator in the secondary proceedings if that measure no longer appears justified, in particular, by the interests of creditors in the main proceedings or in the secondary proceedings.

Article 34

Measures ending secondary insolvency proceedings

1. Where the law applicable to secondary proceedings allows for such proceedings to be closed without liquidation by a rescue plan, a composition or a comparable measure, the liquidator in the main proceedings shall be empowered to propose such a measure himself.

Closure of the secondary proceedings by a measure referred to in the first subparagraph shall not become final without the consent of the liquidator in the main proceedings; failing his agreement, however, it may become final if the financial interests of the creditors in the main proceedings are not affected by the measure proposed.

2. Any restriction of creditors' rights arising from a measure referred to in paragraph 1 which is proposed in secondary proceedings, such as a stay of payment or discharge of debt, may not have effect in respect of the debtor's assets not covered by those proceedings without the consent of all the creditors having an interest.

3. During a stay of the process of liquidation ordered pursuant to Article 33, only the liquidator in the main proceedings or the debtor, with the former's consent, may propose measures laid down in paragraph 1 of this Article in the secondary proceedings; no other proposal for such a measure shall be put to the vote or approved.

Article 35

Assets remaining in the secondary proceedings

If by the liquidation of assets in the secondary proceedings it is possible to meet all claims allowed under those proceedings, the liquidator appointed in those proceedings shall immediately transfer any assets remaining to the liquidator in the main proceedings.

Article 36

Subsequent opening of the main proceedings

Where the proceedings referred to in Article 3(1) are opened following the opening of the proceedings referred to in Article 3(2) in another Member State, Articles 31 to 35 shall apply to those opened first, in so far as the progress of those proceedings so permits.

Article 37 [7]

Conversion of earlier proceedings

The liquidator in the main proceedings may request that proceedings listed in Annex A previously opened in another Member State be converted into winding-up proceedings if this proves to be in the interests of the creditors in the main proceedings.

The court with jurisdiction under Article 3(2) shall order conversion into one of the proceedings listed in Annex B.

---

[7] Note the Declaration by Portugal concerning the application of Arts 26 and 37 ([2000]OJ C183, p 1).

Article 38
Preservation measures

Where the court of a Member State which has jurisdiction pursuant to Article 3(1) appoints a temporary administrator in order to ensure the preservation of the debtor's assets, that temporary administrator shall be empowered to request any measures to secure and preserve any of the debtor's assets situated in another Member State, provided for under the law of that State, for the period between the request for the opening of insolvency proceedings and the judgment opening the proceedings.

CHAPTER IV: PROVISION OF INFORMATION FOR CREDITORS AND LODGEMENT OF THEIR CLAIMS

Article 39
Right to lodge claims

Any creditor who has his habitual residence, domicile or registered office in a Member State other than the State of the opening of proceedings, including the tax authorities and social security authorities of Member States, shall have the right to lodge claims in the insolvency proceedings in writing.

Article 40
Duty to inform creditors

1. As soon as insolvency proceedings are opened in a Member State, the court of that State having jurisdiction or the liquidator appointed by it shall immediately inform known creditors who have their habitual residences, domiciles or registered offices in the other Member States.

2. That information, provided by an individual notice, shall in particular include time limits, the penalties laid down in regard to those time limits, the body or authority empowered to accept the lodgement of claims and the other measures laid down. Such notice shall also indicate whether creditors whose claims are preferential or secured in rem need lodge their claims.

Article 41
Content of the lodgement of a claim

A creditor shall send copies of supporting documents, if any, and shall indicate the nature of the claim, the date on which it arose and its amount, as well as whether he alleges preference, security in rem or a reservation of title in respect of the claim and what assets are covered by the guarantee he is invoking.

Article 42
Languages

1. The information provided for in Article 40 shall be provided in the official language or one of the official languages of the State of the opening of proceedings.

For that purpose a form shall be used bearing the heading 'Invitation to lodge a claim. Time limits to be observed' in all the official languages of the institutions of the European Union.

2. Any creditor who has his habitual residence, domicile or registered office in a Member State other than the State of the opening of proceedings may lodge his claim in the official language or one of the official languages of that other State. In that event, however, the lodgement of his claim shall bear the heading 'Lodgement of claim' in the official language or one of the official languages of the State of the opening of proceedings. In addition, he may be required to provide a translation into the official language or one of the official languages of the State of the opening of proceedings.

CHAPTER V: TRANSITIONAL AND FINAL PROVISIONS

Article 43
Applicability in time

The provisions of this Regulation shall apply only to insolvency proceedings opened after its entry into force. Acts done by a debtor before the entry into force of this Regulation shall continue to be governed by the law which was applicable to them at the time they were done.

Article 44

Relationship to Conventions

1. After its entry into force, this Regulation replaces, in respect of the matters referred to therein, in the relations between Member States, the Conventions concluded between two or more Member States, in particular:

(a) the Convention between Belgium and France on Jurisdiction and the Validity and Enforcement of Judgments, Arbitration Awards and Authentic Instruments, signed at Paris on 8 July 1899;

(b) the Convention between Belgium and Austria on Bankruptcy, Winding-up, Arrangements, Compositions and Suspension of Payments (with Additional Protocol of 13 June 1973), signed at Brussels on 16 July 1969;

(c) the Convention between Belgium and the Netherlands on Territorial Jurisdiction, Bankruptcy and the Validity and Enforcement of Judgments, Arbitration Awards and Authentic Instruments, signed at Brussels on 28 March 1925;

(d) the Treaty between Germany and Austria on Bankruptcy, Winding-up, Arrangements and Compositions, signed at Vienna on 25 May 1979;

(e) the Convention between France and Austria on Jurisdiction, Recognition and Enforcement of Judgments on Bankruptcy, signed at Vienna on 27 February 1979;

(f) the Convention between France and Italy on the Enforcement of Judgments in Civil and Commercial Matters, signed at Rome on 3 June 1930;

(g) the Convention between Italy and Austria on Bankruptcy, Winding-up, Arrangements and Compositions, signed at Rome on 12 July 1977;

(h) the Convention between the Kingdom of the Netherlands and the Federal Republic of Germany on the Mutual Recognition and Enforcement of Judgments and other Enforceable Instruments in Civil and Commercial Matters, signed at The Hague on 30 August 1962;

(i) the Convention between the United Kingdom and the Kingdom of Belgium providing for the Reciprocal Enforcement of Judgments in Civil and Commercial Matters, with Protocol, signed at Brussels on 2 May 1934;

(j) the Convention between Denmark, Finland, Norway, Sweden and Iceland on Bankruptcy, signed at Copenhagen on 7 November 1933;

(k) the European Convention on Certain International Aspects of Bankruptcy, signed at Istanbul on 5 June 1990;

(l) The Convention between the Federative People's Republic of Yugoslavia and the Kingdom of Greece on the Mutual recognition and Enforcement of Judgments, signed at Athens on 18 June 1959;

(m) the Agreement between the Federative People's Republic of Yugoslavia and the Republic of Austria on the Mutual Recognition and Enforcement of Arbitral Awards and Arbitral Settlements in Commercial Matters, signed at Belgrade on 18 March 1960;

(n) the Convention between the Federative People's Republic of Yugoslavia and the Republic of Italy on Mutual Judicial Cooperation in Civil and Administrative Matters, signed at Rome on 3 December 1960;

(o) the Agreement between the Socialist Federative Republic of Yugoslavia and the Kingdom of Belgium on Judicial Cooperation in Civil and Commercial Matters, signed at Belgrade on 24 September 1971;

(p) the Convention between the Governments of Yugoslavia and France on the Recognition and Enforcement of Judgments in Civil and Commercial Matters, signed at Paris on 18 May 1971;

(q) the Agreement between the Czechoslovak Socialist Republic and the Hellenic Republic on Legal Aid in Civil and Criminal Matters, signed at Athens on 22 October 1980, still in force between the Czech Republic and Greece.

(r) the Agreement between the Czechoslovak Socialist Republic and the Republic of Cyprus on Legal Aid in Civil and Criminal Matters, signed at Nicosia on 23 April 1982, still in force between the Czech Republic and Cyprus;

(s) the Treaty between the Government of the Czechoslovak Socialist Republic and the Government of the Republic of France on Legal Aid and the Recognition and Enforcement of Judgments in Civil, Family and Commercial Matters, signed at Paris on 10 May 1984, still in force between the Czech Republic and France;

(t) the Treaty between the Czechoslovak Socialist Republic and the Italian Republic on Legal Aid in Civil and Criminal Matters, signed at Prague on 6 December 1985, still in force between the Czech Republic and Italy;

(u) the Agreement between the Republic of Latvia, the Republic of Estonia and the Republic of Lithuania on Legal Assistance and Legal Relationships, signed at Tallinn on 11 November 1992;

(v) the Agreement between Estonia and Poland on Granting Legal Aid and Legal Relations on Civil, Labour and Criminal Matters, signed at Tallinn on 27 November 1998;

(w) the Agreement between the Republic of Lithuania and the Republic of Poland on Legal Assistance and Legal Relations in Civil, Family, Labour and Criminal Matters, signed in Warsaw on 26 January 1993;

(x) the Convention between Socialist Republic of Romania and the Hellenic Republic on legal assistance in civil and criminal matters and its Protocol, signed at Bucharest on 19 October 1972;

(y) the Convention between Socialist Republic of Romania and the French Republic on legal assistance in civil and commercial matters, signed at Paris on 5 November 1974;

(z) the Agreement between the People's Republic of Bulgaria and the Hellenic Republic on Legal Assistance in Civil and Criminal Matters, signed at Athens on 10 April 1976;

(aa) the Agreement between the People's Republic of Bulgaria and the Republic of Cyprus on Legal Assistance in Civil and Criminal Matters, signed at Nicosia on 29 April 1983;

(ab) the Agreement between the Government of the People's Republic of Bulgaria and the Government of the French Republic on Mutual Legal Assistance in Civil Matters, signed at Sofia on 18 January 1989;

(ac) the Treaty between Romania and the Czech Republic on judicial assistance in civil matters, signed at Bucharest on 11 July 1994;

(ad) the Treaty between Romania and Poland on legal assistance and legal relations in civil cases, signed at Bucharest on 15 May 1999.

2. The Conventions referred to in paragraph 1 shall continue to have effect with regard to proceedings opened before the entry into force of this Regulation.

3. This Regulation shall not apply:
(a) in any Member State, to the extent that it is irreconcilable with the obligations arising in relation to bankruptcy from a convention concluded by that State with one or more third countries before the entry into force of this Regulation;
(b) in the United Kingdom of Great Britain and Northern Ireland, to the extent that is irreconcilable with the obligations arising in relation to bankruptcy and the winding-up of insolvent companies from any arrangements with the Commonwealth existing at the time this Regulation enters into force.

Article 45
Amendment of the Annexes

The Council, acting by qualified majority on the initiative of one of its members or on a proposal from the Commission, may amend the Annexes.

Article 46
Reports

No later than 1 June 2012, and every five years thereafter, the Commission shall present to the European Parliament, the Council and the Economic and Social Committee a report on the application of this Regulation. The report shall be accompanied if need be by a proposal for adaptation of this Regulation.

Article 47
Entry into force

This Regulation shall enter into force on 31 May 2002.

This Regulation shall be binding in its entirety and directly applicable in the Member States in accordance with the Treaty establishing the European Community.

The Annexes are reproduced below as amended by Council Implementing Regulation (EU) No 663/ 2014 of 5 June 2014.

The Annexes are reproduced below as amended by Council Implementing Regulation (EU) No 663/2014 of 5 June 2014.

ANNEX A

Insolvency proceedings referred to in Article 2(a)

Belgique/België
— Het faillissement/La faillite,
— De gerechtelijke reorganisatie door een collectief akkoord/La réorganisation judiciaire par accord collectif,
— De gerechtelijke reorganisatie door overdracht onder gerechtelijk gezag/La réorganisation judiciaire par transfert sous autorité de justice,
— De collectieve schuldenregeling/Le règlement collectif de dettes,
— De vrijwillige vereffening/La liquidation volontaire,
— De gerechtelijke vereffening/La liquidation judiciaire,
— De voorlopige ontneming van beheer, bepaald in artikel 8 van de faillissementswet/Le dessaisissement provisoire, visé à l'article 8 de la loi sur les faillites,

БЪЛГАРИЯ

— Производство по несъстоятелност,

Česká Republika
— Konkurs,
— Reorganizace,
— Oddlužení,

Deutschland
— Das Konkursverfahren,
— Das gerichtliche Vergleichsverfahren,
— Das Gesamtvollstreckungsverfahren,
— Das Insolvenzverfahren,

Eesti
— Pankrotimenetlus,

Éire/Ireland
— Compulsory winding-up by the court,
— Bankruptcy,
— The administration in bankruptcy of the estate of persons dying insolvent,
— Winding-up in bankruptcy of partnerships,
— Creditors' voluntary winding-up (with confirmation of a court),
— Arrangements under the control of the court which involve the vesting of all or part of the property of the debtor in the Official Assignee for realisation and distribution,
— Company examinership,
— Debt Relief Notice,
— Debt Settlement Arrangement,
— Personal Insolvency Arrangement,

ΕΛΛΑΔΑ

— Η πτώχευση,
— Η ειδική εκκαθάριση εν λειτουργία,
— Σχέδιο αναδιοργάνωσης,
— Απλοποιημένη διαδικασία επί πτωχεύσεων μικρού αντικειμένου,

España

— Concurso,

France

— Sauvegarde,
— Redressement judiciaire,
— Liquidation judiciaire,

Hrvatska

— Stečajni postupak,

Italia

— Fallimento,
— Concordato preventivo,
— Liquidazione coatta amministrativa,
— Amministrazione straordinaria,

ΚΥΠΡΟΣ

— Υποχρεωτική εκκαθάριση από το Δικαστήριο,
— Εκούσια εκκαθάριση από μέλη,
— Εκούσια εκκαθάριση από πιστωτές,
— Εκκαθάριση με την εποπτεία του Δικαστηρίου,
— Διάταγμα Παραλαβής και πτώχευσης κατόπιν Δικαστικού Διατάγματος,
— Διαχείριση της περιουσίας προσώπων που απεβίωσαν αφερέγγυα,

Latvija

— Tiesiskās aizsardzības process,
— Juridiskās personas maksātnespējas process,
— Fiziskās personas maksātnespējas process,

Lietuva

— Įmonės restruktūrizavimo byla,
— Įmonės bankroto byla,
— Įmonės bankroto procesas ne teismo tvarka,
— Fizinio asmens bankroto byla,

Luxembourg

— Faillite,
— Gestion contrôlée,
— Concordat préventif de faillite (par abandon d'actif),
— Régime spécial de liquidation du notariat,
— Procédure de règlement collectif des dettes dans le cadre du surendettement,

Magyarország

— Csődeljárás,
— Felszámolási eljárás,

Malta

— Xoljiment,
— Amministrazzjoni,
— Stralċ volontarju mill-membri jew mill-kredituri,
— Stralċ mill-Qorti,
— Falliment f'każ ta' negozjant,

Nederland

— Het faillissement,
— De surséance van betaling,
— De schuldsaneringsregeling natuurlijke personen,

Österreich

— Das Konkursverfahren (Insolvenzverfahren),
— Das Sanierungsverfahren ohne Eigenverwaltung (Insolvenzverfahren),
— Das Sanierungsverfahren mit Eigenverwaltung (Insolvenzverfahren),
— Das Schuldenregulierungsverfahren,
— Das Abschöpfungsverfahren,
— Das Ausgleichsverfahren,

Polska

— Postępowanie naprawcze,
— Upadłość obejmująca likwidację,
— Upadłość z możliwością zawarcia układu,

Portugal

— Processo de insolvência,
— Processo especial de revitalização,

România

— Procedura insolvenţei,
— Reorganizarea judiciară,
— Procedura falimentului,

Slovenija

— Stečajni postopek,
— Skrajšani stečajni postopek,
— Postopek prisilne poravnave,
— Prisilna poravnava v stečaju,

Slovensko

— Konkurzné konanie,
— Reštrukturalizačné konanie,

Suomi/Finland

— Konkurssi/konkurs,
— Yrityssaneeraus/företagssanering,

Sverige

— Konkurs,
— Företagsrekonstruktion,

United Kingdom

— Winding-up by or subject to the supervision of the court,
— Creditors'voluntary winding-up (with confirmation by the court),
— Administration, including appointments made by filing prescribed documents with the court,
— Voluntary arrangements under insolvency legislation,
— Bankruptcy or sequestration.

Annex B

Winding-up proceedings referred to in Article 2(c)

Belgique/België

— Het faillissement/La faillite,
— De vrijwillige vereffening/La liquidation volontaire,

— De gerechtelijke vereffening/La liquidation judiciaire,
— De gerechtelijke reorganisatie door overdracht onder gerechtelijk gezag/La réorganisation judiciaire par transfert sous autorité de justice,

БЪЛГАРИЯ

— Производство по несъстоятелност,

Česká Republika

— Konkurs,

Deutschland

— Das Konkursverfahren,
— Das Gesamtvollstreckungsverfahren,
— Das Insolvenzverfahren,

Eesti

— Pankrotimenetlus,

Éire/Ireland

— Compulsory winding-up,
— Bankruptcy,
— The administration in bankruptcy of the estate of persons dying insolvent,
— Winding-up in bankruptcy of partnerships,
— Creditors' voluntary winding-up (with confirmation of a court),
— Arrangements under the control of the court which involve the vesting of all or part of the property of the debtor in the Official Assignee for realisation and distribution,

ΕΛΛΑΔΑ

— Η πτώχευση,
— Η ειδική εκκαθάριση,
— Απλοποιημένη διαδικασία επί πτωχεύσεων μικρού αντικειμένου,

España

— Concurso,

France

— Liquidation judiciaire,

Hrvatska

— Stečajni postupak,

Italia

— Fallimento,
— Concordato preventivo,
— Liquidazione coatta amministrativa,
— Amministrazione straordinaria,

ΚΥΠΡΟΣ

— Υποχρεωτική εκκαθάριση από το Δικαστήριο,
— Εκκαθάριση με την εποπτεία του Δικαστηρίου,
— Εκούσια εκκαθάριση από πιστωτές, με επιβεβαίωση του Δικαστηρίου,
— Πτώχευση,
— Διαχείριση της περιουσίας προσώπων που απεβίωσαν αφερέγγυα,

Latvija

— Juridiskās personas maksātnespējas process,
— Fiziskās personas maksātnespējas process,

Lietuva
— Įmonės bankroto byla,
— Įmonės bankroto procesas ne teismo tvarka,

Luxembourg
— Faillite,
— Régime spécial de liquidation du notariat,
— Liquidation judiciaire dans le cadre du surendettement,

Magyarország
— Felszámolási eljárás,

Malta
— Stralċ volontarju,
— Stralċ mill-Qorti,
— Falliment inkluż il-ħruġ ta' mandat ta' qbid mill-Kuratur f'każ ta' negozjant fallut,

Nederland
— Het faillissement,
— De schuldsaneringsregeling natuurlijke personen,

Österreich
— Das Konkursverfahren (Insolvenzverfahren),

Polska
— Upadłość obejmująca likwidację,

Portugal
— Processo de insolvência,

România
— Procedura falimentului,

Slovenija
— Stečajni postopek,
— Skrajšani stečajni postopek,

Slovensko
— Konkurzné konanie,

Suomi/Finland
— Konkurssi/konkurs,

Sverige
— Konkurs,

United Kingdom
— Winding-up by or subject to the supervision of the court,
— Winding-up through administration, including appointments made by filing prescribed documents with the court,
— Creditors' voluntary winding-up (with confirmation by the court),
— Bankruptcy or sequestration.

ANNEX C LIQUIDATORS REFERRED TO IN ARTICLE 2(B)

Belgique/België
— De curator/Le curateur,
— De gedelegeerd rechter/Le juge-délégué,
— De gerechtsmandataris/Le mandataire de justice,
— De schuldbemiddelaar/Le médiateur de dettes,
— De vereffenaar/Le liquidateur,
— De voorlopige bewindvoerder/L'administrateur provisoire,

БЪЛГАРИЯ

— Назначен предварително временен синдик,
— Временен синдик,
— Постоянен) синдик,
— Служебен синдик,

Česká Republika

— Insolvenční správce,
— Předběžný insolvenční správce,
— Oddělený insolvenční správce,
— Zvláštní insolvenční správce,
— Zástupce insolvenčního správce,

Deutschland

— Konkursverwalter,
— Vergleichsverwalter,
— Sachwalter (nach der Vergleichsordnung),
— Verwalter,
— Insolvenzverwalter,
— Sachwalter (nach der Insolvenzordnung),
— Treuhänder,
— Vorläufiger Insolvenzverwalter,

Eesti

— Pankrotihaldur,
— Ajutine pankrotihaldur,
— Usaldusisik,

Éire/Ireland

— Liquidator,
— Official Assignee,
— Trustee in bankruptcy,
— Provisional Liquidator,
— Examiner,
— Personal Insolvency Practitioner,
— Insolvency Service,

ΕΛΛΑΔΑ

— Ο σύνδικος,
— Ο εισηγητής,
— Η επιτροπή των πιστωτών,
— Ο ειδικός εκκαθαριστής,

España

— Administradores concursales,

France

— Mandataire judiciaire,
— Liquidateur,
— Administrateur judiciaire,
— Commissaire à l'exécution du plan,

Hrvatska

— Stečajni upravitelj,
— Privremeni stečajni upravitelj,
— Stečajni povjerenik,
— Povjerenik,

Italia

— Curatore,
— Commissario giudiziale,
— Commissario straordinario,
— Commissario liquidatore,
— Liquidatore giudiziale,

ΚΥΠΡΟΣ

— Εκκαθαριστής και Προσωρινός Εκκαθαριστής,
— Επίσημος Παραλήπτης,
— Διαχειριστής της Πτώχευσης,

Latvija

— Maksātnespējas procesa administrators,

Lietuva

— Bankroto administratorius,
— Restruktūrizavimo administratorius,

Luxembourg

— Le curateur,
— Le commissaire,
— Le liquidateur,
— Le conseil de gérance de la section d'assainissement du notariat,
— Le liquidateur dans le cadre du surendettement,

Magyarország

— Vagyonfelügyelő,
— Felszámoló,

Malta

— Amministratur Proviżorju,
— Riċevitur Uffiċjali,
— Stralċjarju,
— Manager Speċjali,
— Kuraturi f'każ ta' proċeduri ta' falliment,

Nederland

— De curator in het faillissement,
— De bewindvoerder in de surséance van betaling,
— De bewindvoerder in de schuldsaneringsregeling natuurlijke personen,

Österreich

— Masseverwalter,
— Sanierungsverwalter,
— Ausgleichsverwalter,
— Besonderer Verwalter,
— Einstweiliger Verwalter,
— Sachwalter,
— Treuhänder,
— Insolvenzgericht,
— Konkursgericht,

Polska

— Syndyk,
— Nadzorca sądowy,
— Zarządca,

Portugal

— Administrador de insolvência,
— Administrador judicial provisório,

România

— Practician în insolvenţă,
— Administrator judiciar,
— Lichidator,

Slovenija

— Upravitelj prisilne poravnave,
— Stečajni upravitelj,
— Sodišče, pristojno za postopek prisilne poravnave,
— Sodišče, pristojno za stečajni postopek,

Slovensko

— Predbežný správca,
— Správca,

Suomi/Finland

— Pesänhoitaja/boförvaltare,
— Selvittäjä/utredare,

Sverige

— Förvaltare,
— Rekonstruktör,

United Kingdom

— Liquidator,
— Supervisor of a voluntary arrangement,
— Administrator,
— Official Receiver,
— Trustee,
— Provisional Liquidator,
— Judicial factor.

APPENDIX 2

Virgos-Schmit Report on the Convention on Insolvency Proceedings

Explanatory note

This Report was produced during the concluding phase of the negotiations for a Convention on Insolvency Proceedings under the auspices of the Council of the European Union. The text was circulated in draft form among the Member States between November 1995 and May 1996, and was revised in the light of resulting comments. A finalized text was produced by the Legal Linguistic Experts' working party and was allocated the EU Council reference 6500/1/96, REV1, DRS 8 (CFC). It was never formally adopted or officially published by the EU Council, however, as the projected Convention lapsed after 23 May 1996, having failed to receive the required signature by all 15 Member States within the time allowed. Because of the close identity of substance between the provisions of the EC Regulation 1346/2000 and those of the Convention, the Virgos-Schmit Report remains an important aid to interpretation of the Regulation. It is reproduced here in the final revision, dated 8 July 1996, which has kindly been made available by its joint author, Professor Miguel Virgos.

EUROPEAN UNION   Brussels, 8 July 1996
THE COUNCIL

6500/1/96

REV 1

LIMITE

DRS 8 (CFC)

_____

NOTE

Subject: Report on the Convention of [sic] Insolvency Proceedings

Delegations will find attached the above text, as finalized by the Legal Linguistic experts' working party.

_____

Report on the Convention on
Insolvency Proceedings[1]

By

MIGUEL VIRGOS

Professor, Universidad Autonoma of Madrid

(who contributed the background and general introduction and the comments on Articles 1 to 26, 43 to 46, territorial application and Article 48)

and

ETIENNE SCHMIT

Magistrate, Deputy Public Prosecutor, Luxembourg

(who contributed the comments on Article 3(2) to 3(4) and Articles 27 to 42, 47, and 49 to 55)

---

[1] The text of the Convention on Insolvency Proceedings was published in Official Journal No L00000 [sic]. The Convention, open for signature in Brussels on 23 November 1995, was signed on that day by the Plenipotentiaries of the following 12 Member States: Belgium, Denmark, Germany, Greece, Spain, France, Italy, Luxembourg, Austria, Portugal, Finland, and Sweden.

Contents

I. Background to the Convention

1. The absence of a Convention on in solvency proceedings within the framework of the Community is viewed as a shortcoming in the completion of the internal market. It seems hard to accept that undertakings' activities are increasingly being regulated by Community law while national law alone continues to apply in the event of the failure of an undertaking. This consideration prompted Community Ministers for Justice, meeting informally in San Sebastian from 25 to 27 May 1989, to express the wish that a solution be found and to relaunch the negotiations on a Convention on this matter between the Member States and to give instructions to that effect to an ad hoc Working Party on the Bankruptcy Convention set up within the Council of the European Communities, as it then was.

A number of national experts (...) was therefore designated. The ad hoc Working Party met from 1991 until the conclusion of the definitive text of the Convention in 1995. Dr Manfred Balz (from Germany) was nominated chairman of the committee of experts. He was also the main author of the various drafts discussed during the negotiations.

2. A limited number of bilateral conventions do indeed exist between some Member States (see Article 48 of the Convention); however, Member States should be linked by a multilateral convention which, through mutual recognition of proceedings opened in each of the Member States, would permit coordination of the measures to be taken regarding an insolvent debtor's assets. To date, attempts to draw up a suitable instrument have been unsuccessful.

3. Bankruptcy, proceedings relating to the winding-up of insolvent companies or other legal persons, judicial arrangements, compositions and analogous proceedings were excluded from the scope of the Convention on Jurisdiction and the Enforcement of Judgments in Civil and Commercial Matters, signed in Brussels on 27 September 1968 and revised for the accession of new Community Member States in 1978, 1982 and 1989 (see OJCE No C 189 of 28 July 1990) hereafter referred to as the '1968 Brussels Convention'. Regarding those proceedings, a committee of experts met, under the auspices of the Commission of the European Communities, between 1963 and 1980 to draw up a first, and subsequently (following the Community's enlargement as from 1973) a second, draft Convention (see Bulletin of the European Communities, Supplement 2/82, containing both the Draft Convention and the explanatory report). The latter Convention was studied by an EC Council Working Party from 1982 until 1985, when work was suspended for lack of sufficient consensus.

That draft Convention provided for single proceedings (with exclusive competence to decree bankruptcy conferred on the Courts of [sc. the] State in which the debtor's centre of administration was located) which would be recognized in the other Contracting States, and parallel local proceedings were not permitted in those other States. The principles of 'unity' (a single proceeding for the whole territory of the Community) and 'universality' (the proceedings comprise all debtor's assets, wherever located) which governed the proceedings were therefore scrupulously followed in this text.

4. In the meantime, negotiations had been initiated within the Council of Europe which culminated in the adoption of a 'European Convention on Certain International Aspects of Bankruptcy', opened for signing in Istanbul on 5 June 1990 hereafter referred to as the '1990 Istanbul Convention' (see the Convention and its explanatory report in Council of Europe, International aspects of bankruptcy, Strasbourg 1990).

It must be pointed out, however, that it is not certain that any Member State will ratify the 1990 Istanbul Convention. Moreover, Article 40 thereof allows scope for reservations on either Chapter 11 (Exercise of certain powers of the liquidator) or Chapter III (Secondary insolvency proceedings), which involves a serious risk of disparity as between Contracting States.

Notwithstanding, the text of the 1990 Istanbul Convention remains important since it introduced more flexibility into the underlying principles of unity and universality.

5. The earlier Community draft ran into a number of obstacles. The principles of unity of the bankruptcy proceedings, on which it was based, led in particular to some complex provisions needed to take account of safeguards and privileges existing only in one or other Member State. Those provisions included the possibility of forming national 'sub-estates' with regard to security interests, privileges and priority claims. Overall, the system proved to be too complicated and ambitious.

For that reason, the new Community Convention on insolvency proceedings offers solutions which are as simple and flexible as possible. Above all, it is based on the principle of the universality of the proceedings limited, however, by the possible opening of one or more sets of secondary proceedings the effects of which are confined to the Member State or Member States in which they were opened.

The parallelism between the main proceedings (recognized elsewhere) and the secondary proceedings (enabling creditors in another Contracting State to invoke a local instrument in order to safeguard their interests) has made it possible to avoid over-rigid centralization, which hitherto appeared to be unacceptable to some Member States. Mandatory rules of coordination with the main proceedings guarantee the needs of unity in the Community.

II. General Introduction to the Convention

A. Scheme of the Convention

6. The Convention is divided into six Chapters with a total of 55 Articles. A Preamble, which contains important information about the scope and character of the Convention, and three Annexes, which form an integral part of it, complement its provisions.

Chapter I (Articles 1–15) defines the scope of application of the Convention (Articles 1–2), lays down the rules of direct international jurisdiction (Article 3), and determines the national law applicable through uniform conflict of laws rules (Articles 4–15).

Chapter II (Articles 16–26) addresses the recognition and enforcement of insolvency proceedings opened in other Contracting States and the recognition of the liquidator's powers.

Chapter III (Articles 27–38) contains the rules on secondary proceedings and on their coordination with the main proceedings and with other secondary proceedings.

Chapter IV (Articles 39–42) introduces several uniform rules on the right to lodge claims, the duty to provide information and the language to be used.

Chapter V (Articles 43–46) confers jurisdiction to interpret the Convention on the Court of Justice of the European Communities.

Chapter VI (Articles 47–55) contains the transitional and final provisions, including those regarding the applicability in time of the Convention (Article 47), its relationship to other Conventions (Article 48) and the procedures to amend the Annexes (Article 54), which list the insolvency proceedings to which the Convention applies and the persons who or organs which may be recognized as liquidator under the Convention.

B. Reasons for the Convention

7. To date, from a Private International Law perspective, the situation in the Community in the field of insolvency has been far from encouraging. There was a conflict of laws at both the internal level, with divergent national substantive rules, and the international level, with different Private International Law solutions.

Unlike contracts, insolvencies do not form an area of the law where private spontaneous cooperation can compensate for the lack of a common legal framework at the international level. Institutional cooperation is needed to provide a certain legal order to avoid incentives for the parties to transfer disputes or goods from one State to another, seeking to obtain a more favourable legal position ('forum shopping'), or to realize their individual claims independently of the costs which this may entail for the creditors as a whole or to the going-concern value of the debtor's firm.

Only a multilateral Convention among all the Member States may discourage the opportunistic conduct of debtors or creditors from taking place and allow for the efficient administration of the financial crisis of firms and individuals within the Community. The Convention on insolvency proceedings provides such a mandatory legal framework of intra-Community cooperation.

The Convention implements Article 220 of the Treaty establishing the European Community (hereafter referred to as the 'EC Treaty') and complements the 1968 Brussels Convention. It also confers on the Court of Justice of the European Communities jurisdiction to rule on the interpretation of its provisions. But, unlike the 1968 Brussels Convention, it also contains conflict of law rules. There are important grounds which justify this difference.

8. Insolvency proceedings are collective proceedings. Collective action needs clearly determined legal positions to provide for an adequate bargaining environment. This is true not only once the insolvency proceedings have been opened, but also before they have been opened (when the debtor is already in economic difficulties), as the rights 'in bankruptcy' will influence negotiations for a possible 'pre-bankruptcy' reorganization.

Furthermore, international insolvency proceedings can be effectively conducted only if the States concerned recognize the jurisdiction of the courts of the State of the opening of the proceedings, the powers of their liquidators and the effects of their judgments. They may accept it only if the rules on conflict of laws are also harmonized, because harmonized conflict of law rules prove [sic] a degree of certainty that, in the event of insolvency, rights created or granted in their jurisdictions will be recognized throughout the Contracting States.

C. Scope

9. The Convention applies to collective insolvency proceedings which entail the partial or total divestment of a debtor and the appointment of a liquidator. Two Annexes to the Convention determine the national proceedings covered by the Convention. These Annexes form an integral part of the Convention.

10. Insurance undertakings, credit institutions, investment undertakings holding funds or securities for third parties and collective investment undertakings are all excluded from the scope of the Convention. Community discussions are under way regarding reorganization and winding-up proceedings for these entities.

11. The Convention deals only with the intra-Community effects of insolvency proceedings. It applies only when the centre of the debtor's main interests lies within the territory of a Contracting State (i.e. the Community, see point 300). Even then, the Convention does not regulate the effect of the proceedings vis-à-vis third States. In relation to third States, the Convention does not impair the freedom of the Contracting States to adopt the appropriate rules.

D. The main and secondary model of insolvency proceedings

12. The Convention tries to provide a 'neutral mechanism' for international cooperation, honouring the basic expectations of the parties, independently of the Contracting State in which they are situated. For this purpose, it follows a combined model of the existing principles of regulation of international bankruptcies (universality or territoriality of effects and unity or plurality of proceedings).

The idea of a single exclusive universal form of insolvency proceedings for the whole of the Community is difficult to implement without modifying, by the application of the law of the State of the opening of proceedings, pre-existing rights created before insolvency under the different national laws of other Contracting States. The reason for this lies in the absence of a uniform system of security rights in Europe, and in the great diversity of national insolvency laws as regards criteria for the priority to be given to the different classes of creditors.

13. In this legal context, the Convention seeks to reconcile the advantages of the principle of universality and the necessary protection of local interests. This explains why a combined model has been adopted which permits local proceedings to coexist with the main universal proceedings.

14. Insolvency proceedings may be opened in the Contracting State where the debtor has the centre of his main interests. Insolvency proceedings opened in that State will be main proceedings of universal character; 'main', because if local proceedings are opened, they will be subject to mandatory rules of coordination and subordination to it, and 'universal', because, unless local proceedings are opened, all assets of the debtor will be encompassed therein, wherever located.

Single main proceedings are always possible within the Community but the Convention does not exclude the opening of local proceedings, controlled and governed by the national law concerned, to protect those local interests. Local proceedings have only territorial scope, limited to the assets located in the State concerned. To open such local proceedings it is necessary that the debtor possesses an establishment in the territory of the State of the opening of proceedings (hereafter referred to as the 'State of the opening'). In relation to the main proceedings, local insolvency proceedings can only be 'secondary proceedings', since the latter are to be coordinated with and subordinated to the main proceedings.

E. The main insolvency proceedings

15. The 'main insolvency proceedings' can be opened only in the Contracting State where the debtor has established the 'centre of his main interests' (hereinafter 'F1 State'). Normally it will be the place of the registered office in the case of legal persons. There can be only one main set of insolvency proceedings.

16. The main insolvency proceedings may be winding-up or reorganization proceedings, as listed in Annexe A to the Convention.

17. The law of the State of the opening (lex concursus) is generally applicable to the insolvency proceedings. It governs the opening of the proceedings, their conduct and their closure.

18. Some aspects are regulated directly by the Convention, which provides a uniform system of individual notification, lodgement of claims and use of language:

(a) Creditors abroad must be duly informed of the opening of the proceedings. An individual notice must be sent to all known creditors domiciled in other Contracting States;

Where necessary, a notice of the opening of the proceedings shall be published in other Contracting States in accordance with their national publication procedures (F2 laws). Contracting States within the territory of which the debtor has an establishment may demand mandatory publication.

(b) Creditors who have their habitual residence, domicile or registered office in a Contracting State may participate in the main proceedings, whatever the nature (public or private) of their claims.

19. Main proceedings are always universal. This has a number of important legal consequences:

(a) Assets located outside the State of opening are also included in the proceedings and sequestrated as from the opening of proceedings on a world-wide basis;

(b) All creditors are encompassed;

(c) Proceedings opened in one Member State will produce effects throughout the whole territory of the Contracting States (ie the Community). The recognition of the effects of the proceedings in other Contracting States is automatic, by force of law, without the need for an exequatur, and is independent of publication;

However, enforcement of judgments will require prior limited control by the national courts, through an exequatur. If the conditions set out by the Convention are satisfied, the national Courts are obliged to grant it.

The Convention follows the model of 'extension' to the other States (to F2, F3, etc.) of the effects laid down by the national law of the State where the main proceedings have been opened (F1).

(d) The liquidator appointed in the main proceedings has authority to act in all the other Contracting States, without the need for an exequatur. He may remove assets from the State in which they are located. In exercising these powers (granted by F1 laws), the liquidator must comply with the laws of the State concerned (F2). This is particularly the case if coercion is necessary to gain control of the assets (he must then request the assistance of the local authorities);

(e) Individual execution is not possible against the assets of a debtor located in any Contracting State;

(f) There is a legal duty to surrender to the insolvency proceedings the proceeds recovered by individual execution or obtained from the debtor's voluntary payment out of assets located abroad.

20. Local insolvency proceedings opened in accordance with the Convention limit the universal scope of the main proceedings. Assets located in the Contracting State where a court opens local insolvency proceedings are subject only to the local proceedings. However, the universal character of the main proceedings reveals itself through the mandatory rules of coordination of the local proceedings with the main proceedings, which include some specific powers of intervention given by the

Convention to the liquidator of the main proceedings (see points 36(3) and 38) and the transfer of any surplus in the local proceedings to the main proceedings.

F. Protection of local interest within the main proceedings

21. The application by the State of the opening of proceedings of its law and the automatic extension of the effects of those proceedings to all Community Member States may interfere with the rules under which local market transactions are carried out in other States. For this reason, in the provisions governing the main proceedings, the Convention gives due attention to important local interests: protection of legitimate expectations and security of transactions.

22. To this end, the Convention excludes certain rights over assets located in another Contracting State from the effects of the main proceedings or declares that those effects must be decided by the insolvency laws of the States concerned, and not by the law of the State of the opening of the proceedings.

23. 1. Exclusion from the effects of the main proceedings:

(a) The opening of insolvency proceedings will not affect pre-existing rights in rem of creditors or other third parties over assets situated in a different Contracting State at the time of the opening of the proceedings. The same rule is also applicable to reservations of title. Firms may obtain credit under conditions which could not be offered without this kind of guarantee.

   If the law of the State in which the security is located permits these rights to be affected, the liquidator (or any authorized creditor) has to request the opening of local insolvency proceedings to achieve this result. The position of the secured creditors will then be the same as in a purely domestic bankruptcy. Only security rights which are in the legal form of a 'right in rem' qualify for this benefit.

(b) Set-off rights governed by the law of a Contracting State other than the State of the opening receive a solution parallel to that of rights in rem.

2. In other cases, the Convention amends the rule that the law of the State of opening (F1) is applicable and provides that the law of the State concerned (F2) shall govern certain specific effects of the insolvency. In this way, the effects in a given State of insolvency proceedings opened in another Contracting State will be the same as in a domestic case.

(a) To protect the local systems of registration of property rights, the admissible effects of the insolvency proceedings on rights of the debtor in respect of immovable assets, ships or aircraft subject to registration are determined by the insolvency laws of the State of registration.

(b) Furthermore, in order to protect bona-fide third-party purchasers the Convention provides that the law of the Contracting State in which the assets are situated applies in the case where the debtor disposes for consideration of immovable assets after the opening of insolvency proceedings in another Contracting State. In the case of aircraft, ships or securities subject to registration, the law of the State of registration applies.

(c) To avoid disruptions in payment systems and financial markets, which may be protected by national law against the normal rules of insolvency law, the effects of the insolvency proceedings are determined by the law of the State the law of which governs the payment system or financial market.

(d) The effects of the insolvency proceedings on contracts conferring rights to make use of or acquire immovable property, and on employment contracts and relationships are governed respectively by the laws of the State in which they are situated and by the law applicable to the contract.

G. Local insolvency proceedings: 'independent' and 'secondary' territorial proceedings

24. Local insolvency proceedings may be opened in the Contracting State where the debtor has an establishment. The effects of local proceedings are limited to the assets located in that State. Local insolvency proceedings are always 'territorial'.

25. The Convention permits the opening of local proceedings both before and after main proceedings have been opened in the Contracting State where the debtor has his centre of main interests.

Local insolvency proceedings are considered as 'independent' territorial insolvency proceedings in the first case (since there are as yet no main proceedings to which they are subordinated) and as 'secondary' territorial insolvency proceedings in the latter case.

Independent proceedings become secondary proceedings once main proceedings have been opened, subject to some special rules (see points 31, 37 and 38).

26. Both types of proceedings are subject to rules of coordination with the main proceedings (in the case of independent territorial proceedings, after the opening of the main proceedings) and with other local proceedings.

27. The law of the State of the opening of the local proceedings is applicable to the local insolvency proceedings (see point 17).

The right to participate in local insolvency proceedings is not limited to local creditors. Once local proceedings have been opened, all creditors (whether local or not) may participate directly or through the liquidator in the main proceedings. This openness guarantees respect for the principle of equal treatment of creditors throughout the Community. As the Community forms an internal market, there can be no restrictions on participation in local proceedings based on the place of origin of the creditor's claim, or on the place of residence of the creditor.

28. The Convention does not restrict the right of any creditor to demand the opening of secondary territorial insolvency proceedings.

29. Secondary territorial insolvency proceedings may only be winding-up proceedings (see also point 31).

30. The right to request the opening of independent territorial proceedings is limited to local creditors and creditors of the local establishment or to cases where main proceedings cannot be opened under the applicable law. The purpose of these restrictions is to avoid the existence of parallel local proceedings which are not coordinated in the framework of the main Community proceedings.

Such limitations would not impair the individual rights of the creditors to recover debts: if no collective insolvency proceedings are opened, they may resort to individual enforcement measures.

31. Independent territorial proceedings may be winding-up or reorganization proceedings as listed in Annexe A or Annexe B to the Convention.

In the case of reorganization proceedings, the subsequent opening of the main proceedings makes them subject to the possibility of conversion into winding-up proceedings, if the liquidator in the main proceedings so requests. It such a conversion is not requested, the local proceedings may continue as reorganization proceedings.

H. Functions of the local proceedings

32. The first function of local proceedings is the 'protection of local interests'. Creditors may request the opening of local territorial proceedings to protect themselves against the effects of the law of another Contracting State. They can thus be certain that, even if the debtor's centre of interests is located in another Contracting State, their legal position will be the same as in domestic proceedings. This possibility makes sense for creditors who cannot rely on the recognition of their rights (or their preferential rank) in proceedings in another Contracting State. Further, it also makes sense for creditors who cannot count on the application of the law of another Contracting State (for instance, small creditors who participated only in domestic transactions with the local establishment of an undertaking of another Contracting State, etc).

33. The second function of local proceedings is to serve as 'auxiliary proceedings' to the main proceedings.

The liquidator in the main proceedings may request the opening of secondary proceedings when the efficient administration of the estate so requires. This may be, for instance, the case where the estate of the debtor is too complex to administer as a unit, where differences in the legal systems concerned are so great that difficulties may arise from the extension of effects deriving from the law of the State of the opening to the other States where the assets are located. It will be always the case where the liquidator in the main proceedings seeks to affect the rights in rem of creditors or other third parties in respect of assets situated in another State at the time of the opening.

I. Coordination of local insolvency proceedings

34. Parallel main and local insolvency proceedings represent an intermediate stage between the individual actions undertaken by the creditors and the 'collective action' in the full sense of the term, represented by single universal proceedings. Cooperation is made easier, since the liquidators' role of intermediary limits the number of parties, reducing the overall complexity.

However, the method of coordination established between the local proceedings is as important as their existence. In order to encourage cooperation, the Convention permits all creditors, irrespective of the State of origin of their claims, to participate in the local proceedings (local proceedings are not reserved for local creditors).

35. Secondary insolvency proceedings are subject to coordination with the main proceedings in a number of ways to ensure that due attention is given to the interests of the main insolvency without encroaching on the specific functions of the secondary proceedings. Some of these rules of coordination apply also to secondary proceedings inter se (see points 36(1), (2) and (5)).

36. 1. The Convention imposes a duty of reciprocal cooperation and exchange of information on all liquidators in both the main and secondary proceedings.

2. All liquidators are empowered to:

(a) lodge in other proceedings the claims already lodged in the proceedings for which they have responsibility; this power is very important for small creditors, whose claims may thus be lodged in proceedings in another Contracting State without great expense, and also for the liquidator in the main proceedings, since it can reinforce his powers to influence the secondary proceedings;

(b) participate in those proceedings.

3. The liquidator in the main proceedings is, as such, empowered to:

(a) request the opening of secondary insolvency proceedings;

(b) make proposals with a view to the winding-up or other use of the assets in the secondary proceedings;

(c) propose any rescue plan, composition or comparable measure in the secondary proceedings or require such arrangements to be subject to conditions, his consent being in principle required to that effect;

(d) request a stay on the liquidation of the assets in the secondary proceedings. Such request may be rejected by the local court only if it is manifestly of no interest to the creditors in the main proceedings. The reason behind this is a desire to provide time for a reorganization or composition to be concluded in the main proceedings, or for the sale of the whole undertaking or establishment.

4. Any assets remaining after winding-up and distribution in local proceedings pass to the main proceedings.

5. Any creditor may keep what he has obtained in secondary proceedings but may not participate in the distribution of the estate in the main insolvency proceedings until the other creditors with the same ranking (according to the law of the main proceedings) have obtained, in percentage, an equivalent dividend. The same rule is applicable when the creditor seeks to participate in other secondary proceedings. A consolidated account of dividends must be drawn up for all of the Contracting States (ie the Community.)

37. Independent territorial insolvency proceedings also become 'subordinated' proceedings as soon as main proceedings are opened within the Community. In this case, the same coordination rules to which secondary proceedings are subject apply to the extent that the progress of the independent proceedings so permits. After the opening of main proceedings, local insolvency proceedings may therefore continue not as independent proceedings but as secondary proceedings.

38. In addition, the liquidator in the main proceedings has the specific right to request the conversion of the previously opened independent territorial proceedings of a reorganizational nature (see points 31, 86 and 210) into winding-up proceedings (with a view to easier coordination with the main insolvency proceedings).

39. The Convention does not address the exceptional situation of two parallel independent territorial proceedings taking place at the same time in the Community, without main proceedings having been opened in the Contracting State where the debtor has his centre of main interests. It should be possible to apply, by analogy, the same conventional rules which serve to coordinate secondary insolvency proceedings inter se (see points 36(1),(2) and (5)).

III. Analysis of the Provisions

A. Preamble

40. The preamble to the Convention contains several important items of information regarding the role of the Convention within the Community system.

41. The first concerns the legal basis of the Convention. The preamble cites Article 220 of the EC Treaty as that basis.

Consequently, the characteristics of the Convention on insolvency proceedings are as follows:
— all Member States must ratify the Convention,
— powers to give rulings on interpretation are conferred on the Court of Justice of the European Communities. Unlike the 1968 Brussels Convention and the Rome Convention of 19 June 1980 on the Law applicable to Contractual Obligations, hereafter referred to as the '1980 Rome Convention', these powers are granted in the text of the Convention itself and not in additional protocols,
— there can be no reservations, except as regards the conferral of powers on the Court of Justice of the European Communities (see Article 46) (see points 57 et seq).

42. The Convention on insolvency proceedings complements the system of international jurisdiction and recognition and enforcement of judgments set up in the 1968 Brussels Convention, which is also based on Article 220 of the EC Treaty.

However, the Convention on insolvency proceedings goes beyond the scope of the 1968 Brussels Convention, since it not only governs international jurisdiction and the recognition of judgments but also contains rules on conflicts regarding the law applicable to the proceedings and effects thereof. A Convention on the mutual recognition of insolvency proceedings would not be possible without the guarantee of respect for acquired rights offered by a uniform system of rules on conflict of laws. Harmonized conflict of law rules guarantee acquired rights so that, in the event of insolvency, rights created in each state will be recognized in other Contracting States.

43. The Convention on insolvency proceedings does not contain any explicit provision regarding its interpretation. In the same way as in the 1968 Brussels Convention and the 1980 Rome Convention, two principles should be followed when interpreting its provisions: the principle of respect for the international character of the rule, and the principle of uniformity.

The Convention is a self-contained legal structure, and its concepts cannot be placed in the same category as concepts belonging to national law. The Convention must retain the same meaning within different national systems. Its concepts may not therefore be interpreted simply as referring to the national law of one or other of the States concerned.

When the substance of a problem is directly governed by the Convention, the international character of the Convention requires an autonomous interpretation of its concepts. An autonomous interpretation implies that the meaning of its concepts should be determined by reference to the objectives and system of the Convention, taking into account the specific function of those concepts within this system and the general principles which can be inferred from all the national laws of the Contracting States.

However, the Convention itself may require the meaning of a concept to be found in the applicable national law, when it does not wish to interfere with the national laws or when the function of a specific provision of the Convention so requires. This is the case, for example, with the concept of insolvency in Article 1 or the concept of rights in rem as laid down in Article 5 of the Convention.

Uniformity of interpretation is required in order to ensure equality in the rights and obligations derived from the Convention for the Contracting States and for the persons concerned irrespective of the Contracting State in which they are located. To this end, the Convention confers powers of interpretation on the Court of Justice of the European Communities.

44. The second important piece of information concerns the territorial framework of the Convention, which covers only the 'intra-Community effects' of insolvency proceedings. The Convention governs only internal conflicts of the Community, with two further limitations:

(a) the [sic] Convention does not govern all intra-Community conflicts. It covers only cases where the centre of the debtor's main interests is located in a Contracting State. When the centre of the debtor's main interests is outside the territory of a Contracting State, the Convention does not apply. In such a case, it is up to the private international law of Member States to decide whether insolvency proceedings may be opened against the debtor and on the rules and conditions to be applied;

   This holds true regardless of whether the debtor has assets or creditors in other Contracting States and whether the question of the effects of such proceedings in other Contracting States is raised (see point 82);

(b) Even when the centre of a debtor's main interests is in a Contracting State and the Convention is applicable, its provisions are restricted to relations with other Contracting States. Where non- Member States are concerned, it is the responsibility of each Member State to define the appropriate conflict rules.

Hence, for example, Article 8 governs the effects of insolvency proceedings on contracts relating to the immovable property of the debtor, as an exception to the general applicability of the law of the State of the opening (ex Article 4), but is applicable only when the immovable property is located in a Contracting State. If the asset in question is situated in a non-Contracting State, the Convention does not govern the case. It is for the State opening the proceedings to decide whether or not an exception to the general applicability of its law is advisable, and under what terms.

45. As the Convention provides only partial (intra-Community) rules, it needs to be supplemented by the private international law provisions of the State in which the insolvency proceedings were opened.

When incorporating the Convention into their legislations, the Contracting States will therefore have to examine whether their current rules can appropriately implement the rules of the Convention or whether they should establish new rules to that end. In this respect, nothing prevents Contracting States from extending all or some of the solutions of the Convention unilaterally on an extra-Community basis, as part of their national law.

46. The third important item of information relates to the relations between this Convention and Community secondary legislation. The Convention represents the general framework of intra-Community cooperation in the area of insolvency proceedings. However, as in the 1968 Brussels Convention (Article 57(3)) and the 1980 Rome Convention (Article 20), the principle of the primacy of secondary Community law is explicitly enshrined in it. For this reason, the preamble stresses that the Convention does not affect the possible application of the provisions of Community law, or of national law harmonized in accordance with those provisions, which govern insolvency proceedings in particular areas.

This principle does not prevent certain rules of the Convention from directly amending the solutions contained in previous Community acts (see Article 12).

47. The fourth item of information concerns the binding nature of the Convention, the provisions of which, including the rules on conflicts of law, should be applied by the court of its own motion even if they are not invoked by the parties concerned.

Although there is no specific mention of this point in the Convention, this was the solution adopted in the 1968 Brussels Convention. Substantial grounds for the binding nature do exist in the Convention on insolvency proceedings, since it deals with collective proceedings which by their very nature are likely to affect multiple interests and individuals. This binding nature is necessary to strengthen the legal protection of individuals established in the Community, since the Convention represents the basic guarantee of their rights vis-à-vis insolvency proceedings opened in other Contracting States.

However, it is for the national law to determine whether the judge is himself bound to establish the facts or whether it is for the interested parties to establish them (see Schlosser Report on the 1968 Brussels Convention, point 22).

B. Chapter I: General Provisions

Article 1
Scope

48. Article 1(1) defines the scope of the Convention by means of the concept of 'collective insolvency proceedings'. Given that it has to encompass widely differing national proceedings, Article 1 restricts itself to providing a very broad framework. Paragraph 1 defines this framework, requiring four cumulative conditions, which will be described below.

It should be pointed out here that, for the Convention to be applied, it is not sufficient that the proceedings in question meet these conditions in a generic way. Under Article 2(a) and (c), for insolvency proceedings to be covered by the Convention the proceedings concerned must also have been expressly entered by the State concerned in the lists of proceedings in the Annexes, which form an integral part of this Convention. Only those proceedings expressly entered in the list will be considered 'insolvency proceedings' as covered by the Convention and will be able to benefit from its provisions. In an area where national laws differ considerably, the lists are aimed at providing legal certainty regarding the proceedings to which the Convention may be applied.

In short, Article 1(1) lays down the conditions which enable proceedings to be added to the lists in the Convention by Contracting States, and only when the proceedings are included in the appropriate list will the Convention be applicable (see Article 2 (a) and (c)).

49. Article 1(1) defines the proceedings to which the Convention applies on the basis of four fundamental conditions:

(a) proceedings must be 'collective', ie all the creditors concerned may seek satisfaction only through the insolvency proceedings, as individual action will be precluded;

(b) the proceedings must be based on the debtor's 'insolvency' and not on any other grounds.

The Convention is based on the idea of financial crisis, but does not provide its own definition of insolvency. It takes this from the national law of the country in which proceedings are opened.

There is no test of insolvency other than that demanded by the national legislation of the State in which proceedings are opened. Thus, if a national law is based on the occurrence of an act of bankruptcy listed in the bankruptcy law or on the evidence that the debtor has ceased to pay his debts, it is sufficient for one of these facts to be established in order that insolvency proceedings be opened and the Convention applied.

By way of exception, it may happen that one of the forms of proceedings listed in Annexe A or Annexe B to the Convention is not confined to bankruptcy law but serves several purposes. Such a proceeding falls within the scope of the Convention only if it is based on the debtor's insolvency (where appropriate the 1968 Brussels Convention will be applied). This is the case with winding-up proceedings under British and Irish law (see points 55 et seq of the Schlosser Report to the 1968 Brussels Convention).

Thus, States which list proceedings which can be used for purposes other than insolvency, must provide sufficient means of identification of the proceedings to facilitate the application of the Convention. For instance, requiring their courts or competent bodies to specify clearly the grounds on which the decision to open proceedings is based, so that these can then be used as an identification 'label';

(c) the proceedings must entail the total or partial divestment of the debtor, that is to say the transfer to another person, the liquidator, of the powers of administration and of disposal over all or part of his assets, or the limitation of these powers through the intervention and control of his actions. It should be remembered that partial divestment, whether of his assets or his power of administration, is sufficient. The legal nature that such divestment may take, depending on the national legislation applicable, has no bearing on the application of the Convention to the proceedings in question;

(d) the proceedings should entail the appointment of a liquidator. This requirement is directly linked to the previous condition. The concept of liquidator used by the Convention is, once again, a very broad concept. Under Article 2(b) it includes any person or body whose function is to administer or realize the assets or supervise the management of the debtor's business. The court itself may fulfil this role. The persons or bodies considered to be liquidators by the Convention are set out in the list in Annexe C to the Convention.

50. All the proceedings listed in Annexe A have two ultimate consequences: the total or partial divestment of the debtor and the appointment of a liquidator. However, distortions would arise if the Convention were to apply only from the time when these consequences occur. The initial stages of insolvency proceedings could be excluded from the Convention's system of international cooperation. These consequences are necessary for proceedings to appear in the lists in Annexe A. However, once the proceedings have been included, it is sufficient to open proceedings in order that the Convention should apply from the outset.

51. Article 1(1) of the Convention does not include in its final version the condition that the proceedings may entail the realization of the debtor's assets.

Limiting the application of the Convention to winding-up proceedings would have had the advantage of simplifying the resulting rules. The disadvantage would have been that it would have excluded from European cooperation very important proceedings in bankruptcy practice in certain Contracting States, such as the 'suspensión de pagos' in Spain or the 'surséance van betaling' in the Netherlands.

Economic analysis shows that retaining the option between two possibilities in insolvency law (winding-up or reorganization) is in itself a sound decision. The same should hold true in the international arena. There is no economic reason to justify the exclusion of reorganization proceedings from international cooperation. The Convention also contains sufficient mechanisms to protect creditors' interests (eg the possibility of opening territorial insolvency proceedings in accordance with national law). For some Contracting States the exclusion of reorganization proceedings would therefore be unjustified.

The outcome of the negotiations was a compromise to extend the Convention system to insolvency proceedings the main aim of which was not winding-up but reorganization.

As part of this compromise, however, local territorial proceedings opened after the main proceedings may only be winding-up proceedings (see points 83 and 86). If opened before, local territorial proceedings may be reorganization proceedings as listed in Annexe A, but are subject to conversion into winding-up proceedings if the liquidator of the main proceedings so requests. The complications of compatibility and coordination between secondary reorganization proceedings (of which there could be several, if the debtor was based in several different Contracting States) and the main proceedings have led to this restriction.

52. The Convention is drawn up on the basis of insolvency proceedings conducted by the courts. This will be the general rule.

However, Article 1 does not require the proceedings necessarily to involve the intervention of a judicial authority (or of an authority with an equivalent role). They must be proceedings (comprising a minimum number of acts and formalities as set down in law) which are officially recognized and legally effective in the State in which the proceedings are opened and which fulfil the four conditions set out in Article 1(1).

The requirement of intervention by a judicial authority was deliberately excluded to allow the Convention to be applied to ordinary non-judicial collective proceedings in countries such as the United Kingdom and Ireland (especially the creditor's [sic] voluntary winding-up). These proceedings offer sufficient guarantees (including access to the courts, for the legality of the proceedings to be supervised and for any questions which may arise to be settled) in order that they be brought under the Convention. Their practical significance justifies this: they represent an important percentage of all corporate insolvency cases. Once again, the Convention has enough mechanisms to defend the positions of the creditors (the possibility of secondary proceedings, public order exceptions, safeguard of acquired rights, etc) to enable these proceedings to benefit from the Convention system.

The fact that non-judicial proceedings are covered in the Convention does not mean that they are dealt with as if they were judicial proceedings or that the decisions adopted in the course of these proceedings are regarded as having the effect of a court ruling. It simply means the rules of the Convention must be applied with flexibility taking into account that they were drawn up on the basis of proceedings conducted by a court.

From this point of view, the Convention guarantees a positive answer to two essential questions:

1. these proceedings have to be recognized as collective insolvency proceedings pursuant to Article 1. Once proceedings have been opened in a Contracting State in accordance with Article 3, the creditors must seek payment of their debts through these collective proceedings, even if they are not conducted by the courts. Any question relating to the conduct of the proceedings or the decisions taken in the course of those proceedings, should be referred to the courts of that State;

2. the appointment of the liquidator and the powers conferred on him by the law of the State where proceedings were opened must be recognized in other Contracting States. However if the liquidator wishes to exercise his powers in another Contracting State, it is necessary for the Contracting States having proceedings of this type (the United Kingdom and Ireland) to introduce into their national legislation a system of confirmation by the courts of the nature of the proceedings and the appointment of the liquidator. This condition is shown in the list in Annexe A which contains the proceedings designated by each country. In both cases these are termed proceedings 'with confirmation of or by a court'.

53. Finally, Article 1(1) does not require that a debtor have a particular status. The Convention applies equally to all proceedings, whether these involve a natural person or a legal person, a trader or an individual (see comments on Article 4).

54. Article 1(2): The Convention does not cover insolvency proceedings concerning insurance undertakings, credit institutions, investment undertakings which provide services involving the holding of funds or securities for third parties, or collective investment undertakings.

Contracting States subject these entities to prudential supervision through national regulatory authorities in order to minimize the risk to the relevant industries and to the financial system as a whole. All these entities are subject to specific Community regulations in the exercise of freedom of establishment and freedom to provide services, which are founded on the principle of control by the authorities of the State of origin of the entity in question. Negotiations are under way for Directives on reorganization measures and winding-up proceedings for credit institutions and insurance undertakings and Directives concerning insolvency proceedings relating to other entities described in this point are expected to follow. It has been agreed, therefore, that insolvency proceedings relating to the aforementioned entities should be excluded from the scope of this Convention.

55. The exclusion of credit institutions and insurance undertakings was agreed to by all Member States only after a statement by the Council and the Commission regarding the need to step up work on insolvency proceedings involving institutions and undertakings referred to in Article 1(2).

56. The excluded entities and undertakings are defined not in the Convention but by other instruments of Community law. The provisions currently applicable are mentioned in points 57 to 60.

The entities and undertakings which fall under the definitions given by the relevant Community Regulations and Directives are excluded from the Convention. Once an entity or an undertaking falls under the said definitions, the fact that the specific rules laid down by those Community Regulations or Directives are not, for any other reason, applicable to them does not alter this rule.

57. An 'insurance undertaking' is any entity covered by the First Council Directive 73/239/EEC of 24 July 1973 on the coordination of laws, regulations and administrative provisions relating to the taking up and pursuit of the business of direct insurance other than life assurance as last amended by

Directive 95/26/EC and by the First Council Directive 79/267/EEC of 5 March 1979 on the coordination of laws, regulations and administrative provisions relating to the taking up and pursuit of the business of direct life assurance, as last amended by Directive 95/26/EC.

58. A 'credit institution' is any entity covered by the definition in the First Council Directive 77/780/EEC of 12 December 1977 on the coordination of the laws, regulations and administrative provisions relating to the taking up and pursuit of the business of credit institutions as last amended by Directive 95/26/EC, which is an enterprise whose activity consists of receiving deposits or other reimbursable funds from the public and granting loans on its own account.

59. An 'investment undertaking' is any entity covered by the definition in Council Directive 93/22/EEC of 10 May 1993 on investment services in the securities field as amended by Directive 95/26/ EC (Article 1); in other words, any enterprise which regularly carries out a professional activity consisting of supplying third parties with an investment service concerning securities (and money-market instruments). Examples of an investment service are: the receiving, transfer and buying or selling of securities on behalf of another person, dealing in these securities on one's own behalf, management on a discretionary and individualized basis of investment portfolios of securities in accordance with a mandate given by the investors.

60. A 'collective investment undertaking' is any undertaking covered by the definition set out in Council Directive 85/611/EEC of 20 December 1985 on the coordination of laws, regulations and administrative provisions relating to undertakings for collective investment in transferable securities (UCITS) as last amended by Directive 95/26/EC; in other words, any body whose sole aim is the joint investment of securities from capital collected from the public, whose operations are subject to the principles of risk sharing, and the shares of which are, on the bearer's request, bought or paid back, directly or indirectly, from the assets of those bodies.

Article 2
Definitions

61. Article 2 provides definitions of a series of concepts which appear throughout the Convention.

62. Article 2(a) indicates that, for the purposes of the Convention, 'insolvency proceedings' refer to proceedings which meet the conditions in Article 1(1) and are included in Annexe A to the Convention which forms an integral part thereof. Hence only the proceedings included in the Annexe may benefit from the system of recognition in the Convention.

Contracting States may amend the list of their proceedings by using the revision mechanism laid down in Article 54.

63. Article 2(b): the concept of 'liquidator' is understood in a broad sense, to encompass any person or body who or which is appointed to administer or realize the bankrupt's assets, or to supervise the management of the debtor's affairs (the full or partial divestment of the debtor being one of the preconditions if the proceedings are to fall under the Convention).

The identification of those persons or bodies of national law who or which may be characterized as 'liquidator' for the purposes of the Convention is established by means of their inclusion in the list of Annexe C of the Convention.

When the court itself performs, according to the national law, functions of administration of the debtor's assets, it may qualify as 'liquidator' within the meaning of the Convention. It is, however, necessary that the State in question states in Annexe C of the Convention that its courts may act as liquidator.

64. Article 2(c): the concept of 'winding-up proceedings' aims to define the type of proceedings acceptable as secondary proceedings.

For the reasons given in point 51, only insolvency proceedings within the meaning of Article 1 which, in addition, may entail the realization of the debtor's assets can be secondary proceedings after the main proceedings have been opened.

The fact that winding-up proceedings may be brought to a close through agreement with the creditors, or in some other way, thus putting an end to the debtor's insolvency, does not alter this qualification if the essential aim of the proceedings is to proceed with winding-up.

The Contracting States must enter in the list in Annexe B those proceedings which serve as secondary proceedings. If a State fails to include specific proceedings in the list in Annexe B, these proceedings may not then benefit from the provisions of the Convention. All Contracting States must include at least one type of proceedings in the list in Annexe B.

65. The Convention does not restrict the types of proceedings which can serve as independent territorial proceedings opened before the main proceedings in accordance with Article 3(4).

These proceedings may be those included in Annexe A (including reorganization proceedings) or Annexe B (only winding-up proceedings). However, once the main proceedings are opened, the liquidator in the main proceedings is empowered to request the conversion of any local insolvency proceedings opened in accordance with Article 3(4) into winding-up proceedings listed in Annexe B.

66. Article 2(d): the expression 'court' is taken in a very broad sense. It covers not only the judiciary or an authority which plays a role similar to that of a court or public authority (as was the case with earlier draft versions of the Convention), but also a person or body empowered by national law to open proceedings or make decisions in the course of those proceedings (see point 52).

This wording brings this Convention close to the concept of 'competent authority' in Article 4 of the 1990 Istanbul Convention, where the explanatory report (in point 23) states that the term 'competent authority' for the opening of proceedings may include the competent body of a legal person which decides on its own winding-up for reasons of insolvency as is the case in Ireland and the United Kingdom.

67. Article 2(e): 'judgment' must be taken in a broad sense to mean 'decision', consistent with what is said in point 66.

68. Article 2(f): 'the time of the opening of proceedings' is very important, since many questions are settled by reference to it. The time of the opening of proceedings is deemed to be the time when the decision begins to be effective under the law of the State of the opening of the proceedings.

The Convention does not require the decision to open insolvency proceedings to be final. It is sufficient for it to have effect in the State of opening and for its effects not to have been stayed.

In the case of non-judicial proceedings of the 'creditors' voluntary winding-up' type, the working party discussed whether, in order to fix the time of opening, the same rule should be used or whether the date of confirmation by the court of the nature of the proceedings and the appointment of the liquidator should be taken as the reference point. Only in order to allow the liquidator to exercise his powers on the territory of another Contracting State would it be necessary to take the date of confirmation by the court as the reference (see point 52). For all other matters, the general rule given above in this point stands.

69. Article 2(g): 'the Contracting State in which assets are situated'. This definition is important in so far as the main proceedings do not affect certain rights on assets located abroad (see Articles 5 and 7) and territorial proceedings can only affect the assets located in the State in which proceedings are opened. To this extent the Convention must help to determine what criteria regarding location are to be followed. In reality, the Convention does no more than stress traditional solutions of private international law which are well known in all the Contracting States.

Thus, tangible property is considered to be located in the place in which it is physically situated.

Property and rights ownership of or entitlement to which must be entered in a public register in order to establish rights in rem over them are considered to be located in the State under the authority of which the register is kept. This provision is applicable, for example, in the case of ship and aircraft registers, and also extends to intangible property, such as patents or securities. The State under whose authority the register is kept is not necessarily the State in which the register is physically situated (eg it may be a consular register or centralized international register).

'Public register' does not mean a register kept by a public authority, but rather a register for public access, an entry in which produces effects vis-à-vis third parties. It also includes private registers with these characteristics, recognized by the national legal system concerned.

In the case of Community patents, trademarks and other similar rights of Community origin, Article 12 states that these can only be included in main proceedings based on Article 3(1) (see point 133).

Finally, claims are deemed to be situated in the State where the debtor required to meet the claim in question (and not the insolvent debtor) has his centre of main interests. The concept of 'centre of main interests' is the same as that specified in Article 3(1) (see point 75).

70. Article 2(h): The concept of 'establishment' is linked to the basis of international jurisdiction to open territorial proceedings. In this regard, it should be mentioned that Article 3(2), in which the jurisdiction to open such territorial proceedings is dealt with, was one of the most debated provisions throughout the negotiations.

Several Contracting States wished to have the possibility of basing territorial proceedings not only on the presence of an establishment, but also on the mere presence of assets of the debtor (assigned to an economic activity) without the debtor having an establishment.

For the sake of an overall consensus on the Convention, those States agreed to abandon the presence of assets as a basis for international competence provided that the concept of establishment is interpreted in a broad manner but consistently with the text of the Convention. This explains the very open definition given in Article 2(h).

In the Convention, the mere presence of assets (eg the existence of a bank account) does not enable local territorial proceedings to be opened. The presence of an establishment of the debtor within the jurisdiction concerned is necessary.

Though defended by one State, the possibility of adopting the same concept of establishment in the Convention as that given by the Court of Justice of the European Communities in its interpretation of Article 5(5) of the 1968 Brussels Convention was ruled out. The majority of States preferred an independent concept to be developed.

Indeed, the Court of Justice of the European Communities emphasized that the special powers laid down in Article 5 of the 1968 Brussels Convention must be strictly interpreted vis-à-vis the general forum of the place of domicile of the defendant. Under these conditions, to import a concept from the 1968 Brussels Convention involved the risk of conveying a possibly restrictive interpretation of the concept of establishment to the Convention on insolvency proceedings, which was precisely the opposite of what most of the working party intended. For this reason, they opted to give the Convention its own definition, which is contained in Article 2.

71. For the Convention on insolvency proceedings, 'establishment' is understood to mean a place of operations through which the debtor carries out an economic activity on a non-transitory basis, and where he uses human resources and goods.

Place of operations means a place from which economic activities are exercised on the market (ie externally), whether the said activities are commercial, industrial or professional.

The emphasis on an economic activity having to be carried out using human resources shows the need for a minimum level of organization. A purely occasional place of operations cannot be classified as an 'establishment'. A certain stability is required. The negative formula ('non-transitory') aims to avoid minimum time requirements. The decisive factor is how the activity appears externally, and not the intention of the debtor.

The rationale behind the rule is that foreign economic operators conducting their economic activities through a local establishment should be subject to the same rules as national economic operators as long as they are both operating in the same market. In this way, potential creditors concluding a contract with a local establishment will not have to worry about whether the company is a national or foreign one. Their information costs and legal risks in the event of insolvency of the debtor will be the same whether they conclude a contract with a national undertaking or a foreign undertaking with a local presence on that market.

Naturally, the possibility of opening local territorial insolvency proceedings makes sense only if the debtor possesses sufficient assets within the jurisdiction. Whether or not these assets are linked to the economic activities of the establishment is of no relevance.

Article 3
International jurisdiction

72. The rules of jurisdiction set out in the Convention establish only international jurisdiction, that is to say, they designate the Contracting State the courts of which may open insolvency proceedings. Territorial jurisdiction within that Contracting State must be established by the national law of the State concerned.

73. Main insolvency proceedings

Article 3(1) enables main insolvency universal proceedings to be opened in the Contracting State where the debtor has his centre of main interests. Main insolvency proceedings have universal scope. They aim at encompassing all the debtor's assets on a world-wide basis and at affecting all creditors, wherever located.

Only one set of main proceedings may be opened in the territory covered by the Convention.

74. Which persons or legal entities may be subject to insolvency proceedings is determined by national law. Where the international jurisdiction rule mentions the debtor, this means the natural persons or legal entity (whether a legal person or not) concerned.

75. The concept of 'centre of main interests' must be interpreted as the place where the debtor conducts the administration of his interests on a regular basis and is therefore ascertainable by third parties.

The rationale of this rule is not difficult to explain. Insolvency is a foreseeable risk. It is therefore important that international jurisdiction (which, as we will see, entails the application of the insolvency laws of that Contracting State) be based on a place known to the debtor's potential creditors. This enables the legal risks which would have to be assumed in the case of insolvency to be calculated.

By using the term 'interests', the intention was to encompass not only commercial, industrial or professional activities, but also general economic activities, so as to include the activities of private individuals (eg consumers). The expression 'main' serves as a criterion for the cases where these interests include activities of different types which are run from different centres.

In principle, the centre of main interests will in the case of professionals be the place of their professional domicile and for natural persons in general, the place of their habitual residence.

Where companies and legal persons are concerned, the Convention presumes, unless proved to the contrary, that the debtor's centre of main interests is the place of his registered office. This place normally corresponds to the debtor's head office.

76. The Convention offers no rule for groups of affiliated companies (parent-subsidiary schemes).

The general rule to open or to consolidate insolvency proceedings against any of the related companies as a principal or jointly liable debtor is that jurisdiction must exist according to the Convention for each of the concerned debtors with a separate legal entity.

Naturally, the drawing up of a European norm on associated companies may affect this answer.

77. Article 3(1) gives the courts in the State of the opening of proceedings jurisdiction in relation to insolvency proceedings. However, the Convention contains no rule defining the limits of this jurisdiction.

This is a fundamental question since it raises the issue of the relationship between the Convention on insolvency proceedings and the 1968 Brussels Convention and their respective scope.

Certain Contracting States recognize a 'vis attractiva concursus' in their national law, by virtue of which the Court which opens the insolvency proceedings has within its jurisdiction not only the actual insolvency proceedings but also all the actions arising from the insolvency.

Although the projection of this principle in the international domain is controversial, the 1982 Community Draft Convention contained a provision in Article 15 which, according to the Lemontey Report, was inspired by the 'vis attractiva' theory. This Article conferred on the courts of the State of the opening of insolvency proceedings jurisdiction over a wide series of actions resulting from the insolvency.

Neither this precept nor this philosophy has been adopted in this Convention. There is no provision in Article 3 of the Convention addressing this problem. However, the Convention's silence on the matter is only partial. Article 25 thereof contains the delimitation criterion between both the 1968 Brussels Convention and this Convention.

This criterion is directly taken from the Court of Justice of the European Communities. It was outlined by the Court of Justice in the interpretation of Article 1(2) of the 1968 Brussels Convention in its Judgment of 22 February 1979 (Case 133/78, *Gourdain v Nadler* [1979] ECR 733).

Article 1(2) of the 1968 Brussels Convention excludes 'bankruptcy, proceedings relating to the winding-up of insolvent companies or other legal persons, judicial arrangements, compositions and analogous proceedings' from its scope. In that Judgment the Court of Justice of the European Communities used the nature of the action taken as the criterion for determining whether or not the jurisdiction rules of the 1968 Brussels Convention applied. According to this criterion, actions directly derived from insolvency and in close connection with the insolvency proceedings are excluded from the 1968 Brussels Convention. Logically, to avoid unjustifiable loopholes between the two Conventions, these actions are now subject to the Convention on insolvency proceedings and to its rules of jurisdiction.

78. The rule on international jurisdiction in Article 3(1) enables the court having jurisdiction to open main insolvency proceedings to order provisional and protective measures from the time of the request to open proceedings.

Preservation measures both prior to and after the commencement of the insolvency proceedings are very important to guarantee the effectiveness of the insolvency proceedings. They may be ordered by the court having jurisdiction according to Article 3(1) irrespective of the Contracting State where the assets or persons concerned (either debtor or a creditor) are located. Such measures may adopt a wide-range of forms, according to the national law of the court ordering them (eg interlocutory orders to do or not to do, appointment of a temporary administrator, attachment of assets).

These preservation measures shall be recognized and enforced in other Contracting States, according to the conditions set out in Article 25 of the Convention (see point 198).

Article 3(1) does not prevent the liquidator, or any other empowered person, from going to the place where the preservation is to be carried out (eg the State in which the assets are located) and asking the local courts to adopt provisional measures available under the national law. This possibility presupposes that the courts of that State enjoy jurisdiction to adopt such measures under their national law (as should usually be the case), and the fulfilment of the subject-matter requirements of that law (evidence of a good prima facie case, sufficient urgency, security to cover damages which may be caused, etc).

These preservation measures are ancillary to the main proceedings. Logically, they remain subordinated to the decisions taken in the course of the main proceedings by the court having jurisdiction under Article 3(1) and which benefit from the system of recognition and enforcement of the Convention. Hence, under Articles 16 and 25, such a court may even stipulate that those preservation measure are to be lifted, modified or continued (see point 198).

The possibility of going to the court of the place where the measures are to take effect is referred to again in Article 38, although with a different purpose. Article 38 empowers the temporary administrator appointed after the request for the opening of main insolvency proceedings, but before such opening, to call directly on the authorities of any other Contracting State to adopt preservation measures provided under the insolvency law of this State for winding-up proceedings on the debtor's assets situated in its territory, as a pre-opening stage of secondary proceedings (see point 262).

79. The Convention does not provide any express rule to resolve cases where the courts of two Contracting States concurrently claim jurisdiction in accordance with Article 3(1). Such conflicts of jurisdiction must be an exception, given the necessarily uniform nature of the criteria of jurisdiction used.

Where disputes do arise, to solve them, the courts will be able to take account of:

1. the Convention's system according to which:
   (a) each court is obliged to verify its own international jurisdiction in accordance with the Convention;

(b) the principle of Community trust, according to which once the first court of a Contracting State has adopted a decision, the other States are required to recognize it (see points 202 and 220).

2. the possibility of a request for a preliminary ruling to the Court of Justice of the European Communities, guaranteeing the uniformity of the contents of the criteria for international jurisdiction and its appropriate interpretation in the given case;

3. the general principles of procedural law which are valid in all Contracting States; these principles include those derived from other Community Conventions such as the 1968 Brussels Convention.

80. Local insolvency proceedings

Article 3(2) enables territorial proceedings to be opened in the State in which the debtor has an establishment, as defined in Article 2(h), under the following conditions.

In cases where the debtor's centre of main interests is located in a Contracting State, the courts of other Contracting States have no power to open main insolvency proceedings.

However, any of these Contracting States may open territorial proceedings, the effectiveness of which is restricted to the assets situated in that State, if the debtor has an establishment in the territory of that State. The mere presence of assets is not sufficient to open territorial proceedings.

Depending on whether or not main proceedings have been opened, the proceedings shall be secondary or independent territorial proceedings.

81. Article 3(2) does not grant jurisdiction to open territorial proceedings to the courts of a State where the debtor does not have an establishment. The assets located in that State cannot, therefore, be included in territorial proceedings, but revert to the main proceedings, if such have been opened.

82. Should the debtor's centre of main interests be located outside the territory of the Contracting States, it is not within the jurisdiction of any Contracting State to open insolvency proceedings within the scope of the Convention. Article 3(1) and (2) assumes [sic] that the centre of main interests is in a Contracting State.

When the centre of main interest does not lie in a Contracting State, national law determines the international jurisdiction of its courts. The effects of such proceedings are not governed by this Convention (see point 44).

83. Secondary territorial insolvency proceedings

Article 3(3) requires that after main proceedings have been opened by the competent court within the meaning of Article 3(1), the subsequent proceedings opened by the court of the State where the establishment is located, in accordance with Article 3(2), are secondary proceedings, subject to Chapter III.

In the event of there being a number of establishments located in different Contracting States, several sets of secondary proceedings may be opened.

The secondary proceedings under Article 3(3) may not be reorganization proceedings, rather they must be winding-up proceedings as mentioned in Annexe B. This rule is reaffirmed in Article 27 (see comments re Article 27 (points 211 et seq)).

84. Independent territorial insolvency proceedings

Article 3(4) deals with situations which exist prior to the opening of main proceedings. This is the result of efforts to reconcile two essentially conflicting approaches.

In line with the philosophy expressed most particularly in Articles 3(1) and (2) and Article 27, the court of the debtor's centre of main interests is the only one having jurisdiction to open main proceedings. These proceedings should naturally encompass all the debtor's assets regardless of the State in which the property is located.

Under the first approach, it is only as an exception to the universal proceedings that territorial proceedings may be opened in advance, in order to satisfy 'local' creditors as to the assets present in that State. Indeed, it is difficult to imagine that 'local' creditors who hold a favourable ranking in the State where the property is located would want to transfer all the assets to another State where their ranking would be less favourable. It is likewise difficult for States without any creditors holding a preferential ranking to accept the transfer of all the assets abroad.

The other approach involves seeking to protect local creditors by allowing national rules on the opening of proceedings to follow their normal course, even in a State where an establishment is located, and even at all times, prior to and regardless of the opening of proceedings in the State of the centre of main interests. This approach takes into account the insolvency of an establishment and the creditors' interest in territorial proceedings or the general interest in territorial proceedings to reorganize an establishment of social and economic importance within that State, and grants less consideration to the principle of the universality of insolvency proceedings.

85. Article 3(4) adopts the following rule:

The courts of a Contracting State having jurisdiction under Article 3(2) may open, prior to the main proceedings, territorial insolvency proceedings called for this reason independent territorial proceedings, in only two cases:

1. The conditions for opening the insolvency proceedings, as set out by the law of the State where the centre of main interests is located, do not allow main proceedings to be opened.

That will be the case if, for example, the debtor cannot be subject to insolvency proceedings, eg where the applicable law requires the debtor to be a trader, and this is not the case, or where the debtor is a public company which the law of the State of the centre of main interests does not allow to be declared insolvent.

2. A local creditor or a creditor of the local establishment, within the meaning of Article 3(4)(b), requests territorial proceedings be opened.

The protected creditor to whom this right to request the opening of territorial proceedings is granted is one:

(a) whose habitual residence, domicile and registered office is in the State where the establishment is located,

(b) or whose claim arises from the operation of that establishment (eg an employee working for that establishment; a person who entered through the establishment into an undertaking which must be performed in that State; the tax authorities and social security bodies).

Outside these two possible cases, the court having jurisdiction to open the territorial proceedings cannot open proceedings prior to the opening of proceedings in the centre of main interests.

86. The territorial proceedings mentioned in Article 3(4) may be winding-up proceedings or reorganization proceedings mentioned in Annexe A or Annexe B.

In the event of the subsequent opening of the main proceedings, independent territorial proceedings become secondary proceedings, in accordance with the special rules of Articles 36 and 37 of the Convention.

Furthermore, reorganization proceedings as mentioned in Annexe A will, at the request of the liquidator in the main proceedings, be converted into secondary winding-up proceedings, in accordance with Articles 36 and 37 (see points 210, 254 to 261). If the liquidator in the main proceedings does not request this conversion, the territorial proceedings may continue as organization proceedings.

Article 4
Law applicable

87. The Convention sets out, for the matters covered by it, uniform rules on conflict of laws which replace national rules of private international law.

When these rules on conflict of laws talk of the 'applicable law', they refer to the internal law of the Contracting State designated by the rule, excluding its rules of private international law.

88. General rule on conflict of laws

Article 4 lays down the basic rule on conflict of laws of the Convention. This Article determines the law applicable to the insolvency proceedings, the conduct thereof and their effects: unless otherwise stated by this Convention, the law of the Contracting State of the opening of the proceedings is applicable (lex concursus).

89. This rule on conflict of laws is valid both for the main proceedings and for local proceedings (secondary or independent territorial proceedings).

To avoid any doubts, Article 28 reiterates this solution for the secondary proceedings. Although Article 28 only considers the secondary proceedings, it is clear that the application of the law of the State of the opening of the proceedings operates as the general conflict of laws rule of the Convention and is also valid for independent territorial proceedings.

90. The law of the State of the opening of proceedings determines all the effects of the insolvency proceedings, both procedural and substantive, on the persons and legal relations concerned.

This law governs all the conditions for the opening, conduct and closure of the insolvency proceedings. It stipulates, inter alia, who may be subject to insolvency proceedings, the requirements to open them and who may present the petition; it determines the nature and the extent of the debtor's divestment and the assets covered by it; it outlines the organization of the administration of the estate and regulates the designation of the liquidator and his powers; it decides the admissibility of claims and the rules on distribution and preferences; it governs the closure of the proceedings and its consequences, etc.

The substantive effects referred to the competence of the law of the State of the opening by Article 4, are those typical of insolvency law, ie effects which are necessary for the insolvency proceedings to fulfil its aims. To this extent, the law of the State of the opening may displace (unless the Convention provides otherwise), the law normally applicable, under the common pre-insolvency rules on conflict of laws, to the act concerned. This happens for instance when Article 4 makes applicable the law of the State of opening of proceedings to invalidate any act (eg a contract) detrimental to all the creditors, even if that act is governed under the general rules on conflict of laws (if a contract, those of the 1980 Rome Convention), by the law of a different State.

91. To facilitate its interpretation, Article 4(2) contains a non-exhaustive list of questions that are governed by the law of the State of the opening.

(a) whether a particular debtor by virtue of his status (eg trader/non-trader, public law company) may be subject to insolvency proceedings (Article 4(2)(a)). This rule is valid for both the main proceedings and for secondary proceedings, where the solution to the case may be different. This paragraph is linked to Article 3(4)(a) and Article 16(2) (see points 85 and 148);

(b) which assets form part of the estate and the treatment of assets acquired by the debtor after the opening of proceedings;

(c) the respective powers of the debtor and the liquidator. This paragraph is linked to Article 14 (see point 141);

(d) the conditions under which set-offs may be invoked. This paragraph is linked to Articles 6 and 9 (see points 107 to 111 and 120 et seq);

(e) the effects of the proceedings on current contracts to which the debtor is party (paragraph (e)). To the extent necessary, the law of the State of the opening displaces the law of the contract determined in accordance with the 1980 Rome Convention. This paragraph is linked to Articles 8 and 10 (see points 116 to 119; 125 et seq);

(f) the effects of the insolvency proceedings on executions brought by individual creditors, their suspension or prohibition after the opening of collective insolvency proceedings. However, the effects of the proceedings on lawsuits pending remain subject to the law of the Contracting State where the lawsuit is pending, ex Article 15 (see point 142);

(g) the claims which are to be lodged against the debtor's estate and the treatment of claims arising after the opening of insolvency proceedings (ie claims arising in the administration and management of the assets which in many systems benefit from preferential payment);

(h) the rules governing the lodging, verification and admission of claims. It must be borne in mind that Chapter IV of the Convention sets out a number of uniform rules on this subject. As regards claims that are admissible, Article 39 acknowledges 'iure conventionis' that Contracting States' public law claims can be lodged in insolvency proceedings opened in other Contracting States. This precept expressly stipulates the right of the tax and social security authorities of any Contracting State to submit their claims in insolvency proceedings opened pursuant to the Convention;

(i)   the ranking (privileges, preferences, etc) and the rules on distribution of the assets realized. As in all main or secondary proceedings the national law of the State of the opening is applicable, the ranking of a claim may vary for each of the proceedings in which it is lodged;

(j)   the conditions and effects of the closure of proceedings, including closure by composition or equivalent measure;

(k)   the rights of the creditors subsequent to the closure of the proceedings, including any possible discharge of the debtor;

(l)   the costs and expenses of the proceedings;

(m)   the voidness, voidability or unenforceability of legal acts that may be detrimental to all the creditors. The applicable national law determines whether action must be taken to obtain their invalidation or whether the decision to open proceedings automatically entails invalidation. To the extent necessary, the law of the State of the opening displaces the law normally applicable to the act in question. This paragraph is to be taken in conjunction with Article 13 (see point 135).

In the case of secondary proceedings, the local rules on invalidation of a detrimental act shall be applicable only in so far as damage has been caused to the debtor's assets which are in this State (eg to the estate of the secondary proceedings). For instance, the act in question (sale, establishment of a right in rem) involves an asset which was located in this State at the relevant time.

92.   Exceptions to the general rule on conflicts of law of Article 4

The application, by the courts in the State of the opening of proceedings, of their national insolvency law and the automatic extension of its effects to all the Contracting States (see Articles 16 and 25) may interfere with the rules under which transactions are carried out in these States.

To protect legitimate expectations and the certainty of transactions in States other than that in which proceedings are opened (for in the latter State all the operators have to count on the application of its laws) the Convention provides for a number of exceptions to the general rule:

1.   In certain cases, the Convention excludes some rights over assets located abroad from the effects of the insolvency proceedings (as in Articles 5, 6 and 7).

2.   In other cases, it ensures that certain effects of the insolvency proceedings are governed not by the law of the State of the opening (F1), but by the law of the State concerned (see Articles 8, 9, 10, 11, 14 and 15). In such cases, the effects to be given to the proceedings opened in other Contracting States are the same effects attributed to a domestic proceedings of equivalent nature (liquidation, composition, or reorganization proceedings) by the law of the State concerned (F2).

93.   The exceptions to the application of the law of the State of the opening (Article 4) are referred to in Articles 5 to 15 of the Convention. Apart from Articles 6 and 14, which by systemic arguments must be interpreted in the same way, the exception is made in favour of the law of a 'Contracting State'.

This does not mean that, by a contrario interpretation, the law of the State of the opening of proceedings is applicable where the State concerned is not a Contracting State. The need to protect legitimate expectations and the certainty of transactions is equally valid in relations with non-Contracting States. The group's intention was simply to regulate these cases in line with the general restriction of the Convention to the intra-Community effect of insolvency proceedings (see point 44). Contracting States are, therefore, free to decide which rules they deem most appropriate in other cases (the same ones as in Articles 5 to 15 of the Convention, or others).

Article 5
Third parties' rights in rem

94.   This provision excludes from the effects of the proceedings rights in rem of third parties and creditors in respect of assets belonging to the debtor which, at the time of the opening of proceedings, are situated within the territory of another Contracting State.

If the assets are situated in a non-Contracting State, Article 5 does not govern the issue (see points 44 and 93).

95. In order to understand the functioning of Article 5, account should be taken of the fact that main insolvency proceedings based on Article 3(1) have a universal scope. All the assets of the debtor shall be subject to the main proceedings irrespective of the State where they are situated unless territorial proceedings are opened. The law of the State of the opening of the main proceedings shall determine which of those assets shall be regarded as forming a part of the estate in the main proceedings and which shall be excluded (see Article 4(2)(b)).

A part of those assets may be subject to third parties' rights in rem. The Convention does not make it obligatory for these assets to be included in or excluded from the estate in the main proceedings. The Convention imposes only an obligation to respect third parties' rights in rem over assets located within the territory of a Contracting State different from the State of the opening of proceedings.

The creation, validity and scope of these rights in rem are governed by their own applicable law (in general, the 'lex rei sitae' at the relevant time) and cannot be affected by the opening of insolvency proceedings.

This means that although the law of the State of the opening stipulates that all assets are part of the estate, the holder of the right in rem retains all his rights in respect of the assets in question. For instance, the holder of the right in rem may exercise the right to separate the security from the estate and, where necessary, to realize the asset individually to satisfy the claim. On the other hand, the liquidator, even if he is in possession of the asset, cannot take any decision on that asset which might affect the right in rem created on it, without the consent of its holder (see also point 161).

96. Article 5 only applies to the rights in rem created before the opening of proceedings. If they are created after the opening, Article 4 shall apply without exception (without prejudice to Article 14).

97. The fundamental policy pursued is to protect the trade in the State where the assets are situated and legal certainty of the rights over them. Rights in rem have a very important function with regard to credit and the mobilization of wealth. They insulate their holders against the risk of insolvency of the debtor and the interference of third parties. They allow credit to be obtained under conditions that would not be possible without this type of guarantee.

Rights in rem can only properly fulfil their function in so far as they are not more affected by the opening of insolvency proceedings in other Contracting States than they would be by the opening of national insolvency proceedings. This aim could be achieved through alternative solutions which were in fact discussed in the working party. However, to facilitate the administration of the estate the simplicity of the formula laid down in the current Article 5 was preferred by the majority: insolvency proceedings do not affect rights in rem on assets located in other Contracting States.

98. The rule does not 'immunize' rights in rem against the debtor's insolvency. If the law of the State where the assets are located allows these rights in rem to be affected in some way, the liquidator (or any other person empowered to do so) may request secondary insolvency proceedings be opened in that State if the debtor has an establishment there. The secondary proceedings are conducted according to national law and allow the liquidator to affect these rights under the same conditions as in purely domestic proceedings.

99. Article 5 states that the proceedings shall not affect rights in rem in respect of assets located in other Contracting States and not that the proceedings shall not affect assets located in another State. As main proceedings are universal (ex Article 3(1)) they encompass all the debtor's assets.

This is important if the value of the security is greater than the value of the claim guaranteed by the right in rem. The creditor will be then obliged to surrender to the estate any surplus of the proceeds of sale.

Without affecting the economic value of the right or its immediate realizability, it also gives the liquidator the power to decide on the immediate payment of the claim guaranteed, and thus avoid the loss in value that certain assets could suffer when they are realized separately.

100. Article 5 refers to 'rights in rem' but does not define what these are. The Convention does not intend to impose its own definition of a right in rem, running the risk of describing as rights in rem legal positions which the law of the State where the assets are located does not consider to be rights in rem, or of not encompassing rights in rem which do not fulfil the conditions of that definition.

The Convention acknowledges the interest of each State in protecting its market's trade, in the form of respect of rights in rem acquired over assets of the debtor located in that country under the law that is applicable before the opening of the insolvency proceedings.

For this reason, the characterization of a right as a right in rem must be sought in the national law which, according to the normal pre-insolvency conflict of law rules, governs rights in rem (in general, the lex rei sitae at the relevant time). In this sense, the Convention adopts a 'lege causae' characterization.

101. The only departure from the above statement is found in Article 5(3), which for the purposes of Article 5, directly and independently of national law, considers as a right in rem any right entered in a public register and enforceable against third parties, allowing a right in rem to be obtained.

102. However, the rationale of Article 5 imposes certain limits to the national qualification of a right in rem. It must be borne in mind that Article 5 represents an important exception as regards the application of the law of the State of the opening and the universal effect of the main proceedings. It must equally be remembered that secondary proceedings are only possible if the debtor has an establishment in that Contracting State. The mere presence of assets is not enough in order to open such proceedings.

An unreasonably wide interpretation of the national concept of a right in rem to include, for instance, rights simply reinforced by a right to claim preferential payment, as is the case for a certain number of privileges, would make the Convention meaningless, and such a wide interpretation is not to be attributed to Article 5.

103. In order to facilitate the application of the Convention and avoid doubts Article 5(2) provides a list of types of rights that are normally considered by national laws as rights in rem.

This list is inspired in two main considerations. The first, that a right which exists only after insolvency proceedings have been opened, but not before, is not a right in rem for the purposes of Article 5 (which protect pre-existing rights).

The second, that a right in rem basically has two characteristics (see also the concept of rights in rem in the Member States in point 166 of the Schlosser Report on the 1968 Brussels Convention):

(a) its direct and immediate relationship with the asset it covers, which remains linked to its satisfaction, without depending on the asset belonging to a person's estate or on the relationship between the holder of the right in rem and another person;

(b) the absolute nature of the allocation of the right to the holder. This means that the person who holds a right in rem can enforce it against anyone who breaches or harms his right without his assent (eg such rights are typically protected by actions to recover); that the right can resist the alienation of the asset to a third party (it can be claimed erga omnes, with the restrictions characteristic of the protection of the bona fide purchaser); and that the right can thus resist individual enforcement by third parties and in collective insolvency proceedings (by its separation or individual satisfaction).

104. A right in rem may not only be established with regard to specific assets but also with regard to assets as a whole. Security rights such as the 'floating charge' recognized in United Kingdom and Irish law can, therefore, be characterized as a right in rem for the purposes of the Convention. Likewise, rights characterized under national law as rights in rem over intangible assets or over rights are also included (see Article 5(1)).

105. This provision is based on non-fraudulent location of the assets.

106. The establishment of a right in rem in favour of a particular creditor or third party could be an act detrimental to all the creditors. In this case, the general rules of the Convention governing actions for voidness, voidability or unenforceability of legal acts are applicable (see Article 4(2)(m), and Article 13).

Article 6
Set-off

107. This Article deals with set-off in the same way as Article 5 dealt with rights in rem. When under the normally applicable rules on conflict of laws the right to demand the set-off stems from a

national law other than the 'lex concursus', Article 6 allows the creditor to retain this possibility as an acquired right against the insolvency proceedings: the right to set-off is not affected by the opening of proceedings.

108. Set-off is a part of the law of obligations governed by the relevant rules of private international law regarding the law applicable to obligations. By including two claims which offset each other, the question arises whether the right to set-off stems from:

(a) the cumulative application of laws applicable to the two claims or

(b) the law applicable to the claim of the debtor ('passive' claim in the set-off) against which the creditor intends to set off his counter-claim against the debtor ('active' claim in the set-off).

The Convention opts for this second interpretation when it derives the right to set-off from the 'law applicable to the insolvent debtor's claim' (ie from the law applicable to the claim where the insolvent debtor is the creditor in relation to the other party).

109. The laws of some Contracting States altogether restrict or prohibit set-off in insolvency. Article 4 subjects insolvency set-off to the competence of the law of the State of the opening of the insolvency proceedings.

If insolvency proceedings are opened, it falls therefore to the 'lex concursus' to govern admissibility and the conditions under which set-off can be exercised against a claim of the debtor.

If the 'lex concursus' allows for set-off, no problem will arise and Article 4 should be applied in order to claim the set-off as provided for by the law. On the other hand, if the 'lex concursus' does not allow for set-off (eg since it requires both claims to be liquidated, matured and payable prior to a certain date), then Article 6 constitutes an exception to the general application of that law in this respect, by permitting the set-off according to the conditions established for insolvency set-off by the law applicable to the insolvent debtor's claim ('passive' claim).

In this way, set-off becomes, in substance, a sort of guarantee governed by a law on which the creditor concerned can rely at the moment of contracting or incurring the claim.

110. Article 6 covers only rights to set-off arising in respect of mutual claims incurred prior to the opening of the insolvency proceedings. After this time, Article 4 is applied without exception to decide whether or not the set-off is admissible. Contractual set-off implies an agreement subject to its own applicable law according to the 1980 Rome Convention. The same rationale on which Article 5 is based explains that in the event of a contractual set-off agreement covering different claims between two parties, the law of the Contracting State applicable to that agreement will continue to govern the set-off of claims covered by the agreement and incurred prior to the opening of the insolvency proceedings.

111. As in the case of Article 5, any actions detrimental to all the creditors may be corrected by bringing actions for voidness, voidability or unenforceability as set out in Article 4(2)(m).

Article 7
Reservation of title

112. In the same way as Article 5, this provision seeks to protect trade by excluding from the scope of insolvency proceedings the reservation of title on property which, at the time the proceedings were opened, was located in a Contracting State other than the State of the opening.

The remarks made with regard to Article 5 apply here mutatis mutandis. The biggest difference between Article 5 and Article 7 concerns Article 7(2) which contains a uniform substantive rule.

113. The first paragraph governs the insolvency of the purchaser of an asset, by allowing the seller to preserve his rights based on the reservation of title. For this to occur, the asset must be located at the time when the insolvency proceedings are opened in a Contracting State other than the one where the proceedings are opened. If its location changes after the opening of the proceedings, this does not affect the application of the provision.

114. The second paragraph covers the insolvency of the seller of an asset after delivery of the asset, allowing the sale to remain valid. If the purchaser continues to make payments, he shall acquire title at the end of the period set out in the contract. For this rule to be applied, it is also a requirement that at

the time the insolvency proceedings are opened the asset is located within a State other than the State of the opening of proceedings.

115. Of course, actions for voidness, voidability or unenforceability, as provided for in Article 4(2) (m) can also be brought against these reservations of title.

Article 8
Contracts relating to immovable property

116. Insolvency law may have an impact on current contracts. Thus, for instance, in the case of mutual obligations pending fulfilment, the liquidator may be empowered to decide either on the performance or termination of the contract. The aim of rules of this kind is to protect the estate from the obligation to perform contracts which may be disadvantageous in these new circumstances.

117. The general rule on conflicts of law is that it falls to the law of the Contracting State of the opening of proceedings to regulate the effects of the proceedings on current contracts to which the debtor is a party (Article 4(2)(e)).

To this extent, the applicable national insolvency law interferes with and displaces the rules applicable to contracts, which derive from the law applicable under the 1980 Rome Convention.

118. This rule, which overall is positive for the general interests of the creditors may be detrimental to other interests. In all the Contracting States, contracts covering immovable property are subject to special rules, both of conflict of laws as well as of international jurisdiction, in order to take into account several interests: those of the parties to the contract (eg tenants) and the general interests protected by the State in which the immoveable property is to be found.

Protection of these specific interests justify [sic] an exception to the application of the law of the State of the opening of proceedings. Hence Article 8 makes the effects of the insolvency proceedings exclusively subject to the law of the Contracting State where the immovable property is located.

Solely means that only the law of the Contracting State of location of the immovable [property] (including its insolvency law), and not the 'lex concursus' under Article 4, is applicable to establish these effects.

119. Article 8 not only covers contracts for the use of immovable property (rental, leasing) but also includes contracts covering the transfer of the immovable property (sale).

Article 9
Payment systems and financial markets

120. The intention of Article 9 is for any effects on transactions subject to a payment or settlement system or to a financial market of insolvency proceedings opened in another Contracting State to be the same as those in proceedings under national law. By making the effects of insolvency exclusively subject to the law applicable to the payment system and the financial market, general confidence in these mechanisms is protected.

The aim of this provision is to avoid any modification of the mechanisms for regulating and settling transactions provided for in payment or settlement systems or on the organized financial markets operating in Contracting States, in the event of insolvency of a party to a transaction which would otherwise result if the 'lex concursus' applied. The relevant mechanisms include closing out contracts and netting, and in so far as the security is situated in that Contracting State, the realization of securities.

Payment systems and markets involve large-scale transactions and as a consequence have been found to require special rules to guarantee their smooth operation and security. That is why the law governing the particular system or market concerned remains applicable.

A financial market is not defined but is understood to be a market in a Contracting State where financial instruments, other financial assets or commodity futures and options are traded. It is characterized by regular trading and conditions of operation and access and it is subject to the law of the relevant Contracting State, including appropriate supervision, if any, by the regulatory authorities of that Contracting State.

121. Article 9 means that only the law governing the system or market in question can be applied to the relevant transactions affected by an insolvency and not the 'lex concursus' as provided by Article 4. Thus, the complex problems of potential conflicts of the two laws are avoided and the certainty of transactions is preserved.

122. For the same reason, any possible voidness, voidability or unenforceability of a payment or transaction carried out under this system or market and which may be detrimental to all the creditors, remains subject to the same solution: the law applicable to the payment system or financial market governs these cases.

123. To determine the law applicable to European payment systems account must be taken of the work in progress in the Community on those systems.

124. The reference to Article 5 means that protection of rights in rem of any kind of creditors or third parties over assets belonging to the debtor is always carried out in the same way under the Convention: by reference to the location of the assets, regardless of the type of creditor or institution which may benefit from its function as a guarantee. Rights in rem affect third parties and uniform treatment of them is essential in order to protect trade.

Article 10
Contracts of employment

125. Article 10 derogates from the general application of the law of the State of the opening of proceedings (Article 4) and makes the effects of the proceedings on employment contracts and on labour relations subject to the law of the Contracting State applicable to the contract of employment, including its law on insolvency.

This Article aims to protect employees and labour relations from the application of a foreign law, different from that which governs the contractual relations between employer and employees. For this reason, effects of the insolvency proceedings on the continuation or termination of the employment relationship and on the rights and obligations of each party under such relationship are to be determined by the law applicable to the contract under the general conflict of laws rules.

126. The 1980 Rome Convention will determine the law applicable to employment contracts (see, in particular, its Articles 6 and 7).

127. The word 'solely' emphasizes that only the law applicable to the employment contract is applied in order to establish these effects and not the 'lex concursus' as provided by Article 4. Any problem regarding possible conflicts between the two laws is therefore avoided.

128. Insolvency questions other than those relating to the impact of the opening of proceedings on contract and employment relationships remain subject to the general competence of the law of the State of the opening, ex Article 4. Thus, for instance, the following would be covered, the question of whether or not workers' claims arising out of their employment shall be protected by a privilege, the prescribed amount protected and the rank of the privilege if any, etc. In the same way as lodgement, verification and admission of claims, all these questions are subject to the law of the State of the opening (Article 4(2)(h)).

Guaranteed payments of workers' claims in cases of insolvency of the employer, ensured by a national institution under a wage guarantee scheme in the event of insolvency governed by the national law of a Contracting State, are subject to the law of that State.

Article 11
Effects on rights subject to registration

129. The application of the law of the State of the opening (F1) to determine the effects of the insolvency proceedings also on the assets of debtors located in another Contracting State may come into conflict with national registration systems, when this law provides for effects or consequences different from or unknown to the system of the State of registration (eg a statutory lien of the general body of creditors over the debtor's property).

130. The Convention does not try to modify the systems either of registration or of rights in rem of the Contracting States. The systems for the registration of property play a significant role in protecting trade and legal certainty. General confidence in its contents and consequences should be protected

under the same conditions, whether the insolvency proceedings are opened in the State of registration or in another Contracting State.

To preserve these systems, Article 11 establishes an exception to the application of the law of the State of the opening. This exception is, however, more limited than the exceptions contained in Articles 8, 9 and 10 of the Convention. Contrary to these provisions, Article 11 does not submit the effects of the insolvency proceedings 'solely' to the law of the Contracting State under the authority of which the register is kept. This means that the general applicability of the law of the State of the opening in accordance with Article 4 is not displaced. Hence, a sort of cumulative application of both laws is necessary.

Under Article 11, the law of the Contracting State of registration will therefore determine the modifications which, required by the law of the State of the opening, may be prompted by the insolvency proceedings and affect the rights of the debtor over immovable property, ships and aircraft subject to registration, the requisite entries in the register and the consequences thereof. In consequence, the law of the Contracting State of registration decides which effects of the insolvency proceedings are admissible and affect the rights of the debtor subject to registration in that State.

However, this rule does have certain disadvantages. While it makes access to different national registers easier, it means that the effects may be different for each Contracting State. The administration of the insolvency proceedings by a liquidator thus becomes more complex, although it increases in certainty. With that in mind, this rule is limited to registers on immovable property, ships and aircraft.

131. Article 11 does not refer to assets but to rights subject to registration in public registers, the purpose of which is to determine who is the holder or which are the rights in rem over the assets. It also includes systems of registration of deeds relating to immovable property to effect priorities such as the Registry of Deeds which exists in Ireland.

Article 11 refers only to the effects on the rights of the debtor over immovable property, ships or aircraft. For rights in rem, whether registered or not, of creditors or third parties acquired before the opening of the insolvency proceedings, see Article 5.

132. For the concept of 'public register', see comments on Article 2.

Article 12
Community patents and trademarks

133. The Agreement relating to Community patents (1989 Luxembourg Agreement), Council Regulation (EC) No 40/94 of 20 December 1993 on the Community trademark and Council Regulation (EC) No 2100/94 of 27 July 1994 on Community plant variety rights all create rights which cover the whole territory of the Community,

This Convention opens up the possibility of insolvency proceedings with universal effect (thus encompassing the whole Community territory) if the debtor's centre of main interests is located in a Contracting State.

However, the Patent Convention contained in the 1989 Luxembourg Agreement (Article 41), the 1993 Regulation on the Community trademark (Article 21), and the 1994 Regulation on Community plant variety rights (Article 25), contain a rule to the effect that a Community right derived therefrom may be included only in the first proceedings (regardless of whether these are main or territorial proceedings) opened in a Contracting State. This rule was logical in so far as common regulations on international insolvency proceedings were lacking. With this Convention it is logical to allocate those Community rights to the main proceedings. Article 12 of the Convention seeks to modify the rule established by the Patent Convention, the Regulation on the Community trademark and the Regulation on Community plant variety rights and to replace it with Article 12.

134. As may be concluded from Article 3(1), Article 12 is operative only when the debtor has his centre of main interests in a Contracting State. In all other cases, ie when this centre is located outside the Community, the provisions of the Patent Convention (Article 41), the Regulation on the Community trademark (Article 21) and the Regulation on Community plant variety rights (Article 25) shall be applied.

Article 13
Detrimental acts

135. This provision must be taken in conjunction with Article 4(2)(m). The basic rule of the Convention is that the law of the State of the opening governs, under Article 4, any possible voidness, voidability or unenforceability of acts which may be detrimental to all the creditors' interests. This same law determines the conditions to be met, the manner in which the nullity and voidability function (automatically, by allocating retrospective effects to the proceedings or pursuant to an action taken by the liquidator, etc) and the legal consequences of nullity and voidability.

136. Article 13 represents a defence against the application of the law of the State of the opening, which must be pursued by the interested party, who must claim it.

It acts as a 'veto' against the invalidity of the act decreed by the law of the State of the opening. This mechanism is easier to apply than other possible solutions based on the cumulative application of the two laws. It is now clear that all the conditions, content and the consequences of the voidability are borrowed from the law of the State of the opening. The only purpose of Article 13 and the law governing the act concerned is to reject the application of that law in a given case.

137. In this respect, Article 13 provides that the rules of the law of the State of the opening shall not apply when the person who has benefited from the contested act provides proof that:

1. the act in question (eg a contract) is subject to the law of a Contracting State other than the State of the opening of the proceedings;

2. the law of that other State does not allow for this act to be challenged by any means. By 'any means' it is understood that the act must not be capable of being challenged using either rules on insolvency or general rules of the national law applicable to the act (eg to the contract referred to in paragraph (1)).

'In the relevant case' means that the act should not be capable of being challenged in fact ie after taking into account all the concrete circumstances of the case. It is not sufficient to determine whether it can be challenged in the abstract.

138. The aim of Article 13 is to uphold legitimate expectations of creditors or third parties of the validity of the act in accordance to the normally applicable national law, against interference from a different 'lex concursus'.

From the perspective of the protection of legitimate expectations, the operation of Article 13 is justified with regard to acts carried out prior to the opening of the insolvency proceedings, and threatened by either the retroactive nature of the insolvency proceedings opened in another country or actions to set aside previous acts of the debtor brought by the liquidator in those proceedings.

After the proceedings have been opened in a Contracting State, the creditor's reliance on the validity of the transaction under the national law applicable in non-insolvency situations is no longer justified. Thenceforth, all unauthorized disposals by the debtor are in principle ineffective by virtue of the divestment of his powers to dispose of the assets and such effect is recognized in all Contracting States. Article 13 does not protect against such an effect of the insolvency proceedings and it is not applicable to disposals occurring after the opening of the insolvency proceedings.

139. This rule covers both the main proceedings and the secondary proceedings (in each case with regard to the law of the State of the opening of the respective proceedings).

Article 14
Protection of third-party purchasers

140. This provision was initially based on the desire to protect the confidence of third parties in the content of property registers when the debtor, after the insolvency proceedings have been opened, disposes for consideration of an asset from the estate, and the opening of proceedings or the restrictions on the debtor have not yet been entered or referred to in the register in question. The final drafting of this Article goes further and covers all acts of disposal concerning immovable assets which take place after the opening of the insolvency proceedings.

To be protected by Article 14, it is necessary that the debtor dispose of the asset for consideration (eg not gratuitously).

141. In principle, any act of disposal by the debtor after the proceedings have been opened shall be ineffective in accordance with the law of the State of the opening (as this law deprives the debtor of his powers of disposal).

However, in order to protect trade and reliance on systems of publication of rights in rem, the protection of bona fide third parties should be no different in respect of proceedings in another Contracting State as compared to domestic proceedings.

If the proceedings opened in another Contracting State do not appear in the local register, the only way adequately to protect confidence in the system of publication regarding rights in rem over assets, without any loopholes, is to make the effects of disposal subject to the law of the Contracting State under the authority of which the register is kept or, in the case of immovable property, to the law of the Contracting State where the immovable property is located.

Property covered by this Article means an immovable asset, ships or aircraft subject to registration in a public register and securities the existence of which presupposes registration (dematerialized securities, see point 69).

An act of disposal must be understood to include not only transfers of ownership but also the constitution of a right in rem relating to such property.

Article 15
Effects of the insolvency procedure on lawsuits pending

142. The Convention distinguishes between the effects of insolvency on individual enforcement proceedings and those on lawsuits pending.

The effects on individual enforcement actions are governed by the law of the State of the opening (see Article 4(2)(f)) so that the collective insolvency proceedings may stay or prevent any individual enforcement action brought by creditors against the debtor's assets.

Effects of the insolvency proceedings on other legal proceedings concerning the assets or rights of the estate are governed (ex Article 15) by the law of the Contracting State where these proceedings are under way. The procedural law of this State shall decide whether or not the proceedings are to be suspended, how they are to be continued and whether any appropriate procedural modifications are needed in order to reflect the loss or the restriction of the powers of disposal and administration of the debtor and the intervention of the liquidator in his place.

C. Chapter II: Recognition of Insolvency Proceedings

Article 16
Principle

143. To recognize foreign judgments is to admit for the territory of the recognizing State the authority which they enjoy in the State where they were handed down.

The Convention accords immediate recognition of judgments concerning the opening, course and closure of insolvency proceedings which come within its scope and of judgments handed down in direct connection with such insolvency proceedings.

Recognition is automatic within the system of the Convention. It requires no preliminary decision by a court of the requested State.

144. Article 16 establishes the general principle of recognition, in the territory of the Contracting States (eg the Community), of a judgment opening insolvency proceedings adopted by the competent authorities of a Contracting State under Article 3 of the Convention.

145. Only insolvency proceedings within the scope of the Convention benefit from the system of recognition of the Convention. To fall within such scope, the proceedings must be listed in the Annexes to the Convention.

Proceedings not listed in those Annexes shall not be eligible for recognition under the Convention nor shall they prevent the recognition of proceedings provided for in the Convention even though they were opened earlier.

146. The general principle of recognition is valid for all proceedings opened in a Contracting State under Article 3, ie for both main proceedings and territorial, either secondary or independent. Obviously, in the second case recognition will be limited to the territorial effects of the proceedings.

147. A judgment opening proceedings need not necessarily be a final judgment (not subject to ordinary appeal) in order to enjoy recognition. Such judgment whether final or provisional shall have effect in the whole territory covered by the Convention as long as it is effective in the State of the opening of proceedings.

The Convention is based on the principle of Community trust and on the 'favor recognitionis', so that national borders are no obstacle to the efficient administration of international insolvency proceedings throughout the Community.

148. The Convention imposes an obligation to recognize insolvency proceedings opened in another Contracting State, even when such proceedings cannot be brought against the debtor in that State, due to his professional capacity or to his public or private nature, as in the case of non-traders in certain States.

Main insolvency proceedings may be opened in a State (F1) in accordance with its own law, although in another Contracting State (F2) insolvency proceedings cannot be brought against the debtor by virtue of his professional capacity (ie a non-trader). The second State (F2) in such a case is obliged to recognize and, where appropriate, enforce the foreign judgment. The State requested (F2) cannot invoke public policy in its territory to oppose recognition on those grounds (under Article 26).

Since the main proceedings can be opened only if the debtor has his centre of main interests in the State of the opening, it seems logical that the decision of the law of that State to allow collective insolvency proceedings against that debtor should be respected by the other Contracting States, whose connection with the debtor is restricted to the existence of an establishment or assets.

However, these other States (ie F2) will not be obliged to open local secondary proceedings against that debtor, since the conditions laid down by their insolvency law, which is applicable pursuant to Article 28, have not been fulfilled.

The opposite hypothesis, ie the impossibility of opening main proceedings because the law of the Contracting State competent under Article 3(1) does not allow it, presents no difficulties. The Convention expressly recognizes the possibility of opening territorial proceedings. Where the law of a State which has jurisdiction under Article 3(2) allows insolvency proceedings against that kind of debtor, it will be possible to open independent territorial proceedings (see Article 3(4)).

Naturally, the territorial proceedings have effects only in the State of the opening of proceedings and do not extend them to the territory of other States (see point 156); they do not therefore affect the situation of the debtor in other States. Only the main proceedings have that effect (see point 212)

149. The relationship between the recognition of main proceedings under Article 3(1) and the possibility of opening territorial proceedings under Article 3(2) is referred to in Article 16(2). The recognition of main proceedings does not preclude the subsequent opening of secondary territorial proceedings (see point 212).

Article 17
Effects of recognition

150. Whereas Article 16 establishes the general principle of the recognition of a judgment opening insolvency proceedings, Article 17 distinguishes between the recognition of main proceedings and that of territorial proceedings.

151. Recognition of the main proceedings

The universality of main proceedings opened under Article 3(1), embracing all the debtor's assets and creditors, implies recognition of the proceedings and their effects in the States in which those assets or creditors are situated. The Convention guarantees this universality through the setting up of a system of mandatory automatic recognition in all Contracting States. The Convention reinforces this by making the consequence of recognition the 'extension' to all other Contracting States of the effects attributed to those proceedings by the law of the State of the opening of proceedings.

152. 'Automatic recognition' means immediate recognition by virtue of the Convention (ipso iure recognition) without any need to resort to preliminary proceedings to declare it effective. Since recognition is not subject to prior proceedings, the authorities of the requested State which may be confronted with the judgment opening proceedings may determine incidentally whether it is a judgment under the Convention and whether grounds for refusal under Article 26 exist.

153. Article 17 lays down a model of recognition based on the extension of the effects of the judgment in a Contracting State to the whole territory covered by the Convention. Proceedings opened in another Contracting State will not, as regards their effects, be equated with national proceedings but will be recognized in other Contracting States with the same effects attributed to them by the law of the State of the opening (= 'extension model').

The law of the State of the opening (and not the law of the requested State) shall be applicable to determine those effects. This shall apply to all the effects of the proceedings in another Contracting State, both procedural and substantive (see point 90). The substantive effects are included by virtue of the general applicability which the Convention attributes to the law of the State of the opening (see Article 4) and they are therefore subject to the same exceptions as are provided for by the Convention in respect of that law (see Articles 5 et seq).

154. The system of automatic recognition and the extension model reinforce the universality of the main proceedings. From the time fixed by the law of the State of the opening, the judgment opening proceedings produces its effects with equal force in all Contracting States. The divestment of the debtor, the appointment of the liquidator, the prohibition on individual executions, the inclusion of the debtor's assets in the estate regardless of the State in which they are situated, the obligation to return what has been obtained by individual creditors after opening, etc, are all effects laid down by the law of the State of the opening which are simultaneously applicable in all Contracting States.

155. The recognition of main proceedings under Article 3(1) shall be limited by the opening of territorial proceedings in accordance with Article 3(2).

The main proceedings cannot produce its effects in respect of the assets and legal situations which come within the jurisdiction of territorial proceedings opened. The territorial proceedings protect local interests and for this purpose the national law applies. However, the main proceedings may influence the conduct of territorial proceedings as a result of coordination and subordination rules which derive from the Convention and to which territorial proceedings are subject.

156. Recognition of territorial proceedings

Territorial proceedings can affect only the assets situated in the State of the opening. Recognition cannot imply, therefore, the extension of the effects of those proceedings to property situated in other Contracting States. Recognition of territorial proceedings means admitting the validity of the opening of the local proceedings and of the effects which they produce over the assets located in the territory of the State of the opening, which cannot be challenged in other Contracting States.

This is the case, for example, where the liquidator in those proceedings has to demand the return of assets belonging to the estate in the secondary proceedings which were transferred abroad without authorization after the opening of proceedings.

Moreover the opening of the territorial proceedings limits the extra-territorial effects of the main proceedings which may no longer include the assets situated in the State where those territorial proceedings were opened, except for the surplus assets in the secondary proceedings under Article 35. The main proceedings must observe that limitation.

157. Article 17(2), second sentence, covers the case of territorial proceedings, either secondary or independent, which may conclude by authorizing the debtor to postpone payment or even by discharging the remaining debt.

It may be clearly seen that, in the case of proceedings under Article 3(2), this reduction of creditors' rights can apply only to the debtor's estate situated in the State of the opening of the territorial proceedings. The creditors concerned will, therefore, be able to seek unlimited satisfaction of all their debts from the assets situated in other Contracting States. Naturally, nothing prevents the creditors from voluntarily agreeing to a further reduction of their rights affecting assets situated outside the State of opening of territorial proceedings. However, that supplementary restriction can be relied on only against creditors who have accepted it personally and not by a majority vote. This principle should be seen in conjunction with Article 34(2).

Article 18
Powers of the liquidator

158. The main effect of the recognition of insolvency proceedings opened in a Contracting State is the recognition of the appointment of the liquidator and of his powers in all other Contracting States. The term 'liquidator' must be understood in the wide sense of the definition given in Article 2 of the Convention.

159. By virtue of that recognition, the liquidator appointed in proceedings in a Contracting State will be able, in other Contracting States, to exercise the powers conferred on him by the law of the State of the opening.

The liquidator's powers, their nature and their scope will be determined by the law of the State of the opening of the proceedings in respect of which he was appointed. That law also establishes the liquidator's obligations.

160. As the Convention provides for a system of automatic recognition of insolvency proceedings, the appointment of the liquidator and the exercise of his powers are covered by that same automatic effect. Neither the exequatur nor the publication provided for in Article 21 is necessary for the liquidator to be able to exercise his powers in other Contracting States.

161. Within the limits laid down in the Convention, the liquidator in the main proceedings may exercise all his powers in the other Contracting States (ie in the whole of the territory of the Community).

In order to remove any doubts, Article 18 expressly stipulates that the liquidator may even transfer assets out of the State in which they are situated. In doing so, the liquidator must respect Articles 5 and 7 of the Convention, since the proceedings cannot affect rights in rem of creditors or third parties over assets situated, at the time of the opening, in a Contracting State other than the State of the opening of proceedings. To the extent that it is required by the right in rem, the removal of those assets to another State may be subject to the consent of the holder of the right in rem.

The creditors can prevent such transfer by requesting the opening of secondary proceedings concerning those assets (provided that the conditions laid down in Article 3(2) and (3) are fulfilled).

162. The powers of the liquidator in the main proceedings are subject to two general restrictions.

163. The first derives from the possible opening of territorial insolvency proceedings in another Contracting State (under Article 3(2)).

This restriction is logical, since the assets cannot be subject to the powers of two different liquidators. Once territorial proceedings have been opened, the direct powers of the liquidator in the main proceedings no longer apply to assets situated in the State of the opening of the territorial proceedings. The liquidator in the territorial proceedings has exclusive powers over those assets. This does not imply that the main liquidator loses all influence over the debtor's estate situated in the other Contracting State, but that that influence must be exercised through the powers conferred on that liquidator by the Convention to coordinate the territorial proceedings and the main proceedings (see Articles 31 to 37).

Article 18 extends this first restriction to cases where provisional protective measures incompatible with the exercise of those powers have been already adopted as a consequence of the request to open territorial proceedings.

The liquidator in the main proceedings is entitled under the Convention to request secondary proceedings (Article 29).

164. The second restriction provided for in Article 18(3) derives from the liquidator's obligation, when exercising his powers, to comply with the law of the State within the territory of which he intends to take action.

(a) The general principle of prohibiting the exercise of coercive power in another State also applies to a foreign liquidator. The latter can take action in other States only if he complies with that principle. Hence Article 18 expressly prohibits direct recourse to coercive measures. Any use of force or coercive action is excluded.

If persons affected by a liquidator's acts do not voluntarily agree to their performance and if coercive measures are required with regard to assets or persons, the liquidator must apply to the authorities of the State where the assets or persons are located to have them adopted and implemented. The Convention allows a foreign liquidator from another Contracting State, on the basis of the automatic recognition of his appointment and his powers, to petition those authorities to adopt distraint measures against such assets or persons in accordance with national law.

(b) The liquidator shall exercise his powers without infringing the laws of the State in which he takes action.

For example, the liquidator may transfer the assets belonging to the estate to another Contracting State. This power may be subject to rules limiting the free movement of goods. Thus, if an asset is part of the historical and cultural heritage of a Contracting State, it may be subject to an export ban protected under Article 36 of the EC Treaty. This prohibition naturally also applies to the liquidator. With regard to this type of asset, he may not exercise his general power to transfer assets.

(c) With regards to procedures for the realization of assets, the liquidator shall comply with the law of the State where the assets are located. The law of the State of the opening shall establish the extent of the powers of the liquidator and the manners in which they may be exercised. Only that law can determine, for example, whether the sale of immovable property can be private (person-to-person) or if sale by public auction is necessary. However, once the form of sale has been decided according to that law, the procedures by which the assets are realized must be in accordance with the provisions of national law. In our example, if the law of the State of the opening requires a sale by public auction, the procedure of carrying out the sale in the State where the immovable property is situated shall be determined by the law of the latter State.

165. The liquidator in territorial proceedings is subject to a supplementary restriction. His powers of administration and disposal have the same scope as the proceedings from which they derive, ie they are territorial. However, assets subject to these proceedings may have been removed to other Contracting States after the opening of proceedings.

In this case, Article 18(2) clearly states that the liquidator may apply to these other Contracting States and request from their courts the return of the asset or may insist on such transfer for any other purpose useful to the local proceedings. He may also bring any action to set aside which is in the interest of the creditors (see point 224).

166. The Convention contains no rule regarding opposition to the exercise of powers by the liquidator. General rules shall therefore be applicable.

Consequently, the authorities of the State in which the powers are intended to be exercised shall have jurisdiction to take a decision if the grounds for opposition lie in the non-recognition, in accordance with the Convention, of the proceedings opened in another Contracting State or of the judgment appointing the liquidator. This is also the case where the grounds for opposition are a breach by the liquidator of the provisions of the Convention which govern the exercise of his powers in other States, for instance, Article 18(1) or Article 3(3).

If the opposition concerns the substance of the exercise of those powers, ie the justification for a measure which the liquidator intends to take, jurisdiction lies with the judicial authorities of the State of the opening of proceedings.

Article 19
Proof of the liquidator's appointment

167. This provision derives from Article 2 of the 1990 Istanbul Convention. In contrast to the draft Community Convention of 1982, it was not thought necessary to establish a uniform model for the certificate attesting the appointment of the liquidator.

168. The proof of the liquidator's appointment may be established by a duly certified copy of the original decision, issued by a person authorized by the State in which the decision originated or by any other certificate issued by the competent court attesting the appointment.

169. The certified copy of the decision or the official certificate of the appointment shall require no legalization or other similar formality, such as the certificate ('apostille') provided for by the 1961 Hague Convention abolishing the requirement of legalization for foreign public documents.

A translation into the official language or languages of the Contracting State in which the liquidator intends to act may be required. This translation shall take into account the requirements established in this State regarding translations of official documents. For example, if we accept the parallel with the provisions of Article 48, second subparagraph, of the 1968 Brussels Convention the translation is certified by a person authorized for that purpose by one of the Contracting States, whether that of the opening of proceedings or that in which the liquidator intends to exercise his powers.

170. The Convention contains no rules regarding the means of proving the scope of the powers of the liquidator.

It seems reasonable that, in the case of doubt or opposition, these powers, based on the law of another Contracting State, are established by the person who invokes them. Proof may be by means of a certificate issued by the Court appointing the liquidator, which shall define his powers, or by any other means of evidence admitted by the law of the State where the liquidator intends to exercise his powers.

Article 20
Return and imputation

171. The Convention considers its geographical scope (the Community) to be a single economic area. The main proceedings shall therefore produce effects within the whole of the territory of the Contracting States. Also for this reason, where the Convention allows for the opening of secondary proceedings, the whole area should be taken as a reference for the distribution of dividends, making it compulsory to take into account the sum obtained in each set of proceedings by means of a sort of consolidated account of the dividends obtained on a European scale. The aim of this Article is to guarantee the equal treatment of all the creditors of a single debtor.

172. Rule regarding return (Article 20(1))

The rule on return is the consequence of the universality of the main proceedings, which encompass all the debtor's assets, wherever they are situated, and affect all the creditors. As a result of this principle of universality, it is evident that a creditor who, after the opening of proceedings, obtains total or partial satisfaction of his claim individually (by means of payment by the debtor or execution of assets situated in other States) breaches the principle of collective satisfaction on which the insolvency proceedings are based. Hence, the obligation to return 'what has been obtained'. The liquidator may demand either the return of the assets received or the equivalent in money.

173. The previous rule operates within the limits of Articles 5 and 7, which exclude from the scope of the main proceedings rights in rem of creditors and third parties in respect of the debtor's assets situated outside the State of the opening of proceedings at that time. As long as these Articles apply, a creditor who obtains satisfaction of claims guaranteed by rights in rem by realization of the security does not enrich himself to the detriment of the estate and does not breach the principle of collective satisfaction (see comment on Article 5).

174. Rule regarding imputation (Article 20(2))

The Convention allows for the opening of parallel insolvency proceedings (see Article 3). Thus, when a creditor obtains satisfaction in insolvency proceedings opened in another Contracting State, he does not breach a law, but simply exercises a right (see Article 32(1)).

For this reason, Article 20(2) allows a creditor to keep what he has obtained in the first proceedings in which distribution took place. Nevertheless, in order to guarantee the equality of all creditors on a Community level, they may not, once this payment has been received, participate in other distributions until all creditors of the same ranking have obtained equal satisfaction.

175. The method of calculation is relatively simple. It comprises four rules:

1. Nobody may obtain more than 100% of his claims.

2. The total original amount of the claim (100% of its initial value) shall be taken into account, and not the remaining amount (satisfaction obtained in other proceedings is not deducted).

If claims were not taken into account in each of the proceedings at 100% of their amount (without deducting the part satisfied in other proceedings), it would not be possible to guarantee the equal treatment of creditors participating in several proceedings.

The only exception to the second rule is that of claims secured by rights in rem or through a set-off, the secured parts of which are not affected by insolvency proceedings (see Articles 5, 6 and 7). The Convention lays down no rule on whether the amount of the original claim or the remaining claim shall be taken into account; this question is left to the rules of the law of the State of the opening (see Article 4(2)(i)).

3. A claim is not taken into account in the distribution until such time as the creditors with the same ranking have obtained an equal percentage of satisfaction in these proceedings as that obtained by its holder in the first proceedings.

For example, if creditor X in proceedings opened in a Contracting State F1 has obtained 5% on an ordinary unsecured claim with an amount of 75, he cannot take part in the distribution in the proceedings opened in another Contracting State F2 (where he has also lodged his claim) until the ordinary unsecured creditors have obtained 5%. If in F2 the percentage of satisfaction attains 8% for ordinary unsecured creditors, creditor X may participate in it only with regard to the difference, ie up to 3% (8% minus 5% already obtained in F1 = 3%). This 3% shall apply to the whole claim (to the 100% of its initial amount of 75), in accordance with the second rule mentioned above.

Conversely, if the first proceedings are in F2 where the creditors obtain a percentage of satisfaction of 8%, despite also having lodged their claims in the proceedings opened in F1, they shall not participate in the distribution in F1, since the ordinary unsecured creditors there obtain only 5%, whereas they have already obtained 8% in F2.

Thus, regardless of which proceedings take place first, the creditors of both F1 and F2 who have lodged their claims in both proceedings shall obtain an equal final dividend (8% of the total claim).

4. The ranking or category of each claim is determined for each of the proceedings by the law of the State of the opening (Article 4(2)(i)). Since different insolvency laws apply to the different proceedings (each is governed by its own national law), the ranking of the same claim lodged in two different proceedings may not be the same in both. The only ranking or category which is taken into account in order to apply Article 20(2) is that given to the claim by the law governing proceedings in which distribution is to be effected.

Hence, for the calculation of the dividend, only the percentage of satisfaction obtained in other proceedings, and not the rank or category which the claim enjoyed in those other proceedings, is taken into account. Thus in our example, if the claim of creditor X is an ordinary unsecured claim in F1 but it benefits from a preference in F2, it follows that it has already obtained 5% in F1, no matter what the ranking was; this percentage is, for the purposes of calculation, compared to the dividend which the rules in force in F2 apply to preferential claims. If these claims obtain a dividend of 25% in F2, creditor X shall benefit from a dividend of 20% in F2 (25% minus 5% already obtained in F1 = 20%).

176. In practice, if a number of claims have been lodged both in the insolvency proceedings opened in F1 and F2, the liquidator in the F2 proceedings may calculate the distribution in F2 by stages, for each rank. In our example, up to 5% (dividend obtained in F1) he will not take into account the claims already satisfied in F1. Once the claims lodged only in F2 have attained 5%, if there are remaining assets to be distributed he will make a further calculation introducing also the claims already satisfied in F1 together with the claims lodged only in F2, in order to determine the new dividend.

Article 21
Publication

177. The publication of the opening of insolvency proceedings in another Contracting State is not a precondition for the recognition of those proceedings or for the recognition and exercise of the powers of the liquidator appointed in such proceedings.

The principal aim of publication is to contribute to the security of trade in the States where the debtor has assets or where he conducts business, by drawing his creditors' and future contracting parties' attention to the legal situation of the debtor.

178. Although recognition is not dependent on publication of the opening of the proceedings, publication may produce significant legal effects in relation to the evaluation of the behaviour of the persons concerned, within the framework of either the Convention (for example Article 24) or the national law to be applied.

179. The initiative to publish in other States is vested in the liquidator. For this purpose, he will have to evaluate all the circumstances (eg individual creditors cannot be identified) and the need for trade security (eg an establishment remains in operation in another State where future creditors should be informed).

This rule shall not prevent the courts of the State of the opening from ordering publication if its national insolvency law provides for this.

180. Any Contracting State in which the debtor has an establishment may provide for mandatory publication of the opening of insolvency proceedings. In no cases may this mandatory publication constitute a precondition for recognition (this would breach the rules of the Convention).

Article 21(2) explicitly states that in the case of mandatory publication, the latter must be arranged by the liquidator or the authority designated by the State of the opening of proceedings. Where necessary, the national law of the State which provides for such mandatory publication will determine the liquidator's liability when the latter has not taken the necessary measures to arrange publication.

181. The Convention establishes no uniform mechanism for publication but stipulates that it should be in accordance with the arrangements laid down by the law of the State in which it is to take place. On the other hand, the Convention does determine what information is to be published: the basic content of the judgment opening proceedings and, where necessary (for example, if there are a number of appointments), the basic content of the decision appointing the liquidator. In both cases, it should always indicate the identity of the liquidator appointed and specify the jurisdiction rule applied (Article 3(1) or Article 3(2)). This does not exclude other items of information which may be of interest to third parties or creditors (deadlines for lodging claims, etc).

In the case of publication as referred to in Article 21(2), the compulsory information required may not go beyond the information mentioned in paragraph 1 of that Article.

Article 22
Registration in a public register

182. Registration in a public register is not a precondition for recognition of insolvency proceedings opened in another Contracting State or for recognition of the powers conferred on the liquidator appointed thereunder. Nevertheless, the registers play a significant role for the trade security. The trust of third parties acting in good faith on the basis of information contained in these registers is protected in all Member States. For this reason, but also to guarantee the full effectiveness of the insolvency proceedings, the Convention empowers the liquidator to request the registration of the judgment opening insolvency proceedings in another Contracting State.

This rule shall not prevent the courts of the State of the opening from ordering the liquidator to register in other States, if its national insolvency law so provides.

The form and content of the registration shall be subject to the law of the Contracting State under the authority of which the register is kept. Such Contracting State should allow registration of proceedings in another Contracting State under conditions similar to those applied for the registration of national proceedings.

183. The Contracting States cannot demand an exequatur as a precondition for access to the registration of a judgment handed down in another Contracting State. Recognition shall be automatic.

Each State may, however, decide if the authority responsible for the register at the time of registration should, incidentally, check whether the decision is recognizable under the Convention.

184. The registration requirement relates to the main proceedings, since by definition the territorial proceedings cannot affect assets situated outside the State of the opening of proceedings.

185. The Contracting States may request mandatory registration in their registers (when the debtor is a holder of registered assets, for example). In no case may such mandatory publication be a precondition for recognition.

Where necessary, the national law of the State of registration will determine the liquidator's liability when the latter has not taken the necessary measures to ensure such registration.

Article 23
Costs

186. The Convention considers the expenditure arising from the publication and registration measures laid down in Articles 21 and 22 as costs incurred in the proceedings. The proposal by some delegations to limit this definition to the expenditure arising from action by the liquidator (Article 21(1) and Article 22(1)) and not to that arising from the mandatory publication or registration requested by a State different from the State of the opening and conduct of proceedings was not approved.

Article 24
Honouring of an obligation to a debtor

187. The automatic recognition of insolvency proceedings opened in another Contracting State, and the lack of any general system of prior publication, guarantee the immediate effectiveness of the judgment opening proceedings in all the Contracting States.

Nevertheless, in some cases, a number of those persons may be unaware of the opening of proceedings and may act in good faith in contradiction with these new circumstances. In this connection, Article 24 provides for a solution to the problem where an obligation is honoured in good faith for the benefit of a debtor, when it should have been honoured for the benefit of the liquidator in the proceedings in another Contracting State. This Article establishes that the person honouring the obligation shall be deemed to have discharged it if he was unaware of the opening of proceedings.

Article 24 is therefore based on a double presumption. If the obligation is honoured before the publication provided for in Article 21 has occurred in the State concerned (eg the State in which the person honouring the obligation is established or the State in which the obligation is honoured, as the case may be), there shall be a presumption of ignorance. If the obligation is honoured after publication has taken place, there shall be a presumption of awareness. These two presumptions are rebuttable, but under each of them the burden of proof shifts from one party to the other. So, for instance, once publication has taken place, it shall be for the debtor honouring the obligation in question to provide evidence rebutting the presumptions.

188. In Article 24(1) the place where an obligation is honoured means the place where the obligation has been performed in fact by the debtor of the obligation.

Article 25
Recognition and enforceability of other judgments

189. Introduction

The Convention refers firstly to the recognition of the opening of insolvency proceedings (Article 16) and to its effects (Articles 17 to 24).

The recognition of judgments relating to the conduct and closure of the insolvency proceedings and of judgments adopted in the framework of those proceedings is dealt with generally in Article 25. This provision also regulates the enforcement of all judgments, including, where necessary, the judgment opening proceedings, as regards all its consequences except the opening itself (see point 143).

190. To enforce is to put into execution. Enforcement implies the exercise of the State's coercive power to ensure compliance.

The principle of exclusive territorial sovereignty precludes the direct exercise of a State's power within the territory of other States. By virtue of this principle, direct application of coercive powers is limited to the authorities of the State where the assets or persons to which this action relates are situated. The Convention has not altered this state of affairs.

As a consequence, the enforcement of judgments of other Contracting States shall depend on prior authorization by the authorities of the State in which it must be carried out. This authorization is obtained by means of a special procedure: the procedure called exequatur.

The exequatur does not deal with the enforcement itself, but with the prior authorization needed for enforcement. Enforcement in the strict sense shall be carried out by the competent national authorities by means of the procedures established by the national law for the enforcement of equivalent domestic judgments. The Convention on insolvency proceedings, like the 1968 Brussels Convention, deals only with the first aspect (prior authorization and its conditions).

If the conditions laid down by the Convention are fulfilled, the authorities of the requested State shall be obliged to grant this authorization, pursuant to the Convention. National law thereafter determines the methods by which the judgment of another Contracting State is enforced by the national authorities. The usual methods of coercive enforcement of the national law will be used, adapted, where necessary, to guarantee the 'effet utile' of the Convention, ie to render effective in other States the specific decision taken by the foreign court.

191. Judgments relating to insolvency proceedings (Article 25(1), first subparagraph)

Judgments relating to the conduct and closure of insolvency proceedings present no specific problem of characterization.

The recognition of these judgments operates in the same way and with the same effects as the judgment opening proceedings which we have already mentioned (see Articles 16 and 17).

The Convention subjects any composition approved by the competent court of the State of the opening to the same system of recognition.

192. As regards the enforcement of all these judgments and, where necessary, of the composition, various possibilities were examined at the negotiations. The idea finally adopted was to use the same system as for the enforcement of judgments in civil and commercial matters provided for by the 1968 Brussels Convention. This explains the reference in Article 25(1) to the rules on enforcement in the 1968 Brussels Convention.

Thus, the simplified system of exequatur provided for in that Convention will be used for the enforcement of judgments adopted in the framework of insolvency proceedings (see Articles 31 to 51 of the 1968 Brussels Convention; for a thorough analysis of that system see also the reports on that Convention).

As under the 1968 Brussels Convention (see Article 31 thereof), in order for enforcement to take effect in the State requested, the judgment should be already enforceable in the State in which it was given (State of origin) and that effect should not have been suspended there. A judgment cannot produce more effects in other States than in the State of origin.

However, grounds for rejection of the exequatur are taken not from the 1968 Brussels Convention (Article 34(2) of the 1968 Brussels Convention is expressly excluded), but from the Convention on insolvency proceedings (see Article 26).

193. It is important to stress that Article 25(3) excludes from the obligation to recognize and enforce those judgments handed down in another Contracting State which might result in a limitation of the personal freedom or postal secrecy of the insolvent debtor or of any other person who may be affected by the limitations derived from the insolvency proceedings.

This is an area which relates directly to fundamental rights and the Contracting States preferred to retain their freedom as to the recognition and enforcement of such decisions, regardless of the Convention on insolvency proceedings. Each State will decide autonomously on the treatment of such decisions when they originate in another Contracting State.

194. Judgments arising from insolvency proceedings (Article 25(1), second subparagraph)

The Convention also governs the recognition and enforcement of judgments arising from insolvency proceedings. These are judgments directly deriving from bankruptcy law which have a direct link to the insolvency proceedings but do not relate to the opening, conduct and closure of insolvency proceedings.

Recognition and enforcement of such judgments are always governed by the Convention whether they are adopted by the bankruptcy court or by an ordinary court, as could be the case under national law.

195. The raison d'être of this provision derives from the Judgment of the Court of Justice of 22 February 1979 (Case 133/78 *Gourdain v Nadler* [1979] ECR 733). Called upon to interpret Article 1(2) of the 1968 Brussels Convention (which excludes the field of bankruptcy, winding-up of insolvent companies, compositions and analogous proceedings from its scope), the Court of Justice

adopted a criterion to define bankruptcy based on the nature of the action undertaken. According to this criterion, actions the direct legal basis of which is the insolvency law and which are closely linked with the insolvency proceedings are not covered by the 1968 Brussels Convention. The character of the judicial body which decides on this action is of no importance.

In accordance with this decision of the Court of Justice, such actions should be subject to the Convention on insolvency proceedings or, otherwise, in the overall Convention rules there might be unjustifiable gaps between the general Convention and the specific Convention. For this reason, Article 25(1), second subparagraph, of the Convention on insolvency proceedings expressly adopts the same criterion of delimitation.

196. In order for the Convention on insolvency proceedings to apply it is necessary that the action undertaken directly derives from insolvency law and be closely connected with the insolvency proceedings.

Such is the case of actions which are based on (and not only affected by) insolvency law and are only possible during the insolvency proceedings or in direct relation with them. It includes actions to set aside acts detrimental to the general body of creditors (see Article 13); actions on the personal liability of directors based upon insolvency law, ie the 'action en combement pour insuffisance d'actif' vis-à-vis the managers of the company provided by the French Law, which the Court of Justice of the European Communities considered as a bankruptcy action in its Judgment of 22 February 1979, Case 133/78; actions relating to the admission or the ranking of a claim; disputes between the liquidator and the debtor on whether an asset belongs to the bankrupt's estate, etc.

However, actions deriving from law other than that relating to insolvency should not be included, even though they may be affected by the opening of proceedings (actively or passively). Such is the case of actions on the existence or the validity under general law of a claim (eg a contract) or relating to its amount; actions to recover another's property the holder of which is the debtor; and, in general, actions that the debtor could have undertaken even without the opening of insolvency proceedings.

197. The purpose of Article 25(2) is to avoid gaps between the Convention on insolvency proceedings and the 1968 Brussels Convention. The exclusion of insolvency proceedings as provided for in Article 1(2) of the 1968 Brussels Convention should be interpreted in accordance with the definition of insolvency proceedings given by the Convention on insolvency proceedings and the criteria incorporated in Article 25 thereof.

198. Preservation measures (Article 25(1), third subparagraph)

The same system of recognition and enforcement shall apply to preservation measures ordered by a court having jurisdiction under Article 3(1) after the request for the opening of insolvency proceedings.

Article 25 covers preservation measures adopted both before and after the opening of insolvency proceedings, Article 25(1) third subparagraph ensures that from the moment of the request of the opening of insolvency proceedings covered by the Convention, all preservation measures necessary to protect the future effectiveness of those proceedings fall under the system of this Convention.

199. The reason for this rule lies in the case law of the Court of Justice of the European Communities. According to the judgment of 27 March 1979 (Case 143/78 *De Cavel v De Cavel* [1979] ECR 1055), provisional orders and protective measures shall be included in the scope of the 1968 Brussels Convention, not by virtue of 'their own nature' but of 'the nature of the rights which they serve to protect'. Since insolvency proceedings are expressly excluded from the scope of the 1968 Brussels Convention (Article 1 subparagraph 2), that Convention cannot apply to measures adopted prior to the opening of insolvency proceedings to guarantee its future effectiveness. In view of the practical significance of preservation measures in insolvency matters it seemed logical to establish a rule expressly including those measures in the scope of the Convention.

200. The resulting system for preservation measures is similar to the one laid down by the 1968 Brussels Convention for preservation measures in civil and commercial matters (see, however, point 207). This solution is of immediate practical importance. There are many examples of preservation measures that should have extraterritorial scope and cover the whole Community (eg after the request for the opening of proceedings and with sufficient grounds, attempted fraudulent concealment of

assets, the judge who has jurisdiction under Article 3(1) issues a provisional injunction prohibiting the disposal of assets by the debtor).

201. To understand the recognition and enforcement system for preservation measures, it must be taken into account that this Convention (as well as the 1968 Brussels Convention) governs both jurisdiction for adopting binding judgments (which is attributed to the courts of the State where the centre of the debtor's main interests is situated (F1)) and the recognition and enforcement of such judgments in other Contracting States.

The court having jurisdiction under Article 3(1) also has jurisdiction to decide, for example, the seizure of the debtor's assets, even though they are situated abroad, or any other preservation measure (see point 78). This decision shall be entitled, according to Article 25, to its recognition and enforcement in the Contracting State where the assets concerned are situated (F2).

Recognition and enforcement of that decision always fall under the exclusive authority of the courts of the State where the measure is to be carried out (F2).

The courts in F2 will only verify that it is a decision covered by the Convention, that it emanates from the judge who claims jurisdiction under Article 3(1) and that the said measure does not breach public policy. It is not necessary, nor may it be requested, that the requirements laid down by the national law of F2 for the direct adoption of equivalent preservation measures be fulfilled.

Once the exequatur has been granted according to the Convention, the enforcement itself shall be done using the mechanisms of enforcement available under the domestic law of F2 (see point 190).

Article 26
Public policy

202. Defences against recognition and enforcement—Introduction

The Convention is based on the principle of Community trust and on the general legal presumption that the judgment handed down in another Contracting State is valid. For this reason it establishes that the only ground for opposing recognition is that the judgment handed down in another Contracting State is contrary to the public policy of the requested State. As a consequence:

1. The foreign judgment cannot be the subject of review as regards its substance (révision au fond). All questions regarding the substance must be discussed before the courts of the State of the opening of proceedings. In the State where recognition or enforcement is requested, the court may only decide whether the foreign judgment will have effects contrary to its public policy.

2. The Convention contains no provisions as to the verification of the international jurisdiction of the court of the State of origin (the court in the State of the opening of proceedings which has jurisdiction under Article 3 of the Convention). The courts of the requested States may not review the jurisdiction of the court of the State of origin, but only verify that the judgment emanates from a court of a Contracting State which claims jurisdiction under Article 3 of the Convention.

It is for the judicial authorities of the State in which the judgment originated (F1) to verify and control its international jurisdiction under the Convention. Any interested party seeking to challenge the jurisdiction of a national court must go to the State of the opening of proceedings to appeal against the decision asserting jurisdiction. The court may refer the interpretation of Article 3 (international jurisdiction) to the Court of Justice of the European Communities for a preliminary ruling (see Article 44).

203. Public Policy

The exception in Article 26 is the traditional exception that a judgment of a foreign court need not be recognized or enforced if such recognition or enforcement is contrary to the public policy in the Contracting State in which recognition or enforcement is sought.

204. The public policy exception ought to operate only in exceptional cases. For this reason Article 26 requires recognition or enforcement of the foreign judgment to be 'manifestly' contrary to public policy.

Furthermore, Article 26 does not require the compatibility with public policy of the rule or principle applied by the foreign court to be ascertained in the abstract, but that the result of recognition or enforcement of the judgment offends against public policy. Verification of conformity with public policy is directed towards the result of the recognition or enforcement, which means that all the circumstances peculiar to the case, including the connection with the requested State, are relevant.

205. Public policy derives from national law, and therefore the concept does not necessarily have a uniform content throughout the Community. Public policy is based on the fundamental principles of the law of the requested State. It involves, in particular, constitutionally protected rights and freedoms, and fundamental policies of the requested State, including those of the Community.

However, public policy cannot be used by Contracting States to unilaterally challenge the system of the Convention. Unreasonably wide interpretations of public policy are not covered by Article 26. (See also point 208.)

206. Public policy operates as a general clause as regards recognition and enforcement, covering fundamental principles of both substance and procedure.

Public policy may thus protect participants or persons concerned by the proceedings against failures to observe due process. Public policy does not involve a general control of the correctness of the procedure followed in another Contracting State, but rather of essential procedural guarantees such as the adequate opportunity to be heard and the rights of participation in the proceedings. Rights of participation and non-discrimination play a special role in the case of plans to reorganize businesses or compositions, in relation to creditors whose participation is hindered or who are the subject of unfounded discrimination.

The 1968 Brussels Convention deals separately, in Article 27, with the conditions concerning the serving of documents and the time necessary to prepare the defence, which form part of (but do not exhaust) the guarantees of the right of defence. However, in view of the special nature of insolvency proceedings, which are collective proceedings with special rules of individual notice (Article 40) and publicity (Article 21), and taking into account that the most important criterion of international jurisdiction is the State of the debtor's centre of main interests, which in principle will normally be that of the domicile or seat of the debtor, the group preferred to leave these conditions to case law.

However, if within the context of insolvency proceedings individual decisions are taken vis-à-vis a specific creditor, it seems reasonable to provide guarantees equivalent to those laid down in Article 27 of the 1968 Brussels Convention.

207. All the Contracting States provide for the possibility of taking, under certain urgent circumstances, ex parte preservation measures without an ex ante hearing of the party concerned. Naturally, for these measures to be constitutional, in most States they are subject to special requirements guaranteeing respect of due process (eg cumulatively, evidence of a good prima facie case, serious urgency, lodging of a guarantee by the applicant, immediate notification of the person concerned and the real possibility of challenging the adoption of the measures).

The Convention does not rule out the possibility of such measures being recognized 'by virtue of their nature'. Whether they are recognized (and, where appropriate, enforced) or not depends on whether or not they are compatible with the public policy of the requested State in which the judgment is to take effect (F2).

208. For the reasons explained in point 193, the Convention excludes judgments affecting personal freedom or postal secrecy from the obligation of recognition and enforcement, so that the States will not be obliged to resort to this exemption clause (Article 25(3)).

Conversely, as stated in point 148, in order to prevent the use of public policy to paralyse such recognition or enforcement, the Convention does not allow the use of the status of the debtor (eg trader/non-trader) to prevent recognition of a judgment handed down in another Contracting State (second subparagraph of Article 16(1)).

209. Public policy may result in total or partial rejection of the judgments handed down in another Contracting State.

210. The Portuguese Republic indicated in a unilateral statement made at the meeting of the Council of the European Union on 25 September 1995 that, under the conditions set out in Article 26, Portuguese public policy might be invoked to defend important local interests against the application

of Article 37, which concerns the conversion of territorial proceedings opened before the main proceedings, where those interests are not sufficiently taken into account in such conversion.

D. Chapter III: Secondary Insolvency Proceedings

Article 27
Opening of insolvency proceedings

211. The Convention permits the opening of local proceedings by the courts of the State where the debtor has an establishment (Article 3(2)).

After main proceedings have been opened in a Contracting State, those local proceedings can only be 'secondary' proceedings.

Secondary proceedings are governed by national law. The Convention, however, modifies the conditions established by the national law for the opening of insolvency proceedings in two aspects:

1. The national law requirement of insolvency of the debtor need not be met, in so far as the judgment opening main insolvency proceedings in another Contracting State is recognized.

2. The right to request the opening of insolvency proceedings is directly given by the Convention to the liquidator of the main proceedings.

The remaining conditions are those of the national law (see Articles 28 and 29(b)) without modifications, ie if local insolvency proceedings can be opened on account of the status of the debtor, persons empowered to request the opening, etc.

212. Let us explain those conditions: the judgment opening insolvency proceedings by the court of the State in which the centre of the debtor's main interests is situated has the specific effect of allowing territorial proceedings to be opened in the State where the debtor has an establishment, without the court of the State in which the establishment is situated having to examine the insolvency of the debtor.

213. The court where the opening of secondary proceedings is requested examines whether the proceedings opened in another Contracting State and by virtue of which the opening of territorial proceedings is requested are covered by Article 16: ie the judgment opens a set of insolvency proceedings as listed in Annexe A, it is delivered by a court which has declared that it has jurisdiction within the meaning of Article 3(1) and it is effective.

Moreover, the court examines its international jurisdiction for opening territorial proceedings, as well as its domestic jurisdiction, and, concerning those aspects not covered by the Convention, the conditions for opening proceedings provided for by national legislation.

214. The proceedings by virtue of which the opening of secondary proceedings is requested must be proceedings included in Annexe A to the Convention.

They must be proceedings based on the debtor's insolvency (see point 49(b), fourth and fifth subparagraphs for the problem posed by winding-up proceedings in Ireland and the United Kingdom).

215. The proceedings by virtue of which the opening of secondary proceedings is requested must be opened by a court of a Contracting State which has jurisdiction, as provided for in Article 3(1): such a court has verified that the centre of the debtor's main interests is situated in that State and it bases its jurisdiction on those grounds to open proceedings which may claim to be the main proceedings.

The court which is required to open secondary proceedings cannot verify the correctness of the appraisal of the first court, whose judgment benefits from the trust placed in judgments delivered by Community courts.

216. The court where the opening of secondary proceedings is requested also examines whether the foreign judgment is effective.

217. If the judgment opens an insolvency proceeding mentioned in Annexe A, acknowledges that it constitutes the opening of main proceedings and has begun to be effective, that judgment is recognized within the meaning of Article 16.

The requirement for opening secondary proceedings laid down by the Convention is thus met.

218. In consequence, the court where the opening of secondary proceedings is requested does not have to examine the debtor's insolvency.

219. Furthermore, the court requested to open secondary proceedings examines its jurisdiction within the meaning of Article 3(2).

The debtor must have an establishment as defined in Article 2(h) on the territory in question. If there is no establishment, no secondary proceedings will be opened.

In the latter case, the main proceedings will produce their full effects on the territory where the debtor does not have an establishment, but does have assets. Chapter II of the Convention comes into play and the liquidator in the main proceedings may exercise all his powers on that territory. Thus, for instance, as the mere existence of a credit balance in a bank account does not constitute an establishment, the liquidator in the main proceedings may, subject in particular to the rights in rem of third parties referred to in Article 5, order the transfer of such money to the State of the opening in order to distribute it amongst the creditors involved in the main proceedings.

220. In examining its international jurisdiction within the meaning of Article 3(2), the court appraises the facts to determine whether the debtor has an establishment in that territory. In fact, the court may be led to consider that the debtor's activities in that territory constitute more than a simple establishment and could have been considered as the centre of the debtor's main interests.

The principle of trust attached to decisions of courts within the Community does not allow those courts to call into question the appraisal of the court that has declared itself competent in accordance with Article 3(1) (see point 215).

A court which establishes that the judgment opening the main proceedings has the quality of a recognized judgment and that the debtor has a place of activity in its territory that can be considered to be an establishment will be led to open territorial secondary proceedings.

221. In accordance with Article 3(3), secondary insolvency proceedings opened after the main proceedings must be winding-up proceedings within the meaning of Article 2(c). Their purpose is to realize the debtor's assets. The proceedings are mentioned in Annexe B to the Convention.

The court cannot open insolvency proceedings the purpose of which is the reorganization of the debtor's business or of his financial situation.

The discussions on the Convention have finally resulted in the inclusion of both winding-up proceedings and reorganization proceedings in the main insolvency proceedings.

In the case of proven insolvency at the centre of the debtor's main interests, it is difficult to conceive, under certain legal systems in the Community, of an establishment dependent on the insolvent person being separately the subject of reorganization. Furthermore, coordination between the main proceedings and the secondary reorganization proceedings was regarded by most Contracting States as so complex technically as to be difficult to carry out.

In order to confer the widest possible scope on the Convention by recognizing not only winding-up proceedings—accepted from the beginning of discussion as proceedings to be recognized—but also reorganization proceedings, it was decided to allow only secondary winding-up proceedings.

This solution shows the dependency of the secondary proceedings vis-à-vis the main proceedings of a universal nature.

222. National legislation determines more specifically the court which has territorial jurisdiction.

It should be noted that the Convention deals with international jurisdiction but does not specify which court has jurisdiction among the courts of the Contracting State in which an establishment is situated.

States shall ensure that their legislation designates the court which has territorial jurisdiction to open secondary proceedings.

223. The court also applies its national law regarding the conditions for opening proceedings which are not the subject of a rule of the Convention (Article 4(2)).

National law determines the persons against whom insolvency proceedings may be brought (Article 4(2)(a)). Where, for example, national legislation does not permit insolvency proceedings against a person who does not have the capacity of a trader, or against a public undertaking, the possibility of secondary proceedings is excluded.

224. In accordance with Article 3(2), secondary proceedings only produce effects with regard to the debtor's assets situated in the territory of the Contracting State where the establishment is situated.

The secondary liquidator has, however, the right to act outside his territory in order to recover an asset moved out of that State after the opening of the secondary proceedings or in fraud against the creditors of those proceedings (Article 18(2)). He is also allowed to bring actions in other States for the voidness, voidability or unenforceability of detrimental legal acts (Article 4(2)(m) and Article 13). The purpose of these actions outside the territory is, in fact, the return of assets which were legally situated in the territory of the proceedings at the time of the opening or which, without fraud, would have been situated in the territory of the proceedings at the time of the opening.

The action of the secondary liquidator in the matter of the return of assets which are actually situated abroad but which should normally be included in the secondary proceedings is to be assessed on the basis of the law of the secondary proceedings, pursuant in particular to Article 4(2)(m), subject to Article 13 (see points 91(l) and 135 to 139).

Article 28
Applicable law

225. This Article expressly stipulates that, save as otherwise provided by the Convention, the law of the State in which secondary proceedings are opened shall apply to those proceedings.

In fact, this reiterates Article 4, which is interpreted as meaning that the law applicable to the main proceedings is the law of the State where the main proceedings are opened, and the law applicable to the secondary proceedings is the law of the State of the opening of the secondary proceedings.

Article 29
Right to request the opening of proceedings

226. The Convention authorizes the liquidator in the main proceedings to request the opening of secondary proceedings. The temporary administrator who, according to national law, may be appointed after the request of the opening of the main insolvency proceedings but before the opening itself, is not covered by Article 29(a) (see point 262).

The liquidator in secondary proceedings has, however, no right derived from the Convention to request the opening of other secondary proceedings.

This rule states the relationship of dependence of the secondary proceedings upon the main proceedings.

227. Furthermore, the persons and authorities empowered by national law to request the opening of the insolvency proceedings referred to in Annexe B are also entitled to request the opening of secondary proceedings.

The right of these persons and therefore the right of the creditors to bring about proceedings is not limited by the requirement of a specific interest.

The provision envisaged in the discussions, whereby only the creditors who would benefit from a more favourable legal status in the secondary proceedings than in the main proceedings (for example, a more favourable ranking) could request the opening of secondary proceedings, has been deleted.

On the other hand, Article 29(b) confers the right to have proceedings opened on any person, without distinction.

It should be noted that the right to request the opening of territorial proceedings before the opening of the main proceedings is limited to those proceedings referred to in Article 3(4)(b) (see point 85).

Article 30
Advance payment of costs and expenses

228. Various legislations rule out the possibility of insolvency proceedings where the debtor's assets are insufficient to cover in whole or in part the costs and expenses of the proceedings.

The Convention takes these legislations into account.

The provision in Article 30 is understood to mean that where national law does not require sufficient assets in order to open insolvency proceedings, it cannot introduce such a requirement for secondary proceedings only.

Should national law rule out insolvency proceedings where assets are insufficient, the Convention upholds this law and allows the court to require from the applicant, including the liquidator, an advance payment of costs, or an appropriate security. The terms 'may require' do not confer a power on the court but mean that national legislation continues to apply.

Article 31
Duty to cooperate and communicate information

229. The main proceedings and the secondary proceedings are interdependent proceedings which concern a debtor with several centres of activity and assets spread over several territories.

The debtor's creditors participate, or may have an interest in participating, in several proceedings. Cooperation and information between the liquidators is thus necessary to ensure the smooth course of operations in the various proceedings.

230. The exchange of information between the liquidators concerns in particular:

* the assets,
* the actions planned or under way in order to recover assets: actions to obtain payment or actions for set aside,
* possibilities for liquidating assets,
* claims lodged,
* verification of claims and disputes concerning them,
* the ranking of creditors,
* planned reorganization measures,
* proposed compositions,
* plans for the allocation of dividends,
* the progress of operations in the proceedings.

231. The duty to communicate information may be limited by national legislation on data exchange, eg by legislation relating to the protection of computerized personal data.

232. The duty of the liquidators to exchange information is complemented by the obligation to cooperate with each other. The liquidators have a duty to act in concert with a view to the development of proceedings and their coordination, and to facilitate their respective work.

233. Article 31(3) expressly mentions a specific obligation of information and cooperation that affects the liquidator in the secondary proceedings, on the grounds of primacy of the main proceedings over the secondary proceedings. The liquidator in the secondary proceedings must give the liquidator in the main proceedings the opportunity to submit proposals on the realization or use of the assets in the secondary proceedings. The secondary liquidator must therefore inform the main liquidator of any use or realization of these assets.

This obligation may enable the main liquidator, for example, to prevent the sale of assets involved in the secondary proceedings, the preservation of which may be deemed advisable from the viewpoint of the reorganization of the business at the centre of main interests and to request a stay of the liquidation through the application of Article 33.

The obligation considered in Article 31(3) refers to important assets or decisions (such as continuation or cessation of the activities of the establishment) in the secondary proceedings. It should not be interpreted in such a broad way as in practice to paralyse the work of the liquidator in the secondary proceedings.

234. Where appropriate, the applicable national law will determine the liquidator's liability when the latter has not respected the duties arising from Article 31.

Article 32
Exercise of creditors' rights

235. Pursuant to Article 4(2)(h), the law of the State of the opening of the proceedings determines the rules governing the lodging of claims.

However, national law concerning the creditors entitled to lodge claims is replaced by the provision in Article 32(1), which entitles any creditor to lodge his claim in the main proceedings and in any secondary proceedings.

The creditor is entitled to lodge claims in the proceedings of his choice, even in several proceedings.

The right to lodge claims of creditors with their domicile, habitual residence, or registered office in a Contracting State other than the State of the opening of the proceedings is restated in Article 39. For comments on the scope of that Article, see points 265–270.

236. Article 32(2) establishes the liquidator's right to lodge in other proceedings claims which have already been lodged in his proceedings. The Convention modifies national legislation concerning the lodging of claims, simply by adding a right for the liquidator to lodge claims (see point 237).

Both the liquidator in the main proceedings and each liquidator in secondary proceedings may lodge claims in the other proceedings.

The aim of this provision is to facilitate the exercise of the rights of those creditors who lodge claims in certain proceedings permitting their claims to be also lodged by the liquidator in other proceedings, and finally, to permit the liquidators to reinforce their influence in other proceedings.

237. The rights of the creditors are preserved in so far as they may oppose the lodging of their claims in other proceedings by the liquidator or withdraw any previous lodgement in other proceedings.

The Convention allows creditors the right to oppose a claim lodged in other proceedings by the liquidator.

On the other hand, the right to withdraw a claim lodged by the liquidator is governed by the law applicable to the proceedings in which the claim has been presented: creditors' rights are subject to the law of the State in which the proceedings are opened and it is a question of determining the rights of creditors in the proceedings in which the claim has been presented.

In so far as the liquidator's claim is lodged on behalf of the creditor, the issue of withdrawal is not a new one, and national laws establish the creditor's right to withdraw the claim lodged.

238. The lodging of a claim by the liquidator has the same effects as the lodging of a claim by the creditor: the liquidator acts on behalf of the creditor and in his stead. The Convention mentions this right of the liquidator to lodge claims.

However, national rules concerning the period for lodging, the consequences of delayed lodging, the admissibility and well-foundedness of the lodging and the expenses linked to the verification of the claims remain unchanged (see point 267).

239. Under Article 32(2), liquidators should lodge in other proceedings claims which have already been lodged in their own proceedings. The obligation to lodge such claims exists only in so far as it is in the general interests of all the creditors or of a class of creditors.

It is effective subject to the individual creditor's right to oppose the lodging of the claim.

The creditor may have various reasons for opposing the lodging of his claim in proceedings other than those he has selected. For example, as the liquidator's claim is lodged on his behalf, and as national law determines the rules for the lodging and verification of claims, including the costs, the creditor may run the risk in the other proceedings of incurring costs which he is not willing to bear.

Appraisal of the specific interest in lodging claims rests with the creditor, who must defend his interests himself. In a way, he has already made a choice when lodging his claim in a certain State.

Specific appraisal of the interest involves an examination in accordance with the law applicable to the claim and, as regards the status of the claim, in accordance with the legislation of the State in which the lodging is envisaged (Article 4(2)(h)).

This specific appraisal for each claim would involve a difficult task for the liquidator, and would be a costly and lengthy procedure.

However, the aim of the Article is different. Under Article 32(2) the liquidator's task to lodge exists only when it is clearly in the general interest of all creditors in his proceedings or of a class of them.

For example, if the liquidator finds that the assets to be distributed in other proceedings are so significant that even the ordinary unsecured creditors in his proceedings may receive a dividend, in competition with the ordinary unsecured creditors lodging claims in the other proceedings, the lodging of the claim may be useful and will take place.

Moreover, he will also lodge a claim where a creditor, rather than lodging a claim himself, has informed the liquidator of the interest of the lodging of his claim.

He will obviously not lodge a claim if the lodgement would be irrevocably delayed and therefore not appropriate.

The liquidator's task, thus delimited, may improve the situation of the creditors, without complicating the proceedings to the detriment of creditors.

240. Article 32(3) empowers any liquidator to participate in other proceedings. The aim of the provision is to better ensure the presence of creditors and the expression of their interests through the liquidator.

In order to resolve the frequent absence of creditors, the Convention allows the liquidator to attend creditors' meetings.

The text stipulates that the liquidator shall participate in other proceedings 'on the same basis as a creditor'. Obviously, the liquidator has the right to express his opinion in the course of the proceedings, and more specifically at the meeting of creditors involved in the other proceedings. However, the Convention does not establish the specific content of the liquidator's right to participate and does not determine how the liquidator shall exercise the rights of the creditors in his proceedings.

It should be noted that the provisions permitting the liquidator who lodges claims already lodged in the other proceedings to exercise the voting right deriving from a claim lodged, and the provisions concerning the simultaneous exercise by several liquidators of the voting right arising from a claim, were rejected in the course of negotiations.

Participation by the liquidator may be regulated by national law.

Article 33
Stay of liquidation

241. At the request of the liquidator in the main proceedings, the process of liquidation in the secondary proceedings may be stayed in whole or in part.

This provision establishes the primacy of the main proceedings, but it equally takes into account the interests of the creditors in the secondary proceedings.

242. The liquidator in the main proceedings submits a request for the stay of liquidation in the secondary proceedings.

The court may not refuse the stay except if it is manifestly not in the interests of the creditors in the main proceedings.

The grounds for request of a stay may be appraised only in relation to the interests of the creditors in the main proceedings.

243. The interests of the creditors in the main proceedings in the stay of liquidation that the court takes into consideration can assume different aspects. For example, the preservation of the estate situated in the State of the secondary proceedings may be useful with a view to selling the main business or the secondary establishment to a purchaser or with a view to a composition. The safeguarding of some of the elements of the assets, useful within a reorganization, or with a view to a sale 'en masse' together with some of the assets involved in the main proceedings may justify a partial stay on the liquidation.

244. The court may take into account the interests of all the creditors in the secondary proceedings, as well as those of certain groups of creditors, imposing on the liquidator in the main proceedings a guarantee which it determines as appropriate, before ordering the stay.

245. The stay is limited to a maximum of three months. Once this period is over, it may be extended for another three months maximum each time. The number of successive extensions is not limited.

The liquidation process which is restarted after a stay can be stayed again, and the stay can be renewed. The number of new stays is not limited.

246. The decision on a stay does not terminate the liquidation process. The effects brought about by the opening of proceedings pursuant to the law of the State of the opening of proceedings, eg as regards the exercise of individual actions, come into play. The liquidation process simply does not continue.

247. Where the stay no longer appears to be justified, the court terminates it. A stay may be terminated at any moment. The court may act:

- at the request of the liquidator in the main proceedings, or
- of its own motion, or
- at the request of the liquidator in the secondary proceedings, or
- at the request of a creditor.

If, in particular, the interests of the creditors in the main proceedings, or those of the creditors in the secondary proceedings no longer appear to justify the stay, it is to be terminated.

Consideration of the interests of the creditors in the secondary proceedings may lead by themselves to an end to the stay.

Article 34
Measures ending secondary insolvency proceedings

248. If the law of the State in which the secondary proceedings are opened allows insolvency proceedings to be closed by means of a rescue plan, a composition, or a comparable measure, all those stipulated by that law, may propose such a measure. In addition, the Convention empowers the liquidator in the main proceedings to propose it himself.

249. Under rescue plans, compositions or comparable measures, the creditors may accept a rescheduling of debts or waive some of their rights and the debtor may undertake to meet certain conditions. All of which may affect the interests in the main proceedings. For this reason, the Convention requires that, to become final, such a measure must obtain the consent of the liquidator in the main proceedings.

In adopting his decision, the liquidator may take into consideration all the interests of the creditors in the main proceedings, including the interests in reorganizing and continuing the main business.

Should, however, the liquidator in the main proceedings oppose the rescue plan, the composition or a comparable measure in the secondary proceedings, the Convention permits his agreement to be waived, and the secondary proceedings may be closed if the financial interests of the creditors in the main proceedings are not affected by the measure proposed.

The concept of financial interests is more restrictive than that of the interest of the creditors in the main proceedings, which may, for instance, justify a stay on secondary proceedings and which is examined in point 243.

The financial interests are estimated by evaluating the effects which the rescue plan or the composition has on the dividend to be paid to the creditors in the main proceedings. If those creditors could not reasonably have expected to receive more, after the transfer of any surplus of the assets remaining in the secondary proceedings (ex Article 35), in the absence of a rescue plan or a composition, their financial interests are not thereby affected.

250. The effects of secondary proceedings are confined to assets situated within the territory of the State in which they have been opened.

Consequently, a rescue plan or a composition restricting creditors' rights may apply only to the assets covered by the secondary proceedings and not to the debtor's other assets situated outside that State.

A composition confined in its effects to the assets involved in the proceedings shall be arrived at under the conditions laid down by the applicable law and, where appropriate, by a majority decision of the creditors. The rights of all the creditors, including the minority creditors who disagree with the measure, would be affected as regards the assets relevant to those proceedings.

A composition restricting creditors' rights may be reached in the secondary proceedings with effects on assets not covered by those proceedings, provided that it is agreed to by every creditor concerned by that measure, ie having an interest affected by the measure.

251. In the event of a stay of the process of liquidation in the secondary proceedings only a measure for a composition proposed by the liquidator in the main proceedings, or by the debtor with that liquidator's agreement, may be put to the vote or approved.

The stay is ordered at the request of the liquidator in the main proceedings on account of the interests of the creditors in those proceedings. During this period, the course of the main proceedings must not be disrupted by measures not agreed to by the liquidator.

Efforts to bring about the reorganization of the main business may have led to a stay. Article 34(3), prohibiting for the duration of the stay any composition not proposed by the liquidator in the main proceedings or by the debtor with his agreement, enables the interests of the creditors who brought about the stay to be taken into consideration (see point 243).

Article 35
Assets remaining in the secondary proceedings

252. If the assets in the secondary proceedings are sufficient to meet all claims allowed in them, any assets not distributed are to be transferred to the main proceedings.

The liquidator shall transfer the remaining assets to the liquidator in the main proceedings.

The transfer of any remaining assets to the main proceedings reflects the primary nature of those proceedings.

253. Assets will be distributed amongst all creditors whose claims are allowed in the secondary proceedings. The Convention allows creditors to lodge claims in any proceedings, so that even creditors with preferential claims in the main proceedings who might be ordinary unsecured creditors in the secondary proceedings will have an incentive to lodge claims in order, at least, to have their claims met in the same way and at the same time as other ordinary unsecured creditors.

The scale of the assets to be distributed will attract creditors. If the assets were such that any surplus remains after distribution amongst all creditors whose claims were admitted to these proceedings, only those claims not lodged or not admitted will remain unsatisfied and may be affected by the transfer of the remaining assets to the main proceedings.

Article 36
Subsequent opening of the main proceedings

254. Should a court in the State in which the centre of the debtor's main interests is located, open insolvency proceedings in accordance with Article 3(1), after independent territorial proceedings have been opened by a court in a State in which there is an establishment, pursuant to Article 3(2), the proceedings opened at the place of the centre of main interests will be the main proceedings, while the proceedings previously opened at the place of the establishment will have to be necessarily regarded as secondary proceedings.

255. In so far as the progress of the independent territorial proceedings, opened first, so permits, the rules for coordination between the main proceedings and the secondary proceedings as laid down in Articles 31 to 35 are to be followed.

Article 37
Conversion of earlier proceedings

256. Pursuant to Articles 3(3) and 27, secondary proceedings opened at the place in which an establishment is situated after the main proceedings, are to be winding-up proceedings within the meaning of Article 2(c), as listed in Annexe B.

Where, prior to the opening of main proceedings, independent territorial insolvency proceedings listed in Annexe A but not in Annexe B are opened, these latter proceedings may be converted into winding-up proceedings listed in Annexe B in the event of main proceedings being opened.

257. Under the Convention, the liquidator in the main proceedings shall be entitled to request that independent territorial reorganization proceedings, as mentioned in Annexe A, be converted into secondary winding-up proceedings.

The Convention does not prohibit the law of a Contracting State competent under Article 3(4) from allowing the liquidator in the main proceedings simply to request the closure of independent territorial reorganization proceedings under the conditions laid down by that law.

258. The court is not obliged to order conversion of the proceedings at the liquidator's request. It is necessary that the conversion proves to be in the interests of the creditors in the main proceedings.

This provision reflects the primary nature of the main proceedings. (See also point 210.)

259. If conversion is not requested by the liquidator or ordered by the court, territorial proceedings may continue as reorganization proceedings.

260. As a result of conversion, the proceedings will be conducted as secondary winding-up insolvency proceedings in accordance with Article 36.

261. Should any territorial proceedings opened prior to main proceedings in a Contracting State where an establishment is situated not be proceedings listed in Annexe A, they will not be covered by the Convention.

Main proceedings that are opened after the territorial proceedings have all the effects laid down in the Convention; the liquidator in the main proceedings is allowed to exercise his powers in other Contracting States and to request the opening of secondary proceedings. Consequently, these territorial proceedings may not continue. The national law must adopt the appropriate solution that would conform with the provisions of the Convention: that could for example be the closing of the territorial proceedings.

Article 38
Preservation measures

262. In order to avoid any change in the debtor's estate to the detriment of creditors from the date on which the opening of insolvency proceedings is requested to the date on which the judgment opening them is handed down, certain laws provide for the appointment of a temporary administrator.

Article 29 authorizes the liquidator in the main proceedings, but not such temporary administrator, to request the opening of secondary proceedings in any other Contracting State where the debtor has an establishment.

However, as a pre-opening stage of secondary insolvency proceedings, Article 38 allows the temporary administrator designated by a court competent to open main proceedings to request measures to secure and preserve the debtor's assets situated in any other Contracting State, provided for under the law of this State for the period between the request for the opening of insolvency proceedings and the opening itself. As a pre-opening stage of secondary proceedings, Article 38 presupposes the existence of an establishment of the debtor in that Contracting State (see Article 3(2)). For the same reason, the preservation measures available will be those which, under the national insolvency law of that State, correspond to winding-up proceedings.

Once appointed, the liquidator in the main proceedings will decide whether or not to request the opening of secondary proceedings.

If the request is made, the national courts of the State of the opening of secondary proceedings will decide on the continuation or modification of such measures. Until that moment or, also, if the opening of secondary proceedings is not finally requested, the preservation measures taken over the assets of the debtor situated in that State will be subordinated to the decisions taken by the court competent under Article 3(1), which benefit from the system of recognition and enforcement of the Convention, in similar terms as those already explained in point 78 of this report.

263. The position of a temporary administrator appointed after the request, but before the opening, of the main insolvency proceedings has to be seen in relation to the provisional task of preserving the assets which is entrusted to him. Such temporary administrator, whose task is more limited, does not correspond exactly with the definition in Article 2(b) of a liquidator in insolvency proceedings and is not necessarily listed in Annexe C.

Article 38 allows the temporary administrator to request in the State where the debtor has an establishment preservation measures of a more general character than those contemplated in point 78, fourth paragraph, of this report.

E. Chapter IV: Provision of Information for Creditors and Lodgement of their Claims

264. Chapter IV specifies the information which the court or the liquidator is required to provide to creditors and the rules for lodging claims.

These provisions are applicable both to main proceedings and to territorial (independent or secondary) insolvency proceedings.

Article 39
Right to lodge claims

265. Article 39 establishes a rule of substantive law, laying down the right of foreign creditors, ie of any creditor who has his habitual residence, domicile or registered office in another Contracting State, to lodge claims in writing in insolvency proceedings. This provision derogates, in the way specified below, from the application of national law, pursuant to Article 4(2)(h).

To clear up any doubts, it is specified that the right of any foreign creditor to lodge claims includes the tax authorities and social security authorities of other Contracting States.

It should be noted that Article 32, allows all creditors to participate in the main or secondary proceedings, as they choose, and even in several proceedings (see point 235).

266. Establishing the right of foreign creditors to lodge claims means that lodgement of their claims cannot be disallowed on the grounds that the creditor is situated in another Contracting State or that the claim is governed by the public law of another Contracting State.

267. However, under Article 4(2)(h), the national law of the State of the opening will govern the time limit for lodging claims, the effect of a late lodgement, and the admissibility and well-foundedness of the lodgement.

268. In addition, the national law of each proceedings determines the costs, to the charge of a creditor, attached to the claim and to the verification of the debts.

The prudent creditor will take into account the rules relevant to the costs, and will appreciate the interest that a claim presents. He will examine the ranking that the law of the proceedings accords to his claim and the importance of the assets that will be distributed.

269. The right to lodge claims for creditors situated in the State in which proceedings are opened is governed by national law.

Moreover, the Convention does not concern itself with the rights of creditors situated outside the Contracting States. The right of creditors from outside the Community to lodge claims is governed by national law.

270. The Convention gives creditors the right to lodge claims in writing, but it does not prevent national law from permitting claims to be lodged in any other more favourable form for creditors.

Article 40
Duty to inform creditors

271. The court having jurisdiction or the liquidator must, without delay, inform known creditors who have their habitual residence, domicile or registered office in the other Contracting States of the opening of insolvency proceedings and of the need to lodge their claims.

The Convention aims to improve the situation of intra-Community creditors situated outside the State in which proceedings are opened.

The liquidator's duty to inform creditors situated in the State in which proceedings are opened is governed by national law.

The Convention does not take into consideration creditors from outside the Community to whom the national law of the State in which the proceedings are opened applies.

272. Article 40(2) lays down the form and the content to be taken by the information provided for creditors.

The liquidator is required to send a notice to each creditor. This notice has to state the time limits for lodging claims, the legal consequences laid down for failing to meet those time limits and the person or body with whom claims must be lodged. It must specify whether creditors with preferential claims or claims secured in rem are required to lodge them.

The compulsory contents of the notice as laid down in the Convention are designed to protect foreign creditors; national laws may not reduce the contents of the notice. A national law may stipulate additional information in the interests of creditors.

Article 41
Content of the lodgement of a claim

273. Under Article 4(2)(h) the lodging of claims is subject to the law of the State of the opening of proceedings.

Article 41 constitutes, together with Articles 39 and 42(2), an exception to that rule in so far as it stipulates the content of claims lodged by creditors situated in another Contracting State.

The requirements set out in Article 41 are intended to identify the claim which is sought to be lodged. As this provision is meant to facilitate the exercise of intra-Community creditors' rights, national legislation may impose no additional conditions on the content of the lodgement of claims by foreign creditors protected by the Convention.

According to the Convention, a creditor may lodge his claim in writing (Article 39), supplying copies of supporting documents, if any, stating:

• the nature of the claim,
• the date on which it arose,
• its amount.

It must also specify any preference, security right or reservation of title alleged, as well as the assets covered by the guarantee invoked.

274. Under Article 4(2)(h), however, national law governs the verification and admission of claims and determines the procedure by which a creditor must establish his claim in order to have it admitted to the proceedings.

Article 42
Languages

275. The information for creditors regarding the opening of proceedings for their debtor's insolvency and the lodging of claims is to be given in an official language of the State of the opening of proceedings.

In order to help those creditors who do not understand the language of the State in which proceedings are opened, the information notice has to be headed 'Invitation to lodge a claim. Time limits to be observed'. This heading is to be given in all the official languages of the Community.

The heading, drawn up by the Secretariat of the Council of the European Union, will be published together with the Convention and the report.

276. Creditors from other Contracting States are allowed to lodge claims in an official language of the State in which they have their habitual residence, domicile or registered office.

However, their written statement must be headed 'Lodgement of claim' in a language of the State in which proceedings are opened.

In order to avoid delay in lodging claims and unnecessary lodgement costs, claims may be lodged in the creditor's language or, to be more exact, in the language of the State in which he lives or carries on his business.

277. Bearing in mind the scale of intra-Community trade and interpretation of economies, especially in border regions, as well as the understanding of one another's languages, a systematic requirement that claims be lodged in an official language of the State of the proceedings may run counter to the interests of creditors without being really necessary.

Use of the creditor's language is therefore the rule; a translation into the official language may be required in the course of the proceedings if this proves necessary.

F. Chapter V: Interpretation by the Court of Justice of the European Communities

278. The conferral of jurisdiction on the Court of Justice to give rulings on interpretation is not an innovation of the Convention on insolvency proceedings. The system of conferral follows the system established by Article 177 of the EC Treaty and adopted by the Protocols of 3 June 1971 concerning the interpretation by the Court of Justice of the 1968 Brussels Convention, and the Protocols of 19 December 1988 concerning the interpretation of the 1980 Rome Convention. Both Protocols were examined in the reports by Mr P. Jenard and Mr A. Tizziano (see OJ No C 189 of 28 July 1990 and No C 219 of 3 September 1990). We refer to those reports for further details.

Article 43
Jurisdiction of the Court of Justice

279. By virtue of this rule new powers of interpretation are conferred on the Court of Justice of the European Communities, supplementing its existing powers. In addition to this Convention and its Annexes, this jurisdiction also applies to future Conventions on accession by States which become Members of the European Union. Article 50 requires the new Members to follow the system of the Convention on insolvency proceedings and to make such adjustments and amendments as may be necessary. This explains the reference to future Conventions.

This jurisdiction covers the actual rules for the conferral of powers, so that it is for the Court of Justice to interpret the rules determining the scope of its jurisdiction or the procedures by which it may be exercised.

280. Jurisdiction in matters of interpretation means that the Court of Justice rules only on the interpretation of the text of the Convention and it is for the national court to apply the rules according to this interpretation and to give a judgment on the substance of the matter.

281. In contrast to the 1968 Brussels Convention and the 1980 Rome Convention, the conferral of jurisdiction to interpret is to be found in the text of the Convention and not in a separate Protocol. This emphasizes the close relationship between this Convention and the Community legal system and the significance of the uniform interpretation of those rules.

282. Both the Protocol on the Statute of the Court of Justice and the Rules of Procedure of the Court of Justice shall apply.

283. The Convention provides for two procedural channels through which the Court of Justice can resolve any problem of interpretation. The first involves preliminary ruling proceedings, as laid down by Article 44 of the Convention following the model of Article 177 of the EC Treaty. The second, included in Article 45 of the Convention, could be termed 'proceedings in the interests of the law'.

Article 44
Preliminary ruling proceedings

284. These are proceedings whereby a national court before which a case is brought requests the Court of Justice of the European Communities to give a preliminary ruling on the interpretation of a provision of the Convention or its Annexes, the application of which in the case in point has raised questions which must be resolved in order for a decision to be given on the substance of the matter.

285. The Convention determines the national courts which make such a request to the Court of Justice. Only the expressly designated courts are duly empowered, ie the higher law courts (such as the Tribunal Supremo in Spain, the Cour de Cassation in France, etc) which are listed in Article 44(a), and other courts when acting as courts of appeal. In the second case it is not necessary for the court to be officially entitled a 'Court of Appeal'. However, it must be involved in hearing appeals against judgments of a lower court. The power to request a preliminary ruling on interpretation is not granted to the courts of first instance.

286. The question must be one raised in a case pending before the court which submits the request for interpretation. The Court of Justice therefore resolves the questions of interpretation concerning cases pending before a national court.

287. It must be a question on which the national court considers a decision on interpretation to be 'necessary' for the judgment, ie it must be a problem of interpretation on which the solution to the case

depends. If the different possibilities of interpretation lead to the same result, this requirement would not be fulfilled. The national court must assess in each individual case whether or not this need exists.

288. National courts have the power to submit questions of interpretation of their own motion to the Court of Justice. A request by a party is not necessary. If such a request is made the national court is not obliged to refer to the Court of Justice.

289. This Convention does not oblige national courts to submit questions of interpretation to the Court of Justice but it simply allows them to make such requests if all the abovementioned requirements are fulfilled.

The need for speed in the conduct of insolvency proceedings explains the choice of a flexible formula which allows the national courts to decide on whether a preliminary ruling is appropriate. The Convention does not impose any criteria.

The national court may take into account the estimated time needed for a ruling by the Court of Justice, the general significance of the question for the proceedings, the formal request of the parties directly affected (as we know, this does not bind the national court), etc.

290. The Convention does not mention a possible suspensive effect of the preliminary ruling on the insolvency proceedings until such time as the Court of Justice settles the problem of interpretation.

The question of the average time for obtaining preliminary rulings is a serious problem in the area of insolvency proceedings.

291. In order to solve the question of suspensive effect, several facts [sic] should be taken into account:

1. The jurisdiction of the Court of Justice derives directly from the powers conferred on it by the Convention on insolvency proceedings and its scope is defined by the latter.

2. This conferral of jurisdiction is aimed at better fulfilling the specific objectives of the Convention on insolvency proceedings. The advantages of uniformity of interpretation must be counterbalanced by the need for efficiency in insolvency proceedings.

3. Time is a crucial factor in insolvency proceedings. They are opened as a consequence of a financial crisis. Promptness of action is imperative in order to avoid a depreciation of existing assets. The suspension of the insolvency proceedings may even preclude the possibility of reorganization. For this reason, many national legislations exclude the suspensive effect of appeals to higher courts in the case of insolvency proceedings. In addition, the collective nature of insolvency proceedings implies that a partial problem should not necessarily alter the main course of the proceedings.

292. In this context, the Convention leaves it to the national law of the State of the opening of proceedings to determine whether preliminary ruling proceedings before the Court of Justice should have suspensive effect. As there is no formal obligation to submit the question of interpretation to the Court of Justice, the most appropriate solution seems to be to confer on the national court the power to decide on whether or not it is necessary to interrupt the insolvency proceedings.

Article 45
Proceedings brought by a competent authority

293. These proceedings can be described as proceedings brought 'in the interests of the law', since the solution to proceedings under way does not depend on the ruling; it is designed to guarantee uniformity of interpretation in the future, when the national courts of different Contracting States have handed down contradictory interpretations of the rules of the Convention.

294. The request to the Court of Justice shall be brought by the Procurators-General of the Supreme Courts of Appeal of the Contracting States or any other authority designated by a Contracting State.

295. In order that this national authority may make a request to the Court of Justice, it is necessary for a national court of the same State to have given a final judgment which contradicts the interpretation given by the Court of Justice or by the courts of other Contracting States mentioned in Article 44 (the higher courts or those acting as appeal courts).

296. The ruling on the interpretation given by the Court of Justice does not affect the judgments which gave rise to it. Its aim is merely to clarify the interpretation for the future, without creating definitive binding precedent.

297. Article 45 incorporates proceedings established by the 1971 Protocols on the 1968 Brussels Convention and by the 1988 Protocols on the 1980 Rome Convention. Further comments may be found in the respective reports (see point 278).

Article 46
Reservations

298. The possibility of entering a reservation is not at the discretion of the State, but depends on the existence of an impediment for constitutional reasons relating to the conferral of jurisdiction to the Court of Justice.

299. The rationale of this reservation is to allow one Member State to minimize the risk of constitutional difficulties at the ratification stage of the Convention, which it felt might arise through the conferral of jurisdiction on the Court of Justice of the European Communities. The difficulties would arise in the event of the Convention being deemed to go beyond the limits of the objectives defined by Article 220 of the EC Treaty.

On the other hand, it was felt by other Contracting States that conferral of jurisdiction for interpretation on the Court of Justice is fundamental to the proper functioning of the system set up by the Convention on insolvency proceedings. A uniform interpretation by this Court is necessary to ensure that the rights and obligations deriving from the Convention are the same for all persons, irrespective of the Contracting State in which the party or person concerned is located. Hence, to mitigate as far as possible such risk, it was agreed that the scope of the Convention should be strictly limited to the intra-Community effects of the insolvency proceedings covered by the Convention. Thus, the perfect adaptation of the Convention to the scope of Article 220 of the EC Treaty would counterbalance the extension of its content to the rules on conflict of laws, without which the system of recognition of insolvency proceedings would distort legal certainty within the Community (see point 42).

G. Chapter VI: Transitional and Final Provisions Territorial Application

300. The Convention has no provisions governing territorial application. Consequently, the general rules of public international law, ie Article 29 of the 1969 Vienna Convention on the Law of Treaties are applicable.

301. This means that, in principle, the Convention on insolvency proceedings applies to the whole territory of the Contracting States. This includes non-European territories which are an integral part of the territory of these States. However, the autonomy of these territories can vary widely. Consequently, the Contracting States may exclude or reserve the application of the Convention to these territories by means of a declaration to that effect. This is the case, for example, with the Netherlands in relation to the Netherlands Antilles and Aruba.

302. For the same reason, the Convention does not apply to those territories whose international relations are assumed by any of the Contracting States, but which are not an integral part of their territory, being a separate entity. In principle, the Convention does not apply to them, no matter whether they are European or non-European territories. Should a Contracting State with such responsibility wish to extend the scope of the Convention to those territories, extension would only take effect if no other Contracting State opposed it.

Article 47
Applicability in time

303. Article 47 establishes two rules concerning the time of the application of the Convention. The Convention is applicable only to insolvency proceedings opened after the entry into force of the Convention. Acts done by the debtor before the entry into force of the Convention shall continue to be governed by the law which was applicable to them at the time they were done.

These two rules were prompted by the concern not to alter existing situations and relations which were governed by specific legal rules at the time of the introduction of the new rules of the Convention into the legal systems of the Contracting States.

304. The Convention applies to insolvency proceedings opened after the entry into force of the Convention; it does not apply to proceedings opened beforehand.

615

The Convention allows the opening of several sets of proceedings some of which may be opened before and some after entry into force.

If proceedings are opened on the basis of the debtor's centre of main interests after the entry into force of the Convention, it could have been thought that, in view of the primacy of the main proceedings in the operation of the Convention, the latter would apply even if proceedings had previously been opened away from the centre of main interests. This solution was not adopted, because it might disturb the course of proceedings opened in accordance with the law applicable at the time of opening. Reorganization proceedings opened in a State where the debtor's centre of main interests is not situated would have to be converted. Rules on conflict of laws would where appropriate have to be modified in the course of proceedings by the application of those in the Convention. Proceedings of a universal nature opened in accordance with the criteria of international jurisdiction laid down in the national law applicable would, where appropriate, be classified as territorial proceedings if, within the meaning of the Convention, the centre of main interests was not situated in the State of the opening of the earlier proceedings.

If earlier proceedings were opened in the State considered by the Convention as being the State where the debtor's centre of main interests is located, those proceedings will not be covered by the Convention. Before the entry into force of the Convention these proceedings may produce effects outside the State of the opening pursuant to the rules applicable under the different national laws. In the case of the earlier opening of proceedings in the State of the centre of main interests, proceedings opened after entry into force in the State where the debtor has an establishment are not subject to the Convention.

The rule in Article 47 has an absolute character: if insolvency proceedings are opened against a given debtor prior to the entry into force of the Convention in a Contracting State, any proceedings opened after the entry into force are not subject to the Convention, irrespective of whether such later proceedings are main or secondary proceedings within the meaning of the Convention.

305. In order to determine whether proceedings are opened before or after the entry into force of the Convention, the concept of the time of opening of proceedings, asestablished by the Convention, applies (see also point 68). Insolvency proceedings opened in advance do not come within the scope of the Convention if the judgment opening proceedings produced effects before the entry into force of the Convention.

306. The law applicable to the acts done by the debtor before the entry into force of the Convention continues to govern these acts.

This rule is prompted by the concern to avoid making the acts of the debtor subject to new rules and is aimed at keeping the relations to which the debtor is party subject to the law which governed his acts.

As regards the purpose of the rule, the determination of the acts done by the debtor and the time at which they are done are governed by the applicable law.

Article 48
Relationship to other Conventions

307. Article 48 establishes the relationship between the new Convention on insolvency proceedings and other international instruments which govern the Private International Law questions of international insolvencies, ie jurisdiction to open insolvency proceedings, law applicable to the proceedings and their effects, and the recognition and enforcement in other States of such proceedings. Article 48 deals with:

1. the relationship between the Convention and Treaties already concluded between certain Contracting States, in Article 48(1);

2. the relationship between the Convention and Treaties already concluded with third States, in Article 48(3).

308. Article 48(1) contains a list of the Conventions which will be superseded after the entry into force of the Convention on Insolvency Proceedings as between the States which are party to it. Such replacement will be subject to:

1. the provisions of Article 48(1) itself, pursuant to which these Conventions will continue to take effect in matters to which this Convention does not apply;

2. the provisions of Article 48(2) relating to insolvency proceedings opened before the entry into force of this Convention, which shall continue to be governed by the Conventions referred to in the list of Article 48(1), where applicable (see also Article 47).

309. The list of previous Conventions superseded, as between the Contracting States, by this Convention includes the 1990 Istanbul Convention, and the Convention between Denmark, Finland, Norway, Sweden and Iceland on Bankruptcy, signed at Copenhagen on 7 November 1933.

310. Article 48(3) concerns the problem of the compatibility of the Convention on Insolvency Proceedings with Treaties already concluded between a Contracting State and a third State.

To the extent that the application of this Convention would be irreconcilable with obligations arising out of Conventions or other international Agreements already concluded with a third State, the Convention on Insolvency Proceedings will not apply. To determine if the application of this Convention is or is not irreconcilable with the obligations arising out of another existing Convention, it should be examined whether they entail legal consequences which are mutually exclusive.

The Convention on Insolvency Proceedings is only applicable when the debtor's centre of main interests is in the territory of a Contracting State. Furthermore, its provisions are restricted to relations with other Contracting States (see point 44). Hence, conflicts with other Conventions will seldom arise.

Article 49
Signature, ratification and entry into force

311. The Convention shall be deposited with the Secretary-General of the Council of the European Union.

312. The decision-making process allowing a State to bind itself by the Convention shall be governed by the national law of each State. The Convention shall be subject to ratification, acceptance or approval by the signatory States.

313. The Convention shall enter into force on the first day of the sixth month following that of the last deposit of the instrument of ratification, acceptance or approval.

Article 50
Accession to the Convention

314. The future Member States of the European Union shall be required to accept this Convention as a basis for the negotiations necessary to ensure the implementation of Article 220 of the EC Treaty.

A special Convention may be concluded between the Contracting States and the future Member State for the purpose of introducing the necessary adjustments.

Article 51
Notification by the depositary

315. The Secretary-General of the Council of the European Union shall notify the signatory States of the deposit of each instrument of ratification, acceptance or approval of the Convention, the date of entry into force, and any other act, notification or communication relating to this Convention.

Article 52
Duration of the Convention

316. The Convention shall remain in force for an unlimited duration.

It does not contain any particular provision governing withdrawal of a State from the Convention. Any withdrawal is subject to the general law of international treaties.

Article 53
Revision or evaluation of the Convention

317. The Convention shall be the subject of a conference for the revision or evaluation of this Convention if any Contracting State so requests.

In the case of such request from a State the President of the Council of the European Union must convene the conference.

318. If no evaluation conference is held at the request of a Contracting State in the ten years that follow entry into force, the President of the Council of the European Union shall convene such a conference.

Article 54
Amendment of the Annexes

319. Each Contracting State may amend Annexes A, B and C which list the insolvency proceedings that may be the subject of main proceedings (list A: reorganization proceedings and winding-up proceedings) or of secondary proceedings (list B: winding-up proceedings), as well as the persons or organs which can assume the functions of a liquidator (list C).

The right of the States to amend the lists is subject to two restrictions.

The new proceedings included in lists A or B must correspond to the definitions of the proceedings given in Article 1(1) and Article 2(a) (list A, see points 48 and 62) and Article 2(c) (list B, see point 64).

320. Each Contracting State may amend the Annexes at any time.

The State shall address to the Secretary-General of the Council of the European Union, the depositary of the Convention under Article 49(1), a declaration containing the amendment which it wishes to make to an Annexe.

321. The depositary of the Convention will notify the signatory States and the Contracting States of the content of any such declaration.

322. The amendment that a State wishes to make to an Annexe must be subject to the acceptance by the Contracting or signatory States. It is not necessary for the States to communicate their acceptance expressly: if any State has not objected to the amendment within three months from the date of notification of the amending declaration, the amendment of the Annexe shall be deemed to be accepted.

Even if the Convention does not expressly stipulate this, the objection of a State should be notified to the depositary of the Convention who received the amending declaration. The depositary shall notify the communicated objection to the Contracting States (see Article 51(c)). Where an objection is communicated by a State, the amendment will not come into force. A solution to a divergence between two States could be sought by convening of [sic] a conference for revision.

323. The declaration for the amendment of an Annexe which was not objected to shall come into force on the first day of the month after the three-month period following the notification of the amending declaration to the Contracting and signatory States by the depositary.

Article 55
Deposit of the Convention

324. The Convention shall be drawn up in twelve languages; all texts shall be equally authentic.

The Convention shall be deposited with the Secretary-General of the Council of the European Union.

618

APPENDIX 3

Regulation (EU) 2015/848 of the European Parliament and of the Council of 20 May 2015 on Insolvency Proceedings (recast)

THE EUROPEAN PARLIAMENT AND THE COUNCIL OF THE EUROPEAN UNION,

Having regard to the Treaty on the Functioning of the European Union, and in particular Article 81 thereof,

Having regard to the proposal from the European Commission,

After transmission of the draft legislative act to the national parliaments,

Having regard to the opinion of the European Economic and Social Committee[1],

Acting in accordance with the ordinary legislative procedure[2],

Whereas:

(1) On 12 December 2012, the Commission adopted a report on the application of Council Regulation (EC) No 1346/2000[3]. The report concluded that the Regulation is functioning well in general but that it would be desirable to improve the application of certain of its provisions in order to enhance the effective administration of cross-border insolvency proceedings. Since that Regulation has been amended several times and further amendments are to be made, it should be recast in the interest of clarity.

(2) The Union has set the objective of establishing an area of freedom, security and justice.

(3) The proper functioning of the internal market requires that cross-border insolvency proceedings should operate efficiently and effectively. This Regulation needs to be adopted in order to achieve that objective, which falls within the scope of judicial cooperation in civil matters within the meaning of Article 81 of the Treaty.

(4) The activities of undertakings have more and more cross-border effects and are therefore increasingly being regulated by Union law. The insolvency of such undertakings also affects the proper functioning of the internal market, and there is a need for a Union act requiring coordination of the measures to be taken regarding an insolvent debtor's assets.

(5) It is necessary for the proper functioning of the internal market to avoid incentives for parties to transfer assets or judicial proceedings from one Member State to another, seeking to obtain a more favourable legal position to the detriment of the general body of creditors (forum shopping).

(6) This Regulation should include provisions governing jurisdiction for opening insolvency proceedings and actions which are directly derived from insolvency proceedings and are closely linked with them. This Regulation should also contain provisions regarding the recognition and enforcement of judgments issued in such proceedings, and provisions regarding the law applicable to insolvency proceedings. In addition, this Regulation should lay down rules on the coordination of insolvency proceedings which relate to the same debtor or to several members of the same group of companies.

---

[1] OJ C 271, 19.9.2013, p. 55.

[2] Position of the European Parliament of 5 February 2014 (not yet published in the Official Journal) and position of the Council at first reading of 12 March 2015 (not yet published in the Official Journal). Position of the European Parliament of 20 May 2015 (not yet published in the Official Journal).

[3] Council Regulation (EC) No 1346/2000 of 29 May 2000 on insolvency proceedings (OJ L 160, 30.6.2000, p. 1).

(7) Bankruptcy, proceedings relating to the winding-up of insolvent companies or other legal persons, judicial arrangements, compositions and analogous proceedings and actions related to such proceedings are excluded from the scope of Regulation (EU) No 1215/2012 of the European Parliament and of the Council[4]. Those proceedings should be covered by this Regulation. The interpretation of this Regulation should as much as possible avoid regulatory loopholes between the two instruments. However, the mere fact that a national procedure is not listed in Annex A to this Regulation should not imply that it is covered by Regulation (EU) No 1215/2012.

(8) In order to achieve the aim of improving the efficiency and effectiveness of insolvency proceedings having cross-border effects, it is necessary, and appropriate, that the provisions on jurisdiction, recognition and applicable law in this area should be contained in a Union measure which is binding and directly applicable in Member States.

(9) This Regulation should apply to insolvency proceedings which meet the conditions set out in it, irrespective of whether the debtor is a natural person or a legal person, a trader or an individual. Those insolvency proceedings are listed exhaustively in Annex A. In respect of the national procedures contained in Annex A, this Regulation should apply without any further examination by the courts of another Member State as to whether the conditions set out in this Regulation are met. National insolvency procedures not listed in Annex A should not be covered by this Regulation.

(10) The scope of this Regulation should extend to proceedings which promote the rescue of economically viable but distressed businesses and which give a second chance to entrepreneurs. It should, in particular, extend to proceedings which provide for restructuring of a debtor at a stage where there is only a likelihood of insolvency, and to proceedings which leave the debtor fully or partially in control of its assets and affairs. It should also extend to proceedings providing for a debt discharge or a debt adjustment in relation to consumers and self-employed persons, for example by reducing the amount to be paid by the debtor or by extending the payment period granted to the debtor. Since such proceedings do not necessarily entail the appointment of an insolvency practitioner, they should be covered by this Regulation if they take place under the control or supervision of a court. In this context, the term 'control' should include situations where the court only intervenes on appeal by a creditor or other interested parties.

(11) This Regulation should also apply to procedures which grant a temporary stay on enforcement actions brought by individual creditors where such actions could adversely affect negotiations and hamper the prospects of a restructuring of the debtor's business. Such procedures should not be detrimental to the general body of creditors and, if no agreement on a restructuring plan can be reached, should be preliminary to other procedures covered by this Regulation.

(12) This Regulation should apply to proceedings the opening of which is subject to publicity in order to allow creditors to become aware of the proceedings and to lodge their claims, thereby ensuring the collective nature of the proceedings, and in order to give creditors the opportunity to challenge the jurisdiction of the court which has opened the proceedings.

(13) Accordingly, insolvency proceedings which are confidential should be excluded from the scope of this Regulation. While such proceedings may play an important role in some Member States, their confidential nature makes it impossible for a creditor or a court located in another Member State to know that such proceedings have been opened, thereby making it difficult to provide for the recognition of their effects throughout the Union.

(14) The collective proceedings which are covered by this Regulation should include all or a significant part of the creditors to whom a debtor owes all or a substantial proportion of the debtor's outstanding debts provided that the claims of those creditors who are not involved in such proceedings remain unaffected. Proceedings which involve only the financial creditors of a debtor should also be covered. Proceedings which do not include all the creditors of a debtor should be proceedings aimed at rescuing the debtor. Proceedings that lead to a definitive cessation of the debtor's activities

---

[4] Regulation (EU) No 1215/2012 of the European Parliament and of the Council of 12 December 2012 on jurisdiction and the recognition and enforcement of judgments in civil and commercial matters (OJ L 351, 20.12.2012, p. 1).

or the liquidation of the debtor's assets should include all the debtor's creditors. Moreover, the fact that some insolvency proceedings for natural persons exclude specific categories of claims, such as maintenance claims, from the possibility of a debt-discharge should not mean that such proceedings are not collective.

(15) This Regulation should also apply to proceedings that, under the law of some Member States, are opened and conducted for a certain period of time on an interim or provisional basis before a court issues an order confirming the continuation of the proceedings on a non-interim basis. Although labelled as 'interim', such proceedings should meet all other requirements of this Regulation.

(16) This Regulation should apply to proceedings which are based on laws relating to insolvency. However, proceedings that are based on general company law not designed exclusively for insolvency situations should not be considered to be based on laws relating to insolvency. Similarly, the purpose of adjustment of debt should not include specific proceedings in which debts of a natural person of very low income and very low asset value are written off, provided that this type of proceedings never makes provision for payment to creditors.

(17) This Regulation's scope should extend to proceedings which are triggered by situations in which the debtor faces non-financial difficulties, provided that such difficulties give rise to a real and serious threat to the debtor's actual or future ability to pay its debts as they fall due. The time frame relevant for the determination of such threat may extend to a period of several months or even longer in order to account for cases in which the debtor is faced with non-financial difficulties threatening the status of its business as a going concern and, in the medium term, its liquidity. This may be the case, for example, where the debtor has lost a contract which is of key importance to it.

(18) This Regulation should be without prejudice to the rules on the recovery of State aid from insolvent companies as interpreted by the case-law of the Court of Justice of the European Union.

(19) Insolvency proceedings concerning insurance undertakings, credit institutions, investment firms and other firms, institutions or undertakings covered by Directive 2001/24/EC of the European Parliament and of the Council[5] and collective investment undertakings should be excluded from the scope of this Regulation, as they are all subject to special arrangements and the national supervisory authorities have wide-ranging powers of intervention.

(20) Insolvency proceedings do not necessarily involve the intervention of a judicial authority. Therefore, the term 'court' in this Regulation should, in certain provisions, be given a broad meaning and include a person or body empowered by national law to open insolvency proceedings. In order for this Regulation to apply, proceedings (comprising acts and formalities set down in law) should not only have to comply with the provisions of this Regulation, but they should also be officially recognized and legally effective in the Member State in which the insolvency proceedings are opened.

(21) Insolvency practitioners are defined in this Regulation and listed in Annex B. Insolvency practitioners who are appointed without the involvement of a judicial body should, under national law, be appropriately regulated and authorised to act in insolvency proceedings. The national regulatory framework should provide for proper arrangements to deal with potential conflicts of interest.

(22) This Regulation acknowledges the fact that as a result of widely differing substantive laws it is not practical to introduce insolvency proceedings with universal scope throughout the Union. The application without exception of the law of the State of the opening of proceedings would, against this background, frequently lead to difficulties. This applies, for example, to the widely differing national laws on security interests to be found in the Member States. Furthermore, the preferential rights enjoyed by some creditors in insolvency proceedings are, in some cases, completely different. At the next review of this Regulation, it will be necessary to identify further measures in order to improve the preferential rights of employees at European level. This Regulation should take account of such differing national laws in two different ways. On the one hand, provision should be made for special rules on the applicable law in the case of particularly significant rights and legal relationships (e.g. rights *in rem* and contracts of employment). On the other hand, national proceedings covering only assets

---

[5] Directive 2001/24/EC of the European Parliament and of the Council of 4 April 2001 on the reorganisation and winding-up of credit institutions (OJ L 125, 5.5.2001, p. 15).

situated in the State of the opening of proceedings should also be allowed alongside main insolvency proceedings with universal scope.

(23) This Regulation enables the main insolvency proceedings to be opened in the Member State where the debtor has the centre of its main interests. Those proceedings have universal scope and are aimed at encompassing all the debtor's assets. To protect the diversity of interests, this Regulation permits secondary insolvency proceedings to be opened to run in parallel with the main insolvency proceedings. Secondary insolvency proceedings may be opened in the Member State where the debtor has an establishment. The effects of secondary insolvency proceedings are limited to the assets located in that State. Mandatory rules of coordination with the main insolvency proceedings satisfy the need for unity in the Union.

(24) Where main insolvency proceedings concerning a legal person or company have been opened in a Member State other than that of its registered office, it should be possible to open secondary insolvency proceedings in the Member State of the registered office, provided that the debtor is carrying out an economic activity with human means and assets in that State, in accordance with the case-law of the Court of Justice of the European Union.

(25) This Regulation applies only to proceedings in respect of a debtor whose centre of main interests is located in the Union.

(26) The rules of jurisdiction set out in this Regulation establish only international jurisdiction, that is to say, they designate the Member State the courts of which may open insolvency proceedings. Territorial jurisdiction within that Member State should be established by the national law of the Member State concerned.

(27) Before opening insolvency proceedings, the competent court should examine of its own motion whether the centre of the debtor's main interests or the debtor's establishment is actually located within its jurisdiction.

(28) When determining whether the centre of the debtor's main interests is ascertainable by third parties, special consideration should be given to the creditors and to their perception as to where a debtor conducts the administration of its interests. This may require, in the event of a shift of centre of main interests, informing creditors of the new location from which the debtor is carrying out its activities in due course, for example by drawing attention to the change of address in commercial correspondence, or by making the new location public through other appropriate means.

(29) This Regulation should contain a number of safeguards aimed at preventing fraudulent or abusive forum shopping.

(30) Accordingly, the presumptions that the registered office, the principal place of business and the habitual residence are the centre of main interests should be rebuttable, and the relevant court of a Member State should carefully assess whether the centre of the debtor's main interests is genuinely located in that Member State. In the case of a company, it should be possible to rebut this presumption where the company's central administration is located in a Member State other than that of its registered office, and where a comprehensive assessment of all the relevant factors establishes, in a manner that is ascertainable by third parties, that the company's actual centre of management and supervision and of the management of its interests is located in that other Member State. In the case of an individual not exercising an independent business or professional activity, it should be possible to rebut this presumption, for example where the major part of the debtor's assets is located outside the Member State of the debtor's habitual residence, or where it can be established that the principal reason for moving was to file for insolvency proceedings in the new jurisdiction and where such filing would materially impair the interests of creditors whose dealings with the debtor took place prior to the relocation.

(31) With the same objective of preventing fraudulent or abusive forum shopping, the presumption that the centre of main interests is at the place of the registered office, at the individual's principal place of business or at the individual's habitual residence should not apply where, respectively, in the case of a company, legal person or individual exercising an independent business or professional activity, the debtor has relocated its registered office or principal place of business to another Member State within the 3-month period prior to the request for opening insolvency proceedings, or, in the case of

an individual not exercising an independent business or professional activity, the debtor has relocated his habitual residence to another Member State within the 6-month period prior to the request for opening insolvency proceedings.

(32) In all cases, where the circumstances of the matter give rise to doubts about the court's jurisdiction, the court should require the debtor to submit additional evidence to support its assertions and, where the law applicable to the insolvency proceedings so allows, give the debtor's creditors the opportunity to present their views on the question of jurisdiction.

(33) In the event that the court seised of the request to open insolvency proceedings finds that the centre of main interests is not located on its territory, it should not open main insolvency proceedings.

(34) In addition, any creditor of the debtor should have an effective remedy against the decision to open insolvency proceedings. The consequences of any challenge to the decision to open insolvency proceedings should be governed by national law.

(35) The courts of the Member State within the territory of which insolvency proceedings have been opened should also have jurisdiction for actions which derive directly from the insolvency proceedings and are closely linked with them. Such actions should include avoidance actions against defendants in other Member States and actions concerning obligations that arise in the course of the insolvency proceedings, such as advance payment for costs of the proceedings. In contrast, actions for the performance of the obligations under a contract concluded by the debtor prior to the opening of proceedings do not derive directly from the proceedings. Where such an action is related to another action based on general civil and commercial law, the insolvency practitioner should be able to bring both actions in the courts of the defendant's domicile if he considers it more efficient to bring the action in that forum. This could, for example, be the case where the insolvency practitioner wishes to combine an action for director's liability on the basis of insolvency law with an action based on company law or general tort law.

(36) The court having jurisdiction to open the main insolvency proceedings should be able to order provisional and protective measures as from the time of the request to open proceedings. Preservation measures both prior to and after the commencement of the insolvency proceedings are important to guarantee the effectiveness of the insolvency proceedings. In that connection, this Regulation should provide for various possibilities. On the one hand, the court competent for the main insolvency proceedings should also be able to order provisional and protective measures covering assets situated in the territory of other Member States. On the other hand, an insolvency practitioner temporarily appointed prior to the opening of the main insolvency proceedings should be able, in the Member States in which an establishment belonging to the debtor is to be found, to apply for the preservation measures which are possible under the law of those Member States.

(37) Prior to the opening of the main insolvency proceedings, the right to request the opening of insolvency proceedings in the Member State where the debtor has an establishment should be limited to local creditors and public authorities, or to cases in which main insolvency proceedings cannot be opened under the law of the Member State where the debtor has the centre of its main interests. The reason for this restriction is that cases in which territorial insolvency proceedings are requested before the main insolvency proceedings are intended to be limited to what is absolutely necessary.

(38) Following the opening of the main insolvency proceedings, this Regulation does not restrict the right to request the opening of insolvency proceedings in a Member State where the debtor has an establishment. The insolvency practitioner in the main insolvency proceedings or any other person empowered under the national law of that Member State may request the opening of secondary insolvency proceedings.

(39) This Regulation should provide for rules to determine the location of the debtor's assets, which should apply when determining which assets belong to the main or secondary insolvency proceedings, or to situations involving third parties' rights *in rem*. In particular, this Regulation should provide that European patents with unitary effect, a Community trade mark or any other similar rights, such as Community plant variety rights or Community designs, should only be included in the main insolvency proceedings.

(40) Secondary insolvency proceedings can serve different purposes, besides the protection of local interests. Cases may arise in which the insolvency estate of the debtor is too complex to administer as a unit, or the differences in the legal systems concerned are so great that difficulties may arise from the extension of effects deriving from the law of the State of the opening of proceedings to the other Member States where the assets are located. For that reason, the insolvency practitioner in the main insolvency proceedings may request the opening of secondary insolvency proceedings where the efficient administration of the insolvency estate so requires.

(41) Secondary insolvency proceedings may also hamper the efficient administration of the insolvency estate. Therefore, this Regulation sets out two specific situations in which the court seised of a request to open secondary insolvency proceedings should be able, at the request of the insolvency practitioner in the main insolvency proceedings, to postpone or refuse the opening of such proceedings.

(42) First, this Regulation confers on the insolvency practitioner in main insolvency proceedings the possibility of giving an undertaking to local creditors that they will be treated as if secondary insolvency proceedings had been opened. That undertaking has to meet a number of conditions set out in this Regulation, in particular that it be approved by a qualified majority of local creditors. Where such an undertaking has been given, the court seised of a request to open secondary insolvency proceedings should be able to refuse that request if it is satisfied that the undertaking adequately protects the general interests of local creditors. When assessing those interests, the court should take into account the fact that the undertaking has been approved by a qualified majority of local creditors.

(43) For the purposes of giving an undertaking to local creditors, the assets and rights located in the Member State where the debtor has an establishment should form a sub-category of the insolvency estate, and, when distributing them or the proceeds resulting from their realisation, the insolvency practitioner in the main insolvency proceedings should respect the priority rights that creditors would have had if secondary insolvency proceedings had been opened in that Member State.

(44) National law should be applicable, as appropriate, in relation to the approval of an undertaking. In particular, where under national law the voting rules for adopting a restructuring plan require the prior approval of creditors' claims, those claims should be deemed to be approved for the purpose of voting on the undertaking. Where there are different procedures for the adoption of restructuring plans under national law, Member States should designate the specific procedure which should be relevant in this context.

(45) Second, this Regulation should provide for the possibility that the court temporarily stays the opening of secondary insolvency proceedings, when a temporary stay of individual enforcement proceedings has been granted in the main insolvency proceedings, in order to preserve the efficiency of the stay granted in the main insolvency proceedings. The court should be able to grant the temporary stay if it is satisfied that suitable measures are in place to protect the general interest of local creditors. In such a case, all creditors that could be affected by the outcome of the negotiations on a restructuring plan should be informed of the negotiations and be allowed to participate in them.

(46) In order to ensure effective protection of local interests, the insolvency practitioner in the main insolvency proceedings should not be able to realise or re-locate, in an abusive manner, assets situated in the Member State where an establishment is located, in particular, with the purpose of frustrating the possibility that such interests can be effectively satisfied if secondary insolvency proceedings are opened subsequently.

(47) This Regulation should not prevent the courts of a Member State in which secondary insolvency proceedings have been opened from sanctioning a debtor's directors for violation of their duties, provided that those courts have jurisdiction to address such disputes under their national law.

(48) Main insolvency proceedings and secondary insolvency proceedings can contribute to the efficient administration of the debtor's insolvency estate or to the effective realisation of the total assets if there is proper cooperation between the actors involved in all the concurrent proceedings. Proper cooperation implies the various insolvency practitioners and the courts involved cooperating closely, in particular by exchanging a sufficient amount of information. In order to ensure the dominant role of the main insolvency proceedings, the insolvency practitioner in such proceedings should be given several possibilities for intervening in secondary insolvency proceedings which are pending at the same time. In particular, the insolvency practitioner should be able to propose a restructuring plan

or composition or apply for a suspension of the realisation of the assets in the secondary insolvency proceedings. When cooperating, insolvency practitioners and courts should take into account best practices for cooperation in cross-border insolvency cases, as set out in principles and guidelines on communication and cooperation adopted by European and international organisations active in the area of insolvency law, and in particular the relevant guidelines prepared by the United Nations Commission on International Trade Law (Uncitral).

(49) In light of such cooperation, insolvency practitioners and courts should be able to enter into agreements and protocols for the purpose of facilitating cross-border cooperation of multiple insolvency proceedings in different Member States concerning the same debtor or members of the same group of companies, where this is compatible with the rules applicable to each of the proceedings. Such agreements and protocols may vary in form, in that they may be written or oral, and in scope, in that they may range from generic to specific, and may be entered into by different parties. Simple generic agreements may emphasise the need for close cooperation between the parties, without addressing specific issues, while more detailed, specific agreements may establish a framework of principles to govern multiple insolvency proceedings and may be approved by the courts involved, where the national law so requires. They may reflect an agreement between the parties to take, or to refrain from taking, certain steps or actions.

(50) Similarly, the courts of different Member States may cooperate by coordinating the appointment of insolvency practitioners. In that context, they may appoint a single insolvency practitioner for several insolvency proceedings concerning the same debtor or for different members of a group of companies, provided that this is compatible with the rules applicable to each of the proceedings, in particular with any requirements concerning the qualification and licensing of the insolvency practitioner.

(51) This Regulation should ensure the efficient administration of insolvency proceedings relating to different companies forming part of a group of companies.

(52) Where insolvency proceedings have been opened for several companies of the same group, there should be proper cooperation between the actors involved in those proceedings. The various insolvency practitioners and the courts involved should therefore be under a similar obligation to cooperate and communicate with each other as those involved in main and secondary insolvency proceedings relating to the same debtor. Cooperation between the insolvency practitioners should not run counter to the interests of the creditors in each of the proceedings, and such cooperation should be aimed at finding a solution that would leverage synergies across the group.

(53) The introduction of rules on the insolvency proceedings of groups of companies should not limit the possibility for a court to open insolvency proceedings for several companies belonging to the same group in a single jurisdiction if the court finds that the centre of main interests of those companies is located in a single Member State. In such cases, the court should also be able to appoint, if appropriate, the same insolvency practitioner in all proceedings concerned, provided that this is not incompatible with the rules applicable to them.

(54) With a view to further improving the coordination of the insolvency proceedings of members of a group of companies, and to allow for a coordinated restructuring of the group, this Regulation should introduce procedural rules on the coordination of the insolvency proceedings of members of a group of companies. Such coordination should strive to ensure the efficiency of the coordination, whilst at the same time respecting each group member's separate legal personality.

(55) An insolvency practitioner appointed in insolvency proceedings opened in relation to a member of a group of companies should be able to request the opening of group coordination proceedings. However, where the law applicable to the insolvency so requires, that insolvency practitioner should obtain the necessary authorisation before making such a request. The request should specify the essential elements of the coordination, in particular an outline of the coordination plan, a proposal as to whom should be appointed as coordinator and an outline of the estimated costs of the coordination.

(56) In order to ensure the voluntary nature of group coordination proceedings, the insolvency practitioners involved should be able to object to their participation in the proceedings within a specified time period. In order to allow the insolvency practitioners involved to take an informed decision on participation in the group coordination proceedings, they should be informed at an early stage of the

essential elements of the coordination. However, any insolvency practitioner who initially objects to inclusion in the group coordination proceedings should be able to subsequently request to participate in them. In such a case, the coordinator should take a decision on the admissibility of the request. All insolvency practitioners, including the requesting insolvency practitioner, should be informed of the coordinator's decision and should have the opportunity of challenging that decision before the court which has opened the group coordination proceedings.

(57) Group coordination proceedings should always strive to facilitate the effective administration of the insolvency proceedings of the group members, and to have a generally positive impact for the creditors. This Regulation should therefore ensure that the court with which a request for group coordination proceedings has been filed makes an assessment of those criteria prior to opening group coordination proceedings.

(58) The advantages of group coordination proceedings should not be outweighed by the costs of those proceedings. Therefore, it is necessary to ensure that the costs of the coordination, and the share of those costs that each group member will bear, are adequate, proportionate and reasonable, and are determined in accordance with the national law of the Member State in which group coordination proceedings have been opened. The insolvency practitioners involved should also have the possibility of controlling those costs from an early stage of the proceedings. Where the national law so requires, controlling costs from an early stage of proceedings could involve the insolvency practitioner seeking the approval of a court or creditors' committee.

(59) Where the coordinator considers that the fulfilment of his or her tasks requires a significant increase in costs compared to the initially estimated costs and, in any case, where the costs exceed 10% of the estimated costs, the coordinator should be authorised by the court which has opened the group coordination proceedings to exceed such costs. Before taking its decision, the court which has opened the group coordination proceedings should give the possibility to the participating insolvency practitioners to be heard before it in order to allow them to communicate their observations on the appropriateness of the coordinator's request.

(60) For members of a group of companies which are not participating in group coordination proceedings, this Regulation should also provide for an alternative mechanism to achieve a coordinated restructuring of the group. An insolvency practitioner appointed in proceedings relating to a member of a group of companies should have standing to request a stay of any measure related to the realisation of the assets in the proceedings opened with respect to other members of the group which are not subject to group coordination proceedings. It should only be possible to request such a stay if a restructuring plan is presented for the members of the group concerned, if the plan is to the benefit of the creditors in the proceedings in respect of which the stay is requested, and if the stay is necessary to ensure that the plan can be properly implemented.

(61) This Regulation should not prevent Member States from establishing national rules which would supplement the rules on cooperation, communication and coordination with regard to the insolvency of members of groups of companies set out in this Regulation, provided that the scope of application of those national rules is limited to the national jurisdiction and that their application would not impair the efficiency of the rules laid down by this Regulation.

(62) The rules on cooperation, communication and coordination in the framework of the insolvency of members of a group of companies provided for in this Regulation should only apply to the extent that proceedings relating to different members of the same group of companies have been opened in more than one Member State.

(63) Any creditor which has its habitual residence, domicile or registered office in the Union should have the right to lodge its claims in each of the insolvency proceedings pending in the Union relating to the debtor's assets. This should also apply to tax authorities and social insurance institutions. This Regulation should not prevent the insolvency practitioner from lodging claims on behalf of certain groups of creditors, for example employees, where the national law so provides. However, in order to ensure the equal treatment of creditors, the distribution of proceeds should be coordinated. Every creditor should be able to keep what it has received in the course of insolvency proceedings, but should be entitled only to participate in the distribution of total assets in other proceedings if creditors with the same standing have obtained the same proportion of their claims.

(64) It is essential that creditors which have their habitual residence, domicile or registered office in the Union be informed about the opening of insolvency proceedings relating to their debtor's assets. In order to ensure a swift transmission of information to creditors, Regulation (EC) No 1393/2007 of the European Parliament and of the Council[6] should not apply where this Regulation refers to the obligation to inform creditors. The use of standard forms available in all official languages of the institutions of the Union should facilitate the task of creditors when lodging claims in proceedings opened in another Member State. The consequences of the incomplete filing of the standard forms should be a matter for national law.

(65) This Regulation should provide for the immediate recognition of judgments concerning the opening, conduct and closure of insolvency proceedings which fall within its scope, and of judgments handed down in direct connection with such insolvency proceedings. Automatic recognition should therefore mean that the effects attributed to the proceedings by the law of the Member State in which the proceedings were opened extend to all other Member States. The recognition of judgments delivered by the courts of the Member States should be based on the principle of mutual trust. To that end, grounds for non-recognition should be reduced to the minimum necessary. This is also the basis on which any dispute should be resolved where the courts of two Member States both claim competence to open the main insolvency proceedings. The decision of the first court to open proceedings should be recognised in the other Member States without those Member States having the power to scrutinise that court's decision.

(66) This Regulation should set out, for the matters covered by it, uniform rules on conflict of laws which replace, within their scope of application, national rules of private international law. Unless otherwise stated, the law of the Member State of the opening of proceedings should be applicable (*lex concursus*). This rule on conflict of laws should be valid both for the main insolvency proceedings and for local proceedings. The *lex concursus* determines all the effects of the insolvency proceedings, both procedural and substantive, on the persons and legal relations concerned. It governs all the conditions for the opening, conduct and closure of the insolvency proceedings.

(67) Automatic recognition of insolvency proceedings to which the law of the State of the opening of proceedings normally applies may interfere with the rules under which transactions are carried out in other Member States. To protect legitimate expectations and the certainty of transactions in Member States other than that in which proceedings are opened, provision should be made for a number of exceptions to the general rule.

(68) There is a particular need for a special reference diverging from the law of the opening State in the case of rights *in rem*, since such rights are of considerable importance for the granting of credit. The basis, validity and extent of rights *in rem* should therefore normally be determined according to the *lex situs* and not be affected by the opening of insolvency proceedings. The proprietor of a right *in rem* should therefore be able to continue to assert its right to segregation or separate settlement of the collateral security. Where assets are subject to rights *in rem* under the *lex situs* in one Member State but the main insolvency proceedings are being carried out in another Member State, the insolvency practitioner in the main insolvency proceedings should be able to request the opening of secondary insolvency proceedings in the jurisdiction where the rights *in rem* arise if the debtor has an establishment there. If secondary insolvency proceedings are not opened, any surplus on the sale of an asset covered by rights *in rem* should be paid to the insolvency practitioner in the main insolvency proceedings.

(69) This Regulation lays down several provisions for a court to order a stay of opening proceedings or a stay of enforcement proceedings. Any such stay should not affect the rights *in rem* of creditors or third parties.

(70) If a set-off of claims is not permitted under the law of the State of the opening of proceedings, a creditor should nevertheless be entitled to the set-off if it is possible under the law applicable to the claim of the insolvent debtor. In this way, set-off would acquire a kind of guarantee

---

[6] Regulation (EC) No 1393/2007 of the European Parliament and of the Council of 13 November 2007 on the service in the Member States of judicial and extrajudicial documents in civil and commercial matters (service of documents), and repealing Council Regulation (EC) No 1348/2000 (OJ L 324, 10.12.2007, p. 79).

function based on legal provisions on which the creditor concerned can rely at the time when the claim arises.

(71) There is also a need for special protection in the case of payment systems and financial markets, for example in relation to the position-closing agreements and netting agreements to be found in such systems, as well as the sale of securities and the guarantees provided for such transactions as governed in particular by Directive 98/26/EC of the European Parliament and of the Council[7]. For such transactions, the only law which is relevant should be that applicable to the system or market concerned. That law is intended to prevent the possibility of mechanisms for the payment and settlement of transactions, and provided for in payment and set-off systems or on the regulated financial markets of the Member States, being altered in the case of insolvency of a business partner. Directive 98/26/EC contains special provisions which should take precedence over the general rules laid down in this Regulation.

(72) In order to protect employees and jobs, the effects of insolvency proceedings on the continuation or termination of employment and on the rights and obligations of all parties to such employment should be determined by the law applicable to the relevant employment agreement, in accordance with the general rules on conflict of laws. Moreover, in cases where the termination of employment contracts requires approval by a court or administrative authority, the Member State in which an establishment of the debtor is located should retain jurisdiction to grant such approval even if no insolvency proceedings have been opened in that Member State. Any other questions relating to the law of insolvency, such as whether the employees' claims are protected by preferential rights and the status such preferential rights may have, should be determined by the law of the Member State in which the insolvency proceedings (main or secondary) have been opened, except in cases where an undertaking to avoid secondary insolvency proceedings has been given in accordance with this Regulation.

(73) The law applicable to the effects of insolvency proceedings on any pending lawsuit or pending arbitral proceedings concerning an asset or right which forms part of the debtor's insolvency estate should be the law of the Member State where the lawsuit is pending or where the arbitration has its seat. However, this rule should not affect national rules on recognition and enforcement of arbitral awards.

(74) In order to take account of the specific procedural rules of court systems in certain Member States flexibility should be provided with regard to certain rules of this Regulation. Accordingly, references in this Regulation to notice being given by a judicial body of a Member State should include, where a Member State's procedural rules so require, an order by that judicial body directing that notice be given.

(75) For business considerations, the main content of the decision opening the proceedings should be published, at the request of the insolvency practitioner, in a Member State other than that of the court which delivered that decision. If there is an establishment in the Member State concerned, such publication should be mandatory. In neither case, however, should publication be a prior condition for recognition of the foreign proceedings.

(76) In order to improve the provision of information to relevant creditors and courts and to prevent the opening of parallel insolvency proceedings, Member States should be required to publish relevant information in cross-border insolvency cases in a publicly accessible electronic register. In order to facilitate access to that information for creditors and courts domiciled or located in other Member States, this Regulation should provide for the interconnection of such insolvency registers via the European e-Justice Portal. Member States should be free to publish relevant information in several registers and it should be possible to interconnect more than one register per Member State.

(77) This Regulation should determine the minimum amount of information to be published in the insolvency registers. Member States should not be precluded from including additional information. Where the debtor is an individual, the insolvency registers should only have to indicate a registration

---

[7] Directive 98/26/EC of the European Parliament and of the Council of 19 May 1998 on settlement finality in payment and securities settlement systems (OJ L 166, 11.6.1998, p. 45).

number if the debtor is exercising an independent business or professional activity. That registration number should be understood to be the unique registration number of the debtor's independent business or professional activity published in the trade register, if any.

(78) Information on certain aspects of insolvency proceedings is essential for creditors, such as time limits for lodging claims or for challenging decisions. This Regulation should, however, not require Member States to calculate those time-limits on a case-by-case basis. Member States should be able to fulfil their obligations by adding hyperlinks to the European e-Justice Portal, where self-explanatory information on the criteria for calculating those time-limits is to be provided.

(79) In order to grant sufficient protection to information relating to individuals not exercising an independent business or professional activity, Member States should be able to make access to that information subject to supplementary search criteria such as the debtor's personal identification number, address, date of birth or the district of the competent court, or to make access conditional upon a request to a competent authority or upon the verification of a legitimate interest.

(80) Member States should also be able not to include in their insolvency registers information on individuals not exercising an independent business or professional activity. In such cases, Member States should ensure that the relevant information is given to the creditors by individual notice, and that claims of creditors who have not received the information are not affected by the proceedings.

(81) It may be the case that some of the persons concerned are not aware that insolvency proceedings have been opened, and act in good faith in a way that conflicts with the new circumstances. In order to protect such persons who, unaware that foreign proceedings have been opened, make a payment to the debtor instead of to the foreign insolvency practitioner, provision should be made for such a payment to have a debt-discharging effect.

(82) In order to ensure uniform conditions for the implementation of this Regulation, implementing powers should be conferred on the Commission. Those powers should be exercised in accordance with Regulation (EU) No 182/2011 of the European Parliament and of the Council[8].

(83) This Regulation respects the fundamental rights and observes the principles recognised in the Charter of Fundamental Rights of the European Union. In particular, this Regulation seeks to promote the application of Articles 8, 17 and 47 concerning, respectively, the protection of personal data, the right to property and the right to an effective remedy and to a fair trial.

(84) Directive 95/46/EC of the European Parliament and of the Council[9] and Regulation (EC) No 45/2001 of the European Parliament and of the Council[10] apply to the processing of personal data within the framework of this Regulation.

(85) This Regulation is without prejudice to Regulation (EEC, Euratom) No 1182/71 of the Council[11].

(86) Since the objective of this Regulation cannot be sufficiently achieved by the Member States but can rather, by reason of the creation of a legal framework for the proper administration of cross-border insolvency proceedings, be better achieved at Union level, the Union may adopt measures in accordance with the principle of subsidiarity as set out in Article 5 of the Treaty on European Union. In accordance with the principle of proportionality, as set out in that Article, this Regulation does not go beyond what is necessary in order to achieve that objective.

---

[8] Regulation (EU) No 182/2011 of the European Parliament and of the Council of 16 February 2011 laying down the rules and general principles concerning mechanisms for control by the Member States of the Commission's exercise of implementing powers (OJ L 55, 28.2.2011, p. 13).

[9] Directive 95/46/EC of the European Parliament and of the Council of 24 October 1995 on the protection of individuals with regard to the processing of personal data and on the free movement of such data (OJ L 281, 23.11.1995, p. 31).

[10] Regulation (EC) No 45/2001 of the European Parliament and of the Council of 18 December 2000 on the protection of individuals with regard to the processing of personal data by the Community institutions and bodies and on the free movement of such data (OJ L 8, 12.1.2001, p. 1).

[11] Regulation (EEC, Euratom) No 1182/71 of the Council of 3 June 1971 determining the rules applicable to periods, dates and time limits (OJ L 124, 8.6.1971, p. 1).

(87) In accordance with Article 3 and Article 4a(1) of Protocol No 21 on the position of the United Kingdom and Ireland in respect of the area of freedom, security and justice, annexed to the Treaty on European Union and the Treaty on the Functioning of the European Union, the United Kingdom and Ireland have notified their wish to take part in the adoption and application of this Regulation.

(88) In accordance with Articles 1 and 2 of Protocol No 22 on the position of Denmark annexed to the Treaty on European Union and the Treaty on the Functioning of the European Union, Denmark is not taking part in the adoption of this Regulation and is not bound by it or subject to its application.

(89) The European Data Protection Supervisor was consulted and delivered an opinion on 27 March 2013[12],

HAVE ADOPTED THIS REGULATION:

Chapter I: General Provisions

Article 1
Scope

1. This Regulation shall apply to public collective proceedings, including interim proceedings, which are based on laws relating to insolvency and in which, for the purpose of rescue, adjustment of debt, reorganisation or liquidation:
    (a) a debtor is totally or partially divested of its assets and an insolvency practitioner is appointed;
    (b) the assets and affairs of a debtor are subject to control or supervision by a court; or
    (c) a temporary stay of individual enforcement proceedings is granted by a court or by operation of law, in order to allow for negotiations between the debtor and its creditors, provided that the proceedings in which the stay is granted provide for suitable measures to protect the general body of creditors, and, where no agreement is reached, are preliminary to one of the proceedings referred to in point (a) or (b).

Where the proceedings referred to in this paragraph may be commenced in situations where there is only a likelihood of insolvency, their purpose shall be to avoid the debtor's insolvency or the cessation of the debtor's business activities.

The proceedings referred to in this paragraph are listed in Annex A.

2. This Regulation shall not apply to proceedings referred to in paragraph 1 that concern:
    (a) insurance undertakings;
    (b) credit institutions;
    (c) investment firms and other firms, institutions and undertakings to the extent that they are covered by Directive 2001/24/EC; or
    (d) collective investment undertakings.

Article 2
Definitions

For the purposes of this Regulation:

(1) 'collective proceedings' means proceedings which include all or a significant part of a debtor's creditors, provided that, in the latter case, the proceedings do not affect the claims of creditors which are not involved in them;

(2) 'collective investment undertakings' means undertakings for collective investment in transferable securities (UCITS) as defined in Directive 2009/65/EC of the European Parliament and of the Council[13] and alternative investment funds (AIFs) as defined in Directive 2011/61/EU of the European Parliament and of the Council[14];

---

[12] OJ C 358, 7.12.2013, p. 15.

[13] Directive 2009/65/EC of the European Parliament and of the Council of 13 July 2009 on the coordination of laws, regulations and administrative provisions relating to undertakings for collective investment in transferable securities (UCITS) (OJ L 302, 17.11.2009, p. 32).

[14] Directive 2011/61/EU of the European Parliament and of the Council of 8 June 2011 on Alternative Investment Fund Managers and amending Directives 2003/41/EC and 2009/65/EC and Regulations (EC) No 1060/2009 and (EU) No 1095/2010 (OJ L 174, 1.7.2011, p. 1).

(3) 'debtor in possession' means a debtor in respect of which insolvency proceedings have been opened which do not necessarily involve the appointment of an insolvency practitioner or the complete transfer of the rights and duties to administer the debtor's assets to an insolvency practitioner and where, therefore, the debtor remains totally or at least partially in control of its assets and affairs;

(4) 'insolvency proceedings' means the proceedings listed in Annex A;

(5) 'insolvency practitioner' means any person or body whose function, including on an interim basis, is to:

    (i)   verify and admit claims submitted in insolvency proceedings;

    (ii)   represent the collective interest of the creditors;

    (iii) administer, either in full or in part, assets of which the debtor has been divested;

    (iv) liquidate the assets referred to in point (iii); or

    (v)   supervise the administration of the debtor's affairs.

The persons and bodies referred to in the first subparagraph are listed in Annex B;

(6) 'court' means:

    (i)   in points (b) and (c) of Article 1(1), Article 4(2), Articles 5 and 6, Article 21(3), point (j) of Article 24(2), Articles 36 and 39, and Articles 61 to 77, the judicial body of a Member State;

    (ii)   in all other articles, the judicial body or any other competent body of a Member State empowered to open insolvency proceedings, to confirm such opening or to take decisions in the course of such proceedings;

(7) 'judgment opening insolvency proceedings' includes:

    (i)   the decision of any court to open insolvency proceedings or to confirm the opening of such proceedings; and

    (ii)   the decision of a court to appoint an insolvency practitioner;

(8) 'the time of the opening of proceedings' means the time at which the judgment opening insolvency proceedings becomes effective, regardless of whether the judgment is final or not;

(9) 'the Member State in which assets are situated' means, in the case of:

    (i)   registered shares in companies other than those referred to in point (ii), the Member State within the territory of which the company having issued the shares has its registered office;

    (ii)   financial instruments, the title to which is evidenced by entries in a register or account maintained by or on behalf of an intermediary ('book entry securities'), the Member State in which the register or account in which the entries are made is maintained;

    (iii) cash held in accounts with a credit institution, the Member State indicated in the account's IBAN, or, for cash held in accounts with a credit institution which does not have an IBAN, the Member State in which the credit institution holding the account has its central administration or, where the account is held with a branch, agency or other establishment, the Member State in which the branch, agency or other establishment is located;

    (iv) property and rights, ownership of or entitlement to which is entered in a public register other than those referred to in point (i), the Member State under the authority of which the register is kept;

    (v)   European patents, the Member State for which the European patent is granted;

    (vi) copyright and related rights, the Member State within the territory of which the owner of such rights has its habitual residence or registered office;

    (vii) tangible property, other than that referred to in points (i) to (iv), the Member State within the territory of which the property is situated;

    (viii) claims against third parties, other than those relating to assets referred to in point (iii), the Member State within the territory of which the third party required to meet the claims has the centre of its main interests, as determined in accordance with Article 3(1);

(10) 'establishment' means any place of operations where a debtor carries out or has carried out in the 3-month period prior to the request to open main insolvency proceedings a non-transitory economic activity with human means and assets;

(11) 'local creditor' means a creditor whose claims against a debtor arose from or in connection with the operation of an establishment situated in a Member State other than the Member State in which the centre of the debtor's main interests is located;

(12) 'foreign creditor' means a creditor which has its habitual residence, domicile or registered office in a Member State other than the State of the opening of proceedings, including the tax authorities and social security authorities of Member States;

(13) 'group of companies' means a parent undertaking and all its subsidiary undertakings;

(14) 'parent undertaking' means an undertaking which controls, either directly or indirectly, one or more subsidiary undertakings. An undertaking which prepares consolidated financial statements in accordance with Directive 2013/34/EU of the European Parliament and of the Council[15] shall be deemed to be a parent undertaking.

Article 3
International jurisdiction

1. The courts of the Member State within the territory of which the centre of the debtor's main interests is situated shall have jurisdiction to open insolvency proceedings ('main insolvency proceedings'). The centre of main interests shall be the place where the debtor conducts the administration of its interests on a regular basis and which is ascertainable by third parties.

In the case of a company or legal person, the place of the registered office shall be presumed to be the centre of its main interests in the absence of proof to the contrary. That presumption shall only apply if the registered office has not been moved to another Member State within the 3-month period prior to the request for the opening of insolvency proceedings.

In the case of an individual exercising an independent business or professional activity, the centre of main interests shall be presumed to be that individual's principal place of business in the absence of proof to the contrary. That presumption shall only apply if the individual's principal place of business has not been moved to another Member State within the 3-month period prior to the request for the opening of insolvency proceedings.

In the case of any other individual, the centre of main interests shall be presumed to be the place of the individual's habitual residence in the absence of proof to the contrary. This presumption shall only apply if the habitual residence has not been moved to another Member State within the 6-month period prior to the request for the opening of insolvency proceedings.

2. Where the centre of the debtor's main interests is situated within the territory of a Member State, the courts of another Member State shall have jurisdiction to open insolvency proceedings against that debtor only if it possesses an establishment within the territory of that other Member State. The effects of those proceedings shall be restricted to the assets of the debtor situated in the territory of the latter Member State.

3. Where insolvency proceedings have been opened in accordance with paragraph 1, any proceedings opened subsequently in accordance with paragraph 2 shall be secondary insolvency proceedings.

4. The territorial insolvency proceedings referred to in paragraph 2 may only be opened prior to the opening of main insolvency proceedings in accordance with paragraph 1 where

    (a) insolvency proceedings under paragraph 1 cannot be opened because of the conditions laid down by the law of the Member State within the territory of which the centre of the debtor's main interests is situated; or

    (b) the opening of territorial insolvency proceedings is requested by:

        (i) a creditor whose claim arises from or is in connection with the operation of an establishment situated within the territory of the Member State where the opening of territorial proceedings is requested; or

        (ii) a public authority which, under the law of the Member State within the territory of which the establishment is situated, has the right to request the opening of insolvency proceedings.

---

[15] Directive 2013/34/EU of the European Parliament and of the Council of 26 June 2013 on the annual financial statements, consolidated financial statements and related reports of certain types of undertaking, amending Directive 2006/43/EC of the European Parliament and of the Council and repealing Council Directives 78/660/EEC and 83/349/EEC (OJ L 182, 29.6.2013, p. 19).

When main insolvency proceedings are opened, the territorial insolvency proceedings shall become secondary insolvency proceedings.

Article 4
Examination as to jurisdiction

1. A court seised of a request to open insolvency proceedings shall of its own motion examine whether it has jurisdiction pursuant to Article 3. The judgment opening insolvency proceedings shall specify the grounds on which the jurisdiction of the court is based, and, in particular, whether jurisdiction is based on Article 3(1) or (2).

2. Notwithstanding paragraph 1, where insolvency proceedings are opened in accordance with national law without a decision by a court, Member States may entrust the insolvency practitioner appointed in such proceedings to examine whether the Member State in which a request for the opening of proceedings is pending has jurisdiction pursuant to Article 3. Where this is the case, the insolvency practitioner shall specify in the decision opening the proceedings the grounds on which jurisdiction is based and, in particular, whether jurisdiction is based on Article 3(1) or (2).

Article 5
Judicial review of the decision to open main insolvency proceedings

1. The debtor or any creditor may challenge before a court the decision opening main insolvency proceedings on grounds of international jurisdiction.

2. The decision opening main insolvency proceedings may be challenged by parties other than those referred to in paragraph 1 or on grounds other than a lack of international jurisdiction where national law so provides.

Article 6
Jurisdiction for actions deriving directly from insolvency proceedings and closely linked with them

1. The courts of the Member State within the territory of which insolvency proceedings have been opened in accordance with Article 3 shall have jurisdiction for any action which derives directly from the insolvency proceedings and is closely linked with them, such as avoidance actions.

2. Where an action referred to in paragraph 1 is related to an action in civil and commercial matters against the same defendant, the insolvency practitioner may bring both actions before the courts of the Member State within the territory of which the defendant is domiciled, or, where the action is brought against several defendants, before the courts of the Member State within the territory of which any of them is domiciled, provided that those courts have jurisdiction pursuant to Regulation (EU) No 1215/2012.

The first subparagraph shall apply to the debtor in possession, provided that national law allows the debtor in possession to bring actions on behalf of the insolvency estate.

3. For the purpose of paragraph 2, actions are deemed to be related where they are so closely connected that it is expedient to hear and determine them together to avoid the risk of irreconcilable judgments resulting from separate proceedings.

Article 7
Applicable law

1. Save as otherwise provided in this Regulation, the law applicable to insolvency proceedings and their effects shall be that of the Member State within the territory of which such proceedings are opened (the 'State of the opening of proceedings').

2. The law of the State of the opening of proceedings shall determine the conditions for the opening of those proceedings, their conduct and their closure. In particular, it shall determine the following:
   (a) the debtors against which insolvency proceedings may be brought on account of their capacity;
   (b) the assets which form part of the insolvency estate and the treatment of assets acquired by or devolving on the debtor after the opening of the insolvency proceedings;
   (c) the respective powers of the debtor and the insolvency practitioner;

(d) the conditions under which set-offs may be invoked;

(e) the effects of insolvency proceedings on current contracts to which the debtor is party;

(f) the effects of the insolvency proceedings on proceedings brought by individual creditors, with the exception of pending lawsuits;

(g) the claims which are to be lodged against the debtor's insolvency estate and the treatment of claims arising after the opening of insolvency proceedings;

(h) the rules governing the lodging, verification and admission of claims;

(i) the rules governing the distribution of proceeds from the realisation of assets, the ranking of claims and the rights of creditors who have obtained partial satisfaction after the opening of insolvency proceedings by virtue of a right *in rem* or through a set-off;

(j) the conditions for, and the effects of closure of, insolvency proceedings, in particular by composition;

(k) creditors' rights after the closure of insolvency proceedings;

(l) who is to bear the costs and expenses incurred in the insolvency proceedings;

(m) the rules relating to the voidness, voidability or unenforceability of legal acts detrimental to the general body of creditors.

Article 8
Third parties' rights in rem

1. The opening of insolvency proceedings shall not affect the rights *in rem* of creditors or third parties in respect of tangible or intangible, moveable or immoveable assets, both specific assets and collections of indefinite assets as a whole which change from time to time, belonging to the debtor which are situated within the territory of another Member State at the time of the opening of proceedings.

2. The rights referred to in paragraph 1 shall, in particular, mean:
    (a) the right to dispose of assets or have them disposed of and to obtain satisfaction from the proceeds of or income from those assets, in particular by virtue of a lien or a mortgage;
    (b) the exclusive right to have a claim met, in particular a right guaranteed by a lien in respect of the claim or by assignment of the claim by way of a guarantee;
    (c) the right to demand assets from, and/or to require restitution by, anyone having possession or use of them contrary to the wishes of the party so entitled;
    (d) a right *in rem* to the beneficial use of assets.

3. The right, recorded in a public register and enforceable against third parties, based on which a right *in rem* within the meaning of paragraph 1 may be obtained shall be considered to be a right *in rem*.

4. Paragraph 1 shall not preclude actions for voidness, voidability or unenforceability as referred to in point (m) of Article 7(2).

Article 9
Set-off

1. The opening of insolvency proceedings shall not affect the right of creditors to demand the set-off of their claims against the claims of a debtor, where such a set-off is permitted by the law applicable to the insolvent debtor's claim.

2. Paragraph 1 shall not preclude actions for voidness, voidability or unenforceability as referred to in point (m) of Article 7(2).

Article 10
Reservation of title

1. The opening of insolvency proceedings against the purchaser of an asset shall not affect sellers' rights that are based on a reservation of title where at the time of the opening of proceedings the asset is situated within the territory of a Member State other than the State of the opening of proceedings.

2. The opening of insolvency proceedings against the seller of an asset, after delivery of the asset, shall not constitute grounds for rescinding or terminating the sale and shall not prevent the purchaser from acquiring title where at the time of the opening of proceedings the asset sold is situated within the territory of a Member State other than the State of the opening of proceedings.

3. Paragraphs 1 and 2 shall not preclude actions for voidness, voidability or unenforceability as referred to in point (m) of Article 7(2).

Article 11
Contracts relating to immoveable property

1. The effects of insolvency proceedings on a contract conferring the right to acquire or make use of immoveable property shall be governed solely by the law of the Member State within the territory of which the immoveable property is situated.

2. The court which opened main insolvency proceedings shall have jurisdiction to approve the termination or modification of the contracts referred to in this Article where:
    (a) the law of the Member State applicable to those contracts requires that such a contract may only be terminated or modified with the approval of the court opening insolvency proceedings; and
    (b) no insolvency proceedings have been opened in that Member State.

Article 12
Payment systems and financial markets

1. Without prejudice to Article 8, the effects of insolvency proceedings on the rights and obligations of the parties to a payment or settlement system or to a financial market shall be governed solely by the law of the Member State applicable to that system or market.

2. Paragraph 1 shall not preclude any action for voidness, voidability or unenforceability which may be taken to set aside payments or transactions under the law applicable to the relevant payment system or financial market.

Article 13
Contracts of employment

1. The effects of insolvency proceedings on employment contracts and relationships shall be governed solely by the law of the Member State applicable to the contract of employment.

2. The courts of the Member State in which secondary insolvency proceedings may be opened shall retain jurisdiction to approve the termination or modification of the contracts referred to in this Article even if no insolvency proceedings have been opened in that Member State.

The first subparagraph shall also apply to an authority competent under national law to approve the termination or modification of the contracts referred to in this Article.

Article 14
Effects on rights subject to registration

The effects of insolvency proceedings on the rights of a debtor in immoveable property, a ship or an aircraft subject to registration in a public register shall be determined by the law of the Member State under the authority of which the register is kept.

Article 15
European patents with unitary effect and Community trade marks

For the purposes of this Regulation, a European patent with unitary effect, a Community trade mark or any other similar right established by Union law may be included only in the proceedings referred to in Article 3(1).

Article 16
Detrimental acts

Point (m) of Article 7(2) shall not apply where the person who benefited from an act detrimental to all the creditors provides proof that:
    (a) the act is subject to the law of a Member State other than that of the State of the opening of proceedings; and
    (b) the law of that Member State does not allow any means of challenging that act in the relevant case.

Article 17
Protection of third-party purchasers

Where, by an act concluded after the opening of insolvency proceedings, a debtor disposes, for consideration, of:
    (a) an immoveable asset;

(b) a ship or an aircraft subject to registration in a public register; or

(c) securities the existence of which requires registration in a register laid down by law;

the validity of that act shall be governed by the law of the State within the territory of which the immoveable asset is situated or under the authority of which the register is kept.

Article 18
Effects of insolvency proceedings on pending lawsuits or arbitral proceedings

The effects of insolvency proceedings on a pending lawsuit or pending arbitral proceedings concerning an asset or a right which forms part of a debtor's insolvency estate shall be governed solely by the law of the Member State in which that lawsuit is pending or in which the arbitral tribunal has its seat.

CHAPTER II: RECOGNITION OF INSOLVENCY PROCEEDINGS

Article 19
Principle

1. Any judgment opening insolvency proceedings handed down by a court of a Member State which has jurisdiction pursuant to Article 3 shall be recognised in all other Member States from the moment that it becomes effective in the State of the opening of proceedings.

The rule laid down in the first subparagraph shall also apply where, on account of a debtor's capacity, insolvency proceedings cannot be brought against that debtor in other Member States.

2. Recognition of the proceedings referred to in Article 3(1) shall not preclude the opening of the proceedings referred to in Article 3(2) by a court in another Member State. The latter proceedings shall be secondary insolvency proceedings within the meaning of Chapter III.

Article 20
Effects of recognition

1. The judgment opening insolvency proceedings as referred to in Article 3(1) shall, with no further formalities, produce the same effects in any other Member State as under the law of the State of the opening of proceedings, unless this Regulation provides otherwise and as long as no proceedings referred to in Article 3(2) are opened in that other Member State.

2. The effects of the proceedings referred to in Article 3(2) may not be challenged in other Member States. Any restriction of creditors' rights, in particular a stay or discharge, shall produce effects vis-à-vis assets situated within the territory of another Member State only in the case of those creditors who have given their consent.

Article 21
Powers of the insolvency practitioner

1. The insolvency practitioner appointed by a court which has jurisdiction pursuant to Article 3(1) may exercise all the powers conferred on it, by the law of the State of the opening of proceedings, in another Member State, as long as no other insolvency proceedings have been opened there and no preservation measure to the contrary has been taken there further to a request for the opening of insolvency proceedings in that State. Subject to Articles 8 and 10, the insolvency practitioner may, in particular, remove the debtor's assets from the territory of the Member State in which they are situated.

2. The insolvency practitioner appointed by a court which has jurisdiction pursuant to Article 3(2) may in any other Member State claim through the courts or out of court that moveable property was removed from the territory of the State of the opening of proceedings to the territory of that other Member State after the opening of the insolvency proceedings. The insolvency practitioner may also bring any action to set aside which is in the interests of the creditors.

3. In exercising its powers, the insolvency practitioner shall comply with the law of the Member State within the territory of which it intends to take action, in particular with regard to procedures for the realisation of assets. Those powers may not include coercive measures, unless ordered by a court of that Member State, or the right to rule on legal proceedings or disputes.

Article 22
Proof of the insolvency practitioner's appointment

The insolvency practitioner's appointment shall be evidenced by a certified copy of the original decision appointing it or by any other certificate issued by the court which has jurisdiction.

A translation into the official language or one of the official languages of the Member State within the territory of which it intends to act may be required. No legalisation or other similar formality shall be required.

Article 23
Return and imputation

1. A creditor which, after the opening of the proceedings referred to in Article 3(1), obtains by any means, in particular through enforcement, total or partial satisfaction of its claim on the assets belonging to a debtor situated within the territory of another Member State, shall return what it has obtained to the insolvency practitioner, subject to Articles 8 and 10.

2. In order to ensure the equal treatment of creditors, a creditor which has, in the course of insolvency proceedings, obtained a dividend on its claim shall share in distributions made in other proceedings only where creditors of the same ranking or category have, in those other proceedings, obtained an equivalent dividend.

Article 24
Establishment of insolvency registers

1. Member States shall establish and maintain in their territory one or several registers in which information concerning insolvency proceedings is published ('insolvency registers'). That information shall be published as soon as possible after the opening of such proceedings.

2. The information referred to in paragraph 1 shall be made publicly available, subject to the conditions laid down in Article 27, and shall include the following ('mandatory information'):
   (a) the date of the opening of insolvency proceedings;
   (b) the court opening insolvency proceedings and the case reference number, if any;
   (c) the type of insolvency proceedings referred to in Annex A that were opened and, where applicable, any relevant subtype of such proceedings opened in accordance with national law;
   (d) whether jurisdiction for opening proceedings is based on Article 3(1), 3(2) or 3(4);
   (e) if the debtor is a company or a legal person, the debtor's name, registration number, registered office or, if different, postal address;
   (f) if the debtor is an individual whether or not exercising an independent business or professional activity, the debtor's name, registration number, if any, and postal address or, where the address is protected, the debtor's place and date of birth;
   (g) the name, postal address or e-mail address of the insolvency practitioner, if any, appointed in the proceedings;
   (h) the time limit for lodging claims, if any, or a reference to the criteria for calculating that time limit;
   (i) the date of closing main insolvency proceedings, if any;
   (j) the court before which and, where applicable, the time limit within which a challenge of the decision opening insolvency proceedings is to be lodged in accordance with Article 5, or a reference to the criteria for calculating that time limit.
3. Paragraph 2 shall not preclude Member States from including documents or additional information in their national insolvency registers, such as directors' disqualifications related to insolvency.

4. Member States shall not be obliged to include in the insolvency registers the information referred to in paragraph 1 of this Article in relation to individuals not exercising an independent business or professional activity, or to make such information publicly available through the system of interconnection of those registers, provided that known foreign creditors are informed, pursuant to Article 54, of the elements referred to under point (j) of paragraph 2 of this Article.

Where a Member State makes use of the possibility referred to in the first subparagraph, the insolvency proceedings shall not affect the claims of foreign creditors who have not received the information referred to in the first subparagraph.

5. The publication of information in the registers under this Regulation shall not have any legal effects other than those set out in national law and in Article 55(6).

Article 25
Interconnection of insolvency registers

1. The Commission shall establish a decentralised system for the interconnection of insolvency registers by means of implementing acts. That system shall be composed of the insolvency registers and the European e-Justice Portal, which shall serve as a central public electronic access point to information in the system. The system shall provide a search service in all the official languages of the institutions of the Union in order to make available the mandatory information and any other documents or information included in the insolvency registers which the Member States choose to make available through the European e-Justice Portal.

2. By means of implementing acts in accordance with the procedure referred to in Article 87, the Commission shall adopt the following by 26 June 2019:
   (a) the technical specification defining the methods of communication and information exchange by electronic means on the basis of the established interface specification for the system of interconnection of insolvency registers;
   (b) the technical measures ensuring the minimum information technology security standards for communication and distribution of information within the system of interconnection of insolvency registers;
   (c) minimum criteria for the search service provided by the European e-Justice Portal based on the information set out in Article 24;
   (d) minimum criteria for the presentation of the results of such searches based on the information set out in Article 24;
   (e) the means and the technical conditions of availability of services provided by the system of interconnection; and
   (f) a glossary containing a basic explanation of the national insolvency proceedings listed in Annex A.

Article 26
Costs of establishing and interconnecting insolvency registers

1. The establishment, maintenance and future development of the system of interconnection of insolvency registers shall be financed from the general budget of the Union.

2. Each Member State shall bear the costs of establishing and adjusting its national insolvency registers to make them interoperable with the European e-Justice Portal, as well as the costs of administering, operating and maintaining those registers. This shall be without prejudice to the possibility to apply for grants to support such activities under the Union's financial programmes.

Article 27
Conditions of access to information via the system of interconnection

1. Member States shall ensure that the mandatory information referred to in points (a) to (j) of Article 24(2) is available free of charge via the system of interconnection of insolvency registers.

2. This Regulation shall not preclude Member States from charging a reasonable fee for access to the documents or additional information referred to in Article 24(3) via the system of interconnection of insolvency registers.

3. Member States may make access to mandatory information concerning individuals who are not exercising an independent business or professional activity, and concerning individuals exercising an independent business or professional activity when the insolvency proceedings are not related to that activity, subject to supplementary search criteria relating to the debtor in addition to the minimum criteria referred to in point (c) of Article 25(2).

4. Member States may require that access to the information referred to in paragraph 3 be made conditional upon a request to the competent authority. Member States may make access conditional upon the verification of the existence of a legitimate interest for accessing such information. The requesting person shall be able to submit the request for information electronically by means of a standard form

via the European e-Justice Portal. Where a legitimate interest is required, it shall be permissible for the requesting person to justify his request by electronic copies of relevant documents. The requesting person shall be provided with an answer by the competent authority within 3 working days.

The requesting person shall not be obliged to provide translations of the documents justifying his request, or to bear any costs of translation which the competent authority may incur.

Article 28
Publication in another Member State

1. The insolvency practitioner or the debtor in possession shall request that notice of the judgment opening insolvency proceedings and, where appropriate, the decision appointing the insolvency practitioner be published in any other Member State where an establishment of the debtor is located in accordance with the publication procedures provided for in that Member State. Such publication shall specify, where appropriate, the insolvency practitioner appointed and whether the jurisdiction rule applied is that pursuant to Article 3(1) or (2).

2. The insolvency practitioner or the debtor in possession may request that the information referred to in paragraph 1 be published in any other Member State where the insolvency practitioner or the debtor in possession deems it necessary in accordance with the publication procedures provided for in that Member State.

Article 29
Registration in public registers of another Member State

1. Where the law of a Member State in which an establishment of the debtor is located and this establishment has been entered into a public register of that Member State, or the law of a Member State in which immovable property belonging to the debtor is located, requires information on the opening of insolvency proceedings referred to in Article 28 to be published in the land register, company register or any other public register, the insolvency practitioner or the debtor in possession shall take all the necessary measures to ensure such a registration.

2. The insolvency practitioner or the debtor in possession may request such registration in any other Member State, provided that the law of the Member State where the register is kept allows such registration.

Article 3
Costs

The costs of the publication and registration provided for in Articles 28 and 29 shall be regarded as costs and expenses incurred in the proceedings.

Article 31
Honouring of an obligation to a debtor

1. Where an obligation has been honoured in a Member State for the benefit of a debtor who is subject to insolvency proceedings opened in another Member State, when it should have been honoured for the benefit of the insolvency practitioner in those proceedings, the person honouring the obligation shall be deemed to have discharged it if he was unaware of the opening of the proceedings.

2. Where such an obligation is honoured before the publication provided for in Article 28 has been effected, the person honouring the obligation shall be presumed, in the absence of proof to the contrary, to have been unaware of the opening of insolvency proceedings. Where the obligation is honoured after such publication has been effected, the person honouring the obligation shall be presumed, in the absence of proof to the contrary, to have been aware of the opening of proceedings.

Article 32
Recognition and enforceability of other judgments

1. Judgments handed down by a court whose judgment concerning the opening of proceedings is recognised in accordance with Article 19 and which concern the course and closure of insolvency proceedings, and compositions approved by that court, shall also be recognised with no further formalities. Such judgments shall be enforced in accordance with Articles 39 to 44 and 47 to 57 of Regulation (EU) No 1215/2012.

The first subparagraph shall also apply to judgments deriving directly from the insolvency proceedings and which are closely linked with them, even if they were handed down by another court.

The first subparagraph shall also apply to judgments relating to preservation measures taken after the request for the opening of insolvency proceedings or in connection with it.

2. The recognition and enforcement of judgments other than those referred to in paragraph 1 of this Article shall be governed by Regulation (EU) No 1215/2012 provided that that Regulation is applicable.

Article 33
Public policy

Any Member State may refuse to recognise insolvency proceedings opened in another Member State or to enforce a judgment handed down in the context of such proceedings where the effects of such recognition or enforcement would be manifestly contrary to that State's public policy, in particular its fundamental principles or the constitutional rights and liberties of the individual.

CHAPTER III: SECONDARY INSOLVENCY PROCEEDINGS

Article 34
Opening of proceedings

Where main insolvency proceedings have been opened by a court of a Member State and recognised in another Member State, a court of that other Member State which has jurisdiction pursuant to Article 3(2) may open secondary insolvency proceedings in accordance with the provisions set out in this Chapter. Where the main insolvency proceedings required that the debtor be insolvent, the debtor's insolvency shall not be re-examined in the Member State in which secondary insolvency proceedings may be opened. The effects of secondary insolvency proceedings shall be restricted to the assets of the debtor situated within the territory of the Member State in which those proceedings have been opened.

Article 35
Applicable law

Save as otherwise provided for in this Regulation, the law applicable to secondary insolvency proceedings shall be that of the Member State within the territory of which the secondary insolvency proceedings are opened.

Article 36
Right to give an undertaking in order to avoid secondary insolvency proceedings

1. In order to avoid the opening of secondary insolvency proceedings, the insolvency practitioner in the main insolvency proceedings may give a unilateral undertaking (the 'undertaking') in respect of the assets located in the Member State in which secondary insolvency proceedings could be opened, that when distributing those assets or the proceeds received as a result of their realisation, it will comply with the distribution and priority rights under national law that creditors would have if secondary insolvency proceedings were opened in that Member State. The undertaking shall specify the factual assumptions on which it is based, in particular in respect of the value of the assets located in the Member State concerned and the options available to realise such assets.

2. Where an undertaking has been given in accordance with this Article, the law applicable to the distribution of proceeds from the realisation of assets referred to in paragraph 1, to the ranking of creditors' claims, and to the rights of creditors in relation to the assets referred to in paragraph 1 shall be the law of the Member State in which secondary insolvency proceedings could have been opened. The relevant point in time for determining the assets referred to in paragraph 1 shall be the moment at which the undertaking is given.

3. The undertaking shall be made in the official language or one of the official languages of the Member State where secondary insolvency proceedings could have been opened, or, where there are several official languages in that Member State, the official language or one of the official languages of the place in which secondary insolvency proceedings could have been opened.

4. The undertaking shall be made in writing. It shall be subject to any other requirements relating to form and approval requirements as to distributions, if any, of the State of the opening of the main insolvency proceedings.

5. The undertaking shall be approved by the known local creditors. The rules on qualified majority and voting that apply to the adoption of restructuring plans under the law of the Member State where secondary insolvency proceedings could have been opened shall also apply to the approval of the undertaking. Creditors shall be able to participate in the vote by distance means of communication, where national law so permits. The insolvency practitioner shall inform the known local creditors of the undertaking, of the rules and procedures for its approval, and of the approval or rejection of the undertaking.

6. An undertaking given and approved in accordance with this Article shall be binding on the estate. If secondary insolvency proceedings are opened in accordance with Articles 37 and 38, the insolvency practitioner in the main insolvency proceedings shall transfer any assets which it removed from the territory of that Member State after the undertaking was given or, where those assets have already been realised, their proceeds, to the insolvency practitioner in the secondary insolvency proceedings.

7. Where the insolvency practitioner has given an undertaking, it shall inform local creditors about the intended distributions prior to distributing the assets and proceeds referred to in paragraph 1. If that information does not comply with the terms of the undertaking or the applicable law, any local creditor may challenge such distribution before the courts of the Member State in which main insolvency proceedings have been opened in order to obtain a distribution in accordance with the terms of the undertaking and the applicable law. In such cases, no distribution shall take place until the court has taken a decision on the challenge.

8. Local creditors may apply to the courts of the Member State in which main insolvency proceedings have been opened, in order to require the insolvency practitioner in the main insolvency proceedings to take any suitable measures necessary to ensure compliance with the terms of the undertaking available under the law of the State of the opening of main insolvency proceedings.

9. Local creditors may also apply to the courts of the Member State in which secondary insolvency proceedings could have been opened in order to require the court to take provisional or protective measures to ensure compliance by the insolvency practitioner with the terms of the undertaking.

10. The insolvency practitioner shall be liable for any damage caused to local creditors as a result of its noncompliance with the obligations and requirements set out in this Article.

11. For the purpose of this Article, an authority which is established in the Member State where secondary insolvency proceedings could have been opened and which is obliged under Directive 2008/94/EC of the European Parliament and of the Council[16] to guarantee the payment of employees' outstanding claims resulting from contracts of employment or employment relationships shall be considered to be a local creditor, where the national law so provides.

Article 37
Right to request the opening of secondary insolvency proceedings

1. The opening of secondary insolvency proceedings may be requested by:
   (a) the insolvency practitioner in the main insolvency proceedings;
   (b) any other person or authority empowered to request the opening of insolvency proceedings under the law of the Member State within the territory of which the opening of secondary insolvency proceedings is requested.

2. Where an undertaking has become binding in accordance with Article 36, the request for opening secondary insolvency proceedings shall be lodged within 30 days of having received notice of the approval of the undertaking.

---

[16] Directive 2008/94/EC of the European Parliament and of the Council of 22 October 2008 on the protection of employees in the event of the insolvency of their employer (OJ L 283, 28.10.2008, p. 36).

Article 38
Decision to open secondary insolvency proceedings

1. A court seised of a request to open secondary insolvency proceedings shall immediately give notice to the insolvency practitioner or the debtor in possession in the main insolvency proceedings and give it an opportunity to be heard on the request.

2. Where the insolvency practitioner in the main insolvency proceedings has given an undertaking in accordance with Article 36, the court referred to in paragraph 1 of this Article shall, at the request of the insolvency practitioner, not open secondary insolvency proceedings if it is satisfied that the undertaking adequately protects the general interests of local creditors.

3. Where a temporary stay of individual enforcement proceedings has been granted in order to allow for negotiations between the debtor and its creditors, the court, at the request of the insolvency practitioner or the debtor in possession, may stay the opening of secondary insolvency proceedings for a period not exceeding 3 months, provided that suitable measures are in place to protect the interests of local creditors.

The court referred to in paragraph 1 may order protective measures to protect the interests of local creditors by requiring the insolvency practitioner or the debtor in possession not to remove or dispose of any assets which are located in the Member State where its establishment is located unless this is done in the ordinary course of business. The court may also order other measures to protect the interest of local creditors during a stay, unless this is incompatible with the national rules on civil procedure.

The stay of the opening of secondary insolvency proceedings shall be lifted by the court of its own motion or at the request of any creditor if, during the stay, an agreement in the negotiations referred to in the first subparagraph has been concluded.

The stay may be lifted by the court of its own motion or at the request of any creditor if the continuation of the stay is detrimental to the creditor's rights, in particular if the negotiations have been disrupted or it has become evident that they are unlikely to be concluded, or if the insolvency practitioner or the debtor in possession has infringed the prohibition on disposal of its assets or on removal of them from the territory of the Member State where the establishment is located.

4. At the request of the insolvency practitioner in the main insolvency proceedings, the court referred to in paragraph 1 may open a type of insolvency proceedings as listed in Annex A other than the type initially requested, provided that the conditions for opening that type of proceedings under national law are fulfilled and that that type of proceedings is the most appropriate as regards the interests of the local creditors and coherence between the main and secondary insolvency proceedings. The second sentence of Article 34 shall apply.

Article 39
Judicial review of the decision to open secondary insolvency proceedings

The insolvency practitioner in the main insolvency proceedings may challenge the decision to open secondary insolvency proceedings before the courts of the Member State in which secondary insolvency proceedings have been opened on the ground that the court did not comply with the conditions and requirements of Article 38.

Article 40
Advance payment of costs and expenses

Where the law of the Member State in which the opening of secondary insolvency proceedings is requested requires that the debtor's assets be sufficient to cover in whole or in part the costs and expenses of the proceedings, the court may, when it receives such a request, require the applicant to make an advance payment of costs or to provide appropriate security.

Article 41
Cooperation and communication between insolvency practitioners

1. The insolvency practitioner in the main insolvency proceedings and the insolvency practitioner or practitioners in secondary insolvency proceedings concerning the same debtor shall cooperate with each other to the extent such cooperation is not incompatible with the rules applicable to the

respective proceedings. Such cooperation may take any form, including the conclusion of agreements or protocols.

2. In implementing the cooperation set out in paragraph 1, the insolvency practitioners shall:

(a) as soon as possible communicate to each other any information which may be relevant to the other proceedings, in particular any progress made in lodging and verifying claims and all measures aimed at rescuing or restructuring the debtor, or at terminating the proceedings, provided appropriate arrangements are made to protect confidential information;

(b) explore the possibility of restructuring the debtor and, where such a possibility exists, coordinate the elaboration and implementation of a restructuring plan;

(c) coordinate the administration of the realisation or use of the debtor's assets and affairs; the insolvency practitioner in the secondary insolvency proceedings shall give the insolvency practitioner in the main insolvency proceedings an early opportunity to submit proposals on the realisation or use of the assets in the secondary insolvency proceedings.

3. Paragraphs 1 and 2 shall apply mutatis mutandis to situations where, in the main or in the secondary insolvency proceedings or in any territorial insolvency proceedings concerning the same debtor and open at the same time, the debtor remains in possession of its assets.

Article 42
Cooperation and communication between courts

1. In order to facilitate the coordination of main, territorial and secondary insolvency proceedings concerning the same debtor, a court before which a request to open insolvency proceedings is pending, or which has opened such proceedings, shall cooperate with any other court before which a request to open insolvency proceedings is pending, or which has opened such proceedings, to the extent that such cooperation is not incompatible with the rules applicable to each of the proceedings. For that purpose, the courts may, where appropriate, appoint an independent person or body acting on its instructions, provided that it is not incompatible with the rules applicable to them.

2. In implementing the cooperation set out in paragraph 1, the courts, or any appointed person or body acting on their behalf, as referred to in paragraph 1, may communicate directly with, or request information or assistance directly from, each other provided that such communication respects the procedural rights of the parties to the proceedings and the confidentiality of information.

3. The cooperation referred to in paragraph 1 may be implemented by any means that the court considers appropriate. It may, in particular, concern:

(a) coordination in the appointment of the insolvency practitioners;

(b) communication of information by any means considered appropriate by the court;

(c) coordination of the administration and supervision of the debtor's assets and affairs;

(d) coordination of the conduct of hearings;

(e) coordination in the approval of protocols, where necessary.

Article 43
Cooperation and communication between insolvency practitioners and courts

1. In order to facilitate the coordination of main, territorial and secondary insolvency proceedings opened in respect of the same debtor:

(a) an insolvency practitioner in main insolvency proceedings shall cooperate and communicate with any court before which a request to open secondary insolvency proceedings is pending or which has opened such proceedings;

(b) an insolvency practitioner in territorial or secondary insolvency proceedings shall cooperate and communicate with the court before which a request to open main insolvency proceedings is pending or which has opened such proceedings; and

(c) an insolvency practitioner in territorial or secondary insolvency proceedings shall cooperate and communicate with the court before which a request to open other territorial or secondary insolvency proceedings is pending or which has opened such proceedings;

to the extent that such cooperation and communication are not incompatible with the rules applicable to each of the proceedings and do not entail any conflict of interest.

2. The cooperation referred to in paragraph 1 may be implemented by any appropriate means, such as those set out in Article 42(3).

Article 44
Costs of cooperation and communication

The requirements laid down in Articles 42 and 43 shall not result in courts charging costs to each other for cooperation and communication.

Article 45
Exercise of creditors' rights

1. Any creditor may lodge its claim in the main insolvency proceedings and in any secondary insolvency proceedings.

2. The insolvency practitioners in the main and any secondary insolvency proceedings shall lodge in other proceedings claims which have already been lodged in the proceedings for which they were appointed, provided that the interests of creditors in the latter proceedings are served by doing so, subject to the right of creditors to oppose such lodgement or to withdraw the lodgement of their claims where the law applicable so provides.

3. The insolvency practitioner in the main or secondary insolvency proceedings shall be entitled to participate in other proceedings on the same basis as a creditor, in particular by attending creditors' meetings.

Article 46
Stay of the process of realisation of assets

1. The court which opened the secondary insolvency proceedings shall stay the process of realisation of assets in whole or in part on receipt of a request from the insolvency practitioner in the main insolvency proceedings. In such a case, it may require the insolvency practitioner in the main insolvency proceedings to take any suitable measure to guarantee the interests of the creditors in the secondary insolvency proceedings and of individual classes of creditors. Such a request from the insolvency practitioner may be rejected only if it is manifestly of no interest to the creditors in the main insolvency proceedings. Such a stay of the process of realisation of assets may be ordered for up to 3 months. It may be continued or renewed for similar periods.

2. The court referred to in paragraph 1 shall terminate the stay of the process of realisation of assets:
    (a) at the request of the insolvency practitioner in the main insolvency proceedings;
    (b) of its own motion, at the request of a creditor or at the request of the insolvency practitioner in the secondary insolvency proceedings if that measure no longer appears justified, in particular, by the interests of creditors in the main insolvency proceedings or in the secondary insolvency proceedings.

Article 47
Power of the insolvency practitioner to propose restructuring plans

1. Where the law of the Member State where secondary insolvency proceedings have been opened allows for such proceedings to be closed without liquidation by a restructuring plan, a composition or a comparable measure, the insolvency practitioner in the main insolvency proceedings shall be empowered to propose such a measure in accordance with the procedure of that Member State.

2. Any restriction of creditors' rights arising from a measure referred to in paragraph 1 which is proposed in secondary insolvency proceedings, such as a stay of payment or discharge of debt, shall have no effect in respect of assets of a debtor that are not covered by those proceedings, without the consent of all the creditors having an interest.

Article 48
Impact of closure of insolvency proceedings

1. Without prejudice to Article 49, the closure of insolvency proceedings shall not prevent the continuation of other insolvency proceedings concerning the same debtor which are still open at that point in time.

2. Where insolvency proceedings concerning a legal person or a company in the Member State of that person's or company's registered office would entail the dissolution of the legal person or of the company, that legal person or company shall not cease to exist until any other insolvency proceedings concerning the same debtor have been closed, or the insolvency practitioner or practitioners in such proceedings have given consent to the dissolution.

Article 49
Assets remaining in the secondary insolvency proceedings

If, by the liquidation of assets in the secondary insolvency proceedings, it is possible to meet all claims allowed under those proceedings, the insolvency practitioner appointed in those proceedings shall immediately transfer any assets remaining to the insolvency practitioner in the main insolvency proceedings.

Article 50

Subsequent opening of the main insolvency proceedings

Where the proceedings referred to in Article 3(1) are opened following the opening of the proceedings referred to in Article 3(2) in another Member State, Articles 41, 45, 46, 47 and 49 shall apply to those opened first, in so far as the progress of those proceedings so permits.

Article 51
Conversion of secondary insolvency proceedings

1. At the request of the insolvency practitioner in the main insolvency proceedings, the court of the Member State in which secondary insolvency proceedings have been opened may order the conversion of the secondary insolvency proceedings into another type of insolvency proceedings listed in Annex A, provided that the conditions for opening that type of proceedings under national law are fulfilled and that that type of proceedings is the most appropriate as regards the interests of the local creditors and coherence between the main and secondary insolvency proceedings.

2. When considering the request referred to in paragraph 1, the court may seek information from the insolvency practitioners involved in both proceedings.

Article 52
Preservation measures

Where the court of a Member State which has jurisdiction pursuant to Article 3(1) appoints a temporary administrator in order to ensure the preservation of a debtor's assets, that temporary administrator shall be empowered to request any measures to secure and preserve any of the debtor's assets situated in another Member State, provided for under the law of that Member State, for the period between the request for the opening of insolvency proceedings and the judgment opening the proceedings.

CHAPTER IV: PROVISION OF INFORMATION FOR CREDITORS
AND LODGEMENT OF THEIR CLAIMS

Article 53
Right to lodge claims

Any foreign creditor may lodge claims in insolvency proceedings by any means of communication, which are accepted by the law of the State of the opening of proceedings. Representation by a lawyer or another legal professional shall not be mandatory for the sole purpose of lodging of claims.

Article 54
Duty to inform creditors

1. As soon as insolvency proceedings are opened in a Member State, the court of that State having jurisdiction or the insolvency practitioner appointed by that court shall immediately inform the known foreign creditors.

2. The information referred to in paragraph 1, provided by an individual notice, shall in particular include time limits, the penalties laid down with regard to those time limits, the body or authority empowered to accept the lodgement of claims and any other measures laid down. Such notice shall

also indicate whether creditors whose claims are preferential or secured *in rem* need to lodge their claims. The notice shall also include a copy of the standard form for lodging of claims referred to in Article 55 or information on where that form is available.

3. The information referred to in paragraphs 1 and 2 of this Article shall be provided using the standard notice form to be established in accordance with Article 88. The form shall be published in the European e-Justice Portal and shall bear the heading 'Notice of insolvency proceedings' in all the official languages of the institutions of the Union. It shall be transmitted in the official language of the State of the opening of proceedings or, if there are several official languages in that Member State, in the official language or one of the official languages of the place where insolvency proceedings have been opened, or in another language which that State has indicated it can accept, in accordance with Article 55(5), if it can be assumed that that language is easier to understand for the foreign creditors.

4. In insolvency proceedings relating to an individual not exercising a business or professional activity, the use of the standard form referred to in this Article shall not be obligatory if creditors are not required to lodge their claims in order to have their claims taken into account in the proceedings.

Article 55
Procedure for lodging claims

1. Any foreign creditor may lodge its claim using the standard claims form to be established in accordance with Article 88. The form shall bear the heading 'Lodgement of claims' in all the official languages of the institutions of the Union.

2. The standard claims form referred to in paragraph 1 shall include the following information:
    (a) the name, postal address, e-mail address, if any, personal identification number, if any, and bank details of the foreign creditor referred to in paragraph 1;
    (b) the amount of the claim, specifying the principal and, where applicable, interest and the date on which it arose and the date on which it became due, if different;
    (c) if interest is claimed, the interest rate, whether the interest is of a legal or contractual nature, the period of time for which the interest is claimed and the capitalised amount of interest;
    (d) if costs incurred in asserting the claim prior to the opening of proceedings are claimed, the amount and the details of those costs;
    (e) the nature of the claim;
    (f) whether any preferential creditor status is claimed and the basis of such a claim;
    (g) whether security *in rem* or a reservation of title is alleged in respect of the claim and if so, what assets are covered by the security interest being invoked, the date on which the security was granted and, where the security has been registered, the registration number; and
    (h) whether any set-off is claimed and, if so, the amounts of the mutual claims existing on the date when insolvency proceedings were opened, the date on which they arose and the amount net of set-off claimed.

The standard claims form shall be accompanied by copies of any supporting documents.

3. The standard claims form shall indicate that the provision of information concerning the bank details and the personal identification number of the creditor referred to in point (a) of paragraph 2 is not compulsory.

4. When a creditor lodges its claim by means other than the standard form referred to in paragraph 1, the claim shall contain the information referred to in paragraph 2.

5. Claims may be lodged in any official language of the institutions of the Union. The court, the insolvency practitioner or the debtor in possession may require the creditor to provide a translation in the official language of the State of the opening of proceedings or, if there are several official languages in that Member State, in the official language or one of the official languages of the place where insolvency proceedings have been opened, or in another language which that Member State has indicated it can accept. Each Member State shall indicate whether it accepts any official language of the institutions of the Union other than its own for the purpose of the lodging of claims.

6. Claims shall be lodged within the period stipulated by the law of the State of the opening of proceedings. In the case of a foreign creditor, that period shall not be less than 30 days following the publication of the opening of insolvency proceedings in the insolvency register of the State of the

opening of proceedings. Where a Member State relies on Article 24(4), that period shall not be less than 30 days following a creditor having been informed pursuant to Article 54.

7. Where the court, the insolvency practitioner or the debtor in possession has doubts in relation to a claim lodged in accordance with this Article, it shall give the creditor the opportunity to provide additional evidence on the existence and the amount of the claim.

CHAPTER V: INSOLVENCY PROCEEDINGS OF MEMBERS
OF A GROUP OF COMPANIES

Section 1
Cooperation and communication

Article 56
Cooperation and communication between insolvency practitioners

1. Where insolvency proceedings relate to two or more members of a group of companies, an insolvency practitioner appointed in proceedings concerning a member of the group shall cooperate with any insolvency practitioner appointed in proceedings concerning another member of the same group to the extent that such cooperation is appropriate to facilitate the effective administration of those proceedings, is not incompatible with the rules applicable to such proceedings and does not entail any conflict of interest. That cooperation may take any form, including the conclusion of agreements or protocols.

2. In implementing the cooperation set out in paragraph 1, insolvency practitioners shall:
   (a) as soon as possible communicate to each other any information which may be relevant to the other proceedings, provided appropriate arrangements are made to protect confidential information;
   (b) consider whether possibilities exist for coordinating the administration and supervision of the affairs of the group members which are subject to insolvency proceedings, and if so, coordinate such administration and supervision;
   (c) consider whether possibilities exist for restructuring group members which are subject to insolvency proceedings and, if so, coordinate with regard to the proposal and negotiation of a coordinated restructuring plan.

For the purposes of points (b) and (c), all or some of the insolvency practitioners referred to in paragraph 1 may agree to grant additional powers to an insolvency practitioner appointed in one of the proceedings where such an agreement is permitted by the rules applicable to each of the proceedings. They may also agree on the allocation of certain tasks amongst them, where such allocation of tasks is permitted by the rules applicable to each of the proceedings.

Article 57
Cooperation and communication between courts

1. Where insolvency proceedings relate to two or more members of a group of companies, a court which has opened such proceedings shall cooperate with any other court before which a request to open proceedings concerning another member of the same group is pending or which has opened such proceedings to the extent that such cooperation is appropriate to facilitate the effective administration of the proceedings, is not incompatible with the rules applicable to them and does not entail any conflict of interest. For that purpose, the courts may, where appropriate, appoint an independent person or body to act on its instructions, provided that this is not incompatible with the rules applicable to them.

2. In implementing the cooperation set out in paragraph 1, courts, or any appointed person or body acting on their behalf, as referred to in paragraph 1, may communicate directly with each other, or request information or assistance directly from each other, provided that such communication respects the procedural rights of the parties to the proceedings and the confidentiality of information.

3. The cooperation referred to in paragraph 1 may be implemented by any means that the court considers appropriate. It may, in particular, concern:
   (a) coordination in the appointment of insolvency practitioners;
   (b) communication of information by any means considered appropriate by the court;

(c) coordination of the administration and supervision of the assets and affairs of the members of the group;

(d) coordination of the conduct of hearings;

(e) coordination in the approval of protocols where necessary.

Article 58

Cooperation and communication between insolvency practitioners and courts

An insolvency practitioner appointed in insolvency proceedings concerning a member of a group of companies:

(a) shall cooperate and communicate with any court before which a request for the opening of proceedings in respect of another member of the same group of companies is pending or which has opened such proceedings; and

(b) may request information from that court concerning the proceedings regarding the other member of the group or request assistance concerning the proceedings in which he has been appointed;

to the extent that such cooperation and communication are appropriate to facilitate the effective administration of the proceedings, do not entail any conflict of interest and are not incompatible with the rules applicable to them.

Article 59

Costs of cooperation and communication in proceedings concerning members of a group of companies

The costs of the cooperation and communication provided for in Articles 56 to 60 incurred by an insolvency practitioner or a court shall be regarded as costs and expenses incurred in the respective proceedings.

Article 60

Powers of the insolvency practitioner in proceedings concerning members of a group of companies

1. An insolvency practitioner appointed in insolvency proceedings opened in respect of a member of a group of companies may, to the extent appropriate to facilitate the effective administration of the proceedings:

(a) be heard in any of the proceedings opened in respect of any other member of the same group;

(b) request a stay of any measure related to the realisation of the assets in the proceedings opened with respect to any other member of the same group, provided that:

(i) a restructuring plan for all or some members of the group for which insolvency proceedings have been opened has been proposed under point (c) of Article 56(2) and presents a reasonable chance of success;

(ii) such a stay is necessary in order to ensure the proper implementation of the restructuring plan;

(iii) the restructuring plan would be to the benefit of the creditors in the proceedings for which the stay is requested; and

(iv) neither the insolvency proceedings in which the insolvency practitioner referred to in paragraph 1 of this Article has been appointed nor the proceedings in respect of which the stay is requested are subject to coordination under Section 2 of this Chapter;

(c) apply for the opening of group coordination proceedings in accordance with Article 61.

2. The court having opened proceedings referred to in point (b) of paragraph 1 shall stay any measure related to the realisation of the assets in the proceedings in whole or in part if it is satisfied that the conditions referred to in point (b) of paragraph 1 are fulfilled.

Before ordering the stay, the court shall hear the insolvency practitioner appointed in the proceedings for which the stay is requested. Such a stay may be ordered for any period, not exceeding 3 months, which the court considers appropriate and which is compatible with the rules applicable to the proceedings.

The court ordering the stay may require the insolvency practitioner referred to in paragraph 1 to take any suitable measure available under national law to guarantee the interests of the creditors in the proceedings.

The court may extend the duration of the stay by such further period or periods as it considers appropriate and which are compatible with the rules applicable to the proceedings, provided that the conditions referred to in points (b)(ii) to (iv) of paragraph 1 continue to be fulfilled and that the total duration of the stay (the initial period together with any such extensions) does not exceed 6 months.

Section 2

Coordination

Subsection 1

Procedure

Article 61

Request to open group coordination proceedings

1. Group coordination proceedings may be requested before any court having jurisdiction over the insolvency proceedings of a member of the group, by an insolvency practitioner appointed in insolvency proceedings opened in relation to a member of the group.

2. The request referred to in paragraph 1 shall be made in accordance with the conditions provided for by the law applicable to the proceedings in which the insolvency practitioner has been appointed.

3. The request referred to in paragraph 1 shall be accompanied by:
   (a) a proposal as to the person to be nominated as the group coordinator ('the coordinator'), details of his or her eligibility pursuant to Article 71, details of his or her qualifications and his or her written agreement to act as coordinator;
   (b) an outline of the proposed group coordination, and in particular the reasons why the conditions set out in Article 63(1) are fulfilled;
   (c) a list of the insolvency practitioners appointed in relation to the members of the group and, where relevant, the courts and competent authorities involved in the insolvency proceedings of the members of the group;
   (d) an outline of the estimated costs of the proposed group coordination and the estimation of the share of those costs to be paid by each member of the group.

Article 62

Priority rule

Without prejudice to Article 66, where the opening of group coordination proceedings is requested before courts of different Member States, any court other than the court first seised shall decline jurisdiction in favour of that court.

Article 63

Notice by the court seised

1. The court seised of a request to open group coordination proceedings shall give notice as soon as possible of the request for the opening of group coordination proceedings and of the proposed coordinator to the insolvency practitioners appointed in relation to the members of the group as indicated in the request referred to in point (c) of Article 61(3), if it is satisfied that:
   (a) the opening of such proceedings is appropriate to facilitate the effective administration of the insolvency proceedings relating to the different group members;
   (b) no creditor of any group member expected to participate in the proceedings is likely to be financially disadvantaged by the inclusion of that member in such proceedings; and
   (c) the proposed coordinator fulfils the requirements laid down in Article 71.

2. The notice referred to in paragraph 1 of this Article shall list the elements referred to in points (a) to (d) of Article 61(3).

3. The notice referred to in paragraph 1 shall be sent by registered letter, attested by an acknowledgment of receipt.

4. The court seised shall give the insolvency practitioners involved the opportunity to be heard.

Article 64
Objections by insolvency practitioners

1. An insolvency practitioner appointed in respect of any group member may object to:
    (a) the inclusion within group coordination proceedings of the insolvency proceedings in respect of which it has been appointed; or
    (b) the person proposed as a coordinator.

2. Objections pursuant to paragraph 1 of this Article shall be lodged with the court referred to in Article 63 within 30 days of receipt of notice of the request for the opening of group coordination proceedings by the insolvency practitioner referred to in paragraph 1 of this Article.

The objection may be made by means of the standard form established in accordance with Article 88.

3. Prior to taking the decision to participate or not to participate in the coordination in accordance with point (a) of paragraph 1, an insolvency practitioner shall obtain any approval which may be required under the law of the State of the opening of proceedings for which it has been appointed.

Article 65
Consequences of objection to the inclusion in group coordination

1. Where an insolvency practitioner has objected to the inclusion of the proceedings in respect of which it has been appointed in group coordination proceedings, those proceedings shall not be included in the group coordination proceedings.

2. The powers of the court referred to in Article 68 or of the coordinator arising from those proceedings shall have no effect as regards that member, and shall entail no costs for that member.

Article 66
Choice of court for group coordination proceedings

1. Where at least two-thirds of all insolvency practitioners appointed in insolvency proceedings of the members of the group have agreed that a court of another Member State having jurisdiction is the most appropriate court for the opening of group coordination proceedings, that court shall have exclusive jurisdiction.

2. The choice of court shall be made by joint agreement in writing or evidenced in writing. It may be made until such time as group coordination proceedings have been opened in accordance with Article 68.

3. Any court other than the court seised under paragraph 1 shall decline jurisdiction in favour of that court.

4. The request for the opening of group coordination proceedings shall be submitted to the court agreed in accordance with Article 61.

Article 67
Consequences of objections to the proposed coordinator

Where objections to the person proposed as coordinator have been received from an insolvency practitioner which does not also object to the inclusion in the group coordination proceedings of the member in respect of which it has been appointed, the court may refrain from appointing that person and invite the objecting insolvency practitioner to submit a new request in accordance with Article 61(3).

Article 68
Decision to open group coordination proceedings

1. After the period referred to in Article 64(2) has elapsed, the court may open group coordination proceedings where it is satisfied that the conditions of Article 63(1) are met. In such a case, the court shall:
    (a) appoint a coordinator;
    (b) decide on the outline of the coordination; and
    (c) decide on the estimation of costs and the share to be paid by the group members.

2. The decision opening group coordination proceedings shall be brought to the notice of the participating insolvency practitioners and of the coordinator.

Article 69
Subsequent opt-in by insolvency practitioners

1. In accordance with its national law, any insolvency practitioner may request, after the court decision referred to in Article 68, the inclusion of the proceedings in respect of which it has been appointed, where:
   (a) there has been an objection to the inclusion of the insolvency proceedings within the group coordination proceedings; or
   (b) insolvency proceedings with respect to a member of the group have been opened after the court has opened group coordination proceedings.
2. Without prejudice to paragraph 4, the coordinator may accede to such a request, after consulting the insolvency practitioners involved, where
   (a) he or she is satisfied that, taking into account the stage that the group coordination proceedings has reached at the time of the request, the criteria set out in points (a) and (b) of Article 63(1) are met; or
   (b) all insolvency practitioners involved agree, subject to the conditions in their national law.
3. The coordinator shall inform the court and the participating insolvency practitioners of his or her decision pursuant to paragraph 2 and of the reasons on which it is based.

4. Any participating insolvency practitioner or any insolvency practitioner whose request for inclusion in the group coordination proceedings has been rejected may challenge the decision referred to in paragraph 2 in accordance with the procedure set out under the law of the Member State in which the group coordination proceedings have been opened.

Article 70
Recommendations and group coordination plan

1. When conducting their insolvency proceedings, insolvency practitioners shall consider the recommendations of the coordinator and the content of the group coordination plan referred to in Article 72(1).

2. An insolvency practitioner shall not be obliged to follow in whole or in part the coordinator's recommendations or the group coordination plan.

If it does not follow the coordinator's recommendations or the group coordination plan, it shall give reasons for not doing so to the persons or bodies that it is to report to under its national law, and to the coordinator.

Subsection 2 General provisions

Article 71
The coordinator

1. The coordinator shall be a person eligible under the law of a Member State to act as an insolvency practitioner.

2. The coordinator shall not be one of the insolvency practitioners appointed to act in respect of any of the group members, and shall have no conflict of interest in respect of the group members, their creditors and the insolvency practitioners appointed in respect of any of the group members.

Article 72
Tasks and rights of the coordinator

1. The coordinator shall:
   (a) identify and outline recommendations for the coordinated conduct of the insolvency proceedings;
   (b) propose a group coordination plan that identifies, describes and recommends a comprehensive set of measures appropriate to an integrated approach to the resolution of the group members' insolvencies. In particular, the plan may contain proposals for:
      (i) the measures to be taken in order to re-establish the economic performance and the financial soundness of the group or any part of it;

    (ii) the settlement of intra-group disputes as regards intra-group transactions and avoidance actions;

    (iii) agreements between the insolvency practitioners of the insolvent group members.

2. The coordinator may also:

  (a) be heard and participate, in particular by attending creditors' meetings, in any of the proceedings opened in respect of any member of the group;

  (b) mediate any dispute arising between two or more insolvency practitioners of group members;

  (c) present and explain his or her group coordination plan to the persons or bodies that he or she is to report to under his or her national law;

  (d) request information from any insolvency practitioner in respect of any member of the group where that information is or might be of use when identifying and outlining strategies and measures in order to coordinate the proceedings; and

  (e) request a stay for a period of up to 6 months of the proceedings opened in respect of any member of the group, provided that such a stay is necessary in order to ensure the proper implementation of the plan and would be to the benefit of the creditors in the proceedings for which the stay is requested; or request the lifting of any existing stay. Such a request shall be made to the court that opened the proceedings for which a stay is requested.

3. The plan referred to in point (b) of paragraph 1 shall not include recommendations as to any consolidation of proceedings or insolvency estates.

4. The coordinator's tasks and rights as defined under this Article shall not extend to any member of the group not participating in group coordination proceedings.

5. The coordinator shall perform his or her duties impartially and with due care.

6. Where the coordinator considers that the fulfilment of his or her tasks requires a significant increase in the costs compared to the cost estimate referred to in point (d) of Article 61(3), and in any case, where the costs exceed 10 % of the estimated costs, the coordinator shall:

  (a) inform without delay the participating insolvency practitioners; and

  (b) seek the prior approval of the court opening group coordination proceedings.

Article 73
Languages

1. The coordinator shall communicate with the insolvency practitioner of a participating group member in the language agreed with the insolvency practitioner or, in the absence of an agreement, in the official language or one of the official languages of the institutions of the Union, and of the court which opened the proceedings in respect of that group member.

2. The coordinator shall communicate with a court in the official language applicable to that court.

Article 74
Cooperation between insolvency practitioners and the coordinator

1. Insolvency practitioners appointed in relation to members of a group and the coordinator shall cooperate with each other to the extent that such cooperation is not incompatible with the rules applicable to the respective proceedings.

2. In particular, insolvency practitioners shall communicate any information that is relevant for the coordinator to perform his or her tasks.

Article 75
Revocation of the appointment of the coordinator

The court shall revoke the appointment of the coordinator of its own motion or at the request of the insolvency practitioner of a participating group member where:

  (a) the coordinator acts to the detriment of the creditors of a participating group member; or

  (b) the coordinator fails to comply with his or her obligations under this Chapter.

Article 76
Debtor in possession

The provisions applicable, under this Chapter, to the insolvency practitioner shall also apply, where appropriate, to the debtor in possession.

Article 77
Costs and distribution

1. The remuneration for the coordinator shall be adequate, proportionate to the tasks fulfilled and reflect reasonable expenses.

2. On having completed his or her tasks, the coordinator shall establish the final statement of costs and the share to be paid by each member, and submit this statement to each participating insolvency practitioner and to the court opening coordination proceedings.

3. In the absence of objections by the insolvency practitioners within 30 days of receipt of the statement referred to in paragraph 2, the costs and the share to be paid by each member shall be deemed to be agreed. The statement shall be submitted to the court opening coordination proceedings for confirmation.

4. In the event of an objection, the court that opened the group coordination proceedings shall, upon the application of the coordinator or any participating insolvency practitioner, decide on the costs and the share to be paid by each member in accordance with the criteria set out in paragraph 1 of this Article, and taking into account the estimation of costs referred to in Article 68(1) and, where applicable, Article 72(6).

5. Any participating insolvency practitioner may challenge the decision referred to in paragraph 4 in accordance with the procedure set out under the law of the Member State where group coordination proceedings have been opened.

Chapter VI: Data Protection

Article 78
Data protection

1. National rules implementing Directive 95/46/EC shall apply to the processing of personal data carried out in the Member States pursuant to this Regulation, provided that processing operations referred to in Article 3(2) of Directive 95/46/EC are not concerned.

2. Regulation (EC) No 45/2001 shall apply to the processing of personal data carried out by the Commission pursuant to this Regulation.

Article 79
Responsibilities of Member States regarding the processing of personal data in national insolvency registers

1. Each Member State shall communicate to the Commission the name of the natural or legal person, public authority, agency or any other body designated by national law to exercise the functions of controller in accordance with point (d) of Article 2 of Directive 95/46/EC, with a view to its publication on the European e-Justice Portal.

2. Member States shall ensure that the technical measures for ensuring the security of personal data processed in their national insolvency registers referred to in Article 24 are implemented.

3. Member States shall be responsible for verifying that the controller, designated by national law in accordance with point (d) of Article 2 of Directive 95/46/EC, ensures compliance with the principles of data quality, in particular the accuracy and the updating of data stored in national insolvency registers.

4. Member States shall be responsible, in accordance with Directive 95/46/EC, for the collection and storage of data in national databases and for decisions taken to make such data available in the interconnected register that can be consulted via the European e-Justice Portal.

5. As part of the information that should be provided to data subjects to enable them to exercise their rights, and in particular the right to the erasure of data, Member States shall inform data subjects of the accessibility period set for personal data stored in insolvency registers.

Article 80
Responsibilities of the Commission in connection with the processing of personal data

1. The Commission shall exercise the responsibilities of controller pursuant to Article 2(d) of Regulation (EC) No 45/2001 in accordance with its respective responsibilities defined in this Article.

653

2. The Commission shall define the necessary policies and apply the necessary technical solutions to fulfil its responsibilities within the scope of the function of controller.

3. The Commission shall implement the technical measures required to ensure the security of personal data while in transit, in particular the confidentiality and integrity of any transmission to and from the European e-Justice Portal.

4. The obligations of the Commission shall not affect the responsibilities of the Member States and other bodies for the content and operation of the interconnected national databases run by them.

Article 81
Information obligations

Without prejudice to the information to be given to data subjects in accordance with Articles 11 and 12 of Regulation (EC) No 45/2001, the Commission shall inform data subjects, by means of publication through the European e-Justice Portal, about its role in the processing of data and the purposes for which those data will be processed.

Article 82
Storage of personal data

As regards information from interconnected national databases, no personal data relating to data subjects shall be stored in the European e-Justice Portal. All such data shall be stored in the national databases operated by the Member States or other bodies.

Article 83
Access to personal data via the European e-Justice Portal

Personal data stored in the national insolvency registers referred to in Article 24 shall be accessible via the European e-Justice Portal for as long as they remain accessible under national law.

CHAPTER VII: TRANSITIONAL AND FINAL PROVISIONS

Article 84
Applicability in time

1. The provisions of this Regulation shall apply only to insolvency proceedings opened after 26 June 2017. Acts committed by a debtor before that date shall continue to be governed by the law which was applicable to them at the time they were committed.

2. Notwithstanding Article 91 of this Regulation, Regulation (EC) No 1346/2000 shall continue to apply to insolvency proceedings which fall within the scope of that Regulation and which have been opened before 26 June 2017.

Article 85
Relationship to Conventions

1. This Regulation replaces, in respect of the matters referred to therein, and as regards relations between Member States, the Conventions concluded between two or more Member States, in particular:
  (a) the Convention between Belgium and France on Jurisdiction and the Validity and Enforcement of Judgments, Arbitration Awards and Authentic Instruments, signed at Paris on 8 July 1899;
  (b) the Convention between Belgium and Austria on Bankruptcy, Winding-up, Arrangements, Compositions and Suspension of Payments (with Additional Protocol of 13 June 1973), signed at Brussels on 16 July 1969;
  (c) the Convention between Belgium and the Netherlands on Territorial Jurisdiction, Bankruptcy and the Validity and Enforcement of Judgments, Arbitration Awards and Authentic Instruments, signed at Brussels on 28 March 1925;
  (d) the Treaty between Germany and Austria on Bankruptcy, Winding-up, Arrangements and Compositions, signed at Vienna on 25 May 1979;
  (e) the Convention between France and Austria on Jurisdiction, Recognition and Enforcement of Judgments on Bankruptcy, signed at Vienna on 27 February 1979;

(f) the Convention between France and Italy on the Enforcement of Judgments in Civil and Commercial Matters, signed at Rome on 3 June 1930;

(g) the Convention between Italy and Austria on Bankruptcy, Winding-up, Arrangements and Compositions, signed at Rome on 12 July 1977;

(h) the Convention between the Kingdom of the Netherlands and the Federal Republic of Germany on the Mutual Recognition and Enforcement of Judgments and other Enforceable Instruments in Civil and Commercial Matters, signed at The Hague on 30 August 1962;

(i) the Convention between the United Kingdom and the Kingdom of Belgium providing for the Reciprocal Enforcement of Judgments in Civil and Commercial Matters, with Protocol, signed at Brussels on 2 May 1934;

(j) the Convention between Denmark, Finland, Norway, Sweden and Iceland on Bankruptcy, signed at Copenhagen on 7 November 1933;

(k) the European Convention on Certain International Aspects of Bankruptcy, signed at Istanbul on 5 June 1990;

(l) the Convention between the Federative People's Republic of Yugoslavia and the Kingdom of Greece on the Mutual Recognition and Enforcement of Judgments, signed at Athens on 18 June 1959;

(m) the Agreement between the Federative People's Republic of Yugoslavia and the Republic of Austria on the Mutual Recognition and Enforcement of Arbitral Awards and Arbitral Settlements in Commercial Matters, signed at Belgrade on 18 March 1960;

(n) the Convention between the Federative People's Republic of Yugoslavia and the Italian Republic on Mutual Judicial Cooperation in Civil and Administrative Matters, signed at Rome on 3 December 1960;

(o) the Agreement between the Socialist Federative Republic of Yugoslavia and the Kingdom of Belgium on Judicial Cooperation in Civil and Commercial Matters, signed at Belgrade on 24 September 1971;

(p) the Convention between the Governments of Yugoslavia and France on the Recognition and Enforcement of Judgments in Civil and Commercial Matters, signed at Paris on 18 May 1971;

(q) the Agreement between the Czechoslovak Socialist Republic and the Hellenic Republic on Legal Aid in Civil and Criminal Matters, signed at Athens on 22 October 1980, still in force between the Czech Republic and Greece;

(r) the Agreement between the Czechoslovak Socialist Republic and the Republic of Cyprus on Legal Aid in Civil and Criminal Matters, signed at Nicosia on 23 April 1982, still in force between the Czech Republic and Cyprus;

(s) the Treaty between the Government of the Czechoslovak Socialist Republic and the Government of the Republic of France on Legal Aid and the Recognition and Enforcement of Judgments in Civil, Family and Commercial Matters, signed at Paris on 10 May 1984, still in force between the Czech Republic and France;

(t) the Treaty between the Czechoslovak Socialist Republic and the Italian Republic on Legal Aid in Civil and Criminal Matters, signed at Prague on 6 December 1985, still in force between the Czech Republic and Italy;

(u) the Agreement between the Republic of Latvia, the Republic of Estonia and the Republic of Lithuania on Legal Assistance and Legal Relationships, signed at Tallinn on 11 November 1992;

(v) the Agreement between Estonia and Poland on Granting Legal Aid and Legal Relations on Civil, Labour and Criminal Matters, signed at Tallinn on 27 November 1998;

(w) the Agreement between the Republic of Lithuania and the Republic of Poland on Legal Assistance and Legal Relations in Civil, Family, Labour and Criminal Matters, signed at Warsaw on 26 January 1993;

(x) the Convention between the Socialist Republic of Romania and the Hellenic Republic on legal assistance in civil and criminal matters and its Protocol, signed at Bucharest on 19 October 1972;

(y)   the Convention between the Socialist Republic of Romania and the French Republic on legal assistance in civil and commercial matters, signed at Paris on 5 November 1974;

(z)   the Agreement between the People's Republic of Bulgaria and the Hellenic Republic on Legal Assistance in Civil and Criminal Matters, signed at Athens on 10 April 1976;

(aa) the Agreement between the People's Republic of Bulgaria and the Republic of Cyprus on Legal Assistance in Civil and Criminal Matters, signed at Nicosia on 29 April 1983;

(ab) the Agreement between the Government of the People's Republic of Bulgaria and the Government of the French Republic on Mutual Legal Assistance in Civil Matters, signed at Sofia on 18 January 1989;

(ac) the Treaty between Romania and the Czech Republic on judicial assistance in civil matters, signed at Bucharest on 11 July 1994;

(ad) the Treaty between Romania and the Republic of Poland on legal assistance and legal relations in civil cases, signed at Bucharest on 15 May 1999.

2. The Conventions referred to in paragraph 1 shall continue to have effect with regard to proceedings opened before the entry into force of Regulation (EC) No 1346/2000.

3. This Regulation shall not apply:

(a)   in any Member State, to the extent that it is irreconcilable with the obligations arising in relation to bankruptcy from a convention concluded by that Member State with one or more third countries before the entry into force of Regulation (EC) No 1346/2000;

(b)   in the United Kingdom of Great Britain and Northern Ireland, to the extent that is irreconcilable with the obligations arising in relation to bankruptcy and the winding-up of insolvent companies from any arrangements with the Commonwealth existing at the time Regulation (EC) No 1346/2000 entered into force.

Article 86
Information on national and Union insolvency law

1. The Member States shall provide, within the framework of the European Judicial Network in civil and commercial matters established by Council Decision 2001/470/EC[17], and with a view to making the information available to the public, a short description of their national legislation and procedures relating to insolvency, in particular relating to the matters listed in Article 7(2).

2. The Member States shall update the information referred to in paragraph 1 regularly.

3. The Commission shall make information concerning this Regulation available to the public.

Article 87
Establishment of the interconnection of registers

The Commission shall adopt implementing acts establishing the interconnection of insolvency registers as referred to in Article 25. Those implementing acts shall be adopted in accordance with the examination procedure referred to in Article 89(3).

Article 88
Establishment and subsequent amendment of standard forms

The Commission shall adopt implementing acts establishing and, where necessary, amending the forms referred to in Article 27(4), Articles 54 and 55 and Article 64(2). Those implementing acts shall be adopted in accordance with the advisory procedure referred to in Article 89(2).

Article 89
Committee procedure

1. The Commission shall be assisted by a committee. That committee shall be a committee within the meaning of Regulation (EU) No 182/2011.

2. Where reference is made to this paragraph, Article 4 of Regulation (EU) No 182/2011 shall apply.

3. Where reference is made to this paragraph, Article 5 of Regulation (EU) No 182/2011 shall apply.

---

[17] Council Decision 2001/470/EC of 28 May 2001 establishing a European Judicial Network in civil and commercial matters (OJ L 174, 27.6.2001, p. 25).

Article 90
Review clause

1. No later than 27 June 2027, and every 5 years thereafter, the Commission shall present to the European Parliament, the Council and the European Economic and Social Committee a report on the application of this Regulation. The report shall be accompanied where necessary by a proposal for adaptation of this Regulation.

2. No later than 27 June 2022, the Commission shall present to the European Parliament, the Council and the European Economic and Social Committee a report on the application of the group coordination proceedings. The report shall be accompanied where necessary by a proposal for adaptation of this Regulation.

3. No later than 1 January 2016, the Commission shall submit to the European Parliament, the Council and the European Economic and Social Committee a study on the cross-border issues in the area of directors' liability and disqualifications.

4. No later than 27 June 2020, the Commission shall submit to the European Parliament, the Council and the European Economic and Social Committee a study on the issue of abusive forum shopping.

Article 91
Repeal

Regulation (EC) No 1346/2000 is repealed.

References to the repealed Regulation shall be construed as references to this Regulation and shall be read in accordance with the correlation table set out in Annex D to this Regulation.

Article 92
Entry into force

This Regulation shall enter into force on the twentieth day following that of its publication in the *Official Journal of the European Union*.

It shall apply from 26 June 2017, with the exception of:

    (a) Article 86, which shall apply from 26 June 2016;
    (b) Article 24(1), which shall apply from 26 June 2018; and
    (c) Article 25, which shall apply from 26 June 2019.

This Regulation shall be binding in its entirety and directly applicable in the Member States in accordance with the Treaties.

Done at Strasbourg, 20 May 2015.

For the European Parliament For the Council

The President The President

M. SCHULZ Z. KALNIŅA-LUKAŠEVICA

ANNEX A INSOLVENCY PROCEEDINGS REFERRED TO IN POINT (4) OF ARTICLE 2

Belgique/België
— Het faillissement/La faillite,
— De gerechtelijke reorganisatie door een collectief akkoord/La réorganisation judiciaire par accord collectif,
— De gerechtelijke reorganisatie door een minnelijk akkoord/La réorganisation judiciaire par accord amiable,
— De gerechtelijke reorganisatie door overdracht onder gerechtelijk gezag/La réorganisation judiciaire par transfert sous autorité de justice,
— De collectieve schuldenregeling/Le règlement collectif de dettes,
— De vrijwillige vereffening/La liquidation volontaire,
— De gerechtelijke vereffening/La liquidation judiciaire,
— De voorlopige ontneming van beheer, bepaald in artikel 8 van de faillissementswet/Le dessaisissement provisoire, visé à l'article 8 de la loi sur les faillites,

БЪЛГАРИЯ

— Производство по несъстоятелност,

Česká Republika

— Konkurs,
— Reorganizace,
— Oddlužení,

Deutschland

— Das Konkursverfahren,
— Das gerichtliche Vergleichsverfahren,
— Das Gesamtvollstreckungsverfahren,
— Das Insolvenzverfahren,

Eesti

— Pankrotimenetlus,
— Võlgade ümberkujundamise menetlus,

Éire/Ireland

— Compulsory winding-up by the court,
— Bankruptcy,
— The administration in bankruptcy of the estate of persons dying insolvent,
— Winding-up in bankruptcy of partnerships,
— Creditors' voluntary winding-up (with confirmation of a court),
— Arrangements under the control of the court which involve the vesting of all or part of the property of the debtor in the Official Assignee for realisation and distribution,
— Examinership,
— Debt Relief Notice,
— Debt Settlement Arrangement,
— Personal Insolvency Arrangement,

ΕΛΛΑΔΑ

— Η πτώχευση,
— Η ειδική εκκαθάριση εν λειτουργία,
— Σχέδιο αναδιοργάνωσης,
— Απλοποιημένη διαδικασία επί πτωχεύσεων μικρού αντικειμένου,
— Διαδικασία Εξυγίανσης,

España

— Concurso,
— Procedimiento de homologación de acuerdos de refinanciación,
— Procedimiento de acuerdos extrajudiciales de pago,
— Procedimiento de negociación pública para la consecución de acuerdos de refinanciación colectivos, acuerdos de refinanciación homologados y propuestas anticipadas de convenio,

France

— Sauvegarde,
— Sauvegarde accélérée,
— Sauvegarde financière accélérée,
— Redressement judiciaire,
— Liquidation judiciaire,

Hrvatska

— Stečajni postupak,

Italia

— Fallimento,
— Concordato preventivo,
— Liquidazione coatta amministrativa,
— Amministrazione straordinaria,

— Accordi di ristrutturazione,
— Procedure di composizione della crisi da sovraindebitamento del consumatore (accordo o piano),
— Liquidazione dei beni,

ΚΥΠΡΟΣ

— Υποχρεωτική εκκαθάριση από το Δικαστήριο,
— Εκούσια εκκαθάριση από μέλη,
— Εκούσια εκκαθάριση από πιστωτές
— Εκκαθάριση με την εποπτεία του Δικαστηρίου,
— Διάταγμα Παραλαβής και πτώχευσης κατόπιν Δικαστικού Διατάγματος,
— Διαχείριση της περιουσίας προσώπων που απεβίωσαν αφερέγγυα,

Latvija

— Tiesiskās aizsardzības process,
— Juridiskās personas maksātnespējas process,
— Fiziskās personas maksātnespējas process,

Lietuva

— Įmonės restruktūrizavimo byla,
— Įmonės bankroto byla,
— Įmonės bankroto procesas ne teismo tvarka,
— Fizinio asmens bankroto procesas,

Luxembourg

— Faillite,
— Gestion contrôlée,
— Concordat préventif de faillite (par abandon d'actif),
— Régime spécial de liquidation du notariat,
— Procédure de règlement collectif des dettes dans le cadre du surendettement,

Magyarország

— Csődeljárás,
— Felszámolási eljárás,

Malta

— Xoljiment,
— Amministrazzjoni,
— Stralċ volontarju mill-membri jew mill-kredituri,
— Stralċ mill-Qorti,
— Falliment f'każ ta' kummerċjant,
— Proċedura biex kumpanija tirkupra,

Nederland

— Het faillissement,
— De surséance van betaling,
— De schuldsaneringsregeling natuurlijke personen,

Österreich

— Das Konkursverfahren (Insolvenzverfahren),
— Das Sanierungsverfahren ohne Eigenverwaltung (Insolvenzverfahren),
— Das Sanierungsverfahren mit Eigenverwaltung (Insolvenzverfahren),
— Das Schuldenregulierungsverfahren,
— Das Abschöpfungsverfahren,
— Das Ausgleichsverfahren,

Polska

— Postępowanie naprawcze,
— Upadłość obejmująca likwidację,
— Upadłość z możliwością zawarcia układu,

Portugal

— Processo de insolvência,
— Processo especial de revitalização,

România

— Procedura insolvenţei,
— Reorganizarea judiciară,
— Procedura falimentului,
— Concordatul preventiv,

Slovenija

— Postopek preventivnega prestrukturiranja,
— Postopek prisilne poravnave,
— Postopek poenostavljene prisilne poravnave,
— Stečajni postopek: stečajni postopek nad pravno osebo, postopek osebnega stečaja and postopek stečaja zapuščine,

Slovensko

— Konkurzné konanie,
— Reštrukturalizačné konanie,
— Oddlženie,

Suomi/Finland

— Konkurssi/konkurs,
— Yrityssaneeraus/företagssanering,
— Yksityishenkilön velkajärjestely/skuldsanering för privatpersoner,

Sverige

— Konkurs,
— Företagsrekonstruktion,
— Skuldsanering,

United Kingdom

— Winding-up by or subject to the supervision of the court,
— Creditors' voluntary winding-up (with confirmation by the court),
— Administration, including appointments made by filing prescribed documents with the court,
— Voluntary arrangements under insolvency legislation,
— Bankruptcy or sequestration.

ANNEX B INSOLVENCY PRACTITIONERS REFERRED TO IN POINT (5) OF ARTICLE 2

Belgique/België

— De curator/Le curateur,
— De gedelegeerd rechter/Le juge-délégué,
— De gerechtsmandataris/Le mandataire de justice,
— De schuldbemiddelaar/Le médiateur de dettes,
— De vereffenaar/Le liquidateur,
— De voorlopige bewindvoerder/L'administrateur provisoire,

БЪЛГАРИЯ

— Назначен предварително временен синдик,
— Временен синдик,
— (Постоянен) синдик,
— Служебен синдик,

Česká Republika

— Insolvenční správce,
— Předběžný insolvenční správce,
— Oddělený insolvenční správce,

— Zvláštní insolvenční správce,
— Zástupce insolvenčního správce,

Deutschland

— Konkursverwalter,
— Vergleichsverwalter,
— Sachwalter (nach der Vergleichsordnung),
— Verwalter,
— Insolvenzverwalter,
— Sachwalter (nach der Insolvenzordnung),
— Treuhänder,
— Vorläufiger Insolvenzverwalter,
— Vorläufiger Sachwalter,

Eesti

— Pankrotihaldur,
— Ajutine pankrotihaldur,
— Usaldusisik,

Éire/Ireland

— Liquidator,
— Official Assignee,
— Trustee in bankruptcy,
— Provisional Liquidator,
— Examiner,
— Personal Insolvency Practitioner,
— Insolvency Service,

ΕΛΛΑΔΑ

— Ο σύνδικος,
— Ο εισηγητής,
— Η επιτροπή των πιστωτών,
— Ο ειδικός εκκαθαριστής,

España

— Administrador concursal,
— Mediador concursal,

France

— Mandataire judiciaire,
— Liquidateur,
— Administrateur judiciaire,
— Commissaire à l'exécution du plan,

Hrvatska

— Stečajni upravitelj,
— Privremeni stečajni upravitelj,
— Stečajni povjerenik,
— Povjerenik,

Italia

— Curatore,
— Commissario giudiziale,
— Commissario straordinario,
— Commissario liquidatore,
— Liquidatore giudiziale,
— Professionista nominato dal Tribunale,
— Organismo di composizione della crisi nella procedura di composizione della crisi da sovrain-debitamento del consumatore,
— Liquidatore,

ΚΥΠΡΟΣ

— Εκκαθαριστής και Προσωρινός Εκκαθαριστής,
— Επίσημος Παραλήπτης,
— Διαχειριστής της Πτώχευσης,

Latvija

— Maksātnespējas procesa administrators,

Lietuva

— Bankroto administratorius,
— Restruktūrizavimo administratorius,

Luxembourg

— Le curateur,
— Le commissaire,
— Le liquidateur,
— Le conseil de gérance de la section d'assainissement du notariat,
— Le liquidateur dans le cadre du surendettement,

Magyarország

— Vagyonfelügyelő,
— Felszámoló,

Malta

— Amministratur Proviżorju,
— Riċevitur Uffiċjali,
— Stralċjarju,
— Manager Speċjali,
— Kuraturi f'każ ta' proċeduri ta' falliment,
— Kontrolur Speċjali,

Nederland

— De curator in het faillissement,
— De bewindvoerder in de surséance van betaling,
— De bewindvoerder in de schuldsaneringsregeling natuurlijke personen,

Österreich

— Masseverwalter,
— Sanierungsverwalter,
— Ausgleichsverwalter,
— Besonderer Verwalter,
— Einstweiliger Verwalter,
— Sachwalter,
— Treuhänder,
— Insolvenzgericht,
— Konkursgericht,

Polska

— Syndyk,
— Nadzorca sądowy,
— Zarządca,

Portugal

— Administrador da insolvência,
— Administrador judicial provisório,

România

— Practician în insolvență,
— Administrator concordatar,
— Administrator judiciar,

— Lichidator judiciar,

Slovenija

— Upravitelj,

Slovensko

— Predbežný správca,
— Správca,

Suomi/Finland

— Pesänhoitaja/boförvaltare,
— Selvittäjä/utredare,

Sverige

— Förvaltare,
— Rekonstruktör,

United Kingdom

— Liquidator,
— Supervisor of a voluntary arrangement,
— Administrator,
— Official Receiver,
— Trustee,
— Provisional Liquidator,
— Interim Receiver,
— Judicial factor.

Annex C Repealed Regulation with list
OF THE SUCCESSIVE AMENDMENTS THERETO

Council Regulation (EC) No 1346/2000

(OJ L 160, 30.6.2000, p. 1)

Council Regulation (EC) No 603/2005

(OJ L 100, 20.4.2005, p. 1)

Council Regulation (EC) No 694/2006

(OJ L 121, 6.5.2006, p. 1)

Council Regulation (EC) No 1791/2006

(OJ L 363, 20.12.2006, p. 1)

Council Regulation (EC) No 681/2007

(OJ L 159, 20.6.2007, p. 1)

Council Regulation (EC) No 788/2008

(OJ L 213, 8.8.2008, p. 1)

Implementing Regulation of the Council (EU) No 210/2010

(OJ L 65, 13.3.2010, p. 1)

Council Implementing Regulation (EU) No 583/2011

(OJ L 160, 18.6.2011, p. 52)

Council Regulation (EU) No 517/2013

(OJ L 158, 10.6.2013, p. 1)

Council Implementing Regulation (EU) No 663/2014

(OJ L 179, 19.6.2014, p. 4)

Act concerning the conditions of accession of the Czech Republic, the Republic of Estonia, the Republic of Cyprus, the Republic of Latvia, the Republic of Lithuania, the Republic of Hungary, the

Republic of Malta, the Republic of Poland, the Republic of Slovenia and the Slovak Republic and the adjustments to the Treaties on which the European Union is founded

(OJ L 236, 23.9.2003, p. 33)

ANNEX D CORRELATION TABLE

Regulation (EC) No 1346/2000	This Regulation
Article 1	Article 1
Article 2, introductory words	Article 2, introductory words
Article 2, point (a)	Article 2, point (4)
Article 2, point (b)	Article 2, point (5)
Article 2, point (c)	—
Article 2, point (d)	Article 2, point (6)
Article 2, point (e)	Article 2, point (7)
Article 2, point (f)	Article 2, point (8)
Article 2, point (g), introductory words	Article 2, point (9), introductory words
Article 2, point (g), first indent	Article 2, point (9)(vii)
Article 2, point (g), second indent	Article 2, point (9)(iv)
Article 2, point (g), third indent	Article 2, point (9)(viii)
Article 2, point (h)	Article 2, point 10
—	Article 2, points (1) to (3) and (11) to (13)
—	Article 2, point (9)(i) to (iii), (v), (vi)
Article 3	Article 3
—	Article 4
—	Article 5
—	Article 6
Article 4	Article 7
Article 5	Article 8
Article 6	Article 9
Article 7	Article 10
Article 8	Article 11(1)
—	Article 11(2)
Article 9	Article 12
Article 10	Article 13(1)
—	Article 13(2)
Article 11	Article 14
Article 12	Article 15
Article 13, first indent	Article 16, point (a)
Article 13, second indent	Article 16, point (b)
Article 14, first indent	Article 17, point (a)
Article 14, second indent	Article 17, point (b)
Article 14, third indent	Article 17, point (c)
Article 15	Article 18
Article 16	Article 19
Article 17	Article 20

(Continued)

Regulation (EC) No 1346/2000	This Regulation
Article 18	Article 21
Article 19	Article 22
Article 20	Article 23
—	Article 24
—	Article 25
—	Article 26
—	Article 27
Article 21(1)	Article 28(2)
Article 21(2)	Article 28(1)
Article 22	Article 29
Article 23	Article 30
Article 24	Article 31
Article 25	Article 32
Article 26	Article 33
Article 27	Article 34
Article 28	Article 35
—	Article 36
Article 29	Article 37(1)
—	Article 37(2)
—	Article 38
—	Article 39
Article 30	Article 40
Article 31	Article 41
—	Article 42
—	Article 43
—	Article 44
Article 32	Article 45
Article 33	Article 46
Article 34(1)	Article 47(1)
Article 34(2)	Article 47(2)
Article 34(3)	—
—	Article 48
Article 35	Article 49
Article 36	Article 50
Article 37	Article 51
Article 38	Article 52
Article 39	Article 53
Article 40	Article 54
Article 41	Article 55
Article 42	—
—	Article 56
—	Article 57
—	Article 58

(Continued)

Regulation (EC) No 1346/2000	This Regulation
—	Article 59
—	Article 60
—	Article 61
—	Article 62
—	Article 63
—	Article 64
—	Article 65
—	Article 66
—	Article 67
—	Article 68
—	Article 69
—	Article 70
—	Article 71
—	Article 72
—	Article 73
—	Article 74
—	Article 75
—	Article 76
—	Article 77
—	Article 78
—	Article 79
—	Article 80
—	Article 81
—	Article 82
—	Article 83
Article 43	Article 84(1)
—	Article 84(2)
Article 44	Article 85
—	Article 86
Article 45	—
—	Article 87
—	Article 88
—	Article 89
Article 46	Article 90(1)
—	Article 90(2) to (4)
—	Article 91
Article 47	Article 92
Annex A	Annex A
Annex B	—
Annex C	Annex B
—	Annex C
—	Annex D

APPENDIX 4

Article 249 EC

In order to carry out their task and in accordance with the provisions of this Treaty, the European Parliament acting jointly with the Council, the Council and the Commission shall make regulations and issue directives, take decisions, make recommendations or deliver opinions.

A regulation shall have general application. It shall be binding in its entirety and directly applicable in all Member States.

A directive shall be binding, as to the result to be achieved, upon each Member State to which it is addressed, but shall leave to the national authorities the choice of form and methods.

A decision shall be binding in its entirety upon those to whom it is addressed. Recommendations and opinions shall have no binding force.

INDEX

.